Europe in 1848

EUROPE IN 1848

Revolution and Reform

Edited by

Dieter Dowe, Heinz–Gerhard Haupt,
Dieter Langewiesche, and Jonathan Sperber

Translated by

David Higgins

Berghahn Books
New York • Oxford

Published in 2001 by

Berghahn Books

© 2001 Friedrich-Ebert-Stiftung

Library of Congress Cataloging-in-Publication Data

Europa 1848. English.
    Europe in 1848 : revolution and reform / edited by Dieter Dowe, Heinz-Gerhard Haupt,
Dieter Langewiesche, and Jonathan Sperber ; translated from the German.
        p. cm.
    Includes bibliographical references and index.
    ISBN 1-57181-164-8 (alk. paper)
        1. Europe--History--1848-1849. 2. Revolutions--Europe--History--20th century. I.
Dowe, Dieter.

D387.E8713 2000
940.2'85--dc21   00-027750

British Library Cataloguing in Publication Data

A catalogue record for this book is available from the British Library.

Printed in the United States on acid-free paper.

CONTENTS

PART II
City and Country

PART III
Revolutionary Politics and Politics in the Revolution

PREFACE TO THE ENGLISH-LANGUAGE EDITION

Jonathan Sperber

The revolutions of 1848 have long been in the shadow of their counterparts of 1789 and 1917. While the latter had seemed successful, bringing about permanent changes in state, economy and society—perhaps even in cultural and intellectual life as well—the 1848 uprisings were ultimately understood as failures, their effects ephemeral. A number of developments, in both public and academic life, have gradually converged over the last several decades to change this picture of the 1848 revolutions.

Certainly the events of 1989 in eastern and central Europe were influential. The way in which demonstrations and disturbances jumped from one country to the next, and the sudden, unexpected and domino-like fall of the communist regimes in the region evoked striking similarities with the circumstances of the middle of the nineteenth century, when revolutions quickly spread from Palermo to Bucharest. The spring of 1848 and the fall of 1989 were suddenly very close, as many of the latter's themes—the demand for unification of the German states, the nationalities' conflict over what had once been the lands of the Habsburg Monarchy—were clearly recognizable as a continuation of issues that had first turned up on a large scale in 1848.

The end of the European communist regimes in 1989/91 also contributed to a revival of 1848, since it brought into question the "success" of the communist revolution of 1917, and again problematized the criteria of "success" for a revolution. Perhaps contributing to this question from a different direction was another international event, albeit a more academic one, the bicentenary of the French Revolution. The lively debate about 1789, the frequently critical tone in which this debate was couched, directed at what was the very model of a modern revolution, once again raised the question of what makes a successful revolution. Undoubtedly, this re-questioning of the "successes" of both the 1789 and 1917 revolutions made it possible to approach the "unsuccessful" ones of 1848 in a different manner.

Contributing to this new understanding of the 1848 revolutions was a gradual shift of focus in historians' interest, already underway for some decades by the

1990s. Seen most broadly (and in so doing, running roughshod over important distinctions and even differing positions in bitter scholarly controversies), this turn involved a re-evaluation of the experiential dimension of the past. Whether in the form of the history of everyday life, or a history from the "bottom up," or a post-structuralist "linguistic turn" that valorized the shaping power of discourse in human affairs, historians found themselves judging less the ultimate outcomes of events and processes, increasingly reluctant to delineate historical winners and losers, with a greater interest in grasping how things were understood, experienced, and articulated as they were happening.

In view of all these developments, the 1998 sesquicentennary of the revolution of 1848 proved to be much more extensive and evoked more interest among scholars and perhaps even the general public than might have been expected. This interest was particularly great in Germany, and among the many conferences and symposia on the 1848 revolution sponsored during and around its 150th anniversary, one in particular stands out, and upon which this book is based: the Friedrich Ebert Foundation's international conference in Würzburg in November 1996, at which thirty-eight historians from nine different countries engaged in a broad and wide-ranging discussion of Europe during the 1848 revolutions. Under the direction of Dr. Dieter Dowe, the director of the Historical Research division of the Friedrich Ebert Foundation, Professor Dieter Langewiesche of the University of Tübingen, and Professor Heinz-Gerhard Haupt of the University of Halle—all experts on the mid-nineteenth century revolutions in their own right—the papers presented at the conference, along with some additional works, were shaped together into a book documenting the political, social and cultural movements of 1848 on a European-wide scale.

This book was published in German in 1998, for the sesquicentennary of the revolution. Thanks to the efforts of the editors of the original German edition, the financial support and good offices of the Friedrich Ebert Foundation, and the patient labors of the translator, Mr. David Higgins, it has been possible to bring out a complete and unabridged English-language version of the book, thus making available to an Anglophone audience the very latest scholarship on the revolution of 1848. Part I of the book contains chapters recounting the events of 1848 throughout the different European countries, and covers the relatively well-known cases, such as the revolutions of France, Italy or Germany, as well as essays on less well known regions, such as the Danubian Principalities of Wallachia and Moldavia. Severeal essays on what the editors call the "reform belt" are also included, covering the areas of peaceful change during the revolutionary year, the Low Countries and Scandinavia.

However, as is frequently and appropriately noted in this book, approaching 1848 as a series of individual national histories is insufficient, and Parts II–IV contain thematic essays on topics spanning the continent: the 1848 revolution in rural areas, the labor movement during the revolution, the role of women and the discourse of gender during the revolution, institutions of civil society, such as the press, public meetings, and political organizations in the revolutionary events, and public discourse in the revolution, whether in the form of parliamentary speech, rumors or public festivals, to name just some of them. The persistent comparative approach in these sections provide another form of European-wide coverage. Two introductory essays offer quite different overviews of 1848, and two concluding ones discuss the traditions left behind by the 1848 revolutions.

Without trying to preempt the introductory and concluding essays, or to offer a systematic account of the many varying and differing views the authors put forth, I would like to outline a picture of 1848 that might reasonably be said to emerge from a consideration of the entire volume. One main point is the place of the peasantry in the revolution. In this volume, the actions, demands, and aspirations of the rural population emerge as central to the revolution—both in the lands where serfdom was still practiced, in the eastern part of Europe, and in the areas of free labor and property in the west. While individual contributions differ on the extent to which different elements in rural society were supporters of revolution or counterrevolution, and, indeed, on the extent and nature of the politicization of the peasantry, there seems to be a broad consensus that 1848 cannot be seen as just an urban event, or one limited to major metropolitan centers, even if crucial struggles of the revolution did take place in them.

If the role of the peasants emerges in magnified form, that of the workers seems somewhat diminished. There are certainly differences of opinion among the contributors. Some hold to a picture of the 1848 revolution as the cradle of the labor movement in continental Europe, seeing the Parisian June Days as the central event of the mid-century revolution. Others, however, are more inclined to note the still strongly artisanal character of the "working class" at the middle of the nineteenth century, to downplay the extent and importance of independent socialist initiatives, and to point to other issues and forms of conflict as more significant. This approach tends to emphasize the discontinuities separating 1848 from the later labor movement, just as recent literature on the English Chartists has stressed their similarity with earlier forms of radicalism, and their differences from future labor organizations.

Nations and nationalism continue to be central to the interpretations of the 1848 revolution put forth in this book. However, in contrast to past views that tended to take the phenomenon of nation for granted and assume the legitimacy and/or natural character of the nation-state as a form of political organization, the authors of this volume problematize the nation, noting its socially and linguistically constructed character. They outline alternative forms of political loyalty and group identity, such as those of dynasty, religious confession or region, and note their role as powerful competitors to nationalism. The connections, especially in eastern Europe, but more generally across the whole continent, between these differing forms of political loyalties and social conflicts are also emphasized. While asserting these newer views, most of the authors continue the emphasis of an earlier historiography on the great diplomatic and military difficulties connected with the realization of nationalist goals in 1848. Together, such a viewpoint makes nationalists appear considerably more embattled and beleaguered, even in the early stages of the revolution, when their goals appeared to be within their grasp.

The question of the immediate and long-term effects of the 1848 revolutions remains controversial, and there is clearly no agreement among the contributors about them. Some see the revolutions as a significant break in previous trends with important immediate consequences; others emphasize the long-term effects of the revolutions, while admitting that in the short term little had changed. Still other contributors are distinctly skeptical about any independent effects of the revolutions, seeing no difference between changes stemming from them and those emerging from long-term socioeconomic or political developments. Needless to say, such judgements vary depending on the country, or on the area of focus since political or cultural consequences can be understood as distinct from socioeconomic ones.

One area of agreement did emerge among the participants of the original conference in Würzburg: the sheer size, multiplicity, and complexity of the events of 1848 on a European scale. The mid-nineteenth-century revolutions and reform movements entailed a broad variety of social and political struggles; they brought forth an enormous range of forms of participation in public life, ranging from chaotic and spontaneous demonstrations in the streets to more organized mass meetings and political-club session, to the highly structured forms of parliamentary procedure. The issues brought into question by this wave of participation in public life covered all aspects of government, society, and economy, from the formation of producers' cooperatives to the formation of parliamentary caucuses, from the liberation of serfs from feudal oppression to the liberation of women from male oppression, from the revamping of the educational system to the revamping of organized religion. The participants were no less varied than the events and organizations in which they participated, and featured, prominently, groups who often had not been previously involved in public life, particularly the rural population, the lower strata of society, and women. It is this continent-wide panorama that perhaps emerges most strongly from a reading of this volume, and might well prove to be its most important feature.

Chapter 1

THE EUROPEAN REVOLUTION OF 1848

Its Political and Social Reforms, its Politics of Nationalism, and its Short- and Long-Term Consequences

Heinz-Gerhard Haupt and *Dieter Langewiesche*

When one spoke of revolution in the nineteenth century, one had 1789 in mind—the great model revolution that shaped the concepts of revolution for people all over the word. Such concepts were never uniform. Competing images of revolution were always available to interpret the past and the present and to set a path toward the future. Only the Bolshevik October Revolution generated a fascination comparable to that of 1789; numerous other revolutions that took place between these two great moments in world history never excited people's imaginations to such an extent. This was also true of the 1848 revolution.

Measured against its aims, it failed everywhere, but in its successes and failures it defined the future of Europe. Still, 1848 produced no myths like those of 1789 and 1917. The "bourgeois era" began with the drama of a new type of revolution and ended, equally dramatically, with the birth of a type of revolution that would become the basic model for revolutionaries in the twentieth century. In between lay a multi-faceted chain of variations—rich in political and social consequences, but poor in myth-making power.

Compared to 1789 and 1917 the revolutions of the nineteenth century appear epigonic. As if under the spell of the great historical model of 1789, nineteenth century revolutions tended either to repeat its course or, more often, to learn from it in order not to slip once again from reform into *terreur* and finally into the dictatorship of one individual. These revolutions lived from their inherited pathos, with whose symbolism they could not compete. Even contemporaries saw this. Karl Marx, for example, with the historical model in mind, called 1848 a "semi-revolution,"[1] and later generations agreed.

Notes for this section can be found on page 23.

Such an assessment is understandable, but unjustified. The year 1848 meant learning from 1789, making use of historical experience to avoid the mistakes of the original model. Revolutionaries, reformers, and counter-revolutionaries were all trying to learn from 1789, to avoid repeating its errors and suffering. But 1848 also covered new ground in its own right: Its geographic extent was unique among all revolutions. The outlines of a new Europe become visible—in terms of the intensity of societal communication across the borders of sovereign states; and in regard to the conflicts of nationalities that arose from the revolutionary alliance in the European "springtime of the peoples." In 1848, the future Europe of nations and nation-states becomes apparent, as well as the fractures which that run through and between individual societies.

Basic Features

In 1848, more states on the European continent were overcome by revolution than ever before and ever since. Revolutionary movements everywhere from France, via the vast central European space of the German Confederation and the Habsburg Monarchy, to the monarchy's southeast European territories and the Danubian Principalities of Moldavia and Wallachia (then under nominal Ottoman suzerainty), from Denmark to Italy placed the reform of the structures of political and social rule on the agenda of history. Nor did things remain quiet in the rest of Europe. Political life was set in motion; there were a few attempts at uprisings, but above all reforms were introduced in order to prevent revolution. Even on the British Isles, the tremors from the continent were felt. The government and the middle class reacted with a vigorous self-defense to the threats they saw emerging from the Chartists and, above all, from the Irish in Great Britain and North America.

Only Russia was not affected by the tremors of the revolutionary earthquake. While there were plans for uprising, they were discovered and had no effect because the tiny conspiratorial circles behind them had little support among the population. A devastating cholera epidemic, major fires in a number of villages and towns caused by a long drought, serious crop failures and a severe economic crisis burdened the countryside in 1848, and peasant unrest rose beyond the usual level. When the first news of the revolutions in Europe reached the country, Russian authorities immediately intensified censorship in the towns, deported conspicuous foreigners as potential troublemakers and, as a preventative measure, increased troop strength on the western border. But while Russia remained peaceful within its borders, it became at the same time one of the central actors in the European revolution. The Tsar was omnipresent in the diplomacy of the counter-revolution. His troops enabled the Habsburg leadership to defeat the Hungarian Revolution militarily and, relieved of this front, to be successful against the Italian and German Revolutions.

Revolution, defense against revolution, and counter-revolution bound the Europe of 1848 into a unity. The continent coalesced into a space of communication and action and reached a new density of information never before achieved in social and geographic terms, but also across the political boundaries that traditionally separated the women's domain from male public life. Access to information for all classes improved abruptly with the revolution—as did the willingness to use it. Never before had Europe been covered by such an extensive information network, from which basically no one was excluded.

The Europeanization of information made the revolutionization of Europe possible. This process was set off by the Paris February Revolution. Shortly before, in January and at the beginning of February, the Italian Revolution had already begun and had celebrated its first victories. However, neither this Italian Revolution nor the Polish Revolution of 1846 (Cracow and Galicia), nor the Swiss Revolution, in the form of the *Sonderbund* War of 1847, set off a chain reaction in Europe or created a European-wide public sphere. The signal came from Paris.

Unlike in 1789, however, France did not export its revolutions into Europe by force of arms (such was the hope of many and the dread of many more). A desire by France to proselytize the revolution, which had led to the collapse of old Europe half a century previously, had been extinguished under the pressure of the enormous military sacrifices which Napoleon had imposed on the country. The French revolution of 1848 did not cross the country's borders. Yet, everyone in Europe was looking to Paris, "this eternally beating heart of Europe" as Fanny Lewald described the city to which she enthusiastically set off immediately after hearing of the February Revolution, in order to witness it herself.[2] In the European capital of revolution, everyone, revolutionaries and their opponents, discovered their hopes and their fears. In February, the political revolution was victorious and four months later, in June 1848, the social revolution was defeated there. Both victory and defeat were significant for all of Europe.

Even while Europe based its conceptions on that which occurred in Paris, the revolutions that shook a large part of the European continent in 1848 were independent, with their own causes, aims, and course. Still, in spite of the complexities of revolutionary events, a common pattern can be recognized. In 1848, all European societies were faced with the challenge of democratizing the political order and finding an answer to the social question. In those countries that were not yet organized nation-states—this was true of most of Europe—the desire for national self-determination added a further major reforming force. The forces active in these three central areas of reform supported each other in part, but also came into conflict with each other.

Reform of the Political and Social Order

Parliamentarization and democratization of the government were everywhere among the core demands of the revolutionary movements. The question of how far this reform should go, however, sparked a bitter debate on fundamental issues between liberals and democrats. This struggle over the form of government was epitomized in the choice: republic or parliamentary monarchy? A new form of monarchy, such as that which had developed in Great Britain, shorn of its aura of divine right and bound politically to a majority in parliament, was still completely rejected by most princes on the continent. Supporters of a parliamentary monarchy hence had to fight on two fronts: against monarchists and against republicans.

From the time of the French Revolution onwards, the republican form of government gave rise to strongly contradictory emotions. Gustave Flaubert brought to life the aura surrounding the word republic in 1848 in his novel *The Sentimental Education.* "The republic has been proclaimed! We shall all be happy now! … we're going to liberate Poland and Italy. No more kings! … The whole world free! The whole world free!" This enthusiasm of a Parisian barricade fighter contrasted with the fears that the republic raised, and not only among conservatives and liberals. Many democrats also preferred a reformed monarchy, for they perceived in the republic the threat of the "schemes of 1793," the revolutionary reign of terror. As brilliantly expressed by Flaubert: "… the sound of the guillotine made itself heard in every syllable of the word 'Republic' …"[3]

Only in France had people already learned by 1848 that, in contrast to the experience of the revolutionary cycle that in 1789 began with the monarchy and led to the republican *terreur*, a republic born of revolution also could be constitutionally and sociopolitically tamed. Other states still faced this experience with the "bourgeois republic." The time was not ripe in 1848. The utopia of a "social republic"—condemned by its opponents as the "red republic," which "means nothing other than freedom with theft and murder"[4]—was overburdened with expectations, including even secularized versions of religious dreams of salvation, which contrasted with no less unreal visions of doom.

It was only in France that the throne collapsed with the first wave of revolutions. Everywhere else, the revolutionary movements sought a compromise with the hereditary dynasties. In those places where the revolution was prepared to risk a republic in its final phases—in Hungary, in parts of Italy and Germany—such a proclamation of the republic was only a futile attempt at saving the revolution. Some revolutionaries saw in it an act of self-defense against monarchs who had rejected reform; others hoped to expand the political revolution into a social one. These contrasting expectations weakened the revolutionary movements' ability to act and contributed to their downfall.

Democratization of the political order in 1848 meant above all expanding the population's chances of participation in public life. For this, the powers of the ruling dynasties had to be cut back and the influence of the old political elite restricted. To have attempted this task by legal means remains one of the central features of the 1848 revolutions. Not the guillotine, but the constitution served as the instrument for approaching the ideal of equality of all citizens. All states seized by revolution or drawn into its reformist wake introduced constitutions or began to liberalize existing ones. Constitutions were no longer granted from above, but founded on the principle of popular sovereignty, embodied in an elected national assembly and couched in a political discourse that was increasingly organized and which contentiously but conspicuously publicized its objectives. Like the discourse, the electorate also changed fundamentally in the years of revolution. It took on a more democratic form, as the franchise was greatly expanded. Never before was the circle of those qualified to vote in Europe socially so broad as in 1848.

The society of citizens, whose outlines were becoming apparent, remained, however, a society of men. Only they were allowed to vote and to be elected or take offices in the state or the municipality. Below this level, however, the revolution begin to have "the potential to disrupt gender relations," as Michelle Perrot quite fittingly expresses it.[5] Women read newspapers and even edited them, they took part in political gatherings, publicly displayed their convictions, with cockades for instance, listened to parliamentary debates and expressed in a variety of forms their views on the political questions of the day. They also made use of an instrument for the formation of political opinion that became almost ubiquitous in the revolution, the voluntary association. The number of women's associations increased rapidly and in those countries where none had existed before, they were founded for the first time—for example in Prague, where in September 1848 two Czech women's associations appeared.

Women thus made use of the expanded possibilities for political participation, but nowhere were they granted legal political equality with men. Only a minority of active women had demanded such equality, and only a few men were prepared to recognize women as equal citizens. The great number of biting caricatures that made fun of women's new found interest and participation in public life shows how uncomfortable the world of men was when women abandoned their traditional roles in the revolution.

Thus the revolution opened new opportunities for women to become active politically, but restricted them to the usual paths of participation in the societal conflicts of interest groups, including collective protest. Women had always taken part in such protests. Social protest contributed greatly to the rapid success of the first wave of revolutions, but then waned as this traditional form of expressing criticism and bringing one's interests to bear lost significance. Revolutionaries and reformers had another sort of politics in mind: as different as their strategies were, they all sought structural changes at the level of constitutional norms and governmental institutions, realms monopolized by men. This did not change when the circle of participants was enormously expanded to include members of previously excluded social groups. The more politics took place in such institutions, the less chance women had of taking part. This basic rule of public life continued to be valid despite the fact that more women than ever before lined up against it. For many, their support of the revolution even led them to the barricades; most, however, kept to peaceful means. In this choice of forms of political action, they were no different from men.

The 1848 revolutions began with violent protests and uprisings, and ended in military struggles. Despite this fact, they were characterized less by the barricade, than by an attempt to reform the political order in non-violent fashion. The focus of political interest hence shifted to the parliaments. They became the place in which society's desire for reform was translated into government policy. The work of the parliaments, which during the revolution concentrated on reform of the constitutional order, was closely related to the extraparliamentary public sphere.

Never before had there been so many newspapers in Europe as there were in 1848. Such newspapers openly took political positions, also in those countries where this had previously not been possible. The political press permeated public life and helped to organize it. The formation of an inter-regional interest organization was dependent on a newspaper as a means of communication. The varied press landscape and the dense network of associations—both the result and the constitutive force of the revolution—were closely woven together. The revolution extended political freedom and thus accelerated the politicization of society. Parties in modern form could arise in places where previously forbidden: they set up permanent organizations, developed programs that they publicly advocated, nominated candidates for elections and attempted to tie together extra-parliamentary organizations and parliamentary caucuses. Associations became centers of political education. Although concentrated in the cities and towns, they also pushed their way into the countryside. The substantial involvement of the rural population in the final phase of the revolution makes apparent a political learning process which never would have been possible without the numerous associations.

Continental Europe was still predominantly an agrarian society in the mid-nineteenth century. To change this society was unavoidable if the revolution was to have permanent success. Here, reform of the governmental and the social orders were directly related. Outside the West European and Scandinavian reform belt, the agrarian program of 1848 can be summed up in a word: defeudalization. The special privileges of the lords and the burdens on the peasants, which varied considerably from country to country and indeed between regions within individual countries, were to be abolished to bring about the realization in the countryside, as well as in the city, of a society of citizens based on personal liberty and individual ownership of property.

Every agrarian revolt was thus both a political and a social revolution—independent of whether one favored or opposed the developing agrarian individualism (Marc Bloch). Peasants acted in revolutionary fashion mostly wanted to liberate the land they cultivated from all seigneurial burdens and usage rights and so did the landless lower class and the smallholders, especially in southern and eastern Europe, who supported a retention or restoration of collective property or the distribution of manorial and church lands. Such a backward-looking vision could also give rise to revolutionary radicalism, a point often misunderstood in the older historiography. It was a radicalism which did not fit with the vision of a future "civil society," but nonetheless radically called into question the existing social order.

Peasants and the rural lower class contributed greatly to the rapid early success of the revolution with their protest and unrest, and they certainly did not withdraw from politics when the agrarian reforms, rapidly approved in a number of European states, fulfilled at least some of their demands. In the final phase of the revolution, when it was a question of rescuing their gains from a reinvigorated counter-revolution, country folk did not stand to one side, but were among the centers of resistance. So while the revolution of 1848 was, to be sure, an urban even—it was in the cities that national demands were raised and the institutions located that were to realize the demands in lasting fashion—the revolution also reached the countryside and initiated learning processes there that reduced the gap between city and country.

Still, a distance remained between the rural and urban revolutions, especially in eastern and southern Europe. Demands of the peasants, and certainly those of social classes below the peasants, which went beyond the agrarian reforms of 1848, could only have been realized in a second revolution, that would have had to have been social in nature. Only a minority, even among the republican left, was willing to risk such a revolution which would have meant going against the majority, against the spirit of the European revolution of 1848.

In European states, the differences between city and country in aims and forms of action were less marked, although the narrow horizons of rural life stood at the forefront for the rural population. It was this life world they sought to change, not the "state" or the "nation." But even, this way of looking at things began to change as well. Country people learned to recognize the connections between the local and the national revolution. Hence the German campaign for the imperial constitution and the French uprising against Louis Napoleon's coup in 1851 also found support in the villages and rural towns. The peasants were most integrated into political events in the Scandinavian societies, where the landowning nobility only played a minor role.

Another group for which the revolution paved a place onto the political stage was the workforce, less so for the workers of developing major industries, than for workers employed in small workshops or in outworking. Their social profile was closer to the sans-culottes of the French Revolution than to the modern industrial proletariat. Challenged by Marxist historiography, which has provided important studies on the revolutionary potential of the proletariat, historians have examined intensively the gradual transitions in condition between small master craftsmen on the one hand, and journeymen, apprentices, and manual laborers on the other. They have also analyzed their orientation toward forms of action, ideals and idioms of the artisan tradition. These artisan workers participated actively in all areas of the revolution. They were part of the public sphere in the streets, and took part in collective protests, founded political associations and drew up codes of law for the crafts, and organized petitions and strikes. They were to be found in all urban uprisings as combatants on the barricades, but also on the side of the counter-revolution.

The Paris June uprising of 1848 offers the most spectacular example of political divisions among this socially heterogeneous *peuple*. The socialism of these common people was impregnated with religious ideas, drew on the collective social images of pre-industrial artisans, and countered the rising industrial–capitalist market society with cooperative forms of property and organization, but was also open to conceptions of the future as proclaimed in the *Communist Manifesto*. In the "right to work," they found a formula that gave the revolution a social vision while at the same time deeply dividing society. In the Paris national workshops they believed to have discovered the future of a social state. When this experiment ended in the June uprising of 1848, bourgeois Europe breathed a sigh of relief. In a less spectacular manner, however, state and municipal job creation programs in many places were begun belonging to such attempts to ease the social consequences of a severe business-cycle downturn that paralleled the revolution. The revolution had politicized this traditional instrument and transformed it into an ideologically loaded sociopolitical program.

Not all sections of the population were equally affected by the revolution, but none remained totally unaffected. These brief sketches of politicization among women, the rural population, and the workers are illustrations of this point. It can be equally demonstrated for other groups, the Jews, the clergy, students and teachers. The contributions in this volume discuss these aspects in detail. In terms of the level of participation in the revolution the general outline seems to be: men participated more than women in political meetings, petitions, organizations and debate, city folk more than country folk, artisans more than peasants, the bourgeoisie more than the aristocracy. However, for all of them the revolution meant an upward lurch in the level of politicization. Those who wished to hold their ground politically and in governmental institutions had to become politically active.

Traditional elites were also not able to evade this necessity, as they could no longer rely on tried and tested means of securing their power. New centers of power had arisen as had new forms of politics. For the first time, representative democracy seemed to have succeeded on the European continent. Liberals and democrats acted in favor of it, but conservatives also turned to the public, founded associations and newspapers, called public meetings and organized petitions, in order not to be excluded from the political opinion market. Those who wished to oppose the revolution had to use the means of the revolution. Among them was the use of violence, but not even the counter-revolution restricted itself to this. Its spectrum of political forms of action was as broad as that of the revolutionaries. Even in the rejection of sociorevolutionary goals—or what were seen as such—distinctions between bourgeois reformers and conservative opponents of the revolution could become blurred.

This was also true of the use of state military force. Everywhere the revolution was defeated by regular troops, but before this revolutionary governments had also not hesitated to use the military and the civil militias if they felt their policies endangered by a part of the revolutionary movement. The forces of the counter-revolution, therefore, should not only be sought within the circles of the old elite.

There were also changes in political alignments during the revolution. Especially in its final phase, when many felt that there was a threat of radicalization along the lines of 1789, a considerable number of bourgeois reformers retreated, greeting the defeat of the revolution as the lesser of two evils. One example of this is provided by Gabriel Riesser. As vice-president of the German National Assembly, he was one of the representatives of reformism during the revolution, and, as a Jew, he personified the sudden expansion in the possibilities for emancipation in Europe. When the moderate majority in the *Paulskirche* refused to take the lead in the campaign for the imperial constitution, he interpreted this as a "declaration of bankruptcy" which only allowed the "dismal choice between the despotism of the princes or that of the so-called democrats." Feeling that he was faced with a hopeless situation he made his decision: "The victory of a despotic, even bloody reaction can be the lesser of two evils, this I can agree with; but I dread no less the rule of a species that can rejoice at such a victory."[6]

The Politics of Nationalism

In terms of the politics of nationalism, the fatherland of revolutionaries was a special case in 1848. France's existence as a nation-state was already well-established. Hence the program of the 1848 French Revolution contained no national demands. Everywhere else, on the other hand, the building of a nation-state or at least the achievement of national autonomy were among the goals of the revolutionaries and the more moderate reformers. Nation-states were part of the catalog of demands of the revolutions in the Italian states, in the German Confederation and, to some extent, in the Danubian Principalities of Moldavia and Wallachia as well. In the Habsburg Monarchy, the plans of the Germans, Hungarians and Italians for the formation of their respective nation-states, and the plans and demands for autonomy by other nationalities, especially Croats and Czechs, overlapped and hindered each other. Polish nationalist revolutionaries were, from the beginning, faced with a package of problems for which the "springtime of the peoples" offered no solution. As a nation without a state they would have had to reverse the partitions of the eighteenth and nineteenth centuries and, at the same time, fend off territorial claims by other nationalities.

In Denmark as well, the revolution set off intense discussions about and conflicts over the politics of nationalism. Should the long road from nordic empire to a Danish nation-state be brought to an end in 1848? Could the Danish nation include in its state the duchies of Schleswig and Holstein, populated mostly by Germans? Intense debate arose on this point in the Danish and German national revolutions, and this led to a war in which the Prussian king sought to enforce the territorial claims of the German nation with armed force. The European Great Powers intervened and forced a truce, which postponed the bloody decision until 1864, when it was finally reached in the Danish-German war.

By comparison, the dispute between the German nationalist movement and the Netherlands over the national affiliation of the duchy of Limburg ended without difficulty. Here, too, however, the explosive power of the nation-state option was unveiled, released in all places where national territorial claims competed. Even in Norway, a liberal state with a strong parliament, voices became louder in 1848 demanding a foreign policy independent of Sweden, to which the Norwegians were tied by a common king. Much more dramatic were the problems in east-central Europe. There, in 1848, the nationalities, with the exception of the Poles, for the first time "ever in their modern history, were perceived from outside as distinct peoples by European public opinion."[7]

The revolution was faced with an enormous task. In order to fulfil the revolutionary program of the European peoples, states needed to be merged and state confederations that included many nationalities broken up. Everywhere the problems were different, but everywhere war threatened. All the core countries of the 1848 revolution waged wars of unification and separation. The only exception was France, where the demands for a nation-state had already been satisfied. However, even the French Republic took up arms; it intervened militarily in 1849 in Italy against the Roman Republic.

In Germany the nationalist revolutionary program demanded a unification of the states of the German Confederation into a united nation-state, but at the same time—if this were to succeed peacefully, as the majority of the Frankfurt National Assembly in the end reluctantly desired—that along all its borders, parts of the Confederation be released from the union of the nation-state. In the north, the question turned on Holstein and on Schleswig, on which claims were also raised, in the west, on Limburg, in the east and the south, on the German and non-German territories of the Habsburg Monarchy. Indeed, a transformation of the entire German Confederation into a German nation-state would have burdened it with the multinational legacy of the Holy Roman Empire and probably provoked a European war, as the interests of too many states and nations would have been violated.

Confronted with this situation, the German national revolution acquiesced in the formation of a small German nation-state. In terms of power politics, this solution would have been acceptable to Germany's European neighbors; it failed because the most powerful German princes refused to be degraded into subordinate territorial rulers in a nation-state. In 1848, a majority of the National Assembly rejected the idea of breaking this blockade by means of a second revolution and a civil war against refractory monarchs, especially the Prussian and Habsburg rulers. In so doing, the assembly's majority remained true to its original stance of seeking consensus with the hereditary ruling houses. Nonetheless, the intra-German war of 1866 and the Franco-Prussian War of 1870 succeed where the 1848 revolution had failed in subordinating the German dynasties to the politics of nationalism.

In Hungary, the problems were different. It was not, as in Germany or Italy, a question of combining existing states. Instead the historical ties to the Habsburgs' multinational monarchy needed to be examined and broken off, or at least loosened. In addition, however, relations of the Hungarian government with non-Hungarian nationalities were also tested in 1848. The Hungarian kingdom was, like the Habsburg Monarchy, a multinational structure. The Magyars dominated their kingdom politically, economically, and socially, but the other nationalities formed a majority of the population. Unlike the Hungarians, they did not wish to leave the Habsburg Monarchy in 1848/49. They demanded, however, national autonomy within the multinational empire which was to be reorganized along federalist lines. Moreover, the Croats in particular exploited the Austrian-Hungarian war for an attempt to separate from the Hungarian crown and to place themselves instead directly under the Habsburg emperor. These national conflicts broke out as soon as the revolution had opened the space for political action by the nationalities. Because political and social revolution were inseparably bound to the national revolution, the brief dream of the "springtime of the peoples" quickly, and permanently, died in the national confusion of eastern central Europe.

In Italy, too, the national revolution inevitably led to a national war, as the individual Italian states could only be united into an Italian nation-state if Lombardy and Venetia were liberated from Austrian rule. The Habsburg emperor was not, however, willing to surrender these states peacefully. In this, he was supported not only by the military leadership and the court, but also by a large part of the Austrian revolutionary movement. Even the Hungarian revolutionary government gave support of a hard line by the Habsburg leadership towards the Italian national revolution, as the Hungarian government did not dare to withdraw its troops from the Habsburg army in Italy.

Hence, in the Habsburg Monarchy all national conflicts overlapped. Individually, the national revolutions in Germany, Italy and Hungary presented a limited challenge, but together they threatened the existence of the massive multinational state, whose historical form would have been erased. It is therefore not surprising that leading groups and all those who attached their futures to the empire did not wish to allow its transformation into an Austrian petty state without a fight. They therefore responded to the national revolutions in their own empire with war and to the nation-state concepts of the *Paulskirche* and of Prussia, which would have separated Germany from Austria, with threats of war. Thus the "springtime of the peoples" of the 1848 revolution ended everywhere in nationalist conflicts. In this, the forces arising from the revolutionary idea of nation became clearly visible for the first time, forces that would transform the European continent in the second half of the nineteenth century and would eventually lead to the First World War.

Effects of the Revolution

Among both contemporaries and subsequent historians, it is undisputed that the revolution influenced the course of the nineteenth century. This radiation of the s implied in the titles of important works that appeared after the Second World War. Hence François Fejtö speaks of the "opening of an era" for Europe, Maurice Agulhon of "apprenticeship of the republic" for France, while 1848 is seen by Raymond Grew as the antecedent of the Risorgimento and by Theodore Hamerow as the preparatory phase of the formation of the German Empire.[8] However, opinions are still greatly divided on the extent, form, and results of this influence on the respective national histories, social classes, and political groups as well as on cultural patterns of perception and interpretation. For some it was a revolution of intellectuals, for others an "uprising of the burghers," here "a bourgeois-democratic revolution," there a "failed bourgeois" one, for some "an intra-Jewish turning point," for others a "historical paradox." These assessments, to which others may be added, depend on the perspective from which the revolution is approached and on the questions one asks of it, but especially on whether one focuses on the individual success of the revolution or on its global failure.

Depending on whether one seeks continuities or breaks between 1848 and the present or one whether one measures revolutionary attempts at solving problems against the complex situation or against the premises of a revolutionary strategy developed ex post, one reaches varying conclusions. If attention is focused on failure, then the social conditions unfavorable to revolution, inadequate organizational forms or the lack of charismatic leadership are placed in the foreground. Looking beyond a revolution that failed everywhere—with the exception of Switzerland—in its immediate goals, however, one begins to focus on the question of its influence on medium and long-term processes of development. On this point an assessment is influenced by whether one concentrates more on short- or medium-term perspectives, the institutional effects of the revolution or its consequences for modes of behavior and expectations, for cultural and political practices. That all these various approaches to the effects of the 1848 revolution are and will continue to be tested indicates the continued strong interest in the subject, but also point to the difficulty in approaching the question in such a disciplined manner that premises of argumentation, and the results dependent on them, become clear.

A study of the effects of a revolution is especially subject to the danger of teleological argument and cause and effect relations that are not very meaningful (as opposed to weighing a given event as a single factor in a comprehensive ensemble). The manifold lines of development that lead from such a complex phenomenon as a revolution may on the one hand be perceived in a linearly narrow way. On the other hand, later structures, processes, and values are often reduced to the influence of the revolution as a "turning-point." Karl Griewank, in his observations of the first long-term anniversaries of the revolution, warned of the dangers of too narrow a line of argument: "The 'forces' which we include among the causes … contain, like the observed consequences, both objective governmental, economical, social and intellectual factors and subjective motivations, and are all interrelated. It is a relatively large complex of facts and motives which have to be drawn out of the interwoven net of the historically effective, as units that act and are acted upon to make visible the essential elements of our investigation."[9]

Rather than an attempt at writing a history of the effects of the revolution, one that raises the question of the lessons and consequences that individual political currents or eras drew from it, the following will consider the relationship between the major processes of change in the nineteenth century and the influence, whether retarding or accelerating, of the 1848 revolution on them. Initially, however, it bears repeating that neither all European societies nor all parts of these societies were equally affected by the revolution. A comprehensive history of effects therefore also needs a differentiated approach to non-effects. The authors of this volume have dedicated their efforts to this difficult task, often neglected or only mentioned in passing in histories of the revolution. It should also be noted that even those areas not directly touched by the revolution did not remain zones of quiescence. No region and no social group could totally evade the pressure to act arising from revolutionary events. This was true, as mentioned above, even for Russia.

A comparison of politically active centers, regions, groups unaffected by the revolution can easily become misleading if it is not kept in mind that Europe grew together into a communication zone in 1848 in which the revolution had consequences even from a geographical or social distance. While England, and the Netherlands, Greece and Russia did not undertake the process of revolutionary changes, influences emanating from Paris and Berlin, Vienna, Naples or Milan were too palpable not to provoke reaction from statesmen, diplomats, and the military. Unrest in many cities and regions was in sum too disquieting not to have an effect on public opinion, among rulers and citizens alike. No less a person than Alexis de Tocqueville observed this mechanism when arriving in his home department of Manche in April 1848: "For although a certain sort of demagogic agitation prevailed among the workers of the towns, in the country all the landowners, whatever their origins, antecedents, education or means, had come together and seemed to form a single unit: all the old political hatreds and rivalries of caste and wealth had vanished. Neither jealousy nor pride separated the peasant from the rich man any longer, or the bourgeois from the gentleman; instead, there was mutual confidence, respect and goodwill. Ownership constituted a sort of fraternity linking all who had anything ...."[10]

Here the fraternity of the revolution is juxtaposed with that of the counter-revolution. Information in general, in fact information in particular—in which the aims and forms of the revolution were distorted and coarsened or deliberately manipulated—set off a reaction among those not actively involved in the revolutionary events. Counter-revolutionary agitation in Vienna in the autumn of 1848 comes especially to mind; illuminating are also the reports received by European public opinion about the Paris June uprising, or the fear in "civilized" Europe of a peasant Jacquerie fostered by rumors of the "Galician massacre" of 1846. Revolutions are much too striking and dynamic events not to leave traces even in those regions and groups isolated from them. Even those who fought against the revolution could not completely evade the dialectic of revolution and counter-revolution. Simply an opposition to, and mobilization against an alleged red danger is one effect of the revolution. Above all one could gain political experience without actively participating simply by looking across the border.

Regarding the Short-Term Failure of the Revolution

One of the standard conclusions regarding the revolution is that 1848 ended in failure. "Both in Germany and in most other countries involved in Europe one did not, admittedly, celebrate the memory of a victorious revolution, but the memory of a failed one," wrote Rudolf Stadelmann in 1948 in his centennial observations.[11] Such a view can be quite plausibly justified. Important aims of the revolution were not achieved. Europe neither became a continent of parliamentary constitutional governments, nor were central civil rights enacted. Freedom of the press, opinion and assembly were not abolished by the post-revolutionary reaction; the governments placed in office by the revolution also restricted them as they restricted personal liberty. The social question became a subject in 1848 which people expected the revolution to answer, but the answers they received were insufficient. The legal status of the peasants was permanently improved in many states, but their social circumstances, and even more, those of the semi-peasants and farm workers, remained precarious. The nationalist hopes of broad sections of the population could not be fulfilled. The bourgeoisie was not able to enforce its claims to power. The ancien regime survived the revolution, but in the long-term it was a Pyrrhic victory. This line of argument, which can be read in thousands of studies, can indeed base itself on evidence from nearly all European countries. The following section will return to this point.

It would be too simple to counter this gloomy balance of failure with the example of Switzerland, in which the old patrician rule was replaced by one of the middle classes, or England, where liberals had strengthened their position by integrating radical protest. References to Belgium and the Netherlands or Norway could also brighten the image of failure. However, the topos of failure should not be differentiated with national success stories from the reform belt of the revolution, but with sectoral examples. Even when the revolution, in a national and pan-European perspective, did not achieve the aims it had set itself, partial successes or—as the revolutionaries would put it—accomplishments should not be forgotten. They are generally not to be found in the macro-structures, but show, nonetheless, why Europe did not return to its prerevolutionary state after 1848.

Sectoral comparisons may be applied in quite different ways. One promising path would be to compare local and regional developments in the various European societies. Some of the studies in this volume take this approach in order to avoid juxtaposing national histories as units with one another, for such a procedure, as a rule, involves the confrontation of different models of interpretation. The debate about the "German *Sonderweg*" is one outstanding example. The 1848 revolution plays a prominent role here: Germany, the country without a successful revolution, is the topos. National comparison here means that German history and the history of Western states—comparisons are almost only made with the West—are reduced to a core interpretation in order to produce, so to speak, a condensed history that allows for comparison. This process has stimulated research as it has directed critical questions at German history.

This achievement remains even if, in the meantime, scholarship has taken leave from the interpretative model of a "German *Sonderweg*" as basically involving the comparison of two fictions: the fiction that the essentials of modern German history can be reduced to the peculiarities of a *Sonderweg* in Europe, and the fiction of a clear, unified Western counter-model. National historiography appears to lag behind new perspectives, inasmuch as the latter are not comprehensive, whether in regard to the state or to society as a whole. Recent work on the revolution has drawn the consequences from this, by following the complexity of the revolutionary processes into the life-worlds of the local level. This current of research, however, has scarcely dared to engage in any cross-European comparisons. A few attempts in this direction can be found in this volume. It is not our intention to present their results here. Rather, a few selected aspects will be briefly examined in which the revolution bequeathed lasting consequences.

Among the greatest achievements of the 1848 revolution was the abolition of feudal domination in the countryside. In large parts of Europe, the rural population only gained accession to the legal structure of "civil society" in 1848. Feudal rights pertaining to persons and compulsory labor obligations duties were abolished without compensation; other encumbrances on the land were abolished with compensation. Property is holy—the revolution respected this fundamental principle in its legislation. In the words of Gustave Flaubert: "Now property was raised to the level of Religion and became indistinguishable from God. The attacks made on it took on the appearance of sacrilege, almost of cannibalism."[12] The eighteen-forty-eighters were not cannibals. They completed the process of defeudalization in most European countries without devaluing chartered titles to property.

The revolution of 1848 was a colossal step forward on the road to a modern agrarian structure, for most of the lands of the Habsburg Empire, but also for regions in Germany, east of the Rhine. Essentially, 1848 marked the concluding points for legal developments. The economic problems of agriculture, and above all rural poverty could not be abolished with an act of legislation. For Italy in general, and for the territories to the west of the Rhine, this success of the revolution was of little importance because the really touchy agricultural problem was rural poverty, and because the French Revolution of 1789 and Napoleonic expansion had already eliminated encumbrances on the land. In the countries of eastern central Europe, on the other hand, abolition of compulsory serf labor and of encumbrances on the land was the central social problem. This change affected that large majority of the population employed in agriculture, improving their personal legal status and the status of their property.

The agrarian reforms of 1848 followed currents of developments that had begun long before. Is this, however, a reason to see in these reforms "no major turning point"?[13] The revolution forced a leap in developments that could no longer be reversed. It shortened the road on which all societies were already traveling without knowing how long the way was. This state of uncertainty was brought to an end by the forty-eighters.

The significance of agrarian reform becomes clear when compared with reforms in non-agricultural production, for which 1848 brought no break. Freedom of occupation remained in those places where it had already existed, but this was also true for the guilds, where they had survived. They would continue to be preserved, even if only for some years. In Germany and Austria, most of them were abolished only around 1860; in Italy, at various times. Seemingly, the strength of the masters' lobby and the power of guild organizational forms to stabilize the urban status quo was so highly rated that authorities and parliaments did not yet dare to abolish them.

For the bourgeois emancipation movement as well, some successes were obtained as an immediate effect of the revolution. A constitutional form of government, to be sure, could not be introduced in all parts of Europe. In the kingdom of the Two Sicilies, in Tuscany, in Parma, and Modena, in the Papal States, in the Habsburg Monarchy and, in the wake of reaction, in Spain as well, the prerevolutionary, antiparliamentary state of affairs was restored. However, in Prussia and in the kingdom of Piedmont-Savoy the power of the ruler remained restricted by a constitution decreed by the monarch and by the monarchical Statuto Albertino respectively.

Hence, at least in a part of Europe, liberal demands for a constitution were fulfilled in places where none had previously existed.

The revolution also showed direct successes in emancipating population groups held in inferior status up to then and in the enactment of freedom of religion. Equal rights for Jews, which had only existed in France, the Netherlands, and Belgium before 1848, were introduced in numerous states through the revolution. In some it was soon reversed—for example in Rome—or only brought in later—as in Switzerland. Not only for this reason are the results of the revolution for Jewish emancipation ambiguous. The revolution began in many societies with antisemitic unrest, which, however, became less significant in the process of the revolution. Nonetheless it must be ascertained: with the surge in emancipation, antisemitism was also strengthened. The two went hand in hand—emancipation and its rejection.

Among the opponents of Jewish emancipation, a number of motives converged. On top of traditional Christian antisemitism came social fears, which become much more prominent in a period when everything seemed to be changing. Against a background of widespread poverty, many saw the Jews as unwanted competitors for scarce social welfare resources of the state and the municipality. Also already apparent was a form of enmity towards Jews of the postemancipation era, for which the new term antisemitism was coined in the second third of the nineteenth century. Nonetheless, in spite of these warning signs for the future, for the Jews of Europe 1848 meant an important step on the road to civic equality and to a self-perception as citizens possessing equal rights.

In France, the February Revolution placed the emancipation of slaves once again on the historical agenda. In the work of the French Revolution of 1789 it had remained an uncompleted project, which Napoleon I then totally eliminated. Republicans had already spoken out against slavery before 1848, and above all Victor Schoelcher had advocated its abolishment. On 27 April 1848, the French national assembly concluded this act of emancipation. And finally, freedom of religion and the decoupling of rights of citizenship from membership in a certain religious confession also belonged to the principles proclaimed in 1848 and anchored in numerous constitutions. As with no other revolution, the ardor for liberty included the demand for freedom of religion.

Among the direct successes of the revolution is finally also an intellectual awareness of problems in society, which led to administrative innovations in many states. Hence the problems of agriculture were given consideration in the ministries of agriculture in France and in many German states, and the great reforming power credited to the education system is shown in the efforts made to increase the powers of the ministries of education. In Paris, the provisional government even proposed the creation of an Ecole d'administration to improve the training of civil servants. The revolution encouraged, among other things, processes of bureaucratization and professionalization both in order to suppress social aspirations and problems, and also in order to deal with them.

This summary of specific accomplishments of the revolution, already visible in the short term and which should not be subsumed by the topos of failure, still requires expansion. At the same time, a systematic and comparative tour of various aspects of politics would make more apparent, but at the same time make clear that numerous civil liberties and rights of participation did not survive the defeat of the revolution. Those areas in which the revolution could be directly effective were greatly restricted both in the range and vehemence of the reaction in nearly all states affected by the revolution,. It was above all the military which, as an institution, resisted constitutional endeavors like a *rocher de bronze* after having everywhere militarily defeated the revolution. Nonetheless, the necessary view towards the medium- and long-term effects of the revolution should not overshadow the short-term ones.

The Medium- and Long-Term Effects of the 1848 Revolution.

There is much to be said for pinpointing an intermediate stage between the middle of the century and the age of mass politics and mass democracy, one that displays the features corresponding to those developed by the social sciences for a period of transition. This period of transition was not equally long in individual European societies. One criterion for measuring it is provided by the franchise, in which the nineteenth century placed considerable political/symbolic value. Taking universal manhood suffrage as a yardstick, the period of transition ended in Spain in 1868 and in 1886, as the franchise was once again restricted in the period between 1879 and 1886. Cisleithenian Austria granted all men the right to vote in 1907, Italy in 1912 and the Netherlands only in November 1917. In Belgium, the circle of those enfranchised was expanded through a pluralistic suffrage in 1893, but the votes of the rich and educated were given more weight. Only in 1918 was this restriction dropped. In the German Empire the period of transition to "mass politics" would end in 1871 according to this criterion, if it were not for a continuation of restrictions on the franchise in the individual states and communes. In France, the universal suffrage for men could not be reversed after 1848, even though Napoleon III restricted it in practice through administrative and manipulative means.

All in all, it may be said that the democratization of the franchise achieved in 1848 could not be defended. The level of 1848 was only achieved decades later in many states. Equality of male voters remained an ideal in many European states before 1914, even if this goal was getting ever closer. The failure of the revolution thus considerably delayed the transition into the age of mass democracy.

Another chronology would emerge if one inquired about the creation of a constitutional-parliamentary form of government. Then the transition can be dated in 1879 in France, when the victories of the republicans in parliamentary and municipal elections put an end to all attempts at political and social restoration. In Austria, one would have to see the 1860s as a first phase, especially the February Charter of 1861 as the beginning and 1867, in which the constitutional monarchy was introduced and reorganized in the Austrian-Hungarian "settlement." In Italy, one could take the 1882 extension of the franchise, primarily the work of the parliamentary left, as a break in the period of transition. The Netherlands, Switzerland, Norway, Great Britain, and Belgium already had significant successes in parliamentarization behind them in 1848.

In contrast to a democratization of the franchise, the success of the forty-eighters in issuing constitutions and strengthening the rights of parliaments could be more quickly taken up again and expanded upon after the end of the period of reaction. In some states, indeed, the end of the revolution did not mean a break in this respect. Except for Tsarist Russia, the prerogatives of the rulers were greatly restricted by constitutions in the decades after 1848 and opportunities for parliaments to participate in the legislative process were codified. Developments thus followed the path that the 1848 revolution had set, but not themselves established. The revolution accelerated and "Europeanized" prerevolutionary beginnings. This may help to explain why the break after the end of the revolution was less severe in this respect.

To measure the period of transition to "mass politics," one could also argue with the condition of civil society, examining possibilities for citizens to organize their interests in associations and parties. Attention would have to be given to both legal provisions and chances of making use of them. In reaction to the enormous number of associations and newspapers that appeared in 1848 and that deeply influenced the course of the revolution, the European states significantly restricted freedom of the press and of association after 1848. They sought to take from "civil society" the possibility of communicative organization. By the 1860s at the latest, this attempt at blockade collapsed. Here, too, the 1848 revolution did not introduce anything fundamentally new. However, it was successful in greatly extending possibilities of communication socially and geographically. A new level of development was reached which the postrevolutionary era could draw on.

The following summary holds true for all three areas that have been used for a brief characterization of the transition to modern mass democracy. The 1848 revolution accelerated and extended the circles of those entitled to and capable of participation. The democratized suffrage of 1848 mobilized politically social groups that had up to then been distanced from politics, despite the limitations on the franchise, which continued to exist in the various states to a greater or lesser degree. It also became apparent that a formally democratic franchise could be combined with an authoritarian non-parliamentary political structure, as Louis Napoleon demonstrated in France.

In order to mobilize increasingly larger sections of the population, propaganda and organization became indispensable. Eighteen forty-eight laid the foundations, on which the political life in the second half of the nineteenth century could be built. Newspapers, flyers, and placards can be named in this respect, as well as festivals, parades, rumors, and songs. Even if the birth of political parties in some places can be dated to the prerevolutionary decades, it was the revolution of 1848 that led to the rise of permanent organizations and the development of programs with which political currents distinguished themselves from one another and stood for elections. This greatly determined the political landscape in the following decades. Especially in France, geographic distribution of central political options remained surprisingly stable. From 1849 onwards, for example, the left, in the broadest sense, has always had its electoral successes in the same areas. This continuity persisted well into the twentieth century. In Germany this effect is less clear, especially as the political scene was made more complex with the Social Democrats and the Catholic Center Party after 1871, and the establishment of the nation-state created new conditions. Above all in Germany, but not only there, the separation of bourgeois and proletarian democracy was a dominant feature of the second half of the century. In France, however, the experience of revolution did not tear apart the ties that bound bourgeois and proletarian supporters of the republic. The republican ideal was such a broad church that quite different standpoints could find a place within it.

For the modern form of party, 1848 was a phase of experiment and trial. Subsequently, however, a period of political persecution and restricted political discourse began in the centers of the revolution. There needs to be a comparison between the different European countries about whether and how the parties, in their structures and programs, accommodated themselves to this new framework set by the state authorities. There is doubtless a typological distinction between the parties that were able to develop under parliamentary forms of government and those that had to adapt to political repression and restricted possibilities of parliamentary influence. England, Belgium, Norway, the Netherlands and, to a certain extent, France of the July monarchy, offer examples of the first type of development; Germany, Austria, Italy and most the east central European states are examples of the second.

Unlike the case of the revolution of 1789, for 1848 there is a lack of studies giving detailed information on oral tradition, the local presence of revolutionaries, and the spread of revolutionary symbols or rituals in the postrevolutionary period. The memory of festivals and flags, parades and slogans, barricades and songs cannot have been totally erased under the pressure of the period of reaction. Whether and how these memories were tied to political organizations, however, or were instrumentalized—as by Napoleon III, for example—still needs to be examined in studies on political culture.

More well-known is the effect of the 1848 revolution in "agenda-setting" for the nineteenth century (Jonathan Sperber). For with the democratic rights of participation and civil liberties, the revolutionaries raised central problems and expressed them in important texts that were then continually discussed in the second half of the century. Reality remained well behind demands, but it was measured against them. To this extent, the 1848 revolution set standards which remained valid well after the failure of the revolution itself.

The year 1848 is held to be an important stage in the history of modern nationalism. Nationalism became a mass movement throughout Europe at the latest during the revolution. It was encouraged by the politicization fostered by the revolution, and the space it created for potential nation-states. Which specific connections can be established between the revolution of 1848 and the phenomena of nationalism, the formation of nation-states, and the internal creation of nations?

In 1848, no nation-state arose through revolution. In Germany and Hungary, Italy and Poland the nation-state was among the central aims of the revolution, but social forces were too weak to overcome domestic and foreign resistance. Above all, the nationalist movements lacked the military power necessary to force through one's own nation-state against the competing claims of other nations, if necessary with military force. Nationalist revolutionaries showed themselves quite willing to make use of force. This was even the case in Denmark.

With the course of the French Revolution of 1789 in mind, contemporaries were as well aware of the close nexus between war and the formation of a nation-state, as they were of the dangerous social dynamic that had developed out of warfare in 1792 and thereafter. Because in 1848, in contrast to 1789, international conflicts could be kept under control and a European war could be avoided, domestic politics in the revolution were much more moderate. This relationship between domestic and foreign policy moderation contributed greatly to the failure of all attempts at forming a nation-state in 1848/49. Nonetheless, decisive steps were taken toward the establishment of a small German empire and toward Italian national unification, although there is no reason to see this as the beginning of an inevitable process. However, in Germany and Italy the nation-state was not only discussed in public and in the institutions as a vision of the future. Its competing configurations and the strategies to realize them were also tested in political practice—from constitutions and draft constitutions via liberal language policies of the "saving deed," up to the limited wars that Prussia, the Habsburg Monarchy and Piedmont, the leading Italian power, waged in the name of their own nation and against the national hopes of others. Thus the nation-state became an aim that did not disappear even after the revolution.

This aim was primarily championed by liberals and democrats in 1848, but monarchs and the old elite also found themselves forced to take up the theme. Especially in eastern central Europe, the idea of the nation, in part still defined in terms of a corporate society of orders, found many defenders among aristocrats and conservatives. The national endeavors of the Hungarian and Bohemian nobility provide a good example of this. Altogether, conservative attitudes remained ambiguous, even if the involvement of the monarchs in the national revolution accelerated a process of adaptation by the nobility and conservatism of the nation and the ideas of nationalism in many states, including Germany and Italy. In the second half of the century the consequences of this development would become apparent when nationalism became a populist ideology whose core had shifted from the left to the right.

In 1848, on the other hand, not only conservatives, but also liberal nationalists distanced themselves from the mass mobilizing power of nationalist slogans. Liberals attempted to socially limit involvement in national unity to the educated and propertied and in its ideas to a liberal program of rights and liberties. Insofar as the idea of nation was bound with national revolutionary aims—as among German democrats, or the supporters of Mazzini or Kossuth—it created a problem for the liberals. Liberalism and "mass politics," as once again became apparent, were counterpoles.

Eighteen forty-eight was also an important stage in the internal process of formation of the nation. National structures increasingly gained acceptance over parochial or local ones. The communication network took on national dimensions, and parties and interest associations were increasingly active at the national level—in general political mobilization in the revolution led to a nationalization of ways of thinking. One need only recall the effect of national parliaments. They spoke to the entire nation, and the circle of voters was greater than ever before.

All this contributed to a nationalization of politics and society. One should not, however, exaggerate this development. The limits of internal nation-building also deserve attention. Thus, for example, even in the western European states a national school system remained a dream for the future. In 1848 it was firmly demanded. The transport network was not yet very dense, but it still helped make it easier for participants to reach large political gatherings than in the years before 1848.

The revolution also made an important contribution to internal nation-building in that social groups up until then not involved in politics were mobilized politically. Nonetheless, there continued to be clear limits on the possibilities for the effects of nationalism as a mass movement. Women were still at the fringe of the nationalist movement, even when there was a rise in the level of participation in 1848. In Germany many Catholics loyal to the church championed ideas of nation which contrasted with those of the Protestant majority. Above all, a distinct gap between city and country remained, even if the revolution and especially the national revolution contributed to bringing a national orientation to the countryside. This seems to be most obviously the case in eastern central Europe, where the national revolution, as mentioned above, became the integrative core of the entire revolutionary process.

As much as the revolution extended the social range of nationalism and advanced internal nation-building, it was only one link in a long developmental process, which continued, even in western Europe, until the end of the nineteenth century, and in eastern central Europe and Italy well into the twentieth. That which developed in the second half of the century—nationalism as a political ideology, which demanded the unconditional priority of the nation—had not yet determined the revolutionary events of 1848. Loyalty to the nation was easily reconcilable with a loyalty to region or dynasty in Germany and Bohemia, Italy and Hungary in 1848—indeed the region and the monarch were held to be important factors in the process of nation-building.

The nation itself was not yet so narrowly defined through a process of inclusion and exclusion that linguistic and ethnic diversity appeared irreconcilable with it. However, the future of an integral nationalism was already apparent in 1848. In those places where it was a question of national existence or self-determination, the appeal to the nation could take on an exclusive character. That was not only the case in regions of clashing nationalisms, such as Schleswig and Posen, but was also apparent in the standpoints of Mazzini or Kossuth. The idea of nation—one promising democratization and progress—was at the center of the revolution of 1848, but its dark side, made up of exclusion, images of national enemies, and a willingness to go to war, also became apparent. The 1848 revolution did not create this Janus face of nationalism, but it did make it more prominent than before and greatly extended its attractiveness geographically and socially.

If dealing with the past—however that past may be conveyed—expresses problems of the present day, then this interest has not past the 1848 revolution by. This has been demonstrated in the reception of events at the time of the revolution's fiftieth anniversary and its centenary. At present, research into the revolution can be connected to both scholarly and political discussions. In historical scholarship, the influence of historical anthropology, the history of everyday life, and cultural history has led to a growing interest in the fundamental processes of mobilization and politicization during the revolution, as well as in the forms of linguistic, ritual, and symbolic expression in which its problems and demands were formulated. These research interests do not necessarily overlap with questions arising from a critical view of the present. These are directed rather toward the difficulties of a renewed process of internal nation-building begun in Germany after the collapse of the GDR or the explosiveness of national exclusion and incorporation in the former Yugoslavia, the territories of the former Soviet Union, as well as in Belgium. An interest in the nationalism of the 1848 revolution is doubtless the result of this present-day experience. At the same time, and in light of the debate on the difficulty of securing and developing democratic structures, and in view of increasing social inequality, the struggles, programs and actions of the revolutionaries of the mid-nineteenth century gain a new meaning. They were faced with serious and interrelated social, political and national problems; the solutions they developed to them would continue to have an effect for a long time afterward.

Notes

We wish to thank the authors of this volume for important insights and information, without mentioning them individually, and without explicitly noting divergent positions. The contributions and the selected bibliography provide the most important secondary literature. References will only be provided here for quotations.

1. *K. Marx/F. Engels,* Werke, Bd. 5, Berlin (Ost) 1959, S. 65 (Neue Rheinische Zeitung, Nr. 14 v. 14. Juni 1848).

2. Fanny Lewald, *Erinnerungen aus dem Jahr 1848,* edited by V. D. Schäfer, (Frankfurt, 1968) 7 (28 February 1848). These "memoirs," which first appeared in 1850, were put together from letters.

3. Gustave Flaubert, *The Sentimental Education,* trans. Robert Baldick (London, 1964), 291, 295.

4. *Der Grenzbote* of 29 November 1851, quoted in Dieter Langewiesche, *Republik und Republikaner. Von der historischen Entwertung eines politischen Begriffs* (Stuttgart, 1993), 38.

5. Michelle Perrot, "Stepping Out," in *Emerging Feminism from Revolution to World War,* trans. Arthur Goldhammer and Joan Bond Sax, (eds.) Geneviève Friasse and Michelle Perrot, 449-81, here 479. Vol. 4 of *A History of Women in the West,* edited by Georges Duby and Michelle Perot, 5 vols. (Cambridge MA, 1992-94).

6. *Gabriel Riessers gesammelte Werke,* ed. by M. Isler, Vol. 1 (Frankfurt. 1867), 574.

7. Rudolf Jaworski, "Revolution und Nationalitätenfrage in Ostmitteleuropa 1848/49," in *1848/49. Revolutionen in Ostmitteleuropa,* ed. by Rudolf Jaworski and Robert Luft Munich, 1996), 371-391, here 375.

8. Francois Fejtö (ed.), *The Opening of an Era, 1848: an Historical Symposium,* trans. Hugh Shelley (London, 1948); Maurice Agulhon, *1848 ou l'apprentissage de la république, 1848-1852,* (Paris, 1973) [*The Republican Experiment, 1848-1852,* trans. Janet Lloyd (Cambridge and New York, 1983)]; Raymond Grew, *A Sterner Plan for Italian Unity. The Italian National Society and the Risorgimento* (Princeton, 1963); Theodore Hamerow, *Restoration, Revolution, Reaction: Economics and Politics in Germany, 1815-1871* (Princeton, 1957).

9. Karl Griewank, "Ursachen und Folgen des Scheiterns der deutschen Revolution von 1848," in *Die deutsche Revolution von 1848/49,* ed. by Dieter Langewiesche, (Darmstadt, 1983), 59-90, here 62.

10. Alexis de Tocqueville, *Recollections,* ed. by J.P. Mayer and A.P. Kerr, trans. George Lawrence (Garden City, NY, 1970), 87.

11. Rudolf Stadelmann, "Das Jahr 1848 und die deutsche Geschichte" in *Revolution,* ed. by Langewiesche, 21-38, here 21.

12. Flaubert, *The Sentimental Education,* 295.

13. Peter Heumos, "Die Bauernbefreiung in den böhmischen Ländern 1848. Anmerkungen zu den ökonomischen, sozialen und politischen Verhältnissen der Agrargesellschaft," in *1848/49:,* ed. by Jaworski and Luft, 221-237, quote on 237.

The explosion is unavoidable and will be terrible! (Anonymous Italian Cartoon)

The giant sea-snake, like many that have appeared in 1848
(Illustrirte Zeitung, Leipzig, no. 287, 30 December 1848, 436)

Chapter 2

"THE HOLY STRUGGLE AGAINST ANARCHY"

The Development of Counter-Revolution in 1848

Roger Price

Revolution involves the armed seizure of power by groups formerly largely excluded from political and/or social power. Counter-revolution in its turn represents an effort to restore their diminished authority by those who have experienced or perceive a threat to their status and vital interests. Each generation of historians has its own particular interests. In the past historians and sociologists have tended to focus on revolution rather than counter-revolution, sharing perhaps some of the dreams that inspired revolutionaries. These dreams have since faded or turned into nightmares and it is time to turn towards the analysis of counter-revolution. Even if one does not accept an entirely negative judgement of revolution, objectively revolution and counter-revolution are clearly inseparable, the historical actors engaged in contention for power. This essay will examine the strategies for resistance to revolution developed by social elites during a period of particularly intense social crisis. It will attempt to develop an understanding of power relationships within diverse European political and social systems, as well as an appreciation of the "multilayered complexity of political reality."[1] What is counter-revolution? When, with respect to the specific circumstances of 1848, did it begin? Who engaged in counter-revolution, whether partially or completely? What were their objectives? What did they actually achieve?

News of the February Revolution in Paris came as a profound shock both in the rest of France and throughout Europe, and this in spite of the severe economic and social crisis and widespread tension that had reinforced criticism of existing regimes and already provoked revolt in Palermo and the mainland provinces of the Kingdom of Naples. As a result existing institutions seemed everywhere to be under assault. Governments invariably thought of resistance and it seems likely that if they had been willing to unleash unrestrained military force this would have succeeded. There were two major obstacles—the first was psychological in nature, of the kind that had prevailed in the Tuileries Palace in Paris on 23 February, where surprise at the scale of the crisis and the rapid deterioration in the regime's position inspired the kind of paralysis shamefully described by such participants as Adolphe Thiers and Charles de Rémusat.[2] Subsequently Joseph Maria von Radowitz in a report to the Prussian King Friedrich Wilhelm from Vienna would note with disgust that "many have the growing feeling that any struggle against the impending doom will be in vain."[3]

The second obstacle was practical/political in nature, namely a reluctance to risk a bloody civil war. The quality of political leadership was of crucial importance. In Britain and Belgium previous liberal concessions, together with an obvious willingness to resort to repressive action, helped to prevent revolution. In Russia and even Spain, repression combined with the weakness of opposition to maintain the status quo. In a crisis, centralized monarchical political systems depended for their effectiveness upon a competent ruler, or at least the effective delegation of power to subordinates. The aging Louis-Philippe, the indecisive Friedrich-Wilhelm and the chronically ill Austrian Emperor Ferdinand, surrounded by squabbling advisors, were not up to the task. To escape the fate of the French Monarchy, governments felt obliged to make concessions to liberal and democratic critics who were willing and able to mobilize popular support. Thus mass demonstrations followed by street fighting led to the collapse of governmental authority in Vienna on 13-15 March and in Berlin on the 18-19th. In Vienna Radowitz saw the departure of Metternich and the emperor's promise of a constituent assembly as symbolizing the collapse of "the most secure dam against the revolutionary tide."[4] With it even such determined old soldiers as King Wilhelm of Württemberg, who had looked for military support from Berlin and Vienna, felt bound to concede. There were widespread promises of constitutions, elections and more immediately the nomination of liberal ministers.

The Revolutionaries' Weakness and Divisions

To a substantial degree counter-revolution would succeed because of the limited support for, and divisions among, those who had initially welcomed political change. The collapse of both constitutional monarchy in France and of absolutist regimes in Austria and Germany created an intense sense of expectancy and encouraged an unprecedented political mobilization. Political clubs, newspapers, street demonstrations, and popular protest in town and country expressed a complex of grievances about low wages, job-threatening mechanization, taxation, restrictions on customary rights of usage of common land and in forests, and throughout central Europe against the last vestiges of serfdom. People were mobilized within "the context of the social networks in which they live[d] their daily lives."[5]

The newly appointed republican ministers in Paris and liberals in Germany, although themselves anxious to secure substantial constitutional reform, came under pressure to make further concessions to demands for political democracy and social reform, including the right to work that took on added significance as unemployment rose with the collapse of business confidence. Within the Austrian Empire they were faced with demands for greater autonomy from the self-proclaimed representatives of a variety of ethnic groups, and most dangerously, given their potential for military mobilization, from Hungary and northern Italy. The democratization of entry into civilian militias and of the right to bear arms threatened the state's monopoly of armed force. The potential for more thorough-going revolutionary change clearly existed.

In the aftermath of the collapse of the old regimes, as new governments struggled to establish their authority, chaos and uncertainty spread throughout the civil and military bureaucracies. The existence of a power vacuum encouraged both internal division within the new ministries and continuous pressure on them from a complex variety of interest groups. In this postrevolutionary situation tensions inevitably emerged between erstwhile revolutionaries, united briefly only through opposition to the previous regime and now in contention for power. They disagreed over fundamental objectives and in particular over the limits to the process of change inaugurated by the revolution. A major political realignment was inevitable as the short-lived revolutionary coalition rapidly disintegrated. Politically aware members of the middle classes were largely satisfied once it appeared that constitutional change and an extension of the suffrage offered them a greater share of political power. In Britain and Belgium this had been the situation for significant groups since 1830/32 and explains the creation of a broad-based alliance of property owners opposed to radical and extra-legal change. This would be substantially enlarged by the threat of social revolution in 1848. Quite clearly, for many moderate republicans in France and for liberals elsewhere, democracy and the threat of a redistribution of property, which granting the vote to the propertyless seemed to imply, were terrifying prospects.

The *Sonderweg* was to be the European rather than simply the German way. Typically the east Prussian newspaper, the *Königsberger Zeitung*, while welcoming the advent of parliamentary government expressed serious doubts about the political maturity of the masses and insisted on the sanctity of private property. Czech intellectuals like Palacky would welcome the eventual defeat of the anti-Slav and "communist" Viennese radicals although this strengthened the likelihood of a general reaction. Similarly, both the Piedmontese Monarch Charles-Albert and the Venetian "revolutionary" Manin, regarded Mazzinian republicanism and the workers' struggle for social reform as threatening a new barbarism. Even in Hungary, after lending their support to the national cause, many gentry easily accommodated themselves to the return of Austrian rule, relieved that revolution and war had not more widely provoked peasant jacqueries. The re-establishment of social and moral order and economic prosperity increasingly appeared to wide sections of all social groups to depend upon the restoration of monarchical authority. The main role assumed by new ministers rapidly became that of "reimposing routine governmental control over the subject population."[6] This inaugurated a relatively brief phase of resistance to revolutionary radicalization that would serve as a prelude to actual counter-revolution. The development of governmental resistance to the perceived threat of social revolution would coincide with a shift in mood amongst the population and the growing mobilization of mass support for more thoroughgoing counter-revolution.

Historians concentrate on the politically active. Indifference to political events was of course another, unmeasurable, factor. Widespread disorder produced a diffuse desire to be left in peace. The economic, structural, and cultural heterogeneity of the various social groups, their localism and the sheer complexity of even individual political behavior clearly make it essential to avoid simplistic class-based assessments of political movements. It does, however, seem safe to claim that middle-class professionals and businessmen, and also many peasants and self-employed artisans and workers who might have welcomed limited reforms, were terrified by demonstrations and the extreme demands made—or rumored to have been made—in the radical clubs and press. The collapse of agricultural prices in many areas following the bumper harvests of 1847 and 1848, and the stagnation of economic activity caused by business uncertainty, encouraged demands for a return to "normality." In terms of gendered responses to political crisis it might be worth considering, although the evidence appears to be rather thin, whether womens' particular responsibilities for the sustenance of their families were likely to dispose them to adopt a similar position, and if so to actively discourage male mobilization.

Respect for monarchy, the church, and for secular elites was undoubtedly widespread among the masses, and for a complex set of reasons including opportunism, material self-interest, and the lack of an acceptable alternative. Conservative propaganda, in the press and from the pulpit, equated democrats and socialists with communism and anarchy, and stressed that demands for equality or the right to work were contrary to the fundamental principles of both religious truth and political economy. It was maintained that degenerates and foreigners were threatening to lead the honest people astray. The fact that artisans and workers made up such a large proportion of those arrested following the June insurrection in Paris or for political crimes in Saxony does not necessarily mean that most artisans unequivocally adhered to the cause of revolution. In Paris even committed republicans felt obliged to support, however reluctantly, the crushing of the popular insurrection that threatened the sovereignty of the Constituent Assembly elected in April by universal [manhood] suffrage. Workers, as well as taking part in the insurrection, were also mobilized against further revolution and fought alongside the regular army in the ranks of the mobile guard and national guard. Similarly in Prussia, particularly in the larger towns, the *Preussenverein* [Prussian Association], appealing to monarchical loyalty and pro-Prussian and anti-German sentiments, was able to recruit members from amongst the ranks of dockers and unskilled laborers and use them to intimidate local liberals. In Bavaria a similar appeal was based upon opposition to Jewish emancipation.

Even where substantial popular grievances existed, these were not necessarily translated into political action. Inexperience, lack of political awareness, the weakness of democratic cadres—especially in the countryside—and dependence on landlords and employers for access to land, work or to charity, promoted conformist values and "deferential" behavior. Local notables frequently appeared to be the only "properly" qualified intermediaries between the community and the outside, particularly the official, world. This greatly inhibited a radical politicization, as opposed to traditional forms of unsustainable popular protest or widespread popular conservatism; the latter a rational response in situations in which conservative politicians seemed to be more successful in offering solutions to popular economic grievances, and were in some cases ready to make substantial concessions to pressure from below. Thus in Austria and much of Germany effective demobilization of peasant protest occurred by means of the abolition of surviving feudal dues and services. With memories of the peasant jacquerie in Galicia in 1846 still fresh, an imperial decree intended both to calm peasants and to reassure landowners, ending compulsory labor service on noble estates (*robot*) but with compensation, was introduced as early as 28 March. In France a similar if unintended political result was achieved when, in an act that revealed budgetary conservatism as well as considerable political incompetence on the part of republican ministers, a 45 percent surcharge was imposed on the land tax.

The potential for successful revolution in central and eastern Europe was further reduced by the very ethnic divisions that had previously weakened established governments. Levels of national self-awareness varied according to a complex of factors affecting the potency of historical myth, including levels of economic development and sociogeographic integration, language, and literacy. The citizens of long-established nation-states like Britain and France possessed a relatively homogeneous culture and sense of nationality created by war and propaganda. Similar sentiments inspired the delegates who gathered for the meeting of the all-German parliament at Frankfurt in May 1848. They were mostly well-educated professionals anxious to establish greater German unity and inspired by Arndt's song—"Where is the German's Fatherland?" and the response—"Wherever rings the German tongue." In achieving greater national unity they were to be obstructed by the conservative defenders of state particularism, and especially that of Austria, Prussia and Bavaria, and by divisions over the contents of a new all-German constitution, with moderates favoring a loose federation and radicals a more unitary one.

The establishment by the parliament of an executive headed by the Habsburg Archduke John as Imperial Regent [*Reichsverweser*], with Prince Karl Leiningen as minister-president and the Prussian General von Peuker as minister of war was symbolic both of the moderation of the majority of deputies and their awareness of the restraints placed upon their freedom of action by the need to reach agreement with the states. There was disagreement too over the place within the new Reich of Austria and its Slav subjects. More generally the debate on a new German constitution revealed fundamental differences between moderate and radical proponents of change and restored the initiative to the conservative defenders of the status quo. The prospect of reforms that might have satisfied some of the aspirations of other nationalities certainly proved offensive to most German speakers regardless of political allegiance.

The Austrian government and army were well placed to exploit a complex of ethnic differences. Approval by the emperor on 8 April 1848 of equality of the German and Czech languages and the, unfulfilled, promise of a common administration and diet for the historic lands of the Bohemian crown appeared perverse to liberals. Rejection by Palacký of the invitation to elect representatives to Frankfurt shocked Germans, previously largely unaware of growing Czech discontent. The leading spokesman for Czech nationalism believed that Bohemia's future lay within a federal Austria in which Slavs could achieve parity with Germans and Magyars and which would offer them protection against both Russian expansion and the danger of being submerged within a greater Germany. In response and following a series of hysterical stories about fanatical Czech hostility towards Germans the radical Viennese newspaper, the *Volksfreund*, would respond by welcoming the ultra-aristocratic Windischgraetz's crushing, in June, of an insurrection in Prague by "the insane or corrupt party of the Czechs," adding that "the victory over the Czech party in Prague is and remains a joyful event … for the Germans bring humanity and freedom to the conquered."[7]

The demands for a federal system based on democratic rights and equality of all the peoples, which was repeated by delegates to the Pan-Slav congress meeting in Prague in June, seemed to most Germans to be nothing less than treason. The German-speaking residents of Bohemia, Moravia, and Silesia, dominant in the official, financial, cultural, and religious spheres, were doubtless greatly relieved by the official rejection of Czech demands. Their contemptuous and condescending attitudes towards the Czechs were, as we have seen, shared by the Viennese radicals who were both the most democratic political group within the Empire and also the most chauvinistically anti-Slav. Such leading German radicals as Marx and Engels firmly believed that Czech demands only reinforced the threat from Russia, already seen as the power-house of the European counter-revolution. Engels would deny that the Czechs had any "historical existence" or "right to independence," in contrast to the Poles who were fulfilling their historical mission in struggling against Russian occupation.

German speakers whatever their political affiliation were also generally anxious to deny the aspirations of Polish nationalists—mainly nobles—whether in Austrian Galicia or the Prussian province of Poznan. A rising in Cracow was easily crushed on 25 April and in Poznan insurgents led by Mieroslawski laid down their arms on 9 May, to the great delight of the Russian government always anxious about developments that might encourage unrest in its own western provinces. The Frankfurt assembly, after heated debate would, on 27 July, vote for final German annexation of much of the Grand Duchy of Posen by 342 votes to 32. Among Viennese radicals there was some sympathy for the Italian cause and rather more for the Hungarian, both being potential allies, but there was little support for granting them full independence and a wider public no doubt gloried in Radetzky's victories in Italy.

Hungarians themselves in their attitudes towards the other peoples of the Crown of Saint Stephen revealed a similar confidence in their own ethnic superiority and an unwillingness to accept that other groups could develop similar patriotic sentiments. The Hungarian leader Kossuth's program involved the creation of an independent greater Hungary that would also include Transylvania, Croatia, and Slavonia. The Serbs and Rumanians seemed to be beneath contempt and, if the Magyars accepted the "historic" validity of Croatian claims for autonomy, concessions were slow in coming and failed to deflect the Croat commander Jelačić from his loyalty to the Habsburgs. Croatian nobles, army officers, officials, and intellectuals, and Serbian and Rumanian officers, priests, teachers, and writers had initially sought autonomy within Hungary. Then, as the determination of the Magyar elite to reinforce its own linguistic and political hegemony became clear, they looked instead to the Imperial court for eventual political concessions as well as an immediate military alliance. They would be poorly rewarded for their efforts, but in the meantime substantial Hungarian forces would be tied down in campaigns against both regular and guerrilla forces that frequently degenerated into vicious interethnic or interclass conflict. Fighting in Transylvania lasted fifteen months and left around 40,000 dead.[8] Clearly, this weakness and division amongst the forces promoting change intensified public anxiety and strengthened the potential for counter-revolution.

The Potential for Counter-revolution

It was hardly surprising, following the collapse of established governments, and in a situation of mounting disorder, that "social elites" should become alarmed. These were people identified by their wealth, education, and life style, as well as the familial connections that provided access to government office. Through this and the informal contacts provided by membership of "high society" they possessed the means of exercising influence over key decision makers. In still predominantly agrarian societies most were landowners—although with dual urban/rural residence—while growing, if often reluctant, recognition was being accorded to the contribution of financiers and major industrialists to the processes of wealth creation and economic and social "modernization," providing of course that the individuals concerned were prepared to conform to established social mores. Traditions of service to the state in both the bureaucracy and army remained strong and with this the commitment to acquiring the classically orientated education and training in the law that were additional characteristics of the gentleman. Although divided by "diverse economic interests, contrasting social backgrounds, and conflicting political agendas,"[9] members of such groups shared a particular "pattern of meanings,"[10] which offered an explanation and justification of their possession of wealth and authority, and both their superiority over and paternalistic responsibilities toward the less fortunate members of society. Their wealth, social roles, and organizational ability ensured that both directly, and indirectly through state and church, they would exercise considerable influence over other social groups.

Nevertheless, even before the outbreak of revolution the habitual self-confidence of members of elite groups had already been replaced by a widespread sense of foreboding. For many, the development of industrial capitalism and of urban concentrations of poverty had seemed to threaten the emergence of a new barbarism. Now the defensive barriers were being destroyed. Fundamental assumptions about the social and political order had been challenged. The violent language so typical of the radical clubs and press, denunciations of the wealthy as "parasites," and the widespread rejection of relationships of subordination, which, it had been believed, the masses had freely entered into, came as a great shock. The social status of established elites and indeed their entire way of life appeared to be threatened. Alexis de Tocqueville compared the situation with that faced by the Roman world invaded by the Vandals and Goths, later remembering Paris "in the sole hands of those who owned nothing" and "the terror felt by all the other classes."[11] Memories of the peasant jacquerie in Galicia in 1846 and the butchery of hundreds of Polish noble families were still fresh, and their impact would soon be reinforced by the myths created around the June insurrection in Paris. The French deputy Beugnot would warn his colleagues about "men who have sworn to destroy our society, its ideas, its morality, its institutions, its religion, in order to construct in its ruins who knows what sort of edifice, in the shadow of which will grow up generations animated by a savage hatred of everything the world has believed and honored since its creation."[12] The introduction of manhood suffrage, of popular sovereignty and equality before the law—major innovations introduced by those moderate republicans and liberals whom Marx condemned for their essential conservatism—appeared to institutionalize the threat. In France the electorate grew from 250,000 qualified by their wealth and gender (about 2.3 percent of adult males) to ten million. How would the masses use their new found political power? The propertied classes feared anarchy, a blood-bath worse even than the French Terror of 1793, followed by the general redistribution of property. Even in Britain, the meeting of the Chartist Convention in London on 4 April caused considerable alarm.

The prospect of an assault on the fundamental values and vested interests of elites previously so confident of their right to rule was virtually bound to provoke a counter-revolutionary response. The existing social order they had conceived of as based on respect for property, family and religion, was threatened by political militants whom they despised and condemned as criminals and whose aspirations for social reform, and greater dignity and status, they were unwilling to recognize. Conservative responses to the revolutionary menace would to a large degree depend on both their self-perceptions and their world-view. Some solace might be gained both from traditional Christian teaching and modern political economy. These combined to assert that wealth was God's blessing and proof of individual energy and ability. The presence of the poor was also God's will or alternatively a result of personal inadequacy. There was nothing to be done to change this situation outside the offering of Christian charity and, to be on the safe side, the provision of more substantial public poor relief at times of crisis. For the poor to demand anything more, for intellectuals to propose measures of social reform, was unreasonable, even blasphemous.

The centrality of this particular conception of order, both social and moral, to conservative ideology is worth stressing. With it went a commitment to strong repressive government, and in particular to monarchy as the only truly natural form of rule, with the king the symbol of a hierarchical social order made up of unequally endowed individuals and of groups bound together by reciprocal interests and mutual obligations. To protect this order, elites would eventually feel justified in resorting to massacre. Monarchs like Friedrich-Wilhelm of Prussia would need little persuading to turn towards counter-revolution, influenced as he was by a closely knit group of courtiers [*camarilla*] including the Gerlach brothers, General Rauch, Count Alvensleben, and Edwin von Manteuffel, all of them determined to protect both the interests of the nobility and the divine right of the king to rule. Friedrich-Wilhelm's move to Potsdam and the flight of the Emperor Ferdinand to Innsbruck insulated them both from liberal ministers and revolutionary crowds, and made it easier for their advisors to rally support. Expressing contempt for the liberal ministers and institutions he had been forced to accept, the Prussian king would come to reject the proposals for a German union coming from the Frankfurt parliament which threatened the integrity of the Prussian state. The revolution would be first contained and then smashed.

That there was considerable potential for counter-revolution should be revealed by analysis of the economic, social, political, military, and ideological bases of social power. A great deal would depend on the specific local context. In France, the German states, and much of the Austrian Empire, the revolutions had involved a partial and incomplete seizure of power by moderate republican politicians in the French case and liberal monarchists elsewhere. Otherwise social elites everywhere retained their property, status, and influence both within the machinery of government and society more generally. Following a moment of paralysis due to the shock of governmental collapse at the center, they would return to the political fray. In contrast, in the Italian and Hungarian provinces of the Austrian Empire dissidents achieved a more thorough-going seizure of the administrative and military apparatus. In these areas local social elites, inspired by a determination to assert their own authority against "interlopers" appointed by the imperial power, played a major role in mobilizing a nationalistic opposition.

In constitutional terms the establishment of the Second Republic in France was unique. Elsewhere, constitutional debate, variously influenced by the precedent of Britain and especially Belgium and Baden, looked towards the strengthening of parliamentary institutions while reserving substantial executive powers for monarchs, including the right to appoint ministers. Even the Frankfurt parliament, in finally agreeing to deprive its proposed German monarch of the ability to reject legislation, recognized the need to reserve extensive emergency powers for the ruler. The French case however illustrates the point that, regardless of constitutional forms, the dominance of government by wealthy members of the property-owning classes limited the scope for revolutionary change. Ministers suddenly and unexpectedly thrust into power, men like the aristocratic poet Lamartine, Marie, Crémieux, Arago, Garnier-Pagès, and Marrast, were essentially liberals despite their republicanism. They were committed to administrative continuity and to the restoration of normal governmental authority. In comparison even with the moderate liberalism of the new Prussian ministers, the Rhenish businessmen Campenhausen and Hansemann, that of Austrian ministers was very mild indeed. The initial appointment of Kolowrat, who had, since 1825, been responsible for internal affairs was nevertheless widely accepted because of his reputation as an enemy of Metternich, the arch-priest of European reaction since 1815.

The task of containment in which these men engaged was extremely difficult. They had to conciliate radicals and limit pressure from the streets by means of a combination of vague promises of political and social reform together with immediate work relief for the masses, thrown out of work by the crisis of business confidence brought on by the revolutions. At the same time they were anxious to reassure moderates and conservatives so thoroughly alarmed by disorder and the prospect of social change. It was probably inevitable, given their own social origins and sympathies, that ministers would give growing priority to the latter objective and that a repressive coalition would come into being, in which a liberalism of fear allied with reaction. The likelihood of such development was reinforced by the dependence of new ministers on established bureaucratic and military structures.

The initial installation of republican or liberal governments had met with little opposition. There was, as a result, no excuse for engaging in a large-scale purge of existing office-holders. Moreover, determined as they were to ensure a smooth transition to new forms of government and to set limits to pressure for further revolutionary change, and concerned as they were about the prospects of war in defense of the Vienna settlement of 1815, ministers were anxious to make use of the skills and experience of established civil servants and military officers. These would provide the essential organizational base and manpower for resistance and subsequent counter-revolution. "The action of the state as an institution depends in large measure on the people who direct it."[13] In general, ministers, together with senior officials and army officers, were drawn from the ranks of the nobility or upper bourgeoisie, often from families with a tradition of service. These conservative officials would gradually regain confidence and a determination to reaffirm their authority. Although one should not ignore differences of opinion within governments, the emphasis given to reformist measures was limited by a growing determination to combat the revolutionary menace.

The repressive strategies pursued by governments would depend upon perceptions of the wider political situation and their own capacity for mobilization. The control of armed force was of crucial importance. However, the initial collapse of governmental authority in February/March had resulted in large part from the provocative use of military force. Among the concessions made by new ministers had been the withdrawal of troops from capital cities and the democratization and armament of a mass civilian militia. Typically, military commanders like the French Marshal Bugeaud or his Austrian counterpart Radetzky tended to blame defeat on the weakness of politicians who had previously starved them of resources and lost their heads at the moment of crisis. For a mixture of social, political, and professional reasons they were anxious for revenge. Withdrawal at least helped to preserve soldiers from political agitation and, from the strictly tactical point of view, facilitated the concentration of strength necessary for an eventual counter-attack.

More immediately, in the face of widespread disorder moderate republican and liberal ministers were increasingly drawn into dependence on the army. In the towns, as political debate spread, the popular classes felt free to demonstrate about all manner of grievances, while in the countryside peasants protested against the vestiges of feudalism, refused to pay taxes, and in upland areas rejected the legal restrictions on the use of the forest resources so important to traditional pastoral agrarian systems. As a result, in France as many as 50,000 soldiers were deployed in the countryside. The situation was quite unlike that prevailing after defeat in a prolonged war, as in Russia in 1917 when the social dilution of the officer corps was followed by the effective disintegration of military morale and discipline. In 1848 only in Baden, and for ethnic reasons in Hungary and Italy, would military units support the cause of revolutionary change. Elsewhere the military-social hierarchy remained intact, and in spite of a short-lived phase of desertion, the rank-and-file remained disciplined.

In France, senior officers drawn from the social elites were committed to the defense of order. In Austria and Prussia, they were additionally dedicated to the monarchy. Military organization—the dispersal of troops in numerous garrisons—reflected a primary concern, prior to the development of a modern police, with internal security. As far as possible the rank-and-file were insulated from politics by long-service and frequent movements designed to reduce contacts with the civilian population. Harsh discipline was combined with the cultivation of an esprit de corps. In France these methods turned even the mobile national guard, recruited from unemployed young workers following the February Revolution, into an effective counter-revolutionary force by June. For conservatives the army offered the way back into power. Evolving political situations and the competing demands of internal security and external defense, as well as the effectiveness of cooperation between the civil and military authorities, would determine the eventual contexts for action. In the meantime, Friedrich-Wilhelm for one was not prepared to make any concessions to his liberal ministers on the question of control of the military.

A distinction ought probably to be made between the organization of resistance to further revolution and overt counter-revolution. Members of social elites, in supporting first the former and then, as their own confidence revived, the latter, possessed the very considerable advantages of a shared ideological commitment to private property and social hierarchy together with access to considerable organizational resources. They combined experience of political activity and close association with the state bureaucracy and army. This was in marked contrast to the "fragmented political identities of the poor."[14] The behavioral norms and multifarious social ties shared by members of elites served as very effective means of communication in a moment of extreme crisis when habitual political and personal differences were subdued. This was the case even in France where elite fragmentation (social and political) seemed most developed.

Prussian Junkers, Austrian nobles, and the French bourgeois were united in their determination to avoid transformative social change. While in the immediate aftermath of revolution they were shocked, confused, and depressed, this initial caution was rapidly succeeded by greater assertiveness. They were able with relative ease and growing momentum to organize strong conservative political movements, employing existing social networks to establish electoral committees, political clubs, and newspapers. As early as the French electoral campaign in April 1848, every effort was made to vilify radicals as communists and anarchists, responsible for the lack of confidence in the future that was to blame for economic stagnation and mass unemployment. The election of a Constituent Assembly that included a majority committed to the preservation of social order considerably strengthened the government's determination to resist pressure from the political clubs and streets.

In the same month a small group of courtiers and east Elbian nobles founded a new newspaper, the *Neue Preussische Zeitung*. Funded by members of the Prussian royal family and the aristocracy, and appearing regularly from the beginning of July, the *Kreuzzeitung*, as it was more commonly known, was dominated editorially by the Pietist Wagener, a man inspired by a paternalist concept of aristocratic responsibility and by the young aristocrat Otto von Bismarck. Confrontational in style, it appealed to the artisanal class by defending corporate ideals against emerging capitalism and above all to landowners by condemning liberal proposals for a land tax. Manhood suffrage was denounced for its abstract egalitarianism and failure to recognize the legitimate interests of both professions and property. The fusion of Prussia into a liberal Germany was decisively rejected. Together with the Society for the Protection of the Interests of Landowners [*Verein zur Wahrung der Interessen des Grundbesitzes*] and branches of the *Preussenverein* active in the larger towns, the *Kreuzzeitung* conducted a major propaganda campaign through the agricultural societies and a variety of patriotic and religious groups. Edwin von Manteuffel, reviewing the situation in May, concluded that conservatives had been "forced back but certainly not defeated."[15] Although not entirely successful, these groups represented the beginnings of a modern conservative political movement.

The Course of Counter-revolution

The Military Response

The transition from the phase of resistance to radicalization which had made the divisions amongst the original supporters of revolution so clear, to that of counter-revolution proper, can clearly be linked to the use of military force. A number of decisive moments can be identified in the development of counter-revolution. As early as 10 April the British government had offered encouragement through its ability to overawe a mass Chartist demonstration in London. The threat of disorder and the violent language of radicalism had been especially pronounced in the British capital and especially in the north, in the Liverpool and Bradford areas, where the cause of political reform was closely associated with the Irish question and the involvement of impoverished immigrants from the famine wracked provinces of the United Kingdom across the Irish Sea. In reaction there occurred a massive enrolment by the middle classes in the special constabulary. Although they shared the widespread antiaristocratic sentiment and dissatisfaction with the limited enfranchisement introduced by the 1832 Reform Act, the middle classes were more concerned to protect their property and social status. The shape of things to come was evident from the government's use of the electric telegraph and railway to improve the transmission of information, and the control and movement of troops. This substantially increased the potential of the limited number of men available.

On 15 May, conservatives throughout Europe received further confirmation that the revolutionary tide was being stemmed with news that King Ferdinand of Naples had unleashed his Swiss mercenaries. For the Habsburgs, the first real victory came in Prague where minor clashes between Czech nationalists and the increasingly assertive garrison occurred on 12 June and was followed by the construction of barricades by some 1,500 insurgents. In the ensuing melee, during which the Austrian commander Windischgrätz ordered an intimidatory bombardment of the city, forty-three insurgents were killed. There then occurred what would soon become a familiar pattern of events with several hundred arrests, the closure of political clubs, and dissolution of the civilian national guard. This firm military response, planned from the end of March, effectively discouraged further protest.

Of far greater symbolic and real significance was the defeat of the June insurrection in Paris. The French capital had seen repeated mass demonstrations, culminating in the unplanned invasion of the newly elected Constituent Assembly on 15 May by crowds demanding social reform and French assistance for the Polish rebels against Russian rule. Although on this occasion the crowds were rapidly dispersed, their demands seemed, as much to moderate republicans as monarchists, to represent proof of the development of a threatening revolutionary international. More immediately, moderate republican ministers were greatly alarmed by the threat posed by workers armed and organized in the democratized National Guard and in the National Workshops. The Workshops had for many workers come to represent the promise of social reform. However, for the moderate republican dominated Provisional Government and its successor, the Executive Committee elected by the Constituent Assembly, they were nothing more than a temporary, and far too expensive, means of providing work relief. The decision to close them would trigger a renewed battle for control of the city and represented a major stage in the transition to counter-revolution. It proved that, in the urban war against the barricades, the military could emerge victorious.

Possibly 40-50,000 insurgents drawn mainly from the working-class quarters of the city fought against the regular army, supported by National Guard units from the wealthier western areas, and the mobile guard recruited from amongst unemployed young workers. Described by Marx as "the first great battle … between the two classes [bourgeoisie and proletariat] that split modern society," the struggle might also be seen as a civil war between workers. The forces of order were placed under the command of the moderate republican General Cavaignac who, in this dire emergency, was also appointed head of government by the Constituent Assembly. Military forces were first concentrated. This was a tactic that allowed the insurrection to spread, but prevented a repetition of February when dispersed groups of soldiers had easily been overwhelmed. Three days of bitter street fighting revealed that with a clear tactical doctrine making use of cannon and outflanking attacks rather than frontal assaults, with determined leadership, high morale, adequate numbers, food, and munitions, regular troops in particular were more than a match for untrained insurgents. Barricade, while they offered protection to street fighters, were no substitute for mobility and clear objectives.

The fighting was followed by 12,000 arrests and the inevitable imposition of martial law and a campaign of mass intimidation. Lord Normanby, the British ambassador in Paris, assessed the importance of the struggle on 25 June and concluded in a report to his government that "I trust that one may now anticipate the defeat of the attempt to establish a République rouge, the success of which in the present feverish state of society would probably have produced dreadful attempts at intimidation throughout Europe." He proposed to offer General Cavaignac "the thanks of the friends of order in all countries."[16] In practice, conservatives still suspected the General's republican proclivities and would be willing to take advantage of the massive popular groundswell in favor of Louis-Napoléon Bonaparte in the December presidential elections and subsequently to support the dissolution of the Constituent Assembly in January 1849 in the hope that the elections would return a more thoroughly conservative assembly. The use of military force against insurgents and the subsequent restrictions imposed on public meetings and the press marked a clear transition from resistance to radicalization towards counter-revolution in a conservative republic presided over from December by an elected Prince-President.

This crucially important victory was soon followed by that of the Austrian marshal Radetzky over the poorly led Piedmontese army at Custozza on 25 July and his re-entry into Milan on 6 August. The Milanese, who had fought so hard to expel the Austrians in March, discouraged by Charles-Albert's defeat and his apparent willingness to abandon Lombardy to its fate, now surrendered without a fight. Victory in Italy released troops for use elsewhere. It decisively altered the balance of power within the empire although Venice, protected by its lagoons, would not capitulate until 25 August 1849. By that time Radetzky's defeat of the Piedmontese at Novara had destroyed any hope of relief. Subsequently a divide-and-rule policy would be implemented by the Austrian authorities. Lenient treatment of former rank-and-file insurgents combined with public relief measures contrasted with the persecution of nationalist leaders drawn from the landowning and professional classes.

In Vienna itself the weakness of the revolutionary alliance that had emerged in March was only too evident when on 23 August students and middle- class radicals stood by as workers protesting about poverty and the lack of reform were brutally dispersed. When the government decided to crush the radicals in their turn, they would enjoy substantially less mass support than they might have expected. This final showdown would occur at the beginning of October. The occasion was the refusal of disaffected troops to leave for Hungary. Together with middle-class and worker national guards, these clashed with soldiers loyal to the government. The subsequent withdrawal of the garrison was followed by the retreat of the emperor and ministers to Olmütz on 7 October. In spite of the competing demands of military commanders, the army under Windischgrätz and Jelačić was reinforced—reaching a strength of 70,000—and established a cordon around Vienna. Reconquest of the capital was opposed by a relatively small number of courageous but poorly trained and badly led civilians and national guards. Resistance was ineffectual, and the last hopes of the defenders disappeared on 30/31 October with Jelačić's defeat of an approaching Hungarian army. In its final assault the army lost around 1,200 men and the insurgents some 3,000.[17] The re-establishment of governmental control was followed by a military reign of terror and over 2,000 arrests.

Furthermore, this success encouraged Friedrich-Wilhelm of Prussia to attempt to restore his own authority. The appointment of his uncle Count Brandenburg as minister-president was announced on 1 November. It was followed by the exiling of the Prussian parliament to the provincial town of Brandenburg, prior to its dissolution on 9 November. At the same time the army under General Wrangel returned in force to Berlin. Wrangel took advantage of his martial law powers to disarm the civilian militia, the *Bürgerwehr*, and close political clubs. Berlin would remain quiet even when, in May 1849, radical anger at the Prussian king's rejection of the all-German constitution prepared by the Frankfurt parliament led to uprisings in the Prussian Rhineland, in Dresden the Saxon capital, which left 250 dead, and in Baden where the insurgents enjoyed the support of part of the army. These movements led, according to Friedrich-Wilhelm, by "devils incarnate, the filth of all nations,"[18] were to be successfully isolated and crushed by local and Prussian troops, reinforcing the status enjoyed by Prussia as the defender of social order throughout Germany.

Finally, in December 1851, Louis-Napoléon Bonaparte's coup d'état would represent the culmination of a lengthy period of intensifying repression in France. In a carefully coordinated movement, military commanders first secured the cities and garrison centers before dispatching mobile columns into the surrounding countryside, particularly in the south-east where insurrections had occurred in defense of the dream of a social and democratic republic. Martial law provided the opportunity for what seemed to be a final settling of accounts with the democratic opposition. Officials welcomed the opportunity to engage in an intense wave of arrests unrestrained by the rule of law. Together with the conservative press they embroidered evidence of "red" activity to create an atrocity myth and justify the coup as resolving a struggle between *la civilisation et la barbarie, la société et le chaos*.

In military terms the greatest problems were faced by Austrian commanders engaged in wars of national liberation in Italy and Hungary. Italy was the key. Failure there would have resulted in the loss of Lombardy-Venetia and a probably enforced compromise with both the greater-German ambitions of the Frankfurt assembly and with Hungarian aspirations. The advance of Italian nationalism was delayed by divisions between the rulers of the independent Italian states and their social conservatism. This they shared with revolutionary leaders from the propertied classes like the Venetian Manin. It made them unwilling to call for a people's war in case it led to demands for a republic and land reform. Sheer military incompetence also eased Radetzky's task. Furthermore, although large parts of the four Italian regiments stationed in Lombardy-Venetia, as well as naval units, defected, the 30,000 Hungarian troops serving in Italy remained loyal.

In Hungary efforts to secure a compromise with Kossuth's government continued until the end of September 1848. Only after the murder of the Imperial emissary Lamberg in Pest on 3 October was war declared on the Magyar regime. In their campaign, the imperial authorities were to be both assisted and obstructed by national divisions. They made full use of often vicious ethnic divisions, and especially Slav and Rumanian hostility to Greater Hungarian ambitions, but remained constantly concerned about the loyalty of the nationalities which made up the army. For as long as the Imperial regime was engaged in a desperate struggle to retain control of German Austria and northern Italy, the Hungarians had time on their side. They were able to create an effective military force from Magyar regiments of the imperial army (c.50,000) and the volunteer Honved (c.120,000).[19] Kossuth was also prepared to appeal to the peasantry on the basis of the abolition of feudalism.

Initial Hungarian successes included the recapture of Buda-Pest in April 1849 after first losing it to Windischgrätz in January. The effort could not however be sustained, particularly after the re-establishment of the imperial regime in Vienna and Radetzky's victories in Italy, which released growing numbers of troops for use in Hungary. Nevertheless it took until August 1849 to force the surrender of the Hungarian armies. By that time Austrian ministers, acting on the overly pessimistic advice of their generals, had taken the humiliating and unnecessary step of requesting a renewal of the Russian military cooperation previously secured by Metternich against the Poles in 1830/31 and in 1846. They were to unite in what the new Emperor Franz-Joseph called "the Holy struggle against anarchy." Tsar Nicholas I was already convinced that Russia alone offered an effective barrier to revolution. Moreover, the prospect of disorder spreading into Russian Poland persuaded the Tsar that instability within the Austrian Empire was a direct threat to Russia itself. Simultaneous Austrian and Russian invasions and a marked inferiority in men and equipment brought Hungarian resistance to an end. Buda-Pest fell on 13 July and the last Hungarian force, besieged in the fortress of Komárom, surrendered on 5 October. Fifty thousand Hungarians and a similar number of Austrians are estimated to have died in the war, along with 540 Russians (although another 11,000 died of cholera), to which ought to be added the unknown thousands slaughtered in ethnic conflict.

International efforts were also necessary to overthrow the Roman Republic inspired by Mazzini and to restore the authority of Pope Pius IX. The behavior of the powers in this case again reflected, in part, a common objective, namely the restoration of a spiritual leader who could be expected to play a vital role in the re-establishment of moral order. Their policy was additionally influenced by their own internal political divisions. In the French case, the never very strong possibility of intervention by the new republic in support of Italian nationalism was ended by the conservative reaction to the June insurrection and the priority given to the employment of the army to protect internal security. Subsequently, Louis-Napoléon's desire to conciliate Catholic elites, as well as to head off Austrian intervention, led to the dispatch of an expeditionary force to support the Pope, although Bonaparte, the former youthful Carbonaro, still hoped to persuade the Holy Father to introduce some political reforms. French, Austrian, and Neapolitan troops invaded the Roman Republic, and on 2 July 1849 the incompetent French General Oudinot finally succeeded in entering Rome after a difficult siege.

These developments highlight the international character of counter-revolution. Although conservative fear of an international revolutionary conspiracy was grossly exaggerated it is evident that both the initial success of revolution and its eventual failure were influenced by perceptions of events elsewhere. These served at first to encourage, and subsequently to demoralize revolutionary activists. Furthermore, the successes of the nationalist movements in Hungary and Italy were rapidly seen to depend upon external support. There had briefly appeared to be a real prospect of a general European war early in 1848. In practice, however, there was considerable support for the status quo established by the Congress of Vienna in 1814/15. The French Foreign Minister Lamartine had realized that, as in 1792, war might radicalize the revolution, an outcome he wished desperately to avoid. He had insisted that the Republic was determined to avoid military adventures. The position of liberal Britain, the other power to which nationalists had looked for support, was explained to the House of Commons by Palmerston. He pointed out that

> Austria is a most important element in the balance of European power. Austria stands in the center of Europe, a barrier against encroachment on the one side, and against invasion on the other. The political independence and the liberties of Europe are bound up, in my opinion, with the maintenance and integrity of Austria as a great European power, and therefore anything which tends by direct, or even remote contingency, to weaken and to cripple Austria, but still more to reduce her from the position of a first-rate power, to that of a secondary state, must be a great calamity to Europe and one which every Englishman ought to deprecate and try to prevent.[20]

Influenced still by Metternich, Austrian ministers were themselves particularly concerned to defend the Vienna settlement of 1815. The restoration of imperial authority in Vienna and that of the Hohenzollern king in Berlin were followed by a clear rejection of the Greater German aspirations of the Frankfurt parliament and by insistence on the need to preserve the integrity and uniqueness of both regimes. The opportunity initially presented to supporters of a (con-)federate Germany by the existence of a political vacuum was lost. While the Frankfurt assembly debated, conservative forces gathered strength. Once the Viennese revolutionaries had been crushed, the new minister Prince Schwarzenberg, in a speech to the Austrian Parliament meeting at Kremsier on 27 November 1848, would make clear his determination to maintain the integrity of the Habsburg Empire and to reject its integration into a federal Germany as well as to secure its dominant position within a revived

German confederation. He too declared that "Austria's continuance as a political unity [was] a German and a European necessity."[21] Growing military success only reinforced this attitude. In a note dated 9 March 1849 Schwarzenberg, in an unrealistic assertion of Austrian supremacy, suggested that the Austrian Empire become part of a Germanic confederation that should have a representative body made up of thirty-eight Austrian delegates and thirty-two from Germany proper, all nominated by their governments.

The Prussian king, although prepared to negotiate a possible reorganization of Germany with his fellow monarchs, was similarly unwilling to accept the subordination of his kingdom's interests to those of a liberal/democratic entity constructed at Frankfurt. Neither was he prepared to risk the conflict with Austria and perhaps Russia which might have resulted from either the continuation of an aggressive policy towards Denmark over the Schleswig-Holstein affair or subsequently from his acceptance of the imperial crown. This shared commitment to the status quo ensured that Austrian and Prussian troops would maintain a presence in some of the minor German states until 1851/52, while in May 1851 Schwarzenberg and the Prussian Minister Manteuffel signed a mutual defense treaty, within the structure of a revived German Confederation, directed essentially against internal subversion, which remained in effect until 1857. Although anxious to limit Prussian expansionism, Schwartzenberg thus appears to have preferred to rely on Prussian assistance in case of another crisis, rather than call for further Russian aid. In contrast to this growing, if often difficult, cooperation between the major powers and the formation of an effective conservative international, revolutionaries everywhere were increasingly demoralized by isolation and the destruction of their dreams of fraternal assistance.

Political Repression

The use of military violence against dissidents seemed perfectly justified to both moderate republican/liberal governments and to conservative elites. It was, however, neither practicable nor desirable to maintain society in a state of permanent mobilization. The search was on for means of social control likely to be more effective in the longer term. Persuasion was to be preferred to coercion. Although the threat of repressive action and the ability to intimidate potential opponents was to be ever present, its intensity would depend upon political circumstances. To be effective, social control required the employment of multifaceted means of enforcement. Power was, as always, to be exercised both through everyday social practices and by means of the action of the state bureaucracy. It would, moreover, be used with greater flexibility than had been the case before the February/March revolutions.

Lessons had certainly been learned. There were obvious priorities. One was constitutional revision in order to limit the impact of the democratic reforms introduced in 1848, without however fracturing the alliance constructed between liberals and conservatives. Efforts would have to be made to develop more effective policing as well as better bureaucratic coordination of police activity. Greater interest would also be shown in satisfying the material aspirations of substantial parts of the population. It was assumed that economic prosperity, resulting from the restoration of order and business confidence would, together with public and private charity, do much to pacify the masses. Although the ability of governments to influence the harvest and business cycle was severely limited, counter-cyclical expenditure on public works and urban renewal would also have a positive impact. Another key factor was the ability of governments to make use of the social influence of landowners and employers, crucially important given the small size of even the expanded bureaucracies and police forces. The traditional influence of religious institutions would be reinforced and substantial resources invested in the development of new networks for the diffusion of conservative ideals through the schools and media. These would promote the legitimacy of state action. In effect then, means were being developed to limit the capacity and increase the risks taken by all those hoping to "subvert, invert, challenge or ridicule"[22] established social and political institutions. Compliance with state policy was to be promoted as a minimum objective with positive approval as the main aim. The label Bonapartism has often been applied to this "combination of traditional authority and force of the police and the state with 'modern forms' of mass appeal,"[23] although of course such developments were not particular to France.

In most cases, existing legislation could be used to eliminate or restrict the activities of political clubs, workers' associations, and the press. In republican France, in the aftermath of the June insurrection and under governments led by both the republican General Cavaignac and his successor, established laws were refined and codified. A 29 July 1848 law subjected all public meetings to prior authorization, ensuring that police agents could halt any discussion "contrary to public order," and prohibiting links between clubs. In August, the practice of requiring political newspapers to deposit a bond from which fines might be paid was revived. In a debate in July 1849, that eminent political figure Adolphe Thiers clearly expressed liberal/conservative views on the freedom of speech and its necessary limits. He maintained that while a government's activities ought to be discussed, its very existence should not be threatened. He attacked "writings full of bile and violence in which the people are told that there is a supreme good which can in a moment put an end to everyone's sufferings, that it needs only a single effort of will by the majority to obtain it, but that we do not wish to make it because we are the wicked rich interested in perpetuating the present situation." The nostrums offered by the left, the "right to work" or cheap credit for cooperatives, were depicted at best as a waste of public money and at worst as communist.[24] An 1850 press law further increased the cost of establishing a newspaper and the ease with which opposition papers could be forced into bankruptcy by means of repeated fines.

Similar measures were introduced throughout Europe. In Austria, sensing the growing conservatism of public opinion, restrictions on the press were reimposed from mid-August 1848 when contributors to the *Studenten-Courier* were arrested for expressing republican sentiments. Officials appreciated the need to control the circulation of information, to repress criticism and to express conservative ideals more forcefully. Although judges might have occasionally infuriated prosecutors and policemen by what they judged to be excessively liberal interpretations of the law, in general, in a period of social tension, the guardians of justice were as frightened as other members of the upper classes. Their judgements offered both retribution and its ideological justification. Thus, in Britain, the definition of an illegal assembly offered by Baron Alderson to a jury in 1839 and which was frequently quoted by constitutional lawyers throughout the Chartist period, might be taken as representative of numerous judicial rulings:

> You will investigate the circumstances under which the assembly took place ... whether they have met at unreasonable hours of the night,—if they have been armed with offensive weapons, or used violent language,—if they have proposed to set the different classes of society at variance the one with the other, and to put to death any part of Her Majesty's subjects. If any ... of those things should appear before you, there will, I think, be little difficulty in saying that an assembly of such persons, under such circumstances, for such purposes, and using such language, is a dangerous one, which cannot be tolerated in a country governed by laws ...[25]

At a time of social anxiety, the principle of the rule of law—or at least a particular interpretation of it—which might in calmer circumstances offer a degree of protection to the powerless, could be employed to justify intense and frequently arbitrary repression, contributing to the creation of an atmosphere of fear and to the effective demobilization of opposition. Membership of suspect groups like political clubs or workers' friendly societies was discouraged and democrats were driven out of public life.

Paranoia ran rampant. Everywhere liberal and moderate republican ministers were replaced with conservatives increasingly dependent upon the head of state. "Unreliable" officials would be purged, and intense repression directed at political suspects. Nevertheless, it was widely accepted, even by conservatives, that a complete restoration of the prerevolutionary situation was impossible. The Prussian Minister Manteuffel, determined as he was to restore the authority of the state to which Prussia owed its historical greatness, accepted that "the old times are gone and cannot return. To return to the decaying conditions of the past is like scooping water with a sieve."[26] Parliamentary institutions and a wider suffrage had been welcomed by broad sections of the community. Even so, there remained considerable scope for restricting the competence of new institutions and for manipulating electoral systems.

Urgent action certainly seemed to be required. In Prussia, the May 1848 elections had made it clear that even the peasants could not always be relied upon to follow the landowners' lead. The dissolution of parliament on 5 December was accompanied—symbolically—by the granting of a constitution by the monarch, from above. In spite of considerable government pressure, the January 1849 elections were, however, no more reassuring. According to the *Evangelische Kirchenzeitung*, manhood suffrage threatened to "destroy piety, submission, obedience and even the sources of public prosperity."[27] A three-class franchise was introduced to replace the more egalitarian voting system introduced since the previous March.

While the right to vote was, in principle, retained, in recognition of the continued strength of democratic pressures, the electorate would be divided into three according to individual tax contributions. In Berlin, for the June 1849 elections, the first class would include 2,000 voters, the second 7,000, and the third 70,000, with each class electing a similar number of representatives. Overall, if around 80 percent of adult males qualified to vote, the 15 percent who made up the first two classes elected more deputies than the 85 percent composing the third class. This would allow, according to the official justification, the "several classes of the people that proportional influence corresponding to their actual importance in the life of the state."[28] It expressed the distaste of Friedrich-Wilhelm and his aristocratic ministers for the new constitutional order and their determination to reject universal suffrage and popular sovereignty as contrary to the traditions of the Prussian Monarchy. Even the recognition of the growing influence of the wealthy grande bourgeoisie implied by their inclusion in the first class of voters would frequently be resented by traditional landowners. The new constitution, which survived in its essential form until 1918, furthermore ensured that ministers were chosen by and responsible to the king. Friedrich-Wilhelm had survived the revolution with most of his prerogatives intact.

Similar developments occurred in the other princely states. In Austria the reaction was more thoroughgoing. The appointment in November 1848, following the defeat of the Viennese revolution, of Prince Schwartzenberg as chief minister administered a severe shock to parliamentarians. The subsequent replacement, on 2 December, of the simple-minded Emperor Ferdinand by the 18-year-old Franz-Joseph was taken to signify the end of the period of liberalization. It made a disavowal of earlier concessions all the easier since the new emperor had not sworn to uphold them. Although the preparation of a draft constitution continued, Schwarzenberg's main aim was to reestablish the emperor's authority and proceed to the centralization, modernization, and Germanization of the empire and the creation of an Austrian-dominated Mitteleuropa. As in Prussia, the grande bourgeoisie was to take its place within the ruling elite alongside the nobility. Schwarzenberg, influenced perhaps by Radetzky, and in this certainly at cross purposes with his brother-in-law Windischgrätz, had decided that there was a pressing need to compensate for what he felt were the dangerous shortcomings of the nobility. Indeed, he wrote that:

> I know of not a dozen men of our class with sufficient political wisdom or with the necessary experience to whom an important share of power could be entrusted without soon having to fear for it. I have thought a great deal about how to constitute the aristocracy of Austria as a body so as to maintain for it an appropriate political influence but the elements out of which this body consists, I have been unable to find. Democracy must be fought and its excesses must be challenged but in the absence of other means of help that can only be done by the government itself. To rely on an ally as weak as our aristocracy unfortunately is, would be to damage our cause more than to help it.[29]

A clash with parliament was inevitable given the determination of many of its deputies to abolish titles of nobility, sequester church property, and affirm the concept of popular sovereignty. A draft constitution that made ministers responsible to parliament and restricted the emperor to a suspensive veto in domestic affairs was clearly unacceptable. On 7 March 1849, the dissolution of parliament was announced and a constitution was promulgated, drafted largely by Metternich's close associate Stadion. The document proclaimed that the "Emperor by the grace of God," was granting a constitution to his subjects, a symbolic return to a form of words that had been abandoned in March by his predecessor. Under its terms, the monarch would retain an absolute right of veto over legislation, ministers would cease to be responsible to parliament, the tax qualification for voting would be raised substantially, and Hungarian autonomy considerably reduced and its former territories in Croatia and Transylvania placed under the direct control of the Austrian Monarch. While the administrative autonomy of the various peoples of the empire was recognized, in practice it would be strictly circumscribed. An Imperial patent confirmed both the abolition of the *robot* and the promise of compensation to landlords. At the same time new laws, severely restricting the freedoms of the press and association were introduced.

Encouraged by the success of Louis-Napoléon Bonaparte's coup d'état, on 31 December 1851, even this constitution, together with its accompanying bill of rights, was replaced by a new fundamental law with the issue of the so-called Sylvester Patent. Equality before the law and the abolition of the *robot* survived. Otherwise, the young emperor was determined to rule, and was effectively supported in his aspirations by Kübeck, head of the Treasury under Metternich. Schwarzenberg was instructed to cancel promises of national autonomy, linguistic equality and trial by jury. There was no mention of parliament. This was the culminating act in the establishment of a centralized, bureaucratic neo-absolutism, something which Metternich had worked towards but had never been able entirely to achieve.

In France, following démocrate-socialiste successes in the May 1849 elections, the conservative majority in the Chamber supported the introduction of an electoral law (31 May 1850) which secured, by means of the introduction of stricter residential qualification for enfranchisement, the disqualification of 30 percent of the electorate at a stroke, with much higher proportions in the larger cities and industrial centers. The prospect of "the communists [being offered] the possibility of becoming kings one day by a *coup de scrutin*"[30] appeared to have been destroyed. Adolphe Thiers saw this as the means by which the "vile multitude" might be excluded from politics. Significantly, however, Louis-Napoléon Bonaparte, elected President of the Republic with massive popular support in December 1848, carefully distanced himself from this legislation.

This unique election of a monarchical pretender, of a man with complete faith in his historical "mission," and determined once having gained power to retain it, had made a coup d'état almost inevitable. Louis-Napoléon would seek to legitimize his eventual seizure of power by restoring manhood suffrage. In the subsequent plebiscite on 20 December 1851, 7,500,000 voters sanctioned the coup, 640,000 voted "no," and 1,500,000 abstained. His program which appeared both to promise the defense of order and national glory, and to confirm the vague reputation for "socialism" he had previously acquired through his pamphlet on the *Extinction du paupérisme*, attracted massive popular support. As in Austria and Prussia, the constitutional structures of a new imperial regime, with an emasculated parliament and system of directed democracy, were then imposed from above. France would receive strong executive leadership as well as a symbolic focus for national loyalty, although Bonaparte would never achieve the degree of legitimacy achieved by other rulers.

In addition to these legal/constitutional measures, efforts were also made to improve the effectiveness of social control through better policing. It was clear that more effective pre-emptive strategies and better crowd control might prevent the development of the cycle of violence that had been initiated in 1848 because of dependence on the efforts of unreliable civilian militias and poorly trained soldiers, equipped with lethal weapons, to clear the streets. The numbers of policemen were increased and their training as well as the coordination of their activities improved. International cooperation sought to curb the activities of political exiles. Developments in France were typical. The monarchist ministers who dominated Louis-Napoléon Bonaparte's first administration assigned the task of reorganizing the police to Léon Faucher, interior minister for an admittedly brief but nevertheless formative period from 29 December 1848 to 16 May 1849. He immediately sought to increase the reliability of the police bureaucracy by means of a purge, particularly of the mayors who performed crucial police functions at local level. He was also concerned to improve the quality and increase the speed of administrative reporting and more generally to control the circulation of information. Lines of authority were clarified and better coordination assured between the various governmental agencies, the police, and the military.

Methods of policing designed to secure the political control of capital cities, through the *gendarmerie* in Paris and the *Schutzmannschaft* in Berlin, were extended to provincial centers, and as far as was practical, into the countryside. In Berlin, the prerevolutionary force of 230 police and *gendarmes* had been expanded to 1,200 by as early as July 1848.[31] The Prussian police law of 11 March 1850, supported by legislation restricting the right of association and freedom of the press, would remain unchanged in its fundamentals until 1918. Although developed essentially in response to the fears of the government and propertied classes, this "new" police was able to strengthen its authority and legitimize its activities by claiming to defend the interests of almost the entire population against whomsoever the authorities chose to identify as criminal elements, thereby promoting a more general "acquiescence to order,"[32] and the creation of a social environment that facilitated police supervision. The growing presence of police on the streets served both as a symbol of authority and as a reminder to citizens of the state's continued capacity for violence.

The Defense of Moral Order

The coercive potential of the state was thus reinforced. However, although the restoration and continued maintenance of order on the streets was a first priority for conservative regimes, long-term stability was believed to depend upon the reimposition of moral order. It needed to be generally accepted that private property, individual liberty, work, the family, and religion were the bases of social order, and that poverty and inequality were part of the natural and divine order of things. The moral as well as the legal basis for the existing social and political order urgently needed to be reaffirmed. In this process of regeneration, religion and education had key roles to play.

The local influence of the clergy varied considerably according to often distant historical experience as well as sociogeographic factors like habitat structures affecting the social role of the churches. Everywhere, however, an established parish organization together with developing new organizations such as the Pius Associations, established in Mainz and spreading to other Catholic regions of Germany from March 1848, promoted clerical influence. In the early stages of the revolution confessional groups appear to have adopted a conservative position where they shared the official faith of the state and otherwise a more radical stance. In France the Protestant minority, concentrated largely in the southeast, had welcomed the revolution as a liberating force. As social conflict intensified, however, at least among the propertied, class became a more significant guide to political behavior than religion. The churches themselves developed agendas that both promoted their own particular interests, with the Catholic Church hoping to gain greater freedom from state control, and the cause of social order. This was hardly surprising, when so many Roman Catholic and Protestant clergy remained traumatized by the secular and often overtly antireligious character of the first French Revolution and were additionally frightened by the obvious anticlericalism of many of the new generation of liberals and democrats.

The Pope himself, once thought to sympathize with liberal aspirations, had been forced to leave Rome by crowds demanding political reform and his support for the war of liberation against Austria. Faced with this threat to his own authority as well as to the unity of the universal church, he had felt obliged unambiguously to denounce liberalism and all its works, thus enlarging the gulf between Catholic and liberal/democratic ideals that had been far less pronounced before 1848. The clergy were required to demand that the faithful respect ruling monarchs and the established social hierarchy. They should teach the poor to resign themselves to their condition and to ignore the sinful advice of those who encouraged greed and envy. In return for accepting God's will during their earthly existence the poor could look forward to a heavenly reward.

If there was a degree of pessimism about the adult population there was also a determination to mould the minds of the young. In this respect both the secular and religious authorities were determined to secure control of the schools, the essential means of indoctrination. However, in this moment of extreme crisis there was also a willingness to cooperate. The new Prussian constitution, while retaining the principle of state control over education, insisted on its confessional character and on the supervisory responsibilities of the Protestant clergy in the east and the Catholic in the western provinces. In France, the education minister, the Comte de Falloux, established an extra-parliamentary commission to prepare legislation. Its most influential figure would be Adolphe Thiers, formally a notorious anticlerical, who was now determined to hand primary instruction over to the church. For practical reasons this would not prove entirely possible. Nevertheless the religious teaching orders were encouraged to expand and suspect lay teachers were dismissed, although the threat posed by supposedly socialistic teachers had been greatly exaggerated. In fact, even before these educational reforms, both lay and religious instruction had already fulfilled essentially conservative objectives. It was further agreed that the curriculum should be restricted to the three R's and that religious teaching should dominate everything. The poor should realize that "man exists to suffer" and not for "pleasure."[33] Childhood socialization would thus, hopefully, ensure normative conformity, and together with the day-to-day experience of subordination within the family, at school, in the work place, and in public places, would promote self-discipline. The parish priest would assume responsibility for supervising the work of the school teacher, although the ultimate rights of the state were preserved. Paradoxically, and with considerable cynicism, Thiers insisted on protecting the classical and secular bases of secondary education for the upper and middle classes, on the grounds that those groups who were not a threat to social order therefore had less need of religion.

In Conclusion

The events of 1848 were obviously shaped by the particular circumstances of time and place. The level of economic development varied from east to west and with it social structures and relationships. Prerevolutionary constitutional systems and political cultures and inevitably the experience of revolution differed considerably between nations and indeed localities within them. The political and constitutional settlements favored by elites would vary as a result of a compromise between perceived pressure for change and the desire to reestablish particular prerevolutionary institutions and political traditions. However, both the outbreak of revolution and subsequent counter-revolution had key features in common, and broad social groups tended to react to events in similar fashion. A decisive element in the success of revolution was ineffective crisis management and a loss of confidence on the part of political leaders. Collapse at the center demobilized both state agencies—bureaucracy and army—and social elites. Recovery would be engendered by social fear. Leopold von Ranke captured the spirit of the times, for conservatives at least, in writing in March 1848 that "the whole order of things on which the further development of mankind depends is threatened by anarchic powers."[34]

It was not only that the republic appeared once again resurgent in France and the centuries-old Habsburg Monarchy on the verge of collapse. That would have been horrifying enough. But where would the revolution end? The decades of upheaval which had followed 1789 were a frightening precedent. Even worse, socialism now appeared to pose a real threat to the entire social order, to the sacred trinity made up of private property, the family, and Christian civilization. The suddenness with which established regimes had collapsed, the very ease with which liberals and democrats had acceded to power, and the resulting absence of civil war had, however, left intact the bureaucratic and military apparatus of the old state. Counter-revolution would be greatly facilitated by the continued control by members of the old social elites of the commanding heights of power, as well as by their ability to mobilize widespread mass support. The bitter divisions emerging over the nature of revolution, amongst liberals, democrats, and socialists as well as ethnic groups greatly contributed to the success of the conservative reaction.

A political restoration occurred throughout revolutionary Europe. It was not, however, complete. Constitutional changes survived in France, Prussia and the smaller German states, with the exception of the Mecklenbergs, and in Piedmont-Savoy, as conservatives accepted that limited concessions to representative government were necessary in order to establish a broader ruling consensus, one which would include liberals willing to accept a strong state as a safeguard against social revolution. Only in Austria was absolutism reestablished and even there equality before the law had been reinforced and the situation of the rural masses improved through the abolition of compulsory labor service—a very effective means of reducing dissidence.

Following such massive societal dislocation the main objective had inevitably been to restore social control. In an absolute sense this was clearly unachievable given finite resources and the continued capacity of the ruled to resist oppression. Moreover prevailing concepts of the rule of law, even if abused, offered at least some protection to subjects and indeed ensured that state repression was far less complete and less brutal than that achieved during the twentieth century. Once organized opposition had been crushed using military force, i.e. "the manifest use of violence," a shift occurred to "the pervasive use of administrative power,"[35] employing growing numbers of civil servants, policemen, the clergy, and school teachers. These were measures more appropriate to the emerging mass society created by industrialization and urbanization. The dominant positions retained within these structures by monarchs and members of old and new social elites nevertheless ensured that they preserved the "ability to set the terms under which other groups and classes must operate."[36]

The political solution to the threat of revolution has often been described as Bonapartist. As Marx suggested, this involved abdication of political power on the part of both traditional elites and their liberal bourgeois competitors for power, in return for protection of their vital interests—most notably private property, the basis of their social power—by the state. Gramsci's prison notebooks suggested a variant of this—Ceasarism—"in which a great personality is entrusted with the task of 'arbitration' over a historical-political situation characterized by an equilibrium of forces heading towards catastrophe."[37] The popularity of the monarch was enhanced by the "invention" of ritual and by the provincial tours, facilitated by railway travel, which sought to "personalize the bonds between ruler and common folk."[38] More dangerously the monarch, invariably wearing military uniform, posed as the symbol of national unity and as the supreme war lord.

This resurgence of the monarchical state in the second half of the nineteenth century was daily exemplified by its judicial and police activities and glorified in school, church, and in the developing mass media. Less frequently, its influence was tested through its ability to use these forms of ideological manipulation, as well as administrative pressure and bribes, to mobilize mass support through elections. In practice, however, the independence of the state would continue to be circumscribed by the power and influence of social elites and its own recruitment of key personnel from within their ranks. Existing elites had managed to retain their predominant social roles. Within essentially transitional societies, the authority of traditional landowning and bureaucratic elites remained substantial in terms of the ownership of wealth creating property, social influence, and access to positions of political and cultural power. The experience of revolution helped promote the ongoing process of fusion between these old and the new elites emerging from the process of economic modernization, an interpenetration based upon the sharing of opportunities for wealth creation, on intermarriage, cultural convergence, the sharing of political power, and on the identification of a common enemy. Together these groups would retain a quasi-monopoly of the leisure time and cultural capital which facilitated control of the state and political organization.

Certainly no political regime or sociopolitical elite can be entirely monolithic. In the mid-nineteenth century neither the technical means nor the political will to impose uniformity existed. The subsequent development of the sociopolitical systems which had emerged as part of the counter-revolutionary struggle depended on a complex of factors. These included the character and quality of political leadership, the effectiveness of institutions and mediating procedures, the pressure for change, and the relationship between internal and external politics. Liberalization and democratization would continue to be promoted through the desire of political groups within the elites to secure a greater share in decision making as well as in response to pressure from below.

Whenever they felt that their vital interests were threatened, however, as during the Paris Commune in 1871, a broadly based alliance of property owners would be mobilized until their fears had subsided. On this occasion, the moderate republican Jules Simon would insist "June 1848, March 1871—the same struggle," and with the same outcome, a blood bath, as politicians and senior military officers seized the opportunity to settle accounts. In 1871, the old imperial army which, in 1870, had been encircled and forced to surrender at Sedan and Metz, would be released from German prisoner-of-war camps to go to the assistance of Thier's liberal-conservative government. The former belligerents could once again agree on the pressing need to smash the international revolutionary menace.

In more normal times, the combination of symbolic authority and occasional police brutality with popular self-discipline, would effectively restrain protest action within the narrow legal limits set for political and trades union activity. The conditions for continued governmental success in an era of accelerating economic and social change additionally included, particularly in periods when fear of social revolution was dormant, an ability to adapt to changing circumstances and to facili-

tate the institutionalization of protest. This might be exemplified by the liberalization of the imperial regime in France in the 1860s, by the concessions forced upon
the Austrian regime by military disaster in 1859 and 1866, and the revival of liberalism within the German states. The balance between reaction and reform varied
over time and between states according to shifting perceptions of the social and
political situation.

State modernization coincided with and partly depended upon capitalistic
growth. Regime legitimacy was undoubtedly promoted by the worldwide economic upturn of the 1850s, which markedly contrasted with the long mid-century
crisis. This upturn was promoted by renewed business confidence in social stability,
by industrial growth, by state support for economic development, by the rural prosperity engendered through rising demand for agricultural produce, at least until the
beginnings of the "great depression" in the late 1870s, and by the rapid creation of
new urban employment opportunities. Together with massive overseas migration,
these developments eased the problems of overpopulation and underemployment
which had previously caused so much social tension. The survival of the counter-
revolutionary settlement established after 1848 depended in the last resort on the
avoidance of delegitimizing crises and, most notably, catastrophic military defeat.

It would, however, be the determination of political elites in 1848 to preserve
the status quo and their inability to satisfy demands for greater German unity,
together with the exacerbation of ethnic rivalries within the Austrian Empire,
which would provoke a series of closely related internal and international crises and
increasingly destructive military conflicts in 1866, 1870, and 1914. The postrevolutionary settlement had failed to solve the problems caused by heightened nationalism. Avoiding these wars would have required political leadership of a very high
standard. Unfortunately France had acquired an emperor, Napoléon III, committed to upsetting the European balance of power; while the Prussian Chancellor Bismarck would be prepared to resort to war to secure Prussian hegemony within
Germany; and the Austrian monarchy would engage in a constant struggle to preserve its integrity. On the one hand, nationalistic ideals inculcated through the
schools and media, and reinforced by the identification of potential enemies, helped
to preserve the internal political settlements and to secure public support for
adventurous foreign policies. On the other, great-power chauvinism stimulated
resistance from minority nationalities whose dreams had been aroused in 1848,
only to be dashed by the—often ungrateful—forces of counter-revolution. Defeat
in war would eventually destroy the regimes constructed by the victorious
counter-revolutionaries between 1848 and 1851—Austrian absolutism in 1859/66,
the French Second Empire in 1870, and both the Austro-Hungarian and German
empires in 1918.

Notes

I am very grateful for the helpful comments made on earlier drafts by Heather Price, John Breuilly of the University of Birmingham, Colin Heywood of the University of Nottingham, Olena Heywood of the Open University, and Peter Lambert of the University of Wales, Aberystwyth.

1. M. Abélès, "Anthropologie politique de la modernité," *L'Homme* 121 (1992): 17.
2. Roger Price, *Documents on the French Revolution of 1848* (New York, 1996), 43-45.
3. Quoted by James Sheehan, *German History, 1770-1866* (Oxford, 1989), 663.
4. Ibid., 665.
5. C. Brochet, "A Protest-Cycle Resolution of the Repression-Popular Protest Paradox," in *Repertoires and Cycles of Collective Action*, ed. by Mark Traugott, (Durham NC, 1995), 123.
6. Charles Tilly, "Revolutions and Collective Violence," in *Handbook of Political Science* ed. by Fred Greenstein and Nelson Polsby (Reading MA, 1975), 536.
7. Quoted by Reuben John Rath, *The Viennese Revolution of 1848* (Austin, 1959), 262.
8. Radu Florescu, "Debunking a Myth: the Magyar-Rumanian Struggle of 1848-9," *Austrian History Yearbook* 12-13 (1976-77): 82.
9. Frances Gouda, *Poverty and Political Culture: The Rhetoric of Social Welfare in the Netherlands and France, 1815-54* (Lanham MD, 1995), 3.
10. Clifford Geertz, *The Interpretation of Cultures* (New York, 1973), 89.
11. *Souvenirs* , vol.12 of *Oeuvres complètes* (Paris, 1964), 91-92.
12. *Compte rendu des séances de l'Assemblée nationale.*
13. Pierre Birnbaum, *The Heights of Power. An Essay on the Power Elite in France*, trans. Arthur Goldhammer (Chicago, 1982), 1.
14. Gouda, *Poverty and Political Culture*, 67.
15. Quoted by David Barclay, *Frederick William IV and the Prussian Monarchy 1840-1861* (Oxford, 1995), 63
16. Quoted by John Saville, *1848. The British State and the Chartist Movement* (Cambridge, 1987), 131.
17. Rath, *The Viennese Revolution*, 195.
18. Quoted by Barclay, *Frederich William IV*, 195.
19. Istvan Deak, *The Lawful Revolution: Louis Kossuth and the Hungarians 1848-9* (New York, 1979), 194-95.
20. Quoted by Alan Sked, *The Decline and Fall of the Habsburg Empire 1815-1918* (London and New York, 1989), 105-6.
21. Quoted by Rudolf Stadelmann, *Social and Political History of the German 1848 Revolution*, trans. James Chastain (Athens, OH, 1975), 131.
22. Gouda, *Poverty and Political Culture*, 1-2.
23. Alf Lüdtke, *Police and State in Prussia, 1815-50*, trans. Pete Burgess (Cambridge, 1989), xiii.
24. Quoted in J.P.T. Bury and R. Tombs, *Thiers 1797-1877: A Political Life* (London and Boston, 1986), 113.
25. Quoted in Saville, *1848*, 168.
26. Quoted in Sheehan, *German History*, 710.
27. 10 January 1849, quoted Jacques Droz, *Les Révolutions allemandes de 1848* (Paris, 1957), 482.
28. Quoted by Robert J. Goldstein, *Political Repression in 19th Century Europe* (London, 1983), 7.
29. Quoted by Sked, *The Decline and Fall*, 133.
30. State prosecutor, Rouen 13, June 1850, in Archives nationales, BB 30 334, Affaires politiques: correspondance 1850-1851.
31. Elaine Spencer, *Police and the Social Order in German Cities. The Düsseldorf District, 1848-1914* (DeKalb IL, 1992), 30-32
32. Max Weber, quoted by Lüdtke, *Police and State in Prussia*, 282.
33. G. Chenesseau (ed.), *La Commission extra-parlementaire de 1849. Texte integral des procès-verbaux* (Orléans, 1937), 33.

34. Quoted by Sheehan, *German History*, 727.

35. John Gledhill, *Power and its Disguises. Anthropological Perspectives on Politics* (London, 1994), 19.

36. G. William Domhoff, *Who Rules America Now?* (Englewood Cliffs NJ, 1983), 2.

37. Quentin Hoare and Geoffrey Nowell-Smith (eds), *Selections from the Prison Notebooks of Antonio Gramsci* (New York, 1971), 219.

38. Barclay, *Frederich William IV*, 12.

Storming of the Palais Royal in Paris on 24 February
(Illustrirte Zeitung, Leipzig, no. 245, 11 March 1848, 176)

Barricade in the Rue St. Martin in Paris on 23 February
(Illustrirte Zeitung, Leipzig, no. 245, 11 March 1848, 177)

Part I

CENTERS OF REVOLUTION AND REFORM

The Origins and Course of Events

*Battle between the people of Palermo and royal troops on 13 January
(Illustrirte Zeitung, Leipzig, no. 242, 19 February 1848, 120)*

*Battle between royal troops and the militia and the people in Toledo street in Naples on 15 May
(Illustrirte Zeitung, Leipzig, no. 259, 17 June 1848, 402)*

Chapter 3

APPROACHING EUROPE IN THE NAME OF THE NATION

The Italian Revolution, 1846/49

Simonetta Soldani

Language and Idioms of a Long Revolution

Why are there so few comprehensive histories of events in Italy in 1848? And why are Italian historians so reluctant to reappraise an age that is of such significance to modern day Italy? These are not merely rhetorical questions. If this were only a recent phenomenon, one could trace its causation to the "revisionist" tendency that aims to downplay the role of revolution in history. The continued influence of this approach is exemplified in a recently published history of Italy, "from the end of the sixteenth century to 1861," that only refers in passing to 1848, as if it were an irrelevant deviation from the course of history.[1]

However, this trend alone is not sufficient to explain why the most recent systematic study on the Italian revolution, by Giorgio Candeloro, appeared no less than forty years ago.[2] Coming at the end of a rich season of local and regional investigations that paid special attention to economic concerns and "social" unrest, Candeloro's work was conceived in a view strictly connected with the centenary of the Italian nation state. Since then very little has been done, partly as a result of a long declining interest in the Risorgimento, apart from a steady trickle of philological contributions (more or less useful in reconstructing events) and some occasional in-depth monographs.[3]

Historiography has traditionally interpreted the Italian revolution of 1848 solely as a "step on the road to unity" and has thus defined it much too narrowly. The revolution was rather the critical, explosive moment in the course of extensive processes of modernization, which began under French rule and which developed along partially diverging lines during the Restoration (1815-1830). Therefore, it defines an age, and not only in the field of politics, but also with respect to attitudes and ways of life. Indeed, in retrospect, it has co me to be identified as a break in the experience of time and space, the first intensely contracted, the second most dilated. Years later, an aristocrat who had participated to the uprising of Milan in March 1848 wrote: "From that moment on all was rapidly changing, in our household habits as in city life, in our customs and in our thoughts."[4]

The profound nature of the revolution's impact was primarily caused by its long duration, which spanned the period from the election of Pius IX in July 1846 to the fall of the Roman Republic in August 1849. "From Rome to Rome," one might say, to name the core problem facing any hope of modernization in the peninsula.[5] Only when keeping in mind this span of three years can one really understand how it was possible for the revolution to bring to maturity changes that would prove irreversible. A national consciousness arose, for once fed from below and based on general principles of liberty, and still respecting both the range of conditions and traditions that the revolution was facing, and the different projects, classes, and interests to which it gave voice.

The revolution was one, but the languages and idioms in which it was articulated between the summers of 1846 and 1849 were many, and continuously changing. Applying a recently proposed model to interpret Italian resistance to fascism during the Second World War, one could say of the 1848 revolution that it was simultaneously a war for national independence, a battle for liberty, and a struggle for improved social conditions, and that the coexistence of these different aspects was sometimes a richness, but more often aroused fears and provoked endless discord.[6]

For all those who wished to change the economic and political condition of Italy, the main problem had long been liberation from Habsburg rule. The entire three years of revolution were characterized by all kinds of hostile demonstrations against Austria, often in the form of genuine mass movements, including assemblies, protests and uprisings, the formation of volunteer corps, and military action. The anti-Austrian movement of 1846/49 was above all characterized by strong popular support and clearly liberal features, namely by its identification with civil liberties and with a constitutional and parliamentary reform of the individual states. The goal on the horizon was no longer "independence at any price," but an independence rooted in freedom. Such a stance implied a direct confrontation with the sovereigns and the world of "aristocratic privileges" they represented, and more generally with the "enemy within, who serves the foreigner." It was also a stand against "conservatives and bogus innovators," perhaps disguised as preachers of cautious harmony, whom Giuseppe Montanelli, one of the most prominent activists of the Italian revolution, denounced in 1851.[7]

For most of the elite who played a central role in 1848, the term "freedom" meant a reorganization of the economy according to the principles of free trade, changes in tariff policies and banking, a modernization of trade and finance laws, as well as the construction of an adequate road and rail network. It also meant the final abolition of communal property and common lands, together with the privileges reintroduced during the Restoration in such fields as church property and inheritance law.

The issues at stake were made more complicated by the active participation of the urban middle classes, pressing for an end to the monopoly of power retained by stagnating courts and the "unchanging urban aristocracies of Italy."[8] Their fight was fought in the name of the *popolo lavoratore* (working people), an expression that typically included all who were not professionals or living off private income, on whom would be bestowed the economic and civil dignity decreed by the triumph of capitalism. This aggressive middle-class presence—independent, at least in part, from well-established networks of aristocrats' and notables' patronage—was not intimidated by the fear of "agrarian communism," a fear that had been roused, primarily in Southern Italy, by peasants occupying the lands usurped by the rich and powerful people. Nor was it intimidated by movements of urban workers in almost every Italian town, demanding higher wages and better conditions of life, and inevitably perceived as manifestations of the hated socialism and of the right to work.

Nation, Freedom and Social Progress were the three registers that organized the discourse on revolution, variously articulated according to time and place, political conditions and social relations: whatever the problem at hand, differences not only between the various Italian states, but also within them, were so great and numerous that the language was inevitably multilayered. It must be added that in the mid-nineteenth century, potential appeals to a common Italian ancestry did not exclude stronger and more tangible loyalties: even those three exceptional years showed that mass mobilization and willingness to fight were all the stronger when local and regional interests could support national issues.

A sense of oneself as Venetian or Milanese, Sicilian or Tuscan, Roman or Bolognese, was still crucial to the concept of being Italian, and this was true not only at a popular level, but also among upper classes. Those who tried to organize mass support for the revolution were driven, as Cattaneo wrote, to raise simultaneously "the flag of the nation and the banners of its one hundred cities." For a long time seeking to represent the Italian nation through a single symbolic image, distinct from those of the urban or regional identities which constituted it, would be an almost hopeless task.[9]

At the same time, some of the most important symbols of the Italian national identity were actually formed, or gained a "patriotic" value, during those years, a real milestone in Italy's shaping as a modern nation. The national anthem, the Battalions of Volunteers, the Lombard League and the Knights of the Cross, Balilla and Ferruccio,[10] the benevolent face of Pius IX and the severe expression of Mazzini, the barricades in Milan and the fierce resistance of Venice, the bell of the Gancia monastery in Palermo and Carlo Alberto's exile, Garibaldi in besieged Rome, the *Camicie Rosse* (red-shirted soldiers) and the dying Anita: all these made up a sort of beloved Pantheon of heroes and role-models for generations of Italians, almost up to the present day.

Today, the world inhabited by such ideals seems to have entered an irreversible crisis, highlighted by recent political movements and historical writing. But just this discontinuity can help us to view the 1848 revolution in a less reductive and restrictive way, as "one of the few moments of an intense collective and unitary life" undergone by a country whose inhabitants, since the Partition of the Roman Empire, had had no common experiences, except for wars, invasions and plagues.[11]

To speak of 1848 as an "Italian revolution" is therefore no historical distortion, or "retrospective definition," as has been claimed in the wake of Benedetto Croce. It was "Italian" because it expressed ideas, plans and aims endowed with a strong national value, though deeply rooted in European culture and experiences, despite the stubborn efforts made by many Italian intellectuals during the Restoration to emphasize the "indigenous" roots of the new national ideology.[12] Even the political structure they planned in 1848, so mindful of the value of the hundred cities of Italy and so far from the centralized state of the "French type" achieved ten years later, was bound to ideas of citizenship and representation inconceivable without the recent experiences of the rest of Europe.

The variety of languages spoken by and expressed in the Italian revolution, was no more than the reflex of the broader European context, whose revolutionary principles had fuelled cultural and political debate for decades, nourishing a dialog both intensive and problematic. The language that came to be used in the course of events fired by ideals of freedom and nation, acquired a growing "foreign flavor" month after month, beginning with the success of the reviled principles of 1789. While at the very eve of the 1848 uprisings moderate opinion held these principles to be inapplicable to Italy, at the close of the three year period they had become a reference point not only for democrats but for the entire range of Italian liberals, with the exception of moderate circles in Tuscany and Sicily. The shift in opinion is all the more obvious when compared to the widespread voices current prior to the revolution, crediting modern Italy with "a revolutionary cycle quite distinct from that of France, ostensibly due to the royal reforms" of the eighteenth century.[13]

This summary of entanglements and effects emphasizes the importance of Italy's involvement in the European revolution in breaking down further parts of the wall that had made Italy a sort of precious "separate niche," and in shifting Italy's political center of gravity from the past into the future, and from the inside to the outside of the peninsula. As examples of these shifts, one can think of the collapse of reform projects based on "urban and regional forms of administration,"[14] of the strongly rooted prejudices against the idea of strengthening the State, and, above all, of the end of neo-Guelph ideology, with its hopes of increasing the political role of the Roman pontiff.

It would undoubtedly be a mistake to underestimate the continued influence of reactionary and municipal powers after order was restored in Italy. Equally, thanks to the experiences of those three years, Italy became more strongly anchored in a European order where the symbols of Christianity and the Roman Empire were being replaced by the principles of a double revolution, economic and political, which had begun to change the world.

A Revolution before the Revolution?

Is it appropriate to consider the events that took place in Italy between the summer of 1846 and February of 1848 as an integral component of the revolution rather than as the "two years of preparation" of the traditional interpretation? In responding to this question, it is certainly legitimate to underline the sharp change in the Italian climate and context that was produced by the collapse of France and of the Habsburg Empire—the two main powers of continental Europe—between February and March 1848. Nonetheless, the course of events in Italy that preceded this watershed highlights the difficulty in clearly separating the spheres of reform and revolution, although a purely ideological approach, shared by contemporaries and historians alike, traditionally interprets reforms and revolution as strictly antithetical.

If we stick to the facts, we must say that all began in Italy with the celebrations marking the election of a reputedly liberal Pope, and his first decisions in office. This election had been long awaited by an inner circle of moderate intellectuals eager to announce it throughout Italy as heralding an end to the opposition between the Catholic Church and modern civilization, which had arisen in the eighteenth century. In great and small cities, all over Italy, celebratory banquets and torch-lit processions were held, prayers were said and the *Te Deum* sung in gratitude, while a multitude of poems and songs were written to honor the Pope of "renewal": the authority that everyone said to be aware of people's desires and willing to fulfil them, even when they became more openly political, and more specifically directed towards the introduction of new principles and political rights. Enthusiasm rapidly reached such a level that it even spread over some rural areas, through the mediation of members of a lower clergy culturally impatient and frequently dissatisfied with its own status. No subsequent retraction or wave of restoration would ever erode the traces of what amounted to a miracle: the possibility of reconciling Catholic orthodoxy to principles of freedom, progress, and nationhood.

The way was opened for creating a strong alliance in the name of religion, thus reducing the danger of mass reactionary uprisings like those which, in the name of the *Santa Fede* (Holy Faith), had plagued the three years of Jacobin rule in Italy (1796-1799).[15] The myth of Pius IX, strengthened and further "legitimized" by the romantic revival of religion and of an imaginary medieval Christianity, favored all over Italy the initiation to politics of the emerging bourgeoisie and lower middle classes, which would prove decisive for the formation of an Italian public opinion. Even the rituals of "reconciliation" and "fraternity" celebrated between traditionally hostile towns and villages, so crucial to the image of restored national unity and so frequent between the summer and autumn of 1847, were largely imbued with the symbolism and emotional impact of religious rites of purification and rebirth.

The effects of such an intense and unusual theocratic-liberal outburst[16] were soon felt. As early as the end of 1846, pressure for domestic reforms had increased considerably in the various Italian states: Metternich's writings of the period reveal his growing unease with the situation.[17] Only the head of the church could fire the imaginations and hopes of the people to so great an extent that as early as the fall of 1846 masses of subjects in all the Italian states had begun to act as potential citizens, determined to affirm the virtue of the word over that of silence, the value duty of active participation over that of passivity. In March 1847, an impassioned witness of the new hopes hovering in the air, Gino Capponi, confessed that he was quite awed by the quick spread of political curiosity, and especially by the speed with which the traditional "neglect of public interest" became perceived as a sign of individual and collective "immorality".[18]

It was in this climate dominated not by a secular idea of modern politics, but by pervasive ideals of religious palingenesis, that important campaigns for freedom of the press, of thought and of assembly took shape, immediately followed by demands for a civic guard, for central consultative bodies, for a strengthening of the role of municipal and provincial governments, for opening their management to wider sections of society, and for a fundamental reform of the legislative and judicial systems. Precisely their being rooted in a heavily religious culture and mentality tended to make these demands more radical, as Metternich observed in the autumn of 1847. Once the threads of the alleged cooperation between princes and subjects had reached breaking point, they were replaced by a devotion to principles of freedom, progress, equality and social justice which, just because lived *sub specie religiosa*, could only fail to meet history's requirements and limitations.[19]

It is hard to determine how significant it was that the election of Pius IX coincided with a series of economic difficulties: the collapse of various international export markets, excessive financial speculations and bankruptcies, food scarcity and high prices of basic necessities. Equally hard is to determine to what extent the general crisis of confidence in the "established order" was influenced by its inability to control the explosive consequences of a market economy strong enough to overturn existing structures of production but too weak to produce a consistent and permanent economic growth.

In Italy as in other countries there has been much discussion on the role played in channeling energies for the outbreak of revolution by the overlapping of two different economic crises: in agriculture in 1846, in the world of trade and banking from the end of 1847.[20]

Providing a clear answer is difficult, particularly as for Italy there is still no satisfactory analysis of their form and extent. It is certain, however, that they affected the entire peninsula. The economic difficulties worsened the disintegration of the "old order," especially in those areas in which isolation and dependence on important European economic centers were dramatically combined; whereas in the few northern innovative areas in which traditional economic structures were gradually being replaced by new ones, the crisis nipped the ongoing transformation process in the bud.[21]

To draw a direct line between economic difficulties, their social consequences, and political tensions would doubtless be an exaggeration. The geography of protest and the geography of most intensive political initiative do not necessarily tally, and the one does not always benefit the other. However, from the hard winter of 1846/47 onwards, sections of rural and urban working classes remained without food or work, while the upper and lower-middle classes dependent on the local economy, living off the processing of agricultural products and small scale commercial activities, had serious problems to face. These upheavals provided specific issues and reference points for those who hoped for political transformation, creating a highly charged situation, noted with apprehension by European diplomats. Moreover, unrest because of the high cost of living, market riots, and attacks on convoys "exporting" local products, had an echo and an effect all the greater in a phase of heightened political sensitivity and an unusually lively press and public life.

The economic crises thus offered the political movement new opportunities, but forced it to "politicize" the crisis to attract more supporters for the struggle in progress, and to channel discontent towards governments rather than the rich. This was no easy task in itself, given the gulf separating the advanced proponents of a liberal individualism and free market economics from the passionate popular defenders of old communal and collective rights. Nonetheless, the attempt was successful, and drove new wedges into the group of the economically powerful, who, aware of their own vulnerability, saw "free competition" as the main threat. What made the miracle of "unifying" the different interests of the educated classes of peninsula was the incredible mass of lectures, articles and pamphlets listing the advantages and successes of economic liberalism, asking for the abolition of protective laws and corporate practices in the name of progress, emphasizing the social aspects of building railways, roads and banks, and the need for a confederation of the Italian states to guarantee their efficiency.

The importance of economic liberalism for proponents of cautious reform is demonstrated by the triumphal receptions for Richard Cobden in a number of cities in central and northern Italy in the spring of 1847, and by the speeches given at banquets held in his honor.[22]

The hymns of praise for the values of "free competition" between states as well as between individuals were raised just when the democrats were rediscovering the political value of solidarity, in the sense of a "support of less fortunate brothers." The common bond of the nation would create solidarity, they argued, between members of different, but no longer antagonistic, social classes.[23]

In considering the dynamics of the so-called "biennium of reforms," one should never ignore the revolutionary potential of its religious and social hinges, that favored the entry into politics of men whose social origins would once have debarred them, and constitutes one of the most important inheritance of those years. What is more, such men—who operated not only in the larger cities, but also in the mid-sized and minor urban centers, so characteristic of the Italian landscape—had a cultural background and a political vision rather different from those of the elite. In a way, their espousal of catch-phrases and slogans derived from the Gospels, made them closer to the popular mentality and culture, and for this reason particularly fit to mediate political ideas and ideals towards the lower social orders.

The mobilization of these spokesmen from the civil service, academic and professional classes as well as from representatives of small and medium size manufacturing and commercial interests was the decisive innovation of 1846/7. It was they who enlivened the squares and coffee houses, who organized demonstrations, who fought for increasingly more sweeping and radical reform programs, and who divulged the significance and aims of the protest in small pamphlets and flysheets, published at first illegally, then legally. As the months passed, the role played by those individuals, who were not from the educated aristocracy and the intellectuals associated with them, grew in importance, especially in steering an ever more restless public opinion, hungry for brief and exhaustive reports on the "events of the day."

Revolutionary Reforms

Naturally, not all the Italian states were affected in the same way and with the same intensity by the wave of a movement ever less open to moderation, or by the increasingly pressing demands that it formulated. Obviously, the states which proved most vulnerable to the pressure of reform were those—the Papal state and the Grand Duchy of Tuscany—that, despite the dignity of their institutions, lacked any real credibility in coping with the intensity of change. This situation was also rooted in the weakness of their administrative, diplomatic and military structures, and in the absence of the power and authority necessary to create consensus. From the spring of 1847 onward, Rome and Florence—though reluctantly and after a series of delays—granted a parallel series of reforms, not in order to prevent the revolution, but to avoid the total collapse of the two states: laws for a cautious freedom of speech and of the press, the institution of a civic guard and of government bodies having at least an advisory power. When a minister of the Grand Duke stated in October that "the permanence of civil servants in their offices seemed to depend on the goodwill of the people only, or rather on that of the leaders of the unrest,"[24] he was only underlining real weaknesses, arising from a substantial lack of instruments of repression. On the contrary, it was just the availability of those instruments that gave strength to the Kingdom of the Two Sicilies. Here, indictments by intellectuals, hunger riots, and conspiracies hatched by old and new secret societies were always dealt with in the same way: imprisonments and deployment of the army. In September 1847, Reggio Calabria and Messina were bombarded.[25]

As to the small duchies of central Italy, they lacked even that minimum of vitality that was necessary to shake off political lethargy, while Carlo Alberto, king of a relatively cohesive state, could allow himself to delay all projects for reform until the last days of October. His hope was that the petitions, appeals and demonstrations in favor of reform would not spread beyond the always discontent and unreliable Genoa, whose past as a maritime republic prompted its inhabitants to resist the pressure of the administrative and aristocratic absolutism of the Savoyard monarchy.[26]

Lombardy and Venetia—integral components of the Habsburg empire, although ruled by a viceroy—were affected by the same troubling and excited atmosphere as the rest of Italy, and by a growing rejection of Austria, which was accused of unjustifiably exploiting the wealth of the region.[27] But it was virtually out of question that the Habsburgs,—grappling with a multinational empire and with the aftermath of the dramatic events in Galicia—could agree to such demands, as was made clear by the bloody attack on the Milanese crowd assembled to celebrate Pius IX and the new Italian Archbishop on 8 September 1847.

Apart from similarities and differences in the reactions of the ruling establishments to the reform movement, what is surprising is the rapid starting up of a national circuit of ideas, proposals, and objectives. No chance was missed to join historical episodes into a common Pantheon of memories, as when the *Tricolore* was reintroduced in the mass demonstrations during December 1847 by Genoese and Tuscan democrats. A sensibility arose in which a success or a failure of the inhabitants of a single Italian state was felt as a success or a failure of all the Italian people; and this tendency of the various segments of public opinion to join together turned even the most moderate opinion into a generalized critique of the establishment. In this framework, calling into question the preservation of that multiplicity of states, which made sense only in a post-Napoleonic perspective of the peninsula's subjugation to Austrian hegemony, sounded like a radical opposition to the current situation.

In this way that "concept of the nation" was strengthened, which, as a Tuscan democratic newspaper recalled, in the 1830s existed only "in the minds of few, [as] a sectarian utopia, an aspiration of the free," and which by now had "reached the common consciousness and set all hearts beating faster".[28] This concept, which grew up in other fields than those worked by the ideas of Mazzini and Young Italy, had acquired overt political connotations even before Massimo D'Azeglio spoke for the moderate party of a program able to support a "*risorgimento* (revival) of the nation" that decades of neo-classical and romantic culture had painted in the colors of a great history. The extremely moderate Cesare Balbo was quite correct in pointing out that whoever promoted "the right and the hope" for a "complete and absolute" independence of Italy, as he had done, was in fact putting forward an extremely radical objective.[29]

Were cautious reforms, therefore, in the service of a revolutionary end? It is hard not to respond in the affirmative, even though the two discourses rely on alternative rhetorical sequences; one entirely practical, interwoven with specific and analytical proposals, the other quite undefined, based as it was on a concept as elusive as that of the nation, impossible to submit to political rationale. It was exactly these aspects that caused Metternich primary concern, as he became increasingly aware that the main danger did not come from what Edward P. Thompson would term "revolts of the stomach," but from ideas, "phantoms" against which he was forced to admit that "material force can do nothing," especially if the ideas were those of freedom and nationhood that drove the movement in an ever more sharply anti-Austrian direction.[30]

Shortly after Pius IX's election, the cry of "foreigners go home" was raised in Rome, and after that no opportunity to exacerbate old tensions and create new grounds for dissent was wasted, beginning with the Austrian occupation of the Papal city of Ferrara in August 1847. This episode emphasized the need to reduce the Austrian presence in the peninsula (or, as one heard more and more, "to free Italy from the Austrian yoke"). A large majority of moderates, as well as of democrats, conceived it as a primary objective. When Papal diplomacy sent out a fact-finding mission in August to explore the possibilities of a defensive alliance between the various Italian states,[31] it was met with enthusiasm in liberal circles, because of the recognition of the existence of a "main enemy" that it implied. References to medieval anti-imperial alliances made the excitement grow to such an extent that neither the Bourbon refusal, nor the hesitation of Tuscany, nor Carlo Alberto's reluctance to sign anything that might imply hostile sentiments toward Austria, were able to dampen the effects of that "need for unity," which negotiations for the formation of a League between individual Italian states had made even more apparent.

Following Vienna's false step in December, when the Duchies of Modena and Parma were forced to sign a treaty allowing the Habsburgs a free use of their military structures and territories, there seemed no alternative but to concentrate all efforts on the goal of independence. This shift in emphasis was shared even by those who were reluctant to pass over in silence the internal responsibilities for the worsening of the crisis. For, by this time, the refusal of the rulers and their advisers to issue a constitution, to grant more generous civil liberties, or to allow new forces into active politics, had made evident the princes' obdurate opposition towards any ideas of constitutional reform and had broken up the myth of an idyll between people and princes that had been blocked by Austrian hostility.

With this background, it was unavoidable that the aftershocks of a new commercial and financial crisis in England—so keenly felt in the more advanced "European" areas—would be ascribed to the governments, accused of being unable to act according the logic of "economic progress." As a consequence, growing difficulties both for the urban manufacturing classes and for the middle classes involved in trade, industry, finance and the professions (who were the driving force of the reform movement), provoked dissatisfaction with the governments, as public opinion became convinced that the crisis was, above all, a political one.

On January 1848—a month marked by uprisings and repression all over the peninsula, by deployment of local troops as well as by further provocation from Austria—in all the milieus the time seemed ripe for a settling of the score. But it took a successful insurrection in Sicily for the sovereigns to become fully conscious of the gravity of the situation. The Bourbon king granted the constitution without trying to resist, so that the other Italian princes were obliged to make the same choice immediately afterwards. "What a miracle this Italian movement is!" Giuseppe Montanelli exclaimed in a letter to Gino Capponi about the latest news, "A constitution in Rome too, allowed by the Cardinals! How can Providence be denied?"[32]

When the texts of those "statutes" (a term meant to emphasize an imagined continuity with indigenous medieval tradition) became available, they were found to be altogether cautiously worded. This partially reflected the role played in drafting them by an extremely moderate elite, who had much to fear from the new political actors appearing on the stage in the course of most recent events.[33] But the very fact that the ruling classes were forced to take such a step—everywhere and simultaneously—was in itself the best proof that Massimo d'Azeglio's "conspiracy in broad daylight" had developed into a revolutionary break, reaching across the entire peninsula even before the uprisings in Paris and Vienna had torn down the two pillars of the European balance of power, bringing up new problems and tasks for people and rulers.

"Italy will Do it Alone"

Even if it would be inappropriate to attribute to Italy an initiating role on a European scale, as historians sometimes did,[34] for once the Italian revolution was not an entirely "passive" one, i.e. not only a projection of ideas, expectations, and breaks nurtured and brought to maturity elsewhere. The need and the desire for a radical upheaval of the situation had indeed sound and diffuse roots in public opinion. What is more, the successful creation of Pius IX as the emblem both of opposition to Metternich's politics and of the new "yearnings of the people" not only overturned the traditional image of the papacy, but severely undermined the organic alliance between throne and altar that was the very basis of Restoration Europe. This fact really opened new vistas across half of Europe, giving fresh hope to those planning more or less radical changes in the political and social situation of the continent.[35]

Nonetheless, there can be no doubt that it took the collapse of the July monarchy and of the Habsburg Empire to drastically change the character, course and perspective of the ongoing political struggle. Now that the revolution had become European, and that the same watchwords suggested realities and perspectives not contemplated in the previous framework, new possibilities opened up, making it necessary to come to terms with the altered dimensions that the political and social problems were taking.

The victory of the revolution in France, and the ideas of a "social republic" that it nourished, reinforced already existing deep fears, fuelled by the massacres in Galicia and the increasing interest in socialist ideas and organizations throughout Europe.[36]

The recently granted statutes—which, it was hoped, would provide protection against revolutionary pressures—were modeled on that French constitution of 1830 which had just been put out of use by a mass uprising. This seemed to increase the danger that someone might wish "to do like in France," advancing ideas of social justice and the right to work, which were increasingly seen as essential corollaries to those of democracy and of the republic. And, in fact, there was a sharp increase in social unrest throughout Italy during February and March, encouraged by the conviction that "a constitution means a just government," and that "new rules" also meant, of necessity, a "new order" as well.[37]

This was manifest in protests against the tariffs and taxes levied on basic foodstuffs; in market riots caused by scarcity of and increases in the price of food; in the occupation and illegal appropriation of woods and common lands; in gatherings of workers and hired laborers calling for secure employment and better wages, in a chaotic overlapping of old and new claims. Episodes of "widespread social crime" differed greatly in severity and intensity across the various regions of the peninsula, but with reference to the new idioms from across the Alps the questions they raised were labeled "class struggle" and "socialist hydra." These labels were applied whether they referred to the division of fallow and common land, to the restitution of lands put to civic uses or illegally privatized into the hands of the community (i.e. of "the communists"), or to measures to limit increases in food prices and to restrict the export of foodstuffs.[38]

The changes within many governments that took place from the beginning of March onwards, were suggested by just this need to confront the unsteady situation, and to make a clean break with the previous royal councils, as a way to respond to the pressure of the working class's demands with something other than simple repression. In any case it became almost a "categorical imperative," accepted by everyone and celebrated by many, "to do without France," both in order to prevent the spread of dangerous revolutionary precedents and not to give the legitimate rulers an excuse for stopping dialogue and cooperation with the reform movement. This imperative became obsessive when, in the second half of March, first Milan and then Venice revolted, trying to take advantage from the revolutionary stream that had struck at the heart the Habsburg empire. From the two capital cities of Lombardy-Venetia, demonstrations and revolts spread across the other towns of the region, leading to the establishment of municipal revolutionary committees and provisional commissions of government, forcing the civil and military authorities of the Empire's "Italian provinces" to quit the field.

All the evidence agrees in pointing out that the manifestations of joy all over Italy following the successful uprisings and the Austrians' flight led to a further radicalization of the political climate, stirred up by a renewed spiral of "pressure from below" on the governments to accept standpoints and reach decisions that did not conflict with a public opinion which was more and more in favor of liberalism. The fevered resumption of negotiations concerning a political league, rightly considered crucial to begin a real "federal war," overlapped with the numerous committees for recruiting the "Volunteers of Lombardy" that arose nearly anywhere, and with severe pressures on rulers to contribute men, arms and funds to the "Holy War of Italy," which began on 23 March when the Piedmontese army crossed the Tessin river.[39]

The strong desire for active involvement felt by the intermediate social classes, who fulfilled the delicate role of social and cultural cohesion in the cities, prevented the "expulsion of foreigners" from being seen as a sufficiently constructive end in itself, regardless of the reasons brought forward, the methods employed, and the solutions contemplated. Accompanied by the usual entourage of songs and verses in praise of war, a flood of flyers, pamphlets, and newspaper articles called to arms all who wished to prove to themselves and others that the Italians were determined and able to fight.[40] The campaign was relatively successful in contrasting its aspirations with the desire of conservative and moderate powers to limit initiative to the army and the diplomatic bodies. Although this "pressure from below" succeeded in maintaining the conviction that the goals of independence, freedom and "social renewal" could and should be pursued in parallel, sustaining and strengthening each other, such a linkage was destined to remain an assertion of principle devoid of concrete consequences. The same thing can be said of the basic unity of the European revolution and of the intrinsic solidarity among the insurgents of the different European countries.

This situation of impasse was confirmed by the dubious success of the motto with which Carlo Alberto ended the speech made on crossing the border into Lombardy: "Italia farà da sé" ("Italy will do it alone").[41] This expression, hovering between warning and encouragement, expressed more than the conservatives' desire to distance themselves from a country wracked by republican and democratic forces, considered little short of diabolical. It also communicated the desire of national and liberal forces to seize this unique opportunity for the Italian people to assert its rights and duties as active players in the "renewal of the nation," fighting for that principle of popular sovereignty, that fed a lively campaign to interpret the recently granted statutes as a first step towards a general constituent assembly.

"Italy will do it alone" meant also calling on the "educational virtues" of the revolution and acting for the construction of national solidarity, so that even Giuseppe Mazzini made the motto his own, repeating it until the beginning of the summer. But it implied too a voluntary isolation from the European context, and a special emphasis on the particular nature and resources of the "Italian case," marked by a national culture of extraordinary value and by the encumbering presence of the Pope. The war would reveal such a path to be a dead end, highlighting the futility of a "separatist" conception of Italian politics and making even the warmest supporters of the national revolution aware of the need to intertwine a constant dialogue with every country and people participating in the revolution, without any provincial idolatry, but also without isolationist tendencies.

The Disasters of the War

Much has been written in praise or criticism of an operation that, from the very beginning, was based on a fundamental misunderstanding: a military campaign, planned and carried out along the most traditional and dynastic lines imaginable, with the usual goal of obtaining new territories for the Kingdom of Piedmont by taking part in the games of the Great Powers, was presented as a national war, fought to bring "the help that a brother can expect from a brother." When Gaetano Salvemini wrote, some hundred years ago, that Carlo Alberto had gone to war "not against Austria, but against the republic" whose proclamation was threatened by the restless crowds in Milan, his comment was a bit exaggerated in tone, but basically correct in its appraisal of the choice made by the Savoyard monarch.[42] Had the republic been proclaimed, it would have excluded Lombardy from Piedmont's plans for annexation, while Carlo Alberto hoped to extend his influence in the fertile Po valley as far as the Venetian border, and to present himself on the national and international stage as the man who could restore order in an area intolerant of Austrian domination, and dangerously inclined to republican sympathies.

In this light, decisions such as only crossing the Tessin once the "popular revolution" had gained Milan appears more intelligible, as does the very slow advance to avoid encountering the imperial rearguard, or—finally—the decision to "act like a customs agent" along the southern shores of Lake Garda to underline Piedmontese respect for Venetian territory.[43] Nor is it surprising that Carlo Alberto tried to extract from the ex-subjects of the Empire a vote which would sound like a request to be annexed to Piedmont, or that he tried to reduce to a minimum contacts between "his" troops and other military units, both the various volunteer corps flooding from furthest and nearest cities (corps which were quite incompatible with an army governed by strict pre-Revolutionary rules), and the "regular" troops which other Italian rulers had promised to send, asking to negotiate forms and goals of their own participation.[44]

On the other hand, the ambiguous attitudes of these princes are also quite evident. Under pressure from the press, demonstrations in the city squares, and advice from government and municipal authorities, the Pope, the Bourbon king and, as far as it was in his power, even the Grand Duke of Tuscany, were forced to come to terms with the revolution, at least temporarily, dispatching some battalions of regular troops to the Po valley. But neither the Savoyard war nor the people's war really fitted into the plans of rulers who had nothing to gain from a strengthening of Piedmont or from a principle as revolutionary as that of the right of the people to independence, to which Carlo Alberto had appealed as he crossed the border. Involvement in the war, moreover, objectively strengthened the "national party" which was most active in demanding broader election laws, extension of the franchise, and greater and better defined powers for parliaments and governments.

The Pope, an authority representative par excellence of pan-national and absolute power, was the first to break out of this spiral, declaring on 29 April that he would never go to war against a Catholic Great Power like the Habsburgs. Immediately after, he began to stand back explicitly from too "liberal" a reading of the Statute he himself had granted two months before, finally declaring himself unprepared to take on the role of a constitutional monarch. The most worrisome signal, however, came from the dramatic events in Naples on 15 May. During a fierce disagreement between the King and the newly elected Parliament, unimpressive barricades were set up in support of the latter which were immediately overwhelmed by hordes of people revolting in the name of the King and the Holy See, while the army opened fire on the civic guard. The government resigned, parliament was suspended and the troops marching north were summoned back.[45]

The revolution was losing pieces and going to pieces, while many wondered if it was really possible to keep such varied goals together, and have a "revolutionary war" led by people who had a horror of "revolutions and revolutionaries" (Cattaneo). This statement was suitable for Carlo Alberto too, who was attempting to put an end to the "temporizing war" he had embarked on, without sacrificing the extension of his realm, or reawakening that terrible stone-guest represented by the armed people of Milan. To succeed in these two aims, he had to avoid being accused of betrayal by those who could influence public opinion in Milan, and who, hostile as they were to the goal of "fusion," asked for the creation of a constituent mechanism at least in the near future.

The obstacle was avoided, as is well known, by a use of the plebiscite that pre-figured its "revolutionary" potential: all adult males were requested to declare whether they preferred to place themselves under the Savoy's aegis before or after the end of the war, according to procedures not yet defined.[46] The plebiscite was accepted, and consent to the immediate fusion given, with the sole exception of Venice, that decided to vote only when directly threatened by Radetzky's advancing troops. But the political price to be paid for the plebiscite was high, and not only with regard to the relationships with other princes of Italy, who in the choice of immediate annexation saw confirmed all the worst suspicions that had already come out during the inconclusive negotiations for the League of the Autumn 1847. Whether one looks at organized political groupings and parties, or at the public mood dominant in urban and rural areas, it is clear that May—the month of the "fusion"—marked a real watershed in Carlo Alberto's fortunes. Opposition came to be voiced even within the Lombard provisional government, which from the beginning was in the hands of the most moderate and pro-Piedmontese forces.[47] Federalists like Cattaneo spoke openly of a boycott, while Mazzini founded a newspaper, *L'Italia del popolo*, to voice opposition to the "strong northern state" prefigured by the plebiscite and by the current diplomatic negotiations. More generally, this solution was vehemently adversed by people and democrats, as a result of agreements between the powers rather than the fruit of the nation's "educational force."[48]

When in mid-June, with the fall of Vicenza, the imperial armies, which had begun marching south some two months earlier,[49] started to threaten the Piedmontese military camp, all the indicators pointed to a political and social collapse of the front. The defeat in the scarcely relevant battle of Custoza (25-27 July) was enough to spread panic through the Savoyard army, so that a withdrawal degenerated rapidly into a ruinous rout. And this time no one opposed the advancing Austrians, neither in the countryside nor in the cities. Even Milan remained generally quiet, if one ignores the dismay and protests at the king's "betrayal," the object of endless debate among contemporaries as well as among historians. However, support by the local population for the few armed volunteers organized by the democrats, proved the existence of willfully ignored potentialities in favor of revolution.[50]

The surrender of Milan and the truce signed on 9 August seemed to seal the fate of the revolution, which in previous months had witnessed the failure of many cherished hopes: the liberal Pope and neo-Guelph movement, the cooperation of the Italian rulers with the war of independence, the national feelings of Carlo Alberto and the value of the Piedmontese army. The gulf created by the ruin of so many myths and aims was not easy to fill up. The offer of the Sicilian crown to Carlo Alberto's second son, which had gained the approval of France and England, had quickly become a dead letter.[51] The union vote teased out of the Lombards and Venetians, and accepted with some difficulty by the Piedmontese parliament on 11 July, was now of only limited value. The plan of territorial reorganization ratified by the Great Powers, with the agreement of civil authorities in Vienna, and based on a "Great Northern State" including Piedmont, Liguria, Lombardy and the duchies of Parma, Piacenza and Modena, was clearly destined not to be realized.

Between 2 and 17 August, the "constitutional" governments of Rome, Turin, Palermo and Florence collapsed like a house of cards under the weight of the Piedmontese defeat, opening the way to cabinets haunted by the fear of not being sufficiently moderate, but determined to ensure public order. While Venice, aware of the impending dangers, chose the path of a civil "dictatorship," in Naples the Bourbon king overcame his initial hesitation and ordered the reconquest of Sicily, after retaking the continental regions of his realm by force and leaving savage destruction and atrocity in his wake.[52] In the meantime, news of the defeat and armistice set off a wave of disruption and protest in many key cities, such as Florence, Rome, Genoa, Venice and Turin itself, while Bologna witnessed a bloody revolt against Austrian occupation on 8 August, followed by a yet more bloody repression, without the Pope lodging any protest against this patent violation of his sovereignty.[53]

Had the revolution run its full course?

Proofs of Sovereignty

"The war of kings has ended, the war of the country begins." With this exhortative assertion Giuseppe Mazzini opened his manifesto *To the Italians* (Agli Italiani), in which he presented a civil and military mobilization "from below" as the only possible way of avoiding an inevitable backlash.[54] The invitation to overcome the current crisis relying on a strengthening of the people's role and its sovereignty must have seemed a pipe-dream, even to militant democrats, at a time in which terms like fraternity and national unity seemed echoes of forgotten sentiments, beguiling remnants of the past rather than cornerstones of the future.[55] This was more true if one considers that in northern Italy, where stragglers and political refugees from throughout the peninsula had gathered, a mood of increasing intolerance towards those "harbingers of discord" was widespread.[56] Who could take seriously Mazzini's demands to France and England in those troubled weeks—"Our Alps and our vote, nothing more, but nothing less"[57]—when the collective body of "the people" on which that claim was based seemed to have disappeared from view? How could one demand that "the nation would retake its "rights," when its champions seemed quite unable to influence a confused and disappointed public opinion?

On the other hand it appeared equally impossible, at least for the moment, to force the ongoing political experiments to a close, without being forced to manage the disrupted machinery of Italian administrations and governments, and the potential threat of an uncontrollable mass reaction. It was absolutely necessary to avoid the risk of stirring up the conflict "between the principle of dynastic property and that of national sovereignty," which—except in France—was at the heart of the European revolution.[58] Even Ferdinand of Bourbon was forced to use some caution, when—encouraged by the success of "his" armies in Calabria against the "rebellious" bands that had gathered there—he suspended once again the sessions of the newly reinstated parliament, but delayed its permanent dissolution until the following March. The extensive network of political clubs and committees for public safety that had sprung up throughout the provinces in the aftermath of the attack on the parliament of 15 May, to defend it and the constitution, was still too strong in August for the problem to be approached directly.[59]

With the exception of the south, where the situation was already seriously compromised, the only feasible approach to get out from this impasse seemed for the moment to restore the credibility of the moderates that lay in tatters because of their too feeble and narrow political behavior both on a social and on a national level. Even this solution however, had a severe drawback, as a falling into disrepute of the moderates could seriously risk the prestige of the liberal institutions and procedures, with their train of voters, members of parliament and governments especially interested in allowing no excuses for "subversion." Moreover, this path proved far from easy to follow. On the one hand, the governments that had resigned because of the disaster in Lombardy had been replaced by equally moderate ones, more mindful of royal power than of the precepts of the constitution, more concerned with the principle of order rather than with that of freedom.[60] On the other hand, it was clear to everyone that support for liberal institutions only made sense, and had a chance of success, if the truce had a positive outcome. Instead, negotiations deteriorated into dilatory proposals for international congresses and exhausting attempts to form an Italian League that might support claims on Austria, which the defeated Piedmont could not credibly advance in its own name.[61]

There was a stark contrast between the hopes with which Italian democrats began, after some hesitation, to approach France, and France's reaction, unmindful of the solemn promises made by Lamartine in the late spring, to provide "helpful assistance" to the brothers across the Alps if "the cause of Italian independence were to be seriously threatened." General Cavaignac and his men now displayed a complete lack of interest in both letters and petitions from Italy asking their aid, and in diplomats sent to Paris "on more or less official missions from stable and provisional governments, from local committees and political parties, and even from units of the national guard."[62] The answers given to these requests were unambiguous, as were those to the heartfelt speeches of Mazzini, and to reserved solicitations from the Piedmontese and Tuscan governments, too anxious to avoid a settlement that would seal Austria's victory to show their deep-rooted hostility for the French "red" government. Like their English colleagues, although with perhaps less conviction, in September the French emissaries let it be known, or even declared openly, that they would advise Austria against returning to the status quo ante, which would be dangerous both for its internal stability and for international peace. They would do nothing beyond that, however, and above all they repeated loudly and clearly that they were quite opposed to any resumption of the war by Piedmont.[63] This advice meant only one thing: Italy had once again relapsed into the periphery of Europe and was unworthy of any serious commitment.

However, the decision of the "mediating powers"—which was already clear by August and fully taken on when the truce ran out at the end of September—did not have the effect that one would have expected. From conviction or fear, instead of relapsing into apathy, Italy saw a new explosion of political activity and debate. Important sectors of moderate opinion spoke in favor of a strong defense of parliamentary institutions and related civil liberties, as well as for the necessity of taking up arms once again, to reaffirm their desire for independence and national pride. Most importantly, the complete indifference of the mediating powers toward the Italian situation lent new vigor to the negotiations between some Italian states that had been underway since the beginning of August. The aim was to bring the national dimension of the political and military struggles to the fore once again, and create permanent federal institutions: a task made more difficult by the current restructuring of the concept of sovereignty, subject to diverse interpretations.

At the beginning of October, a plan for a federal assembly, to be headed by the Pope and composed of delegates elected by the various parliaments, had been patiently worked out by Antonio Rosmini, whose projects had had a preliminary approval both by the Pope and the Grand Duke.[64] At the same time, Piedmontese emissaries were pressing for the unlikely approval of a scheme of an Italian League which would have supported their claims to territorial expansion, while Gioberti convened a congress for the Italian federation in Turin, from 10 to 27 October. Delegates from all over the peninsula came and discussed the issue, although most of them rejected any proposal aimed to establish a "Northern Italian Monarchy."[65] But two days before the opening of that congress, Giuseppe Montanelli, the newly nominated governor of an insurgent Livorno, rebelling against the moderate Tuscan government, spoke out in favor of an Italian constituent assembly. It was, he said, indispensable not only to manage peace, but also to wage war, so that it would be prepared, carried out and perceived as a genuine war of the people and the nation.[66]

The dispute among different hypotheses for the convocation of the assembly—were its members to be nominated or elected? and by what authority? by the parliaments, the governments or the citizens who had the right to vote?—was to rage fiercely until the very last day of the Italian revolution, with continuous recriminations, shifts of emphasis and changes of procedure. The most interesting aspect to point out, however, is that—thanks to these "abstract" controversies—the issue of political nationhood remained on the agenda, and became increasingly closely linked to questions of freedom and democracy, and to public debates on the nature of the state and on the responsibility of citizens for their own future.

It was not by chance that the issue of a constituent assembly attracted the greatest interest in those centers such as Turin, Florence and Rome where it could reorient the country's immediate future. This did not apply to Venice, isolated in the middle of its lagoon, nor to Naples, where the course of the Garigliano river seemed to have become once again "a national rather than a state border";[67] nor to Sicily, where defense of freedom and of privilege came to be considered more and more as synonymous, so that it became impossible to organize an effective resistance to the Bourbon military offensive. On the island, devastated with fire and sword by armed bands of criminals, and held to ransom by municipal, national and private guards in the pay of old and new potentates,[68] not even the bombs, pillages and massacres carried on by the Bourbon troops reconquering Messina[69] could convince the masters of the parliament to call on the popular militias which only a few months previously had allowed the victory of the revolution.

At the decisive moment in spring 1849, Sicily lay in a situation of extremely precarious sovereignty—the consequence of a fragmentation of power against which no steps could be taken. Such a fragmentation was the natural result of the "conservative alliance" between the old and new aristocracies of blood and money, the backbone of the 1848 revolution in Sicily.[70] In a situation characterized by huge problems of territorial control and local domination, any recourse to the Italian nationality looked more like a luxury, rather than an opportunity to keep open the ideals and political possibilities of the beginning of the revolution. Even the government's basic approval of a possible constituent assembly during the month of October had a clearly "passive" character, linked to the wish of ensuring to each participant the possibility of preserving unaltered a character of "free and independent state."[71]

By autumn, half of Italy seemed to have withdrawn from the revolutionary circuit, or to be hovering on its margins, while the other half appeared trapped in the web of confusion and tensions entered after the battle of Custoza. When on 15 November, at the reopening of Roman parliament, a group of conspirators murdered—in the courtyard of the Capitol, and with a collective gesture rife with symbolism and classical references—Pellegrino Rossi, Prime Minister of the Pope and an intellectual of European stature, the situation became explosive.[72] Two weeks later, the Pope's night-time flight in disguise brought the entire Italian political arena in movement once again, and reawakened widespread European interest in events on the peninsula. Though indirect, an attack against the man who embodied sacral power was too dangerous to be tolerated.

Looking to the Future

"A fictional image of Italy exists in the minds of foreigners," wrote the Lombard democrat Carlo Cattaneo in September 1848, after several talks in Paris that made him realize the level of ignorance abroad about the Italian situation and the persistence of a strong stereotypical image of Italy: a country inhabited by a handful of "white people" who—by virtue of their cosmopolitan culture and "foreign travels"—had gained some "lazy and feeble yearnings to freedom and nationhood," and by a "brown race" of natives, a fertile breeding ground for "*lazzaroni* (scoundrels)", who, in their hatred of the "rich and noble," were always ready to rob and kill them, and to plunder and pillage their villas, as well as the surrounding villages and towns.[73] A month later the marquis Cosimo Ridolfi, a Tuscan moderate, wrote from London expressing his surprise at the superficial level of information and opinion existing in England on the Italian situation, even among the most cultivated circles of the capital, too fond of the "land of the dead" stereotype diffused by Lamartine to engage with its realities.[74] The same ignorance could be found in every cross-roads of the European politics of the time, from Frankfurt to Brussels.

The superficiality of views perceivable even among the elite for whom the "travel to Italy" was an indispensable rite of passage sharply contrasted with the obvious desire of the many "special envoys" from Italy to have the *risorgimento* of their nation known and recognized in Europe.

The kaleidoscope of *Commedia dell'Arte* masks that made up the European image of the "Italian character,"[75] made it difficult to conceive that Italians would be capable not only of sudden flames of protest, noble deeds and sudden reversals, but of long-term, patient initiatives aimed at keeping open as long as possible perspectives of change, at consolidating and developing the victories of the previous spring. Hence, when in December the young Franz Joseph was crowned emperor in Vienna and Paris started out its path to empire by electing Louis-Napoleon Bonaparte as president of the republic, no one could imagine that important parts of Italy, beginning with the Papal states, would be swimming against the tide of normalization that was flooding all over Europe. It may even be the case that the Pope's rigid attitude were based on a deliberate, albeit misconceived, attempt to provoke revolt, thus giving him an opportunity for unconditional restoration. In fact, attempts to "break the revolution's back" only hastened the "leftward" shift in the political axis that had already begun.

The first country to join the revolutionary stronghold of Venice—dominated by men whose "municipal" concern caused a fierce opposition towards any moderate political program centred on Piedmont [76]—was Tuscany. Here, a dramatic change of regime took place in October, replacing the moderate colors of the Florentine aristocracy with the "flaming" ones of a ministry led by two leaders of democracy much loved in Livorno, the university professor and former Saint-Simonist Giuseppe Montanelli and Francesco Domenico Guerrazzi, a lawyer and successful novelist.[77] In the first half of December, the increasing difficulties of Piedmont in achieving peace without risking further war brought to the fore the abbot Vincenzo Gioberti. His government's program proposed a "conciliatory democracy" aimed at the "working out of political nationhood" and at the "development of constitutional institutions," but his political ideas and aims were considered little less than subversive even by members of the moderate aristocracy such as Count Cavour.[78]

It was especially in Rome that the constructive and forward-looking aspects of the choice of resisting normalization were tested. The provisional government, formed to lead the country out of the institutional chaos into which the Pope's flight had thrown it, not only achieved this aim but earned widespread approval for the methods used and results gained.[79] Neither accusations of sacrilege nor excommunications flung by the Pope against all who would have favored or were favoring "the current state of affairs" succeeded in damaging the government's prestige. Elections to a constituent assembly that took place under its rule in January 1849 produced a result that was universally considered to have been "remarkable, both for the number of voters and for the quality of the elected."[80]

The transition that the "new men" who just reached the power had to face was not an easy one, as events in France and in some of the German states had already shown. They had to prove that democracy was not necessarily a synonymous with class war, terror or revolutionary dictatorship, but could mean equal opportunities and civil liberties for all citizens, the triumph of right over privilege, of law over despotism, and of "regulated participation" over systematic repression. The main elements of the strategy were to attach importance to the voting system, to ensure the correct functioning of elective assemblies, to give a voice and higher profile to every instrument for the shaping of public opinion, from political clubs to press, in order to anchor in the mind and experience of all the real and potential Roman citizens an idea of Italy whose main strengths were parliament and people.

Despite what one could suppose, Mazzini did not share this opinion. After staying in Milan for several months during the spring of 1848 he had become impatient of the amount of speechifying about elections and governments, constitutions and parliaments.[81] The vote that he called for in the late summer was thought as a decision in favor or against a strengthening of the concept of nationhood, and not as an instrument for the exercise of precisely defined constitutional rights and duties. His disapproval of the Roman assembly's attempts to formulate laws going beyond the immediate emergency and to elaborate a constitution was predictably vehement and clear, from the moment he entered the Capitol on 6 March 1849. On 3 July the disapproval resulted in an invective launched from the benches of parliament against an assembly busy discussing the text of the constitution just while the French army poured into the city.[82] His accusations were all the more incomprehensible when one considers that the prepared constitution was modeled on the French one, i.e. that of the occupying power, and that its clarity and coherence made it a lodestar for Italian democrats up to the constituent assembly debates of 1946.

Not everywhere did it happen that the word democracy was synonymous with voting and delegation of power, or with the formal and informal possibilities and instruments that helped a political apprenticeship, from pamphlets to simple leaflets, from cafés to the ever more numerous clubs, that often united political activity with amusement and general sociability.[83] Nonetheless, the increasing visibility and disputability of the power was a characteristic of this second phase of the Italian revolution, and had important—or better, irreversible—consequences, particularly among those social classes and groupings which had only recently gained the right and possibility to participate in "public discourse."

Even in "collapsed" Tuscany, apart from the unusually lively participation in political life by the middle and lower-middle classes, the documents report the new rulers' constant attention to the proper functioning of institutions and the correct implementation of administrative tasks.[84] This despite difficulties arising from the scant cohesion or integrity of the ministry, the Grand Duke's flight to the amenable coast of Gaeta on 13 January, and an open boycott by moderates, determined not to have "any dealings ever, for whatever reason, not even for an accidental, momentary agreement, with the democratic party."[85] Venice's "democratic experience" was yet more significant, even though Cristina di Belgioioso described the city as one that "lived more in the past than in contemporary Europe," and that had to deal with the Daniele Manin's paternalist centralism and the catholic organicism of Niccolo Tommaseo.[86] Venice's republican tradition is always regarded as the key to understand its long and well organized resistance. Although this accounts for Venice's initial impetus, it does not explain the tenacity shown by the rich bourgeoisie of trade and finance in supporting the provisional government to the last, up to the point of sacrificing their assets. The experience of this long revolution caused ongoing changes in the conception and execution of policies, thanks also to the Italian microcosm living in the city and especially active in journalism and in the parliament.

An oft-repeated interpretation that emphasizes the distance between the 1848 democrats and earlier or later Jacobins—the former fond of harmony and mediation, the latter marked by hard internal struggles and vehement opposition—is an unjustified projection into the past of clashing conceptual pairs reflecting different sensibilities. All the more because the Italian revolution in its full maturity was characterized by a general overcoming of the hypocritical litanies of unity and of the initial, severe phobia toward political parties, together with an attempt to establish political, military and diplomatic initiatives by common consent and with clearly defined aims. This also continued to be the case after the break marked by the departure from the scene of the two heroes from the revolution's early days, Pius IX and Carlo Alberto. On 9 February 1849 a vote of the Roman parliament marked the end of the temporal powers of the Pope, and hence of any theocratic project; on 23 March Carlo Alberto decided to abdicate, as moderate public opinion had long demanded, in consequence of the disastrous campaign followed to the renewal of hostilities (20 March), when the Piedmontese army dissolved like snow in the sun on first contact with the Austrian troops near Novara.[87]

A desperate revolt in Genoa, in response to rumors of surrendering to Austria, was harshly crushed by the same army that had fled before Radetzky's troops, while in the astonishing uprising of Brescia, the poorly armed populace resisted the Imperial army for ten days for the sake of a war that had already ended, in the face of devastation and massacre of unarmed civilians.[88] Such insurrections proved that the instability in Italy was more than the work of a few hotheads, but they could not ease the consequences of defeat. For some time, Piedmont too—its army destroyed, a new king who did nothing to hide his reactionary inclinations, foreign occupation (albeit limited in scale), and a parliament with an uncertain future—left the stage, whereas Venice continued until August to hope that the peace between Austria and Piedmont would not be signed.[89]

In Tuscany, the collapse of any public authority rendered more frightening the reactionary attitude of the countryside and the clashes of hostile bands in the capital, so much so that the moderates of the Florentine municipal administration signed an unconditional appeal for the Grand Duke's return, which paved the way for Austrian military occupation. And if Florence was spared, Livorno was first reconquered by force, with a bloody attack which was welcome by all those who had long feared social subversion,[90] and then subjected to a severe state of siege and a long armed occupation. By the first half of April there were rumors from Gaeta—which had become an important crossroads of international diplomacy since the Pope resided there—of a renewed agreement between the European powers, that were determined to put an end to the scandal of the Pope's loss of power, and collectively take on the burden and honour of reoccupying the "Holy City." The enterprise was largely considered an easy one, for, as the Pope's closest collaborators declared and the *sancta sanctorum* of European public opinion repeated, "Italians are unable to fight" and "even if the Turks came, the Romans would bless them."[91]

Yet the last remaining pillars of the Italian revolution, Venice and Rome, fought until the bitter end, with arms and the instruments of diplomacy and politics. The weakness of the "liberal powers" was thus highlighted, as they proved themselves incapable of obtaining even minimal concessions in favor of a constitution from the reactionary front, and forced even those who had looked with suspicion to the aggressive program of the democrats to recognize the importance of the example of Venice and Rome. "As in the past, Italy lives in her cities," wrote in June Carlo Matteucci, who had travelled to Gaeta two months previously to petition for the Grand Duke's return. "Vicenza, Venice, Brescia, Catania, Messina, Bologna and Ancona all defended themselves bravely. Rome follows their example. All this will remain."[92]

The inhabitants of Venice, whether or not they were actually Venetian, besieged for over a year, resisted to the end, refusing offers of unconditional surrender although the city had been attacked with increasingly well aimed mortar fire since March 1849. To understand such a decision one must assume a really high level of commitment to the reasons and aims of the revolutionary regime.[93] As for Rome, matters were complicated by the high political profile of the "Italian defenders" who joined the city and by the leading role of republican France in the military operation. The *repubblica educatrice* evoked by Mazzini in his speech to the assembly on arrival in the city did not remain a simple ideal, as it is revealed by any eyewitness's reports. Everyone, including Ferdinand de Lesseps, the first commander of the expedition, remembers the solidarity, order and security perceptible in the city right to the end with admiration. This sentiment was matched only by the pride of those who repeatedly succeeded in exposing the flaws in the invaders' reasons: with patient negotiation, like Mazzini, or skilful attacks and "buccaneering" maneuvers like Garibaldi.[94]

On the eve of surrender a young Lombard soldier, with a solemnity made more poignant by his impending death by the hands of those French whom he had seen in Milan as symbols of freedom, wrote: "They will win, but every ruin will be defended … To continue to exist, we must die today," and die in Rome, which seemed to him, in that culminating moment, "as great as its memories, and as the monuments that adorn it, bombarded by barbarians." Some years later, Mazzini confirmed that "damned to die, we had to think of the future in offering up our *morituri te salutant* to Italy from Rome". Mazzini was right, as Cattaneo was when, in the first quiet autumn after the long storm, he declared that thanks to the rising up after the failure of the "fusion," the Italian movement had not been a "fiasco."[95]

Not only "was 1848 not lost," but it had gradually "clearly defined all the problems" that the Italian question implied, and that had led to the rejection of any plan including Bourbons, the Grand Duke, or the Pope as king or president. The course of the revolution had shown that a solution to the Italian question required "struggling for freedom rather than for territorial claims."[96] Many believed that the path had become less troublesome, after the long and active resistance to the tide of normalization had modified the political and ideological background. Firstly the untenability of Italy's political and territorial set up as determined by the Congress of Vienna had become a major theme of international diplomacy. This was due to the numerous groups of utopians, nourished by historical realism, who had occupied the Italian scene during the last year, and who were among the few on the continent who could leave the ruins of revolution with heads held high. Secondly they insisted on choices that would guarantee maximum popular support for the struggle and that would modify not only the structure of the states, but also the reasons and the actors of politics. This determination contributed to preserving the democratic resonance of words like nation and nationhood, interwoven with principles of social justice and solidarity between peoples, long after the revolutionary season had ended. Leaders like Mazzini and Garibaldi thus became human symbols of independence movements halfway across the world.[97]

Today, as this heritage seems to have dangerously crumbled, so that nothing but ethnic conflicts are associated with the word nation, it may be useful to remember its other possible meanings.

Notes

1. See Giovanni Sabbatucci and Vittorio Vidotto (eds.), *Storia d'Italia*, Vol. 1, *Le premesse dell'Unità dalla fine del Settecento al 1861* (Bari, 1994).

2. Giorgio Candeloro, *Storia dell'Italia moderna*, Vol. III, *La Rivoluzione nazionale, 1846-1849* (Milan, 1960).

3. See, for example, Franco Rizzi, *La coccarda e le campane. Comunità rurali e Repubblica romana nel Lazio (1848-1849)* (Milan, 1988), and Enrica Di Ciommo, *La nazione possibile. Mezzogiorno e questione nazionale nel 1848* (Milan, 1993).

4. Giovanni Visconti Venosta, *Ricordi di gioventù. Cose vedute o sapute, 1847-1860* (Milan, 1904), 291.

5. For a general survey of the Italian revolution from this point of view see Simonetta Soldani, *Il lungo Quarantotto degli Italiani*, in Giovanni Cherubini, Franco Della Peruta and Giorgio Mori (eds.), *Storia della società italiana*, Vol. 17, *Il movimento nazionale e il 1848* (Milan, 1986), 259-343.

6. The reference is to Claudio Pavone, *Una guerra civile. Saggio sulla moralità della Resistenza in Italia* (Turin, 1994). Here the author speaks of the Resistance of the years 1943/45 as a war that ran out on three different and often contrasting levels: national liberation, civil war, class struggle.

7. Giuseppe Montanelli, *Introduzione ad alcuni appunti storici sulla Rivoluzione d'Italia* (Torino, 1945), first published in 1851.

8. Leopold von Ranke, "Frankreich und Deutschland" (1832), in von Ranke, *Sämmtliche Werke*, Vol. 49 (Leipzig, 1867/88), 61-76, here 60.

9. Carlo Cattaneo, "Considerazioni sulle cose d'Italia nel 1848" (1851), now in Cattaneo, *Il 1848 in Italia. Scritti 1848-1851* (Turin, 1972), 316, and Ilaria Porciani, "Stato e nazione: l'immagine debole dell'Italia", in Simonetta Soldani and Gabriele Turi (eds.), *Fare gli italiani. Scuola e cultura nell'Italia contemporanea*, Vol. 1 (Bologna, 1993), 385-428.

10. On some of these characters and places of the national mythology (beginning from "Balilla," nickname of the boy who, throwing a stone, sparked off Genua's rebellion against town's Austrian occupation in 1746, see Mario Isnenghi (ed.), *I luoghi della memoria*, Vol. 1 (Rome-Bari, 1996). As for Francesco Ferrucci, the hero of the Florentine Republic struggling against the Imperial army in 1530, collective pilgrimages to the place where he was killed (the village of Gavinana, on the mountains near Florence) began to multiply in summer 1847, and continued until the First World War, organized by Republicans, Radicals, and even Socialists.

11. Antonio Gramsci, *Quaderni dal carcere*, Vol. 3 (Turin, 1975), 2004.

12. See Antonio De Francesco, "Ideologie e movimenti politici," in Sabbatucci and Vidotto, *Le premesse dell'Unità*, 294-320. Di Ciommo, *La nazione possibile*, chapter 1, underlines the considerable homogeneity of the intellectuals in the different Italian states and of their cultural debates in the years before 1848.

13. Montanelli, *Introduzione*, 214.

14. Raffaello Lambruschini, *Dell'autorità e della libertà. Pensieri d'un solitario* (Florence, 1932), 256.

15. On the role played by the myth of the "liberal Pope" in averting a reactionary tide in the countryside and among low people, see Walter Maturi, "L'aspetto religioso del 1848 e la storiografia italiana," in Accademia Nazionale dei Lincei, *Il 1848 nella storia d'Europa*, Vol. 1 (Rome, 1949), 257-80.

16. On the importance of this catholic revival for the success of the Italian mobilisation see Daniele Menozzi, *La Chiesa cattolica e la secolarizzazione* (Torino, 1993). For a rapid description of the atmosphere of that period see Lorenzo Nasto, "Le feste civili a Roma 1846-1848," *Rassegna storica del Risorgimento*, 79 (1992): 312-38.

17. See especially *Mémoires, documents et écrits divers laissés par le Prince de Metternich*, Vol. 7 (Paris, 1883).

18. Giovanni Baldasseroni, *Memorie 1833-1859* (Florence, 1959), 290.

19. See also, for example, Metternich to Lützow, 10 October 1847, in *Mémoires*, Vol. 7, 432.

20. The obligatory reference is to Ernest Labrousse, *Comment naissent les révolutions? 1848-1830-1789* (Paris, 1949). Although dated, these pages still maintain an unquestionable evocative power and offer useful suggestions.

21. A few remarks on the problems connected with the increasing economic disparity North/South in Italy are to be found in Luciano Cafagna, *Dualismo e sviluppo nella storia d'Italia* (Venice, 1989), 187-221. Useful references on the disruptive effects of the market economy on the productive structure of South Italy are in Domenico Demarco, *Il crollo del Regno delle Due Sicilie*, Vol. 1, *La struttura economica* (Naples, 1960), and Mario R. Storchi, *Prezzi, crisi agrarie e mercato nel Mezzogiorno d'Italia, 1806-1854* (Naples, 1981).

22. On the political tone of the speeches given at the banquets in honor of Richard Cobden, during his Italian journey (January to June 1847), see Richard Cobden, *Notes sur ses voyages, correspondances and souvenirs*, ed. by M.me Salis Schwabe (Paris, 1879), 49-79. His advice to the Italian reform movement is well summarized in a letter of 21 May to an Italian patriot: to carry on political reforms in all the Italian states, and to establish a customs league among them like the German Zollverein, but based on free trade: Marco Minghetti, *Miei Ricordi*, Vol. 1 (Turin, 1888), 258-60.

23. An impressive picture of rural Lombardy at the beginning of 1847 is outlined by Franco Della Peruta, *Democrazia e socialismo nel Risorgimento* (Rome, 1965), 66-78.

24. Giovanni Baldasseroni, *Leopoldo II Granduca di Toscana e i suoi tempi* (Firenze, 1871), 258.

25. On the severe crisis of legitimacy of the Boubon dinasty and on the "flight" of the rich and cultured classes towards the idea of a "great nation" see Di Ciommo, *La nazione possibile*, chapters 2 and 4. The dramatic chain of uprisings and repressions in the Neapolitan state of those months is well described in Vittorio Visalli, *Lotta e martirio del popolo calabrese (1847-1848)* (Cosenza, 1928).

26. On the political liveliness and the diffuse democratic attitude in Genua see Edoardo Grendi, "Genova nel Quarantotto. Saggio di storia sociale," *Nuova Rivista Storica*, 52 (1964): 307-50.

27. For an example see Cesare Correnti, *L'Austria e la Lombardia* (Lausanne, 1847), which denounced the discrepancy between taxes raised and investments made in the Lombard area by imperial government

28. *L'Alba*, 2 July 1847, which stressed the "rapid and general crumbling of the political building settled in Vienna."

29. Massimo D'Azeglio, *Proposta d'un programma per l'opinione nazionale italiana* (Florence, 1847), and Cesare Balbo, "Lettere al signor D." (1846), reprinted in his *Lettere di politica e letteratura* (Florence, 1855), 355-70.

30. Metternich to Radetzky, 22 August 1847, in *Mémoires,* Vol. 7, 477, with explicit reference to the unconceivable "spectacle of a Pope playing with liberalism." And shortly after, in a letter to Ficquelmont of 23 October 1847, he added that, as to Italy, it is the morale situation that one m ust keep in mind, because material questions play a minor role there" (Ibid, 436).

31. Fernanda Gentili, "I preliminari della Lega doganale e il protesoriere Morichini," *Rassegna storica del Risorgimento*, 1(1914): 563-639.

32. Giuseppe Montanelli to Gino Capponi, 19 February 1848, in Alessandro Carraresi (ed.), *Lettere di Gino Capponi e di altri a lui,* Vol. 3 (Florence, 1884), 377.

33. Nino Cortese, *Costituenti e costituzioni italiane del 1848/49* (Napoli, 1951), Vols.2, provides much information about the drawing up of the constitutional laws and about their features.

34. A remarkable example is Jacques Godechot, *Les Révolutions de 1848* (Paris, 1971).

35. Till now the subject has been scarcely analyzed. For an overview see Roger Aubert, *Le Pontificat de Pie IX (1846-1878)* (Paris, 1952).

36. On the currency of this theme in the contemporary Italian culture see Gastone Manacorda, *Lo spettro del comunismo nel Risorgimento*, in Manacorda, *Storiografia e socialismo. Saggi e note critiche* (Padua, 1967), 65-88.

37. For some examples of this palingenetic conception of the constitution, which was especially strong in Southern Italy and on the islands, see Giovanna Fiume, *La crisi sociale del 1848 in Sicilia* (Messina, 1982).

38. Simonetta Soldani, "Contadini, operai e popolo nella rivoluzione del 1848-1849 in Italia", *Studi storici*, 25 (1973), 557-613.

39. A vivid collection of documents and reports of the weeks between the end of March and the half of April was published by Carlo Cattaneo, *Archivio Triennale delle cose d'Italia* (1850), now in Cattaneo, *Tutte le opere*, ed. by Luigi Ambrosoli, Vol. 5 (Milan, 1974).

40. Many news on the volunteers, perceived as a litmus test confirming the *Risorgimento* of a fainthearted nation, can be found in Piero Pieri, *Storia militare del Risorgimento. Guerre e insurezioni* (Turin, 1962), who nevertheless does not investigate the social origins of the volunteers, a subject on which there are only few and local studies.

41. Its text has been reprinted in Candeloro, *Storia d'Italia,* Vol. , 180-1.

42. Gaetano Salvemini, "I partiti politici milanesi nel secolo XIX" (1899), now reprinted in Salvemini, *Scritti sul Risorgimento* (Milan, 1961); the quotation is by p. 75. On the interpretation of those events as a "betrayal" of king Carlo Alberto see Adolfo Omodeo, *Difesa del Risorgimento* (Turin, 1951), 156-235, and Guido Porzio, *La guerra regia in Italia nel 1848-49* (Rome, 1955).

43. Carlo Cattaneo, "Dell'insurrezione di Milano e della successiva guerra. Memorie," in Cattaneo, *Il 1848 in Italia*, 177. According to the plans of the Frankfurt National Assembly, the southern border of the German Confederation had to be set at the Lake Garda.

44. Pieri, *La guerra regia*, 278.

45. The most analytical description, avowedly pro-Bourbon, is the one of Giuseppe Paladino, *Il Quindici Maggio del 1848 in Napoli* (Milan and Rome, 1921).

46. In fact, the text written on the ballot-card promised a constituent assembly as soon as possible, "which will discuss the foundations and forms of a new constitutional monarchy with the Savoyard dynasty." But immediately after voting Piedmontese emissaries began to pressure on the provisional government for an immediate "fusion," which led to considerable tensions even within moderate circles: see Antonio Monti, "Il Governo provvisorio di Lombardia e il senso della sovranità," *Rendiconti del Regio Istituto lombardo di scienze e lettere*, 1931: 1201-12 and 1933: 557-74.

47. Leopoldo Marchetti, "I moti di Milano e i problemi della fusione col Piemonte", in Ettore Rota (ed.), *Il 1848 nella storia italiana ed europea,* Vol. 2 (Milan, 1948), 653-723 and Id., *1848. Il Governo provvisorio della Lombardia* (Milan, 1948).

48. *L'Italia del Popolo*, 7 June 1848, in Giuseppe Mazzini, *Scritti editi e inediti*,Vol. 39 (Imola, 1924), 59. Lord Palmerston was highly interested in an international mediation, to prevent France's intervention into Italy and preserve European peace: Alan J. P. Taylor, *The Italian Problem in the International Diplomacy (1847-1849)* (Manchester, 1934).

49. See Alan Sked, *The Survival of the Habsburg Empire. Radetzky, the Imperial Army and the Class War in 1848* (London, 1979).

50. Contemporary democratic pamphlets placed great emphasis on the insurrectionary potential of the situation, as did Gabriele Camozzi, *Cenni e documenti della guerra d'insurrezione lombarda del 1849*, printed in July 1849 in Capolago, in the series of "Documenti della guerra santa d'Italia."

51. On this international guardianship of the island see Ottavio Barié, *L'Inghilterra e il problema italiano nel 1848-49. Dalla rivoluzione alla seconda restaurazione* (Milan, 1965).

52. For a description of the campaign see Benedetto Musolino, *La rivoluzione del 1848 nella Calabria* (Naples, 1903). A general view of the studies can be provided by the *Archivio storico delle province napoletane*, 1947-1949, special issue *Il 1848 nell'Italia meridionale*, and Aurelio Lepre, *Storia del Mezzogiorno nel Risorgimento* (Rome, 1969).

53. As it is clear also in the pro-moderate account of Giovanni Natali, *Cronache bolognesi del Quarantotto*,Vols. 3 (Bologna, 1936).

54. The text of the *Manifesto*, which was widely diffused, is reprinted in Mazzini, *Scritti*,Vol. 38 (Imola, 1923), 213-20.

55. The changing attitude of the public opinion is well pointed out by Montanelli, *Memorie sull'Italia e specialmente sulla Toscana dal 1814 al 1850* (Florence, 1963) 552 (first published in 1853). Captured by Austrians on 29 May, Montanelli could come back to Tuscany only at the end of September.

56. "The Lombardo-Venetians are our trouble, our plague! It is they who have brought this storm over us …" : so a moderate deputy of the Piedmontese parliament wrote on 11 December 1848. Minghetti, *Miei Ricordi*,Vol. 1, 418.

57. The sentence appears several times in Mazzini's writings of that period. See for example: "Ai signori Tocqueville e Lord Minto, rappresentanti la Francia e l'Inghilterra nella Conferenza sugli affari d'Italia," in *Scritti*,Vol. 38, 301-7.

58. Lewis B. Namier, "1848: Seed Plot of History", in Namier, *Vanished Supremacies: Essays on European History 1812-1918* (London, 1958), 21-30, quote on 23.

59. Some remarks on these political committees, mostly made up by people who were interested in strengthening, with the "new order" promised by the constitution, their own politic and economic power, see Gennaro Mondaini, *I moti politici del '48 e la setta dell'Unità italiana in Basilicata* (Rome, 1902).

60. The change was not significant in Florence, where power passed from Ridolfi to Capponi, whose political positions were very close. Much more relevant the change in Rome, where the leadership first passed to a Curia Cardinal and then to Pellegrino Rossi, who favored a restrictive interpretation of the constitution and of the freedom rights. In Piedmont, the "Italian" cabinet of the Lombard Gabrio Casati was followed by clearly dynastic ones, representative of the "Court party." In the same days, the government changed in Sicily too, to include democrats in view of the upcoming campaign of the Bourbons for reconquering the island.

61. See Federico Curato (ed.), *Le Relazioni diplomatiche fra la Gran Bretagna e il Regno di Sardegna*,Vol. 1 (Rome, 1961), and, about the question of the League, the introductions to the first two volumes of: *La diplomazia del Regno di Sardegna durante la prima guerra d'indipendenza* (Turin 1949 and 1951): Vol. 1, Carlo Pischedda (ed.), *Relazioni col Granducato di Toscana*;Vol. 2, Carlo Baudi di Vesme (ed.), *Relazioni con lo Stato Pontificio.*

62. *Introduction* to Mazzini, *Scritti*,Vol. 38, 18.

63. In fact, France and England had acted as mediating powers on the basis of an earlier *Memorandum*, which recognized "the basis of mediation" in the government of Northern Italy "as it resulted from the vote of Lombards": Barié, *L'Inghilterra e il problema italiano*, 161, and Ferdinand Boyer, *La Seconde République et Charles Albert en 1848* (Paris, 1967). But this "factual circumstance" was declared

"completely unacceptable" by Austria, and had to be immediately dropped: Boyer, *La Seconde République*, 251-71.

64. A documented report of this mission was later published by Antonio Rosmini himself, *Della missione a Roma negli anni 1848-49. Commentario* (Turin, 1881).

65. Quotations by Omodeo, *Difesa del Risorgimento*, 138. On the course of the congress see Cesare Spellanzon, "Il Congresso Nazionale di Torino per la creazione di una Confederazione Italiana", *Nuova Antologia*, 85 (1948):39-57. Gioberti's speeches of 27 September and 10 October, in which he outlined this project, are published in his *Operette politiche* (Capolago 1851), 259-63 and 285-93.

66. Long passages of Montanelli's speech are quoted in Candeloro, *Storia dell'Italia moderna*, Vol. 3, 302-5. On the serious fall of confidence in the moderate party that characterised Tuscany in the late summer, see Eugenio Passamonti, "Il Ministero Capponi e il tramonto del liberalismo toscano nel 1848," *Rassegna storica del Risorgimento*, 6 (1919):59-133 and 235-314.

67. Filippo A. Gualterio, *Gli ultimi Rivolgimenti italiani. Memorie storiche*, Vol. 1 (Florence, 1852), 7.

68. On the extent of this social phenomenon see Fiume, *La crisi sociale*, chapters 3-4, and, by the same author, *Le bande armate in Sicilia (1819-1849). Violenza e organizzazione del potere* (Palermo, 1984).

69. Luigi Tomeucci, *Le cinque giornate di Messina nel '48* (Messina, 1953). After Messina, it was Milazzo to be taken up and sacked by the Neapolitan army. On 12 October a truce came into force, due to the intervention of France and England.

70. Rosario Romeo, *Il Risorgimento in Sicilia* (Bari, 1973), 337 (first edition, 1950). Romeo considers the 1848 revolution to be the first display of the "tendency of every liberal regime of the island to degenerate into a dictatorship of the elite for the protection of its privileges" which were originally intended as universal rights. A tendency that is still dramatically lasting.

71. Romeo, *Il Risorgimento in Sicilia*, 339. This feature is reported by many direct witnesses, as Francesco Paolo Perez, *La Rivoluzione siciliana del 1848 considerata nelle sue ragioni e ne' rapporti colla Rivoluzione europea, con una appendice sulla Costituzione italiana*, in Perez, *Scritti vari*, Vol. 3 (Palermo, 1898).

72. A documented description of the murdering of Pellegrino Rossi—who, imbued by the "realism" learnt at the school of French Ideologues, was impatient at any idea of "national independence"—is in Raffaello Giovagnoli, *Pellegrino Rossi e la rivoluzione romana* (Rome, 1898-1911), 3 Vols. For a biographical sketch see László Ledermann, *Pellegrino Rossi, l'homme et l'économiste, 1787-1848* (Paris, 1929).

73. Cattaneo, *Dell'insurrezione*, 13-15. The pamphlet had been written in French and published in Paris in the fall of 1848, to counteract the odd news spread about "Italy's events."

74. See Nicomede Bianchi, *Storia documentata della diplomazia europea in Italia, dall'anno 1814 all'anno 1861*, Vol. 5 (Turin, 1896), 364-65 and 520-24.

75. On the various literature spreading such stereotypes see Giulio Bollati, *L'Italiano. Il carattere nazionale come storia e come invenzione* (Turin, 1983).

76. This feature of the Venetian revolution is stressed by Adolfo Bernardello, "La paura del comunismo e dei moti a Venezia," *Nuova Rivista Storica*, 54 (1970): 50-113, and by Paul Ginsborg, *Daniele Manin and the Venetian Revolution of 1848-49* (Cambridge 1979).

77. See Simonetta Soldani (ed.), *Francesco Domenico Guerrazzi nella storia politica e culturale del Risorgimento* (Firenze, 1975).

78. Vincenzo Gioberti, "Discorso programmatico," in his *Operette*, 307-11.

79. A careful reconstruction of this "soft transition" and of its cautious director, Giuseppe Galletti, can be found in Luigi Rodelli, *La Repubblica romana del 1849* (Pisa, 1955).

80. Quote from Baudi di Vesme, *Relazioni*, xc, which reproduces the notes of a Roman confidant of Gioberti. The deputies elected with the most votes to the Roman constituent assembly would automatically have been the members of the Italian one, once it had been convened: Maria Cossu, *L'Assemblea costituente romana del 1849* (Rome, 1923).

81. However, it was only in the 1850s that this attitude assumed a political coherence, as it has been proved by Cesare Vetter, "Mazzini e la dittatura risorgimentale," *Il Risorgimento*, 46 (1994): 1-45.

82. Mazzini himself recalled this episode in his *Note autobiografiche* (Naples, 1973), 413-14, publishing a letter to Jessie White Mario in 1857: "I jumped out of my skin and used a language quite unsuit-

able to a parliament, I accused the assembly of cowardice and affirmed that people would rise up whenever I wanted, and at the end I ran away." See also Mazzini, *Scritti*, Vol. 43, 176. For the text of the Republican constitution of Rome see Alberto Aquarone, Mario D'Addio, and Guglielmo Negri (eds.), *Le costituzioni italiane* (Milan, 1958), 612-24.

83. An outline of this associational network has been made for the area at the south-east of Rome, on the historiographical model of Maurice Agulhon, by Rizzi, *La coccarda e le campane*, 61-116. The clubs, especially numerous in Romagna, were defined by Aurelio Saffi, one of the Triumvirs of the Roman Republic, an expression of "solidaristic patriotism of the people": Aurelio Saffi, *Ricordi e Scritti*, Vol. 3 (Florence, 1898), 113.

84. A careful analysis of the "diffusion of politics" at a popular level is in Carla Ronchi, *I democratici fiorentini nella rivoluzione del '48-'49* (Florence, 1963). A passionate assertion of the deep correctness of the democratic government can be found in Francesco Domenico Guerrazzi, *Apologia della vita politica, scritta da lui medesimo* (Florence, 1851).

85. Raffaello Lambruschini to Bettino Ricasoli, 9 May 1849, quoted in Paolo Alatri, "I moderati toscani, il richiamo del Granduca e il decennio di preparazione," *Rassegna storica del Risorgimento* 39(1952): 359.

86. Cristina di Belgioioso, *L'Italia e la rivoluzione italiana del 1848* (Lugano, 1849), 359. On "the good Father of the Venetians" see Ginsborg, *Daniele Manin*. Raffaele Ciampini, *Vita di Niccolò Tommaseo* (Florence, 1945), 429, writes that "the republic was for him the form of government closest to, or least distanced from, a good Christian rule."

87. See for example Camillo Cavour, *Epistolario*, Vol. 5 (Florence, 1980), 274 and Vol. 6 (Florence, 1982), 63. On the military management of the war see: Comando del Corpo di Stato Maggiore, *Ufficio storico. Relazioni e Rapporti finali sulla Campagna del 1849 nell'Alta Italia* (Rome, 1911).

88. Cesare Correnti, *I dieci giorni dell'insurrezione di Brescia nel 1849* (Milan, 1953). And Cavour wrote to a French correspondent on 14 March, afterwards the Austrians had denounced the truce: "That which is above all indispensable is to suppress energetically any hint of a republican movement in Lombardy," shooting summarily the first person who would dare to emit "a seditious shout." *Epistolario*, Vol. 6, 72. For the uprising in Genua see Carlo Baudi di Vesme, "Genova dal luglio 1848 all'aprile 1849," *Rassegna storica del Risorgimento*, 37 (1950): 733-86.

89. On the long negotiations that were necessary to extenuate the harshness of the truce, and that demonstrate quite clearly how few sympathies for constitutional and national ideas the young king Vittorio Emanuele had, see Angelo Filipuzzi, *La pace di Milano* (Rome, 1955).

90. See, for example, Bettino Ricasoli, *L'assedio di Livorno. Diario*, published for the first time in *Nuova Antologia* 84(1949): 113-24.

91. Maria Cess Drudi, Contributi alla storia della conferenza di Gaeta," *Rassegna storica del Risorgimento*, 45 (1958): 212-72; quote from 231. Similar information had been given to the heads of the French expedition: Ferdinand de Lesseps, *Ma mission à Rome* (Paris, 1849).

92. Carlo Matteucci to Lord Grove, 29 June 1849, quoted in Nicomede Bianchi, *Carlo Matteucci e l'Italia del suo tempo* (Turin, 1874), 194. As we can notice, there is no mention of Livorno and Genua, whose submission by means of military actions was evidently considered an "internal affair" of Tuscany and Piedmont.

93. Vincenzo Marchesi, *Storia documentata della rivoluzione e della difesa di Venezia negli anni 1848-49. La rivoluzione e la difesa* 2nd ed., (Venice, 1979), 43-77.

94. A somewhat novelistic but very impressive portrayal of the events was provided by George M. Trevelyan, *Garibaldi's Defence of the Roman Republic* (New York, 1907).

95. Luciano Manara to Carlo D Cristoforis, 29 June 1849, quoted in Giuseppe Capasso, *Dandolo, Morosini, Manara e il primo battaglione dei bersaglieri lombardi nel 1848-49* (Milan, 1914), 251; Mazzini, *Note autobiografiche*, 407; Carlo Cattaneo to Enrico Cernuschi, 26 November 1849, in Carlo Cattaneo, *Epistolario*, ed. by Rinaldo Caddeo (Florence, 1949) Vol. 2, 357.

96. Giuseppe Ferrari, "La rivoluzione italiana secondo Machiavelli" (1862), in Giuseppe Ferrari, *I partiti politici italiani dal 1789 al 1848* (Città di Castello, 1921), *Appendix*, 279; Montanelli, *Introduzione*, 72 and 116.

97. Many examples can be found in the congress on *Garibaldi, Mazzini e il Risorgimento nel risveglio dell'Asia e dell'Africa*, ed. by G. Borsa and P. Peonio Brocchieri (Milan, 1985). Their presence is even more prominent in the cultural and political ideas of Eastern Europe and the South American continent.

Inside a worker's rooms during the defense of a barricade in the Rue du Faubourg St. Antoine in Paris on 23 June (Illustrirte Zeitung, Leipzig, no. 263, 15 July 1848, 41)

Elections to the Constituent National Assembly in a provincial town (Illustrirte Zeitung, Leipzig, no. 287, 30 December 1848, 424)

Chapter 4

THE REVOLUTIONARY CRISIS OF 1848/51 IN FRANCE

Origins and Course of Events

Pierre Lévêque

The 1848 revolution in France certainly fits within the framework of the liberal, democratic and social movements that shook Europe in the middle of the nineteenth century, and indeed in the spring of 1848 had given these movements an impetus that was temporarily irresistible. However, it was itself quite unique. In France, and only there, ignoring for a moment the fragile republics in Rome and Venice, a monarchy was replaced by a republic. The "restoration" that followed took the very curious form of a revival of the Bonapartist Empire. The mid-nineteenth-century crisis thus brought forth two new episodes in an already long series of changes of regime begun in 1789. Taken together, these changes constitute the "French exceptional case." Still, socially the French Revolution of 1848 attained a degree of seriousness not seen elsewhere. The uprising in June 1848 and the political appearance of a strong minority of peasants under the influence of a party opposed to the established order was something not to be found on the rest of the continent. Conversely, the national question only played a subordinate role. This chapter aims to emphasize those special features of the French Revolution and, where possible explain them on the basis of the latest research.

Origins

Exclusivity and Immobility

Like the restoration that preceded it, the monarchy of Louis-Philippe collapsed unexpectedly and without any true resistance. Hence Ernest Renan would write:

"So light was the illness which brought an end to the July government, that one must ascribe to it an extremely poor state of health."[1] The regime could neither justify itself on the basis of the traditional conception of the sovereignty of the king (its beginnings lay in radically calling into question this point in 1830) nor on popular sovereignty—which implied universal suffrage, as the republicans called for. Rather it justified its existence with the theory of quasi-legitimacy (July 1830 was no revolution, but in the words of Casimir Périer a "simple change in the person of the head of state") and its exercise of authority with the theory of a sovereignty of reason (only those Frenchmen best able to recognize and realize the common weal should be voters and deputies). Thus the "deeply rooted illiberalism of French political culture,"[2] as Pierre Rosanvallon described it, had great difficulty in coming to terms with this system of a "transaction between monarchy and republic" (Duvergier de Hauranne) based on subtle ideological compromises, such that the July Monarchy "was intellectually moored in a vacuum,"[3] at least in the eyes of its opponents.

Beyond this analysis of political philosophy, it would seem appropriate to evaluate the significance of the various opposition forces. First, let us consider opposition from the right. In spite of attempts at reconciliation—which should not be ignored—legitimists not only remained loyal to the Prince in exile, the Comte de Chambord, but also to the concept of a monarchy both authoritarian and paternal, a hierarchical society, and a true religious restoration. Among the nobility, these views were held by a clear majority and were also to be found within the bourgeoisie. Often such views had the sympathies of a clergy nostalgic for the old monarchy. While legitimism's influence was limited geographically, in the rural districts in the west and in part of the south, it had a solid basis among the population. Thus a regime that saw itself as deeply conservative found itself called into question by a large and influential faction within the elite, whose support it had hoped for. In the 1840s, Guizot's attempts at reconciliation failed, and a refusal by the Chamber to allow a free choice of secondary school led to a further alienation of the church and to a consolidation of a de facto alliance between supporters of Henri V and Montalembert's "Catholic Party."

Nonetheless, the main threat came from the "movement," the opposition from the left. Initially, it was made up of notables who were socially very close to the conservative majority (landowners, businessmen, civil servants, well-off members of the professions), but who remained attached to a "patriotic" ideology strengthened in the struggle against the Restoration. Loyal to the new dynasty, they sought to reinforce it with a prudent and gradual extension of freedoms and the franchise. Hostile to the forces of the "old regime," which they saw embodied in the "Holy Alliance," they supported an active foreign policy in favor of, for example, Poland and Italy. Enfranchised because of their wealth, they formed a minority in the "pays légal" of voters possessing the necessary property qualification. They believed, however, that they could count on the "pays réel," the petit bourgeoisie of businessmen and intellectuals (one spoke at the time of "capacities") who did not pay the requisite tax of 200 FF, and so were excluded from the electorate, and who were unsettled by a new "aristocracy" of banks and big industry.

However, this important part of the "middle class" (in today's sense of the term) was equally attracted to the extreme left of the "movement," i.e. to the republican "party," whose membership was recruited to a great extent from this group. With the exception of a few secret societies, the republicans had given up a strategy of revolt in the 1830s and from that time on had developed legal propaganda activities, especially in newspapers such as *le National* and *la Réforme*. Favorable to universal suffrage, free and compulsory education, justifying an easily excited patriotism by a faith in "France's mission of liberation," republicans were also open, to a certain extent, to a preoccupation with the social question.

Together with England, France had been the cradle of socialism in the first third of the century. In the 1840s, this current found its expression in a multitude of schools and sects. Except for the revolutionary and "insurrectionalist" communism of Blanqui, the heir of Babouvism, all of these aimed for a peaceful creation of a new world through propaganda and their example. In spite of their great variety, they were all united in denouncing the disastrous results of laissez faire and demanding state intervention on behalf of the "most numerous and poorest class," as well as promoting with Victor Considérant, Philippe Buchez, and Louis Blanc the establishment of producers' cooperatives that were to take the place of capitalist firms.

These ideas at first seduced small groups in the middle classes, "capacities," and small businessmen who were hostile to the political monopoly and economic supremacy of the notables. They also found a receptive audience among the elite of the "working class" in the larger cities, that is mainly among traditional artisans (printers, construction workers, cabinet-makers, and textile workers) and among the outworkers, in Paris manufacturers and the Lyon silk trade. Harsh suppression of the revolts of the Lyon silkworkers in 1831 and 1834, and of the great Parisian strikes of 1840 strengthened opposition to the government in these circles and eased the spread of new ideas. On the other hand, the proletariat spread throughout the countryside, like the heavily exploited workers concentrated in large mechanized industries, had only vague contact with these ideas. Still, studies by Villeneuve-Bargemont, Villermé or Buret, describing the fate of workers living in the most impoverished conditions, did awaken public interest in the "social question."

Doubtless many republicans remained true to economic liberalism, and nearly all emphasized the absolute priority of political change. However, many of them saw the problems raised by the different socialist schools as worthy of their attention and some, while not members of these schools, saw in the realization of the right to work and in the encouragement of cooperatives the natural tasks of a future republic.

Republicans continued the democratic tradition of the great revolution and maintained the hopes of egalitarian social change. They were influential within the petit bourgeoisie, the more highly developed level of artisans and a working class the majority of which still worked in small and medium sized firms and was unprotected by any social welfare legislation. As such, the republicans depended on the support of a large sociocultural movement influenced by Romanticism and exalting the role of the people in the history of humanity. Hence they could claim the backing of such varied spirits as the former Saint-Simonians Buchez and Pierre Leroux, the left-liberals Edgar Quinet and Jules Michelet, and Lamennais, one time ultramontanist and later liberal Catholic. Lamartine, who had become quite opposed to conservatism, rehabilitated the Convention in his *Histoire des Girondins* and Alexis de Tocqueville—who was anything but a radical—demonstrated the inevitability of the development of Western societies into democracies. Although they thus had a greater influence than their opponents assumed, the republican party suffered from serious weaknesses. Its organization was rudimentary and sporadic. In rural areas, where memories of Napoleon, raised to mythic status, had eclipsed the largely negative reminiscences of the first republic, the party was almost nonexistent.

In view of this varied opposition, the conservative party, in power since 1831, seemed to have the "pays légal" securely in its hands. The 240,000 eligible voters gave Guizot (and thus also King Louis-Philippe, who agreed with him) a clearer majority in 1846 than ever before. In fact, it was just a fraction of the notables that supported the cabinet in the Palais Bourbon. In opposition were the small groups of legitimists and republicans; to the more consistent ranks of the dynastic left of Odilon Barrot was added the center left, under the leadership of Thiers. Mainly led by higher civil servants and protectionist businessmen, the "ministerial" party gained its strength mostly from electoral backing by the middling bourgeoisie of landowners and rentiers, which, especially in most rural and occasionally archaic arrondissements, inevitably played a mediating role, distinguished by strong clientelism, between the people and the government.

Economic prosperity and peace, the two closely associated, were the decisive political arguments presented by Guizot and his ministers. In their eyes, the electorate, as defined by the law of 1831 had become the upholders of the general interest in a society from which all caste differences had disappeared. There was therefore no reason to enlarge the franchise. Thus an immobility in domestic politics arose, while in Europe the breakup of the *entente cordiale* with England and the desire to preserve the status quo finally led to a rapprochement with the three great absolutist monarchies of Russia, Prussia and Austria, as well as an abandonment of support for liberal and nationalist movements, especially in Poland and Italy.

In the final analysis, this "system" had only a very small social base. Attacked from left and right by a portion of the ruling class, unable to count on the enthusiasm of the clergy, and rejected or little appreciated by the urban middle and lower classes, it also found little support among the peasantry. The major problems of rural society—farm credit, access to property, usage rights, underemployment among day laborers and poverty—were given little consideration. Apart from religion in devout regions, the only living myth in rural districts was a loyalty, not to the "citizen king," and even less to his government, but to the memory of the "great emperor."

The Significance of Economic Cycles

A complex crisis in 1846/47 severely shook this fragile political construction, making it susceptible to even the most minor threat. Ernest Labrousse provided an analysis of this economic crisis in a paper at the 1848 centenary, which was long held to be a classic.[4] Potato blight, widespread from 1845, and the poor grain harvest of 1846, led to a dramatic increase in the price of foodstuffs (100 percent for wheat from the winter of 1844/45 to spring 1847). As poorer consumers had to cut back on spending elsewhere, the high bread price led to a fall in production and to unemployment in consumer goods industries (especially in textiles) and in construction. Simultaneously, excessive investment during the period of growth subsequent to 1840 caused a credit squeeze, especially from the end of 1846 onwards, which hindered commerce and brought the capital-hungry railway companies into difficulties. Bankruptcies rose, with heavy industry (coal and steel) partially affected, and the number of layoffs multiplied rapidly. Reduced tax revenue and a rise in certain expenses (welfare and unusual grain imports) precipitated a worsening of public finances with a dramatic rise in the national debt.

This description of the crisis of 1846/47 has been called into question by more recent studies summarized about ten years ago by Anthony Rowley.[5] In his view, one could not speak of a "decisive agricultural crisis," as the agricultural sector no longer had the same economic weight it held in 1789. The "feeding of the populace was not threatened" and the "price increase (for grain) compensated for reduced harvests (for the peasants)." A shrewd government credit could have braked the mechanism of an "old regime type crisis" which extended throughout the entire economy. It was rather more "an accidental break in the growth of an economy which had reached the stage of industrialization." At the beginning of 1848, when bread prices fell due to an excellent harvest in 1847, an upswing was in sight. The difficulties of 1846/47 did not "carry within them the seeds of revolution."

This thesis, too, gives rise to certain reservations. Even when the period of scarcity was short, it brought with it serious and permanent consequences. In spite of the usual relief programs (bread markets, public works …), the urban lower classes, the rural proletariat, and the peasant smallholders, who became net grain purchasers—that is, the majority of the population—were subject to severe restrictions and suffered under an indebtedness that certainly carried over into 1848. As Ernest Labrousse wrote: "The revolution broke out in an economically damaged world." The sometimes all too obvious hoarding and speculations of large land owners, farmers and grain dealers doubtless contributed in the long term to a worsening of social tensions. More broadly, the crisis, and the various disturbances occurring in its wake, sapped confidence in a government based on prosperity and the maintenance of order among broad circles of the population. As a Catholic provincial newspaper[6] wrote on 3 November 1846: "The members of the government so often seek to take credit for the prosperity of the country that they should not be surprised when one attempts to turn the tables and assign them some responsibility for the public calamities." Certainly, "the revolution of 1848 is neither the result of poverty and hunger nor of the irresponsibility of the tax authorities" (Anthony Rowley). Nonetheless there can be no doubt that the economic and social crises of 1846/47 contributed significantly to a weakening of the July monarchy in public opinion, and this at a time when it was under attack from an opposition disappointed by the results of the legislative elections of 1846.

Even when the effects of dearth and the depression were being felt most bitterly, the government of Guizot and its majority, with the unreserved support of the king, gave proof again of its inflexibility and stubborn conservatism in rejecting two proposals from Duvergier de Hauranne and Charles de Rémusat, deputies of the center left. The first of these two proposals would have meant nearly a doubling of the electorate by lowering the minimum tax payment to 100 F and granting an unrestricted franchise to those members of the "capacities" inscribed on the lists of eligible jurors. The second dealt with the incompatibility of holding a seat in parliament and exercising most public offices.

Very soon after this defeat, part of the opposition decided to bring the conflict to the people by organizing subscription banquets (to get around a ban on political assemblies). After the first of such events in the Château Rouge in Paris on 9 July, the second half of the year saw a further seventy in the provinces. During the banquets, speakers' themes included the necessity of electoral and parliamentary reform as the only possible way to reconcile the "pays légal" with the "pays réel." They also criticized corruption within the ruling circles (with the Affaire Teste-Cubières offering an excellent example, in which two of the Pairs de France accused of embezzlement were involved) as well as an antinational foreign policy that had turned France into a vassal of the Holy Alliance. Slowly, the more dynamic republicans gained the upper hand over politicians from the center left and the dynastic left. They condemned the "system" sharply, occasionally even attacking the king. Their demands for universal suffrage and state intervention in favor of small business and workers were more radical. The level of backing for this movement is not easily assessed. It is estimated that only 17,000 subscribed, but a much larger number heard their speeches, which were then reproduced in the opposition press and as inexpensive pamphlets.

Although government circles gave all outward appearances of calm, the ministry nonetheless felt it appropriate to denounce the opposition's "hostile and blind passions" in the address to the throne at the end of December. Some astute observers repeatedly took up such warnings in January and February 1848 during the debate that followed. This was especially true of Alexis de Tocqueville, who had refused to take part in the banquets, as he feared they would only benefit the extreme left. On 29 January he spoke quite agitatedly of "social" passions that led the "working classes" to call into question even the foundations of society. He found that "in Europe the earth is shaking once again" (the successful revolutions in Palermo and Naples were spreading throughout Italy) and begged his colleagues not only to accept the necessary reforms, but also to change the "spirit of the government," which was leading the country into the abyss. While his words were certainly given scant hearing, the conservative majority nonetheless began to crumble, as the address to the throne was only approved by 228 votes to 185, although "government supporters" had had 291 seats directly after the election. Even when most of those promoting banquets certainly did not wish a revolution and only a few Frenchmen believed in mid-February 1848 that a revolution was around the corner, a vague feeling of unrest and worry had seized a portion of the world of the notables.

Without wishing to deny the role of chance in the events of 23 and 24 February, following the ban of the Paris banquet of the 22nd (the shooting on Boulevard des Capucines seemingly played a decisive role), it is important to emphasize those objective factors that allowed the most militant section of the republican party to successfully follow a strategy of insurrection that had completely failed in June 1832, April 1834 and May 1839; among them: working class hostility toward the regime, reinforced by the harsh suppression of the strikes of 1840 and of the following years and by the difficulties stemming from the economic crisis of 1846/47; embitterment among the petite bourgeoisie due in part to the continual postponement of electoral reform, expressed in the refusal of the Parisian National Guard to work together with the army to restore order.

This blatant rejection of conservative policies by those who had supported them at the beginning of the regime left the monarch and his entourage in disarray, resulting in a totally confused response to the uprising. Guizot was dismissed, thus robbing the executive of its head. At the same time, on the evening of the 23–24 February, Thiers and then Odilon Barrot were requested to form a reform-oriented government, while Bugeaud, who personified antirepublican repression, was assigned the task of suppressing the uprising. Louis-Philippe hastily abdicated on the 24th and fled Paris, without the possibility of retaking power from the provinces being considered. Deputies from the parliamentary majority were disconcerted by Guizot's resignation, paralysed by insurgents slowly forcing their way into the Chamber of Deputies and no longer able to decide on a regency of the Duchess of Orléans.

The rapid spread of the revolution throughout the country is a further demonstration of the July regime's weak foundations in French society. The losers of February did not even attempt to form a core of resistance, for example around the son of the king. Centralization, the habit of following impulses from the capital, eased the tasks of those who had taken power in Paris. No less surprising was a retreat—observed almost everywhere—by civil servants, judges, and notables, once loyal to Guizot, in the face of republicans or the left when they were numerous enough or determined to take over power, without any attempt being made to use police and army. Nearly everywhere, they offered their services to the provisional government when the "movement" was too weak to take their place immediately, before prefects and sub-prefects were replaced by commissars and sub-commissars with little difficulty.

Not being founded on a myth of royalty comparable to that of the legitimists, the July regime was based on a pragmatic support of the monarchy—as reflected in its constitution—and on a satisfaction of "interests." It could not count on sympathy and support from the people and was discredited by the events of 1846/47. Thus this regime, which had identified itself with the conservative party, was not able to mobilize civil society to check the revolution.

The Course of Events

The republic that was founded in February and March 1848 came to an end in theory on 2 December 1852 but in practice a year before. Hence it, too, appears as a weak government, much more short-lived than any of its predecessors since 1792.

In the following an attempt will be made, not to trace the vicissitudes of its short history, but to examine and evaluate the causes, extent, and limits of its failure.

The first period—from 25 February to the end of June 1848—was characterized by an initially latent and then open conflict between moderate republicans, de facto in power, and an extreme left in which were bound together socialist "intellectuals" and a portion of the "working classes" in the large cities and especially in Paris. From the second half of 1848 to 2 December 1851 the retreat of moderate republicans did not leave the field free for that which, at first glance, would appear to be a simple duel between democrats and supporters of the old monarchies, but instead was a three-sided struggle, out of which none other than Louis-Napoléon Bonaparte emerged as victor. The intensity of political and social struggles, which twice led to the brink of a civil war, cannot be understood without consideration being given to the dramatic economic crisis followed by a long depression.

Crisis and Depression

The sudden overthrow of a regime closely connected with the business world, the spread of a revolutionary movement throughout a large part of Europe and more importantly a fear of worker unrest, especially widespread in Paris, almost immediately precipitated a stock market crisis. In view of an uncertain future, investors attempted to "liquidate" securities or claims as soon as possible and an oversupply led to a collapse in market prices after the stock market was reopened on 7 March, causing bank capital to shrink. The banks came under further pressure due to a massive withdrawal from private accounts. Some banks were forced to suspend payment and many could no longer discount bills of exchange, which pushed numerous industrialists and businessmen into bankruptcy. The Banque de France, for its part, was threatened by a steady shrinking of its gold reserves. The provisional government therefore had to fix by decree a compulsory rate for its banknotes, which reawakened memories of the assignat and intensified unrest. As credit and orders were lacking, many factories had to reduce or stop production. The economy, which had begun to recover at the beginning of the year, suffered a spectacular relapse. Compared to 1847, coal production sank by 22 percent, foundry production by 20 percent and iron and steel production by 27 percent. The textile and construction industries were also hard hit. Unemployment reached disturbing levels. A reduction in urban consumption and the paralysis of commercial transactions led to a fall in agricultural prices.

Some reactions by the provisional government were well thought out attempts to revitalize the circulation of money and above all bills of exchange (by founding discount offices, two-thirds financed by public monies). However, a rise of 45 percent in direct taxation (the "45 centimes"), decreed on 16 March, naturally reduced buying power, especially in rural areas. A short time later, plans to purchase the railway companies, which had run into financial difficulties—launched by Duclerc, the Minister of Finance, and supported by Lamartine—with the object of creating construction jobs, were rejected by the constituent assembly. In the period following, the majority in the assembly, reflecting an orthodox finance policy, drastically reduced credits for public works (1849 to 167 million, 1850 to 66 million, 1851 to 65 million).

Moreover, social fears remained even after the victories of "order" in June and December 1848 as well as in May and June 1849, indeed increasing as the election dates in spring 1852 came closer. The crisis was not followed by a general upswing, but by a depression that lasted for more than three years and which was worsened by a fall in prices for agricultural goods caused in part by "too good" harvests. Those branches most closely tied to foreign markets, that expanded rapidly from 1849 onwards, such as merchant shipping or the mechanized textile industry, experienced once again a certain prosperity. However, although railway construction began again, thanks mostly to a return of English investment, heavy industry was not able to regain its 1847 level. In 1851, the coal production index was only 87, foundry production 75, and iron and steel production 69, whereby because of a fall in prices the differences were in fact greater. The construction industry, trade, and most industries in rural areas were worse off because of the financial problems of their peasant customers. In 1850, the price of wheat sank to 14.32 FF per hectoliter, its lowest level in the nineteenth century, and a third below the "normal" price. The wine market was worse still, and the situation for livestock and other main products hardly better. Weak economic performance, due in part to the intensity of the political crisis, in turn sharpened political conflict through related social consequences, increasing the obduracy of supporters and opponents of established order.

"Socialism" and the Repression of the Workers Movement

Three events define the year 1848: a massive strengthening of the labor movement followed by its repression in June; the defeat of moderate republicans led at first by Lamartine and then by Cavaignac; the election of Louis-Napoléon Bonaparte on 10 December.

In the atmosphere of liberty following the proclamation of a republic—which found its expression in the spread of clubs and newspapers—socialism, until then restricted to secret societies and small groups composed of members of the middle class and the working class elite, suddenly forced its way into political life. At the same time, freedom of assembly allowed workers' "corporations" to meet, not only to articulate their demands, but also to discuss a renewal of society to be brought in with the republic and which was to be the task of a government commission on labor questions founded on 28 February. This commission, chaired by the socialists Louis Blanc and Alexandre Martin, a worker known as Albert, met in the Palais du Luxembourg. Its central committee of workers' delegates, founded before 23 March and seen by Rémi Gossez as a true "united front" of the Parisian proletariat, named candidates for the constituent assembly and demanded the creation of cooperative workshops. The most well-known of these would be that of the tailors, in which 1700 people were employed preparing uniforms for the Paris national guard.

The movement even attracted the support of some female workers. Under the leadership of Désirée Gay, once an adherent of Saint-Simon and later of Fourier, dressmakers succeeded in having a national workshop founded, whose hierarchical and authoritarian structure they soon came to criticize, however. On 7 June they presented plans for a true producers' cooperative. A few days later, the central committee published a plan for economic restructuring inspired by the ideas of Louis Blanc in the 15-22 June issue of their newspaper, *Journal des Travailleurs*. Each "corps d'état," which was to be both a trade union and a mutual benefit society, would administer its own social workshops whose directors were to be elected or chosen by a public competition. In each district, consumers would run cooperative shops. An elected central administrative council was to oversee this organization of labor and exchange.

However, relations thus created between the working class and socialism was only an avant-garde phenomenon. Outside Paris one finds something similar in only a few large cities such as Lyon. Workers in the small villages and in rural areas heard nothing of it or, like the rest of the population, had only a vague idea of what was meant (the myth of "dividers"). In Paris itself, unskilled jobless employed in the national workshops were, at first, carefully kept far apart from the labor movement through an almost military leadership and discipline. A further 12,000, and later 17,000 mostly younger people were given paid positions in the garde mobile. It was only in May and June that the "ideas of Luxembourg" were also spread into the national workshops by militant strikers or jobless, in view of rising unemployment. This development, together with financial considerations, led a nervous constituent assembly to harden its positions and on 22 June to disband the workshops, which in turn precipitated an uprising.

The June uprising has been well researched in its entire complexity.[7] It was a true workers' uprising in the contemporary sense of the term. Eighty percent of the 11,642 arrested were manual laborers, including small workshop owners and artisans. The modern proletariat (metal workers and mechanics) was naturally much less present than workers from small and medium-sized firms (construction, furniture, textiles and shoe manufacturing, decorative crafts etc.). Some women also participated in the uprising, who according to Tocqueville "were as actively involved as the men … preparing and bringing munitions and … who were the last" to surrender. In his eyes "they were hoping for victory, in order to make things easier for their husbands."[8]

Nonetheless, it was not simply a revolt of hunger and poverty. Robbed of their well-known leaders (Barbès, Blanqui, Albert, and Raspail were arrested after demonstrators had forced their way into the National Assembly on 15 May), the uprising was led by association activists and was as much an expression of the hopes of February 1848—"to change the social order" (Tocqueville)—as it was of the disappointments that followed. Attacked by the army and by national guard units from the bourgeois quarters of Paris, condemned by the large majority of public opinion—even among republicans, who saw the uprising both as an attack on national sovereignty and as a subversive threat, and even as the result of Bonapartist trouble-making—the rebels could count on the sympathy of the common people in the capital, but not on the entire local working class. They had to fight against the mobile guard, which was not, as long believed, following Karl Marx, recruited from the lumpenproletariat. Rather their ranks were drawn from the youngest workers, who were the last hired and the first fired. The government was able to exploit their resentment of better-off older colleagues and bind them to the status quo with good pay.

Very severe repressive measures[9] meant a rapid end to the revolutionary movement in Paris, but did not have all the consequences previously credited them by historians. They did not strike a decisive blow against the process by which "radicals" conquered a part of public opinion in the provinces. Nor did they turn militant workers, many of whom voted for the democratic-socialist left, against the republic in general, but just against the moderate republicans. Finally, repression did not mean an end to the cooperative movement in the major cities. Theoretically encouraged at the beginning of the constituent assembly, which on 5 July 1848 voted a credit of three million for them, there were still about 300 producers' cooperatives in existence in October 1851, of which two-thirds were in Paris. Nonetheless, this was no longer a real "organization of labor." Most co-operatives were small and were not permitted to work together, as was shown in the court case against the Union of Workers' Associations, which practiced directed exchange and granted interest free loans. Among its founders were the militant feminists Jeanne Deroin and Pauline Roland.

The Failure of the Moderate Republic

Brought to power by the events of February, the moderates provided seven of the eleven members of the provisional government. However, they were among the losers of 1848, just as much as the socialists. At first, deliberating under pressure from the armed "people of Paris," Lamartine and his colleagues made a number of revolutionary decisions. The proclamation of a right to work (25 February), the foundation of a commission for workers (28 February), and a shortening of the working day reflected popular demands. An end to slavery in the colonies and to the death penalty for political crimes, and, above all, a decision to hold an election for a constituent assembly under universal manhood suffrage expressed the fundamental outlook of the majority in the provisional government: namely humanitarianism, rejection of the Terror of 1793, and the desire to move beyond a provisional state of affairs and to give the government indisputable legitimacy as soon as possible.

The question of woman suffrage, raised by the committee for the rights of women, was avoided, in spite of a campaign organized by Eugénie Niboyet in *La Voix des Femmes*. Nor was this problem ever given serious consideration later. The introduction on 16 March of a 45 percent tax surcharge, to which all direct taxpayers were liable, and a refusal, underlined by Tocqueville, to deal with problems of debts, so important to the peasants, especially after the subsistence crisis, are rather expressions of endeavors to spare the rich, even at the price of risking the new government's popularity. A key word for the new government was fraternity, the realization of which was to bring a solution to the social question.

Preparation for elections soon became a central concern. Following a large workers' demonstration on 17 March, elections were postponed from 9 to 23 April. The extreme left would have preferred a later date in order to gain time to "enlighten" the people, especially in rural areas. The government, for its part, hesitated at first to follow the example of its monarchist predecessor and, through the intermediary of its commissars, to support candidates most favorable to the new regime. However, Ledru-Rollin, the Minister of the Interior, a "radical," and Hippolyte Carnot, the Minister of Education and a moderate, followed this line—the former in his circulars and in the *Bulletin de la République*, in part edited by George Sand, the latter in his sending republican publications to public schoolteachers in an attempt to mobilize them in service of the "long-term republicans." Although these initiatives were strongly attacked by monarchist notables and by their press, they still seem to have had no decisive influence. The elections passed generally quietly, although the balloting, held in the cantonal capitals, attracted a substantial number of eligible voters. The high turnout of 84 percent is a demonstration both of the success of the previous half-century in integrating the French into a nation and the importance attached to the elections. It was hoped that they would provide a solution to the crisis, whereby some hoped for a restoration of order and others for a consolidation of the government and an increased possibility of reform.

The large number and variety of candidates, the repeated appearance of the same men on numerous competing lists and their often unclear and undifferentiated statements of political principles makes interpretation of the results difficult. Incontestable, however, is the defeat of the extreme left of "radical" socialists. This group gained fewer than 100 and probably rather only 70 or 80 of the nearly 900 seats at stake. However, should one follow Charles Seignobos in believing that moderate republicans had gained a clear victory with 500 seats compared to 300 for the former monarchists? Detailed examination by Frédérick A. de Luna and George W. Fasel[10] produce another distribution. Only 358 seats were taken by candidates backed by the central committees composed of men of *le National*. Among them were about 50 radicals and approximately 30 conservatives, leaving 270 to 280 moderates. Taking into consideration the 316 victors known as monarchists before February, who then naturally all presented themselves as republicans, there remain only about 200 deputies whose political past is not known exactly, but who had not actively promoted democracy. Even if some of these had since honestly converted to democratic views, the constituent assembly still appears more conservative than previously assumed. Initial predominance of the "veteran republicans" can be explained rather by circumstances than by a solid majority. Its policies continued to develop under pressure from the right, however.

From the start, the two socialist members of the provisional government, Louis Blanc and Albert, were excluded from the five-member executive committee onto which Ledru-Rollin was elected at Lamartine's express recommendation, whereby the former thus took only the forth position, behind Arago, Garnier-Pagès, and Marie. In the dramatic question of national workshops, the compromise plan worked out by Lamartine and Duclerc, that would have involved the employment of workers on the construction sites of railway companies repurchased by the government, was rejected in favor of the much stricter solution propagated by the legitimist Falloux and the moderate republican banker Goudchaux—drafting of young workers into the army and an immediate resettlement of the rest in the provinces. These plans provided the immediate spark for the June uprising.

The insurgents were opposed by the moderates and their adherents among the "capacities" as well as their numerous backers within the petit bourgeoisie. However, the repression was accompanied by a further move to the right. The executive committee resigned in favor of General Cavaignac, who was named chairman of the council of ministers, freedoms of press and assembly were restricted and the most important social gains of February, especially the right to work, abolished. From 15 October onward, two former monarchists belonged to the government. The constitution passed on 4 November was incontestably democratic, but would moderate republicans be able to make use of the positions and powers it created?

And in fact, the dissatisfaction caused by the "45 centimes," the continued economic crisis, the fear of socialism for some and the hope for significant change among others, undermined in a few months the basis of support of the moderate republicans. The monarchist "men of order" now envisaged pushing the "clique of *le National*" out of office and taking their place. "Forthright" democrats distanced themselves from Cavaignac and moved closer to the losers of June in order to defend the achievements of the revolution. In the municipal and cantonal elections of the summer, this polarization had already become apparent.

However, another factor was decisive. The rural population held the moderates responsible for the crisis and believed they had found a savior in the person of Louis-Napoléon Bonaparte. In the presidential elections on 10 December 1848 Cavaignac was still supported by a petit bourgeoisie that was both republican and liberal, hostile to the "reds," and also by a portion of the conservatives and legitimists, who saw in him an effective defender of order and a guarantee against Bonapartist adventurism. Nonetheless, he was heavily defeated by the "nephew of the great emperor."With 19 percent of all votes cast, he only achieved a majority in four departments of Brittany and Provence. Thus moderates lost executive power and soon their administrative positions in the prefectures as well. In elections for the legislative assembly on 13 May 1849 they were attacked both from the left, by the "Montagnards," and from the right, by the "party of order," in the meantime well-established. The judgement of the voters was inexorable. The moderates received only 12 percent of the votes cast and about 70 of the 715 seats. Some of them were only elected because they were included in the lists of the right or the extreme left.

Still, seen in a long-term perspective, this defeat was not irrevocable. Lamartine and the men of *le National* had introduced the political tradition of a democratic, liberal, and socially moderate republic. Although this republic did not succeed in the middle of the nineteenth century because of dramatic crises and the power of Bonapartist and royalist currents, it was able to take its revenge in the last quarter of the century.

Bonaparte's First Victory

At first, Louis-Napoléon Bonaparte was victorious. His massive electoral victory on 10 December, when he received 74 percent of the votes cast, was a spectacular success, the causes and significance of which has been the object of careful historical research in recent decades.[11] In February 1848 Bonapartism, in contrast to the republican party, was not a political force. The notables and intellectuals who admired the emperor felt a return of the empire neither possible nor desirable. The cult of a mythical Napoleon, widely spread especially among the rural population, arose more from a nostalgic yearning for a glorious past than a promise of anything for the future. Nonetheless, he corresponded to the image that most Frenchmen had of statesmen. He should be a man of authority who guaranteed the social achievements of the revolution and the greatness of the nation.

From the spring of 1848 onwards, the ground for the longed-for "Savior" was being prepared by the severe economic crisis in France, a fear of anarchy that possessed some, the severe disillusionment affecting others, and general unrest. From that time on Bonapartist thinking became more and more accepted: Louis-Napoléon Bonaparte was said to be, like his uncle a half a century before, the man who would solve all the country's problems as if by magic. As a patriot he would revenge the humiliation of 1815, without, however, plunging France into military adventurism. As a republican he would continue the inheritance of 1789 and respect constitutional liberties. As a man of unity he would overcome the "rule of cliques" and appeal, like the First Consul, to the "upstanding men" of all parties. As a man of progress he would find a solution to the social question in an atmosphere of concord of capital and labor. As a man of order he would defend the family, propert,y and religion. Hence he was to satisfy the only apparently contradictory wishes of all the French. Supporting him entailed less a political program than identification with a personality that embodied France itself.

Under the leadership of a group of men around Fialin de Persigny, a loyal friend of the prince, Bonapartist propaganda, carefully tailored for universal suffrage, turned above all to the common people. It made use of small, inexpensive newspapers as well as, especially for the illiterates, engravings, portraits and devotional objects, songs and speeches at public meetings, celebrations and annual markets. Even if there was no party structure, apart from the existence of departmental committees, communication was ensured by paid representatives and especially by countless voluntary helpers, including former officers of the Grande Armée, traveling salesmen, businessmen and traveling singers, innkeepers etc. Financing was provided by contributions and large loans taken out by Napoleon and his relatives, as well as by the sale of printed matter, portraits and medallions, sold above the manufacturing price. This propaganda reflected the expectations, fears, and demands of a significant number of Frenchmen.

After being elected in four Departments (including the Seine) on 4 June, he abstained from taking his seat for tactical reasons, and had himself re-elected with better results in the same constituencies (including the Department of the Moselle) on 17 September. Then, in a relative political vacuum, he stood as a presidential candidate. The moderate republicans were discredited; the Party of Order and democratic-socialists were still in a development phase. His candidacy was supported by important Orléanist notables, like Thiers, who believed to be able easily to make use of him, and by a number of legitimists and Catholics (including Montalembert) to whom he had promised the freedom to found religious schools, and the restoration of the temporal power of Pius IX.

His massive victory on 10 December had a complex significance. For many men of order it was a triumph of the conservatives. Advised by the notables, their natural leaders, and led, above all, by their strong common sense, the voters had sought to condemn the "socialists" and save their threatened society. And in fact, Louis-Bonaparte gained his highest share of the vote in western France (from Normandy to the Vendée), in many departments of the Paris basin, in the northeast and southwest, where the Party of Order was given sustained support. However, other observers argued that a vote for Bonaparte was also a vote against Cavaignac, against a "republic of the gentlemen," against a betrayal of the hopes of February. With a high share of the vote in what were later democratic-socialist strongholds (from the region around Nevers to Périgord, in the Lyon region, in the working-class districts of eastern Paris), the nephew of the emperor was also "the representative of the poor." In both cases, the choice was spontaneous, without the intervention of the authorities, who supported Cavaignac, or of the aristocratic or bourgeois notables. Often, it was these groups which, impressed by the élan of the masses, turned to Bonaparte for better or worse. As the legitimist newspaper, *l'Opinion publique,* wrote, "the shepherds have followed the sheep." Bonaparte's voters were naturally unaware of constitutional niceties, and assumed they were electing an all-powerful leader modeled on Napoleon I. ("He will make himself emperor like his uncle," was a commonly held opinion.)

This victory of the people, which often took place in a carnival-like atmosphere, was equally a defeat for democracy, as the voters had surrendered their rights in favor of a man about whom they knew very little and on whom they projected mostly contradictory wishes. It should be mentioned here that his victory was incomplete, as election results were less satisfactory, on the one hand, in legitimist regions, such as Brittany and part of southern France, and, on the other, in those cities in which Cavaignac's and Ledru-Rollin's successes among the middle and lower classes could not be ignored. Thus Bonapartism appears from the beginning as an authoritarian "centerism," whose program, most important adherents, and backers—whom he soon gained from the camp of "order"—gave him a center-right leaning; whereby, however, he did not lose the trust he had ensured himself especially from the left.

Directly following his election, Louis-Napoléon Bonaparte presented himself as an ally of the royalists. As he lacked competent political personnel, he selected his ministers from these circles and struggled with them against a constituent assembly coming to the end of its term. Equally, and for similar reasons, the Bonapartists were only able to present fifteen completely Bonapartist lists in the legislative elections of May 1849. Hindered by the dynamism of the Montagnards and even more by the prestige and influence of the nobles and bourgeois legitimists or Orléanists, they only gained modest results. Even including those who ran on allied lists, among the approximately 450 representatives of the majority in the legislative assembly there were hardly more than twenty truly loyal supporters of Bonaparte.

One of Louis-Napoléon Bonaparte's main concerns was, therefore, to try to escape the tutelage of the Party of Order. He attempted to further develop the structure of his support which had arisen in 1848, but the departmental committees were often split between leftist and conservatives, while the Society of 10 December was hardly more than an acclimation group and occasionally a poorly manned shock troop. He was especially eager to exploit to the maximum his prerogatives as chief executive. From 31 October 1849 he put together a cabinet of second-rate, pliant figures and placed in the prefectures and sub-prefectures dependable people whom he recruited above all among former conservatives and to whom he gave the task of overseeing the other civil servants. Well aware of the personal character of his power, he endeavored to increase his popularity through trips to the Departments, whereby he cleverly tailored his proposals to currents dominant among his public. In the end he exploited a growing division in the Party of Order and created, step by step, an "Elysée Party," which, in the end, had 150 deputies as members. However, the positive results he had gained were no guarantee for a political future, as the constitution robbed him of his strongest weapon, popular Bonapartism, by denying him a second candidacy for 1852. At the time, all things seemed to point to a decisive battle between the two most powerful groups from the election of 1849, the Montagnards and the Party of Order.

The Montagnards: Emergence and Problems

The weakening of moderate republicans—in the spring of 1848 the obviously dominant force—benefited the extreme left, which denounced the moderates' feeble response to monarchist "reaction." After rejecting the mass demonstration of 15 May and taking a clear position against the June uprising, the "radical" group around Ledru-Rollin and the newspaper *La Réforme* increasingly criticized Cavaignac's policies, and, in the fall, some joined the socialist party. Men such as Proudhon, Cabet, and especially the "revolutionary" communists from the Blanqui school kept their distance, unlike the supporters of Louis Blanc and Victor Considérant. Hence a democratic-socialist party appeared, whose members assumed the name "Montagnards" in memory of their predecessors of 1792/95, and often took over the name "the reds" from their opponents, in reference to an attempt by Parisian workers on 25 February to have the red flag adopted. This name enabled them to distinguish themselves from the "blues" of *le National*, and, especially, the "whites," a category into which they placed all the monarchists. In October 1848 the "parliamentary group" of the Montagnards counted 75 deputies. On 4 November Republican Solidarity was founded to develop party structure and propaganda in the Departments. This was the origin of an independent political force, able to withstand three years of repression by Louis-Napoléon and the Party of Order.

In their efforts to give the republican form of government a socialist content, Montagnards rejected communism, which implied state tyranny, but accepted socialism in a very general sense of the term: "It is the opposite of egoism and individualism," and "the principle of mutual love of the people," an impassioned desire to reform for the benefit of the neediest. This "pragmatic socialism," which belonged to no school, inspired in part the very typical program of the "democratic and socialist press," published on 5 April 1849. At the political level the text was defensive, demanding a retention of universal suffrage and the already strictly limited freedoms attained in February. It reflected the left's traditional patriotism, as France was to take on the defense of oppressed peoples in Europe and, especially, was to rescue the Roman republic. Apart from universal and free compulsory education and tax reform (abolition of taxes on salt and beverages and introducing of a direct progressive tax), the program also called for state support for the creation of an agricultural credit system with low interest (which clearly shows a desire to meet specific peasant demands), the demand for associations of all types (producers' cooperatives and mutual benefit societies), centralization and exploitation "for the benefit of the entire society" of the most highly concentrated sectors of the capitalism of the day—in other words, the nationalization of insurance, banks, railways, canals and mines. There was even a demand for the regulation of commerce through state warehouses and state-sponsored markets. With slight variations, a series of projects were presented which would later be taken up by radicalism and then by reformist socialism well into the twentieth century.

These themes were promoted by men of quite different social background. The deputies elected on 13 May 1849, about 200 in total, belonged mainly to the circles of "capacities"—among them were 114 members of the professions, thirty-three mostly lower "civil servants," as against nineteen entrepreneurs from trade and industry and only eleven workers and nineteen farmers. The "statistic of individuals wanted or arrested" after 2 December 1851 was, according to Maurice Agulhon, "less a list of real rebels than a catalog of democratic socialists, whose activity was assumed."[12] Still it provides valuable clues to the make-up of "party" activists. Fourteen percent were from the middle class: people with guaranteed incomes, independent professionals, entrepreneurs, lesser civil servants. In this respect, their social composition was similar to that of the deputies, although mostly from a somewhat lower level. Whether active out of ambition, out of anger at the notables, out of family tradition, democratic idealism or social conscience (and these motives were not mutually exclusive), they were able to exercise a "democratic patronage" because of their education and extensive connections to the working class. These lower classes were represented (at 48 percent) by artisans, shop owners, and wage workers in industry, commerce, and transportation. Even if in the large cities and industrial centers (which were only rarely found in the statistics) factory workers often appeared, most of these were heads of small businesses and journeymen artisans who doubtless were much more willing than peasants (27 percent of the persecuted, as against a share of 57 percent of the working population) to play an active role in rural regions. As heirs of the Jacobin and sans culotte movements of the First Republic, the Montagnards also appear as a sort of "popular front," running from middle bourgeoisie to workers and peasants, although dominated by the petite bourgeoisie. They sought to contest traditional notable claims to political leadership of the people.

To achieve this, they naturally made use of the press. Certainly, many of their newspapers, including *la Réforme*, were forced to close due to persecution by the authorities at every opportunity. However, others appeared to continue the struggle. Among them, the newspaper *La Feuille du Village*, published by Pierre Joigneaux, was especially tailored to peasant concerns. Apart from these, a number of brochures and almanacs appeared. An entire oral propaganda was developed, particularly for the benefit of the illiterate, using songs and public readings. In the autumn of 1848, the Montagnards even attempted to create an extensive national organization, Republican Solidarity. This would have been both a model for a modern political party (with committees at the department, arrondissement, and cantonal level) and a merger of trade union organizations and mutual benefit organizations.[13]

However, Léon Faucher, the Minister of the Interior, and his prefects quickly put and end to these activities, seeing in them preparations for the creation of a "state within a state." The numerous clubs still in existence at the end of 1848, in spite of ever more careful surveillance, disappeared almost completely after the very restrictive law of 19 June 1849 was passed. The election committees, unobtrusively maintained after the elections of 13 May 1849, were still able to function as coordination centers at the department level. The rank-and-file activities of the Montagnards were carried out above all in sociable organizations, which, in theory, were apolitical: certain Masonic lodges, mutual benefit societies, entertainment circles, some "closed" and more bourgeois, others "open" and intended more for the lower classes. This included the "chambrées," the drinking and social clubs, attended by artisans and peasants in the large villages of the south, as well as cafés and inns, many of which took in "red" newspapers from Paris or the departmental capitals. As shown especially in the work of Maurice Agulhon on the Department of Var[14] and Peter McPhee on the Pyrénées-Orientales[15] the democratic socialists were very clever in making use of traditional popular events (Mardi Gras, festivals of patron saints, farewell parties and charivaris) to bring their message to the people. Suppression of such traditional events often backfired, as it was seen as an attack on popular customs. It also contributed to forcing activists into clandestine action or the creation of secret societies (of which more later).

In the spring of 1849, the Montagnards were concentrating above all on preparing for the election on 13 May, the results of which are extremely significant. With 2,300,000 votes (34.8 percent of votes cast) and about 200 deputies, they had done much better than the extreme left in April 1848 (70 to 80 seats) and, especially, better than Ledru-Rollin on 10 December (5 percent of the vote). They gained a majority in lower class districts in the east of Paris and in numerous industrial cities, where they received the backing of workers disappointed by the moderates, as well as in traditional towns, where they found significant support among unpropertied "capacities," artisans and shop owners. However, the main reason for their success was their conquering a part of rural France. In about forty departments, nearly all of which lie south of the line Bordeaux-Orléans-Strasbourg, their results were above their national average. In sixteen of these—with the exception of the Department of the Rhône they were all rural areas—they won an absolute majority, and in the Departments of the Saône-et-Loire and the Pyrénées-Orientales they had record results with nearly two-thirds of the votes cast.

This was a protest vote, often a continuation of the vote for Louis-Napoléon of 10 December, and the result of a complex of motives. Dislike of the "whites" and the Catholic Church, which after a short idyll as supporter of the republic was once again seen as a close ally of the former, certainly played a role. However, many "blue" regions, where people were indifferent towards, or rejected religious practice (Ile-de-France, Champagne, Charentes), voted conservative. The red success seems especially to reflect the extent of a social revolt against the notables; on the basis of a "patriotic" tradition, or a more recent rallying to that tradition, with its integrating effect, and following dramatic economic developments—a revolt by sharecroppers and small tenant farmers against estate owners and their managers in the regions of large estates in central France, or in the wine producing region of Burgundy; a revolt of heavily indebted peasants against profiteers in the towns and villages in the economically backward regions of the Alps and the Massif Central or in the populated areas of Bresse and Alsace. In all these regions the dreams of agricultural reform, abolition of debt or indirect taxes won the day over a fear of the "levelers." This rise of a "red" peasantry was, at the time, a purely French phenomenon, and one that would be long-lasting. After being submerged between 1851 and 1870 beneath a massive support for Bonapartism, this electoral geography of the rural world was confirmed in numerous elections well into the twentieth century.

In 1849, however, the Montagnard Party was defeated, and its leaders worsened their parliamentary position further by mistaken tactics. A demonstration planned for 13 June, intended as a peaceful protest against an attack by the French expeditionary corps on the Roman Republic, degenerated into a failed attempt at insurrection. Ledru-Rollin was forced to flee, and a number of deputies lost their seats. In the period following, the democratic- socialists restricted themselves to legal actions and propaganda activities and hoped for victory in the elections of 1852. After their relative success in the by-elections of March and April 1850, and the subsequent vote on the law of 31 May, that mutilated the democratic franchise, a split occurred. A large majority of the deputies remained loyal to a legal strategy.

The twenty-four deputies of the Nouvelle Montagne, together with the deputies in exile, however, encouraged the development of secret societies, which in fact had never really disappeared. These were organized along military lines, preparing armed actions to defend the republic or to force the reintroduction of universal suffrage, and gained even more support in central and southern France after the discovery and suppression of the "conspiracy of Lyon" in the autumn of 1850, which aimed at a merger of secret societies in southern France. In parts of "red" France, thousands of petit bourgeois and common people[16] were recruited in this way, especially in rural districts, which was less easily controlled than larger cities.

The Montagnards of 1851 thus presented a complex and unique appearance: on the one hand, a parliamentary party, newspapers and meetings of officially apolitical hiding their real activities; on the other hand, the formation of clandestine groups which continued and renewed—with their democratic and less urban oriented recruiting practices—the tradition of the Charbonnerie and certain republican associations during the July monarchy. The two branches of the movement naturally maintained close contact. The same men belonged to both. They shared the same beliefs: a conviction of being the only true representatives of popular interests, a romantic religiosity,[17] the cult of France, the revolution and humanity, messianic expectations for the year 1852, in which all accounts open since 1848 would be settled. They were, all in all, a powerful political force, which, nonetheless suffered from one serious weakness, "the lack of a workable central structure."[18] Their existence, the secrecy that surrounded some of their actions and led to an over-estimation of their strength, increased fears among all "friends of order." The revolutionary crisis that ended in central Europe at the end of 1849 with the defeat of the Badenese republicans, the capitulation of Hungary and the surrender of Venice, thus continued in disguised form in France until the end of 1851.

The Party of Order: Victory and Impotence

In view of the dangers that abruptly manifested themselves in the events in the spring of 1848, a broad movement of conservatives of all currents arose for the first time, in which Orléanist liberals united with traditionalists. Although the latter had nothing against an overthrow of the usurper, as they viewed Louis-Phillippe, they shared their fears with his former supporters. Both feared—in spite of the provisional government's reassuring stance—a return to dictatorship along the lines of the Year II and the Reign of Terror, and were equally afraid of a brutal implementation of socialist and communist theories, which in their eyes meant a general plundering of the property owners for the benefit of the proletariat. Naturally they saw the cause of the financial, industrial, and commerical crisis in the "insane" demands of the workers in Paris and Lyon. Neither the election of a moderate constituent assembly in April, nor the election of Louis-Napoléon in December, nor their own victory in May 1849, could completely dispel their fears. The "demagogues" continued to act both underground as well as legally, the economic depression continued, and the dreaded election date of 1852 clouded their perception.

To defend their property and perhaps even their lives, legitimists and Orléanists attempted to form an alliance based on their shared values, which they saw endangered. First came property, which, according to Tocqueville, leant "a form of fraternity ... to all who enjoyed it." Absolute respect for property as well as for the concomitant entrepreneurial freedom and a renunciation of plans that threatened property (for example the right to work ...) were held to be the conditions for renewed prosperity. The family, endangered by plans of some socialists for the emancipation of women, also needed protecting. Some even believed that the community of women was intended.

Against such dangers, order had to be defended unyieldingly. Freedoms of press, assembly, and association had to be strictly limited. In the long-term, only a solid moral and religious education could finally bring an end to "base passions"—envy of the upper classes, immoderate desire for social advancement. For this reason the church needed to regain its influence in education and society—something which it never should have lost—and "proclaim the admirable philosophy that man is on earth in order to suffer" (Thiers). Finally, France had had to beware of supporting European revolutions, which were just as dangerous as its own, all the more as a war would play into the hands of extremists. In this alliance, which was oriented in part not only towards conservative goals, but literally reactionary ones, legitimists and adherents of the former center-right had to sacrifice few of their principles. The same cannot be said either of the center-left, nor of supporters of the dynastic left, who had once appeared as champions of freedom against Molè and Guizot, held quite anticlerical views and felt themselves part of the "emancipatory mission of France." Their alliance with the Party of Order meant therefore that Orléanism shifted to the right and ended its struggle on two fronts.

To deal with the new circumstances of universal suffrage, which had increased the number of voters by a factor of forty, the notables created an organization. At first, the Republican Club for Electoral Freedom was founded on 10 March 1848, which allied its endeavors with Montalembert's previously established Committee for the Defense of Religious Freedom. With the beginning of the constitutent assembly there followed the "meeting of the Rue de Poitiers," which 300 members of the assembly soon were attending. This informal parliamentary caucus published brochures and circulars via a Commmittee of the Electoral Union and monitored preparations for the elections of 13 May 1849. With the help of a group of senior parliamentarians (the "Burgraves") it dominated the legislative assembly and founded an association, led by Molé, for antisocialist propaganda. At the departmental and local level it was supported by election committees which, in principle only temporary, generally became permanent institutions.

From the winter of 1849 onwards, they were also supported by the associations of the Friends of Order, which were organized along military lines and wanted "to provide the national guard and the army active assistance." Like some mutual benefit and fraternal societies, they recruited a part of their membership from the lower classes—who were also the target of a press with large print runs, the coordination of which, from September 1848 onwards, was the responsibility of a committee arising from a congress in Tours. Cheap brochures and annuals written in part in a familiar style where "common sense" condemned the socialist utopia, and, in part, in apocalyptic jargon (the monstrous plans of the reds, credited to the "dangerous classes"), served the same aim. For the rural population, two rather traditional instruments proved to be useful: "patronage" (which, however, was only effective when the estate owner lived on the estate or was usually present and when the peasants really accepted his influence) and the support of the clergy, who justified existing order in the name of the will of God.

While the revolution of 1830, directed against the "party of the priests," was accompanied by violent anticlerical demonstrations, during the July monarchy the church and the democratic movement moved closer together, a rapprochement aided by the appearance of liberal Catholicism, the development of social Catholicism and the evangelical and romantic religiosity of many republican and socialist activists. Directly following events in February, there was a short romance between the new powers and the clergy, which hardly mourned the regime that had been overthrown, and hoped to achieve from the republic freedom of education. Need one be reminded of the classic image of the priest blessing the tree of liberty? However, this convergence was only short-lived. By the fall of 1848, at the latest, bishops and priests, worried by threats to the social order, shocked by the Roman revolution against Pius IX, and traditionalist in their majority, joined the Party of Order without hesitation, and condemning the "Christian democrats," personified by men such as Professor Frédéric Ozanam and Abbé Maret, editor of *l'Ere Nouvelle*, to a minority role. Hence, a return was made to a confrontation—begun more than a half-century previously—between a Catholicism, now supported by a Voltairean bourgeoisie worried about its property and the spirit of revolution, now embodied in the "democratic and social republic." It was hoped that the clergy would provide a decisive counterweight to this. However, its sympathies lay above all with the legitimists, and its political intervention was not always appreciated, in the strongholds of the "blues."

In March and April 1848 most of the conservatives around Guizot retreated temporarily, while legitimists and the old opposition of left and center-left voiced their approval of the republic, which, however, they wished to see as "honorable and moderate." Whether they stood on the same lists as the moderate republicans or not, they still won at least 300 seats, including about sixty seats for the adherents of Comte de Chambord, who were thus much more strongly represented than in the parliament of the July monarchy. Among them were numerous experienced parliamentarians, such as André Dupin, Odilon Barrot, Rémusat, Tocqueville, Falloux, and Thiers (elected in June 1848) who had considerable influence in the committees and public sessions. All of them naturally supported Cavaignac in his suppression of the June uprising and restriction of freedoms of press and assembly. With their solid local base, they achieved dazzling successes in the municipal and canton elections in most departments.

The presidential elections, however, proved an embarrassment, as they had no candidate who was well-known and popular enough. On 5 November, the committee of the Rue de Poitiers avoided deciding between Cavaignac and Louis-Napoléon. A minority of legitimists opted for the former, which explains, in part, his good results in a number of "white" departments. Others, such as Berryer and Falloux, preferred Louis-Napoléon and allied with Montalembert, who remained true to his support of the temporal power of the pope and of liberty of education, as well as with a number of the most important leaders of the Orléanists—Thiers, Odilon Barrot, and Léon Faucher—who believed they could easily influence the nephew of the emperor. It should be mentioned that little credit for Louis-Napoléon's massive victory can be given to the royalist notables. They claimed, at least, to be able to exploit him. As he, like they, intended to be rid of the moderate republicans as soon as possible, he also chose men from their circles for his first cabinet.

Thus it was important to achieve a solid majority in the legislative assembly. To this end, the Party of Order attempted to make use of the popularity of the president. Quite often they placed Bonapartists on their lists, which generally included both legitimists and Orléanists, except in certain "white" departments, where the former felt strong enough to present homogeneous lists, or, inversely, in "blue" regions, where the presence of legitimists would have offended moderate but anti-clerical and "patriotic" voters. On 13 May the electoral victory of the Party of Order was indisputable: 53 percent of the votes, 450 of 715 seats including 150 legitimists and a handful of Bonapartists. Like with the Montagnards, the geographical distribution of the votes is equally complex and significant. Success was total in aristocratic and upper class residential areas, like the west of Paris, but also in more modest urban centers, in which, because of the organizational weakness of the democratic-socialists, a clientele relationship between notables on the one hand and middle and lower class on the other remained intact. In rural districts, a distinction can be made between the Catholic and legitimist strongholds of Brittany and several departments in the south, and those regions where victory was due mostly to the Orléanists (and Bonapartists): the areas of the "capitalist hierarchy" (Ile-de-France, Haute Normandie), in which landowners and rich peasants controlled village society: the "democracies" of the northeast (Champagne, Lorraine) and west central France (Charantes), where numerous peasants feared above all those who would divide up their property. In both these cases the clergy often played an only modest role.

Master of the legislature, the Party of Order was able to carry through its program: reinstatement of the pope in Rome; restoration of the "moral order" by a purge of the public school teaching staff; extension of control by the church and "social authorities" over public education, privileges for the teaching orders;[19] "cleansing" of universal suffrage with the statute of 31 May 1850, where 29 percent of the voters lost their right to vote because of criteria, in part related to tax payments.[20] However, although members of the majority were nearly unanimous in their determination to fight the threat of "socialism" with the help of a repressive policy that showed little interest in civil liberties, they were deeply split on the question of what form of government should replace the republic.

For legitimists, the only possibility seemingly existed in the return of Henry V, as in their view, only a traditional monarchy supported by the church could heal the malady under which France suffered. But how was this goal to be achieved? For the *Gazette de France* and above all for the "Committe of the National Right," led by the Marquis de La Rochejaquelein and strongly supported in the south, a referendum in the sense of a plebiscite was necessary. This group was therefore known as "the white Montagnards." This method was officially rejected by the pretender to the throne and by Berryer and Falloux, because they hoped for a "fusion" at some time in the future: Orléanists would recognize the legitimist pretender as king, but in the absence of a direct heir the Count of Paris would be his successor.

This solution was preferred by most conservative supporters of Louis-Philippe—especially after his death on 26 August 1850—among others, by Guizot, Molé, Victor de Broglie, and the Duke of Nemours. It was, however, received with reservations by the Duchess of Orleans, the Duke of Aumale, by Thiers and former members of the dynastic opposition. Both wished certain minimal guarantees from the Count of Chambord (respect of the principles of 1789, recognition of the contractual character of the monarchy, the Tricolor). As he refused to make these guarantees, the "fusion" failed at the end of 1850. Was it then necessary to alter the constitution so that Louis-Napoléon could stand again and thus prevent any success by the "reds"? Thiers, who preferred a candidacy by the Duke of Aumale or the Prince of Joinville as a preparation for a return of the Count of Paris, was opposed to this solution. He and his group voted with the republicans and thus helped to stop the amendment, which required a three-fourths vote. As this discussion led to unrest among conservatives and paralyzed the Party of Order, the constellation played into the hands of Louis-Napoléon as the elections of 1852 approached. Numerous Orléanists in the assembly and in the country turned, for example, to the Elysée Party.

The Bonapartist Outcome

Louis-Napoléon was determined to remain in power. At first he employed legal means. To this purpose, prefects pressured the general councils to voice their approval for a constitutional amendment and supported a major petition campaign to this end, begun in the spring of 1851. When the amendment failed in the National Assembly, however, he began working towards a coup. He continued to place his loyal followers in key military and civil positions. To prepare the ground politically, the Elysée and the publicists and committees it directed made perfect use of the ambiguity of Bonapartism. In view of the Assembly's disunity and impotence, Luois-Napoléon was presented as the only possible guarantee of order. Were not administration, justice, police and gendarmerie daily active at his behest in order to contain the "reds"? Was he not the only one who, as Romieu showed in *Le Spectre Rouge de 1852*, could thwart their abominable subversive projects? In his statement of 4 November, he confirmed that "antisocial hopes are getting out of control as the weakened organs of state approach the end of their period of office."

At the same time he endeavored to appease public opinion on the left. If he was not always able "to do good and improve the condition of the population," he stated in Dijon on 1 June 1851, this was because the Assembly "had refused to cooperate." And in the autumn he proposed to repeal the statute of 31 May 1850, i.e. to reintroduce the universal franchise mutilated by the monarchist majority. Thus, simultaneously he claimed to be able to save the "welfare of society," threatened by "demagogues" and ruined by an incapable and divided parliament, and to restore completely the principle of popular sovereignty disparaged by retrograde parties. Thus the foundations for his successful coup were laid.

The events of December 1851 are thus easily understood. From the "men of order," hardly 200 deputies provided resistance (they were arrested in the mayor's office of the X arrondissement), and a part of the Paris bourgeoisie showed its passive sympathy. The president's initiative, in contrast, was received with relief by a large part of the notables and conservative peasantry, who later saw themselves confirmed in their stance by the official version ("the jacquerie") of republican attempts at resistance. This met with only limited success in Paris. About 1500 people (ten to fifteen times fewer than in June 1848) answered a call to resistance by some of the Montagnard deputies. As the people had been disarmed, the superiority of the police and army was overwhelming. Moreover, the president had dissolved the reactionary Assembly and reintroduced universal suffrage. In some "red" districts (the larger cities monitored by their garrisons hardly reacted) relatively significant uprisings broke out. In central France, in central southwest France, in the Mediterranean and Alpine Departments especially strong revolts occurred. These powerful local movements (Digne, the capital of the Department of the Basses-Alpes, was occupied by six to seven thousand armed republicans for a number of days) were quickly and brutally suppressed by the army—with the occasionally assistance of spontaneously organized "men of order."

These revolts have given rise to contradictory interpretations. The Bonapartists, their press and, following them, a large part of a very one-sidedly informed public opinion, saw in them an intrusion into politics by the "dangerous classes," by people who dreamed of murder and plundering. This thesis was easily refuted by republican historians following Eugène Ténot.[21] Most of the violence alleged by official or semi-official propaganda never took place. Rather the insurrections were legalistic and spontaneous uprising for the defense of the republic and its violated constitution.

Research in the last decades has produced a much more strongly nuanced version. The uprisings were organized locally by Montagnard secret societies (in the "red" regions such as southern Burgundy or Limousin, where there were few such organizations, the uprisings were very weak), but national coordination was lacking. It was a mass movement of the people—peasants, artisans, journeymen and shop owners under the leadership of activists from their circles and minor notables—people from independent professions, dismissed civil servants, entrepreneurs. Finally, it was typically "democratic and social." Solely (or almost solely) the most educated of the leaders wanted to keep the movement a strictly legalist one, replacing mayors and state officials who had accepted the coup d'État. Most of the insurgents rose up to defend the "good" and "true" republic, the republic that was to bring an "end of misery" in 1852. For them, the people, once they had regained their sovereignty, could immediately take measures to the benefit of the poor—for example, abolishing indirect taxes. Hence in the uprising, "the intellectuality of the republican notables and activists" was bound with "the primitivism of the masses with their traditional mentality (Maurice Agulhon)"[22] on a common foundation of passionate loyalty to the republic.

Reflected in the extent and failure of this uprising are, moreover, the limits of the democratic-socialist party's influence. It remained restricted to individual regions. In three-fourths of the departments, the proclamation of the coup met with general approval, and many "red" voters, still susceptible to the Bonapartist myth, saw no reason to oppose the "Napoleon of the people," who had dissolved the monarchist Assembly in order to return sovereignty to the totality of the citizen body.

Directly following the coup, the presidential republic that arose from the events of 2 December and the restored empire that succeeded it clearly leaned to the right. Political freedoms disappeared, and the referendums of December 1851 and November 1852 as well as the legislative cantonal and municipal elections in between were no longer free. Massive and arbitrary sanctions, demanded by conservatives desirous of revenge, extended not only to the particularly "guilty" rebels, but also to the more well-known Montagnards: nearly 27,000 arrests were made and almost 10,000 were sentenced without trial to transportation to Guyana (239) or, above all, to Algeria. The republican party was practically destroyed. At the same time, the church and conservative forces (with the exception of some of their political representatives who remained true to legitimism and liberalism) placed great trust in the new regime, which had prevented the elections of 1852, eliminated "anarchy" and created the conditions for a strong economic upswing.

Thus, after only a few years, the movement of 1848 ended in a parliamentary, liberal monarchy with a class-based franchise being replaced by another monarchy uniting a democratic principle with the personal power of a man sent by Providence, who saw himself as the only one "chosen by the people." Was the Second Republic therefore only a short and fruitless intermezzo? In fact, it played a decisive role in the process of politicization of the French people, especially of the rural population. Frequent recourse to universal suffrage, the development of propaganda to previously unknown levels and the fact that the people became aware of the national import of their actions in a continuous situation of crisis led to a strengthening of already existing collective attitudes, and occasionally to their fundamental transformation, and, above all, to their metamorphosis into political standpoints. Their revival in the last phase of the Second Empire and in the Third Republic show the extent to which experiences of the third of the nineteenth century had left their traces.

Through universal suffrage, tested for many years and blessed in principle by Napoleon III, the problem of the hegemony of the notables, who had had a monopoly of power under the constitutional monarchy, appeared in a new light. They were forced to see how their traditional influence over the broad masses was called into question by politicians who came for the most part from the middle or petite bourgeoisie, the "capacities," and small businessmen. Is that not already the "new social strata" as extolled by Gambetta some twenty years later? The peasants, for their part, were seen until then as a "silent majority" fundamentally submissive to the established order and only capable of local expressions of displeasure, which could be quickly appeased or suppressed. Thanks to their numbers, they had become the arbiters of the competition of the parties. Politicians would have to stay in touch with them, listen to their demands and try to obtain their votes. The peasants became used to expressing their opinion with the ballot. As far as the "working class" is concerned, it was its avant garde, especially in Paris, succeeding for a few months in having its voice heard and even placing itself in the spotlight of politics. Rallying around a both cooperative and state interventionist "socialism," it raised great fears among all property owners and its movement was destroyed in the June repression. However, the idea which had inspired it continued to live beneath the surface, even after the coup of December 1851. As Jacques Rougerie has shown, it sparked the "socialism of the Commune," which "resembled in many respects the experiments of 1848."[23] In more general terms, the labor question had placed itself so emphatically to the fore that from then on no government could react with the indifference or lack of understanding of the monarchy with its class-based franchise.

The Second Republic provided a stage in the development of political currents that had already appeared, destined to mark the history of modern France. At first, let us consider Bonapartism. After becoming a simple myth at the end of the July Monarchy, it reentered the political arena with all its complexities (it reassured conservatives but was also able to seduce democrats because of its basic principle of popular sovereignty) and in a new form (it adopted for good the universal franchise and stressed its social content). At first dictatorial and clearly oriented to the right, but from 1860 increasingly more liberal and aiming for economic growth, the Second Empire unintentionally—in modernizing society and accustoming the French to voting—prepared the ground for a return of the republic while remaining the model for an antiparliamentarianism, often directed against the republic.

Legitimists and Orléanists sought to bring an end to the republic as soon as possible, but the republic allowed them, for the first time, a common government for the retention of social order. Thiers and his friends from the center-left never forgot this lesson during the 1870s. After seeing the impossibility of restoring the monarchy, they offered their support once and for all for a republic, hoping it to be a conservative one, and contributed to its permanency in voting for the constitution of 1875. Thus the experience of the middle of the century led, with some delay, to a reconciliation of the right with the republic.

At the time their focus lay elsewhere. The two largest monarchist currents agreed to a close alliance with the Catholic Church, something up to then sought above all by the followers of the older branch of the Bourbons, while many Orléanists, as the heirs of 1789, displayed a certain distrust of the clergy. The Party of Order was, as the Loi Falloux showed, a clerical party. The church accepted this conservative alliance in spite of the danger of being instrumentalized by it. Shortly after, it sided with the coup and the authoritarian empire. It is hardly surprising that it appeared to the republicans of the second half of the century, much more than those of 1848, as a relentless opponent, as the most important "ideological apparatus" of their opponents. The "religious question" long remained on the agenda.

The "rebellious" extreme left believed at first that it would be successful in replacing the bourgeois order, continued by the moderates in a new form, with a "socialist" or "communist" society. Without giving consideration to the new government's growing legitimacy provided by universal suffrage, they remained true to their project, even after their defeat in June, of forcing on an "alienated" majority a dictatorship of a "conscious" and active minority. In spite of the painful experience of the Commune, this strategy was long preserved by their disciples: "Blanquists," anarcho-syndicalists, "orthodox" or Leninist Marxists.

A much more numerous group in the camp of the forty-eighters drew quite different lessons. The republic, based on universal suffrage, civil liberties and the rule of law ("the ballot replaces the gun") appeared to them the ideal framework for an emancipation of the people. The tasks of the backers of such a policy was to win over public opinion and to achieve the necessary changes step by step: enlightenment of a people subjected to the influence of the church, which had proved itself reactionary once again, social reform for the benefit of the most disadvantaged groups. However, even when united on the strategy for achieving power and maintaining legality, differences of opinion very quickly appeared, as in the middle of the century, as to the speed and extent of reforms desired. The "opportunists" intended, like the moderates of 1848 (whose romantic illusions they criticized, however) to stagger changes over time and to restrict them. The radicals, who saw themselves as heirs of the democratic-socialists, sought at first to advance further and more quickly, before they "became reasonable" after gaining power. Jaurès would attempt to prove that socialism was the logical result of a democratic republic. But were not the Montagnards, in this respect, his predecessors? Thus the short experiment of 1848/51 weighed heavily on the future political evolution of France.

Notes

1. Ernest Renan, "Philosophie de l'histoire contemporaine. La monarchie constitutionelle en France," *Revue des deux mondes*, 1 November 1869, 84-85.
2. Pierre Rosanvallon, *La monarchie impossible. Les Chartes de 1814 et 1830* (Paris, 1994), 179.
3. Ibid., 174.
4. "1848-1830-1789. Comment naissent les révolutions," in *Actes du congrès historique du contenaire de la révolution de 1848* (Paris, 1948), 1-29; "Panoramas de la crise," in *Aspects de la crise et de la dépression de l'économie française au milieu du XIXe siècle* ed. by Ernest Labrousse (La Roche-sur-Yon, 1956), iii-xxiv; *Le mouvement ouvrier et les théories sociales en France au XIXe siècle* (Paris, 1952), 183-89.
5. Anthony Rowley, "Deux crises économiques modernes: 1846 et 1848?" *1848, Révolutions et Mutations au XIXe siècle* 2 (1986): 81-89.
6. *Le Spectateur de Dijon*, 3 November 1846.
7. Thanks to the work of Rémi Gossez: "Diversité des antagonismes sociaux vers le milieu du XIXe siècle," *Revue économique* VII (1956); and *Les ouvriers de Paris, Livre I: L'organisation (1848-1852)* (La Roche-sur-Yon, 1967); Pierre Caspard, "Aspect de la lutte des classes en 1848: le recrutement de la garde nationale mobile," *Revue historique* (1974, pt. 3): 81-106; Mark Traugott, *Armies of the Poor: Determinants of Working-Class Participation in the Parisian Insurrection of June 1848* (Princeton, 1985). This author rejects the thesis of generational conflict and points out the weakness of legalistic leadership of the national guard from the end of May onwards.
8. Alexis de Tocqueville, *Souvenirs* (Paris, 1964), 152.
9. Thousands of dead and wounded in the battles, approximately 1,500 executed on the spot, 4,000 sentenced to deportation to Algeria, not fully carried out.
10. Frederick A. de Luna, *The French Republic under Cavaignac, 1848* (Princeton, 1969); George W. Fasel, "The French Election of April 23, 1848. Suggestions for a revision," *French Historical Studies* 5 (1968): 285-98.
11. Especially worth mentioning: François Bluche, *Le Bonapartisme. Aux origines de la droite autoritaire (1800-1850)* (Paris, 1989), and *Le Bonapartisme* (Paris, 1981); *Le Bonapartisme, Phénomène historique et mythe politique, Actes du colloque franco-allemand de Paris (1975)* (Munich, 1977); Adrien Dansette, *Louis-Napoléon à la conquête du pouvoir* (Paris, 1961); Bernard Ménager, *Les Napoléons du peuple* (Paris, 1988). One could also include most dissertations on regional history in the mid-nineteenth century.
12. Maurice Agulhon, *1848 ou l'apprentissage de la République, 1848-1852* (Paris, 1992), 258. [This exact quote does not appear in the English edition, *The Republican Experiment, 1848-1852*, trans. Janet Lloyd, (Cambridge and New York, 1983), but see 163.]
13. Raymond Huard, *La Naissance du parti politique en France* (Paris, 1996), 97-101.

14. Maurice Agulhon, *The Republic in the Village: The People of the Var from the French Revolution to the Second Republic*, trans. Janet Lloyd (Cambridge, 1983).

15. Peter McPhee, *Les Semailles de la République* (Perpignan, 1995).

16. 50,000 to 100,000 according to Ted W. Margadant, *French Peasants in Revolt: The Insurrection of 1851* (Princeton, 1984).

17. Remarkably well presented by Edward Berenson, *Popular Religion and Left-wing Politics in France 1830-1852* (Princeton, 1984).

18. R. Huard, *La Naissance*, 109.

19. This was the object of the statute of 15 March 1850, the so-called Loi Falloux.

20. Inclusion in the electoral rolls required residence in the canton in question for at least three years. As proof of this, entry in the list of those liable to pay income tax was necessary, and the poorest were exempt from this tax.

21. Eugène Ténot, *La province en décembre 1851* (Paris, 1865).

22. Agulhon, *Republic in the Village*, 294.

23. Jacques Rougerie, *Paris libre* (Paris, 1971), 186.

Chapter 5

REVOLUTION IN GERMANY
Constitutional State—Nation-State—Social Reform

Dieter Langewiesche

All the issues of the European revolutions of 1848 came to the fore simultaneously in the states of the German Confederation. As in France, demands were raised for a German constitutional regime, with a democratic franchise, a strong parliament, a free press, and an unlimited right to political association, all of which would offer male citizens much greater possibilities of political participation than they had previously enjoyed. The assumption that such a reformed regime would also enable social reform to be carried out was common to both the French and German Revolutions, as were arguments about the nature and extent of these reforms. In contrast to France, however, the German Revolution faced the challenge of establishing not only a parliamentary, constitutional regime open to the possibility of social reform, but a nation-state as well.

While the overthrow of the French king opened the door to reforms that broke with the country's monarchical past, the German revolutionary movement was confronted by the inertia of thirty-nine states, thirty-five of which had dynastic rulers. There was no one capital city where a revolution could be decided centrally and in which national institutions existed that could be taken over by a revolutionary regime. Simply changing elites and reforming the constitution by themselves would thus not suffice to fulfil the revolution's aims in Germany. Together with the nation-state aspired to by the revolutionaries, a new state central authority also had to be created—over the heads of the thirty-nine states, as these showed little willingness to become impotent provinces. The civic regimes of the four city-states of Bremen, Frankfurt am Main, Hamburg, and Lübeck were no less resolute in their desire for self-preservation than were Germany's royal dynasties.

Notes for this section begin on page 142.

Large portions of the population also felt ties to the states in which they lived. This often led to conflicting roles, as every future German citizen was equally a citizen of a state and of a locality. Those who insisted for instance, in their capacity as German citizens, that every German must be allowed to choose his place of residence freely and to work in whatever part of Germany he wished, might, in their capacity as citizens of individual states and municipalities, have had a quite different opinion. In his role as citizen of an individual German state, the "progressively" minded national citizen saw the right to unlimited freedom of movement as socially dangerous in an age of pauperism. As citizen of a municipality that had to fight the effects of mass poverty daily, he rejected this progressive gift from the nation all the more decidedly.

Other cases were analogous. The national citizen might possibly have approved of a guarantee to the basic right of marriage and the full emancipation of the Jews, while many state and municipal citizens continued to try to limit both. One important reason for this attitude, if not the only one, was to avoid burdening still further the already strained state and municipal social welfare budgets. Such dissonance between actions at the national, state, and municipal levels are partly explain the fact that only a minority in the revolutionary movement wanted a unified German republic. The feeble response to the two Badenese uprisings of April and September 1848, which sought to impose a German republic by force, can also be interpreted as an implicit plebiscite against a German nation state that broke with the federalist and simultaneously dynastic tradition.

A German national revolution could only succeed when revolutions were victorious in the individual states as well—at least in the larger and militarily powerful ones, Austria and Prussia, as well as in the four medium-sized monarchies of Bavaria, Saxony, Hanover, and Württemberg. Reforms had to take place simultaneously at the national level and at the level of the individual states. This, however, created a complexity of problems that no one before 1848 had foreseen. Only in the course of the revolution did these problems come to light, and there were no obvious solutions for them.

The difficult double task of forging both a parliamentary constitutional state and a nation-state was doubtless a central aim of the German Revolution, but by no means the only one. Older scholarship placed it center-stage and it has remained firmly anchored in the German conception of history down to the present day. However, there was more to the revolution. Besides the institutional revolution that sought to establish a nation-state and with it a society of citizens, and to ensure their permanence through institutional reforms at the municipal, state, and national level, there was the primal revolution. In it, the lower classes, both urban and rural, predominated. They had other goals and other forms of action; they were not permanently organized, and did not coordinate their activities beyond the local level. Since neither the nation-state nor the creation of new, permanent constitutional institutions were part of their primal revolution, it remained as foreign to the actors of the institutional revolution as it did to later historians.

Only in more recent years have scholars begun to include the distinct logic of the sociopolitical behavior characteristic of this primal revolution in their broader picture of the revolution. Doing so does not mean calling into question the central importance of the national and constitutional revolution, but it does make the fractures within the revolutionary process visible in a way different from before. The revolution regains its complexity; its image becomes more diverse. This does not make it any easier to answer the question of why the revolution failed in the end, despite all its partial successes, but it does exclude simple answers to that question.

Legalization, Parliamentarization, Institutionalization

These three key words bind together the central strands of development in the two years of revolution in Germany. They combine to form the basic decision already reached by an overwhelming majority of the adherents of the revolutionary movement in March and April 1848: to channel the revolution as quickly as possible into a reform process. For this, institutions were required which would be recognized both by the political nation and by that core of governmental authority that had everywhere survived the first wave of revolution. Two institutions stand out in this work of limiting a revolution by promises of reform: the March Ministries in the individual German states and the German National Assembly. They legalized and parliamentarized the revolution and thus transformed it into a process of institutionally led reform.

Through the so-called March Ministries, the German princes evaded the revolutionary pressure from the street. The monarchs appointed leaders of the liberal opposition to office in March and April 1848 when the authority of the old power structure threatened to collapse under the impact of mass movements in the cities and the countryside. That the dynasties "quickly grasped the need to cover themselves with the popular shield of liberal government ministries," as the Badenese liberal Ludwig Häusser astutely noted in 1851 "was most responsible for disarming the revolution at its most dangerous moment."[1] Naming liberal ministers meant striving to unite "freedom" and "order," two key words of the German revolution. The old rulers gained allies among the reformers and the reformers gained governmental power.

The military, however, remained everywhere at the disposal of the princes.[2] In July 1848 the National Assembly was unsuccessful in its undertaking to have state armies swear an oath of loyalty to the provisional head of the future nation-state. The creation of a national fleet, for which the national movement assiduously collected money, never got very far, in view of the short time available for the effort. The military was neither nationalized nor brought under constitutional control in the individual German states. This proved to be a decisive weakness for the revolutionary movement and its work of reform. Supported by the military power of their states which they alone controlled, the Prussian and Austrian Monarchs could reject the German National Assembly's concept of governmental unity and in the end militarily defeat the revolution both at home and abroad. The provisional national government created by the Frankfurt Assembly did command a federal army with a strength of about 300,000 men. Because it consisted of units from the individual states, it could only be deployed to crush revolutionary uprisings. And it was used for this purpose. As a weapon against rulers who resisted national central power, it would have been useless.

The nature of the German Revolution is reflected in the weakness of the provisional central government. A creature of the revolution, the German National Assembly simultaneously represented a majority wish for continuity. In March 1848, the revolution had not only ceased at the foot of the thrones, it had also not touched the individual German states and their institutions. Thus, a German nation-state could only come into existence with the agreement of the individual states and their princes. This was something they were not prepared to do voluntarily. The Federal Diet, the steering committee of the German Confederation, had appointed a committee of well-known liberals in March to prepare a revision of the old confederate constitution. However, when after only a few weeks, this committee presented the draft of a constitution that would transform German Confederation into a federal nation-state, by reform from above, the monarchs rejected it.

They did not dare resist, however, elections to a German National Assembly demanded by the so-called pre-parliament. This body consisted of 574 spokesmen of the German national movement who met on 31 March in the *Paulskirche* [St. Paul's Church in Frankfurt, the meeting place of the German National Assembly—ed.], legitimating themselves by revolutionary "rights" since they had no commission from any state institution. A minority of determined radicals proposed a motion to name an "executive committee" but failed in this attempt to force through a German national republic. The "one and indivisible republic, with a president at its head" could only have been arrived at along "a path soaked in German blood," as stated in the introduction to the constitutional draft the committee produced for the Federal Diet.[3] Not only did liberals reject such a path, but so did moderate democrats as well, opting for peaceful reform, legalized by the traditional dynasties and legitimized by an elected national assembly. Their ambition to find a middle way between "anarchy" and "reaction" also determined the pre-parliament's decision to leave the drafting of a constitution "exclusively and solely" to a national assembly.

Republicans around Freidrich Hecker could not accept this decision. In a second revolution of April 1848, starting from their base in Baden, they sought to create a republican nation-state by force and violence. They were defeated for two reasons: The population offered them too little support, the people voting with their feet against a violent republican revolution, and the liberal March cabinets and the Federal Assembly did not hesitate to employ federal troops against the revolutionaries.

After this revolt against the path of reform had collapsed, the Frankfurt National Assembly became the central parliamentary decision-making body in the process of constraining the revolution to reform—but not the only one. With the Prussian National Assembly in Berlin, the Austrian Reichstag in Vienna and, somewhat later, the parliaments of the other German states, additional centers of reform came into existence. Even while the *Paulskirche* quickly developed a functional parliamentary party system,[4] in all these parliaments the fundamentally decentral characteristic of German history asserted itself, one opposed to a unitary nation-state. The political decision on success or failure of the national revolution would, however, be made in conjunction of events between Frankfurt, Berlin, and Vienna. In this triangle composed of two established monarchies and a nascent nation-state, the weight of power and influence was unequally distributed.

The monarchies were anchored in history and state power, while the political authority of the German National Assembly, on the other hand, was based solely on the legitimacy it possessed as the elected representative of the German nation. The assembly had no instruments of governmental power that it could employ to enforce its will. The extent to which it was able to influence national political events is therefore all the more surprising. Its deputies first met in the *Paulskirche* in Frankfurt on 18 May 1848. Chosen in elections where about 80 percent of adult men had the vote they had an unusually broad basis of legitimation, in comparison to other European countries. Based on this legitimation, they energetically went about their historically unprecedented task: creating a constitution that would form a liberal nation-state out of thirty-nine illiberal individual states. This constitution would not eradicate the existing states, but subordinate them to a federal state and simultaneously encourage the process of their liberalization, already begun by their March Ministries and state parliaments. This immense task could not be completed by the National Assembly alone; it required the assistance of a political public sphere and the consent of Germany's monarchs.

When at the beginning of the revolution all the barriers erected by the states against the politicization of society collapsed, a political public sphere, with an unprecedented breadth and intensity, evolved very rapidly. People gathered in larger and smaller meetings, demonstrated and protested, pleaded and threatened, drew up resolutions and petitions, passed out handbills and caricatures, brought out a great number of new newspapers and in established ones did not mince their words. Politicization was centered in the cities, but the countryside was affected as well. Men set the tone, but women were also active. This public sphere became a politically creative force because it was rapidly organized and could thus constantly influence the process of political decision-making.

Although observed distrustfully by the state authorities, numerous voluntary associations had already become schools of civic action in the preceding decades. During the revolution, this process paid off: now, great numbers of political associations originated, as the early forms of modern political parties. These associations passed statutes to give themselves a permanent form, formulated programs according to which they strove to shape politics, came together in regional and national congresses, acquired newspapers with which they communicated with each other and influenced public opinion, and cooperated with the parliamentary parties whose viewpoints they shared in order to influence government policy.

In the course of the first year of revolution a network of associations developed which evolved into five large party groups.[5] Continuing the developments in the prerevolutionary decades, they anticipated the party system that— interrupted by a relapse during the postrevolutionary decade of reaction—reached its completed form in the 1860s and survived in its essential features into the Weimar Republic: labor movement, democrats, liberalism, political Catholicism, and conservatism. During the years of revolution, however, the borders between these groups remained partially fluid. In contrast to the circumstances of its refounding in the 1860s, the labor movement in 1848 was exclusively non-parliamentary and cooperated politically with democrats. The 1848 conservatives who were also organized exclusively in extraparliamentary fashion, were, in many places, active in liberal or Catholic associations. Only in their stronghold of Prussia were they successful in making the transition to an independent, modern interest group. Political Catholicism also built up a broad organizational network, but two striking differences separate it from its successor in the German Empire of 1871. In 1848, there was no Catholic parliamentary caucus; only when religious questions were discussed did the Catholic deputies in the *Paulskirche* gather into a separate group across caucus lines. Secondly, political Catholicism did not possess in 1848 an organizational monopoly on politically active Catholics. Indeed, in many places more Catholics were active in democratic associations than in Catholic ones.

Liberals and democrats held the greatest influence both in parliament as well as in the landscape of extraparliamentary associations. The democrats surpassed by far other political groups in numbers of associations and membership, while liberals dominated in the *Paulskirche*. They benefited from the fact that the organizational separation of democrats and liberals had not been completed at the time of the elections. Elected as well-known representatives of the reformist middle-class, they quickly split into two camps, becoming bitter enemies.

While foreseeable before 1848, it was only in that year that the middle-class reform movement diverged into two hostile camps over the question of "republic" or "constitutional monarchy." In this conflict of principles more was at stake than simply the shape of the future nation-state. Ever since the French Revolution, the term "republic" had become ever more highly charged, and by 1848 had reached its highpoint. For liberals and conservatives the word set loose fears of doom and destruction. They equated "republic" with mob rule, which would destroy morality and property, dissolve family ties, and, ultimately, demolish bourgeois life. From the "vain hopes of roast dove, which the republic would drive into their mouths" they drew a direct line to "the much worse trust in so-called socialism, which, in the current state of humanity, would mean nothing less than freedom with robbery and murder."[6]

In contrast to this anxiety syndrome were the quite diverse, hopeful visions of the democrats. Extreme examples of these visions were secularized versions of religious expectations of salvation, when the "red race of republicans" was placed semantically as the successor to the passion of Christ, burdened with the "sins of the bourgeoisie" and marked by the "scourge of thorns" approaching the death of atonement.[7] The new labor movement remained more sober. It placed its hopes in the socially reforming powers of a democratic republic. Such an attitude helped bridge the gap between the workers movement and the democratic bourgeoisie. There was a common understanding of the "republic" as a society of citizens which would openly discuss all problems, social ones as well, and bring them into a constant process of reform. This led to a demand for more state activity, but less state bureaucracy, through voluntary self-government. Such a demand echoed the old ideal of a community of burghers which administered itself and therefore had no need of a bureaucracy. However, the republicans' opponents were unable to hear this echo of prerevolutionary innocence in their goals. For them, every call for a republic, in Germany or elsewhere, revived the bloody "schemes of 1793." No one in the society of 1848 expressed this fear of a repetition of the French revolution better than Gustave Flaubert: "… the sound of the guillotine made itself heard in every syllable of the word 'Republic' …"[8]

The nightmare of a "red republic" became the line of division between liberals and democrats, although the large majority of democrats would have been satisfied with a "democratized monarchy." A "king without characteristics," as Rudolf Virchow called rulers deprived of their powers by a constitution, was, however, rejected by the liberals.[9] They believed that in 1848 they had peered into the abyss of a social revolution. In order to be armed for the social revolutionary emergency, they resisted every temptation to demote aristocratic heads of state to hereditary presidents. As a further barrier against the bid for power of the uncultivated "masses," they sought to install a social filter in the election laws. In so doing, they did not surrender their goal of a society of politically equal men, but they banished this vision into the future. Until that time, they preferred a temporary bourgeois class society. Both liberals and democrats sought to prevent a social revolution, but that which the liberals praised as prophylaxis was seen by the democrats as spurring on the revolution, and vice versa.

This dispute within the middle class about the correct path into the future considerably weakened the constructive strength of middle-class reform policy in the two years of revolution. It split not only political associations, but also gymnasts and many different kinds of social clubs; in Berlin even salons went their separate ways, and in many families it split old from young in a conflict of generations. In the end, however, liberals and democrats proved themselves capable of compromise in the *Paulskirche*. In the imperial constitution of 28 March 1849 their demands merged into a work that promised to block a retreat into the past and to institutionalize a future order capable of reform.

The deputies began their work on the constitution with a careful and lengthy debate on basic rights, reflecting their bitter experience of the prerevolutionary years. The catalog of basic rights guaranteed above all individual rights to freedom and private property against state arbitrariness. There would no longer be a state church, and civic rights were detached from religious confession. Thus the imperial constitution also awarded full citizenship to the Jews. Up to then, even liberals who were determined proponents of legal and political equality for Jews, had understood emancipation of the Jews as a long-term, educational process. "De-Jewing the Jews," was how contemporaries described this program of assimilation.[10]

The imperial constitution dropped this program. It provided for equality to be granted in one act without demanding a sociocultural alignment to the Christian majority. Ethnic minorities were also promised respect for their cultures. Article XIII guaranteed all "their national development" and "equal standing for their languages … in the church, schools, domestic administration and justice." The *Paulskirche* did not surrender territories in areas with a non-German majority (see section 2), but its deputies anchored an extensive protection for minorities in the constitution.

Pressing demands among the broader masses for fundamental social rights were opposed by the majority of the German National Assembly, although the pre-parliament had also recommended an innovative expansion of basic rights: "Protection of labor through institutions and measures to prevent poverty among those incapable of working, creation of gainful occupation for the unemployed, adaptation of the structure of employment and factories to the needs of the current day." Even the liberal president of the pre-parliament, Karl Mittermaier, had in his opening speech called for measures on behalf of "that majority of the people who arduously earn their daily bread with the sweat of their brows, and who demand that their need for an improvement in social conditions now finally be satisfied."[11] Various proposals for social policy, which might well have been acceptable to liberals at the beginning of the revolution, fell, in the following months, under suspicion of preparing the way for the "red republic." The "right to work" was part of this menacing construct, associated by the European public with the failed French experiment with "national workshops" and with the great Paris uprising of June 1848. When the lower classes in Germany also took up this slogan and became actively involved in the revolution, this contributed to liberals and many democratic delegates backing the guidelines of the influential constitutional committee: "We will leave the development of our social relations to the power and the genius of our people."[12]

At the same time, the constitution produced by the German National Assembly was not blind to social issues. In recognizing the universal right to education it anticipated developments far into the future. Tuition was not to be charged for attending primary schools and "lower vocational schools," and the "impoverished" should also have free access to other "public educational institutions." The definitive conclusion of defeudalization, required by the imperial constitution, was also a great achievement for society as a whole and for peasants in particular. To be sure, they had to pay compensation for "dues and services imposed on the land, especially the tithe (¶ 168)," but after the revolution, conditions set by the German states for the redemption of feudal and seigneurial obligations were more favorable to the peasants than they had been before. The committee on industry of the National Assembly discussed proposals to provide for codetermination for factory workers, and a rejection of tax privileges was also socially significant. The debates were steeped in a "basic tone of social welfare." This tone remained long unobserved; as did the long-term effects on society that could be expected from the principles of equality contained in the imperial constitution. In the long-term they aimed at a "reconstruction of the political and social constitution."[13]

In regard to the division of powers within the state, a central problem of every constitutional structure, the reformist majority of liberal and democrats reached a compromise open to future possibilities. The democrats ensured the acceptance of a universal, equal suffrage for all men as well as a merely suspensive veto for the executive. Parliamentary parties were not mentioned in the imperial constitution, but a parliamentary system of government was already practiced in the *Paulskirche*; parliamentary parties led the debates, and they decided on the political composition of the government. Formally, the Imperial Regent, the provisional head of state, named and dismissed ministers, but when the government lost the confidence of the National Assembly, a change of ministers corresponding to the new majority always took place. Thus a parliamentarism evolved that broke with the past and, after the failure of the revolution, only again reappeared in the Weimar Republic and in the Federal Republic of Germany.

The imperial constitution thus confirmed that which had been achieved in the revolution, and was a magnificent work that opened up the future. But to give it life, the agreement of the German rulers was needed, above all the approval of the Prussian King Friedrich Wilhelm IV, whom the National Assembly had elected German emperor by a narrow majority on 28 March 1849. When he rejected the parliamentary crown—a "dog's collar" is what he called it behind the scenes—the policy of cooperation endorsed by the National Assembly and the entire reform movement collapsed.[14] Even recognition of the imperial constitution as valid law by twenty-eight German governments did not help. Without the Prussian Monarch, the small German nation-state agreed to by the National Assembly could not be peacefully realized. Some delegates quietly slipped from the political stage in the following weeks. Among those who stuck it out, a narrow majority of 190 risked an appeal to the nation and its institutions on 4 May 1849. They called on "the governments, the legislative bodies, the communities of the individual states, the entire people to recognize the constitution of the German Empire of 28 March and to bring it into force."[15]

With this began the last phase of the German Revolution, the so-called *Reichsverfassungskampagne*[the campaign for the imperial constitution]—an attempt to force recognition of the imperial constitution on those governments and princes that had refused to recognize it, a group including all of Germany's kings, except for the King of Württemberg. Not everyone participating in this campaign wanted to save the work of the *Paulskirche*, the federal nation-state as parliamentary monarchy. Some republicans hoped to overthrow the thrones after all and a still smaller minority believed in the possibility of a social revolution. The large majority, however, supported the National Assembly. Their object was to join in imposing on the unconstitutional rulers its work of reform, and in defending the newly created nation-state and its constitutional order. In their own eyes they were not revolutionaries, but were defending the law.

New political associations were founded in waves, raising to an enormous level the already high degree of organization, and reaching into rural areas. Even in the smallest village, large public meetings took place. The democratic "March Association" in the town of Kitzingen in lower Franconia, for example, managed to found affiliated societies in the surrounding villages and from March 1849 onward held numerous meetings with several thousand participants. In these associations and in public meetings the political situation was debated, resolutions were passed, and oaths of loyalty to the imperial constitution sworn. The Bavarian government, its parliament and town councils were urged to act in its favor and members of an elected committee of the Würzburg militia declared it their duty to defend it. An appeal by forty-eight Bavarian deputies to the *Paulskirche* and the state parliament in May 1849 even declared rejection of the imperial constitution to be "high treason against the German nation," which all citizens were legally bound to oppose.[16]

Political life was in a state of flux—much more so than at any point since the outbreak of the revolution—but there was no central instance that could have directed the movement in favor of the imperial constitution and endowed it with legitimacy to state authorities and in the eyes of the more cautious citizens. Only the National Assembly and the institutions of the empire, the government, and the Austrian Archduke Johann as Imperial Regent, could have taken on this task. However, Johann refused to support the government when it spoke out—with Prussia in mind—against state suppression of movements favoring the imperial constitution. When, in response to this, Heinrich von Gagern, the leading liberal figure in the *Paulskirche*, resigned his ministerial post on 10 May, the National Assembly lost its cohesion. A renewed legalization of the revolution, as in March 1848, was no longer possible, especially as a number of states had recalled their deputies and thus publicly demonstrated that they no longer recognized the National Assembly.

The national central power thus split into three parts, each pulling in different directions. The Imperial Regent and the new government he appointed, which no longer had the confidence of the majority of the deputies in the *Paulskirche*, remained in Frankfurt and supported military suppression of the revolutionaries in southwest Germany. Some of the delegates quietly slipped away, while the remainder, the "rump parliament," moved to Stuttgart on 30 May to preserve the "rights of the revolution." When the government of Württemberg dissolved it under military threat, the parliamentary strand of the German Revolution came to an end—but the revolution itself continued.

Under pressure from the popular movement, the monarch in Württemberg recognized the imperial constitution. After the king of Saxony fled, a provisional government, attempting to seize power, also recognized the imperial constitution, with the support of twenty-four cities. Events in Saxony, the Bavarian Palatinate and Baden demonstrated that the civil service and the regular military could certainly not be deployed against the campaign for the imperial constitution in every state. A precondition for this attitude, however, was the formation of new governmental institutions, that could give law-abiding citizens the feeling of being on the side of the law against the illegal actions of the princes. That was the case in Saxony, as in the Bavarian Palatinate, where a provincial defense committee had the civil servants take an oath to the imperial constitution and called for the distribution of weapons to the people.

The revolutionaries in Baden were the most successful. There it became most obvious, that the refusal of the princes to recognize the imperial constitution strengthened the republicans and threatened to push the revolution beyond the previously maintained limits of reform. After the Grand Duke had fled, a state committee of the People's Associations installed a republican government, to which the civil servants swore an oath and which was supported by most of the common soldiers—but not by their officers—and which organized the election of a constituent assembly. As in Saxony, this last wave of revolution in Baden, which, in spite of all republican sympathies and social revolutionary undercurrents apparent in it was aimed primarily at the defense of the imperial constitution, could only be stopped by the deployment of Prussian troops.

The hopes for a nation-state were destroyed by the bayonets of the soldiers of the same king of Prussia who was to head that state, whose dynasty the National Assembly had wished to proclaim the hereditary "Emperor of the Germans." A majority of the parliamentary representatives of the German national and constitutional revolution refused to respond to this governmental demonstration of force with a call for revolutionary counter-violence. Thus they remained true to the same principle they had consistently followed: to transform the revolution into a program for legally enacted constitutional change. Using force and violence to realize their aims was not part of their program, and the majority of citizens did not want to do so either.

The German National Revolution

The task of having to weld together a nation-state from a multitude of existing states was shared by the German and Italian revolutionary movements. However, the situation in Germany was much more intricate, as the German Confederation was an ethnically heterogeneous, multinational league of states. To transform it into a nation-state inevitably led to conflicts with members of other nationalities living, entirely or partially, within its borders, who rejected inclusion in a German nation-state.

The two leading powers of the German Confederation, Austria and Prussia, were equally diverse in their national composition. The Kingdom of Prussia possessed in the provinces of Posen, West Prussia, and East Prussia, large territories outside the German Confederation and the old German imperial power of Austria was a multinational monarchy. Any reorganization along national lines would have meant its destruction. Its Hungarian, Polish, and Italian territories did not belong to the German Confederation, but included nearly six million inhabitants of other nationalities: especially Czechs and Slovenes, but also Poles, Croats, and over 400,000 Italians. In many portions of the Habsburg Monarchy, which, in the tradition of the defunct Holy Roman Empire of the German Nation, were part of the German Confederation, a majority of the inhabitants belonged to non-German nationalities—for example in Bohemia, Moravia, Silesia, Carniola, Görz and Trieste.

Nearly every European nationality that had not yet formed its own nation-state was present in the German Confederation, and especially in its main centre of power, the Habsburg Monarchy. Hence, any attempt to transform the German Confederation from a multinational confederation into a federal German nation-state would be harmful to the interests of these nationalities. Equally, every attempt by members of these nationalities to form their own nation-states, could lead to conflict with the German national movement. When the European revolutions broke out in 1848, these previously latent conflicts emerged in dramatic fashion.

The quickly fading dream of a European "springtime of the peoples" was the work of all national groups that sought to fulfil their yearning for their own nation-state in the revolution. But for the German nation it was especially difficult to create a nation-state whose territorial expanse was acceptable to a future Europe organized along national lines. It was an enormous task, involving the simultaneous unification and dissolution of states, with no precedents for a peaceful solution. If the step from multinational confederation to German nation-state was not to lead to a great European war, the act of founding a German state would have to involve renouncing territories on which Germans could make historical claims.

Like other European nations, the Germans also showed little willingness for such voluntary self-limitation. In imperial dreams of power, visions were conjured up of a future German hegemony from the North Sea and the Baltic to the Adriatic and Black Seas. In the end these dreams of becoming a great power remained fantasies of revolutionary euphoria. Ultimately, the German national movement proved itself to be flexible. The small-German nation-state which was endorsed by a majority of the Frankfurt National Assembly would in fact have been acceptable to Germany's European neighbors and to the Great Powers. Their objections did not thwart its realization; such a nation-state could have been peacefully inserted into a future Europe organized along national lines. (This would have been a unique achievement as all other European nation-states were born of war.) German nationalist revolutionaries also did not shy away from limited wars, leading to a powerful nation-state, possessing a maximum of territory. But when a military intervention by the Great Powers in the Schleswig-Holstein conflict threatened, they gave way.[17]

No other crisis-ridden site of national conflict stirred up nationalist emotions in Germany as much as the conflict between Denmark and the German nation over the duchies of Schleswig and Holstein; no other led so close to the brink of a great European war; and no other makes so plain the inter-relationship of decisions about national and domestic policy. Elections for the German National Assembly were held not only in Holstein, part of the German Confederation, but also in Schleswig, which had been incorporated into the Danish state on 22 March 1848. Prussia fulfilled the wishes of the German national revolution and occupied Schleswig militarily. However, when Prussian troops retreated to southern Schleswig, because of British mediation, a storm of indignation broke out in Germany. A British proposal to divide Schleswig along linguistic lines was rejected by both Germans and Danes. Territorial "integrity' was more important to them than the self-determination for the respective populations. The National Assembly, by a large majority, declared the Schleswig-Holstein "a question of honor for the German nation." It had, however, also become a problem of European diplomacy and a question of power in Germany.

The militarily weaker Denmark occupied the high ground in European politics. It was defending its territory, while the German nation was trying to expand into an internationally sensitive point, the "Bosporus of the north." Neither Russia nor Great Britain were willing to permit that. Bending to their pressure, Prussia agreed to an armistice in Malmö on 26 August 1848, which was a de facto renunciation of German claims.

The German nationalist movement reacted with outrage, and the National Assembly demanded that Prussia conquer all of Schleswig for the German nation-state. In a second vote, a majority in the *Paulskirche* accepted the refusal of the Prussian king to risk a European war for Schleswig, but the Assembly felt betrayed. "Through the national war to external and internal freedom" was their slogan. The left was most active in its protest. Accepting the Malmö armistice meant not only bowing to pressure from the Great Powers; it also meant publicly documenting the impotence in domestic politics of the revolutionary movement and the governmental institutions it had created. The nation and its new institutions, the imperial government and National Assembly in Frankfurt am Main, had rattled their sabers, but the king of Prussia would not draw his.

Those who engaged in an ex post facto ratification of the armistice were placing the task of German national unification in the hands of a king who would not subordinate himself to the decisions of the highest authorities in the nascent nation-state and who would soon scornfully reject the title of German Emperor by grace of parliament. The German national revolution thus had already lost, in August 1848, the monarch who was to crown the work of national unification. Without this crowned head, the path to domestic political reform taken by the National Assembly and the great majority of the entire revolutionary movement came to a dead end. Therefore many, especially on the left, hoped a national war would set off a new wave of European revolutions, which would decisively weaken the old elite in Germany and would bring together the nations of Europe in a struggle against Tsarist Russia, the stronghold of reaction.

The alternative was either to end the German-Danish conflict and thus avoid the threat of a European war, or to unleash anew the revolution in Germany and in Europe with such a major war. The majority of the German national movement decided against a second wave of revolution and thus in favor of peace. This stance has always been interpreted by German nationalist historians—seconded by the historians of the former German Democratic Republic—as a betrayal of the German nation or of the revolution. Such an interpretation, however, involves a misunderstanding of the dilemma faced by contemporaries: to defend the revolution against the growing strength of the old elite in Germany, or preserve peace with the European Great Powers.

Where territorial claims could be achieved without risk of a major war, the German nation hesitated as little as other European nations in using military force to reach its goals. The European freedom movement had always championed a restoration of the Polish nation-state, but when this became a realistic possibility in 1848, international assistance failed to appear. In Frankfurt am Main and in Berlin the majority of the German and the Prussian National Assemblies stood behind Prussian government's decisive opposition to the efforts of the Polish national movement to construct a Polish state in the Grand Duchy of Posen. Prussian troops were militarily supreior to the Polish militias and the latter could expect no help from the European Great Powers.

Neither did the Frankfurt National Assembly wish to renounce those parts of the Austrian Empire—Bohemia, Moravia, and Silesia—which belonged to the German Confederation. Measured by their position towards Polish demands in Posen and those of the Danish in Schleswig, the deputies were more restrained in this case. They renounced nothing, but passed, almost unanimously, a declaration of minority protection of all foreign nationalities. For practical purposes however the problem was left in the hands of the Habsburg Monarchy—for a military "solution." When Austrian troops suppressed the Prague uprising in June 1848, they did so to the applause of both the German and Hungarian national movements. National interests—or what was understood as such—triumphed over a solidarity of peoples so often celebrated before 1848.

The situation was comparable in northern Italy. "Not an acre of sacred German soil may be surrendered," resolved the Frankfurt National Assembly in regard to the Tyrol. The deputies also refused to release Trent, Rovereto, and Trieste from the German Confederation. All further action they left to the Austrian government. What this meant was clear, as Austria had already won its first important military victory against the Italian national revolution on 25 July 1848. As previously with Prince Windischgrätz in Prague, the victorious Austrian general Count Radetzky was celebrated as a defender of German national interests, although both soldiers were vehement opponents of the revolution.

The victories of the Austrian troops settled the dispute between great Germans and the small Germans about the form of a future German nation-state. A greater German nation-state would have been the heir of the German Confederation, with essentially the same territory, perhaps shed of the areas on its southern and south-eastern borders populated by a majority of other nationalities; and perhaps without Limburg as well, which belonged to the Confederation, but was, however, treated by its Grand Duke, the king of the Netherlands, as a Dutch province. This greater German nation-state would have fitted into the territorial framework developed by the Congress of Vienna. The Great Powers therefore could not have rejected it as contrary to the terms of the peace treaties ratified at that Congress. The Habsburg Monarchy would have been split, however, into a German and non-German part.

No one could have predicted the consequences of such a development, nor can they be clearly estimated in retrospect. On the other hand, it is quite clear what such a policy would have meant for the German Revolution. Any attempt to dissolve the old German imperial power in favor of a greater German nation-state would have entailed—at the latest following Austrian victories in Bohemia, in Italy, and in October 1848 over insurgent Vienna—a war against a militarily stabilized Habsburg monarchy. A greater German national revolution would have sparked a German national war. Even proponents of a greater German nation-state wished to avoid this. Hence the Frankfurt National Assembly voted for a small German nation-state in March 1849—a state without the traditional German imperial power of Austria, and with a Prussian king as the new emperor of the Germans. The small German nation-state thus broke with the historic tradition of the Holy Roman Empire. For this reason it only gained the approval of a narrow majority in the National Assembly. Most deputies understood the exclusion of Austria as merely a temporary solution or hoped that the Habsburg Monarchy would become a German outpost beyond Germany's borders.

It is impossible to say whether the Habsburg Emperor would have accepted a small German nation-state without military resistance. No decision ever had to be made as the Prussian king brusquely rejected the crown offered him by the German National Assembly. In so doing, Friedrich Wilhelm IV decided against a parliamentary monarchy tied to a recognition of the imperial constitution by the German nation-state, and, in the final analysis, by the individual German states as well. In refusing the imperial crown, he also rejected a constitutional taming of the monarchy and its power base, the royal army. This united him with the Austrian emperor and assured both of them the loyalty of the old elites.

With the Prussian king's refusal to become the head of a German nation-state, the work of the German national revolution collapsed. The national revolution was to revolutionize Germany, but in a continuous process of reform. The national revolutionaries sought to reach agreement with the rulers of the individual states. Only a minority of them demanded a radical break with the past, to which the states and their dynasties belonged. The vast majority of the revolutionary movement, however, wanted to create a democratic, federalist, nation-state in cooperation with the individual German states and their princes. When Prussian monarchy refused the terms of this reformist alliance, the basis of the German national revolution shattered. It disintegrated into its politically disparate components, when a part of the revolutionary movement attempted in 1849 to force the creation of a German nation-state against the opposition of refractory rulers.

In addition to the alternative of a greater Germany or a small Germany, discussed in the German National Assembly and among the entire nationalist movement, there were two other programs of national unification, devised by the two German Great Powers to compete against each other. Their programs involved both bringing the revolution to an end, but also inheriting its nationalist aspirations by means of a national reform from above. Only the Prussian scheme pointed the way to the future. It aimed for a small German federal state, with a common constitution and an elected parliament, and bound to Austria in a broader confederation. However, Prussia's attempt to continue the work of the National Assembly in a less democratic and less unitary form failed, primarily because of Austria's decisive resistance. A renewed flare up of the Schleswig-Holstein crisis in 1849/50 was enough to isolate Prussia in European politics. In November 1850, when war threatened and Russia appeared to take Austria's side, Prussia abandoned its plans for German national unity.

Austria failed in its national policy as well. Prime Minister Prince Schwarzenberg's designs of integrating the entire Habsburg Monarchy in a German state meant, ultimately, bringing together central Europe, northern Italy, and a large part of southeastern Europe in a giant confederation. It would have totally destroyed the territorial order of Europe and its balance of power. His intentions were opposed by the Great Powers and rejected by the German princes as well. When finally, in May 1851, for lack of better alternatives the German Confederation was restored at the Dresden Conference, both governmental aftermaths to the German national revolution of 1848/49 came to an end.

The Primal Revolution

The question of the victory or defeat of the revolution would be decided in the arena of the national and constitutional revolution—both at that time and in the struggle over the memory of the revolution. For it was only this strand of the revolution that found its way into German historical interpretation. Only recently has research begun to survey a second arena: the primal revolution. It founded no traditions; no one referred back to it in the struggle over the interpretation of German history; school books did not pass the memory of it on to future generations. Even in the memory of the liberal bourgeoisie and socialist workers movement, it was ignored or devalued. From the very beginning, the socialists placed a different emphasis in their recollections of the revolution than did middle-class liberals or democrats[18] (to say nothing of the conservatives, who generally referred to the revolution as the "crazy year")—and in the controversy between East and West Germany over their historical inheritance, this rivalry about the "correct" historical interpretation continued. However, everyone was in agreement on one point. They only saw fit to pass down that part of the revolution that sought to create a modern state and to form this state into an institutional structure appropriate for the future developments of society. The primal revolution did not fit into this understanding fo the revolution as a process of modernization.

The primal revolution is difficult to describe, as it had no center and developed no common institutions and aims in the course of events. Rather it was defined mainly by its inconsistency and by its disunited actions. Anchored in disparate local life-worlds, it certainly showed itself capable of effectively imparting its wishes, but could not be reconciled with a policy aimed at creating permanent interest groups and in establishing legal institutions. The "nation" was not a legitimating instance for it, and the nation-state was not the framework for its actions. Nonetheless, the two strands of the revolution were closely tied to one another. The primal revolution learned from the national revolution, and the potential of the national revolution for effective action depended to a great extent on the pressure exerted by the primal revolution.

We can see this, for instance, in the agrarian unrest with which the revolution began.[19] A good deal of the rapid initial success of the more urban constitutional and national revolutions were a result of these rural disturbances. The old elites would hardly have abandoned the bastions of the authoritarian state with so little resistance, would hardly have taken middle-class reformers into government and agreed to an election of a national assembly had the agrarian revolutionary movement not made them pliable. Nonetheless, the agrarian revolt followed its own logic, which cannot be grasped when measured against the constitutional and national political mainstream of the revolution.

Peasant demands were not directed to the "nation," but to the noble landlords and to the princes. The press, handbills, and associations played little role initially and never developed the central importance that they had in urban areas from the very beginning. In the villages, the standard repertoire of enforcing interests was employed—above all public meetings and petitions—but peasants also applied traditional means of protest, and many villages used violence and the threat of violence as an efficient means of collective action. Not only villagers' methods, but also their demands contradicted at least in part bourgeois ideas of modernization. Urban reformers looked on with incomprehension when the peasants sought to reverse the enclosure of common land, when they used the ending of seigneurial hunting rights for an offensive against game, when they invaded the forests en masse to supply themselves with wood, or became nostalgic for "the good old days" and even had recourse to violent self-help to bring them about.[20] Some of their demands were socially conservative but politically radical insofar as they opposed a society based on the rationality of , a utopia created from images of the past, and at the same time revealing social problems of the emerging "bourgeois society."

The peasants did not remain stuck in their policy of revolt. They learned to use all forms of modern interest politics in the course of the two years of revolution. Protests in the countryside declined, but petitions increased. Of the c. 12,000 petitions received by the Prussian parliament in 1848 nearly half of them dealt with conditions in the countryside and many were sent collectively by village communities. The peasants also learned to recognize the value of the imperial constitution as a permanent guarantee of concessions they had forced from their lords at the beginning of the revolution. While they took little part in the violent struggles of the campaign for the imperial constitution, the campaign found non-violent support in many villages, via public meetings and the founding of associations.

These beginnings of peasant participation in national politics did not survive the end of the revolution, but this should be not understood as the result of peasant backwardness. Rather, the peasants were acting rationally. For a long time, they would no longer need the nation as an arena of action, because they did not have to give up what they had harvested in the revolution. The conclusion of the process of the "emancipation of the peasantry" achieved in 1848/49 was preserved, even without the nation-state and the imperial constitution.

The logic of the primal revolution and its learning process can be observed in the cities as well. There, a lower-class alternative public sphere flourished, part of everyday life in the revolution, but largely rejected by the organized revolutionary movement. Traditional forms of censure such as *Katzenmusike* (German charivaris) were revived and politicized; bakers whose loaves were said to be too small or of poor quality were censured in ritual fashion, and in many places a yearning was expressed for a "world turned upside down." "So, now things are going to change!

Now you women will have to wash and clean, and we'll move into your house!" a washerwoman yelled at her mistress, the wife of a businessman.[21]

A public sphere arose in the streets, in which strata of the population participated that had previously been regarded as incapable of political activity. Above all a wave of protests ran through the cities, with quite different aims, but in agreement on one point: they contradicted the forms of politics long become established in the "bourgeois public sphere" and practiced by all wings of the organized revolutionary movement regardless of their particular political positions. The middle classes were frightened, above all, by the willingness to use violence, but also by the unplanned character of the course of the protests. It was a form of interest politics that the middle classes rejected as uncivilized and outdated. "Nothing should happen unplanned," reprimanded a left-wing Hamburg newspaper, when, in August 1848, the attempt failed to build a barricade in the wake of a street disturbance. The incompetent barricade builders were seen by the newspaper as "a confused mass, which hadn't a clue about what it wanted."[22]

The protests contributed considerably to many of the middle class equating the "republic" with "mob rule" and "anarchy." At the same time they opened up the public sphere to portions of the population not yet ready or capable of using the possibility of representing their interests in organized fashion. The "collective occupation of the streets" in the space for action provided by the primal revolution created opportunities for participation not offered by the constitutional and national revolution.[23] Women from the lower classes also used these opportunities extensively.

Lines of Development and Contradictions—Bourgeois Character and Emancipation

Was the German Revolution of 1848/49 a bourgeois revolution? This common label can mean one of two things: members of the bourgeoisie made up a majority of the revolutionary movement or determined its course and aims, or the revolution was for the purpose of bringing into existence a "bourgeois society," conceived of as bringing an end to the corporate society of orders, and creating a liberalized state. On the basis of these two criteria, as has been properly emphasized in recent scholarship, the total process of the revolution cannot be characterized as bourgeois.

Bourgeois circles only dominated in the arena of the highly organized national and constitutional revolution. In the non-parliamentary strand of the revolution, they were often in the minority, outnumbered in many public meetings, political associations, and petition lists by participants from social strata below or on the margins of the bourgeoisie. But for these events or organizations, members of the bourgeoisie acted as the spokesmen. In the primal revolution, on the other hand, non-bourgeois social circles clearly dominated, and the bourgeoisie could not even articulate the intellectual bases for action.

Those who were active in the national and constitutional revolutions were able to agree with their political opponents, despite fierce confrontations with them, on the goal of a "bourgeois society." This goal was not, however, shared by the participants in the primal revolution. Their criticism of the existing state of affairs, primarily as expressed in their protests and revolts, was, to be sure, anticapitalist, but was radically different from the critique of capitalism of the nascent workers movement, which welcomed "bourgeois society" as a stage that needed to be reached first in order then to advance progressively beyond it. The anticapitalism of the primal revolution, on the other hand, drew its expectations for the future from images of the past. These, too, contradicted present conditions, but were aimed in the other direction. Bourgeois contemporaries therefore spoke of a "conceptual confusion" by those who called for "freedom" but did not mean the freedom of "bourgeois society." Those involved in the primal revolution were not necessarily in favor of a democratization of state institutions, and the nation-state as vehicle of progress was generally not what they envisaged.

The term "bourgeois" does not therefore fully characterize the German Revolution, even though it did evolve ever more in this direction, and in its final phase was more "bourgeois" than at the beginning. Traditional protests did not disappear, but their number decreased, as did traditional forms of censure such as cat musics. Other forms of interest politics, above all organization in associations, petitions, and public meetings also became more important for those who had at first made use of the possibilities of the primal revolution. This did not change when violence increased in the final wave of revolution in April-May 1849. For the violent forms of the primal revolution did not recur, and its aims also did not determine the violent, final phase of the revolution. Where those active in the campaign for the imperial constitution employed violence, they did so in organized military formations, in order to fight against the Prussian army for a democratic nation-state. These activists had no common expectation of this nation-state. But no matter whether they wanted to see it realized as parliamentary monarchy or as republic, their aim was a "bourgeois society," which was understood more decisively and in broader social circles as a counter-model to the existing order of state and society than had been the case at the beginning of the revolution. To this extent the German Revolution was more "bourgeois" in 1849 than it had been in 1848, but in its total process it was not a bourgeois revolution.

The complexity of the revolution, the forms it took in its course and its aims prohibit unilinear characterization. Its multifaceted character also becomes visible when one asks about the significance of the revolution for the process of emancipation of the Jews.[24] "The special position of the Jews in Germany ... has now been eliminated," wrote Zacharias Frankel, chief rabbi in Dresden, in 1851 in the introduction to the *Monatsschrift für Geschichte und Wissenschaft des Judenthums*.[25] This conviction of having lived through a giant leap forward in development was generally shared and also popularized by Jewish historiography. "Unexpectedly and stunningly, the hour of liberation struck for European Jewry with the February and March (1848) uprisings in Paris, Vienna, Berlin, Italy and other countries. An intoxication of freedom came over the European peoples, more exciting and wonderful than in the years 1789 and 1830. ... In western and central Europe, up to the borders of Russia and to the territory of the Papacy, the chains of the Jews have fallen," wrote Heinrich Graetz, one of the most important Jewish historians of the nineteenth century and an eyewitness of the revolution, still full of enthusiasm, four decades later.[26]

In France, a Jew became a member of the government in 1848; in Germany, Jews were elected to parliament for the first time. Delegates of the Frankfurt National Assembly honored the best-known of the Jewish advocates of Jewish emancipation, Gabriel Riesser, with the office of second vice-president. Serving with him, at first as first vice-president and then from December 1848 as president, was Eduard Simson, a baptized Jew. This sequence may have reflected expectations the Christian majority held of the Jews—emancipation as a first step away from Jewishness. However, the National Assembly did not tie civic equality for the Jews to any conditions, and the numerous state parliaments that in 1848 did the same, also did not set any conditions. Nonetheless, the direct revolutionary experience of the Jews was as ambiguous as the long-term effects of a revolutionary advance in emancipation for Christian-Jewish relations and for Jewish life.

At the level of the constitutional and national revolution, the long drawn out road of an assimilatory "emancipation by education," which the German states had followed up until then and which was generally recommended even by liberal supporters of emancipation among Christians, was replaced in 1848 by a legal act that decreed equality immediately and without any preconditions. What consequences this act of emancipation would have for the German Jews, whether the "tradition bound, primarily religiously oriented Jew" would be transformed into "a culturally assimilated German citizen of Jewish confession"[27] or whether orthodox communities would develop a new self-confidence, was left to the future. The revolution determined nothing, but simply removed barriers to development.

It made apparent, however, how strong resistance within German society to such an "emancipation from above" still was. This resistance was carried out violently by those involved in the primal revolution, but in the form of newspaper articles, caricatures, speeches at public meetings or petitions, articulated in a completely different field of action. In many cities and also in the countryside, the revolution had begun with violent antisemitic riots. In these riots, traditional Christian anti-Judaism overlapped the attempt, in a period of mass poverty, to ward off new competitors for the already much too scarce sociopolitical resources of municipalities and the state. Jews were held liable for everything their opponents disliked. Some defamed them as helpers of reaction, the others denounced the revolution as a "Jewish conspiracy." In reality Jews did not behave any differently than the Christian majority: there were opponents and supporters, moderates and radicals, and the majority probably remained quite passive.

The revolution of 1848/49 not only brought a significant step forward in the realization of the equality of the Jews and thus a closer approach to the ideal of a legally and politically egalitarian "bourgeois society." It also revealed the social resistance that was to be expected when these ideas were given life. In 1848, most Jews reacted calmly and with confidence to the antisemitic unrest, and in some places they defended themselves collectively. The orthodox newspaper *Der Treue Zion-swächter* spoke of a "bloody consecration of freedom,"[28] and Leopold Zunz, co-founder of the *Wissenschaft des Judentums* [the scholarly study of Judaism], and, at the time, an active democrat, was convinced that "the storm of the rabble against the Jews in isolated areas will pass away without a trace, like other mischief, and free-dom will remain."[29] For this reason, not only liberal congregations, but also spokes-men of orthodox circles appealed for to Jews to become active politically in the two years of revolution. Nonetheless, they placed quite different hopes in the revolution.

In their expectation of being able to use the revolution for their own ends, lib-eral and orthodox Jews were no different from Catholics and Protestants. Insofar as they were rooted in their church, Christians of both confessions saw in the revolu-tion not only a political event, but also as "a turning-point in the history of salva-tion." "Freedom" could take on quite a different meaning here than in the non-parliamentary political association movement, in public meetings and in par-liament, as well as in the actions of the primal revolution: the revolution as a "judge-ment of God on the Enlightenment"[30] and at the same time as a chance to anchor a Christian understanding of freedom in the state.

The experience of the revolution weakened liberal reformers in both churches. In Catholicism, ultramontanism came to the fore, as did among Protestants those who wanted to erect a religious bulwark against the revolution in close coopera-tion with the state authorities. However, religious life and participation of the faithful in it was also strengthened by the revolution, as shown in the beginnings of the Inner Mission and the Catholic Congresses during the revolution and in the popular missions, which, after the revolution, brought together more people than any other movement.

The intensive participation of the churches and the religious mobilization also extended possibilities for women in the revolution.[31] Churches and religion created public spaces that were traditionally more accessible for women than those of pol-itics. Most open to women was the free church movement, in which at least a part of the members assumed that society could only be transformed when relations between the sexes were changed. Criticism of religion and criticism of society were bound together in a comprehensive reform program that united men and women. Liberation from the "triple tyranny of dogma, convention and the family"—although not everyone shared the radicalism of these demands by Malwida von Meysenbugs[32]—and a strong desire for reform, which women shared, connected all currents within the free church movement. In this respect they were far in advance of all political groups, including the democrats.

The state is male—most men agreed with this, no matter the political current they belonged to. During the revolution, however, greater changes appeared than ever before. While women were still not allowed to vote or to stand for office under the new election laws, they entered into public space previously closed to them or where access had been more difficult for them to achieve. They took part in public meetings and a few even spoke at them, participated in revolutionary festivals and corresponded with parliamentary deputies. They wrote and signed petitions, read newspapers and wrote articles for them, donated money and jewelry for the national fleet or promoted the purchase of German-made goods, organized lotteries to finance national claims in Schleswig and Holstein and to arm civic guards, and helped refugees and the wounded. Women symbolically demonstrated their political convictions in the streets by wearing, for example, sashes or carrying umbrellas in the "national colors" of black-red-gold—the female counterpart, so to speak, to the political profession of faith made by the male democrat's beard. The many new political associations remained men's clubs, but some—both conservative and democratic—let in women as guests to their meetings, and women also founded their own associations. These were the start of the organized women's movement. Nonetheless, the revolution had two faces for women.

The primal revolution offered women a space for participation traditionally open to them, since even prerevolutionary protests had occurred with considerable female participation. This did not change during the revolution, when protest became more explicitly political and when clashes on the barricades introduced a form of violence that went beyond the violence in traditional protests. With the decline in the significance of the primal revolution, and as the revolution overall became more "bourgeois" in its action and aims, women's spaces for action, especially for women from lower and lower middle class circles, were circumscribed.

It was above all middle-class women who made use of the new chances for political participation which became available; the more institutionalized the politics, the more exclusively male it became. Women could not annul this basic rule in the revolution, but they were making progress in hollowing it out and, in many areas, overcoming it, by taking part in all levels of the revolutions, either as active participant or as observer when their participation was prohibited. Lower class women, on the other hand, lost traditional possibilities of public activity as the process of organizing, legalizing, and parliamentarizing the revolution advanced. To this extent, the revolution also did not provide women with a single experience, but some of them worked at ending the exclusively male character of the future project of a "civil society."

Contemporaries, as seen here, experienced the revolution in all its aspects as a contradictory event. It included a complex mixture of potential for modernization and barriers to modernization, of different to contradictory models against which the present was to be measured and the future formed. Equally contradictory were individual and collective experiences of gain and loss. This range of problems could not be solved by the revolution—neither in Germany nor elsewhere. But although the revolution failed, it brought with it permanent results.[33] Most importantly a "bourgeois society" as a model for the future not only survived the revolution's failure, but was even more broadly accepted than before. Exactly how this society was to be constructed and expanded remained the greatest controversy for the future. However, the entire society shared the experience that this contoversy could not be resolved by revolutionary violence. This experience united liberals, democrats, and socialists, the middle class and the workers. The socialist workers' movement still spoke of a "social revolution," but its model of a revolution approximated the path of reform, just as had been the case with the liberals in the first half of the century. Among the effects of the revolution of 1848/49 was that in the future German society would fulfil its hopes of reform non-violently. Socially approved violence was banished to war, where it, was however, endorsed. The revolution of 1848/49 in no way changed this endorsement of warfare. It was the experience of war, as well, which brought violence back as a means of domestic policy seven decades later.

Notes

1. Ludwig Häusser, *Denkwürdigkeiten der Badischen Revolution* (Heidelberg 1851),110-11.
2. For greater detail see the chapters by Langewiesche and by Pröve, in this volume.
3. Printed in Ernst Rudolf Huber (ed.), *Dokumente zur deutschen Verfassungsgeschichte,* Vol. 1 (Stuttgart 1978), 352-59.
4. For greater detail see the chapter by Heinrich Best, "Structures of Parliamentary Representation in the Revolution of 1848," in this volume.
5. For more details Michael Wettengel's chapter "Party Formation in Germany: Political Associations in the Revolution of 1848," in this volume.
6. Quoted in Dieter Langewiesche, *Republik und Republikaner. Von der historischen Entwertung eines politischen Begriffs* (Essen, 1993), 38.
7. Quoted in ibid., 41.
8. Gustave Flaubert, *The Sentimental Education,* trans. Robert Baldick (London, 1964), 295.
9. Quoted in Dieter Langewiesche, "Republik, konstitutionelle Monarchie und 'soziale Frage.' Grundprobleme der deutschen Revolution von 1848/49," in Dieter Langewiesche (ed.), *Die deutsche Revolution von 1848/49* (Darmstadt 1983), 341-61, here 358.
10. The expression was used in the emancipation debate of 1828 in the Württemberg lower house, quoted in Dieter Langewiesche, "Liberalismus und Judenemanzipation im 19. Jahrhundert," in P. Freimark/A. Jankowski/I.S. Lorenz (eds.), *Juden in Deutschland. Emanzipation, Integration, Verfolgung und Vernichtung* (Hamburg, 1991), 148-63, here 149.
11. *Verhandlungen des Deutschen Parlaments,* Teil 1, Frankfurt 1848.
12. Franz Wigard (ed.), *Stenographische Berichte über die Verhandlungen der deutschen Nationalversammlung zu Frankfurt a.M.,*(ed.) Vol. 2, 1334 (speech of deputy Beseler).
13. The basic work on this question is J.D. Kühne, *Die Reichsverfassung der Paulskirche. Vorbild und Verwirklichung im späteren deutschen Rechtsleben* (Frankfurt a.M., 1985), quotes on 240, 331.
14. Quoted in Wolfram Siemann, *Die Deutsche Revolution von 1848/49* (Frankfurt a.M, 1985), 203.
15. Huber, *Dokumente zur deutschen Verfassungsgeschichte,* 418-19.
16. Quoted in Dieter Langewiesche, "Die politische Vereinsbewegung in Würzburg und in Unterfranken in den Revolutionsjahren 1848/49," *Jahrbuch für fränkische Landesforschung* 37 (1977): 226.
17. See chapter 12 by Steen Bo Frandsen, "1848 in Denmark. The Victory of Democracy and the Collapse of the State," in this volume.
18. See Beatrix Bouvier's chapter, "On the Tradition of 1848 in Socialism," in this volume.
19. See chapter 18 by Christoph Dipper, "Rural Revolutionary Movements: France, Germany, Italy," in this volume.
20. Quoted in Bernd Parisius, *Von Groll der "kleinen Leute" zum Programm der kleinen Schritte. Arbeiterbewegung im Herzogtum Oldenburg 1840-1890* (Oldenburg, 1985), 39.

21. M. Scharfe, "… Die Erwartung, daß "Nun alles Frei Sey" … Politisch-rechtliche Vorstellungen und Erwartungen von Angehörigen der unteren Volksklassen Württembergs in den Jahren 1848 und 1849," in K. Köstlin and K.-D. Sievers (eds.), *Das Recht der kleinen Leute* (Berlin, 1976), 188.

22. Quoted in Dieter Langewiesche, "1848/49: Die Revolution in Hamburg—eine vergleichende Skizze," in Arno Herzig (ed.), *Das Alte Hamburg (1500-1848/49)* (Berlin and Hamburg, 1989), 187.

23. For greater detail see Manfred Gailus, *Straße und Brot. Sozialer Protest in den deutschen Staaten unter bes. Berücksichtigung Preußens, 1847-49* (Göttingen, 1990), and his essay, "The Revolution of 1848 as 'Politics of the Street,'" in this volume.

24. See chapter 31 by Reinhard Rürup, "Progress and its Limits: The Revolution of 1848/49 and European Jewry," in this volume.

25. Quoted in Dieter Langewiesche, "Revolution und Emanzipation 1848/49: Möglichkeiten und Grenzen," in F.D. Lucas (ed.), *Geschichte und Geist. Fünf Essays zum Verständnis des Judentums. Zum Gedenken an den fünfzigsten Todestag von Rabbiner Dr. Leopond Lucas* (Berlin, 1995), 12.

26. Heinrich Graetz, *Volkstümliche Geschichte der Juden*, Vol. 6 (Munich, 1985) (first edition, 1888), 345.

27. Jacob Toury, "Die Revolution von 1848 als innerjüdische Wendepunkt," in Hans Liebeschütz and Arnold Pauker (eds.), *Das Judentum in der deutschen Umwelt 1800-1850* (Tübingen, 1977), 376.

28. Shulamit Volkov, *Die Juden in Deutschland 1780-1918* (Munich, 1994), 40.

29. Nachum N. Glatzer, "Leopold Zunz and the Revolution of 1848. With the Publication of Four Letters by Zunz," *Leo Baeck Institute Yearbook* 5 (1960): 132.

30. Stefan J. Dietrich, *Christentum und Revolution. Die christliche Kirchen in Württemberg 1848-1852* (Paderborn 1996), 405.

31. See chapter 26 by Gabriella Hauch, "Women's Space in the Male Revolution," in this volume.

32. Cited in Sylvia Paletschek, *Frauen und Dissens. Frauen im Deutschkatholizismus und in den freien Gemeinden 1841-1852* (Göttingen, 1990), 233.

33. See the chapter by Hans-Gerhard Haupt and Dieter Langewiesche, "The European Revolution of 1848: Its Political and Social Reforms, its Politics of Nationalism, and its Short- and Long-Term Consequences," in this volume.

*Proclamation of new concessions on Constitution Square in Vienna on 15 May
(Illustrirte Zeitung, Leipzig, no. 257, 3 June 1848, 363)*

Publication of the Pest Twelve Points (Illustrirte Zeitung, Leipzig, no. 254 13 May 1848, 314)

Chapter 6

REVOLUTIONS IN THE HABSBURG MONARCHY

Jiří Kořalka

The great heterogeneity of socioeconomic and political circumstances was not peculiar to the Austrian Empire in comparison to many other countries on the European continent before the middle of the nineteenth century. The need, however, in historical evaluation, to deal with not just one but a number of revolutions in the Habsburg Monarchy is directly related to the fateful interconnection between liberal and democratic aspirations and the complicated process of the formation of nations in the region between Germany, Russia, and the Balkan territories of the Ottoman Empire. The question was posed, and no longer just theoretically observed, as in the *Vormärz* [lit. "pre-March," the period before the revolution of March 1848—ed.], but also in political practice, of whether—and if so, to what extent—Austria was part of Germany; and whether the Habsburg Empire should be preserved, divided or destroyed. German and Italian ideas of national unity, efforts to recreate Poland, and attempts to transform multi-ethnic Hungary into a Magyar nation-state were opposed to the interests of the Czechs, Croats, Slovenes and other national movements in constructing a reformed, multinational monarchy.

Aspirations for Political Reform

In the three decades before 1848, the system of government in the Austrian Empire suffered from inflexibility and fundamental antipathy towards reform. The Council of State was governed by rivalry and a lack of direction; highest priority was given to fighting liberal and democratic ideas. Most of the important problems, even the pressing need for agricultural reform, remained unsolved. Enlightened minds among senior Austrian bureaucrats were well aware of the ills of the *Vormärz* government and played a significant role in the modernization of the judiciary and the school system, especially in the enforcement of compulsory universal education. It was not by chance that some reformist ministers of the Austrian governments in 1848 came from the senior bureaucracy, for example Prime Minister Freiherr Franz Pillersdorf, who began his state service as a finance expert in the court council in 1809, and from 1832 onwards had been a privy councilor in the united Bohemian-Austrian court chancellery. Moderate liberal ideas, in the sense of support for a constitutional monarchy, were widespread among Austrian civil servants of both common and noble background before 1848.[1]

In some provincial diets, corporatist opposition on the part of the nobility to the conservative system of government in Austria and bureaucratic centralism also grew. The liberals, with Lajos Kossuth at their head, had solid support in the Table of Deputies of the Hungarian Diet. In their program of June 1847 they demanded national sovereignty for Hungary under a Habsburg Dynasty, ministers responsible to the Hungarian Diet, extension of the franchise, freedom of the press and of assembly, as well as other reforms.[2] In the Lower Austrian Diet, some nobles gave their support to moderate liberalism, in both economic and political questions, and advocated greater representation for cities and peasants in the Diet, which in turn was to be given increased powers vis-à-vis the absolutist state administration.[3] Similar signs of corporatist opposition appeared in Upper Austria, in Styria, Moravia, and especially in Bohemia. Moderate reform proposals were not restricted to gaining a right to approve taxes and control of public finances; they also included agrarian and tax reform. Additional demands were raised in March 1848: freedom of the press and of assembly and a general introduction of constitutionalism. In most of the smaller Crown Lands, the leading political forces remained fixed on this March program.

Before 1848, bourgeois reformers in Vienna and Lower Austria gathered in the private salons of open-minded civil servants, jurists, doctors and academics, where opposition writings circulated that had generally been printed abroad. Reformers demanded the transformation of the absolutist and bureaucratically governed police state into a constitutional state with a parliament, a responsible government ministry, an independent judiciary, freedom of the press and of assembly, publication of the state budget, and free municipal governments. Three petitions were produced by these circles and from university students in Vienna in the first half of March 1848 insisting on constitutional freedoms. In Bohemia as well, especially in Prague, a self-confident and active bourgeois vanguard appeared before 1848, consisting mainly of academics, writers, and jurists, who aspired to a bourgeois transformation along the path of reform and not by revolutionary means. From the first public assembly in Prague on 11 March 1848 onwards, this group dominated politics in Czech areas of Bohemia, as was reflected in all the elections of that stormy year. From opposition circles of Polish attorneys, administrators of feudal estates, and the lesser nobility of Galicia came the equally reform-oriented petition of 18 March 1848 that demanded a political amnesty, ending of censorship, equal rights for all citizens, and the convening of the Galician Diet.

In some provincial centers of the multinational Austrian state, new governing bodies were established with the declared aim of strengthening and securing the way to reform. They were, however, not recognized by the existing governments in Vienna and Pest. On 11 March 1848 the Prague citizens' committee, also known from its meeting place as the Saint-Wenzelbad committee, was constituted. On 10 April 1848, it was transformed into a powerful national committee. A national council was formed in Lemberg, in Galicia, on 13 April 1848, which continued to function in quasi-conspiratorial fashion after its dissolution by the government in Vienna. The Ban of Croatia, Josip Jelačić, who took office on 14 April 1848, shared his responsibility with a Banal council, composed in equal parts of Croatian conservatives and liberals, which de facto exercised state power and rejected any subordination to the Hungarian government. The Bohemian governor, Leo Thun, justified forming an eight-member provisional government in Prague on 29 May 1848 by pointing out that Pillersdorf's ministry in Vienna was crippled by revolutionary events in the capital and no longer free to reach decisions.[4] In the end, only the Ban of Croatia was successful, by exploiting the Austrian Imperial court's antipathy to radicalism in Vienna and Pest, in gaining autonomous administration for its country, while in Bohemia and Galicia the Austrian government was able to regain the upper hand with the aid of the military.

Opposing Conceptions of the Nation

In the multinational Habsburg state, 1848 was marked by the rise of relatively small groups of resolute activists who expressed their demands in the name of their nations. These demands were based, alternatively or simultaneously, on natural and historic rights of their nation, which in most cases did not exist as a modern social structure. A development of national bonds and national ideologies seems to be an unavoidable concomitant of the formation of civil society, with its reconciliation of corporate and regional differences. Conflicts between nationalities, which broke out throughout almost the entire Empire in 1848/49, were only in part related to unequal levels of social development and to ethnic-linguistic overlaps. The decisive factor was that territorial and political claims of individual national movements were unreconcilable with those of their direct neighbors, leading at best to misunderstandings and more often to open political and even armed clashes.

In the spring of 1848, the idea of a pan-Austrian state nation was only acceptable to a thin stratum of reformist conservatives of the prerevolutionary government. The national pride of these Old Austrians, as expressed best in the *Constitutionelle Donau-Zeitung* edited by Karl Ferdinand Hock, was based not only on their well-known loyalty to the Emperor, but also on Austria's past and, as they hoped, future international standing. Political "Austrianness" was defined as supra-ethnic in nature and promised to respect the ethnic-linguistic differences of individual peoples within the Habsburg Empire, as long as these did not seek to interfere at the level of national politics. Only the German language was to be used, however, in a uniform state administration and in higher culture and education. In international relations, Old Austrians demanded the preservation of the unconditional supremacy of Austria in the German Confederation, and, if possible, the expansion of Austria's sphere of influence in the Balkans as well. The antiliberal stance of political "Austrianness" alienated a large part of politically active Austrian Germans, but after the military suppression of Vienna at the end of October 1848, reformist-conservative Old Austrians gained ever more influence.[5]

In most Austrian Crown Lands, provincial consciousness was still stronger in 1848 than a loyalty to the monarchy as a whole on the one hand, or to German nationalism, on the other. Among those delegates sent to the Frankfurt National Assembly by the Austrian lands belonging to the German Confederation, there were many advocates of a leading role for Austria in Germany. However, just as many deputies were German nationalists who wanted to assert the political premises of a future German nation state vis-à-vis Czechs in Bohemia and Moravia, vis-à-vis the Slovenians in Carniola and vicinity, and vis-à-vis Italians in Trieste and South Tyrol. In this respect, German Bohemian liberals and democrats were especially interested, in view of escalating national conflicts in their province, in breaking up the Austrian Empire and excluding not only Hungary and Lombardy, but also Galicia, with Bukovina and Dalmatia, in order to give Germans a secure majority vis-à-vis Czechs and Slovenes in a rump Austria.[6] In this context, their claims were based on the views of the Frankfurt National Assembly, which applied historically-based arguments of international law toward the non-German population in the countries of the German Confederation and sought to improve their status to that of German citizens with equal rights, while in the case of a division of the Grand Duchy of Posen, ethnic-linguistic and economic arguments were employed.[7]

The same territorial-political concept of nation provided the leaders of the pre-1848 Hungarian national movement appropriate assistance in transforming aristocratic patriotism into the political influencing of and rule over other ethnic-lingustic groups. Before 1848, the originally supra-ethnic Hungarian political nation had already undergone a successful process of "Magyarization." Lajos Kossuth compared the Slavs, Rumanians, and Germans in the territory of the Kingdom of Hungary with the Bretons in France, Welsh and Irish in Great Britain or Kashubians in Prussia, who were able to retain their own customs and language in their private life, but owed their loyalty to the state-nation in the area of politics and higher education.[8] Revolutionary developments in 1848/49 strengthened the belief that only a Hungarian nation existed in Hungary, containing elements of non-Magyar ethnic groups or nationalities. The Polish national movement also raised a claim on the loyalty of non-Polish peoples in its struggle for national unity and reconstitution of the Polish state. The Polish petition from Galicia of March 1848 promoted the concept of a political nation of the Poles, to which the "Polonized" Ruthenians also belonged. Numerous representatives of the Polish aristocracy denied the Ruthenians the character of an independent nationality.

By way of contrast, Bohemian aristocratic patriotism in 1848/49 proved to be weak and less convincing in its struggle with German and Czech bourgeois nationalism. In the Prague national committee a few Bohemian, German-speaking aristocrats were active for two months, but they were not able to exert any fundamental influence on the political movement. Czech nationalist claims in the spring of 1848 oscillated between historically based concepts of international law and natural law. While the first Prague petition of 11 March 1848, edited by František August Brauner, primarily emphasized the constitutional unification of the lands of the Bohemian Crown—Bohemia, Moravia and Austrian Silesia—with a common body and a common administration, František Palacký, in his letter of refusal to the Frankfurt Committee of Fifty on 11 April 1848, professed a belief in the natural right to equal treatment for all nationalities and religions.[9] Czech politicians were no more successful in gaining the support of German Bohemians for a common bilingual patriotism, than were Germans in persuading Czechs to become "Slavic-speaking Germans" in a German nation-state. Croatian resistance to the claims of the Hungarian Revolution was based on the century-old constitutional independence of Croatia, but a desire for a merger with Dalmatia and possibly even with Slovenian territory went beyond all historical-constitutional ideas. In the case of both Czechs and Croatians, the concept of a national linguistic unit was met with resistance by the elected representatives of Moravia and Dalmatia respectively.

National claims and wishes were also raised by many smaller ethnic-linguistic groups, which had no tradition of political independence in the modern era, and which lacked the support of an aristocratic provincial patriotism. Slovenian petitions demanded the formation of a "united Slovenia" across the borders of the Austrian Crown lands. Such petitions had less support in the cities and market towns than among the rural population, students, and people with a higher education.[10] The Ruthenian-Ukranian national movement in Galicia and Bukovina, and to a lesser extent in north-east Hungary, found its main support in the Greek Catholic Church and among the clergy. Its supporters demanded a partition of Galicia into Polish and Ruthenian territories. The Slovak national movement sought independence not just from "Magyarized" Hungary and German Austrian centralism, but also from the plans of Czech nationalists, who often regarded the Slovaks as just the Hungarian branch of their own nation. The conflict of nationalities in the kingdom of Hungary was sharpened still further by nationalist and confessional resistance against the Hungarian Revolution from Serbs in Vojvodina and Croatia, as well as by Rumanians, Saxons and Swabians in Transylvania.

Parliamentary Representative Bodies

Even before March 1848, the Hungarian Diet in Pressburg had far outdistanced all other corporate representative bodies in the Habsburg Monarchy in terms of political experience, definition of aims, and determination. In the Table of Deputies elected in October 1847, the liberal opposition could count on about half of the votes, with the Table of Magnates playing the role of conservative opposition. Kossuth's fiery speech in the Hungarian Diet on 3 March 1848, in which he accused the Vienna government of being responsible for the monarchy's economic problems and called for wide-ranging reforms and a separate government for Hungary, was the curtain-raiser on dramatic changes throughout the entire monarchy. Within a few weeks, the Hungarian Table of Deputies passed thirty-one liberal laws, the so-called April laws, which became valid after their approval by the Conference of State in Vienna and by the emperor—whom the Hungarians insisted on calling their king. Under pressure from revolutionary events in the Hungarian capital Budapest, the parliament in Pressburg approved equal voting rights for the previously second-class representatives of the cities for the rest of the session and passed, before its dissolution on 11 April 1848, a new election law for a Hungarian national assembly.

In most of the Crown Lands of the Austrian Empire, with the exception of the Kingdoms of Bohemia and Galicia, the old corporate, provincial diets met again in March and April 1848 and were prepared, in view of the revolutionary events in Vienna, to agree to an expansion of the membership to include representatives of bourgeois estate-owners, the cities and industry, and to a limited extent also representatives of the peasants. In the mostly agricultural provinces, widespread demands for liberation from feudal dues, abolition of serfdom, and ending of patrimonial rule predominated in the proceedings of the diets. The Styrian and Moravian Diets declared their backing for equal rights for Germans and Slavs in their provinces, but the language of their sessions was almost exclusively German.[11] Only in Tyrol was their no common provincial consciousness among German and Italian delegates, so that the Italians rejected sending representatives to a common Tyrolean Diet. In most cases, new parliamentary election laws were set, in general in a reformist-conservative direction. Demands for the representation of landowners, industrial and commercial bourgeoisie, and the educated classes were raised and generally granted, but, overall, peasants also gained significant representation. The Moravian Diet in Brno, whose session lasted through the end of January 1849, the longest of any such body in one of the Austrian Crown Lands, became known as the "peasants' parliament."[12]

The main reason that neither the Bohemian nor the Galician Diets were convened in 1848/49 lay in the antipathy of the Austrian central government towards aspirations of autonomy in the two largest non-Hungarian Crown Lands, where strong national movements of the Czechs and the Poles set the tone. The Imperial Cabinet communication of 8 April 1848 promised to convene a newly elected Bohemian Diet in the near future, after the governor of the region, Graf Rudolf Stadion, had cancelled the meeting of the old diet originally set for 30 March 1848. The Prague national committee declared the preparation and implementation of elections to the diet as its most important task. In the rural areas and in the cities of Bohemia, a total of 178 Czech and 106 German representatives were elected, reflecting more or less their share in the population; in addition to them would be the members of the old diet.[13] The new governor, Count Leo Thun, summoned the Bohemian Diet for 7 June and then 14 June, but in the meantime a state of siege was declared for Prague. Despite of the urgent requests of the Czech delegates, the Vienna government refused to convene the elected diet, arguing that the Austrian Reichstag would soon be sitting, although numerous other provincial diets would be having parallel sittings. Unlike in other crown lands, the Galician Diet had not met since 1845, and even the attempt of the governor president, Count Franz Stadion, to summon it to Lemberg (Lwów, L'viv) on 26 April 1848 was rejected by nationalist Polish politicians. Four different proposals to reform election laws were made, but none were put into practice.[14]

In Croatia, the Ban Josip Jelačić, whose authority was not recognised by the Hungarian government, originally summoned the diet to Zagreb for 19 June, but in his confrontation with Budapest and Vienna brought the date forward to 5 June 1848. This move was intended as a response to partially successful attempts by the Hungarian government to remove Jelačić from his influential posts. The Croatian Diet ignored the emperor's decision to grant Kossuth's request to dismiss Jelačić, and voted him dictatorial powers. In its stance, which Pest denounced as illegal and revolutionary, the Croatian Diet was allied with the Austrian conservatives, especially with the Minister of War in Vienna, Count Baillet de Latour, and other leading officers.

Invited to participate in the sessions of the diet were dignitaries of the Roman Catholic and Greek Orthodox churches, members of the high nobility, alongside elected or appointed representatives of the counties, the cities, and the military borderland. The Diet was originally intended as a display of unity within the triune Kingdom of Croatia, Slovenia, and Dalmatia. These plans came to naught, however, when the Dalmatians refused to come to Zagreb, since they did not wish to become involved in a conflict between Croatia and Hungary, preferring instead direct representation of the province in Vienna. The Croatian Diet published a manifesto to all the Slavic peoples in Austria and called for a political reorganization of the Habsburg Monarchy along ethnic-linguistic lines. Ban Jelačić, however, did not want to share his power. He declared the Diet on 9 July 1848 to be in permanent session and in view of the fighting suspended it for an indefinite period.[15]

Elections, on a limited franchise, to the lower house of the new Hungarian national assembly lasted more than a month, from the beginning of June to mid July 1848. The influence of the previously liberal opposition under the leadership of Kossuth was so strong that more than half of the 414 representatives were elected unopposed. The Table of Magnates remained unchanged as the upper house of the national assembly. After its festive initial session on 5 July 1848, the lower house worked intensively. Meeting nearly every day and sometimes several times a day, it acted with self-confidence even towards the ruler. In a dispute with the government in Vienna about financial matters and approval of recruits for the regular Austrian army, the Hungarian lower house supported national Hungarian interests more stubbornly than did the government of Count Batthyány.

After fighting between Croatian and Hungarian military units had broken out, Kossuth persuaded the national assembly to name a permanent defense committee on 21 September 1848. On 8 October 1848 the delegates granted this committee, under Kossuth's leadership, full executive powers. Of all the parliaments of continental Europe in the revolutionary year of 1848, the Hungarian lower house took on the greatest amount of power between the end of September 1848 and mid-April 1849 and in this respect displayed many similarities to Jacobin France of

1793/94.[16] Under pressure from the Austrian offensive, the majority of delegates decided at the end of 1848 to transfer the seat of the national assembly to Debreczen in eastern Hungary, where, however, the left wing radicals were isolated from the public discourse of the capital. In the end, the lower house returned to the capital in June/July 1849 for a single session, which was then followed by a move to Szeged; there resolutions were passed, much too late, on equal rights for all nationalities and emancipation of the Jews. In any event there were still 200 Hungarian representatives gathered in Szeged at the end of July 1849.[17]

Of all the parliamentary representative bodies in the Habsburg Monarchy during 1848-49, the first Austrian Reichstag would be the only one with a multinational composition. While the Imperial Charter of 15 March 1848 was predicated on the continued existence of the provincial diets, the new charter of 25 April 1848 promised a Reichstag consisting of two houses, senate and house of representatives, which together with the emperor would exercise legislative powers. A senate was planned as the upper house, consisting of representatives of great landowners and princes of the Imperial house, together with members named by the emperor for life, as a conservative safeguard. A strong wave of protest arose against this two-house system and equally against tying the franchise for the lower house to a minimum level of tax payments. This forced a declaration on 15 May 1848 that the first Reichstag would be a unicameral, constituent assembly, and would be elected by an almost universal manhood suffrage. From the start, the government in Vienna assumed that the kingdom of Hungary, with Croatia and Transylvania, and the North Italian provinces would be absent, although all provinces belonging to the Austrian Empire were to form an indivisible constitutional monarchy.[18]

When the Austrian Reichstag met in Vienna on 10 July for its first unofficial consultations and then on 22 July 1848 for the festive opening, the great diversity of the representatives became quite clear. More than a quarter of the elected delegates were peasants, mostly from Galicia and the inner Austrian Crown Lands, while the Czech districts of Bohemia sent mostly educated men, jurists, doctors, academics, writers and civil servants, to Vienna. With the exception of Polish nobles from Galicia, aristocratic representation was surprisingly low. In the first weeks, delegates dedicated much time to examining their credentials and devising rules of order, as well as posing parliamentary questions to the minister, who was not always present.

The most important deliberations of the Reichstag up through the Viennese uprising of October 1848 were those over the motion by the German Silesian Hans Kudlich on 26 July 1848 to end serfdom. After long discussions on questions of compensation, the Reichstag approved this important law on 7 September 1848. Great arguments arose over the requests by four deputies of the Croatian parliament and by a delegation of the Hungarian national assembly to be received and heard by the Austrian Reichstag; in both cases this was rejected by a majority of delegates. During the armed struggles in and around Vienna on 6 October 1848 some members of the Reichstag, above all most of the Czech delegates, left the capital and achieved the transfer of the Reichstag to the peaceful Moravian city of Kremsier (Kroměříž).[19] There, the elected representatives of various nationalities, under pressure from the approaching counter-revolution, were successful in reaching a remarkable compromise, which, however, was made worthless by the forced dissolution of the Reichstag on 7 March 1849.

Extensive democratization of social and political life in 1848-49 revealed in the parliamentary bodies of the Habsburg Monarchy new, difficult problems of oral communication. There can be no doubt that Croatian was spoken in the Diet in Zagreb, and that the proceedings of the Hungarian national assembly, meeting in several different cities, were held exclusively in Hungarian. A German-speaking representative from the mountain cities of central Slovakia was turned away by the Budapest parliament because he was not able to speak Hungarian and was given two months to acquire the language skills he lacked.[20] In the Croatian delegation to the Imperial Court and to the Austrian Reichstag, serious thought was given as to whether its members, as representatives of a sovereign people, could be allowed to speak in any language other than the Croatian. Speeches held in Czech in the Moravian Diet were not recognized until they had been translated into German.[21]

Most difficult, however, was the situation in the Austrian Reichstag. Most of the Galician peasant representatives spoke and understood no German, so that they were described as "deaf and dumb," and in vain they demanded an official interpreter. Dalmatian representatives claimed the same rights for their Italian as for the German language, and a proposal was made that, at the request of at least ten delegates, every question voted on had to be translated into Polish, Ruthenian, Czech, Rumanian, and Italian.[22] Problems of understanding in the multi-ethnic state served to support calls by Czech and other non-German representatives for a federalization of the Habsburg Monarchy.

Constitutional Proposals

The term constitution was one of the most popular and widespread words in the various languages of the Habsburg multinational empire in the spring of 1848. Almost overnight everything was constitutional. Hats, ties, umbrellas, biscuits, and even a constitutional polka appeared.[23] Constitutions were demanded, proposed, and drawn up in the individual provinces and for the monarchy as a whole, in which state power was to be limited in favor of citizens' basic rights. In an imperial patent of 15 March 1848, the emperor promised the preparation of a constitution, and, until his abdication on 2 December 1848, he held the title of Constitutional Emperor of Austria, King of Hungary and Bohemia etc. Not only state authorities, but also some liberal politicians thought it advisable to point out that a constitution entailed a fair distribution of both rights and duties, in contrast to the idea of the constitution as unlimited freedom and arbitrariness.[24]

The constitutional charter of the Austrian Imperial state, issued on 25 April 1848, which did not extend to Hungary and northern Italy, was modeled in part on the Belgian constitution, especially in its view of civil liberties and relations between the crown, ministers, and parliament. This so-called Pillersdorf Constitution, named after the Interior Minister and provisional Prime Minister Freiherr von Pillersdorf, was rejected by the people of Vienna as undemocratic and by the Prague National Committee as centralistic, but it served nonetheless as the legal basis for calling of the Austrian Reichstag. For the first time, all peoples were guaranteed the inviolability of nationality and language, whereby, however, these equal rights, in the Old Austrian sense, only concerned the non-political sphere. For the individual crown lands, the Pillersdorf Constitution was predicated on a strengthening of existing provincial diets, which in turn were to make suggestions to the Reichstag for modernizing their provincial constitutions. The great heterogeneity of the multinational monarchy was given little consideration in this work of the highest state bureaucracy.

A contrasting view was put forward in a draft constitution for Bohemia presented to the Prague National Committee on 7 June 1848. This envisioned limiting Imperial legislative and executive powers to military matters, the Imperial budget, international treaties and trade agreements, and all other matters of foreign relations, as well as to unified legislation and administration of the economy, transport, and justice. Everything else was to be left to the provincial parliament and to the governor, who would be responsible to it, and his cabinet of five councilors for individual branches of the administration. Furthermore, this draft foresaw direct elections with nearly universal manhood suffrage, with members of parliament then electing one sixth of the senate each year and sending delegates to an Imperial Assembly.[25]

Nearly all the Austrian provincial diets of the year 1848 showed a broad indifference to the interests of the state as a whole and often sought to block off their province from outside influence. The provincial constitutions approved by the newly constituted diets of Upper Austria, Moravia, and Styria, although not sanctioned by the emperor, declared individual crown lands to be indivisible and independent, insofar as this was consistent with the constitution of the empire. A proviso in the Moravian draft constitution, that the province was tied solely to the constitutional Austrian Empire, was seen as a rejection of claims by the Czechs of the unity of the lands of the Bohemian Crown.[26]

The Austrian Reichstag, which began its deliberations in July 1848, viewed the conclusion and implementation of a liberal Imperial constitution as its foremost task. In agreement with the Pillersdorf Constitution, Hungary (including Croatia and Transylvania), Lombardy, and Venetia were not represented. Arguments arose on just the question of receiving a delegation of the Croatian Diet in July 1848 and one from the Hungarian National Assembly in September 1848. In both cases it was decided against receiving outside representatives. Czech and South Slav representatives did not disguise their interest in having constitutional restructuring apply to the entire Austrian Empire, assuming thereby a strengthening of Slavic elements, but war in North Italy and the outbreak of fighting in the south of Hungary showed that these wishes were illusory. With the formation of a constitutional committee in the Reichstag, a fierce argument broke out between the German-speaking adherents of centralism, and the mostly Slav federalists. In the thirty-member constitutional committee, both large and small crown lands were represented by three members of parliament each, but the predominance of centralists that this entailed was balanced out to a great extent by the energetic work of the federalists, especially the Czech politicians František Palacký and František Ladislav Rieger, in the smaller sub-committees on the basic rights of citizens and the constitutional form of the monarchy.

The work of the constitutional committee of the Austrian Reichstag and its two sub-committees went on for months, from August 1848 to the beginning of March 1849, in Vienna and Kremsier. The result of this work was the emergence of remarkable constitutional proposals, whose value lay primarily in being the result of a voluntary agreement between the elected representatives of all nationalities of the non-Hungarian and non-Italian crown lands of the Habsburg Monarchy; nothing similar was ever to occur again up to the collapse of the multinational state in the fall of 1918.[27] Twice, on 26 September 1848 and on 21 December 1848, the Reichstag was presented with a complex of constitutional rights, including equality of all citizens before the law, the abolition of aristocratic privileges, a public system of justice, ending of the death penalty for political crimes, freedom of movement both domestically and abroad, freedom of religion and equality of all confessions, freedom of speech and assembly, and, not least, equal rights for all nationalities and customary languages.

Rieger's fiery defense of the first paragraph of the constitution, which stated that the power of the state came from the people, led to a rapprochement of German-Austrian and Czech liberals; one cannot fail to recognize the influence of French and North American ideas of freedom in it. Palacký presented two drafts, in October 1848 and January 1849, on the constitutional subdivision of the multinational state, whereby he always gave due consideration to the interests of the central government. At the highpoint of the struggle between centralists and federalists, Palacký was even prepared to accept a division of the monarchy along ethnic-linguistic lines, if Hungary were to be so subdivided as well. The resulting constitutional draft of the Kremsier Reichstag, which combined historic-political and ethnic-linguistic subdivision, was presented to the chamber, but never gained approval as the Reichstag was dissolved by force on 7 March 1849. At the same time the government published the so-called decree constitution, which applied to Hungary and North Italy as well.

Serious constitutional problems arose during the war between revolutionary Hungary and the regular Austrian army. At the end of September 1848 relations between the Hungarian government and the Imperial Court broke down for good, after Count Franz Lamberg, named by the Emperor as Imperial Commissioner and Commander-in-Chief of all armed forces in Hungary, was killed in Pest. Following this, Emperor Ferdinand, as King of Hungary, dissolved the Hungarian parliament and declared the country to be in a state of martial law. After Franz Joseph ascended to the throne on 2 December 1848, some Hungarian politicians were prepared to seek a compromise with the ruling house, but the national assembly declared, on Kossuth's motion, that the change in the person of the monarch was inconsistent with the constitution.

Prince Windischgrätz, as Commander-in-Chief, insisted the Hungarians surrender unconditionally, but military success once again increased Hungarian desire for independence. The Austrian decree constitution of March 1849 was unacceptable to Hungarian politicians as it did not recognize Transylvania, Croatia and Slavonia, the Adriatic coast, the military borderland, and Vojvodina as belonging to Hungary and revoked the Hungarian constitution of 1848. Their direct response was a declaration of independence by the Hungarian National Assembly in Debreczen of 14 April 1849, announcing as well that the throne of the "faithless House of Habsburg-Lothringen" was forfeit.[28] Lajos Kossuth was elected governor-president, but outside intervention, together with growing opposition from within the country, brought an end to this unique constitutional experiment.

Associations

Even before March 1848 a few officially permitted associations in Vienna, Prague, and other territorial capitals evolved into centers of political information and discussion for the wealthy, propertied, and educated bourgeoisie. The Lower Austrian Trades Association in Vienna and the Association for the Encouragement of Industrial Spirit in Prague were concerned mostly with questions of economic policy. The fierce debates that occurred in their monthly assemblies before 1848 doubtless served as good preparation for later disputes in the Austrian Reichstag. Lajos Kossuth, as opposition journalist, proposed the formation of a trades association in Pest and similar associations in other Hungarian cities to work towards the economic independence of the country. The Legal-Political Reading Club, founded in Vienna in 1840, like the Citizens' Resource founded in Prague in 1846, provided both its members and a broader middle class public with a wide choice of foreign and domestic newspapers and magazines.[29] Associations of this sort, including Concordia, a society of artists and writers in Vienna, became unofficial political centers, where the events of the day were debated. It was not by chance that the March petitions of Vienna and Prague were presented for signature especially in these clubs.

In general, it can be said that strong and influential associations appeared during the months of revolutions in 1848-/49 primarily in those instances in which a portion of the politically interested public felt itself insufficiently represented by the newly formed organs of power and representative bodies. In Pest, the largest city in Hungary, a committee of public security emerged in March 1848, but in the following weeks the Hungarian government, together with the diet, completely controlled the political stage and no Hungarian association was able to take over the political initiative. In the Czech areas of Bohemia the Prague National Committee enjoyed such an unshakeable authority that there was no need to found political associations. To oppose Czech claims, however, the Associations of the Germans of Bohemia, Moravia, and Silesia, for Preservation of their Nationality was founded in Vienna at the beginning of April 1848 in Vienna.[30] In German Bohemian cities, constitutional clubs appeared which pressed for a close association of Bohemia with German-Austrian crown lands on the basis of a common constitution. On the other hand, Czech associations were founded where Czechs were a minority or where they felt discriminated against; for example the Bohemia-Moravian-Silesian Association in Vienna, the Slavic Association in Olomouc or the Moravian National Association in Brno.[31] For the protection of Slovenian national interests, associations of the same name, Slovenija, were founded in Vienna, Graz, Klagenfurt, and Ljubljana, because the division of the Slovenian region among various crown lands made common national representation of the Slovenians more difficult.[32] The Ruthenian central committee in Lemberg, with a predominance of Greek-Catholic clergy, state servants, and adminstrators of feudal estates, functioned in a gray area between unofficial power structure and association.[33] Liberal demands, especially for a liberal reform of municipal government, were also propagated by the Società dei Triestini, founded in April 1848.[34]

After the first wave of enthusiasm had receded, new associations slowly appeared which were no longer distinguished by ethnic or national criteria, but by sociopolitical and ideological ones. Small clubs, often competing among themselves, appeared in Vienna, such as the Society of the Friends of the People in the second half of March and the German Eagle in April 1848, which were critical of moderate liberalism. Especially influential was the Vienna Committee of Citizens, National Guard and Students for the Maintenance of Order and Security, and for the Preservation of the Rights of the People, known as the committee for public safety for short, which has been aptly described as a political debating club, a petition site, advisory body and, from mid-May 1848 onwards, an executive organ, administrative, and judicial authority in one.[35] Following the results of the Reichstag election, which were unfavorable for the democrats, the committee for public safety lost influence, and was dissolved in August 1848.

After a split in the Society of the Friends of the People, the Democratic Club in Vienna organized in June 1848 gained considerable influence in the struggle with the liberal-conservative majority in the Austrian Reichstag, especially due to its support for the Hungarian Revolution. Parallel to this, the Hungarian Society for Equality appeared in Pest in July 1848, which demanded from the Hungarian government radical action against enemies of the revolution on the model of the French Jacobins. There were indeed no lack of plans to overthrow the government and introduce a radical dictatorship.[36] The Society for Equality, with a membership of about 1,000, including thirty deputies in the Hungarian National Assembly, collapsed at the end of September 1848, because some of the leadership joined the war effort and others were working intensively in various parliamentary committees.

The defensive attitude of Catholic conservative circles towards political changes in the spring of 1848 was only overcome after some months. Markedly Catholic conservative associations arose in the provinces earlier than in Vienna. At the end of April 1848 the Catholic-Constitutional Association for the Tyrol and Voralberg was founded in Innsbruck, expanded quickly throughout the entire province, and very soon had more than one thousand members.[37] In the east Bohemian county seat of Chrudim, a Czech-patriotic Saint Wenceslaus Association was established, probably at the end of May 1848, and only later reformed into a branch association of the Czech *Katolická jednota*. In Czech society during 1848, the Catholic association movement was closely tied to reform endeavors by the lower clergy, although radical demands, such as an end to clerical celibacy, free discussion of church matters, election of clerical superiors or an easing of the strict discipline in the theological seminaries appeared in the Czech press earlier than in the associations.[38] This contrasts with the Catholic Association for Faith, Freedom and Decency founded in Vienna in June 1848, which was considerably more conservative and was oriented, apart from its educational activities, towards social work.[39] It was mainly the Catholic Association of the Tyrol which presented itself as a dedicated defender of the rights of an independent Catholic church against the alleged tyranny of the state.

At the turn of the year 1848/49, the Slavic Linden [*Slovanská Lípa*] rose to become the strongest association in the entire Habsburg monarchy. From its modest start at the beginning of April 1848, when its founders, from the younger generation, certainly did not wish to be active in opposition to the Prague national committee, the activities of the Slavic Linden expanded in the autumn months into most of the Czech cities in Bohemia and into two Moravian cities, so that at the end of 1848 it had between 2,500 and 3000 members in thirty-six local associations.[40] The Prague central office organized, in cooperation with the Citizens' Resource, the decisive Czech victory in the Prague municipal elections, protested against the results of the military investigation into the uprising of June 1848, collected and distributed contributions for Croatians and Slovaks, fighting the Hungarian government.

From the beginning, the Prague Slavic Linden sought contact with the other Slavic groups in the monarchy, especially with the Slovenes and Croats. While the central leadership in Prague increasingly came under radical influence, the majority of the members in the branch associations belonged to the liberal or even the national conservative minded Czechs. At the Slavic Linden congress at the end of December 1848, delegates from most of the Bohemian and the two Moravian branch associations participated; one guest came from the Slovanian Society in Laibach. The Croatian Slavic Linden in Zagreab developed into an independent and influential organization, which carried on from where the adjourned Croatian parliament left off.[41] In February 1849 the Slavic Linden encouraged a broad petition movement to support the Austrian Reichstag in Kremsier and was able to collect more than 40,000 signatures in 722 cities and villages in Bohemia and Moravia. On 6 March 1849 more than 12,000 signatures from a further 298 communities were presented.[42] In July 1849, the Slavic Linden ended its activities both in Prague as well as in Zagreb before it could be closed down by the authorities.

Social Movements

While a reform of the relationship between the serfs and the great landowners, and the related question of ending seigneurial administration, was long overdue, nothing happened in this respect through the spring of 1848. This made the liberation of the peasantry into one of the fundamental questions of the revolution throughout the Habsburg Monarchy. A recognition of the unproductive nature of the system of serfdom extended well into the ranks of the aristocracy, but neither the government in Vienna nor the feudal lords were willing to risk more than a territorially limited relief of serfdom up to 1848. Overall, the Habsburg Monarchy was still a predominantly agrarian country, but the economic level of the rural population and its mentality varied considerably among the different regions of the multinational state. In Galicia, Ruthenian and even Polish peasants trusted the state bureaucracy far more than they did the Polish nobility, and a patriarchal belief in the good, distant emperor was more effective there than in the Bohemian lands, to say nothing of Hungary. There, the abolition of feudal dues and labor services, and the liberation of the peasantry rebounded to the benefit of the Hungarian Revolution. In Bohemia, the national committee enjoyed an extraordinary authority from April to mid-June 1848 among different strata of the rural population, as witnessed by the 580 petitions it received from peasants and poor villagers of more than 1,200 communities.[43] Although the original Imperial Charter set the ending of feudal obligations for 31 March 1849, serfs refused to perform their labor services in the spring and summer of 1848, and, with a few exceptions, there was no effort to force them to do so. In Moravia and in Croatia peasants sent their petitions to their parliaments; only a few petitions dealt with political questions.[44]

Indicative of the relatively independent attitude of peasants' representatives in the parliamentary bodies, especially in the Austrian Reichstag in Vienna and Kremsier, was that democrats and German-Austrian liberals suspected most of them of being the tools of reaction, while some conservatives saw them as allies of the left.[45] Peasant ideas of justice were based to a great extent on customary rights. Peasants appealed to a past time, when they were free men, but also aimed at an adequate representation of peasants' interest in civil society. Even before acceptance of the act of 7 September 1848 on peasant emancipation, there was little understanding among the rural population of the Bohemian regions and of Inner Austria for any radical slogans, not least due to social tension between well-off peasants and the rural lower classes.[46]

Some Hungarian counties, however, did experience peasant unrest, during which villagers seized control of land that had been expropriated from them, occupied the former common land, refused to pay the rent to landowners and began cutting down forests owned by the lords. It was not an isolated phenomenon for rebels to confiscate or destroy the hated property registers. In agricultural areas inhabited by other nationalities, even the manor houses of Hungarian aristocrats were torn down and their families attacked.[47] There was an uprising of Ruthenian peasants in Bukovina and in north-east Hungary in the autumn of 1848 to defend the common lands.

Skilled factory workers and artisans in Vienna, Prague and Pest drew on their organizational activity of the previous years in the spring of 1848. They felt their existence threatened by the introduction of machines and the spread of female and child labor and took up collective resistance, which had already reached a high point in June and July 1844 with attacks on machines in Prague and other industrial centers of Bohemia. Worker unrest in the suburbs of Vienna on 14 and 15 March 1848 took on the character of planned attacks on machines: nothing was plundered, nothing stolen, but the factory halls with machines were destroyed and some were set on fire.[48] Prague cotton printers renewed their old demands in mid-March 1848 and presented the generally recognied SaintWenzelsbad-Committee a petition against the introduction of printing machines and for a ban on taking on new apprentices.[49] At the same time, various groups of workers in Pest called for an end to the guilds, a reduction in work hours and an increase in pay. Because these demands were not granted, strikes broke out. In Vienna and its surroundings, stoppages occurred in a number of industries and crafts, especially among bricklayers and journeyman tailors, weavers, clothmakers, and blacksmiths. Even apprentices joined the movement and demonstrated in Vienna on 6 April 1848.

Leading liberal groups, the real beneficiaries of the revolutionary events in the spring of 1848, viewed the social movement as a disruption of a united front against the powers of the old system. For this reason, some liberals and moderate democrats attempted in certain places to develop contacts with the workers and to influence their actions. The management of the Vienna-Gloggnitz Railroad Company granted their machinists, the best paid among railway workers, a ten-hour day.[50] The Prague citizens' committee entrusted the democratically-minded doctor František Cyril Kampelík with the task of establishing contact with dissatisfied printers and to publish a journal, *Hlásník* [The Messenger], for them. However, it seems likely that only one issue of it ever appeared.[51]

The nobles who had taken power in Hungary felt themselves less threatened by the workers. They decreased the working day to eleven hours and, among similar measures, allowed journeymen to participate in guild meetings. The Hungarian government was successful in persuading the print-shop owners and workers to hold wage negotiations and to work out a collective bargaining agreement. In Vienna, as well, journeymen and laborers in various trades for the first time secured such collective bargaining agreements, which set a reduction of working hours and an increase in wages. In view of rising unemployment, public works in Vienna were reorganized.

It was only in Vienna that the spontaneous development of the workers movement during the year 1848 led to the beginnings of working-class political organization. On 24 June 1848, journeyman artisans and skilled workers joined together to form the Vienna Workers' Association. At its high point, the group had between 7,000 and 8,000 members, making it the largest of Vienna's associations.[52] Through the association's president, the journalist Friedrich Sander who had originally worked as a journeyman bookbinder, the Vienna Workers' Association established contact with the Berlin Central Committee for Workers and with the General Assembly of Saxon Workers' Associations.

The Vienna Workers' Association clearly supported freedom of occupation and emphasized the necessity of a political combination of workers beyond the framework of trade union associations. Its protest against the exclusion of workers from the Reichstag elections was followed by an invitation to elect representatives to prepare a workers' parliament in Vienna. Other demands of the group were political rights for workers equal to those in other occupations, workers' representation in the Ministry of Labor, freedom of settlement, establishment of educational institutes for workers and of health and disability insurance, the introduction of courts of arbitration, staffed equally by representatives of employers and workers, an end to passport requirements, and unlimited permission to marry.[53] All other worker associations, based on bourgeois-philanthropic principles, such as the Concordia Society, or the Vienna General Journeymen's Association for Mutual Assistance, Organization of Labor, and Preservation of Civil Rights, were less influential.

Social demands of master craftsmen belonging to guilds in Vienna, Salzburg, Prague, Brno, and many other cities of the Habsburg Monarchy were filled with deeply rooted mistrust of factory industry and workers. The Minister of the Interior in Vienna presented the Austrian Reichstag with a petition in July 1848 which protested in advance against any resolution on freedom of occupation. In September 1848 it was moved in the Reichstag that the state grant an interest free loan to the craftsmen of Vienna, but Czech representatives could not agree to the privileged position it gave the capital, to the disadvantage of other cities.[54] In Prague, many artisan guilds had already begun sending petitions to the national committee in the spring of 1848 with complaints against unfair competition and against a possible customs union with Germany. In August 1848, the artisan association in Prague published fifteen demands, which together would have meant stricter control and decision-making powers for the guilds in the individual crafts. A committee of all guild associations in every city and an administrative council in the entire province were to oversee the enforcement of guild restrictions.[55] Active participants in the artisans' movement saw with horror, in the difficult social position of the workers, an anticipation of their own fate.

Everyday Life in the Revolution

Contemporaries were still able to recall decades later the series of lovely sunny days in mid-March 1848 and were all convinced that the lovely weather also contributed to general enthusiasm and relief. "Everyone, drunk with the strong wine of freedom (which had never passed their lips before), wore their heart on their tongue, and whatever they wished for they immediately put into practice," commented one astute Czech observer in retrospect.[56] For Austrian circumstances, where compensation for official repression of any free expression of opinion before 1848 was found in a relatively generous attitude towards private life, it was doubtless a great change. People felt themselves liberated from hypocrisy and servility, liberated from censorship and bureaucracy. In a conservative monarchy, in which up to March 1848 not one single daily political newspaper had been tolerated, suddenly dozens of large and small daily and weekly newspapers of the most varied political currents appeared. Previously semi-official papers fell into the hands of the opposition within months; new papers, like the *Národní Noviny* [National Newspaper] under the editorship of Karel Havlíček in Prague, the

Jutrzenka [Morning Star] in Cracow or the *Slavenski Jug* [Slavic South] under the editorship of Dragutin Kušlan in Zagreb, developed into highly respected organs of their national movements.

A quite noticeable difference existed, however, between most of the large cities, on the one hand, and the smaller cities, market towns and villages on the other. With the exception of eastern Galicia, Bukovina and the minority regions of the kingdom of Hungary, revolutionary activity was concentrated almost totally in the imperial metropolis of Vienna and in some (certainly not all) provincial capitals. In Vienna, Prague, and Pest, numerous marches took place, with flags and torches, crowds and mobs. One characteristic accompaniment to the revolutionary spring of 1848 in these cities was cat music [charivaris] at night, beneath the windows of unpopular individuals, upsetting not only the immediate victim, but also the entire neighborhood. There were always many people in the streets. Even the smallest excuse or spurious pretext was sufficient for the energy of the masses to be discharged in a protest against the property owners.

Numerous handbills and placards accused Jews primarily of exploitation and usury. Antisemitism had already played a part in the machine breaking in the suburbs of Vienna in March 1848, but it was most widespread among guild artisans. A rash of antisemitic violence broke out on 21 March 1848 in Pressburg, where Jewish shops were destroyed and Jewish residents assaulted, and peaked on 24 April 1848 with plundering and attacks, resulting in fatalities in Pressburg and southern Hungary.[57] On 1 and 2 May 1848, antisemitic unrest continued with an attack on the Prague Jewish quarter, in which no shots were fired, but people on both sides were injured.[58] In contrast to that, a secure shelter from the revolutionary unrest was granted to the royal court by Innsbruck the conservative capital of the Tyrol, from 17 May to 12 August 1848 and in the archbishop's residence of Olomouc in Moravia after 6 October 1848.

Everyday life in the revolution in the Austrian multinational state seems to have been quite colorful. Different newly designed suits and uniforms, cockades and ribbons, ties and colorful caps expressed membership in a club, occupation, or support of a national ideal. The delegation of the Hungarian parliament inspired the people of Vienna on 15 March 1848 not only with their political demands, but also with their colorful Hungarian costumes, richly decorated sabers at their sides and herons' feathers in their caps.[59] In the streets of the Bohemian capital of Prague people admired the unusual costumes and uniforms of the participants of the Prague Slav Congress in the first weeks of June 1848. The example of the Polish, Croatian, Serbian, Ruthenian, and Slovak costumes led Czech artists, writers, and academics to form a committee to consult on the Slavic national costume and to design a Czech national costume for men and women. The *Čamara*, the Czech buttoned jacket, which appeared at the time, remained a national political symbol beyond the revolutionary years 1848/49.[60] Because frock coats, top hats, and bewigged pigtails were seen as symbols of the old system and of reaction, supporters of the Czech national movement attempted to make popular a bourgeois national costume, differing from traditional peasant costume, but without success.

A significant novelty in this year was the active participation of mostly younger women and girls in various spheres of public life, primarily in Vienna and Prague, where the formation of civil society was most advanced. In the two major cities one could observe similar, and sometimes almost identical events and symbols, but with contrasting national political connotations. This was seen in the public wearing of the German or Bohemian (or Slavic) colors in clothes and jewelry, in the consecration of flags and in charity events. The young women who fought on the barricades in Vienna in May 1848, and in Prague in June 1848, were unanimously called amazons.

Perhaps the Democratic Women's Association, founded in Vienna on 28 August 1848, was more overtly political than the *Spolek Slovanek* [Association of Slavic Women] and the *Slovanská Dennice* [Slavic Morning Star] established in Prague in September 1848, which placed greater emphasis on educational activities for women and girls.[61] Similarly, the Democratic Women's Association, established in Cracow in December 1848 on the model of the Berlin and Vienna associations, attempted to spread literacy among bourgeois women and servant girls.[62] It cannot be overlooked that many politically active men did not wish to tolerate women in their clubs and meetings, much less in elections. There are, however, contrasting examples, where women followed the political activity of their husbands with great unease and openly spoke out against it. The leading Czech historian and politician František Palacký, when Reichstag representative in Kremsier, was constantly reproached by his wife Therese to think of his family, put an end to his politicking, and return home. This antirevolutionary attitude among women in the years 1848-1849 was doubtless not an isolated one.[63]

Armed Struggle

The revolution in the Habsburg Monarchy was not only a competition of ideas and plans, not only a confrontation of petitions and electoral candidates; it was, above all, a relentless struggle for power, in which street fighting with barricades, uprisings and, finally, military operations were the decisive factors. The Austrian army under the experienced commanders Count Josef Wenzel Radetzky in northern Italy and Prince Alfred Windischgrätz in Prague, Vienna, and Hungary, intervened repeatedly in political developments during the almost one and half years of the revolution to defend the unlimited power of the emperor, sometimes even against the decisions of the ruler and his government. The situation was, however, much more complicated, because not only the regular army, but also the national guards and student corps represented armed power. "In large and small cities almost everyone of the male sex who was beyond childhood wore uniforms and carried arms," remembered a well-informed contemporary.[64] Apart from the diplomatic service, which despite domestic developments continued in its traditional manner, the Austrian army (with the exception of a few Hungarian units) was by far the strongest support of the counter-revolution in the Habsburg multinational state.

The first, and for the following weeks, decisive, armed clash took place on 13 March 1848 in the center of Vienna between demonstrators and the military, and the death of five demonstrators set the masses in motion. The Vienna national guard and the academic legion preserved their bourgeois character, even when some journeymen artisans, day laborers, and apprentices also forced their way into the civic armory. Parallel to this, worker unrest occurred in the suburbs of Vienna, which was put down by armed civilians together with the military. Between forty-eight and sixty of the victims of the fighting in March, a large majority, were journeymen and workers.

Early in the morning of 15 March 1848, Hungarian democrats, with Sándor Petöfi at their head, led a large demonstration of Pest citizens and students from the National Museum to the City Hall and to the Hungarian viceroy's office, where they succeeded in forcing an end to censorship and the release of some political prisoners, as the military garrison was seen as unreliable. On the same day, the first companies of the national guard were formed in Pest to protect private property and the new political gains, and in the next few days national guard units were set up in nearly the entire Magyar area of Hungary, not least for the struggle with resisting nationalities. From the permanent battalion of the National Guard arose gradually the core of the Hungarian national Honvéd army.

The success of the Hungarian Revolution encouraged Serbs in southern Hungary and in the military borderland to go beyond petitions to enact their originally moderate demands, since they could depend on good soldiers and weapons, and in part on the backing of the Principality of Serbia and from Croatia. On 13 May 1848 a representative assembly of Hungarian Serbs in Karlowitz [Sremski Karlovci] responded to the state of martial law ordered by the Hungarian government with the establishment of an autonomous Serbian province of Vojvodina and with the naming of the orthodox Metropolitan Josif Rajačić as patriarch of "all Slavs, Serbs, and Wallachians." Within a few days, on 25 May 1848, armed resistance to the Hungarian Revolution began, with officers and soldiers of the Habsburg army fighting on both sides, and with both sides proclaiming their loyalty to the king (not to the Austrian emperor). In the first battle, the Serbian border troops were successful.[65]

The army commanders stationed in nearly every Austrian crown land sought to repair their temporary loss of prestige vis-à-vis the almost independent Hungarian government with actions taken on their own authority, which the government in Vienna only found out about later on. Nearly all armed clashes between democratic radicals and the army in the most important centers of the Austrian Revolution were more or less consciously provoked by the military. The successful advance of the Austrian counter-revolution began in the Polish city of Cracow, which had been an independent free city until the spring of 1846. After the governor of Galicia, Count Franz Stadion, had banned production of weapons in the city and the return of Polish emigrants from France and other countries, the army tried to disarm the Polish national guard. The response by the dissatisfied section of the Cracow population was a mass demonstration on 25 April 1848, with an attack on the government building and the building of barricades. Johann Castiglione, the commanding general, withdrew his soldiers from the center of the city and forced the city to capitulate with a massive bombardment. The Cracow national council was dissolved as well as the national guard while emigrants who had previously returned were expelled. The city of Cracow played no role in the rest of the revolution.

Prince Alfred Windischgrätz an open enemy of constitutional developments, made nearly the same challenge to the Bohemian capital of Prague in June 1848. To oppose the rise of a radical mood in the city, the army gave a show of power, with a parade of troops and deployment of artillery on the hills around the city. On 12 June 1848, the Prague uprising began with a clash between grenadiers and demonstrators, continued with the construction of around 400 barricades, and ended, in spite of mediation efforts from Vienna, five days later, with the capitulation of the bombarded city.

From late summer 1848 the Hungarian Revolution had to fight a war on many fronts. The fighting, commencing in a clash with Serbian border troops and interrupted after a few weeks, began anew on 7 September 1848 after the Imperial Court in Vienna had guaranteed its backing of the Croatian Ban Jelačić in his struggle with the Hungarian government. Jelačić was not acting in support of Croatian national claims, but as the adherent of a unified and centralized multinational monarchy. The Croatian army was neither so numerically superior nor well enough armed to be able to achieve a decisive victory. Equally unsuccessful was an advance of a corps of volunteers, led by Slovak Protestants, in the second half of September 1848. Constant unrest was reported in Transylvania. In a very difficult situation the Hungarian Revolution, under Kossuth's leadership, succeeded in continuing a months-long campaign, against the regular Austrian army and against resisting nationalities. While going through a mixture of victories and defeats, the Hungarians held off all their opponents into the summer of 1849. From a purely military point of view, the success in raising and supplying the Hungarian Honvéd army, along with the volunteer corps, was doubtless unique in the history of the European revolutions of 1848-49.

For the fate of the revolutions in the Habsburg Monarchy, however, the developments in the metropolis of the multinational empire were decisive. Starting in the spring of 1848, Vienna experienced repeated armed clashes, in which three different forces, the Austrian army, the national guard with the academic legion, and the workers, opposed one another. Deployment of the legion and a large part of the national guard on 15 May 1848, under the influence of which the Ministerial Council in Vienna gave in to all the demands of the demonstrators, took place without gunfire, even when calls were heard to construct barricades on the French model.[66]

Only eleven days later, military occupation of the assembly hall of the University of Vienna led to about 160 barricades being thrown up in the streets and squares of the center of Vienna, where, apart from students, numerous workers offered resistance and opposed the withdrawal of the troops from the narrow lanes. A journeyman tanner was shot dead, the only victim of the May days in Vienna. The three days from 21 to 23 August were quite different. Week-long tensions between the Vienna bourgeoisie and those employed in public works projects led to large wage cuts, demonstrations, and clashes between workers and the municipal police and national guard. The result of the so-called "battle of the Prater" left eighteen dead workers, one dead policeman, one dead national guardsman and 350 injured. Finally, the popular uprising of 6 October 1848, apparently provoked by the counter-revolution, on the model of previous events in Cracow and Prague, brought a unique armed clash between the regular army on the one side and the national guard, allied with journeyman artisans and workers, on the other. Contemporary estimations of 2,000 civilian victims and 189 dead soldiers seem rather too low.[67] One can only agree that: "Through the victory of the military counter-revolution over Vienna more was destroyed than just human lives: the hope of a further development of democracy in Austria."[68]

Results and After-Effects

Despite the political defeat of the revolutionary and reformist forces in the Habsburg Monarchy, 1848/49 was an important step in the process of modernization of the Austrian multinational state.[69] Liberation of the peasantry opened the way for capitalist development of agriculture and made possible the formation of an integrated economy on the basis of free enterprise. A general reform of state economic policy, initiated in 1848 and continued in the postrevolutionary decade, encouraged a strong upswing in industrialization, at least in the western lands of the Habsburg Monarchy. For the first time, the principle of the equality of all citizens was recognized on the territory of the monarchy and put into practice in elections at various levels, held with only a few restrictions. It took nearly six decades, until the electoral reform of 1907, until universal male franchise was once again accepted in the non-Hungarian crown lands; in Hungary, even longer. Broad strata of the population of all nationalities of the monarchy were drawn, more or less voluntarily, into social and political activity and organized at different levels. In 1848/49, the Habsburg multinational Monarchy played a pioneering role in the legal confirmation of the principle of linguistic and political equal rights for different nationalities.[70]

The disunited, indeed conflicting nature of individual national political movements in central Europe during the years 1848/49 was continued in tradition and historical interpretation.[71] The Austrian conservative view sought to dismiss 1848 as a "crazy year," as, so to speak, a period of temporary insanity of otherwise worthy and loyal subjects. The name Reichstag fell into disrepute in Austria and was never again rehabilitated; with the return of constitutionalism in 1860/61, the term Reichsrat [Imperial Council] was apparently used to stress the advisory role of parliamentary representatives. Hence the emphasis of the tradition of the March, May, and October uprisings in Vienna shifted to the Austrian workers' movement.

In contrast to this, the year 1848 left deeper traces in the Hungarian public discourse than in all other nationalities of the monarchy. Even today, 15 March is a Hungarian national holiday, and every Hungarian looks back with pride to March and April 1848. Even though the year 1848 does not belong to the high points in

Czech historical understanding, emphasis was given alternatively to the liberation of the peasants, to the revolutionary determination of the youth, and above all to the level-headedness and the supranational view of leading liberal groups. It is no coincidence that nowadays the Kremsier Reichstag is much more popular than the Prague barricades. The tension that existed 150 years ago between freedom and nationality, between civic and national emancipation, is integral to other national interpretations as well. But the experience of 1848/49 deeply influenced all subsequent attempts at finding solutions to the problem of the coexistence of nations mature enough for self-government in the geopolitically exposed region between Germany, Russia, and the Balkans.

Notes

1. Waltraud Heindl, *Gehorsame Rebellen, Bürokratie und Beamte in Österreich 1780 bis 1848* (Vienna, Cologne and Graz, 1991), 200-9.

2. Istvan Deak, *The Lawful Revolution: Louis Kossuth and the Hungarians, 1848-1849* (New York, 1979), 56.

3. Viktor Bibl, *Die niederösterreichischen Stände im Vormärz. Ein Beitrag zur Vorgeschichte der Revolution des Jahres 1848* (Vienna, 1911), 249-74.

4. Friedrich Prinz, *Prag und Wien 1848. Probleme der nationalen und sozialen Revolution im Spiegel der Wiener Ministerratsprotokolle* (Munich, 1968), 46-67.

5. Jiří Kořalka, *Tschechen im Habsburgerreich und in Europa 1815-1914. Sozialgeschichtliche Zusammenhänge der neuzeitlichen Nationsbildung und der Nationalitätenfrage in der böhmischen Ländern* (Vienna and Munich, 1991), 27-37.

6. *Verhandlungen des österreichischen Reichstages nach der stenographischen Aufnahme,* Vol. 1 (Vienna, 1848), 157. The motion was widely discussed in the daily press.

7. Günter Wollstein, *Das "Großdeutschland" der Paulskirche. Nationale Ziele in der bürgerlichen Revolution 1848/49* (Düsseldorf, 1977), 135-88.

8. Deak, *The Lawful Revolution*, 45.

9. Jiří Kořalka, "Palacky und Österreich als Vielvölkerstaat," *Österreichische Osthefte* 28 (1986): 22-37.

10. Stane Granda, "Das Verhältnis zwischen nationaler und sozialer Frage bei den Slowenen im Jahre 1848/49," in Robert Jaworski and Rudolf Luft (eds.), *1848/49. Revolutionen in Ostmitteleuropa* (Munich, 1996), 245-57.

11. Jindřich Dvořák, *Moravské sněmování roku 1848-1849* [The Moravian Parliamentary Proceedings, 1848-1849] (Telč, 1898), 148-49.

12. Stanley Pech, *The Czech Revolution of 1848* (Chapel Hill, 1969), 349.

13. Jan Heidler, "Český sněm ústavodárný 1848 [The Constituent Bohemian Diet of 1848]," *Český časopis historický* 13 (1907): 36-59.

14. Peter Burian, *Die Nationalitäten in "Cisleithanien" und das Wahlrecht der Märzrevolution 1848/49. Zur Problematik des Parlamentarismus im alten Österreich* (Graz and Cologne 1962), 108-10.

15. Anton Springer, *Geschichte Österreichs seit dem Wiener Frieden 1809. Teil 2: Die österreichische Revolution* (Leipzig, 1865), 455-56.

16. Deak, *The Lawful Revolution*, 174-78.

17. Burian, *Die Nationalitäten in "Cisleithanien,"* 27-47.

18. As in ¶1 of the constitutional charter of 25 April 1848. Heinz Fischer and Gerhard Silvestri (eds.), *Texte zur österreichischen Verfassungs-Geschichte. Von der Pragmatischen Sanktion zur Bundesverfassung (1713-1966)* (Vienna, 1970), 4.

19. Andreas Gottsmann, *Der Reichstag von Kremsier und die Regierung Schwarzenberg. Die Verfassungsdiskussion des Jahres 1848 im Spannungsfeld zwischen Reaktion und nationaler Frage* (Vienna and Munich, 1995).

20. Springer, *Geschichte Österreichs* 2: 468.

21. Dvořák, *Moravské sněmování*, 183.

22. *Verhandlungen des österreichischen Reichstages nach der stenographischen Aufnahme*, Vol. 2 (Vienna, 1848), 627.

23. Josef V. Polišenský, *Aristocrats and the Crowd in the Revolutionary Year 1848*, trans. Frederick Snider (Albany, 1980), 112.

24. František Palacký, "Co jest konstituce?" [What is Constitution?], in *Spisy drobné* [Short works] vol. 1. *Spisy a řeči z oboru politiky* [Writings and speeches from the area of politics], ed. Bohus Rieger, (Prague, 1898), 9-11.

25. Jan M. Černý (ed.), *Boj za právo. Sborník aktů politických u věcech státu a národu českého od roku 1848* [The struggle for justice: a collection of political documents in the matter of the Bohemian state and the Czech nation], Vol 1., (Prague, 1893), 287-90.

26. Dvořák, *Moravské sněmování*, 253.

27. Josef Redlich, *Das österreichische Staats- und Reichsproblem. Geschichtliche Darstellung der inneren Politik der habsburgischen Monarchie von 1848 bis zum Untergang des Reiches*, Vol. I/1 (Vienna 1920), 92-93.

28. Deak, *The Lawful Revolution*, 260-62.

29. Wilhelm Brauneder, *Leseverein und Rechtskultur. Der Juridisch-politische Leseverein zu Wien 1840 bis 1990* (Vienna, 1992), 157-247; A. Stompfe, *Devadesát let Besedy měšťanské v Praze* [Ninety years of the Citizens' Resource in Prague](Prague, 1936), 3-11.

30. Ernst K. Sieber, *Ludwig von Löhner. Ein Vorkämpfer des Deutschtums in Böhmen, Mähren und Schlesien im Jahre 1848/49* (Munich, 1965), 58-67.

31. Jan Kabelík, "Moravská národní jednota [The Moravian National Association]," *Časopis Matice moravské* 33 (1909): 225-52, 321-55.

32. Jera Vodušek-Starič, "Program Zedinjene Slovenije in leto 1848 [The Programme of the United Slovenes in 1848]," *Prispevki za zgodovino delavskega gibanja* 25 (1985): 3-30.

33. Jan Kozik, *Między reakcją a revolucją. Studia z dziejów ukrainskiego ruchu narodowego w Galicji w latach 1848-1849* [Between reaction and revolution: studies on the history of the Ukrainian national movement in Galicia in the years 1848-1849] (Cracow, 1975).

34. Camillo De Franceschi, "Il movimento nazionale a Trieste nel 1848 e la Società dei Triestini," in *La Venezia Giulia e la Dalmazia nella rivoluzione nazionale del 1848-1849. Studi e documenti*, Vol. 1 (Udine, 1949), 263-315.

35. Wolfgang Häusler, *Von der Massenarmut zur Arbeiterbewegung. Demokratie und soziale Frage in der Wiener Revolution von 1848* (Vienna and Munich, 1979), 243.

36. Laszlo Deme, *The Radical Left in the Hungarian Revolution of 1848* (Boulder CO, 1976).

37. Josef Fontana, "Das Sturmjahr 1848," in *Geschichte des Landes Tirol*, Vol. 2 (Bolzano, Innsbruck, and Vienna, 1986), 709.

38. František Roubík, "České kněžstvo v roce 1848 [The Czech clergy in 1848]," *Akord* 5 (1932): 62-70.

39. Häusler, *Von der Massenarmut*, 342-43.

40. Jan Novotny, "Slovanská Lípa 1848-1849. K dějinám prvního českého politického spolku," [The Slavic Linden 1848-1849: on the history of the first Czech political association] pt. 1, *Acta Musei Pragensis* (1975): 71.

41. Jaroslav Šidak, "Družtvo Slavenske Lipe na slavenskom Jugu" [The Slavic Linden Association in the Slavic south], in Jaroslav Šidak, *Studije iz hrvatski povijesti za revolucije 1848-49* [Studies in Croatian history during the revolution of 1848-49] (Zagreb, 1979), 291-321.

42. Jan Novotny, "Slovanská Lípa 1848-1849 [The Slavic Linden 1848-1849]," pt. 2, *Acta Musei Pragensis* (1976): 48.

43. František Roubík (ed.), *Petice venkovského lidu z Čech k Národnímu výboru z roku 1848* [The petitions of the rural population from Bohemia to the National Committee of 1848] (Prague, 1954).

44. Jiří Radimsky and Milada Wurmová (eds.), *Petice moravského lidu k sněmu z roku 1848* [The petitions of the Moravian people to the parliament of 1848] (Prague, 1955); Jaroslav Šidak, "Seljačko pitanje u hrvatskoj politici 1848," [The peasant question in Croatian politics of 1848],in Jaroslav Šidak, *Studije iz hrvatske povijesti*, 145-74.

45. Roman Rosdolsky, *Die Bauernabgeordneten im konstituierenden österreichischen Reichstag 1848-1849* (Vienna, 1976), xi.

46. Peter Heumos, "Die Bauernbefreiung in den böhmischen Ländern 1848. Anmerkungen zu den ökonomischen, sozialen und politischen Verhältnissen der Agrargesellschaft," in Jaworski and Luft (eds.), *1848/49. Revolutionen in Ostmitteleuropa*, 221-37.

47. Deak, *The Lawful Revolution*, 116-17.

48. Häusler, *Von der Massenarmut*, pp. 147-51.

49. Karel Novotný, "Účast dělnictví v buržoazní revoluci roku 1848-1849 v českých zemích," [Worker participation in the bourgeois revolution of 1848-1849 in the Bohemian regions] *Slovanské historické studie* 13 (1982): 143-64.

50. Häusler, *Von der Massenarmut*, 179.

51. Karel Novotný, "Prvníčeský časopis pro dělnictvo," [The first Czech journal for workers] *Novinářský sborník* 10 (1965): 173-79.

52. Häusler, *Von der Massenarmut*, 316-17.

53. Gustav Otruba, *Wiener Flugschriften zur Sozialen Frage 1848, Arbeiterschaft, Handwerk und Handel*, Vol. 1(Vienna, 1978), 134, 141.

54. Palacký, *Spisy drobné* 1: 55-56.

55. *Národní Noviny* (Prague), Nr. 103, 12 August 1848, 407.

56. Josef Pekař, Review of Heinrich Friedjung, *Österreich von 1848-1860*, Vol. 1, *Český časopis historický* 14 (1908): 100.

57. Deak, *The Lawful Revolution*, 113.

58. K. Kazbunda, *České hnutí roku 1848* [The Czech movement of 1848], (Prague, 1929), 168.

59. Deak, *The Lawful Revolution*, 74.

60. Mirjam Moravcová, *Národní oděv roku 1848. Ke vzniku národně politického symbolu* [National dress of 1848: on the development of a national political symbol], (Prague, 1986), 87-95.

61. Gabriella Hauch, *Frau Biedermeier auf den Barrikaden. Frauenleben in der Wiener Revolution 1848* (Vienna, 1990); Mirjam Moravcová, "Die tschechischen Frauen im revolutionären Prag 1848/49," in Jaworski and Luft (eds.), *1848/49. Revolutionen in Ostmitteleuropa*, 75-96.

62. Josef Alexander Freiherr von Helfert, *Geschichte Österreichs vom Ausgange des Wiener Oktober-Aufstandes 1848*, vol. 2: *Revolution und Reaction im Spätjahre 1848* (Prague 1870), 430.

63. Archive of the National Museum of Prague, Papers of František Palacký, Inv. no. 826. Palacký's reply to his wife Therese of 9/9, 16/9, 2/10, and 15/12/1848 and 9/1, 1/2/1849.

64. Helfert, *Geschichte Österreichs* 2: 294.

65. Deak, *The Lawful Revolution*, 129.

66. Häusler, *Von der Massenarmut*, 226.

67. Ibid., 395-96.

68. Ibid., 397.

69. Otto Urban, "1848—Eine Modernisierungsetappe in der Habsburgmonarchie," *Der Donauraum* 35 (1995): 6-14.

70. Gerald Stourzh, *Die Gleichberechtigung der Nationalitäten in der Verfassung und der Verwaltung Österreichs 1848-1918* (Vienna, 1985), 17-28.

71. To the point is Wolfgang Häusler, "Zur sozialen und nationalen Problematik der Revolution von 1848/49 in der Donaumonarchie," in Erich Zöllner (ed.), *Revolutionäre Bewegungen in Österreich* (Vienna, 1981), 110-28.

Chapter 7

THE POLISH NATION IN THE REVOLUTION OF 1846-49

Hans Henning Hahn

Introductory Remarks

"The Cracow uprising of 1846 and the movement in Poznań [German: Posen] were the beginnings of the European 'springtime of the peoples.' Two years later the revolution began in the Grand Duchy of Poznań, in Cracow, and in Galicia. After its military suppression the situation for the Polish nation and liberal forces in Europe worsened."[1] These sentences, taken from the 1972/75 joint German-Polish schoolbook of recommendations, express what the Poles often regarded as self-evident: the interdependence of their destiny with that of Europe. Revolutionary events in the mid-nineteenth century were no exception. In Polish historical tradition, they began before 1848, as a "springtime of the peoples" (Wiosna Ludów) in February 1846 in Poznań, Cracow, and Galicia—with a widespread conspiracy directed from exile and a failed uprising—and did not end until August 1849/April 1850 with the flight of Poles involved in the Hungarian uprising into the Ottoman Empire and with the banning of the Liga Polska in Prussia, a legal organization of national solidarity. In between there were numerous revolutionary events and activities: attempts to exploit revolutions affecting two of the partitioning powers, Prussia and Austria, for the benefit of Poland and to take power in the Polish provinces they controlled; hopes of a national war of liberation to restore the Polish state; violent suppression of all these endeavors; revolutionary, military, and diplomatic participation by Poles in all revolutionary events in Europe; parliamentary activities of Polish delegates in Vienna, Kremsier, Berlin, and Frankfurt (albeit there deliberately reduced to one deputy); and finally, participation in the Prague Slav Congress. This wide range of activities reflects the entire spectrum of strategic options for national politics.

Notes for this section begin on page 184.

The revolutionary events in Europe of 1848 can be understood as three synchronous revolutions with different aims and opponents. There were political, social, and national revolutions, aimed at political participation, social emancipation and national separation and/or integration, and directed against three existing states of affairs: the exercise of power and domination within existing states, the prevailing social structures, and the international relations of sovereign states, in the diplomatic system of the Pentarchy. In Poland, the highest priority was given to the national revolution. There was no dissent among social and political elites on the final goal of Poland's restoration to its prepartition boundaries of 1772. "National reorganization," promised for Poznań by Friedrich Wilhelm IV and never fulfilled, postulated in Galicia and never implemented, was viewed only as a first step. The course of events left no time to define its extent and limits.

The most important arena for Polish politics after the quashing of the November uprising of 1830/31 in the Russian partition—the kingdom of Poland—was located in exile beyond the reach of the three partitioning powers. There, the political and intellectual elite of the Polish nation could advance all the possibilities of national emancipation. The political-ideological range of this so-called "great emigration" extended from early socialist groups to the clergy, whereby the Polish Democratic Society and the constitutional-monarchical Hôtel Lambert under Prince Adam Jerzy Czartoryski formed the two largest, loudest, and most active camps. Common to all of them, however, was a pursuit of the strategy of insurrection as the only possible means of restoring Poland. This strategy, based on the old Polish Rzeczpospolita that perished in the eighteenth century, implied a predominantly political understanding of the nation, in which ethnic elements were rarely included.

Despite all the differences in vision of the constitution and social structure of a future Poland, the partition of the Polish nation among the three European Great Powers meant that the national revolution had to be more radical than its social or political counterparts. The objectives of the latter two were always weighed against their usefulness in achieving national independence. Radicalism and close European involvement in the so-called Polish question was mutually dependent, as realistic chances for a restoration of an independent Poland could only arise from a radical transformation of the European status quo. Consequently, the revolutionary drama of "Poland in the springtime of the peoples" can be presented on three levels: the role of the Polish question in European events, the revolutionary events in formerly Polish territories, and the revolutionary activities of Poles in Europe. But first a few words to the revolutionary beginnings of the "springtime of the peoples."

Events of 1846 or Problems of a Rural Revolution

Measured by their journalistic echo in Europe, the events of February 1846 came as a shock, notably the discovery of an extensive Polish nationalist conspiracy in the Prussian partition (Poznàn and West Prussia), whose existence did not reflect well on to the allegedly so well-ordered Prussian state; an urban revolution, successful in the short-term in the (nominally independent) Free City of Cracow, during which some radical views on the interdependence of national and social revolution were put forward (more specifically on the necessity of radical social reform as a condition of a successful national war of independence); and above all the "massacres of Galicia," when an uprising of aristocratic conspirators with nationalist revolutionary aims came to a bloody end in the Galician peasants' jacquerie, in the course of which the Austrian bureaucracy played a dubious role that has not been completely explained, down to the present day.

This last event seemed to interest European public opinion, especially German journalists, much more than the simultaneous mass death by starvation of Irish peasants, and calls into question the notion that a national revolution in Poland was prioritized. It can hardly be overlooked that the Galician jacquerie was a social revolution, meant to overthrow aristocratic landwoners' oppression of peasantry. In addition, reference is often made to an extra cause—a parallel, national contrast of Polish landowners vs. Ruthenian (Ukrainian) peasants and an alleged natural monarchism on the part of the peasants.[2]

Doubtless, rural social conditions in Galicia were extremely tense. Their explosiveness was intensified by the European agrarian crisis of the 1840s. Reforms, held by many contemporaries to be long overdue, did not get out of the starting blocks. Austrian bureaucracy and aristocratic Polish reformers blocked each other in their (quite timid) attempts at reform. This was due, on the one hand, to the bureaucratic immobility of the Metternich system and to the fact that moderate aristocratic reformers were (still) in the minority. On the other hand, both adversaries (at least their enlightened protagonists) were well aware that the national political dimension involved, among other issues, a question of whom the peasants would thank for reforms, and/or of whether a peasant Polish national identity could be created. In other words, it was a question of gaining peasant support for the "national cause." It must be noted, nonetheless, that national differences between Ruthenian peasants and Polish landowners, reflected in language and confession, existed only in eastern Galicia, while the bloody unrest of February 1846 occurred exclusively in western Galicia where peasants were without exception Polish speaking Catholics.

The "monarchism" of Galician peasants, the existence of which was asserted by all sides, was based on specific hopes. And those social tensions that so crassly exploded in 1846, including the lack of interest of a large part of the peasantry in the objectives of national revolutionaries, and their ideas on a constitution, remained unchanged in 1848/49, albeit without the bloodletting. However, it should not be overlooked that peasants in the republic of Cracow, living as hereditary leaseholders, had already taken sides with the national uprising, seemingly without reservation.

The abolition of the *robot* [servile labor services] was one of the few achievements of the revolution of 1848/49 in the Habsburg Empire which was not reversed. This might lead one to conclude that the Austrian bureaucracy was victorious in the struggle that led to peasant emancipation. In fact, it had little influence on Galician peasant identity. In the long run, the Polish-speaking peasantry of Galicia emancipated itself into a Polish national society in the second half of the nineteenth century and not, for example, into an "Austrian society," which did not exist in Galicia and hardly could have existed. Eugen Weber's "Peasants into Frenchmen" thus had its Polish parallel.

The 1846 attempt at a national revolution was begun by democrats in exile, both aristocratic and bourgeois. In view of the generally agrarian character of Polish society, they were faced with a practically insoluble dilemma in program and strategy. An inter-relation between a national uprising and the immediate social emancipation of the peasants was an irrevocable credo for all democrats, as only a mass movement could secure independence and a modern Polish republic and thus fulfil the mission of the Polish nation—implementation of the slogans of the French Revolution in Eastern Europe. Contrasting this was the understanding that a national uprising without the patriotic aristocracy, as the leading class in society, could hardly succeed. Thus, at least a partial consideration of their social and political interests seemed advisable. It was also felt that their military know-how could not be sacrificed in the planned revolutionary people's war.

At the same time, in light of the conditions of an agrarian society without large cities and with a generally illiterate lower class (only 20 percent of the children in Galicia attended school in 1848, compared to 95 percent in Bohemia), effective agitation was only possible through the spoken word, which often proved impossible, for reasons of conspiratorial secrecy. Moreover, considerable problems of communication existed between democratic intellectual emissaries from the Polish Democratic Society, working from Paris, and the peasants. The only go-betweens were apparently local aristocrats or clergy. Unlike the cautiously maneuvering exile organizations, which were working towards a longer, more realistic preparation of an uprising, conspirators in Poland pushed for a rapid start, not least because of the constant threat of discovery and arrest. Their patriotic-revolutionary conviction that all needed doing was to gather the peasants in one place and present them with a manifesto promising them ownership of the land proved to be a fateful illusion as this was to be done by the peasants' former "exploiters," the local aristocrats, or by unknown emissaries. Many patriotic aristocrats recognized that existing social conditions were untenable and in desperate need of reform, but let themselves be fooled by the external traditionalism of peasant life, not understanding that the existing social abuses had undermined the legitimacy of their claims to political and social leadership.

The course of events will not be presented in detail here.[3] In Poznań, the uprising was betrayed by one of the conspirators, who thought it poorly prepared and who feared its social revolutionary aspects. The arrest of, among others, Ludwik Mierosławski, the intended leader of the uprising, led to a mass trial with 254 defendants in 1847. The open court proceedings created quite a sensation, since they gave the conspirators an opportunity to present their aspirations to a broader public. In Galicia, the attempt to begin with the rebellion in spite of the news from Poznań cost 1,000—2,000 aristocrats their lives in the ensuing jacquerie. Most of the victims had nothing to do with the conspiracy. It is generally accepted as proven that the Austrian authorities deliberately exploited peasant dissatisfaction in order to suppress the national uprising, although the details and extent of their actions will probably forever remain unclear. The question raised above of whether the uprising in Galicia in 1846 was a national or a social revolution thus seems incorrectly formulated; it seems rather that an attempt at a national revolution was faced with considerable hurdles during its preparation, as it was rooted in the social tensions of agrarian society, and was suffocated by a peasant social revolution, which was in turn exploited by Austrian authorities.

In Cracow, a "classic" urban revolution was successful at first and was able to drive off the limited number of Austrian troops sent to suppress it. An attempt to spread the revolution outside the city failed—despite support from peasants in the Republic of Cracow and miners in Wieliczka—because of decisive action by the Austrian troops under Ludwig Benedek. The national government under Jan Tysowski recognized the untenability of its situation and stepped down. Cracow was occupied and in November 1846, after longer negotiations between the three partitioning powers, was annexed by Austria—a blatant violation of the Treaty of Vienna of 1815, which caused a scandal throughout Europe.

Polish events in 1846 prefigured the nature of the problems and the course of events that would be of significance for the entire revolutionary period in Europe in the following years, notably the splits in the revolutionary movement due to various political and social antagonisms; attempts (successful in this case) by the "reaction" to exploit rural social conflicts for its own ends against the revolutionary aims of the social elite; the initial weakness of the military when confronted by the outbreak of an urban revolution; the role of determined, vigorous military leaders in suppressing the revolution; the weakness in practice of political radicalism and the political left; the fragility of the international order and the vanishing validity of the European status quo of the treaties of 1815.[4]

These seem to be reason enough to consider the events of 1846 in Galicia and Cracow not only as a curtain-raiser for the revolutionary year of 1848, but as the revolutionary overture and first act of the European revolutionary drama of 1846/49.

The "Polish Question" in Europe

The long life of the "Polish question"[5] in the nineteenth century is a result of both the fact that each of the three partitioning powers of Poland had "their" Polish question, making the areas of the partition internally destabilizing factors for 120 years, and especially to its pan-European dimension. The latter arose from the consequences (which lasted for the entire century) of Poland's "general, definitive and irrevocable dismemberment"[6] for the European balance of power and from cross-border attempts by Poles to reverse this partitioning and to restore Poland as an independent state. The political will to live felt by the Polish nation, or more exactly by its politically conscious strata, was also an absolutely necessary precondition for keeping the Polish question alive in the minds of Europeans, friends, and foes alike.

The explosiveness of the Polish question for Europe was a consequence of the fact that maintaining the partition and preventing the re-emergence of a Polish nation-state were fundamental conditions for preserving the European balance of power and the system of states founded in 1815. For the Polish nationalist movement this meant that an evolutionary option for national emancipation was, in principle, out of the question or, at best, acceptable only as a temporary strategy. All protagonists were aware of the necessary sociorevolutionary implications of a strategy of insurrection, even when many tried to minimize them.

A restoration of Poland would have meant a simultaneous extensive revision of the European status quo. It was therefore only conceivable in the context of an international solution resulting from a radical change in the European state system, which meant via the path of a major European war in combination with a pan-European revolution—an idea not strange to anyone as the relation between revolution and war belonged to the formative experiences of an entire generation of politicians from the 1790s onwards. As a collaborator of Prince Czartoryski wrote in 1836: "In the diversity of our diplomatic systems for the deliverance of Poland, it was only possible to consider two extreme means: either a volcanic disruption of all of Europe, which would even bring down the power of Russia; or individual or collective action by the Great Powers with the aim of reducing the predominance of Russia, for which the surest guarantee would be the restoration of Poland."[7] What he saw as alternatives were also conceivable ten to twelve years later, then perhaps only in combination.

In March/April 1848 many politicians and journalists awaited, with quite different motives, a major European war for the restoration of Poland[8]—some as a result of a Polish uprising in the Russian part of Poland, others as an answer to expected counter-revolutionary intervention by the Tsars, still others as a safety-valve to prevent a sociorevolutionary explosion in Germany.[9] The Prussian Foreign Minister Arnim, to secure his German policy plans, included in them the possibility of a war against Russia to restore Poland, but received both evasive and clearly formulated rejections from his potential allies, France and England, and met with equally effective resistance from his king and the Prussian military.[10]

The option of a foreign war concerning Poland as a safety-valve for domestic tensions in Germany disappeared rapidly, this safety valve function being taken over by the Schleswig conflict. An awareness remained that a war concerning Poland would have meant a surge of radicalization of the revolution, and thus the Polish question became ever more a domain of the left, at least in France and Germany. Attempts by radical Parisian clubs on 15 May 1848 to reverse their defeat in the elections of the constituent national assembly were undertaken, not by chance, under the pretext of supporting Poland, although without Polish participation. With the defeat of this attempted putsch, the possibility of a radicalized European power making the Polish question its own disappeared, voluntarily or of necessity. The restoration of Poland as a lever, or the instrument of a radical reformation of international relations proved infeasible; the only really far-reaching conceivable alternative to the prevailing system did not come into play.

This does not mean, however, that this vision did not continue to remain the subject of political debate and part of revolutionary plans or counter-revolutionary action. Thus, for example, the threat arising from the Polish national movement was one main reason for Tsar Nicholas I giving in to requests for help from the Austrian government and intervening in Hungary.[11] His actions also confirm the thesis that the Polish question was immanently radical, on a European level. All contemporaries, on both sides of the barricades, were aware of this; historians, looking back can hardly avoid it.

Revolutionary Events in Poland 1848/49

Revolutionary events in the Polish partitians were largely shaped by the position of the Polish question in Europe, that is, by the real possibility of a war of liberation against Russia and later by resignation when it became clear that such a war was not going to occur. This affected not only Polish attitudes, but also those of the partitioning powers, obviously well aware of the key role played by the Polish question. In the Russian region of Poland, (the Kingdom of Poland and the eastern part of the so-called "stolen areas" [ziemie zabrane]) conspiratorial associations were emerging. In view of a mobilization of the Russian army in March 1848, however, these had no possibility of taking action and did not therefore let themselves be pushed into acts of desperation.[12]

Stefan Kieniewicz, in an essay published posthumously on "the springtime of the peoples"[13] names three causative factors for events in Poznań and Galicia in March 1848. Apart from the above-mentioned atmosphere of expectation of a general war by revolutionary "Europe" against Tsarist Russia, he includes as a factor the imitation of European revolutions beginning in January 1848, and the decline in the pressure exercised by the partitioning powers following the outbreak of the March revolutions in Vienna and Berlin, allowing protagonists of the Polish national movement greater room for maneuver. Tensions between the bureaucracies of the partitioning powers and the indigenous social elites of the Prussian and Austrian regions—that is Poznań and West Prussia as well as in Galicia—had certainly not lessened since 1846. Hence, it was not surprising that the revolutions in Vienna and Berlin—where the conspirators of 1846, convicted a few months before, had been freed by the people in March 1848—had their corresponding effects. Despite considerable differences between the two German powers, in view of both their previous policies towards Poland and the revolutionary events of 1848/49, certain parallels do exist in relation to the course of events in Poznań[14] and Galicia.[15]

Neither in Poznàn nor in Galicia did the revolution of 1848 begin as an uprising, but, rather, as a bloodless seizure of power, since the state bureaucracy had become more or less incapable of acting in the wake of the Berlin and Vienna Revolutions. Civilian governmental power passed into the hands of national committees, national guards were formed, freedom of the press announced, delegations were sent to the capitals to implement demands for a "national reorganization," but above all to search for governmental allies in the struggle for Poland's restoration.

While the civilian bureaucracy was, to a great extent, eliminated (in Poznań apparently more so than in Galicia), the military remained. At the same time, the rebels armed themselves, especially in Poznań, where under the leadership of L. Mierosławski, a "war department" of the National Committee coordinated these activities. With the permission of the government, emigrants began returning from France and Belgium to Poznań and Galicia. All this took place in the expectation of the imminent outbreak of war with Russia.

The delegations received a promise of a "national reorganization" in Berlin and Vienna, and in Berlin probably also delphic references to a coming war that had to be prepared for, but nothing more. Both the Austrian and the Prussian governments made concessions, which at first were no more than indirect recognition of a fait accompli, without, however, losing their temporary character. They sought to keep the Polish nationalist movement as a potential ally for any eventuality, without, however, committing themselves to anything specific. In Prussia, the king ordered, behind the back of the government, a military attack on the Polish movement while General v. Willisen, as "royal commissar for the national reorganization" at the behest of the government, but without military command, was to negotiate and coordinate.

In both provinces the bureaucracy sought to provoke and exploit clashes between the nationalities: in Galicia between Poles and Ruthenians, when on 2 May 1848 the Polish National Council gained an adversary in the Supreme Ruthenian Council (Holovna Ruska Rada) supported by the provincial governor, Count Stadion; in Poznań as early as late March/early April between Poles and Germans, whereby the German National Committee, at first willing to cooperate with the Poles, soon took a stand against the Polish movement, with considerable support from state officials, and thus against a Polish "national reorganization" of the entire province.

In both cases, Polish concepts of nation, based on politics and history, ran up against two generally ethnically conceived and argued concepts, whereby Poznań Germans (about 30 percent of the population) referred not only to Berlin, i.e. Prussia, but at the same time to Frankfurt, i.e., Germany. In other words, as long as it was a question of a (constitutional) political revolution (in the first days), Poles and liberal Germans were united. In view of the obvious priority of the national revolution on the Polish side, this common front quickly collapsed. In Galicia, in the Ruthenian movement, which was quite differently socially structured, there was little reference to Russia, but all the more to Vienna.

The protagonists of the Polish national movement had experienced the events of 1846 as a "moral defeat"[16] insofar as it became obvious that the peasant "masses," for whose emancipation they wanted to fight (among other causes), were not behind them. The ideas raised in a brochure[17]—which caused quite a sensation— that Polish aristocrats should give up for good their aspirations toward national independence in order to maintain the prevailing social structure and should voluntarily submit to the Russian Tsar, were generally rejected with indignation. However, awareness of their own weakness and knowledge of how much they were playing with fire, in view of social tensions, inhibited revolutionary élan both in Galicia and Poznań. This, however, had different effects in the two provinces. In

Galicia, peasants generally did not support the Polish nationalist movement, and in a discussion of how and under what conditions the *robot* should be eliminated, considerable conflicts of interest became apparent which could not be bridged by common national concerns. What was lacking was a common enemy. The actions of Provincial Governor Stadion contributed no small amount to this state of affairs. While forbidding the great landowners to free peasants from the *robot* on their own authority, he had the government in Vienna grant him special powers and announced on 22 April 1848 its abolition in all of Galicia. He did not seek to disguise the national political dimension of this agrarian policy coup, as "the purpose of the entire regulations" were "to secure the loyalty of the servile rural population to the government, and deprive the supporters of Polish nationalism this important means of gaining the support of the rural population for their interests."[18] The situation was different in Poznań, where the movement received support from peasants, who were apparently much less interested than the aristocratic officers in preparing for a war of liberation against Russia and more in fighting against the Prussian military, against the Prussian bureaucracy, against the Germans.

It is a reflection of the European significance of the Polish question that the first victories of the counter-revolution against an initially successful revolution occurred in Poznań and Galicia. In both provinces, the position of the military remained unchallenged, so that it basically was left to the initiative of higher officers when they saw the best opportunity to employ military force.

In Poznań, General Peter von Colomb had already begun in April to bring troops together (about 30,000 men) and to impede the formation of armed Polish units allowed by the government.[19] On 3 April 1848 he declared martial law for the province of Posen. Action by the Prussian troops initially led to concessions on the Polish side. In the convention of Jaroslawiec of 4 April, negotiated by General Karl Wilhelm von Willisen, the Poles promised to reduce their troop strength from 8,000–9,000 to 3,000. Implementation of the convention, however, ran into difficulties. Under the pretext that they were not keeping to the agreement, Colomb attacked the Polish positions. While many Polish officers held further military action for pointless in view of unequal strength, other wanted to continue fighting, apparently above all the "scythe men," the poorly armed peasants.

In the meantime, as the result of numerous petitions from German Committees in Poznań, among other causes, two cabinet orders (14 and 26 April) were announced, according to which the Grand Duchy of Poznań was to be divided into a larger German section, to be included in the German Confederation, and a Polish section, where a national reorganization would take place.[20] With the publication of these orders, the Polish national committee saw that the basis for any further cooperation with the Prussian government was lost and dissolved itself officially. The Prussian troops crushed (after a few defeats) the rapidly disintegrating Polish units, which finally capitulated on 9 May 1848.

In Cracow, a disagreement arose between the Polish movement and the Austrian district commander Wilhelm Krieg von Hochfelden in the second half of April. The commanding Lieutenant Field Marshall Heinrich Graf Castiglioni made use of this situation and as his troops were not successful in fighting at the barricades, he had the city bombarded, forcing an unconditional capitulation.

The counter-revolution was successful for the first time, in the countryside and in a city. Behind this success was, on the one hand, a desire by the military both in Prussia and in Austria to erase the humiliating defeat of March—namely for having had to abandon the capital to the "revolution"—and, starting in the provinces, to defeat the revolution. On the other hand, the crucial question arose for constitutional order in Prussia, involving the relationship between the army and the crown. In Poznań it was answered—one is tempted to say in a manner indicative of the future—in favor of a retention of the royal prerogative in military matters. To this extent, the suppression of the Polish movement was at the same time a defeat for Prussian liberalism.

Finally, the "national reorganization" of both Poznań and Galicia, promised in March but never exactly defined, was basically condemned to failure from the beginning. On paper it contained little more than the promises made to the Poles in 1815. Stefan Kieniewicz is therefore completely justified in his remarks concerning Poznàn: "Concession of territorial self-administration was too little for the Polish nationalist movement, but too much for Prussian reasons of state if peace was to be preserved. The conflict [between the Poles and Prussia] was unavoidable, it could only have been avoided by a war against a common enemy."[21]

As a war with Russia did not occur, the national revolution did not have a chance. The revolutionaries had to be content with legalistic activities. This occurred primarily in the parliamentary arena, in Vienna, Kremsier, and Berlin, There, apart from working on constitutional drafts, the Polish deputies were most interested in achieving at least a national autonomy for their province—in the end in vain. Elections for the Frankfurt National Assembly were boycotted by the Poles in Poznań, who were under martial law, in any event. Only one deputy, Jan Janiszewski, represented the Poznań Poles, and after an impressive appearance in the famed debate on Poland of 24-27 July 1848, he resigned his seat.

In Poznań, a new form of nationalist political activity was developed with the founding of the Liga Polska in June 1848, an organization of national solidarity which soon counted 37,000 members in 300 branches. Working strictly legally on the explicit model of the Irish Repeal Association, the Liga was especially intended to fulfil national educational tasks, to protect the Polish nationality and contribute to the national shaping of Polish society in Poznań. To this end, a path of national self-organization was chosen which, despite the prohibition of the Liga on 8 April 1850, substantially defined the further development of the Polish national movement, and not just in Poznań.

Stormy Pretels of the Revolution

The way that the Polish question was interwoven with the revolutionization of Europe, repeatedly emphasized above, and the recognition that every chance at a change in the status quo needed to be exploited for the political aims of Polish nationalism meant that many Poles, above all those in the "great emigration," sought to bring a change of fortune from outside Poland. These actions commenced at the beginning of the revolution and were intensified following May 1848, when revolutionary action in Poznań and Galicia was practically out of the question. While it is often and quite justifiably remarked that there was hardly a barricade or battlefield in Europe between 1830 and 1870 where no Poles were fighting, this is especially true (except for the conflict in Schleswig) for the revolution of 1848/49. Poles were particularly active in Italy, Hungary, and Germany. Participants were not only democratic Polish revolutionaries, but also supporters of Prince Czartoryski. All camps of Polish exiles contained numerous professional soldiers, whose abilities were in demand everywhere; their numbers were increased in 1848/49 by refugees from Galicia, Poznań, and from the Russian partition.

In 1846 Prince Metternich wrote "*Polonismus* is only a formula, a wording, behind which stands the revolution in its most crass form; it is *the revolution* itself, and not only a section of it; this is demonstrated by statements by Polish emigrants which have become public. '*Polonismus*' does not declare war against the three powers in possession of former Polish territory; it declares war against all existing institutions, it preaches the overthrow of the entire foundation on which society is based. To combat it is therefore not a matter for the three powers alone, it is a general duty."[22] As if the Polish emigrants wanted to confirm in retrospect this total denunciation of the Polish national movement by the elderly Austrian Chancellor, nearly all their activities were directed against the Habsburg Empire in 1848/49. At the Prague Slav Congress in May 1848,[23] they had not yet completely burned their bridges, as the predominantly Austro-Slavic mood there aimed foremost at a defensive position vis-à-vis German and Russian hegemonic aspirations. Even there, they had not hidden their quite ambiguous relation to Austro-Slavism. Later, however, after Austrian troops had broken up the Slav Congress—and at this point they consciously distinguished themselves from Czech, Slovak and Croatian, and in part also the Galician Poles—they saw in the breakup of the Habsburg Empire and the formation of a Slav, or still better, a Slav-Magyar federation the only possibility of effectively changing the European status quo.

The living tradition, between the end of the eighteenth century and the Second World War, of Polish legions in foreign service was founded on three different points. The legions were seen as the core of a future Polish army of liberation, symbolizing the idea of Polish action and presence within the framework of European events and which contributed to gaining allies, and pushing forward the revolution in 1848. A legion formed by the romantic poet Adam Mickiewicz, founded in April 1848 in the Papal States, fought in northern Italy, in Tuscany, and in the end was one of the defenders of the Roman Republic in May-July 1849. Apart from a number of Polish officers in the Piedmontese army, General Wojciech Chrzanowski, close to Czartoryski and highly respected by the British, was given command—through Palmerston's agency—after its first defeat in the summer of 1848 without, however, being able to prevent a further loss at Novara. L. Mierosławski, called to Sicily in December 1848, had no better luck there and had to leave the island again after its conquest by Naples.

In October 1848 General Józef Bem found himself more or less by chance in Vienna in order to negotiate with Hungarian delegates; at the request of Austrian democrats he took on command of the defense of Vienna against Habsburg troops, supported by further Polish officers. After Vienna was taken, he fought through to Hungary. There he commanded an army in Transylvania, together with other Polish colleagues who were active above all in the northern Hungarian army. In Hungary, the rest of the revolutionaries from throughout Europe "gathered" to defend the last bastion (apart from Venice) of the revolution.[24] The share of Poles was quite high and indeed founded a tradition.[25] Polish revolutionaries also played an important role in the Saxon and Badenese revolutions of 1849, especially Mierosławski, who was once again given command of the troops.[26]

This list of the highlights of revolutionary condottieri could give the impression that their activities were in the end only the culmination of an unexploited revolutionary actionism. Opinions may vary on the practical military value; the symbolic value of this active international solidarity of national revolutionaries should not be underestimated and must be seen in the context of the thesis—widespread especially in German works and otherwise a historiographic platitude—that, especially in this revolution, relations between national movements often turned into bloody conflicts practically overnight. It can often be demonstrated that such a development was in no way unavoidable and more or less fated, but rather at least in part a conscious machiavellian creation by the powers of the ancien regime. Also opposing this argument was the high level of consensus demonstrated at the Prague Slav Congress.

Finally, the endeavors of Polish diplomacy deserve mention. From the autumn of 1848 onwards, numerous diplomatic agents and officers, at the behest of Prince Czartoryski, tried to establish an Italo-Hungarian alliance, as well as to mediate in the conflict between Hungarians and South Slavs and Rumanians. On 18 May 1849 Czartoryski arranged a Hungarian-Slav conference in Paris where the Austrian Slavs were represented by the Czech František L. Rieger. However, the agreement reached at this conference could no longer be brought into force. The benevolent reception that revolutionary refugees found in the Ottoman Empire was to a great extent due to the mediation of the Hôtel Lambert, which had some access to unofficial channels.

It is certainly an open question whether all these activities—including representation of Polish interests in Western capitals and in Frankfurt as well—are best described as "diplomacy of the people," a term that is, in any event, difficult to define. That they failed does not make them any less interesting for historians. Certainly, in their principal concepts and in their incomplete realization they indicate that the history of European nations and their relation to one another was not a one-way street, but that alternatives existed.

The Consequences

Apart from the abolition of the *robot* in Galicia, the events of 1846/49 changed little in Poland, when examined superficially. In this there is little to distinguish between Polish regions and the rest of Europe. A restabilization of prerevolutionary conditions was nearly intact; in spite of a pan-European revolution and a number of wars between countries, not a single border in Europe was altered. In retrospect, however, it is evident that Europe after 1849 was nonetheless not the same as before the revolutions. For the Polish nation, apart from numerous details, the following aspects appear significant.

With the defeat of the revolution, a large part of the nationally minded strata of Polish society came to the conclusion that the previously quasi-compulsory strategy of insurrection for national independence had failed. Although the great January uprising of 1863 in the Russian region would again see a new generation attacking the status quo, and again unsuccessfully, a rejection of an ideology of uprisings, especially in the Prussian and Austrian territories, belongs to the most important lessons drawn from the frustrated "springtime of the peoples." Also, the belief that an international brotherhood of peoples emancipating themselves would be in a position to overthrow the old system lost many of its supporters.

The task, indeed the challenge, came to be seen more and more as one of preserving the nation as a social body; building it up and modernizing it so that it could survive conditions of accelerated change; integrating the "lower" classes and thus as a modern nation resisting increasing pressure to assimilate from the partitioning powers and their equally nationalizing societies. To do this, required "work at the foundation" (praca od podstaw), an "organic work" (praca organiczna). While restoration of the nation-state remained the final aim, priority was given to more immediate conscious steering of an inner process of nation building. At the same time, exile groups lost their previous roles as tone-setters, suppliers of ideas and dominant providers of impulses and were forced to be satisfied with the role of serving the nationalist movement in the homeland.

Tied in with this—initially, not a very well-perceived consequence both of the ideology of the praca organiczna and the direct experience of 1846/49—was a gradual "ethnicization" of an understanding of the nation. That is, Polish identity was no longer understood primarily in political and historical terms, but was increasingly considered to have ethnic content. The Polish concept of nation became a characteristic mixture, and whether this discourse on national identity is to be more ethnically or more politically defined has not yet been decided, even today.

This development, this change in national political strategy, was hardly noticed outside Poland. Metternich's damning "*Polonismus*" stereotype (quoted above) lived on, and the activities of the "*Sturmvögel der Revolution*" seemed to confirm it: the image of a united nationalist movement, the goals of which—unlike those of Romania, Italy, and Germany—could not be achieved through a partial modification of the state system, but only through total change, and because of this very radicalism could not be integrated, and thus became the incarnation of revolution and revolt. Contributing to this was a mental process that did not simply target a few revolutionaries, but the entire Polish nation. Not only did the nightmare of the "Polish scythemen," a "Sicilian vespers," and a "born anarchist" belong from then on to the canon of stereotypes, replacing the image of "noble Polish martyrs for freedom," but also the stereotype of a nation incapable of modernization, with its specific mixture of Catholicism, socialism, political revolt, and good-for-nothing nobility, remained for bourgeois Europe, and especially for German society, the absolute image of horror.

The year 1848 clearly meant the end of liberal German friendship towards Poland. In Wilhelm Jordan's infamous speech in the Frankfurt National Assembly against the Poles, one finds all seeds of German anti-*Polonismus* and anti-Slavism which were to became a requirement for several generations of German publicists. The door to a growing German-Polish antagonism was deliberately pushed wide open, a "healthy national egoism" was preached especially in this context. From this time on it became a matter of faith that German and Polish interests were incompatible and that both nations found themselves in a "life or death struggle"[27]— words which would have consequences well into the twentieth century and which continually found people willing to carry them out.

In the historical tradition of the Polish nation, the images of the revolution of 1846/49 pale somewhat in comparison to the two great uprisings of the nineteenth century, the November uprising of 1830/31 and the January uprising of 1863. While the latter, seen by contemporaries as true Polish-Russian wars, achieved an unchallenged, prominent place in the national pantheon and have become a national myth, the events of 1846/49, while being important dates for regional Galician and Poznanian traditions, are only of secondary importance for the national gallery of heroes. The fact that Warsaw and the Russian region were not included doubtless plays an important role here. The history of Poland in the twentieth century confirmed the location of tradition, indeed probably established it. The major pioneering "lieux de mémoire" are concentrated in Warsaw, and also national myth-forming without reference to Warsaw is only possible to a limited extent. Even the important role of Gdańsk in the history of resistance to the communist regime has quickly paled.

However, there are—and in this, the "springtime of the peoples" and the decade that preceded it provided the starting point—many national "lieux de mémoire" located outside Poland. The myth of the solidarity of freedom-loving peoples"— "Za waszą i naszą wolność" ["For your freedom and ours"]—for which so many Polish emigrants fought and died, which arose from a belief in real possibilities, and which was seemingly buried in 1849, has, despite all failures and bitter experience, remained to the present a part of the national canon: today it is no longer understood as a national mission, while often denounced as an illusory and romantic ballast, it remains part of the discourse of national identity—an appealing part, one that points the way toward the future.

Notes

1. *Gemeinsame deutsch-polnische Schulbuchkommission, Empfehlungen für die Schulbücher der Geschichte und Geographie in der Bundesrepublik Deutschland und in der Volksrepublik Polen,* new expanded edition (Braunschweig, 1995), 21.

2. Examples of such arguments include Roman Rosdolsky, *Die Bauernabgeordneten im konstituierenden österreichischen Reichstag 1848-1849* (Vienna, 1976), 12, 40, 70; Brigitte Biwald, *Von Gottes Gnaden oder von Volkes Gnaden? Die Revolution von 1848 in der Habsburgermonarchie: Der Bauer als Ziel politischer Agitation* (Frankfurt, 1996), 44ff.

3. See Wolfgang Häusler, "Österreich und die Polen Galiziens in der Zeit des "Völkerfrühlings" (1830-1849)," in Walter Leitsch and Maria Wawrykowa (eds.), *Polen—Österreich. Aus der Geschichte einer Nachbarschaft* (Vienna and Warsaw, 1988), 125-80; Gernot Seide, "Wiener Akten zur politisch-revolutionären Bewegung in Galizien und Krakau," *Mitteilungen des Österreichischen Staatsarchivs* 26 (1973); Arnon Gill, *Die polnische Revolution 1846. Zwischen nationalem Befreiungskampf des Landadels und antifeudaler Bauernerhebung* (Munich and Vienna, 1974); Stefan Kieniewicz, *Ruch chłopski w Galacji w r. 1846* (Wroclaw, 1951); Marion Żychowski, *Rok 1846 w Rzeczypospolitej Krakowskiej i w Galicji* (Warsaw, 1956); Marcel Szarota, *Die letzten Tage der Republik Krakau* (Breslau, 1911); Witold Jakóbczyk (ed.), *Dzieje Wielkopolski,* Vol. 2, *Lata 1793-1918* (Poznań, 1973), 186ff.

4. See Hans Henning Hahn, "Die Revolution von 1848 als Strukturkrise des europäischen Staaten-systems," in Peter Krüger (ed.), *Das europäische Staatensystem im Wandel. Strukturelle Bedingungen und bewegende Kräfte seit der Frühen Neuzeit* (Munich, 1996), 131-52.

5. See Hans Henning Hahn, "Polen im Horizont preußischer und deutscher Politik im 19. Jahrhun-dert," *Jahrbuch für die Geschichte Mittel- und Ostdeutschlands* 35 (1986): 1-19, here 3-6.

6. From the Petersburg Convention of 15/26 January 1797, quoted in Fjedor de Martens, *Recueil des traités et conventions conclus par la Russie,* Vol. 2 (St. Petersburg, 1875), 291.

7. Karol Sienkiewicz, "Dyplomacia Emigracii," *Kronika Emigracyi Polskiej* V/1 of 8 August 1836 (Paris), here quoted in Hans Henning Hahn, *Außenpolitik in der Emigration. Die Exildiplomatie Adam Jerzy Czartoryskis 1830-1840* (Munich and Vienna, 1978), 86.

8. So even before the March Revolution, the Russian Ambassador in Berlin wrote: "Now begins for us the decisive moment: the struggle against a Poland supported by all of Europe, France, Germany, Hungary, etc. etc. ....,"- P.v. Meyendorff to Nesselrode (Russian Foreign Minister) 25 Feb./8 March 1848, in Otto Hoetzsch (ed.), *Peter von Meyendorff. Ein russischer Diplomat an den Höfen von Berlin und Wien. Politischer und privater Briefwechsel 1826-1863* Vol. 2 (Berlin and Leipzig, 1923), 42.

9. A range of German press opinions are found in Józef Feldman, *Sprawa polska w roku 1848* (Cra-cow, 1933), 106-8. Also writing on this point were Gervinus, "Deutschland und Preußen," *Deutsche Zeitung* 91, 31 March 1848, and the Gagern brothers in Ludwig von Pastor, *Leben des Freiherrn Max von Gagern 1810-1889. Ein Beitrag zur politischen und kirchlichen Geschichte des 19. Jahrhunderts* (Kempten and Munich, 1912), 229-34; Heinrich von Gagern, *Das Leben des Generals Friedrich von Gagern,* Vol. 2 (Leipzig and Heidelberg, 1856), 775.

10. This episode is dealt with in greater detail in my essay cited in note 5 above.

11. Ian W. Roberts, *Nicholas I and the Russian Intervention in Hungary* (New York, 1991), 112 and pas-sim; Uwe Liszkowski, "Rußland und die Revolution von 1848/49. Prinzipien und Interessen," in *1848/49—Revolutionen in Ostmitteleuropa,* ed. by Rudolf Jaworski and Robert Luft (Munich, 1996), 343-69, here 364.

12. Ama Minkowska, *Organizacja spiskowa 1848 roku w Królestwie Polskim* (Warsaw, 1923); David Fajn-hauz, *Ruch konspiracyjny na Litwie i Białorusi 1846-1848* (Warsaw, 1965). A collection of sources can be found in *Wiosna Ludów w Królestwie Polskim. Organizacja 1848 roku,* ed. by Wlodimir A. Djakow, Stefan Kieniewicz and Wiktoria Śliwowska (Wrocław, 1994).

13. Stefan Kieniewicz, "Wiosna Ludów na ziemiach polskich," in *Wiosna Ludow,* ed. by Dyakow, Kieniewicz and Śliwowska, 3-18, here 3.

14. On Poznań in 1848 see also the still useful work of Hans Schmidt, *Die polnische Revolution des Jahres 1848 im Großherzogtum Posen,* (Weimar, 1912); from a very German nationalist viewpoint, see Wolf-

gang Kohte, *Deutsche Bewegung und preußische Politik im Posener Lande* (Poznań, 1931); Karl Heinz Streiter, *Die nationale Beziehungen im Großherzogtum Posen (1815-1848)* (Bern, 1986), 125ff.; Stefan Kieniewicz, *Społeczeństwo polskie w powstanie poznanskim*, 2nd revised ed. (Warsaw, 1960) (first edition, 1935). A very useful collection of sources is Hans Booms and Marian Wojciechowscki (eds.), *Deutsche und Polen in der Revolution 1848-1849. Dokumente aus deutschen und polnischen Archiven*, (Boppard, 1991), and Marek Rezler, *Wielkopolska Wiosna Ludów (1848 roku). Zarys dziejów militarnych* (Poznan, 1993). A good summary of the state of research can be found in Krzysztof Makowski, "Das Großherzogtum Posen im Revolutionsjahr 1848," in Jaworski and Luft (eds.), *1848/49* (Munich, 1996), 149-72.

15. Besides the works of Häusler and Seide cited above note 3 and those of Rosdolsky and Biwald cited in note 2, see Wolfgang Häusler, "Die österreichische Revolution von 1848 und die polnische Frage bis zur Einberufung des Reichstags," *Studia Austro-Polonica* 1 (1978): 107-127; Jan Kozik, "Galizische Ukrainer im konstituierenden Reichstag von Wien und Kremsier (1848-1849)," *Studia Austro-Polonica* 1 (1978): 129-55; Jan Kozik, *The Ukranian National Movement in Galicia: 1815-1849* (Edmonton, 1986), 177ff.

16. Stefan Kieniewicz, *Wiosna Ludów* , 4.

17. *Lettre d'un gentilhomme polonais sur les massacres de Galicie adressée au Prince de Metternich* (Paris, 1846). The author was Marquis Aleksander Wielopolski, who would later play a significant role in Russian Polish policy.

18. Wolfgang Häusler, "Die österreichische Revolution" 121.

19. He could refer back to the express orders of the king, that "You in all seriousness and with all your power by means of mobile columns and all means available to you should aim to restore legal order and obedience in the Province" (quoted in Otto Hoetzsch, "Die Stellung des Generals von Colomb zur Revolution in Posen und zu Willisen 1848," *Zeitschrift für Osteuropäische Geschichte* 4 (1914): 338-74, here 370). This order was in flagrant contradiction to the orders of the Minister of War, for restraint and to avoid bloodshed at all costs.

20. This and other partition plans, often modified to the disadvantage of the Poles, were given considerable discussion in the Berlin government and the Berlin and Frankfurt National Assemblies. In general they remained without consequence and were shelved in 1851 (see the literature cited in note 14, above). There were also plans to partition Galicia into eastern and western portions.

21. Stefan Kieniewicz, *Spoleczenstwo* 171.

22. Fürst Richard Metternich-Winneburg (ed.), *Aus Metternichs nachgelassenen Papieren*, Vol. 7 (Vienna, 1883), 206 (emphasis in original).

23. Lawrence D. Orton, *The Prague Slav Congress of 1848* (Boulder, 1978).

24. Kathrin Sitzler, *Solidarität oder Söldnertum. Die ausländischen Freiwilligenverbände im ungarischen Unabhängigkeitskrieg 1848-49* (Osnabrück, 1980).

25. Even in 1956 a demonstration at the monument to József Bem was one of the triggers of the Budapest uprising.

26. Ama Owsińska, *Powstanie palatynacko-badeńskie 1849 r. oraz udział w nim Polaków.* (Wrocław, 1965).

27. Jordan's remarks are taken from Franz Wigard (ed.), *Stenographischer Bericht über die Verhandlungen der deutschen constituirenden Nationalversammlung zu Frankfurt am Main*, Vol. 2 (Frankfurt, 1848-1849), 1143-51.

THE REVOLUTION OF 1848 IN MOLDAVIA AND WALLACHIA

Lothar Maier

On 20 March 1848 a group of Rumanian students and intellectuals living in Paris met in the apartment of Nicolae Bălcescu, who had called them together. With news of the revolution in Vienna fresh in their ears, they decided to set off a revolution in their homeland as well. They then agreed on a program, which included land reform with compensation for the large landowners, a guarantee of civil liberties, and a constitutional regime under the continued sovereignty of the Sultan. The Wallachians and Moldavians could not fully agree on a plan of action. The course of events, in any case, passed them by.

Their decisions had been preceded by weeks of debates on programs and strategies, in which moderates opposed the radicals who had a dominating position, thanks to Bălcescu's persuasiveness. Rumanian students had taken part in the demonstrations and fighting at the barricades of 22-24 February. In the rooms of their "Rumanian Library" they had set up a first-aid station for wounded street-fighters. Bălcescu sent his friend, Vasile Alecsandri, the most well-known poet of Rumanian romanticism, a piece of velvet that he himself had torn from Louis Philipp's throne during the storming of the Tuilleries. A delegation of Rumanians then appeared before the provisional government, carrying their own blue-gold-red tricolor with the motto "Dreptate-Frație" (Justice-Fraternity), to congratulate its members and to solicit their assistance.

Several days after the meeting of 20 March, Bălcescu and Alexandru G. Golescu traveled through Germany, Austria, and Hungary to Wallachia as the first delegates of the Paris revolutionaries. Rumanian students had long maintained contacts with Polish emigrants in Paris. Bălcescu and Golescu took the same train through Germany as Prince Adam J. Czartoryski, the leader of the moderate Polish exile organization, who was traveling with his staff to Berlin. Czartoryski promised to send Polish officers as military advisers and to arrange weapons shipments from the republican government of France.

This start might create the impression that the revolution of 1848 in Moldavia and Wallachia had its beginnings in the Quartier Latin, that it was set off by a mixture of voluntarism and romantic adventurism. And in fact, superficial or unfavorable observers have sought to explain away the Rumanian Revolution as a conflict of generations. However, the young intellectuals who were hurrying home from France in the spring of 1848 articulated a profound dissent that had arisen and accumulated through economic, social, political and cultural changes throughout the preceding decades.

Prehistory and Preconditions

Unlike other countries under Ottoman control, Moldavia and Wallachia had retained a Christian ruling elite and, well into the nineteenth century, political institutions modeled on the Byzantine Empire. The boyars, nobles divided into ranks, held government and administrative posts, for which they received landed estates in payment. Peasants were required to pay rents and provide limited labor service, generally transformed into a rent payment, in return for which they had the customary right to the use of the entire manor. The cause of more severe exploitation was a pyramid of sale of offices, extending up to the princes at the top. Every office was insecure, and the Porte in Istanbul, the end of the food chain, was becoming ever more demanding. It was therefore very important to amortize expenses as quickly as possible and to make a profit.

As a consequence of the Greek uprising, which began on Rumanian soil in 1821, the native boyars, many of whose families also came from throughout the entire Christian Orient, were finally rid of their Greek-Phanariotic competitors. However, the crucial break only came with the Treaty of Adrianople of 1829. Russia, as victor, became "protective power" and introduced a strict limitation of the rights of the Ottoman ruler. It is one of the paradoxes of Rumanian history that the two principalities were granted constitutions under Tsar Nicholas I, otherwise seen as the embodiment of reaction. These were written by Nikolai D. Kiselev, an extremely competent, enlightened bureaucrat, together with representatives of the major boyars. The intention behind this move was to win the favor of the native elite for Russia by granting a well-ordered administration in order to prepare the ground for an annexation, a Russian aim since the eighteenth century. However, it was those organs of government, modeled on Europeans ones, which probably saved the two Danube principalities from the fate of, for example, the Czerkessians, whose "political and ideological idiom" was incomprehensible to the leading great powers.[1]

In May 1831 in Wallachia and in January 1832 in Moldavia, two nearly identical "Organic Statutes" went into effect. The rather cumbersome terminology is easily explainable: the word "constitution" had to be avoided in Nicholas I's sphere of influence. However, the beginnings of constitutional government were modest. Only boyars elected the "Adunarea obsteacă" [general assembly] in two curias, and the major boyars held a majority over those of the second and third ranks. The prince, elected for life from among the major boyars, held a significant share of legislative powers; the ministers he named were not responsible to the "assembly." Justice and administration were separated; the sale of offices once again became the practice, but tax-farming remained abolished. Personal income of the princes and the state treasury were distinguished, and a proper budget was planned. Boyars and clergy were freed of direct taxes. In "constitutional reality," constant interference by the protective power was a decisive factor. The great advance consisted of a rationalization of institutions and a reduction in arbitrariness. There was an unmistakable tendency towards oligarchy in the dominant influence the boyars received.

In other respects as well, boyar handwriting could be seen in the Organic Statutes. In agrarian legislation, they were able to exert their influence over that of Kiselev, who was pushing forward the abolition of serfdom in Russia. Peasants were given small parcels of land. The exact size of these parcels depended on the peasant's ability to provide labor-services, but were generally too small to support a family. The peasants' land was burdened with both labor services and a tithe. The remaining manorial land, probably at least a third of the total, became the unrestricted property of the boyars; the peasants previous usage rights to it were abolished. The boyars were no longer entitled *Stăpíni de mosie* [lord of the manor] but *Proprietari* [owners], while the peasants came to be known officially as *Locuitori* [residents], with no rights to the land. Although labor services remained de jure the same at twelve days per year, it was de facto increased considerably through a written recording of obligations. Because the land assigned them was not sufficient to support them, and certainly too small to maintain the still high level of livestock that was their basis of prosperity, peasants were forced to lease further estate property in "free contracts." The leases were paid with labor services. About a quarter of the peasants still lived in free villages. Their situation is not relevant here.

The causes of these changes lay in new possibilities for export. After the Treaty of Adrianople, the Porte's monopoly on foreign trade and its right of first refusal for the purchase of farm products, never totally enforceable, were abolished and Danube harbors and the Straits opened to international shipping. In the Habsburg Monarchy, as well as in England and France, demand for agricultural products was rising. The boyars had created the legal basis with which they could employ unpaid peasant labor and the peasants' own farm equipment to produce wheat for export on those parts of their manors freed from the peasants' usage rights.

This concept could not, however, be easily implemented. First, peasants rebelled in many parts of the country against the new regulations. Russian troops were sent to quell the uprisings. However, a relative lack of labor in relation to exploitable land, as well as a lack of capital and of know-how among the boyars, favored the peasants. Only in Moldavia were estate owners able to start production on their land reserve under their own control and in part with their own equipment. In Wallachia, peasants were able to maintain control of the manors. They successfully resisted surveying, which would have separated their lands from those of the boyars. Rent for the lease of extra land was transformed from labor services into cash payments.

Some peasants were therefore able to profit from the export boom at first, although lease prices rose rapidly and they found themselves at a disadvantage in dealing with wholesale traders in the Danube harbors. In Wallachia, estate owners sold that share of the harvest which they received as tithe. In Moldavia, on the other hand, they produced considerably more grain and livestock for export on their reserves than the peasants, who were generally limited to subsistence agriculture. Around 1843, pressures on the peasantry increased in Wallachia as well. Administrative measures were brought in to support the endeavors of estate owners to have their reserves worked by labor services. The struggle for the control of export production, in which the state, dominated by the boyars, promoted the interests of the estate owners, created a great potential for unrest in the 1840s.

The legal security offered by the Organic Statutes, despite all their problems, and the increasing demand from the European grain markets, precipitated social changes. Somewhat delayed in comparison to Western Europe, there was a rapid growth in population in Moldavia and Wallachia, which increased still further due to immigration from neighboring countries. Urban growth was over-proportional because of movement from the land. The population of both Bucharest and Iaşi reached 60,000 at the end of the 1840s. In the nineteenth century, there were no comparable urban centers in the Balkans with the exception of Saloniki. Furthermore, there were the Danube harbors, which until the Treaty of Adrianople, were fortified Ottoman bridgeheads with generously measured environs. They profited from the grain export trade and attracted Greek traders especially, among whom British subjects from the Ionian islands had the most advantageous conditions. Changes in the structure of domestic trade gave rise to the development of market towns, spread evenly across both principalities.

Previously farmers had made up the vast majority of the urban population, but in the 1830s and 1840s, their share declined, and the number of small traders, and of artisans especially increased. The Organic Statutes spoke of free trade but did not abolish the guilds, which were becoming increasingly restrictive. The vast majority of town dwellers belonged to the lowest of the three tax classes into which the Organic Statutes divided non-farm businesses. Among them, and even more so among the wholesalers, the share of foreigners was high. Because of the Ottoman Empire's capitulations to the European powers, many of these stood under the protection of foreign consulates. One the one hand, this engendered a need for integration, giving the national idea an important function (which meant either the exclusion of foreigners, as was the case of Jews in Moldavia, or their integration, as was the case of Bulgars in Wallachia). On the other hand, the existence of the capitulations, from which economic competitors benefited, promoted the desire for independence from Turkish rule. The Organic Statutes had created the preconditions throughout the 1840s for the appearance of members of the educated professions in urban areas, such as teachers, doctors, and pharmacists, but also lawyers and surveyors. The latter were important for the boyars because of a rise in the value of land due to the boom in grain exports.

As a consequence of these economic and social changes, a potential for discontent gathered in the towns, which could be politically mobilized. Neither in the severity of complaints, nor in numerical strength, was this potential to be compared with the condition of the peasants. But opposition in the main cities and even more so in the suburbs could be more quickly directed against the government because of its proximity to centers of power. In the period of the Organic Statutes, and reaching a high point in 1848, a culture of public political discourse began to develop, fostered through newspapers, pamphlets and mass meetings with speeches, that, in the form of large demonstrations and street disturbances, could be employed in the struggle against the ruling powers.

There was a considerable rise in the number of boyars after the Treaty of Adrianople. The economically successful bought their way into the class, and they also preferred to invest in landed estates, where grain exports promised secure profits. The new entrees, while having many interests in common with the old elite, did not share their value system. They were given the unflattering sobriquet "*ciocoi*," which means unscrupulous nouveau riche. One or two generations later, the term came to be applied by peasants to all estate owners. Tensions also arose between large estate owners, who owned latifundia and who, because of the grain boom, saw no reason to change their method of exploiting their estates, and second and third class boyars, who were more likely to be interested in increasing productivity on their smaller estates and in processing their farm products themselves. The interests of these more innovative boyars were closer to those of the wholesalers and entrepreneurs. There were, however, only a few factories, which produced mostly foodstuffs from the raw materials provided by local agriculture. Free trade policies towards the end of the century reduced their numbers still further.

The Organic Statutes granted extensive political powers to the first class boyars. However, because the prince himself came from their ranks and built up his own clientele, heated political struggles sometimes broke out between "ins" and "outs." The losers of these struggles would sometimes then make use of liberal and national ideas and programs, which possessed the potential to burst the bounds of the existing political system. In this way, the old ruling elite had once again lost the homogeneity it had so recently gained by the expulsion of phanariotic Greeks; additionally, the families of the major boyars began to be broken up by generational conflicts. Their sons, returning from their studies in Western Europe, could no longer share their fathers' political and cultural world view. Young intellectuals, who corresponded with French early socialists, came home to estates where Gypsies were still held as slaves. The new generation took up the conflicts of a changing society and articulated them in the language of liberalism and nationalism which they had absorbed.

Following the Treaty of Adrianople, the shift in cultural orientation from the Byzantine Christian Orient to the West accelerated. French replaced modern Greek as the language of the educated. Even in the eighteenth century, a narrow stratum of the educated had become acquainted with the works of the French Enlightenment in Greek translation. At the beginning of the nineteenth century the system of higher education in both principalities was reorganized by Rumanian academics from the Habsburg Monarchy. They introduced the ideas of the "Transylvanian School," which made an ideology of the "Latinness" of the Rumanian language, an important precondition for the rise of a Rumanian national idea. Even before the Greek insurrection, Greek as a language of teaching was being replaced by Rumanian and the curriculum reformed along Western lines.

Rumanian Orthodoxy was thus faced with the task of uniting religion with secular scholarship. The Metropolitans of Moldavia in particular made use of the experiences of the Russian church, which had faced this problem one hundred years previously, by sending young clergy to study in Kiev. Through these connections, and through Rumanians from Bessarabia who had studied at Russian universities and moved to the two principalities, the Rumanian intelligentsia took up the ideas of the Slavophiles, which promoted the development of a romantic nationalism. While this Russian influence is much less important than the French one, it should not be totally ignored, as is common to both Rumanian and Western scholarship.

As foreign travels became easier under the Russian protectorate, a first generation of sons of boyar families began to study in Western Europe, generally in Paris. There, they became more aware of how much Moldavia and Wallachia had in common politically and culturally, strengthening a desire for unification. In the meantime, an opposition group was active in Bucharest and Iaşi, which called itself the "national party" and worked towards such aims as unification of the two principalities and independence from Russian influence—in both conspiratorial and legal fashion. Czartoryski's Polish exile organization in Paris began to develop an interest in the exploitation of the potential of the two Danube principalities for a Polish uprising, offered guidance to the Rumanian students in Paris. In 1838, Czartoryski sent Janusz Woronicz, one of his closest colleagues, to Rumania. Together with the leader of the "national party," Ion Câmpineanu, and supported by the British Consul Robert G. Colquhoun, he drew up a national program that included unification of Moldavia and Wallachia under a hereditary monarchy, independence from the Ottoman Empire, and an end to interference by the Russian protectorate. This was followed by a draft constitution rather advanced for the time.

Quite remarkable are the parallels to the Serbs, who would also develop their national program with the assistance of Czartoryski's organization, six years later. With the second war between Muhammed Ali, the viceroy of Egypt, and the Sultan setting off an Eastern crisis, the activities of the "national party," supported by the Poles, reached their highpoint. At first, the two princes had nothing against exploiting the movement to create greater freedom of action for themselves in foreign policy, but then, under pressure from Russia, had its leaders arrested or expelled from the country.

Following this fiasco, leadership of the opposition transferred to the students in Paris, whose circles expanded up to 1848 and who maintained close contacts with former students. A clearly defined group arose, with common experiences, a common cultural orientation, and common political aims. Because their finances were generally assured by family estates, the Rumanian students had little need of a degree. They therefore, mostly frequented the Collège de France, where no exams were given, but which offered the chance of coming into contact with the French opposition to the July Monarchy and exiled representatives of central and eastern European national movements. Intellectually, the Rumanian students were influenced by the lectures of Jules Michelet, Edgar Quinet, and Adam Mickiewicz.

The ideas of romanticism, which they absorbed from this milieu, made a powerful impression on this whole generation's intimately inter-related conceptions of aesthetics and politics. History, folklore, and their native landscape became the subject of a literature assigned political and didactic tasks. The "nation" became a term that also legitimated demands for political participation. However, these demands were no longer restricted to ensuring a share of power for second and third rank boyars, as had been the case a generation earlier, but extended to include new bourgeois classes and even peasants, with their specific concerns.

The paradigm of the "nation," borrowed from the West, needed to be filled with indigenous meaning. Using inspirations from Paris, and in part, from the Russian Slavophiles, Rumanian intellectuals began a search for their own popular culture. In this, they lagged considerably behind comparable movements among the Serbs and Greeks. The recording of folksongs, for example, and their adaptation for contemporary poetry was not anywhere near completion in 1848. Boyar sons returning from Paris were totally oriented towards Western models in their thinking and aesthetic judgements. The cultural gap that separated them from the peasants was hardly any smaller than for their fathers, but a romantic interest in folklore offered at least a bridge towards understanding.

In the 1840s, the national opposition was making itself heard both in Paris and in the two principalities. In the country, its leading members were attempting, with the help of newspapers and legal organizations—constantly hindered by the censor—to establish and spread a national historiography and literature. After his involvement with the unsuccessful movement of 1840, Nicolae Bălcescu was imprisoned in a monastery. Shortly after his release in 1843 he founded, with Ion Ghica (one of the first Rumanians to study in Paris), a secret political organization, "Frăţia" [Fraternity], modeled on the Freemasons. Their intention was to be prepared in case the possibility for revolt arose. Although in part beyond student age, the brothers Dumitru and Ion C. Brătianu, C.A. Rosetti, Alexander C. Golescu (the cousin of A.G. Golescu, who traveled from Paris to Wallachia at the end of March 1848), Mihail Kogălniceanu and the agricultural expert Ion Ionescu de la Brad founded the "Society of Rumanian Students in Paris" in December 1845. When Bălcescu arrived in Paris in July 1846, he took over leadership of this society, which led to its radicalization. From then on, majority opinion held that economic and social changes necessary in the Danubian principalities could only be achieved through revolution and that the masses therefore had to be won over through intensive propaganda. However, at first the group's endeavors were directed rather towards making their national claims known and gaining sympathy for their cause throughout Europe. A library was founded; reading and meeting rooms were rented near the university. The poet Alphonse de Lamartine, after the revolution of 1848 the first French foreign minister, accepted the post of honorary president. The approximately thirty founders and original members of the society included most of the Rumanians from the two principalities who would play a role in the 1848 revolution there.

The Petition Movement in Iaşi and Reaction in Moldavia

As the first Moldavians sought to return from Paris to their homeland, they were turned away at the border, as the reaction had already been victorious in their country. In Moldavia, the domestic situation was especially tense in the spring of 1848. Prince Mihail Sturdza, after an opportunistic flirt with the "national party," had founded a corrupt and authoritarian regime, angered large landowners, trade and industry and crafts, as well as the peasants, and had long since abandoned the legality of the Organic Statutes. Elections for the general assembly in the summer of 1847 took place under compulsion, with fraud and arbitrary arrests. Complaints to the Russian protectorate were ignored.

The Moldavians Costache Negri, Iancu Alecsandri (the brother of the poet) and Nicolae Ionescu only left Paris on 8 April as events in Iaşi had already begun to advance rapidly. There have been conjectures that this delay was related to a postponement of a Polish uprising, originally planned for 15 April. After the unsuccessful uprising of 1846, Polish émigrés were present in large numbers in Moldavia and well organized. Even if they were not aware of such deliberations, it is clear that members of the "national party" in the country would not begin anything before their co-conspirators arrived from the West. Certainly, in the broad movement which had begun in Moldavia at the end of March, they played no significant leadership role.

During this period, opposition boyars met to discuss aims and strategies. In view of the tense situation, Guéroult, the French Consul, and Richthofen, the Prussian Consul in Iaşi, advised the prince to agree to compromises, in order to check the obviously growing resistance movement. Sturdza rejected this advice and announced that he would oppose demands for change with force, if necessary. A circular from Nesselrode, the Russian Foreign Minister, declaring that Russia would maintain the old order in that part of the Ottoman Empire controlled by it militarily, and doubtless also assurances from the Russian Consul, encouraged him in his stance. After the revolutions in Vienna and Berlin, however, Russia seemed isolated and internationally weakened.

Some months before, in view of the commercial interests of the German Customs Union, Prussia had distanced itself from Russia's policies in the Danubian Principalities, and Richthofen, overstepping his authority, openly favored the opposition in Iaşi. The French Consul felt that the prince's position had been so weakened that his opponents among the boyars would have had no difficulties in removing him from office and declaring Moldavia's independence and its unification with Wallachia. In his view, the prince only had a chance of staying in office if he placed himself at the head of the movement. Instead, Sturdza prohibited all meetings and banned the leaders of the opposition from the capital.

This did not prevent the moderate boyar opposition from laying the groundwork for peaceful protests throughout Moldavia. With the broadest petition campaign possible, they sought to bring an end to misgovernment. In response, the prince gave the appearance of being willing to compromise in order to bring his opponents out into the open. On the evening of 8 April about a thousand people gathered in the Hotel Petersburg in Iaşi: boyars, intellectuals, traders, and craftsman from the capital. There were no peasant representatives present. The prince sent his Minister of the Interior and his Chief of Police. The presence of a large number of people, a feeling of solidarity which extended beyond class borders, and the impression of being carried along by the advancing revolutionary movements in Europe gave the meeting a sense of strength. The mood was such that the participants felt themselves to be a national assembly with a right to direct the government along the correct path. It was not subdued by a threatening speech from the Minister of the Interior, who attacked the "revolutionary spirit" in the hall. But instead of using their position of strength, the assembly resolved to break up and assign a commission of sixteen people the task of bringing together and formally posing the demands raised in the assembly.

Representatives of the Paris organization were also active in the commission. Apart from the chairman, the poet Vasile Alecsandri, Alexander Cuza, later prince of a united Moldavia and Wallachia, was involved. The petition movement apparently came as surprise to the intellectual revolutionaries. Alecsandri neither approved of its peaceful methods without any power base, nor of its modest aims. Nonetheless, he took part in order not to lose control, but also in the hope that the petition movement could set off an uprising of the lower classes, especially the peasants.

The demands of the Hotel Petersburg assembly were put together, in some haste and not very well ordered, making thirty-five points. Central to these demands was a restoration of legality on the basis of the Organic Statutes, as well as the elimination of corruption and violent abuses of the administration, and a more humane criminal law. The "general assembly," whose current complexion was due to violent government interference in the elections, was to be dissolved and new fair elections held. Moreover, the legislative branch was to be strengthened by public sessions, a right to legislative initiative and a right of petition. Noticeable were the numerous wishes for improvements in trade and industry: export duties, which had greatly angered estate owners, were to be abolished, the Galati horbor extended, a trade bank and a national bank founded, a commercial court established, and French commercial law introduced. An improvement in the situation of the peasants was called for, but only in very general terms.

As far as the interests of the intelligentsia were concerned, demands for an ending of censorship were only made for domestic affairs, and teaching in the upper schools was to be in the language of the country and not in French. Shortly before, the government had introduced French as the language of instruction with the intention of later making it more difficult to study abroad. The opposition had condemned these measures as an attack on national values. No mention was made of the larger national goals of unification and independence.

By the evening of 9 April, 800 signatures had been gathered for this list. Even the metropolitan of Moldavia, who was ex officio president of the "general assembly," gave his support. Through the offices of the Minister of the Interior, a delegation presented its demands in a petition to the prince on 10 April. Sturdza was under pressure from both the general unrest in the country and from the Russian Consul. He must have feared that conceding to these demands would have been the beginning of an erosion of his power. In his predicament, he pretended to be willing to make compromises while at the same time preparing a suppression of the movement. Because there was a danger that the Moldavian militia would take sides with the movement, he had already armed a private army of about 1,000, composed of Serbs, Bulgarians, and especially Albanians. He promised the delegation to grant thirty-three of their demands, but rejected a dissolution of the "general assembly" and a reintroduction of Rumanian as language of instruction. When the delegation pressed for acceptance of all their demands in threatening tones, it provided an excuse to break up the meeting. The following night, about 300 participants in the petition movement were arrested and mistreated. Leading members of the "national party" were able to escape abroad. The counter-revolution had gained its first victory on the margins of Europe.

While suspects were being hunted down throughout the country, leading Moldavian revolutionaries met in Cernăuti [Czernowitz], near the border, and founded the "Moldavian Revolutionary Committee," which kept in close contact with its allies in Transylvania and in Wallachia. For this committee, Mihail Kogălniceanu wrote a brochure in August, "Demands of the National Party in Moldavia," in which were summarized the most important programmatic writings of Rumanian revolutionaries. He ended his list of demands with the "keystone, without which the entire national construction would collapse … *the unification of Moldavia with Wallachia.*"[2]

Nonetheless, at the same time he wrote a draft constitution just for Moldavia, the only totally worked out and applicable one to appear in the revolution of 1848 in Rumania. He based his work on the usual models, above all the Belgian constitution, on the program of his fellow revolutionaries, published in the meantime, as well as on knowledge gained in his study of law in Lunéville and Berlin. Remarkable in the "Draft Constitution for Moldavia" is the extremely strong position assigned to the legislative branch, so that one could speak of a parliamentary system rather than a constitutional one. While the unicameral parliament was to be elected on a franchise based on property and education, a gradual transition to universal suffrage was foreseen. Parliament was to elect a prince for five years to sanction the laws passed by it, but who had no right of veto. The prince was to appoint and dismiss government ministers, who were responsible to the parliament. Although elected councils were to play a role in local administration, a centralist tendency was recognizable. Great care was given to a separation of administration and justice and to a four-tiered court system. Abolition of labor services and a distribution of estates among the peasants with compensation for the estate owners was included, as were demands for economic and administrative reforms, which reflected the interests of the business community. Human rights and civil liberties were called for in a detailed catalog.

Perhaps because the revolutionary movement in Moldavia was suppressed at its outset and the Moldavian leaders of the "national party" were therefore not confronted with practical political and administrative problems, we have it to thank for the most, and the most weighty, theoretical statements. In this respect, constitutional demands and above all Kogălniceanu's draft constitution are especially important, as in the further course of events, forms of constitutionalism became more important for the Rumanian "forty-eighters" than socioeconomic principles. While Kogălniceanu was able to dedicate his time to the formulation of a detailed program, the energies of revolutionaries in Wallachia were absorbed by the practical experiment of establishing a new government.

The Experiment of a Revolutionary Government in Wallachia

When the two emissaries from Paris, Bălcescu and Alexandru G. Golescu, crossed the border into Wallachia on 8 April, they found all strata of the population, from officers to peasants, in a state of excited expectation of a revolution. Even before they reached Bucharest, they had worked out a plan for a revolt with Christian Tell, a major in the Wallachian militia. In March, members of the Frăția, among others C. A. Rosetti, Ion Ghica, and the Golescu brothers (the cousins of Alexander), had founded a secret revolutionary committee. On 20 April, the two newly arrived emissaries proposed to this committee to begin the revolt three days later, on Easter Sunday. The majority rejected this date as premature. Playing a role in their decision, apart from the awareness that their preparations had not yet been completed, might have been a wish to wait for the Polish Revolution. On 21 April, the brothers Dumîtru and Ion C. Brătianu arrived in Bucharest and reported that the French Foreign Minister, Lamartine, had promised assistance. Their arrival strengthened the radical faction. As compensation, Ion Heliade Rădulescu, a writer and teacher, and other moderates were co-opted.

The British General Consul in Bucharest, Robert Colquhoun attempted to dissuade the Prince, Gheorghe Bibescu, from applying repressive measures and advised him to accommodate the reform demands of the "national party." He also tried to persuade his Russian colleague, Kotzebue, to follow the same line. However, on 8 April Kotzebue showed him an official note in which Nesselrode stated that the Russian government would continue in its policy of noninterference in the internal affairs of states in which revolutions had broken out, but that it would seek to prevent any change in the status quo in those parts of the Ottoman Empire to which Russia had been granted a protectorate in international treaties, by force if necessary.

This statement, intended for publication, raised fears that the Tsar intended to exploit the momentary weakness of France, Prussia, and Austria to find an excuse to occupy and annex the two principalities. The first principle of Palmerston's Eastern policy, on the other hand, was to protect the integrity of the Ottoman Empire. Hence, Colquhoun advised the Wallachian opposition to seek reforms as concessions from the Porte and to respect its sovereignty. As, however, the Turkish government was de facto incapable of action without the "protective power" Russia in Moldavia and Wallachia, the situation was contradictory and foreign policy options were relatively limited.

In the meantime, the Russian government had completed preparations for a military intervention in the two principalities. Tsar Nicholas I sent his adjutant, General Alexander O. Duhamel, on a special mission to Iaşi and Bucharest. In Wallachia, he attempted to persuade the prince—who was of two minds, not being totally opposed to reform—to have liberals arrested, using a combination of threat of intervention and promise of assistance. He publicly showed his disdain for the country's dignitaries and clearly distanced himself from the British and French General Consuls. At the behest of the Russians, the Porte also sent a special envoy, Talaat Efendi. Despite Duhamel's protests, Talaat also contacted members of the revolutionary committee and maintained good relations with representatives of the Western powers. Like Colguhoun, Talaat tried to hold Bibescu back from provocation and to persuade the liberals of the disadvantages of a violent revolt.

The committee made intensive efforts to maintain good relations with the Western powers and the Porte and at the end of May sent Ion Ghica to Istanbul. He had good contacts with supporters of the Ottoman reform movement and was friends with Czartoryski's representative to the Porte. With Polish, English, and French support, he was to try to convince the Porte that reforms, indeed even abolition of the Organic Statutes was not directed against the sovereignty of the Sultan, but rather that it was constant Russian intervention in the Danubian Principalities which violated Ottoman interests. His final aim, however, was to secure neutrality of the Porte towards a revolt. Outside encouragement came with the announcement that a Polish officer from Czartoryski's organization would serve as military adviser, and with the arrival of a special emissary from Lamartine. The success of the Transylvanian Rumanians also had a stimulating effect.

The revolutionary committee formed an executive, consisting of Bălcescu, A.G. Golescu, and Rosetti. Heliade Rădulescu and Bălcescu drew up a program in the form of a proclamation. Three thousand emissaries of the committee fanned out through the entire country. They engaged in intensive propaganda work, especially among the peasants. The large majority of merchants and artisans in Bucharest already stood behind the revolutionaries. An uprising was to begin simultaneously in Bucharest and various sites in the provinces. Although Bibescu, under Duhamel's influence, no longer seemed open to compromise, he was to be kept as prince and forced to support the program.

In Oltenia, the western region of Wallachia, support for the revolutionaries was especially strong. In this region, they could also count on the backing of the militia.

On 21 June, a crowd, composed primarily of peasants and soldiers of the militia, gathered in Islaz, a small Oltenian town on the Danube. Heliade Rădulescu, Gheorghe Magheru, the head of a Oltenian district administration, Tell, another officer, and the priest Radu Şapca had called the meeting. Heliade read the program of the revolutionary movement as the "proclamation of Islaz," and the priest had the crowd swear by it. The organizers had themselves confirmed as a provisional government.

The proclamation of Islaz became the most influential program of the Rumanian Revolution and in the following three months it was treated as a provisional constitution. In regard to foreign relations, the proclamation showed itself very open to compromise. The Porte was practically courted. Its sovereignty was recognized, but it was emphasized that this sovereignty was based on protective treaties from the time of Ottoman expansion which allowed the principalities to form their laws and administration independently. This old right of "internal sovereignty" had been violated by the Russian protectorate. Its restoration, therefore, also meant securing the integrity of the Ottoman Empire. While the one national goal, independence, was thus surrendered, another, unification, was hinted at towards the end. A nation consisting of over eight million souls would know how to defend itself against attacks from outside. This figure of eight million included not only the Moldavians, but also the Rumanians in the Habsburg Monarchy.

Nonetheless, unity was the great theme, a unity of the nation above and beyond all social barriers. Every Rumanian of every class was a part of the people, from whom sovereignty arises. At nearly every point in the program it was reiterated that for this reason nobody's rights were to be violated; that the demands were raised for everyone's benefit. Entreaties of social harmony permeated the entire appeal. However, the individual points, insofar as they referred to a reorganization of domestic relations, were anything but moderate. The Organic Statutes were to be abolished. A parliament was to be chosen in a "broad, free, just" election.[3] A prince was to be elected for a five year period; eligibility for this office was not to be restricted to members of a particular social order. The prince's civil list was to be modest so that he had no possibility of corruption. Ministers and civil servants were to be held responsible for their actions. Every district was to have the right to elect its civil servants. An equality of political and civil liberties, abolition of ranks, of capital and of corporal punishment, liberation of Gypsy slaves, freedom of the press, freedom of assembly and speech and equal rights to education were decreed. Taxes were to be proportional to the property owned by the taxpayer. Bălcescu succeeded in having included what was probably the most momentous point, number thirteen: serfs were to be freed, given land, and their former lords compensated. On the basis of these points, resolved by the Rumanian people, a constituent assembly, in which all interests of the nation had to be represented, was to work out a constitution.

A march from Oltenia to Bucharest was not necessary. The prince had had some members of the committee arrested on 22 June. However, he found no support, either among the militia or among the city's business community, for a suppression of the revolution. The lower classes of Bucharest and its suburbs joined the revolution, supported by peasants who poured into the city with the proclamation of Islaz in their hands. Still shaken by an attempted assassination the day before, the prince received a delegation of revolutionaries on 23 June, signed the "constitution" of Islaz, and named a provisional government consisting of members of the revolutionary committee. The Russian Consul General, Kotzebue, accused him of violating his duties as head of state and favoring the revolution, and left the country in protest. Between pressure from the revolution and Russian threats, the prince's position had become intolerable. In the night of the 25th to 26th of June he abdicated and fled across the border to the Transylvanian city of Braşov [Kronstadt]. Following this, the governments formed in Izlas and Bucharest were united to form a provisional government under the nominal presidency of the Metropolitan Neofit.

The government demonstrated its ability to mobilize the masses by organizing a celebration on 27 June on the Filaret field near Bucharest said to have been attended by around 30,000 people. The field was renamed "field of freedom." In the following months, the government regularly assembled the lower classes from the city and peasants from the surrounding areas on this field in times of crisis to engage their support. The radicals Bălcescu, Ion C. Brătianu, A.G. Golescu, and Rosetti were only given the office of "secretary" in the government, but nonetheless played a significant role because they were able to mobilize the masses. Bălcescu and Rosetti immediately made use of the freedom of the press and published two newspapers with which they spread the program of the revolution among the petit bourgeoisie of the cities as well as among the peasants.

Parts of the program, such as a guarantee of political liberties, abolition of ranks, capital and corporal punishment and liberation of Gypsy slaves, were put into practice by decree immediately after the new government had been formed. Political prisoners were freed and steps were taken to establish a national guard. The government's most important task to secure its new position, the organization of elections for a constituent assembly, quickly led to public disputes in the press between moderates around Heliade and radicals around Bălcescu. On 10 July, moderates proposed dividing 300 seats equally among "interests." This proposal was quickly denounced in the radical press, which argued that it would mean that 7,000 major landowners, 50,000 businessmen, artisans and intellectuals, and 1,850,000 peasants would each choose 100 deputies. In the end, the radicals carried the day. A decree of 26 July provided for 250 deputies to represent 10,000 people each. Seats were distributed according to population among the seventeen districts and the two cities of Bucharest and Craiova. Unlike in the cities, representatives of the countryside were to be elected indirectly. Electors were to be chosen on the 21, and deputies on 30 August, and the assembly opened on 6 September. Especially in rural districts, campaigning was quite lively. In some places, the date of the first round of voting was moved up, so that the initial balloting had already taken place by 16 August, when elections were suspended under pressure from outside threats.

Threats to the new government became obvious immediately after the revolt. Conservative boyars had support in the militia. They reckoned with an intervention from abroad and openly resisted the new government. On 1 July, Colonel Ioan

Odobescu, commander of the militia, who had been given a seat in the government, together with Ioan Soloman, commandant of a regiment of the Bucharest garrison, staged a putsch. Ministers were held captive, but immediately freed by an armed crowd, who in turn arrested the rebels. This counter-strike had been organized by the radicals. That a woman, Ana Ipătescu, armed with two pistols, inspired the masses from the front lines became part of a national legend. Representatives of the revolutionary government, looking for support in Hungary, Germany, and England, quickly made use of this image for propaganda purposes.

On 7 July, Russian troops crossed the border of Moldavia and occupied Iaşi on 10 July. Conservative boyars were able to stir up a feeling of panic, and the government precipitously fled to the Carpathians. Its nominal president, the Metropolitan Neofit, then revealed his true political sympathies by proclaiming the restoration of the old government and appointing an administration consisting of reactionary major boyars. However, once again the masses from the lower classes of Bucharest and its suburbs, reinforced by the peasants, foiled a restoration and made possible the provisional government's return.

Conditions for a military defense of the revolution were not favorable. The militia, formed along the lines of the Organic Statutes, was not trustworthy. Nearly all programs demanded the establishment of a national guard, on the French model. In the course of the three months left to the government, about 20,000 national guardsmen were enlisted, of them over 10,000 in Bucharest. But there were only 700 rifles available for the guardsmen of Bucharest. In district centers, and all the more so in the villages, the national guard had almost no firearms. It played only a modest role as honor guard and in securing domestic order.

Already at the beginning of 1848, the prince had named Gheorghe Magheru, administrative head of a district in Oltenia, commander of irregular troops—the Dorobrantzes and Pandours—to defend against an attack which, according to obscure rumors, threatened from Transylvania. Magheru had distinguished himself as leader of the Pandours in the Russian-Turkish War of 1828/29. Dorobrantzes were generally recruited from among the serfs and assigned to the district administration. They served the preservation of the old order. Magheru strengthened these units and converted them into protectors of the revolution. The Pandours had a long tradition in the mountainous northern border region of Oltenia as voluntary units formed above all from local free peasants. They had taken part in Austrian and Russian wars against the Turks, especially with their own liberation as their aim.

In Oltenia, the recruiting campaign was successful. Near Rîureni on the upper Olt, these irregular units were put together in a camp and trained with the help of Polish military advisers. Because Wallachia had no arms production and all attempts up to the end of the revolution to purchase arms abroad failed, these units were extremely poorly equipped. Old rifles, which had been confiscated from the peasants by the authorities because of a fear of an uprising, were gathered and repaired. These, however, could not have amounted to over one thousand weapons. Shortly before the final Turkish and Russian intervention, there were about 12,000 Pandours and a few thousand Dorobrantzes gathered in Rîureni, consisting mostly of highly motivated peasants, who were supported by the civilian population. They knew the region well, whose terrain, had they been sufficiently armed, would have allowed long resistance against numerically superior troops.

It was impossible for the government in Bucharest to know that Nicholas I did not wish to intervene in Wallachia as developments in Western Europe still seemed unclear. Even the invasion of Moldavia had not been intended by St. Petersburg and certainly did not fit into the plans of Russian diplomacy. In a circular note of 31 July, Nesselrode, the Russian foreign minister, explained that Russian intervention was justified by international treaties, that it took place in agreement with the Porte, and that it was only temporary. The entire note was apologetic in tone and was meant to ease Great Power worries about Russian intentions. However, for the provisional government in Wallachia, the announcement that neither the Turkish nor the Russian government would allow changes in the political system along the lower Danube must have appeared extremely threatening.

An existential threat for the entire Rumanian national movement for 1848 and beyond, was, however, contained in the official statement by the "protecting power" that the revolutionaries were drawing on "an alleged nationality, the origins of which are lost in the darkness of centuries," and "the historical basis of which never existed."[4] The "Moldo-Wallachians" were denied the ability to found and maintain a stable, independent state. Kogălniceanu, in his "Demands of the National Party of Moldavia," filled pages disputing Nesselrode's claims. The denial of a right to existence of the Rumanian nation they contained makes understandable the revolutionary obsession with ideas of nation and a constitutional state in decades following 1848.

Even if Nicholas I did not wish to intervene in Wallachia, there was still a real danger of a Turkish invasion as a consequence of diplomatic pressure from Russia. The provisional government sent prominent representatives to Paris, Vienna, Budapest, and to the National Assembly in Frankfurt to gain foreign protection, and courted above all the British Consul General, Robert Colquhoun. Most important were Ion Ghica's endeavors to convince Ottoman dignitaries that abolition of the Organic Statutes did not affect the sovereignty of the Sultan. From him came warnings that the Porte did not approve of the radicalism of the new government's measures.

In the end, the Porte succumbed to Russian pressure and sent Suleiman Pascha to replace Talaat Efendi—together with a 20,000-man-strong army of occupation. A representative of the provisional government assured Suleiman that Turkish sovereignty would not be infringed upon. Nonetheless, on 31 July the army crossed the Danube and occupied Giurgiu. Suleiman announced that he intended to restore the old order on the basis of the Organic Statutes. His government had, however, also assigned him the task of giving a hearing to the complaints of the revolutionaries. These in turn made use of differences between Russian and Turkish interests and accepted Colquhoun's mediation.

After lengthy negotiations, led in Bucharest by a representative of Suleiman, a compromise was reached. The provisional government resigned, to be replaced by a "princely regency" [*Logotenenţa domnească*], made up of Heliade Rădulescu, Christian Tell, and Nicolae Golescu, moderate members of the government. They agreed to suspend the "constitution" of Islaz until it had been confirmed by the Sultan. On 16 August the regency sent a note to the Sultan containing twenty-two points, and asking for his approval. At the same time, elections for a constituent assembly were suspended. When the compromise had been reached, Suleiman, who had up until then avoided direct contact, came to Bucharest to meet the new government on 10 August. This was generally understood as official recognition of the revolutionary government by the Porte, and representatives of the Great Powers took up official contact with the regency at Suleiman's invitation.

During this crisis, as the Turkish army stood ready in Giurgiu to march into Bucharest, the conservative boyar opposition was preparing a coup. A propaganda war began for Suleiman's opinion and favor, in which Magheru used his irregular units to keep conservatives away from the Turkish camp. At the same time, the government was able to mobilize peasants with a large-scale propaganda campaign. In the villages, meetings were called by government commissioners and delegates sent to Bucharest to announce their satisfaction with the new state. Around 15,000 met on the Filaret field and remained in the city during negotiations with Suleiman. The Ottoman commissar allowed 100 peasants to come and respectfully declare their agreement with the new government.

The paramount importance of the peasantry as support for the new government forced the revolutionaries to take their interests very seriously. However, expectations that an immediate ending of labor services on the estates would severely impair grain production led to a postponement of the thirteenth point of the proclamation of Islaz, which foresaw the liberation of the peasants and their being granted land, immediately after it had been presented. On 27 June, peasants were requested to continue to fulfil their services. Changes were to be postponed until the end of October, that is after the end of the growing season.

Many barriers stood in the way of fulfilling the promises to the peasants. Agrarian reform provoked bitter resistance to the new government among the boyars. A large proportion of the revolutionaries themselves lived from their estates. Soon doubts were raised as to whether such fundamental changes could be implemented by decree instead of leaving them to the planned constituent assembly. It was open to interpretation whether the peasants should receive only the small parcels of land for cultivation to which they were entitled according to the Organic Statutes. A transfer of property required complicated, lengthy surveying, as the land was not divided between peasant and estate cultivation. Compensation for estate owners by the government also required long preparation, and its financing was in any case unclear.

Hence, only the circle around Nicolae Bălcescu insisted that point thirteen had to be put into practice. The tactic of sticking to point thirteen of the "constitution" while postponing its implementation satisfied neither large landowners nor the peasants. Despite attempts by the government to reassure the peasants, they refused to comply with their feudal obligations. At the behest of the ministry of the interior, local authorities even employed violent repressive measures. The government was forced to admit that it was itself responsible for raising expectations. Even before the revolt, the revolutionary committee needed to assure itself of peasant support. The peasant movement had made possible the revolutionaries' seizure of power, and the constant threat of a counter-revolution by conservative boyars within the country and intervention from abroad made the revolutionary government even more dependent on the peasants as a base of support. Bălcescu saw more clearly than most that the peasantry had to substitute for the still weak bourgeoisie. In mid-July, after the crisis that led to the hasty retreat of the revolutionaries, a systematic propaganda campaign was organized in the countryside under his direction. Commissars held speeches in village meetings, discussed the revolution's program and administered a solemn oath to the peasants.

Although this propaganda was conciliatory, corresponding to the harmonizing nature of the revolution, it contributed to a radicalization of the peasants, who viewed themselves as free and feudal burdens as abolished. Eventually, peasants ceremonially burned the agrarian rules of the Organic Statutes and the leases for extra parcels of land. The provisional government not only had to fear the loss of the most important part of its social base, but perhaps even a jacquerie. The events of 1846 in western Galicia, when the peasants had massacred the estate owners who had called on them to join their uprising, was certainly on the minds of the revolutionaries, as various statements showed. Hence the situation necessitated decisive measures in order to bring the agrarian question out of its cul-de-sac.

At Bălcescu's initiative, the government decreed on 21 July that one representative each of large landowners and peasants from each of the seventeen districts should form a "property commission," which was to work out a temporary compromise to the agrarian question until the constituent assembly had been established. The boyars attempted to delay the appointment of their delegates, but peasants began enthusiastically with their election campaign, which included mass meetings and discussions, and precipitated a further radicalization of the villages. At the same time, the government attempted to gain an overview of those parts of the estates cultivated by the peasants. It was discovered that the division of peasant land as provided for in the Organic Statutes had hardly been carried out and that peasants, as a rule, cultivated the entire estates against a rent payment.

Because of these delays, the commission only met on 21 August. It was chaired by a boyar, but his assistant was Ion Ionescu de la Brad, who was closer to the radicals. The beginning of the sittings was unfavorably influenced by outside forces. Suleiman Pascha, in Bucharest at the time, declared property to be inviolable, thus strengthening the dilatory resistance by large landowners to a solution of the problem. In their program and actions, the revolutionaries held private property in no less respect. Conservatives efforts to turn the government's attitudes about property into a propaganda weapon were based on a misjudgment.

Landowners based their actions on the assumption that they were owners of the entire estates in the sense of the term as used in the Code Civil, which was certainly wrong. They and the peasants had common rights and mutual responsibilities.

The boyar delegates accepted, after some resistance, abolition of labor services and tithes, but resisted, with all means possible, a distribution of property to the peasants. Expropriation, even with compensation, was condemned as a violation of the sacred right of property and they accused the government of "communist" ideas and intrigue in their propaganda. A "liberation of labor" alone, however, would have left peasants dependant on purely private leases. Thus labor services and tithes could have been reintroduced into the agrarian regulations through the back door, if perhaps under new names, or the peasants would have been degraded into agricultural laborers, assuming that landowners would have been able to cultivate the land on their own account. Reform only made sense when the manors were divided into large estates and viable parcels for the peasants. This would, however, have prevented large landowner's uncompensated exploitation of the peasants' labor and farm equipment, which they wished to use in order to start producing, on their own account, for the profitable export market.

After heated discussion, the peasants reported the amount of land necessary to feed a family. Depending on the region, they demanded between four and eight hectares. The other side countered with a proposal to grant each serf one hectare against a compensation payment. On 31 August, the government dissolved the commission, which obviously was no longer capable of reaching agreement. Its sessions had been accompanied by heated public discussion, which caused severe tensions in domestic politics, while an intervention from abroad once again threatened to bring the revolution to an end.

Russian diplomacy had applied all its influence at the Porte to prevent a recognition of the compromise negotiated by Suleiman in Bucharest. A high-level delegation from the regency arrived in Istanbul on 22 August, but was generally kept isolated. Neither the sultan nor the grand vizier received them. Representatives of the reactionary boyars worked together with Russian diplomacy against the new government in Wallachia and often spread outrageous slanders. As a consequence, Suleiman fell into disfavor, was recalled and replaced by Fuad Efendi, who was given strict instructions to intervene militarily and restore the old order of the Organic Statutes. In reality, however, the situation in the Ottoman government was not unfavorable for the Wallachian revolutionaries. During Suleiman's mission, the reformers Reşid and Ali Pascha had once again taken positions in the government as grand vizier and foreign minister. They were not especially opposed to the Wallachian reform experiments, but in their relations with the Russian government they were just as helpless as their predecessors. The Porte hoped to preempt Russian intervention with Fuad Efendi's mission. Once successful, he would probably have allowed modest and politically less noticeable changes.

When it became known in Bucharest on 18 September that the new Turkish commissar, Fuad, then on his way to the Turkish troops in Giurgiu, had been given the task of restoring the Organic Statutes, this led to a remarkable ceremony. Organized behind the scenes by Ion C. Brătianu, a radical who in the meantime had become chief of police in Bucharest, a crowd demanded that the regency hand over the original copies of the Organic Statutes and the "Archondologie," the official listing of boyar ranks. After a solemn procession, in which the two books were carried on a bier, all the church bells of the city were rung and funeral marches played, about 10,000 people gathered in front of the palace of the metropolitan. He appeared on the balcony—doubtless not entirely voluntarily—in ceremonial regalia and cursed both books, which were then burned by the peasants. Finally he pronounced an anathema on the supporters of the Organic Statutes (of which he was one) and blessed the new order. Among the speakers was Brătianu. Similar ceremonies followed throughout the country.

On 23 September the Turkish intervention army stood at the gates of Bucharest. Duhamel accompanied it as Russian representative to ensure that no agreements were made with the revolutionaries. Without arms and equipment, Magheru's irregular units in Oltenia were no more able than the national guard to defend the capital and the revolution. Probably to secure a continuity of legitimacy, he was given the administration of Oltenia and the adjacent mountain region. Stationed in positions difficult to attack, the revolutionary army strengthened resistance in the countryside. The revolutionary government decided on a course of passive resistance and once again mobilized the peasants for this purpose. Organized according to their village, carrying church flags and candles, led by priests in their robes with prayer books in their hands, and unarmed, they pressed on the Turkish troops in Giurgiu, and continued to do so during their advance towards Bucharest. On 23 September, 30,000 peasants united with the crowds from around Bucharest and attempted to immobilize with their numbers the army, which, after carefully circling the city, was stationed at the Cotroceni Monastery on a hill to the west.

On 25 September, Fuad received 300 delegates of the revolutionary regime from Bucharest on the square in front of the monastery. He declared the princely regency to be deposed. The Organic Statutes were to be valid once again. He named as Caimacam (the sultan's representative) Constantin Cantacuzino, a Russophile major boyar. It was characteristic of the situation that among the revolutionary delegates was his son, who protested loudly and without respect until he was arrested. When Turkish troops then marched into the city, they were blocked by masses of peasants who had assumed an attitude of prayer in the streets and who had to suffer the kicks of horses and blows from the flats of sabers. In an emotional situation, which became more and more confused, a bitter fight broke out between firemen and a Turkish unit in Dealul Spirii. Against a professional, fully equipped and numerically superior army, the fireman were without hope. But the incident was very suitable for providing the stuff of national legends.

At the behest of the British General Consul, Fuad sent the leaders of the revolution over the Austrian border, and a trial, as desired by the Russians, did not take place. In order to avoid any excuse for a Russian intervention, Colquhoun successfully prevented Magheru's troops in Oltenia from beginning armed resistance. The Russian invasion had, however, already been decided on. Fuad was told of the upcoming invasion on the day he marched into Bucharest. On 27 September a Russian army crossed the border between Moldavia and Wallachia.

Summary: Western Form and Eastern Substance

When liberal students and young intellectuals from Moldavia and Wallachia unfurled their own tricolor from the Paris city hall after the February Revolution, when they decided on 20 March to follow the examples of Paris and Vienna and "to make" a revolution in their homeland as well, and when they furthermore formed an alliance with the Polish exile organization, the international avant garde of revolution—at first glance all this seems like irresponsible and thoughtless adventurism. But we have seen how broad the base of the revolutionary movements in Moldavia and Wallachia was. There was no lack of indigenous traditions of a national program and of a struggle for institutions with broad-based participation. The Paris episode at the beginning of the Rumanian Revolution of 1848 only shows the close relation with Western models.

Liberal intellectuals, who in the coming decades came to be known as *Paşoptiştii* [forty-eighters], brought strategies, modes of behavior and revolutionary symbolism from the culture of political opposition in the Paris of the July monarchy. On the lower Danube, however, these were imbued with indigenous social and cultural contents. In Wallachia, a propaganda brochure, which borrowed heavily from Abbé Sieyès's "What is the Third Estate?" was very influential from March 1848 onwards. Its anonymous author obviously had problems finding a suitable equivalent for "Third Estate," but chose the word "*mesieraşi*," which meant artisan, subsuming within this term the peasants as well, whose concerns were given more space. In general, the Rumanian Revolution had its difficulties with terms which in France were as self-evident as the objects they described. As we have seen, a quite differentiated middle class already existed. The word "*burghez*" as a translation of "bourgeois" first appeared in 1848. "*Cetatean*" was used to describe city-dwellers from the sixteenth century, but the word gained a new meaning in 1848 with reference to "citoyen."

Methods of propaganda and mass mobilization needed to be made applicable to serfs. To attract support from among the educated classes in the planning phase required the secret societies and illegal propaganda writings tested in the West, and these were widespread. However, the immediate preparation for the revolt necessitated establishing contact with the peasants. In this respect, Magheru's recruiting activities for the Dorobantzes and Pandours were very effective. With their help, he was able to overcome the regional, clientelist power structure of large landowners in Oltenia, and install there revolutionaries from the center of the movement as civil servants and judges. (The underlying conflict remained long acute and influenced, as did French institutional models, the tendency among Rumanian veterans of 1848 towards centralism.) Recruitment for the irregular units was always paralleled by targeted propaganda in the villages, and broad participation of peasants in endeavors to defend the revolution strengthened their self-confidence and spread national and revolutionary myths. The provisional government systematically sent propaganda commissars, "priests of the constitution,"[5] out into the countryside, equipped with instructions and money. Linguistic and cultural gaps that separated peasants and boyars doubtless contributed to the penetration of a national idea into the rural population, an idea that would be successful in the long-term.

In the West as well, it was quite normal for liturgical forms, such as the repeated auto-da-fé of the Organic Statutes in the villages, to be tied to revolutionary symbolism. This form of action was particularly useful for reaching the peasants. Conspicuous in their mobilization, village priests often played a major role and themselves generally came from a peasant milieu. Characteristically, a national guard on the French model, demanded in most political programs, was much less important than the Panduras, which drew on local peasant tradition and gave the peasants their own myth.

Other myths, such as the unequal fight of the firemen of Dealul Spirii, were actively expanded upon, as had been the case with Western models. A good example of the creative shaping of a revolutionary myth was the heroism of Ana Ipătescu. C.D. Rosenthal, the historical painter of the Rumanian "forty-eighters," described the scene two years later when sending a friend material for a series of articles in *The Times*. The image he painted with words seems to be reminiscent of Delacroix's celebrated painting, composed under the impression of the July revolution, "Liberty Leading the People on the Barricades."[6]

It would be too simplistic to see in the peasants, as mass basis, and in the intellectual boyars' sons, as leadership elite, only a "substitute" for an underdeveloped bourgeoisie. The boyars' sons introduced Western ideology, forms of resistance, and rituals and gave the starting signal as the European revolutions appeared to have weakened the old powers sufficiently. But both peasants and boyars had their own complaints and demands, and hence, in spite of many similarities and parallels, the revolution on the lower Danube was different from the one in France.

The counter-revolution also borrowed ideologically from the West. Boyar resistance was mobilized by the attempt to implement agrorian reform. Its battle cry was "property," which was threatened by the devilish, "communistic" intrigues. Thus conservatives had, on the one hand, found a phrase with which they could plead for intervention on the international stage. On the other, they had reinterpreted traditional legal conditions in their favor. In reality, their rights to their estates were limited by the peasants' usage rights. They claimed, however, absolute ownership as defined in the Code Civil. This position could be explained to European cabinets and gradually gained acceptance. That also meant, however, a claim to sole control of the soil, a means of production whose value was steadily increasing due to the booming grain exports.

Even if economic and social reforms benefiting peasants, trade, and commerce had a prominent place in the catalog of liberal demands, decisive elements in these demands were the civil and political liberties and institutions established along Western lines with a constitution as focal point. Constitutionalism did also have its tradition in the Danubian Principalities, extending back to the Constitution of the Carbonari of 1822, as its opponents called it, with which lower ranked boyars in Moldavia had sought to secure for themselves a share of power. Later, while the oppositional portion of the political elite in Moldavia and Wallachia impatiently

chafed at the constitutional inadequacies of the Organic Statutes and composed radical counter-proposals, the younger generation experienced a more advanced constitutional system in France. They perceived it, however, mainly from the viewpoint
of the French opposition. Political thinking and action within a constitutional framework would also become self-evident after 1848, well beyond the circle of supporters of liberalism.

In this respect we can see two contrasting tendencies that crossed paths in
Rumania in 1848. Western institutions, which allowed broad participation in decision-making, became ever more important in political thinking and, after a short
setback, increasingly defined political reality from 1856 onwards. At the same time,
however, agrarian relations were developing in the opposite direction. In the 1840s,
the peasants, especially in Wallachia, struggled to preserve traditional usage rights in
the entire manor and a share of profits in the booming grain export trade. Despite
their bitter resistance, their conditions gradually worsened after 1848, so that by the
last third of the nineteenth century they were reduced to subsistence agriculture on
a small part of the manor and, on the rest, produced export goods in dependence
on the estate owner. At the same time, they were excluded from political participation. The well-developed constitutional system and political liberties therefore did
not de facto apply to four-fifths of the population.

In 1848, the struggle of the liberal intelligentsia for Western institutions and the
struggle of peasants for control of the soil reached their highpoints. The two strands
of development were knotted together in 1848. It this respect, the latter strand was
a greater danger to the revolutionaries in Wallachia than the Damoclean sword of
foreign intervention. The revolutionaries had promised the peasants both the abolition of feudal burdens and the gain of a title to their own land. Had these measures
been consistently carried out, they would have given the peasants a decisive advantage over the large landowners, who were dependent on the peasants' farm equipment and their labor. However, at the latest with the failure of the Property
Commission, it became obvious that the revolutionary government's agrarian policy had reached a dead end.

Radicals had, in the meantime, had great success in mobilizing the peasants and
making them into their most important base of support—not least in their struggle
for a constitutional system. Peasants participated actively in political activities in the
capital and were extremely capable of articulating their interests. In 1848, they gained
a level of political influence that they would never again reach. For the revolutionaries, dangers arose when they were not able to fulfil the counter-demands of their
peasant allies, because of the relation of forces, internally and in foreign affairs. They
were well aware of the fate of rebellious Polish nobles in western Galicia in 1846. The
possibility can therefore not completely be ruled out that foreign intervention saved
the revolutionary government from more than one political impasse.

In the last analysis, Rumanian "forty-eighters" gave less importance to social
reforms than to political liberties, rule of law, and a constitutional system. This
approach was strengthened in the following decades. It was based on the expectation that liberal institutions would create their own social base. A consequence of

this was the corruption of Rumanian constitutionalism through the exclusion of a majority of the population from de jure guaranteed, but de facto withheld rights of participation. The revolution of 1848 and the following eight years of exile became the shaping experience of a generation which thereafter would determine the fate of their country through the 1880s. The "forty-eighters" created a united, independent Rumanian nation-state, introducing institutions along Western lines and beginning a process of pseudo-modernization, that, in the end, would lead them into an oligarchy.

Notes

Although the Julian calendar was still valid in nineteenth century Rumania, all dates are given using the Gregorian calendar of Western Europe.

1. Kenneth Jowitt, "The Sociocultural Bases of National Dependency in Peasant Countries," in Kenneth Jowitt (ed.), *Social Change in Rumania 1860-1940: A Debate on Development in a European Nation* (Berkeley, 1978), 1-30, citation from 20.
2. Cornelia Bodea (ed.), *1848 la Români. O istorie în date și mărturi*, Vol. 1 (Bucarest, 1982), 663. Emphasis in original.
3. Ibid., 534.
4. Ibid., Vol. 2, 817
5. Ibid., 694
6. Ibid., 1165.

Chapter 9

SWITZERLAND 1847/49

A Provisional, Successful End of a "Democratic Revolution?"

Thomas Christian Müller

An interrelation exists between the two, Germany and Switzerland 1847, 1848, 1849, despite their differences, or perhaps even because of them. Differences will make themselves felt: German radicalism in Switzerland, Swiss history and the Swiss present from the German point of view. That opposites attract is possible under certain circumstances, is in fact under certain circumstances quite fruitful. And very fruitful indeed can be a comparative history. Here and there are broadcasters and receivers—once the correct wavelength is found, the reception is clear in the historical atmosphere.

These programmatic sentences appear at the beginning of a slim volume that appeared in 1929 under the title, *Switzerland in the German Revolution. A Chapter in Swiss-German Relations in the Years 1847-1849*. Its author was Werner Näf,[1] at the time a thirty-five-year-old professor of universal history at the University of Bern. Two years after Marc Bloch's plea for a "comparative historical view of European societies" at the Oslo History Conference, Näf developed his first ideas on a comparative "European history of Switzerland"—a concept that would come to occupy his entire career. During my research for this essay and other projects concerning the revolution of 1847/49, I became aware of the many difficulties of Swiss historiography concerning crossborder and comparative theses, despite Näf's work.

For decades, a "Schweizergeschichte" prevailed, that is a historically based, both methodically and thematically narrow national history. Only recently has the comparative perspective experienced a renaissance. Especially in Germany and France, it has been rediscovered by historians—in part via the prompting of other social sciences. Not least for a social history of politics and the political, it has provided new, fruitful research fields and perspectives. This starting-point—not to mention the theoretical reflections on possible forms of comparison and topologies—has seldom been employed by contemporary Swiss historians and also applies to the history of Switzerland in the 1840s, to the German *Vormärz*, and to the events and consequences of the 1848/49 revolution.

In this essay, an attempt will be made to place events in Switzerland in the 1840's within a European, and especially a German context. At the same time I would like to sketch some out points from which a cross-border discussion could start, and offer some comparisons. These considerations ought not to thought of as a definitive synthesis. Rather I will propose five theses, all of which deal the question of why the establishment of a Swiss federal state proved successful.

A first comparison of historical developments in Switzerland, Germany and other European countries produces the following results. The outcome of the revolution of 1847/49 in Europe, especially in the German states, was in many though not in all respects negative. Switzerland, however, provides the exception, where after a civil war in 1847/48 the Restoration-era Confederation of 1815 was transformed into a federal and democratic state with a bicameral parliament and an advanced constitution open to change. This specific Swiss "road to modernization" (Eder), i.e., to the inner formation of a nation-state, lasted a number of decades; the process included numerous crises, breaks, continuities, and structural changes in society, economy, politics, and culture. Alexis de Tocqueville aptly described this development in January, 1848: "In effect, Switzerland has been, for the last fifteen years, a country in revolution."[2]

In my thinking I have been inspired by the writings of Karl W. Deutsch—including his well-known lecture "Switzerland as a paradigmatic case of political integration."[3] In it, Deutsch applies to Switzerland his idea of integration as a communicative learning process, sustained by the social elite. His thesis ties in well with categories proposed by Klaus Eder, who—in relation to the development of political culture in Germany—has examined the structural possibilities and conditions of collective and institutional learning processes.[4]

At the beginning of my considerations is the founding of a federal state in 1848.[5] Why did it take place? What were the political, institutional, and collective learning processes in Switzerland? Can aspects be found for the period between 1815 and 1848 that allow comparison between developments in Switzerland and in Germany?

My arguments concerning the "unique Swiss development from the July to the February revolution" (Koselleck) relate to political development, the role of the bourgeoisie, the economy, national consciousness, and Swiss foreign relations. At the end of my paper I will summarize the individual sections and attempt to explain why the founding of the Swiss federal state in 1848 can be seen as an important, provisional stage and a consequence of a process of transformation with a revolutionary character.

Political Change between Breaks and Continuity

The establishment of a federal state in 1848 resulted from a historical learning process accompanied by numerous conflicts. Switzerland was successful in combining cantonal claims of sovereignty and democratic rights of the population with new federal structures, and in so doing created a unique form of government, linking various political and institutional traditions with the idea of a liberal and federal constitutional state. At the same time, the founding of a national federal state was the result of a fundamental process of reform, which worked from bottom to top—i.e., it was carried from popular movements into the communities, into the cantons, and finally onto the federal level.

Phase 1: The Failure of the Helvetian Republic (1798-1802)

In 1798, the French revolutionary army marched into Switzerland, declared it a protectorate and established the Helvetian Republic. This meant the end of the *Alte Eidgenossenschaft* [Old Confederation of Jurors] and the beginning of an attempt, short-lived and in the end a failure, to form a modern economic, social, and governmental structure.[6] Paris imposed on Switzerland a new constitution and thus a new form of government—a centralized and representative democracy modeled on the constitution of the French Directory. While providing numerous political and cultural impulses, this artificial structure failed, because it did not sufficiently integrate existing, long-term traditions. The upshot was a period of political instability, numerous coups, and constitutional struggles. Moreover, the War of the Second Coalition, 1799-1801, between Russia, Austria, and France also meant ravaged countryside and devastated villages for Switzerland as well. The second Helvetian constitution of 1802 was also unable to restore peace, although it once again granted the cantons greater competence.

Phase 2: The "Mediation" (1803-1813)—A First Attempt at Compromise

Napoleon ended the failed "Helvetian" experiment by at first withdrawing his troops from Switzerland, well knowing that troubles would break out throughout the country, against which the central government would be helpless. The chaos was in fact total. Only the "act of mediation" (1803), introduced by Napoleon, restored peace. Switzerland returned to the political traditions of the old regime, while preserving some of the civil liberties of the Helvetian Revolution. The country was once again a league of states with a weak central government [*Tagsatzung*] and sovereign cantons of three different types: rural community cantons (Uri, Schwyz, Unterwalden, Glarus, Zug, the two Appenzells), former urban cantons with corporate-aristocratic systems (Basel, Bern, Freiburg, Lucerne, Schaffhausen, Solothurn, Zürich), and newly formed cantons (St. Gallen, Aargau, Thurgau, Tessin, Waadt), with representative democracies limited by a very high property qualification. The population remained generally excluded from political decision-making. Power lay in the hands of a small class of property-owners, aristocrats, and notables whereby—and this is remarkable—the gap between old aristocracy and a new rising bourgeois elite narrowed considerably.

Phase 3: The "Restoration" (1815-1830)—Deadlock and Liberal Awakening

With Napoleon's defeat in 1813, this experiment, too, came to an end. Switzerland began once again a "search for a new state" (Andrey). Peace negotiations and the

Congress of Vienna of 1815 created a new political map of Europe, with Switzerland also assigned to a new place in this system. The second Treaty of Paris of 20 November 1815 declared that "the neutrality and unassailability of Switzerland, as well as its independence from all foreign influence, accords with the true interests of all European states."[7] From the time of the Congress of Vienna, the Great Powers sought to recognize and guarantee the "perpetual neutrality of Switzerland within its new borders." At the level of domestic politics, the *Tagsatzung* instituted a new treaty of confederation [*Bundesvertrag*] on 7 August 1815, and thus cemented the "restoration" of prerevolutionary conditions. The Swiss Confederation now included twenty-two cantons (Neuenburg, Geneva, and the Valois had been included); it reestablished the sovereignty of the individual cantons and thus also the rule of the old educated and propertied elite. The *Tagsatzung*, a body of cantonal representatives that met once a year, was powerless, as was the *Vorort* [steering committee], which rotated among Zürich, Bern and Lucerne every two years and was "not much more than a letter-box" (Andrey) for foreign correspondence. These two institutions, together with an "itinerant" chancellor's office, took care of the few confederate areas of activity, such as the army, diplomacy, and the conclusion of alliances and trade agreements.[8]

Moreover, the treaty of confederation neither defined church-state relations, nor did it establish under which conditions under which significant changes to it were possible. These defects and the "inherent inflexibility of the confederate authorities"—Tocqueville's analysis—underline the intent of the restoration: to preserve the status quo. Its effect proved fatal, as the political system was not able to keep pace with accelerating developments within society. Political reform at the confederate level was blocked. Here lay the roots of all major conflicts and political crises of the following decades.

Even when legal historical research is not united in its estimation, the confederate agreement of 1815 presents an important stage in the development of Swiss politics and theory of state. In the cantonal constitutions, and in their legal and administrative systems, were to be found remnants of an earlier, freer constitutional law. The press and the political public sphere were also preserved to an extent, and a few cantons maintained freedom of the press. In the welfare, school, and penal systems, there were individual improvements, which, however, could not disguise the fact that everyday life was encumbered by a confusion of legal contradictions, obstacles and erratic regulations—especially in the postal system, coinage, rights of domicile and residency, customs regulations, weights and measures, and in the army. Divisions within the country had consequences for foreign relations. Especially after the Carlsbad Decisions (1819), the restoration powers under the leadership of Metternich continually found reasons to intervene in Switzerland.

Phase 4: Awakening in the Cantons, Stagnation at the Confederate Level

Towards the end of the 1820s, signs of a political awakening increased. A new generation of liberal oppositionists arose and began to organize. When the revolution in Paris broke out on 17 July 1830, these liberals believed the time for political change had come. In Zürich and elsewhere a liberal movement directed against the rule of the urban elite developed in rural centers of early industrialization. In numerous cantons, mass meetings and assemblies of all cantonal citizens were held; brochures, petitions, and "memoriale" demanded political reform. The cantonal governments more or less quickly yielded to popular political pressure. Constitutional councils were formed or elected. Alfred Kölz speaks of "revolutionary acts" as the restoration-era constitutions did not provide for such change. The *Tagsatzung* was also quick to act, passing a resolution at the end of 1830 which was to prove very significant for further developments. It stated that "Every confederate state is free, due to its sovereignty, to make those changes to its cantonal constitution which it feels necessary and useful, in as far as these do not conflict with the confederate agreement."[9]

This resolution represents an important stage in the political learning process in Switzerland. The *Tagsatzung* reconfirmed cantonal autonomy and approved, moreover, the breakthrough of liberal demands and principles—well aware that the reform movement would not stop at the cantonal level but would come to encompass the confederate treaty, as well.[10] The resolution of 27 December 1830 was a turning point and symbolized a specifically Swiss road to political modernization and nation building, confirming as it did popular sovereignty, the principle of subsidiarity, and thus the movement from below.

Within a year, eleven cantons[11] had introduced new constitutions, establishing representative-democratic systems with popular sovereignty and separation of powers. Of decisive influence for the so-called "regeneration" were the works of the Swiss-French political theorist Benjamin Constant and the German constitutional law expert Ludwig Snell.[12] Change did not occur peacefully everywhere. In Basel, for example, tensions between city and rural districts burst forth into a bloody war of secession which ended in 1833 with a division into two half-cantons (Basel-Landschaft, Basel-Stadt).

Liberal reforms in the cantons were introduced very rapidly. At the confederate level, however, two attempts at constitutional reform failed in 1832/33 due to insurmountable differences between federalists and centralists, between conservatives and progressives. The strongest opposition to a federal solution came from the Catholic cantons as they feared a loss of sovereignty and thus their cultural and religious autonomy. After this failure, the national question remained open for over a decade. Indeed, differences became ever more entrenched. Catholic-conservative and seven liberal cantons organized themselves into special alliances in 1832, the Sarner Bund on the one hand, the Siebner Konkordat on the other.

Phase 5: Radicalization and Civil War (1840/47)

At the end of the 1830s the liberal movement slipped into a deep crisis because it had not been able to fulfil the expectations of a large part of the rural population in the "regenerated" cantons. Moreover, liberal modernization policies led to a great amount of insecurity among many Swiss. In Zürich in 1839, a protest march from rural districts—led by a Protestant pastor—entered the city and overthrew the liberal government. The causes of this *Züriputsch* lay not only in social tensions but also in religious differences. The offer of a chair to the theologian David Friedrich Strauß at the University of Zürich raised the ire of an already doubtful population.[13] In Lucerne, the conservatives took power (1840/41) and introduced a new, theocratic-conservative constitution.

In Aargau there were uprisings that came close to a civil war when, following a referendum, equal representation of Catholics and Protestants in the Great council was ended. Shortly thereafter, the liberal government (with a radical Catholic at its head) banned the monasteries because in the eyes of the Protestants, they had played a significant role in the Catholic revolt. Such a move was, however, clearly against the confederate treaty, and the Aargau Cloister Controversy of 1841/43 became a national affair. During negotiations, the impotence of the *Tagsatzung* and the contradictory nature of the 1815 confederate treaty were again made painfully obvious. The *Tagsatzung* condemned the dissolution and demanded that the ban be rescinded. Supported by other radical cantons, however, the Aargu government remained stubborn at first and only followed the confederate resolution on second request.

The events and disturbances described above sharpened the conflicts between the political blocs in Switzerland—that is, between liberal/radicals as proponents of a democratic-progressive order, and conservatives as defenders of clerical claims to truth. This tension had already made itself felt in the 1820s. Recent work has shown that differences cannot, however, be reduced to a "Protestant/Catholic" dichotomy. Rather they must be examined in light of the relation between progress and tradition. Accelerated development and its far-reaching consequences raised both fears and hopes among many people, urban and rural. A search for orientation and truth increased; questions of education and confession became especially charged in the 1830/40s, as the strife over the appointment of David Strauß in Zürich demonstrates. Furthermore, it must be remembered that supporters of progress as well as defenders of tradition were to be found in both Protestant and Catholic cantons.

Back to the run of events, the Catholic cantons were not willing to accept *Tagsatzung* policy and began discussions of a mutual defense pact. Supported by the Austrian envoy, acting under Metternich's orders, representatives from seven cantons (Lucerne, Zug, Uri, Schwyz, Unterwalden, Freiburg, Wallis) met to plan their next move—negotiation of a separation of Catholic Switzerland. In 1844, tensions rose further. In Wallis, the conservative government forcibly repressed a liberal rebellion, and the Lucerne government stoked the fire still further in entrusting leadership of the seminary to the Jesuit Order; Lucerne thus became an "outpost" (Biaudet) of ultramontane powers. The "Jesuit question" made the gap between the various positions almost completely unbridgeable; as reconciliation became increasingly less likely, much less so did any domestic political compromise.

Radicals, for their part, armed themselves, organized large mass meetings and attacked anything related to the Jesuits in the press. In the following months, events began to develop very quickly throughout the country. In December 1844 there was a failed coup against the Lucerne government. This rebellion went down in history as the first "march of the volunteers " [*Freischarenzug*]. Reprisals by the government of Lucerne exacerbated the crisis. In March 1845 about 3,000 volunteers again marched on Lucerne, armed with weapons taken from confederate arsenals. This second march of the volunteers also ended in defeat.

Gottfried Keller, himself one of the volunteers, described the anti-Jesuit mood that prevailed at the national sharpshooters' festival in Basel. The Jesuits provoked "a strong and highly productive hate and anger." It would not have taken much should they have decided "to set off en masse, wearing their festival costumes, with festival wine in their blood, to plug up the Jesuits' hole and destroy their insane theocracy."[14]

The spiral of violence increased ever more. In Lucerne, Joseph Leu, the leader of the conservatives, was murdered by a former volunteer. In the same year, the liberal-conservative government of Bluntschlis was overthrown, and in Waadt and Bern radicals took over the government following coups. When it became known in June 1846 that seven Catholic cantons had formed a defense pact, there were violent reactions everywhere. In the *Tagsatzung*, liberals failed in their attempt to declare this separate league [*Sonderbund*] as an opposition to the confederate treaty and force its dissolution. Only after a successful radical rebellion in Geneva and new elections in St. Gallen were liberals and radicals able to form a majority in the *Tagsatzung*. Following a fierce debate, the delegates passed a motion on 20 July 1847 with votes of twelve cantons and two half cantons: "1. The separate alliance of the seven cantons Lucerne, Uri, Schwyz, Unterwalden, Zug, Freiburg, and Wallis is incompatible with the clauses of the confederate treaty and is correspondingly declared to be dissolved. 2. The above-named cantons are responsible for the fulfillment of this resolution, and the *Tagsatzung* reserves the right, if conditions demand it, to take further measures to ensure its respect."[15]

When a final attempt at mediation had failed, the *Tagsatzung* decided in Bern on 24 October 1847 to dissolve the *Sonderbund* militarily. One aspect of this decision must be underlined as it was indicative of further developments. The liberal ambassadors followed clearly limited war aims; they sought "only" to dissolve the *Sonderbund* and not, for example, to conquer militarily and to subjugate completely the seven rebel cantons. As uncertain the result and duration of the civil war was, the progressive powers were well aware that taking up arms endangered the continued existence of the confederation. On the other hand, they saw the war as a stage towards the road to a federal government and thus consciously accepted the great risks they were running.

Things moved more rapidly than was expected both domestically and abroad. The civil war ended after twenty-six days, "during which there were more maneuvers than fighting" (Biaudet).[16] The troops of the *Sonderbund* cantons, clearly inferior to the confederate army, both militarily and strategically, capitulated on 29 November 1847. Despite the sharpshooters' societies, firepower discipline on both sides was catastrophic and the use of munitions immense. Obviously the troops did not fight with the fiercest of determination against their fellow countrymen.

Sonderbund hopes of intervention from abroad (France and Austria) proved to be an illusion. The war's rapid end, the small number of dead and injured,[17] and an absence of major attacks and greater humiliations by confederate troops "contrasted sharply with the outbreaks of hate and violence" (Andrey) before the civil war and paved the way for a quick re-integration of the defeated *Sonderbund* cantons. At the confederate level as well, the civil war had encouraged a willingness to compromise, integrate, and cooperate among the various camps and led to the nation coming closer together.

Phase 6: Federal Reform, Drafting a Constitution, and Establishing a Federal State (1847/48)

Clausewitz's maxim that war is the continuation of politics by other means could almost serve as a paradigm for the period before and after the Swiss *Sonderbund* War. The *Sonderbund* had hardly capitulated when the *Tagsatzung* began anew with its revision of the confederate treaty, starting where the first revision commission had left off in the summer of 1847—before the outbreak of the civil war. In the former *Sonderbund* cantons, liberal minority governments took over. It soon became obvious that the *Tagsatzung* had learned something from the cantonal constitutional struggles of the "regeneration" and the double failure of the confederate revision in 1832/33. It was decided to form a commission of cantonal representatives instead of having the people elect a constitutional council, a body that the cantons would have greeted with skepticism or outright rejection. Thus federal interests and the powers of the cantons were bound together.[18]

The twenty-three-member commission was staffed exclusively by liberals, liberal-conservatives, and radicals—all men who supported confederate reform. They belonged to the young liberal generation that had been involved in the political troubles of the 1830s in the cantons and who brought this experience into the negotiations. On 17 February 1848 "power-hungry, liberal politicians" (Kölz) and pragmatists met for the first sitting and produced, within eight weeks(!), their first draft. The commission had recognized and made use of a "uniquely favorable moment" (Bucher), as a week after they had begun their work revolution broke out in Paris, followed by "the springtime of the peoples" throughout Europe. These events abroad gave Switzerland the necessary breathing space to overcome the consequences of the civil war. In the words of Henri Druey, a Waadtland radical and member of the constitutional commission, they were able "to bring ideas to life which some would have viewed at other times as utopian." As the negotiations were reaching their conclusion, the Bern radical Ulrich Ochsenbein remarked: "We have made amazing progress, due to the events around us,"[19] in other words: the victors of the civil war had the "Zeitgeist" behind them.

After a lengthy debate, a narrow majority of delegates approved a modified draft on 27 June 1848, on which the people in the cantons then voted. Fifteen and one-half cantons voted in favor, six and one-half against the new constitution. Turnout was around 55 percent of eligible voters, that is about 19 percent of the total population. In two former *Sonderbund* cantons, liberals used questionable means to ensure victory. In Lucerne, those not casting a vote were simply included among the ayes, and in Freiburg the Great Council voted on the constitution instead of the people. Both cantons would otherwise have rejected the constitution. On 12 September 1848, the decisive vote took place in the *Tagsatzung*, which unanimously declared the constitution as accepted. The delegates from the former *Sonderbund* cantons abstained.[20]

The new constitution contained 114 articles, ordered into three sections, and was remarkable in "that it contained traditional liberties in modified form, that it founded new institutions and defined their tasks and that it provided a framework for future development."[21] In what were often tough negotiations, the commission managed to tie the past (i.e. legal traditions and experience from earlier constitutional struggles) to the future, to limit the sovereignty of the cantons, to increase popular representation, and to establish centralized institutions as uniting elements.[22] For this purpose, various models of government were examined and in part adapted in a pragmatic process. Thus one finds in the constitution attributes of the American bicameral legislature, traces of French constitutional law, parts of the regeneration-era cantonal constitutions, and elements of those direct democratic practices that predominated in rural cantons.

The decisive compromise, and a constitutional novelty, was a bicameral legislature, both of whose chambers, the National Council, representing the people, and the Council of the Estates, representing the cantons, were legally equal. This legislature was supplemented by a seven member Federal Council (the executive) and the Federal Court (the judiciary). These federal bodies were assigned the task of "securing the league of the comrades of the oath [*Eidgenossen*], of maintaining and supporting the unity, power, and honor of the Swiss nation," and, simultaneously, of securing "the claim of the independence of the fatherland against foreign powers, preserving peace and order domestically, protecting freedom and the rights of the comrades of the oath and furthering their common welfare."

From the perspective of constitutional history, apart from the specifically Swiss form of the bicameral legislature, two further points deserve mention: unlike the constitution of the Frankfurt National Assembly, the Swiss constitution of 1848 contained no separate declaration of basic rights. Furthermore, the commission established regulations for future constitutional reforms. In so doing, they hoped to stabilize the political situation in Switzerland and to integrate the various interests. At the same time they took into account future changes in society, changes which might call into question existing constitutional law.

The "path of political development" in Switzerland between 1798 and 1848 can be described as an institutional and political learning process, and can be divided into six phases, marked by breaks, continuities, and conflicts. The "French period" ("Helvetik," "Mediation") was followed by the "Restoration"—equally strongly influenced from abroad—and by the new treaty of confederation (1815), which restored the conditions of the old regime and to a great extent blocked political development at the national level. In the "regeneration" that followed, constitutional conflicts took place at the cantonal level, political "experimental laboratories" (Ruffieux). The next stage was distinguished by increasing tension between "regenerated" and conservative cantons [*Sonderbünde*], by a crisis in the liberal movement, radical coups, and an increase in the pressure of the European Powers. In the autumn of 1847, the conflict over organization and legitimation of political control escalated into a civil war between the *Sonderbund* cantons and confederate troops. Thereafter, the situation became clearer insofar as the victorious liberals, together with the radicals, were able to push through the establishment of a federal government.

The modern theories of constitutional law developed at the end of the eighteenth century influenced the entire process, but so did traditions of the organization of domination and legitimation in the communities and cantons that dated back into the middle ages. In 1798, the ideas of the French Revolution were imported into Switzerland in the first national constitution. This meant the end of the old confederation and the beginning of a "struggle over forms of the legalization of political rule" and a "legal institutionalization of political freedom"[23] in which supporters of modern forms of government were opposed by proponents of the old order. In the final analysis, it was a question of which form of government would best secure the freedom of individual citizens, cantonal claims to sovereignty, and fundamental democratic liberties.

In conclusion a few thoughts on a comparison between Switzerland and Germany: from 1815 onwards both formed a league of states with a confederate structure, sovereign member states (with constitutionally different systems), and weak central administrations (*Tagsatzung*, German Confederate Diet). While the Swiss were successful in establishing a federal state—after a number of intermediate stages and numerous conflicts—a simultaneous attempt in Germany failed. In the German Confederation, as constituted in 1815, both the long-lasting power struggle between Prussia and Austria and the "multifaceted consequences of German polycentralism and differences in regional levels of development" (Wehler) hindered a transformation into a federal and nation-state. Political and national integration, as sought for in the Frankfurt National Assembly, foundered not least on the "different intentions for a German nation state"—namely on the resistance to a greater German or small German solution.[24] Concerning this point, Werner Näf remarked: "It was necessary to unite two Great Powers in one federation, or to expel one of them, it was necessary to take into consideration the claims of mid-sized states and the doubts of the small ones; one could count on the envy of Europe, Germany was oddly intertwined with its neighboring powers, it had no set external borders, not even the division of the individual states among themselves had been arranged completely and to everyone's satisfaction."[25]

The situation in Switzerland was similar in certain respects. However, in spite of the many sovereign states of which it was composed, Switzerland had set internal and external borders from the time of the Vienna treaties onward. The confederate treaty of 1815 was a mixture of traditional and modern theories of government and was, despite its faults, an important and long undervalued stage on the road to a federal state. Differences (urban/rural, confessional, linguistic), special interests, and economic disparities existed between the cantons. In comparison to Germany, one can agree with Werner Näf when he writes that, in Switzerland, constitutional differences between the cantons were considerably smaller. "No Swiss canton could exist in an isolated position; they all were dependent on unification in a federation in order to survive."[26]

Social Change: "Middle Classes as Sovereign"

The history of the rise of the bourgeoisie and the historical development of liberalism in the nineteenth century cannot be separated from one another in the case of Switzerland. This "affinity between bourgeois culture and early liberal thought" (Kocka) can be found in other European states; in Switzerland, however, social, cultural, and political ties between bourgeois social formation and an early liberal movement could already be observed at the beginning of the nineteenth century. The old, established aristocratic and patrician families had to cede the social and political supremacy they had held since the seventeenth and eighteenth centuries to a politically and economically heterogeneous, but socioculturally "relatively homogeneous social group" (Tanner). This new bourgeois elite was, at the same time, the class that promoted liberal and progressive ideas. Between 1830 and 1848 the connection between the bourgeoisie and liberalism experienced various phases of crisis, radicalization, differentiation, and polarization. In the end, liberals and radicals came together in 1847/48. This alliance held its own against conservatives and pushed through the establishment of a federal government.

Albert Tanner's work *Arbeitsame Patrioten und wohlanständige Damen* [Industrious Patriots and Respectable Ladies] is the first large-scale analysis of the social and cultural history of the bourgeoisie in Switzerland. Taking Zürich and Bern as examples, Tanner describes the rise of the most important social group in Switzerland—a rise that nowhere else in Europe occurred so rapidly and without hindrance. The primary cause of its rise was a loss of significance and general disappearance of the nobles in the fifteenth century and a comparatively early end to the feudal system in the old Confederation.

In the seventeenth and eighteenth centuries, a new upper class took over political leadership in the cities (Bern, Freiburg, Lucerne, Solothurn, Basel, Zürich, Schaffhausen, St. Gallen, Geneva), as well as in rural towns. This self-contained social group originated from rich urban-bourgeois/rural-agricultural families and developed into a new aristocracy whose privileges and rule were based on lineage, property, and education. In the old regime -against the backdrop of proto-industrialization and the growth of commerce and finance—a "bourgeoisie consisting of merchants, outwork-manufacturers, entrepreneurs and bankers" arose within the aristocratic-bourgeois upper class, and pressed for more power. The capital of this early landed and commercial bourgeoisie, which adopted an aristocratic lifestyle, resided less in lineage and land ownership than in economic success.

In 1798, the Helvetian Republic brought the supremacy of patrician and aristocratic families to a temporary end. The commercial and educated elite that had up until then beem excluded from politics—in rural towns, former subject regions (Thurgau, Aargau, Waadt), and the outworking districts (Zürcher Oberland, Appenzellerland)—took on administrative and governmental offices in the new central state.[27] This new elite supported revolutionary principles imported from France, but rejected political participation by the masses. In 1803 and 1815 respectively, the "Mediation" and the "Restoration" largely re-introduced the old order and the supremacy of patricians and aristocrats. Only a few rich members of the landed and commercial bourgeoisie could jump the high hurdles of a property franchise: "The state [became] the monopoly of the rich property owners."[28]

Democratization of the political order in 1830/31 finally ended the supremacy of the "periwigged aristocrats." Support for the liberal movement in the cantons came from the "middle classes"; they fought for a representative-democratic constitution that guaranteed freedom and basic civil liberties and at the same time laid the foundations of a modern liberal state and civil society. The "middle classes" arose from the "small town and village upper and middle class" and included "apart from farmers, traders and master craftsmen, manufacturers in outwork, factory owners, and merchants as well."[29] Among them were also the "bourgeoisie of the talents" (Tanner) and their various occupations: intellectuals, professionals, civil servants and university trained jurists, journalists, doctors, pastors, and professors. As in the period of the federal revision of 1847/48, jurists and lawyers played a decisive role in the cantonal regeneration struggle, as constitutional experts, as members of the new executive and legislative organs or as civil servants.

The movements of the 1830s were thus neither politically nor socially homogeneous. The further course of the decade saw the shattering of this "coalition" of petit bourgeois circles in the country and the middle class business and professional bourgeoisie in the cities, who increasingly distanced themselves from the uneducated and troublesome masses and rejected their participation in all levels in politics.[30] As in Germany, the liberal bourgeoisie in Switzerland also separated itself first from the old powers (aristocracy, patricians). Later they cut themselves off from the lower classes—out of "fear of the rabble, the proletariat and communism" and from an "aversion against the anarchic character of popular movements" (Wehler). "Six years ago we fought the fight against aristocracy and privileges; in the next six years we will have to fight against the brutality and rule of the rabble."[31]

As early as 1830/31, a new group within the liberal movement began to form in the western and French speaking parts of the country, under the leadership of a younger generation of intellectuals—radicals.[32] Its adherents were often "unpropertied, self-employed intellectuals of petite bourgeois or agricultural background" (Tanner). Discord between liberals and radicals broke out into the open in 1832/34 on the question of a revision of the constitution. The radicals were committed to a transformation (in revolutionary fashion, if necessary) of Switzerland into a democratic, centralized nation-state with universal suffrage.[33] Little research has been done into the differences in political aims and ideas between liberals, mostly active in German speaking Switzerland, and radicals, heavily represented in western Switzerland. In this context it is important to remember that linguistic borders did not correspond to the political ones. In educated and politically active circles, an orientation towards political tradition played a more important role in defining political attitudes than did language.[34]

At the beginning of the 1840s, a political triangle had thus formed in Switzerland which would define politics for the next decade: radicals, liberals and conservatives. Parallel to the rise of the radicals, moderate liberals experienced a crisis at the end of the 1830s. With their elitist and commercially oriented domestic policies, they lost the support of the rural population. In addition came increasing pressure from the European powers, who sought to influence events in troubled Switzerland and its refugee and asylum policies. As for the conservatives, the rise of the radicals led to the foundation of the *Sonderbund*.

Only when the domestic situation became still worse was there an amalgamation of the liberals and the radicals, who were now setting the tone. The threatening civil war, as well as Protestantism and the anti-Jesuit mobilization, led to a the "formation of a bloc" (Andrey) between radical powers in the west, liberals in the industrialized east, and liberal-conservatives of the upper bourgeoisie as well. This great coalition achieved success in the *Sonderbund* war and then used its majority to push through the long-desired constitutional reform. The spokesmen of the bourgeois "middle classes" held power from 1847 onwards at the national level as well— a position they would maintain well into the twentieth century.

While radicals had been the driving force behind the dissolution of the *Sonderbund* and governmental reform in the context of the civil war, during the debates of the revision commission in the spring of 1848 "liberal and moderate radical forces from the landed and educated bourgeoisie, from the commercial and industrial bourgeoisie proved stronger than the representatives of the radical petit bourgeoisie and the peasants."[35] The first legislative elections produced a very clear picture: both houses were dominated by the *Freisinn*, a coalition of the radical and liberal bourgeoisie. This bourgeois-liberal hegemony was maintained until 1919, when proportional representation was introduced.[36]

In the second volume of his history of German society Hans-Ulrich Wehler puts forward various reasons for the failure of the March Revolution in Germany, which I would like to discuss here briefly in relation to Switzerland.[37] One argument relates to a "split between liberals and democrats." It was not so much that this split itself had a negative effect on the course of the revolution. Rather, because of "a lack of intimate familiarity with the art of parliamentary compromise," it had taken too long for the two camps to agree on a common plan of action. A further assessment relates to the role of liberalism in inhibiting the revolution. Wehler describes the liberals "as revolutionaries against their will." Thirdly, he finds that in Germany in 1848/49 there was no "class capable of acting," which could have formed a "powerful coalition."

And in Switzerland? There the bourgeoisie had played a dominant role from the end of the old confederation onwards; there, old aristocratic families and new, bourgeois powers (rural, landed, and commercial bourgeoisie) were intertwined from the Mediation era. "In Switzerland it was the Helvetik, and especially the liberal revolution of 1830/31 and the federal state of 1848 which helped to bring about the breakthrough of civil society, in almost ideal-typical fashion, and thus to establish a new economic, social and political order."[38]

The liberal movement, which had taken over the government in a number of cantons, collected parliamentary, executive, and legislative experience. Moreover, rural cantons contributed their experience of direct democracy to the debate. The constitutional revision of 1832/33, which failed due to the inability of various political forces to compromise, also provided an valuable example. Later, liberals were forced to recognize that in a democratic state, changing majorities and conservative setbacks were possible. Furthermore, radicals and Catholic-conservatives came to understand that marches of volunteer corps and secessionist separate leagues were not useful political instruments, leading at best to less of a willingness to talk and to greater violence.

Liberals, liberal-conservatives, and radicals entered the decade of civil wars divided. However, the threat of civil war, the threat to the nation, the belief in progress, and even the anti-Jesuit mood bridged the gaps between the three groups. From then on, this "coalition"—strengthened by its victory over the *Sonderbund* and its majority in the *Tagsatzung*—set the course for a revision of the constitution. The defeated cantons, on the other hand, had no choice; they had to accept a number of proposals. Nonetheless, the members of the commission recognized that finding compromises was an unceasing task and that self-interest and "petty cantonal particularism [*Kantönligeist*]" needed to be put aside in favor of an integration of all politically relevant groups.

Economic Change, Industrialization

Economic development and the political learning process influenced each other in the first half of the nineteenth century. Between 1800 and 1820, Switzerland was one of the leading countries in continental Europe in terms of economic development. The Helvetic Constitution of 1798 introduced freedom of trade, occupation and settlement, with positive results for economic development. This could be seen above all in the textile industry, especially cotton textiles, the economy's real leading sector. The partial mechanization of textile production marked the beginning of the production of industrial machinery, although output at first was still quite modest. Because the textile industry was dependent on exports, international trade and tariff problems persistently remained live issues. Between 1819 and 1849 there was a very lively debate about free trade and protectionism, reflected in the constitutional controversies of the 1830s and 1840s between "centralists" and "federalists." Railway construction—an important motor of industrial development—only began in Switzerland in the 1850s, comparatively late.

Before 1848, Switzerland lacked the governmental-institutional framework for an economic policy; industrial modernization was well in advance of that of the nation-state. Domestic conflicts in the 1840s, the economic crisis of 1846/47, and increasing competitive pressure from abroad, however, made palpable the close relation between economic development, tariff policies, and national unity. The establishment of a federal state thus formed an important basis for the upswing in Swiss industry and economy in the following decades.

In his economic history of Switzerland, Jean-François Bergier proposes a model to describe the course and the specific preconditions of the so-called "industrial revolution" in Switzerland.[39] He attributes industrial growth in Switzerland at the beginning of the nineteenth century to a "lack of potential resources," which circumscribed the potential range of entrepreneurial activity and made the cotton industry the leading sector between 1800 and 1820. The consequence of this concentration of "industrial revolution" on the textile industry was a slow rate of economic growth and an increase in general affluence. A second characteristic mentioned by Bergier is Switzerland's geographical restraints. This prevented the "sudden expansion" to be observed in other states. At the same time, tiny Switzerland was separated "into still smaller independent states," which in turn differed significantly from one another "in their resources, population, mentality and even in their institutions." These differences had the effect of restricting the breakthrough of industrial production to only a few cantons.

What were the preconditions in Switzerland for the transformation from a preindustrial to an industrial-capitalist economy? Population statistics for the years between 1798 and 1850 are very incomplete. Switzerland's population rose by about 41 percent in this period, corresponding to an annual rise of approximately 0.65 percent.[40] Such an increase put Switzerland somewhere in the middle of the ranks of all European countries, behind the German Confederation, and naturally behind England, whose population doubled between 1800 and 1850. The reason for the population increase lay in the increase of life expectancy, as the balance of migration remained negative for this period. For many, emigration to neighboring countries, and later to the USA, Russia, and South America, afforded the only possibility of escaping misery at home.

Demographic changes had little influence on economic development; less, certainly, than technological progress, which had a lasting effect on the occupational structure. Cheap and—thanks to a relatively good school system—well-qualified workers were in good supply. This lowered production costs on the one hand and allowed competitive prices; on the other hand, entire regions were impoverished by the mechanization of production, famines and the severe economic and agricultural crises of 1816/17 and 1845/47 when thousands lost their jobs. In the new factories, children and adult workers of both sexes were exploited in two-shift work—just as one might expect in an early industrial economy with little government regulation.[41]

Industrialization occurred mainly in the rural districts (Zürcher Oberland, Glarus) where cheap water power was available for the machines, as was a large supply of rural outworkers. According to Rudolf Braun, in many places one cannot really speak of an "industrial revolution" because the "machine and factory system" had grown "organically out of outworking."[42] In the first half of the nineteenth century there was a "symbiosis of agriculture and industry" (Andrey). Many farming families improved their income with outwork. In 1820, outworkers made up half of the industrial labor force and in 1850 more than a third.[43]

The most important economic sector in Switzerland was agriculture, which employed around 60 percent of the population in 1850, but also changed fundamentally in this period. The Helvetic period and the Mediation dealt the final blow to the system of feudal rents and tithes, affecting agricultural production: common land was divided up, the three field system came to an end. Nonetheless, despite new methods of planting, despite an upswing in fruit growing, in animal raising and, to some extent, in milk production, Swiss agriculture was never completely able to meet domestic requirements.

The years 1798 and 1848 are turning points in the development of the economy. The Helvetian Revolution brought an end to the guild system and introduced freedom of trade and occupation. For a short time Switzerland was a unified market. In 1801, the first mule-jennies were put into operation in a former monastery in St. Gallen. Within a decade, almost all cotton spinning was being done by machine, as Swiss producers profited from Napoleon's continental system banning English imports. In the 1820s the end of the import ban and the mechanization of cotton spinning brought about the final collapse of hand spinning in Switzerland. This phase saw the founding of numerous companies, an increasing polarization between large and small firms, strong competitive pressures, and numerous bankruptcies.[44] It was a period in which technologically oriented businessmen were more successful than commercially oriented ones.

There followed an upturn from 1828 to 1837, with new technological advances but also with new demands on entrepreneurs' ability to innovate. Technological know-how also increased, and growing requirements for capital made new ways of raising it necessary. Small firms, lacking the means to obtain new and better machines, disappeared; production was concentrated in the larger factories in Zürich, St. Gallen, Aargau, Glarus, and Thurgau. The canton of Zürich was the "reservoir for spinning firms in Switzerland" (Dudzik) because one third of all Swiss spindles were controlled by Zürich firms in 1836.

Between 1838 and 1853 the cotton industry experienced a recession. Stagnation was related to a general lack of confidence about the future, due to the intensification of political and social conflicts in the 1840s, the economic crisis of 1846/47, the great agricultural crisis, and the European revolutions. This development in the cotton industry reflected the contentious, mutually dependent structural changes in economy, politics and society. Only after some measure of calm was restored after 1848 did the industry find firm footing again, and did trust in the future and a willingness to invest increase. Economic and technological diversification, which was only slowly beginning in the 1830s and was stymied in the 1840s, became more evident after 1848. Gradually new industries arose, such as mechanical engineering, and the metallurgical and chemical industries. Other (traditional) branches, such as silk and clock production, continued their expansion and, with some delay, the construction of a rail network in Switzerland began.

Countless problems of commercial policy inherited from the old regime, such as domestic customs, and road and bridge tolls, hindered domestic trade. At the beginning of the 1840s there were about 180 customs stations on cantonal borders, 147 on national borders.[45] A variety of coinages, measurements, and weights exacerbated the problems, while foreign trade was confronted by the German Customs Union. Following the "regeneration," liberal industrial cantons in particular argued for economic integration. At the same time, debate between free traders and protectionists about customs policies intensified. A number of expert commissions brought forward different proposals, whereby the business community was especially interested in foreign trade aspects.[46] Export-oriented companies began to work more closely with the authorities when they concluded trade agreements or set up consular representation, which strengthened the relation between the state and business community.[47]

In the 1840s, representatives from the business community and politics sought a step-by-step rapprochement at the national level. Entrepreneurs organized themselves into the first national chamber of commerce (1843), and scheduled the first inter-regional industrial and commercial exhibitions. The great agricultural and economic crisis of 1845/47 not only affected food supply, but also export industries and caused political and economic leaders (often enough the same people) to think more seriously about a national economic policy. In 1847, delegates from twelve cantons, including the industrial cantons, met to discuss the creation of a customs union. These negotiations were interrupted by the civil war, as were those on the revision of the constitution.

Of all European countries, Swiss industry was more developed than any other, after England. The upswing in the Swiss cotton industry succeeded without an expanding domestic market or relevant political, social or institutional structures. In Germany, economic development and integration were also in advance of political ones, but apart from a few regional exceptions industrialization only really began in the 1850s.[48]

Ulrich Menzel examines the question of "why Switzerland, or individual cantons reached such an advanced state of industrialization in spite of significant political and economic barriers." He advances the thesis that the role of the state can remain minimal as long as a country is "a forerunner and not a late arrival in the industrialization process." Even the "petty federalist particularism" [*föderalistische Eigenbrötelei*] need not have had a negative effect on developments, because hardly any government intervention relative to further advanced foreign competitors would have been necessary if the industrial lead were preserved.[49] This assumption is to a great extent true for Switzerland for the period between 1800 and 1840. In the 1840s, however, foreign competition increased; domestic confusion and a European-wide agricultural crisis occurred simultaneously in the first major modern-style economic crisis. In this period of transformation and new departures, politicians and businessmen were forced to recognize that a certain level of economic and government integration was necessary. Here, too, attention must be paid to a "movement from the bottom up." Before the institutional framework for a modern economy was created at the federal level, trade and economic policies were being introduced by the cantons.

For Jean-François Bergier it is obvious that industrialization, "perhaps more than any other factor," contributed to political integration and the establishment of a federal state.[50] Hansjörg Siegenthaler, on the other hand, in a "calendar of crises" for the 1840s, describes the years before 1848 as an open "context of fundamental insecurity" in which individual and collective actors sought agreement on new political strategies in a communicative exchange. In this interactive process, "Helvetian Nationalism" [Siegenthaler] influenced the actors' willingness to communicate, their ability to learn and played, together with economic, social or political interests, a significant role in the founding of the federal state.[51]

Hence Switzerland experienced both an economic as well as a political learning process. Both paths of development ran separate from one another through the 1830s. It would therefore be a mistake to explain the founding of the federal state as the result of economic interests. It would be an equal mistake, however, to argue that economic interests played no role or only a marginal one.

Cultural Change: National Consciousness, Forms of Communications, Public Discourse

Beginning in the eighteenth century, a national consciousness arose in Switzerland which had a range of effects on the individual phases of political and institutional learning processes between 1798 and 1848. In 1848, the various forms of Swiss nationalism constituted important integrative factors in the founding of a national federal government. Swiss nationalism was promoted by and institutionalized in diverse cultural, social, and state institutions, which at first were determined by a bourgeois elite. Only from the 1830s onward were national ideas disseminated among the rest of the population via associations and educational institutions, the press and public discourse, historiography and the schools. In a lengthy process involving new forms of communication and public discourse, these institutions contributed to a gradual "nationalization" of everyday life and of the population. They were based on cultural traditions, but were also a side-effect and result of the "new and modern," that is, of structural change in the entire society. Above all the dense network of voluntary associations, the school system and the press helped to overcome linguistic and confessional barriers.

Voluntary Associations and Educational Institutions, Festival Culture, Schools

In the "era of popular education and voluntary associations," according to Rudolf Braun, an interdependence existed between industrialization and the rise of a complex and socially broad range of clubs, educational institutions and organizations.[52] These clubs, open only to men, have been well researched; however, there exist considerable gaps in the research into women's roles and women's "space," and in works that have taken on a gender-oriented perspective.[53]

Men's clubs contributed not only to the origination and group practice of leisure-time activities in industrial societies, they also slaked a middle class-petit bourgeoisie thirst for education and reading. Depending on the nature of the club, they offered their members different forms of sociability, culture, popular education and physical training.

One institution without which village life would be unimaginable, even today, is the choral and music society. These clubs arose at the end of the eighteenth century out of church choral schools. Their collection of songs reflected not only enlightened concepts of education and self-cultivation, but also a "new fatherland-patriotic consciousness" (Braun). Patriotism became a civil religious force which mobilized the populace in village clubs, then at regional and cantonal choral meetings, and finally at

regularly occurring confederate choral festivals. In 1842 the Confederate Choral Association was founded, the statutes of which contained the following goal: "Cultivation
and refinement of popular singing, awakening of higher feelings for God, freedom and
fatherland, unification and fraternization of the joy in art and on the fatherland."[54]

The choral festivals were (and still are in part today) both social and political
events. Their programs were arranged like a church service; political speeches, joint
singing and moments of prayer alternated. In various texts by Gottfried Keller one can
read that, apart from patriotism, social elements were seldom absent (in other words,
wine). According to Braun, the phenomenon of a choral societies cannot be understood
"without its political-patriotic functions for the period." Conversely, as "spiritual-psy-
chological foundations" of the Swiss Federation, the clubs greatly influenced a growing national consciousness. The political phase of choral societies with a middle-class
membership, and an atmosphere in which men bonded together to boast of their
strength [*männerbündisch-kraftmeierisch*] lasted into the middle of the nineteenth century.
Subsequently, there followed a period of "depoliticization" and social broadening.[55]

A comparable development occurred among sharpshooting and gymnastics
societies. The Swiss Sharpshooters' Association was founded in 1824, the Confederate Gymnastics Association in 1832. Another significant national political integration
factor was the confederate militia with its regular training camps, the confederate
military school in Thun, founded in 1818, and the Swiss Officers' Society (1833). The
project, begun in the 1830s to produce a cartographic record of Switzerland, also
played an important role in the formation of state and nation. Swiss territory and its
borders were measured, recorded and established on exact maps (Dufour-Karten)—
an act of integration both internally and vis-à-vis foreign countries.[56]

From the end of the eighteenth century onwards, the struggle for control of
school between the church—Catholic or Protestant—and state institutions
increased in intensity. A "people's school" and the right to education and knowledge
were among the central planks of the liberal platform around 1830. The regeneration constitutions transferred responsibility for education to the cantons. Thus
Zürich gained its first teachers' college in 1832 and a "school system almost revolutionary for European conditions" in which the same basic education for boys and
girls was planned.[57] The "professionalized" teachers brought voluntary associations
to the communities where they taught and spread new knowledge and bourgeois-
liberal values. Naturally all of these decisive reforms were not introduced without
problems. There was considerable resistance to such innovations among the populace. The school reform debate, moreover, widened the gap between liberals and
democrats. Thus fierce conflicts arose again and again during the 1830/40's with the
introduction of new pedagogical concepts, key expressions of which were teaching
materials instead of catechism, thinking instead of memorization.

Historiography

The upswing in Swiss national historiography also reaches back into the eighteenth
century, a historiography that was not only part of the field "of academic research,
but also the object of national devotion."[58] Intellectual and social elites cultivated

this national feeling in reading circles and other societies such as the Helvetic Society, founded in 1761.[59] Around 1800, the "history of the foundation" of Switzerland, with the oath of Rütli Field, formed an incontrovertible integrative factor that was supplemented by Johannes von Müller's "myth of the Alps." Later joining these was the "myth of the pillar builder": according to it, the history of Switzerland had begun in ancient times. It is here that one finds the beginnings of the mental construct of a free and independent "Switzerland as an island in an unstable Europe." Together with the "neutrality myth," which also reaches back into the nineteenth century, the Alpine myth and the island concept still (unfortunately) belong today to the rhetorical and embarrassing standard set phrases of those politicians who oppose Swiss integration into Europe.

Contemporary historiography deems the period between 1798 and 1848 as the final fifty years of a long tradition. But the period between the 1291 oath of Rütli Field of and the founding of the federal state—the framework of the patriotic historical teleology—was a dark chapter of wars of the Reformation and the old, degenerate Confederation, that only ended in 1798. There followed until 1848 an agitated period of transformation, often influenced from abroad; in 1848, the federal state arose like a phoenix from its ashes.

Press and the Public Sphere

The "communications revolution" (Borchardt) began earlier in Switzerland than elsewhere in Europe. Improved levels of education and a legal guarantee of freedom of the press in the regenerated cantons led to the founding of many newspapers after 1830. Freedom of the press had already been established in the Helvetian Constitution of 1789; this basic right had to yield temporarily to a repressive press policy in the Mediation and Restoration periods. In 1829, after a historical debate on freedom of the press, the *Tagsatzung* annulled the "Presskonklusum," which Switzerland had introduced in 1823 under pressure from the European powers. The founding of the radical *Appenzeller Zeitung* (1828) had a signal effect throughout the country; it brought a turning point in press policy and simultaneously presaged the Regeneration.

Pushed forward by progressives in the printing industry and in many places freed from censorship, the print media (newspapers, books, journals) offered politics a broad forum. Regional distribution of newspapers was very uneven; in 1830, of the thirty-seven newspapers, twenty appeared in the wealthy industrial cantons of eastern and northwestern Switzerland; in 1848, sixty-seven of 110. In 1848 there was one newspaper for every 21,800 Swiss.[60] In comparison, in Prussia in 1845 there were forty-two political newspapers for a population of about 15 million; i.e., one for every 360,000 inhabitants.[61]

In Switzerland, the numerous political newspapers and journals worked, in fact, as a political forum, open to different political opinions that tied politics, state, and society together. In the period of accelerated political, economic and social upheaval and new departures (1830-1848), political positions were polarized between conservatives, liberals, and radicals. Moreover, class contrasts began to become more obvious. Sociopolitical changes were accompanied by a "structural change in the public sphere"; a complex field of competing and interacting partial public spheres arose that served the individual interests of social groups as public arenas.[62]

The rise of modern nationalism in the nineteenth century was a pan-European development and not just limited to the Swiss Confederation. In Germany, the Rhine crisis of 1840 brought about the breakthrough of modern nationalism as a mass phenomenon. In the following decade "national mobilization" achieved a "new quality" (Siemann) in its consequence and aims.[63]

In Switzerland, the countless clubs, the school system and the rapidly expanding press landscape were among the most important integrative factors in the "search for a new state." Other aspects of social communication and integration such as theater, literature, performing arts also played a role. Transport, as well, by "shortening" distances and accelerating the passage of information (the postal system) contributed to the forming of a nation. Only in the 1850s did Switzerland begin with the construction of a railway network—nearly twenty years after Germany. Federalism, competing projects, and financial problems prevented its rapid completion.[64]

In the "great integration crisis of the 1840s" (Mesmer) it was less national defamation than mutual defamation of religious confessions which led to a radicalization and mobilization of the masses.[65] The successful federal integration of Switzerland, therefore, should not lead one to conclude that in 1848 a national integration had succeeded in one stroke. Considering both Germany and Switzerland, Werner Näf stated that in the 1840s it was a question in the "nature of national consciousness of something unusually complex and complicated," because the original rational and liberal-enlightened elements of a national idea had been drowned out through the "addition of political-power political tendencies."[66] The losers of the civil war, the gap in development between cantons, and rising social antagonism ensured that a specific Swiss identity at first "only" existed in the heads and within the circles of the political and social elite, as before 1848.

Hansjörg Siegenthaler believes, certainly quite justifiably, that "nationalism was involved" in the founding period of the federal republic.[67] Between 1842 and 1848 a "fundamental insecurity" at first appeared; later, nationalism came to the fore. Individual actors were more approachable and open to communication because of the crisis, which drove forward "in the final analysis the run of events to their climax." And in fact there was at the time a "new networking."[68] As I have shown above, this process had already begun in the 1820s. And even after the founding of the federal state, the "cultivation of nationalist sentiment among our people"[69] still remained a concern of the schools, national politics, and numerous patriotic clubs.

Foreign Relations: Switzerland in Europe, Europe in Switzerland

Despite its specific path of development, Switzerland was no island, but tied to Europe in many respects. The integration and learning processes in Switzerland described above also need to be examined for their European dimension. The difficult political conflicts of the 1830/40s were accompanied by a constant "interplay of domestic and foreign relations"; they were equally "indicator[s] of the general European situation."[70] Cross-border relations affected not only foreign policy and diplomacy, but they also made themselves felt in the economy, in cultural exchange, and in the spread of political ideas.

While in the previous section I dealt with the influences "internal to Switzerland" which contributed to the rise of a national consciousness at the end of the eighteenth century, there existed external influences that stimulated the thinking of patriotic or national issues—at first within the bourgeois elite, and then, during the course of the nineteenth century, among the rest of the population as well. I would like to present these external factors briefly using two examples.

Political Relations among States, Diplomatic Pressure

The Helvetian Republic only lasted a short time. It failed not least because it subordinated long-developed regional and cantonal traditions to a unitary state, that was planned and designated by outsiders. Military occupation and the devastation of entire regions during the War of the Second Coalition, were followed by Napoleon's Mediation. The Congress of Vienna and the Paris treaties finally established the borders of Switzerland and guaranteed the Confederacy "perpetual neutrality." This neutrality was not clearly defined by either side, the reason for which the "Holy Alliance" continually intervened, directly or indirectly, between 1815 and 1848, and exerted at times considerable diplomatic and economic pressure.

In the 1820s, the shock-waves of the Carlsbad Decrees of 1819 reached Switzerland. Metternich wanted to integrate the Confederation into his European defensive system against revolutionary movements. He had especially targeted press and asylum policy, i.e., political refugees and the Swiss press. In 1823, under enormous pressure from abroad, the *Tagsatzung* approved the introduction of a "Press und Fremdenkonklusum," to prevent the misuse of the press and the right of asylum by political refugees. At the end of the 1820s, the situation had become calmer. The "democratic principle" that Metternich had fought with all means had become established in a number of cantons.

After the revolutionary unrest of 1830, after the Hambach Festival and the abortive Frankfurt insurrection in Germany, the conservative governments prepared a massive counter-strike. Throughout Europe, thousands of oppositionists—Germans, Poles, Italians—had to flee police persecution. A large number of them—mostly young, university educated radicals and members of the professions who were early socialists, but artisans and journeymen as well—were received in the regenerated cantons in Switzerland. In clubs, with newspapers, pamphlets, "literature in exile," and with armed attacks such as the so-called march on Savoy, these refugees continued their political struggle from Swiss soil.[71]

In 1834, one of these refugee militias, led by Giuseppe Mazzini, marched into Savoy from Switzerland. The attack was a complete failure and set off an avalanche of diplomatic protest. Metternich presented Switzerland with an ultimatum, threatening a blockade of Swiss borders, which in the end led to the expulsion of the activists. Directly following this "episode," Metternich was confirmed in his belief that Switzerland was the center of the revolutionary party by the Bern Steinhölzli gathering of German workers and artisans. In order to appease him, the *Tagsatzung* passed a second *Fremdenkonklusum* in 1836, thus severely limiting cantonal jurisdiction. Once again, numerous foreigners suspected of political agitation were expelled.

All of these events—mention should also be given to the affair of the naturalization of Louis-Napoléon (the future Napoléon III) in the canton of Thurgau, which almost led to war between France and Switzerland—underline the weak position of the *Tagsatzung*, under pressure from foreign powers, but also required to consider commitments under international law. Domestically, the *Tagsatzung* had to respect cantonal autonomy and was dependent on the voluntary cooperation of the cantons. Regenerated cantons often publicly supported the refugees. In view of this impasse, and of the contradictions and anachronisms, dissatisfaction increased among Swiss radicals—in the eyes of Friedrich Wilhelm IV a "godless and lawless sect"— as did the wish to push for the long overdue revision of the confederate treaty of 1815. In other words, refugee agitation and intervention from abroad had strengthened the reform movement in Switzerland.

The *Sonderbund* crisis of 1846/47 also had its international dimensions. Some foreign powers supported the *Sonderbund* with money and weapons, but could not agree to a common policy: Austria wanted to act, France hesitated, and England viewed the events in Switzerland rather favorably.[72] By the time a common plan had finally been agreed upon on 28 November 1847, the civil war was already over. The *Tagsatzung* announced that there was no longer anything to mediate.

In the middle of January, the great powers threatened military intervention if Switzerland were to revise its constitution. Once again the reply from the *Tagsatzung* was clear and definite: Switzerland had been "in its various forms independent for hundreds of years" and would itself decide about such revisions. Moreover, it was argued that the principle of neutrality of 1815 was not related to a "specific form of government structure."[73] Paris, Vienna, and Berlin had other problems shortly thereafter, and Switzerland was able to carry through its constitutional revision without interference from abroad. This foreign policy calm after the storm was not long preserved. In the summer of 1848, 22,000 Risorgimento activists pushed their way from Italy into the canton of Tessin after the battle of Custozza. This Lombardian "refugee affair" developed in 1848/49 into the first foreign policy conflict of competences between the new federal administration and a Tessin government that sympathized with the Risorgimento. Similar problems arose on the Rhine border, when after each of the three revolts in Baden rebels escaped into Switzerland.[74] Especially in 1849—after the defeat of the third revolt in Baden, when about 10,000 people fled from the Prussian troops into Switzerland—the Federal Council was faced with a very delicate foreign policy problem. It decided to transfer the refugees away from the border region, to divide them among the cantons, and to expel their political leaders.[75]

Exchange on the Political-Intellectual and Cultural Level

> While our enemies have bombs and canons, we have—pamphlets, small, very small
> pamphlets! Believe me, a single pamphlet against the violence is sometimes as fearsome
> a weapon as an entire artillery battery is against freedom.[76]

In the 1820s some of the German early liberals who had taken part in the Wartburg
festival, and had therefore been driven out of the country, found positions at the new
cantonal schools, teachers' colleges, and universities as teachers or professors.[77] At
first this "intelligentsia in exile" moved especially to Basel; later, the new universities
of Zürich (1833) and Bern (1834) became institutions of political action and teaching. In the 1830s the next "wave of refugees" (Urner) arrived in Switzerland. The-
ologians, constitutional law experts, doctors, and jurists took on important posts at
the universities. German pedagogical theorists played a major role in school reform.

In this period, the German worker and artisan movement also began in
Switzerland.[78] In Geneva, Zürich, Biel, Lausanne, Bern, and St. Gallen artisans' associations were founded which maintained close contacts to the secret society Young
Germany. After the "refugee witch-hunt" [*Flüchtlingshatz*] in the early summer of
1836—as a result of the second *Fremdenkonklusum*—the entire Swiss network of
artisans' associations was disbanded. Only Geneva and Waadt did not participate in
measures against refugees and artisans' associations. At the beginning of the 1840s
the movement experienced a second wind; once again artisans' associations arose, at
first in western Switzerland, then later in German-speaking Switzerland, mostly at
the initiative of individual people. They distributed newspapers, brochures, and
pamphlets with early socialist and communist ideas.

For their "literary guerrilla warfare" (Näf) the "censorship refugees" were
dependent on Swiss publishing houses and printers. In the 1840s, Switzerland was,
along with Belgium and England, the most attractive place for oppositional literati.
Here they found that which they had fought for in Germany: freedom of opinion
and of the press. Only a few authors succumbed to the illusion that from Switzerland one "could set off a revolution simply with pamphlets." Nonetheless, many
hoped that "a single pen that could reach a repressed people from a secure point
would in the end be able to overthrow every reaction."[79] In the 1840s, there were a
good dozen printers and publishers especially in German-speaking Switzerland who
produced the political pamphlets of the writers in exile.[80] Their works sometimes
appeared anonymously or under assumed publishers' names. At first, they reached
Germany through book trade routes; after 1846, when German customs confiscated
entire consignments, the goods were smuggled across the border along secret paths.

The actions of the political émigré publishers had consequences on both sides
of the border. In the German states, the works of writers in exile gave rise to an
enormous press and state police apparatus, whereby it soon became clear to the
authorities that the existing press and censorship policy, based on sweeping prevention and control, was no longer up to the developments in publishing and
could not prevent the spread of political writings. In 1846/47 a debate began in the

German Confederation about possible reforms of its press policy. In Switzerland, which once again found itself in a dilemma between rights of freedom, asylum, and international law, the authorities were forced to take action against exile publishers and literati.

This asylum policy led to a lengthy debate in Swiss newspapers, which made two points clear. On the one hand was the position of the liberals. Thinking along the lines of what would later be called *Realpolitik*, they saw in the behavior of the refugees a misuse of the right of asylum and a violation of international law and therefore approved of the expulsion of the Germans. On the other hand, radicals supported the exiled literati; Switzerland, with its liberal-democratic traditions, bore a European responsibility and was morally bound to support the refugees. A few refugees (Herwegh, Snell among others) also received Swiss citizenship. The debate also shows that Switzerland was struggling both for domestic integration and for an international position—European integration—for the country.

What did the writings of the political refugees mean for relations between Switzerland and Germany? Many emigrants not only expounded on the political conditions of their homeland in their pamphlets, but often equally critically followed the crises and events in their land of refuge. Swiss radicals remained in contact with the refugees, despite certain tendencies to distance themselves, a "hatred of Germans" in certain circles and the severest political controversies. This expanded communicative space affected both sides.

"High in the mountains, the first shot fell"—this line begins a well-known poem by Ferdinand Freiligrath from 1848. The poet describes the *Sonderbund* War as presaging the March Revolution. Not only writers in exile but also radical opposition movements throughout Europe followed spellbound the civil war in Switzerland. The *Tagsatzung* received around fifty addresses with over 5,000 signatures (including those of all the leading figures of the forthcoming 1848 revolution) from Germany as well as from Paris, Brussels, and London. With their letters, the signatories sought to provide moral support for the *Tagsatzung* and its troops in their fight against the *Sonderbund*; the civil war was thus transformed into a model of republican struggle for freedom. The victory of the radicals in Switzerland strengthened the self-confidence of their German fellow radicals and their belief in the possibility of a political upheaval.[81] One can, however, hardly say—and here I agree with Werner Näf—that new, pioneering political ideas arose in Switzerland or that the *Sonderbund* War "had carried Germany with it." "With few exceptions, the struggles in Switzerland functioned only as spark, as movement."[82]

Switzerland was (and is) not an island: Werner Näf's statement that the Switzerland of 1848 was of "European importance"[83] is certainly true, but in my view it must be extended to the entire period between 1798 and 1848 and beyond. Here one should not ignore the fact that developments in the confederation were informed by events and processes abroad. A good example for my thesis are the refugee and press policies, because they run like an unbroken thread through the entire fifty years; both represent border-crossings, expanded communicative spaces and mutual relations between Europe and Switzerland. Beginning in Switzerland, new political ideas were propagated which were of major import for the labor movement and the social question in the second half of the nineteenth century. The confederates thus also played a significant role here. On the other hand, during the Regeneration they profited from exile German intellectuals. And finally the March Revolution had its effect on developments in Switzerland.

Wolfram Siemann writes that the formation of the German nation took place "in exchange and in contact with its European neighbors,"[84] and this statement could equally be applied to Switzerland, although the confederation experienced its own specific development and the establishment of a nation-state succeeded in 1848. The social, institutional, and national learning processes were equally an international relations learning process; "the process of differentiation and integration" repeated itself "at a higher level" (Siemann). The founding of the nation state against domestic opposition also meant a demarcation with respect to the outside. Of this, the liberal victors were sure, when they pointed out to the European Powers the neutrality of Switzerland after the conclusion of the *Sonderbund* War of 1847/48. The Swiss federal state began to engage in active foreign relations. The national integration of Switzerland should not be understood in terms of a separation from the external world, but as a process of international integration.

Conclusion

Why was the founding of a national and federal state successful in Switzerland in 1848? I began with two assumptions. First, events in Switzerland need to be viewed in both a geographically and temporally expanded context. For this reason I have not limited myself to Switzerland, but instead occasionally glanced across the borders, especially towards Germany and I expanded the time period to that between 1798 and 1848. Second, integrative processes were occurring in Switzerland at various levels, which can be described as a learning process in the sense of the term employed by Karl W. Deutsch and Klaus Eder. I have attempted to define these learning processes in five sections.

1. In politics, the long political traditions and range of political experience had an integrating effect. This integrative process, which in the final analysis was always about the creation of new forms of legalizing and institutionalizing political domination, can be divided into six phases. The real key phase was the period between 1830 and 1848—the period of the long "democratic revolution" (Tocqueville), fierce conflict, and the civil war. Then, the central issue was the reform of the deadlocked confederate 1815 league of states and the formation of a federal state out of petty cantonal particularism [*Vielstaaterei*], different governmental traditions, various political standpoints and cultural diversity.

This constitutional structural change occurred in Switzerland from bottom up. It began in the communities, continued in the canton, and finally reached—after fierce conflict—the federal level. This "historical constant" (Andrey) and the "familiarity with the politics of parliamentary compromise" (Wehler) are two central points that distinguish Switzerland from the *Vormärz* German states. The federal constitution of 1848 is therefore the result of a specifically Swiss road to a federal state; a temporary result, however, because the new constitution contained regulations for its reform and conflicts continued. The political learning process certainly did not end in 1848, quite the opposite. This openness made possible—again after long and hard conflict—the continued learning process and integration of new political ideas at the end of the nineteenth the beginning of the twentieth century.

2. The early rise of the bourgeoisie was another aspect of specifically Swiss development. From the time of the Regeneration, the bourgeois "middle class" was the most important social group and the social stratum that carried forth political and economic progress. The new bourgeois-liberal elite was on the one hand "relatively homogeneous" (Tanner), but on the other, open below and above, according to Deutsch a central condition of sociopolitical integration. The liberals had hardly occupied the governments of the cantons in the 1830s when they began with their "policy of circumscribing the revolution" (Langewiesche) and a consolidation of power. Sixteen years later their German "colleagues" pursued the same policy in the summer of 1848, as they directed the March Revolution onto a reformist-legal course.

It was only the conservative counterattack, the successes of the radicals and the intensification of the *Sonderbund* conflict that led the liberals in Switzerland to continue with political reform. The great bourgeois-liberal "coalition" emerged as the victor of the civil war and was able to carry through long desired constitutional reform within a few months. This success was certainly also based on the liberals' pragmatic, moderate, and integration-oriented outlook. It must be added, however, that this dominant "bloc" hindered further political reform in the decades after 1848 and thus had a disintegrative effect. It delayed the solution of important political questions -equal rights for women,[85] the "civic emancipation" of the Jews or protection of minorities for example.

3. Economic developments were in advance of political modernization; the upswing of the export-oriented cotton industry took place without the existence of a united state administration or a customs union. Nonetheless, it would be wrong to suggest that the two areas developed independently of one another. Especially in the regenerated cantons, more and more businessmen entered politics and worked towards economic integration (customs debate). The great crisis of 1846/47, growing competition, and trade barriers abroad encouraged interest in connection between the economy and the federal state in business circles, and the founding of a federal government gave the economy an extra boost.

4. Voluntary associations and educational institutions, a dense network of newspapers and journals, as well as national institutions such as the army exercised, along with new forms of communication and new versions of the public sphere, a great influence on sociocultural development. They contributed to a gradual nationalization of everyday life and of the population, to an overcoming of linguistic and confessional barriers, and, finally to the formation of a Swiss identity. National integration was, however, not completed in 1848, and remained a constant challenge.

5. Switzerland went through its political and institutional learning process with a constant exchange and in a constant struggle with its neighboring countries. International relations played an important, perhaps even a central, role in all areas. National integration of Switzerland was thus related to events and changes abroad. Switzerland was seen by many as a model, as a utopia on earth, so to speak—and not only because it "was the sole republic in Europe" (Näf). According to Reinhart Koselleck there was "something paradigmatic for all of Europe" in the "Swiss special development" between 1830 and 1848. "The dismantling of the patrician-corporate constitutions, the breakthrough of the liberal and industrial bourgeoisie, equal rights for city and country, the extension of voting rights downwards, the gaining of national unity against all attempts at intervention in the name of supranational claims to legitimacy: all this took place during the *Vormärz*. Switzerland thus took a road which was soon to become the program of the revolutionaries of 1848."[86]

Finally, the question arises of whether one can describe the events 1847/48 in Switzerland as a revolution. As the following three examples show, historians are not in agreement in this point. Wolfram Siemann states that Switzerland experienced—earlier than the German Confederation—an "analogous process of inner formation of state and nation"; "the *Sonderbund* War of 1847 was the successful revolution there, which legitimized and anchored the structural change."[87] Albert Tanner also speaks of a "bourgeois revolution"—sometimes with, sometimes without quotation marks.[88] Dieter Langewiesche, on the other hand, points to the acceleration of the political reform movement in Switzerland, "without its turning into a revolution."[89]

I prefer the term "transformation," common in recent social science discourse, to the controversial term revolution. This term is indeed useful, as it includes various developments, different forms of sociohistorical change, as well as political and institutional learning processes. In January 1848, before the establishment of the federal state, when Tocqueville spoke of an, apparently oxymoronic "democratic revolution" in Switzerland in the period between 1830 and 1848, he precisely had in mind this processual character of Swiss development—the political, social and cultural transformation process. Still, from today's point of view, there is something "revolutionary" in the founding of the federal state in 1848.

Notes

I would like to thank Hansjörg Siegenthaler, Andreas Suter, Martin Leuenberger and especially Marietta Meier for their criticism, patience, and never-failing support during my work on this chapter.

1. Werner Näf, "Der schweizerische Sonderbundskrieg als Vorspiel der deutschen Revolution von 1848," *Basler Zeitschrift für Geschichte und Altertumskunde*, 19 (1921): 1-105 (= Diss. Munich 1917); and by the same author, *Die Schweiz in der deutschen Revolution 1847-1849. Ein Kapitel schweizerisch-deutscher Beziehungen in den Jahren 1847-1849* (Frauenfeld, 1929); W. Näf (ed.) *Deutschland und die Schweiz in ihren kulturellen und politischen Beziehungen während der ersten Hälfte des 19. Jahrhunderts*, (Bern, 1936).

2. Alexis de Tocqueville, "Etudes économique, politiques et littéraires," *Oeuvres complètes*, Vol. 9 (Paris, 1866), 86.

3. Klaus W. Deutsch, *Die Schweiz als ein paradigmatischer Fall politischer Integration* (Bern, 1976). See also, by the same author, *Nationenbildung-Nationalstaat-Integration*, ed. by A. Ashkenasi/P. Schulze (Düsseldorf, 1972).

4. Klaus Eder, *Geschichte als Lernprozeß? Zur Pathogenese politischer Modernität in Deutschland* (Frankfurt, 1985).

5. To a certain extent I take the results of a historical process in Switzerland as given and then ask about its specific structural conditions. In view of the "150 years of the Swiss Federation," the "Allgemeine Geschichtsforschende Gesellschaft der Schweiz" organized numerous conferences in 1997. These appear in: A. Ernst, A. Tanner and M. Weishaupt (eds.), *Die konflikthafte Entstehung des schweizerischen Bundesstaates 1798-1848* (Zürich, 1998); Th. Hildbrand and A. Tanner (eds.), *Im Zeichen der Revolution. Der Weg zum schweizerischen Bundesstaat 1798-1848* (Zürich, 1997).

6. See H. Böning, *Revolution in der Schweiz. Das Ende der Alten Eidgenossenschaft. Die Helvetische Republik 1798-1803* (Frankfurt, 1985); Gordon Craig, *The Triumph of Liberalism: Zürich in the Gold Age* (New York, 1988), 32-39; F. de Capitani, "Beharren und Umsturz (1648-1815)," in *Die Geschichte der Schweiz und der Schweizer* (Basel, 1986), 508-525; A. Kölz, *Neuere schweizerische Verfassungsgeschichte. Ihre Grundlinien vom Ende der Alten Eidgenossenschaft bis 1848* (Bern, 1992); by the same author, *Quellenbuch zur neueren schweizerischen Verfassungsgeschichte* (Bern, 1992).

7. Quoted in Kölz, *Quellenbuch*, 204.

8. Kölz, *Verfassungsgeschichte*, 177-207.

9. *Repertorium der Abschiede der eidgenössischen Tagsatzung 1814-1848*, Vol. 1, (Bern, 1874), 402.

10. Kölz, *Verfassungsgeschichte*, 221-22.

11. Tessin, Thurgau, Aargau, Lucerne, Zürich, St. Gallen, Freiburg, Waadt, Solothurn, Bern, and Schaffhausen.

12. See Kölz, *Verfassungsgeschichte*, 235-64.

13. Craig, *Triumph of Liberalism*, 54-59.

14. Quoted in Edgar Bonjour, *Die Gründung des schweizerischen Bundesstaates* (Basel, 1948), 53.

15. *Repertorium*, 1: 463.

16. On the *Sonderbund* War see Näf, "Der schweizerische Sonderbundskrieg"; E. Bucher, *Die Geschichte des Sonderbundskrieges* (Zürich, 1966); Joachim Remak, *A Very Civil War: The Swiss Sonderbund War of 1847* (Boulder, 1993).

17. In the literature there is some confusion about the exact number of victims—one mentions 98 dead and 493 injured, another speaks of 104 dead and 374 injured.

18. E. Bucher, "Der Werdegang der Verfassung," in *Handbuch der Schweizer Geschichte*, Vol. 2 (Zürich, 1977), 989-1017; Kölz, *Verfassungsgeschichte*, 543-613.

19. Quoted in Bucher, *Werdegang*, 992.

20. On constitutional revision see *Repertorium*, 1: 387-396.

21. De Capitani, "Beharren," 643.

22. For the following section see Kölz, *Verfassungsgeschichte*, 543-630; and his *Quellenbuch*.

23. Eder, *Geschichte als Lernprozeß*, 354-55.

24. Hans-Ulrich Wehler, *Deutsche Gesellschaftsgeschichte*, Vol. 2 (Munich, 1987), 764-65.

25. Näf, "Der schweizerische Bürgerkrieg," 23.

26. Ibid., 23.

27. Rudolf Braun, *Das ausgehende Ancien Régime in der Schweiz* (Göttingen, 1984; by the same author, *Sozialer und kultureller Wandel in einem ländlichen Industriegebiet* (Erlenbach-Zürich, 1965); Craig, *Triumph of Liberalism*, 41-42.

28. Albert Tanner, *Arbeitsame Patrioten und wohlanständige Damen. Bürgertum und Bürgerlichkeit in der Schweiz* (Zürich. 1995), 485. See also by the same author, "Bürgertum und Bürgerlichkeit in der Schweiz. Die 'Mittelklassen' an der Macht," in Jürgen Kocka (ed.), *Bürgertum im 19. Jahrhundert*, Vol. 1, (Munich, 1988), 193-223; M. König, "Neuere Forschungen zur Sozialgeschichte der Schweiz," *Archiv für Sozialgeschichte* 36 (1996): 395-433.

29. Tanner, *Arbeitsame Patrioten*, 487-88.

30. Craig, *Triumph of Liberalism*, 53-59.

31. Quoted in Tanner, *Arbeitsame Patrioten*, 489.

32. Kölz, *Verfassungsgeschichte*, 276-89.

33. J.-C. Biaudet, "Der modernen Schweiz entgegen," in *Handbuch der Schweizer Geschichte*, Vol. 2 (Zürich, 1977), 924.

34. Hansjörg Siegenthaler, "Supranationalität, Nationalismus und regionale Autonomie. Erfahrungen des schweizerischen Bundesstaates—Perspektiven der europäischen Gemeinschaft," *Traverse, Zeitschrift für Geschichte / Revue d'Histoire* 3 (1994): 127-28.

35. Tanner, *Arbeitsame Patrioten*, 494.

36. On this process, see Erich Gruner, *Die schweizerische Bundesversammlung 1848-1919*, 2 vols.(Bern, 1966).

37. Wehler, *Deutsche Gesellschaftsgeschichte* 2: 761-770.

38. Tanner, *Arbeitsame Patrioten*, 11-12.

39. Jean-François Bergier, *Die Wirtschaftsgeschichte der Schweiz* (Zürich, 1983), 191.

40. H. Ritzmann (ed.), *Historische Statistik der Schweiz* (Zürich, 1996); see also G. Andrey, "Auf der Suche nach dem neuen Staat (1794-1848)" in *Geschichte der Schweiz und der Schweizer* (Basel, 1986), 534-38.

41. See Braun, *Sozialer und kultureller Wandel*; Erich Gruner, *Die Arbeiter in der Schweiz im 19. Jahrhundert: Soziale Lage, Organisation, Verhältnis zu Arbeitgeber und Staat* (Bern, 1968); Albert Tanner, *Spulen, Weben, Sticken. Die Industrialisierung in Appenzell Ausserrhoden* (Zürich, 1982); P. Dudzik, *Innovation und Investition. Technische Entwicklung und Unternehmerenstscheide in der schweizerischen Baumwollspinnerei 1800-1916* (Zürich, 1987); E. Joris and H. Witzig, *Brave Frauen—Aufmüpfige Weiber. Wie sich die Industrialisierung auf Alltag und Lebenszusammenhänge von Frauen auswirkte (1820-1940)* (Zürich, 1992); U. Pfister, *Die Zürcher Fabriques. Protoindustrielles Wachstum vom 16. Bis zum 18. Jahrhundert* (Zürich, 1992).

42. Braun, *Industrialisierung und Landleben*, 16.

43. G. Andrey, "Auf der Suche nach dem neuen Staat (1798-1848)," 542.

44. For the following section, see Dudzik, *Innovation und Investition*.

45. Ulrich Menzel, *Auswege aus der Abhängigkeit. Die entwicklungspolitische Aktualität Europas* (Frankfurt, 1988), 118.

46. Ibid., 108-36.

47. G. Andrey, "Auf der Suche nach dem neuen Staat," 551-52.

48. Wolfram Siemann, *Vom Staatenbund zum Nationalstaat. Deutschland 1806-1871* (Munich, 1995), 167ff.

49. Menzel, *Auswege aus der Abhängigkeit*, 38-39.

50. Bergier, *Wirtschaftsgeschichte der Schweiz*, 210.

51. Siegenthaler, "Supranationalität," 117-42.

52. Braun, *Industrialisierung und Volksleben*, 297-362; See also H.U. Jost and A. Tanner (eds.), *Geselligkeit, Sozietäten und Vereine* (Zürich, 1991).

53. See B. Mesmer, *Ausgeklammert—Eingeklammert. Frauen und Frauenorganisationen in der Schweiz des 19. Jahrhunderts* (Basel, 1988); Joris and Witzig, *Brave Frauen*; R. Jaun and B. Studer (eds.), *Weiblich-*

männlich. Geschlechterverhältnisse in der Schweiz: Rechtssprechung, Diskurs, Praktiken (Zürich, 1995); E. Joris, "Die geteilte Moderne. Individuelle Rechtsansprüche für Männer, ständische Abhängigkeit für Frauen," *Schweizerische Zeitschrift für Geschichte* 46 pt. 3 (1996): 306-331.

54. Quoted in Braun, *Industrialisierung und Volksleben*, 328.

55. Ibid., 329-33.

56. D. Gugerli, "Politics on the Topographer's Table. The Helvetian Triangulation of Cartography, Politics, and Representation" in Timothy Lenoir (ed.), *Inscribing Science. Scientific Texts and Materiality of Communication* (Stanford, 1996).

57. B. Fritzsche and M. Lemmenmeier, "Die revolutionäre Umgestaltung von Wirtschaft, Gesellschaft und Staat 1780-1870" in *Geschichte des Kantons Zürich*, Vol. 3 (Zürich, 1994), 134. See also Braun, *Industrialisierung und Volksleben*, 296-306.

58. De Capitani, "Beharren," 507. See also, by the same author, "Die Suche nach dem gemeinsamen Nenner. Der Beitrag der Geschichtsschreiber" in F. de Capitani and G. Germann (eds.), *Auf dem Weg zu einer schweizerischen Identität 1848-1914. Probleme, Errungenschaften, Mißerfolge* (Freiburg, 1987), 25-38.

59. Ulrich Im Hof, *Die Entstehung einer politischen Öffentlichkeit in der Schweiz. Struktur und Tätigkeit der Helvetischen Gesellschaft*, (Bern, 1983); Ulrich Im Hof and F. Capitani, *Die Helvetische Gesellschaft. Spätaufklärung und Vorrevolution in der Schweiz*, Vol. 1 (Frauenfeld, 1983).

60. R. Ruffieux, "La presse politique en Suisse durant la première moitié du XIXe siècle. Esquisse de ses caractéristiques socio-économiques," in *Festschrift Gottfried Bösch* (Schwyz, 1980), 231-44.

61. The figures are from Wehler, *Deutsche Gesellschaftsgeschichte* 2: 10, 528.

62. For Switzerland, see the essays on the subject of the "public sphere" in *Schweizerische Zeitschrift für Geschichte*, Vol. 46, Pt. 1, 1996.

63. See for Germany: Wehler, *Deutsche Gesellschaftsgeschichte* 2: 394-412; and Siemann, *Vom Staatenbund zum Nationalstaat*, 353-62.

64. See R. Ruffieux, "Die Schweiz des Freisinns (1848-1914)," *Geschichte der Schweiz und der Schweizer* (Basel, 1986), 661-63. On Germany: Siemann, *Vom Staatenbund zum Nationalstaat*, 209-213.

65. B. Mesmer, "Nationale Identität. Einige methodische Bemerkungen" in de Capitani and Germann, *Auf dem Weg zur Schweizerischen Indentität*, 17. See also D. Frei, "Die Förderung des schweizerischen Nationalbewußtseins nach dem Zusammenbruch der Alten Eidgenossenschaft 1798," (Ph.D. Diss., Zürich 1964).

66. Näf, *Die Schweiz in der deutschen Revolution*, 11.

67. Siegenthaler, "Supranationalität," 123.

68. Ibid., 128, writes that the liberal elite of the regenerated cantons, both German and French speaking, had united beyond the language barrier, because they wanted "to make their revolutionary government permanent."

69. So ran the theme of the annual conference of the Swiss charitable society in 1889. Quoted in Mesmer, "Nationale Identität," 22.

70. Reinhart Koselleck, "Die Julirevolution und ihre Folgen bis 1848" in Louis Bergeron, François Furet, and Reinhart Koselleck, *Das Zeitalter der europäischen Revolutionen 1780-1848* (Frankfurt, 1969), 281.

71. See L. Lenherr, "Ultimatum an die Schweiz. Der politische Druck Metternichs auf die Eidgenossenschaft infolge ihrer Asylpolitik in der Regeneration (1833-1836)," (Ph.D. Diss., Zürich 1991); H. Reiter, *Politisches Asyl im 19. Jahrhundert. Die deutschen Flüchtlinge des Vormärz und der Revolution von 1848/49 in Europa und den USA* (Berlin, 1992). See also Hans Henning Hahn, "Möglichkeiten und Formen politischen Handelns in der Emigration" *Archiv für Sozialgeschichte*, 23 (1983): 123-61.

72. See Bonjour, *Die Gründung des schweizerischen Bundesstaates*, 122-52; Biaudet, "Der modernen Schweiz entgegen," 960-61.

73. *Repertorium* 1: 190.

74. Craig, *Triumph of Liberalism*, 81-89; M. Levenberger, *Frei und gleich ... und fremd. Flüchtlinge im Baselgebiet zwischen 1830 und 1880* (Liestal, 1996).

75. J. Frei, "Die schweizerische Flüchtlingspolitik nach den Revolutionen von 1848 und 1849," (Ph.D. Diss., Zürich 1977).

76. Karl Heinzen, *Weniger als 20 Bogen* (Herisau, 1846), 48.

77. See K. Urner, *Die Deutschen in der Schweiz. Von den Anfängen der Kolonienbildung bis zum Ausbruch des Ersten Weltkrieges* (Frauenfeld, 1976).

78. Wolfgang Schieder, *Anfänge der deutschen Arbeiterbewegung. Die Auslandsvereine nach der Julirevolution von 1830* (Stuttgart, 1963).

79. Karl Heinzen, *Erlebtes, Zweiter Teil: Nach meiner Exilierung* (Boston, 1874), 108-9.

80. This aspect of relations between Germany and Switzerland forms the center of my doctoral dissertation: Thomas Christian Müller, "Schmuggel politischer Schriften, Bedingungen exilliterarischer Öffentlichkeit in der Schweiz und im Deutschen Bund (1830-1848)," (Ph.D. Diss., Zürich 1997).

81. See Näf, *Die Schweiz in der deutschen Revolution*, 24-45, 106-207 (texts of the petitions).

82. Näf, "Der schweizerische Sonderbundskrieg," 96-97.

83. Ibid., 95.

84. Siemann, *Vom Staatenbund zum Nationalstaat*, 16.

85. See also Joris, "Die geteilte Moderne," 331, who describes the founding of the federal repbulic as a "compromise among men at women's cost." Liberal men "saw women neither as citizens nor as part of the people who needed to be liberated."

86. Koselleck, "Die Julirevolution und ihre Folgen," 284. Early industrialization could be added to this list.

87. Siemann, *Vom Staatenbund zum Nationalstaat*, 326.

88. Tanner, "Bürgertum und Bürgerlichkeit in der Schweiz," 199; Tanner, *Arbeitsame Patrioten*, 493-94.

89. Dieter Langewiesche, *Europa zwischen Restauration und Revolution 1815-1849* (Munich, 1985), 71.

Chapter 10

THE WATERLOO OF PEACE
AND ORDER

The United Kingdom and the Revolutions of 1848

John Belchem

To contemporaries and subsequent generations of historians, Britain's immunity from revolution in 1848 confirmed her cherished extra-continental "difference." Geographically in Europe but not of it, Britain managed to escape such continental horrors as revolution, as alien forces stopped short at the English Channel. Britishness, however, acquired an additional defining characteristic in 1848. Superiority over the external continental "other" was reinforced by ethnic-like denigration of an internal "other," the wild and violent Irish. To understand the meaning of 1848, its importance in the construction and projection of national identity, it is necessary to study events within the complex "multinational" framework of the United Kingdom.

An exercise in deconstruction, this chapter is concerned less with the extent of British exceptionalism in Europe than with the stresses and strains within the United Kingdom itself, points of tension accentuated by the year of revolution. The traditional defining juxtaposition with continental Europe, still an article of faith in some political quarters, has long withered under historical interrogation. Admittedly as the first "industrial" nation, Britain enjoyed comparative advantage and a different economic rhythm. Having endured its worst trough during the cyclical crisis of 1839/42, the economy, boosted by a number of growth factors, was carried through the commercial crisis of 1847 with resilience and strength. Continental Europe, by contrast, was ravaged by old-style distress, the combustible conjuncture of famine and high unemployment. The political response, however, was remarkably similar. Moderation and constitutionalism were not uniquely British. On both sides of the Channel, popular pressure for constitutional reform, not revolution, was the hall-

---

mark of 1848.[1] Recently, a more critical attack on British distinctiveness has come from within: by challenging Anglocentricity, the new "four nations" historiography of the United Kingdom has undermined the traditional representation of Britain as moderate, consensual, and unitary.[2]

The inclusion of Ireland in studies of Britain and 1848 does not necessarily imply a revisionist historiographical project. For some historians, Ireland has proved a useful point of comparative reference, serving to confirm, not to subvert, traditional interpretations. Events in Ireland were more violent and confrontational, but even so protestors and authorities (not least the new police) displayed moderation and toleration. By comparison with continental Europe, W.J. Lowe observes, events in both England *and* Ireland were "rather sedate."[3] While a welcome development, this comparative approach has a number of flaws. The disregard of Scotland and Wales is unfortunate but perhaps not inappropriate: as Roy Foster, the leading Irish historian, has recently observed, "'England' carries a historical charge, an implication of attempted cultural dominance, an assertion of power, which is not conveyed to the Irish ear by 'Britain.'"[4] A more serious weakness is the static geographical framework: for purposes of comparative case study, England and Ireland are treated as discrete entities. Even the major studies by Stanley Palmer and John Saville fail to take adequate account of the complex interconnections between the British and Irish within the United Kingdom and throughout the wider Irish diaspora.[5] It was this very fluidity—the lack of clear boundaries of revolutionary threat—which so disturbed the authorities, prompting them to take massive precautions to ensure the political and geographical integrity of the United Kingdom.

While arguing for the importance of the Irish dimension in 1848 this paper does not offer a "revolutionary" re-interpretation of events in Ireland itself. Despite opportunistic conversion to republican separatism, democracy, Chartist alliance, and insurgency, Irish nationalism lacked the program, strategy, and popular following for revolutionary challenge. John Mitchel's amendment of James Fintan Lalor's rent-strike proposals took account of famine distress, but in upholding the property-holding rights of the "peasantry," nationalist discourse privileged the small tenant-farmers, leaving landless laborers and cottiers unprotected. Mitchel's scheme, however, had considerable tactical potential: premised on pervasive passive resistance and defensive violence, it could develop into guerilla warfare or mass insurgency. It was embraced with enthusiasm by middle-class nationalist leaders in the immediate aftermath of revolution in Paris. Thenceforth the Irish Confederation sought to provoke the government into repressive action that would delegitimize its authority and rouse the masses from political dormancy, O'Connellite obeisance, and traditional "non-political" forms of "outrage" protest.[6]

As it was, the Confederates attracted little support. Battered by disease, starvation, forced migration and emigration, the famined Irish lacked the strength and will for popular nationalist insurgency. Agrarian "outrage," however, rose dramatically: the ratio of such "protest" crime to indictable crime in general reached 17.7 percent in 1848, more than double the highest figures ever recorded in England and Wales.[7] The Confederate leaders chose not to ally with those inured to such violence, the peasant secret societies. Even so, most of the Catholic clergy, loyal to the memory and methods of the late Daniel O'Connell, cautioned their parishioners against involvement with the Confederates.

In the absence of popular backing, and confronted by a coercive over-reaction by the authorities, Confederate leaders belied their intimidatory rhetoric by acting in ways and means which, as Stanley Palmer notes, "seem more confused and timid than dangerous."[8] As the authorities gained confidence, even perhaps provoking the hapless Confederates into insurgency, the Irish "Revolution" collapsed in farcical confrontation in Widow McCormack's cabbage-patch in Ballingarry, County Tipperary in late July. This unplanned incident, Palmer notes, "was just another in a long line of constabulary affrays in early nineteenth-century Ireland. But contemporaries in the year of European revolution, like some subsequent scholars, elevated it to the status of a rebellion."[9]

Events in Ireland seemingly conform to the norms and tropes of mainstream British history. In their dislike of violence, Irish Confederates appear little different from moral-force English Chartists, although Smith O'Brien, the leader of the "rising," was ultimately driven to an act of "symbolic protest." While more coercive than their English counterparts, the Irish authorities still operated with restraint and within the spirit of the law—and without recourse to continental-style military intervention and its disastrous consequences. There was one slight difference: in Ireland the professional police lacked civilian assistance. Restrained or not, coercion bred feelings of resentment to British laws and practices in Ireland, hence the absence of special constables.[10]

In their "colonial" isolation, the authorities feared they might lose control should the nationalists gain "external" assistance, whether in the form of an Irish-American army of invasion or simultaneous and diversionary insurrection coordinated by the new alliance between the Irish Confederates and the British Chartists. In Dublin and London the fears and anxieties of the authorities centered on the threat posed by Irish migrants.

Flushed with the excitement of the "springtime of the peoples," Irish migrants in Britain and the United States displayed greater nationalist fervor than their compatriots at home. Consciousness of being Irish, it seems, was more readily appreciated at a distance. Migration helped to construct a national identity, to superimpose a wider "invented" affiliation upon traditional and instinctive sub-national loyalties, to unite socially heterogeneous groups. In sure expectation of a popular rising back in Ireland, migrants were to infringe the codes and conventions of public space and political behavior, overstepping the limits of what was possible and permissible within the political culture of their new lands of residence. By the end of the year, they were forced into embarrassing retreat, shamed by the humiliating turn of events in Ireland. These cultural and behavorial tensions, dramatically revealed by the gap between expectation and eventuality in 1848, established the Irish as different and alien, an identity subsequently confirmed by pseudo-scientific racialism.[11]

Electrified by news of revolution in Europe, Irish-Americans pledged immediate support for active republican insurrection, promising to supply funds, arms, and

American "military science": an "Irish Brigade" with an officer corps drilled in the militia, the latest firearms technology (including colt revolvers) to supplement the native pike, and battle-hardened veterans of the Mexican war.[12] In the revolutionary excitement of 1848, Irish-American nationalism was to be carried forward, far ahead of "Young Ireland" itself, by identification with the American mission of republicanism. Ireland was projected as the privileged site for American aid and intervention, *the* test-case for America to fulfil its historic promise through international expansion of its republican liberty. It was in 1848, indeed, that Irish-American nationalism acquired its "Fenian" characteristics: republican separatism and physical force.

The British authorities took the new threat extremely seriously. Elgin, the governor general of Canada, entered "extra official correspondence" with the British chargé d'affaires at Washington to gain early intelligence of any invasion plan by Irish nationalists, acting on their own or in concert with Papineau's French republicans and "Yankee" expansionists. In New York an informer, funded by the British Consul, posed as an "Emigrant Runner" to provide accurate descriptions of the Irish Brigade as the squads set sail. Ships were searched upon entering British waters. New telegraphic links were established between Dublin Castle and Liverpool docks where specially-trained police (working in conjunction with detectives from Dublin) kept a close watch on all American arrivals. A police circular memorandum in Ireland, where returning emigrants were regarded with particular suspicion, ordered that all "persons coming over from America are to be immediately arrested, and searched for treasonable papers." A couple of members of the advanced guard of the brigade were eventually spotted in Liverpool, tailed to Dublin, arrested and held without charge. Otherwise all was quiet and uneventful, except for sustained diplomatic protest by the United States at the mistreatment of its citizens. Palmerston reacted with predictable vigor:

> I beg to observe that it is notorious to all the world that proceedings of the most hostile character toward the British government have of late taken place in the United States; that not only private associations have been formed, but that public meetings have been held for the avowed purpose of encouraging, assisting and organizing rebellion in Ireland, with a view to dismember the British empire ... these associations and public meetings have been composed not only of Irish emigrants, but also of natural born citizens of the United States ... these conspirators in the United States have sent to Ireland, to assist the rebellion which they had intended to organize, money, arms, ammunition and active agents ... some of the agents have been arrested, and must be dealt with according to their deserts.[13]

While American politicians were prepared to exploit Irish issues for electoral or diplomatic advantage, they shunned the direct intervention espoused by Irish nationalists. By the autumn of 1848 it was clear that Irish-American nationalists had miscalculated badly. Oblivious to the fragile opportunism of republicanism in Ireland itself, they had failed to acknowledge the fundamental isolationism of republican America.

This transatlantic dimension (curiously overlooked by John Saville) helps to explain why Liverpool, notoriously resistant to Chartist implantation, occupies the largest single file in the Home Office Disturbance Papers for 1848.[14] The Irish population, calculated at 90,000 to 100,000, posed a serious physical threat, compounded by the alarming intelligence reports from New York, pointing ominously to Liverpool as the landing-stage for the first squads of the Irish Brigade. Having abandoned residual O'Connellite restraint, the local middle-class Confederate leadership—shipping agents, doctors, tradesmen and publicans—turned to the Ribbonite culture of secrecy to penetrate deep into the migrant community, establishing a network of clubs in sympathetic pubs, temperance hotels, and private houses. In Irish-Liverpool, indeed, middle-class nationalist leaders enjoyed greater success than their counterparts in Ireland itself in enlisting their less fortunate fellow-countrymen in the Confederate cause.[15] Relations with the Chartists, however, proved increasingly problematic as Confederates soon lost patience with their new allies' insistence on strict observance of constitutional ways and means.

According to Matthew Somers, a Liverpool-Irish provisions dealer renowned for "hyperbolical speaking," such "moral force" was nonsense. They should petition "on the point of a bayonet … with a musket over the shoulder and a pike in the hand," implements available from the new "ironmongery business" opened by his colleague, Dr Lawrence Reynolds. On the Chartist platform, Reynolds introduced himself as a "Young Irelander—one of that class of men who detested and hated, and spurned the word 'petition.'" Nevertheless, he committed himself to the traditional radical strategy of "forcible intimidation," looking to the mass platform to mount a combined and irresistible display of strength: "Let the Chartists of England and Irish Repealers unite in one grand body, and all the powers of England, and foreign assistance to help them, could make no impression upon the phalanx they would present." While Reynolds and other Confederate orators rejuvenated the time-worn language of mass pressure from without—Somers warned of "skies reddened with the blaze of the Babylons of England"—the Chartists hesitated to apply the politics of menace.[16] At first a great boost to Chartism in 1848, the Irish alliance was soon to expose debilitating deficiencies in radical tactics.

"For now thirteen years," Feargus O'Connor reminded the Saint Patrick's Day audience in the Manchester Free Trade Hall, "I have been advocating the very union which you have thus tardily confirmed." So began "three glorious days" of joint Chartist-Confederate celebration in Lancashire, culminating in a monster demonstration on Oldham Edge where the assembled thousands swore a solemn oath to set England and Ireland free. For many Irish migrants, formal approval from Dublin may have made little difference. Those that settled in the industrial districts seem to have participated in Chartism at levels similar to native inhabitants, little restrained, as Dorothy Thompson has shown, by either O'Connellite proscription or structural factors: in the fastest-growing industrial areas the Irish were not a single out-group facing a stable population, but simply one such group among many.[17] Even so, formal alliance with the Irish was a welcome psychological and physical boost for the Chartists as they took to the mass platform again *faute de mieux*, without much confidence in the success of "forcible intimidation." The government, however, was deeply disturbed by the security implications: military resources might be overstretched by simultaneous and diversionary insurrectionary activity; and there were new anxieties about the loyalty of the army which contained large detachments of Irish troops, previously deployed in Chartist trouble-spots, a Habsburg-type strategy to prevent fraternization with disaffected workers.[18]

While keen to exploit the excitement generated by European revolution, Chartists were determined to display constitutional good order and discipline, to establish their credentials in respectable and legal extra-parliamentary agitation. Here was the irony that disabled the Confederate-Chartist alliance. While events in Europe prompted Irish nationalists to abandon previous restraints and proscriptions, in taking to the platform the Chartists affirmed their identity as true and respectable constitutional Britons.

Aware of their "image" problem, Chartists hoped to reverse their steady decline in popularity and support by a scrupulous concern for legitimacy. Recent research on Chartism has rightly drawn attention to the movement's remarkable persistence, facilitated through a democratic counter-culture of Chartist schools, chapels, cooperative stores, burial clubs and temperance societies. Coordinated through the National Charter Association, this cultural provision held the movement together during the lean periods, ready to reactivate the mass platform at the first suggestion of cyclical depression or social tension.[19] Each revival, however, registered a drop in numbers, excitement, and expectation. Crude economic explanations of this progressive decline have now fallen from favor. Chartism, historians contend, was undermined less by socioeconomic change than by the rigidity and obsolescence of its public political language. According to the linguistic "rethinking" of Chartism, the old populist predictions of ever-worsening political immiseration, oppression and exploitation steadily lost resonance and appeal as the "moralized" Peelite state introduced beneficent reform. However, this much-vaunted policy break was halting, begrudging, delayed in impact and punctuated with repression.[20] Furthermore it is difficult to reconcile the argument for a major discursive break in the 1840s with the recent volume of revisionist writing in which populist "visions of the people" remain the dominant motif in the mainstream current of political radicalism extending from Chartism through liberalism to the revival of socialism and beyond. Taking Stedman Jones as their point of departure, revisionists insist on the continued dominance of liberal values and absence of class specific language and demands.[21]

Prompted by Stedman Jones's "linguistic turn," historical attention has shifted away from the structural foundations of collective action to examine the ways in which radical political formations deployed rhetoric, narrative and other discursive practices to construct identities, to create constituencies of support, to forge alliances among heterogeneous social groups. Whatever its ideological deficiencies, the Chartist language of popular constitutionalism stood above economic, ethnic, and party division. Recast as popular melodrama on the radical mass platform, the nation's "master narrative" became a people's history of a lost golden age, heroic struggle against privilege, faction and "Old Corruption," and the promise of an imminent utopian future consequent on the instauration of the pristine constitution.[22] Identities merged in a wider solidarity: assembling behind banners and bands in trade, locality, family, ethnic and other groups, the crowd joined together in proud display as the sovereign, but unrepresented, people. In the name of the people, Chartism was able to attract workers whose material experience of industrialization diverged considerably. In seeking political inclusion in the civic nation, residency not ethnicity was the essential consideration. English liberties were to be restored throughout the United Kingdom. While campaigning for social justice in Ireland—a policy which would stem emigration—the Chartists had always welcomed Irish migrants into their midst. Extending across the "four nations," the Charter promised political citizenship for all adult males resident in the United Kingdom.

Standing above economic and ethnic division, Chartism repudiated partisan affiliation. Feargus O'Connor, the "lion of freedom," personified and guaranteed this cherished extra-parliamentary independence. Like "Orator" Hunt before him, the "demagogic" O'Connor was an independent gentlemanly leader in the best constitutional tradition, embodying an integrity above the factionalism and apostasy of party politicians and the specious independence of other parliamentary Radicals.[23]

As a radical extra-parliamentary movement, Chartism faced a more difficult task than other political formations: it sought not merely to construct an audience—to find a language that resonated with people's material and other needs and grievances—but to mobilize for change. Here options were limited as they had to conform to the rhetorical, organizational, and agitational norms of constitutional culture in order to attract popular legitimacy and support. It was at this point—where rhetoric became language in action—that Chartism found itself in increasing discomfiture in the 1840s.

The bluff and bluster of the mass platform was falling from fashion. While imposing order on the crowd (often portrayed by wearing Sunday best), the "constitutional" platform had also to raise the specter of menace, and hence did not discourage the presence of rough and rugged workers, "the fustian jackets, blistered hands and unshorn chins." At the beginning of the 1848 campaign, G. J. Harney specifically looked to extend the platform's outreach to the physically strong, to railway laborers, miners, soldiers and the like, "those masses of physical force, which, even at present, though deplorably wanting in moral power, strike alarm into the minds of the supporters of the existing system."[24] To attract such crowds, the Chartist platform relied on an atmosphere of escalating excitement and impending confrontation, fueled by ominous predictions of a great defensive rising, of spontaneous and invincible armed resistance to government repression. Having grown wise to the tactics, the authorities, backed by the quickly-acquired crowd control expertise of the new police forces, refused to be drawn. In the absence of some Peterloo-like act of outrageous provocation, Chartists lacked a universally agreed point at which resistance—as sanctioned by history, Blackstone, and other constitutional authorities—was deemed to be justified. While leaders hesitated and deliberated, mass support dwindled, excitement was squandered and the agitation collapsed.

Despite this recurrent critical flaw, Chartists persisted with the open-access tactics they had inherited from the great post-Napoleonic radical campaigns. Middle-class radicals proved more flexible. Abandoning the old "brickbat argument" of the Reform Bill agitation, they developed new and more "respectable" forms of "pressure from without." They were the pace-setters in a wide and fundamental change in political culture and communication.

The open-access procedures of the past—the ritual and street theater of open elections, the open-air carnival of the radical mass platform—were being challenged by more organized and disciplined forms, and by more efficient policing that restricted access to public space.[25'] Meeting indoors, but not in the pub, the new formations were male-dominated but not gender exclusive: seeking to banish disorder, to project an image of respectability, they specifically encouraged the (passive) attendance of women and family groups. Politics was domesticated, as it were, by ticketing, direct mailing, door-to-door canvassing, and other mechanisms that excluded the crowd, while the growth of the press encouraged personal and political development in the privacy of the home. A new political culture was in the making, based on a common respectability extending across public and private spheres.

The respectable individual replaced the riotous freeborn Englishman as the emblematic figure of popular politics. Disaffected Chartists, dismayed by the empty bluster of forcible intimidation, found common ground with middle-class radicals in behavioral reform. As a necessary first step in the cultivation of the self-respect necessary for the attainment and exercise of the franchise, "new movers" distanced themselves from the vainglorious demagogues and volatile crowds of the platform. "Respectable" and exclusive, new-model forms of collective mutuality gained what the National Charter Association was denied: public approval, legal recognition, and financial security. Still jealous of its extra-parliamentary independence, Chartism remained committed to the streets and to members unlimited, bad risks (and the Irish) included. Unable to stem seepage to new model forms, Chartists had yet to establish a "respectable" alternative to the unruly mass platform of monster open-air demonstrations, mass petitions, and the empty threat of physical force.

Through constitutional good order the Chartists of 1848 sought not simply to distinguish the British platform from European revolution but also to comply with new standards of respectability. Unhappily, the first mass meetings called in the wake of revolution in Paris were the occasion for unseemly disorder, as the vulgar adventurism of "butterfly reformers" such as G.W.M. Reynolds allowed free rein to trouble-making youths, pickpockets, criminals and other members of the "dangerous classes."[26] Satirical publications refused to distinguish between rioter, revolutionary, Chartist, and criminal: *Punch*, an accurate barometer of middle-class opinion, "felt it to be its duty to exert all its powers of ridicule, even to a pardonable exaggeration, in the cause of order and loyalty." In secret, platform militants like Harney shared Bronterre O'Brien's misgivings about the monster demonstration planned for 10 April, fearing it would "let loose hundreds of rogues and thieves upon society, thus bringing down upon themselves the indignation of the reflecting people of this country." A sustained press campaign accompanied the excessive security precautions for the ill-located demonstration on Kennington Common, portraying Chartism as criminal, unconstitutional, unEnglish and, most damning of all, Irish. "The present movement," *The Times* warned on the morning of 10 April, "is a ramification of the Irish conspiracy. The Repealers wish to make as great a hell of this island as they have made of their own." Quite as much as the fear of continental "red republicanism," it was the specter of Irish violence that impelled the middle classes to protect the established order.[27]

Confronted by what John Saville has described as the three-pronged threat of revolutionary Paris, insurgent Ireland, and revitalized Chartism, the authorities mounted a massive display of coercive power, coordinated by the Duke of Wellington, to defend English freedom and constitutional liberty. With considerable numbers of troops, enrolled pensioners, and police strategically placed in reserve, they shrewdly allowed front-line prominence to the special constabulary on the decisive day. Immortalized by Palmerston as "the Waterloo of peace and order," the events of 10 April became the stuff of instant mythology, a day when "men of all classes and ranks were blended together in defense of law and property."[28] In this victory of civil society, the special constables acquired emblematic status, exemplifying the "sterling qualities of the English character." As the *Times* prophesied, Chartism was routed and humiliated, dispatched to oblivion by "a firm, peaceful, and almost majestic union of all classes in defense of constitutional liberty and order."[29]

Among the 85,000 or so special constables assembled in London in the middle-class *levée en masse*, there was some working-class representation, but few workers seem to have enrolled voluntarily. Subject to quasi-military discipline at the best of times, railway employees were in no position to object when conscripted by their employers, an example followed by the gas companies. Domestic servants were similarly powerless to protest when enrolled along with their masters: in some instances, crackshot gamekeepers were brought up to own from country estates specially for the purpose. The burly Thames coal-whippers, darlings of the anti-Chartist press, were the exception. Their services were lauded as a mark of gratitude and loyalty following the introduction of legislation in the trade. When the demonstration was over, however, they demanded full compensation for their loss of earnings, a payment which the much-embarrassed government decided to meet. Voluntary enrollment was limited, but some workers who refused to serve were prepared to act within their own works to protect premises against attack.[30]

The consensual glow surrounding the 10 April 1848—a forerunner, as it were, of the spirit later elicited by Dunkirk and the Blitz[31]—needs further historical deconstruction. Key elements of the narrative have not withstood critical scrutiny. Contrary to mythology, Feargus O'Connor served Chartism well on 10 April: it was "Feargoose" indeed who ensured that the day's events were not a fiasco. Considerable crowds (including a substantial Irish contingent) were attracted to Kennington Common. Acting on police instructions, the anti-Chartist press reported the total as 15,000, a figure ten times lower than the latest historical estimate. Thanks to O'Connor's oratorical skills, unpropitious confrontation was avoided: the right of assembly was asserted, but the mass procession to present the national petition was wisely abandoned. Having salvaged some self-respect for the movement on Kennington Common, O'Connor was nevertheless forced to withdraw the motion for the Charter when the Commons Committee reported (with undue haste) that the national Petition had not been signed by 5,706,000 as the Chartists claimed, but by 1,975,496, a figure that included many bogus, fraudulent, and obscene signatures

In these embarrassing circumstances, O'Connor refused to sanction an escalation in extra-parliamentary pressure. No longer prepared to appear more insurrectionary than he actually was, he abandoned forcible intimidation to promote discussion of the Land Plan, his practical (non-socialist) solution to the "labor question." Some of the more ardent Chartist spirits proceeded to convene a National Assembly, only to be drawn into languishing discussion of tactical and constitutional niceties. A sparsely-attended, dispirited affair, it marked a sorry end to the "anti-parliament" in radical politics, replaced in mid-Victorian agitation by the stage-managed conference.[32]

By this time, the Irish Confederates in Britain had lost all patience with their Chartist allies and their debilitating self-doubt. Where their presence was strong, as at Bradford, the town with the highest concentration of Irish-born in the West Riding, they were to boost Chartist morale and activity. A Chartist "National Guard," primarily composed of woolcombers threatened by machinery, drilled openly on the streets until military reinforcements arrived. Investigation revealed that half of the Bradford Chartists were Irish, nationalist radicals preparing to "make a diversion should Mitchel be convicted, in order to prevent the government from sending more troops to Ireland." News of John Mitchel's conviction and transportation, the first victim of the new Crown and Government Security Act, enraged Irish migrants, prompting them to abandon the restraints of open Chartist alliance for a secret conspiratorial framework linked to Dublin. The Chartist rump, however, hoped to channel the anger over Mitchel's fate into renewed platform agitation. Supported by prominent Irish-Chartists, Ernest Jones planned for an exact count of heads to be taken at simultaneous Whitsun meetings, a combined display of Chartist and Confederate numerical strength to stand in lieu of the withdrawn petition. These plans were thwarted when the authorities, alarmed by the unrestrained language and ominous new tactics of the Confederates, introduced repression.[33]

After Mitchel's conviction, there was much unguarded talk of "private assassination and Moscowing," while the tactic recommended by Doheny from Dublin—unannounced nightly silent protest processions through town centers—soon turned into running battles between Irish migrants and the police. Refusing to distinguish between the Chartist platform and violence on the streets, *Punch* portrayed Chartism transmogrified into Irish rapine, pillage and massacre; *The Times* was appalled by "that extravagance of wild sedition which, for want of any other adjective, must be denominated 'Irish'"; London, it warned, was endangered by "the Irish love of knife, dagger and poison bowl." Assured of public support, the government finally crushed the Chartist challenge: the Whitsun demonstration was declared illegal and warrants were issued against Jones and other leaders.[34]

As in the past, repression and arrests pushed some militants towards physical force, notwithstanding the absence of support throughout the nation. Speaking at Halifax, George Webber called on the forward areas to take independent regional action: "If a similar sentence should be passed on Jones as had been done on Mitchel, though they should stand alone, they would erect barricades and bid defiance to the bloodthirsty government of England … and if necessary proclaim the republic of Yorkshire and Lancashire."[35] Beneath this rhetorical defiance, however, there was little coordination between Chartists and Confederates in the underground politics of conspiracy and insurrection.

In Liverpool, the Confederates thrived in self-enclosed secrecy. Here ethnicity and class were in apparent contradiction. Reynolds, indeed, denounced Chartist "class politics," as he abandoned the platform to prepare for physical force within a paramilitary framework of Confederate Clubs:

> Every street in Liverpool and every town ought to have its club; every club its president, and other commanding officers; every club ought to take care of defending itself; every officer ought to have his rifle, every committee man his musket, and every member ought to have his pike. (Great cheers)[36]

Alarmed by the rapid spread of such clubs, the local authorities placed the town under a state of siege. Having petitioned in vain for the Suspension of Habeas Corpus in Ireland to be extended to include Liverpool, they set legal objections aside to raid club premises. By chance, they stumbled across the Confederate minute book, a detailed record of committee membership and meetings.[37] With its leaders in flight and most of its weapons seized, Confederate conspiracy was rendered powerless on the eve of the Irish rising, unable to provide either the direct assistance or diversionary activity in Liverpool which Terence Bellew McManus had promised Duffy in secret discussions in the wake of Mitchel's trial.[38] Bitterly disappointed, McManus made personal amends at Ballingarry, proving himself "the boldest fellow among the entire body of insurgents."[39]

Elsewhere in the north of England, there was some overlap between Chartist and Confederate underground politics, but no common timetable for insurrection. When news came that Ireland was "up," Confederates insisted on "an immediate outbreak of a serious nature." They were criticized for precipitate haste by Chartists who had yet to complete plans, coordinated by Cuffay and the "Orange Tree" conspirators, for simultaneous risings in London and Manchester. In the interim, as relations deteriorated, the authorities prepared for decisive action.[40] Come the day, they arrested the conspirators, and then issued "monster" indictments, as at Manchester, listing "all the leading agitators who have for some time past infested this City and the neighboring Towns." Cuffay, the veteran black radical, was an easy target for the cartoonists, but *Punch* and the press preferred to highlight the Irish element in the August conspiracy, a dastardly affair involving the likes of "MOONEY, ROONEY, HOOLAN, DOOLAN."[41] The trials followed a standard format well summarized by Harney:

> Place *Fustian* in the dock, let *Silk Gown* charge the culprit with being a "physical force Chartist," and insinuate that he is not exactly free from the taint of "Communism," and forthwith *Broad Cloth* in the jury box will bellow out "GUILTY."[42]

Conducted within the constraints of popular constitutionalism, the Chartist-Confederate alliance proved mutually disadvantageous. The volume and nature of anti-Irish propaganda underwent significant change. Paddy appeared in new and defamatory guise, denied his former benign and redeeming qualities. Unable to conform to British political and cultural norms, Paddy was depicted as racially inferior, more ape-like than man, a despised simian with ludicrously exaggerated prognathous features.[43] Popular Toryism flourished as the volume of propaganda increased, rallying freeborn Englishmen to protect the protestant constitution from the enemy within. In mid-Victorian Britain, the Irish were the internal "other" against whom identity and respectability were defined. Thenceforth the Irish were forced into defensive segregation: even in mixed streets in the cotton districts there was a strong tendency towards ethnic clustering with distinct Irish and non-Irish ends.

A shadow of its former self, Chartism entered a final period of revision and adaption, a brief coda characterized by both ideological advance and reformist pragmatism. The initial impetus came from across the Channel. Since the mid-1840s, Harney had been trying to re-invigorate the Chartist platform by incorporating "red republicanism," the creed of revolutionary European artisans exiled in Britain. Known to Marx and Engels as "Citizen Hip-Hip Hurrah!" he managed to unite diverse nationalities and social philosophies in the Fraternal Democrats, a pressure group formed to hasten the necessary changes: "henceforth mere Chartism will not do, ultra-democracy, social as well as political, will be the object of our propaganda."[44] Ironically, progress was curtailed by the outbreak of revolution: the repatriation of the political refugees and the introduction of a tough new Alien Act in 1848 deprived Charter-Socialists of their continental red-republican allies.[45]

In response to events in "revolutionary" Europe, a pronounced ideological and class gulf developed within British radical discourse. Chartists displayed their working-class credentials, prioritizing events in France where Louis Blanc's "Organization of Labor" pointed to social as well as political rights, towards a positive social-democratic view of liberty and the state. Middle-class radicals, by contrast, remained committed to classical political economy and a negative definition of liberty. Insisting on the distinction between the social and the political sphere, they condemned socialist revolution in France while applauding liberal and nationalist revolution in Germany, Italy, and later Hungary.[46] Class polarization, however, should not be overdrawn. Mazzinist ideals, emphasizing respectability and the "inward conscience of the Universal Duty of the Suffrage," exerted a powerful cross-class appeal, embracing a new generation of working-class radicals disillusioned with unruly (and unsuccessful) platform agitation.[47]

On return to Britain after the collapse of revolution, republican exiles—heroic in defeat—enjoyed considerable prestige. Their presence, however, may have constrained the process of change, hindering the transition from green flag to red. Respected voices in the stock-taking that followed in the wake of 1848, Mazzini and Kossuth deflected attention away from "démoc-soc" experiments—red republicanism, socialism and the organization of labor—back towards more traditional radical concerns.[48] Their impassioned condemnation of centralized state power encouraged some radicals to reject "mongrel Socialism" imported from "the Parisian school of philosophers." Implacable opponents of "Communistic Chartism," the Manchester-based National Charter League, continued to campaign against "Old Corruption," henceforth identified with government centralization. Unable to support the Charter-Socialists or the National Charter League, O'Connor, the "worn-out warrior," was left stranded in political isolation, vainly seeking the illusive "union of the veritable middle classes and the working classes … an alliance between mental labor on the one hand and manual labor on the other."[49] Chartism lost its sense of national perspective as each aspect of O'Connor's centralized leadership—command of the platform, control of movement's newspaper, and grip on the administrative apparatus of the National Charter Association—finally collapsed. When Harney captured control of the Executive, the initiative, he was forced to admit, had passed to the "respectable" agencies of collective self-help:

> We are at this time passing through another period of "Reaction"—reaction in favor of social, or rather industrial reform. The masses aspire to progress, and accomplish the amelioration of their condition, by means of Labor Associations, Co-operative Societies and Trades Unions.[50]

In an effort to engage their support, he joined with middle-class progressives in a single-issue campaign for the suffrage. By an irony of the times, advocacy of "the Charter and Something More" ended with the sacrifice of the six points, the original "whole hog," abandoned in favor of "respectable" and rational gradualism, moderation, and expediency.[51]

Although the events of 1848 widened the cultural and ideological distance between middle-class radicals and the Chartists, there was gradual rapprochement thereafter, encouraged by joint involvement in constitutional campaigns to advance continental nationalism and by the steady politicization of the skilled workers. To simplify what was a complex, problematic, and far from complete process, Chartists were to amend their ways and means while middle-class radicals modified their program. Forced to abandon the independent mass platform, Chartists re-entered what most historians consider the mainstream of radical endeavor: the attempt to reconstruct the class cooperation and parliamentary support which, having secured the passage of the 1832 Reform Act, was necessary to ensure liberty, retrenchment, and reform. Determined to eradicate the Hanoverian "fiscal-military" state, middle-class radicals were jolted into action early in 1848, before the spread of revolution, to protest a rise in income tax to finance an increase in national defenses. While prepared to defend the established order on 10 April, middle-class radicals were reinforced in their commitment to franchise reform: in the parliamentary session 1847/48, no less than 7,350 petitions were presented calling for the extension of the suffrage.[52] Considerable energies were expended on devising a formula to incorporate the lower middle-class heroes of 10 April, the young clerical workers living in lodgings who had so conspicuously proved their respectability and worth by enrolling as special constables. Hence there was considerable dissatisfaction when the veteran Joseph Hume proffered household suffrage, the traditional talisman of middle-class radicalism, as the basis of his "Little Charter" movement. Some middle-class radicals were already looking to the skilled workers in their respectable new-model associations of collective self-help. John Bright sought to "garrison" the constitution by enfranchising the aristocracy of labor, the "industrious, intelligent and provident members of the working class." Incorporated within the political nation, they would be rewarded for their virtue and drawn away from dangerous and contaminating contact with those below them.[53]

Similar reasoning was gradually to extend to the ranks of the political establishment. Having protected his Chesham Place home against the expected mobs on 10 April by lining the windows with parliamentary blue books, Lord John Russell, the Whig prime minister, was soon emboldened to abandon his "finality" stance over the 1832 Reform Act. Others were soon to follow suit. Parliamentary reform worked its way onto the political agenda of all the major parties and governments during the 1850s.[54] Complacent conservatism, so much in evidence after 10 April, gave way to cautious reformism. Having stood firm against revolutionary and violent challenge, Britain could move forward, distancing itself from other alien forces such as reaction and inertia. A liberal version of constitutional history grew steadily in influence: a chronicle of progressive improvements founded on English concepts of liberty and the rule of law, it justified continued but moderate reform, benefits to be extended throughout the United Kingdom and the empire. No longer a matter of constitutional balance, taxation entitlement or citizenship right, franchise reform was a question of character, of moral entitlement. The special constables, heroes of the Waterloo of peace and order, pointed to a wider "participation ratio" in which all who exemplified Anglo-British constitutional respectability were entitled to full membership of the body politic. Citizenship was the reward for all males (irrespective of class, creed or language) whose public behavior conformed to British values. In putting national identity to the test, 1848 underlined the "rules of the game." It was a lesson that some "outsiders" within the United Kingdom were quick to learn.

Notes

1. Roland Quinault, "1848 and Parliamentary Reform," *Historical Journal* 31 (1988): 831-51.
2. Raphael Samuel, "British Dimensions: Four Nations History," *History Workshop Journal* 40 (1995): iii-xxii.
3. W.J. Lowe, "The Men in the Middle: A Social and Occupational Profile of English and Irish Policemen in 1848," *Consortium on Revolutionary Europe* 2 (1989): 290.
4. Roy Foster, *Paddy and Mr Punch: Connections in Irish and English History* (London, 1995), xii.
5. Stanley Palmer, *Police and Protest in England and Ireland, 1780-1850* (New York, 1988). John Saville, *1848: The British State and the Chartist Movement* (Cambridge, 1987). For a sharply critical review of Saville, see Dorothy Thompson in *History Workshop Journal* 28 (1989): 160-66.

256 | *John Belchem*

6. Dorothy Thompson, "Seceding from the Seceders: The Decline of the Jacobin Tradition in Ireland, 1790-1850," in Dorothy Thompson, *Outsiders: Class, Gender and Nation* (London, 1993), 134-63. Richard Davis, *The Young Ireland Movement* (Dublin, 1987), 140-52, 189, 255-57.

7. George Rudé, "Protest and Punishment in Nineteenth-Century Britain," *Albion* 5 (1973): 1-23.

8. Stanley H. Palmer, "Power, Coercion and Authority: Protest and Repression in 1848 in England and Ireland," *Consortium on Revolutionary Europe* 2 (1989): 285.

9. Palmer, *Police and Protest*, 500-1.

10. Palmer, "Power, Coercion and Authority," 274-89.

11. John Belchem, "Nationalism, Republicanism and Exile: Irish Emigrants and the Revolutions of 1848," *Past and Present* 146 (1995): 103-35.

12. For a full account, see John Belchem, "Republican Spirit and Military Science: The 'Irish Brigade' and Irish-American Nationalism in 1848," *Irish Historical Studies* 29 (1994): 44-64.

13. For a convenient summary of the major correspondence on this affair, including Palmerston's letter of 30 September 1848, see *New York Commercial Advertiser*, 15 January 1849, enclosed in Barclay to Palmerston, 16 January 1849, Foreign Office Papers, Public Record Office, FO 5/502.

14. Kevin Moore, "'This Whig and Tory Ridden Town': Popular Politics in Liverpool in the Chartist Era" in John Belchem (ed.), *Popular Politics, Riot and Labour: Essays in Liverpool History 1790-1940* (Liverpool, 1992), 68-97. Bewilderingly, the file at the Public Record Office, Kew, has recently been renumbered as H.O. 45/2410B, although the material in it (now in a state of chaotic disorder) is clearly marked as H.O. 45/2410A.

15. John Belchem, "'Freedom and Friendship to Ireland': Ribbonism in Early Nineteenth-century Liverpool," *International Review of Social History* 39 (1994): 33-56. My findings differ from two earlier studies: W.J. Lowe, "The Chartists and the Irish Confederates: Lancashire 1848," *Irish Historical Studies* 24 (1984): 172-196; and Louis R. Bisceglia, "The Threat of Violence: Irish Confederates and Chartists in Liverpool in 1848," *Irish Sword* 14 (1981): 207-15.

16. John Belchem, "Liverpool in the Year of Revolution: The Political and Associational Culture of the Irish Immigrant Community in 1848," in Belchem (ed.), *Popular Politics*, 68-97.

17. Dorothy Thompson, "Ireland and the Irish in English Radicalism before 1850," in James Epstein and Dorothy Thompson (eds.), *The Chartist Experience: Studies in Working-Class Radicalism and Culture, 1830-1860* (London, 1982), 120-51. For a contrasting view, see J.H. Treble, "O'Connor, O'Connell and Attitudes of Irish Immigrants towards Chartism in the North of England," in John Butt and Ignatius F. Clarke (eds.), *The Victorians and Social Protest*, (Newton Abbot, 1973), 33-70.

18. Saville, *1848*, 107-12.

19. Eileen Yeo, "Christianity in Chartist Struggle 1838-1842," *Past and Present*, 91 (1981): 109-139.

20. Gareth Stedman Jones, "Rethinking Chartism," in Gareth Stedman Jones, *Languages of Class: Studies in English Working Class History 1832-1982* (Cambridge, 1983), 175-78. Saville, *1848*, 217-29. See also, Anna Clark, "The Rhetoric of Chartist Domesticity: Gender, Language and Class in the 1830s and 1840s," *Journal of British Studies*, 31 (1992): 62-88. For a useful introduction to these controversies, see Miles Taylor, "Rethinking the Chartists: Searching for Synthesis in the Historiography of Chartism," *Historical Journal* 39 (1996): 489-90.

21. Patrick Joyce, *Visions of the People: Industrial England and the Question of Class* (Cambridge, 1991). Eugenio F. Biagini and Alistair Reid (ed.), *Currents of Radicalism: Popular Radicalism, Organized Labour and Party Politics in Britain 1850-1914* (Cambridge, 1991). Jon Lawrence, "Popular Radicalism and the Socialist Revival in Britain," *Journal of British Studies* 31 (1992): 163-86.

22. James Epstein, "The Constitutional Idiom: Radical Reasoning, Rhetoric and Action in Early Nineteenth-Century England," *Journal of Social History* 23 (1990): 553-74. James Vernon, *Politics and the People* (Cambridge, 1993), 295-330.

23. John Belchem and James Epstein, "The Nineteenth-Century Gentleman Leader Revisited," *Social History*, 22 (1997): 174-93.

24. "The War of Classes," *Northern Star*, 19 February 1848.

25. Vernon, *Politics and the People*. Martin Hewitt, *The Emergence of Stability in the Industrial City: Manchester, 1832-67* (Aldershot, 1996). See also Frank O'Gorman, "Campaign Rituals and Ceremonies:

The Social Meanings of Elections in England 1780-1860," *Past and Present* 135 (1992): 79-116. For the new efficiency of the Metropolitan Force in crowd control, see David Goodway, *London Chartism, 1838-48* (Cambridge, 1982), 99-105.

26. Taylor, *Decline of British Radicalism*, 108.

27. For a full account of the 1848 campaign and the press response, see John Belchem, "1848: Feargus O'Connor and the Collapse of the Mass Platform," in Epstein and Thompson (eds.), *The Chartist Experience*, 269-310.

28. Quinault," 1848 and Parliamentary Reform," 836.

29. Henry Weisser, *April 10: Challenge and Response in England in 1848* (Lanham, 1983), 58.

30. Saville, *1848*, 109-16. At the time of the Irish rising, 500 Irish dock laborers were dismissed from employment in Liverpool when they refused to be sworn in as special constables.

31. Weisser, *April 10*, 58.

32. Goodway, *London Chartism*, 72-80; Weisser, *April 10*, 105-25; Belchem, "Feargus O'Connor," 281-83.

33. Belchem, "Feargus O'Connor," 289-93.

34. *Punch*, Nr. Xiv, 1848, 240. *The Times*, 2 June and 8 July 1848. Belchem, "Feargus O'Connor," 291-93.

35. *Halifax Guardian*, 17 June 1848.

36. *Liverpool Mercury*, 13 June 1848.

37. Belchem, "Liverpool in the Year of Revolution," 89-95.

38. T.G. McAllister, *Terence Bellew McManus* (Maynooth, 1972), 11-12.

39. For McManus's own narrative of events, see Denis Gwynn, *Young Ireland and 1848* (Cork, 1949), Appendix 3.

40. The provincial ramifications of the August conspiracy are difficult to unravel, see John Belchem, "The Spy-System in 1848: Chartists and Informers—an Australian connection," *Labour History* 39 (1980): S.15-27. For events in London, see Goodway, *London Chartism*, 91-96.

41. *Punch*, Nr. xv, 1848, 154-5. *The Times*, 18 August and 29 September 1848.

42. *Northern Star*, 23 December 1848.

43. S. Gilley, "English attitudes to the Irish in England, 1780-1900," in C. Holmes (ed.), *Immigrants and Minorities in British Society* (London, 1978), 81-110. M.A.G. Ó Tuathaigh, "The Irish in Nineteenth-Century Britain: Problems of Integration," in Roger Swift and Sheridan Gilley (eds.), *The Irish in the Victorian City* (London, 1985), 13-36. The racial emphasis of L. Perry Curtis, Jr, *Apes and Angels: the Irishman in Victorian Caricature* (Newton Abbot, 1971), is best refuted by Denis G. Paz, "Anti-Catholicism, Anti-Irish Stereotyping, and Anti-Celtic Racism in Mid-Victorian Working-Class Periodicals," *Albion* 18 (1986), which contends that anti-Irish stories began to fade out of the gutter press in the mid-1850s.

44. Harney to Engels, 30 March 1846, in F.G. and R.M. Black (eds.), *The Harney Papers* (Assen, 1969), 239-45.

45. Henry Weisser, *British Working-Class Movements and Europe 1815-1848* (Manchester, 1975), 154-71.

46. Margot Finn, *After Chartism. Class and Nation in English Radical Politics, 1848-1874* (Cambridge, 1993), chapter 2.

47. Francis B. Smith, *Radical Artisan: William James Linton 1812-97* (Manchester, 1973), chapter 5.

48. Gregory Claeys, "Mazzini, Kossuth and British Radicalism, 1848-1854," *Journal of British Studies* 28 (1989): 225-61.

49. Belchem, "Feargus O'Connor," 299-304.

50. *Friend of the People*, 18 January 1851.

51. Gregory Claeys, *Citizens and Saints. Politics and Anti-Politics in Early British Socialism* (Cambridge, 1989), chapter 7.

52. Taylor, *Decline of British Radicalism*, 105.

53. John Belchem, *Popular Radicalism in Nineteenth-Century Britain* (London, 1996), 102-27.

54. Quinault," 1848 and Parliamentary Reform," 840-51.

Triumphal March of the Poles through Berlin, drawn by J. Kirchhoff
(Illustrirte Zeitung, Leipzig, no. 250, 15 April 1848, 258)

Chartist march after the Kennington riots in London on 10 April
(Illustrirte Zeitung, Leipzig, no. 253, 6 May 1848, 303)

Chapter 11

THE NETHERLANDS AND BELGIUM

Notes on the Causes of Abstinence from Revolution

Horst Lademacher

Introduction

Two adjacent states, united until 1830, stand out in a revolutionary European environment by their abstinence from revolution. Apart from relatively insignificant demonstrations here and there, lasting just a few days, it would be true to say that neither the social nor the governmental order was ever endangered. Thus one cannot examine the type of revolution, cannot analyze causes, course, and consequences: it is, rather, a question of analyzing the factors that suppressed possible revolutionary forces, that led to an immunity to revolutionary models from abroad, that indeed prevented the idea of revolutionary acts from even being given consideration.

Theoretically, this question is no different from that of the search for the cause of revolutions. Eric Hoffer made that clear in 1968 when he wrote: "We are usually told that revolutions are set in motion to realize radical changes. Actually it is drastic change which sets the stage for revolution. The revolutionary mood and temper are generated by the irritations, difficulties, hungers and frustrations inherent in the realization of drastic change. Where things have not changed at all, there is the least likelihood of revolution."[1] This relationship between change and the outbreak or lack of revolution is certainly one possible starting point for this analysis. Chalmers Johnsen enlarges upon this point, when he writes, in relation to T.H. Wintringham's examination of military revolutions, that revolutions can be "rationally contemplated" only in a society that is experiencing structural change and in which further change is necessary.[2]

The Netherlands

The validity of this relationship needs to be examined for the case of abstinence from revolution in both countries, with the understanding that an "analysis of causes and configurations of change in a society" will not provide a full explanation of either the occurrence of a revolution or of its non-appearance.[3] Thus the question arises, beyond social and economic processes, of further causes of the outbreak or lack of revolution. Such an analysis would emphasize the importance of leadership figures, in cases of both inertia and transformation, would pay attention to the extent that political activity was present in public opinion, would consider openness to influences from abroad as well as the country's position in international relations—an especially relevant factor for the new Belgian state.

Therefore, we will begin with a brief analysis of state and society in the Netherlands and Belgium from the founding, in 1815, of a state in which the two countries were united. The end of the Napoleonic era brought with it the beginning of a qualitatively new period in both domestic and foreign affairs for the Low Countries, the entry into the world of modernization and modernity with its shifts and faults in economic and social structures, as well as new constitutional forms, in which the two countries were involved quite early on. After a good two centuries as a sovereign republic and a fifteen year-long French interlude, the Netherlands became a monarchy, a "United Kingdom." The unification with the formerly Spanish, then Austrian Netherlands remained, however, an episode, a result of outdated maxims of policy based on a European balance of power.

This unity of two separate parts emerged in 1815 from a concerted action on the part of the Powers and shattered after one and a half decades of an existence, that, in its last years, was rich in discord. At the end of the United Kingdom was the Belgian Revolution. It unfolded and succeeded following—and clearly under the influence of—the French July Revolution of 1830, because the Great Powers, which generally had set the guidelines for a remodeling of Europe, had little difficulty in replacing the continental block of small powers intended as a defense against France with an institution of international law, a Belgium of guaranteed neutrality.

The Belgian Revolution, which can be defined as an early consequence of economic innovation and aspirations toward political modernization, broke out just as the inhabitants of the northern half of the Low Countries set out to cultivate a new identity—an identity which, after centuries of republican fame, had become somewhat obscured under French influence and then under French rule. The end of French sovereignty did not entail a "rediscovery" of their own country, especially as the French withdrawal could easily be interpreted as the result of the work of others. Certainly, a new identity can be constructed not only as a result of one's own merits, but also on the strictures of international relations, as determined by foreign powers. G. von Hogendorp, the author of the early constitution of 1815, wrote that: "It is absolutely necessary for the Netherlands to remain a naval power and a Protestant state ... The Netherlands will remain a naval power and a Protestant state as long as the center of power lies in the provinces of Holland, Seeland and Friesland ... The

Belgians can be allowed everything not contrary to these principles, but one should not grant them more if we wish to harvest the fruits of our own efforts."[4] About one and a half years before Belgium's revolutionary secession, the foreign minister of the Netherlands, Verstolk van Soelen, had the presumption to claim that his country was a Great Power—in a somewhat chimerical lack of appreciation of the true situation—and registered a claim to the annexation of the Prussian Rhineland.

This somewhat hybrid self-validation deserves attention because the relatively rapid collapse of the Congress of Vienna led to a general political and cultural hangover, perhaps even a mood of defeatism among the leading political and intellectual circles in the north. This attitude was to shape thinking for nearly two decades, because the imagination of Dutch politicians, with the exception of King Wilhelm I, was quite clearly oriented to the status of the former republic. Rather symptomatic of the attitudes of Dutch politicians and intellectuals was the response of Johan Rudolf Thorbecke—perhaps the central liberal figure in the Netherlands' *Vormärz*—to a book by the German historian Heinrich Leo in which the latter had argued for a German-Netherlands association: "We are a member of a Germanic Europe, but a free member ... We see our place as in the middle between Germany and England. While Germany concentrates rather on an abstract, subjective view and can take pleasure in a world so created, we find ourselves, as consequence of our natural-ethical and political structure, always under the influence of the material, the external, the objective aspects of society and practice."[5]

These were words written against potential interference from the outside world, but also in defense against a skeptical view of the Dutch—at times extending up to parody and malice—dominant in the first half of the century. That was the most noticeable symptom of a period in which the Netherlands retreated from the status of middling to that of a small power. Political and literary observers from the rest of Europe sneered, at times vaingloriously, at times pompously, at the Dutch lifestyle and character. They invented a whole flood of stereotypes or abstruse constructs to deal with matters that outsiders did not properly understand and about which the country had been unable to present itself properly. The time of fame and fortune, of great admiration, of a rich bourgeoisie, was past. A number of observations were made which tended towards the droll. In this context they are of little interest.

There were, however, those who sought to present serious reports and judgements on the country's position in an international context. They were observers in the manner of the geographer and politician Johann Georg Forster, who, as early as the era of the French Revolution, had spoken of the Netherlands as the refuge of a democratic confession of faith—certainly not without justice considering the Patriots of 1787, a revolutionary movement whose readiness to act would thereafter never be equalled. The British ambassador in the 1820s wrote of the appearance of Dutch politicians: "the old gentlemen in the Dutch city halls with black coats and collars and floppy hats," thus classifying and caricaturing a paragon of conservative attitudes.[6] They were certainly not those with floppy hats, long beards. and fluttering coat tails described by Eric Hobsbawm in prerevolutionary Europe.[7]

And in fact the Netherlands was a state without eruptions —excluding the revolutionary secession of Belgium—in a period which Hobsbawm has characterized as the "springtime of the peoples." This country knew no aroused student movements, no *Hambacher Fest*, no *société des saisons* and, almost as a direct consequence, needed during the period of unrest in middle and western Europe around 1848 neither a Grapeshot Prince nor a General Cavaignac. It does not come as a surprise that the Westphalian poet Annette von Droste-Hülshoff classified the Netherlands under terms such as tradition, peculiarity, eccentricity. She wrote: "The Netherlands ... this ... patch of land ... preserves in its national character a hoard of all-explaining uniqueness which offers better protection than mountains."[8] Three generations later, Richard von Kühlmann, envoy in The Hague, drawing on his own experience and supported by the observations of his colleagues, confirmed the poet's words when he spoke of a "unique and distinct nation," whose dogged attachment to the time-honored appeared to be its most conspicuous characteristic.[9] But even those with mockery on their lips, identifying the Netherlands with windmills, cheese, and canal boats, classifying the Dutch simply as the "de-pigtailed" Chinese of Europe, spoke of the unique, the special way of their neighbor in northwest Europe.

When the romantic poet Annette, with a talent for identifying the typical and unique, and generations later an astute diplomat, emphasize such characteristics, that is, when the same observation remains so conspicuously constant over such a long period of time, the question still remains of what it actually means. It could mainly refer to the powers of inertia, to persevering traditions. Observations from abroad were paralleled in the writings of Dutch authors on the special values of their own country. As the above-mentioned Thorbecke had done, they swore by their republican tradition, not the republican form of government, but the contents and characteristic forms of political life and of life in general in the Netherlands, connected to this tradition.

This past condition was constantly recalled, especially from the 1830s onward, whenever it was necessary to defend against ostensible threats from abroad or to re-emphasize the fact of the country's current weaknesses in view of the secession of Belgium. Thorbecke and others quite justifiably believed that the republic had already achieved a standard of liberality and general political thought long before these became universal as a result of the Enlightenment, and the American and French Revolutions. It was in agreement with this "tradition of the republic" that modern, basic rights were included in the constitution with little controversy—not as a unified block, but scattered through its text: the inviolability of the individual, sanctity of the home, the right to property, freedom of the press, freedom and equality of religion, equal rights in appointments, equality before the law, public and oral judicial proceedings, the right of petition.

In the final analysis, the unique tradition, the uniqueness, lay in the early bourgeois character of the country, which, in regard to political authority, can be characterized as distinctly oligarchical. In view of the decline in international standing, the power of this tradition lay in the memory of the uniqueness of a republic whose inhabitants were able to achieve fame and fortune in every respect, in the midst of an environment of monarchical Great Powers. A connection between republican glory and the transposition of early liberal, corporate freedom into individual rights made possible a certain initial recognition of the limitations to the principle of legitimacy that were anchored in the constitution [*grondwet*].

On the other hand, it certainly cannot be overlooked that this early constitution involved a break with the process of democratization that had been completed in the Batavian Republic under the influence of the French Revolution. The new constitution, written by Gijsbert Karel van Hogendorp, involved a clear rejection of the radicalism of the constitution of 1798. The term "popular sovereignty," as used by Hogendorp in the years before the transformation into a kingdom or in the period after its establishment, was so inconsistent and poorly-defined that it could have referred to a corporatively structured decision-making authority. In any case, high property qualifications and indirect elections had little in common with democracy. In the north, today's Netherlands, there were about 80,000 voters; in the south, in Belgium, some 60,000. The new constitution included a restricted franchise, a limited control of the executive through a legislature no longer bound by an imperative mandate, as well as the transformation of the freedom of privileged groups into constitutionally guaranteed individual rights. All these elements were characteristic of early liberalism. If one wishes to search for predecessors, the constitution corresponded to the moderate government and structural principle of 1795/96 and the post-1798 tendencies modelled after the French Directory, "when a natural relativism and particularism resisted the extreme unitarians." Reference to unitarian currents in the constitution of 1798 is necessary here because from that time onward a unitarian constitutional structure, admittedly also viewed under the aspect of increased efficiency, was associated with the success of democratic ideas.[10]

As noted above, there was a connection between the new national self-consciousness in need of encouragement and the tradition of the free republic, but contemporaries felt that a nation should not nourish itself on memories of past glories alone; rather, it should also grow in its acceptance of the constitution. A man like Thorbecke expected the rise and maturing of civic consciousness—and was at first disappointed. There was no automatic relationship between a guarantee of civic freedoms and civic consciousness in the Netherlands. Even the acceptance of the constitution of 1815 took place relatively unobserved because broad strata of the population showed little interest in it, due to the economic stagnation oppressing them.

The country developed an extreme class and caste society, with a high level of pauperism and traditional economic relations. This point was quite astutely raised in 1820 by Barthold G. Niebuhr, in his early years a bank director in Copenhagen, then employed by the Prussian state and finally historian of the ancient world in Berlin and Bonn and an eminent judge of the Netherlands: "It is the natural path of the development of monetary wealth, that while the rich become ever richer, not only a countless mass of poor—desperately poor—arise, but that the middling and comfortably well-off founder, and in the end hardly anyone remains in the middle between the enormously rich and ever richer, and the destitute. Then the heart has been removed and the nation is forever lost ... The rich are then totally without any moral value; and the poor none the better."[11] Today's economic historians give this phase of socioeconomic development no better grades.

And within the country a remarkable political calm indeed dominated, which some saw as lethargy. Evaluating the first twenty-five years of political-cultural mentality in the Kingdom of the Netherlands, Thorbecke wrote, out of clearly disappointed liberal optimism: "The constitution has touched on citizenship, the most noble mainspring of our century, as little as possible ... Down to the present day, the middle class does not have the consciousness to participate in government. But without such consciousness the state is not based on the power of the nation, and without a highly developed power of the nation no state can presently be maintained. Such a consciousness is given the people through a genuine, simple representation at the local, regional and national level."[12] One can assume that his critique, which we will take up again below, was directed both at the inadequacies of the constitution and the lethargy of the population.

However, the question arises of who within Dutch society could have developed an early critical consciousness. The notable elite of the old republic's ruling stratum was quite satisfied with the results of 1814/15, even though they had to pay a price for the idea of efficiency with a certain centralization of authority. A large percentage of the population employed in the agricultural sector offered no basis from which ideas on a greater say in politics might grow. The middle class, retailers or artisans, was much too weak economically to provide the impulse for a re-orientation of the economy and of politics.

The main emphasis of the economy was on traditional forms of commerce. It was there that capital gathered, which, however, was not innovatively used, as the times demanded, but rather sought potential investment abroad. And when, moreover, the authorities, especially in the ministry of commerce, held the view that it was mainly trade that contributed to the affluence of the country, then there were few chances for the encouragement of industry. In view of this limited openness and receptiveness towards technological change, the activities of King Wilhelm II appear extremely progressive, but these were concentrated in the south of the country (Belgium).

Foreign observers remarked upon a conspicuous lack of knowledge about technological-industrial and management issues during the entire first half of the century, and spoke of inward-looking professors and merchants. These observers were well-positioned to make such judgements as it was they who helped to set up at least the beginnings of a Dutch industrial sector. It is not surprising that as late as the 1851 London Industrial Exhibition it was reported: "Sad would be the word to describe the sight of the Dutch section; something dead, something naked dominated the area reserved for the Netherlands ... A lack of visitors and the calm in this section showed that everyone felt the unfavorable climate which dominated there."[13] Similar statements on inadequate Dutch competitiveness, past and future, were made by the French ambassador at the Paris Exhibition of 1868.

Certainly, in the decades after French rule, measures were taken to improve the infrastructure, and steamships came increasingly into operation. However, the spread of steam engines was sluggish, and if the textile industry did experience a certain growth, it was only through investment by Belgian industrialists who wanted to preserve their market in the Indonesian archipelago after the 1830 Revolution. A combination of self-satisfaction, lethargy and a clear lack of willingness to be innovative in the industrial sector created—besides the very low social mobility, and the permeability of the "estates"—a climate of total inertia, something also reflected in politics.[14] In any case, developments were not comparable to those in Belgium, nor to those in the neighboring Prussian Rhineland, and the liberal Prussian economic policy had no counterpart in the relevant ministry in The Hague. There was no one corresponding to Hansemann, the Camphausens or other Rhenish industrialists in the Netherlands.

The inertia of economic traditionalism, just discussed, and the modest amount of reflection on the country's political constitution admittedly did not prevent the gradual crystallization of a liberal opposition, after members of distinctly non-liberal circles had already criticized the quality of the system. Real doubts on the contemporary character of the system came from the church, of all places, from both Protestants and Catholics. The Protestant Church [Hervormde Kerk] functioned, in contrast to the public church of the republican period, as nothing short of a state church. In the 1830s, a number of congregations left it, turning against its rationalism—arising from a combination of secular scholarship and theology—and seeking instead a return to the beliefs of the republican period.

Concentrated in the northern provinces, it was not a mass movement, but certainly large enough to push the government and the official church to the limits of their tolerance and sending police and troops against the congregations—a quite exaggerated response to be explained by government insecurity following the secession of Belgium. These apostates [Afgeschiedenen] belonged to the lower classes, but there was nothing to indicate that these "Church Splitters" were also seen as a social threat. Their congregations did not have forces in their membership capable of turning a religious struggle into a political one. Those preachers who supported the movement certainly lacked the ability for such action. Furthermore, a possible alliance with members of the upper classes, who were adherents of a similar theological-philosophical awakening movement, never came to pass.

Theirs was certainly one critique of the existing system and thus of the close relation between church and state, with the consequence of a rather inward-looking and isolated organized opposition. It was, however, less remarkable than the Catholic opposition, which had been "rebelling" from the 1820s onward against the established order of 1815, because the Catholic Church, tolerated again since the Batavian Republic of 1796, felt it did not have equal rights. In fact, the mood in the country was against tolerance. Belgian secession provoked fears about the future of the country and also intensified memories of the Republic and its society, creating a national self-conception in which nationhood and the Reformed faith were linked. Under these conditions, Dutch Catholics were simply equated with rebels. The result was a process of social exclusion based on the tortured memories of past enemies. Catholicism had already transformed itself into a political force in the

1820s—through newspapers, clubs and, not least, under the influence of Lamen-nais—in order to help overcome "the mark of a former slave, who has been set free, but who however, feels like an inferior person compared to the free-born." The Catholic movement grew as public discussion on the constitution increased—a dis-cussion carried out by liberals of various colors. In the political struggle over the constitution, the Catholics supported the liberals.[15]

Catholic support meant in any case a strengthening of the reform front in the constitutional question. From the late 1830s onwards, liberals regarded it as the most pressing political problem, and approached it with varying degrees of radicalism. Leading the reformers was Thorbecke, whose ideas had been shaped by Savigny's and Eichhorn's Historical School of Law. For him, liberal demands as political prin-ciple did not arise from individual claims based on natural rights, but from the growth of a collectively sovereign nation as a historical entity. His starting point was a people developed through language and culture. He appeared then as a deeply his-torical thinker, who assumed developed structures and thus developed unique national characteristics. Like Savigny, he saw in history the most important ingredi-ent for the intellectual existence of a people. Language, culture, people, nation took precedence for Thorbecke—liberalism and liberality were related to them. His atti-tude falls under the definition of romantic liberalism as formulated by Thomas Nipperdey: "Romantic liberalism was … was closely bound to classical liberalism. The emphasis on national culture had a self-cultivated, individualistic, a liberal char-acter. References to history were references to old national liberties; references to the spirit of the people turned into demands for 'popular,' i.e., liberal institutions."[16] Embedding new, liberal thought in history was especially easy for Thorbecke, because he, for all his critique of the history of his own country, simply required the application of the principles of the French Revolution. He found his liberal poten-tial in the history of the republic of the united Netherlands, which in contempo-rary European thinking had been seen as a refuge of liberality, both collective and individual, despite all its undeniable faults.[17]

The groups that finally formed around Thorbecke in the 1840s, and that never included more than five to nine members of parliament, were quite heterogeneous in their intellectual starting points, but generally unified in the political consequences they drew from them. Included in the group were Dirk Donker Curtius, a lawyer in The Hague, Joan Melchior Kemper, constitutionalist and international law expert from Leiden, J.M. Kempenaer, a member of parliament, Th. M. van Roest van Lim-burg, the editor of the liberal newspaper *Arnhemsche Courant*, and the jurist L.C. Luzac. Roest van Limberg had, already in 1837, published a pamphlet entitled *Liber-alisme* thus really introducing the term into the Netherlands; Donker Curtius and Luzac were not as historically oriented as Thorbecke, stressing more the realization of individual rights; but all were united in their desire to bring to an end an "aristocratic rule of cliques" as reflected in the government and, in the final analysis, in the parlia-ment of this "distinguished society of notables" as well. They were concerned with transparency, with greater public knowledge of state finances, thus leading to a struc-tural change in the public sphere in the direction of greater political participation.[18]

The saying that "The king reigns but does not rule" was to be realized by instituting ministerial responsibility, proposed in 1839/40. In 1840, legal responsibility was introduced for the case of abuse of office, as was ministerial countersignature, approval of the budget every two years and the regulation that every minister must defend his budget in parliament. This was too much certainly for an autocrat such as Wilhelm I, who abdicated in favor of his son. He recognized the trend of the age when he commented, at the time of his abdication, that while he would probably regret his move, he would doubtless have regretted even more having to make new concessions daily "to satisfy what cannot be satisfied." The autocrat did not want to continue because he could no longer do as he wished. Whether his son operated out of sympathy or opportunism is an open question. In any case he stated: "On must march along with one's century; it is necessary to enter sincerely, onto the constitutional path. ...."[19]

It certainly sounded convincing when the liberals around Thorbecke talked of getting rid of the "aristocratic cliques." However, all the energy expended in the constitutional question, as reflected in the draft constitution introduced by nine liberal representatives in December 1844, cannot hide the fact that liberal debate on constitutional changes, which were also advocated to a certain extent by conservative-liberals, was at a rather abstract level. Their actions resemble more a game in a political arena, in which the basis, the "pays légal" as it were, was temporarily absent from the discussion or at least did not speak. There was neither a real constitutional movement nor associations that supported or could have supported the policies of these liberal intellectuals. Absent was a visible grouping of specific interests. References to citizenship remained as vague as the defense of free trade. The distance to that which was called "the people" remained quite great for this group from the upper bourgeoisie [*fatsoenlijke stand*] whose writings seldom stooped to the level of general comprehensibility.

This was reflected, as well, in these liberals' understanding of political participation—and, in the final analysis, of citizenship—as a matter of degree. Certainly, Thorbecke had seen the close relationship between the introduction of universal suffrage and the implanting of civic ideas in the general population. In his 1844 brochure on "citizenship" he even wrote that the principle of universal suffrage followed the trend of the nineteenth century.[20] When he stated on 11 April 1848, in an explanation of constitutional changes, that the state, unlike in the past, must "absorb" the power of the people "in its veins," his use of the term "people" referred at most to the more or less well-situated farmers and urban middle class. This was, however, not a question of principle, rather more a threshold designed to hinder an all too rapid introduction of radical democratic thinking at first, but which was to be eventually overcome. Thorbecke, a member of the educated middle class, saw quite clearly, however, that the gradualism he envisioned could quite easily be circumvented were the franchise to remain bound to property. He showed such insight when he raised the possibility of a deep split between rich and poor in a social order based on capital and with the danger of a demand for a citizenship applicable to everybody decaying into a formalism.

It is hardly surprising that this group of parliamentarians, with its rather academic disposition, left a gap which a series of radicals, who saw themselves as closer to the people, sought to fill. Especially after 1844 there certainly were a few liberal newspapers that either shared the standpoint of the group around Thorbecke or in certain points struck a more radical tone. However, from the early 1840s onward, journalists began to appear who acted less from theoretical principles and more from their own disquiet with an altogether lethargic society, politically dominated by a monarchy and bourgeois aristocracy and increasingly impoverished, as well as with their own position within it. In part they were simply adventurers who enjoyed causing a scandal. Their only possible means of expression lay in the printed word.

To avoid a stamp tax based on size, they published newspapers in a small format, the so-called "Lilliputters," which were a curious mixture of yellow journalism with a political coloring and social consciousness. Taken together, these papers never reached a print run of more that 10-15,000, but as they were readily available in the pubs, readership was doubtless considerably higher. Aimed at the broadest mass of the population, they never defined clearly whose participation in politics they would welcome. Apparently limits existed, and—in spite of all complaints about pauperization—tramps, for example, remained excluded from the area of political opinion. However, there were a few among the journalists, such as Eilert Meeter, Adriaan van Bevervoorde or Jan de Vries and P.J.W. de Vos, whose radicalism did not stop even before the royal house and indeed—not least under the influence of Belgian radicals such as Adolphe Bartels or Lucien Jottrand—proclaimed the republic as a possible form of government.[21]

Perhaps the general aim of these journalists was to scandalize society into overcoming its lethargy. Still, it appears doubtful whether they succeeded in the end, either with the petite bourgeoisie, who were their direct targets, or with the workers. It would, however, be wrong to assume that these journalists refrained from approaching the early forms of organization of the social classes they targeted in their "newspapers." Organization in this sense simply meant a call for public meetings, a gathering of the masses, in order to elect a spokesman to approach the mayor of Amsterdam, for example, about the distress of the "lower" population. Only the above-mentioned van Bevervoorde, who maintained close contacts with the Democratic Association in Brussels (led, by Karl Marx, among others), hoped for a real organization of democrats in the sense of a modern party. Van Bevervoorde was himself one of the founders of the Association, but was well aware of the difficulties such organizations entailed, as he tried to explain when speaking to association members at a meeting in Brussels on 14 November, 1847: "Holland, gentlemen, is not as far advanced on the road of liberalism and progress as France, Belgium, England, and even a large portion of Germany. The problem is in its political institutions, which tend to weaken the public spirit and perpetuate the reign of the aristocracy."[22]

In the same year, repeated appeals were made to the Dutch by the editor of the newspaper *Waarachtige Physiologie van Amsterdam* to organize or to arrange protest meetings against poverty. Unemployed demonstrations were planned—for example, on 1 January 1847 on the Amsterdam dam—with slogans such as free work, job creation by the communities, ending of forced labor in the poor colonies: "Work in order to stay alive or die at the door of our bloodsuckers."[23] However, these demonstrations never took place. An examination of the political demands made in this context show that they corresponded to those of the liberal opposition, which had been presented from the beginning of the 1840s in more or less radical terms: a modified or new constitution, changes in taxes, direct elections, free trade, right of dissolution for the lower house. As Stein has shown, Meeter and van Bevervoorde, the main representatives of radicalism, also had high hopes of improving social conditions through the political changes they demanded.[24] Among the workers, which included factory workers and day laborers, market helpers and dock workers, as well as journeymen—who were nearly all suffering economically—clubs began to appear in 1847. These were fostered more by foreign journeymen, mostly German, and less by native tradesmen. It was the former who set up an organization modeled on those in Switzerland, France and other countries—the Amsterdam workers' educational association [*Vereeniging tot zedelijke beschaving der arbeidende klasse*].

The association was intended to form an organizational core for all workers living in the Netherlands. It was aimed much less at strengthening liberal opposition than at the cultural existence of the workers altogether. As its name implies, it was part of the education and training repertoire of journeymen communism and belonged to the objectives of early socialistic circles; naturally, value was placed on political education. Subjects extended from arithmetic, through geography and history, to questions of democracy and socialism. Under the motto "all men are brothers" the association developed those ideas expressed in the debates in London with Wilhelm Weitling in 1845/46. Those workers aspiring to "freedom, equality and justice" were first to be intellectually and morally prepared and enlightened for the "great task," as Karl Schapper said in London. The way there remained hidden, however, and the governor of Nordholland, who was quite concerned about such developments, quite correctly put a question mark behind "the great task."

The activities of the workers' association need not concern us here further, but two revealing accounts deserve mention. Christian Gödecke, a German turner and wood dealer who lived for a number of years in Amsterdam, regretted the immaturity and low levels of education of Dutch workers during a police interrogation at the beginning of 1848. He, in turn, was held by the responsible police commissar to be mentally deranged in view of his aims.[25] Karl Hanke, a dyed-in-the-wool agitator and journeyman who had already been active in Paris, attempted to exploit the radical democratic Lilliputian press for the workers' association. The chance arose when, after serious hunger riots (in Groningen, Leeuwarden, and Harlingen in the summer of 1847) many of those involved were arrested. A petition movement, led by Hanke among others, was begun in their support. Estimations of the number of signatures collected range from 150 to 200.[26]

Neither these local riots of 1847 nor the police and military measures taken to repress them, were serious enough to spark a revolutionary mood in the country or even preserve an existing one. They were spontaneous, unorganized and in the end geographically not wide spread enough to generate broader echoes. While impoverishment continued, reaching a high-point in 1847, the perceptible social and political lethargy of the previous decades, which had also infected ordinary citizens, clearly had its effect. For this reason, radical or workers' association press campaigns seem imported into a situation without any real base of support. One cannot overlook the fact that from 1844/45 Dutch authorities at various levels showed a certain concern about potential sedition, but such concerns were in the end only a consequence of a highly cultivated sensibility, which had become accustomed to a political harmony of souls, the people's silence and to peace and order in general.

Only events abroad brought movement into the political scene in the Netherlands again. On 11 March 1848 the liberal *Arnhemsche Courant* wrote quite aptly that if the government continued to support itself with an artificial majority in parliament, it would suffer the same fate as the former Charles X in 1830 and his successor Louis Phillippe in February. If the existing system were not changed then the people would be driven to extremes, leading to a revolution.[27] This opinion was not shared by all liberals who had set their sights on changing the constitution. Some felt a little dust should be allowed to settle after the events in Paris before any reforms were made.[28] Certainly, the events in France, and later in Germany and Austria, were not without their echo among the native population. The electric shock of which the Groningen liberal jurist spoke in his description of the events and their effect also applied to the Netherlands. Press reaction was that only reform could prevent a revolution.[29]

The significance of the unrest in Amsterdam and the Hague in March 1848 should not be overestimated, however, as neither spontaneous riots nor demonstrations called for by the radicals with the support of the Amsterdam workers' educational association led to mass meetings. The meeting on the dam in Amsterdam on 24 March degenerated into plundering by people taking advantage of the troubles, was thus given no chance for political statements and was quickly repressed. In The Hague, van Bevervoorde placed himself at the head of a larger demonstration, though not without having agreed with the liberal Donker Curtius beforehand to keep the demonstration under control, even though it would not hurt if a few windows were smashed. This was understood as the liberal form of public pressure from the streets. Altogether, in respect of the popular movement one can agree with the Amsterdam correspondent of the *Neue Rheinischen Zeitung* who wrote on 27 June 1848: "… here we have no barricades or grape-shot; here we have neither Marseilles nor shrapnel; here we have neither national assemblies nor revolutionary clubs: the old tulip bulb Holland pushes out its young shoots just as leisurely as a hundred years ago. And yet if we sometimes awake with a start, if we sometimes jump up from our teapots and almost smash our earthenware pipes, it is not because we perhaps are storming out into the streets for a riot, for an insurrection—no, it happens because we are startled by the wild carryings-on of our dear neighbor."[30]

Nonetheless, in combination with events abroad, the relatively limited echo of the demonstrations was at least strong enough to help the liberal reform movement win a quick victory. In the same month, the apparently extremely flexible king established a constitutional commission that was to introduce those changes held to be necessary. In this process, the lower house, controlled by conservative and conservative-liberals, was simply bypassed. Apparently it was felt there was no time to waste. Thorbecke headed the commission. The draft was presented to the king on 11 April, with an explanation from Thorbecke's pen, including the passages on citizenship cited above. The draft was promptly published.

The quickness of the work can be explained in that the new proposal was practically pre-written in the December proposal of 1844. It would seem that the European events of the spring of 1848 had also defeated Dutch lethargy, at least in part. This was not because liberal members of the provincial or national legislatures became especially active—throughout the 1840s they had never really been quiet—but because after publication of the proposed changes a true flood of handbills and petitions covered the country, the large majority, moreover, in support of the liberal draft. In the months of May and June 838 petitions arrived in The Hague, and another 700 were received by the end of the year. Those who rejected the draft spoke of an unacceptable plea for a republic and of the a priori corrupt mass of the broad population; the authors aimed especially at the proposed direct elections as many would lose their seat and vote in the national legislature after its introduction.

Most of the supporters were located in the northern provinces of Groningen, Friesland, and Nordholland, as well as in Geldern. These changes were also endorsed in Catholic Nordbrabant, which like all the Catholics politically allied with the liberals, calculated on their improving their position, although difficulties could be expected because numerous supporters of the draft were turning against freedom of religion. Explicit opposition to the proposals came from Amsterdam and Utrecht. There were a few short-term political difficulties before the approval of the lower house could be attained, which was then granted in October 1848.

The Dutch drew up the framework of a constitutional monarchy once and for all: direct election of the lower house, inviolability of the king and thus full ministerial responsibility, annual budgets, considerable influence in colonial policy for the house (which had not existed until then), right of parliament to establish commisions of inquiry and to amend submitted legislation. Thorbecke's desire to allow total freedom of education, which would have benefited the Catholics, did not gain acceptance. Public—state financed—education was given preference. This would prove to be a serious domestic problem in the coming years.

All in all, the revolution brought the Netherlands a greatly changed constitution, whose basic elements are still in force today. It arose above all under the influence of events abroad, which were perceived as a threat, and less from domestic pressure, which simply was not consistent enough. It arose as well because there was an energetic and, in its tactics, politically shrewd group of liberals, able to take advantage of developments at the right moment. Another reason was that the existing system, with its aristocratic structure of rule by the notables, was only based on past practice, and in view of socioeconomic backwardness, and political reforms beyond the borders, had reached its limits. Finally, there was a monarch who offered no resistance. Moreover it can be assumed that a lack of any transition to industrialization, even whose beginnings were not in sight, lethargy, caused by foreign political reversals as well, and a lack of an elite also capable of leading the broader middle and lower classes prevented greater unrest. And not least, the mostly Protestant character of the country, despite a high percentage of Catholics among the population, reduced the unrest to a peripheral matter in the political life of the society.[31]

Belgium

Just a few days before the outbreak of the February revolution in France, the Belgian Foreign Minister d'Hoffschmidt felt it advisable to report in a circular to Belgium's diplomatic representatives the absence of unrest in their country. He took this step in view of the country's quite special international position, which was one of guaranteed neutrality. Unlike neighboring countries, he wrote, including neutral Switzerland, nothing had happened in Belgium that was not legal and proper. Everyone was making the effort to protect the constitution of the country. "The way things are going," he wrote, "we will soon be one of the most conservative governments of the age." In Belgium, he continued, there was neither a radical nor a republican party. Extreme political ideas were limited to a few persons who remained without influence and who had no common organization and no means of action.[32] His statement was an expansion—certainly also helped by wishful thinking—upon the words of W. A. Arendt, professor in Löwen and well-informed advisor of the king and the government when he had spoken, three years previously, of a consolidated internal order as an important condition for the security of the neutral state.[33]

Although two weeks later the Belgian representative in Paris sought to downplay alarming reports from France by underlining the efforts of Lamartine's provisional government to restore order,[34] he felt it necessary, shortly after, to add: "I know that the dominant idea among the men of movement who have overthrown the July Monarchy is the union of Belgium with France."[35] As before, when the Belgian Revolution of 1830 had broken out in the wake of the Paris July Revolution, thus leading to fundamental changes in the international constellation in Europe, so it was now feared both at home and abroad that a similar development was in process.

Potential for revolt in Belgium, or the conditions for an effective transfer of revolutionary events into Belgium, must be especially examined in respect of an altered constellation of international relations, undesirable in the opinion of the Great Powers. First it must be stated that the Congress of Vienna's experiment of reuniting north and south Netherlands into a united kingdom on the model of the former Burgundian-Habsburg territories did not fail on account of the economic policy of The Hague government, but because of its linguistic and religious policies. A policy of state unity in which people, culture and language were topoi of integration could not be so easily implemented in this region. This was all the more true as the French-speaking population was seen as second class. Moreover, in the course of centuries they had developed another cultural experience and, parallel to that, a deeply rooted Catholic Church had defined politics, culture, and daily life. Furthermore, cultural influence from the south increased—despite a linguistic policy favoring Dutch, which was intended to promote integration—to which especially the influential classes of Belgian society ascribed and which gained acceptance in the1820s among a new generation of Belgian liberal intellectuals. And liberal meant nothing less than achieving a constitution that did justice to individual freedoms.

The personal and fundamentally autocratic policies of the Dutch king, informed by good will and dedicated to promoting the south, suffered in their execution from their own discrepancies. Especially the new liberal demands made in Belgium could easily be combined with general dissatisfaction because of the government's church and language policies. Contrary to these was the royal industrial policy that was certainly up to date or even, in comparison to the rest of the continent, ahead of its time. But its effect was to bolster the position and self-confidence of an industrial, commercial and financial bourgeoisie, whose leading element, at least, spoke French and was unwilling to accept the king's linguistic policies. Apart from this economic bourgeoisie a young intelligentsia arose—publishers, political publicists, jurists, teachers and book sellers—which, under the influence of French old Jacobins and Bonapartists, cultivated a French life-style and culture. The influence of conservatism, the ruling force of the United Kingdom of the Netherlands up to the revolution of 1830, limited freedom of the press in Belgium as well. Such limitations resulted in press trials, which led young Belgian intellectuals to an increasing rejection of the regime.

Together with the Catholics of the country, the liberals created a constitution for themselves- a result of the revolution, as it were—which for many years was seen as the epitome of liberal constitutions. Direct elections allowed access to political participation in parliament. Restrictions lay in the property qualifications, which were placed so high that the petite bourgeoisie remained excluded. Later on, a simple election law added a difference between town and country in the property qualification for voting.

The new state which arose from a revolutionary coalition of intellectuals, the middle class, aristocrats, and the Catholic clergy was a constitutional one, with a clear division of powers. Freedom of assembly and association, freedom of the press, opinion and religion belonged as much to the fundamental liberal principles as did the introduction of ministerial responsibility, before both parliament and criminal law. The Catholic Church was, moreover, no longer subordinated to state control and could develop freely, of great significance in view of the guaranteed freedom of education. A certain conservative balance against the authority of the parliament was ensured by the introduction of a senate, the seats in which could only be taken by the richest of the great landowners, because of a high property qualification for membership.

However, after 1831 a whole series of restrictive regulations were introduced which considerably narrowed the sector of "fundamental civil liberties." As long as the newspapers were subject to a high stamp tax, freedom of the press was limited. Freedom of association was limited as long as workers' coalitions were banned.

While democrats fought the autocracy of the Dutch king together with the liberals in the revolution of September 1830, this coalition quickly shattered after their success. Thus, liberals and conservatives immediately rejected democratic demands for a republican form of government, and the franchise laws hindered the entry into politics of the lower classes, including the lower middle class. Demands for democracy and a republic, however, were not to die away in the following years.[36]

These years were characterized above all by changes in the Belgian economic structure, prepared by earlier developments in the eighteenth century and now all the more intensively implemented. This change involved, more than anything else, the expansion of one very important sector, that up until then had ranked third behind agriculture and commerce: the iron industry and coal mining. One important impulse was a decision by the cabinet to invest in a national railway network. In mining near Mons (Bergen) the number of miners rose in the ten years after 1834 by 23 percent, coal production by 43 percent; in Charleroi the figures were 55 percent and 209 percent; in Liège, they were 38 percent and 72 percent. In the provinces of Liège and Hainault the metal industry thrived and steam power came to dominate the entire Belgian industrial region.

If this development already clearly distinguishes Belgian industry from its stagnant Dutch counterpart, the difference is all the more apparent in the capital sector. While Dutch businessmen profitably invested their money abroad, the Société Générale, founded by Wilhelm I in 1822, granted large loans to industry and set up investment trusts, contributing to industrial expansion. In 1835 the Banque de Belgique and other consortiums were established, bringing French capital into the country. Joint-stock corporations were the preferred form for these newly founded industrial enterprises. Still, agriculture remained the leading economic sector. The percentage of those living from agriculture was 54.6 percent in 1846. However, especially because of poor competitiveness in the non-mechanized, outworking textile trade, migration from the country rose, leading to a growth of an urban proletariat and also, because the new workers could not be given jobs in the early phase of economic change, to a growth in the urban poor.[37]

Politically, Belgium never really came to rest between 1830 and 1848, and in this respect, political activity, especially outside government and parliament, more closely paralleled developments in France than the lethargy of the Netherlands. Nonetheless, the continuation of the liberal-Catholic union of 1828 ensured conditions in which the new nation could develop with a self-assurance that gained an extra boost with the successful end of the war against the Dutch in 1839. Even though the war served as a nucleus for a liberal-Catholic union, covering over their divergences, this union was nonetheless preserved even after the end of the war and was only replaced by a purely liberal government in 1847. As early as the 1830s, Catholic ultramontanists had already attempted to deter those liberal Catholics, who were partially under the influence of Lammenais, from participating in the new regime. Liberals, however, only really began expressing doubts about cooperation with the Catholics in the subsequent decade, even though the ultramontanist efforts to influence Catholic liberals had failed.

The liberals complained of an all too great conservative influence, and a preference for big landowners, who were, in fact, successful in resisting free trade policies desired by the liberals. Moreover, liberals regretted an all too great Catholic influence on the education system. There were repeated instances of friction, which were continually patched over, "but they ate away at the initial commonalities."[38] On the one hand, this development was surprising, since those Lamennais-Catholics opposed to the papal encyclical "Mirari vos" based themselves totally on the Belgian constitution with all its freedoms and possibilities. On the other hand, it was understandable, as the church increasingly supported the conservative policies of the king and L. Delebecque, named Bishop of Gent in 1840, and placed the liberal-Catholic clergy under great pressure.[39]

Resistance to the church was also useful—in mediated form, so to speak—in the struggle against the large landowners and against obsolete forms of textile production in the countryside. It involved the entire spectrum of liberals, who after the end of the war in 1839, had been strengthened by the anti-Catholic Orangists. The former called for laicization and a greatest possible liberalization of the economy. Among the liberals was the group around Paul Devaux, Charles Rogier, and Josef Lebeau, who had been among the leaders of the 1830 Revolution, and who were most concerned with limiting monarchical power without promoting a doctrinaire anticlericalism. Other liberals included spokesmen for the middle class, representing the interests of industrialists, bankers, and large merchants, who still felt themselves disadvantaged by policies in favor of the special interests of agriculture and the rad%tional trades. From this class came the demand for a gradual sinking of the property qualification, to allow political participation by the lower classes and also to improve the conditions of the working class. Humanitarian motives and utilitarian considerations doubtless played a role. This wing of liberalism maintained some contacts with the democrats, who had been active ever since the 1830 Revolution, without, however, really gaining much ground.

It should be noted—typical for developments in Belgium—that the call for an established organization—a party—arose from the opposition of a broad spectrum of liberals to conservative-Catholic predominance. The groundwork was prepared by the Masonic Lodges, widespread in Belgium and in general quite powerful. Politicization of the Freemasons began in 1836/37. Even earlier, in the era of French rule, as well as during the long period of the United Kingdom of the Netherlands, the Freemasons had been prominent in their support of a laic state.

Local liberal organizations, politically active from 1842 onwards, merged to form a nationwide liberal party in 1846. In the journalistic preparation for the Belgian liberal congress, the common thread uniting everyone was, above all, anticlericalism, the fear of the church capturing the state. However, there was more in the program that the congress promulgated. Extending the franchise by lowering property qualifications belonged as much to the liberals' political objectives as did ousting Catholics from the education system by budgeting sufficient funds for state schools. Seemingly in honor of the participation of intellectuals in the birth of the nation, those members of those professions requiring a diploma for their exercise were also to be granted voting rights. At the last moment the congress also added that measures to improve the living conditions of the working class and other needy must unquestionably be introduced.[40]

Previously, social deprivation had not really been the object of more detailed political reflection. Naturally, people were aware that the number of paupers was growing in both the city and the country, especially after spinning machines had gradually begun to supersede outworking, the means by which the large majority of the rural population had, until then, earned their meager income. Migration from country to city meant the spread of poverty, increased still more by the appearance of entire bands of beggars in urban areas, where the indigenous proletariat lived in scarcely better conditions. It is not surprising that the liberals included in their 1846 program a reference to the plight of a large part of the population, because the years 1844/47 were ones of serious agricultural depressions (potato blight, failed harvests) with corresponding consequences for the already meager conditions of the workers and the poor.[41]

In this early phase of industrialization, that was also an era of agricultural crises accompanied by the restructuring of the rural linen industry, what was the political potential of the proletariat or, more broadly, of the poor in general? The workforce of the early factories was recruited mainly from an untrained rural proletariat; the needy and paupers certainly could not be counted as a class-conscious proletariat, based on its self-organization. Moreover, a ban on coalition existed for workers, so that they could gain no "practice in organization." In the crafts, the initial conditions were more favorable. While the ban applied here too, the law tolerated the creation of mutual benefit funds, which can be viewed as early forms of organization. Furthermore, craft workers could generally read and write, so that political agitation and theoretical debate on the necessary changes in society could develop. There was, however, the difficulty that the journeymen rarely looked beyond their own craft and, certainly had no interest in demonstrating solidarity with factory workers, but preferred to keep their distance from them.[42]

The political work was taken on by the Belgian democrats who, unlike their Dutch neighbors, had played an active role in the political spectrum since the revolution, but who were not able to bring about the introduction of a republic. The democrats' ranks included every possible variation from liberal-democrat to social revolutionary—from Adelson Castiau, via Lucien Jottrand, Adolphe Bartels, Charles Louis Spilthoorn, to Jacob Kats. These were some of the leading figures, representing both the old democrats of the revolution of 1830 as well as the new activists from intellectual and craft circles and from the middle class of industrial cities such as Ghent, Verviers and Liège. The demand for a republic was common to most; an end to the property franchise was part of the repertoire. Their efforts were concentrated on the lower middle class, as well as on the workers.

The democrats' social program, as published in the newspapers *Le Radical, Le Patriote Belge*, or in *Le Débat Social*, included the introduction of progressive taxes in place of indirect ones, a gradual breaking up of great fortunes through a high inheritance tax, workers' co-determination in large firms, free schooling, unemployment assistance, and an old age pension. With respect to the question of property, however, differing views were held. The instruments for spreading political demands included newspapers—with, however, only a limited press run—organizational and financial assistance and so-called "meetings" (they used the English word) organized especially by Jacob Kats, an adherent of the ideas of Buonarotti, organized on the model of the Chartists. These "meetings" were suppressed by the police as much as possible.[43]

While some of the democrats maintained close contacts with the left-wing liberals, they had to distance themselves from the liberals in general. A. Delhasse expressed it most clearly in 1838 when he wrote:

> Question: What is the doctrine opposed to democracy? Answer: it is liberalism, oldest son of Girondist federalism, descended in a direct line from the philosophical school whose high priest was Voltaire. Liberalism puts for the principle of the sovereignty of individual reason and of wealth, and it works from this antisocial principle to establish the pre-eminence of the bourgoisie over the classes called inferior, to make the immense majority vassals subject to the whim and dictatorial omnipotence of a privileged caste. In other words, it begins with individualism, to end with egoism and the exploitation of man by man.[44]

This was also the basic attitude of the Democratic Association, founded in November 1847, on the initiative of Jottrand. Its leadership group was international, and included Karl Marx as deputy chairman. This was to provide the basis for a "democratic International." The association immediately took up contacts with the Fraternal Democrats in Great Britain, which were maintained by Friedrich Engels and George Julian Harney. Together with Ledru-Rollin, the most important French democrat of the time, and J. Flocon, editor-in-chief of *La Réforme* [a leading Parisian, left-wing daily, ed.], Harney was preparing an international democratic congress for 1848.

The Democratic Association had as much the character of an early international society as the "Fraternal Democrats," or the London Communist League. Marx introduced into the Association Carl d'Ester and Mikhail Bakunin. Admittedly, the latter was of the opinion that in the vicinity of Marx and Engels it was impossible for anyone else to breathe freely. If Marx's attention was primarily fixed on his work in the London Communist League, he also remained active in Brussels, where his 9 January 1848 speech on free trade made some impression. He stated: "But in general, today protectionism is conservative, while the free trade system has a destructive effect. It undermines the existing nationalities and pushes the contrast between proletariat and bourgeoisie to extremes. In a word, the system of free trade accelerates the social revolution. And only in this revolutionary sense, gentlemen, do I support free trade." Although Marx's presentation was well received, it nonetheless appears questionable whether the relationship between economic development and a revolutionary uprising in the form presented to the ordinary association members could have provided an basis for discussions among them.

Marx was valued more as a theoretician by those in the Communist League than by those in the association, an altogether heterogeneous mixture that included representatives of the workers (e.g., J. Kats and J. Pellering) as well as bourgeois intellectuals (L. Jottrand, A. and F. Felhasse, Ch. Spiltoorn, A. Bartels). The necessity of social and political reform was a common belief, and while the members of the association did not cut themselves off from ideas about the creation of a future society, drawing mostly on Fourier, Saint-Simon, Robert Owens, and Louis Blanc, most of their interest was concentrated on immediate political measures such as suffrage and tax reforms, compulsory schooling, abolition of the standing army and the establishment of a civic guard, and trade associations. Little attention was given to theoretical constructs, such as those being developed at the time by Marx and Engels in the *Communist Manifesto*.[45]

Before the government under Charles Rogier could begin implementing its program, purely liberal from 1847 onwards, and before the democrats could begin to establish themselves beyond their central office in Brussels and a few provincial cities, the revolution broke out in Paris. On 26 March Moses Heß, at the time co-editor of the *Deutsche Brüsseler Zeitung*, wrote to Andreas Gottschalk in his somewhat hypertrophied "revolutionism" that Belgium would introduce the republic within two weeks. Possibly he had been impressed by the numerous banquets held in Brussels and the Wallonian industrial region by the pro-French "Fraternal Reunion," calling for a democratic republic on the French model. Moreover, all of Hainault was teeming with French propagandists.[46]

One can wonder, however, whether the ground was prepared for a revolution with aimed at the introduction of a republic. Certainly, the consequences of the years of crisis of 1844/46 were not yet overcome; the extreme poverty of factory workers and the rural population working in the textile sector had not yet been alleviated. Still, there was no more than a few disturbances in Brussels, Ghent, and in the province of Hainault. The police had little difficulty maintaining order in Brussels; they had more trouble in Ghent, where many workers were involved in the rioting. At no time did a real danger exist for the entire country, or at least a large part of the population, of developing a readiness to take part in a republican upheaval.

This would soon become apparent. Nonetheless the liberal government introduced measures that certainly appeased the majority of the politically dissatisfied. It took to the path of reform with noticeable haste. In lowering the property qualification for the entire country, up to then staggered, to a minimum of BF 42 (HFL 20)—which translated into a 70 percent increase in the electorate—it met the desires of the left-wing liberals and thus also a part of the democrats. This occurred in the middle of March. In April the stamp tax was cancelled. On top of this, postal fees for printed matter were lowered—although only in December—which, in effect, facilitated political campaigns. In May 1848 civil servants were banned from taking seats in parliament, in order to ensure a clear separation of the executive and legislative. Up until then the numerous civil servants with seats in the lower house and the senate had provided conservative government policy the necessary support. Of considerable importance was the loan floated by the government. It was used to stimulate industry and to avoid, in any event, a dangerous increase in unemployment.

Extending the franchise was a clever move because it drew petit-bourgeois circles, generally associated with the democrats, into the liberal government camp. For moderate progressives, who had never contemplated overthrowing the monarchy, this was certainly a victory. Its consequences are reflected in the results of the parliamentary elections of June 1848. In the lower house, the liberals took eighty-three seats to the Catholics twenty-five. Thus the first half of 1848 turned into a catastrophe for the Belgian republicans—into a catastrophe that reached its nadir in the town council elections of August of that year. "A few months after February 1848," wrote Els de Witte, "the movement died a quiet death." While in France Cavaignac was forced to use the army to restore public order, in Belgian things more or less carried on as usual, without there ever being a revolutionary threat.

Some preventive measures were taken. The government, for instance, expelled radical foreigners—Karl Marx among them. A middle of the road policy, involving the accommodation of democratic demands and, at the same time, firmness against the appearance of extremism, characterized the actions of the government. It not only turned its back on every republican demand using the police to close down meetings, it also used the army against the "Belgian Legion." This was a group of Belgian emigrants returning from France who crossed the border near Quiévrain and Risquons-Tout (25 and 39 March) to offer armed assistance to the founding of a Belgian Republic. Little effort was required to thwart these adventurers. But these events deserve to be examined in greater detail.

The "Belgian Legion" was the work of the Franco-Belgian Democratic Club, located in Paris, whose formation was probably supported by French government officials with extreme left-wing sympathies. Other political forces in Paris certainly looked upon this recruitment process favorably, seeing in it the possibility of getting rid of impoverished Belgian immigrants who had been laid off from factories and workshops in the French capital. The Belgians did not join the "Legion" spontaneously, but did so under the influence of the political propaganda of French republicans, who also promised to make foodstuffs available for the trip. In Belgian itself, leadership of the "Legion" was to be taken on by Ch. Spiltoorn, a lawyer and radical politician, together with Jottrand and other founding members of the above-mentioned Democratic Association, who were awaited in the west Flanders city of Kortrijk (Courtrain).

However, it proved to be quite a disorganized movement, which apparently counted on considerable reinforcement by supporters in Belgian, but was itself too heterogeneous to allow the rapid development of a unified republican consciousness. Certainly, on 24 March the "revolutionaries," still waiting in Paris, gathered in front of the Belgian embassy, to give three cheers for the republic. The following day, about 800 to 900 members of the "Belgian Legion," consisting of Belgians, Frenchmen, and Poles, caught the train north, outfitted with tickets and food for the trip. When reading the reports of the Belgian Ambassador in Paris and the related correspondence between him and the Belgian foreign minister, it is noticeable that official nervousness, obvious at the beginning, while easing later, grew at first because of the general unrest throughout Europe, especially as it was to early to judge the developments in Belgium itself. News that the "Belgian Legion" awaited reinforcements of about 3,000 to 4,000 men with arms and munitions in Rijssel (Lille) and Moescroen (Mouscron), which would then head off towards Gent where they were counting on about 20,000 workers, also contributed to their disquiet. The fact that on the following day, the government had to pay careful attention to developments in Brussells itself only increased the tension still further. From The Hague came the news that members of the Democratic Association had approached the affiliated Amstel Society in Amsterdam with an invitation to start a common popular movement in the two capitals and to proclaim the republic in both countries.

However, events on the Belgian-French border reduced to a minimum the prospects of the realization of revolutionary (republican) wishes. In Quiévrain those arriving were met by armed troops, supported spontaneously by residents of neighboring towns armed with hunting rifles. The French were expelled on the spot; those Belgians with identity papers were sent home under armed escort; and those without papers were handed over to the authorities. Diplomatic reports pointing out that the majority of Belgian workers had arrived without any political intentions and had only made use of the opportunity of a free trip home seem thoroughly believable.

Apparently such failures did not prevent other groups from setting out for the Belgian border. Several thousand gathered in the town of Seclin, near Lille and the Belgian border. Foreign Minister d'Hoffschmidt wrote to van de Weyer, the Belgian envoy in London: "The French authorities provide foodstuffs to this kind of military camp just as one would for regular army units." The note was intended for Lord Palmerston, whom the Belgian government expected to intervene with the provisional government in Paris. For a moment, danger seemed in the offing when, on 29 March, 2,000 men crossed the border near Lille, heading for Moescroen. This rather large group was met at the appropriately named border town of Risquons-Tout [Risk-All] by a Belgian infantry unit of 200 men, twenty-five mounted riflemen, and two field howitzers, and was beaten back in less than two hours. If there were a common republican will among this vanguard, then after this brief armed confrontation its realization was just one of the utopias of the day. In this context it needs to be stressed that here, as in Quiévrain, Belgians were not alone among the advance troops, but these were made of an internationally mixed society. According to statements made by some deserters, it seems that a number of Belgian workers were forced to take up arms.

On the one hand, we can ascertain that propaganda in favor of a Belgian republic began quite early in February, and was certainly carried out by a number of Belgian republicans and finally found support from like-minded Frenchmen. On the other hand, it is almost impossible to answer questions about the effectiveness of such propaganda for revolutionary ideas—especially among those workers who had become unemployed in their host country and simply wanted to return home. Spontaneity, a poor substitute for necessary preparation time, did not suffice to form an armed body with a unified will. Hence, the impact of events in Paris and vicinity on a potential revolutionization of Belgian remained stuck in a state of improvisation.

In other words, the Belgian Revolution only took place in Paris, because the merger with republican forces in Belgian projected in Paris did not occur as such republicans were too few in numbers and even the most convinced republicans of the Democratic Association, those around Louis Jottrand, were no way near prepared to start a violent uprising. Even among this group, there were fears of French annexation, in view of the strong expressions of Franco-Belgian cooperation in Paris. In addition to that, while there was indigenous unrest, mostly in Gent where Kats, Spilthoorn, and Pellering had carried out a lot of propaganda for the republic, prorepublican street demonstrations in mid-March brought forth counter-demonstrations for the monarchy, organized and supported by Flemish activists. Even though the Flemish movement at that time should not be seen as especially strong or wide-ranging, the identification of republican ideas with the French Revolution was, nonetheless, a disadvantage in trying to spread such ideas among the mass of the Flemish population. The numerous counter-demonstrations were accompanied by patriotic, that is anti-French, songs and poems, which Hermann von der Dunk felt betrayed quite clearly German influence.[47]

Let us now return to considering the behavior of the government and its motives. The hasty reform policy served not only to stabilize public order and secure property, but was also motivated by the knowledge that the internationally guaranteed Belgian neutrality required the preservation of the form of government introduced with the revolution of 1830/31. This relationship between domestic and foreign policy, part of the intellectual presuppositions of the Congress of Vienna and the Restoration, was still accepted by the leading statesmen of the time. For Belgian, geographical proximity to France weighed double, because the 1830 Revolution had already obtained the reputation of being carried out on the basis of a French model and in the years immediately following that revolution there had been enough calls for the annexation of Belgium by France. Moreover, before the 1848 revolution it was clear that relations between Belgian and French republicans existed within the framework of an international "democratic" movement. A change in the form of government, as the Belgian government knew, in the direction of a Franco-Belgian republican cooperation, could have meant intervention by the Great Powers that were the guarantors of Belgian neutrality.

That was known from the start in Paris as well, where Lamartine denied connivance both by his government as well as by subordinate authorities or their representatives in recruiting the troops advancing toward Belgian. In any event, he seems in April 1848 to have sounded out the situation in Belgium in view of possible international consequences. It appears that the government in Paris was prepared to support a Belgian republic if necessary, were it to be threatened from abroad. For this purpose Lamartine sent Bellocq, a plenipotentiary, to Brussels, a political moderate who had previously served in the French embassy there.

Bellocq raised the question "Does Belgium want a republic?" The envoy demonstrated not only a very discerning eye for modes of political behavior within Belgian society, but also recognized the close relation between a strong national consciousness aiming at independence from foreign powers and the constitutional structure: "... the great obstacle to the establisment of the republic is the conviction that a republican Belgian could never lead an independent existence, that it would inevitably be absorbed by France. This nationalist sentiment is much stronger than people might think."

However, what had France to offer constitutionally which was not in practice already available in Belgium? All individual freedoms were guaranteed in the constitution. It was only that there was a monarch as head of state, a position elsewhere called a president, and this monarch clearly personified the results of the national revolution. The share of the republican party in the total population was extremely small, quite a long way from becoming a majority. The relationship between rich bourgeoisie and nobles, on the one hand, and the working classes and the common rural population, on the other, gave no cause to suspect tensions. Bellocq answered his introductory question with a clear no. Accordingly he advised against any attempt to push through or even promote a Belgian Revolution, because such a move would not only have been opposed by Belgians, but also by Great Britain.[48]

Bellocq also pointed out that Belgium could also foster friendly relations with France even with its current form of government and that a Franco-Belgian union would only lead to friction with competing industries in the Department Nord. Bellocq's considerations raise the entire "revolutionary" events to a general European level. This is understandable enough, considering that in 1848 as well the concept of revolution included not just social confrontation, but also a justification for expansion across international boundaries, as members of the Holy Alliance had already understood.

In and of itself, the decisive stance of the liberal government in Brussels against any revolutionary change made it evident that Paris needed to demonstrate clear reserve. The liberal government itself took the initiative, not only in its domestic reform policy but also by informing the great powers that it expected unconditional support in the case of a French invasion.[49] Leopold I, as well, who was seen in the country by both liberals and democrats—especially by the latter—as rather conservative, approached Metternich in this spirit.[50] To reduce the danger of a French attack even further, the government pleaded for a rapid recognition of Ledru-Rollin's provisional government—an attitude that did not please all the guarantee powers. Diplomatic developments need not be followed further here. It should only be mentioned that both Vienna and Berlin approved of the domestic political measures in Belgium as a successful reform policy.[51]

In understanding political developments in Belgium since the preceding revolution of 1830, it is quite clear that a comparatively deep-seated socioeconomic change had occurred, with all the consequences for the conditions of existence for the upper classes. The period before the revolution of 1848 should be characterized primarily as one of a continued public discussion on the meaning of modern liberal order. While such a discussion also developed in the Netherlands, it took place more peripherally, and not on the broader basis on which the Belgians could build. Furthermore, liberal principles were already well established and in the end needed only to be secured from attacks by conservatives and parts of the Catholic Church.

At the moment when a revolutionary upheaval threatened, it turned out that broad democratic popular movement was just a chimera, because it had no support from a working class without the sufficient consciousness. In the end, a hastily developed rapid reform policy sufficed to calm the situation, to politically undermine the spokesmen for disturbances and to let the call for a republic, as had just come from France, die away unheard.

My final remarks lead back once again to the definition of revolution given at the beginning of this paper, which emphasized the relationship between change and revolutionary upheaval, or, conversely, between lack of change and abstinence from revolution. Developments in the Netherlands exemplified this converse. One cannot speak of socioeconomic change in view of the behavior of the Dutch capital, which was not directed at innovation but at investment abroad. The era of modern industrial policy had not yet begun. One can assume that despite an early constitutional order no civic consciousness arose, as Thorbecke regretted in the spring of 1848, and furthermore it is worth noting that the concept of "rank" or "order" clearly prevailed over the more modern term "class," only introduced into the discussion relatively late.

This situation was quite different in Belgium. There, the above-mentioned simple equation of change and revolution is not immediately valid. Despite clear socioeconomic change, there was unrest but no revolutionary upheaval. It should be noted that the transformation of Belgium into an industrial country advanced rapidly, but was still far from completion. Agriculture, with its social structures, still played a significant role. However, a number of other factors also existed which possibly justify the question of whether it does not seem idle—in view of a number of relevant elements that change from country to country—to present a theory of the revolutionary potential of any given era. In any event, change as precursor to revolution should always mean change in consciousness in the sense of a political redefinition of one's own (class) identity, in this case as a redetermination of one's political location in the process of industrialization. Such had not occurred at this early point in Belgium. In the great collection of essays on the history of the Belgian workers' movement edited by J. Dhont this point is made over and again.[52]

Apart from the above-mentioned, rapidly implemented governmental reform program, special reference must be made to the factor of the "nation." The concept of a Belgian nation had been brought to life by the successful and successfully defended revolution of 1830, and its positive reception should not be underestimated. This recently acquired independence, anchored in international law by the guarantees of neutrality, was to be defended on all sides. Thus, support for a revolution, as offered to Belgium by the French republicans, could not be a recommendation, in view of the memory of the consequences of the French Revolution of 1789, especially as, in the final analysis, a "republic" had no more and no less to offer constitutionally than the "real existing" Belgian monarchy. The above-mentioned French plenipotentiary, Bellocq, stated this quite clearly. In view of the strong presence of a combined constitution and monarchy, republicanism appeared an inopportune idea, one that did not have an electrifying effect on political will, especially as the mass of the population was clearly under the influence of the Catholic Church, which was, quite simply, more popular or even more "every-day" than the bourgeois intellectual members of the Democratic Association.

Notes

1. Eric Hoffer, *The Ordeal of Change* (New York, 1963), 4-5.
2. Chalmers Johnson, *Revolutionary Change* (Boston, 1966), 59-60. He refers to T.H. Wintringham, *Mutiny* (London, 1936), 10.
3. Johnson gives as an example the United States during the Great Depression.
4. *Brieven en Gedenkschriften van Gijsbert Karel van Hogendorp*, Vol. 5 ('s-Gravenhage, 1900), 498 (translation from the Dutch by the author of the essay).
5. Thus in the review from 1837: J.R. Thorbecke, "Onze betrekkingen tot Duitsland," *Historische schetsen*, 2nd ed. ('s-Gravenhage, 1872), 21.
6. Cited in Horst Lademacher, *Die Niederlande. Politische Kultur zwischen Individualität und Anpassung* (Berlin, 1993), 406.
7. Eric J. Hobsbawm, *The Age of Revolution, Europe 1789-1848*, 3rd. ed. (London, 1969).
8. Anette von Droste Hülshoff, *Sämtliche Werke*, ed. by J. Schwering (Berlin, undated) Vol. 5, 194.
9. Here, in general, see Horst Lademacher, *Zwei ungleiche Nachbarn. Wege und Wandlungen der deutsch-niederländischen Beziehungen im 19. und 20. Jahrhundert* (Darmstadt, 1989), chapters 2 and 3.
10. Later, a fierce argument on the negative role of the constitution in the realization of democratic principles arose in Dutch historiography between the adherent of democratic thought, C.H.E. de Wit and the older Pieter Geyl. See "Oligarchie en proletariaat," (Ph.D. Diss., Amsterdam 1965), later published under the title *De Nederlandse revolutie van de 18e eeuw, 1780-1787. Oligarchie en proletariaat* (Oirsbeek, 1974), and *Geschiedenis van de Nederlandse stam*, 6 vols. (Amsterdam, 1952), respectively. For a balanced analysis Ernst Heinrich Kossmann, *The Low Countries, 1780-1940* (Oxford and New York, 1978), 65ff.
11. Barthold G. Niebuhr, "Circularbriefe aus Holland," in Niebuhr, *Nachgelassene Schriften nichtphilologischen Inhalts* (n.p., 1842), 449ff.
12. Cited in Lademacher, *Die Niederlande*, 435-36
13. Quoted in W.J. Wieringa, "Economische herorientiering in Nederland in de 19e eeuw," in *Economische ontwikkeling en emancipatie*, 2 (The Hague, 1977), 35.
14. In summary, see the contribution by Wieringa cited in the previous note, and in *Algemene Geschiedenis der Nederlanden*, Vol. 10 (Haarlem, 1981), 106ff., the section written by J.H. van Stuivenberg; in addition, Th. van Tijn and M. Zappey "De negentiende eeuw 1813-1914," in J.H. van Stuivenberg (ed.), *De economische geschiedenis van Nederland*, 2nd ed. (Groningen, 1979), 201ff.
15. On the development of the two churches, see L.J. Rogier and N. de Rooy, *In vrijheid herboren. Katholiek Nederland 1853-1953* (The Hague, 1953); M.E. Kluit, *Het protestantse Réveil in Nederland en daarbuiten 1815-1864* (Amsterdam, 1970).
16. Thomas Nipperdey, *Nachdenken über die deutsche Geschichte* (Munich, 1986), 123.
17. On Thorbecke, see H.G. Beuckers, *Rober animi. Niederländische Liberalität des J.R. Thorbecke und positivistischer Liberalismus* (Frankfurt, 1983); J.B. Manger, *Thorbecke en de historie* (Utrecht, 1986). See also Thorbecke's correspondence which is being prepared for publication and has in part already been published: G.J. Hooykaas (ed.), *De briefwisseling van J.R. Thorbecke*, vols. 1-4 ('s-Gravenhage, 1975-1993).

18. See first chapter in J.C. Boogman, *Rondom 1848* (Bussum, 1978), 9-49. The volume is naturally also concerned with Thorbecke´s policies; also the recent work of S. Stuurman, *Wacht op onze daden. Het liberalisme en de vernieuwing van de Nederlandse staat* (Amsterdam, 1992), 45-134, concentrating on Donker Curtius.

19. Quoted in Kossmann, *The Low Countries*, 181.

20. "Over het hedendaagsche staatsburgerschap" (1844).

21. See for an overview M.J.F. Robijns, *Radicalen in Nederland (1840-1851)* (Leiden, 1967); for the "Lilliputters," see J.J. Giele, *De pen in aanslag. Revolutionairen rond 1848, Fibulareeks 40* (Bussum, 1968).

22. Quoted in Hans Stein, "Der Amsterdamer Arbeiterbildungsverein von 1847 und die Vorläufer der modernen sozialen Bewegung in Westeuropa," *International Review for Social History* 2 (1937): 128. Although an older work, this extensive essay should be considered along with the discussions of the radicals mentioned in the previous footnote.

23. Ibid.: 135

24. Ibid.: 137.

25. Ibid.: 142.

26. Ibid,: 144ff.

27. Quoted in S. Stuurman, *Wacht op onze daden*, 135. An English version of chap. 4 of the book, " Het wonderjaar," appears in *European History Quarterly* 21 (1991): 445-480.

28. On this point see B.D.H. Tellegen, "1848. Het voorspel van de herziening der Grondwet," in *De Gids*, IV Series, Vol I, 1883, 1-37, with excerpts from the *Journaal van Luzac*.

29. Stuurman, *Wacht op onze daden*, 145.

30. Quoted in Stein, "Amsterdamer Arbeiterbildungsverein," 155. On the development of unrest see also Giele, *De pen in aanslag*, 69ff., as well as *Algemene Geschiedenis der Nederlanden*, Vol. 12 (Haarlem, 1977), 333ff. (essay by J.C. Boogman). More recently, see also Stuurman, *Wacht op onze daden*, 145ff.; for greater detail, especially on van Bevervoorde and his activities, see Robijns, *Radicalen in Nederland*, 249ff.

31. On the Protestant nature of the country see A.J. van Dijk, *Groen van Prinsterer´s Lectures on Unbelief and Revolution* (Ontario, 1989).

32. See in A. de. Ridder (ed.), *La crise de la neutralité belge de 1845. Le dossier diplomatique*, Vol. 1 (Brussels, 1928), d`Hoffschmidt's circular to the diplomatic representatives of 9 February 1848, 1ff. Quote on 1.

33. See Horst Lademacher, *Die Belgische Neutralität als Problem der europäischen Politik, 1830-1914* (Bonn, 1971), 122ff. and 126.

34. Letter of the Prince de Ligne to d´Hoffschmidt 25/28 February, in De Ridder, *La crise*, 4, 11-12.

35. Letter of Lignes to d´Hoffschmidt of 26 February, ibid., 26ff. Quote on 27.

36. See on this point in condensed form in E. Lamberts, "Belgie sinds 1830," in J.H.C. Blom and E. Lamberts (eds.), *Geschiedenis van de Nederlanden*, (Rijswijk, 1993), 253; (English language edition: *History of the Low Countries*, ed. by J. C. H. Blom and Emiel Lamberts, translated by James C. Kennedy [New York and Oxford, 1999]). See also, E. de Witte, in E. de Witte and J. Craeybeckx, *Politieke geschiedenis van Belgie sinds 1830. Spanningen in een burgerlijke democratie*, 3rd ed. (Antwerp, n.d.) 9ff.

37. See the overview in de Witte and Craeybeckx, *Politieke geschiedenis*, 31ff.; also in Kossmann, *The Low Countries*, 176ff.; see additionally, M. Erbe, *Belgien, Niederlande, Luxemburg. Geschichte des niederländischen Raumes*, (Stuttgart, 1993), 212ff.

38. Quotation from Erbe, *Belgien*, 215. On Belgian ultramontanism see E. Lamberts (ed.), *De Kruistocht tegen het Liberalisme. Facetten van het ultramontanism in Belgie in de 19e eeuw* (Leuven, 1984), especially 38-63, the essay by Lamberts on the period 1830-1914.

39. Lamberts, *Kruistocht*, 42.

40. See A. Miroir, "Het liberaal Congres van 1846," in A. Verhulst and H. Hasquin (eds.), *Het liberalisme in Belgie. Tweehonderd jaar geschiedenis* (Brussels, 1989), 67ff.

41. On this point, see the detailed description by K. van Isacker, *Mijn land in de kering, 1830-1980*, Vol. 1 (Kapellen, 1978), 67-79. This work is also useful for the lifestyle and level of consciousness of, above all, the middle classes.

42. Analysis in de Witte and Craeybeckx, *Politieke geschiedenis*, 45 ff.; similar results in Robijns, *Radicalen*, 43. Further on this point, remarks J. Dhondt, *Algemene Geschiedenis der Nederlanden*, Vol. 10, (Utrecht, 1955) 314:

   > The material and spiritual rise of the Belgian proletariat from animal-like living conditions in the early industrial period to a level fit for human beings is one of the most significant developments in the nineteenth and twentieth centuries. Such a development is, however, difficult to comprehend in detail. It is necessary that the historian—and, even more so, the layman—avoid gross simplifications. Although these may conform to real developments in general, they can, however, prove false for individual cases or, in view of short development intervals, become misleading. For a workers' movement to develop in the first place, the existence of workers is a prime condition. Furthermore, these workers, or at least a large part of their class, must be placed in an ideological, organizational framework or at least a leadership cadre must make an appearance, that can make a battering-ram out of the many fragmented and powerless efforts. In regard to these elementary conditions, the first half of the nineteenth century in particular is different from that which the layman, for reasons of simplicity and often schematically, imagines.

43. On this point see Robijns, *Radicalen*, 44ff.; as well as de Witte and Craeybeckx, *Politieke geschiedenis*, 46-47.

44. Quoted in Robijns, *Radicalen*, 46. Kats and Spilthoorn also devoted themselves to the Flemish problem, and supported Flemish demands because to a great extent they saw in the language question a social conflict. In their view, the gap between the upper and lower classes broadened because of greater French influence north of the language border.

45. See A.W. Schoyen, *The Chartist Challenge, a Portrait of George Julian Harney* (London, 1958), 154ff.; L. Bertrand, *Histoire de la démocratie et du socialisme en Belgique depuis 1830*, Vol. 1 (Brussels, 1906), 211.

46. Moses Heß, *Briefwechsel*, ed. by Eduard Silberner ('s-Gravenhage, 1959), 175ff.

47. On the sequence of events see Erbe, *Belgien*, 218ff.; de Witte and Craeybeckx, *Politieke geschiedenis*, 45ff., the quotation from 51. More generally, see the essay of L. Wils in *Algemene Geschiedenis der Nederlanden* Vol. 12, (1990), 1268-83. Somewhat older but still worth reading in regard to the gradually developing Flemish question, Herman von der Dunk, *Der Deutsche Vormärz und Belgien 1830/48*, (Wiesbaden, 1966), 330 ff.; the reference to German influences in the antirevolutionary outpourings of the Flemish is on 365. Reports on the affairs of Quiévrain and Risquon are published in de Ridder, *La Crise*, vol. 1.

48. See Lademacher, *Belgische Neutralität*, 144. Lamartine's denial of complicity of the French government can be found in de Ridder, *La Crise*, vol. 1 296-304, and memoranda on 199 and 200.

49. See de Ridder, *La Crise*, vol. I, de Ligne to d'Hoffschmidt, 28 February 1848.

50. See Lademacher, *Belgische Neutralität*, 127-28.

51. In general, ibid., chapter 4.

52. J. Dhont (ed.), *Geschiedenis van de socialistische arbeidersbeweging in Belgie* (Antwerp, 1960).

Proclaiming Frederick VII King of Denmark on the square in front of Christiansburg
(Illustrirte Zeitung, Leipzig, no. 242, 19 February 1848, 121)

Friedrich VII, King of Denmark, enters Flensburg
(Illustrirte Zeitung, Leipzig, no. 251, 22 April 1848, 266)

Chapter 12

DENMARK 1848

The Victory of Democracy and the Shattering of the
Conglomerate State

Steen Bo Frandsen

On the evening of 20 March 1848, the commission formed by the king to draw up a constitution for the existing Danish-German conglomerate state met for its final sitting. Its members could not suspect that their work would become obsolete by the next morning. On that same evening, a meeting of liberals was held at the Casino in Copenhagen that formulating an appeal calling for a constitution and nation-state. The next morning a long parade of Copenhagen inhabitants presented these demands to the king. Friedrich VII explained that he had already dismissed the previous government ministers. Thus absolutism was abolished; the King had set the course toward a nation-state.

The result of a head-to-head race between these two different concepts of the state made March 1848 a turning-point in Danish history. The losers included those supporters of an absolutist reform policy who strove for a controlled expansion of political participation in a constitutional monarchy and wanted to preserve the unity of the state. Victorious were supporters of a national liberal form of democracy in the boundaries of a nation state that consciously renounced portions of the former absolutist realm. Usually honored as a key date on the road to Danish democracy, 21 March 1848 meant above all an abandonment of an inherited multi-ethnic state. The end of absolutism and the introduction of a constitution, even if conservatively colored, was soon to come—even without the effects of the evolutions in Europe. The dissolution of the state, on the other hand, was considerably accelerated by developments abroad.

While national liberals only set the course for a short time, it is their version of events that decisively shaped the judgements of posterity, due not least to the suc-

---

Notes for this section can be found on page 311.

cess in discrediting the losing side—absolutist state power—as not only incompetent and undemocratic but also as unnational. Proponents of the victorious political course, the advocates of a moderate-liberal nation-state, presented the change in system as a peaceful one, carried through by thoughtful men who acted when the time was ripe. This would prove to be of long-term significance for Denmark's national self-awareness and political culture. The festive parade of citizens to their king and their coming to power in non-contentious fashion was seen as characteristic of the peaceful nature of the Danish March.

The peaceful revolution in Copenhagen on 21 March 1848 was simultaneously the start of a three-year civil war, fought with the sometime participation of the German Great Powers. The transition to democracy and a nation-state was also certainly not so smooth as the chronology would sometimes lead one to believe. Neither of the two forms of state organization achieved a final victory in 1848. In the following years, democratic development experienced setbacks and the nation-state suffered teething troubles. Many difficulties stemmed from the national liberals' lack of political experience, but also revealed the inability of the old powers to adjust to a new era. Neither the king nor the state officials knew the ground rules of a constitutional state, and often bowed to dominant political ideas only reluctantly and half-heartedly.

The Process of Politicization in the Danish Monarchy

Following the Congress of Vienna, the monarchy included numerous territories that were tied to the Danish crown by right of inheritance. Apart from the Kingdom of Denmark, the realm included the duchies of Schleswig, Holstein and Lauenberg, the North Atlantic possessions of Iceland, the Faroe islands, and Greenland as well as other overseas territories, among them three West Indian islands. In this respect, the Danish Monarchy was no more heterogeneous than many other states of the period, and the coexistence of different peoples within it had a centuries-old tradition.

One of the most important aims of Danish central government was to remove the remnants of the traditional structures and rights which granted some of these territories, above all the duchies, a special position in the state. During the one-and-a-half centuries of its rule, Danish absolutism had succeeded in ending many of these special rights, and the chances of integrating the Duchies further into the state were felt to be good. The conglomerate state, under whose roof the Danes and Germans lived, was inconsistent with the ideas of adherents of a nation-state, who had been gaining influence since the middle of the century.

The revolutionary wave of 1830 also reached the Danish Monarchy, but did not have the power to set off political changes. Nonetheless, events awakened interest in political questions and brought ideas of reform into circulation. In the two most important political centers of the realm, Copenhagen and Kiel, members of the urban middle class, under the influence of liberal ideas, began to look beyond their private sphere and to think about the welfare of the community. Indicative of the mood was the appearance of a small publication on the liberalization of political life written by an official in the government of Holstein, Uwe Lornsen.[1] While later interpreted as a manifestation of Schleswig-Holstein separatism, the book was greeted by contemporaries, not only in Kiel, but also in Copenhagen, as a courageous proposal for reform. The Danish king saw things differently and had Lornsen prosecuted, although his book had been passed by the censors. Together with events in other countries, the interest Lornsen created led the King and his advisors to begin contemplating political reform.

After careful and long deliberation, so-called Consultative Provincial Diets were summoned in 1834. The Congress of Vienna had already required the Danish king to establish diets in Holstein and Lauenberg. In finally meeting this requirement, such institutions were also erected throughout the entire monarchy with the aim of co-opting the most able and respected men of the realm into the political decision-making process.[2] In total, four provincial diets were founded, two for the duchies and two for the kingdom—a distribution intended to provide unity to the realm. Neither the division nor the institution as such meant a weakening of the absolutist regime, nor did they endanger the cohesion of the realm. Modeled on Prussia, the Danish provincial diets differed from those in Prussia in their taking into account the countries' different social structures. Peasants had much greater representation, as the Danish aristocracy was relatively weak and the bourgeoisie in the few cities of any size quantitatively insignificant. Holstein, with its greater share of nobles and larger cities, was the exception.

Friedrich VI had accepted reform policies only with a certain reluctance. Once the policy was in place, he showed himself determined to make constructive use of the new institutions. One of the most important personalities of Danish late absolutism, the jurist and minister Anders Sandøe Ørsted, in his capacity as Royal Commissioner, expressed the state's organic reformist position at the opening of the Danish diets.[3] The king and his advisors were prepared to take up central problems of the state, albeit always under the premise of strengthening the conglomerate state in its existing boundaries and forming a homogeneous unity from its different parts. As an important step in this direction, wide-ranging proposals for a common customs policy were presented to the diets at their first sittings in 1834.

Establishment of the diets gave political life a strong boost. Lively debates in the press and numerous associations quickly became part of everyday life. In the capital, the liberal opposition was very rapidly able to dominate "public opinion," presenting its own standpoints as representative of the entire society. Tone-setting liberals were moderate in their political ideas. They admired Guizot and were soon entitled doctrinaires by their radical critics. They were, however, impatient and felt themselves strong enough to attack the government for its inefficiency. From the mid-1830s onward, they also put forth proposals for the further development of the institutions of the diets. They were all the more active in this respect in the belief that summoning the diets was only a first step toward the rapid fulfillment of their main demand, the introduction of a constitutional monarchy. As it became apparent in the course of the 1830s that the state did not share their views, they reacted with growing resentment and increasing frustration. The king had no intention of surrendering his decision-making powers and repeatedly rejected petitions from the diets on central political questions.

In Copenhagen, the liberal opposition was more active in making demands of principle than in pressing for specific reforms. This stance, in turn, ran diametrically opposite to the intentions that the king and his advisors had had in establishing the diets. To the government's frustration, the dominant tendency in the duchies was the demand for the preservation of traditional provincial rights vis-à-vis the crown. Nonetheless, the diets in Schleswig and Holstein proved themselves by and large more flexible than the one in Copenhagen and spent less time drawing up fruitless petitions on questions of principle. Altogether, however, the government received little thanks from the tone-setting section of the opposition throughout the monarchy for its willingness to discuss specific reforms. A growing disappointment in the government's stubbornness was heightened by the very slow increase in the interest for political questions among broad sections of the population.

Christian VIII's accession to the throne in December 1839 triggered a serious crisis in the ranks of the opposition. In 1814, as prince, he had given Norway a free constitution, but, against liberal expectations, he was unwilling to grant the same in Denmark. As a believer in an organic and uniform development of society, he had become more conservative over the years and by the time he took over the reins of government he had developed very clear ideas on how reform policies should be continued.

From the very beginning, he met with greater opposition than any of his absolutist predecessors had experienced. Reform measures of the past years provided the opposition with the opportunity to call even the absolutist form of government into doubt. Still, liberal politicians were unable to form a united front against the new king. After having flooded the government with petitions for constitutional reform, the opposition split more and more. While the liberals continued to see themselves as representatives of an overwhelming majority of the population, this was a continuously self-orchestrated process that had little to do with reality. In spite of their facility for controlling public opinion, they were also not able to set the political agenda. Instead, for important questions, they found themselves forced to await the initiative of the king.

In many respects, government views did not differ from those of moderate liberals, but the climate was still more one of confrontation than cooperation. The government and conservative forces did not credit liberals with enough maturity for responsible participation in government, while opposition leaders believed that they could do without pedagogical control from above. They felt that the tempo of reform had to be stepped up. Hence they did not even wish to discuss government proposals, concentrating instead on demands of principle which the king could not accept. More than once it became plain that the opposition had not thought through the consequences of their reform schemes. Moreover, they often represented the interests of individual groups while the king's officials sought to place themselves above these particular demands. Liberals were especially bitter when the king rejected their demands—always presented as in the interest of the people as a whole—on the grounds that he also had to give consideration to interest groups that were not part of the liberal camp.

Constant defeats on questions of principle, such as the right to approve taxes, freedom of the press, and the unification of the two Danish diets gave rise to a great amount of liberal pessimism about the future. It would only be a slight exaggeration to say that when all the important programmatic points had been worn out by political controversy, liberal politicians brought up one final point, with broad mobilization potential, raising a question that could put the absolutist state on the defensive: the national question. As the astute journalist Johan Ludvig Heiberg wrote, the national embodied the eternal, while the political was only finite. "A government can therefore reject political desires without placing itself in contradiction to the nation, but it cannot reject national desires without becoming unnational."[4]

The moderate liberal mainstream's turn toward national liberalism at the beginning of the 1840s had wide-ranging consequences. From then on, absolutism was no longer rejected exclusively as a political system. Its territorial state tradition and thus the coexistence among different national groups was repudiated in favor of the idea of a homogeneous nation-state. It soon turned out that for national liberals the national question was not simply one platform plank among many; their supporters were increasingly willing to subordinate liberal demands to national ones.

The national question split the liberal camp. A small minority, increasingly isolated, rejected giving this theme decisive weight. They argued that a constitution and significant democratic reforms should continue to be at the center of liberal demands. In their view, the national question would rapidly prove to be secondary once a liberal constitution had been introduced. Specifically, German citizens could then be proud of living in a political system that offered them more freedoms and rights than they could expect in Germany in the near future.

The turn of Danish liberals to national liberalism also led to a break with their fellow liberals in the duchies. There, at first regionalist and then German-nationalist positions gained ground. Relative to sociopolitical development, moderate liberals in Copenhagen and Kiel continued to follow the same line—only the national question separated them.

Danish and German

The national question placed relations with the duchies at the center of Danish political debate in the 1840s, becoming of major significance for the events of 1848. As an ally of Napoleon, the Danish king was able to fulfil an old wish with the annexation of Holstein in 1806. He was allowed to retain these spoils after the end of the Napoleonic wars, while Norway was lost as punishment for having backed the defeated Napoleon. As part of the well-known territorial horse-trading during peace negotiations, the Danish monarch was also able to pick up the small duchy of Lauenberg on the Elbe river, thus shifting the monarchy's center of gravity far to the south after 1814.

One difficulty, which, however, only became acute with the rise of nationalist thought, was that Holstein and Lauenberg belonged to the German Confederation. While the Danish king took part in meetings of the Confederation, he had to accept that its decisions also applied to Holstein and Lauenberg. While not presenting an existential threat to the absolutist state, this restriction of sovereignty was seen as a serious danger in nationalist political theory. It became possible that the absolutist monarch, as a German prince, would have to lead an army into the field in a war declared by the German Confederation but, in his capacity as King of Denmark, maintain neutrality. Such a division of roles conflicted with ideas of a sovereign nation-state. The two duchies' continued ties to the German Confederation went from being a theoretical to a practical question in the German-French crisis of 1840. Danish liberals were afraid that the country could be drawn into a war. Equally, they were alarmed by a German offer for Denmark to join it as its "maritime state," a proposal that made foreign policy ties between the two countries the subject of a heated debate.[5]

More serious than foreign policy problems was the internal balance between Danes and Germans. Schleswig became the focus of the debate as it contained both German- and Danish-speaking groups. The fluid borders between German and Danish language areas were ignored by nationalists from both sides—who were mostly outsiders to Schleswig. They sought rather to present the people of Schleswig with a clear choice: were they Danes or Germans? A separate Schleswig identity, neither Danish nor German, did not fit into nationalist ideas and was soon forgotten in the heated debate.

Danish nationalists demanded an incorporation of all of Schleswig into a Danish nation-state. While the duchy's ties to the Danish crown were beyond doubt, Schleswig had not been a part of Denmark for centuries. However, on the Danish side, nationalists spoke of an old Danish territory which advancing Teutonism slowly threatened to conquer. Those demanding Schleswig's integration did not take into consideration that there were many in the duchy who thought in German, Schleswig or Schleswig-Holstein terms and rejected a unification of their land with Denmark. The nationalists had no second thoughts about excluding Holstein from the state because, as a clearly German land, it did not fit into the Danish nation-state they sought.

Schleswig-Holsteiners and Germans, on the other hand, demanded that the duchies remain together and be separated from the kingdom. Here too, Schleswig was the problem, as a significant part of the population spoke Danish and, unlike Holstein, the duchy had no constitutional ties to Germany. German agitators therefore continually made reference to a famous medieval charter, wrung from the Danish king in questionable circumstances, in which was declared that the duchies should remain *up ewig ungedeelt* [forever united]. The debatable legal value of this document made it all the more useful as a slogan in the political struggle.

Both sides treated Schleswig as an indivisible unit. While there were other voices, they were seldom able to gain a hearing. Historical rights counted more than the opinions of the people affected and a partition under the principles of international law lay well beyond the intellectual horizon of that time.

Although the king wanted to preserve and extend the unity of the state, he could not completely ignore nationalist voices, as can be seen in the king's declaration on the problem of a successor on 8 July 1846. The heir to the throne was childless and the uncertain future of the Danish royal house also weakened Christian VIII's position. To bring to an end continuous public discussion of the problem he published a letter declaring that the succession for Denmark and for Schleswig should be the same. In so doing, he satisfied to some extent the demands of Danish national liberals but raised the ire of the German side as he contradicted the idea of an unbreakable tie between Schleswig and Holstein. His open letter brought more unrest than clarity and gave the Schleswig-Holstein movement a considerable lift.

A Revolution from Above: The Program of the Constitutional Conglomerate State.

The year 1847 was the least successful for the liberals since the awakening of political life. Although the diets planned to meet the next year, there was little hope of quick reforms. The unexpected death of Christian VIII on 20 January 1848 changed perspectives overnight. In between the lines of the pious tributes in the press could be read both liberal disappointment with the dead king's policies and the hopes they placed in his successor. Even before the old king had been laid to rest, the first petitions demanding a constitution arrived. Two leading national liberal politicians composed a memorandum that immediately refreshed the public's mind about the desires of the opposition.[6]

On his deathbed, Christian VIII advised the crown prince to have a constitution quickly drafted, which would continue the previous process of cautious democratization, while preserving the unity of the state. Immediately upon ascending the throne, Friedrich VII made known his willingness to pursue reform policies. In an open letter he promised to codify and organize the condition of the realm and to preserve the independence of its individual lands, while simultaneously bringing them together into an ordered totality. At the end of January, the king underlined his interests in reform by ending censorship and abandoning pending trials.

In the press, Friedrich VII's accession to the throne set off a lively discussion on the future of the state. National liberals included with their demands for a constitution a call for the integration of Schleswig and a separation from Holstein. Their opponents accused them of ignoring the German part of the population in Schleswig which in the case of integration would require the government to introduce censorship and police action, against all liberal ideals.[7] In conservative circles there was a deep distrust of the "constitutionals," as they saw no reason to limit royal power and they found the thought of ending the conglomerate state alarming.

On 28 January, the king presented more precise ideas on the future development of the state.[8] In opening the doors to a constitution for the entire state he was attempting to steal the initiative from both the nationalist forces in the capital and the separatists in the duchies. His declaration of 28 January 1848 in fact provides excellent proof of the willingness for reform of Danish late absolutism. Its author, Carl Moltke, a strong proponent of the conglomerate state, managed to give consideration to different political currents in his formulations and not to appropriate, in one-sided fashion, the views of a single group. It fulfilled the most pressing demands of the opposition and in a few decisive points went beyond them. If this declaration had not appeared only a few weeks before the revolutionary disruption in Europe, Danish history might have taken a different course.

The king was prepared to fulfil important constitutional wishes but rejected all demands for renouncing portions of the state's territory. The declaration was infused with the spirit of the conglomerate state. There was no mention of either the Eider state of the Danish nationalists nor of a united Schleswig-Holstein.[9] The state was to be bound together by the introduction of democratic elements. Provincial diets were not to be abandoned, but were to be supplemented by a common assembly with legislative powers for matters concerning the entire monarchy, as well as for taxes and finances. This common assembly was to be made up of the same number of members from the kingdom and the duchies, and its regular sittings were to alternate between the two parts of the country.

As previously in the formation of the provincial diets, the king wished at first to summon experienced men to discuss the new structure of the state. They were to be in part elected, and in part named by the king himself. Moreover, the king retained the right to present further proposals concerning, for example, universal military service, the reorganization of coinage, and the order of business of the provincial diets. In publishing his declaration on Friedrich VI's birthday, the king consciously placed his reform work in the tradition of that begun by his predecessor.

The declaration split the opposition. The left liberal wing greeted the new program as a promising basis for the establishment of a constitutional monarchy.[10] On the other hand, both Danish nationalists and Schleswig-Holsteiners were appalled. They perceived the planned common assembly as a threat to their aims. Danish nationalists saw their nation endangered if the Holsteiners participated. It was unfair, they argued, to grant the predominantly German-speaking regions the same number of representatives as the Danes, since the Danish population in the monarchy was much greater than the German. In their view, this disadvantage for the Danes was another indication of the pro-German stance of the king's advisors. The Schleswig-Holsteiners, on the other hand, feared a Danish majority and insisted on the traditional separation of the two duchies from the kingdom. They raised the point that the king had recognized the traditional rights of the lands and could not therefore alter the duchies' constitutions. Neither the nationalists in the Kingdom nor the Schleswig-Holstein regionalists were prepared to find an agreement within the framework of a conglomerate state; they were determined to destroy the unity of the state.

The intense criticism of the king's declaration could not hide the fact that his initiative had, in a way, taken the nationalist and regional opposition by surprise, as it offered the prospect of the constitutional regime the liberals had demanded for so long. In presenting a concrete program, the government succeeded in turning public debate toward technical points, such as voting procedures, the number of representatives per section of the country and, to a certain extent, the contents of the constitution. As the government, however, accommodated the opposition in constitutional questions, attacks concentrated above all on the conglomerate state structure of the royal initiative.

In early February, Anders Sandøe Ørsted, Carl Moltke, and Peter Georg Bang, three men especially trusted by the king, began to work out the final draft of the constitution. They followed the outline set in the declaration: among other matters, the introduction of civil liberties, the abolition of privileges, and ministerial responsibility to a high court of the realm. Their proposal also gave no consideration to national differences and thus received greater praise from radical liberals than from the nationalist section of the opposition in Copenhagen and Kiel. In both places a conglomerate state constitution was feared, albeit from contrasting interests.

Once again petitions were drawn up. The national liberal opposition in Copenhagen demanded the Eider state and a renunciation of the project of a conglomerate state constitution. In Schleswig and Holstein, as well, developments were followed with suspicion. When delegates of the duchies met on 17 February in Kiel to elect those men who were to advise the King on constitutional matters, it was decided by thirty-nine votes to twenty-one to proceed with the election. At the same time, the assembly passed a resolution rejecting a conglomerate state constitution. The delegates demanded independence for Schleswig and Holstein and a constitutional regime in the duchies. As the voting results showed, German subjects of the Danish king were also not of one mind. As in Copenhagen, opponents of the king's proposals came from the national camp, which wished to see the duchies tied to Germany. Representatives of this camp included, among others, Wilhelm Beseler and Johann Gustav Droysen. Support for participation in the constitutional process came from the radical liberals, led by the editor of the *Kieler Korrespondenzblatt*, Theodor Olshausen, and from the noble owners of "knights estates," who had been guaranteed their privileges in the king's draft.

Under the surface, social conflicts were at work which threatened to undermine united action as soon as concrete demands had to be made. Differences of opinion between constitutionalists and nationalists, liberals and conservatives, estate-owners, the urban middle class, and peasants seemed to improve the long term chances of the government winning the struggle for the duchies. In Denmark as well, representatives of the diets met and elected, according to the wishes of the king, delegates to the constitutional deliberations. Despite all dissatisfaction, developments continued to run in the direction set by the government.

Revolutionary Unrest: The Mood Suddenly Shifts

At the end of February news of the unrest in Paris reached the monarchy and the political mood suddenly shifted. Political positions became more radical, as the various opposition groups had renewed hopes of greater concessions than those proposed by the king. Very quickly the perspectives altered. Friedrich VII's reform initiatives, once seen as a major advance, seemed to have become worthless by March.

In the duchies, above all the victories of revolutions in the German states raised emotions, strengthening the position of the separatists. With international events in mind, radicals abandoned their previous position in favor of the conglomerate state. Olshausen shifted his allegiance to the German movement, as revolutionary Germany promised a freer constitution than the Danish Monarchy. In the first days of March, Olshausen's newly founded civic union rapidly gained membership. The situation in Holstein threatened to slip out of control. Unlike in Kiel, radicals did not join with nationalists in Copenhagen. National liberals, on the other hand, saw the chance to put an end to the constitutional draft produced by the conservative government commission in the revolutionary unrest in Europe and a potential revolt in Holstein and an opportunity to prevent the conglomerate state they so vehemently rejected.

Schleswig remained the bone of contention. The declaration of 28 January had sharpened the conflict between the national wings. In Denmark, nationalists began to awaken greater interest in Schleswig by demanding a constitutional unification of the duchy with the kingdom. This problem was also the focus of a large meeting in the Casino in Copenhagen on 11 March, intensively reported in the press and attended by all the leading figures of the national liberals. Their speeches were immediately printed, with the aim of spreading national liberal ideas and, if possible gaining, predominance in public opinion.[11]

Zealous nationalists such as Henrik Nikolai Clausen and Orla Lehmann issued sharp attacks on the Schleswig-Holsteiners. In a moderate passage of his speech Clausen underlined what would prove to be the Danes' strongest argument in the struggle: Holstein could have its freedom and leave the realm, but not Schleswig, to which the Germans had no historical rights. Lehmann marked the priorities of the national liberals. Freedom in the form of a constitution was important but the nation had precedence.

One of the most important, and at the same time, most ambivalent, leading figures of the nationalist movement, the officer Anton Frederick Tscherning, made a symptomatic remark: "If I were there [in Schleswig], I would be a Schleswig-Holsteiner," thus admitting how similar the two movements basically were. As he said himself, he had taken a "position of passion," one which he, unlike most of his fellow contenders of 1848, would surrender in favor of a more sober attitude several years later.

That the Danish public also held other opinions than those of the nationalists came to the fore in the Casino meeting as well. The peasant agitator Rasmus Sørenson, completely unimpressed by the fiery speeches, took a stand against any attempt at making the differences between nationalities, completely outdated in his view, into the object of political struggle and at fanning the flames of nationalist hostility. Differences in language were no reason to go to war and the average Schleswiger certainly gave no thought to begin fighting because of a charter from 1460 or the annexation of Holstein in 1806. The people, in any event, had no interest in a conflict between different parts of the state. Sørenson's words no doubt represented the opinions of a section of the population which, at the time, was presumably much larger than that which dominated public opinion. Although nationalism experienced an upswing in the years that followed 1848, many examples show that by no means everyone was infected by nationalistic thinking. Such non-nationalists were unable, however, to exert any lasting influence either on developments or on their later representation.

Sørenson's criticism of nationalist ideology showed not least that social questions also demanded political consideration. In those hectic days of March artisans in particular, who met under the auspices of the political radicals in the Copenhagen Hippodrom, demanded that extensive social reforms and universal suffrage be constitutionally adopted. National liberals were not exactly enthusiastic about these demands, but they were aware that the opposition had to present a united front if it was to achieve anything.

At a meeting at the Hippodrom on 12 March, Orla Lehmann, the leading opposition spokesman at the time, promised that the national liberals would back demands for universal suffrage. It was his due that the confusion and arguments that had broken out in the ranks of the opposition because of the declaration had eased somewhat. Lehmann and other nationalists knew that the government still had greater leverage. Their efforts were therefore aimed at forcing the king and his government onto a nationalist course. It was this aim that Lehmann had in mind at the meeting at the Casino on 11 March, where claims to Schleswig were renewed, the reason for his appearance at the Hippodrom.

The journalist Meir Aron Goldschmidt, a sharp critic of both the government and the national liberal leadership, printed in his paper on 20 March—shortly before the dramatic events that led to a victory for the nationalists and the abolition of absolutism—the following shrewd judgement on the chances for Danish and German extremists: "Nothing can save the Schleswig-Holsteiners as a party, if we Danes do not act unjustly towards the Schleswigers and lead them to violence through our threats. Nothing can save the ultra-Danes as a party and prove them right unless the Schleswig-Holsteiners succeed in causing unrest and disturbances."[12] Both Danish and Schleswig-Holstein opposition to the proposed constitution could only win their game if the other side broke with the rules in the absolutist state.

Goldschmidt was not the only one to perceive this constellation. It was probably the reasoning behind the actions of the national liberal leadership in Copenhagen on 20 and 21 March. Reports of stirred up feelings in the duchies and of the wave of revolution coming from the south made it at least probable that the Schleswig-Holstein party would provoke a dramatic break with the monarchy at a meeting called for 18 March in Rendsburg, a move that would justify Danish national demands for the annexation of Schleswig. In spite of the tense atmosphere and Olshausen's severe attacks on the Danes, however, events took a different turn. The moderate wing was victorious and succeeded in arranging that a delegation be sent to Copenhagen to present the king with a petition listing the demands of the inhabitants of Schleswig-Holstein. The moderates knew well that the king would not respond to these demands, but their action showed both their willingness to avoid open conflict as well as their expectation that experienced government representatives would be able to find an answer that left room for further negotiations.

This was, as Goldschmidt had foreseen, an extremely unfavorable result for the plans of nationalists in Copenhagen, such that Orla Lehmenn and the national liberal leadership, although knowing better, acted in the following days as if the duchies were already in revolt. As the private correspondence of the national liberals as well as their public appearances showed, they were not only well aware of the results of the Rendsburg meeting, but also held a revolt to be improbable. This correspondence contradicts the public description of events offered by contemporary participants and later repeated by historians. In this respect, the decisive meeting of the opposition on 20 March in the Copenhagen Casino appears in a completely different light.[13]

The Abolition of Absolutism on 21 March

The meeting, scheduled in fact for 22 March, was pushed up to the evening of the twentieth at Lehmann's initiative. This should be seen as an attempt to exploit insecurity relating to developments in Rendsburg arising from slow communication. As soon as the news that the Schleswig-Holsteiners had approved a delegation reached the capital, it would no longer have been possible to maintain that a revolt had already broken out. In the afternoon the leaders of the opposition gathered, zealous nationalists and skeptical moderates, in the offices of the leading national liberal newspaper *Faedrelandet* and planned the agenda for the evening. Lehmann, rhetorically talented, quickly put together a resolution for approval.

At the meeting, the nationalists had the crowd under their control. Even before the meeting, the most important radical newspaper, *Kjøbenhavnsposten*, had complained that it had been arranged in advance for the opponents of the national liberals to be a minority in the Casino.[14] Hence it was hardly surprising that only Francke, a German-speaking councilor of state, risked casting doubt on nationalist versions of events in Holstein. He expressed optimism with respect to the chances of moderate elements to prevent an uprising against the king. This troublesome voice was quickly silenced by the organizers. National liberals spoke as if the revolt in the duchies were an established fact.

The meeting was presented with Lehmann's text, which had already been approved by the Copenhagen Citizens' Committee and published. It demanded that the king immediately dismiss his old advisors, who no longer had the confidence of the people. The resolution ended with a barely veiled threat: "We beg of your majesty not to drive the nation out of desperation to take matters into its own hands." With enthusiasm the assembly approved the resolution and decided to accompany the delegation the next day which was to present the resolution to the king in Christiansborg Castle.

In the past, the opposition had often, and usually in vain, drawn up petitions with demands for changes in the state. Although the situation was more dramatic this time, their success was certainly not ensured. The king did not have in mind a dismissal of his advisors, who still had great hopes, in spite of all difficulties, of successfully implementing the January program. Within the government, little credence was given to the idea that either Schleswig-Holsteiners or Danish nationalists would "out of desperation [take] matters into their own hands." It was in this sober estimation of circumstances that the possibility of the government maintaining control of the situation existed.

That the old system was indeed undermined was due in large part to the weak Minister of Justice, Carl Emil Bardentleth. As a childhood friend he was trusted by an insecure Friedrich VII. On the evening of 20 March, the king categorically rejected giving in to the Casino petition, but by noon of the following day he had changed his mind, after listening to Bardentleth's arguments. He informed the ministry that unrest in the country was due to a lack of trust in the old system and demanded that the conglomerate state envisaged in the January program be abandoned in favor of a nation-state. As a consequence, the entire government, with the exception of Bardentleth, resigned. When the demonstration arrived at Christiansborg in the early afternoon of the 21st, the King declared that the old government had been relieved of its duties and promised to ensure that Schleswig remain part of Denmark.

The March Ministry

How far the revolutionary upheaval would go was the question asked in forming the new government after the resignations on 21 March. A new government could not be brought in immediately as the national liberals lacked suitable personalities. While wanting to get rid of the old system, they had said little about what should be put in its place. Many national liberal leaders were held by conservative circles, which included most of the civil servants, to be hot-heads and frivolous troublemakers. Conservatives found no basis for cooperation either in the liberals themselves or in the program they put forth.

Hence, civil servants quickly blocked Bardentleth's attempt to form a coalition of veteran politicians and Eider state nationalists. Following his intrigues against the old government, he had become extremely unpopular. Then, the opportunist P.G. Bang sought to form an interim government in which adherents of the conglomerate state had a de facto majority. Surprised by their sudden success and unprepared for the new situation, the liberals accepted Bang's proposal.

Bang's endeavors, however, also quickly came to nothing, because in the meantime the experienced Minister of Finance, Adam Wilhelm Moltke, had been persuaded to form a government on the basis of the Eider state program, as demanded by the national liberals. After brief negotiations, he offered positions in his cabinet to the national liberal leaders Orla Lehmann, Ditlev Gothart Monrad, Lauritz

Nikolai Hvidt, and Anton Frederik Tscherning. The so-called March Ministry can therefore not be seen as a result of a national liberal seizure of power. Rather, the opposition had forced a change in government policy on 21 March and was then given a share of the responsibility for it.

Ministers immediately had to prepare themselves to receive the Schleswig-Holstein delegation traveling to the capital. On the morning of 22 March the delegation arrived in Copenhagen with a steamer from Kiel. They only narrowly escaped the clutches of an angry crowd waiting for them on the quay. Since their departure, the political situation had changed dramatically. The old government would probably have sent the furious Germans back to Holstein with a calming response. Denmark now had a government, however, that was neither able to confront the delegation with the superiority of veteran, experienced civil servants, nor to gain its trust. Just as the political program of some radical members of the delegation, including Olshausen, was totally unacceptable to the Danes, ministers such as Lehmann and Hvidt were a like a red rag to a bull for the Germans. The representatives of the Danish nationalists and German separatists had exchanged so many insults about the others' nationality that agreement was highly improbable.

Although national liberals did not believe there would be an uprising in the duchies, it was in their own interest to ensure this did not happen. The assumption, however, that the Schleswig-Holsteiners stood alone in their radical demands and could not expect help from outside boosted the position of hard-liners in the Danish government and helped their representatives, Lehmann and Monrad, to carry the day in the cabinet meeting of 23 March. They insisted that all important Schleswig-Holstein demands be rejected, and called for a demonstration of military strength that would also underscore the decisive attitude of the government. Ministers responsible for the duchy and German civil servants pleaded in vain for a compromise solution of granting Schleswig its own constitution while insisting on its separation from Holstein and the German Confederation. This would have recognized Schleswig's constitutionally unique status while rejecting the Schleswig-Holsteiners' intolerable demands for a unification of the two duchies. The King's response to the delegation, written by Lehmann, stated however, "… that we have neither the right, the power, nor the desire to integrate our duchy of Schleswig in the German Confederation, that we wish instead to strengthen Schleswig's indissoluble ties with Denmark through a common free constitution."[15]

This was the response that the delegates from Schleswig-Holstein delegation were forced to carry back with them. The departure of the steamer to Kiel was held up for a day to ensure their rapid return. This meant, however that the steamer reached Kiel a day late and its delay led to considerable unrest and was, in fact, the trigger for a revolt. German civil servants left the capital together with the delegation—an unmistakable sign that the German-Danish system of government was breaking up.

The news of the course of the meeting in the Casino and the ending of absolutism reached Kiel before the delegation, and led to the formation of a provisional government for the duchies on the evening of 22/23 March. In Kiel, radical forces understood immediately that the influence gained by national liberals in Copenhagen had destroyed any chance of reaching a compromise.

Not even in this situation were all Holsteiners in agreement. Just taking the step of beginning an armed rebellion was a risky business. Radical separatist options were limited all the more by the extraordinary loyalty of the population of the duchy to the king. Quite justifiably, therefore, it has been repeatedly emphasized that the Holstein aristocrat Reventlow-Preetz, rescued the Schleswig-Holstein movement with his assertion that the king was no longer a free man but rather the captive of national liberals in Copenhagen, thus giving legitimacy to claims of acting in place of the king. If resistance by loyal forces had not been thus overcome, the provisional government would have been forced to flee to Hamburg within three days, confessed Beseler, a lawyer and a key figure in the government.[16] Hasty action by national liberals had already set a fatal development in motion in Copenhagen. Now the same occurred in Kiel. The potential prince of the new state, the duke of Augustenburg, was in Berlin as the crisis broke. From there he secured himself backing for a legalistic policy directed against both the Danish nationalists and the liberals in the duchies. On his return, Schleswig-Holstein was already in revolt.

Nationalists had had decisive influence on the course of events both in Copenhagen and in Kiel without completely taking power. The men of both movements, irreconcilably opposed, were basically cast from the same mould. From the beginning of the process of politicization, liberals in the two most important political centers of the realm had been in contact and had followed the same aims. Only following 1840 did they take separate roads in letting their liberal program be eclipsed by national and national-regional views. Tschernig's declaration at the Casino meeting that he would be a Schleswig-Holsteiner if he lived in Holstein, hit the nail on the head. The same was true for most of his fellow nationalists in Copenhagen, and conversely for liberal leaders on the other side. People such as Beseler and Olshausen would have felt quite at home among the national liberals in the Copenhagen Casino were they not Holsteiners.

The Civil War

At the beginning of the conflict, which was to become a three-year civil war, an enthusiasm marked by nationalist passions prevailed on both sides. The monarchy experienced a wave of national popularity as never before. Patriotic and martial songs were widespread. In speeches and in print, agitators expended the entire arsenal of emotive phraseology of the time. National honor, national rights, the right of independence, threats to the nation, and a danger of being absorbed by an expansive neighbor were repeatedly raised.

Unfortunately it was not a unifying, but a divisive frenzy that dominated emotions. Two competing nationalisms were mobilized within the realm. The level of hysteria that this triggered could be seen above all in rural areas. Peasants were driven into panic by rumors that criminals, allegedly released from jail by Schleswig-

Holstein insurgents, were rampaging through the countryside, and in some areas it was even said that prominent rebels were in hiding there. Completely innocent Holstein and German tenants, workers, and servants were affected by the general excitement and the inflamed mood. They were accused wholesale of being traitors and treated in correspondingly hostile fashion. While a nationalist fervor encompassed broad sections of the population, social and regional differences were noticeable, in spite of all the nationalist fraternization. National enthusiasm was strongest among the liberal bourgeoisie in the capital. Among conservatives, artisans, and peasants, on the other hand, critical words toward the nationalist fever could often be heard. They took to the battlefield above all for the king.

A debate in the press, demonstrating the Copenhageners' distrust of the Jutes, reveals that the 1848 national liberals themselves did not totally believe in their own reiterated assertions of the homogeneity of the Danish nation and its interests. The Prussian invasion had brought troubled times to the Jüte mainland. Certainly the Jutes did not lack patriotic fervor. Nonetheless, it was said that not only did the Jutes personally suffer most from the fighting, but that they also experienced heavy financial losses as Jute trade relations were traditionally with the south. Not a few politicians and journalists in Copenhagen believed a danger existed that the Jutes would soon switch sides. Considerable fear was expressed that the Jutes could feel abandoned by their fellow countrymen on the islands. Even the king felt it necessary to issue a proclamation in which he reminded the Jutes that it was Copenhagen that had stood in flames in the last war.[17]

While concerns in Copenhagen about the Jutes were totally unjustified, the situation in Schleswig, the causus belli, was completely different. There, many inhabitants wished to be united with Holstein, many wished to be Danes and a third large group, those who wished to remain Schleswigers, were stuck in the middle. Indicative of the situation, one spokesman for the Danish side in Schleswig demanded of the Minister of War that the Danish army in Schleswig no longer ask natives whether they were "Danish or German," but rather "Schleswiger or Schleswig-Holsteiner," or "loyal to the king or a rebel."[18] A lack of understanding of the duchy's special character led to serious mistakes made from the beginning and was hardly suitable for building up a pro-Danish stance among the Schleswigers.

The people of the kingdom had little experience of war. Only the oldest among them could remember the fighting of 1814, which had been especially destructive for the country. Glorious episodes during the battle of the Copenhagen Reede in 1801 or of Sællands Odde in 1807 were transformed into heroic tales and led the Danes to forget the bitter defeats they had suffered at the time. Hardly anyone could realistically imagine the upcoming long and bloody war—certainly not in the turbulent days in March. Moreover, it was expected that the Great Powers, the British in particular, would soon put the rebels in their place.

When the military conflict began, both sides had to raise an army, a task led on the Danish side by Tscherning, the new Minister of War. A large part of the army was made up of draftees. Their experience of war—not only for the soldiers personally, but also as presented in their letters, in popular martial songs, and later in monuments and artists' representations—became an important factor to spreading the national program, even when experiences of many in the field or the home front had little to do with the heroism, sacrifice, and patriotic enthusiasm praised by nationalist propaganda.

The first phase of the three-year war ran from spring to early summer 1848. Early military actions took a peaceful course. On 24 March, the Schleswig-Holstein rebels took control of the strategically significant fortress of Rendsburg, thus finally clearly opting for violent conflict. When the Danish army marched into the duchy of Schleswig via the Königsau a short time later, the first skirmishes occurred. On 9 April there was a clash with poorly organized rebels near Bau, north of Flensburg. The Danes won the day, but did not completely route their opponents, something an experienced commander should have managed. Then the Danish army occupied Flensburg, the center of Danish support in Schleswig.

The Danish army advanced to the line Schlei-Danewerk. From there they were pushed back by a numerically superior German unit—the insurgent free corps had in the meantime been strengthened by Prussian and Confederate troops. Schleswig had to be abandoned and on 1 May Prussian troops marched over the Königsau into Jutland. Thus the war had reached the territory of the kingdom itself and began attracting international attention. Under pressure from Russia, the Prussians soon retreated. Sweden-Norway and England sought to mediate. Ending the conflict proved, however, to be difficult—on the German side because of tension within the Confederation and on the Danish side because the negotiators rejected up front any discussion of a division of Schleswig.

On 2 July, during negotiations in Malmö, Denmark and Prussia agreed to a truce that was neither recognized by the provisional government in Kiel nor by the troops of the German Confederation under General Wrangel. Prussia's solo efforts led in the end to a Danish-Prussian agreement to set up a common government for the duchies, but they were unable to force its acceptance. The conflict with Denmark and the problem of the future of the duchies was also the cause of heated discussion in the *Paulskirche* and was to play a significant role in the further course of the German Revolution.[19]

During peace negotiations, the Danes sought to organize an agreement among the great powers with the intention of creating a guarantee for a Danish Schleswig. When this failed, the British government took on the role of middleman, and Palmerston presented a new proposal for a division of the duchy. It foresaw a border running somewhat south of today's, namely from south of Flensburg to the North Sea coast near Föhr. As such, it met Danish demands to a great extent and would have left nearly all Danish-minded Schleswigers in Denmark. Still, the Danish government rejected it. Because of nationalist enthusiasm, national liberals, in the meantime part of the government, could hardly retreat from their loudly declared demands for a Denmark-Schleswig, and incessantly repeated claims of historical rights to all of Schleswig in favor of a compromise. A solution to the conflict was not made any easier by Friedrich VII, who was still not comfortable in his new role as constitutional monarch. Regarding a possible division of Schleswig he declared publicly "That cannot be allowed" and required of the negotiators in London that they stick to claims on all of Schleswig, despite instructions from the government that the diplomats should negotiate concerning a partition if an incorporation of the entire duchy proved to be impossible. For this reason, among others, there was a change of government in November. The new ministers were determined to work towards an Eider state.

The Road to a Constitution

At first, nationalistic fervor eclipsed latent domestic political conflicts. It was a period in which even "the most complete cosmopolitan" had to be a nationalist and patriot, as the literary critic Peder Ludvig Møller wrote in his "Letters from the Elbe" in *Kjøbenhavnsposten*. The articles in this radical organ make especially plain how difficult the times were for those who did not see the nation-state as the promised land. Conservatives and radical liberals were faced with a government that was under the influence of men and views they completely distrusted. When the king also decided to ride the wave of nationalist feelings and back claims for an Eider state, it was no longer possible to change course.

To fight for king and country was understood as a natural and self-evident duty, but for which country, with which borders and organization, was not clear. Under the surface coursed competing ideas on the future form of the country. Although the national liberals were successful, with abiding consequences, in presenting their polit-ical vision as the only true one and their opponents as poor patriots, they in turn did not feel themselves to be anything but true patriots. Neither conservatives nor radi-cals could easily surrender their dream of a conglomerate state. However, they could not agree on a common alternative. Conservatives were bound by tradition and only came to accept the king's new program some hesitation. Radicals still preserved the idea that with a new constitution all national problems would solve themselves.

The fighting in the spring and summer of 1848 interrupted political develop-ments, which had reached their first high-point with the end of absolutism. The war did not prevent the ministers, however, from reorganizing the central powers: the collegial system of absolutism was abolished in favor of independent, functional ministries. Otherwise little changed. The confirmation of freedom of the press, the introduction of compulsory military service, some improvements for cottagers, and an end to the right to set up entailed estates were the most important reforms.

In April 1848 work on drafting a constitution began. At first, however, a con-stituent assembly had to be summoned. It was to be completely separate from the provincial diets, contrary to the plans of the prerevolutionary government in which the liberals had used the opportunity to abolish regional interest representation. Ever since its creation, the independent diet of Jutland had been a thorn in the eye of the liberal leadership in the capital. As convinced centralists, who drew their model of governmental organization from France, they rejected this creation of late absolutism. Both the kingdom as well as Schleswig were to be uniformly and centrally governed.

Preparations for the constituent assembly dominated political debate in the second half of the year and brought national unanimity to an end. After the truce with Prussia it became possible to express different political convictions once more. Difference of opinion arose above all on the question of the extent of democratic reforms and the future organization of the state. For both aspects of this question, quite different views were held to the left and right of the national liberals.

At first, the government produced a draft election law for the constituent assembly. Disagreement among ministers was finally overcome with a compromise solution. The king was to name a quarter of the deputies. The government did not feel strong enough to resist the ever louder demands for universal suffrage, so the men selected by the king were to ensure a certain moderation in the assembly. The draft was promptly presented to the two provincial diets, which were summoned one last time specifically for this purpose. In both diets, discussion became heated on the question of an electoral system. The peasant movement and the radicals of the Hippodrom, both in the assembly and in public, strongly resisted the king's right to choose deputies. They interpreted these plans as an expression of distrust in general elections. Nonetheless, the king received his prerogative as planned. Furthermore, the electoral law gave a vote to all men of good reputation over the age of thirty with their own household and without debts to the poor relief.

Elections for the constituent assembly took place on 5 October and the course of events confirmed all the fears held by moderates and conservatives about universal suffrage. Opponents of the royal prerogative directed their campaign against its supporters, and especially the national liberals had to accept bitter defeats at the hands of peasant candidates. The well-known national liberal "peasants' friend," Johan Christian Drewsen, only received thirty votes in Holbæk on Seeland, while his opponent, a farm tenant, received 778 of the 911 votes cast. Nonetheless, the royal prerogative fulfilled its purpose. When the prominent national liberal H.N. Clausen was beaten by a simple weaver in Praestø, he received a mandate as a delegate named by the king. On 23 October 1848 the 148 members of the constituent assembly met for their opening sitting in Christiansborg. Deliberations lasted until 25 May 1849 and on 5 June 1849 Friedrich VII signed the constitution. At first it applied only to the kingdom of Denmark and was to be introduced in Schleswig later.

The political process in Denmark had its parallels in developments in the duchies, where the provisional government simultaneously endeavored to introduce reforms and to safeguard the new state. Like the March Ministries in Copenhagen, the new government was a compromise between conservative and liberal forces, and like in the kingdom, champions of democratic reforms were at first victorious. Accompanying the Schleswig-Holstein delegation returning from Copenhagen on 24 March were a number of German civil servants of the absolutist government who set to work to form a provisional government. A series of laws on civil liberties were quickly passed.

As with their adversaries in Copenhagen, the future of Schleswig also occupied the minds of liberals in Kiel. When the diets of the two duchies met in Rendsburg on 3 April, Danish-minded Schleswigers were absent. The assembly approved a request that Schleswig be accepted in the German Confederation and invited the provisional government to produce an electoral law for a constituent assembly. This law, which was oriented toward the regulations approved by the Frankfurt pre-parliament on 7 April, could be presented on 18 April. A number of prominent personalities were elected to the constituent assembly, who in past years had promoted Schleswig-Holstein demands in Germany. Among them were an impressive number of well-known German historians: Friedrich Christoph Dahlmann, Georg Waitz, Andreas Ludwig Jakob Michelsen, and Gustav Droysen.

Not least in order to forestall the Danish-Prussian agreement in Malmö, the assembly rapidly set to work and was already able to present its draft constitution in September. According to this draft, Schleswig-Holstein was to remain in personal union with Denmark until the death of Friedrich VII while at the same time belonging to the German Confederation as an indivisible state. Furthermore, the constitution met democratic demands to a great extent. In the question of voting rights, however, moderate to conservative forces were successful. The three class franchise it planned clearly benefited landowners.

The provisional government continued its work until the autumn of 1848, in spite of the burdens of social tensions, such as those requiring landed estates in eastern Holstein to be protected by the military in the summer of 1848. The governments' efforts were also weakened by the resignation of leading members—first Olshausen in August and then in September Prince von Noer, brother of the duke of Augustenburg and one of the leading figures in the uprising in the duchies. According to the agreement between Denmark and Prussia in Malmö, the provisional government was to be replaced by a common government, consisting of five members, two from Schleswig, chosen by Denmark, two from Holstein, named by Prussia, under the leadership of the Danish civil servant Carl Moltke. This common government was not really able to establish itself in Schleswig-Holstein and soon proved to be non-viable. Schleswig-Holsteiners attempted for another two years to set up their own state until the reaction was firmly in place and the Danish government regained the initiative in the civil war.

Concluding Remarks

The process which began with the death of Christian VIII in January 1848 had not reached its conclusion by the end of that year. The civil war extended to October 1850, with changing fortunes, when the Schleswig-Holsteiners made a last, desperate attempt to gain the upper hand. In the treaty of Olomouc of November 1850, however, Prussia and Austria forced the Schleswig-Holsteiners to surrender. The two powers occupied Holstein for a year, before the duchy was returned to the Danish king. Denmark had already dropped national liberal demands for Schleswig's integration in its peace treaty with Prussia. Thus the two sides mainly responsible for the conflict ended as losers. At the end of the civil war, the conglomerate state was restored, and in May 1852 the status quo was sanctioned by an agreement of the Great Powers in London.

Even in the 1850s it became clear that the revival of the conglomerate state was a lost cause. Both in the kingdom and in the duchies, distrust of the other side could not be overcome. Moreover, the events of 1848 had introduced an irreversible conceptual change in the direction of the nation-state. An attempt made at the beginning of the 1850s to form a coalition between conservatives and radical liberals against the nationalist program failed in the end, as the conservatives would not accept peasant politicians and radical demands for a more extensive democratization. Later, the majority of the peasant movement came to back a nationalistic course and in coalition with the national liberals led the country into the catastrophic war of 1864.

In spite of all endeavors by conservatives to revive the "good old days," the abolition of absolutism in 1848 was irreversible. This was due, despite the limited extent of reform and an only partial shift in power, to a decisive political change. Denmark was one of the states in which the victory of the liberal movement was permanent, even when in the years following there were relapses in the process of democratization.

Particularly in Germany, however, developments in Denmark are not judged as an example of a successful liberal revolution primarily because of the war, but also because of Denmark's cooperation with Russia. In the view of the deputies of the Frankfurt National Assembly, and of other German observers, such as Marx and Engels, this made Denmark appear as a reactionary power, against which the German revolution was directed. Their negative judgement is based not on rejection of a reform program but on nationalist motives.

In its national liberal form, constitutionalism in Denmark was closely related to ideas of a nation-state. While it proved impossible to introduce the constitution of 1849 in Schleswig—nationalist forces were glad to surrender Holstein—in the borderlands of the kingdom the constitution contributed to paving the way for a nation-state. At the same time, through the war, the image of Germans as aggressive neighbors, so often raised by the national liberals, was securely anchored in the minds of the populace. Even in 1848, national liberals dreamed of a Scandinavian alliance. "Scandinavianism" had taken root within academic circles not only in Denmark, but also in Sweden and Norway and was the cause of a wave of expressions of sympathy at the beginning of the war. Norwegian and Swedish volunteers came to Denmark to defend the southern Scandinavian border against advancing Germans. Scandinavia came to be seen as the great fatherland that could substitute for broken ties to Germany. Although Danish nationalists were willing to surrender Holstein voluntarily and wished to cut themselves off from Germany, they feared that their country could become too small and unable to survive.

In historiography and in collective memory, the "spirit of '48" was closely tied to the national enthusiasm of that troubled spring. Despite all justified skepticism about the formation of national myths and their idealization of consensus and creation of simplified objects of hostility, it must be said that important elements of Danish national tradition developed in this period, for example, the close relation between the people and the royal house and the lax attitude of the Danes towards their national symbols, especially their flag, the Dannebrog. Denmark developed into a prime example of an integrated nation with a comparatively homogenous society. This development, however, was not only paid for with the bloody civil war and the conflicts with Germany which later followed, but also paralleled the formation of a state whose citizens were welded together not least by a hate-filled images of foreigners. Such a state hardly corresponded to the ideas of absolutism and of critics of a nation-state from either the left or the right.

If the victory of the national liberals is viewed as a surprising success—a surprise, as well, to the national liberals themselves—of a last-ditch attack on an unpopular conglomerate state, then the events of March 1848 can be represented quite differently than the liberals might have preferred. The situation was open and its end uncertain. The course of events in March 1848 indeed demands hypothetical questions. What would have happened if absolutism had been able to resist national liberal attacks? And if news technology had been able to supply reliable information about the situation in Holstein, as was possible only a few years later? It is not impossible that Denmark could have received an conglomerate state constitution based on the ideas of absolutist reformers and that a war could have been avoided. Basically, the take-over of power by the liberals only anticipated a reform policy that the king had already introduced and which would have led to a constitutional form of government, even if it would have been more conservative than the national liberals wished.

However, much points to the fact that constitutional reform attempts from above came too late. The government did not agree to demands by the opposition for a constitution in time, and thus the chance disappeared of combining constitutional reform with a conglomerate state program. It is in no way guaranteed that the state would have succeeded, in calmer circumstances, in implementing its program against the resistance of strong nationalist and regionalist forces, as its initiative was made in a period in which nationalist fever had already overtaken the Danish and German subjects of the Danish king. Nonetheless, it was without doubt revolutionary unrest in France and Germany which created the decisive condition in March 1848 for a victory of national forces in Copenhagen and Kiel. In 1848, the nationalist wave undermined both conservative reform policy and a radical liberal concept of providing the existing conglomerate state a new foundation through extensive democratization. Hence, events in Copenhagen in March 1848 opened the door to both a constitutional state and a nation-state.

Notes

1. Uwe J. Lornsen, *Ueber das Verfassungswerk in Schleswig-Holstein* (Kiel, 1830).
2. H. Jensen, *De danske Staenderforsamlingers Historie*, 2 vols.(Copenhagen, 1931-34).
3. *Tidende for Forhandlingerne ved Provindsialstaenderne for Ostifterne*, 1835, col. 1 ff.
4. "Dansk og Tydsk," *Intelligensblade*, Nr. 20, 1 January 1843.
5. T. Fink, "Admiralstatsplanerne i 1840'erne," in *Festskrift til Erik Arup* (Copenhagen, 1946), 287-303.
6. J.P. Schouw and H.N. Clausen, *Ved Thronskiftet* (Copenhagen, 1848).
7. "En fri Forfatning," *Kjøbenhavnsposten*, Nr. 22, 27 January 1848,
8. *Collegial-Tidende*, Nr. 5, 29 January 1848, 89-92.
9. The Eider is a river in southern Schleswig, flowing through Rendsburg into the North Sea (translator's note).
10. See, for example, *Kjøbenhavnsposten*, 7 February 1848.
11. *Forhandlinger om Danmarks og Slesvigs constitutionelle Forening, udgivne af Comiteens Formand, N.L. Hvidt, 1848*.
12. M.A. Goldschmidt, in *Nord og Syd*, 1848, 111. Cited in H. Vammen, "Casino 1848," *Historisk Tidsskrift* (1988): 253-79, on 256.
13. Ibid.
14. *Kjøbenhavnsposten*, Nr. 67, 20 March 1848.
15. Quoted in C. Bjorn, "Fra reaktion til grundlov 1800-1850," in O. Olsen (ed.), *Danmarks Historie* Vol. 10, (Copenhagen, 1990), 331.
16. L. Rerup, *Slesvig og Holsten efter 1830* (Copenhagen 1982), 121.
17. Steen Bo Frandsen, *Opdagelsen af Jylland. Den regionale dimension i Danmarkshistorien 1814-64* (Aarhus, 1996), 370-82.
18. Rerup, *Slesvig og Holsten efter 1830*, 123.
19. Günter Wollstein, *Das "Großdeutschland" der Paulskirche. Nationale Ziele in der bürgerlichen Revolution 1848-49* (Düsseldorf, 1977).

*The Prussian storming of the Danewerk in Schleswig on 23 April
(Illustrirte Zeitung, Leipzig, no. 256, 27 May 1848, 346)*

*Danish troops leaving Copenhagen by train for Roeskilde to be transported to Schleswig-Holstein
(Illustrirte Zeitung, Leipzig, no. 260, 24 June 1848, 414)*

Chapter 13

THE REVOLUTION OF 1848 ON THE NORWEGIAN SCENE

Anne-Lise Seip

The Political System—A Model Democracy?

Two themes dominate European history in the nineteenth century: liberalism and nationalism. Political groups fought to obtain either a constitution, or national recognition for their territory, or both. In this picture, Norway, a country of one and a half million inhabitants in 1855, nine-tenths of whom lived in the countryside, was in a unique position. Within the span of some months in 1814, the country went from enlightened absolutism to constitutional liberalism, and from being part of a territorial state to being a nation state. In January, the union with Denmark, that had lasted for 400 years, was dissolved. In May 1814 a constituent assembly adopted a liberal constitution. A unicameral parliament that met every third year was set up. The power of the king was curtailed, limited to a suspensive veto on legislation. The vote was given to all tax-paying property-owners and tenant farmers, however small the property, people who were registered as tradesmen or artisans in the towns (burghers), and to higher civil servants. The so-called dependent people, that is servants, recipients of poor relief, people without property and, of course, women were excluded.

When the union with Sweden was concluded in November, the king accepted this arrangement, although he struggled for more than twenty years afterwards to change it more to his monarchical liking. The union with Sweden was to be a personal one, the two countries having only the king and foreign policy in common. In 1837 the country also introduced local government, based on the same suffrage as for parliament.

This political framework had several implications. The constitution was democratic: parliament could overrule the king. It had a broad social base: the farmers, many of whom were small, were integrated into the political system. In their local communities, the farmers were masters. In parliamentary politics they could dominate, if they had the political will. For all practical purposes they were a major political force to be taken into consideration by the ruling élite, that is the bureaucracy. The aristocracy was insignificant in number, and had been stripped of its privileges in 1821.

Norway had thus in 1848 already reached the two goals set by political groups in other countries. It was a nation, and defined itself as such both culturally, in an upsurge of national romantic manifestations of folklore, art, and history, and politically in a constant struggle with Sweden over symbols of independence and for more influence over foreign policy. It had a democratic constitution, which was envied by and served as a model for both Swedish and Danish liberals. Could the revolutions of 1848 have any effect on this seemingly peaceful and politically advanced society on the fringe of Europe? It had. A new voice was heard in Norwegian politics, that of the laboring class. In a few years a movement numbering 30,000 people had been organized to change political conditions.

The growth of the population by half a million between 1815 and 1855 meant that the laboring class had increased both in absolute numbers and in proportion. The Norwegian working class was, on the whole, not of the modern, industrial type. The towns were few and mostly small, with only 12 percent of the population living in them in 1845. The urban laboring class consisted mainly of servants, especially female ones, and, to a lesser degree, of day laborers. Most belonged to the artisan class, many of whom owned their own house, and could thus vote. Industry consisted mainly of the older ironworks, sawmills, and mines, with mechanical works and textile industry still in its infancy. Taken together, this meant that the proletariat was rural rather than urban, consisting of cotters, particularly in the eastern, grain-growing districts, and farm laborers. The economic and social fabric of the country explain two distinct features in the workers' organization in Norway: the rural element was strong, and the movement was not confined to the proletariat proper, but included in both rural and urban areas members of better off social strata who were already included in the political system.

The voice of the workers was not, however, the first to be heard. The cry for reform initially came from the radical opposition in Parliament. Notwithstanding the democratic constitution, it wished for more, and set out to get it.

Radical Opposition in Parliament

The session of the twelfth Norwegian Parliament was solemnly opened on 1 February 1848. The liberal newspaper of the capital Christiania, *Morgenbladet*, welcomed the representatives, urging them to pursue a radical political course which would be in accordance with the "spirit of the Constitution."

After some weeks the farmer Ingebrigt Sæter wrote to inform his brother and thus his local constituency of strong political activity in Parliament. "I was scared that the representatives should show themselves as weak Democrats. I was wrong. Radical ideas seem to be very well represented." Discussions were vivid all day long in "my circles," he wrote.[1]

This discussion stemmed from domestic problems. The Paris Revolution was not yet known in Norway. But the parliamentary opposition, consisting of two groups, the urban liberal representatives and the radical democratic farmers, had its own political program. The liberals wanted constitutional reforms that would strengthen parliament vis-à-vis the government; the farmers desired stronger local self-government.

On 8 March news of the upheavals in Paris in February finally reached the pages of *Morgenbladet*. They arouse enthusiasm: "Once more France has shown the world that the people can and shall govern itself," the editorial stated. In Parliament the opposition felt freshened up by the revolutionary breeze. In April Ingebrigt Sæter again wrote home: "Events in the South have given the Democrats courage."

The opposition tested their courage in an attack on the government. Models could be found all over Europe, but particularly in Sweden. On 10 April the king reshuffled his Swedish government, upon demand of the farmers in the fourth Estate of the Swedish parliament. All but one of the old guard had to leave. What could be more natural than to call for a reshuffling of government in Norway as well?

The demand for new ministers was not restricted to the opposition. Inside the government itself the man who was later to become a famous prime minister, Frederik Stang—"our youngest, much too young minister," as the Governor Løvenskiold wrote to the king—maintained that the government needed fresh blood.[2] On 19 April two new ministers were appointed. Both were men in whom parliament, including the opposition, had confidence. Still, the opposition was not satisfied. A general reshuffling was demanded, except for the young Frederik Stang, that is. The opposition wanted new policy and new men: "reform of principles and system." Only thus could the confidence of parliament and the people be ensured.

What exactly did the opposition want? It was split. The liberal bourgeoisie wanted constitutional reform, that is a parliamentary system in which ministers would partake in the debates in Parliament. The farmers, feeling unsecure, feared such a formidable and awe-inspiring presence. What they wanted was democracy, which meant less influence of central government in local affairs. But all could agree on a demand for a government that paid more attention to the wishes of the people, that is to the Parliament. In a state of radical intoxication, stronger words were used. The government was accused of contempt for Parliament, which it considered, it was said, as consisting of "an aggregate of farmers and people for whom it had no concern."[3] The opposition threatened not to vote the budget if the government did not submit.

To indicate this procedure, and at the same time point to the revolutions in Europe, was to go far. The opinion in the capital went against the opposition. The Governor Løvenskiold could assure the king of the loyalty of the students. Some of them had already started to train for an armed conflict with "domestic enemies." Moderate members of Parliament became anxious. The address to the king calling for reform was withdrawn, and a new one was introduced, so modest that it was ironically suggested to submit it to the committee for religious matters. Discussion of the address was postponed to the day before Parliament was dissolved, and then it was quietly shelved. The so-called "revolutionary party" had suffered a humiliating defeat.

Parliament also felt that it failed in the field of legislation. "All important legislation is obstructed by the obstinate government," it was maintained by a member of the opposition. In reality forty out of forty-nine new bills were sanctioned by the government, but among the nine were the issues most important to the opposition.

Unrest in the Capital

The February Revolution released emotions outside Parliament as well. The news and the positive reaction to it in the liberal newspaper caused unrest. Supporters of the government, mainly students, arranged a pro-government demonstration, complete with hissing, outside the house of the editor. The next day journeymen and small shopkeepers staged a counter-demonstration. They demanded back their old right to do business on Sundays. Some thousands took to the streets. The highest official in Norway, the Governor Severin Løvenskiold, sent the soldiers to meet them, and made it clear that the troops would be used if necessary. But the crowd broke up. Some were arrested, but were let free after having tasted a "well deserved corporal punishment," the Governor told the king. The March "Revolution" in Christiania was over. In Stockholm there had also been riots, with loss of life.

The enthusiasm did not die at once. In Paris the famous Norwegian violinist Ole Bull gathered visiting Norwegians and marched to the Town Hall, presenting a Norwegian flag to Lamartine. In Christiania a new military corps was founded in opposition to the conservative Academic Corps, but since it was denied weapons, it quickly broke up. Political clubs were formed, in imitation of reform societies abroad. Their demands included universal manhood suffrage, universal conscription, self-government for the local communities, legal reform, including the introduction of trial by jury, and lower duties on grain. The clubs were rather impotent. But the radical current manifested itself in the parliamentary elections, in which many alleged radicals were elected, and above all in the formation of a new political movement—the first labor movement in Norway.

The Struggle Between "Capital and Labor" Begins

News of the February Revolution reached the village of Modum in March. Modum had the largest industrial labor force anywhere in the country, producing cobalt for the European market. Due to the international economic crisis, the works were short of capital, and could not pay wages.

The workers' distress was witnessed by a young teacher, Marcus Thrane. He was the son of a rich merchant who had gone bankrupt after the Napoleonic wars. Friends and family had looked after him, but still he was left with social uncertainty

and social hatred. He left school, he left a secure, but tedious job, he left his benefactors. Traveling in Europe he probably acquainted himself with modern revolutionary literature. The only socialist tract that had been published in Norway before
1848 was Wilhelm Weitling's *Guaranties of Harmony and Liberty*. Coming home,
Thrane married a gifted teacher, Josephine Buch, got a job as a teacher for the
workers' children at the Modum Works, and planned to study theology.

The February Revolution released his energy. He had suffered want himself; he
had witnessed it among farm laborers before, and now he witnessed it among the
workers at Modum. He had long studied radical theories. Now he felt that the
opportunity had come to alter the conditions of the laboring classes. Revolution
abroad could facilitate reform at home. Thrane left Modum, went to the town
Drammen, got a job as editor of a newspaper, *Drammens Adresse*, a paper in which
he propagated his radical ideas. After five months he was sacked. But at that time he
had established his own platform, founding a newspaper, *Arbeider-Foreningernes Blad*,
and organized the first labor associations. In the span of a few years he headed a
movement counting about 30,000 members.

What was his aim? First to start a political movement. "Laborers, wake up and
unite!" were the opening words of his newspaper on 5 May 1849.[4] Associations
were to be the main instrument. The goal was to improve the lot of the working
classes. In economic terms it meant a fight between rich and poor, while socially, it
was a struggle for equality and justice. Politically, it would mean a confrontation
between the groups that the constitution had included in the political system, the
farmers, the property-owners, and the bureaucracy on one side, and the laboring
poor on the other. The language of the agitation was partly aggressive, partly conciliatory. There would be struggle, but no bloodshed. The struggle was to be fought
with words, "the words of truth," and in a true Christian spirit.

A more detailed political program was developed in the years 1849 to 1851. It
was influenced both by general European slogans, and by the policy of the radical
opposition at home, taking up demands that had long been part of its policy, and
thus trying to forge a link between the parliamentary and the extra-parliamentary
opposition. The catchword was "liberty," but understood as the right to subsistence,
and more specifically the right to work. This right was "the new right now bang-
ing on the door of the social Constitution," wrote Thrane in 1850. This claim was
later to be called "the claim of 1848" in Norwegian debate.

The central point was, of course, the right to private property. Thrane did not
attack this right directly. Property was not considered theft, but on the other hand
it could not be an absolute right. It had to be restricted, and Thrane found that the
poor law taxes already involved admitting the validity of this ideological stance.

How to strike a balance between opposing interests, and reduce inequality?
First of all, universal (male) suffrage must be granted. This claim was not unrealistic
at the onset. There was sympathy for the claim in democratic circles, and Denmark
in 1849 showed the way. Among the economic demands were reduced duties on
imported grain. The conditions of the cotters needed to be investigated. Demands
were also directed at the cultural improvement of the laboring class: trade in liquor

was to be restricted, and the schools improved. The importance of the latter claim was demonstrated when the petition to the king was to be signed. Many of the petitioners could not write their names.

As time passed, more radical measures were urged. The laborers should form production cooperatives, as in France. There ought to be an upper limit to property in arable land. Free land should be distributed to cotters, who should also have compensation for the improvement they made on rented land. The law should protect debtors from being totally ruined in the case of bankruptcy. All these demands were put forward in oral agitation, and, above all, in Thrane's newspaper. Thrane's agitation was popular and witty. He often staged a little dialogue between for instance a laborer, a cotter, and a priest, and let the latter try to explain why God could let all this unjust usurpation go on. Thrane's relationship with the church and religion deteriorated as the policies he advocated became more radical.

The Character of the Movement

Thrane's ideas and program voiced the dissatisfaction and frustration of both urban and rural workers. The movement grew fast. The associations were bound together through the newspaper. They levied dues, which financed the paper and Thrane himself as editor. Thrane was from the onset the central figure: he was the agitator; he established new associations; he corresponded with local followers. After a while, a central committee was set up; others took over agitation in the districts or looked after the finances, and Thrane's role was restricted to that of chief ideological leader.

Political work was directed partly towards local communities, and partly aimed to influence high politics. Petitions were the main instrument. A petition to King Oscar I asked for universal suffrage; a petition to the county council of the town of Drammen asked for tax reductions.

The movement was geographically confined to the eastern, southeastern, and northeastern parts of southern Norway. People in the towns and the densely populated areas along the eastern coast first joined the movement. In spring 1850, the associations spread to the rural areas in the eastern part of the country, and went as far north as Trondheim and its vicinity. On the west coast there were only a few associations; none existed in the northern part of the country. It was thus a characteristic of the richest part of Norway, the trading areas and the grain-producing rural areas, that class conditions were permeated with inequality and dependency on the part of the cotters.

Who joined the associations? Did the members all belong to what can be called a proletariat? In later years many of the rural associations were studied. The country policemen were asked in 1851 to draw up lists of local members. Even if they are not totally reliable, they give an approximate picture of which social groups joined the movement. Cotters were in the majority, but many small farmers also joined, although no big farmers. There were local variations. In some parts, mainly in Trøndelag (around Trondheim), many farmers were members. In the eastern part of the countryside, the cotters dominated. Economically the members represented an average of the rural population. Among members in Ullensaker one fifth can be classified as well off, one fifth were in poor circumstances, while the rest, three fifths, were rather well off.

Studies of local associations also show the economic reasons for joining the movement. The economic slump which followed the crisis in 1847/49, affected those living from activities connected to sawmills, timber trade, and shipbuilding. Workers were laid off. The farmers and cotters lost their income from forest labor and timber transport. The effects spread to the grain districts: the farmers had no buyers for their products.

When one man joined an association, his family and neighbors tended to follow. Kinship and neighborhood played a decisive role in recruitment. This social mechanism can be a complementary explanation of the fact that so many farmers followed Thrane's movement. A third reason is of course that the political program incorporated so many of the claims of the opposition.

The Practical Policy of the Thrane Movement

Where and how were the practical political aims formulated? As the movement grew, the need to coordinate policy was felt. In August 1850 the first national convention of workers gathered in Christiania. One hundred two representatives met. There was a discussion about the nature of the movement: should the members consider themselves as radicals or moderates? Thrane spelled out the difference to the audience. To be moderate was to accept the status quo, to be radical meant to change society, and to "liberate labor from the tyranny of capital." The delegates agreed with their leader to choose the radical course, whatever it meant in practice.

But Thrane's leadership was no longer uncontested. His chief rival for leadership, Theodor Abildgaard, urged the national convention to collaborate with the opposition in Parliament, and in the end this line was agreed upon. The parliamentary opposition consisted mainly of farmers, some of whom were wealthy. It was uncertain whether they had many interests in common with the small farmers, the workers, and particularly the cotters in the Thrane movement. The leadership nevertheless decided to play this card.

After the king had rejected the petition of the movement in November 1850, Abildgaard offered to the opposition to support an attack on the government in Parliament by arranging a big demonstration in town. The plan was that the joint push should take place on 24 February, the third anniversary of the revolution in France. The king, who normally resided in Stockholm, would be in town, and the workers planned to march to his palace. But the plan was betrayed by spies in the movement; military forces were mobilized; the police went to Thrane's house in the night, and he was forced to call off the march to the palace. Instead the workers went in procession to the premises of the Worker's Association in the capital, shouting "Hurrah" for the leader of the parliamentary opposition. This opposition did not deserve the cheers. The attack on the government was blown off. Parliament decided instead to set up a special committee to handle the labor question. The members were mostly of a conservative leaning; some were wealthy farmers.

The second national convention of workers met in June 1851 in a gloomy and warlike atmosphere. The politics of rapprochement with Parliament had failed. Revolution was discussed. Thrane, who had already lost control of his newspaper to his rival Abildgaard, also lost control over the meeting. Revolution was agreed to by vote. Thrane was not present. The next day the vote was reversed, and it was instead decided to send a delegation to Parliament to present a new petition. In the written document, revolution was not mentioned directly, but hints were given of "unruly masses" who would act if the wrongs were not remedied. The revolution had boiled down to empty threats.

This was the moment for the authorities to act. The convention broke up. Shortly afterwards Thrane, Abildgaard, and other leaders were arrested. In the following weeks supporters in the countryside were arrested, some 200 in all. They were held responsible for unrest and rebellion in their local communities. With these arrests, the activities in the local associations quickly died away.

Local Activities—Peaceful or Subversive?

The activities of the local associations were mostly peaceful, and closely followed the pattern set by similar clubs and associations formed by students, journeymen or other groups in these years, both in Norway and other countries. Some associations started schools to teach their members to write. Small banking institutions were established, some of which later developed into ordinary saving banks. Celebrations and processions were arranged, especially on 17 May, the anniversary of the Constitution. Musicians followed the procession. Banners had beautifully embroidered symbols. Most associations had their own choir, and a special workers' songbook was published. The press reported that the feasts were held in the traditional style: "The evening was spent in a merry mood, embellished with beautiful national songs," was how one such event was described. All in all, the local workers' associations can be seen as the labor class variant of the new community life that spread all over Europe.

But in some places the activity had a more revolutionary ring. There were several reports of unrest. In some instances, it was a protest against workers being laid off. In other places, workers tried to prevent forced sale of property. In Romedal, the execution of such a sale in the house of a watchmaker was prevented by the worker's association. When the watchmaker was nevertheless arrested, the workers went to the jail to free him. They did not succeed, and twenty-three persons were convicted in this case. The worst episode happened when a gathering of workers really succeeded in freeing one of their arrested leaders. He went to the Aadalen valley, gathered his followers, and marched to the town of Hønefoss to attend the trial of one of the other workers' leaders. On the road they were met by military force, and were arrested. Eighty persons were later convicted.

Did they aim at revolution? In that case they were ill equipped. None brought weapons. Here as in many other instances, the language was revolutionary, but there was little violence. But in a Europe where there had been so much bloodshed, both authorities and ordinary people were easily scared.

Reaction to the Revolutionary Threat

In the first months of 1849 the conservative press wrote rather kindly about the workers and their cause. When the government in the spring of 1850 expelled the European revolutionary Harro Harring from the country, who had participated in both the Greek and Polish uprisings, but had done nothing wrong in Norway except to publish a radical paper, a protest meeting was arranged in the capital. Several respectable citizens with democratic sympathies took part, including the twenty-two-year-old poet Henrik Ibsen—not so respectable at that time. But this sympathy of the bourgeoisie soon evaporated. In Europe the revolutionary movements were repressed. In Norway the labor movement still made progress for some time, but resistance was mobilized.

The Governor, reporting to the king, had confidence in his government and his "trustworthy soldiers." Wherever unrest was reported, troops were at hand, he assured. Also the state officials did their duty. One of the ministers told a friend that he had, in private letters, asked senior officials in the districts to report, privately as well, any suspicious circumstances in his district, and to act forcefully, if necessary.

The activities of the Thrane associations, and particularly the association in the capital, were undermined by spies. They reported dutifully what was said and done, both on the peaceful choral festival in 1851 where people met "particularly well dressed and proper," to the more unruly national convention that same month. No information seemed too unimportant, and the authorities could follow the situation from day to day.

The bourgeoisie also mobilized. One means was to found philanthropic and unpolitical labor associations whose aim was to reconcile capital and labor within the framework of the established order. In the capital, one priest, particularly well known among the workers for his thundering against the rich, went in person to a Thrane meeting, urged the workers to put their trust in God and follow him into a new association. Many did, the new association soon had 2,000 members against Thrane's 1,000. This was a hard blow to Thrane's work in the capital. The new association was abundantly funded by the rich, whose money now came handy, and soon it had built its own house, and had its own choir and saving bank.

In other places, the policy was to destroy the labor organizations. In Stavanger, all members of the county council appeared at the founding meeting of a Thrane association, and prevented its establishment. Another attempt to take over the Thrane association in the capital by infiltration did not succeed. But the man who tried, the founding father of Norwegian social sciences Eilert Sundt, started his own non-political worker's association in the capital in 1864, an association that still exists, now attached to the Labor Party.

Thrane's labor movement was broken when the leaders were arrested. They sat in custody for four years before the final verdict fell. Thrane himself lived in rather poor conditions, but was allowed some freedom. Most important was that his wife were permitted to see him. Through her he kept in touch with the movement. But the rivalry that had started before the leaders were arrested continued. For a short period Josephine Thrane took over the newspaper, and became the first woman editor in Norway. But in 1856 the paper folded.

The verdicts had then been pronounced by the High Court of Justice. A cousin of Thrane's presided over the court, and read the verdicts aloud. They were rather severe. Thrane and his rival Abildgaard were sentenced to four years. The time they had already spent in custody was not to be included. Worse fared the leader of the Aadalen uprising, who got nine years. On his way to jail he died. Thrane supposed he had taken poison.

Compared to the horrors in Europe, both the activities of the movement and the reactions of society may present a picture of innocence and idyll. But in Norway it was taken seriously. The workers shunned political activities for years, and the ruling class never forgot the experience of a revolutionary threat. In posterity the verdicts have been called miscarriage of justice.

Prosperity through Economic Growth?

The Thrane movement had grown strong because its message reached the laboring class in a time of economic hardship. The crisis had opened the eyes of other classes to the fact that the distribution of national wealth was uneven, some would say unjust. Poverty and pauperism was the political problem of the day. Social investigations were introduced. The conditions of the cotters were looked into by a royal commission, and Parliament granted money to the above mentioned Eilert Sundt to travel around in the country and report on the conditions of the laboring class both in the mining community Røros, and in the eastern countryside.

In Parliament the special committee worked on its answer to the labor movement's claims. Parliamentary elections in 1850 had been influenced by a democratic atmosphere, and many radical members had taken their seats. Would they respond to the claims of the workers? They would not. In Europe the political reaction prevailed. In the economy a boom was on its way, easing living conditions, weakening radicalism.

The answers given to the workers were thus cementing the ideological position of the elite. The Labor Committee in Parliament gave a condescending answer. The workers' claims to liberty and equality were "immature" and against nature. Inequality was in accordance with "natural law." The state could not do more than had already been done without violating this law. The committee recommended trust in God and prudence, and advised strongly against "communist and socialist madness," which had been so disastrous in the rest of Europe.

As far as specific demands were concerned, they were said to have been dealt with already, or a vague promise was given about future consideration. Some minor reforms were also adopted. The most important demand, universal manhood suffrage, was voted down. Only twenty-one out of 106 representatives voted for the reform. The majority agreed with the conservative leader who stated with Cicero that "Power must rest in good hands." After this, the question of suffrage reform was shelved for another decade. The government had won the day, supported by a Parliament that had been frightened out of being in opposition. But the middle classes sought for lasting solutions. How could the laboring class be reconciled with the existing social order?

The answer was sought and found in economic theory. Before 1848 a growing interest in the theory of distribution could be observed in the lectures of the most outstanding economist at the university, Professor Anton Martin Schweigaard. The uneven distribution of national wealth was considered a problem. After 1848 this "problem" was dismissed, and the theory of "harmony liberalism" held the field. Supporters of this theory replied to demands for a more just distribution of existing wealth with a call for expanding the total amount of distributable wealth. Economic growth would bring prosperity to all, also to the working class. Social harmony would automatically follow. The means to raise productivity was education of the working class. Thrane himself had pointed to this measure. The middle class came to see education as the panacea for all evils, the main road to economic growth and social harmony.

The Labor Question Buried and Revived

The traces of the 1848 revolution are not easy to find. The boom in the 1850s that lasted until 1857 meant prosperity for all, and made it easy for both the middle and the working class to proceed with business as usual. The number of cotters reached its high point in 1855, and after that year, this class gradually declined. Emigration started to ease the population pressure in the countryside. The 1860s, which were disastrous years in agriculture, nevertheless offered other economic outlets, and the first wave of industrialization, which started in the 1850s, created new opportunities.

The impact of 1848 on parliamentary politics was negligible. The most obvious result was that suffrage reform was taken off the agenda. When it was discussed again in the 1860s, the memory of the revolutionary potential in the working class was evoked, and suffrage reform had to wait until 1884.

The workers themselves turned their back on Thrane. The organization broke up. Those of the working class who were organized either went into philanthropic associations or joined friendly societies or cooperatives. Thrane went to America after coming out of jail. When he returned in the 1880s to lecture in the countryside, no workers turned up to listen. Thrane was taken care of by members of the upper class. This was the élite from which his family stemmed, and whom he had once fought.

Thrane's movement pointed towards the past as well as to the future. It was the last revolt of an old type in the tradition of farmers' uprisings in the past: born out of immediate crisis, voicing claims of "old rights." But it also presented new ideas, and an organizational structure that anticipates the modern labor movement.

In the beginning of the 1880s trade unions and political labor associations were again founded. The government felt the pressure. In 1884, the suffrage was extended. The following year, a commission was set up to discuss social security for workers. The prime minister was the man who, in 1851, as a young radical, had introduced the universal suffrage bill that had been defeated. After thirty years the labor question again presented an urgent problem to society, but the ways and means to handle it had changed. Organized pressure from below was met with political action from above. Interests were institutionalized. A modern labor movement could present its demands in a new setting.[5]

Notes

1. Inge Krokann, *Då bøndene reiste seg. Ingebrigt Sæter,* 197, 203.
2. The reports of the Governor to the king are in Riksarkivet, Oslo. They are currently being published. Quotations are from the original reports.
3. *Storthingsefterretninger 1848-51,* 471.
4. This and following Thrane quotations from *Arbeiderforeningernes Blad.*
5. A selection of literature on politics and society in mid-nineteenth century Norway would include the following works. More general studies are Francis Sejersted, *Norges historie. Den vanskelige frihet 1814-50.* Vol. 10, (Oslo. 1978); Hans Try, *Norges historie. To kulturer. En stat 1851-1884,* Vol.11 (Oslo, 1979); Jens Arup Seip, *Utsikt over Norges historie.* Vols. 1 and 2 (Oslo, 1974-81); Anne-Lise Seip: *Aschehougs Norgeshistorie. Nasjonen bygges 1830-1870,* Vol. 8 (Oslo, 1997); and Edvard Bull, *Arbeiderbevegelsens historie i Norge. Arbeiderklassen blir til 1850—1900,* Vol.1 (Oslo, 1985). Specialized works include Oddvar Bjørklund, *Marcus Thrane, sosialistleder i et u-land,* (Oslo, 1970); Rolf Grankvist, *Thranitterbevegelsen i Trøndelag,* (Trondheim, 1966); Tore Pryser (ed.), *Thranerørsla i norske bygder,* (Oslo, 1977); Tore Pryser: *Klassebevegelse eller folkebevegelse? En sosialhistorisk undersøkelse av thranittene i Ullensaker,* (Oslo, 1977); and Einhart Lorenz (ed.), *Marcus Thrane. Arbeidere, forén dere!* (Oslo, 1969).

Chapter 14

SWEDEN 1848—ON THE ROAD TO THE "MIDDLE WAY"

Göran B. Nilsson

The sociopolitical upheaval in Sweden 1848 was minor compared with continental Europe and even with that of its Scandinavian neighbors, Norway and Denmark. Nevertheless, the European development was followed with keen interest and inspired political participation to a degree unseen since the revolution of 1809. Reform activity was concentrated in two discontented groups, Stockholm's working class and Sweden's upper middle class. The working class's plan was unclear; it demanded political rights, but was also concerned about the negative social consequences of the recently implemented freedom of internal trade (1846) that threatened the paternalistic guild system. The followers of the plan had to pay with their blood during the so-called March riots in Stockholm 1848, where some thirty participants were killed by the police and the army.

The riots took place outside the building where the other reformers, the discontented middle class, were having dinner at a Reform banquet on the Paris pattern, paying in cash. Their program for constitutional reform had been a standing political issue for some years, but was now rapidly becoming more radicalized with the encouragement of events elsewhere on the European continent. The program demanded the abolition of the old fashioned Swedish parliament, where the four estates—nobility, clergy, burghers and peasants—shared power. The liberals recommended a unicameral system on the Norwegian model, with equal male suffrage adopting the "principle of personality" endorsed by the great Swedish historian and philosopher Erik Gustaf Geijer (1783-1847).

Demands for a liberal reform of parliamentary representation had already gained support from the two lower estates, but now acquired more weight through a brand new political platform, the so called Reform Societies [*Reformsällskap*], which (formally against the law) sprang up all over the southern half of Sweden. The members of the twenty-nine societies consisted mainly of middle class people from town and countryside. A central inspiring and coordinating role was played by the Stockholm Society that freely used the resources of *Aftonbladet*, Sweden's biggest daily newspaper, founded in 1830 by the liberal politician and industrialist Lars Johan Hierta.

The agitation made some impression. King Oscar I reorganized his cabinet, giving it a more left-wing composition. The new cabinet impiously spent all of Easter 1848 working out a Parliamentary Reform Bill proposing a two-chamber system with severely restricted universal male suffrage and strong guarantees against a threatening "peasant domination" [*bondevälde*] in the lower chamber. The proposal was unanimously accepted by the four estates to be pending for final treatment at the parliament's next session in 1850.

Although radical liberals were not at all satisfied, public opinion soon calmed down along the lines of European developments. The threat from below, "the red specter," raised its head in Paris and aroused horror in Stockholm. And another disrupting factor, nationalism, had made its impact more directly felt with the outbreak of the Danish-German war over Schleswig-Holstein in April 1848, raising hot pro-Danish sympathies among many Swedish liberals ("the Scandinavists"). Oscar I did not miss the opportunity, and his proposals for active intervention took—as L. J. Hierta bitterly stated—the parliamentary reform issue out of mainstream politics.

Reaction was already on its way, here as elsewhere in Europe, albeit with the important difference that very little violence was needed or used in Sweden. At the parliament's session in 1850 the pending Reform Bill had been transformed from a liability into an asset for the liberals, but it was turned down by the king and parliament, with the exception of the burgher estate. The numbers of and activities in the Reform Societies had already shrunk considerably. A last, poorly attended meeting was held 1853 in Örebro.

King Oscar's second worry, the working class of Stockholm, was a less serious threat, lacking in organization and competence. Like the liberals the workers had access to the new political platform, constituted by the daily press, "the Third Power of the State," as Geijer had succinctly put it. But Oscar I knew how to handle the radical (so called scandal) papers well: either the editor could be bought or—cheaper—prosecuted for breaking the albeit rather liberal press laws.

Götrek and Wallenberg

The revolutionary movements in Sweden 1848 may seem to have been of little significance, entailing few consequences. Nevertheless I will argue that the February Revolution of 1848 gave a significant impulse to Sweden's initial choice of "the Middle Way," alluding, of course, to the international slogan of the 1930s, when Sweden made a more well-known one in a series of historic "fundamental compromises, where conflicts of class and organized interests were reinstitutionalized rather than fought out in open and exclusive power struggle."[1]

In order to illustrate and analyze this thesis I will make a comparison between two individuals, who both got new and unexpected chances to make a political career with the upheavals of 1848, Pär Götrek (1798-1876) and André Oscar Wallenberg (1816-1886). They are appropriate symbols for the two above mentioned progressive groups, Götrek representing the proletariat of Stockholm and Wallenberg Sweden's discontented upper middle class. Both were born in the town of Linköping, Götrek as a son of a journeyman glover (his biological father possibly an officer), Wallenberg as a son of a teacher of Greek, soon to become bishop of the Linköping diocese. At the time of Wallenberg's birth the talented young Götrek was working as a private tutor for Wallenberg's elder brothers (on his way to study at Uppsala University); their ways parted after a year.

At the outbreak of the 1848 revolution Götrek made his living as a bookseller, editor, and writer in Stockholm. His intellectual and personal connections with different socialist and communist ideas and groups in Europe would make him a central figure in the unexpected revolution. At that time Wallenberg described himself as "a poor sub-lieutenant" in Sweden's naval center, the town of Karlskrona on the periphery of southeastern Sweden. His passionate aspirations to have a political and financial career in Stockholm were to be facilitated by the coming of the Reform Societies.

By 1851 their roles were reversed. Götrek's political activities had ended in failure and he accordingly moved his bookstore from the center to the periphery, from Stockholm to Karlskrona. At the same time Wallenberg in 1850 had moved from Karlskrona and established himself as a wholesaler merchant in Stockholm (formally Sundsvall). Such remained their way in the future. In 1876, Götrek died in Karlskrona as a respected but a bit eccentric small-town citizen, known for his philantrophic engagement in improving the situation of the lower classes through diverse associations such as cooperative, temperance, and educational societies. Wallenberg, on the other hand, was by then at the peak of his power and influence, leader of the great Stockholm's Enskilda Bank, member of the parliament´s upper chamber, elected chairman of the Stockholm city council, a prolific writer in newspapers and journals, internationally known as an expert on monetary politics. Such were the long-range consequences of 1848 in Sweden. Socialism and communism had still to wait for its future; middle class liberalism reaped a rich harvest.

Working Class Efforts

Pär Götrek was a jack of many trades, all of them rather dreamily handled.[2] For him, the July Revolution of 1830 and above all Saint-Simonianism had become the "great experience of his life" (Gamby). Götrek spread the gospel in his book *The Religion of the Future, as Revealed by Saint-Simon*[3] which had notable success in liberal-minded circles. From this starting-point Götrek took a rather small but significant step in the summer of 1846, when he converted to Cabet's Icarian communism. In so doing, he made himself a spokesman for a handful of Swedish tailor

journeymen who had just begun to introduce European communist ideas and organization in Stockholm. Their inspiration came from vocational travel experiences in
London, Hamburg, and above all Paris, where in 1845 a politically active Scandinavian Society had been founded. In this milieu, Götrek was destined to be a leading
figure, thanks to his education and abilities as a skillful journalist. However, in the
autumn of 1847 he got competition: two young graduates from Lund University,
C. W. Bergman, Fredrik T. Borg, and the worker Nils Persson-Nordin, began to
campaign for a more radical program.

The first organizational basis for socialist work, Stockholm's Educational Circle [*Stockholms Bildningscirkel*], had been founded in 1845 by two tailor journeymen,
Olof Renhult and Sven Trägårdh, although power was soon to be taken over by the
bourgeoisie. A new and more successful basis was then created in March 1847 with
the Scandinavian Society of Stockholm [*Skandinaviska Sällskapet i Stockholm*]. On
the surface, this was an innocent organization, whose official aim was to "awaken
the spirit of true citizenship" and to work for friendship between Danes, Norwegians, and Swedes. In reality, however, its aim was to serve as a recruitment base for
a small branch of the Communist League in London, committed to secretive and
advanced political cell work.

However, the Scandinavian Society was a short-lived organization, with seventeen meetings in 1847, thirty-four meetings in 1848 and nine in 1849 (2 April
probably being the last date). The visible results were minimal. The connections
between the March riots and communist activities are unknown and uncertain. The
attempt to use Stockholm's Reform Society as a platform failed (facing clever resistance from Wallenberg, among others), as did the attempt to create Reform Societies only for workers.

The most spectacular achievement came in December 1848, when Pär Götrek
began to distribute the first printed translation in any language of Marx-Engels'
famous *Communist Manifesto* under the title of *The Voice of Communism* (*Kommunis-
mens Röst. Förklaring av det kommunistiska partiet, offentliggjord i februari 1848*). But this
achievement was more so for a distant future than for contemporary consumption
and needs. Not least, Pär Götrek must have been bewildered by the new message:
his lawful and religious icarian communism had suddenly been replaced by a revolutionary and irreligious one. His bewilderment is illustrated in a couple of changes
in the translation. The motto: "Proletarians of all countries, unite!" was altered to
"The Voice of the People is the Voice of God." And the means of obtaining the
communist goals had in the Swedish text been modified from "through a violent
overthrow" to "through a radical reorganization" of the existing social order.

After the death of the Scandinavian Society in 1849 an alternative was sought
in a Reading Society, soon transformed into the Worker's Society, both connected
with two newspaper projects, *The Voice of the People* (*Folkets Röst*) and *Reform*. The
tougher communist eggs led by Borg and Persson-Nordin now made interesting
efforts to get in touch with and imitate the successful Norwegian example set by
Marcus Thrane.[4] But already in May 1850 the atheist Borg was prosecuted for blas-
phemy and he and Persson-Nordin left the board of the Worker's Society. It was time

for the more peaceful Götrek to make one last effort. In October 1850 he managed to set up a newspaper called *The Democrat (Demokraten)* that survived for a year. Here Götrek edited more entertaining and less socialistic messages than had been seen in its forerunners. Nevertheless, the political and economic situation continued to worsen and Götrek was forced to give up his political work in the capital. On 5 October 1851 he delivered a final speech on "The Man as Citizen" at the Education Circle and the Worker's Society . In return he obtained a golden ring from the thankful members and, with that memory, he headed for tranquillity in Karlskrona.

Middle-Class Dissatisfaction

For A. O. Wallenberg the tranquillity of Karlskrona (= The Crown of King Charles) had been an ordeal during the 1840s, and accordingly he and his subaltern colleagues in the so-called "Young Fleet" called the town Karlspina (= The Pain of King Charles). They also had good reasons to be dissatisfied with their social, economic, and political situation. For historical reasons, the authorities were still paying much more attention to naval equipment than to naval personnel (the remaining battleships from last century still being upheld as a maritime version of Potemkin villages). The salary was low, the chances of promotion bad and getting still worse during the 1840s. The social reputation gave some compensation, but it did not give a corresponding amount of political influence in the old fashioned estate's parliament. Captain-lieutenant P. E. Ahlgren summarized the situation in a letter to Wallenberg (14 March 1848) as follows:

> I am not entitled to choose persons who make our laws, but that is my neighbor the shoemaker, who scarcely earns his daily bread, that is a farmer, who on selling a load of wood or a stone of meat will fall on his knees if he gets a dram in connection with my payment. Such persons are electors …
>   In regard to *our* profession I consider it being in a such deep decay that it never could be helped off with the means that our country can provide. Consequently I will resign my appointment as soon I can retire on a pension …[5]

Beginning in the mid-1840s, this discontentment had prompted Wallenberg and some other talented young naval officers to form an inner circle within the Young Navy, writing anonymous articles in the press and lobbying in the corridors of the parliament. Wallenberg also acted as the "banker," taking care of the deteriorating economic situation of his colleagues, thereby making use of his background and his own autodidactic zeal for the science of finance. He also learned to exploit the silver lining of the dark naval skies, taking advantage of the fact that it was very easy to get leave from duties in Karlskrona, which on average called for only one year out of four. Wallenberg used his spare time to build up relations with liberal-minded business men in Stockholm, eventually also including Lars Johan Hierta.

Just before the outbreak of the revolution of 1848 Wallenberg had managed to get his first articles published in *Aftonbladet* (concerning naval politics and currency questions), and, of course, did not miss the opportunity to climb the brand new political platform provided by the Reform Society of Stockholm, where he made his maiden speech in March 1848. Wallenberg associated himself with the right-wing minority of the Society, although he was exceptionally radical in his recommendation for women's suffrage (but not eligibility for elective office). His staunch supporter in Karlskrona, sub-lieutenant A. Herkepe, member of "the inner circle," was deeply impressed and satisfied, but gave a small warning: "You are a mariner and consequently cannot be an ultra-liberal. It is an impossibility that the impressions of order and discipline, which are connected with life on board, ever could give ground for a political idea that does not acknowledge these principles as a foundation."[6] Yet, so it remained, in spite of the increasingly agitated state of public opinion. Even A. O. Wallenberg's mother, the bishop's widow Laura, was infected by this mood and (for a short while) she ended up in sympathy with the radical Norwegian ideas and laws.[7]

Wallenberg's moderation and cold-bloodedness would, however, have repercussions when reaction made its impact felt in Sweden. Wallenberg's participation in the Stockholm Reform Society was now standing in his way; it was again considered improper for an officer to engage in public politics on behalf of his own opinions. Even worse, Wallenberg had together with four other young liberals in December 1848 founded a weekly newspaper, *Bore* (Bore being a symbol for the fresh northerly wind), propagating oppositional views, including a critique of the official naval policy. Under these circumstances the Minister of Naval Affairs in April 1849 pointed out the desirability for Wallenberg to join the Danish armed forces as a volunteer in the ongoing war. Wallenberg, an ardent pro-Scandinavian [*skandinavist*], could not refuse. But he did so when after his return he again was gently pushed out of politics with an unwarranted "promotion" in May 1850 to a naval post in Sundsvall, 420 kilometers north of Stockholm. His sly reply was to formally obey but in reality establish himself as a wholesaler. In October 1850 he surprised the world by taking the oath as a burgher of Sundsvall, ostentatiously dressed in naval parade uniform. The authorities could no longer hamper his bright economic and political career.

Harmony Liberalism

Bore proclaimed itself as a "child of a new age" and was a pioneer of a new variety of liberalism that can be characterized as "association liberalism" or "harmony liberalism." The new epoch had begun with 1848, when, said the paper, new conceptions had awakened among the peoples of all Europe, and when new problems had been put, "which sooner or later *must* be solved. It cannot be denied that a new enemy has arisen in all societies, communism; and might it be defeated by just restoring the old order?" Of course not![8]

As undoubtedly sound and relevant as the analysis was for all governments after the return of peace and order, what did *Bore* propose that could be met with enough approval in ruling conservative circles? Three leading figures among the harmony liberals will help to answer this question: Wallenberg we have already met, and in the future he was to cooperate closely with J. A. Gripenstedt (1813-1874) and C. F. Bergstedt (1817-1903). The subaltern artillery officer Gripenstedt had, like Wallenberg, risen on the small tidal wave of 1848. From being an inexperienced but promising orator in the House of Nobility he had then been surprisingly promoted and appointed minister in King Oscar's hastily refurbished government. Gripenstedt was later to become minister of Finance (1856) and the leading man in the Cabinet for the next ten years. Bergstedt was a senior lecturer in Greek at Uppsala University, where he also edited a literary journal before he succeeded L. J. Hierta as editor of *Aftonbladet* (together with some of the "Boreads") in 1851. Bergstedt was a keen scholar but also, like Gripenstedt, a practical man engaged in the iron industry and in farming.

The harmony "liberals of the fifties" turned, as Victor Svanberg has put it, from politics to the economy, from rhetoric to matters of fact. They had an open eye for social evils in Sweden and abroad. *Bore* depicted the situation of the French working class and of Swedish women with an acerbity that came close to the Marxist style. But as to the remedy a gulf was, of course, separating the two. The liberals saw the future in the development of capitalist institutions, not in their demolition. Their fundamental starting-point was that economic progress is the necessary and even sufficient condition for all other types of progress: moral, political, and social. Improving the economy would thus become the main instrument for reaching the great goal: the progress of humankind towards an ever level of higher civilization

This rather odd union of crass materialism and lofty idealism was especially striking in Bergstedt's theories and in Wallenberg's practice. In public life, Wallenberg worked for great ideas to the benefit of humankind at the same time as he used the same ideas in business to achieve the greatest possible private profit. And Bergstedt was always eager to give idealistic dimensions to every economic reform, like in 1851 when in his journal he asked: "What tremendous moral weight does not lie in the demand for facilitating correspondence by means of a low postal rate and numerous post offices?"[9]

Indeed, the demand for improved communications, material as well as spiritual, became something of a magic formula for the new liberal generation. It was a logical consequence of the old liberal belief in the blessings of the free exchange which now could and should be drawn in practice. For here as elsewhere, science and technology had given modern man hitherto unseen infrastructural possibilities to make free exchange easier, for instance through newspapers, railways, and banks. Bergstedt, Gripenstedt, and Wallenberg acted as eager workers and reformers in all three areas, although they had to grapple with rather formidable political, economic, and social obstacles. But the harmony liberal program gave ample room for concessions to the right in a leftish manner.

Classical liberalism had often been criticized for being too individualistic, too atomistic, and thus for having disastrous anarchical consequences for united action in state and society. No wonder the Swedish liberals of the 1830s became interested in Saint-Simonian ideas. But of greater importance was probably the conversion of E. G. Geijer from conservatism to liberalism in 1838, when he provided an authoritative defense of liberal ideas. Liberal reform would not lead to anarchy but to eager voluntary cooperation in different associations, which would be more effective than any corporate, guilded cooperation initiated from above through the authorities.

Geijer died in 1846 but his message was carried on by pupils and admirers like C. F. Bergstedt. And Wallenberg had learned the same lesson the hard way from his experiences in the Young Navy. To his coleader of the inner circle Axel Adlersparre he wrote in 1851: "Nobody who trusts only himself is strong enough to break his way through the solid rocks of ignorance and prejudice, but by united action and by fervent conviction that your cause is rightful, nothing will be impossible."[10]

The common European belief in voluntary associations certainly was a characteristic for the Swedish harmony liberals (as it would become a Swedish characteristic for the future). As *Aftonbladet* put it in an editorial in 1857: "the association is a fundamental pillar for higher civilization."

As we have seen Wallenberg did not neglect political associations, but the most important for him were, of course, the economic ones. In the early 1850s Wallenberg was busy setting up steamship companies in order to improve the traffic between Swedish coastal towns. These firms, however, were based on the traditional model, in which every partner was liable for company debts to the whole extent of their individual fortunes. But much more could be done with the modern joint-stock company, where liability was limited to the partner's share of company capital. By not risking their whole fortune, both small and large capitalists would be much more willing to invest in bigger projects that would be more promising for future economic development.

Sweden passed its first law on limited liability corporations in 1848, but it was applied very restrictively by the government until 1856, when Gripenstedt was appointed minister of finance. The following years saw a flood of new corporations. The associational way thus showed its effectiveness, but when really big projects were at stake, this solution did not suffice in a poor country. An alternative then was to invited foreign capitalists or entrepreneurs, but that would move the project out of national control, which the harmony liberals were rather reluctant to do. Their classical liberalism was also modified by nationalism.

Moreover, important infrastructure projects offered little direct profit and could not be expected to attract foreign or domestic capitalists. In these circumstances, Gripenstedt did not hesitate to launch a huge railway program under government auspices in 1856. Similarly, he gave a governmental helping hand to the regional Swedish mortgage institutions, when in the crisis of 1857 they could not obtain enough credit in the German financial market. This faiblesse for state intervention was not altogether to Wallenberg's taste. But on the other hand he gladly— and to the horror of his banking colleagues on the continent—accepted and even propagated a regular state inspection of the Swedish banks. The reason was the need to induce the public to make deposits in these banks, and then public control would serve as an important risk reduction factor in the depositors' perception. The harmony liberals were shrewd practical men, prepared to apply their doctrine in a pragmatic way.

As we have just seen, the Swedish harmony liberals deviated from classical liberalism by being pragmatically open to intervention on the part of the nation state when the preferred private solutions of vital economic problems through associations did not suffice. The result here, as in Norway, was what has been called "a liberalism chastened by the state." It would ultimately guarantee the (almost fated) coming of the welfare state.

It was the harmony liberals' general belief that such an outcome could be achieved without strong social conflicts. This general belief was connected to their belief in modern science, not least in the science of the so-called harmony school of economics, which maintained that there did not exist any fundamental contradiction between the interests of capital(ists) and work(ers). The doctrines in that respect of the American economist H.C. Carey and, still more, those of the French economist Frédérique Bastiat served as guidance for Wallenberg and Gripenstedt.

But these optimistic views did not prevent Swedish liberals from educating the people to embrace industriousness and thrift. These two fundamental virtues were important conditions for the future well-being of the society but of course also for every individual. Or as Gripenstedt put it in a famous speech in the House of Nobility in 1856:

> Everything has been improved! And I greet with pleasure that day when you shall see how, little by little one class of society after the other is elevated and betakes of the privileges, spiritual as well as material, which we the more well-favored have, unfortunately enough, enjoyed almost alone.[11]

Everyone was welcome to enjoy the benefits of the future welfare state, although the main social target group was the middle class, of course. As Bergstedt pointed out in 1851 England here had set a splendid example, worthy of imitation.

This new ideal called for a good deal of rethinking and revaluation. In 1856, the former military officer Gripenstedt shocked the House of Nobility with his eloquent praise of the tradesman, in an analysis that could have been borrowed from Marx and Engels's *Communist Manifesto*. This frequently scorned profession, Gripenstedt said, was in fact of immense importance for civilization compared with the military system of violence and conquest, on which old-time politics was based and whose:

> aim was the plundering and oppression of the weaker. Not only was this system basically unrighteous and hostile to all true humanity. It inevitably lead to hatred and separation between the different countries of the world, free trade relations on the contrary aiming at mutual advantage, forming ties of friendship and of interests in common ... Once more, therefore: glory be to the magnificent profession of trade, working to the benefit of mankind![12]

A more down-to-earth way of taking care of middle class needs was to erect a modern insurance and banking system. Wallenberg's reform program, for instance, aimed at mobilizing the unused monetary resources of the middle class in commercial banks that would then direct them toward loans for the building up of Swedish industry. In that way one would bring about social safety and economic growth for the depositor (not least, for economically ignorant women), increased possibilities for industrial entrepreneurs, and growing welfare for the whole nation. Industriousness and thrift thus would get their ample reward, as well as the intermediary Wallenberg. His calculation were correct and Stockholm's Enskilda Bank became a great success from its founding in 1856.

The Liberal Boom

In his standard work *Swedish History*, Sten Carlsson rightly refers to the period between 1856 and 1866 as the "Liberal boom."[13] All sorts of laws were modernized in a harmony liberal way. Domestic passports were abolished; every woman was granted majority at the age of twenty-five and got permission to seek public appointments; Jews were permitted to settle anywhere in the country; civil marriage was allowed. A new banking law, a new fiscal law, a new maritime law, and a new criminal law were proclaimed. The freedom of domestic trade was increased and the principle of free foreign trade guaranteed for the future by a trade agreement with France. In the final stage new political foundations were laid with the law on local government (1862) and the long-desired reform of parliamentary representation (1866), which replaced the four estates with a bicameral parliament, modeled on the royal proposal of 1848, but now somewhat radicalized.

The question here is how it was possible for the harmony liberals to get such a response for their program, provided that the ruling classes shared Bore's judgment that something had to be done after the experiences of 1848. Firstly, let it then be said (but not commented upon) that the alternative was increased repression. This Austrian-style solution was never brought to the fore in Sweden.

On the contrary, the conservative House of Nobility was won over for more liberal ideas already in the parliamentary session of 1853/54, when the so-called young conservatives deserted their more old-fashioned leaders in the free trade question and took control. The younger conservatives (nicknamed "the Junkers") had a more open mind and supported cautious reforms in, for instance, public health and local government. They were also willing to exploit the possibilities that liberal reforms opened for securing the economic standing of the nobility. The landed gentry supported the modernization of the mortgage institutions. And the noble bureaucrats saw with pleasure how Gripenstedt's tariff reductions resulted in increased state revenues, allowing for a sizable raise in their salaries.

On the other hand, the conservative majority in the two upper Estates had been quite willing to back King Oscar's policy of restricting freedom of the press. Nevertheless, his proposal to that end met unanimous and stubborn resistance from Burghers and Peasants in the Riksdag 1854 and was rejected by all four Estates in 1856. The steady expansion of the newspapers in number and circulation went on as before, and the vast majority was sailing under liberal flag.

A notable exception was the biggest daily paper, *The Native Country (Fädernes-landet),* the mouthpiece of the Stockholm Worker´s Association. But its radical colors now had changed considerably. "Instead of the excommunicated socialism as uniting idea and future goal, nationalism was emphasized—a programmatic regression brought about by the failures of the labor movement and by the broken socialist illusions." [14] During the Crimean War the paper even propagated active Swedish participation on the side of England and France, true champions of freedom and progress. This idea was, of course, repugnant to the peaceful harmony liberals. In their keen use of the possibilities of the press, most notable is the campaign (through anonymous articles) of royal minister J. A. Gripenstedt to thwart his superior's, King Oscar's, rather desperate plans of entering the war, at the same time perhaps carrying out an internal coup d'état.

Indeed, the Crimean War of 1854/56 constituted an important external factor for internal Swedish development. First, the war was accompanied by a boom, from which Sweden's economy (and even the lower social groups) profited to a great extent. Second, this war also signified a definitive change in the orientation of Swedish foreign policy, from east to west, from isolationism to internationalism. From now on, the royal family with King Oscar and his follower Charles XV (reigning 1859/72) could give free rein to their admiration for France and, above all, for Napoleon III. The political system of Napoleon was certainly not to the harmony liberals' taste, and the emperor's use of universal suffrage in the plebiscite of 1851 had made them very reluctant to grant the franchise to the uneducated. But in economic questions the gap between Saint-Simonian inspired French politics and the program of Swedish association liberals was not very wide, the latter being unusually open to technocratic solutions in their admiration of science and technology. New banks on the model of the Pereire brothers' Crédit foncier and Crédit mobilier were erected in Sweden (1861 and 1864). And in monetary questions Wallenberg made friends with the formerly ardent Saint-Simonian Michel Chevalier, the architect of Napoleon III's free trade policy.

The Fate of the Liberal Program

On the whole, the harmony liberal program can be said to have succeeded well. Such was, in any event, the impression that Sweden made on the famous author Arthur de Gobineau arriving 1872 from a Paris newly harrowed by foreign and civil war, on his (unintended) last diplomatic mission as French minister in Stockholm. As a doctrinaire he already had praised the Nordic race, yet his high expectations were now surpassed.

> You cannot imagine how pleasant it is here, how sensible, industrious and intelligent the Swedish people are. No revolution, no question of barbarian outrages from the mob. You live and let live ... True independence and personal freedom shine through everything. There exists no class hatred here; the nobility lives free and easy with the bourgeoisie and the people... Imagine workers who agree with their employers without strike

threats, employers who understand that the workers have to eat and raise their salaries without being asked; and both parties wouldn't care a fig for the International.[15]

Even if you make a substantial reduction—Gobineau being a welcome guest in the families of Bergstedt and Wallenberg—enough is left to substantiate Jean-Hervé Donnard's observation that you are meeting a forerunner of the social-democratic welfare state of the 1930s (by the way then "discovered" by another French diplomat, Serge de Chassin). The idyllic circumstances were, if anything, strengthened by the hitherto unseen economic boom of the years 1870/1875, years which saw the first breakthrough of industrialization in Sweden.[16]

The Great Depression, the slump that began in Austria in 1873, did not reach Sweden until 1878/9. But then the crisis became very sharp and deep. The first big strikes broke out. And as for the overoptimistic Wallenberg, his bank was brought to the brink of bankruptcy. He had to humiliate himself by asking for some (reluctantly given) state support. He never won back his political and economic positions. The harmony liberal program had here as elsewhere in Europe definitely lost its credibility, and time had come for the tailor August Palm to spread socialistic propaganda, soon resulting in the founding of the Swedish Social-Democratic Party in 1889. By then and long afterwards the pioneer work done by Pär Götrek was completely forgotten.

Conclusion

This chapter has treated the revolutionary and revolutionizing events of 1848 as something of a traumatic experience, making a lasting imprint for the future on a whole generation of leading politicians. As such its consequences in Sweden have been traced right up to the end of the 1870s. However, even if one focuses on influential diehards like Wallenberg, this approach may perhaps appear too sophisticated. In that case an alternative and less Scandinavian ending should be sought and found in 1870/71 with the watershed of the Franco-Prussian war. By then the red specter of Paris in 1848 was outstripped by the red specter of the Commune, and the liberal dreams of peaceful international cooperation and negotiation were distinctly overtaken by the Bismarckian principle of "Blut und Eisen." This change of times was clearly seen and commented upon by Wallenberg in his newspaper, *Stockholms-Posten*, when he wrote the following in December 1870:

> We saw an emperor's throne raised in France, founded on indecent actions. Its durability was short. Now we see an emperor's throne raised in Germany, and its glory begins with sacrificing hecatombs of men to the idol of the war of conquest. If France fails to obtain a tolerable peace, but Germany on the contrary will alone dictate the conditions after the war, then the freedom of the German people is lost and cannot be regained with less than a revolution of 1789 in Germany. But before then the German people will have to suffer much, and the power of the German unity will be employed to many misuses. This great change ... is not for the benefit of Freedom, and much energy that could better be used in the service of Civilization, will now be spent for the unproductive occupation of keeping guard against intruders.[17]

Notes

1. T. Nybom, "The Swedish Social Democratic State in a Tradition of Peaceful Revolution," In *Konflikt og samarbejde. Festskrift til Carl-Axel Gemzell* (Copenhagen, 1993), 303-35, here 325.
2. E. Gamby, *Pär Götrek och 1800-talets svenska arbetarrörelse.* (Stockholm, 1978), 102-7.
3. *Framtidens religion, uppenbarad av Saint-Simon*, 1831, (revised ed. 1833)
4. See the chapter on Norway in this volume, by Anne-Lise Siep.
5. G. B. Nilsson, *André Oscar Wallenberg*, 3 vols (Stockholm, 1984-94), vol. 1, 160.
6. Ibid., vol. 1, 173.
7. Letter of 29 March 1848, ibid.
8. Ibid., vol. 1, 211.
9. *Tidskrift för Litteratur* 1851, 320.
10. Nilsson, *Wallenberg*, vol. 1, 410.
11. Ibid., vol. 2, p. 88.
12. Ibid., vol. 2, 89.
13. Sten Carlsson, *Svensk historia*, vol. 2 (Stockholm, 1961), 401.
14. Å. Abrahamsson, "Ljus och frihet till näringsfång. Om tidningsväsendet, arbetarrörelsen och det sociala medvetandets ekologi - exemplet Stockholm 1838-1869," (Ph.D. Diss., Stockholm 1990), 368-69.
15. Letter of Gobineau, of 27 June and 6 September, 1872, printed in Nilsson, *Wallenberg*, vol. 3, 157.
16. J-H.Donnard,"Gobineau et le 'modèle suédois.'" *Acta Regiae ... Gothoburgensis, Humaniora*, 29 (1988): 220-21.
17. *Stockholms-Posten*, 30 December 1870, as cited in Nilsson, *Wallenberg*, vol. 3, 54.

Part II

CITY AND COUNTRY

Shot-maker behind a barricade [in Berlin], drawn by R. Kretschmer
(Illustrirte Zeitung, Leipzig, no. 250, 15 April 1848, 254)

The Palais des Prinzen von Preußen in Berlin
(Illustrirte Zeitung, Leipzig, no. 251, 22 April 1848, 267)

Chapter 15

THE EUROPEAN CAPITAL CITIES IN THE REVOLUTION OF 1848

Rüdiger Hachtmann

Revolutionary events in the European capitals at the beginning of 1848 sealed the fate of the Ancien Régimes. This is true, with reservations, for the prelude to the European revolutions of 1848/49, the short Swiss civil war, which has gone down in history as the *Sonderbund* war. With the entry of the troops of the Swiss majority cantons into Lucerne on 24 November 1847—the third Swiss capital, along with Zürich and Bern, and in that year of crisis the political center of the separatist seven conservative, "Jesuitical" minority cantons—the *Sonderbund* war found its de facto end. This is true, without reservations, for the Italian beginnings of the European revolutions as well as for the February and March Revolutions: the uprising in the Sicilian (provincial) capital of Palermo in mid-January and the mass demonstration in Naples at the end of January 1848 forced the king of the two Sicilies, Ferdinand II, to grant a constitution and to complete, temporarily, the transition to a constitutional monarchy.

After struggles on 22 and 23 February in Paris, the "roi bourgeois," Louis Philippe, was driven from the French capital on 24 February and France was declared a republic. The events in Vienna on 13 and 14 March and the barricade fighting on 18 March in Berlin turned the two German hegemonic powers into constitutional monarchies. On 15 March, with a large demonstration and the formation of a "committee of public safety," the first phase of the Hungarian revolution began peacefully. The Milan uprising of 18 to 22 March and the revolution in Venice on 22 March led to the entire north of Italy temporarily liberating itself from Habsburg rule.

The European revolution of 1848 was a chain reaction, above all (if one ignores revolts and movements in the agrarian sector) a chain of revolutions in the capitals.

Palermo and Naples provided the prelude—including the "train of constitutions" (Engels) which in the other Italian states followed the revolution in Naples. The Italian "little revolutions," as they were described in Central Europe, remained, like the Swiss *Sonderbund* war, without direct consequences for the other European states. The February Revolution in the capital of France, on the other hand, had the effect of a signal, a "bolt out the blue," as contemporaries frequently put it. The events in Paris from 22 to 24 February gave the decisive thrust to the March Revolutions in Vienna and Berlin, even when the Berlin March movement ran parallel to meetings, petitions and unrest in the capitals of the provinces (especially in Breslau and Cologne), and the Viennese March revolution was preceded in the Hungarian half of the empire, particularly from the beginning of 1848 onwards, by demands, presented ever more loudly, for more autonomy and greater political freedom. Only with the bloody events in Paris, Vienna and Berlin did the revolution of 1848 gain a European dimension. Metternich's fall, on the other hand, set off the Venetian and Milan Revolutions.

Among the larger capitals, only Rome presents a special case in this context. In the capital of the Papal States, the revolution had already begun two years previously with a reform phase—the election of the Bishop of Imola as Pope Pius IX in mid-June 1846 and the amnesty for political prisoners and exiles which followed, the easing of censorship, the introduction of freedom of association allowing the formation of political organizations, the calling of a diet (only a consultative body, however, with few rights), and the creation of a civic guard open to members of all social classes. The conservative turning point in Rome, introduced by the Pope when he named Count Pellegrino Rossi as Prime Minister in August 1848 after the waning of the first wave of European revolutions, remained an episode in contrast to developments in other European capitals, especially the June uprising in Paris, the events of October in Vienna, and those of November in Berlin. Rossi's assassination in mid-November 1848 and the Pope's flight marked rather the beginning of a second wave of revolution in Rome, that only ended in the summer of 1849.

Just as the revolutions of 1848 brought an end to the political systems handed-down from the *Vormärz*, events in the capitals between the summers of 1848 and 1849 were decisive for the overall defeat of the European revolution. In its course, the counter-revolution resembled only to a limited extent a chain reaction of the capitals: until autumn it ran parallel in the centers and the periphery. Of fundamental importance was the total defeat of the insurgents in the Paris "battle of June," interpreted by many contemporaries as the start of a second, social revolution, as a "class war." It encouraged counter-revolutionary forces in the Habsburg and Hohenzollern Monarchies to "clear away" the "revolutionary fuss" in their capitals as well.

Even before the bloody fighting of 22 to 26 June in the French capital, events in three other European capitals had given a preliminary decision to the question of success or defeat of the revolutionary movements in favor of the established powers in these countries. The clever actions of the British government in advance of and during the demonstration of 10 April 1848 in London put an end to a growth of the English Chartist Movement. With the failure of the London Chartist demonstration, Great Britain remained immune to a revolutionary coup. Two weeks later, on 26 April, the Austrian Commandant in Cracow, the old center of Poland (until 1611 the capital of Poland, and, until the first half of the eighteenth century, the coronation city of the Polish kings) had the town bombarded to kill off an attempted revolt in its infancy and to subjugate the town for a second time after 1846 to the Habsburg Monarchy. In the second week of June, Austrian troops under the command of General Windischgrätz suppressed a revolutionary uprising in Prague, thus destroying Czech and other Slavic nations' hopes of autonomy and giving rise to a conservative turning-point throughout the Habsburg monarchy.

The occupation of Milan on 6 August 1848 crowned the success of General Radetzky and his troops over the poorly functioning Italian national army. The total defeat of the Viennese revolutionary movement at the end of October and beginning of November and the taking of Berlin without a fight by General Wrangel's troops in the second week of November led to the German speaking part of Austria and Prussia dropping out of the European revolutionary movement. With the bloody repression of the revolutionary uprising in Dresden in May 1849 by Prussian troops, Saxony, too, was "pacified." The conquest of Rome on 30 June 1849 by French troops ended the Italian Revolution. Venice's capitulation on 22 August 1849 was only an echo of these events and was atypical to the extent that the Venetian mainland had already been re-subjugated by Austrian troops in the summer of 1848, so that the capitulation of the capital did not decide the "fate" of the revolution.

The capital cities put their stamp on the face and the course of the European revolutions. All capital cities, however, were not equal. In 1848, there were more than sixty cities in Europe which could quite justifiably claim to be a capital. Among them were towns such as the residences of the three Anhalt duchies, Bernburg, Köthen, and Dessau (the largest of the three with a population of about 13,000) in the center of the German Confederation, as well as the major cities of London and Paris. First (1), the characteristics of "capital cities" in 1848 will be investigated. What distinguished them from other cities and among each other? Following (2), is a sketch of the demographic and socioeconomic framework without which the specific developments and constellations in the capitals during the revolutionary years would be nearly impossible to understand. Themes of the next sections are (3) the differing basic political attitudes of the inhabitants, primarily of the three revolutionary metropolises, Paris, Vienna, and Berlin, (4) the multilayered and tension-laden political constellations in the capitals, especially with regard to political associations, and (5) the especially sharp social polarization, at least in the three revolutionary capitals, and the politically important role of the labor movement in the three European revolutionary metropolises. In the final section (6) the concept of a "municipal polycracy," will be used to sketch out the process of the creation of new institutions and centers of power in the capitals during the year of revolution, in addition to and in competition with the previously existing ones. Reference will also be made to the conclusions the authorities reached from the February and March Revolutions, and in this context the modernization of law enforcement in the capitals will be discussed at somewhat greater length.

Given the complexity of the subject, it is obvious that the above-mentioned aspects can only be dealt with roughly, and that at times it will be necessary to simplify matters schematically. Other important themes must be put aside, for example the diverse and not easily categorizable periodical press of 1848, that would develop quite differently in the capitals than in the provinces.[1] Equally, all European capitals cannot be dealt with in the same depth—quite apart from the fact that for some nations, for example Slovenia, the question of which city should be the capital had not yet been decided in 1848/49. In view of the many capitals, their differential significance for the total course of the European revolution, as well as, finally, the uneven state of research, the following remarks will concentrate on the revolutionary capitals of Berlin, Vienna, and Paris. Also included will be "second class capitals," especially Rome, Venice, Milan, and Budapest, which as Hungarian capital only overtook Bratislava in 1848.

Characteristics of "Capital Cities" around 1848

The first thing that distinguishes capitals from other types of cities is that the central state institutions are located there: the government of the entire country and national or statewide legislatures, whether a parliament or a corporate legislative body. In general, the king and his court also reside in the capital. This, however, was not always the case. At the end of the seventeenth century, the kings of France had transferred their residence to Versailles, a Paris suburb. Numerous Prussian monarchs, as well, only occasionally resided in their Berlin palace. Especially Friedrich Wilhelm IV spent much of 1848 and later in Potsdam, in the palace there or in Sanssouci.

This does not naturally alter the fact that it was and is typical for capital cities to house a number of individuals with the authority to take political action, frequently in competition with each other. In addition to the prince and his court, along with the ministers of state, were added the municipal officials, as well as specific civilian and military authorities, such as the chief of police, or the military governor. During the revolution (we will return to this point below) other institutions or individuals able to take action and centers of power developed: political associations, organizations of the early labor movement, civic and national guards as well as the politicized lower classes, that were not integrated into any formal structures, either organizationally or institutionally.

Capital cities usually had a heavy military presence, in part from a fear of "disturbances of domestic tranquility." Often the largest garrison of the country was located there. But capitals were not only sites of troop concentrations and centralization of the authorities; they were not only the political-administrative, but also, usually, the cultural centers of the country. They had, as a rule, more theaters, opera houses, concert halls, libraries etc. than other cities. Moreover, they possessed a higher than average number of institutions of higher education, at least well-known and often the largest universities.

However the model "university city" is certainly not identical with the model of a "capital city." European universities with long traditions were often located in smaller cities, such as Oxford, Cambridge, Bologna, Toledo or Halle and Göttingen. Just in view of disparate sizes it is not surprising that students and lecturers generally played a more important role in the smaller university cities than in the revolutionary capitals. (Vienna was the most prominent exception to this rule.) Still, the universities in the capitals also had a high status: as educational institutions for the new state bureaucracy, as crystallization points for intellectual-cultural life, and, in view of revolutionary events, as centers of political-ideological criticism, as "suppliers" of new ideas and theoretical concepts. The intellectual opponents of the revolutionary era, who determined the political-ideological confrontations, had often experienced a similar socialization at the university and stemmed from the same academic milieu.

In central and western Europe, the capitals had gained a further important function from the end of the 1830s onward. They were a central junction of a developing railway network. The railway did not just stimulate initial development of industry, it also decisively influenced the thinking and feeling of bourgeois and lower class contemporaries. Above all, it revolutionized feelings for time and space because of its continual and, as many contemporaries felt, "planetary speed." "Nation" and "Europe" could be tangibly experienced. With a totally altered relation to time and space, political horizons were also expanded. In Paris, Vienna, and Berlin, which were becoming the focal point of a rapidly expanding spider's web for this new form of transportation, broad circles of the population had doubtless already been seized by this change of consciousness by 1848, especially as not only the bourgeoisie, but also some of the lower class had been taken by a quite marked wanderlust.

Moreover, the railway transported current information. It was, apart from the equally new telegraph, the reason why new ideas, news, and rumors spread much more rapidly in the 1840s than in previous decades. Without the railway, the revolution of 1848 would not have grown into a European one. This modern means of transport made communication possible between capitals: from there, information, opinions, and rumors generally slowly seeped "into the provinces."

Even if one glances only at the larger European cities, not all capitals were the same in the mid-nineteenth century. There were old cities—Rome, thousands of years old, or Vienna, Paris, and London, which for centuries had been the unchallenged centers of powerful states—and parvenus with little tradition, such as Berlin and St. Petersburg. Above all, however, the capitals of the larger European states had, so to speak, a varied political reach. In a period in which the nation-state was rather the exception and important nations (Germany, Italy) were fragmented into numerous larger and smaller states, and where, on the other hand, the premodern type of multinational Great Power played an important role (the Habsburg Monarchy, and to a certain extent, Russia and Prussia as well), this different political reach of the capital city was of considerable consequence.

The most important capital of the European continent was Paris. In the first half of the nineteenth century it remained the "capital of Europe" (Willms) and in 1848, after 1789/1794 and 1830, was once again the starting point and center of a European revolution. Only the "thunderbolt" of the Paris February Revolution made contemporaries aware that the political break already prefigured in Switzerland and Italy would take on European dimensions. In 1848, events and developments in the capital of France outshone events in all other scenes of the revolution and influenced directly or indirectly the political constellation in the rest of Europe as well.

The extent to which the eyes and ears of contemporaries were directed towards events in Paris and France, and the insignificance of other European revolutionary events in comparison, was shown in 1848 by "the most reliable barometer of political weather," the stock market. With the February Revolution, the value of all share on European stock markets crashed. The proclamation of the overthrow of Lamartine's government and the temporary occupation of the constituent assembly on 15 May initially set off, according to a report in the *Vossische Zeitung* on the mood in the Prussian capital, "a panicked shock among the speculators, and there was a rush to sell, in which the prices of numerous funds and railway companies came under great pressure." After the news had arrived by telegraph that "Paris is quiet again, the national guard remained loyal and its commander and many other people, mostly communists, have been arrested," the market breathed a collective sigh of relief. The "military parade of 20,000 bayonets" in Paris on 21 May stabilized the stock market at a low level. The victory of the "forces of order" in the June uprising, the news "that in Paris … after a hard struggle, the workers' uprising has been ended and peace restored," put the market in a better mood and drew prices out of the cellar.

Ten days later, when it had become clear that the forces of order had established themselves permanently, the market reports in the Berlin press described "a persistent upswing" and "a very lively rise" in the price of railway stock, bank and state bonds: "a feeling of security restored [is gaining] more and more the upper hand." From July onwards, nothing could upset the market any more. "Even a catastrophe of world historic order" remarked the *Vossische Zeitung* at the end of October laconically "as is happening at this moment under the walls of Vienna, [is] no longer able to shake the calm of the market."[2]

Next in importance were the capitals of the two other European Great Powers shaken by the revolution, Berlin and Vienna. Berlin was not only the Hohenzollern residence and the Prussian metropolis, but also took on a further role between 1848 and 1850. In the summer of 1848 the city on the Spree became the informal capital of Germany due to the increasing political significance of Prussia and its monarch. This had already become apparent on 21 March 1848. Three days after the fighting at the barricades, Friedrich Wilhelm IV rode through the streets of his capital and declared that he had "placed himself at the head of the German people," "for the days of danger."

More important than this early "German" initiative with which the Hohenzollern monarch wished to redirect domestic political pressure was an increasing orientation by the most important political currents in Germany—above all the democrats—toward Berlin as "the capital of the largest German country"; "the German people [must] see Berlin as the source of its future."[3] With the resolution of the *Paulskirche* to offer Friedrich Wilhelm IV the German imperial crown, Berlin moved even closer to the center of political events in Germany. And even after 28 April 1849, the Prussian king's clear rejection of the German "crown of dirt and clay" and the dissolution of the lower house of the Prussian parliament, Prussia's final withdrawal from the revolutionary movement, Berlin remained the pivot of aspirations for German national unity, until the declaration of Olmütz on 29 November 1850 marked the definitive failure of a policy of national unity from above [*Unionspolitik*] initiated by the Prussian crown (and, in the eyes of many contemporaries, beyond).

In 1848/49 Berlin ousted Frankfurt as well as Erfurt (a city, which because of its geographical position in the center of Germany was chosen by many, during the public debate of the revolutionary period, as the future German capital) from their role as political centers of Germany. The failure of the German National Assembly and the provisional central power of the Reich crowned this development, even when Frankfurt once again became the seat of the German Confederation from 1849 to 1866. Although Vienna was held to be, after Paris, the "intellectual capital of Europe," one only seldom finds the name of the Austrian capital mentioned in discussions of which city should become the future capital of Germany.[4] This was not by chance. The numerous nations within the Habsburg Monarchy, in which German speaking Austrians formed a minority, and the Habsburgs' reaffirmation, observable from 1849 onwards, of their role as a traditional, multinational, European Great Power, made it appear improbable for most contemporaries that Vienna would be able to fit the role of capital of a homogenous German-speaking nation-state.

Of more limited political import than Paris, Vienna and Berlin were the capitals of the German mid-sized states, those of the crown lands of the Austrian Empire and those on the European periphery. Within this type of capital city, Budapest, as the center of the Hungarian national movement and the Hungarian nation-state, Venice, in the spring and summer of 1848 (until the reoccupation of the Lombardo-Venetian mainland by Austrian troops), and Milan and Prague (with certain reservations, until the summer of 1848), as well as Dresden, Karlsruhe and Stuttgart (during the spring and summer of 1849 in the context of the campaign for the imperial constitution and the second round of German uprisings) held a certain status. Frankfurt am Main, although only a city-state, was, apart from Berlin, the political center of Germany from the beginning of March 1848 to the spring of 1849—and once again after 1850, as the seat of the German Confederation. The two Sicilies, although already shaken by revolutionary movements in January 1848, and with them their capitals of Naples and Palermo, had, on the other hand, from the very beginning, only a peripheral import in a total European context.

Rome played a special role. The Pope was not only the ruler of an Italian state, but at the same time the spiritual head of all Catholic Christians. Rome, first, the traditional focal point of Catholicism and, second, the capital of the papal states, lived, third, from its fame as the center of a world power of classical antiquity, and was seen by many as, fourth, the capital of a future united Italy. It was therefore not by chance that the Pope was also earmarked for a further role. Pius IX, since he had taken office in the autumn of 1846, personified the hopes of Italian liberals and democrats for national unification. The constellation of being, on the one hand, the head of all Catholics and, on the other, having been raised up as a figure of national identification, made the position of the Pope and the Vatican admittedly somewhat precarious in the spring and summer of 1848 in view of the Italian national war against Catholic Austria and gave political developments in Rome from the autumn of 1848 their own momentum. The Pope fled, the national-republican movement under the leadership of Mazzini proclaimed Rome as the (ideal) capital of a democratic Italy, with the reconstitution of the former papal states as a republic.

Greater or lesser political influence, and thus the significance of a capital city for the European or the respective national revolutionary events, was dependent to a great extent on whether the state was centralized or federal. In France, the city of Paris embodied the entire nation-state. The cultural and political gap between capital and the "provinces" was especially marked, as (according to the publicist Hermann Hauff, the older brother of the German poet Wilhelm Hauff, in his *Sketches from Life and Nature* of 1840) "basically public life [was concentrated] exclusively in the capital." In Germany, on the other hand, Hauff continues, "Everything on which intellectual life develops is spread throughout the country; nowhere is there a German Mecca … nowhere a commanding point."[5]

As a consequence the gap between the capital and the "provinces" was not as wide in the German states. While everything in France was concentrated in Paris, developments in the Prussian capital did not have so strong an effect on the periphery. The more distant a province was from the center and the weaker its historical ties to the Hohenzollern monarchy, the more marked its own political life. The Rhine Province was influenced as much by developments in southwestern Germany as it was by events in Berlin. Other provinces with a difficult past, especially Silesia, could also only with difficulty be kept on a tight leash by the central government. Vienna's influence was broken most by independent "regional" developments, especially in the non-German areas of the Habsburg monarchy. In the east and south of the empire, the March revolutions were not set off solely by the February revolution, but also by developments in the Hungarian half of the empire.

To comprehend the significance of capitals for all the events of the revolution, one needs to differentiate not only according to capital type, but also according to time period. Until October/November 1848, Vienna and Berlin were, apart from Paris, the most important revolutionary centers. Thereafter, the Austrian and Prussian capitals dropped out of the direct course of the revolution. Paris played a decisive role as a center of revolutionary stimulus only until the June uprising. In the second phase of the revolution, the capitals of the "midsized" states (that is, "second-class" capitals) made a greater impression on events. However, even the Roman republic—in spite of Rome's great confessional and ideological importance—had only a limited and no longer European-wide significance. Apart from Rome, the role of capitals in general for revolutionary action in the respective states or regions was reduced in comparison to the first phase of the revolution. The previous centers of the revolution became centers of conservative action, in which the old powers (or, in France, the newly formed "Party of Order") coordinated their counter-revolutionary activities at various levels. The following remarks on the internal structure of the metropolitan revolutions and on their socioeconomic preconditions concentrates, therefore, on the first phase of the revolution, the period from February to November 1848.

The Demographic and Socioeconomic Framework

As a rule, cities that are capitals and royal residences cannot be precisely distinguished from other types of cities. They were generally the largest cities in their countries, industrial centers, educational center, and transportation junctions. The extent to which the specific demographic and socioeconomic characteristics sketched below were the result of other functions than that of capital can therefore not be stated with certainty.

The population of most European capital cities grew in the first half of the nineteenth century at a rate that was faster than the average for other cities in their respective countries (table 1). However, there were considerable differences: in Berlin and, starting at a very low level, in Budapest as well as in Munich, one could speak of a population explosion. In the three cities, the population more than doubled in the first half of the nineteenth century, if not tripled. Only in the major ("pure") British industrial towns was the increase in population more rapid. Somewhat slower, but still above average, was the growth of population in Paris and Vienna in the period between 1800 and 1850. Population growth in Milan, Naples, Frankfurt, and Prague reflected the general trend of urbanization. Quite against the trend, on the other hand, were Rome, hardly affected by industrialization, and, especially, Venice, whose economic development was considerably hindered by the Habsburg Monarchy.

It seems reasonable to assume that the respective growth in population of the various capitals can be attributed to differing levels of industrialization. Berlin, for example, developed in fact into one of Prussia's most important industrial centers. The slow growth of population in Rome and the fall in Venice on the other hand were due, to a great extent, to a lack of industrial enterprises. In Venice, the once important ship building industry, like the textile industry, only played a marginal role; more important was manufacturing for the production of glass goods and wax products. Tourism had, quite tellingly, become the leading economic branch in the city.[6] Modern industry had avoided Rome even more; the high intra-Italian trade barriers also played a role. In Milan, however, the prosperity of the craft and industrial sectors that continued until 1846/47 in spite of all restrictions was remarkable for Italian circumstances. It was doubtless greatly responsible for the relatively rapid growth in population. The same is true of Frankfurt, which saw a rapid expansion in early, mostly craft-based, industrialization, and for Munich, which had a true major industrial company in the Maffei Maschine Factory, with its 370 employees.[7]

A survey by the Paris chamber of commerce in 1847 put the number of craft and industrial "workers" at about 343,000, hence about a third of the entire population. Berlin, according to the occupational census of 1846, had about 77,000 wage

Table 1: The Growth in Population of European Capital Cities, 1800-1850

	1800	1850	Population Growth, 1800/50 (in percent)
Berlin	172,000	419,000	+144%
Buda-Pest	54,000	178,000	+230%
Frankfurt a.M.	38,000	60,000	+58%
Milan	170,000	242,000	+42%
Munich	40,000	96,000	+140%
Naples	350,000	449,000	+28%
Paris	547,000	1,053,000	+93%
Prague	75,000	118,000	+57%
Rome	153,000	175,000	+14%
Venice	137,000	122,000	-11%
Vienna	247,000	444,000	+80%
In comparison (a)			
Birmingham	71,000	233,000	+228%
Glasgow	77,000	345,000	+348%
Liverpool	82,000	376,000	+359%
London	1,117,000	2,685,000	+140%
Manchester	75,000	303,000	+304%
St. Petersburg	220,000	485,000	+120%

a. European cities with particularly rapid population growth

Figures (1800 and 1850 respectively) except Venice, Frankfurt, and Munich in: B.R. Mitchell, "Statistischer Anhang 1790-1814," in Carlo M. Cipolla and Knut Borchardt (eds.), Europäische Wirtschaftsgeschichte Vol. 4, (Stuttgart, 1973), 490. Estimates for Frankfurt an Main in: R. Koch, Grundlagen bürgerlicher Herrschaft. Verfassungs- und sozialgeschichtliche Studien zur bürgerlichen Gesellschaft in Frankfurt a.M. (1612-1866) (Wiesbaden, 1983), 185. Figures for Munich in Karl-Joseph Hummel, München in der Revolution von 1848/49 (Göttingen, 1987), 261, and C. Zimmermann, Die Zeit der Metropolen. Urbanisierung und Großstadtentwicklung (Frankfurt, 1996), 123. Figures for Venice (1797 and 1845) in: Paul Ginsborg, Daniele Martin and the Venetian Revolution of 1848-49 (Cambridge, 1979), 30.

laborers in crafts and industry. On top of that came another 18,000 small masters, nominally self-employed but who had in fact sunk to being outworkers. However, the leading sectors of early industrialization only played a secondary role in the two cities. In Paris, only about 6,600, or just 2 percent of all "workers" were employed in engineering, and about 25,000, or 7.3 percent in other iron or metalworking industries. In Berlin, 7.8 percent of waged workers were employed in engineering or tool making and another 12 percent in other metallurgical industries.[8]

In spite of a number of major industrial firms and manufacturers, Paris and Berlin remained characterized by small shops. In the capital of France there were only a few firms with more than fifty employees in the 1840s. While industrialization in Berlin moved at a quite respectable pace from the early 1840s onward, modern industry in Paris was slow to develop. Prefects, state officials, and municipal politicians in Paris were somewhat cautious. They were afraid that potentially revolutionary masses of workers could concentrate in large factories and could (once again) bring an end to the established order, and therefore renounced any sort of government industrial policy that could have given a boost to such a development—quite unlike the Prussian and Berlin civil service, without any experience of revolution, who knew no such inhibitions. In regard to the pace of industrialization, Vienna stood between Berlin and Paris. How little population growth had to parallel industrialization was shown by the example of the Hungarian capital. Pest and Ofen (Buda) had, apart from 10,000 journeymen, 7,000 messengers, and 2,200 construction day laborers, only 3,000 "factory proletarians" together within their borders.[9]

It was not so much the available jobs in industry and crafts, as the often illusory hope of being able to "make one's fortune" better in the big city than in the provinces, that made most capitals and major cities into centers of a population explosion. Vienna, Berlin, Paris and other European major cities became "magnets" that "attract the poor."[10] As this population growth took place within a closed urban region (the cities did not expand their territory in the 1830s and 1840s), the three European capitals also became centers of urban pauperism. A shortage of apartments, high rents, and homelessness were chronic. Pauperism was a general phenomenon in the *Vormärz*, but it was particularly oppressive in the capitals and major cities because of above-average increase in population expansion and a simultaneously overtaxed system of poor relief.

Because social want was ever-present, the impoverished were more directly confronted with the aristocratic world of splendor and abundance than in other cities. Pauperism in the capitals thus had greater political consequence than elsewhere. Easily inflammable lower-class embitterment as well as political precautionary measures—for example attempts by the Paris city administration to keep the price of bread stable at the beginning of 1847 and thus to prevent hunger riots that could quickly escalate into an uprising—express this quite clearly. The crisis in the agrarian and craft sectors from 1846 to 1849, with its serious consequences, not least for the major cities, condensed in the minds of contemporaries into the feeling of permanent crisis. The good harvest of 1847 brought no relief. The revolution at the beginning of 1848 was fraught with hopes and fears.

In view of developments during the revolutionary period, it is significant that the capital cities had strong ties to the developing industrial society, even if crafts still clearly dominated. However, early capitalism had established itself in the three centers of the 1848 revolution in different ways: especially strong in Berlin, weaker in Vienna, and only to a limited extent in Paris. The Prussian capital had not only a number of genuine large factories, but some craft workshops had also attained a respectable size. This led (to be brief) to relations between journeymen and masters becoming increasingly impersonal. It was not by chance that, in the Prussian capital—and in contrast to Vienna—money wages were the rule, and room and board the exception.[11] Moreover, numerous journeymen switched back and forth between crafts and industry, thus gathering work experience in both forms of production. Thus, the waged status of the journeymen was more noticeable here than elsewhere; boundaries between occupational groups were also breaking down more and more.

One consequence of this weakening in differentiation was that in the revolution a "modern" form of social polarization could develop more clearly. Distinctions between the trades tended to be reduced in favor of a more abstract employer/employee dichotomy. It was this altered socioeconomic constellation that explains to a great extent why the organized labor movement was able to establish itself in Berlin in the spring of 1848 and in Vienna in mid-summer, also finding a strong echo in broad sections of society. The range of travels of some journeymen—many of whom reached Switzerland or France, where they came into contact there with revolutionary ideas—as well as journeymen's educational associations—such as, for example, the Hedemann Craftmen's Association in Berlin with over a thousand members, in which rationalist theology and early socialist theories could circulate—further encouraged this process of forming a rudimentary "class consciousness." In comparison especially with Berlin, industrialization progressed rather more slowly in Paris in the 1840s; forms of work and experience also changed more slowly. In Paris, however, revolutionary tradition and greater freedoms for workers' associations, by comparison to Vienna and Berlin (in spite of all restrictions) in the years before the revolution, explain why social conflict was more charged in Paris than elsewhere and why the soil for early socialist ideas was especially fruitful.

Basic Political Attitudes of the Inhabitants of Paris, Vienna, and Berlin

While in Paris there existed a broad societal consensus about the replacement of the monarchy by a republic in February, and in Rome (equally a traditional stronghold of republicanism) this also occurred, at the second attempt, at the end of 1848, "the revolution" in most other capitals stopped "at the foot of the throne." Especially in the three European revolutionary capitals, political assumptions and mentalities were often quite distinct. Certain events directly after the February Revolution and the March Revolutions highlight these distinctions.

In Paris, with the flight of the roi bourgeois, Louis Philippe, the monarchy was totally repudiated. Its symbols were "desecrated" and became the object of the ridicule and insults of the "rabble." After the Royal Guard had surrendered, the "people" streamed into the Tuileries. Initially they found the dressing chamber of the royal family and began a sort of spontaneous masked ball: housewives paraded past in salon robes, workers in tails. A somewhat older Parisian had put on the king's morning gown. "The mob dressed itself mockingly in lace and cashmere, golden fringe was wrapped around the arms of their blouses, hats with ostrich feathers decorated the heads of blacksmiths, and Legion of Honor sashes served as belts for prostitutes … In the anteroom a prostitute stood like the Statue of Liberty on a pile of clothes, with eyes opened wide, frightening."

The court life of Louis Philippe was parodied, a wild "court concert" was given in original costumes and some enjoyed the rest of the still warm food left by hastily fleeing ministers. In the center of events was the throne room. Everyone wanted to sit on the symbol of the past monarchy. Men, women, and children from all social classes stood in long lines, waiting for their turn to finally arrive, so that they could take their place on the throne covered in red velvet. Many imitated Louis Philippe's affected behavior. A few youths jumped around on the throne like on a trampoline. A few hours later, in the afternoon of 24 February, the throne was "picked up and passed unsteadily from hand to hand across the room…to the accompaniment of hisses and boos," it was thrown out the window. Four "workers" raised the damaged throne on their shoulders and carried it, at the head of a large crowd, like a casket, to the Place de la Bastille. There the throne was smashed to pieces and then burned.[12]

That was a symbolic act unthinkable in Berlin or Vienna. The extent to which the majority of the population in the Prussian capital remained attached to the monarchy and the person of the king was shown a day after the barricade fighting, on 19 March, when Friedrich Wilhelm IV bared his head to the numerous corpses, which, in a sort of demonstration of mourning (like in Paris on 23 and 24 February) had been driven on hand-carts, decorated with flowers and sashes, through the streets of the city and finally in front of the palace. What then took place was experienced as follows by an unnamed bourgeois eyewitness, quoted by the chronicler of the Berlin revolution, Adolf Wolff. The king's gesture of removing his hat before the fallen barricade fighters was a scene "which outdoes all the tragic pathos ever offered the shaken souls in the tragedies of antique and romantic art." Paris, the "mother" of continental revolution, was the scale against which to measure the experience.

> Louis XVI was called "le roi martyr" when he mounted the guillotine; how modest the atonement appears which the people of Paris … imposed upon him compared to the penance which the people of Berlin prepared for their king … From this hour on, there has been a transformation in the heart of the king like that which had occurred in the hearts of the people. The Prussian kingdom had risen, irrevocably, from the absolute throne; the staircase leading to constitutionalism had been put in place. The people of Berlin had completed their revolution in a greater and more dignified fashion than the people of Paris. There, they had broken the king's throne into pieces and tossed them into the flames; even Napoleon had called the throne only a piece of wood covered in velvet. Here [in Berlin] a great victory was celebrated; here the king's heart was broken and tossed onto a fire of purification, out of which the king's heart and his salvation rose up again.[13]

This eye-witness and with him probably a large majority of the people of Berlin did not think that the monarchy had been called into question; quite the opposite, they believed that the ties between people and king had been strengthened. They felt confirmed in this stance by events on the following days: by Friedrich Wilhelm's nationalist ride through the city on 21 March and, at the "state funeral from below" (Hettling),[14] one day later, by the king's gesture of paying his respects. Every time a wagon with the body of a barricade fighter drove past his palace, he "remov[ed] his helmet and with bare head" remained on the balcony "until the casket had passed."[15]

In the Austrian capital, political attitudes were similar to those in Berlin, although the mentally retarded Kaiser Ferdinand, forced to abdicate at the beginning of December 1848, was not suitable as an identification figure, as a "people's king." Instead of orienting themselves to the living monarch, the people turned to historical myth. In Vienna, the "public" had to express its desire for a constitutional monarchy open to reform by applauding a historical myth. On 14 March a statue of the reforming emperor Joseph II received spontaneous applause from a large crowd.

In Berlin, early enthusiasm for a constitutional monarchy—something seen in the beginning even among many Berlin democrats and people from the lower classes—began to fade in the summer and early autumn of 1848. Not only did the extremely disliked person of the Prince of Prussia, designated successor and later king and emperor Wilhelm I, become the target of criticism, but also the person of Friedrich Wilhelm IV, originally the "people's king." Cries of "Republic!" were an oft used slogan in demonstration.

Support for the Habsburgs in the Austrian capital was long preserved, however, in spite of particular criticisms. Well-known are the words that a Viennese worker was said to have called out while building a barricade against advancing troops on 6 October: "This is what we have to suffer for our Emperor!"[16] These words expressed the widespread feeling that the insurgents were not fighting against the "good" emperor but against his "bad" advisors and a treacherous military. Only in the second half of October did the trust of Viennese revolutionaries in the emperor disappear. The majority of mobile guards refused to swear an oath to protect the constitutional throne. Like in Paris in February, when the color red temporarily became the national color, next to the tricolor, and in Berlin, where from the early summer of 1848 onwards, ever more red flags were seen in the demonstrations, the color red finally also became the symbol of the Viennese October uprising.[17]

Political Constellations in the Capital Cities

Apart from the central question of "monarchy" or "republic," the course of the revolutions in the capital cities and the political constellations there show remarkable similarities. In the capitals, the monarch, the parliament, and the barricade were united in a very confined space. A wide range of forms of action and organization existed side by side. They overlapped and reinforced each other, thus giving the revolutionary stage of the capital city a unique, dramatic impact.

Barricade fighting in the capitals was the event that shaped most lastingly the image of "revolution" for contemporaries, and for future generations formed the basis of later myths of revolution. Without barricades, no revolutionary break. Barricade construction and fighting, indeed physical violence in general, were generally the forms of action of the lower classes. Thus arose in the capitals a very marked, and at first glance paradoxical constellation. People from the lower classes mounted the barricades, above all to help bring about a breakthrough for "bourgeois freedoms." A second glance, admittedly, resolves this paradox. The struggles were for freedoms that were as much those of citizens as of the bourgeoisie for the implementation of equal rights and freedoms for all men, independent of the social class to which they belonged.

The parliaments were the result of the barricade fighting. Even when many deputies did not wish to see it this way, the national and statewide assemblies, together with the bourgeois February and March Ministries, represented a new, "revolutionary" legality. Not least because the parliaments met in the capitals of their respective countries, local and national or state-wide events were more closely dovetailed than in "normal" times. Parliamentary and extra-parliamentary forms of action did not remain unconnected, two separate revolutionary stages; rather, they existed in an extremely tension-laden relationship to another.

On the one hand, parliaments and government ministries reacted very sensitively to events in the capital cities. They frequently engaged in immediate "local politics." At the same time, the "revolutionary nightmare," that was the capital city, in the authorities' point of view, shaped the national policies of the leaders of the state. Conversely, parliament, deputies, and governments were often subject to "pressure from the streets." This pressure could escalate into insults and violent attacks on individual members of the Prussian National Assembly, as in Berlin on 9 June and 31 October, into uprisings, as in Frankfurt am Main on 18 September because of the consent of the *Paulskirche* to the Malmö armistice, two days previously, or into an occupation of parliament, as in Paris on 15 May.

The deputies, whose decisions greatly determined the fate of the entire country, were subject, so to speak, to constant intensive, and sometimes turbulent "observation" by the public in the capital, which included those who followed parliamentary debates with lively interest from the galleries. Members of parliament and parliamentary parties were forced by a bourgeois and "proletarian" public sphere, especially present in the capital cities, to formulate political programs precisely and in plain language, and to justify parliamentary decisions. As the democrats had their most important bastions in the major cities but were under-represented in many parliaments because of an exclusion of a part of the lower classes through a restrictive franchise and because of indirect voting, they were often more successful in this manner in placing deputies under considerable pressure.

Other actors had decisive influence on political events in the capitals. Ignoring for the moment Paris and from November Rome, and the regional capitals of the Habsburg Monarchy, the prince was a decisive figure, usually surrounded by influential advisors. Typical was a tense relation of the princes to their capitals, often a sort of love-hate relationship. This was especially marked with Friedrich Wilhelm IV, who, after the March Revolution, initially flattered his "dear burghers of Berlin" only to describe a few weeks later, to Prime Minister Camphausen, his capital as an "inflamed boil" that needed to be "lanced."[18]

A fourth central actor, after prince, parliament, and the street, that gave each capital its own particular profile during the revolution, was the political association. Especially in Paris and Berlin a quite varied range of associations existed. Just the total number of associations is impressive. In Paris there were more than 200 clubs in 1848; the majority of them were, admittedly, only short-lived. If one includes the approximately 100 neighborhood associations and the organizations of immigrants from different regions, all with different political affiliations, Berlin counted around 150 political associations in the summer and early autumn of 1848. Altogether, political associations organized between twenty- and fifty-thousand members in the Prussian capital (including the neighborhood associations and the relatively open membership structure typical of them), and the political clubs in Paris almost twice as many.[19]

Less differentiated and with fewer members were the political associations in Vienna and in the other European capitals. In Rome, the political camps crystallized around two large associations, the moderate "Circolo Romano" and the radical "Circolo Populare." In Venice, some radical clubs existed, although too little is known about their membership figures and internal life. Moreover, shortly after the founding of a republican government under Manin they were dissolved—without Manin's popularity suffering. In Budapest, on the other hand, two radical democratic clubs appeared—the "March Club," founded at the beginning of May and renamed the "Democratic Club" in July, and the "Society for Equality," founded in mid-July, and becoming an important political factor in the summer and early autumn of 1848. In the relatively small Frankfurt am Main, four clubs from the democratic and liberal camps played a politically significant role in 1848, but in the larger but more conservative Munich there were only three associations until November of that year.[20]

A large number of political associations were seemingly a special characteristic of Paris and Berlin, corresponding to a broad range of political currents in the two cities. In Paris, this spectrum extended from moderate republican organizations up to radical socialist associations. In Berlin, the democratic associations especially showed a high level of shading. Which form of government was preferred by the associations in the different capitals was naturally dependent on the respective specific political constellation. In the French capital, support for the republic was self-evident even for moderate associations; royalist organizations were just a vanishingly small right-wing oppositional minority. In Berlin, as in Vienna, on the other hand, even most of the democratic associations voted at the beginning for a constitutional monarchy as short-term political objective.

Because at least in the three European revolutionary metropolises the political contrasts were much more extreme than in the "provinces," the political center was quickly worn down between two poles, the democrats on the one hand and the conservatives on the other. This process can be especially clearly followed in Berlin. The Constitutionalist Club, the only organization of the Berlin liberals, had, in its beginnings, a membership comparable to that of the radical Political Club and the later Democratic Club. Organizational splits to the left and the right as well as a constant decline in membership permanently weakened the liberal association, to the point that it had become completely insignificant by the end of the revolution.

The "red" capitals were faced with a rather conservatively tinged "black" surrounding countryside. The political gap between capital and "the provinces" was recognized by democratic contemporaries as a central problem for the survival of the revolution. The Paris Club of Clubs carried out election campaigns, although with little success, and in general sought to influence the provinces in a revolutionary direction. Like the radical republicans of the French capital, who sent many hundred organizers into the provinces, the Berlin democrats with equally limited success, also sought to reach an "agreement with the provinces" by publishing statements and founding associations of immigrants from specific provinces [*landsmannschaftliche Vereinigungen*]. Admittedly, the political gap between center and periphery did not change the fact that associations in the capital city, no matter what their political viewpoint, served as models, and "parties" in the provinces often patterned themselves on the organization in the capital.

The democratic movement had its social basis mainly in the lower classes in Berlin, Paris, Vienna, Milan, and numerous other cities. "The workers," remarked the Berlin Chief of Police, made up the "main population" of the democratic clubs, which in general exert an influence on the lower classes, "as great as it is pernicious" while having "fallen into discredit" among the bourgeoisie since the summer of 1848.[21] A similar change of mood can be observed for Vienna.

Admittedly, this should not be misunderstood as indicating that the bourgeoisie played no role in the democratic movements in the capitals. The bourgeoisie in the social sense, especially professionals and the "academic proletariat" also set the tone in the democratic associations and republican clubs of the capitals.

Table 2: Social Composition of the Executive Committees of the Parisan Revolutionary Clubs and the Berlin Democratic Associations

	Paris	Berlin
Bourgeoisie (without the lower middle class)	68%	73%
Sub-categories of the bourgeoisie		
Businessmen, including rentiers	21%	9%
Journalists, writers, university teachers[a]	22%	41%
Students	5%	10%
Workers and artisans	23%	7%
Others[b]	9%	20%
Total number of persons	178	59

a. In Berlin, above all lecturers [Privatdozenten]

b. Because of different categorization, only partially comparable.

Sources: Peter Amann, "The Paris Club Movement in 1848," in Price (ed.), Revolution and Reaction, 119; Hachtmann, Berlin 1848, 277.

In Paris, a good two-thirds of all members of the executive committees of political clubs whose occupation is known belonged to the bourgeoisie in the narrow sense (without the lower middle classes). Journalists, writers, and university teachers provided the largest bourgeois group; and the percentage of students was also relatively high for a city of over a million inhabitants. In Berlin, the corresponding percentages lay somewhat higher. Three-quarters of all identifiable members of democratic clubs' executive committees were bourgeois, most of them journalists, artists, university teachers (mostly younger academics at the beginning of their careers) and students (cf. Table 2). The same social classes provided the leadership of democratic associations in Vienna, Milan, Venice, Rome as well as most other capitals, regional centers (for example Cologne), and also many smaller cities.

In the liberal and conservative associations, not only of the capitals, but of most cities, the bourgeoisie also dominated. However, it provided not only the executive committee but also, together with members of the petit bourgeoisie, the majority of members. "Workers" and journeymen, on the other hand, were almost totally absent. Unlike in the democratic associations, in the liberal and conservative associations other bourgeois strata apart from educated professionals played a significant role, especially state officials and businessmen, and, in conservative associations, aristocrats and high-ranking army officers as well.[22]

A "proletarian" basis for democratic associations on the one hand, and the bourgeoisie and petit bourgeoisie as preferred recruiting grounds for liberal and conservative associations (in the major cities) on the other, directly expressed a rejection by a majority of the bourgeoisie and petit bourgeoisie as a social class of "revolution" and radical democracy, and this all the more the "older" the revolution became. Many bourgeois desired wide-ranging reforms, but were, however, decisively non-revolutionary. However, "bourgeoisie" as a social class needs to be differentiated. A considerable portion, above all of the educated, professional bourgeoisie sympathized with the democrats or with left-wing liberalism.

Moreover, a decision for or against a political tendency could well reflect a conflict of generations. In Vienna, Berlin, Budapest, Munich, Frankfurt, and probably in most other capitals as well as numerous smaller towns the tendency was: the younger they were, the more radical. For the Prussian capital, this can be demonstrated with figures. The founding and executive committee members of conservative associations (Patriotic Association and Prussian Association) were forty-seven years old on average and those of the liberal clubs were thirty-nine. Leading members of the four largest democratic associations in Berlin, on the other hand, were thirty years old on average; among them, the board members of the radical Democratic Club, at twenty-eight, were the youngest.

The democratic-revolutionary movement, at least in the capital, also contained features of an anti-authoritarian revolt against the established parental generation, socialized by the "terrors" of the older (French) revolution. Young, radical Berliners also demonstrated their protest against the "establishment" in their behavior: long goatees and black Calabrian hats with red feathers were the "main symbol of democratic party members." In the capital of Austria, the revolutionary enthusiasm of academic youth found its expression in the prominent role played in revolutionary events by the "Aula" and the "Academic Legion" during the entire period from March to October 1848. The conflict of generations in Paris and probably also in the Italian capitals was not as marked as in Berlin and Vienna. Instead, revolutionary veterans from the July Revolution and the uprisings at the beginning of the 1830s also played a leading role in 1848, while in Paris some of the rebellious youths could be recruited for the mobile guard.

Social Polarizations and the Role of the Labor Movements

Apart from the liberals, the democrats, and the conservatives (all of whose groups could be strongly differentiated internally) as well as political Catholicism that was less significant in the major cities, the labor movement was the fifth political current in the European revolution of 1848. Together with some industrial centers, such as Leipzig (in Germany), the capitals were the most significant bastions of the early labor movement. With the Luxembourg Commission and the Workers' Central Committee versions of early workers' parliaments were formed in Paris and Berlin that set as their goals an improvement in the working and living conditions of the lower classes.

The Central Committee, in which delegates from most of the relevant trade branches were already represented at the time of its founding in mid-April 1848, remained limited in its organization to the Prussian capital, in contrast to the aims it had set itself. However, it formed the core of the first national workers' organization in Germany, the Workers' Fraternization. Moreover, the Berlin Central Committee functioned as a model for corresponding initiatives in the Austrian capital. A Workers' Association was founded in the second half of June; at its high point, it would have between seven and eight thousand members, making it the largest organization in Vienna. At the end of September 1848 it began preparations for a "workers' parliament." An institution comparable to the Berlin Central Committee was never formally constituted in the capital of the Habsburg Monarchy, however, because of the rapid turn of events that started in early October.

The founding of workers' organizations across occupational lines resulted in an intellectual reorientation of workers and journeymen. This was especially clear in Berlin. In the first weeks after the March revolution, workers and journeymen sent in numerous petitions containing demands that betrayed a strong orientation toward guild ideals and were similar to demands raised in other cities, such as restrictions on or prohibition of women's work, or the use of machines, and restrictions on the number of apprentices. In contrast, the objective of the Central Committee, according to its program, was the creation of a modern welfare state, including state care for "all those who cannot help themselves" and for "all invalids of labor," the establishment of a minimum wage and maximum working hours as well as the creation of joint commissions of workers and employers to negotiate a sort of collective bargaining agreement. Demands for "employment of the unem-

ployed in state workshops" reflect, like those for the establishment of national workshops and the foundation of a "ministry of labor" raised in many journeymen's petitions and "workers' meetings," the paradigmatic role played by the French capital.

There, at the end of February 1848, a "'ministry of labor" had been established,
headed by the worker Albert (Martin), and the first attempts at a socialist "organization of labor" were made in national workshops. Unlike the Parisian socialists,
Born and his friends, although members of the Communist League, did not aim at
the redistribution of property along socialist lines, but (initially) rather at developing industrial capitalism and at ending the remnants of guild restrictions, especially
by extending freedom of occupation and liberalizing restrictions on commerce.
Demands like those for the abolition of indirect taxes or for a progressive income
tax served to make modern industrial capitalism "socially tolerable." The establishment of a socialist society, in the view of the leading members of the Central Committee, was only possible in the long run.

The Vienna Workers' Association also put together a "modern-sounding trade
union program." Like the Berlin Workers' Central Committee, it recognized the
principle of occupational freedom while "totally rejecting the spirit of the guilds."[23]
Trade union demands and demands for a (bourgeois) welfare state, however, did not
exclude, either in the Prussian or in the Austrian capital, strong support for the radical left, as was the case in France, as well. Characteristic for the organized labor
movement in the two cities as well as in numerous other cities of the German Confederation was, furthermore, a relatively close alliance with the local democrats.

The rapid expansion of the labor movement exacerbated an already pronounced political polarization in Berlin, Paris, and Vienna. Simply the demand for
welfare-state measures to protect the proletariat, and for equal rights to political participation raised fears of social decline, of "communism," and of a redistribution of
property among the bourgeoisie and petit bourgeoisie. In Paris and Berlin, "entire
caravans" of aristocrats and the well-to-do left the city directly following the February and March Revolutions, while in Vienna this was seen "only" in the first half
of May, after the imperial court had abandoned the capital of the Habsburg Monarchy for Innsbruck.

In order to defuse the politically charged nature of the "social question," especially in view of the high rates of unemployment, municipal and state authorities
introduced massive job creation schemes in the capital cities. In Paris, in the end,
more than 110,000 of the unemployed were put to work at public expense, in
Vienna 20,000, and in Berlin over 8,000. Admittedly, they were employed in senseless excavation jobs whose character as "employment therapy" was obvious. In
Venice, 700 of the jobless were employed in public construction sites in April 1849.
In Rome at the beginning of 1849, a large number of the unemployed began to
restore churches, to strengthen the banks of the Tiber, and to build roads along its
banks, all paid for by the state. Job creation schemes were, of course, not the privilege of larger capitals. In smaller towns attempts were also made to get the jobless
off the streets with public means. Dessau, the capital of the small state of Anhalt-
Dessau, for example, employed 1,200 jobless workers in excavation work in 1848;

relative to population, that was as many unemployed as those registered in the national workshops in Paris in June.[24]

In the French capital, quite unlike Berlin and Vienna, job creation schemes were, moreover, not only and not even primarily intended to defuse the political explosiveness of the "social question." The Paris national workshops were seen as an attempt, planned above all by Louis Blanc, to implement early socialist concepts of state organized cooperative production. The implementation of this concept, between March and June 1848, failed because of the huge number of jobless who required public employment, because of poor organization, and because of (the related) prejudice and rejection by the bourgeoisie and the new bourgeois-republican government.

The status of the "social question" in the capitals is shown in the involuntary central role played by those employed in public works in the three revolutionary metropolises. Excavation workers did not gain political significance because they were especially "class conscious," but because they became an incarnation of bourgeois fears. All the political fears that terrified the bourgeoisie were projected onto Berlin Rehberger, the Viennese excavators, and the workers employed in the Parisian national workshops. Just their great number caused the bourgeoisie to fear the worst. On top of this, came their ragged appearance, their pleasure in celebrating, an often excessive consumption of alcohol, and probably presumptuous behavior towards authority. The excavators did not even need to approach the bourgeoisie. Simply their poor dress, different modes of behavior and, in general, their "culture" (in the broadest sense of the term), that was foreign to the upper strata of the population, raised deep resentments.

Bourgeois and petit bourgeois, for whom saving time, work discipline, moderation, and frugality were central values, felt themselves mocked by the excavators' work ethic. In Berlin, Paris, and Vienna, conflicts escalated when the authorities, in agreement with the majority of bourgeois public opinion, attempted to subject those who were allegedly idle at public expense to bourgeois work discipline or to end job creation schemes altogether. Disciplining of the Berlin Rehberger was relatively mild. At the end of May there were repeated demonstrations by excavators who had been laid off because they had resisted the introduction of piece work. The demonstrations caused a lot of unrest, but the authorities did not give in. In Vienna, government and municipal plans to lay off many workers and to reduce pay drastically for those who remained ended on 23 August with the Praterschlacht, a bloody struggle between demonstrators and the national guard which cost the lives of seven workers and, it should be mentioned, was started by female excavators. In Paris, finally, a plan to disband national workshops culminated in the June uprising, which was interpreted by contemporaries as a "class war," although it was rather more an act of desperation and the combatants on opposite sides of the barricades differed little in their social background.[25]

In the less influential capitals, tensions between workers and journeymen on the one hand, and employers on the other, did not escalate into great "tumults" and bloody struggles. In these cities, socioeconomic interests and tensions faded in importance compared to self-assertion against an external enemy and the goal of national sovereignty. In the capitals of Italy, and in Budapest as well, the national question eclipsed intra-municipal conflict structures. If especially in Venice, Rome, and Budapest, social conflicts and political differences played a secondary role in the revolutionary movement compared to Paris, Vienna and Berlin, and considerable portions of the upper social strata remained involved in "the revolution," this was also due to the prominent status of charismatic "revolutionary leaders": Lajos Kossuth, initially Hungarian Minister of Finance, then Chairman of the National Defense Committee and finally provisional head of state of Hungary; Daniele Manin, the Venetian "dictator"; and Giuseppe Mazzini, member of the triumverat and spiritus rector of the Roman republic. The revolutions in Vienna, Berlin, and Paris did not produce a comparably prominent and above all uncontroversial leader—in spite of a Louis Blanc and Auguste Blanqui in Paris, who only personified specific tendencies within the revolutionary movement. Political differences in the February and March movements in the French, Austrian, and Prussian capitals reduced the possibility of a "great" leader appearing, which in turn meant that in the three metropolises the tensions and divisions in the revolutionary movement were certainly not reduced.

Municipal Polycracy and the Modernization of Law Enforcement

Especially in Berlin, Vienna, and (with reservations) Paris, job creation schemes were the central pillar of the authorities' antidote to the revolution conceived in view of the numerous and politically powerful lower classes. Modernization of law enforcement was the other side of the same coin. Job creation schemes and new forms of police were a carrot and stick to reduce pressure coming from socially and politically dissatisfied lower classes, and to prevent a further radicalization of the revolution. Above all, three institutions were used for law enforcement during the year of revolution in the capital cities: civic and national guards, constabularies and mobile guards, and the regular military, initially removed from public view after the February and March events.

With the outbreak of revolution at the beginning of 1848, urban militias appeared (or were reactivated) in many European capitals. In Vienna, the *Bürgergarde*, which had led a shadowy existence since 1815 as a guard of honor, was armed, its numbers increased, and was renamed the "national guard." The Vienna municipal militia, with a nominal strength of 30,000 to 40,000 men, the Berlin civic guard with more than 25,000 members and most other civic guards were, quite literally, guards of the bourgeoisie. Only those who possessed municipal citizenship rights, that was the minority of male residents who owned a house and/or had a sufficiently high income, could be a member.

One prominent exception to this rule was Rome. The civil guard founded there was open to all classes. In Venice, the "Arsenalottis," workers in the arsenal workshops, had their own independent armed formations parallel to the bourgeois civic guard. The Berlin civic guard with its "armed engineers," the mobile corps of shop clerks, and the artisan associations had at least a proletarian element. Nonetheless, the civic guards of the capital cities were, in view of their social composition almost exclusively bourgeois militias. In Vienna, the national guard was dominated in the beginning by "mature men from all classes, wealthy citizens from the inner city, merchants, bankers, but also aristocrats, courtiers, senior state officials, attorneys and doctors." In Berlin as well, during the first weeks after the March Revolution, service in the new militia was performed, apart from merchants and master craftsmen, many "patriotic court suppliers," among them, especially by "privy councilors of all classes" and, in general, people "whom the [government] office and the green table [at which state officials held their meetings] had kept from public view."[26] Civic guards were founded to fill the law enforcement vacuum that arose after the military had retreated, to reduce lower class influence, which had played a key role in the uprisings, and to avoid a general arming of the people. Moreover, the presence of a large civic guard was intended to deflect criticism of the regular military, that also had to function as domestic law enforcement body and had involuntarily become a midwife of the revolution.

The civic guards were established as institutions against the revolutionary movement from the mostly proletarian suburbs. However, as bourgeois-conservative notables and state officials quickly left, especially in the Vienna National Guard and the Berlin Civic Guard, the petit bourgeois strata gained preponderance, democratic currents became more influential and the guards became ever "less dependable" for law enforcement from the authorities' viewpoint. The government and the authorities found themselves faced with the same problem that had led to the overthrow of the French "roi bourgeois" in February. The Paris national guard, founded in 1789, was no longer willing to support the discredited monarchy of Louis Philippe, turning instead to the revolutionary movement.

The extent to which the political self-perception of the municipal militias of the Austrian and (to a lesser extent) Prussian capitals had changed was already apparent a few weeks after the March Revolutions. On 7 May the Viennese National Guard elected a Central Committee, a kind of assembly of delegates of the municipal militia, that was in opposition to what had been until then the rather conservative leadership of the National Guard. More than two months later, on 18 July, a similar body, the Permanent Civic Guard Committee, was formed in Berlin for the same reasons. The Civic Guard Committee especially the Central Committee of the Viennese National Guard gained political influence because the municipal parliaments were elected only by the bourgeois minority of male residents, or in Vienna only by a minority of the bourgeoisie. Especially in the summer of 1848, the organs of municipal government in the two German capitals experienced a crisis of legitimacy. While the Berlin Civic Guard Committee not able to exploit this constellation and disappeared from the political stage without a trace in mid-September, the Central Committee of the Viennese National Guard was successful in becoming, temporarily, a center of power in competition with the institutions of municipal government.

The Viennese Central Committee dissolved itself after a short time. However, a committee of safety was founded in the Austrian capital, a new municipal center of power, in which the National Guard had considerable influence. In the "Committee of Burghers, National Guardsmen, and Students for the Maintenance of Quiet, Security and Order, and for the Preservation of Rights and Nations," as the new body was officially entitled, students, national guardsmen, and members of the city council worked together and thus filled, temporarily, the political vacuum that had arisen with the March and May Revolutions in Vienna. The group's two hundred member strong security committee was dominated by members of the National Guard, and armed students, the Academic Legion, with more than a thousand men.

Although the old powers were not put as much on the defensive in Berlin and were able to preserve their structures to a great extent, municipal polycentrism, the parallel existence of many new and old institutions competing against each other certainly did not come to an end with the disbanding of the Permanent Civic Guard Committee. An agile civic guard leadership, drifting politically leftwards from June 1848 onwards, and neighborhood associations loudly raised demands for rights of political participation.[27] In a number of other capitals, (unstable) polycratic structures also arose at the municipal level, against a background of a chronic crisis of identity and legitimacy of especially traditional city government institutions. In Paris, apart from city institutions, new government bodies as well as parliament, including the Luxembourg Commission, the national workshops, the national guard, police headquarters, and the radical clubs exerted considerable influence on events in the city, and the same was true in Rome (up to the beginning of 1849) especially for the quite independent civic guard and the influential radical *Circolo Popolare*.

Even though the Viennese National Guard and the Berlin Civic Guard did not stand solidly behind the "revolutionary camp" towards the end of the revolution and found themselves between the fronts in everyday conflicts, the authorities, for reasons of self-preservation, must have been interested in disbanding the polycratic structure in the capitals in their own favor. An important step in this direction was establishing absolutely loyal law enforcement organizations that did not develop an independent political existence. New organizations were also unavoidable from the authorities' viewpoint because the old gendarmes were numerically weak and had shown themselves totally overtaxed in revolutionary situations. A start was made in Paris with the mobile guard, a police-like militia, which was established on 26 February and consisted finally of 15,000 young men, mostly previously unskilled laborers. The Berlin police headquarters, directly responsible to the Prussian Minister of the Interior and thus in a politically rather strong position, followed this example, and established a 2,000 strong body of guards and constables. In Vienna, there was no comparable modernization of the police, as traditional authority was more greatly weakened and the situation more unstable.

The term constable, generally used by contemporaries for the new Berlin police force, awakens, not by chance, associations with the English police force. Police experts and the bourgeois public in the central European cities, especially in Berlin, were extremely impressed by the English police's response, especially their effective deployment of constables during the London Chartist demonstration on 10 April 1848. The British capital had had a modern police organization since

1829. At the beginning of 1848, with movements on the continent in mind and a new upswing in the Chartist movement, the number of constables was, however, increased to 4,800.

The Chartists planned a demonstration in front of parliament for 10 April to hand over to the M.P.'s a People's Charter, the third after 1838 and 1842. The demonstration was banned, but Chartist meetings allowed as long as they kept a respectable distance from parliament. This anti-Chartist policy was successful because many thousand constables, some armed, made a show of force (and the leader of the Chartists wanted to avoid an armed conflict). The military, with around 7,000 troops stationed in the direct surroundings of the Houses of Parliament, were kept in readiness, but were shielded from public view. "You will not see one soldier or one canon if it is not really necessary," was the Duke of Wellington's explanation of his tactics to the Prussian envoy Bunsen two days before the demonstration. Only if there is a defeat of the constables, as "the force of law" threatened, "then the troops will advance, then it is their time. But it is not good for any side when they are used instead of the police—the military should not be confused with the police, nor transformed into police."[28]

Moreover, the British authorities provided themselves with extra insurance in creating a sort of voluntary police reserve. Above all in March and April 1848, more than 80,000 males, mostly from the "middle class," were sworn in as special constables in London and surroundings. It was less the—very doubtful—military value of this militia that was important, but its political-psychological effect: the large number of special constables was an expression of the willingness of the bourgeoisie and middle class to suppress revolts by the lower classes, with force if necessary.

The constables, which had attracted a lot of interest even before 10 April 1848,[29] became an element in preventing revolutions. Apart from the civic guard, which continued to appear as police reserve during larger "excesses" (in the Prussian capital on 16 and 31 October), the regular army retained its central function as a potential weapon. Even before General Wrangel entered the city at the head of about 15,000 troops on 10 November, bringing to an end the Berlin Revolution, the garrison in the city was continually enlarged. At the end of March 1848, the first 2,500 soldiers returned; by mid-April the number increased to 6,000, and by mid-July to 11,000. In Paris, as well, the number of troops was successively increased, in view of possible future bloody conflicts, from around 10,000 men at the end of February to about 25,000 men directly before the beginning of the June uprising.

Improved civil war tactics, in which the military continued to play a central role, were, in general, an important consequence, which the old and new authorities drew from the experience gained during the revolution, especially in the capital cities. In Vienna, the old city walls were demolished in 1857, and replaced with a ring road, lined with a number of massive barracks. The new military fortresses—to guard train stations and main routes of entry—were planned to be strong enough to hold out until extra troops could be called in from the surrounding countryside to oppose (potential) revolutionaries. The Max II Barracks begun in 1860 in Munich—which had hardly been disturbed by the revolutionary unrest—resembled a "fortified castle" (Junkelmann) and was also the result of considerations arising from 1848. The thirty-three kilometer Paris city wall, with ring road and a circumferential railway, had already been built between 1841 and 1845, also as a result of older considerations of civil war tactics. The ring of forts surrounding the French capital survived the wall's dismantling, for similar reasons, and would play an important role in 1870/71.[30]

Considerations of military tactics, the modernization of the police (including the establishment of a political police), and furthermore an attempt at state control of the press were not the only as aspects of a post-1849 effort at preventing revolutions that were drawn, above all, from experiences gained in the revolutionary uprisings in the capital cities. Continental governments attempted to learn in other respects from London and England, as well as from Belgium, with its liberal constitution of 1831. Great Britain, as a constitutional monarchy with century old parliamentary traditions, had long granted a bourgeois class (even if a small one) rights of participation. Openness to reform among the English aristocracy and the upper "middle class" had turned the British Isles into a bulwark against revolution, socially as well. The Ten-Hours Bill, passed in 1847, but admittedly controversial until the outbreak of revolutions on the continent, may serve as an example of this.

Especially the Prussian crown, more open to these lessons than the Habsburgs, were aware that it had to gain the support and loyalty of the urban bourgeoisie and petit bourgeoisie to survive politically, in the long run. The Prussian Constitution of December 1848 and January 1850 (like the Austrian constitution of 1849 modeled on the Belgian constitution of 1831), the revised production code of January 1849, which increased the rights of guilds and thus fulfilled the demands of master artisan, or the three-class franchise, which met the wishes particularly of the liberal bourgeoisie for a suffrage system in which votes were weighted by the amount of taxes a voter paid, were the most important results of this willingness to learn. Constitutions, franchises and production code applied, of course, to the whole country. The trauma of "the revolution"—which forced the crown (in Austria) into temporary or (in Prussia) permanent concessions to the new elite, thrust the bourgeoisie and the middle classes in most European states into the arms of the old powers and assisted Louis Bonaparte in becoming president and then emperor—were decisively marked by developments and events in the respective national capitals. For this reason as well, the revolutions in the capitals produced long-term results.

Notes

For criticism and encouragement I would like to thank (apart from the participants in the Würzburg preparatory colloquium for this volume) Michael Grüttner.

1. See also (for the French and Prussian cities) the overview of Ursula E. Koch in this volume.
2. Quote from *National-Zeitung*, 19 April 1848; *Königlich privilegierte Berlinische Zeitung von Staats- und gelehrten Sachen*, better known as the *Vossische Zeitung*, of 28 June, 7 July, and 22 October 1848.
3. Thus the explanation of the delegates of the second congress of German democrats for their resolution to transfer the future national parliament from Frankfurt a.M. to Berlin. *Verhandlungen des 2. Demokraten-Kongresses in Berlin, Beilage zu den "Volksblättern"*, 32. In general, see W. Hardtwig, "Nationsbildung und Hauptstadtfrage. Berlin in der deutschen Revolution 1848/49," ini *Nationsbildung und Bürgerkultur in Deutschland 1500-1914* (Göttingen, 1994), 163-64
4. A summary of the debate on the German capital 1848/49 is in Wolfram Siemann, "Die deutsche Hauptstadtproblematik im 19. Jahrhundert," in H.-M. Körner and K. Wiegand (eds.), *Hauptstadt. Historische Perspektiven eines deutschen Themas* (Munich, 1995), esp. 252-56.
5. Quoted in ibid., 250.
6. See Paul Ginsborg, *Daniele Manin and the Venetian Revolution of 1848-49* (Cambridge, 1979), 32 n. 61.
7. See Karl-Joseph Hummel, *München in der Revolution von 1848/49* (Göttingen, 1987), 416. In comparison, the three largest Berlin engineering firms of A. Borsig, C.A. Egells, and F. Wöhlert respectively employed a good 1,000, nearly 800, and 380 people in 1848/49.
8. Figures for Paris, from Heidrun Homburg, "Kleingewerbe in den Hauptstädten Paris–Berlin. Wirtschaftliche Rahmenbedingungen und konjunkturelle Entwicklung im Vorfeld der Revolution von 1848—eine Skizze," in Ilja Mieck, Horst Möller, and Jürgen Voss (eds.), *Paris und Berlin in der Revolution 1848* (Sigmaringen, 1995), 142; for Berlin, Rüdiger Hachtmann, *Berlin 1848. Eine Politik- und Gesellschaftsgeschichte der Revolution* (Bonn, 1997), 71-79, esp. tables 2 and 3.
9. Among them (1847) were 1,600 workers in the shipyard of the Danube Steamship Company in Old Ofen. See Wolfgang Häusler, "Soziale Protestbewegungen in der bürgerlich-demokratischen Revolution," in Rudolf Jaworski and Robert Luft (eds.), *1848/49. Revolution in Ostmitteleuropa*, (Munich, 1996), 193; by the same author, *Von der Massenarmut zur Arbeiterbewegung. Demokratie und soziale Frage in der Wiener Revolution von 1848* (Munich, 1979), 70-71, 92; Laszlo Deme, *The Radical Left in the Hungarian Revolution of 1848* (New York, 1976), 51.
10. *Augsburger Allgemeine Zeitung*, 9 March 1847.
11. See Jürgen Kocka, *Arbeitsverhältnisse und Arbeiterexistenzen. Grundlagen der Klassenbildung im 19. Jahrhundert* (Bonn, 1990), 330. On the size of enterprises in Berlin crafts, Jürgen Bergmann, *Das Berliner Handwerk in den Frühphasen der Industrialisierung*, (Berlin, 1973), 158ff. On industrial production in the Prussian capital of Prussia: apart from Borsig, Egells and Wöhlert (n. 8) and the Royal Institute of Engineering and Iron Foundry in Moabit, which belonged to the Prussian *Seehandlung* (a sort of state company), in engineering alone, a leading sector of early industrialization, another five firms with between 100 amd 300 employees were in existence in 1848/49.
12. Quotes from Gustave Flaubert, *Sentimental Education*, trans. Robert Baldick (London, 1964), 289.
13. Adolf Wolff, *Berliner Revolutionschronik. Darstellung der Berliner Bewegungen im Jahre 1848 nach politischen, socialen und literarischen Beziehungen*, Vol. 1 (Berlin, 1851) (Reprint Leipzig 1979), 249-50.
14. Manfred Hettling, "Das Begräbnis der Märzgefallenen 1848 in Berlin," in Manfred Hettling and Paul Nolte (eds.), *Bürgerliche Feste* (Göttingen, 1993), 105.
15. *Vossische Zeitung*, 23 March 1848.
16. Quoted in Häusler, *Massenarmut,* 386.
17. Ibid., 392-93.
18. Friedrich Wilhelm IV to Camphausen on 1 June 1848, in Erich Brandenburg (ed.), *König Friedrich Wilhelms IV, Briefwechsel mit Ludolf Camphausen* (Berlin, 1906), 138.

19. More precise estimates are not possible because of high membership fluctuation and the instability of many associations. A number of associations existed only as "letter box companies," i.e., published a few flyers and disappeared again. On Paris and Berlin associations see the survey in Peter Amann, "The Paris Club Movement in 1848," in Roger Price (ed.), *Revolution and Reaction. 1848 and the Second French Republic* (London, 1975), 115-32 (estimates of total membership, 123); Hachtmann, *Berlin 1848*, 272-88 and 605-41. The organized womens' movement is not included here; on it see the essay by Gabriella Hauch in this volume.

20. On Venice, see Ginsborg, *Daniele Manin*, 236, 310-13; on Rome, Henry Hearder, "The Making of the Roman Republic, 1848-1849," *History* 60 (1975): 177; for Budapest, Deme, *The Radical Left*, 57, 77ff.; on Frankfurt, Michael Wettengel, *Die Revolution von 1848/49 im Rhein-Main-Raum* (Wiesbaden, 1989), 107ff., 205-12 as well as Ralf Roth, *Stadt und Bürgertum in Frankfurt am Main* (Munich, 1996), 419-20; on Munich, Hummel, *München*, 209-15. If the existence of a relatively large number of political associations in German (capital) cities is known, that may well be the result of the comparatively extensive level of research.

21. Berichte des Berliner Polizeipräsidenten an den preußischen Innenminister vom 20. Juli bzw. 27 Okt. 1848: Brandenburgisches Landeshauptarchiv, Rep. 30, Tit. 94, Nr. 14377, Bl. 4 u. Rs. bzw. Bl. 27 Rs. u. 28. On Vienna see Häusler, *Massenarmut*, 208.

22. Admittedly, this can only be maintained with (a high degree of) certainty for German associations.

23. Summary according to Häusler, *Massenarmut*, 312. On the Berlin Workers' Central Committee see the detailed account of F. Rogger, *"Wir helfen uns selbst!" Die kollektive Selbsthuilfe der Arbeiterverbrüderung 1848/49 und die individuelle Selbsthilfe Stefan Borns—Borns Leben, Entwicklung und seine Rezeption der zeitgenössischen Lehren* (Erlangen, 1986), esp. chapters 5 and 10. In German-speaking regions the comparatively early development of the labor movement in Berlin and Vienna (as well as in Leipzig and, with reservations, Cologne) was, however, rather an exception. On the workers movement in Frankfurt a.M., which varied in content and in organizational structure, see Wettengel, *Revolution in Rhein-Main-Raum*, 121-38, and on the admittedly marginal workers' education associations in the Bavarian capital, which joined the Workers' Fraternization, founded some two months previously in Berlin at the end of October 1848, see Hummel, *München*, 511-18.

24. On the revolution of 1848/49 in the three Anhalt duchies see Rüdiger Hachtmann, "... die Autoritäten haben einen Knacks erhalten"—Anhalt in der Revolution von 1848/49," in Hachtmann and G. Ziegler, *Parlamentarismus in Anhalt I: Die anhaltischen Landtagsabgeordneten und die Abgeordneten zur Deutschen Nationalversammlung 1848-1851* (Dessau, 1996), 3-23, esp. 12.

25. See, in summary, Rüdiger Hachtmann, "Die sozialen Unterschichten in der großstädtischen Revolution von 1848. Berlin, Wien und Paris im Vergleich," in Mieck, Möller and Voss (eds.), *Berlin und Paris*, esp. 125ff.

26. Quotes from J.A. Freiherr v. Helfert, *Geschichte der österreichischen Revolution im Zusammenhange mit der mitteleuropäischen Bewegung der Jahre 1848-1849*, Vol. 1 (Freiburg i.Br. and Vienna, 1907), 263; P. Boerner, *Erinnerungen eines Revolutionärs. Skizzen aus dem Jahre 1848*, Vol. 2 (Leipzig, 1920), 11; (Anon.), *Personen und Zustände Berlins seit dem 18. März 1848. Ein Beitrag zur künftigen Geschichte Preußens*, Vol. 1 (Leipzig, 1849), 7. (Helfert was a conservative deputy in the Austrian Reichstag, Boerner a spokesman for the democratic student body in Berlin.)

27. On Vienna, see also the survey by M. Seliger and K. Ucakar, *Wien, Politische Geschichte 1740-1934. Entwicklung und Bestimmungskräfte großstädtischer Politik,* Part 1: 1740-1895 (Vienna and Munich 1985), 216ff., 226; on Berlin, see Hachtmann, *Berlin 1848*, esp. 588-91, 635-41.

28. Chr. K.J. Freiherr von Bunsen, *Aus seinen Briefen und nach eigener Erinnerung geschildert von seiner Witwe*, Vol. 2 (Leipzig, 1869), 415.

29. During the 11 March 1848 session of the Berlin municipal parliament, a deputy, later a leading member of the conservative Patriotic Association, introduced a motion for the modernization of the municipal police along English lines. The motion was received with much applause, but it was never voted upon and implemented.

30. See M. Junkelmann. "Die Präsenz des Militärischen in der Hauptstadt," in Körner and Weigand (eds.), *Hauptstadt*, 130-33, quote on 132.

Assembly in tents on 20 April in Berlin (Illustrirte Zeitung, Leipzig, no. 253, 6 May 1848, 302)

Dissolution of the Prussian Constitutional National Assembly in Mielentz'schen Saale in Berlin, on 14 November (Illustrirte Zeitung, Leipzig, no. 283, 2 December 1848, 365)

Chapter 16

THE REVOLUTION AS URBAN EVENT

Hamburg and Lyon during the Revolutions of 1848-49

John Breuilly and *Iorwerth Prothero*

Second Cities as a Particular Site of Revolution

Defining Second Cities

Broadly speaking one can distinguish second cities from capital cities, large towns, "home towns" and the countryside. Capital cities were the sites of the most intense conflicts during the revolutions of 1848. However, the initial revolutions of the capitals could only be taken further if the majority of the population, located in the countryside, could be persuaded to support of the revolution, or at least to not support the counter-revolution. In this, the important role for large towns and "home towns" becomes clear. These served as a clearing-place for agricultural products, local administration, and the supply of goods and services and, during the revolution, frequently provided the leadership and rallying points for rural action.

This rough and ready classification leaves aside what could be termed "second cities," by which we mean very large cities (by contemporary standards) of 100,000 inhabitants or more which were not capitals of territorial states. There were some twenty such cities in Europe in 1848: nine in Britain, three in France, two in Germany, three in Italy, and three elsewhere. Against this one can note some twenty-one capital cities with over 100,000 inhabitants. The average size of these capital cities was much larger than that of these second cities, which means that the total population of capital cities was much higher than that of second cities. This continued to be the case for all countries, with the notable exception of the United Kingdom (despite a London population of over two million). Second cities in continental Europe were demographically inferior to both capital cities and the countryside.

The experiences of these second cities in 1848/49 varied enormously. Some witnessed violent conflict comparable, given their smaller size, to that of capital cities such as Paris, Berlin, Vienna, and Milan. Some were fairly quiet. These second cities were also very diverse, some owing their existence primarily to their function as a regional capital, some to their central position in networks of communication and trade, some to the growth of new manufacturing.

All these negative points might suggest that the concept of the second city can hardly be used as a positive type for the study of revolution in 1848. Yet, arguably, it is precisely this diversity that offers an opportunity for the comparative historian. If there are common patterns within this group of cities, this would suggest a distinctively urban dimension to revolution. There are three major grounds on which second cities can be compared: demographic, sociological, regional.

Demography

Second cities represented the most dense clusters of population outside the capital cities. Given that these cities did not have the political significance of the capitals, and so did not attract as much state-wide attention (e.g., through the convening of parliaments and the work of government), one could explore how far such population densities encouraged particular kinds of politics without the complications of the capitals. Did second cities, whether violent or quiet, exhibit types of collective action that were not possible in villages, "home towns," or even larger towns, but lacked the national significance of such action in the capital cities? Could they sustain similar kinds of political communication (posters, pamphlets, street oratory) to those of the capital cities? Were there particular kinds of conflict over law and order (e.g., the role of soldiers, disputes over a citizen's militia) in second cities?

Sociology

Whatever the specific functions of second cities, they exhibited many occupational similarities. "Core" occupations vary with the type of city. Where trade dominates these will be merchants and clerks; in manufacturing centers, entrepreneurs and their workforce; in ports, ship owners, sailors, and dock workers. However, there was a mixture of these occupations. Furthermore, these occupations only constituted a minority of the whole population. Running a second city required large numbers of artisans, shopkeepers, street traders, professional people, an army of casual laborers to fetch and carry in an age before the electrical and internal combustion engines; a mass of domestic servants for the elite as well as many of the middling ranks. These groups were largely immune from the influences of the central political apparatus of capital cities and the notables of the surrounding countryside. Arguably one can get a "purer" view of the interests, values, and modes of action of urban social groups in second cities than anywhere else.

This has implications for the social dimensions of revolution. If artisans, a mass of retailers and petty traders, domestic servants and casual unskilled laborers made up much of the "popular" classes in second cities, were these reflected in group interests and forms of action? Or did they take their lead from the "core" occupations? Generally speaking, bourgeois elites dominated second cities. But did domination vary with the type of elite and did this shape the relationship between elites and popular classes? Were there similar problems for the maintenance of order whatever the particular make-up of the urban elite? Did different kinds of elites respond to challenges from below in different ways?

Regional

The second city could act as a center for its region. If there was a regional dimension to revolution, the provincial city could become its center. The second city, with its larger supply of political activists and resources (printing presses, access to national and international news) compared to the rest of the region could supply leadership and a focus for action and organization. Conversely, second cities might feel isolated from the surrounding countryside.

Lyon and Hamburg

Why these Two Cities?

We are engaged in a research project comparing the cultural history of mid-nineteenth century Hamburg, Lyon, and Manchester.[1] These cities are comparable as second cities, with similar growth rates, and dominated by a merchant/manufacturer elite. They were centers of liberal opinion. They offer opportunities to compare bourgeois and popular cultures across national boundaries in a focused way.

We do not place these cities within narrower typologies (textile center, port) because we do not believe that such cities easily fall into such types or that comparison requires one to compare "typical" cases. Lyon and Hamburg are not "typical" of anywhere else. Rather, we contend that similar sizes, growth rates, and the dominance of international trade in the life of these cities makes them comparable. Such comparisons should point up differences as well as similarities.

About the Cities

LYON

Lyon is located where the Rhône and the Saône meet and form a peninsula. In 1848, it was one of the chief manufacturing centers on the Continent, its economic life centered on the import, weaving, and export of silk, mainly abroad. While silk-weaving was scattered throughout the city, the biggest concentration was in the Croix-Rousse, the high plateau north of the peninsula looking down on the city. But the greatest expansion of the city in the century was across the Rhône, particularly in the Guillotière, an area of industry and working-class dwellings.

The boundaries of the official city enclosed the peninsula and the right bank of the Saône. With the Piedmontese frontier not far away, Lyon was an important military center. After the 1831 uprising, when the silk-weavers of the Croix-Rousse defeated the troops and took over the city, and the 1834 uprising, which was more widespread, the government constructed a ring of forts, which marked the real limits of the conurbation, including the three fast-growing suburbs that were not officially part of the city but had their own municipal government—Vaise, Croix-Rousse, and Guillotière.By mid-century the total population of Lyon and its suburbs was about 270,000, nearly double what it had been in 1800.This was due to a massive immigration, mostly from southeastern France, especially the Dauphiné, but also including many from Savoy and North Italy, Switzerland, and southern Germany.

The size of the city promoted geographical specialization. The aristocratic, rentier class tended to live in the rich and fashionable Bellecour/Ainay area, the center of the luxury trade.The Terreaux area further north was the administrative and business center, the area of bourgeois firms and dwellings (also found across the Rhône at the Brotteaux). Unpleasant and noxious industries tended to be in the suburbs, and the old, poor parishes on the right-bank of the Saone were inhabited by impoverished plain silk-weavers.The skilled fancy-weavers concentrated in the suburbs, especially the Croix-Rousse, where the sale of religious properties in the revolution had led to extensive settlement using the new big Jacquard looms in large rooms in apartment blocks on the slopes of the hill.The Guillotière had recently been transformed into a poor working-class suburb, containing a variety of industrial occupations, especially metallurgical, chemical, glass, and candle and soap manufacture, as well as docks and boatyards.There was therefore a general distinction between a commercial center and industrial suburbs where workers lived and worked.

The dominant economic elites were in the silk industry. Silk merchants bought thrown silk, and sold it to manufacturers [*fabricants*] who had it woven and then sold the finished goods. The importance of credit meant that many merchant firms were also bankers, and there were close commercial, credit and social links between merchants/bankers and manufacturers. There were other important industries, notably dyeing (closely connected with silk), chemicals (closely connected with dyeing), and engineering.

The silk-manufacturers did not have weaving done on their own premises but gave work out to master-weavers [*chefs d'atelier*], on whose looms the weaving was done by themselves, family members, journeymen [*compagnons*] or other wage-earners. The main industrial conflicts in the industry pitted the manufacturers against the masters and journeymen. In such a large city there was a large service sector, an extensive petit bourgeoisie, and many workers in clothing (hatters, tailors, and shoemakers) and building, all tending to live in the suburbs. There were also many laborers, including those working on river navigation.

Lyon was the economic center of an extensive region, and its domination grew in the century. Large numbers were involved in rearing silk-worms (as far afield as northern Italy), producing raw silk, and throwing it.The putting-out of plain silk-weaving to cheaper proto-industrial rural weavers, as well as the employment of female labor in unmechanized rural factories, grew steadily from the 1820s, and by 1840 over half the looms working for Lyon manufacturers were rural. Lyon was a transport center and river navigation was crucial to the region. Lyon acted as a market center and entrepot for regional products. The profits from the trade in silk financed transport developments, and made Lyon a great capital market and stock exchange center that promoted industrial development and coal and iron extraction in the region, and Lyon bankers had close relations on equal terms with Paris and Geneva bankers

All this made Lyon the center of its region, exerting great influence on the countryside and neighboring towns. The local population that flocked to the city retained their local links and there was much two-way mobility. Many rich Lyonnais owned rural land and provoked local opposition. Peasant proprietors were often hostile to Lyon bankers and merchants who lent to them, and appropriated or forced the sale of the land of debtors.

HAMBURG

Hamburg was a republican city-state, one of only four non-monarchical states within the German Confederation. It prided itself on having no officially defined, privileged upper class. The city-state lived by entrepôt trade. The general pattern was the importation of colonial and British manufactured or semi-manufactured goods (especially cotton), and the export of food and raw materials from a hinterland that extended beyond the German states. Hamburg's position at the mouth of the Elbe and on the western side of the landmass of Schleswig-Holstein that juts north, dividing the North Sea from the Baltic, placed the city in an ideal position for land and river-borne trade to and from the south and east and sea-borne trade to and from the west. The expansion of trade since the end of the Napoleonic wars, especially between Britain and the continent, the liberalizing, by Britain, of third-party trade with its colonies, and the opening of trade with the newly independent states of South America, all contributed to Hamburg's economic growth.

Around 1840, the city-state of Hamburg had a population of at least 140,000. By 1866, a more accurate census than earlier ones estimated the population of the city with the two suburbs of St. Georg and St. Pauli at some 220,000, to which one must add about another 80,000 living in the rural hinterland that belonged to the city-state. There had been rapid growth since the end of French occupation. Growth was fastest in the suburbs where land and housing was cheaper and the initial population less dense.

Demographic growth was accompanied by geographical specialization. The area immediately by the river and the suburbs housed the increasingly dense and poorer classes. The areas around the lake stretching north of the Elbe, the Innen-Alster and the Außen-Alster, were where richer inhabitants of the city lived, if they had not built themselves villas in the rural parts of the city-state or further afield. Nevertheless, there was still much intermixing within particular districts where social differences were registered through type of dwelling or location within buildings.

A merchant elite dominated the city, unchallenged by landowners, state officials or manufacturers, and aided by a subordinate professional class. This dominance was organized through the constitution of 1712 (restored after the removal of French occupation in 1814) in which executive power lay with a self-selected Senate consisting mainly of merchants. There was a good deal of intermarriage between the chief merchant families. The Hamburg "parliament," the *Erbgesessene Bürgerschaft*, was not an elected body but consisted of owners of real estate in the city and had little political power. Day-to-day government was in the hands of "deputations" confined to members of the Lutheran church. The accent was on cheap and minimal government. As in Lyon this elite was unostentatious and little given to enthusiastic charity.

Arrayed beneath the tiny minority of rich merchants and their interlinked families was a complex social and institutional structure. There were the "core" occupations associated with a trading city: sailors, dockers, and clerks. But these were outnumbered by the kinds of occupations one finds in any large city of the time: domestic servants, artisans, casual laborers. There was little in the way of an industrial labor force; indeed, Hamburg had lost most of the shipbuilding, brewing, and sugar-processing industries it had possessed in the previous century. A large section of the workforce was nominally independent—petty traders, small masters, various professional people. Whereas the trading sector of the economy was subject to minimal restriction, the rest of the economy was regulated through guilds, tolls and controls over movement [*Torsperre*].

The "hungry forties" had reduced even many of the middling orders to desperate straits, leading to expressions of anger against those both higher and lower in the social scale. "Citizens' Associations" demanded more open and accountable government. Among artisans there developed both occupational and general organization, demanding guild reform or abolition. There had been some sporadic disorder, for example expressed against Jews who had their own communal institutions and were excluded from government and the guilds. Some of the conflicts divided the popular classes, e.g., masters and journeymen, residents and foreigners, Jews and Christians, but there was also scope for a common hostility to the oligarchic and exclusive institutions of government.

Hamburg was separated politically from the surrounding territory as it was an independent city-state. In economic and demographic terms the region mattered more. Population growth was based on immigration from neighboring states. Surrounding agrarian areas were oriented towards supplying Hamburg with food. Hamburg was concerned with the policies pursued by neighboring states, especially anything that might threaten trade routes, but it relied on diplomacy and economic influence. Hamburg was a cultural center, with its reputation as a liberal publishing center and as a conduit for the introduction of English fashions and manners into Germany. People with disposable income came to Hamburg to spend it on luxury goods. The growing tensions between Danish and German speakers in Schleswig pulled Hamburg opinion into the national question.

The Course of Revolution in Lyon and Hamburg

Lyon

Legitimism was weak in Lyon and Orléanist members of the elite ran the city and were elected to the Chamber of Deputies. However Orléanism lacked popular support. There was a growing liberal opposition to Orléanism, leading to local electoral successes, and sometimes taking the form of moderate republicanism. Campaigns among the silk-weavers had led to uprisings in 1831 and 1834, the latter being largely republican, and Lyon remained a center of popular radical republicanism.

The revolution in Paris led to local changes and transfers of power. As in other large cities there was a municipal revolution. While the Prefect handed over his powers to a self-appointed committee of journalists connected with the moderate republican newspaper, the *Censeur*, a group of liberals and moderate republicans took over at the town hall, with Laforest as the new mayor. However, in contrast to other French cities, popular action was also important; a crowd came down from the Croix-Rousse, paraded through the city, gathering numbers as they went, and enforced the immediate proclamation of a republic at the Town Hall. The following day similar action imposed a substantial enlargement of the municipal central committee to include radicals and workers. Similar revolutionary committees were established in the suburban communes. The red flag flew over the Town Hall and for three days the crowds were in control of Lyon. Workers on the Croix-Rousse formed armed militias, especially the notorious "Voraces," took over the forts and seized the cannon from the troops.

On 28 February Emmanuel Arago arrived as the commissioner appointed by the Provisional Government, removed the red flag and tried to restore order with the cooperation of the Central Committee, increasingly dominated by moderates. He established public relief works in National Workshops, secured a government order for silk flags, set up a Labor Commission to settle disputes between employers and workers, and formed a Mobile Guard to strengthen his authority and take young men off the streets. But in general he proved ineffective. Radicals grew increasingly disillusioned with the moderate Central Committee, built up an opposition movement centered on a Democratic Association, and Arago failed to suppress or disarm the workers' militias or retrieve cannons seized on the Croix-Rousse, while the national workshops were a drain on finances. The elections of National Guard officers produced conservative victories, and the new officers campaigned against the Central Committee.

The republican veteran of secret societies, Martin-Bernard, arrived as Arago's deputy and then replacement, and the elections to the Constituent Assembly in April, in which there were rival but overlapping slates, were surprisingly favorable for the conservatives. Lyon was part of the Rhône constituency, and while the city voted radical, the rural areas voted conservative. The result was the election of seven conservatives, three moderates, and four radicals. This success encouraged the conservatives. There was a conservative campaign against the Central Committee and the expense of the national workshops, which secured the election of a new, conservative-dominated municipal council.

An uprising in Lyon in June to accompany the Paris one was narrowly averted, because of a concentration of troops and because Martin-Bernard had delayed the implementation of the changes at the national workshops which caused disturbances elsewhere. In July, Ambert became prefect and dissolved and disarmed all the local National Guards, ended the National Workshops, suppressed the Mobile Guard, extended Lyon police authority to the suburbs, purged local officials, and engaged in systematic repression of radicals for the rest of the year. But radical strength remained undiminished, and was repeatedly demonstrated in local elections, producing a strong minority in the city municipal council and overwhelming domination in the Croix-Rousse and Guillotière. While a conservative, Rivet, won a Rhône by-election in September, the radical Raspail secured a majority in Lyon, Croix-Rousse, and Guillotière, and although in the presidential election Louis-Napoleon obtained most votes, Raspail and Ledru-Rollin did well.

After Napoleon's victory repression intensified, especially with the arrival in February 1849 of Bugeaud as military commander. He forbade commemorations of the February Revolution, the wearing of red bonnets or the planting of trees of liberty, harassed the radical press and dissolved clubs. But the elections to the Legislative Assembly in May 1849 produced a stunning radical victory, including the election of five workers, with almost the whole of the garrison voting red. However, a uprising on the Croix-Rousse in June, to accompany the Paris one, was easily crushed, and martial law was imposed, which continued in Lyon after it was lifted in Paris. This enabled more intense repression, especially after Napoleon's appointment of a non-parliamentary government in October 1849, and the arrival in May 1850 of Castellane as military commander. Political clubs and cafés were closed, the opposition press was ended, and every radical institution was destroyed except for the municipal councils, to which radicals were regularly re-elected, despite franchise restrictions. The continuing strength of popular radicalism was revealed in the by-election in July 1849 and the refusal of the Rhône council in September 1850 to support a revision of the constitution to allow the president to stand for reelection. There was hardly any organization or means of public expression left for Castellane to suppress when he enforced the coup d'état in December 1851.

Hamburg

Already in January 1848 demands for political reform had been submitted to the Hamburg Senate, and before the February Days well-attended meetings of the Real Property Owners' Association [*Grundeigentümer-Verein*] had called for the separation of justice from administration and reform of the deputations. News of revolution in Paris and concessions made in late February in the southern and western German states aroused popular responses in Hamburg and stimulated the Senate to declare on 1 March that it would place a comprehensive reform program before the *Bürgerschaft*. However, it was too late to head off challenges, a number of reform meetings took place in different parts of the city, involving crowds and clashes with the militia, and the Senate was losing control.

To head off opposition, it announced the formation of a reform deputation, but a mass meeting on 10 March in the *Tonhalle* in the neighboring town of Altona criticized the basis of the reform deputation and agreed upon a twelve-point program which went beyond the reforms the Senate had been prepared to consider. On 11 March the Citizens' Association [*Bürger Verein*] at a well-attended meeting supported the twelve-point program, adding a thirteenth demanding abolition of the guilds. Democrats began to consider the need for more direct action, although they thought peaceful pressure and use of new freedoms would suffice. There was a good deal of hope in the reform deputation, especially as a leading liberal, Baumeister, was a member.

But political divisions were emerging, for example, in the Real Property Owners' Association, over the issue of a representative constitution. Conversely many merchants thought the twelve-point program went too far. The *Commerz-Deputation* [commercial delegation], a merchant body, did not oppose a representative assembly but only if elected on a class franchise, with the Senate having life-long office, some degree of self-renewing powers, and an absolute veto.

April was fairly calm as political groups devoted energies to the elections to the German National Assembly. Within the Reform Deputation Baumeister trod a delicate line, suggesting that the deputation confine itself to issuing an electoral law (with a weighted franchise) and leave subsequent work to a constituent assembly and the German National Assembly. The deputation submitted three draft constitutions in June—two of which largely kept to the present arrangements. Baumeister proposed another, more democratic program. Only once it had become clear that most of the "liberals" on the Deputation were opposed to significant reform did a movement grow demanding that Hamburg have its own constituent assembly.

Democrats by now had developed various techniques of organization and agitation. Already in April protests concerning restrictions on the franchise for elections to the German National Assembly had secured the right to vote of all adult males deemed to be members of the city-state. Waning interest by early summer in the work of the National Assembly led to a renewal of demands for state reform. From July this was coordinated through the *Zentralkomitee der verbundenen Vereine* [ZVV; Central Committee of the Affiliated Associations], which, by August, was demanding a constituent assembly. This was too much for two of the members—the *Deutsche Klub* [German Club] and the *Bürgerverein St. Pauli* [St. Pauli Citizens' Association] which withdrew from the ZVV. Three of the leading figures at the 7 August meeting, that had demanded the constituent assembly, were arrested. This led to an escalation of pressure as protest meetings formed demanding the release of those arrested and the calling of a constituent assembly. By the middle of August even the stock exchange had taken up this demand and the Senate agreed to it at the beginning of September.

The end of September and most of October was taken up with the elections of the *Konstituante*. "Advanced" liberals and democrats won a majority in the elections and proceeded with the work of drawing up a constitution. However, this work proceeded as counter-revolution gathered pace elsewhere. Only by June 1849 did the assembly have a draft constitution prepared, the central feature being a sovereign representative assembly elected on the basis of universal manhood suffrage but also stipulating that the state take on a range of social tasks, including the free provision of elementary education.

In August 1849 Prussian soldiers entered the city on the way back from Schleswig-Holstein. The real purpose was to intimidate the popular movement. Opposition was forcibly repressed. In September freedom of association was removed and a commission to consider the draft constitution established by the Senate. The Senate waited until June 1850 before it dissolved the *Konstituante*. The revolution was over in Hamburg.

Second Cities and the Politics of Revolution

The Politics of the Street

LYON

The republic was ushered in by street demonstrations. These were largely free of violence and took the form of processions, drawing on models that had been put to political use in 1830. The same characteristics marked the actions during the next few days to destroy the looms at establishments employing cheap labor, particularly the religious Providences. These were not riots but disciplined, premeditated, and ritualized actions.

Street actions drew on established practices like Carnival; a ceremony of the funeral of legitimism on 12 March drew on the Shrovetide wickerman. One model for street action was provided by fairs held in the suburbs, organized by volunteers, funded by voluntary subscriptions, and announced by a parade around the whole city. This was the model for a ceremony on 12 March in the Croix-Rousse, with a parade of the whole city behind a red bonnet. There were similar ceremonies to plant Trees of Liberty in other suburbs; their radical tone was shown by the red bonnet, and the absence of priests and the army.

However, a private initiative to commemorate the 1834 uprising was taken over by Arago and the municipal authorities, and combined with the planting of a Tree of Liberty at a huge official ceremony on 9 April in the city, involving a procession, military bands, pupils, and staff from the municipal educational institutions and faculties, and speeches. Over the following weeks there was a spate of tree plantings all over the city, but their character changed from the more plebeian earlier ones, as they now involved musical bands, the local National Guard in the place of honor, speeches, and the participation of the clergy. This marked an attempt to tame the threatening character of earlier tree-planting ceremonies.

However, all were ended by the municipal authorities in mid-May. While conservatives saw them as threats to work, trade, and order, and as rowdy occasions for drunkenness and sex, radicals also saw them as wasting money and time, and recognized the growing manipulation by the clergy and the rich. Nevertheless, some street demonstrations had a clearly radical character. A huge crowd on 30 March, including National Guardsmen and mutinous troops, saw off the volunteer legion departing to liberate Savoy, a ceremony reminiscent of official departures from the city. Later that day, the crowd forced the liberation of a man seized by the military authorities for spreading radical propaganda, and the next day he was paraded around the city in a triumphal procession.

The central radical organization did organize three great demonstrations of its own: a petition to Arago on 27 March, a procession on 22 April to publicize the names of radical election candidates, and a protest on 1 May against election frauds. These were publicized through the political club delegates, and engaged in a traditional tour of the city with the emphasis on discipline, a band at the head and the participants marching in the appropriate place as members of political clubs, trades or national workshops, each with its flag. The only shout allowed was "Vive la République."

The 1 May demonstration was the last one, and was overshadowed by a great military review by the new army commander. Radicals were uneasy about street politics. They felt such actions associated radicalism with anarchy and disorder, alienated the small property owners that they were trying to win over, were of doubtful effectiveness, and carried risks of disorder or repression. With the law in June against processions, the radicals therefore called a halt to demonstrations. Radicalism was not necessarily in favor of street activity, and radical organization was meant to be a substitute for it.

However, the radical leadership did not have complete control of popular action, while growing repression weakened radical organization and provided more occasions for resentment. Thus local and national elections saw spontaneous demonstrations, and the burning in effigy of enemies like Rivet in September and Cavaignac in December. After the closure of the National Workshops, unemployed workers staged sit-ins in fashionable areas and cafés run by conservatives and refused to pay or budge, and clashed with troops sent to disperse them. Crowds resisted the re-imposition of tolls on the river bridges. The start of rebuilding the toll wall at the top of the hill between the city and the Croix-Rousse, which the local population had begun to demolish after February, provoked resistance, processions including youths and women, and effigy-burning. The traditional processions of those drawn to be conscripted into the army were also turned into political demonstrations.

The election of Louis-Napoleon in December provoked greater unity and discipline among radicals, while the intensified repression led to greater radical control of popular action. Dinners were held, as family occasions involving males and females, to commemorate the execution of Louis XVI and the February Revolution, and in connection with the national election in May 1849, when there were fewer demonstrations than previously.

The possibilities of radical action were undermined by the martial law after the June uprising. Republican newspapers were banned, all but election meetings prevented, cafés used by radicals closed down, associations persecuted. Yet radicals maintained popular support, as the success of Favre in the July by-election showed. Crowds gathered to cheer the lawyers defending radicals on trial, and in 1851 they discovered a new means of public expression in the form of a series of radicals' funerals in February and March 1851, when huge crowds paraded through the city to the cemetery for a civil burial without priests. In the end, on dubious legal authority, Castellane forbade even this and so removed the last remaining manifestation of outdoor expression.

HAMBURG

Compared to Lyon there was far less in the way of street politics in Hamburg, and what there was seems less organized and less indebted to traditions of collective action. At the beginning of the revolution there were two demonstrations, on 3 and 13 March, the second of which led to the first killing of a demonstrator. However, the decisive political step forward came with an indoor meeting on 10 March at the *Tonhalle* in Altona. Some subsequent street actions came about for less directly political reasons, as when a crowd gathered at the railway station on 27 March to greet Prussian soldiers on their way to support the German cause in Schleswig-Holstein, or the unrest that followed a song-festival on the *Sternschanze* on 1 April.

More political in intent were demonstrations in early April protesting against planned restrictions on elections to the German National Assembly. Later demonstrations, sometimes leading to violence, seem less obviously political, for example the attack on a police watch and the burning of a gatehouse on 9 June, following a popular festival in St. Georg, was an expression of resentment against the *Torsperre*. A demonstration on 11 August about abuses in a mental hospital ended up as a protest against the *Torsperre*.

August saw a revival of more focused political assemblies as democrats demanded a constituent assembly. Where such pressures led to attempts at repression, as with the arrests of three leaders figures on 10 August, this triggered further street protests. By September there were instances of violent conflict between the militia and crowds. September and October were dominated by elections to the constituent assembly, with many speeches and the posting of numerous election placards in the open-air. With polarization in the city and examples of counter-revolution elsewhere, workers' groups started to engage in ostentatious drilling and there were demands for an arming of the people. This polarization culminated in the protests over the entry of Prussian soldiers in August 1849 but the display of force by the authorities forced politics off the streets.

There was a narrower repertoire of traditions of collective action to call upon in Hamburg compared to Lyon. After an event, political or not, brought people out on to street, crowds of some hundreds might gather at the entrances to the city and attack the gates, or march through the streets, or perform a *Katzenmusik* [German charivari] at the homes of well-known reactionaries. There were a few examples of barricade building, but these appear symbolic rather than serious attempts to achieve popular control. Often it was onlookers who got involved, as happened when the militia attacked with bayonets, and members of the crowd responded with stone-throwing and sticks.

There were no massive demonstrations and no "uprisings." In Hamburg, there was neither a radical leadership prepared to organize such a politics nor a core of popular support for such actions. The only example of intimidation was the demonstration organized on 10 September to force the release of people arrested at an earlier demonstration. Insofar as there was a consistent target of crowd action it appears to have been the *Torsperre*. The democratic press usually condemned such actions. Indeed, the St. Pauli Citizens' Association organized a security watch to help the militia.

Such unrest as there was appears to have largely ended by September. Organized workers moved increasingly into occupational and general labor associations with links beyond the city-state. The capacity of democrats to win support in elections to the constituent assembly and to dominate that assembly meant they felt no need to resort to direct action. There was a brief renewal of crowd action and violence on 13 August 1849 as all forms of politics were threatened by the entry of Prussian soldiers.

The Development of Political Organization: Elections and Clubs

LYON

One distinctive feature of second cities is the extent of political organization. This partly reflects the prior existence of organizations, including unpolitical ones like voluntary associations, professional and literary clubs, convivial circles, and freemasonry, all present in Lyon. Political organizations were not new in Lyon, but after 1834 they became clandestine, or took other forms, like friendly, trade, educational, and cooperative societies. These could provide models for political organization in 1848, and some radical leaders during the Second Republic had been involved in earlier organizations. The notorious Voraces was a breakaway club from the main journeymen silk-weavers' organization, with strong convivial functions, while the Carbonari were a former secret society. Trade organizations were an important element in mobilizing radical activity in 1848 and 1849.

Initially most political groups looked to the new Central Committee and its sub-committees, and to the government commissioner, to restore order and security, and to meet the pressing needs of the poor. But soon those opposed to the drift of policy of the Central Committee turned to other theaters of action, while radicals, fearful of the continuing influence of enemies of the new republic, pushed organization as an alternative to spontaneous street action. National Guard formations appeared, particularly in the richer quarters, where members were able to buy their own uniforms and arms, and they quickly mobilized to put pressure on Arago over arming workers, interference in religious establishments and financial policies. When regular elections of National Guard officers were held, a conservative committee organized the victory of conservatives, and these then engaged in a campaign against the Central Committee and ultimately secured its dissolution to be replaced by a regularly elected conservative municipal council.

The weaver Joseph Benoît on 26 February established a Democratic Society to influence the Central Committee and neutralize the enemies of the new republic. However, the principal concern was the forthcoming elections to the new Constituent Assembly, and these were the main impetus to political organization, in the form of clubs seeking to win over new voters. The Democratic Society expanded and established links with suburban clubs to form a Central Democratic Club, which adopted a radical platform of manhood suffrage, election of all officials, free and equal education for all, progressive income tax, state credit, and nationalization of transport, mining and insurance. A separate Workers' Electoral Committee, grouping forty trade societies, soon merged with the Central Democratic Club. One hundred thirty-eight clubs were founded in Lyon of which three quarters were affiliated to the Central Democratic Club and United Trades, totaling 8,700 members. It established its own newspaper, the *Tribun du Peuple*, formed clubs in neighboring towns, and prepared an election slate.

A conservative General Committee of Clubs grouped thirty-one clubs, including National Guard ones, and worked out a common slate with a General Committee of Rural Cantons and, through local landowners, conducted propaganda and formed rural clubs. As a result, Arago's hope of electing moderate republicans was defeated; in a high poll Lyon voted for the radicals and the countryside for conservatives, to produce a mixed representation.

After the election, the number of clubs dropped, and the Central Democratic Club disbanded. Although it was re-established for the Lyon municipal election in June, it had only fifty club delegates and was poorly organized, and lost. It was revived again for the regular municipal elections in July, and this time as many radicals as conservatives were elected for Lyon, while in the suburban municipalities, radicals won overwhelmingly. This was repeated in new suburban and departmental elections in August, and in Raspail's support in the by-election in September. It was the large number of elections in 1848 that was responsible for the clubs. However, repression in the latter part of 1848 led a number of radicals to retreat into secret societies, especially the Society of the Rights of Man, and into cooperative trading societies, mainly on the Croix-Rousse, largely as front organizations.

Radicals were split between Ledru-Rollin and Raspail in the presidential election. Louis-Napoleon won easily, but afterwards radical activity increased and radicals participated in the national campaign led by Republican Solidarity centered in Paris to unify the left for the elections to the Legislative Assembly. As political clubs were shut down, new ones were opened to replace them, or instead they formed educational clubs [*cercles*]. After electoral success, the political clubs declined, and with martial law and the law against clubs after the June uprising, radical organization focused on the defense of those put on trial for the uprising, election committees, cooperative societies, private or secret political societies and convivial clubs [*chambrées*]. With the intense repression of the first half of 1850, organization became more secret and informal.

Political organization thus built on established groupings and figures, and the form depended on the extent and nature of political freedom or repression. The chief impetus to formal open organization was elections, with the result that such organization was not continuous but episodic. To a large degree political action rested on informal and enduring trade, cooperative and convivial bodies, and centered on café meetings.

HAMBURG

As in Lyon, there existed a network of associations, mainly non-political, which could form the nucleus of political action in the revolution. The merchant elite already had close informal connections, control over governmental institutions, and formal organization in such bodies as the *Commerz-Deputation*. Those seeking moderate reforms could be found in the *Patriotische Gesellschaft* [Patriotic Society]. More radical petit bourgeois opinions—small merchants, master artisans, retailers—organized in such bodies as the Citizens' Association and the Real Property Owners' Association [*Grundeigentümer-Verein*]. Labor concerns were voiced through the *Bildungsverein für Arbeiter* [Workers' Educational Association] and the *Verein zur Hebung des Gewerbestandes* [Association for the Advancement of the Trades].

With the outbreak of the revolution these organizations expanded, grew explicitly political, and patronized the formation of other, similar associations, especially in the less well organized suburbs. Typical was the deliberate break the Workers' Educational Association made with its patron, the Patriotic Society. Elite groups had been less formally organized, and they founded new associations, such as the German Club representing moderate liberal views.

Nevertheless, the elections to the German National Assembly are what primarily stimulated explicit and polarized political organization. Hamburg could elect three deputies. Very quickly a "merchant," a liberal and a radical "slate" formed, although it is typical that one man, the prominent moderate liberal Heckscher, figured on both of the first two. The merchant slate won easily, indicating a consensus that Hamburg had to ensure that its interests as a trading center were properly defended at the national level.

When it came to internal politics, consensus disappeared. By July, those demanding reform were frustrated by the lack of progress at Frankfurt or on the part of the Hamburg Senate. This sparked off a new wave of political organization, partly to channel and partly to control popular discontent. In that month the Central Committee of Affiliated Associations [ZVV] was formed to push forward the stalled reform program. There had been some prior attempts to coordinate oppositional politics but these had never been important. The ZVV consisted of seven organizations: the German Club, the *Gesellschaft für die politischen und sozialen Interessen der Juden* [Society for the Political and Social Interests of the Jews], *Erste politische Assoziation* [First Political Association], the St. Pauli Citizens' Association, the Citizens' Association, the Association for the Advancement of the Trades, and the Workers' Educational Association. The first four were moderate liberal, looking to the German club for a lead, while the other three represented democratic and labor interests. In August, with demonstrations in favor of a constituent assembly and arrests by the authorities, these seven were joined by more associations. By January 1849 there were thirteen affiliated organizations. These affiliated clubs represented a shift to the left as moderate liberal bodies such as the Deutsche Klub left the ZVV.

Political organization thus developed more belatedly than in Lyon and was also less extensive in terms of the number of organizations and members. It is difficult to estimate membership as records are incomplete and because of the practice of affiliating organizations rather than individuals. In any case, attendances are better indicators of popularity. One estimate is that something like 3,500 people were active in the associations, perhaps 2,000 of them as formal members. About two-thirds of these 2,000 activists were in the more democratic associations and about one-third in the moderate liberal ones. The figure of 3,500 represented about 10 percent of the electorate.

Political organization reached its high point during the elections for the *Konstituante* in September/October 1848. New organizations were formed; meetings held; placards and leaflets distributed. Even at this stage, however, one finds the same prominent figures appearing on the election lists of rival organizations. The idea of binding candidates to a particular political line as the price for "adopting" that candidate was proposed but poorly articulated and ineffectively enforced. The election result was a victory for oppositional liberals but it was not clear just how far this majority would go with democratic as well as liberal reforms. There was a minority that also wanted "social" measures but they exerted little influence except in less controversial fields like education.

There was another direction for organization, principally among the artisan trades, which involved taking up links with similar groups in other parts of Germany in order to press for reform in Frankfurt or create associations that could support extensive and widespread forms of action, including cooperation, education and collective bargaining as well as political action. Some of the leaders involved also participated in city-state politics. Occasionally labor associations became directly involved, as when members of the Workers' Educational Association drilled, but generally the two forms of organization went their separate ways, especially with the onset of counter-revolution. Since October 1848 people had tended to look to the *Konstituante* to help tackle issues of reform. From mid-1849, except for a small minority of extreme radicals who shifted to secret societies and hatched conspiratorial plans for a second revolution, the tendency was to focus on non-political organization such as education and cooperation.

Public order

LYON

The February Revolution established a power vacuum in Lyon. The army could not be used by the new authorities, and recourse was had to the new unofficial workers' militias. The Carbonari provided a small Civic Guard that guarded the Town Hall, while other militias, notably the Voraces, operated openly as military bodies with flags and drums, seeking recognition by the new authorities. They saw themselves as embodiments of revolutionary legality, and maintained order, checking, for instance, riotous crowds hostile to Savoyard workers. As defenders of the revolution they took over forts on the Croix-Rousse and began to destroy fortifications.

The War and Police Committee, a sub-committee of the Central Committee, was filled by radicals. Radicals saw a people in arms as the best defense of the republic against counter-revolution, while propertied groups were horrified at the prospect of arms been given to workers. There was no National Guard in Lyon, and the War and Police Committee was determined to establish democratic security forces. It replaced the army commander, established radical bodies in the suburbs, and began to distribute weapons as a step towards a general armament, but failed to secure a new Republican Guard to replace the old police force, as happened in Paris. Furthermore, the Central Committee kept the existing police, and Arago founded a Mobile Guard as a counterweight to the militias.

Spontaneous National Guard units began to appear, their character varying with the locality, but those in the richer areas tended to predominate, and the failure of workers to register in the Guard meant that the officers elected tended to be from the propertied classes. Thus the War and Police Committee never succeeded in establishing a democratic National Guard, and generally the National Guard was not a threat to the authorities. While Arago secured the withdrawal of the Voraces from the forts in favor of the Croix-Rousse National Guard, he failed to get the Croix-Rousse to give up its weapons to the army, which was not allowed to regain its posts. With spreading insubordination and mutiny in the army, Arago was forced to rely on the Voraces and other paramilitary groups that operated as regular police forces and maintained order, but also conducted searches of religious and other houses for arms, which inflamed opinion.

Nevertheless, Arago took over the powers of the War and Police Committee and stopped the distribution of rifles, except to his new Mobile Guard. In the end, only about two-fifths of the National Guard ever had rifles, and few of them were workers, so Lyon never had an armed popular National Guard as in Paris. After April military insubordination ended, and half of the Voraces were merged with the National Guard, and the rest were dissolved in May after attacks on looms bound for a rural employer. Arrests were made, the Voraces tried to release those arrested and clashed with police and National Guards. During the June uprising in Paris, a large concentration of troops overawed the workers, and the authorities were able to disarm them quite easily, and restore control for the first time since February. Thus the plurality of armed power was fairly short-lived, there was no general arming of the people, and the control of force by the authorities was never in doubt after June 1848.

HAMBURG

There were two major institutions for the maintenance of order. The garrison formed part of the Hanseatic contingent of the German Confederate Army and stood at about 1,000 men. Since the mid-1830s there had been a slow shift from a professional body to one based on conscription. However, conscription from those obliged to serve was by lot and there was provision to pay for a substitute. The result was that richer inhabitants were largely absent from the rank-and-file, but they dominated officer positions. The garrison supported authority reliably.

Then there was the civil militia in which all adult males who belonged to the city-state were obliged to serve. This had an elaborate arrangement of battalions and companies. In addition to drilling, the militia discharged other tasks, such as the twice-yearly census. Workers were under-represented as they could buy themselves out of service for a sum significantly less than the cost of a uniform. Rank within the militia mirrored social position, even though officers were elected after a fashion.

The forces of order did not have too many challenges to confront in 1848/49. Militia were used in the disturbances of 3 and 13 March, in the second of which there was shooting and at least one demonstrator was killed. Different militia behaved differently—for example, the 7th battalion drawn from the opulent St. Georg district had a reputation for brutal action against demonstrators.

The militia was unreliable. On 13 March, garrison troops finally intervened to restore order. The disturbance of 9 June, which involved the storming of a gate-watch, saw militia disarmed (though they only carried bayonets). Most ominously, the disturbances on 9 August 1849, when crowds sought to obstruct the entry of Prussian troops, saw militia and demonstrators making common cause. Only the intervention of the garrison restored order. With the entry of the Prussian soldiers it was clear that a new and more formidable force would ensure effective repression.

No alternatives were developed. This may have been due to reform of the militia, which secured more democratic elections of officers in 1848, linked to the formation of a militia association that supported the democratic cause. Taken together this may have made the opposition think it unnecessary to form other armed groups. Volunteering to serve in Schleswig-Holstein deprived the city-state of committed democratic nationalists prepared to fight for their cause. The militia, even when democratized, tended to exclude workers. Although the idea of arming workers was floated it was never acted upon. More effective, in fact, was a private force organized by property owners [*Knüppelgarde*] that conducted itself in a quite brutal manner in defense of property but was tolerated by the authorities.

Political Communication

LYON

Lyon's population had a relatively high literacy level, and there was a fair number of different newspapers. Several of these—including workers' newspapers—were around during the July Monarchy. With the political freedom it ushered in and its removal of press restrictions, the February Revolution encouraged the establishment of newspapers with varying political outlooks. Most of the new ones were radical papers. The Democratic Club started its own paper, the *Tribun du Peuple*, and by 18 April there were other radical papers. The forthcoming elections were the main impetus here, and the number fell afterwards, and in the second half of the year there was only one radical paper, the *Peuple Souverain*, with a sale of 8,500. Harassment of the press, including a law early in 1849 against street-hawkers, led to a decline in its sale, but it was joined in the radical revival before the elections of April 1848 by the daily *Républicain*, with a sale of 6,400. Copies of both were given free to troops and had an effect on the army vote in the 1849 election. The radical success led to a rise in the *Républicain*'s sale to 10,000, but after the June 1849 uprising the *Censeur* was the only republican paper left, and it was soon suspended. A republican press re-appeared in early 1850, but did not last out the year.

The newspaper press seems to have had a limited political impact in Lyon. More important were books, pamphlets, tracts and, especially, radical adaptations of that old staple, the almanac. But their circulation was harmed by a clampdown on hawking and selling.

Oral communication was crucial, and it was the club meetings and discussions in 1848/49 that were important in arousing and mobilizing action, and the dinners of late 1848 and 1849, and café discussions and celebrations, were all adaptations to the more repressive situation. In Lyon these were more important than demonstrations.

Nevertheless, more spontaneous events like processions, the planting of Trees of Liberty, and the burning of effigies were also important means of making political messages, and songs played a prominent role in them as the most effective form of oral communication.

The importance of symbols like caps and trees of liberty led to conflicts. In May 1848 the decision of the Central Committee to remove the equestrian statue of Louis XIV from Bellecour Square, the chief open place in the city, led to gatherings in this and other squares anxious to defend it, partly in the name of pride in the work of a local artist. The planting of a Tree of Liberty at the southern suburb of Perrache on 16 April was accompanied by the erection of a statue of the Sovereign People, unusually depicting a man instead of the usual female Marianne. The statue was of a working man, with bare arms, of great muscular strength and brutal energy, one hand holding a gun and the other pointing to a crown trampled underfoot, with the inscription "Who will dare to raise it again? 24 February 1848, on the barricade." The erection of this symbol of the social republic was seen as a popular triumph, as it was on the edge of the white district of Ainay and looked north towards Bellecour

The arrival of Bugeaud in February 1849 was followed the next day by a grand military review, and the conservatives regained their courage. A few days later the mayor ordered the removal of red bonnets and other figures at the Trees of Liberty, and a rumor spread that the Man of the People, as the statue was known, was in danger. A guard formed spontaneously for several days, and led to clashes with the police and a dragoon charge that killed a demonstrator, the first death of the revolution, and the crowds remained for several days more. Gradually and cautiously the red bonnets were removed surreptitiously at night-time, starting in the least radical districts, but for the Croix-Rousse there was full-scale daytime military operation.

HAMBURG

Hamburg already had a varied range of newspapers, from established organs of the government and merchants, to democratic newspapers such as *Freischütz*. There were few additions to these during 1848, the most notable being the democratic paper *Reform*. Some new periodicals were published, such as the satirical *Mephistopheles* (actually founded in 1847). People also subscribed to new newspapers and journals published elsewhere in Germany. Artisanal associations took copies of the *Das Volk* published by the Workers' Fraternization; radicals might have subscribed to the *Neue Rheinische Zeitung*.

As in Lyon, more important than newspapers and periodicals were the ephemera of placards and pamphlets. Only a fraction of these survive, in police files or the papers of political activists. Demonstration would be advertised by placards. Such poster literature was especially important at the outbreak of the revolution, during the two elections in 1848, and in moments of unrest.

This new publicity was not merely literary. It was possible to be more uninhibited in the use of caricature and symbol to make political points, drawing upon a tradition of caricature that had been used for personal and moral criticism. Most of the caricatures published in Hamburg that have survived focused attention upon events outside Hamburg, namely Schleswig-Holstein, Frankfurt, the larger German states and events in France, especially Paris, suggesting that for many the local revolution was not as interesting or important as events elsewhere. However, once a Constituent Assembly existed both the issues under debate and the emergence of a class of local political activists taking up public stances on a day-to-day basis provided the material for local caricature and reportage. This period of relative freedom of expression came to a halt with the entry of Prussian soldiers into the city in August 1849.

Most difficult of all to assess is the power of the spoken word. Hamburg was not a place of many large outdoor meetings and demonstrations. Popular politics was more energetically pursued at the more closed settings of club meetings, usually taking place indoors during the evenings. Neither radicals nor moderates had any desire to see politics taken over by crowds that were difficult to control or predict and often ended up pursuing their own objectives. We have no examples, as for example from Berlin, of well-known crowd orators who drew large numbers to regular meetings at recognized outdoor sites.

Second Cities and the Sociology of Revolution

Elites

LYON

Lyon had had no resident military or judicial aristocracy, though its elites included landlords, merchants, bankers, industrialists, officials, professionals, and clerics. But the chief element was the commercial elite of about 550 merchants, bankers, and manufacturers. Men from this group had run the city in the July Monarchy, and a key institution was the Chamber of Commerce, which had come out in favor of free trade in the interests of the silk-industry. They were characterized by a private and unostentatious culture, and did not engage in the extensive private charity that characterized some other towns, while the structure of the silk-industry did not favor paternalism and control of the workforce.

This elite was naturally alarmed at the revolution, the collapse of authority, the apparent power of crowds in the streets, and the prospect of an armed working class. Many rich Lyonnais fled Lyon, and even France. Members of the elite looked to Arago to restore the situation and were disappointed, while the National Workshops he established were not only extremely expensive but attracted large numbers of workmen from the neighboring areas, which seemed to worsen the situation. However, fear of the workers made the elite accept the provision of relief, despite privately expressed intransigence and hatred of the workers.

However, members of the elite were keenly interested in their own fortunes and businesses, and the export nature of their industry, and its ramifications in northern Italy led to a great interest in the events in Italy in particular and Europe in general, political developments, and the state of the markets. The silk-industry, dependent on luxury and foreign demand, was subject to changes in fashion and great fluctuations. The revolution, coming after a severe depression, hit business confidence, and the Lyon silk industry was devastated, suffering from a lack of orders, financial crisis, and an absence of credit, which led to runs on banks that suspended cash payments. The letters of a merchant like Arlès-Dufour reveal as great an interest in business matters as in political questions, and, in contrast to Paris, there was as much interest in the government's economic policy as its political actions.

The dominance of the silk industry made it easy for the elite to plausibly portray their own business interests as those of the whole population. They approved of the orthodox and conventional financial policy of the government and the municipal finance committee, and the latter's aid to the Lyon savings bank, while about 150 local merchants combined to establish a discount bank to help local businesses, with funds from the Chamber of Commerce. They pressed the government for aid, and gained an order for silk flags for national guard units. They expressed the widespread discontent at the costly National Workshops in Paris, but rather because Lyon should get more of this help than to object to the principle as such. When the idea of a patriotic subscription in Lyon to relieve the poor was mooted, a group of merchants, led by the two chief figures on the Chamber of Commerce, Brosset and Arlès-Dufour, successfully insisted that Arago impose a compulsory levy for this purpose, and there was anger when the Provisional Government imposed a new national tax on top of this. These measures had some success in that there were few industrial conflicts in the silk industry, and no attacks on property except for religious and rural firms.

Many of the elite supported Cavaignac in the Presidential election, but the improvement in economic confidence afterwards affected the silk industry and 1849 proved prosperous for Lyon, and so members of the commercial elite ceased to argue a particular economic line. They approved the conservative policy of the Legislative Assembly, and supported parliamentary government against the suspected designs of the president. While few were in favor of the coup d'état, once it began most hoped it would succeed as quickly as possible to avoid appalling conflict.

HAMBURG

In retrospect, it appears that the power of the merchant elite in Hamburg was never severely under threat. In the April elections to the German National Assembly the merchant interest was able to convince the electorate that its understanding of the city-state's interest was the one that needed to be taken to Frankfurt. Even radical newspapers, disillusioned with the National Assembly by the summer, argued during a by-election that the principal duty of a deputy from Hamburg was to defend the trading interests of the city against possible adverse national policies.

It was more difficult to control the local revolution. Fortunately for the elite, the opposition satisfied itself first with a reform deputation and subsequently with the work of the Constituent Assembly. The executive branch of the government, the Senate, remained unchanged throughout. The elite lacked the skill to engage effectively in either repression or a populist manipulation of opinion, and the Constituent Assembly drew up a radically different constitution for the city-state. But the continued existence of the Senate, combined with an ability to appeal for outside assistance once the broader process of counter-revolution had begun, enabled the elite to regain control by the second half of 1849.

The Labor Movement

LYON

Silk-workers were seen as the shock troops of the revolutionary city. It was the fancy weavers, mainly living and working in the suburbs, who were mostly involved in industrial and political action. Fancy weavers from the Croix-Rousse imposed the declaration of the republic, formed the Voraces and other militias, organized the destruction of looms in low-paying religious and charitable institutions, and sought to confine silk-weaving to the conurbation, and initiated the first plantings of Trees of Liberty.

After the February Revolution there were actions against other industrial targets, such as attacks on sawmills and steamboat construction yards. There were also movements among trades active under the July Monarchy: tailors and shoemakers, as well as other artisan trades and some hitherto unorganized groups, like female silk-throwers. Employers felt constrained to adopt conciliatory attitudes. Industrial conflicts worried the authorities as threats to order and economic recovery, and Arago set up a Committee to Organize Work to mediate in disputes and arrange settlements, with a fair degree of success, so that industrial peace returned in April. The trades were also important bases of radical mobilizing for political clubs, demonstrations, and elections. With the restoration of order and control by the authorities in June 1848, employers felt confident enough to break agreements made in March. There were a number of strikes in the autumn, all unsuccessful.

Growing repression discouraged industrial combinations, and there were few disputes during the rest of the republic. There was tendency in France for trade organizations to retreat into cooperative production societies, one of the few forms of organization allowed, and even encouraged. However, the main impetus behind the growth of cooperative societies at the end of 1848 was a political one, as a refuge for radical activists faced with repression. In Lyon, they mainly took the form of cooperative trading, not production, as radicals thought the latter tended to prolong divisions between trades that they were seeking to break down. Cooperative trading flourished most in areas dominated by a single industry, especially textile ones, and the proliferation of cooperative stores among silk-weavers on the Croix-Rousse made Lyon the chief center of cooperation. These co-operative societies had a strong radical affiliation and played a role in the uprising of June 1849, and suffered in the consequent repression, but cooperative trading continued in Lyon and new stores were opened until Castellane closed them all down in the coup.

HAMBURG

Whereas the "core" labor force of silk-weavers played a leading role in the labor movement and revolution in Lyon, there was no equivalent in Hamburg. Dockworkers were divided into various groups and were poorly organized (with the exception of the lightermen). Clerks developed social and self-help activities in the 1850s but had no corporate organization during the revolution. Sailors were too dispersed to play any role.

Rather it was the artisans, especially from the "mass" demand trades such as shoes, clothing, furniture and building, to a lesser extent from food industries, along with the special cases of printers and tobacco workers, who provided the organizational base of a labor movement. In part, they could build on pre-existing occupational organizations such as benefit societies and the shadowy trade unions of the building trades. The early part of the revolution saw a relatively large number of strikes and concessions by employers but many of these gains were being reversed by the end of the year. Some more general associations that existed before 1848, such as the Workers' Educational Association and the Association for the Advancement of the Trades, quickly formed the basis for both general demands for reform of the trades as well as for a number of occupational organizations that sprang up. Some of these remained occupationally fairly distinct, notably the printers and, at least initially, tobacco workers. Others played a role in more general associations both at the local and at the regional/national level.

However, it was master artisans who took the initiative with the summoning of a north German artisan congress in June 1848. That in turn formed the basis for a general congress (known as the masters' congress because of its exclusion of journeymen) that met in Frankfurt and put a series of demands to the National Assembly. Smaller masters and journeymen responded by forming their own associations that were not just the organization of petitioning meetings but attempts at a wide range of actions (cooperation, education, collective bargaining) articulated through occupations but under a general, umbrella organization.

With the onset of counter-revolution these organizations began to turn away from dangerous political activity. By mid-1849 the Workers' Educational Association was declaring its concerns to be purely educational, even if a minority resisted this tendency. Activists turned their attention toward cooperation as well as playing a part on the left of the Constituent Assembly. Education and cooperation were not simply blinds for political activity but also regarded as embodying worthwhile ends in and of themselves. By the end of 1849 it was increasingly difficult and dangerous to run regional, let alone national associations of any kind, and police supervision and censorship were being effectively imposed at the local level. There were some who counseled a move towards secret, conspiratorial and even insurrectional activity, but these represented a small, ineffective minority. Nevertheless, the arrest and trial of such figures served to maintain an atmosphere of repression for some years to come.

Maintaining Social Order

LYON

High unemployment led the local authorities to see official action as essential to get workers off the streets and to avoid further disturbances. With the February Revolution there were demands for food, work, and relief, made more intense as unemployment shot up, and a new municipal Provisioning Committee tackled the huge problem of destitution through control of bakeries and a new organization of relief, distributing food tokens. Public works were an established recourse in Lyon in periods of unemployment, and the Committee for the Organization of Work proposed extensive schemes for public works, such as on roadworks and a water-system. The moderate Central Committee only approved two small schemes, which attracted destitute workers from neighboring areas and thus worsened the problem. Arago established a Mobile Guard to mop up some unemployment, secured an order for republican flags, and opened new National Workshops, so that in the end there were twelve such works, employing 17,000 men. These were expensive and Arago exceeded his mandate and levied a special tax equal to the total of the ordinary direct taxes, an extra burden on top of the government's raising of property taxes by 45 percent.

The National Workshops were controversial. The numbers employed were greater than in any other French town except Paris, and the men were paid above the standard daily rate in addition to food vouchers, so the cost was large. All were employed to do unpleasant and unproductive earthwork, with lax supervision and much absenteeism. They provided a focus for organization, and were an important element in radical mobilization. Every morning, workers gathered at meeting points in the city and marched in groups of a hundred or so behind flag and drum to the work sites on the edges of the city. The process was repeated every evening and payday, and meant that these were the workers most likely to demonstrate in street processions over pay issues, almost the only ones to display written demands, and were prominent in the few demonstrations organized by the radical Central Committee. Nevertheless, they helped secure public order and peace. It was towns without such workshops that had the worst disturbances in April. Arago's successor, Martin-Bernard, wisely delayed trying to implement the government order to impose task-work in June, an important factor in Lyon's not uprising like Paris and Marseille. Thus, despite Lyon's revolutionary reputation and the unique strength of radicalism there, the city had a low level of disturbances, partly because the very strength of radicalism worked against street demonstrations and riots, and partly because of the unusually extensive and generous provision of public work.

HAMBURG

There was no strong tradition of public works as in Lyon and nothing like the same level of popular threat to order which might have stimulated large-scale provision of employment by this means. Yet during the "hungry forties" there had been demands both for the "organization of work" and financial assistance to small employers. These had sometimes been received sympathetically by those in authority but not acted upon. Democrats and social reformers took up similar demands in 1848. The democrat, Hagen, for example demanded national workshops along the lines of Paris. Insofar as such demands were seen as part of a "socialist" movement they were firmly and effectively rejected. Even many in the democratic movement, drawn from the ranks of the professions and the small property-own-ers and businessmen, had little time for schemes that would raise their tax burden.

That does not mean nothing was done. Specific cases of hardship, such as the unemployment of some 1,500 warehousemen caused by the blockade of the Elbe during the Schleswig-Holstein conflict led to renewed demands for special employ-ment measures. The democratic activist Gallois wrote an open appeal "To Hamburg's Lords of Commerce and Aristocrats of Money," demanding a large unemployment fund. Another idea that floated was that of cheap rented land. However, the only practical measure of significance was that enough funds were brought together to employ some 500 people as earth diggers in the summer of 1848. Typical of Ham-burg, however, was that this was collected as a private rather than a public initiative, even if it was given to the police authority to distribute.

The City and the Region

LYON

Lyon's dominant position in the region provided the opportunity for political influ-ences in the Second Republic, but initially there was a political contrast. In the elec-tions to the Constituent Assembly in April 1848 Lyon voted radical and the countryside voted conservative, and this was repeated in the September by-election, when Rivet beat Raspail. Nevertheless the Central Democratic Club established clubs in neighboring towns, and in the August local elections some radicals were elected. Under pressure from Republican Solidarity, Lyon became the center of reg-ular correspondence between radicals in neighboring departments, and, starting in December 1848, determined efforts were directed at the rural populations

Propaganda countered accusations that the radicals were hostile to private property, the family and religion, condemned reactionary notables, fueled anticler-icalism, and advocated reduction of taxes and the provision of cheap credit so as to safeguard small landed properties from expropriation by creditors and enable poor people to buy land. The movement of republicans spreading the message was assisted by the constant mobility between Lyon and local towns and countryside. The Lyon newspaper press played a central role in the Ain and Lower Dauphiné, and tracts were circulated and given away free. A network of political clubs was established, centered on Lyon.

Thus in the elections to the Legislative Assembly in May 1849, four-fifths of the electorate in the Rhône voted, and the rural vote was decisive in the radical victory. Moreover, in great contrast to the year before, the reds won in a number of rural departments over a wide area centered on Lyon. In the by-election in July, Favre was the compromise candidate of the left, and gained an absolute majority of votes. This Lyon radicalization of the rural population lasted for the rest of the Second Republic.

HAMBURG

There is less of a regional role for Hamburg. The independent city-state had a more autonomous revolution and, through the National Assembly, had a role in national events, but missed out on the regional level. The Schleswig-Holstein affair did dominate opinion in the city, especially during moments of crisis. Hamburg was a good jumping off point for reporting and comment on the question, and the gathering of volunteers and supplies, but it did not offer political leadership. The city-state was surrounded by more powerful territorial monarchies and neither the Senate nor liberal politicians wished to challenge that. At most the city-state took up links with the other city-states of Bremen and Lübeck in order to defend its free-trade interests at a national level.

More important was the way in which labor and radical movements could furnish a regional leadership. The north German trades' congress and the beginning of north German organization among more dependent artisans was centered on Hamburg, even if Bremen with Pastor Duon acquired a more radical reputation. From the middle of 1849 on, the Hamburg authorities were closely in touch with Prussia and other north German states to ensure that its own local revolution did not get out of hand. At the same time, the mildness of counter-revolution in Hamburg made it a temporary refuge for radicals fleeing from other states, although this in turn led to pressure from those states upon Hamburg to enforce control measures more effectively. Hamburg was more acted upon by surrounding areas than acting upon them.

Comparative Conclusions

The scale of revolution and counter-revolution was much greater in Lyon compared to Hamburg. There are some obvious reasons for this. Lyon had a tradition of revolution and counter-revolution that was absent in Hamburg. The core labor force of silk-weavers provided a nucleus for a popular and radical movement that was lacking in Hamburg. The closer links between the urban revolution, the regional revolution, and the national revolution in the single territorial state of France also gave politics in Lyon a significance that was lacking in Hamburg. With more experience and concern with confronting revolution, and also a capacity to draw upon national assistance, the Lyon elite was also more skilled and inventive in its manipulation of popular customs and symbols, in the extent and organization of such measures as work-creation schemes, and in the organization of repression.

All this meant that there was a much higher level of politicization in Lyon, as measured for example by the number of elections and the level of organization and participation involved in those elections. There was also a higher degree of polarization, as indicated for example by the capacity of the popular and labor movement to take control of parts of the city and the subsequent scale of measures taken by the authorities to wrest that control back.

Yet if anything, there was less violence and bloodshed in Lyon than in Hamburg. Arguably this was because the conflicting parties in Lyon were more used to and skilled in handling their conflicts. Political leadership was more adept at bringing its followers under control. The sheer level of organized power one or the other side had at any particular moment of conflict made the eventual outcome obvious and discouraged resistance from the weaker party. By contrast in Hamburg violence broke out because crowds pursued "non-political" ends and the militia or garrison panicked in response.

These differences can be linked to the very different political context of the two cities—a provincial city in a centralized territorial state compared to an independent city-state in a federal German political system. They can also be linked to the difference between a city with a core manufacturing activity and labor force that formed the basis of a radical tradition, compared to the more open and diffuse economy of an entrepôt trading center without a core labor force. Finally the differences can be registered as national ones—France with a history of revolutions and counter-revolutions and Germany where established authority was never subjected to the same kinds of challenges.

The differences are fairly obvious. Less obvious and more interesting are the similarities that can be linked to the status of the two cities as second cities. In demographic terms the sheer density of population provided a prerevolutionary nucleus of networks, formal and informal, that quickly provided the basis of political action during the revolution. The major stimulus to a much greater development of political organization and communication were elections, both local and national.

Within this political process there were also similarities. Political leaderships, both conservative and democratic, had no wish to see uncontrolled popular action and sought instead to channel politics through the oral culture of clubs and relatively closed political meetings. Radicals generally proved more adept at mobilizing support in these ways. The overriding concern of the merchant elite was the maintenance of order and of the economy where they represented the business interest as identical with that of the city as a whole. Within the popular movement, the most prominent part was played, both occupationally and at a more general level, by a limited range of artisan trades. As the counter-revolution closed in these trades moved towards more clearly non-political forms of action such as cooperation and conviviality. However, insofar as these also served as covers for continuing political activity, in a subsequent phase these associations were also subjected to repression and control.

Lyon is often caricatured as the red city, second only to Paris in its history of violent revolution and counter-revolution. Hamburg is often caricatured as a city of consensus, where revolution was introduced from outside and which only became polarized after its incorporation into a unified Germany. Clearly there is something in these two images. Yet one can also find other images of the two cities—for example, the depiction of the merchant elite as philistine and grasping, unconcerned with the general interest or in higher goals—which point to similarities linked to the common dependency of the two cities on highly competitive international trade. Above all, in demographic and sociological terms, these two second cities had a good deal in common and this was reflected in their experience of revolution in 1848.

Note

1. We have decided not to include Manchester here because of space limitations, and not simply because there was no revolution in Manchester. A comparison would have been interesting for that reason precisely, but also more difficult.

Public Assembly at the Franciskanerkeller in the Au district of Munich (Illustrirte Zeitung, Leipzig, no. 271, 9 September 1848, 165)

Chapter 17

POLITICAL QUIET ZONES

Karl-Joseph Hummel

For the years 1848 and 1849, contemporary sources throughout Europe report a "revolutionary storm," a phrase that has almost become proverbial. Accordingly, the revolutionary calendar of the European "springtime of the peoples" begins with the Paris revolution at the end of February 1848, and goes on to record a European chain-reaction, rapidly spreading from west to east. "Never before and never since has there been such an intensive and widely strewn concert of revolutionary forces in Europe, nor a comparable interdependence of various revolutionary centers, which in 1848/49 were closely connected in a feedback system."[1] Throughout Europe, many contemporaries, whether enemies or supporters of the changes in the "crazy year," agreed in describing them as a dramatic experience: "A major, fateful turning point has occurred in the history of the world. Indeed, every day we experience all too much that we are living through an age of general, earth-shattering movement, sweeping changes, the castigation of God's judgement, miraculous undoings. What incalculable changes are brought every day, indeed nearly every hour? ... Where could one find in Europe a clod of earth which has not been shaken, strongly or lightly, by the massive shocks and struggles that rage in the foundations of our society?"[2]

Guido Görres's rhetorical question was neither answered by his contemporaries, nor did it later stand at the center of academic attention. In a critique of Jacob Burckhardt's thesis—that the period from 1789 was basically "nothing but ages of revolution" and that we now know "that one and the same storm which has taken hold of mankind since 1789 bears us onwards as well"—Theodor Schieder has raised some doubts.[3] Nonetheless, even modern scholarship on revolutions has only occasionally offered a critical re-examination of the myth of a ubiquitous European-wide revolution of 1848/49. "Does not," as Schieder wrote, "the greatness of the past century lie in its overcoming, almost without catastrophe, enormous tensions—technical, social, economical, and ideological—all bearing within themselves explosive power? Does it rather not appear to us, eyewitnesses of revolutionary world crises, more as the century of elastic adaptation to abruptly changing conditions, that is as the century of evolution and not of revolution?"[4]

Richard Cobb coined the phrase "life on the margins" to describe the situation of the non-participants in the French Revolution, that is the majority of the French "who did not 'live' but only lived through the Revolution."[5] Michel Vovelle commented further: "Evidently, there is something like 'conservatories,' not touched by the collective shock."[6] For the 1848 revolution, investigation of the differential revolutionary mobilization, the distribution curve between "revolution" and "life on the margins" is still in its infancy. This chapter, a first approach to the subject, will not deal with the everyday lives of those not involved. Rather it will serve as an introduction to a geography of revolution, to identify "quiet zones" in Europe, states of political peace amid the revolutionary hurricane.

Let us begin with Switzerland. For Metternich, Switzerland had become—at the latest, with the admission of numerous political refugees after 1830—the "center of the revolutionary party" in Europe. Following 1830, the major domestic political issue was the revision of the confederate constitution of 1815. When the new federal constitution was adopted by the *Tagsatzung* on 12 September 1848, it marked Switzerland's success in transforming itself from a confederation into a federal state, in the eye of the European revolutionary storm, and without the intervention of the European Great Powers. "This federal constitution," wrote Jonas Furrer, Mayor of Zürich and the first president of the Swiss federation, "is the first among those which our fatherland has had in the last fifty years that is free of any foreign influence ... We are the only people in Europe that, in this stormy age, have completed the difficult task of its own political restructuring, in calm and peace, as well as in legal fashion."[7]

In 1847 the road had seemed to lead in another direction. Swiss domestic politics was subject to constant observation by the European Great Powers. In their interpretation of the proceedings of the Congress of Vienna, a "contractual interrelation" existed between them and Switzerland, that tied guarantees of Swiss neutrality to a particular order of confederate institutions. Following the *Sonderbund* war of November 1847, the Great Powers, in disagreement among themselves about policy towards Switzerland, quickly came to terms with the new state of affairs. Diplomatic assistance from Great Britain undermined an intervention note from Austria, France, Prussia, and Russia of 18 January 1848. The *Tagsatzung* unequivocally rejected France's offers of mediation on 7 February 1848 and ruled out "any other form of intervention." "The decisiveness of Furrer's reply helped to bring an end to foreign discussion about the Swiss affair. Even before the outbreak of revolution had made any further interference impossible, Guizot had agreed with his envoy in Berlin to simply drop the matter. Nor was Metternich willing to take up immediate counter-measures. Only the Tsar still rattled his saber a bit."[8]

The rapid end of the *Sonderbund* war, after only twenty-six days, left the Great Powers no time to agree on a common policy. When Austria, Prussia, Russia, and France finally decided to act together, the European crisis brought on by the February Revolution in Paris necessitated their concentrating on their own domestic problems. "At the most favorable moment for Switzerland a tidal wave of revolution broke over Europe, sweeping away old governments and shaking the thrones of kings, thus saving the *Tagsatzung* from further demands from abroad. The Great Powers simply did not have the time to worry about the Swiss. Unobserved, Switzerland was able to restructure itself. And the manner in which it reconstituted itself robbed the Great Powers of any plausible reason to intervene."[9]

Switzerland was surrounded by a great number of neighboring states—France, Piedmont-Savoy, Lombardy-Venetia, Austria, Bavaria, Baden and Württemberg—but was nonetheless generally successful in steering clear of revolutionary influences. In April 1848, during the war between Piedmont-Savoy and Austria, King Carl Alberto offered Switzerland a mutual defense pact—which, however, the *Tagsatzung* rejected. Observance of the obligations of neutrality took precedence over engagement out of solidarity. From Tessin, closely tied to the Risorgimento, came armed volunteers for the Italian unification movement. In July 1848 , after the battle of Custozza, 20,000 refugees entered Switzerland, and after the uprisings in Baden of the spring of 1848, October 1848 and May 1849, many defeated revolutionaries retreated to this country.

Thus, Switzerland was involved in numerous conflicts regarding its policy on the right to asylum with Austria, Baden, Prussia, and France and not totally isolated from events in Europe. However, the concentration of the Great Powers on their own domestic problems allowed Switzerland, as well, to concentrate on working out its constitution without outside interference, as long as the Swiss restrained themselves from intervening on behalf of solidarity and popular liberty in Europe. As Gottfried Keller wrote in March 1848: "How calmly, collectedly, almost literally as looking down from a mountain, we poor, small Swiss are able to watch the spectacle."[10]

The revision commission made use of the opportunity presented it and within a few weeks, from 17 February to 8 April 1848, drew up a new constitution on the basis of the drafts of 1832/33, which was then approved by the *Tagsatzung* in June of that year.[11] The diplomat and publicist Adolphe de Circourt, who was in the French foreign ministry from February 1848 until the fall of Lamartine, traveled through Switzerland in September 1848 and was quite surprised to find "this seat of European revolution so quiet and peaceful."[12] "We found the Swiss laughing and relaxed. This calm was due above all to the overexertion of energy in the two years past ... Everything rested in that, luckily not very bloody, grave of the *Sonderbund*."[13]

"The Confederation ... knows the secret of never going beyond a certain level of political moderation. It therefore has absolutely no need to fear the disintegration taking place in the rest of Europe today." [14] Switzerland was not suitable as "a tool of absolute state powers, nor equally as a tool of foreign revolutions."[15] "Switzerland," Tocqueville predicted in summary, "in spite of the chronic low fever of its democracy, appears to me to enjoy a more robust health and to have a more peaceful future than the majority of the states surrounding it."[16]

As in Switzerland, Bavaria also experienced a prerevolutionary crisis in 1847, one defused by a reform from above of the constitutional monarchy, before revolutions began elsewhere in Europe. "By some remarkable providence, the burghers of Munich gathered and demonstrated their strength before there was any incitement from outside to do so."[17]

It has often been observed that the fate of the old regimes was decided between January and March 1848 by revolutionary events in the European capitals— Palermo, Naples, Paris, Vienna, Berlin, Milan, and Venice.[18] In Bavaria, this role was played by the capital city and royal residence, Munich. "Through these events, Munich has become a political capital."[19] However, in Munich "the March movement, in the sense presented by political propaganda [found] no breeding-ground … The character trait of a resident of Old Bavaria is too down-to-earth to be led astray. He will not throw a good thing away before he is convinced that its replacement will be better."[20] "I have observed this harmless revolution in the streets from the beginning to the end," wrote one of Metternich's secret agents, "and have deeply regretted the blindness of a monarch who irritates such a people to the extremes of bitterness. Nonetheless, in the entire movement of these three days there has been no trace of revolutionary attitudes, no rebellious call has been sounded."[21] In Munich "things worked differently than elsewhere in Germany," including the six Bavarian provinces and their capitals, Nuremberg, Augsburg, Würzburg, Regensburg, Bayreuth, and Passau.[22] Veit Valentin even went so far as to characterize "revolutionary" events in Munich as a "dramatic anecdote" in a "royal village."[23]

Count Montgelas's reforms at the beginning of the nineteenth century had strengthened the Bavarian Monarchy, even if Ludwig I later interpreted these policies as "antimonarchical," and refused to come to terms with the idea of "the monarch as state official." Ludwig I kept the final say in all matters for himself and would not accept his influential minister Karl von Abel (1837-1847) becoming a leading minister along the lines of a Metternich. State reform initiatives to strengthen the monarchy had noticeably slowed after 1830, and after von Abel's resignation on 1 March 1847, they completely lost direction. In the fifteen years from 1832 to 1847 there had been a total of sixteen government ministers in Bavaria; in the three years from 1847 to 1849, however, twenty-seven ministers were named and dismissed. Of the fourteen ministers in the period between March 1847 to March 1848, only three were definitively appointed, the other eleven functioned as interim administrators. In January, Ambassador Freiherr von Brenner reported to Metternich: "For all the apparent changes in the system, the king's principle of government, the concentration of power almost exclusively in his hands, has remained unchanged. Hence the conservative sentiment, which is the foundation of this governmental principle, can still inspire the same trust. Nonetheless, the actions of the government during the last eleven months have had a lasting effect on the situation in general. The series of ministries, still simply the tool of the king's will, were formed less by the course of public business than by the needs of the moment."[24]

This rapid exchange of the political elite aimed, on the one hand, at maintaining a system of government directed by the monarch himself and not by his ministers. On the other hand, it was closely related to the "needs of the moment," fulfilling King Ludwig's personal wishes regarding his relationship with the Spanish dancer Lola Montez. Following King Ludwig's decision to grant Senora Lola Montez Bavarian citizenship by royal decree and to elevate her to Countess Landsfeld, Abel and Ministers Gumppenberg, Seinsheim, and Schrenk tended their resignations in the so-called "memorandum" of 11 February 1847 "with deepest respects and unshakeable loyalty and devotion," because "the most ignominious anecdotes and most disparaging attacks on your royal majesty" had in the meantime spread throughout Europe. "It is the monarchy's cause which is at stake."[25]

After this letter of resignation had been published, King Ludwig formed an investigative commission that spent months searching, in vain, for the source of the leaks. Ernst von Lasaulx, a nephew of Joseph Görres and son-in-law of Franz von Baader, proposed that the university, as the first moral corporation, should express its respect for all that Abel had done to preserve the royal dignity in 1847. As a result of this proposal, eight professors were dismissed and pensioned off. From this, and from the criticism of the king's personal moral behavior, a conflict developed with the new Archbishop of Munich, Karl August Graf von Reisach, who had been ceremonially installed in office on 25 January 1847. The king's constant endeavors on behalf of his favorite, anger in the army and the state bureaucracy about transfer and promotion policies influenced by his relations with Lola Montez, stubborn resistance from diplomatic circles and conservative nobles all accelerated the inexorable loss of Ludwig's authority. His abdication on 20 March 1848 was applauded not so much by those seeking an end to the monarchy altogether as by supporters of the monarchy who saw in Ludwig's resignation the preservation of the crown.[26]

When in February/March 1848 the situation in Bavaria escalated to the alternative of abdication or revolution, this was not due to republican agitators or to a third estate demanding reform, but the consequence of widespread insecurity and anger in civilian and military circles, in the state administration as much as in the army and the Catholic Church, among the conservative nobility or the middle class of the capital city and royal residence, caused by Ludwig I's "system." Successful conservative politics in Bavaria in 1848 consisted of change through reform, of modernization controlled by the crown. When the king broke with this policy, conservatives among the high and lesser nobility, and those among the urban middle-class who represented the interests of the state in opposition to the government and above all to the king, saved the institution of the monarchy by advising the monarch to abdicate.

King Ludwig's abdication strengthened rather than weakened the monarchy in Bavaria. The new king, Max II, gained immediate support as there was no serious competition to his rule, even in the spring of 1848. In a retrospective report to the government of Upper Bavaria in the autumn of 1849, the mayor of Munich, Dr. Jakob Bauer, denied the events in Munich any sort of political quality. "The removal of that demon [Lola Montez] was the only thing the masses intended, they had no political intentions." This situation had then been exploited for political propaganda, but the "revolutionary party" in Munich had not even made up 5 percent of the population and, "it must be said in the honor of Munich," that two thirds of them certainly did not come from old Bavaria.[27]

Nor are there any signs of fundamental social conflicts in Bavaria—and certainly not in Munich—in 1848/49 that would have forced the liberal middle class to reach a compromise with the old ruling strata in order to defend the status quo against the lower classes. From Guido Görres to Franz Spengler, the Munich member of the Communist League, everyone agreed that one could not speak of any sort of threatening, politically active proletariat in Munich or in Old Bavaria. Spengler wrote to the central committee of the Workers' Fraternization in December 1848: "The large majority of the workers here is conservative, and, one can assume, in Upper and Lower Bavaria as well … In no other city are there so many hurdles facing organization, and, even more, association."[28]

Post-1830 economic development in Munich had generally followed a positive course.[29] The increase of 21.5 percent in the Bavarian population, between 1818 and 1848 was noticeably lower in comparison to 49.7 percent in Prussia and 53.4 percent in Saxony. While the population of Munich had grown by 76.7 percent, from 53,672 in 1818 to 94,830 in 1848, the major share of this increase, 35,233 inhabitants, had occurred in the period between 1818 and 1832. The year 1834 marked a decisive break. In a revision of three laws concerning community of residence, settlement, and marriage, the municipalities were granted the right to a veto, of which Munich made extensive use. Suffering most from these new regulations were applicants for a trading license. The percentage of successful applications sank in the period between 1834/35 and 1843/44 by 56.2 percent compared to that between 1824/25 and 1833/34; the percentage of other non-impoverished applicants fell by 31.1 percent; the group of house- and landowners, on the other hand, rose by 165 percent. A decisive factor for Munich's social peace was a regular use of the municipal veto, which did much to protect indigenous tradesmen from unwanted competition.

Altogether, Munich's share of Bavaria's total population remained constant at 1.9 percent. Statistical analysis of professions does, however, produce some interesting deviations.[30] While the total number of people in Bavaria living from industry, trade, and crafts fell by 7.8 percent between 1840 and 1852, it rose in Munich by 1.5 percent. Among the self-employed in these areas, the difference is even greater: a decrease of 8.7 percent for all of Bavaria, compared to an increase of 10 percent in Munich. Apart from an increase in self-employment in Munich, there was also a noticeable reduction in the group of assistants, journeymen, trainees, servants, and day laborers. In 1852, 15.4 percent fewer people in Munich worked in this group than in 1840. Moreover, Munich experienced a favorable development in the group of registered poor. While the total number of poor in Bavaria rose by 16.9 percent, it fell in Munich by 8.6 percent.

The situation in Munich was thus quite distinct from that of Cologne or Berlin. "Only out of desperation did unemployed journeymen attempt self-employment at that time," is Aycoberry's diagnosis of the situation in Cologne, "and search out customers for their own businesses. This change in status from dependence to independence therefore no longer meant liberation, but decline and proletarization."[31] In Berlin, the number of both self-employed and wage-earners rose in the period before the revolution of 1848, the number of journeymen, apprentices, factory workers and day laborers clearly more than that of the self-employed. In Munich, the self-employed increased in number, the economically dependent decreased in number. For the personal servants of the nobles, clergy, pensioners, retirees, academics, doctors, and artists, moreover, the alternative of pseudo-self-employment did not exist. When the size of this group alone fell by 25.8 percent and the number of poor sank by 8.6 percent, this meant a reduction in that part of the population which, because of economic and social problems, would have been most likely to join a revolutionary movement.

An analysis of Munich police statistics underlines this conclusion.[32] The number of registered crimes in Munich in 1848, 13,783, was almost the same as the annual average of the years 1841/50, (13,540). Admittedly, the 1848 figure was a noticeable drop compared to 1847's 16,548. During 1848 itself, the months of revolutionary élan show below-average figures: February (896), March (993), April (965), September (973). In the Munich police statistics for the years 1846/50 there was only one other month with a figure below 1,000.

Johann Casper Bluntschli, an expert on constitutional law, who came from Zürich to Munich at the beginning of March 1848 and who, as political advisor to King Ludwig, had directly played an influential role, wrote in 1864 in the *Deutsches Staats-Wörterbuch*: "Revolution is always a relatively stateless condition … even a moderate and mild revolution limits for a moment the effect of legitimate authority."[33] Police authority was certainly not in control of the situation, temporarily at least. This was due above all to the troubled relationship between the people and the gendarmerie from the days of Lola Montez; for a time no gendarme could walk the streets "without being insulted."[34] The police director complained that in eight weeks no one had been charged for serving after hours, although as often as not noisy entertainment was occurring long past midnight in the taverns of Munich. The Minister of the Interior commented that "recently" daily reports had registered only one or two arrests for begging, while daily experience offered sufficient evidence of "an increasing in the pernicious practice of begging."[35] The internal difficulties suffered by the police and their tense relations with the populace—"The police con us, the police are in on it together with Lola"—lasted only a short while, however.[36]

When the police had been completely restaffed in 1849, the number of arrests increased again from 13,783 to 17,769. And even more importantly, an analysis of arrest records shows that in both 1848 and 1849 the majority of crimes fell in only four categories: begging, vagabondage, violating servant regulations, and the rules of the aliens branch. The concentration of police work in those areas, which were not necessarily a threat to the state—1848, 57.36 percent; 1849, 67.74 percent—was not unusual in comparison to the rest of the 1840s. An analysis of the rest of the cases handled by the police shows, moreover, that their authority was certainly sufficient in every month of 1848/49 to follow up over 3,300 trivial cases such as offenses against regulations concerning dogs, traffic, and cab regulations, smoking where banned, drunkenness, concubinism, and crimes against public morals, altogether 12.2 percent (1848) and 9.3 percent (1849).

On 24 November 1849, the district governor of Upper Bavaria reported to the Ministry of the Interior: "In the Old Bavarian districts daily wages are high, as a rule at a level with food prices; there is no lack of work and he who wishes to work … will have his income and the basis of a comfortable existence … Altogether the working class in Upper Bavaria is quiet and satisfied and not very open to political tendencies."[37] In a book about poor relief written in 1850, the Mayor of Munich came to a similar conclusion about the relationship between income and living standards in Bavaria. "The [political] movement [of the 1848 revolution] has a deeper cause, and those who believe that it is the result of the poverty of the country are obviously mistaken, as a large proportion of the affluent were in the leadership of the movement and purchased the help of those who fought with them."[38] Guido Görres wrote in 1848: "Another bit of fortune, for which we cannot be thankful enough, is that Bavaria, especially in its old provinces, has almost no proletariat compared to other German states."[39] "The workers are good, and wish order and peace, so that they can earn their money."[40]

The workers in Munich's largest factory, Joseph Anton von Maffai's locomotive works, were so upset about a rumor that they were planning a public disturbance that they protested against it in an advertisement in the *Polizei-Anzeiger Münchens*: "Declaration. To counter the repeated chatter, apparently only started by the nasty-minded and passed on by the simple-minded, that any of us ever intended a public disturbance, or that our participation in similar disturbances planned by others could be expected, we feel forced to make this public statement that hardly any of us could hope to keep his place if justifiably accused of such intent, whereby we would request those involved who claim to find the originators of such disturbances among us to have a look elsewhere."[41] Even the democrat Franz Sensburg, editor of *Vorwärts*, printed in Munich, regretted that the equilibrium in wage and price trends prevented the intensification of political confrontations in Munich that he hoped for, and wrote, disappointedly: "Those who govern you believe that because hops and barley are cheap, you would cheaply surrender the other things, this rubbish of liberty, not absolutely necessary for living as you see daily from slaves and chained dogs. It is up to you to show whether they are right or not."[42]

Based on a basket of goods put together by Teuteberg it can be demonstrated that the cost of living in Bavaria fell after the peak of grain prices in in May 1847 till 1850. In November 1847 District Governor von Godin saw no "reason to worry about dissatisfaction and disorder … according to all available indications and observations the public mood is good and satisfactory, although food prices are still unusually high."[43] In Munich, action by numerous charitable organizations was in part responsible for preventing acute poverty. In critical situations, the Bavarian government itself intervened, in pay and price policies, in supply and demand, sometimes against the wishes of the Munich municipal authorities, and implemented job creation measures. If, for example, the mean price of a Scheffel of corn exceeded 28 Gulden, then daily 25,000 pounds of bread were baked and sold three days later for 6 Kreutzer. In the spring of 1847 King Ludwig suspended all debt payments to him by the Munich municipality for two years to provide for extra means for aid programs. When the price of beer—in Bavaria always a politically sensitive point—exceeded a certain price, payment of a short-term, cost-of-living supplement to the gendarmerie for example, to lower level civil servants, chancellory clerks, or to the troops, offered a countermeasure. Minister Abel claimed publicly to have invented these preventative measures. "Even the word cost-of-living supplement in its current general use throughout Germany is of Bavarian origin."[44]

King Ludwig's ambitious construction plans functioned like a government countercyclical job creation program. "Furthermore, where is the misery of the lower classes—a result of the unpredictable and unavoidable conditions of the times—brought to an end by the proven means of public works in a like or similar manner as in Bavaria?"[45] "In order to assist crafts and manufacturing, and the working class tied to them ... an amazing amount was done in Bavaria, and especially in Munich, where this help was needed most urgently. The like has not been seen in any other country ... King Ludwig has dedicated his entire attention, indeed nearly his entire private fortune, to this purpose."[46]

The Munich municipality set up an "inquiry office," which proved to be "an institution of extreme usefulness for the workers," and which offered day laborers a wage of 24 Kreutzer so that they could earn at least the minimum subsistence.[47] This policy was continued by King Max II, who, as early as April 1848, instructed his Interior Ministry, "The improvement of the situation of the working classes will always be an object of my prime concern ... I commission you herewith to begin all rail, water, and street construction projects, as far as the public purse allows, to ensure their unhindered continuation and to ensure, furthermore, that sources of employment be expanded in all possible ways."[48]

In general, mid-nineteenth century Munich was certainly in a state of political equilibrium—"an oasis in the middle of the desert, or perhaps more accurately a desert in the middle of an oasis."[49] At the same time, this equilibrium was fragile and naturally not every conflict could be defused in advance. "Among the German capitals, Munich is distinctive in preserving its respectable composure. Individual, more or less trivial incidents, however—clashes of the police with journeyman shoemakers ...—show how incautious it would be to rely, in foolish confidence, on the continuation of these peaceful conditions, in view of the feverish irritability of all of Europe, or even to succumb to the absolutist superstition that the movement of the revolution could be limited and repressed by the mere power of the police."[50] The most serious troubles, during which 127 people were arrested, took place on 17–18 October 1848 and cost the district governor of Upper Bavaria and the commandant of the Munich garrison their jobs.[51]

The authorities evaluated the violence of these days as a dangerous political provocation, for which they held Viennese students primarily responsible. The Minister of the Interior requested the strictest of control by the Bavarian envoy in Vienna, and customs officials did not admit any Viennese students to the University of Munich for the winter semester 1848/49 and expelled those Viennese already studying there. In the considerable destruction caused by about 150 drunks—the brewer Pschorr later sued for over 24,000 Gulden worth of damage—the *Neue*

Münchener Zeitung saw a barbarian attack on civilization, instigated from Paris and supported from Vienna. "One has to have seen these people to understand the scandalous behavior of which they are guilty. It was mostly young lads whose faces were quite clearly stamped by moral decay and dissolution … Up to now their appearances seem to have a strong communist coloring: because on the *Thal* … these good friends of the citizens took beer from the brewer, bread from the baker, and tobacco and cigars from the shops without thinking that they might pay for them."[52] "On the 6th of October, people were betting in Paris that on the same day a bloody revolt would break out in Vienna: on 6 October Latour was murdered in Vienna. On the thirteenth, Parisian radical papers announced the outbreak of revolt in Berlin for the fifteenth. On the sixteenth, it took place. On the seventeenth, the disorder and troubles began in Munich: everyone is free to reach his own conclusion."[53]

The troubles were, in fact, the usual misbehavior following the fixing of the winter beer price, well-known in Munich, an "excess of dearth" without revolutionary character. Those involved "mostly young men with limited incomes and without family ties in the capital, who vented their resentments towards the well-to-do and influential brewers when the alcohol had its effect, through violent exhibitionism and by taking matters into their own hands. These disturbances did not aim at any change of the existing order," were not resistance of a political nature, and were normally limited to only one day.[54] By way of apology, the district governor of Upper Bavaria in fact raised the point that experience did not lead one to expect troubles on two successive days, especially not in the middle of the week. Thon-Dittner, the Minister of the Interior, had propagated the same view a few days before the troubles started. In his September report on the public mood, written on 12 October 1848, he noted for the district of Upper Bavaria: "during the month of September, nowhere has a serious disturbance of the peace occurred. Even poaching has stopped. The district governor ensures me that the large majority of the population is tired of all the subversive agitation."[55]

The inhabitants of Munich and their representatives were constantly "tired" and notably distanced during these politically active years. In March 1848, the town council could steadfastly refuse to make available the town hall for further "discussion of general political questions" as long as the kingdom's parliament was meeting, a decision that met with no great opposition.[56] The municipal authorities sent no delegates to the preparatory discussions for the German parliament, because they preferred to concentrate strictly on local administration. Even in the spring of 1848, the majority of the people of Munich showed only modest interest in the debates of their municipal representatives and had no desire for them to deal with broader political questions. When demands for public city council meetings, which had been raised from the beginning of 1848, were finally fulfilled in the autumn of that year, "a spectator only now and again [wandered] into the chambers." Twelve burghers made for an "unusually numerous visit."[57]

The People's Association for Discussion of Patriotic Issues, set up at the beginning of April 1848, already had at its third (and final) meeting "difficulties, due to lack of participation in the meeting, to bring the evening tolerably to an end"—and this in the middle of the election campaign for the Frankfurt National Assembly.[58] In the first round of elections for the *Paulskirche* in Munich on 25 April 1848, 6,901 people (42 precincts) voted.[59] In the second round, voter participation sank to 2,825 (30 precincts) and in the third only 715 voted (8 precincts). With about "34,000 enfranchised men" this implies a turnout rate of only 20.3 percent in the first round.[60]

During the summer of 1848, political inactivity in Munich became a theme in the press: "The consequences are inestimable," *Der Volksrath* warned, "if Germany's most robust tribe, the Bavarians, were to withdraw indifferently into themselves during these birth pangs of a new age … All of Bavaria is looking to Munich, it is the metropolis and if it is insipid, then so is the entire land … What horrible consequences this political indifference of Bavaria will have!" [61] Repeated public appeals—"Every good citizen must take sides"—remained without much echo among the people.[62] In the elections to the Bavarian parliament of 30 November 1848, for example, turnout was once again quite low: "Hardly half of the total number of the active voters appeared."[63] In the Munich suburb of Au, the *Deutsche Zeitung* wrote, "there was such half-heartedness during the elections that they tried to call the voters together with church bells, but still did not reach their target in all precincts."[64]

An examination of the two European peripheral powers in 1848, England and Russia, under the rubric of "political quiet zones," would be worthwhile, but cannot be undertaken here. As to events in the Netherlands and Belgium, a detailed review of which is presented in another contribution in the volume, only a few points need be raised.[65] Both states remained peaceful within a revolutionary Europe. While some demonstrations took place in a few cities, they threatened neither the social nor the governmental order.

The reasons for the Dutch King Wilhelm I's (1815-1840) abdication in October 1840 in favor of his son Wilhelm II (1840-1849) and the constitutional reform policies of his successor show remarkable parallels, down to the choice of words, to the changes in Bavaria in 1847/48. When King Ludwig I saw that the position of the monarch within a constitutional monarchy had been qualitatively transformed by events in February/March 1848, he was no longer prepared to continue to govern on the basis of what he saw as an unacceptable circumspection of royal prerogative and decision-making powers. As he wrote in his diary, "I will have stopped governing in any case, whether I retain the crown or not."[66] Instead of "Just and Steadfast," his son Max II chose as his watchword "For Freedom and Legality." With "wise moderation and clever obligation," he placed himself at the forefront, to control the revolution from above and to direct it into the paths of legal constitutional reform.[67]

While the autocratic Wilhelm I feared that he would soon come to regret his abdication, nevertheless this step seemed to him the lesser of two evils compared to the daily concessions that he would have otherwise been forced to make "to satisfy that which cannot be satisfied." His son, on the other hand, chose a reform policy "with one's century, it is necessary to pursue, frankly, the constitutional path."[68] The overall governmental order of the Netherlands was not threatened in 1848, and local disturbances in 1847 also remained without further echo. While pauperization reached a high-point in 1847, social and political lethargy among the lower middle class as well prevented the creation of a revolutionary mood. Unlike the Netherlands, Belgium never really settled down in the period 1830/48. There as well, however, revolutionary developments, like in France, did not occur. In 1848, a hastily introduced reform policy was sufficient to calm things down and to finally put an end to all those republican hopes that had looked to France.

Research on the revolution has concentrated mostly on events in the capital cities. The correction of a provincial perspective needed for an accurate total picture is therefore seldom made appropriately. In the provinces of territorially larger states such as Prussia and Austria, for example, "political quiet zones" developed at the same time as the revolutionary struggles in Berlin and Vienna, because news of the revolution spread only with great delay. Thus considered, a calendar of the revolution which only considers events in the capitals would produce a rather distorted image. For example, in the town of Letschin only eighty kilometers from Berlin, nothing had been heard of the revolution in the capital until Theodor Fontane reported the events in great detail in a letter to his father on 19 March 1848: "Of the events of Saturday in Berlin not a whisper had been heard, even, 'rumor,' which otherwise flies so quickly, had failed, and hence the excitement caused by my letter was immense. Messengers walked and rode into all the neighboring villages to announce the great events, of which I do not know whether they were received with sadness or jubilation."[69]

By this time, news had already reached Lemberg. Anton v. Borkowski, a surveyor from Czernowitz, the capital of the Crown Land of Bukowina in eastern Galicia, reported on this in a letter of 18 March 1848 to his son Carl, who, as a student legionnaire, was actively involved in the revolution in Vienna.[70] In Czernowitz itself, constant rain apparently prevented "acts of indulgence in freedom."[71] On 22 April 1848 Anton v. Borkowski wrote to his son: "No one is able to act himself. In matters of revolutions, like in questions of fashion, Czernowitz looks to Lemberg and Lemberg in turn to Cracow … Our mayor (Alfred Suchanek) pretends not to have heard anything about a revolution and continues to act like in the old days."[72] Only a vague impression of events in Vienna could be gained through the press. In his letter of 10 August 1848, Borkowski complained about the meager flow of information: "Only very seldom does a small bit of world history wander into our country."[73] However, by this time an outbreak of cholera had pushed any interest in the revolution well into the background. "At the moment the revolution has been totally forgotten; for everybody, their own health is more important than the higher goals of freedom."[74]

By mid-May 1848, the revolution had been victorious in Vienna, but "for the provinces, for the rural population, for the foreign nationalities, the revolutionary leaders in Vienna were without authority."[75] The royal court's "move" from Vienna, via Salzburg, to Innsbruck (17 May to 12 August 1848) shifted even further the relative weights of the capital and the provinces. "At that moment when Vienna was no longer the royal residence, it was no longer the capital. Austria's center of gravity had shifted."[76]

The provinces competed against each other, "as everywhere hopes were raised of the blessing of a royal visit." "Vienna has been quiet for a time,"[77] but also "the provinces—especially Graz—began to present themselves again as a 'refuge of peace and tranquillity' far from stormy Vienna, where the clocks kept a different time—above all, a slower one."[78] In August 1848 the revolution in Graz appeared to have "fallen asleep"; political life seemed to have come to a standstill.[79] Diplomatic life from May to August took place in Innsbruck, where numerous diplomats had followed the court, flooding the town—and still nothing happened in Innsbruck! "Innsbruck in 1848—believe me, you could hardly choose a less fertile subject. In Paris, in Madrid, Naples, Milan, Berlin, and Baden, in Vienna, Budapest, Prague—you could say in nearly all of Europe quite exciting things happened in 1848—but in Innsbruck of all places, nothing, but absolutely nothing, took place."[80]

Notes

1. Rudolf Jaworski, "Revolution und Nationalitätenfrage in Ostmitteleuropa," in Rudolf Jaworski and Robert Luft (eds.), *1848/49 Revolutionen in Ostmitteleuropa* (Munich, 1996), 375.
2. Guido Görres, "Die Gründung des Münchener Vereines für constitutionelle Monarchie und religiöse Freiheit, sein Programm und seine Statuten," *Historisch-politische Blätter für das Katholische Deutschland* 22 (1848): 225.
3. Jacob Burckhardt, *Historische Fragmente* (Stuttgart 1957), 26, 270.
4. Theodor Schieder, "Das Problem der Revolution im 19. Jahrhundert," in Theodor Schieder, *Staat und Gesellschaft im Wandel unserer Zeit* (Munich 1958), 11.
5. Richard Cobb, *The Police and the People. French Popular Protest (1789-1820)* (Oxford, 1970).
6. Michel Vovelle, *Die Französische Revolution—Soziale Bewegung und Umbruch der Mentalitäten* (Munich 1982), 143.
7. Quoted in *Das Werden der modernen Schweiz*, Vol. 1 (Lucerne, 1986), 112.
8. Edgar Bonjour, *Geschichte der schweizerischen Neutralität*, Vol. 1 (Basel, 1970), 302-3.
9. Ibid., 303.
10. Gottfried Keller to Eduard Dössekel, 25 March 1848, in Gottfried Keller, *Gesammelte Briefe*, ed. Carl Helbling vol. 2 (Bern, 1951), 454.
11. See the chapter by Thomas Christian Müller in this volume.
12. S. Widmer, *"Das ist die Freiheit!" "Das ist Barbarei!", Sonderbundskrieg und Bundesreform von 1848 im Urteil Frankreichs* (Bern, 1948), 99.
13. Ibid.
14. Arthur de Gobineau, 1849-1854, French ambassadorial secretary in Bern, quoted in ibid., 135.
15. *Schweizerisches Bundesblatt*, Nr. 15, 7 April 1849, 285.
16. Cited in Widmer, "*Das ist die Freiheit!*", 125.
17. F. Rohmer, *Der vierte Stand und die Monarchie*, quoted in Karl-Joseph Hummel, *München in der Revolution 1848/49* (Göttingen 1987), 17.
18. See the chapter by Rüdiger Hachtmann in this volume.
19. Johann Caspar Bluntschli, *Denkwürdiges aus meinem Leben*, Vol. 2 (1848-1861) (Nördlingen, 1884), 39.
20. Dr. Jakob Bauer, Mayor of Munich, in a report to the Ministry of the Interior, Staatsarchiv München, RA 15879, 10 September 1849.

21. Report dated 14 February 1848, published in A. Fournier, "Lola Montez und die Studenten, unedierte Berichte," *Deutsche Revue* 39 (1914): 290.
22. Veit Valentin, *Geschichte der deutschen Revolution 1848-1849*, Vol. 2, (Cologne and Berlin, 1977), 435.
23. Ibid., Vol. 1, 105, Vol. 2, 436.
24. Freiherr von Brenner on 3 January 1848 to Metternich, in A. Chroust (ed.), *Gesandtschaftsberichte aus München 1814-1848, Abteilung II: Die Berichte der österreichischen Gesandten*, Vol. 3 (Munich, 1942), 511-12.
25. Quoted in Hummel, *München in der Revolution von 1848/49,* Anlage 1, 526-28.
26. For this and following points, see Hummel, *München in der Revolution.*
27. King Max II asked for an exact report on the situation in Bavaria on 30 August 1849. Dr. Bauer's report is to be found in Staatsarchiv München, RA 15879 (fasz. 1153).
28. Cited in Horst Schlechte, *Die Allgemeine Deutsche Arbeiterverbrüderung 1848-1850,* Doc. 247 (Weimar, 1979), 402.
29. On this point, see Hummel, *München in der Revolution,* 253-77.
30. Ibid., 278-88.
31. Pierre Aycoberry, "Der Strukturwandel im Kölner Mittelstand 1820-1850," *Geschichte und Gesellschaft* 1 (1975): 83-84.
32. On this point, see Hummel, *München in der Revolution,* 362-77.
33. *Deutsches Staats-Wörterbuch,* ed. by Bluntschli and Brater, Vol. 8 Stuttgart and Leipzig, 1864), 609.
34. Quoted in *Jahrbuch der Stadt München, 1848,* 42.
35. On this, see Hummel, *München in der Revolution,* 37.
36. *Der Generalmarsch in München am 16 März 1848* (Munich, 1848), 1.
37. Bayerisches Hauptstaatsarchiv München, Mlnn. 45404.
38. J. Bauer, *Die Armenpflege in Bayern, insbesondere in der königlichen Haupt- und Residenzstadt München* (Munich, 1850), 23.
39. Guido Görres, *Über die Gefahren der Gegenwart und die Gründung politischer Vereine,* (Munich, 1848), 49-50.
40. Point six of Dr. Bauer's report of 10 September 1849 to the government of Upper Bavaria, Staatsarchiv München, RA 15879.
41. *Polizeianzeiger München,* Nr. 45, 7 June 1848, 593, quoted in Hummel, *München in der Revolution,* 414.
42. Supplement to *Vorwärts,* August 1848, in Bayerisches Hauptstaatsarchiv München, Mlnn 45185.
43. Report of the government of Upper Bavaria to the Ministry of the Interior of 26 November 1847, Bayerisches Hauptstaatsarchiv München, Mlnn 46424.
44. *Münchener politische Zeitung,* Nr. 45, 22 February 1847, 173.
45. *Münchener politische Zeitung,* Nr. 45, 22 February 1847, 173-74. See also Bayerisches Hauptstaatsarchiv München, Mlnn 45001.
46. J. Bauer, *Die Armenpflege,* 138.
47. Announcement of 24 March 1847, *Polizei-Anzeiger,* Nr. 25, 28 March 1847, 279-80.
48. Handwritten note from King Max II to Minister of the Interior Thon-Dittman on 9 April 1848, printed in *Münchener politische Zeitung,* Nr. 92, 10 April 1848, 368.
49. J. Gotthelf, *Historisch-dogmatische Darstellung der rechtlichen Stellung der Juden in Bayern* (Munich, 1851), v. (This was the prize-winning essay in a competition organized by the law faculty of the University of Munich.)
50. J.C. Bluntschli, in *Blätter für politische Kritik,* second issue, 30 June 1848, 79.
51. See Hummel, *München in der Revolution,* 193-208.
52. *Neue Münchener Zeitung,* Nr. 97, 19 October 1848 (special supplement).
53. *Neue Münchener Zeitung,* Nr. 99, 21 October 1848, 398.
54. Hummel, *München in der Revolution,* 199.
55. Bayerisches Hauptstaatsarchiv München, Mlnn 46129.
56. *Münchener politische Zeitung,* Nr. 71, 20 March 1848, 283.
57. *Zopf und Scheere,* Nr. 20, 9 May 1849, Nr. 30, 15 June 1849, 225.
58. *Allgemeine Zeitung,* Augsburg, Nr. 112, 21 April 1848, 1779.

59. On these elections, see Hummel, *München in der Revolution*, 112-159.
60. *Augsburger Postzeitung*, Nr. 120, 29 April 1848, 473.
61. *Der Volksrath*, 26 June 1848, 5.
62. *Der Bayerische Landbote*, Nr. 296, 21 October 1848, 1265.
63. *Neueste Nachrichten*, Nr. 243, 7 December 1848, 2935.
64. *Deutsche Zeitung*, Nr. 322, 6 December 1848, 2456.
65. See the chapter by Horst Lademacher on the Netherlands and Belgium in this volume.
66. Hummel, *München in der Revolution*, 24ff.
67. Recommendation of the Bavarian Government to all outlying authorities in March 1848.
68. Quoted in Lademacher, "The Netherlands and Belgium," (chapter 11 in this volume), n. 19.
69. Theodor Fontane, "Von Zwanzig bis Dreißig, Autobiographisches nebst anderen selbstbiographischen Zeugnissen," *Sämtliche Werke*, Vol. 15 (Munich, 1967), 351.
70. P. Frank-Döfering, *Die Donner der Revolution über Wien. Ein Student aus Czernowitz erlebt 1848* (Vienna, 1988), 145-50.
71. Ibid., 147.
72. Ibid., 50.
73. Ibid., 112.
74. Ibid., 115.
75. Valentin, *Geschichte*, Vol. 2, 76.
76. Ibid., Vol. 2, 77.
77. Ibid.
78. Gerhard Pfeisinger, *Die Revolution von 1848 in Graz* (Vienna, 1986), 124.
79. Ibid., 195-96.
80. Roda Roda, "Wohnung in Innsbruck," quoted in ibid., 1.

Chapter 18

RURAL REVOLUTIONARY MOVEMENTS

Germany, France, Italy

Christof Dipper

In 1848, peasants in many countries of continental Europe became restless. They plundered castles, set fire to archives, mishandled officials and money-lenders, invaded forests, and marched in large numbers into administrative centers to present their demands. In some places, albeit only in 1849 or later, small scale campaigns took place against the state. The clergy had little influence in such cases and at best were able to prevent greater violence; sometimes they, too, were the targets of peasant anger. Elites were surprised and shocked, especially those who had brought about the uprising generally under the slogan "revolution without revolution," as Robespierre had scoffed in 1792. In Germany, people remembered the Peasants' War of 1525, in France the "Great Fear" of 1789, and in Italy the unrest that accompanied the withdrawal of the French in 1799 and 1813/14. Although the individual peasant uprisings of 1848 never extended beyond a local or, at best, a regional setting, contemporaries not only viewed them as very significant, but even as particular examples of a single broad phenomenon. It was feared—or hoped (depending on political stance)—that they would have consequences for the revolution in general.

When the outbreak of collective violence came to an end and the revolution became history, political calculation was replaced by a need for explanation. Why did the rural masses revolt? More explicitly, did the unrest follow a common pattern? Was it a political or social movement? Who were the opposing parties? What was achieved? Why was it the last rural uprising (apart from Italy's)? As far as I can see, such questions have been answered from very different methodological starting points, but almost always from the perspective of regional or national history. As such, the image of a European peasant revolution within the "bourgeois" revolution constantly gained new nourishment, if only implicitly. But even if it's true that all peasant movements had rural origins and that they were violent, are these commonalities enough to endow them with a unitary character across national boundaries? Only comparison can provide an answer. A comparison will show firstly that the particular political contexts caused the movements to go in very different directions, but that secondly a specific constellation of overpopulation and structure of ownership did in fact provide a common trait. In other words, while varying aims such as ending feudalism, tax and tariff reform, the franchise, and the rejection of the modern state led the rural movements of 1848 to take a variety of different forms, a large portion of the society of estate owners in continental Europe was faced with a uniform, desperate, and final attack by the "partageux" (to use a contemporary term).

Modernization theories do not help keep unity distinct from diversity any more than "peasant society" theories do. There are, as Alan Corbin argued, no universal explanations: the violence had many different rationales. Therefore, the three countries under discussion should first be presented for discussion and then, in a second analysis, compared.

Germany

Rural society in Germany was traversed by many dividing lines. Therefore, the number of features and experiences that could serve as a source of unity among all denizens of the countryside had become few, although some not insignificant ones remained. The three most important divisions concerned property-ownership structures, agrarian development and level of emancipation. Through their mutual restrictions these made for a highly fractured village society but one that, however, was not always perceptible at any given time in the same way. In periods of crisis, the fractures could break apart, and in fact, in 1848/49 a range of different modes of behavior and aims are apparent, which can only be summarized here.

The rural population—apart from the privileged and the estate owners—can fall into three clear-cut groups—not belated constructions, but ones all too well-known to contemporaries as they defined their daily life. In modern terms the three groups would be described as full-time peasants, part-time peasants, and day laborers—the last of these possessing at most a small plot of land. Depending on inheritance laws, the latter were better or less well situated socially, but everywhere the class division between them and owners of agricultural enterprises had widened. In contrast to a widespread misapprehension, the number of peasants dependent on subsidiary employment considerably outweighed those who were full-time farmers, although substantial variation existed between individual regions. In some areas, day laborers had already become the large majority.

This social differentiation was accompanied by an economic one. The two could be, but were not necessarily, related. Using trends in farm prices as a criterion, their rise and fall had quite different consequences for those enterprises that were net sellers in the market and those dependent on purchases there. Further distinctions arose in the form of market relationships. Differences in location had not only been a factor since the introduction of the railway and liberal market structures. Around the middle of the nineteenth century a dynamic and market-oriented agricultural economy existed alongside one that was backward and unaware of market forces, although nothing more exact can be said of the numerical relation between the two.

The third division arose from the level of redemption of the land from feudal burdens or *Grundentlastung,* as contemporaries put it. On the eve of the revolution the extent of this redemption varied greatly in the individual parts of Germany. It had been completed in those areas belonging to France until 1814, that is, on the left bank of the Rhine. After 1816, Prussia no longer had the strength to carry through a transformation for the entire state. Hence, Silesia in particular was quite backward. Moreover, Prussia in the interest of more productive large estates, had excluded small-scale land owners from this right to a redemption of their feudal obligations, or had left them at the mercy of the economic calculations of the owners of large estates, ensuring that the latter had access to sufficient labor. The work of emancipation, as it was later positively termed, ended on the class line described above and left hundreds of thousands of families in their old dependent state.

States containing the former high nobility of the Holy Roman Empire, especially in south Germany, were forced to respect another line of division. In those states, peasant emancipation generally only began with the July Revolution, but could not be extended to the ownership complex of these nobles, who with the aid of the Diet of the German Confederation blocked any further loss of privileges. Emancipated and non-emancipated villages often lay close together, and the different levels of emancipation provoked no less a sense of injustice than they affected the purse.

The difference between Southern Germany and Mecklenburg was that in the south neither property structure nor legal situation threatened the existence of peasants as such. On the Baltic Sea, the nobility retained the right to expropriate the peasants' land well into the nineteenth century; they made considerable use of this right, so that in this region there were hardly any peasants to emancipate. In central and northern Germany, on the other hand, a medium and large peasantry had been preserved, which up until 1848 had been emancipated on relatively favorable conditions and was only subject to patrimonial justice.

Apart from these three decisive factors of peasant existence, others contributed to a considerable differentiation in peasant living conditions. Regions with a higher urban density contrasted with those far distant from town-dwellers and transportation routes. Regions where land was passed on as a unit alternated with those where it was divided among the surviving siblings; proto-industrialized zones presented a totally different picture from those in which there was no alternative to agriculture. Overpopulated territories, especially in the southwest, in the Rhineland, and in Saxony, contrasted with regions in which the young could still find land and thus make a living.

Much of what influenced the horizons of rural society was directly dependent on these conditions which, in spite of the influence of conscious human action, still contained a perceptible residue of nature and tradition. Social differences therefore appeared to be within the bounds of the overall, natural experience of the world and so remained legitimate. Admittedly, the state had already entered the scene with its plans for ending the feudal burdens on the land, and had intervened in rural conditions to a degree never seen before. No other social group was subject to such intervention. In the eyes of the peasantry, this intervention did not violate justice. Quite the opposite, numerous local uprisings and countless petitions and court cases were intended to accelerate the slow and incomplete emancipation process or bring about better conditions for the redemption of feudal obligations. The feudal system was totally discredited, and assistance was expected from the government.

The government's involvement, however, followed its own logic, not necessarily reflecting the wishes of the peasant population. This was all the more true for other areas of intervention, including military service, customs borders, taxes, systems of justice, village government and, not least, the common lands. In spite of all the differences in detail, the trend of a growing presence of the state in the villages was as widespread a phenomenon as it was new. It affected every rural resident, especially those from the lower end of society, as the emphasis was not on social justice, but, by necessity on the amortization of state and village debts and on increasing agricultural productivity.

The northern, eastern, and central German states therefore tied the abolition of feudal and seigneurial rights and duties to a division of common lands and the abolition of legal restrictions on individuals' free use and disposition of their farm property, thereby ending, with the stroke of a pen, one thousand years of cooperative practices. That which liberal commentators cautiously criticized as the "tutelage" of the rural population was, in the eyes of day laborers and others in the ranks of the poor, an official declaration of war, as the most important support of their existence had been removed. A considerable amount of local resistance therefore accompanied the process of the so-called agrarian individualization in these parts of Germany.

The south took the opposite road. There the state implemented equal rights of use for common land and hence preserved common village property. Admittedly, land hunger was at best alleviated, and the unfulfilled desire for a division of remaining demesnes shows that the state, here too, followed its own logic.

Its intervention threatened the harmony of the village. In the past, this unity was based on a view of the world which centered on the integrity of peasant economy and way of life, and emphasized extensive autonomy vis-à-vis lords and rulers. Internally and externally, relations were subject to a "justice" that was difficult to define specifically but was as such undisputed. This view of the world, however, lost its integrative power to the degree that the village came to be included in the circulation of money characteristic of the market economy, and to the degree that administrative and political incorporation of the countryside raised problems for which no one had an answer. In the village, it became ever more difficult to speak with one voice and to react as one to challenges. Combativeness was, however, not reduced; indeed quite the opposite.

The rural movement began with the participation by villagers in the revolution in the cities where monarchs resided or other larger urban centers in the early days of March. Returning home, their experience of fundamentally transformed conditions was immediately transferred into collective action, in which they vented their displeasure at the "unreasonable demands" to which they felt they had been subject in the past. This lent the entire action a uniformity that overtaxed law enforcement and led the educated classes to believe that the Peasant Wars were repeating themselves.

Peasant action had many facets, which may be divided into the categories of violent protest and petition. Both were always collective as, under the conditions of village life and economy at the time, individual action certainly could not achieve its aim. Hence the events described below allow, more or less, for generalization. They occurred in Vogelsberg, Wetterau, Odenwald (divided among a number of states), the Main Valley, the Hohenlohe, and parts of the Kraichgau and middle Neckar Valley. In the southern Black Forest, Donaueschingen—the seat of the Fürstenbergs—formed the center, as did the capitals of the Hohenzollern sections of the country in the Alb. The other regions of the south German higher nobility were less affected.

Protest began in the villages themselves. Under threat of violence, mayors were removed, foresters chased away, Jewish traders, peddlers and "usurers" intimidated and subjected to extortion. Actions such as these were often followed by traditional rituals such as kangaroo courts, charivaris and parish festivals—the character of this part of the revolution as a public festival contributed greatly to its early popularity. However, conflicts with the nobility, the next stage, displayed other forms.

A number of villages, indeed entire regions, acted together, and violence played a much greater role. Together with unfavorable structural conditions—a consequence of land division, overpopulation, and moderately mountainous topography—the decades-long refusal of the nobility to make almost any concessions created an especially conflict-laden mixture. As soon as a number of villages had banded together, the mobs set off. They threatened the nobility's administrations, plundered bursaries, sought to set archives on fire, tore down symbols of authority and, in the end, arrived in front of administrative offices or their castles where they forced concessions from chancellory directors or the lords: as a rule the renunciation of dues, jurisdiction, hunting rights, and the right to name pastors and mayors. While material damage was generally limited, the mental, legal, and political consequences were considerable, even if often only short-lasting. In the countryside, "1848" never entered the collective long-term memory to the extent that it did in the cities.

The authorities were generally paralyzed in March, and the only thing they could do was to send government commissioners into the unsettled regions. These commissioners, however, were neither given special powers, nor did they have at their disposal the means to restore public order. The first two to three weeks in March belonged more to the rural areas than the cities. In these circumstances, the higher nobility had little choice but to renounce its privileges more or less unconditionally in official statements to the governments. The lesser nobility was forced to do this on the spot, as mentioned above.

It was only in April that the ministries once again began to function properly. They sent troops into the countryside to restore peace; that was not difficult as the local revolts had ended on their own and the rural population avoided direct confrontation with the military. At the same time, they quickly introduced interim ordinances, and even permanent legislation, allowing the peasants subject to the direct overlordship of the nobility the possibility of redeeming their feudal burdens and in general accelerating the redemption of the land, and on much better conditions. The parliaments of the individual states passed the relevant bills between April and June 1848, thus pulling the rug out from under a large part of the potential unrest.

The spark of revolution was not limited to southern Germany. Still in March, it sprang over into Silesia—very backward in regard to emancipation—and in April it reached that part of Saxony in which noble property was concentrated. The focus was the Schönburg reserved lordship where on 5 April town and the country demonstrated together, setting the Waldenburg castle on fire. In Silesia, protest was less violent, not least because the Prussian military, following the French model, was on the spot surprisingly quickly with their mobile columns. Rich peasants and mayors marched together on government offices and demanded a total end to the feudal system by issuing formal "letters of freedom." In this they were not successful, and thus Silesia became the most unsettled Prussian province: no other province sent more radical deputies from the rural population to the Berlin National Assembly, nowhere else did villagers more willingly flock to the mass organizations led by the democrats—the Silesian "Rustics Association" founded in August counted 200,000 members—and no other province experienced so many waves of protest, which continued into 1849, although participants and aims often changed.

Up to this point the account has dealt primarily with the peasants; while they were not the only ones protesting, they determined the course of events in the countryside in the spring of 1848 and they were the ones who benefitted most from the new laws. Their aims could be summed up in the decade old slogan "liberty and property," coined by the liberals and taken up and implemented by the bureaucratic elite. That peasant demands could be read as bourgeois ones ensured their gaining acceptance. Peasants were forgiven the method chosen for enforcing their demands once the unrest had died off.

Other aims, other methods, other regions, and above all other times come into view when turning to the rural lower classes. While peasant rebellion was focused in southwestern Germany and had its center in the Odenwald, violent protests of the village poor arose above all in Hanover, Prussia, and Mecklenburg. These were directed against the "rich" in general and correspondingly made little distinction between peasants, estate owners, and demesne leaseholders. They lasted up into August and are a secondary phenomenon of the 1848 revolution, as they were rather "fragments of a social skirmish,"[1] which had its beginnings in the eighteenth century and did not necessarily end in 1848.

The southwest, too, did not remain free of such events, but the practice of equal inheritance mitigated social distance among the inhabitants of the village, so that the object of their actions was different. The "state" was much more their target, and this explains their greater participation in the campaign for the imperial constitution in 1849. In any case, there was a series of local protests from Nassau into the Main and Neckar valleys in the spring of 1848 which did not so much aim at emancipation but rather demonstrated clear traits of a religiously colored movement of the poor. Its participants wanted, on the one hand, the restoration of extinct seigneurial duties—access to meadows and forests, the right to gather fallen leaves and to take wood for construction, etc.—on the other hand, they had an almost chiliastic hope "that soon everything will be divided up."[2] In the north and east aims were similar and here and there demands were underlined with thefts from fields and forest and poaching, but seldom with occupation of land, although the latter was by far the main problem.

As lower class protest was less likely to take violent form than anti-feudal peasant movements, petitions provide better information on its extent and aims. Although it has been comparatively rare up to now that those petitions relating to agrarian questions have been systematically analyzed, the images from them fit together into a snapshot of rural poverty and distress.

Like the peasant petitions, those of the tenant-laborers [*Heuerlinge*], cottagers and day laborers were distributed across a large part of 1848 with a majority in the second and third quarters. However, those model petitions written, circulated, and presented to parliament by lawyers and deputies only contain lower class demands in the southwest. In their demands, the wishes of the lower classes went against the mood of the era—such as the request of a rural worker in Oldenburg "that the good old days be brought back."[3] Democrats and communists, on the other hand, politicized the programmatic catalog of the rural poor so that the latter's wishes functioned only as means to an end. This did not lead to a long-term alliance.

Most of these petitions were, like the ones on ending feudalism, addressed to the parliaments and governments of the individual states where decisions had to be taken. Nonetheless, so many petitions found their way to Frankfurt that the constitutional committee saw itself moved to restrict the autonomy of village governments so that they would not irresponsibly distribute their property among the local poor. The poor saw in such a redistribution their escape from poverty. Liberal and conservative observers, however, saw in it a renunciation of prevailing social norms.

Consequently one could hear the accusation of "communism" from this side, the most severe judgement possible in the 1840s. In Westphalia, Hanover, and the Prussian provinces east of the Elbe, "division" specifically meant a revision of enclosure or of the distribution of the common lands—undertaken at the same time as emancipation—from which the lower classes were left empty-handed. The opposite was true in the southwest, where there were extensive common lands that were to be distributed among the villagers equally and without compensation. On top of this came other demands designed to relieve distress in subsistence farming, especially rights to the forests; just how short the supply of land was for these production units is shown, not least, in petitions for the agricultural use of roadsides and pathsides. The desire for emancipation among Prussian peasants, still subject to compulsory labor services shows, on the other hand, that all these demands did not aim at a return to the feudal system, but at a safeguarding or restoration of traditional forms of earning a living within the framework of a "moral economy."

While the parliaments of the south German states and the Frankfurt National Assembly, and, following an almost two-year-long delay, the Prussian parliament, met peasant demands to the extent that they were consistent with the ideas of civil society, the hopes of the poor were not fulfilled. The common lands were not distributed in the south, nor was their privatization reversed in the north and east. Given the doctrinaire economic liberalism in Prussia, such a step was certainly out of the question. In the southwest, where a different point of view prevailed, the pauperism of the 1840s had shown that intensively exploited small holdings were particularly subject to crisis, which led to a government change of heart in agrarian policies. Not only were common lands not to be distributed, even the "slaughter of farms," which, in places, had reached a considerable level, came to be seen in another light, without, however, leading to serious legislative action. A solution to the social question in the countryside in the sense of alleviating village poverty was therefore not attempted by the German governments, either in 1848 or later.

The rural population's alternatives for action in 1848/49 were, however, not limited to a choice of protest or petition. As far as the press is concerned, while no peasants have been shown to have been journalists, they were active readers. Even if a history of reading in the 1848 revolution has not yet been written, a relation between the level of general dissatisfaction and reading habits emerges from the many local studies. The existence of rural reading circles has been demonstrated, and they appear to have been no rarity in those unsettled times. The same applies to political associations.

A jump in the level of politicization had already occurred in Germany in the winter of 1847/48. This had also included the "little people" as can be seen from protests of urban and rural poor and of the younger generation against their exclusion from elections for the National Assembly. At least a large part of male adults was able to take part for the first time in the spring of 1848 (not including elections for village councilors). Participation levels, however, varied. Political mobilization, as well as the expectations projected on this new possibility of articulation, can be seen in the Rhein-Main area, where voter participation "was especially high in the countryside."[4] Elsewhere, in Westphalia for example, the lower classes, at least, did not show much interest in the elections.

The case of political associations was similarly differentiated. Two features deserve mention here. The first is that the association as such was not a form of rural sociability; it had to be imported into the countryside. That was, apparently, only possible where the level of political agitation was high, but also depended on the willingness of those villagers not from the peasant milieu to take on a leading role. The second is that not all political currents put the same amount of effort into gaining a presence in the countryside. The constitutionalists, as the liberals called themselves at the time, remained generally an urban phenomenon. (Prussian) conservatives were able to make the first step into the (Protestant) countryside, but did not penetrate into the ranks of the peasantry. Catholics did not require a political organization in the villages.

The democrats, on the other hand—who understood popular sovereignty as a democracy made practicable through parties, with social reform as its most important task—endeavored from May/June 1848 onwards to extend their organization into the countryside. In the course of the next twelve months, they achieved considerable success. This has been well demonstrated for specific cases in the Rhein-Main region, Lower Franconia, and Silesia. For Baden and Württemberg, parts of the Rhineland and Ries, there are good reasons to assume their achievement was equally successful

Reasons for the affinity between democrats and the rural population differed, depending on the region. The Silesian Rustics' Association, founded by the democrats, demanded the abolition of feudal burdens without compensation and an end to tax privileges for owners of noble estates. Their program hence expressed the maximum expectations of large peasants and the favored hereditary tenants. No mention was ever given to a redistribution of land. Even after the Brandenburg government in Prussia promised improved conditions for emancipation (but naturally not without compensation) in December 1848, problems were discussed in association meetings which interested above all the upper strata of rural society: village government, improved schools, and especially the founding of rural credit institutions. An alliance with market-gardeners and allotment holders, that is with the majority of villagers, did not occur, although the editor of the *Schlesische Dorfzeitung* [Silesian Village News], the journal of the Rustics Association, made an effort in this direction in the spring of 1849.

In the southwest, the picture was different. In Nassau and Hessen-Darmstadt, where the associations only reached the villages after the legislatures had already passed new laws on emancipation, it was above all their activity in questions of local government, especially their defense of village autonomy, that made the democrats popular among the rural population. That they were the only ones, apart from the Catholics, demanding universal suffrage naturally contributed to the positive response they received as well. However, questions of "high politics" were also discussed in countless association meetings. In short, the democrats broke through the system of the notables and exploited a ground-swell of politicization.

In the southwest, conditions were especially favorable to the democrats' efforts to encompass the countryside: weak class divisions, greater urban density, at least in Protestant areas a lower level of political religiosity and, in part, a longer and acknowledged tradition of social revolt. It was reactivated for the last time in the campaign for the imperial constitution in 1849, which also reached the villages. Once more, defeudalization without compensation and total autonomy of village government appeared in the catalog of demands passed by mass meetings in Reutlingen, Offenburg and Erbach/Odenwald. In the military action, which took place during the hay and grain harvest, there was little peasant participation. Farm workers and day laborers, possibly without work because of the extremely poor market, were, however, among the captured and dead. Democratic-peasant affinity did not end with a retreat by the peasants into a quasi-natural conservatism. The cause lay rather in the democrats' loss of prestige in the early summer of 1849 and was then formally ended with the ban on associations and abolition of universal suffrage in the wake of the counter-revolution.

Seen as a whole, this affinity remained the exception. In comparison with France, for example, it can be seen that the social and political conditions for a long-term mobilization and politicization of the rural population were rather unfavorable. The dynasties were not overthrown; universal suffrage could not fully develop its potential; repression began earlier; and, above all, the peasants, in spite of the agrarian crisis, were nowhere near so close to ruin as their fellow farmers across the Rhine.

France

In France, as in Germany, various lines of division traversed the rural population, and here, too, there were certain unifying elements that could compensate for the differences to a certain extent. From the German point of view, most noticeable is the quite different form taken in the distribution of property. French peasants not only competed with noble estate owners for land, but also with the bourgeoisie; relations with the latter were especially tense, because of their tendency to invest as much money as possible in real estate. It was not the peasants but the bourgeoisie that was the biggest winner in the land sales following the French Revolution of 1789. Approximately 75 percent of the rural population owned, before 1789, about 30 to 40 percent of the productive land; afterwards, no more than fifty percent.

A second peculiarity, still in comparison with the German case, was that only a small proportion of the nobility and an even smaller one of the bourgeoisie directed the exploitation of their landed property, or even turned this exploitation over to an agent. Property was instead generally leased to peasants, in a block, or per field, the proverbial parcel of land. Rural society in France therefore had a different physiognomy than the German. Some one million rentiers, who owned about half the land, shared the majority of countryside with the comparatively few landowners who worked their property themselves and the large tenants, the "fermiers."

The mass of the agrarian population consisted of "cultivateurs," and of "manouvriers," the so-called parcel peasants, who did not themselves own sufficient land and therefore had to lease additional fields and often had to seek further sources of income as seasonal or migrant workers or in outwork. Unlike in Germany, however, a class of landless day laborers hardly existed. The "cultivateurs," owners of farms that provided a full time occupation who played an important role in the villages, mediated between rich and poor in many respects, insofar as a castle with resident nobleman did not shift the weight of influences.

The economic lines of divisions traversing rural society can thus be gleaned. They were, however, not equally distributed throughout France. Structurally, the northern and northeastern regions were generally more modern than the west, the southwest, and the south. In those regions, overpopulation, short-term leases, and the predominance of small farms provided for continual tensions. The hunger crisis of 1846/47 affected the so-called "archaic France" less than the modern one, because the south's diet was different and Russian grain helped to ease distress.

Much more intensively than in Germany, French agrarian society was tied together by monetary relations: a minority were creditors, the majority debtors. With money, peasants paid for foodstuffs, craft products, taxes, interest and debts. The proverbial indebtedness of parcel peasants as a consequence of the lack of land and higher direct taxes has often been described; especially drastically by Karl Marx, who saw in their situation a clear analogy to the industrial proletariat and drew from this the hope for a successful revolution.[5] In this, as is well known, he was mistaken.

Clearly high indebtedness increased a dependency on stable farm prices. The depression that began in 1848 and extended to 1851 hit especially hard those parts of France that came through the previous crisis comparatively well. This time, the lack of land was especially noticeable, because on top of an unfavorable ownership structure came the abolition of common meadows and pasture rights and the division of common lands—energetically pushed through by Guizot's government— which had until then served as a land reserve for the village poor.

With this, we have reached the fourth determining factor of conditions in the countryside. Louis-Philippe had not seen himself as the protector of peasantry, and thus the villages played their part in the "mania of revolt"[6] during the July Monarchy. From the mutually supportive village community, peasants sought to defend themselves against "violations of the norms" by large estate owners intent on modernization, but especially against the forest administration that enforced the "Code forestier" of 1827. Relations between the government and peasant communities can be described as troubled even during the July Monarchy; if there was not a complete break, it was due to the mediating role of notables.

State intervention in the villages was extensive, and from the peasant point of view it was unjustified and indeed unjust. As there were no agrarian experts within the bureaucracy, nor among the opposition, the government lacked any idea of its image among the rural population and of rural demands. Problems included high taxes on land, home ownership, salt and alcoholic beverages, closing off of woods, elimination of collective use rights privatization of the common land, appointment rather than election of mayors, military duty as a "special tax" on the poor; in addition to these, the land register (completed in 1850) was conceived as a uniquely precise instrument of surveillance, and included every single parcel of land, and a very exact census that took place every ten years.

To the peasants, the "state" meant tax collectors, gendarmerie, foresters and bailiffs. The personified enemies of the villagers included the mayor, often named by the government, who, for his part, had command of the field watchmen, and naturally, the money lenders as well, notorious for being "usurers," who were generally members of the agrarian bourgeoisie and often also notaries, and, not least, the landowners from whom parcels were leased. It is no surprise that the regime of the July Monarchy had little support in the countryside.

The February Revolution was totally unexpected in the provinces and temporarily robbed representatives of the state of their power. Immediately violent conflicts concerning the forest broke out in Alsace, in the sub-Alpine regions and in the Pyrenees. Many "usurers" were also threatened and forced to release people from their debts, which led in Alsace to antisemitic attacks much like in neighboring southwestern Germany. In many places, collective practices were revived, in more or less violent fashion. In other places, day laborers forced through higher pay. But nowhere—and this is significant—did the protests take on a mass character as they did on the right bank of the Rhine.

Altogether, French peasants experienced 1848 quite differently than their German counterparts. The decisive difference arose first in that the republicans who had come to power were not seriously interested in rural distress and did not make one single peasant demand their own. Instead, they remained fixated on urban and especially Parisian unemployment, which in spring and summer threatened the existence of the government.[7] Second, by introducing universal suffrage, applied three times in 1848, the republicans did place themselves at the mercy of the village—where, as mentioned above, 75 percent of the population lived. The "sleeping giant" thus suddenly became a referee, quickly adapted itself to this role and, following that, actively intervened in politics. This intervention requires closer examination.

The elections to the constituent national assembly, held on Easter Monday 1848 in the cantonal seats, had the character of a festival in many places. The villages marched united, sometimes with the priest, the mayor or even the lord at their head and voted against the "Quarante-huitards" [forty-eighters]. This had nothing to do with the 45 percent surcharge on direct taxes introduced by the provisional government on 16 March to finance its ambitious job creation scheme, as, up to 23 April, enforcement, which especially affected landowners, had not really gotten going. Tax strikes and unrest only began in the second half of the year. Election results reflected much more a shock effect. Widespread dissatisfaction in the countryside had not yet been translated into (party) politics so that local notables decided the race among themselves. This was repeated in municipal and departmental elections in the summer of 1848.

French peasants recognizably became aware of their own interests only in the presidential election of 10 December 1848, in which the large majority voted for Louis-Napoléon and thus helped him to victory. It was a protest against representatives of the Second Republic who ignored agriculture, not an expression of shared convictions with the prince, who lacked as much an agrarian program as his main opponent, Cavaignac. However, the impoverished classes of the rural population—at the time suffering a crisis of price depression on top of the structural crisis and who were the poorest group in France—saw in the name Bonaparte the embodiment of their wishes. They sought shelter with the nephew of the person who represented the guarantee of revolutionary achievements and better times. It was a victory of the Napoleonic legend.

The vote for Louis-Napoléon was in truth, however, politically polyvalent. This had already become obvious in May 1849 when the countryside split into "white" and "red" regions in the parliamentary elections—a result of attempts begun in the meantime to include the provinces in party politics. The right had stirred up fear of upheaval, declared order, property, and religion to be inviolable and put its money on the influence of the notables. The left had only just discovered the countryside, and developed an agrarian program which spread among the population with clever propaganda—founding the *Feuille de village*, politicizing rural forms of sociability and issuing tens of thousands of copies of an appeal "To the Peasants of France."

This program of the left promised repayment of the 45 Centime surcharge, abolition of the tax on salt and alcoholic beverages, cheaper credit, and free elementary schools—all themes that affected each and every class of the rural population. This was less true of "Montagnard" demands to open the forests for woodcutting, pasturing, and hunting and even more so concerning the occasionally raised question of a redistribution of land. That leftists suggested the necessity of a second revolution that was to take place in a strictly legal form, supported only by the ballots of the "ordinary people." The left thus presented itself as the protector of the constitution while simultaneously aiming at a different republic. The Bonapartist state reacted with increasing harshness to this program and its adherents, but did not reap approval everywhere. Quite the opposite: through its reliance on justices of the peace, police, and gendarmerie, whose presence in the cities and in the countryside was becoming ever more tangible, the government was creating itself its own opponents.

In the elections of 13 May 1849, rural France no longer spoke with one voice. South of La Rochelle-Metz the provinces voted "red." This was not a random outcome, as the electoral geography of the twentieth century has shown: the same regions have provided stable majorities for the left up through the early years of the Fifth Republic. There has been much speculation about the causes of this political development. It is fairly certain that it was not a matter of specific historical landscapes nor that religious dissent or the social structure of the population determined their electoral behavior. In other words, "red" France was neither especially poor or Protestant, nor a region of the Occitaine dialect nor backward. It was mostly the France of villages and towns situated close together, where communication networks had long been dense and a specific sociability had formed. Admittedly, social tensions also played a role in transforming these structural preconditions into the political sphere.

In the "red" provinces, the peasants had dissociated themselves from their traditional spokesmen, the notables and the clergy, and placed their trust in the republican bourgeoisie of lawyers, journalists, doctors, and teachers. In sixteen departments the candidates of the left achieved an absolute majority; altogether the opposition gained thirty-five percent of the vote.[8] There is some disagreement as to the reasons for the electoral behavior in the "white" provinces; religiosity, systems of leasing, and the geographic nature of settlement are most often named as causes. They had suffered no more than the "red" regions from over-burdening, lack of land, and agricultural depression.

This was also the reason that the agrarian question continued to remain on the agenda. It must be all the more emphasized that the uprising against Louis-

Napoléon's coup, which shook especially central and southern France from 5 to 10 December 1851, did not have agrarian aims as its first priority.[9] Rather the rebels defended their republic, no less that had been the case in the campaign for the imperial constitution in Germany two and a half years before. One can therefore not speak of a peasants' war, also because peasant participation remained below their share of the population.

Nonetheless, agrarian conditions played a decisive role in mobilizing the rural population. The important factor in these conditions was not so much the collapse in prices at the time, but, rather a more structural crisis of property ownership, the question of the future direction of agriculture: strictly individual and capitalistic or with a cooperative element and to this extent subsistence oriented. In 1851 the old struggle for forests and meadows could also set off a revolt of entire communities. In this respect, much appeared antiquated, above all, of course, an idea of a "justice" that the rebels sought to restore by violence. A new element appeared, however, in that the village did not enter the fight as a cooperative but as a political collective, that it placed its trust in a politically schooled opposition in consultation with the world outside instead of acting autonomously. It was a matter of "high politics," the one side of which was social tensions within the village, and the other side increasing intervention by the state.

Up until the coup, the left had promoted a strictly legal course that the rural population had followed; both placed their hopes in the parliamentary elections scheduled for 1852 that were anticipated with almost chiliastic expectations. This they did not want to lose. Bonaparte's coup offered an unexpected opportunity for getting the regime, which had little to do with the popular image of the "republic," off their backs. The authentic republic, "la Bonne," as it was often called in the countryside, was a self-governing commonwealth of artisans and peasants without gendarmerie, bailiffs, conscription, tax collectors and, naturally, without the "rich." That the democratic elite had another idea of the "republic" was not a problem as long as armed revolt delayed having to make a choice. Defeat, severe repression, and twenty more years of mostly clandestine political education ensured that the system established in 1871 then indeed became something like a "republic of the peasants," admittedly one oriented toward a more modern content.

In view of the most pressing peasant demands, the uprising was as unsuccessful as the German campaign for the imperial constitution. That is not surprising in view of their defeat. But the rural population of those regions that did not revolt in 1851 also gained nothing. Land remained the great problem, one which in the following years, however, was not dealt with collectively and politically but rather individually. Experts have long attributed the stagnation of French agriculture between 1840 and 1880 to investment in land purchases instead of in increasing productivity. This was possible due to continually rising prices for agricultural products, on the one hand, and a more limited interest by capital in land investment in light of industrialization. Because of reduced demographic pressure and an increasing number of jobs outside agriculture, conditions in fact eased, until in the 1880s a new crisis would hit French, and European, agriculture.

Italy

In Italy, conditions were different in three respects. The change of system, to begin with political events, had already commenced in 1847, in Piedmont, Tuscany, and the papal states. These three states formed a customs union in November, the political significance of which was far greater than its economic import. Very significant for the course of events in 1848 was that Pius IX, who had taken office in 1846, awakened the impression that he sought to be a national leader. Above all, this stance prevented the clergy and the rural population from immediately rebelling against the liberal estate owners as had happened in 1799 and 1813/14. The change of system thus retained its anti-Austrian tone.

It should not be forgotten that a wave of uprisings that threatened the existing regimes also began on the Italian peninsula in Messina in September 1847. It quickly spread to Reggio Calabria in January 1848 and then to Palermo and ended with the expulsion of the Neapolitan administration and army. The uprising in Palermo directly triggered a constitutional movement that led to the granting of constitutions in mainland Naples and Tuscany in February, and Piedmont and the papal states in March. Only the Habsburg regions remained excluded from these reforms, which led the oppositional "moderati," the aristocratic and bourgeois estate owners, to the conclusion that the constitutional question and the national question were inseparable.

If Italy was a pioneer from the political point of view, socially it brought up the rear, at least when measured by industrialization. This was not by chance, conforming instead to the declared will of the landowning elite, who did not wish to lose control over the lower classes. The countryside was, namely, subject to the city, and had been so for centuries. Its legal and social structures were tailored completely to the needs of the urban population. For the countryside, the city had a contradictory mixture of contempt and patriarchal care and moreover basked in the glow that domestic and foreign writers and travelers spread concerning the condition of the peasantry. In reality this situation was anything but idyllic; it continued to worsen through the nineteenth century because of demographic pressure, falling wages, rising lease prices, and reduced land reserves.

In the nineteenth century Italy became a peasant country without peasants. Below 500 meters, that is in the zone of fertile land, rentier landowners, whether individuals or companies, had the property more or less to themselves. The rest of the land was divided among a million-strong army of dwarfholders, who were also tenants or farm workers or who had a supplementary occupation, such as silkworm raising, particularly prevalent in the north. The paradoxical observation of 1884 that the countryside was populated by "a veritable proletariat of proprietors,"[10] hits the nail on the head. In the course of a process that had begun shortly after 1800, the rural classes had to a great extent lost their claims to what had been until then comparatively extensive common land. Under pressure from estate owners, wasteland and underbrush as well as meadows and parcels of arable were surveyed, divided, and auctioned off. The heavily indebted, impoverished rural population received almost nothing. The estate owners had forced this step on reluctant governments who feared unrest—quite justifiably as it would prove—in the hope of compensating for a fall in rents caused by a decade-long decline in farm prices. From 1820 onwards, prices for wheat fell and they did so from 1830 onwards for rice, oil, and wine—that is, with the exception of raw silk for all the important marketable products. The agrarian crisis was therefore worse in Italy than elsewhere, related, on the one hand, to agriculture's more restricted buying power, and, on the other, to its greater dependence on the market as a consequence of an unusually high level of urbanization.

The two factors taken together produced constellations that, in this form, were seen nowhere else in 1848. The large liberal-conservative landowners had to prevent the government from making concessions to the rural population, whose increasing distress was (re-) discovered in the 1840s and whose situation worsened dramatically in the subsistence crisis of 1845/47. In those states where the landowners had taken power in 1847, such worries were unfounded. In Lombardy-Venetia, on the other hand, with its troubled relations especially between aristocratic landowners and the Austrian administration, high-level state officials, especially Field Marshall Radetzky, occasionally thought out loud about a "Galician solution," that is a peasant uprising tolerated to a certain extent by the government. No less threatening from the point of view of landowners was an attempt by the government to change lease rights and the law on village government and to transform the military into a peasant militia. The agrarian question especially in upper Italy, could therefore have been turned into an instrument against a national movement controlled by the landowners, all the more since plebeian loyalties to the royal houses still functioned among the population. The restoration regimes could not play this card.

The uprising broke out, corresponding to the logic of this constellation, in Venice on 17 March and in Milan on 18 March 1848 after the news of Metternich's fall had been received. During the five-day street fighting in the Lombard city, major landowners were successful in wresting leadership from the democrats and in forming a provisional government on 21 March. They called on the Piedmontese for help, who were successful in pushing Radetzky back to the fortified quadrilateral in upper Italy. Led by rural doctors, students and above all by priests, who had spread neo-guelf ideas into the most remote villages, the parcel peasants rose up in the hill zones and even more in the Alpine valleys and streamed into the provincial cities where they formed military columns and marched through Milan.

The mood was joyful, as it was generally believed that the high taxes had been abolished with the Austrian retreat. In the plains, where there were practically only landless leaseholders and, above all, agricultural laborers, the unrest took on an anti-landowner character from the beginning. This was all the more threatening as deserting soldiers had brought their weapons into the villages. In all cities, therefore, civic guards were set up to protect the social order and estate owners living in the provincial cities retreated to Milan.

In April, when the "Germans" had left the country, the uprising in the countryside changed in nature. In the foothills of the Alps—where a large proportion of the inhabitants were small peasants dependent on leasing or supplementary occupations—there were ever louder calls for a return of the common lands that had been privatized by the law of 1839. Refusal to pay taxes, turnpike tolls, and rents in the hill zones of Brianza became so widespread that the Archbishop of Milan made a tour to calm the population. The head of the provisional government, Count Casati, saw in the peaceful action the work of Austrian emissaries, who were aiming for a "communist uprising."[11] The rural population, excluded from the militia, set up their own formations, sometimes consisting of hundreds of people, occasionally led by a mounted and crowned stable lad, signifying reverence for the Pope and the Piedmontese king. After the farm workers in Lower Lombardy had also risen up in June and July with a call to redistribute land and fight against the militia, it was finally clear that modern agrarian structures were open to debate in this especially progressive part of Italy.

Only a very few participated in the war of the "lords"; an attempt to raise an army in June and the "levée en masse" announced at the beginning of August for the defense of Milan were met with shouts of "Viva Radetzky," which were not pro-Austrian, but antiseigneurial. However, even when Radetzky followed a determined antielite policy after retaking Milan at the beginning of August, he did not intend a change in property ownership. In this respect everyone was in agreement—the "moderati" and the Austrian administration as well as the democrats around Cattaneo, the spokesman of the Lombard educated elite and entrepreneurs, who represented urban interests no less than their liberal-conservative opponents. Insofar as any attention was given to rural problems, the furthest they went was to recommend the government to take up the task of improving the leaseholds in a "spirit of evanglical fraternity."[12]

The situation in the Veneto was no different, where, with Daniele Manin, control had remained in the hands of a republican bourgeoisie who had paid no attention to agricultural questions. Especially in the northern and eastern parts of the Terra ferma, in which an antiquated agrarian system with a relatively high level of peasant ownership had been preserved, the revolution could have taken another course, one leading to broad social support for the total expulsion of the Austrians. The law of 1839, which required the privatization of the common lands, had also led to considerable tensions in Veneto, including even land occupations, common elsewhere and highly ritualized. But here, in 1848, a number of preconditions were lacking. First, there was no military conflict, which always undermined public order; second, the peasants with better leases were taken into the civic guards; and, third, the new government, in immediately abolishing the poll tax, reducing salt prices and releasing conscripts, disposed of three significant sources of general dissatisfaction. Due to these measures and because of anti-Habsburg activities by the clergy, at least a significant portion of the rural population sympathized with the revolution. The revolutionaries, however, trusting in a Piedmontese victory, decided against establishing their own forces and were therefore rapid victims of the Austrian counter-offensive in the summer of 1848; only the city of Venice itself kept up resistance until August 1849.

Initially, central Italy was spared a continuation of the revolution; instead, it returned to its starting point in the south. In April, disturbances began in the mainland portion of the Kingdom of Naples, which reached renegade Sicily in August. Not for the first time, the rural population rebelled. Their protests were directed against the "rich" in general, which in the south also often included the priests. The rebellion was spontaneous, large-scale and violent and turned above all on the question of land, as from 1806 onwards the extensive common lands had been privatized in this region as well. Armed bands, led by a "capitano del popolo," [captain of the people] occupied lands, tore down border markers, set fire to hedges and devastated the fields. They then marched into the main towns or provincial centers where they destroyed land and tax registers and rent rolls.

In carrying out these actions, the peasants shouted out cheers for the constitution, which did not spare them an imputation of "communism" by the educated.[13] The rebels believed in all seriousness that the social order had been overturned by the constitution. This led the landowners to hastily establish militias, which were occasionally involved in outright battles with the rebels. Nonetheless, peasants in parts of Basilicata and Apulia began with a distribution of land after the collapse of Bourbon authority in May 1848. In some places this was not restricted to the former common lands; instead all land was equally distributed among the villages. In such cases, a semantic recasting of "communista" was practically forced upon bourgeois observers.[14] The rebels only found sympathy in Calabria, where republicans, due to their long-existing secret societies and their legal arm, the political associations, had successfully taken control of the entire province. However, even the Mazzinians were, of course, unwilling to overturn the entire order of property; redistribution was to be limited to common lands because these had been "usurped" by the "rich."[15] Actions by the rural classes showed all the traits of a "jacquerie." The fear and horror that they caused bore no relationship to that which they actually achieved, namely nothing. The army, called back from the north, restored control of the mainland provinces in the autumn and winter, and in April 1849 it reconquered Sicily.

A second wave of revolution, with much more radical features, hit previously peaceful central Italy in the fall of 1848. There, the democrats took power after Pius IX and the Tuscan Grand Duke had fled to Gaeta. While in Tuscany the agrarian question was raised neither by share-croppers nor by the new government, the Roman Republic reacted to political and social tensions between farm workers and small peasants on the one hand, and landowners on the other with an agrarian political program. It was unique in its form and was oriented toward the first Roman Republic of 1789/99, also in relation to the anti-clericalism of the measures.

In order to tie the rural population to the revolution—the municipal elections of 21 March 1849 once again showing the pressing nature of their pacification—the triumvirate led by Mazzini issued a number of decrees in April 1849 ordering church property—which had been expropriated in February—to be distributed among its present leaseholders and farm workers against payment of a moderate rent. This was not uncontroversial and took place against the protest of rural notables, who controlled the militias and municipal administration—whose influence, however, did not extend to Rome because of the lack of a constitution and parliament. The government, for its part, was supported in this matter by many political clubs, which were aware of their sociopolitical responsibility, although neither small leaseholders nor certainly day laborers could afford membership. The municipalities controlled by the democrats began immediately to implement the program, but this experiment with redistribution could never be completed because of the fighting beginning in May around the capital. At the very least, it shows that in the late phase of the 1848 revolution in Italy—when the "Moderati" who had set the tone in the north had already been eliminated—with Saffi, Crispi, and even Garibaldi, those forces within the democrats had been successful which viewed the national and social questions as equally important and closely bound together.

In his *Prison Writings*, Gramsci placed the blame for what he considered an unsuccessful unification on the fact that there was no agrarian revolution in the Risorgimento; since their publication in 1949, his arguments have been the subject of much discussion in Italy.[16] It is undisputed that the Italian nation-state founded in 1859/60 was based on an alliance of major landowners and democrats, which ignored social aspirations (and the Catholic identity) of the majority of the population and therefore could not survive without repression. On the other hand, however, Gramsci's theses, which Marx had already put forward,[17] are without foundation.

None of the aims of the 1848 revolution were shared by the rural population. The contrast between city and country, greater in Italy than elsewhere, was an insurmountable barrier to the political inclusion of the rural population, who saw themselves quite justifiably as victims of urban interests, while, on the other hand, the revolutionaries remained dependent on existing agrarian structures. A mobilization through elections was also lacking—with the exception of the Roman Republic—as there was no parliamentary tradition on the peninsula and therefore other things seemed more pressing to the revolutionaries of 1848. Thus all political conditions for an uprising comparable to the campaign for the imperial constitution or the insurrection against Louis-Napoléon's coup were absent.

Moreover, insofar as the limited research available allows for such a conclusion, ownership structure as such was not attacked by the rural population. They were united in their protest against the privatization of the common land reserves of woods and pasture, while the few experts in agrarian conditions complained about the worsening of lease conditions and high taxes. That leaseholders and day laborers underlined their demands for redistribution with marches and occupation of land—which could not be really prevented by the hastily formed civic guards—strengthened the determination of the elite to continue to exclude the rural population from their political calculations in the future. The nation-state was founded without the participation of the rural population; in the south its founding was in fact seen as a declaration of war. The greatest peasant uprisings in Italian history had not yet occurred in 1848/49.

A Comparative Balance Sheet

Comparison is a recognized part of historical scholarship. If it is to be more than simply a stringing together of individual examples, it requires methodological foundation. This is more difficult in the case under discussion than would seem at first glance, as no useful theory is available. Hardly anyone would today speak of some historic mission of the rural masses and an examination of whether they fulfilled this mission in the 1848 revolution. The seemingly value-neutral theory of "peasant society" also does not offer much help, as social divisions within the central and western European rural population generally led to a dearth of the united action demanded by this theory. Modernization theories, finally, do not provide much more than a formalized pattern of categories, with the help of which differences can be measured and evaluated. However, the assumptions and values implied have proven ever less useful in the recent past. The range of theories generally offered is therefore rather poor.

It is thus necessary to find a middle way between naive narrativity and an obsession with theory to delineate reality. Success here is most likely if the range of facts is historically interrogated, so to speak, with questions arising from the events described. Thus, perhaps, a guarantee is provided that the events are neither forced into the procrustean bed of some theory, nor that they, so to speak, roam freely, answerable only to God. Mixed forms are nonetheless possible, indeed necessary. The two questions that seem suitable to me are therefore: how do these empirical observations on peasant movements during the revolution of 1848 fit in long-term agrarian history, and what is their relation to the revolutionaries' logic?

As far as the first question is concerned, there can be no doubt that agrarian structures—not only in the countries examined here—experienced an enormous transformation between 1770 and 1870, in which the necessity of circumstances (lack of foodstuffs, increase in population) and human will (independence or, expressed in the style of the time, "property and liberty") acted in combination. Transformation was two-pronged, suggesting a certain parallelism, and aimed at the ending of common rights of ownership and forms of usage. For our theme it appears that participation by the rural classes in the 1848 revolution depended to a great extent on the state of these two secular processes. Some used the revolution to accelerate developments, because blockades had fallen, others sought to make use of the revolution with the intent of stopping or even reversing these developments. Members of the crafts-industrial sector were, incidentally, just as divided between progress and traditionalism in 1848.

Defeudalization, to become more specific, only played a role to the east of the Rhine. This was the result of German backwardness. Those affected by it suffered, but it was also a thorn in the side of bourgeois revolutionaries, who were dedicated to a modern understanding of property as the basis of an up-to-date form of economy. Agrarian structure and revolutionary logic complemented each other much more than in other cases, and the problem was therefore eliminated within a few weeks. The state's involvement in defeudalization was, admittedly, a contributing factor, as was its subsequent behavior in permitting no doubts about its guarantee of the accomplishments of the spring of 1848. This was of inestimable significance for the question of whom the peasants would credit with the dividends of emancipation.

In France the situation was somewhat different. Defeudalization remained inviolable after 1814, but was called into question. Hence, in suggesting that the "lords" planned the restoration of the Ancien Régime, one could go a long way politically in the countryside. Louis-Napoléon owed his electoral victory of 10 December 1848 as much to this reflex of rural voters as did the left their surprisingly large number of votes five months later in the elections for the national assembly on 13 May 1849. The comparison with France—not possible with Italy because of its quite different circumstances—hence allows for the conclusion that the form of defeudalization implemented in Germany in 1848 was perhaps too successful to allow those emancipated to continue to be tied to the revolution. In political terms, the royalist mechanism (king and peasant together against the nobility, an opposition that was in any case part of the standard inventory of the villagers' view of the world) were once again reinforced by the emancipation of the peasantry, and revolutionaries did not gain in prestige. While not making political incorporation of the countryside in Germany impossible in the future, it doubtless made it more difficult.

It was not only the victims of a delayed peasant emancipation who used the revolution to carry through their aims. The same was attempted by the victims of abolished forms of collective usage. Only seldom did these groups overlap. If there was one common feature of rural action in 1848/49, then it was a defense of a traditional lifeworld. This defense was able to mobilize the largest masses; it followed identical patterns; and it failed in all three countries. Day laborers and parcel peasants could find allies in the camps of the revolutionaries at best among the extreme left, and this only as long as the revolutionaries ignored pre-modern tones in the key word "distribution" and instead read into it a struggle against the "rich."

The continental European omnipresence of the "partageux," as the proponents of collective usage forms for forests, pastures, and water and of the distribution of fields soon came to be known in France shows, on the one hand, how unpopular and lacking in broad support agrarian individualism was at the time, and exposes, on the other, the dilemma of the national revolutionary movements. If they had allied with the "partageux," they would have been unbeatable, but at the same time would have pulled the rug out from under their feet. It therefore was not a question of whether or not the revolutionaries themselves upheld agrarian interests, as was the case in Italy, an alliance was impossible from the start.

A second hurdle was a (bourgeois) conceptual confusion. One saw in the "distributors" the gravediggers of bourgeois society, because they were suddenly seen as "communists," and this in the modern sense of the term. In the French and especially the Italian specialized literature on agrarian law, the users of common lands had in fact long been known as "communistes" or "comunisti."[18] Even in *Vormärz* Germany authors spoke of a "certain communistic"[19] use of the land. That the demand for distribution came from the poor made the semantic switch more plausible.

However, these agrarian "communists" had, apart from the same name, nothing in common with the modern political movement, which, moreover, protested against any such comparison.[20] It was therefore possibly the democratic socialists, who, trying to integrate the land-hungry population, coined the neologism "partageux," to avoid the accusation of wanting to overthrow the social order.[21] "Partageux" was admittedly a neologism in decline, which only gained use in France, as it fit the logic of those revolutionaries who did not surrender their hopes even after the June uprising and the presidential elections.

Thus we have returned to the political conditions for relations between revolution and agrarian protest. To them are dedicated two final passages. It is not banal to point at first to the urban origins of the revolution. That a social question also existed in the countryside, and indeed a quite severe one, was totally unknown to the revolutionaries of 1848 when their course was set. In Italy, the paramount influence of Romagnosi prevented a recognition of the economic and social causes of the severe crisis. Generally the existence of a serious crisis was denied, with reference to Sismondi. In France, people could only find dependable information on the dramatic situation of parcel peasants and day laborers before the revolution in novels, such as Balzac's *Les Paysans* of 1844 or Michelet's *Le Peuple* of 1846. The provisional government completely ignored the carefully prepared reports of its representatives in the provinces. None of the sociopolitical resolutions between 25 February and 2 March related to the rural population.

The parliaments of the constitutionally governed German states often discussed the redemption of the land even before 1848. The Heppenheimer program of 1847 also endorsed it. The parliaments of the revolution, including the National Assembly, fulfilled these demands quickly, as described above, but that was the limit of their agrarian political catalog. Journeymen and workers had a lobby; the peasants did not.

It was precisely this that would change in the course of the revolution. In all three countries, mass protests in the villages made obvious the necessity of an agrarian policy. In those places where the rural population could vote, there was increased motivation. Italy can, therefore, remain excluded from the following, because all institutional and political conditions for putting the findings of such shrewd observers as Cantoni into practice were absent. The impoverishment of the countryside progressed rapidly. A specially coined term "bracciantizzazione"[22] accurately describes the situation. National unity, successful the second time around, set off the worst "peasant" unrest in Italian history. In France and Germany, however, the view held sway that the countryside needed to be helped. This required an amount of political patience that the revolutionaries lacked, to the advantage of the governments. The revolution of 1848 marked, in summary, the beginning of agrarian politics in Germany and in France, something already reflected in the new ministries of agriculture. Up until then, bourgeois legal and economic structures were introduced in the countryside, without consideration of social consequences; such structures would not be called into question in the future. However, apart from this, from then on there was not only crisis management in periods of hunger—emergency works, trade barriers, subsidized grain—but also measures for a long-term improvement of the situation: loans, road-building, education, exhibitions, to name the most important.

The question of politicization remains. It is often stated that the rural population inevitably became more conservative due to these favors from the state—an assertion that is incorrect. Where no natural conservatism held sway, as in Westphalia, or where a system of notables did not survive the shocks, as it did in northern and western France, the democrats had good chances of bringing together the village and the revolution. However, this assumes a reciprocal process of education. The village had to learn modern political procedures—associations, elections, political education—and the democrats had to translate the needs and wishes of the rural population into agrarian political demands.

Both worked much better than a popular view of history would lead one to believe. The campaign for the imperial constitution of 1849 and the insurrection in southern France in 1851 provide extreme examples of the extent of politicization in the countryside by the left, but, at the same time, also demonstrate its limits. A victory of the insurgents would have produced a republic supported by the "little people" in both cases, whose economic order would have respected the needs of artisans and the "partageux." Defeat, at least in France, did not end relations between the left and the peasants; electoral geography shows that the alliance formed at the time lasted into the early years of the Fifth Republic. In Germany, the democrats survived in the cities, if that, and rural protest had to be articulated by others in the future.

The 1848 revolution broke out as the order of property and of society in the countryside was in the middle of a process of rapid transformation and had become illegitimate for a majority of the rural population. There is nothing to suggest that the revolutionaries were aware of this, as the strategies they developed in the spring of 1848 took no notice of it. The spontaneous uprisings in the villages caught them unprepared. The rural population acted differently, did not speak with one voice and sometimes followed aims that the revolutionaries could not make their own. These were very poor preconditions for cooperation.

This is the first result of a comparative examination. The second is that one would be ignoring European conditions in suggesting that the revolution failed for this reason alone. The third, finally, is that one of the unexpected, but long-term significant byproducts of the revolution was that the rural population for the first time successfully gained a hearing and had their problems dealt with- through protest, petitions and elections. Historical research should, in the future, pay more attention to this inter-relationship.

Notes

1. Manfred Gailus, *Straße und Brot. Sozialer Protest in den deutschen Staaten unter besonderer Berücksichtigung Preußens, 1847-1849* (Göttingen, 1990), 121.

2. Quoted in Michael Wettengel, *Die Revolution von 1848/49 im Rhein-Main-Raum* (Wiesbaden, 1989), 72, 301.

3. Quoted in Bernhard Parisius, "'Daß die liebe alte Vorzeit wo möglich wieder hergestellt werde.' Politische und soziokulturelle Reaktionen von oldenburgischen Landarbeitern auf ihren sozialen Abstieg," in Heinrich Volkmann and Jürgen Bergmann (eds.), *Sozialer Protest* (Opladen, 1984), 198-211, here 202.

4. Wettengel, *1848 im Rhein-Main-Raum*, 102.

5. Karl Marx, *The Eighteenth Brumaire of Louis Bonaparte* (1852) in Karl Marx and Friedrich Engels *Collected Works*, Vol. 11 (New York, 1979), 103-97, here 189ff.

6. W. Giesselmann, *"Die Manie der Revolte." Protest unter der französichen Julimonarchie (1830-1848)* (Munich, 1993), 194ff. According to Giesselmann, however, the countryside was underrepresented, see 604-5.

7. None of the sociopolitical measures decreed between 25 February and 2 March 1848 concerned the countryside.

8. J.-P. Houssel (ed.), *Histoire des paysans français du XVIIIe siècle à nos jours* (Roanne, 1976), 251-52.; E. Juillard (ed.), *Histoire de la France rurale*, Vol. 3 (Paris, 1976), 167ff.

9. Here I am following Maurice Agulhon, *The Republic in the Village: The People of the Var from the French Revolution to the Second Republic* trans. Janet Lloyd (Cambridge, 1982). The analysis by Ted Margadant, *French Peasants in Revolt: The Insurrection of 1851* (Princeton, 1979), is an overly mechanistic attempt to ascribe the uprising to a crisis of modernization.

10. St. Jacini, *I risultati della inchiesta agraria* (1884), (Turin, 1976), 109.

11. Quoted in Franco Della Peruta, "I contadini nella rivoluzione lombarda del 1848," in his *Democrazia e socialismo nel Risorgimento* (Rome, 1973), 59-108, here 92.

12. G. Cantoni, "Sulle condizioni economico-morali del contadino in Lombardia," *L'Italia del popolo*, 60, 27 July 1848. Reprinted in C. Lacaita (ed.), *Campagne e contadini in Lombardia durante il Risorgimento. Scritti di Giovanni Cantoni* (Milan, 1983), 3-14, here 3. Cantoni, a doctor, was a leading member of the democrats and had mobilized the peasants in Brianza in March. He saw the worsening of agrarian conditions as a moral problem that could be solved by educating both sides, that is through instruction. Only in 1850, in exile in Switzerland, did he begin to see things from a sociocritical standpoint and criticized agrarian conditions correspondingly sharply. "Sulle sorti dei contadini in Lombardia," see 27-88.

13. As, e.g., by the Mayor of Rionero in Vulture, quoted in T. Pedío, *Contadini e galantuomini nelle provincie del Mezzogiorno d'Italia durante i moti del 1848* (Matera, 1963), 61. It is worth noting that from the movement of the "comunisti" an idea had already arisen, namely "comunismo."

14. More on this point in the last section.

15. Quoted in Franco Della Peruta, "Aspetti sociali del '48 nel Mezzogiorno," in Della Peruta, *Democrazia*, 120.

16. Antonio Gramsci, *Il Risorgimento* (= *Quaderni del carcere*, 3) (Turin, 1972), 95-104, here 103-4.

17. Karl Marx to Joseph Weydemeyer, 11 September 1851, in Karl Marx and Friedrich Engels *Collected Works*, Vol. 38 (New York, 1982), 453-55.

18. Greater detail in Wolfgang Schieder, article "Kommunismus," Section II 2. and 3., in Otto Brunner, Werner Conze, and Reinhart Koselleck (eds.), *Geschichtliche Grundbegriffe*, Vol. 3, (Stuttgart, 1982), 455-529, here 462-68.

19. G. L. W. Funke, *Über die gegenwärtige Lage der Heuerleute im Fürstentume Osnabrück* (Bielefeld, 1847), 28; quoted in Josef Mooser, *Ländliche Klassengesellschaft 1770-1848* (Göttingen, 1984), 129.

20. At least in France, where the modern communists were already a well-established ideological community. A reference for 1847 in Ahlrich Meyer, "Die Subsistenzunruhen in Frankreich 1846/47," *Francia* 19/3 (1992): 1-45, here 26, n. 100.

21.   As a glance through the relative special dictionaries reveals. J. Dubois, *Le vocabulaire politique et social en France de 1869 à 1872* (Paris, 1962), 178–79. *Trésor de la langue française. Dictionaire de la langue du XIXe et du XXe siècle (1789-1969)*, Vol. 12 (Paris, 1986), 1046.

22.   From "bracciante," day laborer.

Scene from the riots at the Waldenburg Castle
(Illustrirte Zeitung, Leipzig, no. 251, 22 April 1848, 271)

Scene from the Magyar camp (Illustrirte Zeitung, Leipzig, no. 278, 28 October 1848, 277)

Chapter 19

THE AGRARIAN QUESTION IN SOUTHEASTERN EUROPE DURING THE REVOLUTION OF 1848/49

Wolfgang Höpken

Introduction

If there is any consensus among historians at this point then it is that the revolution of 1848/49 can be understood as both "European" and regionally very distinct, as an event in which particular scenes of the revolutionary action had their own specific characteristics. Recent research especially has repeatedly pointed out that there were many "centers of the revolution" requiring "many perspectives" in order to make apparent both the common and the individual aspects of the year 1848/49.[1] In the meantime, in view of such a multifaceted survey of the complexity of revolutionary events, warnings have been raised "not to lose sight of the unity of the revolution."[2] Democratization, the nation, and the social question mark the "the objective total context of revolutionary themes."[3] Each of these three common elements, as well as their "mixture" is admittedly influential in a different way in individual revolutionary centers. The course of revolution, programmatic aims, and the groups that carry forward the revolutionary process are thus given by those individual characteristics of the separate revolutions.

The still central role of the national question is one of those special traits that can be attributed to the "revolutionary paradigm" of east-central and southeastern Europe (and of Italy as well). The significance of the agrarian question—which gave the revolutions in these areas a totally different social dimension than in France or Germany—may be viewed as a second defining element. Their interaction and tensions, their mutually reinforcing, but also neutralizing effects, greatly determined the results of the revolution. Other actors than those in the central European revolutions come into view.

While Priscilla Robertson could still assert, at the beginnings of the 1950s, that it was the rise of the working class and the labor question that lent the revolution its explosive nature,[4] the inclusion of east-central and southeastern Europe in a comparative history of the revolution has certainly qualified such an interpretation. Even the social question in the villages had a considerable dynamic effect on the course of the revolution in southeast European agrarian society. Not only the leading role played by aristocrats in the Hungarian and Croatian revolutions, shattering the image of a "bourgeois revolution," but also the importance of the peasantry, make up the revolutions in these regions.[5] In this sense, Hans Rothfels' argument that the social question "played nearly no role" in the revolutions of east-central and southeastern Europe requires some qualification.[6]

Even contemporaries made judgements on the significance of the agrarian question and the role of the peasantry in the revolution, which later research took up unquestioningly. The agrarian question was interpreted as a field neglected by the influential classes, and the peasants seen as a revolutionary potential disregarded by nobles, bourgeoisie, and intelligentsia, a behavior understood as the cause of the failure of the revolution from within, so to speak. This thesis was then united with the verdict, for a long time equally unshakeable, of a "betrayal of the revolution" by the peasants. The accusation that they turned their backs on the revolution for reasons of crude class egoism, that indeed they often drifted into the "counter-revolutionary" camp after their elementary aim of the abolition of feudalism had been achieved was already raised by contemporaries. Even a revolutionary activist such as Hans Kudlich, who sympathized with the peasants, and whom the Austrian peasants had to thank for the introduction of decree of emancipation, did not disagree that the peasants "[lay back] in satisfaction on the oven bench as soon as the tithe, the *robot* and military quartering had been rolled off them."[7] However, more recent authors have also ascertained that the peasants were only revolutionary as long as they felt their immediate social interests could be accomplished in the revolution. Once that had happened, they withdrew, satisified, from politics.[8] Here too, one could not miss the accusation that the peasants contributed to the failure of the revolution.

Only recently has there been a change in perspective; less of a new description of peasant behavior than a reinterpretation of the assumptions behind understanding peasant revolutionary behavior in the tradition of "peasant studies." Attention is directed toward the very specific peasant rationality, toward their endogenous goals—which did not fit with bourgeois demands—and toward the conditions of agrarian life that determined behavior as an explanatory framework of rural revolutionary events. "The horizons of peasant experience," argues Wolfram Siemann, "were limited to the peasant environment."[9] Such a point of view seems fundamentally more suitable for approaching the peasantry in the revolution, especially for southeastern European agrarian society, with a peasant life-world and experiential space, much less affected by the modernization processes than in central Europe.

Admittedly however, very few studies have examined the agrarian movement in southeastern Europe from such a methodological perspective.[10] Not only has the historiography of the revolution been dominated by the perspective of the "national movements" and their actors, in which history and transformations in rural areas received much less attention, but when a glance was given to peasant revolutionary activities, it was almost always dictated by the dominant perspective of the "national question." Often peasant protest is unquestioningly interpreted as part of the "national movement," and when it does not fit into categories of national endeavors it is either ignored or misunderstood as "antirevolutionary." Even more seldom are attempts at a comparative representation that transcend the horizons of the national revolution.[11]

One final point must also be considered. Just as the European revolutions are characterized by both common and very individual features, the agrarian question and the peasants' role in the revolutions in individual regional centers were quite divergent. In the Hungarian context, where social conflict took place within a single ethnic milieu, it was distinct from that in Transylvania or in Upper Hungary, with their ethnic-social class divisions between Magyar nobility and Rumanian or Slovak peasants. The Croatian revolutionary events with the special Hungaro-Croatian divisions were different yet again, as were the events in Serbian South Hungary and in the military borderlands with their unique agrarian social conditions. Still different was the agrarian and peasant question in the Slovenian regions where events in Vienna had a much more immediate influence and the importance of the course of the revolution in the German Confederation was much greater. Hence one cannot speak of *the* role of the agrarian question and the peasantry in the revolution even for southeastern Europe.

The Agrarian Question in the Hungarian Revolution

Like the entire Dual Monarchy, Hungary was one of the "latecomers" to agrarian social change in Europe, particularly in regard to a solution to the agrarian question, as it was only the events of 1848 that brought the peasants their emancipation from feudal dependence. This "delayed" peasant emancipation reflects the dilemma of an accelerated "path of modernization" in east central and southeastern Europe.[12] Nonetheless, the revolution was preceded by more than two decades of continual discussion of the agrarian question, which prepared the peasants' emancipation from feudal dependence long before the March Laws of the revolution put this into practice in 1848. Two currents opened the way for peasant emancipation: peasant dissatisfaction rooted in their class condition on the one hand, and endeavors toward reform among the nobility on the other.

The peasant situation in prerevolutionary Hungary was full of tension. In 1765, Maria Theresa introduced a reform of land encumbered by feudal obligations; the subsequent Josephine agrarian reforms were enacted only fragmentarily and at a late date—1785—in the Hungarian half of the empire because of the bureaucratic and centralistic attempts at circumscribing the corporate autonomy of the nobility connected with them. Together, these reforms regulated relations between the nobility and the peasantry and considerably improved the legal standing of part of the peasantry, set dues, and increased peasant mobility.[13] The peasantry's social standing did not change to a great extent, however.

The introduction of a standing army and the wars of the eighteenth century had led to a strong increase in farm prices, that was combined with growing social pressure by the nobility on the peasants. While the peasantry was able to evade this pressure during the period of repopulation after the end of Ottoman rule, the possibility of escaping to unsettled land decreased appreciably in the second half of the eighteenth century. The Napoleonic wars brought a renewed surge in demand, in the wake of which noble landowners—with a growing interest in marketing their produce—turned increasingly to the instrument of expanding their private holdings at the expense of encumbered land. The extent of these measures is still controversial, as is their immediate consequence for the peasants' social situation.

In the transformation of encumbered land into private holdings, seen by peasants as an attack on customary rights, an area of conflict arose that would remain virulent both during the revolution and beyond statutory emancipation in 1848. Similar effects developed out of an increased reorientation by many noble estates towards sheep rearing for wool production—an aristocratic reaction to the end of the wartime high prices at the conclusion of the Napoleonic wars. The resulting transformation from cultivated land to grazing land and encroachment on fields and meadows up to then used by the peasants was also seen as a violation of "customary rights."[14] This, too, sowed seeds of discontent in relations between nobility and peasantry, which would continue to have an effect into the revolution and the postrevolutionary implementation of emancipation laws.

These developments in agriculture in the decades before 1848 also meant an increasing differentiation in peasant status. A switch to money rents in place of rents in kind, a growth in leases and day labor also removed a section of the peasantry economically from the traditional feudal system.[15] In total, this certainly did not mean a mass impoverishment of the peasants. Their material situation, however, continued to be marked by strong regional differences. There were no upward limits on their standards of living, and some peasants could live as well as nobles did. Leases, *robot*, and a more or less traditional economy—not very innovative and not open to innovation—restricted improvements in peasant life even under favorable economic conditions. "It was not serfdom, but pauperism" that characterized the lot of the mass of Hungarian peasants, even when they were said to be better off than their fellow peasants in Galicia, Transylvania or Bohemia.[16]

Peasant protest was thus not unknown in Hungary, especially in the eighteenth century. It remained, however, generally within the framework of traditional peasant forms of resistance: regionally limited, usually not involving an exaggerated intensity of violence, and aimed more at ending abuses and relieving the burden of the *robot* than in completely changing the agrarian order. In spite of peasant dissatisfaction with continual encroachment on encumbered lands and disagreements on the right to use meadows and woods, the first decades of the nineteenth century remained relatively quiet. One exception, admittedly, is provided by the so-called cholera unrest in 1831, which went beyond the usual pattern of peasant protest in extent and militancy.

While peasant dissatisfaction therefore did not directly threaten the social order in the *Vormärz*, it was enough to raise fears among the nobles. As elsewhere throughout Europe, the "fear of revolution" in Hungary was above all a fear of the peasants—a circumstance that did not fail to influence noble tendencies toward reform. Especially the cholera unrest, and even more the Galician peasant uprising in 1846, encouraged the nobility in this respect. Both eruptions of peasant disobedience gained their threatening effect not least, from the Hungarian noble point of view, in their seeming to unite for the first time that fateful coalition of social and national dissatisfaction, as it was above all peripheral territories of Hungary, settled by Slovaks, Ukrainians, and Rumanians that were the centers of the cholera uprising. The behavior of the Ruthenian peasants in 1846 had shown how easily social dissatisfaction could be mobilized into ethnic violence.

While one can agree with Wolfgang Häusler that the agrarian laws of the 1848 revolution are unimaginable without peasant willingness to protest in the spring and summer throughout the monarchy,[17] in the final analysis it was not so much peasant protest that led to emancipation. Even the well-known example of the so-called peasant march to the outskirts of Budapest in March 1848, whose cause lay in attendance at traditional markets and not in social mobilization, was simply cleverly exploited by Petőfi and the radicals to put pressure on the Bratislava Diet and was less an expression of peasant-revolutionary dissatisfaction. It had a direct effect only in that it accelerated decision-making processes in the Diet. The impulse for changes in agrarian order arose from liberal discussion of reform from the 1820s onward. This discussion had provided a milieu that allowed a relatively conflict-free emancipation of the peasants even in the context of revolutionary change.

This was a discourse of reform in which the initial debate certainly did not have as a goal the abolition of the existing agrarian system, but rather, as in the rest of Europe, "improving the peasantry" through enlightenment. Even a Kossuth, in the 1820s, did not look forward to an abrupt transformation of agrarian order, seeking instead to improve the peasants' fate without upsetting the nobility. Peasant impatience that went as far as revolt seemed rebellious to him as well.[18] Even when it did not condense into an effective reform program, nonetheless, the idea that "it is no doubt one of the greatest hindrances of the peasant and the town-dweller living from working the fields to possess no land" became more and more accepted.[19]

An awareness that subjectively-felt backwardness in their country could only be abolished through a social change that went beyond the structures of the existing order became, from the 1830s onward, a concern of the middle-ranking nobility. The idea of agrarian reform hence became the core of a wide-ranging project of economic and political modernization. Szecheny saw the emancipation of the peasantry as a precondition of economic progress. For the young Deák, his desired goal of transforming a nation of nobles into a Magyar political nation was unimaginable without changing peasants into property-owners.[20] The social-reformist literature of an Eötvös not only heightened the awareness of Hungarian liberal society of the problem, but also pointed a warning finger at the nobility—that they could only preserve their position in the long-term through a willingness to reform.[21]

For those nobles supporting reform, the agrarian question was, however, not only a part of a liberal project of modernization, but also a tactical variable in their relations with Vienna. Only with the backing of the peasantry was it possible to implement their demands for more autonomy for the Hungarian nation in its relations to Vienna, and this backing could only be gained by means of agrarian reform.[22] In this sense, the social and national questions were closely bound together from the start, not only in Slovakia, Croatia, Serbia, and Transylvania, which will be examined in greater detail below, but also in the Hungarian revolution.

The reform discourse carried on by reform-minded nobles was increasingly able to approach a consensus that extended beyond liberal circles. Without a doubt, willingness to contemplate agrarian reform within the conservative camp was much less pronounced. The aristocracy remained reserved, hoping to limit reforms to changes in the status of encumbered land and endeavored, up to the beginning of the revolution, to deal with specific steps in a dilatory manner or to block them completely, using their veto in the upper house of the Hungarian Diet. If without enthusiasm, here, too, an awareness grew that changes in agrarian relations could not be avoided in the medium-term.[23] From the radical side as well, the common sense of a reform that demanded concessions and renunciations of old rights from the nobility but which did not seek to endanger them either politically or economically was never really called into question.

Practical consequences certainly did not go as far as the liberal reforms under discussion. Debates on the agrarian question in the Diets reflected a complex mesh of disparate noble interests, acceptance of reform, as well as a fear of revolution and of the peasants kept alive both by European eruption, such as those of 1791 and 1830, and by continual outbursts of peasant unrest. Finally, the stance of the provincial Diets also reflected relations between the Hungarian estates and the government in Vienna, as both sides constantly exploited the agrarian question to modify their mutual relations. All these factors affected the tempo and radicalism of agrarian policy measures and, in their mutual dependence, explain the distinctly limited progress made in dealing with this question in the Diets from the end of the eighteenth century. Even when their resolutions up into the 1840s aimed more at improvement than change, the agrarian question nonetheless became more and more something which, while perhaps dealt with in a dilatory manner, could not to be ignored.

Early debate on the agrarian question in the Diet of 1791/92 was submerged in the fear of revolution triggered by events in France. The two Diets of the 1820s and 1830s dealt with the agrarian question in a rather dilatory manner and did not achieve much more than selective improvements aimed at easing the status of encumbered land. More far-reaching proposals—like those, for example, pursued by Ferenc Deák—failed because of the resistance of the conservative upper house. Especially in the Diet summoned in 1832, it was once again fear of peasants and revolution, raised by the cholera unrest and events in Paris in 1830, that sharply limited the aristocracy's readiness to engage in reform. In both Diets, moreover, Vienna presented itself in its usual manner as the representative of an Imperial-paternalistic "protector of the peasantry" and sought to discipline the Hungarian nobility with demands of relief for the peasants.

During the sessions of the Diet in the 1840s, however, the situation began to change. The increasing success of the liberal project of a "politically Magyar nation"—which took a great step forward in the 1840 Diet with the permanent establishment of Hungarian as official language and increasing demands towards Vienna for autonomy—led to a growth in acceptance of agrarian reform among noble circles, without which a Hungarian "political nation" was unimaginable. The specific resolutions passed by the Diet, that made possible agreements on a voluntary dissolution of seigneurial obligations, with monetary compensation for the lord, had little effect in practice, as the large majority of peasants lacked the capital to take this step.

At least some peasants did succeed in ending their feudal obligations in this manner. The Hungarian agrarian historian J. Varga has discovered fifty-one dissolution contracts for the years between 1840 and 1848.[24] Above all, however, such a resolution doubtless had "considerable symbolic meaning"[25] on the road to an agrarian reform. Possibly, the Diet that began in November 1847 would have again attempted, under the influence of the upper house, to preserve the existing agrarian order with superficial improvements. That it only required the news of events in Paris at the beginning of 1848 for the abolition of peasant obligations to be set on the agenda was also the result of the fact that the Diet had been slowly but irreversibly moving in this direction in the previous two decades.

The feudal order had lost its legitimacy; it was, as is often emphasized quite justifiably, attacked from within.[26] Even when reform discussions in the 1830s and 1840s and the first, doubtless hesitant, changes by the Diets had not solved the agrarian question, this "preparation" had "softened it up." It had already taken much of the edge from the agrarian question before the revolution and thus contributed to a relatively conflict-free compromise that appeared astoundingly quickly in the early phase of the revolution. This compromise certainly did not satisfy the peasants completely and may have seemed to some of the nobility as a necessary evil, but it did not turn a majority on both sides truly against the revolution.

The "April-Laws," rapidly passed by both houses in face of events in Vienna and Pest, were certainly a "partial reform." All peasants were freed personally; patrimonial jurisdiction, which had in any case long been in a process of transformation into institutional jurisdiction,[27] was abolished. However, less than half the peasantry truly benefitted from these reforms, those namely who fell under the encumbered land system: 43.7 percent or about 568,000 of the 1,366,746 peasants. After their lords received compensation, which was to be paid by the state, they became owner of their land. This arrangement did not extend to those peasants who lived on the personal property of the nobles. They, too, were spared the *robot* in future, but they did not become owners of the land and continued to have to provide the estate owner with goods and services. The effects of the April Laws was certainly restricted by questions left unanswered: the preservation of the wine tithe, as well as the noble privilege of wine sales, and most hunting and fishing rights, and, moreover, many questions concerning encumbered land transferred to private property in the decades before the reform.[28]

In the end, however, there was no alternative. Kossuth himself had remained within the framework of the earlier discussions of 1847 in his ideas, and neither "left" nor "right" fundamentally went beyond them. The circle of Budapest radicals around Petőfi basically did not go beyond the position of the liberals and the agrarian laws in their twelve-point program.[29] And, in fact, proposals which transcended the consensus, such as those of the peasant leader Tancics, who was not only more radical in the question of compensation, but was also open to changes in the structure of property ownership, remained a fringe position.[30] While doubtless held in high regard by the peasants because of his background and his social commitment, it is not certain if even the peasants gave consideration to such ideas touching on questions of ownership.

The loyal higher aristocracy grouped around the conservative committee functioning as a sort of shadow cabinet in Vienna, in view of the revolutionary changes in Budapest, while complaining about the economic consequences of agrarian reform for the nobility and about compensation, also viewed a return to the previous status quo as extremely unlikely, since they did not wish to turn the peasants against them. "As long as peasant interests remain untouched, limited power is sufficient to keep the cowards in check," was the conclusion of the Vienna committee. "If his interests are affected, then a peasant war will occur."[31]

The imperial government, for its part, in view of events in its own capital, was unable either to hinder the resolutions or to influence their content. An attempt to postpone a sanctioning of the resolutions until questions of compensation had been clarified,[32] pointing out the allegedly ruinous consequences for Hungarian nobility, was unsuccessful. In any event, resolutions on financial autonomy and army administration were much more serious for Vienna than the agrarian reforms.

With the March Laws, the Diet did no more than necessary, as György Spira quite aptly concluded, but it did what was necessary to avoid conflict with the peasantry.[33] Peasant dissatisfaction with the limits and weak points of the laws were obvious in the first weeks after their approval. There was unrest in many places, sometimes requiring the application of the military force and the proclamation of martial law. To make of this, however, a "powerful movement" with the social potential to endanger the revolution, is a contention that can hardly be maintained.[34] The number of villages that experienced unrest indeed fell noticeably from April on into the summer.[35] Hungarian research, under the influence of Marxist-Leninist theory, originally over-emphasized the extent and character of peasant protest against the agrarian laws but has in the meantime retreated to a more cautious evaluation.

Furthermore, more important than the quantitative dimension of agrarian protest after the passing of the April Laws is the fact that there certainly were a number of protests. Peasants residing on estate owners' private property, not affected by the laws, refused to make lease payments, and in some places peasants occupied nobles' lands. More common, however, were peasant attacks on the so-called controversial land, which had been transformed by the nobles into their private property in the decades before the reform, or a reclaiming of usage rights for woods and meadows.[36] This was an attempt to recover "customary rights," which peasants saw as violated by the nobles and which they hoped would be reinstated in the reforms. Less common was the desire to push reform up to the total abolition of all "feudal relics." In the final analysis, the villages did not break with the consensus on reform, in spite of some disappointments.[37]

Reforms did not fulfil all wishes, but they accommodated peasant interests to the point that the peasants were pacified. Thus, admittedly, the revolution found itself in an unsolvable dilemma in relation to the peasants: its reform measures prevented a peasant social eruption against the revolution, but they were a long way from encouraging peasants to commit themselves unconditionally to the revolution. Hence, it also seems questionable whether, as alleged in some of the literature, restrictions in the agrarian laws had robbed the revolution of a major base, i.e. that a more radical statute would have turned the peasants into active supporters of the revolution.[38] A more precise definition of the agrarian reforms, which would have clarified them and extended the circles of those who benefited—something which Ferenc Deák in particular worked for in a follow-up to the April Laws[39]—certainly would have eliminated peasant dissatisfaction. However, the decision to abolish the wine tithe in September 1848, made under the pressure of a lack of military commitment on the part of the peasants, the ending of other bonds and duties, and the inclusion of tenants in the reform laws—all measures which in any case would become lost in the confusion of the autumn crisis of the revolution in 1848 and showed little if no effect in practice—also did not permanently influence peasant attitudes towards the revolution.

The ambivalence of peasant attitudes is nowhere so clear as in the military commitment of the peasants toward the defense of the revolution. Peasants certainly did not refuse to fight on the side of the revolution. Especially the confrontation with Jelačić after his invasion in September 1848 found the peasants on the side of "the defense of the fatherland." According to Peter Hidas, peasants made up 55-60 percent of the army in August 1848, much less than their share of the total population, but too many to allow one to speak of mass refusal to serve. On the other hand, one cannot speak of a peasant "levée en masse," as Helmut Rumpler writes. Over time, the revolution had ever greater difficulties in making peasants into a base of its military support.

Peasants continued to give precedence to safeguarding their basic social interests over a commitment to the revolution. Hesitation in joining the national guard, seen as a revival of the former draft, resignation during harvest time, etc. became ever more common, especially in 1849, "among the large mass of peasants" as Mór Jókai complained, an activist from Petröfi's circles, as early as May 1848. "He [the peasant] does not understand the national colors; for him a law is not a law as long as the seal of the emperor with the great two-headed eagle is not affixed. He does not take up arms for us, he does not trust our words …"[40] A general "arming of the people" could not be carried through by Kossuth in the decisive moments of the struggle in the summer of 1849.[41] As long as the agrarian laws were not withdrawn, the Rubicon had not been crossed for the peasants. Vienna, with its tradition of a paternalistic policy toward the peasants, recognized this immediately and continually emphasized the unassailablility of the April Laws.[42]

It has been quite rightly pointed out that the traditions of the peasant life-world did not fit into the ideas of the "bourgeois" revolution.[43] "… [O]nly a radical theoretician, who doesn't know anything about the peasants" as Hans Kudlich pointedly remarked at the time, could have expected peasants to go to battle unreservedly for the aims of the urban bourgeoisie.[44] What appeared to the noble and bourgeois leaders of the revolution as indifference and social narrowness was in the end an expression of the peasants' traditional life-world, but also a necessary strategy for safeguarding their existence. Only in those places where social protest overlapped with national conflicts, such as in Serbia, Croatia, Transylvania, and in Slovakian "Upper Hungary" could this dilemma be avoided in part. National conflicts could, at least for a time, be employed to mobilize the peasants for the revolution. In these regions, as well, the revolution was not immune from peasants withdrawing their commitment to the abstract aims of national emancipation and bourgeois transformation when their own elementary interests suggested doing so. Even here, relations between peasant and revolution, as will be shown below, were much more varied than the theses of a national historiography—which claims peasant revolutionary activity unreservedly as an element of "national aspirations for emancipation"—would have one believe.

The Agrarian Question and Revolution among the Non-Magyar Nationalities

The Initial position

Among the southeast European nationalities of the dual monarchy, the significance of the agrarian question and the role of peasants in the revolution were defined by common features but also by individually specific ones. The idea of an "overall thematic of the revolution" realized in very individual facets thus also applies to the context and regions under discussion here. The agrarian question played an important role everywhere, and everywhere peasants played a significant role in revolutionary events. Beyond all ethnic and regional differences, similar interests produced similar peasant aims and behavior. At the same time, however, the role of the peasants was also marked by regional distinctions, which distinguished revolutionary events in the countryside in southeastern Europe not only from those in Hungary, but also produced remarkable variations between individual revolutionary centers in southeastern Europe. The special manner in which the agrarian question gained relevance for the revolutionary events among the southeast European nationalities began with the diverging agrarian legal and social conditions in the individual regions.

In Croatia-Slavonia, lines of social conflict were in some respects similar to those in Hungary. Here, too, members of the same ethnic community formed the opposing groups: Croatian peasants directed their expectations, demands, and protests towards a native, Croatian nobility. Beyond these parallels, however, agrarian legal and social conditions even within Croatia-Slavonia were quite varied, and the exact nature of the agrarian question varied with them. Slavonia, where land ownership was concentrated in large noble estates, had already been subject to the Theresian reforms from 1756 onwards, something introduced in civil Croatia, with its very fragmented land ownership structure, only a quarter of a century later. The nature of land encumberment in Croatia resembled that in Hungary to a great extent; in Slavonia, by contrast the Theresian reforms had formulated the land provisions and rights of the serfs comparatively favorably.[45]

The legal status of the Serbs of "South Hungary," that is in Bǎcka, the Banat, and Srem, differed little from conditions in Croatia-Slavonia. Here, too, the Theresian reforms and the legal regulation arising from them also applied. However, the much greater overlap of social and ethnic conflict distinguished conditions here considerably from those in Croatia. Even when substantial social disparity between Serbian peasants and "Serbian" land ownership of Orthodox monasteries existed, "class lines" ran primarily between a *Hungarian* nobility and a *Serbian* peasantry; circumstances that did not remain irrelevant for social conflict. Moreover, there was a confessional division between Orthodox and Catholic peasants, which in confessionally mixed regions such as Srem would be drawn into the wake of national confrontation during the revolution.[46]

In ethnic-social polarization, but also in relation to confessional heterogeneity, the Serb situation tresembled that existing in Transylvania. Here, too, a mostly Rumanian subject peasantry faced a mostly Hungarian nobility. Admittedly, the situation in Transylvania was complicated by the fact that Theresian reforms had not been extended to the region. This government attempt at regulation, which, in the spirit of absolutist protection of the peasantry, had codified the burdens and obligations for peasants and lords in the rest of the monarchy, had never applied to Transylvania. The Josephine emancipation patent, which applied initially to Transylvania as well, met with the resistance of Transylvanian nobles and was not long lasting. While the Diet of 1791 allowed the peasant the possibility of mobility, this had little consequence for the peasants' de facto dependence on the estate owner. Further regulatory attempts, like the encumbered land reforms in Hungary and Croatia in the 1830s, had not been implemented in Transylvania up to the time of the revolution. An attempt to establish a Transylvanian encumbered land system in 1847 never got off the drawing board. The legal situation, and above all social conditions for Rumanian peasants in Transylvania, were thus clearly worse than in the southern Slav regions of the monarchy. Those Rumanian peasants living on the "Saxon Land" were in part in a clearly better legal position, at least those who lived as agricultural workers or free peasants, but this had little influence on their social position.[47]

Still another unique development is to be found in the military borderlands, whose ethnically and confessionally divided peasant population was, as is well known, subject to a special agrarian legal status. The situation of peasants in the borderlands was not determined by a clash betwen nobles and peasants, but by the military-feudal obligations of the peasants toward the ruling dynasty. The property status of farmland, as well as the considerably more extensive practice of raising livestock and the still widespread family and economic combinations of the communal joint-family, the so-called *zadruga*, clearly distinguished this region from both civil Croatia and South Hungary.[48]

Finally, revolutionary events among the Slovenes of the monarchy occurred under their own special regional conditions. Feudal ties also burdened the peasants here, although in those areas that had belonged to the Illyrian provinces at the beginning of the century, the Napoleonic reforms had brought some improvements. The social conflicts here were, naturally, however, much more greatly influenced by Viennese agrarian policies, and in relation to the national problem, the question of being included in the German Confederation presented a special problem.[49]

Peasants in the above-mentioned regions were affected to various degrees by the agricultural price developments from the late eighteenth century onwards in the Hungarian half of the empire. Problems of the structural modernization of agriculture were more serious, however, especially in Croatia, but also in Serbian regions, than in Hungary itself. Early attempts at improvements, starting in the late eighteenth century, that aimed at enlightenment and not at reform, had little effect on the low level of agricultural productivity, serious technological backwardness, and an anti-innovative attitude among peasants as well as among a large part of the nobility.[50]

Nonetheless, the cyclical turning point of the Napoleonic wars, which contributed to a greater market integration of the noble estates, also made itself felt here. Especially the large estate-owners in Slavonia were able to profit from this. As in Hungary, attempts were made to ease the postwar collapse in farm prices in part through a shift to sheep raising. The tendency toward transforming encumbered land into private property and attempts to restrict peasant usage rights for meadows and woods were noticeable here, too, in the first half of the nineteenth century; the extent is admittedly unclear and controversial.[51]

Equally controversial is the extent to which this development can be understood as a worsening of conditions for the peasants. The earlier-held view of intensified "feudal exploitation" during the *Vormärz* has recently been countered in regional case studies with substantial arguments that the condition of the peasantry was changeable, but in general did not seriously worsen in the first half of the nineteenth century.[52] Nonetheless, a whole series of peasant uprisings did occur in the late eighteenth and early nineteenth centuries, at the center of which stood worsening of peasant feudal burdens and transformation of peasant land.[53] Improvements in the status of encumbered land, introduced by the Hungarian Diets in the 1830s and 1840s, had little influence on the peasant social situation. Only in Slavonia did peasants make use of the possibility of purchasing an end to their feudal duties. The possibility of voluntary withdrawal, announced by the Bratislava Diet of 1836 and certainly to be seen as one of the first, even if mostly theoretical, steps in a preparation of agrarian reform, was not applied at all in Croatia.

Hence specific agrarian legal structures, but also common social problems, characterize the agrarian question in the non-Magyar regions of the Hungarian half of the empire. This had a considerable influence on peasant aims and protest in the revolution. Quite apart from this, there is one common feature of revolutionary events in all these regions: the way that the social and the national elements were closely interwoven. The image used by Hans Rothfels of a "communicating network" [less literally, a feedback relationship—ed.] [54] to sketch the mutual influence of the European revolutions can also be transferred to the connection of social and national questions in the southeast European revolutions. Both strands of the revolution influenced each other; both retained, however, their own dynamic and internal logic. They moved like two currents, which for a time flow together, but which, however, can flow apart again. In the individual formation of this relationship, the "special paths" of the course of revolution in the particular revolutionary centers are recognizable.

Peasant Reactions to the Agrarian Reforms

The news of events in Vienna and even more so of those in Pest spread quickly along the frontiers of Transleithenia. The March Laws in particular could not long be kept hidden from the peasants. In the last days of March and in April, there were a number of peasant uprisings and revolts everywhere. Their immediate aim was the fastest possible emancipation of the peasantry, regardless of the particular agrarian legal conditions in the individual regions. In those regions with an encumbered land structure, peasant action aimed at a rapid implementation of the Bratislava agrarian laws, even when the peasants were not aware of their details. Hence, peasant uprisings in Croatia—where the Bratislava Laws, for constitutional reasons, only became valid after a corresponding resolution by the Croatian Sabor—sought to pressure the nobility into rapid acceptance of the March Laws through the normative force of creating a de facto situation. [55]

Spontaneous unrest also arose among the Serbs in South Hungary during the second half of March; they sought to anticipate the emancipation laws before they were announced and defined. [56] In Transylvania, peasant unrest which broke out at the end of March was directed at having the region included in peasant emancipation laws. [57] In the military borderlands, where peasant action began somewhat later, demands reflected the region's special status. Introduction of civil administration, abolition of feudal dues, and the end of existing restrictions on mobility and the possibility of division of the *zadruga*, which had become an economic hindrance, lay at the center of peasant concerns. [58]

Independent of the thoughts of using the Hungarian Revolution as the starting-point of their own emancipation, peasant unrest was also directed, from the beginning, at the weak points of the March Laws. [59] With their protest actions, the peasants sought to interpret the laws as they understood them. Nearly everywhere—and quite like their fellow Hungarian peasants—they were concerned with the same complaints. The question of the use of the meadows and the forests, a precise regulation of which had not been provided in the agrarian laws, was one of the points that led to massive clashes between peasant and nobility in the months of the revolution. Even well into the 1850s, this would lead to numerous legal battles as well as to violent confrontations. Inclusion of vineyards, rights of sale for wine and the question of licenses to keep a tavern, which in some regions provided peasants important extra income, were also constant subjects in these disputes. Overshadowing all other issues, however, was the question of whether land transformed by nobles into their personal property in previous years would be included in the agrarian reforms. This was one of the most significant peasant complaints, and they felt that the agrarian laws did not deal with it sufficiently.

The social dynamics of this agrarian unrest was, however, quite different in individual regions. In civil Croatia, there were a whole series of peasant protests and uprisings, especially in the spring and autumn of 1848, which led to the military being called out in various locations and martial law being declared by the Ban. Following a first wave between March/April and the beginning of May, protests fell off with the forthcoming session of the Croatian Diet, the Sabor, from which the peasants hoped for a consideration of their complaints. After what was for them a disappointing resolution by the Sabor in June 1848, the level of protest reached a new highpoint in the autumn of 1848. Even when there were conflicts in the course of 1849, the agrarian movement increasingly lost in intensity and import. Furthermore, in Croatia there were considerable regional differences. In some counties, such as Požega, protest ebbed relatively quickly or became less radical, while in other, as in the well-documented county of Virovitrica, the struggles lasted much longer. Well into 1849 a "lawless spirit, a 'virus anarchiae,'" held sway, as was said in the complaints of landowners who were continually calling on the ban for military support against the peasants.

Agrarian conflicts among the Serbs of South Hungary seem to have had a much greater social dynamic than in Croatia. Not only practically throughout the entire year 1848, but also, to a greater or lesser extent in 1849, there were continual peasant uprisings in many areas, such as Srem, which, it was complained, led at times to conditions of "anarchy" in relations between estate owners and peasants. Demands here were quite the same as in Croatia and even interior Hungary, although the radicalism of peasant action was obviously much greater. Especially on the monastic estates, where a particularly high number of contract peasants were living who did not profit from the agrarian laws, there were a considerable number of clashes.

The struggles in Transylvania, especially after the assembly in Blaj in April 1848, were marked by similar, if not greater radicalism and violence. For all practical purposes, the peasants ceased paying their feudal dues and performing their compulsory labor services. They also demanded the return of their "old lands"— sometimes simply occupying it. The announcement of the abolition of serfdom on 18 June could not ease this protest, especially as this abolition was slow to be implemented. Severe military suppression of peasant self-help was the result.[60]

The extensive appearance of peasants as revolutionary actors in southeast European revolutionary centers has led some historians to speak of an "agrarian revolution," which, unlike the case in other parts of the monarchy, was directed at the total abolition of feudalism. Although the sometimes quite considerable social dynamic of peasant protest should not be underestimated, doubts must be raised about such an interpretation. Certainly, such a qualification applies to the agrarian movement in Croatia. In spite of the number of "open" revolts by peasants, there were essentially no "serious" and truly threatening uprisings—a point already raised by Aleksije Jelačić in his 1925 analysis of the agrarian movement, still the only work of its kind. Even if one sets the level of peasant protest considerably higher than Jelačić, it would be true to say that peasants "generally remained within the law." There were naturally attacks on noble lands and violent action by the peasants, but they were not decisive.[61]

Moreover, peasant actions generally remained regionally isolated protests. However, even for Serb and Rumanian peasants in Transylvania, with their higher level of radicalism, it is questionable whether the term "antifeudal revolution" is suitable to properly capture the quality and character of peasant action. Not least, peasant demands themselves raise doubts in this respect. Quite apart from the fact that—unlike in Croatia and Hungary—demands were greater for land and there were violent attacks on noble and church property, the mass of peasant protest was concerned with maintaining "customary rights": reversal of the transformation in legal status of land, use of meadows and woods, to which they believed they had documented legal claims and which, in their moral interpretation of the law, had been stolen from them by nobles flouting their obligations.

The myth that one finds among the peasantry in all of southeastern Europe— that it was the emperor who was to be thanked for the emancipation of the peasants—may also be conceptualized in the unbroken traditional understanding of law and less in a nationalist conflict of nationalities with Budapest. To consider "customary rights" simply as simply rhetorical references continually raised in peasant petitions, by which the peasants sought to hide their true aim of overthrowing the feudal order in legalistic terminology,[62] is to attribute to the peasants an understanding of revolution that was foreign to them. Also in economically further developed revolutionary centers, with a higher level of "bourgeois order," this was not the case, as has been shown, for example, by Peter Heumos.[63]

The Agrarian Question, the Peasants, and Nationalist Movements

Everywhere peasant protest was initially a spontaneous eruption, motivated only by elementary social interests. Political aims in general, to say nothing of nationalist programs in particular, were absent. In ethnically relatively homogeneous regions such as Croatia-Slavonia, peasants turned against their own nobility. In ethnically mixed regions peasants united across ethnic lines, as, for example, when Serb and Hungarian peasants in South Hungary at the beginning of the revolution refused, in common action, to perform their feudal obligations.[64]

Against the backdrop of a national question which from the beginning of the revolution became ever more prominent, the agrarian question and peasant movements were everywhere quickly drawn into the wake of escalating national struggles. The literature often does not do justice to the complex web of inter-relationships between the national and social levels of action which thereby arose. While the historiography of southeast European nationalities deals with the social movement without reservation as part of the national movement, especially in Hungarian historiography the peasants are denied any nationalist motivation and the agrarian movement is often reduced to the role of a simple object of manipulation for nationalist elites in their struggle against a "politically Hungarian nation." As far as both attitudes and policies toward the peasants of the social strata who were the bearers of nationalism and, conversely, concerning the "nationalization" of the peasants, a very nuanced picture exists. Here, too, it would be true to say that revolutionary events in southeastern Europe did not follow one set pattern but were extremely varied.

If one first examines the policies toward the peasants on the one hand and the social question in the countryside with respect to those social strata who were the bearers of nationalist ideas, one discovers a high level of ambivalence. Completely fixed on fulfilling their claims of national emancipation, nobles, the narrow group of the urban middle class, and, especially, the nationalist intelligentsia had a troubled relationship with the peasantry. On the one hand, the virulence of agrarian conflict demanded that peasant expectations of emancipation not be ignored. As everywhere in the European revolutions, nobility and governments in southeastern Europe rapidly showed a willingness to make concessions concerning agrarian reform, with which they also sought to channel rural social explosiveness along a legal path.[65]

Already in March, the Bratislava Laws were being implemented in South Hungary and de facto peasant emancipation went into force in Croatia in April. The delay in Transylvania before the Klausenburg Diet announced emancipation in June shows, on the other hand, how quickly the level of conflict could rise. Moreover, independent of these social motives, in southeastern Europe the social strata that were bearers of nationalist ideas could not do without the loyalty of the peasantry if they wished to realize their national aspirations. It was therefore necessary to mobilize the peasants, about whose lack of "national consciousness" they held no illusions, for the nation.

On the other hand it is obvious that the leading elite in the nationalist movements maintained a considerable distance from spontaneously arising peasant social action. Consideration of the interests of the nobles played a role here, but also the fact that peasant endeavors all too often did not fit, either in form or in aims, in the canon of liberal or at least non-conservative revolutionary expectations. Everywhere, the social question was clearly of secondary importance in the programs and policies of nationalist activists; it could not be completely dropped, for the above-mentioned reasons, but it could not be allowed to get out of hand. And certainly the activists did not wish to become leaders of agrarian revolutionary transformations that threatened to go beyond the scope of Hungarian reforms.

This is especially clear in Croatia, where the noble basis of the national movement created social barriers to the inclusion of the peasantry. Even before the revolution, the Croatian nobility had shown little interest in agrarian policy reform. This reflects less sociopolitical intransigence and more the fact that except for Slavonic nobles and the few large estate owners in Croatia, the mass of medium and minor nobility was dependent on the *robot* and on feudal dues and had to fear the economic consequences of an agrarian reform. In the Hungarian Diet, it was above all Croatian nobles, totally in agreement with their Hungarian colleagues, who were unwilling to consider anything more than cautious improvement of the encumbered land structure.[66] However, the Illyrian movement and the nationalist intelligentsia gathered around it also showed an astounding lack of interest in the agrarian question before the revolution. The primacy of the national question made it indispensable for them to avoid bringing up social conflicts as much as possible in order not to endanger a "national unity" that was certainly not well-secured.

Some of that which stimulated debate on the agrarian question in Hungary, in the rest of the monarchy, and in the rest of Europe in the *Vormärz*, was echoed in Croatia—efforts towards an increased "enlightenment" and "education" to improve social and economic conditions in the countryside and to raise the technological level in agriculture. However, comparable "preparation" of a broad liberal reform discourse, such as in Hungary, did not take place. Only the news of the Galician peasant uprising of 1846 wakened a sensibility among Croatian nobility and the national movement for the agrarian question. Even the revolution itself did not basically change the secondary position of the agrarian question. Social and national political reasons forced the nobles and national intelligentsia, however, to react quickly to the Bratislava resolutions. The social reasons arose from the above-mentioned unrest among peasants, who were on the way to bringing about agrarian reform themselves; the national political reasons lay in the political influence that pro-Hungarian "Magyarones" threatened to gain in large parts of Croatia and Srem. Pointing to the Bratislava resolutions, they could present peasant emancipation as the work of Hungarian nobles. The peasantry threatened to become alienated from Croatian nationalist forces.[67]

For both these reasons, a rapid implementation of agrarian reform in Croatia was necessary, although it had to appear both legally and politically as their own "Croatian" reform. However, Croatian nobles did no more than was necessary. Thus, demands for peasant emancipation were included in the "narodno zahtijevanja," the Croatian national demands, in which Croatian claims to autonomy were presented to the Hungarian crown on March 25.[68] Such social aspects did not stand in the foreground of these demands, although they naturally could not be altogether avoided. Even when, a month later, Jelačić, implemented the de facto abolition of feudal dues, labor services and church tithes, before a corresponding resolution by the Hungarian Diet,[69] this was more a defensive attempt to work against continuing peasant unrest and the danger of Magyarone exploitation of it.

In the sessions of the Sabor in June, the agrarian question remained a subordinate point on the agenda, and raised little interest. Conservatives no longer denied the necessity of agrarian reform in the spring of 1848, but neither for them nor for liberals nor even for the minority of so-called "radicals" was the agrarian question of paramount importance. In the middle of the struggle on the extent of agrarian reform, even a group such as the "Slavenska Lipa," whose spokesmen claimed to have the interest of the peasants at heart, could do without an explicit agrarian program.[70] Debate in the Diets was governed by a general consensus, as in Hungary, which in principle did not call into question the framework of the March Laws. Various standpoints concerning the wine tithe or use of woods and meadows did not go beyond the framework known from Bratislava; the question of the signing over of peasant land without compensation or including private property in the reform excited only a minority, and even for them, there was no question of attacks on the rights of property. We have Jaroslav Šidak to thank for pointing out that no side put forward a truly radical agrarian program.[71]

In the end, the Croatian legislation, which bore to a great extent the stamp of the liberal People's Party, went, in fact, only slightly beyond the Bratislava regulations. It, too, restricted reforms to encumbered lands, but defined more narrowly the range of remaining royal privileges and promised greater concessions to Slavonians in use of woods and meadows.[72] Hence it fit in the picture of agrarian reform which had been successful elsewhere in the monarchy, with all the benefits, but also the half-measures. It reflected the liberal revolution, but to describe it as the "most decisive and consistent" solution to the agrarian question within the dual monarchy, as Šidak does, is to exaggerate its social radicalism.[73] Practical attempts by peasants or by local administrations supportive of them to interpret the Sabor resolutions to the benefit of the peasants were then generally thwarted.[74]

From the viewpoint of nobles and the nationalist intelligentsia, agrarian reform was initially a necessity that could no longer realistically be refused in the face of the Hungarian resolutions and peasant social expectations. "We have done that demanded by shrewd politics," the editor of the Illyrian *Narodne novine*, Bogoslav Sulek, commented in regard to the resolutsion of the Sabor on peasant emancipation. "We have given that which we could no longer refuse—we have granted concessions at the proper time and with them saved the order and secured general peace."[75]

Apart from this, the agrarian question was only of interest to the nobility and intelligentsia to the extent that it would not endanger their nationalist aims and if possible, support them. Concessions in the agrarian question, liberal representatives argued as well, could, as long as they did not go too far, be offered to the peasants "in order to win them over to the idea of the nation."[76] Jelačić's policies always reflected this instrumental role for the agrarian question, both in the relatively rapid acceptance of agrarian reform in Croatia and in setting clear limits for the social movement. In this spirit, Jaroslav Šidak quite justifiably pointed out that one could not speak of one "national-social movement" in Croatia. The two were related, but in the final analysis there was a nationalist movement supported by the nobility and the intelligentsia, and a peasant movement.

Much more closely woven together were the social and national movements in Transylvania and among the Serbs. In both regions, peasant activity was at first exclusively in the service of social interests. Spontaneous action in March among the Serbs of South Hungary, for example, showed practically no national political preferences and absolutely no nationalist aims. The peasants sought social emancipation. As in civil Croatia, the Magyarones profited more from this, for example in Srem, than the Serb people's party. The first Transylvanian "mass meeting" in Blaj, in which thousands of peasants took part in a remarkable act of political activism, was also understood by peasants more in terms of transethnic social interests than Rumanian nationalist aims.[77]

The early program of national activists from the intelligentsia and the clergy and their relations to the agrarian movement were also marked by moderate reservation. The demands made by the Serbs of Pest on 17 March, and the program of Neusatz proclaimed shortly thereafter were characterized by Serb nationalist claims on the Hungarian crown for recognition and self-goverment. Demands for the abolition of serfdom could not be avoided, but they received the same secondary consideration as in the Croatian "national demands." The national assembly in Karlovac in May also repeated demands for social emancipation, but focused on national demands for the establishment of a Vojvodina that would include the Serbs in the Banat, Bačka, and Srem.[78]

The clerical-conservative leadership of the Serb movement around Bishop Rajačić was not alone noticeably distanced from peasant social aims. From the beginning of the peasant movement, he called on the peasants for moderation, and criticized all attempts to go beyond the Bratislave agrarian resolutions by refuing to pay feudal dues without authorization, or occupying disputed lands. He even called on the Hungarian military for assistance against peasant attacks on monastic lands. Also on the part of the small urban and, with all qualifications, "bourgeois" liberal camp, there was a complete lack of interest and understanding for peasant social concerns. From the same standpoint of legality and enlightenment, national Rumanian leaders in Blaj sought to keep peasant protest on ordered paths.[79]

However, the social and national movements increasingly flowed together from both sides. The overlapping of ethnic and class lines offered fertile ground for this. Especially the adherents of nationalism saw in the peasant movement, with its considerable social dynamic, a political and military resource for a nationalist struggle that threatened ever more to turn into an open military confrontation with Hungary from the spring of 1848 onwards. However, for the peasants as well, the sharpening of nationalist political conflict seemed to make it possible for them to realize their social interests only within the framework of a clash of nationalities. Hence, peasants accepted the nationalist program, but they gave it "an agrarian substance," according to Slavko Gavrilović, who has devoted his attention to the agrarian movement in Croatia and Vojvodina like no other.[80] Doubtless the early nationalist connection between language and the Orthodox confession in a developing Serbian "confessional nation"[81] encouraged a liaison between social and nationalist revolutionary themes. In Transylvania, on the other hand, it was not only cumulating ethnic-social conflicts, but equally the sociopolitical intransigence of Hungarian policies that favored the confluence of these two strands of the revolution. Initially not part of the areas covered by the Bratislava Agrarian Laws, the government made peasant emancipation dependent on an agreement to a union of Transylvania with the Hungarian crown and thus underestimated the autonomous force of the social question. Military suppression of peasant efforts from March onwards to throw off their feudal burdens, hesitation by the Hungarian nobility in Transylvania to agree at least to the status quo of the Bratislava laws, de facto ineffectiveness of the resolutions of the Klausburg Diet of June 1848, in which serfdom was formally abolished, but certainly not in practice—all this made peasant protest more radical and brought it together with an equally radicalized nationalist movement. The result was a conflict expanding into an open war, in which concessions had no chance either from the national or the social point of view.

The example of Transylvania more generally shows how much Hungarian policy favored the convergence of the two strands of revolution. The Hungarian government perceived peasant social claims primarily as part of the nationalist movement. Social concessions were therefore seen as an accommodation of what was, from the Hungarian point of view, "secessioninst" aspirations, and thus as a blow to the unalterable credo of an inflexibly defined "political Hungarian nation." Hungarian minority policy, often described as the "weakest point" of Hungarian policy,[82] was thus, for its part, unable to decouple nationalist and social movements, although these were in practice less inseparably bound than was believed in Pest.

Although both in the Serbian and Rumanian cases social and national movements were closely bound, this should not unreservedly be understood in the sense of a "nationalization" of the peasantry. Even when peasants joined in the national struggles, they remained in the final analysis less interested in national integration than in the fulfillment of their social demands. Peasant petitions therefore generally contained no national demands and if so, then the qualification is quite justified that these were placed in their mouths by leaders of the national movements. Complaints about a lack of national patriotism could be heard everywhere. And behind the superficial acceptance of national-political programs by the peasants were often hidden social expectations. This was true of the Serb goal of a Vojvodina, from which the peasants expected above all a diffuse framework for the solution of the agrarian question.

It can also be seen in another example, up to now only touched upon here, namely that of the Slovenes. The Slovene national leadership, that seemingly appeared from nowhere with the revolution, also found little room for peasant social demands in their national program, which aimed for Slovenian unity, national recognition, and rejection of incorporation into the German Confederation.[83] Indeed they were totally absent from the catalog of demands of the Viennese "Slovenija." Even if the Slovenian peasants were, in fact, remarkably open to the national program in the months of the revolution, here too this was only because social expectations could be incorporated. Hence, as has more recently been emphasized, one can no longer speak without reservation of peasant voting behavior in selecting electors for the Frankfurt National Assembly being only an "agrarian question."

Still, peasants also judged national programs on the extent to which they reflected demands for peasant emancipation. The clearest rejection and dislike of the German Confederation could be found in those places where the peasant social conditions were the most severe. A desire for Slovenia to be closely tied to the kingdom of Croatia, for example, which was also well received by some peasants in particular regions of Styria and Carniola was most widespread where the peasant social situation was the worst. Hence, behind a wish to unite with Croatia stood less a desire for national "Yugoslav" programs than the hope of being able to enjoy the emancipation already announced in Croatia.[84]

Especially in those places where peasants were called out to support the revolution militarily, such as Croatia, among the Serbs, and in Transylvania, ambivalence of peasant attitudes toward the national concerns of the revolution was obvious. Among Croatian peasants, there was an indifference to military commitment similar to that among Hungarian peasants, and especially in 1849, when the Hungarian-Croatian war was becoming an ever greater economic burden for the peasantry, complaints about recruiting problems increased. In any case, Jelačić was rather skeptical about including the peasantry, in placing the "nation in arms."[85]

However, even where the peasants were successfully tied to the nationalist movement and integrated into armed confrontations, as was the case among the Serbs, peasant commitment was always contradictory. Their "traditional radicalism" (Langewiesche) also made peasants susceptible to militant forms of action, as Rumanian and Serbian peasants demonstrated in their revolts and attacks on Hungarian nobles. This militant radicalism could not necessarily be translated in the long-term into military action in the service of the nationalist movement. Desertion, refusal to be conscripted, and the abandonment of units during harvest time were common occurrences. Especially in the course of 1849, when the Serb military situation vis-à-vis Hungary became ever more untenable, the number of such cases rose rapidly. In the spring of 1849, about a third of the peasants drafted into the army were on the run from military service.

And even in Transylvania, where peasants took part in the struggle against the Hungarian army, it was not the revolutionary "levée en masse" but the Imperial army that mobilized the peasantry, as especially here it was the monarchy, and not the "bourgeois revolution" that was credited with their social emancipation. Peasant resistance and refusal made no distinction between Hungarian and "their own," "national" institutions. Complaints about peasant refusal to pay taxes were to be heard from the new institutions of the Serb "national committees," which temporarily replaced the old administration during the revolution.[86] To interpret such behavior as "class struggle" (Gavrilovic) is hardly sufficient; rather it marks those traditional peasant modes of behavior that fit as little into the allegedly new national obligations than into the "old" ones that had been seen as "unjust." Especially here one can see that in southeastern Europe, admittedly like elsewhere in the revolution, the peasants were a long way from being integrated into an emerging nation.[87]

Conclusion

In the final analysis, an examination of the agrarian question and the role of the peasantry in southeastern Europe confirms that an interpretation of the 1848 revolution in terms of "parallel" and "asynchronic" revolutionary processes and actions.[88] Perhaps more than in central Europe, the social movement in southeastern Europe took place within the framework of national revolutionary events, characterized by a "mainstream" aiming at "bourgeois" transformation and oriented towards modernization. Nonetheless, it formed a separate strand, which adapted to this mainstream only temporarily, partially and with many breaks. The social movement in the countryside followed its own aims and rationality, even when it came together with the nationalist movement.

When comparing the individual southeast European revolutionary regions, a common fundamental pattern appears, but also distinctive features for each region. Among the common fundamental patterns are the important role played by the social movements in the countryside for the revolution throughout southeastern Europe. They were more than a "distant, muffled roll of thunder," more than only "sheet-lightning in the distance" with no decisive influence on the "major" revolutionary events, as Emil Niederhauser alleged.[89] Peasant emancipation was a concern of the revolution which could not even be circumvented by political forces outside the liberal camp. Peasant movements were everywhere important actors in revolutionary events, although with different degrees of intensity and radicalism.

Unlike in central Europe, their activities did not peter out with the introduction of agrarian laws, but remained a part of the revolution—here, too, with various intensities. Much less than in central Europe, peasants gained access to the circle of leading actors in the revolution. Organized reinforcement of peasant activities occurred much less often in southeastern Europe than in central Europe; the peasants had no access to the leading strata of the revolution, made up of the nobility, the clergy, and the intelligentsia. Their "plebiscitary" role in revolutionary events, however, achieved a remarkable significance regionally, as for example in the "mass meeting" of Blaj in Transylvania or in Karlovac among the Serbs and Croats of the monarchy. Their role was certainly not limited to providing decoration for the staging of national movements. Rather the leaders of the individual revolutions reacted to the peasants' presence by including social aspects in their catalog of demands.

Finally, one final common element is, above all, that unique rationality, reflecting the peasant life and experiential worlds, which shines through all the peasant movements in the region. Their demands and aims show everywhere an astounding conformity, and they can be summed up under the heading of restoration of "customary rights," not under bourgeois transformation or national unity. One may accept different levels in the formation of confessional–ethnic identities; one can, however, nowhere speak of the ideal of national integration playing a role for peasants. Political demands were also not part of their revolution. At best, they understood national and political movements as a basis for their social aims. Their relation to the aims and activities of the "major" revolution thus remained fractured. In this, the southeast European revolution proves itself to a part of the larger European one.

This fundamental pattern of peasant participation in the revolution displays special features in nearly every respect when examining the individual regions. Even the dynamics of peasant movements show considerable variation. In Hungary, and in Croatia, the agrarian laws led peasants to a more moderate course relatively quickly. Here, too, there was dissatisfaction and protests in reaction to the emancipation decree. Altogether, however, they remained restricted in number and in radicalism. In this respect, they were closer to the revolutions in central Europe, even when the situation in the countryside was much more troubled than in the German states or in Cisleithenia. Attempts by the national leadership of the revolution to tie the peasants to the nationalist movement was also much less successful here.

The situation was different where social and ethnic lines of conflict crossed and hence the chance for an accumulation of the movements arose for both sides, the nationalists and peasantry. This is true, for example, of the Serbs of the monarchy, but also especially for Transylvania. The peasants there were generally much more radical, both in their demands and in their forms of protest, and nationalist and social protest movements were much more intertwined. Nonetheless, peasant activity retained its own rationality and logic. Here too, especially in the attitude of peasants to military service, the relations between the two levels of the revolution were not free of breaks.

The peasants accused of "class utilitarianism" and "betrayal" of bourgeois and national revolutionary objectives can, however, claim one thing for themselves. More than in central Europe, in southeastern Europe it was particularly the peasants whose activities in the revolution produced results that lasted beyond the end of the revolution. Naturally, one cannot overlook the fact that in the follow-up to the agrarian laws of the revolution various matters were only implemented with delay and insufficiently defined. On a few issues the nobility was able to reinforce its position in a climate of neo-absolutism; and, of course, peasant social dependency had not been ended with the agrarian reforms.[90] In this sense, the revolution indeed produced a "half-answered agrarian question."[91]

Nonetheless, not only did emancipation remain inviolable, but in other respects a sociopolitical "rollback" in the countryside could no longer be carried out—something which, in any case, was not even desired even by the neo-absolutism of the postrevolutionary era. Neither did the debacle of Világos have consequences for agrarian reform in Hungary, nor was agrarian reform in Transylvania, which originally had not even fallen under the jurisdiction of the March Laws, reversed. Thus the events of the "agrarian revolution" distinguish themselves not only from the political results of the revolution, but especially from its nationalist aims, which, in southeastern Europe, ended, at best, in disappointment. The economic consequences of the revolution were certainly ambivalent: the structural weaknesses of the individual economic regions continued to have their effect beyond the agrarian reform. However, in this respect as well, there were considerable differences between the various regions. In Hungary the reforms did not lead to modernization in the short-term; they were not the watershed to a rapid breakthrough in productivity, and the peasant economy also was not immediately transformed.[92]

In the medium-term, however, conditions had been created for the modernization that rural districts would experience in the following decades, at first under the dominance of Viennese neo-absolutism and then in the era of the Austro-Hungarian compromise.[93] For the South Slav regions, the economic balance was more sobering. In Croatia-Slavonia the modernization impulse of the revolution remained modest in respect of the economy, at least far from the breakthrough of capitalism that older literature would have one believe.[94] The same is true of agriculture in Transylvania and South Hungary. Even with much less significant structural consequences, the revolution in southeastern Europe, especially in view of the agrarian sector, was part of an irreversible process of modernization. In this sense as well, it has its place in a overall European thematic of these events.[95]

Notes

1. Dieter Langewiesche, *Europa zwischen Restauration und Revolution 1815-1849,* revised and expanded edition (Munich, 1992), 72-73, 275ff.; Wolfram Siemann, *Die Deutsche Revolution von 1848/49* (Frankfurt, 1985), 15-16; Horst Stuke and Wilfried Forstmann, "Einleitung," in Stuke and Forstmann (eds.), *Die europäischen Revolutionen von 1848* (Königstein/Ts, 1979) 4ff.
2. Wolfram Siemann, "Der König lügt!" *Die Zeit*, Nr. 47, 14 November 1997, 9.
3. H.H. Brandt, "Ungarn 1848 im europäischen Kontext. Reform-Revolution-Rebellion," in Karl-Heinz Mack (ed.), *Revolution in Ostmitteleuropa 1848-1849* (Vienna, 1996), 44.
4. Priscilla Robertson, *The Revolutions of 1848. A Social History* (Princeton, 1952), 4.
5. Charles H. Pouthas, "Die Komplexität von 1848," reprinted in Stuke and Forstmann (eds.). *Die europäischen Revolutionen von 1848,* 26; furthermore G. Palmade et al. *Das bürgerliche Zeitalter* (Frankfurt, 1974), 46-47; Friedrich Prinz, "Nationale und soziale Aspekte der Revolution von 1848," in U. Haustein et al. (eds.), *Ostmitteleuropa. Berichte und Forschungen* (Stuttgart, 1981), 192-216; György Spira, "Über die Besonderheiten der ungarischen Revolution von 1848-49," *Österreichische Osthefte* 12 (1970): 168-77; Dieter Langewiesche, "Die Agrarbewegungen in den europäischen Revolutionen von 1848," in *Wege in der Zeitgeschichte. Fs zum 65. Geburtstag von Gerhard Schulz,* ed. y J. Heideking et al. (Berlin and New York, 1989), 275ff.; Rudolf Jaworski and Robert Luft (eds.), *1848-49—Revolutionen in Ostmitteleuropa* (Munich, 1996), 8-9.
6. Hans Rothfels," Das erste Scheitern des Nationalstaates in Ost-Mitteleuropa 1848/49," in Dieter Langewiesche (ed.), *Die deutsche Revolution von 1848/49* (Darmstadt, 1983), 223.
7. Hans Kudlich, *Rückblicke und Erinnerungen,* Vol. 2 (Vienna, 1873), 104. In this sense also K. Grünberg, *Die Bauernbefreiung und die Auflösung der gutsherrlich-bäuerlichen Verhältnisse in Böhmen, Mähren und Schlesien,* Vol. 1 (Leipzig, 1893/94), 388ff.
8. F. Seibt, "Das Jahr 1848 in der europäischen Revolutionsgeschichte," in Jaworski and Luft (eds.), *1848/49—Revolutionen in Ostmitteleuropa,* 22.
9. Siemann, *Die deutsche Revolution,* 184 (quote); Langewiesche, "Agrarbewegung," 276ff.
10. See for the development of historiography of the revolution in relation to Croatia, Wolfgang Kessler, *Politik, Kultur und Gesellschaft in Kroatien und Slawonien in der ersten Hälfte des 19. Jahrhunderts. Historiographie und Grundlagen* (Munich, 1981), esp. 22-106; Jaroslav Šidak, "Historiografija hrvatske povijesti od 1790-1883," [On the Historiography of Croatian History 1790-1883] *Historijski zbornik* 31/32 (1978/79): 68ff.; by the same author, *Studije iz hrvatske provijesti za revolucije 1848-49* [Studies in Croatian History in the Revolution of 1848-49] (Zagreb, 1979), 323-58. On the Hungarian historigraphy of the agrarian and national questions in the revolution see among other items, F. Szakály et al., *Hungary and Eastern Europe, Research Report* (Budapest, 1980), 76ff.
11. For what has been up until now a rather rare example of a comparative view of Southeast European agrarian movements, see E. Arató, "Die Bauernbewegung und der Nationalismus im Frühling und Sommer 1848," *Annales Universitatis Scientiarum Budapestiensis. Sectio Historica* 9 (1967):

61-103 and 11 (1970): 45-68. Further, a brief synthesis can be found in E. Niederhauser, "Seljastvo i nacionalno pitanje u burzuaskim revolucijama," [The Peasants and the National Question in the Bourgeois Revolution]," in SANU (ed.), *Srbi i Madjari u revoluciji 1848-1849 godine* [Serbia and Hungary in the Revolution 1848/49] (Belgrad, 1983), 179-86. On southeastern Europe and beyond, see Di. Langewiesche," Die Agrarbewegungen," 275ff.

12. Andrew C. Janos, *The Politics of Backwardness in Hungary 1825-1945* (Princeton, 1982).

13. See, among others, C.M. Knatchbull-Hugessen, *The Political Evolution of the Hungarian Nation*, Vol. 1 (London, 1908), 202ff.; E.H. Balász, "Die Lage der Bauernschaft und die Bauernbewegung 1780-1787," *Acta historica* 2 (1956): 292ff.

14. See Bela K. Király, *Hungary in the Late Eighteenth Century. The Decline of Enlightened Despotism* (New York and London, 1969), 56ff.; Istvan Deak, *The Lawful Revolution: Louis Kossuth and the Hungarians, 1848-1849* (New York, 1979), 48-50.

15. Peter Hanák, "Die gesellschaftlichen Voraussetzungen der Revolution in Ungarn," in Jaworski and Luft (eds.), *1848/49—Revolution in Ostmitteleuropa,* 242-43.

16. For a description of the ifestyle and economy of Hungarian peasants in the *Vormärz*, see J. Varga, *Typen und Probleme bäuerliche Landbesitzes in Ungarn 1767-1849*, (Budapest, 1965). I. Orosz, "Die landwirtschaftliche Produktion in Ungarn 1790-1849," *Agrártörténeti Szemle* 13 (1971): 1-24, provides a differentiated picture of agricultural productivity and attempts at modernization. A contemporary description can be found in P. Magda, *Neuste statistische-geographische Beschreibung des Königreiches Ungarn, Croatien, Slavonien und der ungarischen Militärgrenze*, Vol. 1 (Leipzig, 1832), 57, 230; A. von Féynes, *Stastik des Königreichs Ungarn, zweyter und dritter Theil* (Pest, 1843), 121; M. von Schwartner, *Statistik des Königreich Ungarns, Ein Versuch, Zweyte, vermehrte und verbesserte Auflage* (Ofen, 1809), 339.

17. Wolfgang Häusler, "Soziale Protestbewegungen in der bürgerlich-demokratischen Revolution der Habsburgermonarchie 1848," in Jaworski and Luft (eds.), *1848/49-Revolutionen in Ostmitteleuropa,* 191ff.

18. Györgi Spira, *Kossuth and Posterity* (Budapest, 1980), 7-8.

19. Magda, *Neueste statistische-geographische Beschreibung*, 58.

20. From the extensive literature on liberal discussion of the agrarian question before the revolution, see Bela Király, "The Radical Liberal Phase of Ferenc Déak," *Südostforschungen* 34 (1975): 196ff.; by the same author, "The Young Ferenc Déak and the Problems of the Serbs," *Südostforschungen* 29 (1970)" 95-127; P. Sándor, *Déak und die Frage der Hörigen auf dem Reichstag der Jahre 1830-1836* (Budapest, 1977), 45ff.; Deak, *The Lawful Revolution*, 40-41; A. Gerö, "Count Széchenyi and the Conflicts of Modernity," in A. Gerö, *Modern Hungarian Society in the Making: The Unfinished Experience* (Budapest, London and New York, 1993), 60ff.; Janos, *The Politics of Backwardness*, 40ff.; Edsel Walter Stroup, *Hungary in Early 1848: The Constitutional Struggle against Absolutism in Contemporary Eyes* (Buffalo, 1977).

21. On this, see Steven Bela Vardy, *Baron Joseph Eötvös. A Literary Biography* (New York, 1987); Paul Bödy, *Joseph Eötvös and the Modernization of Hungary, 1840-1870* (New York, 1985).

22. Sandor, *Déak*, 17.

23. On the attitudes of Hungarian conservatism, see among other works, Erzsébet Andics, "Der Widerstand der feudalen Kräfte in Ungarn am Vorabend der bürgerlichen Revolution des Jahres 1848," *Acta historica* 4 (1955): 170ff. (accents the resistance by conservatives too highly); by the same author, "Erste Reaktion der ungarischen Konservativen auf die Revolutionsereignisse und ihre Abwartungstaktik im Frühjahr und Sommer 1848," *Annales Universitatis Scientiarum Budapestiensis. Sectio Historica* 21 (1981): 39-60; and "The Plans of the Hungarian Conservatives to Suppress the Hungarian Revolution 1848-49," *Etudes historique hongroises* 16 (1985/pt. 1): 3ff. Underlining more the understanding of unavoidability of agrarian reform in principle, see Deak, *The Lawful Revolution*, 54; Spira, *Kossuth and Posterity*, 13; somewhat too uncritical toward conservative policies is Stroup, *Hungary in Early 1848*, 41.

24. Varga, "Typen und Probleme," 36.

25. Stroup, *Hungary*, 56-57.

26. Deak, *The Lawful Revolution*, 40; A. Gergeley, "The Liberalization of Hungarian Political Life 1830-1848," *Etudes Historique Hongroises* (1985/ pt.1): 241-57; Hanák, "Die gesellschaftlichen Voraussetzungen der Revolution in Ungarn," 239-44.

27. On the development of partimonial jurisdiction: J. Kállay, "Patrimonialgerichtliche Jurisdiktion im 18. und 19. Jahrhundert in Ungarn," *Etudes historique Hongroises* (1985/pt. 1): 500-20.

28. For an account of the laws and the measures to be taken, see Schwatner, *Statistik*, 200ff; on the effects of the laws, see Janos, *The Politics of Backwardness*, 85ff.; E. Niederhauser, *1848. Sturm im Habsburgerreich* (Vienna, 1990), 97ff.; P. Hidas, "The Emancipation and the Impact on the Hungarian Peasantry in 1848-1850," in Joseph Held (ed.), *The Modernization of Agriculture and Rural Transformation in Hungary 1848-1975* (New York, 1980), 8ff.

29. See the "Twelve Points" reprinted in K. Nehring (ed.), *Flugblätter und Flugschriften zur ungarischen Revolution von 1848/49* (Munich, 1972), 71-74. Spira interprets the Twelve Points as going much beyond the statutes: György Spira, "Die Linke in der Revolution, in Manfred Kossock (ed.), *Revolutionen der Neuzeit* (East Berlin, 1982).

30. Laszlo Deme, *The Radical Left in the Hungarian Revolution of 1848* (Boulder, 1976), 17-18.

31. From a report by László Czinday to Windischgrätz of 6 April 1849, in: E. Andics (ed.), *A nagybirkotos arisztokrácia ellenforradalmi szerepe 1848-49-ben*, Vol. III (Budapest, 1965), 155. Additional sources on conservative attitudes can be found there and in H. Schlitter, *Versäumte Gelegenheiten. Die oktroyierte Verfassung vom 4. März 1849* (Zürich, 1920), 130ff.

32. *Archiv des ungarischen Ministeriums und Landesvertheidigungsausschusses*, Vol. 1 (Altenburg, 1851), 19ff.

33. Spira, *Kossuth*, 15.

34. Thus Walter Schmidt et al., "Die europäische Revolution 1848/49," in Kossock (ed.) *Revolutionen der Neuzeit*, 307.

35. I.I. Orlik, "Krest´janskoe dvizenie v Vegrii v pervye mesjacy burzuaznoj revoljucii 1848-1849" [The Peasant Movement in Hungary in the First Months of the Bourgeois Revolution in Hungary 1848/49], *Novaja i novajsaja istorija* 3 (1959/pt. 4): 90.

36. György Spira, *A Hungarian Count in the Revolution of 1848* (Budapest, 1974) 160-68; Deme, *The Radical Left*; Deak, *The Lawful Revolution*, 116-17; Niederhauser, *1848*, 86ff.

37. Similarly in Hidas, "The Emancipation," 14.

38. A. Klima, "The Bourgeois Revolution of 1848-1849 in Central Europe," in Roy Porter and Mikulas Teich (eds.), *Revolution in History* (Cambridge, 1986), 91-92.

39. Bela K. Király, "Ferenc Déak, the Social Reformer in the Revolution of 1848-1849," *East European Quarterly* 14 (1980): 411-22; by the same author, "The Radical Phase of Ferenc Déak's Career," *Südostforschungen* 34 (1975): 195-210.

40. Quoted in Arató, "Die Bauernbewegung," Vol.11, 73; similar reports also in *Archiv des ungarischen Ministeriums* Vol. 2, 247.

41. On the question of military commitment: ibid., 13; Helmut Rumpler, *Eine Chance für Mitteleuropa: Österreichische Geschichte 1804-1914* (Vienna, 1997), 304; Z. Barcy, "The Army of 1848-1849 Hungarian War of Independence," in Bela K. Király (ed.), *East Central European Society and War in the Era of Revolution 1775-1856* (New York, 1984), 439-72; Laszlo Deme, "The First Soldiers of the Hungarian Revolution: The National Guard in Pest in March-April 1848," in Király (ed.) *War and Society in East Central Europe during the Eighteenth and Nineteenth Century*, Vol. 1 (New York, 1979), 81-95; Dieter Langewiesche, "Die Rolle des Militärs in den europäischen Revolutionen von 1848/49," in W. Bachhofer and H. Fischer (eds.), *Ungarn-Deutschland. Studien zur Sprache, Kultur, Geographie und Geschichte* (Munich, 1983), 276ff.; A. Urbán, "Die Organisierung des Heeres der ungarischen Revolution vom Jahre 1848," *Annales Universitatis Scientiarum Budapestiensis, Sectio Historica* 9 (1967): 105ff.; G. Handley, "Revolutionary Organization in the Context of Backwardness: Hungary's 1848," *East European Quarterly* 6 (1972): 46ff.; Deme, *The Radical Left*, 56; E. Niederhauser, *1848*, 125; E. Stroup, *1848*, 141.

42. *Archive des ungarischen Ministeriums, Dritter Band*, Vol. 2, 27.

43. Langewiesche, "Agrarbewgung," 276ff.

44. Kudlich, *Rückblicke*, 106.

45. For agrarian legal structures, see M. Gross, *Počeci moderne Hrvatske. Neoabsolutizam u civilnoj Hrvatskoj i Slavoniji 1850-1860* [The Beginnings of Modern Croatia. Neoabsolutism in Civil Croatia-Slavonia 1850-1860] (Zagreb, 1985), 155ff.; Kessler, *Politik, Kultur und Gesellschaft in Kroatien*, 234-40; I. Karaman, "Postanak i značenje privremenog urbara za Hrvatsku g. 1755," [Origin and Significance of the Provisional Encumbered Land Status for Croatia 1755] *Radovi Filozofkog Fakulteta, Odsek za povijest* 4 (1962): 51-78; I. Erceg, "Die Theresianischen Reformen in Kroatien," in *Wege und Forschungen der Agrargeschichte* (Frankfurt, 1967), 146-52; on the conditions in Slavonia above all, see F.W. von Taube, *Historische und geographische Beschreibung des Königreiches Slavonien und des Herzogsthums Syrmien*, II. Buch (Leipzig, 1777), 73ff.; J. Bösendörfer, *Agrarni odnosi u Slavoniji* [Agrarian Relations in Slavonia], (Zagreb, 1950), 82ff. For a brief summary, see R. Ritter von Pfeiffer-Hochwalden, "Die Entwicklung der Landwirtschaft in Slavonien," Ph.D. Diss., (Leipzig, 1897), 31-35; G. Harms, *Bevölkerungsstruktur und Agrarverfassung Slawoniens. Der wirtschaftliche und soziale Aufbau einiger Dörfer im Poscheger Kessel* (Leipzig, 1942), 401-7; M. Ivsic, *Les problèmes agraires en Yougoslavie* (Paris, 1926), 53-73.

46. On the agrarian legal and social situation in these regions see, among others, Slavko Gavrilović, *Srem u revoljuciji 1848-49* [Srem in the Revolution 1848/49] (Belgrade, 1963), 19-23; *Istorija Srpskog naroda*, [History of the Serbian People] Vol. 2 (Belgrade, 1984), 511ff.

47. Keith Hitchens, *The Rumanian National Movement in Transylvania 1780-1849* (Cambridge, 1969), 136ff.

48. R. Ritter von Pfeiffer-Hochwalden, *Die Entwicklung*, 31-32; Gavrilović, *Srem u revoljuciji*, 55ff.

49. See for the social condition of Slovenian peasants on the eve of the revolution, B. Grafenauer, "Slovenski kmet v letu 1848," [The Slovenian Peasant in 1848] *Zgodovinski časopis* 2-3 (1948/49): 7-69. A summary of revolutionary events in J. Prunk, *Slovenski narodni vzpon* [The Rise of the Slovenian Nation 1768-1992] (Ljubljana, 1992), 51-69.

50. To cite just a few of a number of similar contemporary reports: Taube, *Historische und geographische Beschreibung*, Vol. 1, 44-45; J. v. Csaplovics, *Slavonien und zum Theil Croatien*, pt. 1, (Pest, 1819), 103ff.

51. With some reservation see Slavko Gavrilović, *Agrari pokreti u Sremu i u Slavoniji pocetkom XIX.veka* [The Agrarian Movement in the Srem and in Slavonia at the Beginning of the nineteenth Century] (Belgrade, 1960), 67-68; by the same author, *Srem u revoluciji*, 20ff., 85.

52. J. Čapo, "Economic and Demographic History of Peasant Households on a Croatian Estate, 1756-1848," Ph.D. Diss. (University of California at Berkeley, 1990); an increase in "feudal exploitation," on the other hand, is emphasized in, among others, V. Bogdanov, *Ustanak Srba u Vojvodidi i Madjarska revolucija* [The Revolt of Serbs in the Vojvodina and the Hungarian Revolution 1848/49] (Subotica, 1929), 19ff.; by the same author, *Društvene i politicke borbe u Hrvatskoj 1848/49* [The Social and Political Struggle in Croatia 1848/49] (Zagreb, 1949) 105ff., I. Karaman, "O nekim osnovnim problemima ekonomskog socijalnog razvoja ne području Slavonije u Srejema pocetkom XIX. Sto," [On some problems of Economic-Social Development in the Region of Slavonia and Srem at the Beginning of the nineteenth Century] *Historijski zbornik* 14 (1961): 243-60.

53. S. Gavrilovič, *Agrarni poketi u Sremu i u Slavoniji*; by the same author, "Prilogi istoriji seljackih nemira u Hrvatsckjoj i Slavoniji 1778-1848," *Historijski zbornik* (17) 1964: 115-80, and "Agrarni pokreti u Sremu, Slavoniji i Moslavini pocetkom XIX.v." [The Agrarian Movements in the Srem, in Slavonia and in Moslavina at the Beginning of the Nineteenth Century] *Historijski zbornik* 10 (1957): 71-82.

54. Rothfels, "Das erste Scheitern," 225.

55. On early peasant unrest in Croatia-Slavonia, see Aleksije Jelačić, *Selijacki pokret u Hravtskoj i Slavoniji godine 1848-1849* [The Peasant Movement in Croatia and Slavonia 1848/49] (Zagreb, 1925), 17ff.; S. Gavrilovič, "Agrarni nemiri u Križevačkoj i Varaždinskoj Županiji 1848-1850," [Agrarian Unrest in the Counties of Križevic and Varaždin 1848-1950] *Historijski zbornik* 13 (1960): 47-52; by the same author, "Virotvitrička županija u revoluciji 1848-1849," [The County of Virotvitrička in the Revolution 1848/49] *Historijski zbornik* 14 (1961): 1; Jaroslav Šidak, "Seljačko pitanje u hrvatskoj politici 1848," [The Peasant Question in Croatian Politics of 1848] *Jugoslovenski istorijski casopis* 2 1(963): 10ff. (an English language version of this essay can be found in *Acta Iugoslavia his-*

torica 1 (1970): 94ff.); by the same author, *Studije iz hrvatske povijesti za revolucije 1848-49* [Studies From Croatian History on the Revolution](Zagreb, 1979), 62ff.

56. V. Bogdanov, *Ustanak Srba u Vojvodini*, 66ff.; Gavrilović, *Srem u revoluciji*, 108ff.; by the same author, *Srbi u Habsburškoj monarchiji 1792-1849* [The Serbs in the Habsburg Monarchy 1792-1849] (Novi Sad, 1994), 34.; A. Radenić, "Suštinska sporna pitanja srpskog pokreta 1848-1849 godine," [The True Disputes of the Serbian Movement 1848-49] in SANU (ed.), *Srbi Madjari*, 103-4, 133-34.

57. Hitchens, *The Rumanian National Movement*, 199.

58. Gavrilović, *Srem u revoluciji*, 144ff.

59. See on the problem of peasant unrest: Jelačić, *Seljački pokret*, 73ff.; B. Stojsavljević, *Šuma i pasa u borbi sela u Hrvatskoj i Slaviniji poslije 1848* [Woods and Meadows in the Struggles in the Villages of Croatia and Slavonia after 1848] (Zagreb, 1961); Gavrilović, "Agrani nemiri," 60ff.; by the same author, "Virovitrička županiji," 26 and "Agrarno-socijalno zbivanja u Požeskoj županiji 1848-1849," [The Agrar-Social Movement in the County of Pozega 1848-1849] *Godišnjak Filozofskog Fakulteta u Novom sadu*V (1960): 35-71; M. Gross, *Počeci moderne Hrvatske*, 159ff., 196 ff.; Gavrilović, *Srem u revoluciji*, 118ff., 252ff., 272ff., 321ff., 347ff. On the initially spontaneous agrarian unrest among the Slovenes with helpful references to further literature also: J. Prunk, *Slovenski narodni vzpon,* 53.

60. Hitchins, *The Rumanian National Movement*, 240-43.

61. Jelačić, *Seljački pokret*, 23; Šidak, "Seljačko pitanje," 14f.

62. Thus again see, Gavrilović, *Srbi u Habsburskoj monarchiji*, 58; and by the same author, *Srem u revoluciji*, 118 and "Virovitrijska županija," 26; see also I.I. Leščilovskaja, *Obščestvenno-političeskaja bor'ba v Charvatii 1848-1849* [The Social-Political Struggle in Croatia 1848-1849](Moscow, 1977), which evaluates peasant actions as part of the "bourgeois-democratic" quality of the revolution.

63. Peter Heumos, "Die Bauernbefreiung in den böhmischen Ländern 1848," in Jaworski and Luft (eds.), *1848/49—Revolutionen in Ostmitteleuropa,* esp. 226-37.

64. György Spira, "Na pragu bratoubilačkog rata. Razvoj nacionalnich pokreta u Ugarskoj u dova revolucije 1848," [On the Brink of a War between Brothers. The Development of National Movements in Hungary in the Course of the Revolution 1848] in SANU (ed.), *Srbi i Madjari*, 21.

65. See Langewiesche, "Agrarbewegungen," 284.

66. Jaroslav Šidak, "Prilozi historiji stranačkih odnosa u Hrvatskoj uoci 1848," [Contributions to the History of Party Relations in Croatia on the Eve of the Revolution of 1848]*Historijski zbornik* 13 (1960): 67-207, esp. 188ff.

67. Šidak, "Studije," 62ff.

68. Reprinted in ibid, 51ff.; in German, see W. Behnschnitt, *Nationalismus bei Serben und Kroaten 1830-1914*, (Munich, 1980) 152. On Croatian-Hungarian relations the two sides have in the meantime produced an amount of literature that can be reviewed only with difficulty. For the most recent contribution which makes use of the available literature see T. Markus, "Madjarski nacionalizam i hrvatska," *Časopis za suvremenu povijest,* (1997/pt. 1): 41-68.

69. Reprinted in St. Pejakovic (ed.), *Aktenstücke zur Geschichte des kroatisch-slavonischen Landtages und der nationalen Bewegung vom Jahre 1848* (Vienna, 1861), 4.

70. Šidak, "Studije," 191-299.

71. Šidak, "Seljačko pitanje," 18ff., in contrast to the older interpretation of V. Bogdanov, who speaks of a "left" in the revolution: V. Bogdanov, *Društvene i političke borbe u Hrvatskoj*, (Zagreb, 1949). In spite of Šidak's convincing critique, the Russian historian Leščilovskaja also keeps to a three-way division of the political spectrum into conservative, liberal, and radical camps: I.I. Leščilovskaja, *Obščestvenno-političeskaja bor'ba,* 102ff.

72. The resolutions are reprinted in: *Hrvatski pokret u ljetu godine 1848* [The Croatian Movement in the Summer of 1848](Zagreb, 1899), 134ff.

73. Šidak, "Studije," 213. In this respect, Šidak was quite justifiably more reserved in his 1963 essay "Šeljačko pitanje," 22.

74. Gavrilović, "Agrarno-socialno zbivanja u Požežkaj zupaniji," 40ff.

75. Cited in Šidak, "Šeljačko pitanje," 10.

76. The liberal Antun Nemcic in the debates in the Sabor, quoted in Gavrilović, *Agrarni nemiri*, 60.

77. V. Cheres,tesiu, *Adunarea na,tionala de la Blaj* [The National Assembly of Blaj], (Bucharest, 1966), 40ff.; Stefan Pascu, *A History of Transylvania*, trans. Robert Lad, (Detroit, 1982), 196; Hitchins, *The Rumanian National Movement*, 204ff.

78. Cf. R. Petrović (ed.), *Gradja za istoriju srpskog pokreta u Vojvodini 1848-1849* [Materials on the History of the Serb Movement in the Vojvodina 1848-1849], (Belgrade, 1952), 255ff. Furthermore: A. Lebl, *Revolucionarni pokret u Vojvodini 1848-49* [The Revolutionary Movement in Vojvodina 1848-49], (Novi Sad, 1960); Gavrilović, *Srbi u Habsburskoj monarchiji*, 52ff.; most recently: L. Krlkjus, "Misao i stvarnost autonomije srpske Vojvodine 1848 i 1849 godine," [Idea and Reality of a Serb Vojvodina 1848/49]*Jugoslovenski istorijski časopis* 24 (1996/pts. 1-2): 95ff.

79. Hitchins, *The Rumanian National Movement*, 242ff.

80. Gavrilović, *Srem u revoljuciji*, 185.

81. E. Turczynski, *Konfession und Nation. Zur Frühgeschichte der serbischen und rumänischen Nationalbildung* (Düsseldorf, 1976).

82. As opposed to a reference to the vast amount of literature on Hungarian national policy in the revolution, reference is made here to the brief attempt at explanation in Gerö, *Modern Hungarian Society in the Making*, 92–105.

83. See the reprinted source material in J. Prunk, *Slovenski narodi programi* [The Slovene National Program], (Ljubljana, 1991), 152–59; J. Mal, *Zgodovina slovenskega naroda, najnoejša doba* (Celje, 1934), 605ff.

84. St. Granda, "Das Verhältnis zwischen nationaler und sozialer Frage bei den Slowenen im Jahre 1848/49," in Jaworski and Luft (eds.), *1848/49—Revolutionen in Ostmitteleuropa*, 245–55; P. Korunić, "Prilog poznavanju hrvatsko-slovenskih političkih odnesa 1848," [A Contribution to an Awareness of Croatian-Slovene Political Relations 1848]*Historijski zbornik* 31/32 (1978/79): 165–93.

85. On the problem of the inclusion of the peasantry, see above all J. Adamczek, "Narodne straze 1848-1849," [The National Militia 1848-1849]*Radovi Filozofskog Fakulteta u Zagrebu. Odsjek za provijest* 5 (1963): 27-108; further references in Gavrilović, "Virovitrička županija," 51, 54, and his "Agrarmi nemiri," 69.

86. Gavrilović, *Srem u revoluciji*, 236 ff.

87. Langewiesche, "Die Rolle des Militärs," 277.

88. Langewiesche, "Agrrarbewegungen," 276; Siemann, *Die deutsche Revolution*, 176.

89. Niederhauser, *1848*, 183.

90. Rumpler, *Geschichte Österreichs*, 349.

91. Häusler, "Soziale Protestbewegungen," 192.

92. Richard Rudolph, "Economic Revolution in Austria? The Meaning of 1848 in Austrian Economic History," in John Komlos (ed.), *Economic Development in the Habsburg Monarchy in the Nineteenth Century* (New York, 1983), 165–87; John Komlos, "The Emancipation of the Hungarian Peasantry and Agricultural Development," in Ivan Völgyes (ed.), *The Peasantry in Eastern Europe*, Vol. I (New York, 1979), 109–18; A. Varos, "The Age of Preparation: Hungarian Agrarian Conditions between 1848-1914," in Held (ed.), *The Modernization*, 30.

93. G. Szabad, *Hungarian Political Trends between the Revolution and the Compromise 1848-1867* (Budapest, 1988); P. Gunst, "Die Marktlage der ungarischen Landwirtschaft im 19. Jahrhundert (1814-1918)," *Akademie der Landwirtschaftswissenschaften der DDR: Tagungsbericht* 173 (1979): 116–28; K. Dinklage, "Die Landwirtschaft," *Die Habsburger Monarchie 1848-1918*, Vol. 1: *Die wirtschaftliche Entwicklung*, ed. by A. Brusatti (Vienna, 1973), 415ff.

94. See also Gross, *Počeci moderne Hrvatske*, 155ff.; I. Karaman, *Priveda i društvo Hrvatske u 19. stoljecu* [Economy and Society in Croatia in the Nineteenth Century] (Zagreb, 1972); for older views especially R. Bičanić, "Industrijska revolucija u Hrvatskoj i godina 1848," [The Industril Revolution in Croatia and the Year 1848] *Historijski zbornik* 1(1948): 67-101.

95. Siemann, *Die deutsche Revolution*, 15.

Part III

REVOLUTIONARY POLITICS AND POLITICS IN THE REVOLUTION

Sitting of the preparatory parliament in the St. Paulskirche in Frankfurt a.M.
(Illustrirte Zeitung, Leipzig, no. 255, 20 May 1848, 330)

Clearing of the rostrum in the national assembly hall after the attack by the clubbists on 15 May
(Illustrirte Zeitung, Leipzig, no. 257, 3 June 1848, 371)

Chapter 20

STRUCTURES OF PARLIAMENTARY REPRESENTATION IN THE REVOLUTIONS OF 1848

Heinrich Best

Comparative Starting Points and Perspectives

$\mathbf{R}$esearch on the revolutions of 1848 has long since shifted its focus from the business of state, cabinets, and parliaments, to actions in public space, the groups involved, the organizations, and the course of mass movements. The older historical tradition, focused on the upper layers of the societal organization of power and domination, and the persons acting in them, remains unrelated to a social history of the revolution from the bottom up. This is a shortcoming, especially as revolutions are distinguished by a plasticity of institutional order, in which previously separate areas of activity are bound together, the borders between system levels become blurred, and groups of actors intermingle. For a historical moment it is uncertain what is the top and what the bottom, or where the core of the societal organization of power and domination is located. A diffuse situation of dual power forms the starting point for a new differentiation, consolidation, and institutionalization of power structures.

In this essay, when parliaments in revolutionary processes are discussed, emphasis shall be given to processes of collapse and formation of power, social opening and closing of access to power, and the dissolution and consolidation of institutional orders. Empirical access to these themes comes from a consideration of the processes and structures of parliamentary representation, conceived as the connecting link between society and politics, in which social structures of conflict and power are projected into the arena of political decision-making.

It is somewhat surprising that Karl Marx, who could not otherwise be said to have had a friendly relationship to the institutions of parliamentary representation, can be called upon as a witness for such a view of things. However, with the Parisian constituent assembly in mind, he remarked that the general election of April 1848 had brought, in place of the "imaginary people," "the real people to light," "that is, representation of the various classes into which it falls." In this respect, the National Assembly represented "the nation."[1] The "real nation" of the voters distinguished itself not only from the imaginary figure of a disinterested and enlightened *citoyen*, the dream of "republicans of the old school," but also, and more clearly still, from the militant groups of mass protest and revolutionary uprisings.

Not only in France was the position of parliament in the revolutionary process of the years 1848/49 characterized by the conflictual antitheses of mediating representation and direct action, legitimation through procedure and violent pressure, delay through procedural protraction and acceleration through mass protest, protected preparation of decisions in the back rooms of power and exposed staging of political discourse, moderating compromise and radical extremism, stabilization through development of institutions from above and dynamization through self-organization from below, realpolitik and utopia, rostrums and barricades. Parliamentary assemblies soon lay athwart the revolutionary currents of 1848/49; this was both their dilemma and their raison d'être. To this extent they indeed formed elements of a "political reconstruction, the political reconsolidation of bourgeois society"—as Marx ascertained in reference to the Paris constituent assembly.[2]

But this is only one side of the coin, as such, parliamentary assemblies were, at the same time, the core of a political order which prefigured the modern European state—if only temporarily. A number of elements of modern political life were present in 1848: political mobilization, one expression of which was a radically expanded franchise; freedom of association, which heralded the beginnings of organized political parties; public debate free of censorship; and an increase in the power of parliaments, from which governments were drawn, and which were given the power to decide on fundamental outcome and the institutional framework of politics. Together, these formed a constellation in which the important elements of a representative democracy appeared for the first time in Europe. The question arises of why this configuration, which would become the successful model of the organization of political power in the second half of the twentieth century, remained ephemeral in the mid-nineteenth century and gave way to the restored monarchical regimes and, in France, to the authoritarian empire of Napoleon III. Some significant explanatory aspects, though perhaps not the entire answer to this question, arise from a reconstruction of the structures of parliamentary representation in 1848, in which can be traced the tensions and fractures in the embryonic order of a new form of government.

This will be done via a comparison between the Frankfurt and Paris national assemblies. This perspective reflects not just the author's research interests and the greater availability of sources compared to other parliaments; it is also based on systematic considerations.[3] The study encompasses a broad swath of central and western Europe, which in today's political geography reaches from Kleipeda in Lithuania to Perpignan in France, from Tönder in Denmark to Ljubljana in Slovenia. In addition, the contrast between both polities along the lines of J.S. Mill's "method of differences" proves to be an ideal constellation for concepts of comparison.[4]

The institutional form of the constitution, their mandates for action, and the time limits in which the two assemblies had to carry out their work were largely identical. Both were to produce constitutions for large territorial states; their members were elected on a universal or nearly universal male suffrage; both met at nearly the same time, from May 1848 to May/June 1849. Both also were placed under a great deal of public pressure, which was expressed, among other ways, in broad petition movements and in extra-institutional interventions in the sphere of parliamentary deliberations.

Broad differences, on the other hand, existed in the general sociocultural context. The population of the divided territory of the German Confederation was multi-ethnic and multi-confessional. In the polycentric structure of its myriad of states—before simplification of the conflict by Austria's exit—the "querelles allemandes" were still palpably present. France, on the other hand, embodied in its self-representation and in the perception of foreigners the archetype of a "nation une et indivisible," in which ethnic-cultural and religious diversity had been leveled in a rigorous process of standardization. This standardization is said to have been overarched by a centralization of state authority completed during the French Revolution. The use of indirect quotation, however, indicates a cautious distancing from this concept; for as will be shown below, the territorial diversity of the old regime still shone through the structures of political conflict in 1848/49. Nonetheless, it remains true to say that the two cases represent different stages in the process of nation- and state-building, something directly reflected in the agendas of the respective national assemblies: while the Paris constituent assembly's task was to remodel the established structure of an existing nation-state, its Frankfurt counterpart sought to create this power structure for the first time, via a laborious process of setting up foreign boundaries and forming the internal structures of the state.

The Establishment of the Field of Parliamentary Action

The attempt to bring the territories of the German Confederation into a nation-state by common agreement, through parliamentary deliberation and an act of superordinate constitution-making was encumbered by extreme problems of coordination, as had already become apparent in the immediate prehistory of the Frankfurt National Assembly. The road to a pan-German parliament went through many stages, marked by a rapid succession of assemblies, (parliamentary in form but private in legal status), which completed the transition from the (semi) conspiratorial and informal organizational forms of the *Vormärz* opposition to the "improvised parliamentarianism" of the Frankfurt National Assembly.[5] The Heidelberg Assembly and the committee of seven, the pre-parliament and the committee of fifty, all arose within a matter of weeks through cooptation and delegation in and from the circles of the *Vormärz* opposition movement.

In view of rigorous repressive measures and the territorial division of the German Confederation, this coordination was a remarkable achievement. It demonstrated just how much progress had been made in the formation of a civil society, reaching across and beyond existing state structures in Germany, in spite of all governmental restrictions. The basis of this civil society was a tightly knit and widely extended network of the German propertied and educated middle class. An important factor here was a high level of mobility, as can be reconstructed from the biographies of the deputies to the Frankfurt National Assembly, for example. The practice of traveling considerable distances for a higher education and job-related migration, especially of civil servants, had led to the establishment of interregional arenas of communication and action. Eighty-seven percent of the deputies had received a higher education, making universities nodes of politically exploitable communication networks and points of the crystallization of oppositional organization.[6]

The "cultural nation" in Germany formed a communicative space in which the "political nation" was prepared. Although we have found the business middle class as a group somewhat more "rooted," they also had access to a wide-ranging network through its commercial relations. Large trade fairs, as the most important meeting points and arenas for the establishment of the first special interest groups of the business middle class, were the functional equivalents of the universities, which were shaped by the educated middle class.[7] When Karl Marx commented in 1845 that the German bourgeoisie was only "provincial, urban, local and private," he ignored the true extent of supra-local and interregional contacts.[8]

Nonetheless, it would be premature to conclude that, through the interlocking [*Verflechtungen*] of positions of civil society, the elite structural conditions already existed for a German nation-state based on representative institutions. To do so would ignore the decisive condition for further development—that these relations only led to partial integration, to the formation of second order segmentations. This can be seen clearly in the spatial mobility patterns of the deputies to the Frankfurt National Assembly before they took their seats. In their movements, three territorial blocks stand out, within which exchange was concentrated, between which, however, barriers existed to mobility: Old Prussia, Austria, and a third Germany expanded to include the Prussian Rhine province. This pattern appears in an analysis of exchange between areas of residence and it structures—even more clearly—areas of communication in the movement between universities during individuals' education. Especially noticeable was the exclusion of Austrian deputies, who in turn show a centripetal pattern of exchange centered on Vienna. Important here is that the borders of these communication areas anticipated the splits in territorial conflicts of elites and starting points for alternative attempts at consolidation of a nation-state.[9]

This pattern had also appeared in the constitutive phase of the Frankfurt National Assembly. Members of the preparatory assemblies were recruited at first exclusively (and, in the later course of events, to a considerable extent), from southern and central Germany—regions that were territorially fragmented, but advanced in their constitutional development. They were the heartland of the recently collapsed Holy Roman Empire and last bastions of a residual "imperial patriotism," clearly distanced from the two "secession states" (S. Rokkan), Austria and Prussia. Even in the pre-parliament, where greater efforts were made on maintaining a regional balance, the southern and central German small- and medium-sized states (excluding Old Bavaria) were still massively over-represented with 63 percent of the delegates, compared with the 23 percent share in the Frankfurt National Assembly, where regional representation was based on population.[10] Prussia provided only a quarter of the delegates, although here in turn a disproportionally large share (two-thirds) came from the western provinces. Austria sent only two delegates to the pre-parliament and thus continued to take little part in the preparation of a German national representation.

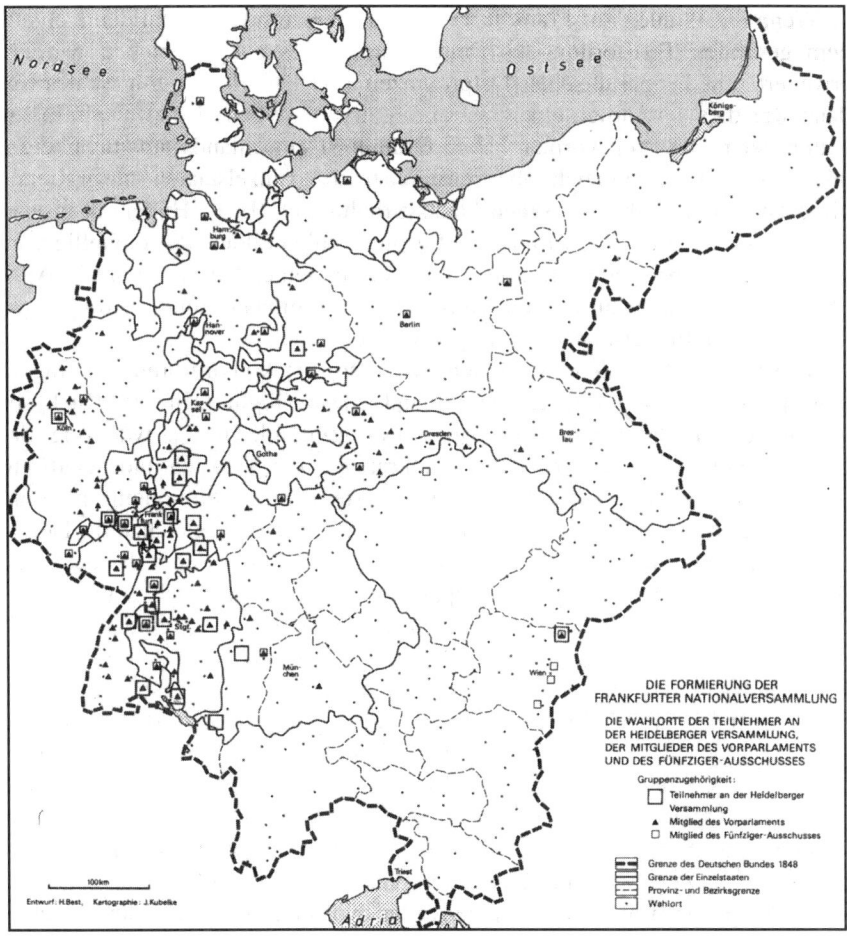

Formation of the Frankfurt National Assembly Constituencies of Delegates to the Heidelberg Assembly, Pre-Parliament and The Committee of Fifty

If elections to the Frankfurt National Assembly were called nonetheless for the entire territory of the German Confederation, expanded to include Prussia's eastern provinces and the Duchy of Schleswig, this was due to the German Confederation, which was highly discredited as the incarnation of the repressive *Vormärz* order in Germany, but which could claim a "legal continuity of German governmental conditions" (E.R. Huber) above and beyond the individual states. The formal basis for the elections was provided by the Federal Election Statute in its version of 7 April 1848, unanimously approved by the Diet of the German Confederation. The implementation of the statute and its adaptation to regional special conditions was given to the individual German states.[11]

Just how important it was to be able to revert back to an established authority extending beyond the individual states for all conflicts between competing agencies of a politically newly organized Germany is shown in the example of Italy, where attempts by democrats in Tuscany and the Roman Republic to call an Italian constitutional assembly failed. As in Germany, both democratization and national unity were on the agenda. However, in Italy, existing relations between opposition groups were weaker and much more strictly segmented territorially.[12] Above all, however, there was nothing beyond the individual Italian states, that might have served as an institutional reference and starting point for Italian state formation. To this extent, Italy was in fact only a geographical term, as Metternich disparagingly put it.

Connections between the centers of the revolution also remained weak in 1848/49: the Kingdom of Naples, was preoccupied with particularist developments in Sicily; in Upper Italy, where Piedmont's attempt to create a territorial power base for the incorporation of the rest of Italy under a dynasty failed militarily; and, finally, central Italy, the democratic "counter-model" of dynamizing and coordinating the process of building a nation-state through the summoning of a parliamentary representative body for all of Italy was equally unsuccessful. Against this background, the gathering of the German constituent national assembly can be seen as a remarkable success, perhaps the greatest success the opposition movement had in 1848/49, even if it was accomplished at a time when the dynamics of revolution in Germany were still unbroken and it was achieved with the aid of established powers, for which a high price would soon have to be paid.

In France, the challenge of forming the constituent assembly was met within the clearly marked paths of an established nation-state with precisely defined borders and a dominating capital. While in Germany the parliamentary elites could only amalgamate gradually and incompletely to represent the broad area between the Meuse and Memel, the Adige and the Belt, political activity in France during the phase which preceded the meeting of the constituent assembly was focused on the narrow space between the Palais Bourbon, the seat of the Chamber of Deputies of the July Monarchy, and the Hôtel de Ville, the meeting place of the revolutionary leaders. Only the meeting of the constituent assembly brought the French regional leadership groups into play politically once again.

Unlike in Germany, in France neither the social nor the territorial extent of the franchise for the National Assembly was publicly controversial. While in Germany universal manhood suffrage was implemented with the social restriction of independence, which, depending on the individual state, excluded between 5 percent and 25 percent of adult men, the franchise for adult men in France was unrestricted.[13] This consensus formed the basis for cooperation between moderate republicans and radical democrats in the provisional government of 24 February 1848. Only the date of the elections was controversial. The radical democrats attempted to postpone them, to gain time for the revolution to penetrate the countryside, while the moderate republicans sought to direct revolutionary events onto the well-ordered path of parliamentary procedure as soon as possible.[14]

The perspective here was "the political reconsolidation of bourgeois society" and a surmounting of the "divorce between the revolution and the country,"[15] which denotes both the weak points and the lines of conflict that burdened the process of consolidation of the Second Republic. Certainly the establishment of the "Provisional Government of the French Republic" meant investiture in the power of a real state, shaken as it might have been by the change in regime and violent uprising in the capital. The army had generally remained intact, one reason being that considerable portions of it were engaged in Algeria. The administration of the Departments continued to work and—after the prefects of the July Monarchy were replaced by "Commissars of the Republic"—followed the instructions of the new government in Paris. The judicial system was hardly affected by the revolution, as only fourteen judges were suspended and nine senior prosecuting attorneys removed from office. Judicial officials were quite willing to start proceedings against ministers of the previous regime.[16] Nonetheless, it would be premature to credit the provisional state of the Second Republic with revolutionary omnipotence, although this would have been justified formally before the new constitution had been passed. In fact, however, the governments in the early phase of the Second Republic were bound in a pre-constitutional system of "checks and balances" that severely limited room for maneuver and played a determining role in the course of events.

The most important actors on the stage up to June 1848 were the "people of Paris," who occasionally appeared in the plenum and in the cabinet chamber.[17] Mass uprisings, which were repeated at intervals of a few weeks between February and June 1848, provided the potential for intimidation and intervention for the democrats of the extreme left. In coalition with the radical clubs, they were partially successful in establishing a revolutionary counter-power, which, until the suppression of the June uprising, gave the political constellation of forces some of the characteristics of a situation of dual power. The ambivalence of the situation also influenced the formation of the provisional government, which may be described as the fusion of two cliques, grouped around the two leading newspapers of the opposition left in the July Monarchy: the radical *Réforme* and the moderate *National*.

In the foundation of the Second Republic two strains of legitimacy crossed—one based on the established state and one proceeding from the revolutionary sovereignty of the people. Seven members of the provisional government were designated by the Chamber of Deputies of the July Monarchy as it was dissolving, and four by the acclamation of a crowd in front of the Hôtel de Ville. Later, four experts were coopted as ministers, but they were never to belong to the narrow circle of fully legitimated members of the government.[18]

The changing composition of the subsequent governments documents the dynamics of a transformation of the power structure in the process of a revolutionary transition of regime. The fact that members of the democratic left were displaced from the government until none were left in President Bonaparte's Barrot-Falloux government is hardly surprising.[19] What is more unexpected, and indeed striking, is that the number of individuals residing in the capital city declined, whether for personal or political reasons. All fifteen members of the provisional government, but only six of the eleven ministers of Barrot's government, had their main residence in Paris. Eight members of the provisional government represented Paris in the national assembly, but none of President Bonaparte's ministers.

Belonging to the political personnel of the capital—which, in a situation of open rebellion, was a necessary condition for taking on a government office—became a handicap during a phase in which the notables of the provinces were again able to make good their claims to participation in the new political order and to central positions of power. The detachment of the provinces from the revolutionary leadership in Paris manifested itself in the change in the social composition of those in leading political positions. Restoring peace in the capital also ended the rule of Parisian leaders of the revolution, whose system of support was decisively weakened through a ban on political clubs, restriction of freedom of the press, and stationing of front-line troops in Paris. All things pointed to a return to a rule of the notables as practiced in the July Monarchy, characterized by a symbiosis of central and local representatives of power.

Recruitment and Circulation of Parliamentary Leadership Groups

The foundation and the lead-in to the restitution of the traditional arrangements of power in France were the elections for the national assembly—although the electoral system was designed to dissolve the political effects of social hierarchies and personal ties. Voting was, for the first time in human history, on the basis of universal manhood suffrage at the national level. Compared to the July Monarchy, the share of voters in the population jumped from 0.7 percent to 23.1 percent. To lessen local influences, constituencies were based on the departments. Voting was by an open list procedure; a plurality sufficed for election. Turnout was extremely high at 83.3 percent, a rate only exceeded in 1928.[20]

In spite of a dramatic change in the formal conditions for gaining a mandate, the extent of elite circulation at the level of parliamentary elites was rather moderate and less far-reaching. Twenty-one percent of the members of the national assembly had already held seats in the chamber of the July Monarchy; whereby it should not be forgotten that the national assembly had almost twice as many seats as its predecessor.[21] Moreover, the second rank of local and regional politicians in the July Monarchy made use of the opportunity to appear on the national political stage. Thirty-seven percent of the members of the national assembly had held office in local or regional administration before 1848, for example as mayors, city councilors, and *conseillers généraux*—all of these are functions for which a property qualification was necessary. A further 9 percent may be regarded as "dignitaries" with public status—for example as lay judges or those having leading functions in corporations, colleges, and associations.

These figures thus lead to the conclusion that about half of the delegates had held elective office during the July Monarchy and about two-thirds had sworn an oath of loyalty to Louis Philippe as state employees or political functionaries. According to other estimates, about three-quarters of the delegates paid a direct tax of at least F 500, thus belonging to that 0.13 percent of the population who were eligible for election as parliamentary deputies before the February revolution.[22] Equally, the socioprofessional composition of the assembly, in which landowners, rentiers, independent professionals, and businessmen made up 72 percent of the deputies, points to a dominance of an economically "unassailable" (M. Weber) propertied bourgeoisie.[23]

The petit bourgeoisie, semi-proletarians, and "unpropertied intellectuals," with a share of 12 percent, formed a rather fringe category, about as large as that of businessmen. The picture that appears then is one of a remarkable ability to resist on the part of the existing social organizations of power after a fundamental change in the formal conditions of their reproduction. The "pays légal" of the July Monarchy had retained preferred access to positions of political leadership—even without the assurance of a property franchise and the intervention of a royal patron.

Alexis de Tocqueville's well-known description of the April elections in his home region of Normandy points to the remolding of democratic practices by the loyalties, dependencies, and hierarchies of authority in traditionally influenced life-worlds. Together with Tocqueville (the local lord) the male residents of the village went to the polling station. There, after being warned by Tocqueville, "not to let themselves be accosted or diverted by people who might … seek to deceive them, but rather to march as a united body with each man in his place, and to stay that way until they had voted," nearly all votes, Tocqueville surmised, were cast for him.[24]

This was a frequently repeated occurrence, according to contemporary observers, even if often in a less seigneurial form and with more tangible means of manipulation. The republican left was also not inactive, making use especially of the machinery of government to influence elections in its favor.[25] In general, and well beyond April 1848, it would be true to say that in spite of formally secret ballots the act of voting was not the result of individual reflections, but rather an element of local culture. The "true people" of the voters, many illiterate, to a great extent not French-speaking, and, since the end of the First Republic, mostly excluded from the arena of institutional politics, initially remained bound up in parochial networks and structures of authority, relations of patronage and loyalty, which formed the core of local notable rule. This situation had been recognized by some of the political protagonists of the pre-February period, which explains why the universal franchise was already a plank in the program of a part of the legitimist opposition against the July Monarchy and why, for the provisional government, combating localism in politics became the central point in its preparations for the election.[26]

While in France, the representative body chosen in universal suffrage was shaped by the propertied bourgeoisie, interspersed with functionaries of the July Monarchy, its German equivalent was marked by the educated middle class and the servants of the state: 87 percent of the deputies had completed a university course of study or attended an equivalent educational institution; 56 percent belonged to the public service when taking their seat, and 83 percent of them had been state officials in the past. These are figures which would never again be achieved in the later history of German national parliaments (although the Bundestag of the past two decades has approached its Frankfurt predecessor in both respects).[27]

In view of the vehement criticism of the bureaucracy in the *Vormärz* and against the backdrop of a liberal constitutional theory, whose core feature was the idea of the separation of powers, a high percentage of state officials among the deputies to the Frankfurt National Assembly must seem paradoxical. In a "bourgeois revolution, which was directed constitutionally against the precedence of the state officials,"[28] it is precisely the state officials themselves who became the protagonists of constitutional change. This is a contradiction which can perhaps be mitigated if one takes into consideration that parliamentarianism of state officials was not a specialty of the Frankfurt National Assembly, defining as it did the parliaments of individual German states well into the last third of the nineteenth century. Thus, for example, in the state parliament of Württemberg in 1845, state officials, including municipal government officials and professors, held 75 percent of the seats, with more than the half of them in direct state service.[29] However, especially in southwest German small- and medium- sized states, with a constitutional tradition reaching back to the years after the Napoleonic wars, the share of state officials among the deputies to the National Assembly was only 34 percent, while reaching 65 percent in the Old Prussian provinces.[30]

Attempts have been made to explain the strong position of government officials in the early parliaments in Germany in terms of a lack of specific and autonomous political elites, which predestined members of the state service to become a "substitute elite" because of their specialist knowledge, their proximity to power, and their high social prestige. The share of government officials in parliamentary elites thus becomes a gauge of the maturity of a political system and an indicator of the level of differentiation in sectors of state organization of power.[31] A closer look shows, however, that the duration of constitutional and parliamentary traditions is not sufficient to explain variations in the proportion of state officials. This is true in international comparison, where, for example, in the Netherlands, with a long constitutional tradition, the share of civil servants in the lower house reached about 46 percent in 1848.[32] It is also true of inter-regional comparison within Germany, where, for example, Old Bavaria and Franconia, which had long been constitutionally governed, had an disproportionately high level of state officials among their Frankfurt deputies, and the Prussian Rhine Province, without a constitution, a disproportionately low share.

A further division according to sector and level of function of public service points, rather, on the other hand, to local conditions of recruitment, which were only indirectly related to the existence or lack of a constitutional tradition. In those places where the position of the office holder gained an element of personal rule through a fusion of jurisdictional, police, and administrative functions, and often through a simultaneous control of economic goods (for example, as an estate owner, managing his own estates or as caretaker in the absence of an estate owner from the high nobility), a disproportionate share of such office holders gained seats in the Frankfurt parliament. This is true of Austria, Prussia east of the Elbe, and some small- and medium-sized states north of the Main. The share of this type of government official parliamentarian, personified in Prussian *Landräten*, Austrian *Pflegern*, Saxon *Patrimonialrichtern* and Hanoverian *Amtmännern*, reached 22 percent—23 percent in its strongholds but only 6 percent in the constitutional states of southwestern Germany.[33]

Their success in elections to the Frankfurt National Assembly can hardly be explained by manipulative influence of state machinery or direct pressure (although this also occurred occasionally), since the electoral process was indirect, which meant handing over the actual election of the deputies to a group of relatively independent notables.[34] In addition, the general political situation in April 1848 was less favorable for the exercise of such pressures. Rather, what these results confirm is a paternalist site of power, based on control over various aspects of the rural life-world and a position of intermediary between citizen and state. To this extent, this social figure was an equivalent of the French notable, only more directly involved with the state, through an oath of office, a body of law concerning state servants, through a salary, and a career ladder. All of these involved a close and binding tie to the ruling monarch.

In respect to the sociopolitical anchoring of parliamentary representation, however, regional differences were much stronger than national ones. In Germany, as in France, approximately every fifth delegate had had parliamentary experience before 1848, if one includes the Prussian and Austrian provincial diets. However, this level of experience increases for delegates from the third Germany with its constitutional and parliamentary structures already well-developed before 1848. Fifty percent of the deputies from Württemberg, Baden and the Bavarian Palatinate had parliamentary experience, while only 3 percent of those from Bohemia did.[35] These figures demonstrate a parceling of the space of political experience, arising from a different pace of political modernization in *Vormärz* Germany. In the individual states that already had constitutions before 1848, one can see the progress in the differentiation of an autonomous field of political action, connected to the shaping of a cadre of individuals tested in elected office, while in the rest of Germany one finds rather an anchoring of delegates in the power structures of the bureaucratic state and traditional society.

In France on the other hand, it was the "stamp of Paris" (N. Elias) which structured the deputies' experiential space. The concentration of political power and the focusing of political discourse on the capital city also reshaped the profile of its parliamentary representation. A third of the delegates from the Parisian region, but only every tenth from the Massif Central, were journalists and publicists by profession, compared to an overall average of 11 percent. The share of Parisian deputies active before 1848 in crypto-political organizations also lay clearly above the rest of the country.[36] This recalls the ephemeral February alliance between representatives of the parliamentary opposition in the July Monarchy and an extra-parliamentary counter-elite of journalistic circles which formed the basis of the provisional government. We have been able to show that this remained a very specific constellation, restricted to the capital.

In an interim summary of results at this point, it can be concluded that both in Germany and in France the extension of the franchise generally led to a confirmation of established social organizations of power and order of authority. Those enjoying the privileges of education and property more or less had both assemblies to themselves, although in France it was more the propertied and in Germany the educated who qualified for a mandate. However, while these were necessary they were not sufficient in themselves for election to a constituent assembly: rather, these conditions were connected to the specific political significance of their respective social positions. In Germany this was mostly membership in the state service; in France it was a position in the middle level of municipal or regional offices in the July Monarchy, or at least a significant position in the informal network of ruling notables. While the German situation shows an extension of the "rule of state officials" (R. Koselleck) into parliament, one can observe in France rather a socialization of political power by private parties.

In contrast, the members of the prerevolutionary counter-elite remained mostly excluded from parliament. It is as true for the Paris constituent assembly as for its Frankfurt counterpart that neither were assemblies of martyrs of the previous regime. In both parliaments, conflicts with officially valid norms of political behavior before 1848 can be demonstrated for only every eighth delegate and only every twentieth had suffered serious sanctions such as arrest and imprisonment—including repression of a right wing patrician and legitimist opposition.[37]

Thus the scenario of opportunities, risks, and challenges existing in the social structure of parliamentary leadership groups in Germany and France is outlined. In the former, it was above all territorial divisions and ties of loyalties to existing states that needed to be overcome in order to found a nation-state in representative form. In the latter, it was a question of combining local clientelism and the mechanisms of a hierarchically layered elite communication with the concepts of participatory democracy, whose protagonists were largely concentrated in the capital city. In both situations, a tension soon arose between the principles and dynamics of revolution and those of representation, which raised the dilemma of radical democrats described by Alexis de Tocqueville for revolutionary leaders in Paris, but which also blocked their German counterparts in many respects:

There may have been more mischievous revolutionaries than those of 1848 but I doubt if there have been any stupider. They did not know how to make use of universal suffrage or how to manage without it…they handed themselves over to the nation while doing everything best calculated to alienate it; they threatened it while they put themselves at its mercy; they frightened it by the boldness of their plans and the violence of their language, while the feebleness of their deeds invited resistance; they flaunted the airs of instruction at the very moment when they put themselves at the nation's disposal. Instead of opening their ranks after the victory, they jealously closed them; in a word, they seemed bent on solving this insoluble problem: how to govern through the majority but against its inclination.[38]

4. The Shaping of Political Conflict Groups

With this reference to majorities the perspective shifts from the patterns of recruitment to the internal structures of the parliaments, the front lines and organizational forms of conflict groups in both national assemblies. In this respect, too, 1848/49 provides a phase of anticipatory transformation, in which the ephemeral conflict patterns of traditional parliamentarianism of existing chambers of deputies changed under the pressure of ideological polarization and mass mobilization into a more rigid structure, differentiated more sharply by programmatic standpoints. Thus 1848 was, in this respect, not a "zero hour:" rival concepts for the ordering of state and society and the groups related to them had already formed into a party of inertia and a party of movement before the revolution. However, only the actual experience of the parliamentary context provided the incentive for a process of differentiation and fusion, which led in both assemblies to the rise of a right wing and left wing and made it possible for the majority of delegates to decide their own position in these coordinates. Both in Germany and France, similar patterns of voting behavior were related to various forms of the formation of intra-parliamentary organizations.

The Assemblée nationale constituante was a parliament without parliamentary caucuses, voting discipline, and formal organization. Deputies of similar convictions and interests joined together in "réunions," whose memberships fluctuated and partially overlapped. Paul Bastid characterizes the ensemble of political groupings in the assembly as "rather confused," giving the impression of "variety, imprecision and fluctuation."[39] Nonetheless, this situation became the starting point for a development of parliamentary frontiers, which heralded those political camps that have defined the party landscape in France through the present day.[40]

With the Réunion de la rue de Poitiers, formed on 20 May 1848, just two weeks after the national assembly had opened and only a few days after an attempt by insurgents to break the assembly up, there came together a conservative coalition of Orleanists, legitimists, and conservatives without express ties to either of the two branches of the French royal house. Bonapartists at the time were not yet differentiated as a distinct group. It is revealing that the initiative for the founding of the Réunion de la rue de Poitiers arose from a meeting of delegates from Lot-at-Garonne: a first indication of the continuing importance of regional ties for the formation of political conflict groups and simultaneously an expression of a provincial defensiveness against radical political leaders in the capital and their clientele. May 20 was also the beginning of the debate on the future of national workshops, which one month later would lead to their closure and the outbreak of the June uprising. Coordination of the right wing took place within a framework of loose organizational structures and with fluctuating membership, as revealed in membership figures for the group, which were between 200 and 400 deputies. Such fluctuation, however, should not be equated with inefficiency.

Adolphe Thiers, who, after his belated entry into the national assembly, became a director of the Rue de Poitiers, praised it as an effective instrument for influencing the national assembly. Its recommendations were increasingly followed by non-member deputies in the right wing and in the center. The end result of this development was the formation of the Party of Order, comprising a wide-ranging alliance of the right, moderate republicans, and the Bonapartists, who were now publicly appearing much more clearly as the clientele of the "Prince-President." The Party of Order formed the parliamentary backbone of the first cabinet of the new president, albeit with a precarious majority, and was the starting point of an electoral organization extending into the provinces.

In contrast to this process of aggregation and consolidation, which led to the formation of a governing right, the Réunion du Palais National—an alliance of moderate republicans around the newspaper *Le National*—suffered a process of erosion. Between 100 and 260 delegates took part in its meetings, which hardly supports the claim that there was a strong and coherent center in the national assembly. For six weeks, between 9 May and 26 June 1848, it formed the parliamentary backbone of the executive commission. However, because of increasing polarization in the national assembly after the suppression of the June uprising, it lost most of its significance. By January 1849 it had shrunk to just 60 members.[41]

The alliances of the parliamentary left, on the other hand, had a much more well-defined profile and a more binding concept of membership. This was the case with the Société des représentants républicains, whose name alone indicated a rigid organized structure. In its restrictive rules for membership and procedures it displayed elements of the conspiratorial pre-February secret societies. Thus, for example, acceptance of new members was decided by secret ballot, and participation in the meetings of other parliamentary associations required the approval of the other members. In spite of this form of organization and a publicized definition of its political stance, the extreme left wing was also unable to introduce voting discipline. Even after its reconstitution as the Montagne, in reference to its historical model, in November 1848, its parliamentary membership was not clearly defined. A core of 56 registered members were joined more or less regularly by about 20 further deputies during votes.[42]

In the Frankfurt National Assembly, unlike in its French sister parliament, parliamentary caucuses with relatively rigid structures formed almost immediately—a fact that requires explanation.[43] Already at the beginning of June 1848, just two weeks after parliament had first met, one could speak of "complete, constituted and organized parties," meaning, of course, parliamentary parties.[44] In September 1848, the first phase of their programmatic definition and organizational consolidation had concluded. Nine parliamentary parties or caucuses had formed by this time, to which 80 percent of all deputies belonged by October 1848.[45] With just some small differences, all parliamentary parties' memberships were acquired through a formal act of signing a program and statutes. Dual membership was naturally not allowed. Membership fees were collected and regular participation in caucus sessions, which took place several times a week, was expected. All caucuses had executive committees, which usually had extensive authority—for example, when rapid decisions needed to be made during parliamentary debates. If necessary, even previous caucus resolutions could be set aside.

At the core of the regulation was party discipline: every parliamentary party had the possibility of declaring an issue a party issue. In this case, no deputy was allowed to vote against the party resolution in the chamber, unless he wished to risk a formal suspension hearing. At most, abstention was possible. The level of discipline reached this way can be reconstructed using roll call votes. In October 1848, when the parliamentary parties had consolidated and the conflict about the greater-German or small-German solution to the question of unity had not yet had its disintegrative effect on the party system, 7.4 percent of the votes of deputies bound to parties were made against the wishes of their party—whereby the parties of the extreme left and right wings showed the greatest coherence, while the center party frayed at both ends.[46]

Although the forms of institutionalization differed, the parliamentary conflict groups in both assemblies had completed a similar process of structural formation by the beginning of 1849, something most succinctly reflected in the constellation of roll call votes. In the Paris and Frankfurt assemblies—after a phase of consolidation and amalgamation that lasted until the end of 1848 in France and was temporarily concluded in Germany in September of the same year—a right and left wing faced each other, presenting a relatively united front in the parliamentary arena, in spite of internal differentiations and conflicts. In both cases, the right wing formed the backbone of the government. Coordination of voting behavior took place in Germany through agreements between parliamentary caucus leaders, which was also formally constituted in inter-party commissions. Thus, for the first time, the entire repertoire for the order of business in modern parliamentarism had come into use.

At the same time, there were signs of a re-formation of parliamentary caucuses in the final phase of the Frankfurt National Assembly in order to create new large groups. The left was united in the Central March Association—which, as the first parliamentary party in Germany parliamentary history, was able to call on the support of a party organization outside parliament with about 950 local associations and approximately 500,000 members. The vast majority of deputies from the center-right, remnants of the center-left, and break-aways from the right formed the major parliamentary party Weidenbusch.[47]

The process of simplification and consolidation of parliamentary conflict structures into a polarized pattern, essentially similar in both assemblies, was prefigured by older conflict constellations. The confrontations between a party of movement and a party of inertia before 1848 continued in the struggle over the extent and guarantees of social and political rights of participation, which formed the core of the disagreement between the two rival political camps in both assemblies. However, only in the hectic business of parliamentary decision-making, under the pressure of having to find majorities and simplifying reality under the eyes of an extra-parliamentary public opinion (and in Germany also under massive pressure from reconsolidated individual states), did an amalgamation of comprehensive voting formations take place on the basis of the smallest common denominator of agreement and a temporary setting aside of greater ambitions.[48] This was true of the diverging loyalties of supporters of the two branches of the French royal house and an imperial restoration, united under the auspices of the "involuntary republic" in the Party of Order, and it was equally true of the left in the Frankfurt National Assembly, whose democratic wing postponed its project of an extensive republican transformation of the German state system.

Much more clearly than in Germany, where confessional conflict would permanently change the party system after 1870, in France 1848/49 was a historical crossroads, which set political options for a time to come. As a consequence, the Second Republic became the common root of the two political currents which would endure through to the present day: "...[the Second Republic] was the true ancestor of the ideology of the left, while, through its *burgraves* and other conservative leaders, it provided a precedent and model for all the center-rightists of the future."[49] Internal conflict, however, did not prevent both assemblies from successfully completing the parliamentary process of drafting a constitution—in France after only six months of hearings and in the final vote against a minority of less than 5 percent of the votes cast.[50]

In Germany, on the other hand, starting at the end of 1848 and beginning of 1849, the process of finding a constitution was burdened by a new confrontation, that cut across the left-right scheme of previously existing caucuses and political coalitions. The decision to include Austria in a future German territory opened a new conflict front, which led to a split in the existing camps. As early as the May 1848 elections for the National Assembly, after a boycott of the elections in many constituencies with a large Slavic majority and after all of central Bohemia returned no deputy to Frankfurt, the special position of those areas of the Austrian empire belonging to the German Confederation became obvious.[51] More sharply than in Prussia, where parts of the mostly Polish province of Posen had not been incorporated into the German Confederation and therefore did not participate in the elections, this raised questions of the compatibility of ethnic affiliation and loyalty to a German nation-state. In view of the Austrian composite state, there was an inconsistency between its supranational-dynastic character and the program of consolidation of German-speaking Central Europe into a nation-state.

For the Austrian deputies to the National Assembly, this had already led to conflicts of orientation and loyalty before the constitutional debates on the territorial boundaries of the proposed German national realm, which manifested themselves

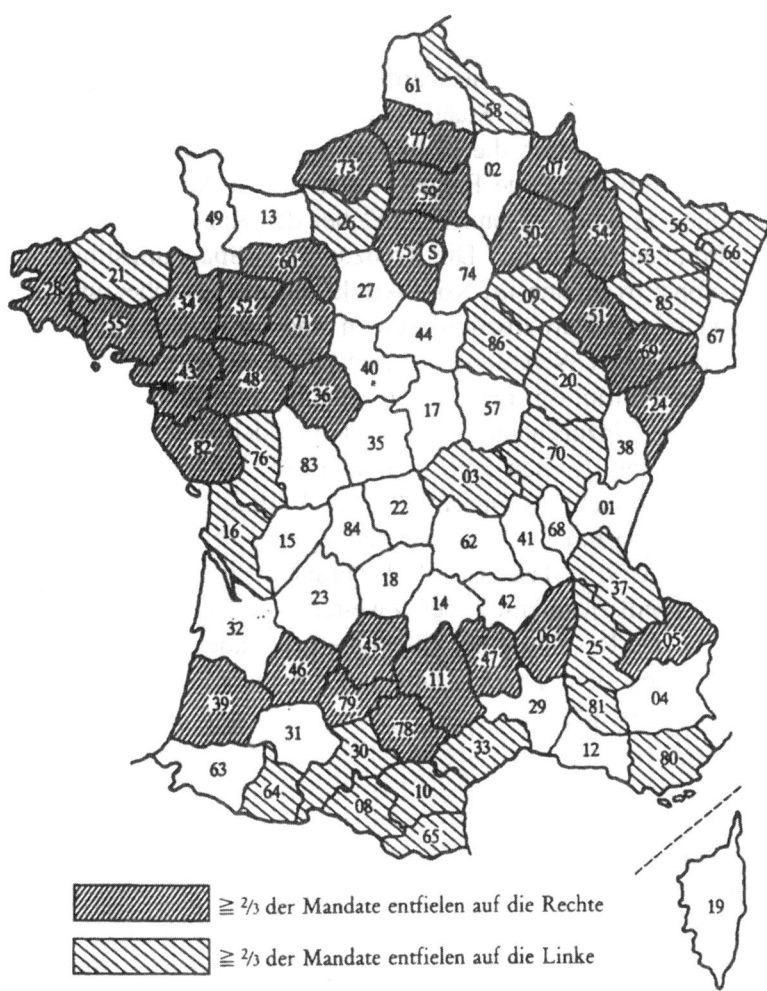

≧ ⅔ der Mandate entfielen auf die Rechte

≧ ⅔ der Mandate entfielen auf die Linke

Linke Departements
03 Allier; 08 Ariège; 09 Aube; 10 Aude; 16 Charente-Inf.; 20 Côte-d'Or; 21 Côte-du-Nord; 25 Drô-me; 26 Eure; 30 Garonne (Haute-); 33 Hérault; 37 Isère; 53 Meurthe; 56 Moselle; 58 Nord; 64 Pyrénées (Hautes-); 65 Pyrénées (Orient.-); 66 Rhin (Bas-); 70 Saône-et-Loire; 76 Sèvre (Deux-); 80 Var; 81 Vaucluse; 85 Vosges; 86 Yonne; 88 Überseeische Bes.;

Rechte Departements
05 Alpes (Hautes-); 06 Ardèche; 07 Ardennes; 11 Aveyron; 24 Doubs; 28 Finistère; 34 Ille-et-Vilaine; 36 Indre-et-Loire; 39 Landes; 43 Loire-Inférieure; 45 Lot; 46 Lot-et-Garonne; 47 Lozère; 48 Maine-et-Loire; 50 Marne; 51 Marne (Haute-); 52 Mayenne; 54 Meuse; 55 Morbihan; 59 Oise; 60 Orne; 69 Saône (Haute-); 71 Sarthe; 73 Seine-Inférieure; 75 Seine-et-Oise; 77 Somme; 78 Tarn; 82 Vendée; 87 Algérie;

Indifferente Departements
01 Ain; 02 Aisne; 04 Alpes (Basses-); 12 Bouches-du-Rhône; 13 Calvados; 14 Cantal; 15 Charente; 17 Cher; 18 Corrèze; 19 Corse; 22 Creuse; 23 Dordogne; 27 Eure-et-Loir; 29 Gard; 31 Gers; 32 Gironde; 35 Indre; 38 Jura; 40 Loir-et-Cher; 41 Loire; 42 Loire (Haute-); 44 Loiret; 49 Manche; 57 Niévre; 61 Pas-de-Calais; 62 Puy-de-Dôme; 63 Pyrénées (Basses-); 67 Rhin (Haute-); 68 Rhône; S Seine (Paris); 74 Seine-et-Marne; 79 Tarn-et-Garonne; 83 Vienne; 84 Vienne (Haute-);

Quelle: Best, 1984: 199

Strongholds of the Right and Left in the Assemblée nationale constituante in deviating behavior patterns. Their ties to their mandate in the National Assembly were already considerably weaker in the spring and summer of 1848 than those of the other deputies. In the key committees in the *Paulskirche*, in the parliamentary party leadership, and in the provisional German central government, they were markedly under-represented.[52]

These findings correct the appearance that the transfer of the Imperial Regency to a Habsburg grand duke and a temporary entrusting of an Austrian with the office of Prime Minister of the Empire might have awakened. In fact, the break which had already existed before the convening of the National Assembly continued in the parliamentary arena and led to a rapid "Austrianization" (E. Bruckmüller) of delegates from the Habsburg Monarchy.

On the other hand, dynastic loyalties and ties to the political world of *Vormärz* Germany were also mobilized and undermined the coherence of groups sharing common convictions. This had consequences that appear paradoxical—for example, when the delegates of the radical democratic Donnersberg caucus voted for the election of Friedrich Wilhelm of Prussia as German emperor.[53] The crossing of lines of cleavage and overlapping loyalties in the conflicts concerning the decision about the extent within society of rights of participation and the territorial extent of the future German nation-state reduced the forcefulness of the parliamentary elite in Germany vis-à-vis established authorities in the individual states. On the other hand, however, it eased a somewhat antagonistic confrontation and opened room for new solutions. The "historic compromise" involved in combining a hereditary, small-German emperor with universal manhood suffrage was the most significant constitutional bequest of the Frankfurt National Assembly and prefigured a fundamental constellation in the founding of the Second Empire after 1867. It was the result of a reshaping of political camps, beginning in January 1849, that transcended left and right, and was a marked expression of parliamentary realpolitik.

The Sociostructural Foundations of Structures of Political Conflict

At this point the question arises of the sociostructural foundations of political conflict in the two assemblies. In his studies of the Second Republic, Karl Marx formulated an explanation of these questions in terms of interest theory, according to which the different "forms of property" and the "social conditions of existence," found their political expression in parliamentary struggles—an interpretation which Friedrich Engels also applied to Germany with his somewhat coarse slogan of the "betrayal by the bourgeoisie" of the aims of the revolution.[54] However, if one considers the recruitment of parliamentary conflict groups in terms of this interpretation, then only a weak connection with socioeconomic interests appears in both assemblies.

An "economic interpretation of the constitution" as Charles Beard proposed for the United States, is not applicable to the constituent assemblies in Paris and Frankfurt. This is also true of the French deputies who supplied Karl Marx with the empirical material for his theory of interests and who also, according to the theory of political modernization, should have long ago completed the transformation from a "territorial" to a "functional," i.e., class determined, pattern of action. Findings of statistical research indicate, however, that the political arena in the two assemblies had a considerable inner logic and momentum, which was affected by quite different interventions than economic interests.[55]

The entrepreneurs at the core of the "bourgeoisie" were in particular spread haphazardly through the right and left wings—which, as we have seen, were the dominant conflict groups in both assemblies. The same is true for the representatives of "landed interests," which in most research inspired by modernization theories are held to be the social base of political reaction. If we hold constant the influence of membership in the aristocracy, which in fact was disposed to the right, landed interests were then equally divided among the left and right wings in the two assemblies. For this political indifference among propertied bourgeois delegates there is an explanation. It was precisely economic saturation that opened up opportunities for action and allowed the freedom to select political standpoints from a broad spectrum. "Bourgeois interest" placed no limits on their political options, since, to quote J. Schumpeter, "there is no policy—apart from the destruction of the bourgeoisie—of which it cannot be said that it serves the interest of the bourgeoisie, at least in the sense that it fends off worse things."[56]

In both assemblies, however, there was a disposition towards the right among state officials. They were most closely tied to existing governmental orders and after the reconsolidation of the government, from the autumn of 1848 onwards, they were most directly subject to its disciplinary intervention. This was basically true for France as well; in spite of the retention of a republican form of government, as under the President Louis-Napoléon Bonaparte, the pre-February elite regained decisive leadership positions with regard to personnel policy. The level of dependence on disciplinary and career-related intervention by state administration provides the best prediction of the political orientation of the deputies in both assemblies, if one chooses occupation as a predictor.

However, this influence should not be overestimated. Altogether, the effect of occupation as a determinant of political position is limited. In this respect, the "failure" of the Frankfurt National Assembly cannot be attributed to its large proportion of state officials among the deputies. When strong demands were once again placed on loyalty to the state, in the greater-German/small-German conflict, and in the violent struggles of the campaign for the imperial constitution, the alligence of the deputies to the individual states disrupted the context in which the Frankfurt National Assembly carried out its actions, whether those involved were state officials or not.[57]

Thus it can be seen that class and economic interests are not suitable categories to describe the reasons for political group formation. Only after 1848 did the era of class politics and the rise of labor parties commence. A transformation of the social order began in which interest ties took the place of traditional loyalties and paternalistic dependencies. If it is true that we are currently experiencing the end of class

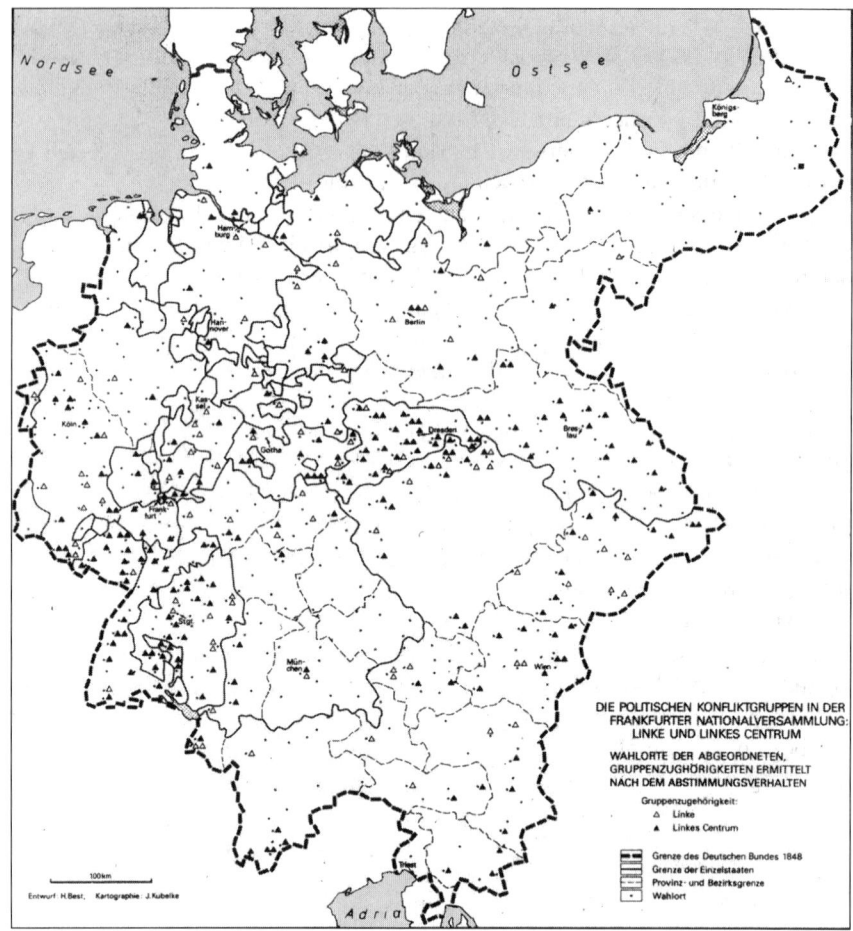

Political Conflict Groups in the Frankfurt National Assembly:
Left and Centre-Left: Constituency of the Delegate: Group Membership as per Voting Behavior

politics in the democracies of Western Europe something which is discussed under the rubrics of postmaterialism and individualization—then this development can be understood as the completion of a secular cycle which had its beginnings in the pre-materialistic situation in the mid-nineteenth century.

The results of comparison converge again, whereby, in the determining influence of territorial ties on the political orientation of members of both assemblies.[58] This is a complementary finding to the refutation of the interest theory. Region, not class, is the decisive variable explaining the political behavior of deputies. This finding can only with some difficulty be reconciled with theories of political modernization—which expect, as a consequence of state and nation formation, social mobility and growing communication between communities and regions, an erosion of regionally based loyalties and their replacement by alliances between groups or individuals with similar value orientations.

With regard to the regionalization of political conflicts, although France was a long consolidated nation-state, that had experienced a wide-ranging centralization and the mobilizations of three revolutions with the abolition of intermediary structures and territorial special rights still existing in the old regime, it did not differ to a great extent from Germany, where the divided territorial structure of the Holy Roman Empire had survived. The modern forms of political participation introduced in the spring of 1848 translated the archaisms of what was still, in many significant respects, a traditional social order into parliamentary representation in both countries. Thus the findings from the level of elites confirm the observations and conclusions of Eugene Weber in his micro-analysis of structures of power and conflict in rural France.[59]

Electoral Geography and Political Regionalism

Not only the extent but also the forms of territorial basis of political conflicts were similar in France and in the territory of the German Confederation, in spite of differences in tradition and in the course of state- and nation-building. As can be seen from the map on p. 491, the strongholds of the right were in western France, in Brittany and in the neighboring departments—including the traditional royalist reserve of the Vendée—in eastern Normandy, Champagne and the Massif Central, while those of the left were in Languedoc and Provence, Haput-Bourgogne and Limousin, in northern Alsace, Lorraine and in the Department of the Nord. This is a division of strongholds across larger regions that in its basic form, has survived until today as the landscape of France's "political temperaments" (A. Siegfried).

In Germany, the left had its strongholds in a heavily jointed, but territorially connected belt that stretched from southwest Germany (Baden, the Palatinate, and Württemberg) the Grand Duchy and Principality of Hessen, the Thuringian states, the Kingdom of Saxony, and Bohemia up to Austrian Silesia and Moravia. Eighty-seven percent of the deputies from these areas belonged to the left; 46 percent of their deputies were elected in these regions, although they only sent 23 percent of all the representatives to the *Paulskirche*.[60] This area was to a certain extent surrounded by the strongholds of the right: the province of Westphalia and the Kingdom of Hanover in the northwest, Old Prussia in the northeast, Old Bavaria and the Alpine regions of the Austrian Empire in the south and southeast. Along the seams of these core areas there were zones of overlap and heterogeneity, such as the Rhine province, parts of the provinces of Saxony and Silesia, the New Bavarian districts of Swabia, and Upper and Middle Franconia. A pattern of sectional division thus appears that simultaneously prefigures the intervention zones of the counter-revolution: Prussian and Austrian militaries pushed into the core regions of left-wing representation in 1849 and 1850 (Principality of Hessen). In Saxony, the Rhine Palatinate and in Baden, the conflict took the form of a civil war.

In the question of the modus operandi that mediated between the characteristics of the represented regions and the political orientation of their representatives, a explanatory model has been confirmed which connects social structural and polit-ical-institutional factors. The differences in regional regimes of power, based on agricultural property structures, and in the traditional patterns of opposition and observance towards the traditional holders of state power, resulting from the fate of regions during the process of state formation, colored the political map of 1848/49 in both Germany and France.[61]

In the case of France, where these assumptions could be tested with the instru-ments of ecological regression analysis, distribution in size of agricultural enterprise and ownership conditions in agriculture prove to be especially powerful explanatory factors. A high proportion of farmland taken up by large agricultural enterprises of over one hundred hectares favored a high proportion of right-wing representatives; a high share of small agricultural enterprises—and this is especially true of regions with specialty crops such as vinicultural—favored the left. Equally, the number of left-wing deputies grew with increasing population density, but independent of the share of the population living in cities. This is a connection which relates to Emil Durkheim's argument that increasing density of population produces intensifying social differentiation and more wide-ranging chains of communication, which in turn weaken patrimonial ties and loyalties towards traditional authorities. In an overview, these findings coalesce into a contrast of two rural worlds. While in the "France des campagnes" the social hierarchy was dominated by large estate owners with a fundamentally conservative outlook, and often from the nobility, the "France des villages" provided the milieu of a "left-wing" representation oriented towards an ideal of equality. Or, as Maurice Agulhon succinctly phrased it: "it was possible to be a red because he [a peasant] was independent."[62]

In Germany a similar relation can also be discovered. In those regions in which parliamentary representation was based on a local power structure, in which exercise of authority was bound, formally or informally, to the possession of the land by a few individuals (typical in regions where large landed estates, run by their proprietors, dominated, and where regional representation was controlled by the estate-owning nobility) deputies tended towards the right. The left had its strongholds in southwest and central Germany where equal inheritance prevailed, resulting in a large number of small farms, but too many to support the rural population. These were simultane-ously the regions with the largest rural population density.

The spatial patterns of parliamentary representation are, however, not suffi-ciently determined by the socioeconomic regional structures. Institutional processes of state formation had a strengthening, weakening, or even sometimes reversing effect on these correlations. In Germany, this was especially true of changes in the territories of individual states within the German Confederation. Only in the core zones of the territory they controlled in the mid-nineteenth century did the Ger-man dynasties have a right to rule which extended back to the Holy Roman Empire. The secularization of ecclesiastical territories, the mediatization of the smaller units of the Holy Roman Empire, and the redistribution of land through the Congress of Vienna, dissolved over a wide range of areas "inherited" dynastic ties and led to the rise of "accidental states," especially in southern and western

Germany. In these areas, conservative observers such as Wilhelm Heinrich Riehl discovered "advancing social decay" and the "most pathologically excited, strife-torn part of our fatherland."[63]

This was certainly true to the extent that opposition was provoked when absorption of the newly won territories was connected to economic decline, restriction of rights of participation, increased pressure of taxes, reduced chances for gaining state offices, or changes in existing legal codes. On the other hand, as shown in the course of the Napoleonic wars, ties to the dynasties had remained a source of loyalty and observance in the core areas of the individual states. The effect of these dynastic ties continued up to 1848 in regions such as Old Bavaria, Old Prussia, and German Tyrol, which were strongholds of right-wing representation. The left was primarily successful in those regions strongly affected by shifts in borders after 1789, or in those, such as in the Thuringian states, where the highly divided territorial structure of the Holy Roman Empire had survived.

The stronger representation of the left in Bohemia and Moravia, the Rhine province, Silesia and New Bavaria, compared to the core areas of the individual states, also can be interpreted from the viewpoint of regional tradition—which means, in this case, from their status as secondary territories of dynastic state structures. A defense of regionally specific legal traditions and forms of local government against the leveling pressure of a central bureaucracy, a rejection of discriminatory administrative practices, and a representation of economic special interests were, even in the *Vormärz*, starting points of bourgeois-opposition movements, whose more radical representatives joined the left-wing of the Frankfurt National Assembly in 1848.

In France as well, patterns of parliamentary representation may be identified which were based on special conditions arising in the course of expansion of French territory during the old regime and politicized in the process of national integration. In the complex state formation of the monarchy before 1789, the seventeen pays d'etat and the provinces gained from the Holy Roman Empire and from Spain since the end of the seventeenth century were granted provincial estates, autonomous administrative authority, and the right to approve and apportion taxes. The affected—or perhaps better, the favored—provinces lay like a belt around the core area of the old kingdom. This is an important condition, as these were simultaneously those areas of France in which regional cultural traditions—up to preserving their own language—continued to exist.[64]

The continued strength of these traditions after the institutional leveling following the French Revolution is shown in representation patterns in 1848. The explanatory power of the existence of provincial estates up to 1789 is at the same level as sociostructural factors, whereby a tradition of regional autonomy in the old regime tended to favor left-wing representation in 1848. Nineteen of the 24 departments in which the left dominated lay in the territory of the provinces that had possessed estates until 1789.

There is some evidence to suggest that it was the regional elites who mediated between obsolete institutions of the ancien regime and the electoral geography of

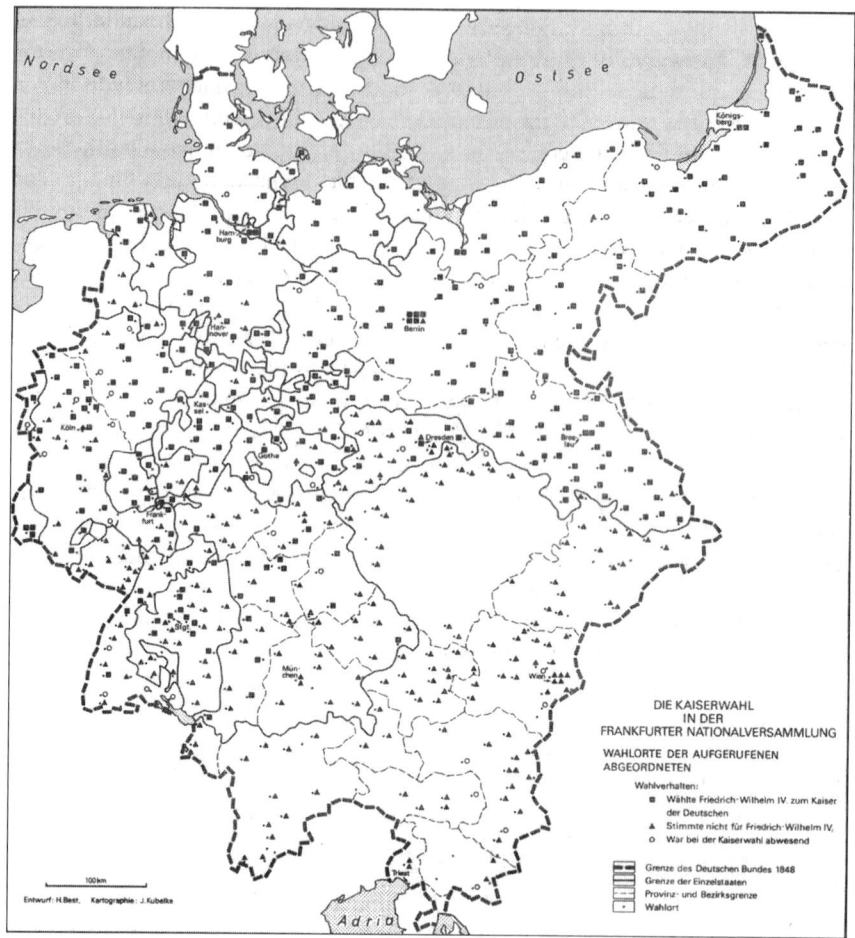

Election of the Emperor in the Frankfurt National Assembly. Constituency of delegates summoned

1848. Paul Bois and research from the circles around Michel Vovelle have shown, for example, that "white" and "red" notable dynasties were able to tie political clientele to themselves over generations.[65] They confirm that which the social history of intermediary elite in France has often shown: a remarkable stability through the various changes of regime.

Up to this point, the religious factor, which can be counted among the more significant deciding moments in the formation of political cultures and especially political regionalism, has not been given due consideration. This is true of Germany, where confessional division promoted a sharp, often hostile division of historical-political regions, while in France the confrontation between a clerical and a laicistic camp belonged to the formative conditions of political conflict groups, the origins of which extend back into the old regime.[66] In the pattern of parliamentary representation in 1848/49, religious orientation is also manifested—even if rather hidden as a structure behind the structure. Thus in the Frankfurt National Assembly confessional standpoints hardly affect left-right contrasts which formed the dominant conflict front in 1848.[67] This picture of confessional indifference changed, however, when, from January 1849 onwards, the question of territorial extent of a future German nation-state led to a reformulation of conflict groups. The confrontation between the two hegemonic powers in the German Confederation in this question took state power rivalries into the parliamentary arena, and also favored a confessionalization of the controversy, as Austria was seen as the protector of Catholicism and Prussia as a future leading power of Protestant Reich.[68]

This can clearly be seen in the election of a German emperor on 28 March 1849. With 94 percent of the deputies present, the Frankfurt National Assembly met for the last time as a complete representation of the entire territory from which it had been elected.[69] In the deputies' voting behavior, loyalty to their home-states, confessional orientations and the residues of left-right contrasts overlapped. The topography of the vote reproduced the confrontation between greater-German and small-German camps, in which the Main River and the southern Prussian border provided a marked dividing line. But it also shows an independent significance of confessional factors—this above all in those areas in which the minority confession of the large, confessionally mixed individual states was a regional majority, such as in the Catholic Rhine province or in the mostly Protestant regions of the Kingdom of Bavaria. In these regions, the politicization of confessional conflict manifested themselves first, without, however, having already become a dominant orientation pattern in the process of state formation in Germany.

In France, in the mid-nineteenth century, the religious color of regions is more difficult to record than in Germany, where confessional division provides a comparatively strong indicator. The share of priests who had refused to swear an oath of loyalty to the constitution of the First Republic, or the density of the supply of priests in the departments have therefore been introduced to provide measures for churchbound religiosity.[70] When using such indicators to explain the genesis of political regions, one finds a weak positive relation between clericalism and right-wing representation—which, however, disappears to a great extent when the other explanatory factors are considered. This leads to the conclusion that church-bound religiosity tended to be effective when it coincided with power structures at the local and regional levels which favored right-wing representation. Sociostructural factors were, therefore, decisive, while the influence of clericalism, in as far as it can be recorded with our indicators, remained rather subsidiary.

Overall it can be seen that the distribution of strongholds of political conflict groups in Germany and France during the years 1848/49 were based on similar structures of ownership and authority and reflected both historically older and in part obsolete conflicts of state formation. In both societies, it was the network of local elites that were able to bind traditional political loyalties and transfer these into the era of mass politics. The ramifications of 1848/49, however, also provided the starting point for a "confessionalization" of politics in Germany, in which parties anchored themselves in sociocultural milieus and changed themselves into agents of ideal interests with universalist claims. In France, the organization of power remained much more strongly marked, up through the Fifth Republic, by the transfer mechanism of regional clientelism and the binding power of patronage with a reduced party coherence and organizational strength.

Revolution and Representation: Résumé and Outlook

If one asks, finally, and in view of the results so far, about the significance of the constituent assemblies for the revolutionary process of 1848/49, two lines of consequence can be distinguished. On the one hand, the parliaments instigated and focused the course of development in that they simplified conflicts in their area of competence, placed on the agenda the great controversies of the extent of social and political rights of participation and contributed to a politicization of the public by being a reference point for election campaigns, petition movements, reports in the press, and the formation of party organizations. It is therefore not by chance that their meeting places became the central point of attack for extra- and anti-parliamentarian insurgencies during the uprisings in Paris and the September disturbances in Frankfurt. On the other hand, the parliaments had a conciliatory and stabilizing effect daring the revolution of 1848/49. After they were convened, decisions were transferred into the arena of institutionally defined politics, thus becoming once again the object of compromise formation and regulated balance of interests.

Of all the collective actors in the revolution, they had the most convincing democratic mandate and an incontrovertible brief to form institutions. This gave them a very powerful legitimacy. In the critical phase after the revolutionary movement of the spring of 1848, they therefore became crystallization points of an established provisional state, consummated in Frankfurt in the election of an imperial regent and the establishment of a provisional central power for the Reich, and in Paris through the transfer of executive power to the president of the council of ministers. In France, the assembly's position was first seriously and permanently undermined by competition from the Prince-President, elected in December 1848 by plebiscite, while in Germany it was weakened by a reconsolidation of the individual states and the monarchical regime starting in the fall of 1848. In the end, it was not the revolutionary mass movements, but the executives, that either had established themselves through the constitutional assemblies of 1848 or had consolidated themselves behind its protective shield, which ended the experiment of representative democracy in western and central Europe.

The parliaments had already lost much credit with the population due to the slow process of parliamentary decision-making and thier failure to meet the peoples extremely high expectations. In Paris, as in Frankfurt, the deputies had attempted to separate society and parliament in order to reduce pressure on the process of parliamentary decision-making while not simultaneously losing their position as the focus of public discourse. It was demonstrated to the voters that the representation of the people was not the source of salvation but rather a clearing house which, in often non-transparent processes of compromise formation, attempted to find political solutions. The unavoidable disillusionment was exploited by a radical critique of parliament, that, especially in Germany, would define the anti-parliamentarian repertoire of the coming century. It showed remarkable parallels at the extremes of left and right. When, for example, Friedrich Engels attacked the "Frankfurt humbugs," who lustfully played in the "airy realms of dreams," and spoke of the "lucubrations of the Frankfurt collective tomfoolery," which was only of interest for "the collector of literary and antiquarian curiosities," this derisory invective could almost literally have been taken from the Borussian-conservative *Kreuzzeitung*, in which events in Frankfurt were described as an amalgamation of immaturity, philistinism, and comedy.[71]

In such statements, we can hear the doctrines and movements that saw themselves as executors or guardians of historically powerful forces, whose claims to validity could not be domesticated by majority decisions and the provisos of a liberal constitutional state. The binding utopia of the monarchical principle and the emancipatory utopia of a classless society stood in irreconcilable contrast to the principles and processes of representative democracy, with its ideas of a correspondence between social and political pluralism, the pacified competition of political conflict groups, a strict hewing to the principle of legality, and the restriction of political power through electoral processes and strong institutional control. This was (and is) a form of the organization of power that demands an extraordinarily large number of preconditions, which asks of participants a knowledge of the mechanisms and effects of procedural regulation, thoroughly tested by experience, a setting aside of ambitions of power, and a trust in political opponents' conformity to accepted norms.

In the mid-nineteenth century, representative democracy was a mostly untried model; the question of whether an order of social inequality can be stabilized under the conditions of political equality was still unanswered. This may go some way to explaining the half-heartedness, errors, and insecurities the protagonists were accused of. This is demonstrated by the contradictory construction of the constitutional figure of the president by the Assemblée nationale constituante, in which extensive authority was unclearly combined with its restriction, and by the rapid reorientation to the established state among the large majority of the Frankfurt National Assembly after the rejection of the imperial crown by Friedrich Wilhelm IV.

The revolution of 1848 remained a painful, though certainly not inconsequential, "apprenticeship" (M. Agulhon) for representative democracy. An "oath of the tennis courts," which is a celebratory act of self-assertion by parliament towards competing centers of power, did not occur in Europe after 1848. The violent dissolution of the rump parliament in Stuttgart was preceded by an erosion of the National Assembly to about one fifth of its original members—to a great extent from the south German left. In the struggles of the campaign for the imperial constitution in the early summer of 1849, the rump parliament and its imperial regency played only a peripheral role.[72]

In France, where, after the dissolution of the constituent assembly in May 1849, the Assemblée nationale legislative was elected on the basis of a universal manhood suffrage (even if only with a 68 percent turnout), the erosion of republican order had already begun under the auspices of the November constitution of 1848. Two weeks after the opening of the new parliament, exponents of the parliamentary left were already being arrested after their participation in a mass demonstration, or were going into exile. The freedoms of the press and assembly were restricted in the following months in a way that their limitations approached those of the July Monarchy. A revision of the franchise reintroduced de facto property qualifications and reduced the electorate from some ten to some seven million voters. It is characteristic that directly before the violent dissolution of the national assembly by Louis-Napoléon, a vote for an amnesty for deputies from the far left arrested in June 1849 did not gain a majority. Thus, here too, there was no coordinated and overarching resistance in the defense of the republic: the large majority of the members of the National Assembly remained passive during the coup. A few dozen deputies from the extreme left went underground and about 200 monarchist and moderate republican deputies formed the French parallel of the German rump parliament which half-heartedly attempted legal resistance, but which was also dissolved after a few hours.[73]

Neither in Germany nor in France could a consensus elite have formed after the revolution of 1848, which, according to the most recent theories of democratic elite rule, is the condition for stable representative institutions.[74] In both cases parliamentary leadership groups had little to counter the re-establishment of authoritarian state power. Nonetheless, it was not the experiment of representative democracy, but the authoritarian Caesarism of Napoleon III and the restitution of monarchic regimes in Germany which were episodic. In the long run of historical development, that which had defined the expectations of voters and the representatives they elected in the constitutive phase of the two national assemblies was successful as the dominant organizational principle of political order in complex societies: the legitimation of political organizations of power and their representatives through elections, the conciliation of elite conflicts through an institutionally regulated competition for power, and a relation between society and politics through the transfer mechanism of parliamentary representation.

Notes

1. Karl Marx, *The Class Struggles in France* in Karl Marx and Frederick Engels, *Collected Works*, Vol. 10 (New York, 1975-), 65; Karl Marx, *The Eighteenth Brumaire of Louis Bonaparte* in ibid., Vol. 11, 109.
2. Marx, *Class Struggles in France* Vol. 10, 66.
3. Heinrich Best, *Die Männer von Bildung und Besitz. Struktur und Handeln parlamentarische Führungsgruppen in Deutschland und Frankreich 1848/49*, (Düsseldorf, 1990), 34ff.; idem, "Politischer Regionalismus in Deutschland und Frankreich in intertemporal-interkulturellen Vergleich," in: K.-H. Reibend, Franz Urban Pappi, and Heinrich Best (eds.), *Die deutsche Gesellschaft in vergleichender Perspektive. Festschrift für Erwin K. Scheuch zum 65. Geburtstag* (Opladen, 1995), 137-57.
4. Theda Skocpol, "Emerging Agendas and Recurrent Strategies in Historical Sociology," Theda Skocpol (ed.), *Vision and Method in Historical Sociology* (Cambridge, 1984), 397.
5. Ernst Rudolf Huber, *Deutsche Verfassungsgeschichte seit 1789*, Vol. 2 *Der Kampf um Einheit und Freiheit 1830-1850*, 2nd ed. (Stuttgart, 1968), 594.
6. Heinrich Best, "From the 'Kulturnation' to the 'Staatsnation': Universities and National Integration in Mid-Nineteenth Century Germany," in G. Janitz, H. Kropaç, and P. Teibenbacher (eds.), *The Art of Communication: Proceedings of the Eighth International Conference of the Association for History and Computing* (Graz, 1995), 109-17.
7. Heinrich Best, *Interessenpolitik und nationale Integration 1848/49. Handelspolitische Konflikte in frühindustriellen Deutschland* (Göttingen, 1980), 81-104.
8. *Marx-Engels Gesammtausgabe*, Vol. 8 (East Berlin, 1960), 10.
9. Heinrich Best, "Der 'Ausschluß'—Elitenstruktur und kleindeutsche Lösung 1848/49. Ergebnisse einer kollektiven Biographie der Abgeordneten der Frankfurter Nationalversammlung," in *Bericht über den sechzehnten österreichischen Historikertag in Krems/Donau 1984*, (ed.) Verband österreichischer Geschichtsvereine (Vienna, 1985), 609-19.
10. Best, *Bildung und Besitz*, 249.
11. Huber, *Verfassungsgeschichte*, Vol. 2, 595ff.
12. Stuart Woolf, *A History of Italy 1700-1860. The Social Constraints of Political Change* (London, 1986), 361ff.
13. Manfred Botzenhart, *Deutscher Parlamentarismus in der Revolutionszeit 1848-1850* (Düsseldorf, 1977), 141-60.
14. Paul Bastid, *Doctrines et institutions politiques de la Séconde République*, Vol. 1 (1945) 142; Charles Seignobos, *La Révolution de 1848—le Second Empire (1848-1859)* Vol. 6 of *Histoire de la France contemporaire depuis la Révolution jusqu'à la paix de 1919*, ed. Ernst Lavisse (Paris, 1926), 72.
15. Marx, *Class Struggles in France*, 66; Bastid, *Doctrines*, 157.
16. Roger Price, *The French Second Republic. A Social History*, (London, 1972), 100; Bastid, *Doctrines*, 158-62; Félix Ponteil, *Les institutions de la France de 1814 à 1870* (Paris, 1966), 290.
17. Price, *Republic*, 95-155.
18. Bastid, *Doctrines*, 104-19; Peter H. Amann, *Revolution and Mass Democracy. The Paris Club Movement in 1848* (Princeton, 1975).
19. Heinrich Best, "Pariser und Berliner Abgeordnete im nationalen Handlungsfeld der Jahre 1848/49," in Ilja Mieck, Horst Möller, and Jürgen Voss (eds.), *Paris und Berlin in der Revolution von 1848—Paris et Berlin dans la Révolution de 1848* (Sigmaringen, 1995), 195-96.
20. G. Medzeg and D. Nohlen, "Frankreich," in: Dolf Sternberger and Bernhard Vogel (eds.), *Die Wahl der Parlamente und anderer Staatsorgane* Vol. 1 (Berlin 1969), 458, 514-15.
21. Heinrich Best, "Kontinuität und Wandel parlamentarischer Repräsentation im revolutionären Frankreich 1848," *Francia* 11 (1984): 667ff.
22. Best, *Bildung und Besitz*, 169ff., 279, n. 8.
23. Ibid., 68-69.
24. Alexis de Tocqueville, *Recollections*, trans. George Lawrence (Garden City, 1970), 95.
25. Robert Huard, *Le suffrage universel en France 1848-1946*, (Paris, 1991), 19ff.

26. André-Jean Tudesq, *Les grands notables en France (1840-1849). Etude historique d'une psychologie sociale*, 2 vols.(Paris, 1963); Bastid, *Doctrines*, 72ff.

27. Best, *Bildung und Besitz*, 66, 146; A. Hess, "Statistische Daten und Trends zur Verbeamtung der Parlamente in Bund und Ländern," *Zeitschrift für Parlamentsfragen* 1 (1976): 34–42; Heinrich Best, "Politische Modernisierung und Elitenwandel 1848-1996. Die europäischen Gesellschaften im intertemporal-interkulturellen Vergleich," *Historical Social Research* 24 (1997).

28. Reinhart Koselleck, *Preußen zwischen Reform und Revolution. Allgemeines Landrecht, Verwaltung und soziale Bewegung von 1791 bis 1848*, 2nd ed.(Stuttgart, 1975), 447.

29. G. Grünthal, H. Brandt, and K.E. Pollmann, "Social Aspects of German Constitutionalism: Prussia, Württemberg and the Norddeutscher Bund in the Mid-Nineteenth Century," *Parliaments, Estates and Representation*, No. 1 (1989), 66–67.

30. Best, *Bildung und Besitz*, 62, table 2.

31. Werner Conze, "Das Spannungsfeld von Staat und Gesellschaft im Vormärz," in Werner Conze (ed.), *Staat und Gesellschaft im deutschen Vormärz 1815-1848*, 2nd ed. (Stuttgart, 1970), 207ff.

32. W.P. Secker, "Representatives of the Dutch People. The smooth transformation of a parliamentary elite in a Consociational Democracy," in Heinrich Best and M. Cotta (eds.), *The European Representative 1848-1998. 150 Years of Parliamentary Representation in Comparative Perspective* (Oxford, 1998).

33. Best, *Bildung und Besitz*, 64.

34. Botzenhart, *Parlamentarismus*, 142ff.

35. Best, *Bildung und Besitz*, 173, table 28.

36. Ibid., 174, table 29, 177.

37. Ibid., 185ff.

38. Tocqueville, *Recollections*, 96–97.

39. Bastid, *Doctrines*, 216.

40. Maurice Agulhon, *The Republican Experiment, 1848-1852* trans. Janet Lloyd (Cambridge, 1983), 192. On the formation of réunions in the Assemblée nationale constituante see, among others, Frederic A. de Luna *The French Republic under Cavaignac* (Princeton, 1968), 108ff.; Bastid, *Doctrines*, 215 ff.; D. Stern (pseud.: Marie. d'Agoult), *Histoire de la Révolution de 1848* (Paris, 1985) 505; J.Tchernoff, *Associations et sociétés secrètes sous la Deuxiéme République* (Paris, 1905).

41. Agulhon, *The Republican Experiment*, 50–51.

42. Bastid, *Doctrines* 216.

43. Cf. H. Kramer, *Fraktionsbildung in den deutschen Volksvertretungen 1815-1849* (Berlin, 1968), 74-133, and, summarizing the current state of research: Botzenhart, *Parlamentarismus*, 415-41.

44. Karl Biedermann, *Erinnerungen aus der Paulskirche* (Leipzig, 1849), 11; J.G. Eisenmann, *Die Parteien der deutschen Reichsversammlung. Ihre Programme, Statuten und Mitgliederverzeichnisse* (Erlangen, 1848).

45. Best, *Bildung und Besitz*, 326, table 64.

46. Ibid., 331, table 65.

47. Michael Wettengel, "Der Centralmärzverein und die Entstehung des deutschen Parteiwesens während der Revolution von 1848/49," *Jahrbuch zur Liberalismus-Forschung*, 3 (1991): 34–81; Dieter Langewiesche, "Die Anfänge der deutschen Parteien. Partei, Fraktion und Verein in der Revolution von 1848/49," *Geschichte und Gesellschaft* 4 (1978): 324ff.

48. Heinrich Best, "'Disorder Yields to Order Fair the Place': The Emergence of Political Parties in Western and Central Europe," *Parliaments, Estates and Representation* 15 (1995): 133.

49. Agulhon, *The Republican Experiment*, 192.

50. Voting results documented in: Heinrich Best, *Die Abgeordneten der Assemblée Nationale Constituante 1848/49. Sozialprofil und legislatives Verhalten* (Köln, 1983), 97.

51. Botzenhart, *Parlamentarismus*, 41-160; Frank Eyck, *The Frankfurt Parliament 1848-1849* (London, 1968), 62-73.

52. Best, *Bildung und Besitz*, 263, table 50, 287-88, table 55.

53. Heinrich Best and W. Weege, *Biographisches Handbuch der Abgeordneten der Frankfurter Nationalversammlung* (Düsseldorf, 1996): entries for E. Grubert, C. Meye,r and E. Zimmermann; Gunter

Hildebrandt, *Parlamentsopposition auf Linkskurs. Die kleinbürgerlich-demokratische Fraktion Donnersberg in der Frankfurter Nationalversammlung 1848/49* (East Berlin, 1975).

54. Marx, *Eighteenth Brumaire*, 128; Friedrich Engels, *Revolution and Counterrevolution in Germany*, in ibid.,Vol. 11, 3-96, esp. 42, 66.

55. Best, *Bildung und Besitz*, 350ff.

56. Joseph A. Schumpeter, *Kapitalismus, Sozialismus und Demokratie*, 3rd ed. (Munich, 1985), 97.

57. Best, *Bildung und Besitz*, 451, table 86.

58. Ibid, 434ff., table 81.

59. Eugen Weber, *Peasants into Frenchmen: The Modernization of Rural France, 1870-1914* (Stanford, 1976).

60. Best, "Regionalismus," 148.

61. Data and findings in: Best, *Bildung und Besitz*, 407ff.

62. Agulhon, *The Republican Experiment*, 106.

63. Quoted in Theodor Schieder, "Partikularismus und Nationalbewußtsein im Denken des deutschen Vormärz 1815-1848," in Conze (ed.), *Staat und Gesellschaft*, 14.

64. Xavier de Planhol (with the collaboration of Paul Claval), *An Historical Geography of France*, trans. Janet Lloyd, (Cambridge, 1994).

65. Paul Bois, *Paysans de l'Ouest* (Le Mans, 1960); Michelle Vovelle, "Midi rouge, Midi blanc: une problématique," *Provence Historique* 34 (1987): 337-47.

66. René Rémond, *The Right Wing in France: From 1815 to de Gaulle*, trans. James M. Laux (Philadelphia, 1968).

67. Best, *Bildung und Besitz*, 391ff. and table 72. Members of various caucuses belonged to a "Catholic Club" formed in the Frankfurt National Assembly in 1848. No Catholic parliamentary caucus was formed. See also H.H. Schwedt, "Die katholischen Abgeordneten der Paulskirche und Frankfurt," *Archiv für mittelrheinische Kirchengeschichte* 34 (1982): 143ff.

68. Ruldolf Lill, "Großdeutsch und kleindeutsch im Spannungsfeld der Konfessionen," in Anton Rauscher (ed.), *Probleme der Konfessionalismus in Deutschland seit 1800* (Paderborn, 1984), 29ff.

69. Voting results in Heinrich Best (with the collaboration of R. Kuznia), *Die Abgeordneten der Frankfurter Nationalversammlung. Datenhandbuch* (Cologne, n.d.), mimeograph, Sec. 9, 76.

70. See, among other works, Hervé le Bras and Emmanuel Todd, *L'invention de la France. Atlas anthropologique et politique* (Paris, 1981). Findings in: Best, *Bildung und Besitz,* 421.

71. Engels, *Revolution and Counter-Revolution*, 42; Veit Valentin, *Geschichte der deutschen Revolution 1848-1849*, 2 vols. 2nd ed.(Cologne, 1970),Vol. 2, 557ff.

72. Heinrich Best, "'Que faire avec un tel peuple?' Karl Vogt et la révolution allemande 1848/49," in F. Dubusson et. al., *Actes du colloque Carl Vogt* (Geneva, 1997).

73. Agulhon, *The Republican Experiment*, 117-44.

74. See also Lowell G. Field and John Higley, *Eliten und Liberalismus, Ein neues Modell zur geschichtlichen Entwicklung von Eliten und Nicht-Eliten* (Opladen, 1983).

Lamartine's victory over the red flag through a speech to the people on 25 February
(Illustrirte Zeitung, Leipzig, no. 246, 18 March 1848, 187)

Sitting of the provisional government of the French republic in the Paris city hall
(Illustrirte Zeitung, Leipzig, no. 249, 8 April 1848, 238)

Chapter 21

TO SURVIVE THE REVOLUTION OR TO ANTICIPATE IT?

Governmental Strategies in the Course of the Crisis of 1848

Giovanna Proccacci

When revolution broke out in Paris in February 1848 and social struggles raged in the streets, the fate of the government was decided. The attempt by the monarchy to save itself via a regency was only short lived. After the monarchy had disappeared, the republic was solemnly proclaimed. After that, it was only a question of its organization, that is, of finding a politically acceptable way out of the social crisis. What was the role of the government in this turning-point and which paths could the political institutions take to keep pace with the changes and still end the revolution?

This question necessitates not restricting oneself to a point of view in which the state, frozen in its repressive function, opposes, as an institution, the revolutionary movement. Rather the positive substance of a process of institutional transformation and the preventative strategies this implies need to be examined. The question of the state in 1848 is, indeed, not easily dealt with in itself. The revolution brought with it a phase of instability in which the authority of the state lurched from side to side between those groups that happened to be in power and that could only with difficulty evade numerous pressures and influences. The state was less an independent political subject than a strategic aid for those who were successful, again and again, in exploiting it for their aims. It was, above all, a battlefield. But which war was taking place there?

It was not a matter of choosing a form of government, as it soon became clear that the republic was an inevitable consequence of the revolution, something not even called into question by its opponents. "We did not want the republic, but we accept it," said Thiers.[1] On the other hand, the war becomes discernible in questions of the republic's specific form. This demanded a new definition of political institutions, to adapt them better to the society that had resulted from the social crisis. The republic was, as Lamartine remarked, "not only a form of government, but a principle: practical democracy, equality of rights, fraternity through the institutions."[2] It was from this principle that the new authority of the government had to be drawn.

It was above all a matter of translating a new political order into a sum of strategies for directing social and economic processes. However, in the transformation of institutions, as well, a clash inevitably arose with the expectations raised by the revolution in respect to the role the state would play in freeing society from its problems and especially in solving the social question. These expectations were defined not only by the revolution, but equally by the economic and political crisis which had derailed the dogma of laissez-faire and the neutrality of the government in relation to social processes. At the core of the process of political renewal, innovative ideas and reality overlapped in shaping new political institutions.

In other words, in 1848 there was no political debate that was not fundamentally determined by its social implications and vice versa. The place where this mutual fusion took form was in the law. On the one hand, simply the principle of a republic meant that its legal and institutional form had extensive social consequences. On the other hand, through a juridical language, every social demand became a direct political petition. In fact, law is a political compromise, and the insurgents of 1848 called into question the political compromise achieved in France. The notion of rights lost the unifying vocation it had gained in the course of the French Revolution, when it came to express a means of attacking the privileges of the ancien regime. In 1848 rights were accused of having been used as "a means of deceiving the people since 1789."[3] It was now time for rights, instead of being an instrument of political exclusion, to become a means for inclusion—hence demands for the right to vote, and the right to work and to welfare support.

These demands caused a form of politicization of juridical language; they demonstrated that such language no longer simply expressed the formal equality of natural rights of the individual. In 1848, claims for rights did not, as Agulhon[4] or Nicollet[5] seem to believe, collapse together with legalism; in the demands of the excluded, "right" itself became illegal. "This obscure and mistaken concept of rights, which was bound to brutal violence, lent this violence an energy, a stubbornness, and a power which it of itself would never have possessed."[6] Rights were was certainly no means to unity, but instead made from then on, the social break clearly recognizable. The awareness of such a break deeply influenced thinking and the entire process of political renewal. Hence the "war" within the state took place in the area of law.

I intend to follow these political transformations in the period between the formation of a provisional government and the proclamation of the new constitution. Under pressure from a rebellious population, the provisional government approved the franchise demanded as well as the right to work. In the course of the process of establishing a new constitutional order which followed, the first of these rights was firmly anchored and the second revoked. This was, however, not an unambiguous development. Strategies addressing these two kinds of rights, did differ in the attempt to create a coherent institutional framework for them. In the one strategy, the revolution was equated with an extension of the franchise, and the republic was to be organized on this basis. In the other strategy, it was a question of a revolution "beyond the franchise" and the struggle was aimed at gaining more than simple access to additional representation from the republic. A closer analysis shows, moreover, that the political fates of these rights could cross, that extension of the franchise was grist to the mill for those who rejected a right to work. The two types of rights were thus reflected, from the beginning, in different political strategies. An examination of their interplay can contribute to an interpretation of France's capability for political innovation in 1848, and its limits.

I shall eventually compare this capability to a totally different, indeed contrasting case, in which the shock of the Paris February revolution was absorbed by reformist activities which made institutional transformation avoidable. In Belgium, a republican transformation was successfully resisted. Moreover, the Belgian example reveals interesting overlaps because of the role it played in the French constitutional debate—in which it was often raised as an example. Above all, a form of institutional transformation can be observed in Belgium, which was also actively championed by opponents of centralization in France, who saw in decentralization a strategy for solving the social problem that did not include the right to work. As decentralization was rejected in the French constitution of 1848, the entire question of work remained outside the framework of political-institutional transformation.

Harmony Instead of Civil War

February or June? The entire political history of 1848 is embedded in the contrasts of these two central events. The one is juridical, the other military. The juridical aspect, generally seen as a continuation of 1789, is normally overwhelmed by the military. Nonetheless, the momentum of this revolution can only be understood when one rejects a contrast of June and February.

In the eyes of contemporaries, the revolution had a special character, which, in fact, distinguished it from 1789. As Tocqueville said "it had a unique, popular character."[7] The people, said Lamartine, is a moral idea which characterized the events of 1848.[8] However, this term "people" was certainly not used uniformly. For some it was the nation, the third estate—that is, reference was made once again to 1789 and any gap between the social classes denied. "Only the nation remains," said Lamartine.[9] For others, especially for Tocqueville, something totally new politically had appeared on the political scene. "The classes which work with their hands," had never been capable of controlling the state. Therefore the revolution, in his mind, should not only be characterized as a people's revolution, but also as taking place "outside and against the bourgeoisie."[10]

From February to June the meaning of this people's revolution crystallized. In February, the popular revolt took place in the spirit of the Grand Nation; it directed itself at the national assembly and placed, in the words of the worker Marche, poverty "in the service of the Republic." However, the rights demanded placed the people outside the nation, indeed outside the law. From here a break appears, which for the first time, and long before June, was expressed in terms of class, a break implicit in the use of juridical language. These two aspects of the popular character of the revolution can also be found in the close relation between political and social demands. Not only the socialists established such a relationship—rather, this was the core of the revolution.

Tocqueville recognized the danger inherent in such a relationship, when—in his famed "Discours" in the national assembly in January—he had accused Guizot's government of not wishing to see the consequences of its policies. He analysed the collapse of public morals and denounced political apathy that arose because the *pays légal* of the government had been reduced to a minority, while the larger part of society had been excluded from any form of participation. "The people feel themselves excluded and thus not responsible," and what they could not demand via the ballot took the form of social demands. "Can you not see that man's political passions have become social ones?"[11] Guizot had not wanted any reform of a property-based franchise. "Enrichissez-vous" he replied to those who demanded such reform,[12] and he had lost all control over the masses. However, this apathy should not deceive: rights of property were no longer guaranteed, as Tocqueville had stated, while property had become more accessible and thus more open to attack. The most important political questions from then on would deal with changes in the right of property. Consequently, one must "ensure the people all equality of rights, which are consistent with individual property rights and the inequality arising from them."[13]

For these reasons it became pressing to break through the interchangeability of political and social passions: both had in fact a common significance, cast in the form of rights. The right to work and to support were the social equivalent of the franchise. It was necessary to lead the social desires of the people back to politics. The franchise agreed to by the provisional government, under pressure from the revolutionary uprising, presented itself as a strategic instrument for the implementation of this program.

The decree of 5 March, which ended the property qualification and introduced universal manhood suffrage, described this franchise as the "first of all civil rights." The franchise was thus based on legal equality, becoming practically a natural right.[14] In reality, the franchise was always two-sided. It was a natural right, while at the same time credited with a social function. The restriction through property qualification had strengthened this latter feature of the franchise and weakened the former without, however, modifying the nature of the right which made every citizen a voter.[15] However, in 1848 universal suffrage seemed to have no more opponents. It was once again interpreted as a natural right of the individual, this time, however, in respect to the principle of equality and no longer in view of the nation as abstract construction.[16] Hence it was once again discovered that political equality, already in existence in 1789, had remained subliminal in the actual theories of the republic.

Lamartine's report[17] provides, in spite of its solemn tone, a realistic image of a government that was barricaded in the city hall as a prisoner of the people for six days before its members were able to gain access to the building of its foreign ministry. Outside, the crowd protested, discussed, yelled, and called for the ministers. The people were already ruling, one could say. The decree only meant a recognition of this. From this time on, political power only had to be organized so that it corresponded to its new basis and gained a lawful character. For this, a revaluation of the franchise was necessary, which was used to direct the desires of the people again towards politics and distract them from the social question.

The people had to be convinced that the franchise, in itself, fulfilled demands by the popular classes for greater participation, so that they would no longer expect political equality to be translated into social equality. "The French Revolution had desired that there be no more classes, certainly not in society ... that politically there be no more classes."[18] All in all there was nothing threatening about the franchise: very quickly its association with chaos and revolutionary radicalism disappeared, and it became nearly an orthodox postulate, so heavily concentrated were the problems in other areas. This meant, furthermore, less a recognition of a new individual right to vote than an inclusion of every citizen in a holy collective unit of the nation with the aid of nationalistic rhetoric à la Lamartine.[19]

Such rhetoric was, however, less significant for the process of standardizing the franchise than the idea that it could contain a general model of reconciliation and thus a solution to the revolution. The franchise appeared as a mould in which the unity of the people took form, developed further and thus counteracted social division and contradictions. "Elections belong to everyone without exception. Since this law was passed, there is no longer a proletariat in France," was stated in a declaration by the provisional government, written by Lamartine.[20] And Dupin[21] declared that since the formation of the French people in 1789 "there were no more privileged individuals."

Everywhere, the franchise dominated political debate and was certainly not separated from expectations of social equality. Rather, it appeared to be a cure-all for all problems, especially social ones. In this sense it was employed in most of the government's responses to demands by the people and provided the basis for an organizational model of collective consultation, with the help of which, as Regnault remarked in his judgement of the Luxembourg Commission, "a population armed for war" could be transformed into "a consultative corporation."[22] The franchise thus lends a specific form to the central political idea: "harmony" in place of "civil war." In this perspective, the only recently shattered national unity could already be restored. The franchise seemed to offer more than access to political representation. It also displayed a possible strategy for the settlement of social conflict.

However, the franchise, for its part, would create more problems than it could solve. Initially, the franchise was bound up with demands for a right to support and to work and thus strengthened popular demands to extend political equality into the social domain instead of weakening it. On the other hand, through the franchise, the necessity of centralization increased, in order to ensure the unity of state power which could be endangered by the sudden extension of the franchise to all men. As we will see, this destroyed any hopes of being able to get social demands under control through a politically less dangerous strategy of decentralization.

Socialists and radicals, for their part, feared the franchise and insisted on giving it only a limited import. They sought to postpone its introduction until later, and above all they maintained their doubts. Their distrust proved to be justified to the extent that the franchise was part of a strategy directed mostly against them. Ledru Rolin expressed his doubts thus. "If elections do not lead to a triumph of social truth, when they become the expression of the interests of a caste ... then the elections, meant to serve the welfare of the republic, will mean its end."[23] Socialists and radicals were practically incapable of politically exploiting the success achieved with the franchise, and continued to contrast it with the real demands of the people for a right to work and support. This strategy was perceived as a "dangerous mistake, which would reintroduce revolutionary violence into politics, just at the time when the republic was granting every citizen the peaceful weapon of the ballot."[24]

Living through Labor

The strategy of these parties was concentrated on demands for a right to work: "The people did not fight to achieve a franchise and reform of parliament ... what the people demand are economic reforms," wrote *La démocratie pacifique* on 28 February. Through the political influence which the masses had achieved with their access to political representation, the right to work was put on the agenda. This demand worked in two directions. On the one hand, it took up the difficulties of the industrial revolution and implied a series of specific measures such as job creation and guarantees of working conditions and job security. For L. Blanc[25] it even included the idea that individuals should be paid according to their needs.

On the other hand, however, the right to work was understood as a structural solution to the social question. When work, and not charity, is the only legitimate way of securing one's living, then working was justly a right of every citizen. The only way to counter the inequality of the propertied and the propertyless, without this in turn becoming an injustice, was to ensure the latter the right to work, just as the former were ensured a right to property. Thus, however, the right to work runs up against a revolutionary understanding of a right to support which included welfare support and labor policies.

The idea that poverty was a result of unemployment was quite natural from the liberal point of view. On the other hand, the right to work, if it were to become a right of the individual, had anti-liberal consequences. "Those who speak of rights, are thus saying that those who have this right ... can demand society and the government representing it guarantee this support."[26] "The right will be claimed from the state, because a right is a right," wrote Gaulthier de Rumilly.[27]

The right to work would have meant significant institutional changes, especially because of different interpretations of the term property, whose individualization would have been called into question by the principle of cooperative work. Such a right would also have led to an altered role for the state, that, in a democracy, should reflect the tensions and divisions of society. The state therefore had to protect the interests of the weakest as an increase in power they gained through collective organization in order to counterbalance their inferior position. And in fact, L. Blanc demanded the creation of a new governmental administrative bodies in which such state care should be put into practice: a ministry of progress and a ministry of public welfare, through which the right to work and the right to support could be effectively organized.

The decree with which the provisional government formally recognized the right to work was dated 26 February and preceded the decree on the franchise. With it came a series of institutional measures: the creation of national workshops under the administrative control of the ministry of labor instead of social workshops, as well as a state commission for labor instead of the ministries of labor and progress demanded by supporters of the right to work. These were all part of a strategy to control politically the insurgent movement, in which old policies were bound to new techniques. These measures endured only a few months. Instead of overcoming the social crisis, they shifted the conflict to the legal sector.

While in the "social workshops" of L. Blanc worker profit-sharing was planned, in the national workshops of 1848 there was only an investment of capital by the government. Just in the term "national" instead of "social," the intention becomes apparent of using them to demonstrate the unity of the nation while denying social conflict, which was, however, the reason for their existence. De facto, the national workshops resembled more, in the final analysis, a government policy of public works which had been repeatedly taken up from the time of Turgot's "charitable workshops" to overcome periods of intensified crisis.[28] Nonetheless, they were set up this time in reference to work instead of charity. This distinguished them from their predecessors and thus they could be understood as an attempt to solve the social crisis revealed by the revolution.

And, in fact, the workers saw in the national workshops an accomplishment of the revolution which offered tangible proof that task of organizing work was incumbent on the nation and that it had to take on the responsibility for this. Later on, Lamartine[29] would counter that the workshops were never intended to be more than a temporary measure. Herein lies the error of the popular movement, as Spuller remarked.[30] They did not realize that the workshops were a temporary measure for easing tensions between the classes. There is a certain ambiguity in the one side believing the right to work had been put into practice while the other was reviving older political strategies. Nonetheless, it led to something new.

Furthermore, the workshops embodied a new political rationale in which the organization was understood as a form of government. They eventually represented an attempt to organize the mass of unemployed, to encourage discipline, and above all to strengthen moral influence. This factor has been especially emphasized by Émile Thomas. "Moral influence remained the most effective lever with regard to public opinion and popular action."[31] Moral influence was the core of the provisional government's strategy with regard to the new demands connected to the introduction of universal suffrage. On the one hand this could, in regard to moral incompetence (the traditional defence of property qualifications) legitimize influencing the public. On the other hand, it allowed acting to create a public opinion a pressing necessity given the new emancipation of the people. "The currents of democracy drive us on. Our only chance is to successfully develop the virtues of independence among the working population."[32] The popular classes had to be introduced into political life.

The establishment of a government commission in the Luxembourg Palace, which had no decision-making powers was in turn also the result of a compromise. The insurgents demanded a ministry, so that the state would surrender its neutrality and take the initiative in organizing the economy along the principle of association. With this commission, the provisional government attempted, on the other hand, to restrict governmental responsibility and the effects of demands for a right to work. The commission steered debate on the cooperative principle in a very pragmatic direction, which related only to the organization of work in the workshops. This pragmatism and above all a much too narrow outlook for the workshops led in the end—in view of the dilemma of increasing unemployment and the need to counter the oppressive power of employers in the workshops—to an undermining of the cooperative principle.

Hence commission debate was limited to the horizons of the guilds. Sewell[33] has pointed out the paradox of a workers' revolution which aimed at a reform of society but whose language and most important concerns were generally restricted to the traditional guild framework. Mutual aid, conditions of work, and pay negotiations were, under the influence of former guild artisans, the typical themes of discussion. Hence a gap appeared between the generations of workers which separated the older workers in the commission from the younger—generally concerned about unemployment and who only followed the debates in passing and tended to frequent more the national workshops.[34]

This new republican guild distinguished itself considerably from its predecessors. Its public nature made it into a microcosm of the democratic and social republic. Consequently it transferred to the commission its desire to gain a political hearing and thus developed two tendencies in the discussion about work. The one emphasized greater independence for the workers, the other appealed to the state against the power of the employers. Thus, to the guild tradition was added a statist component, which for its part was of revolutionary origin.

The idea of L. Blanc consisted of combining voluntarily formed associations of workers with state intervention, whereby the latter was, however, not understood as a nationalization of work, but rather simply strengthening a society organized on a collective basis.[35] This principle of association was as unacceptable for liberals as was a demand for a subjective right to work. Against it, that which Craveri[36] has called the "individualistic prejudice" predominated, which ensured that associations did not long enjoy favor. Once the element of collective organization was rejected, the right to work was marked by the stigma of statism, even when its supporters continually emphasized the local character of its realization.

In the end, the commission did support the neutrality of the state, which had remained in the background in their work, but it transformed the principle of association, potentially subversive for liberal order, into a technical problem of workshop organization. "The idea of an organization of labor subdues thoughts of war among the masses," Lamartine recognized in his memoirs.[37] This discussion did not bring about any new subjective right to work, creating instead *Chambres syndicales*, in which workers' delegations could express their views about occupational aims. Corporation became, in general, the basis for a new form of discipline, self-control, and negotiation, through which the state gained other means of taking action against the lack of discipline of a new worker generation that had taken refuge in the national workshops.

The Fraternal Republic

The provisional government decided to take up the republican tradition and, instead of having a commission issue a "Charta," as was done during the restoration, it had a constitution drafted by a constituent assembly. On 17 May the constituent assembly named an eighteen man committee, whose members were chosen from different parliamentary groupings on a proportional representation basis. The majority of the members, headed by Cormenin, were national republicans and Orléanist liberals; socialists were only represented by Victor Considérant. The committee presented its first draft on 19 June, which was then modified by the assembly's *Bureaux*. The final draft was presented to the assembly for discussion on 30 August by Marrast[38] and debate began on 4 September. While regulations for state institutions remained the same, the two drafts differed considerably from each other—above all in their preamble and guarantees for the right to work, support and education.

Work on the constitution of 1848 did not dispose of some fundamental uncertainties. In 1848, that is, at the end of the "Charta" era, the belief that the constitution could establish an ideal form of government also came to an end.[39] In the course of the revolution of 1789, even the most controversially discussed drafts had a common root: a "pouvoir constituent" founding a new society and a constitution as a rational expression of the revolution. Social crisis in 1848 called into question both Siéyès's Third Estate representing the nation and the Jacobin theory of popular sovereignty as legitimizing power. Hence it was a matter of reconciling every individual's sovereignty with the sovereignty of all, as Leroux remarked.[40]

As a common frame of reference was lacking, the idea of a constitution itself was criticized. This criticism was based on a disputed comparison of a democracy of form and one of substance, something the revolution had underlined with its ideas on real equality, political control of production and distribution of society's wealth. The committee met in June, and the noise from the street battles could be heard through the windows, as Odilon Barrot recalled in his *Mémoires.*[41] The committee was faced with a society torn by contrasting interests, which the government sought to unify—something that society itself was not capable of. The social fracture, which also carried along the institutions, distanced revolution and constitution from one another. What place should a constitution take, which did not form the basis of the principles of political organization, but instead expressed assumptions on a restoration of a dissipated unity of society and politics?

Hence the work of the committee was caught between constitutionalizing political relations and state authority on the one hand and administrative codification of civil liberties on the other.[42] Apart from a constitutional tradition—of revolutionary origin—two other fundamental traditions of modern France had to be taken into consideration: the administrative from the Napoleonic era and the parliamentary from the restoration.[43] However, these increased the significance of the social question, which forced the integration of a further specific outlook from 1848 in the work on the constitution: the "fraternal republic."

Fraternity was seen—as in the work of Hyppolite Flandrin, which was selected in a competition as image for the new state—as a symbol of the revolution. In it flowed all hopes, disappointments, and misunderstandings of 1848 together, distinguishing this year from 1789. The Great Revolution had been given the task of creating freedom and equality. Fraternity, a direct result of the new revolution's popular character, lived uneasily with the new social order based on individual liberties, the consequences of which could not be corrected by bourgeois equality. Seen by the insurgents as a principle of organization, it was reinterpreted by the government as "fraternity through the institutions,"[44] and as a guideline for the political reform of the state.[45] But how was this to be achieved?

Fraternity was a controversial term in legal theory, difficult to define normatively, but which nonetheless played an important role in the establishment of public law in France.[46] Failure in 1848 to make fraternity the permanent basis of social rights and duties devalued the definition of this concept, and social rights were eventually legitimized by "solidarity," a "more scientific" and "more positive" term. In spite of the relative juridical weakness of the term fraternity, public interest nonetheless often forced through political measures which contradicted the dogma of laissez-faire and a minimal state.[47] Whether for the prevention of disturbance of public order or for the maximization of workers' participation in productive labor, the government was often forced to become involved administratively in questions of expropriation, education, labor laws for women and children, public hygiene, etc. Such involvement had only a weak political legitimacy and had rather a more moral base. Nonetheless, they were unavoidable in order, for lack of a better alternative, to place some limits on the worst effects of industrialization, even though they were felt to be inadequate.

This is also shown in the ambivalent character of the committee debate, which oscillated between the principles of promulgating rights and the question of rights as governmental strategy. The debates concentrated generally on the relations between social questions, fraternity, and form of government. In particular, a group formed of deputies from different political currents (Barrot, Lamennais, Tocqueville) proposed a model of administrative decentralization as a possible way out of the political cul-de-sac and as a solution to the social question by other means than a right to work. In view of the attack on the state implied in demands for a right to work, they held the view that institutional change could be effected through decentralization. Mannoni's[48] remark that the beginning of a new phase of constitutional debate in France always meant a favorable climate for a revaluation of local liberties also applies to this debate. It is true that this theme was already in the air. Guizot[49] himself was forced to confess that centralization alone was not sufficient in a democratic system. Tocqueville, in his work *Democracy in America,* had strongly denounced this: "I believe that in the democratic century which is beginning now, individual independence and local liberties will always be artificial products. Centralization will be the natural form of government."[50] The fight against centralization was a point of controversy through the entire political spectrum, which at least in part might explain the weaknesses and finally the failure of the decentralization project.[51]

It remains true that the constitutional committee intensively studied a proposal from Lamennais and Odilon Barrot to introduce the new text of the constitution with a section on the organization of municipal administration.[52] The two proposed a second chamber elected by the municipalities, which was to look after local interests and thus weaken the effects of "general will." Tocqueville naturally supported this idea. "In my view it is an outrageous principle that the state should be the trustee of the governed, that is, has the right to force an individual to put his house in order."[53] It was a question of one's own freedom to "take care of one's own affairs," that is, the idea of self-government, for which Tocqueville argued in matters of administration. Separation of politics and administration was a major element in this strategy. Administrative decentralization was to parallel political centralization.

Behind this strategy of decentralization, another answer to the social question than the right to work appeared. It would allow an improvement in the situation of the lower classes being placed in the center of public measures without, however, altering the political role of the government. While an individual right to work would make every individual a creditor of the state and would place the state in the very uncomfortable position of being indebted to its citizens, administrative decentralization would allow the creation of intermediary levels at which the necessary measures to reduce excessive poverty could be taken. According to Tocqueville's model, this would contribute to an anchoring of democracy not only by law, but also by custom. As Béchard would later say in a debate in the Assembly, "only municipal liberty and freedom of religion together can make possible a fulfillment of the promise of support."[54] Such a mixture of local liberties, which corresponded to the project of a "Christian and democratic republic" in Tocqueville's sense of the term, could rescind the political responsibility of the state and return the solution of the social question to public charity, the organization of which needed to be improved.

Most republicans in the committee were nonetheless opposed to decentralization. They feared that such an acceptance of local variety would threaten the principle of equality, which they always linked with a centralized state. "The republicans of 1848 loathed the possibility of local influence, which they held to be counter-revolutionary."[55] For them, decentralization meant, on the one hand, potential for "influence just in petty local politics," on the other, for the influence of worker's associations, citizens' committees, and mutual benefit societies, etc. that is, they understood decentralization would become political and not purely administrative. Basically, they feared the normative dynamic of democratic institutions.[56]

Associations were only tolerated because they had the advantage of accustoming the individual to organization, as this contributed to a disciplining of the masses, corresponding to the requirements associated with the new franchise. However, this abrupt transformation from property qualification to universal suffrage made an extension and consolidation of the political classes and a unified organization of power an imperative for the constituent assembly. Convinced of the necessity of a strong executive and administrative centralization, they quickly founded a central administration school to train state personnel in unified regulations.[57] Furthermore, from June 1849 onwards, the clubs were successively abolished.

This may serve to explain Tocqueville's severe judgment of his colleagues in the committee, when he compares their lack of political conviction with the political courage of the men who, under the direction of George Washington, had written the American constitution.[58] Nonetheless, he was forced to modify his strategy. In the debates in the Assembly, he concentrated his attacks on social rights.

"A Good Constitution is Less Required Than Simply Any Constitution"

When the text of the draft was finally presented to the Assembly, the right to work had disappeared. However, a debate on this right broke out immediately in discussions on the preamble. In it, the rights of the state and those of the individual, in other words the contents of a social contract, were defined. As Lamartine[59] remarked, the "totally moral conditions" created by the revolution necessitated making explicit the "social discoveries" of 1848. The "philosophical" character of the preamble had to transform the spirit of the revolution into principles of government.

Governmental organizations had to assume that "from now on all power comes from the people, that is from this mass of male citizens, who in their sum form the only sovereign."[60] However, the effects of popular sovereignty on the organization of power were unclear. "Everything lies in the hands of popular sovereignty, but this still must be organized," remarked Pierre Leroux.[61] This was all the more necessary as universal suffrage proposed political power to public opinion's consensus. Hence the government had to be sensitive to the needs of the people, but equally had to escape their pressure, in order to avoid limits to its autonomy. Universal suffrage forced the government to be flexible—that is, restricted in time and easy to be changed.

The discussion took place between those who understood a constitution as only about the rights of the individual, and those who felt that a constitution also had to organize a system of duties, that limited state power vis-à-vis society. "What does one want from a republican government?" asked Goudchaux, the Minister of Finance: no one could ask "the impossible" of it.[62] There were natural limits to a government's ability to act and no moral obligation to popular sovereignty could place it under unbearable constraint. The idea that the state was a responsible individual with rights and duties remained exclusively a socialist idea.[63]

Nonetheless, for a solution to the political problem of the organization of the state, it was not sufficient to reject the obligations of the state. The social question was unavoidable; one did not have to be a supporter of the right to work to recognize that "the middle classes had gained everything from the revolution that they could expect. But have the lower classes gained from the revolution what they could legitimately strive for?"[64] In other words, political attention and legislative measures needed to be directed towards "the fate of the popular classes."[65] This, however, required breaking the links between the social question and centralization. "The central administration has at its disposal the entire social instrumentation and receives further power when progress leads to new needs."[66]

Despite the intentions of supporters of the right to work such as Pelletier, L. Blanc, and Pierre Leroux, who all insisted on a decentral implementation of it, it seems that the state should inevitably gain power when social inequality became a political affair. Socialist theories, complained Tocqueville, glorified the role of the state and thus led back to the Ancien Régime, in that they kept the citizens in tutelage. "The French Revolution did not raise the absurd claim of creating a social power, which itself directly cared for the welfare of each citizen, which replaced the practical and well-rooted wisdom of the ruled with a very questionable governmental wisdom; it did believe it sufficient to fulfill its task by granting every citizen enlightenment and liberty."[67]

The emphasis on individual rights was proportional to a "natural" tendency of government to penetrate without restriction into the sphere of personal liberty. On the other hand, creating obligations for the state meant the implicit recognition that it should become involved in social processes and thus favored such a tendency. Once again attempts were made, especially in Béchard's[68] amendment to defend the "principle of cooperative organizations" through local associations and extra rights for the communities, whereby decentralization was, furthermore, seen as the best countermeasure to electoral abstention. However, the idea of decentralization experienced a new defeat. If the tendency of the state to expand could not be countered by these means, another strategy was required. This consisted of attacks on social rights, and in this supporters of decentralization were united with those of centralization.

When Mathieu (representative from the Drôme) presented an amendment to paragraph eight of the preamble—which dealt with rights—in order to reintroduce the right to work, an impassioned debate arose, in the course of which thirty-two speakers took the floor. The debate centered on the following questions. Can work be recognized as an individual right? Should this be made a responsibility of the state?

What would be the political consequences? Very quickly a general strategy appeared behind the pros and cons. Should one, or not, as Tocqueville remarked, separate politics, which is the sphere of rights, from morals, which is the sphere of obligations?

The right to work, said Mathieu, was nothing more than the "right of hunger" and thus an obligation that the constitution could not evade. Ledru Rollin added, "The right to work is the republic in action." For Lamartine,[69] the conflict between property and work could only be solved by a growth of property, and the right to work meant to recognize the worker's ownership of his work. To separate politics from morals would lead in the end to rescinding the fraternity of political organization: rights and duties had to remain united in politics, the "moral and legal spheres" had to permeate each other. "The new truth lies in there not being two moralities," concluded Lamartine.[70]

Property, however, responded Tocqueville, had been not only guaranteed from the time of the "Great Revolution," but had been widely distributed. "Because the French Revolution populated this land with ten million property owners, one can safely bear this [socialist] teaching taking place in the tribune."[71] The right to work had, as consequence, the idea that not only should the state steer society, but also "that it [should] so to say become the teacher of every individual, his preceptor, his pedagogue." Even more dangerous, this right would make the state an economic actor. "Either the state will be forced to become, step by step an industrialist ... and soon to become the sole entrepreneur of industry ... or it will become the largest and only organizer of labor."

The revolution had to be sober, Tocqueville said, so that it remained the final one and therefore work had to be prevented from becoming a right of the individual. Moreover, the state's political task was something else than its moral obligation to offer support. Politics concerned only rights; support was a moral obligation that belonged to the sphere of public charity. The committee "had not wanted to create something totally new: it had wanted to expand, specify, and regulate public charity."[72] Thiers was of the same opinion. Association could only be a principle of government. In production, on the other hand, only personal interests could function. The right to work was a procedure to reward the idle, one in which the wealth of society was only being used for the benefit of one group. Who could say, moreover, that charity was humiliating? Either the right to work described charitable assistance or "if it is a right, be warned. One cannot joke with rights! A right allows no exceptions, this is true for all classes."[73]

In the final text of the constitution, nothing is said of the moral obligation of society to aid its members through providing work. "The National Assembly avoided the difficulties in not announcing the right of the impoverished to support and instead proclaiming the moral obligation of society to support them. As this detour via social obligation replaced individual claims, the same course was taken with the right to work. It was said to this point that there were obligations to which no rights corresponded."[74] The strategically important separation of politics and morals was thus sealed. Hence, the deputies avoided that the concept of rights ends up in the idea, implied in the right to work, of the ability to enjoy a right. Instead, they resolved to transform such rights into a more reassuring moral obligation. Such a strategy, moreover, would continue well beyond 1848. The report on charity presented to the Assembly by Coquerel in February 1849 was adapted to the separation made in the constitution. This also allowed for the possibility of renewed cooperation between politics and the social sciences, as was reflected in the numerous commissions of the provisional government and Cavaignac to the Academy of Moral and Political Sciences.[75] Thus began a governmental strategy which would become more significant during the Second Empire, especially thanks to Frédéric Le Play and the world's fairs.

On the other hand, moral reform depended to a greater extent on the factor of education. A government legitimized by popular sovereignty had a direct interest in forming public opinion, in everyone earning the title citizen—and this not only on the basis of some elementary knowledge, but rather through moral education. Therefore, in the public interest it was necessary to provide a free and obligatory basic education, which was both a right and a duty, shown by punishment for a father who did not send his son to school. The government retained a decisive role in the organization of public schools, for example, in hiring teachers and supervising the schools.

Although the pressure of centralization had allowed other, less politically dangerous solutions to be found to the social question than the right to work, the separation of politics and morals legitimized the idea that necessary reform must above all be moral reform. The political education that the decentral organizations would have supplied therefore had to be provided by a reform of morals, which remained the only means of ensuring that the voters behaved responsibly. In the end, the electoral law remained the only clear success within the framework of the institutions created in 1848. The people, at least its male segment, had found access to political representation. For this, it had to surrender the claims to change politics in its consequence for their own living conditions. The people were released from the juridical-political tutelage of property qualification, to find themselves under a moral tutelage. Political innovation in 1848 thus approached the Second Empire, which would rid itself of the right to vote and take over the tutelage.

The Advantages of Decentralization

As Kergolay reported in his introduction to his examination of "The Municipal Institutions of Belgium," published in the *Revue provinciale* in 1848 and 1849, the constituent assembly, in its session of 18 October, had made a number of references to the Belgian constitution during the debate on decentralization or centralization. Thus the paths of the two countries crossed in 1848 in a different way than as an export of the republican revolution, dreamed of by some in Paris. The effects of the February revolution in Paris, namely, led to a radicalization of the liberal regime that had been governing Belgium since the elections of 1847 rather than to the success of the radical, republican, and socialist movements.

A severe financial and economic crisis had hit the country and especially the flax industry in Flanders, leading to a rise in an already noticeable industrial pauperism. It strengthened critics of industry from the Catholic milieu and from circles open to the influence of foreign refugees, especially republicans and socialists. It is therefore understandable that the February revolution awakened hopes of an extension of the popular uprising, especially among those Belgian workers who had had to emigrate to France in search of work. The association of the Rue de Menilmontant, which met under the leadership of Splithoorn, soon became the "Belgian Legion," which marched off to the north to prepare armed action on Belgium territory in support of Belgian republicans.

Although Ledru-Rollin made no secret of his support, the provisional government, as a whole, took an ambivalent stance, including Lamartine, as shown in the dispatches of the Prince de Ligne, the Belgian ambassador in Paris.[76] The Belgian government's diplomatic situation was difficult; hence it was constantly attempting to persuade the provisional government to distance itself formally from Legion activities. In any case, the Belgian republicans remained small in number and were isolated. Operations on Belgian territory by rebels coming from France were limited to a few skirmishes with the army, the most well-known of which were the incidents in Quievrain and Risquons-Tout at the end of March. They were, however, quickly brought under control.[77]

The cause of their lack of success doubtless lay in the political measures quickly taken by the Belgium government in view of the danger of French intervention. Property qualifications for voters were reduced to the minimum set in the constitution and property qualifications for political office abolished. Furthermore, the government forbade deputies from holding public offices, introduced a 1 percent tax on direct inheritance—a concession to the radical definition of property—approved extensive public works as well as the establishment of training workshops, as a measure against the disastrous effects of the flax crisis in Flanders. These were radical measures which ran counter to the spirit of the doctrinaire group in the government,[78] but the various political currents within the Belgian bourgeoisie were united in their support of the measures.

In the question of public order, the government resolved to depend on the energy of the provincial governors and municipal authorities. They released a reassuring circular in which they pointed out that the civil guard, which could only be called up by the mayors, was sufficient to preserve order. This all the more so as the government intended to renew the city councils with a new electoral law, so that they better reflected "the mood of the country," as Rogier put it before the Senate.[79] This mood hindered the government from reinforcing troops on the French border to face possible mutineers, but did not mean their having to be deployed inside the country to preserve order. The government also made use of anti-revolutionary propaganda, which extended even to liberal newspapers.[80]

On the other hand, relations with Paris demanded intensive diplomatic activity. Belgium recognized the French provisional government on 3 March and maintained strict neutrality. The Belgian government emphasized that "the King in

Belgium has very limited prerogatives" and that the Belgian constitution was fundamentally not very much different from a republican form of government. This was suggested to the ambassador in Paris with the intention of "awakening the understanding that a people which enjoys the full range of civil liberties does not and could not have the least intention of abandoning the regulated and measured course that it has taken with success and determination."[81] Leopold I, in a letter to Thiers a year later, had to describe his country as one that "is much more republican than most of those countries which feel it appropriate to see themselves as such."[82] In general, the fear that moderate voices in Paris could be replaced by more radical ones, and that Lamartine's position could be undermined, led to a reserved reaction to the provisional government's involvement in the propaganda activities of Belgian republicans.[83]

Hence not only the proclamation of a republic was avoided. Rather, the run of events had strengthened the constitutional monarchy because it had been able to withstand the revolution, which had broken out so close to its borders, and to survive the collapse of the French monarchy. As Pirenne[84] has emphasized, Belgium was a model country which secured its place among the nations of Europe with its demonstration of independence and stability. Belgium, which resisted the revolution, appeared to offer proof that liberal institutions were compatible with a monarchy, and the country's constitution became a much imitated model. Very quickly the idea became accepted—as Lamartine wrote to his ambassador in Brussels, Sérurier—that the liberties enjoyed by the Belgians did not drive them to armed revolt[85] and the French came to believe that the Belgians were a step ahead of them in their peaceful conquest of liberties.[86]

They were especially envious of—to use Hofschmidt's[87] words—the "mass of provincial and municipal liberties" which the Belgian government could draw on to preserve order in the face of a threat of revolution. Its trust in them was, moreover, well placed, as the mayors were in fact able to maintain order. The forerunner of these local liberties extended back to the independent municipal tradition, which had allowed a peaceful separation from the central government and which was not seriously impaired by the centralizing efforts of the Duke of Burgundy and the House of Habsburg. The sovereign had, in fact, no essential rights; his central authority arose from the special rights of the individual princes.[88] The constitution of 1831 continued in this tradition, confirming the rights of the provinces and municipalities and assigning to the monarch the task of organizing the state at the central level. Thus it contrasted with the principle, taken from the Italian republics, of making the municipalities into a sort of state within the state. This principle appeared in Belgium as a threat to the independence of the municipalities.

In view of the rights of the municipalities, it was stated in article 108 of the constitution that "the exclusively municipal and provincial interests shall be managed by the provincial and municipal councils." This aim was underlined by the municipal law of 1838. The affairs of the provinces and municipalities thus fell, from the administrative point of view, into the area of responsibility of provincial and municipal councils in Belgium, which were led by the governor of the province or the mayor of the municipality, whereby both were representatives of the king in the exercising of the power of the executive. The constitution allowed the direct election of members of the council, public sessions, budgets, and accounting. Interference by the king or the government was only possible in order to prevent provincial or municipal councils from overstepping their competence or violating public interest.[89] Furthermore, at the same time as the February revolution broke out in Paris, the Belgian parliament was discussing a draft law to restrict the rights of the central government in naming and recalling of mayors. It was resolved that these could only be named in consultation with the provincial governors.

Kergolay held no illusions. The friend of Tocqueville was well aware that the municipalities in Belgium were not the decisive element of power. Moreover, after the French revolution and in the Napoleonic era, Belgium had had to suffer the same bureaucratic despotism as France. The union with Holland had meant a certain increase in local liberties, and the revolution of 1830 had given them a greater boost because the clergy, "the true political power" in Belgium, held local liberties "as the only solid guarantee for religious education," in their defense of freedom of education.[90]

Such an increase did not, however, prevent the municipalities from being both autonomous institutions and delegates of central power. Certainly, the events of 1848 had strengthened their autonomy, especially because of the successes of the civil guard, a true army under the command of the mayors. The law of March 1848 restricting the prerogatives of the government in naming mayors was a measure which aimed at "weakening the after-effects of the February revolution among the population."[91] The generally representative system enacted moreover, gave, the local authorities "a certain very modern touch, that even looks a bit like a government."[92]

Nonetheless, both in France and Belgium the councils were "under the tutelage"[93] of a superior authority; the American idea of a certain municipal independence was lacking in the relevant laws. According to article 87 of the law of 1836, the king even had the right to annul all council decisions if these violated public interest. In this, one can see that we are in Europe. However, customs were more independent in Belgian than the law, municipal thinking stronger than the liberties allowed by the laws on municipal government. Public sessions and the right to summon the council strengthened this feeling. The mayors played an important role as they had considerable influence on the public. Resolutions were collective; the mayor was only the head of a council of jurors. The law of 1836 had lowered limitations of collective administration.[94]

The similarities of the two countries inevitably led to an increased interest in Belgian legislation, as it demonstrated that it was also possible in Europe to bring about the independence of the municipalities without totally surrendering European customs. Belgium was "a region of transformation between today's constitution of our French society and a complete development of liberties which we could hardly have dreamed of in advance." Belgium took a position between the ideal conditions of American democracy and the European distrust of local liberties. The interest in the Belgian experience, according to Kergolay, was also based in its similarity to French tradition. This interest would prove to be very valuable about twenty years later when, towards the end of the Second Empire, the question of local liberties again became topical and republican policies regained the strength to reconcile themselves with morality through the institutionalization of solidarity.

Notes

1. Adolphe Thiers, *Discours à la Assemblée sur la constitution* (Paris, 1848).
2. Alphonse de Lamartine, *La France parlementaire*, 5 vols. (Paris, 1865), Vol. 5, 250.
3. Louis Blanc, *L'organisation du travail* (Paris, 1848), 17.
4. Maurice Agulhon, *The Republican Experiment, 1848-1852*, trans. Janet Lloyd (Cambridge, 1983).
5. C. Nicolet, *L'idée républicaine en France* (Paris, 1982).
6. Alexis de Tocqueville, *Souvenirs*, (Paris, 1978), 213.
7. Ibid., 123.
8. Lamartine, *Histoire de la révolution de 1848*, 2 vols. (Paris, 1849).
9. Ibid., vol. 1.
10. Tocqueville, *Souvenirs*, 124.
11. Tocqueville, *Écrits et discours politiques. Oeuvres complètes*, 5 vols. (Paris, 1962) Vol 3/2, 750.
12. Jacques Godechot, *Les constitutions de la France depuis 1789* (Paris, 1979), 253.
13. Tocqueville, *Écrits et discours politiques*, 737.
14. Pierre Rosanvallon, *Le sacre du citoyen. Historie du suffrage universel en France* (Paris, 1992).
15. E. Spuller, *Historie parlementaire de la Seconde République*, (Brussels, 1891), 28.
16. P. Craveri, *Genesi di una costituzione. Libertà e socialismo nel dibattito costituzionale del 1848* (Naples, 1985), 52. In the appendix: "Comité de constitution. Comptes-rendus des travaux."
17. Lamartine, *Histoire*.
18. *Compte-rendus des séances de l'Assemblée nationale constituante*, Vol. 3 (Paris, 1850), 968.
19. Rosanvallon, *Le sacre du citoyen*, 300.
20. *Bulletin de la république* (Paris, 1848), 4.
21. C. Dupin, *Discours sur la constitution* (Paris, 1848), 107.
22. E. Regnault, *Histoire du Gouvernement provisoire* (Paris, 1850), 127.
23. *Bulletin*, 16.
24. Spuller, *Histoire parlementaire*, 28.
25. Louis Blanc, *Histoire de la révolution de 1848*, 2 vols.(Paris, 1849), Vol. 1, 148.
26. J. Garnier (ed.), *Le droit au travail à l'Assemblée nationale* (Paris, 1848), xvii.
27. *Compte-rendus*, Vol. 3, 956.
28. H. Maillard, *La théorie du droit au travail en France* (Paris, 1912).
29. *Compte-rendus*, Vol. 4, 414.
30. Spuller, *Histoire parlementaire*, 123.
31. Quoted in Mark Traugott, *Armies of the Poor* (Princeton, 1985), 138.
32. Michel Chevalier, *Questions politiques et sociales* (Paris, 1850), 20.
33. William H. Sewell, Jr., *Work and Revolution in France* (Cambridge, 1980).
34. Robert J. Bezucha, "The French Revolution of 1848 and the Social History of Work," *Theory & Society* 12 no. 4 (1983): 469-84.
35. E. Girardin (ed.), *Discours à la Commission du Luxembourg*, 2 vols. (Paris, 1849).
36. Craveri, *Genesi*, 78.

37. Lamartine, *Histoire*, Vol. 2, 26.
38. Armand Marrast, *Rapport à l'Assemblée nationale sur le projet de constitution* (Paris, 1848).
39. Craveri, *Genesi*, 7ff.
40. *Compte-rendus*, Vol. 4, 41.
41. Odilon Barrot, *Mémoires posthumes* (Paris, 1875), 32.
42. Craveri, *Genesi*, 69ff.
43. Nicolet, *L'idée républicaine*, 138.
44. Lamartine, *La France*, 250.
45. Marrast, *Rapport*, 16.
46. M. Borgetto, *La notion de fraternité dans le droit public français* (Paris, 1992).
47. Giovanna Procacci, *Gouverner la misère* (Paris, 1993).
48. S. Mannoni, *Une et indivisible*, Vol. 2 (Milan, 1996), 204.
49. François Guizot, *De la démocratie en France* (Paris, 1849), 119.
50. Tocqueville, *De la démocratie en Amérique*, Vol. 1, 303.
51. Mannoni, *Une et indivisible*, Vol. 2, 193-99.
52. Craveri, *Genesi*, 100ff.
53. Ibid., 115.
54. *Compte-rendus*, Vol. 4, 982.
55. Spuller, *Histoire parlementaire*, 200.
56. I. Tchernov, *Associations et sociétés secrètes sous la Deuxième République* (Paris, 1905), 5.
57. Carnot, *D'une école d'administration*, 1878.
58. Tocqueville, *Souvenirs*, 255.
59. Lamartine, *La France*, 395.
60. Marrast, *Rapport*, 22.
61. *Compte-rendus*, Vol. 3, 790.
62. Ibid, Vol. 4, 26.
63. Renouvier, *Manuel républicain de l'homme et du citoyen* (Paris, 1848), 7.
64. Tocqueville, *Écrits et discours politiques*, Vol. 3, 744.
65. Ibid., 737.
66. Ibid., 129.
67. *Compte-rendus*, Vol. 3, 967.
68. Ibid., Vol. 4, 980.
69. Lamartine, *La France*, 410.
70. Ibid., 423.
71. *Compte-rendus*, Vol. 3, 965.
72. Ibid., 964.
73. Thiers, *Discours*, 46.
74. Garnier (ed.), *Le droit au travail*, xvii.
75. Adolphe Blanqui, *Des classes ouvrières en France pendent l'année 1848* (Paris, 1849); Seillière, *L'Académie des sciences morales et politiques et le redressement moral de la France après les événements de 1848* (Paris, 1941).
76. A. De Ridder, *La crise de la neutralité belge de 1848*, 2 vols. (Brussels, 1928).
77. Henri Pirenne, *Histoire de la Belgique*, 7 vols. (Brussels, 1909-32), Vols. 4-5.
78. A. Erba, *L'esprit laïque en Belgique sous le gouvernement libéral doctrinaire* 2 vols. (Louvain, 1967).
79. L. Hymans, *Histoire parlementaire de la Belgique*, 2 vols. (Brussels, 1858) Vol. 2, 624-26.
80. M. Dessal, *L'accueil fait en Belgique à la révolution de 1848* (Rennes, 1939).
81. De Ridder, *La crise*, Vol. 1, 327.
82. Ibid., 325.
83. B.D. Grooch, *Belgium and the February Revolution* (The Hague, 1963).
84. Pirenne, *L'Europe et l'indépendance belge* (Brussels, 1990).
85. Grooch, *Belgium and Februry Revolution*, 34.
86. Pirenne, *Histoire*, Vol. 4, 425.

87. De Ridder, *La crise*, Vol. 1, 326.

88. V.A. Waille, *Essai sur l'histoire politique et constitutionnelle de la Belgique* (Brussels, 1838), 149.

89. P.A.F. Gerard, *Études historiques et critiques de la constitution belge* (Brussels, 1869).

90. L. Kergolay, "Des institutions communales de la Belgique," *Revue provinciale* (1849), 325.

91. Ibid., 331.

92. Ibid., 328.

93. Ibid., 426.

94. Ibid., 434.

Festival parade of Berlin clubs to Kreuzberg on 6 August
(Illustrirte Zeitung, Leipzig, no. 270, 2 September 1848, 149)

Chapter 22

PARTY FORMATION IN GERMANY

Political Associations in the Revolution of 1848

Michael Wettengel

"Our age is the age of associations!"[1]

Even contemporaries described the *Vormärz* as a period in which people joined together in voluntary associations, from individual motives for specified reasons, or to settle their affairs. Unlike earlier corporate groups, associations were freely organized combinations of individuals, each of whom had, at least formally, equal rights in the group. The association existed for specific purposes, determined by the association's members.[2] French and English examples as well as reading circles and patriotic clubs from the Enlightenment period in Germany provided models for associations in the nineteenth century. In the spirit of a still unbroken belief in progress, associations appeared to be the "means of self-mobilization" most appropriate for society to solve the many problems of the age.[3] This optimism was only shaken by the revolution of 1848, in which associations failed as a "universal formula for conflict-resolution."[4]

As early as the beginning of the nineteenth century, decidedly political associations were formed, whose members aimed their activities outside of the groups themselves and sought to win public opinion over to their aims. National, liberal, and radical convictions dominated in these early political associations, that provided a training ground, above all, for the younger generation of the bourgeois-opposition in the *Vormärz*. From the proclamation of the Karlsbad Decrees in 1819, or, at the latest, with the Confederate Decree of 5 July 1832, political associations were systematically suppressed throughout the entire German Confederation. Political combinations therefore had to be created in secret or in the disguise of seemingly apolitical associations. Nonetheless, during the *Vormärz*, numerous associations were

---

founded with more or less political aims. Among them, the Press and Fatherland Association of 1832/33 represented "a relatively highly developed prototype of a party organization."[5] The group had aspirations to spread throughout Germany and was able to gain support among the members of the lower-middle and lower classes. Political associations were a new form of social organization, one which sought to integrate broader strata of the population into the political process. Because of repressive measures by the various governments, however, attempts at political organization during the *Vormärz* were never long-lasting.

With the March uprising of 1848, the existent ban on associations and restrictions on assembly came to an end. At the same time, the revolution brought about a mobilization and politicization of a large portion of the population. Political associations were an expression of this development, appearing in numbers directly following events in March and multiplying rapidly thereafter. In comparison to their predecessors, the political associations of the revolutionary period included a more socially diverse membership and were present over a much wider geographical area. In organizing public meetings, writing petitions, providing political education, putting up candidates for parliamentary assemblies and municipal governments, organizing election campaigns, and carrying out political agitation among the general public, the associations became the focal point of local political life. They brought the "great" political events into a local context. Formed separately for each major political tendency, these groups organized and channeled the process of the formation of public opinion, expanded the radius of civic action, and created a self-organizing public sphere. Associations arose even before the corresponding parliamentary parties could form.

Quite early on, groups of each political tendency began to organize, also separately, on a super-regional basis. They developed numerous federations at the provincial, state, and national levels, led by the association in one particular locality or by an established central body. Thus, local party organizations were loosely tied together in federalist structures. These federations were closely tied to the parliaments and their parliamentary parties, but extra-parliamentary organizations were the central element in early party formation. At the national level, the democrats' Central March Association was indeed a party in the modern sense of the term. In this respect, the practice of political parties was in advance of theory, since "party" was usually still understood in the *Vormärz* as meaning individuals sharing the same general views, without necessarily having any organizational connection. Increasingly, however, the necessity of organization was recognized, and a theoretical distinction was made between communities of individuals sharing the same beliefs and organized political parties.[6]

The subject of this chapter will be extra-parliamentary organizations, the "party associations" of the revolution of 1848/49: in particular, their organizational forms, political currents, regional concentration, range of activities, and development. This excludes parliamentary parties and those associations whose primary purpose did not lie in political education and the organization of political opinion, such as the many special interest groups, as well as the gymnastic associations of the revolutionary period, although many of these groups also had political aims and occasionally merged with political associations. However, they did not represent an independent political force nor were they designed to have the organizational form of a political party. The aim of this contribution is to describe the importance of political associations for the formation of parties as well as their structure and the spectrum of the effects of their activities in the German states.

1. Organization and Development of the Party System

Political associations did not appear out of thin air in 1848. Directly following the outbreak of the revolution, they were formed in the cities from public meetings, electoral committees, informal circles, or local associations. Even in the *Vormärz*, different political currents were recognizable, but it was only in the revolutionary period that they were able to find full organizational expression. Political associations developed statutes, that established parliamentary practices for their meetings; they created a permanent organization and political programs. The various political currents organized themselves in new political associations. Thus a "five party system" arose, similar to the modern party system, with the following political associations.

- The labor movement, which was not represented in parliament and which was organized into workers' associations. In spite of differences between individual associations and regardless of the fact that their programs were still in a state of flux, the workers' associations generally desired fundamental social reforms, political equality, and a republican form of government.
- The democrats, who also demanded a republic or at least a parliamentary democracy with a weak monarch, but who were open to compromise in questions of forms of government. While not rejecting the sociopolitical claims of the workers' associations, they tended to give precedence to the postulate of political equality.
- The constitutional liberals, who were striving for a constitutional monarchy and who felt threatened by the political and social claims of the workers' associations.
- Political Catholicism, which defended the claims of the Catholic Church in society on the basis of a strictly confessional orientation. In the Pius Associations, it created a broad non-parliamentary organization.
- The fifth political current was the conservatives, who had a broad social base of support, but did not set up their own associations in many regions, but joined constitutional associations instead, and operated from within them.

Political currents were not always so organizationally distinct as they are in the ideal types presented here. The boundaries between the democrats and the liberals, the labor movement and the democrats, but also between the liberals and the conservatives as well as between political Catholicism and all other political groups, were often vague and indistinct. Although various political currents had already developed in the *Vormärz*, both in political theory and in the activities of their protagonists, this only had a gradual effect on political organization in 1848/49. The revolutionary period was distinguished by a process of differentiation and formation of distinct political parties. This is especially obvious in the split in the liberal-democratic spectrum.

Even during the *Vormärz*, constitutionalists and democrats had begun to organize themselves as independent political forces. On 12 September 1847, Badenese democrats formulated their own program in Offenburg, as did southwest German and Rhineland constitutional liberals in Heppenheim on 10 October of that year. Still, at the beginning of the March revolution in the German states an almost totally unified liberal-democratic movement existed at the local level, with a common organization. In many regions, the process of organizational differentiation extended well into the middle of 1848. Splits occurred especially early in Baden, Saxony, and some Rhineland cities, and especially late in Schleswig-Holstein, Mecklenburg, and Pomerania. But even in southern Germany, constitutionalists and democrats only formed separate organizations relatively late, in Würzburg, for example, only in December 1848.[7] Common action and temporary agreement between constitutionalists and democrats was still possible in many places even after the split.

The first political associations formed in March/April 1848 were, as a rule, joint liberal-democratic associations which sought to integrate the entire bourgeois spectrum. Characteristic for this phase of organizational development were efforts to unite liberals and democrats at the local level as well as to merge associations at the national level. Especially southern German associations, such as the Monday Circle in Frankfurt am Main and the Fatherland Association in Darmstadt, were active in this respect. The public meetings in Offenburg on the 19 March and in Michelstadt on 30 March 1848, which called for the formation of "fatherland associations" and "patriotic committees", might be included here, although they already clearly bore the stamp of the democrats.[8] These efforts were often illusory, quickly fading because of emerging conflicts between democrats and constitutionalists.

The main point of conflict in liberal-democratic associations, even at this early stage, was the question of the form of government—whether a republic or a constitutional monarchy was preferable for the German nation-state that was to be created. Closely related to this were fears among large sections of the middle class, for whom the unrest at the beginning of the revolution seemed to be a harbinger of a "red revolution." As one example among many, a Darmstadt liberal wrote in March 1848. There are:

> two dangers … to Germany's better order, freedom, and morals:
>
> 1) the Republic with its transition to civil war, reign of terror, and tyranny,
>
> 2) *the war of the propertyless against propertied* with its transitions to barbarianism and also tyranny. Against these two dangers, all right-thinking people must unite and organize in time.[9]

The democratic left responded more flexibly to claims toward greater political participation and demands for social reform on the part of artisans and workers. The constitutional liberals, on the other hand, were worried by the appearance of an organized labor movement: "They no longer ask, they defy and insist," wrote one shocked constitutionalist publicist, perceiving this as an expression of moral collapse.[10] These different attitudes toward the form of government and the social question led, sooner or later, to a split in the liberal-democratic movement.

In spite of the controversy it caused, the question of creating a nation-state served rather as an integrating factor, occasionally even bridging the gap between liberals and democrats. Hence the majority of democrats accepted the small- German solution and moderates among them were even willing to tolerate a Prussian hereditary emperor in a nation-state with free governmental institutions, even if only "as the good Lord [tolerates] evil."[11] While the greater- German/small-German controversy influenced the realignment of parliamentary parties, it was almost without import for extra-parliamentary organizations. Only where the national question was eclipsed by confessional differences, as was the case with the Pius Associations oriented toward a greater Germany, did it play a role.

As early as the elections in the spring of 1848, liberal-democratic electoral committees, which put forward both constitutionalist and democratic candidates, were already competing with committees of specific political tendencies that put up their own candidates. With a few local exceptions, the democrats led the way. Supported by the democratic caucus of the pre-parliament, a "Democratic Central Committee for Elections to the Constituent Assembly" published a 13 point election platform in Frankfurt am Main on 4 April 1848, calling, in addition, for the organization of a democratic election campaign. Characteristically, a public declaration of support for the republic was avoided. This call, however, found little echo.

The first Democratic Congress, which met in Frankfurt am Main from 14 to 17 June 1848 and was attended by 234 delegates under the chairmanship of Julius Fröbel, was an important step in the formation of a democratic "party." It was the first national congress of political associations in Germany to declare itself openly in favor of the republican form of government. However, more than two-thirds of the delegates came from the Hessian states, the Palatinate, Baden and Württemberg: there were also a number from the Prussian Rhine province. At the time of the congress, democratic organization was still in its inception. The alleged 89 associations represented at the congress were a colorful mixture of associations of Germans living in foreign countries, democratic associations, gymnastic associations, workers' associations, and liberal-democratic committees and associations uniting different political tendencies. Some delegates apparently only attended in the name of a democratic caucus within a broader association.

The congress resolved to organize and centralize democratic associations under the leadership of a central committee in Berlin. Although this was never achieved, the congress did result in the formation of a democratic "party" and a wave of new associations. Certainly, numerous district federations of democratic associations were set up in many regions which allied themselves with the central committee. Furthermore, the congress pushed forward the process of the differentiation of political associations and of the development of a democratic program. A democratic and plebiscitary understanding of popular sovereignty, a unicameral legislature and general, equal, and direct elections were fixed components of democratic associations' catalog of demands. Moderates among them were willing to accept a "weak" monarch in a parliamentary government, while radical republicans wanted to institute the republic, with force and violence if necessary. To resolve the social question, these radicals raised demands for a ministry of labor, the right to work, a progressive income tax, and national workshops. Common among all democrats was a high regard for associations as a "lever of political enlightenment."[12]

Plans for a strictly disciplined democratic organization divided into districts and regional federations led by a Berlin central committee came to nothing, however. Especially for rather moderate south and southwest German democrats, later calls by the central committee, e.g., the creation of a counter-parliament to the National Assembly, were too radical. Just a day after the congress, the Mainz republican, Ludwig Bamberger, concluded that in view of the democratic party's weakness: "I believe that more harm than good will come of this congress. It may well be pleasant to express your views quite coarsely, but it unnecessarily weakens effectiveness."[13] There was little contact with the distant Berlin central office.

A second turning-point came with the failure of the second Democratic Congress, which met in Berlin from 26 to 30 October 1848. Attended by more than 230 delegates, the congress was unable to find solutions for the lack of organization, internal communication, and finances of the democratic party. Delegates were literally overrun by counter-revolutionary events in Vienna and Berlin, and were unable to develop realistic strategies in response to the new situation. Equally serious differences arose among delegates about ways to solve the social question. A committee report presented by radical delegates on the social question appeared to many bourgeois democrats to be an "absurd communistic program."[14] The "catastrophe in Berlin"[15] and the growing strength of reaction in the late summer and autumn of 1848 encouraged the formation of a moderate democratic unity movement as reflected in the establishment of the Central March Association.

The rejection of the tax boycott appeal of the Prussian National Assembly by a majority of the deputies to the German National Assembly finally gave rise to coordinated activity among the different left-of-center caucuses in the Frankfurt National Assembly. At a meeting on 23 November 1848, the parliamentary caucuses Donnersberg, Deutscher Hof, and part of Westendhall merged to form the Central March Association, in order to create a center for extra-parliamentary agitation for the minority in the *Paulskirche*, as deputy Jakob Venedey put it.[16] The Central March Association called for popular sovereignty, a parliamentary form of government, defence of the accomplishments of the March revolution, and a constitution approved by the people with a democratic franchise and liberal basic rights. However, nothing further was said about the form of government.

A central committee, composed of members of the National Assembly, served as a mixture of parliamentary party committee and umbrella association at the national level. Associations allied themselves with it either individually or as regional federations under the leadership of central committees. The Central March Association did not have the power to control its member organizations. Only a congress of association delegates—which, however, met only once (6 May 1849)—could pass binding resolutions. This loose, decentralized federal structure was generally based upon already existing district (or regional), provincial, and state federations. With its institutionalized connection between local associations and the parliamentary party, the Central March Association represented the most highly developed party organization of the revolutionary period. At the state level, as well, close relations often developed between parliamentary caucuses and democratic district or regional associations. For correspondence, the Central March Association made use of the franking privileges of deputies to the National Assembly, and a network of newspapers allowed the dissemination of the association's declarations. The Central March Association is said to have even had an office and a proper register.

The Central March Association expanded rapidly, becoming the largest federation of associations in the revolutionary period. By March 1849 it included more than one thousand associations; its membership has been estimated at up to a half million.[17] With its propaganda work aimed at a broad public and its extensive membership, it already had the characteristics of a modern mass political party. Its success was due above all to its organizational structure, which was quite suitable for revolutionary-era associations—as can be seen in the regional variety of local association names, which were never unified. This strength was at the same time its greatest weakness, because effective leadership was not possible.

It was at least successful in providing impulses and coordinating associational activities, as became clear in the mass petitions and other mass actions for the recognition of the Declaration of Basic Rights and later the German Constitution drawn up by the National Assembly. The Central March Association became the party of moderate democrats, but at least for a time they were also joined by constitutionalist associations, and, in February/March 1849, even by the republican Central Committee of German Democrats, although it had sharply attacked the Central March Association as late as January of that year. The Central Committee did, however, only join "while reserving its party principles and party positions."[18]

Relations with the republican wing of the democratic movement remained tense. After the Prussian king, Friedrich Wilhelm IV, had rejected the Imperial crown, strict republicans were willing to dispense with a hereditary emperor as head of state, while moderate democrats wanted to stick to all points of the Imperial Constitution to preserve its legal foundations. On 11 April 1849 a group of 28 delegates from the extreme left of the National Assembly therefore withdrew from the Central March Association, as it "threatened to endanger the decisiveness of the democratic party and to make more difficult the decisive, uncompromising implementation of democratic principles."[19] The radical left's appeal to the rank and file to leave the Central March Association was followed by only twenty-five democratic clubs. An attempt, in conjunction with the Central Committee of German Democrats, to create a federation of republican associations, failed. Factional disputes between republicans and moderates did not, in the end, lead to an organizational split in the "democratic party."

Most constitutionalist liberals were opposed to the Central March Association. Their reasons included both the group's openness to republicanism and its character as a political party. Heinrich Jaup, constitutionalist minister in the government of the Grand Duchy of Hesse-Darmstadt accused democratic associations in general of forming "their own government apart from the legal government, a government which mocks all laws and rules through terrorism. This state of affairs, leads to the collapse of societal conditions: not just political and religious ones, but social ones as well."[20] Liberals had fundamental reservations about a "club system," which reminded them of past events in France, and about the "confusion wrought by party obsession."[21]

This attitude also had repercussions for the organizational efforts of constitutionalist liberals. Heinrich von Gagern had already declared himself a "party man," in 1834,[22] but in spite of such professions of leading liberals, liberal-constitutionalist extra-parliamentary associations developed only falteringly. Liberal-constitutionalist associations were often formed quite early on, especially in cities where a royal family resided. At times, they had very impressive membership figures—for example the Constitutional Club in Berlin with 2,000 members, the Patriotic Association in Frankfurt am Main with 2,500 members, and the Consitutional-Monarchical Association in Darmstadt with 2,300 members.

As a rule, though, constitutional associations were set up in reaction to democratic activities and remained well behind these in extent, numbers and organizational effectiveness. Their members' activity was also comparatively weak. For Wilhelm Heinrich Riehl, this was an expression of a phlegmatic "philistinism" totally fixated on economic interests: "And if the fear of material losses, of violence and excesses did not lead many to support the constitutionalist party, what a meager band of supporters it would then count! Of a hundred, certainly ninety-nine would prefer the old political indifference and apathy."[23]

As with the democrats, the constitutionalist "party" also experienced its share of factional disputes. Many conservatives, who subscribed to a "fanaticism for order,"[24] joined constitutional associations, forming a strong element within these organizations. They were "dangerous friends"[25] in the eyes of many constitutionalists, especially those in the southwestern states, as they endangered the internal unity and the cohesion of the constitutionalists: "The constitutional party, which has now become conservative to a certain extent, always has to absorb patiently, without examination, all elements which do not side with the opposition; and so it had to come that a few Sauls have entered our ranks who date their road to Damascus to the 6th of March ... and these people falsify and confuse the stance of the party ... Pressing and repeated is therefore our call to the entire party: Keep your ranks pure, unsullied by reactionaries, the self-satisfied, and fanatics!"[26] Such appeals were of little use, however, as many constitutionalists were not disinclined to a conservative alliance against allegedly republican and social revolutionary forces. Occasionally the constitutionalists even split into liberal-constitutionalist and conservative-constitutionalist associations, as happened, for example, in Saxony, Nassau, and Darmstadt.

Tendencies toward a closer union of constitutionalist associations at the state and national level appeared at an early date. From 22 to 24 July 1848, a constitutional congress met in Berlin "to counter republican endeavors."[27] Even in these early stages, conflicts arose between a liberal and a conservative wing, and latent competitiveness existed between the Berlin association and the German Association in Leipzig. At the invitation of the Citizens' Association in Kassel, another congress of liberal-constitutionalist associations took place from 3 to 5 November 1848. Because the invitation was vague as to program, democratic associations also took part at first, but left the meeting, as they disagreed with its resolution that the National Assembly should be the only legal expression of popular sovereignty.

At the congress, the National Association was founded as a federation of constitutionalist-liberal associations in Germany. A majority, following the lead of the Saxon associations, demanded the inclusion of a constitutional-monarchist form of government in the National Association's program. As this led some associations to threaten their withdrawal, the congress waved inclusion of such a statement. Support of the National Assembly remained a lowest common denominator, that was to be defended against "anarchistic" and "reactionary" attacks.[28] For many constitutionalists, this result was unsatisfactory. The congress ended "like the Hornberger shooting contest," commented Riehl.[29] An attempt by the German Association in Leipzig to set up a principled constitutionalist federation at the national level failed, however, in spite of support from Hesse-Darmstadt and Braunschweig.

The Citizens' Association in Kassel was chosen to be the steering committee of the National Association for the following year. It was assigned the administrative management of the association, which in general was limited to correspondence with state associations and, from February 1849, publishing the *Newsletter of the German National Association* as well. The committee had no power to set policy, and the association's organization was extremely loose. This was also quite typical of state-level federations of associations. They, too, had a comparatively loose structure and low level of organization. Institutional ties to parliamentary parties were almost unknown for constitutional associations. Relations between individual associations and the parliamentary deputies existed mostly at the personal level.

However, a lack of organization was felt to be a deficiency by some constitutionalists. Hence Riehl's complaints about conditions in Nassau: "What effect could an efficient organization of Nassau associations have had on the proceedings of the legislature, if we had *prepared in advance* the questions that were to deliberated in parliament, *debated them in advance*! Is our voice not the voice of the people? Thus some disastrous decisions have been made, simply because our party in the chamber [of deputies] lacked courage from the beginning and believed itself *without support from outside*."[30] As the party of the governing March ministries, constitutionalists had more difficulties than democrats in "organizing a party from the bottom up."[31]

With about 160 affiliated societies, the National Association remained well behind its democratic competition. Noticeable, too, was a low level of associational density. In general, the National Association remained limited to small- and medium-sized cities in northwestern, central, and southwestern Germany. Absent were the numerous Prussian associations as well as those of Bavaria and Württemberg, to name but the most important. The regional steering committees in Stuttgart and Nuremberg based their refusal to affiliate with the National Association on its lack of a declaration in favor of constitutionalism.

In view of the Prussian king's rejection of the imperial crown and against the backdrop of a struggle for acceptance of the imperial constitution, the question also arose for the National Association of whether to ally with the Central March Association. This triggered serious controversy at the "National Congress" that met in Frankfurt am Main on 14 May 1849 under the chairmanship of Heinrich von Sybel—a controversy which led in the end to the dissolution of the National Association. The poor attendance of deputies to the National Assembly at this congress was noticeable. Many constitutionalist-liberal deputies had already left the National Assembly. The Kassel steering committee attempted in vain to hold the National Association together. During the course of July, the group dissolved itself.

While in the southwestern and central German states, conservative forces striving to preserve the monarchical principle and the social and political status quo mostly joined constitutional associations or the Catholic Pius Associations and only seldom gathered in outspokenly conservative associations, conservatives in Prussia took another path. Prussian conservatives close to the *Kreuzzeitung* [the *Cross News*— from the Iron Cross on its masthead (ed.)] recognized the relationship between a constitutional system and party struggles, and developed from that a tactical view of political associations. As Ernst Ludwig von Gerlach wrote: "The greater the people's share in the direction of government, the more necessary is their grouping according to political tendencies, *in other words* the organization of political parties. The formation of a party has the purpose of uniting in common action all adherents of the general principles of a political tendency, thus bringing victory of this tendency over diverging ones."[32] From May 1848 onwards, conservative organizations, in the form of Prussian Associations and Patriotic Associations were created in Berlin and neighboring provinces. The "Association for the Preservation of the Rights of Landed Property and the Upholding of the Interests of All Classes of the People" served to represent the interests of Junker estate-owners.

The Association for King and Fatherland, founded in Berlin in July 1848 at the initiative of leading conservatives close to the *Kreuzzeitung* and the court camarilla, such as Leopold von Gerlach, Victor Aimé Huber, and Bismarck, was intended to set the stage for a coalition of all conservatives and the formation of a "party." It was not able to fulfill these ambitious goals to the extent desired, as conservatives also held different positions and, for example, the *Kreuzzeitung* and The Association for the Preservation of the Rights of Landed Property disagreed on some points. Prussian conservatism drew its strength especially from locally and regionally oriented interests, which balked at being organized in a party.

Finally, in May 1849, the General Committee of the United Monarchist-Conservative Associations was established, to which more than 200 associations belonged and which had connections to the conservative parliamentary party in the state parliament. The League of Loyalty to King and Fatherland, on the other hand, founded in the spring of 1849, was not a political association in the narrow sense of the term, having more of a conspiratorial—masonic nature. By the summer of 1849 there existed under various names more than 300 conservative associations with at least 60,000 members. On top of that came more than 250 military associations which, with the *Deutsche Wehrzeitung* [Germany Army News] as their mouthpiece, represented a decidedly counter-revolutionary mass movement and an independent force within the conservative camp.[33]

The Association for a Constitutional Monarchy and Religious Freedom established in Munich in May 1848, is a non-Prussian example of tendencies toward the formation of a conservative party. With its 1,600 members in Munich and approximately 60 affiliated associations, the Bavarian group remained well behind its Prussian counterparts, in terms of organization and activity as well. It was counted as one of the Catholic associations rather than a conservative one, but stood out among the Catholic groups by its openly political stance and pronounced loyalty to dynastic authority. The "Saxon Associations," "Protective Associations," "Associations for Order and Security," and usually veterans' groups as well were located in the conservative spectrum.

Catholic associations, generally named Pius Associations, provide a special case among political associations of the revolutionary era. Unlike all other political currents of the time, with their wide-ranging political aims, political Catholicism concentrated mostly on relations between church and state. As extra-parliamentary organizations, the Pius Associations strove to safeguard the interests of the Catholic Church in times of political and social change. In this context, religious freedom demanded by the Pius Associations meant corporate autonomy and independence of the church from the state.

The Pius Associations were often initiated and supported by "ultramontane"-anti-rationalist circles in the Catholic clergy. Among them, there was no clear view as to how far the Pius Associations should become politically active. The statutes of the Mainz association, founded in March 1848, clearly rejected general political tendencies. "Such objects of politics which do not touch on religious freedom are—as such topics will be discussed in citizens' meetings—excluded from association meetings."[34] On the other hand, the influential Catholic associations in the Prussian Rhine provinces and in Westphalia followed quite openly broader political aims. Especially the Cologne association was characterized by a general interest in politics and in sociopolitical questions, and the above-mentioned Association for a Constitutional Monarchy and Religious Freedom represented a decidedly political conservatism.

Like the other political associations, the Pius Associations also participated in election campaigns and political controversies during the revolutionary period, supported their candidates at elections, and maintained relationships to "their" parliamentary deputies and politicians. Thus, in March 1848, the Limburg association called for the formation of a Catholic association for the entire Duchy of Nassau, "in order to prevent the splitting of the votes of voters and electors, [and] to make it easier for Catholic voters and electors to fulfil their highly important duties through the naming of candidates enjoying the confidence of Catholic citizens."[35] Catholic associations were especially successful in organizing mass petitions to the National Assembly and parliaments of the individual German states. Sometimes circulating pre-printed resolutions, theirs was one of the biggest petition movements of the revolutionary period. After elections, however, Catholic association activity generally declined, and some associations even dissolved themselves.

The first Catholic Convention, which, following the initiative of the Mainz Pius Association, took the form of a gathering of Catholic associations in Mainz from 3 to 5 October 1848, was an important stage in the development of Catholic associations into a political party. The Pius Associations united at the national level to form the Catholic Association of Germany, with a rotating steering committee, that was to be located in Mainz until the next Catholic Convention. This was only a loose federation, with a steering committee to carry out current business and implement decisions; nonetheless, participation by deputies to the National Assembly delegates indicated a close relation between Catholic associations and the Catholic Club, an inter-party group in the *Paulskirche*. The Catholic Convention was also the starting point for a second wave of formations of Pius Associations. While the first half year saw the establishment of seventeen central associations with numerous branches, following the convention thirty main associations allied with the Mainz headquarters up to January 1849, and the numbers continued to rise.[36] With its 2,600 members and another 110 affiliated associations in May 1849, the central association in Breslau was probably one of the largest Catholic associations in Germany.[37] Regional examination indicates a shift from short-lived clubs in the spring of 1848 to more permanent organizations.

Still, the exact extent of Catholic associations is especially difficult to estimate. It is certainly true, however, that the movement was one of the largest extra-parliamentary organizations of the revolutionary period, with hundreds of associations. In the organization of Catholic associations, an influential main or central association played a decisive role. One larger inter-regional federation of Catholic associations was the Rhenish and Westphalian Pius Associations, which united in April 1849 under the leadership of the Cologne association.

Compared to other political currents, political Catholicism included the widest range of views. One can, however, discover regional distinctions. The Pius Associations of the Diocese of Limburg, under the influence of the anti-liberal and reactionary Moritz Lieber, and the Munich association displayed quite conservative traits, coupled with a strict traditionalism in religious matters. The Catholic associations in the Prussian Rhine province, on the other hand, often showed quite radical and democratic tendencies, most clearly in Trier and Koblenz, where the Catholic People's Association split on the question of whether to ally with the local democratic club. In July 1849, the Wiesbaden association even demanded "that the *Trier Pius Association*, which has recently become known for its political radicalism, be expelled from the federation of Pius Associations."[38]

This motion must be seen in the context of a public conflict in the summer of 1849 on the question of taking political positions, in which the Breslau association, which acted as steering committee for the Catholic Association of Germany accused the influential Cologne Pius Association of working against "both the general resolution [of the second Catholic Convention in Breslau] and the admonitions of His Holiness" in its political activity.[39] During the second Catholic Convention, held in Breslau, from 9-11 May 1849, the majority had expressly resolved: "The official participation of Catholic associations in *purely political issues* is totally out of the question ... The steering committee is instructed to ensure that individual associations respect this decision."[40]

This should not be misunderstood as a "withdrawal" from politics by Catholic political associations. Rather, it involved preparation for an expected government ban on associations. And, in fact, the "politicized" associations of the Rhineland suffered especially from repressive measures during the Reaction Era. Moreover, as the Rhenish example shows, political activity had proven to have ambivalent effects on Catholic associations, since it threatened to split their supporters along political lines. A retreat to ecclesiastical and educational affairs and to religious and charitable activity in the summer of 1849 favored the influence of the clergy on the Catholic associations and strengthened their conservative orientation.

At the start of the revolution, the organized labor movement in the German states was still in its inception. Only slowly did it take on programmatic profiles and organizational structures, which were, however, heterogeneous and diverse. Efforts to unite workers' associations were encumbered above all by internal differences on the one hand and, on the other, by opposition from portions of the middle class, who feared such groups were conspiring to carry out a "red revolution." As the factory workforce in the German states in 1848 was small in number and still in the earliest stages of development, the early labor movement had a strongly artisanal character. Local workers' associations developed against the background of a network of artisans' organizations, journeymen's clubs, and trade associations, but in contrast to such groups, they had sociopolitical and general political aims that were not specific to a particular occupation.

The Communist League had the most highly developed program. With the *Communist Manifesto* of February 1848, it offered the prospect of a socialist transformation of society. Early attempts by Karl Marx and the Cologne central office he headed to gain influence within the workers' organizations with the help of local affiliates of the League were generally unsuccessful. This was true even in Cologne itself, which had one of the largest workers' associations of the revolutionary period, which counted, for a while, 5,000 members. Its chairman, the physician Andreas Gottschalk, wrote on 26 March 1848 that "the name 'republic' is quite unpopular and the proletariat, at least here, is not strong enough to act on its own."[41] An appraisal of the situation by the Mainz association, which had been selected by the Communist Legue to be the "provisional central committee" of a federation of German workers' associations, was even more drastic. League member Johannes Schickel wrote to Karl Marx on 14 April 1848 that: "If a communist appeared here, he would certainly be stoned to death, even though these cattle do not even have the faintest idea of what communism is."[42]

Especially in the south and southwest, advocacy of guilds and other corporate institutions was widespread in workers' associations. At the Frankfurt General German Workers' Congress in August-September 1848, which arose from a journeymen's congress, Karl Georg Winkelblech, a trade school instructor from Kassel, got endorsement for his "federal system," which postulated the existence of common interests among masters and journeymen and saw in the "monied powers" their common enemy. Among Winkelblech's central demands were compulsory guilds and the governmental "organization of labor" through a "social parliament" and a "social ministry." The congress resolved further to establish a general German workers' association and elected a central executive, primarily from members of workers' associations in the Rhine-Main region.

The consequences of the September uprising in Frankfurt, in which members of the Frankfurt workers' association also took part, and Winkelblech's return to his trade school, however, considerably hindered the organizational efforts of the General German Workers' Association. An *Allgemeine Deutsche Arbeiter-Zeitung* [General German Workers' News] was also brought out by the "federalists," but only the first issue, of 4 January 1849, appeared. On 14 January 1849, a regional association of "federalist" workers' associations in the Rhine-Main area was finally established in Hanau.

It was Stephan Born's Workers' Fraternization that first succeeded in creating a lasting, independent national federation of workers' associations. On 11 April 1848, the Workers' Central Committee was formed in Berlin under his direction. Its program, passed in June, included among other things, demands for a minimum wage and limits on working hours, introduction of a progressive income tax and ending of indirect taxes, state care for invalids and "the helpless," free education for youth and an end to all restraints on "the movement of workers."[43] Parallel to the Frankfurt Workers' Congress, the Central Committee, together with Saxon and north German associations, organized a workers' congress, which endorsed self-help through production associations and mutual benefit funds: "We workers must help ourselves; that was the point of departure for the Berlin congress."[44]

However, like the Frankfurt congress, the Berlin congress avoided any confrontation with masters: "The General German Workers' Congress in Berlin does not assume an antagonism between masters and journeymen as preserved in the medieval guild system; for it, there are the only modern social antagonisms between capitalists and workers."[45] Under the direction of a central committee in Leipzig, acting as an independent executive body, the Workers' Fraternization was founded as a organization of workers' associations. The committee published a journal, *Die Verbrüderung* [The Fraternization]. The Workers' Fraternization was also strongly influenced by artisans' views.

The Workers' Fraternization quickly developed into a national federation of German workers' associations. At the workers' congress in Heidelberg on 28/29 January 1849, Stephan Born won out against Winkelblech, and most of the workers' associations in the southwest joined the Workers' Fraternization. Regional congresses in Hamburg (February 1849), Halle (March 1849) and Nuremberg (April 1849) were further stages in its development. In the spring of 1849, the Workers'

Fraternization had more than 15,000 members in about 170 workers' associations.[46] Thus, in comparison to other federations of associations in the revolutionary period, it achieved an astoundingly high level of organization, which compensated for the fact that there were in total fewer workers' associations than democratic, Catholic, or even constitutionalist ones.

Decisive for the organizational success of the Workers' Fraternization was its practical, sociopolitical orientation, especially its system of traveling assistance funds. However, the Workers' Fraternization, like the other groups, was not tightly organized. Rather, through contacts with regional and local associations and through *Die Verbrüderung*, the central committee encouraged solidarity and the formation of a common opinion. Regional and local associations, on the other hand, remained organizationally and programmatically independent; a homogeneous sociopolitical program was lacking among workers' associations.

The workers' associations were closely connected with the democratic movement during the revolutionary period. Joint memberships were common as was mutual support of activities, regular cooperation in federations of associations, and the establishment of joint committees at the local and regional levels. The political aims of the workers' associations did not differ fundamentally from those of the democrats, although because of their social demands and strong republicanism they often formed a radical element within the democratic "party." The organizations of the labor movement remained extraparliamentary in 1848–49; the labor movement had no parliamentary representatives. Nonetheless, the organizations of the labor movement supported the work of the National Assembly during the campaign for the Imperial Constitution.

A characteristic of workers' associations was particularly extreme fluctuations in membership. The Cologne association had 5,000 members in May 1848 and 120 at most in October; in Frankfurt the figure sank from 2,000 in May 1848 to 303 in July, only to rise again to 2,000 in September of that year. This was a reflection of the especially severe repressive measures to which these associations were subjected, as well as the travels of the journeymen who made up the largest part of the membership.

The party associations of the revolutionary period, which indeed developed into mass organizations, found their precedents above all in England and in Ireland. During consultations leading to the foundation of the Central March Association on 22 November 1848, Jacob Venedey used the examples of the Anti-Corn Law League, the Catholic Association, and the Reform Association.[47] In general, parallels were drawn over and over again with the mass mobilization of the English Chartist movement and its goals of a constitution with democratic franchise. Fergus O'Connor, the famed Chartist leader, was well known in German democratic and republican circles, and many articles on the history of the Chartists had been published. The Catholic associations saw the Catholic Association and the Irish Repeal Movement for ending the union between Ireland and Great Britain in particular as models for the establishment of associations and for initiating a petition movement. This went so far as to include a great respect for the charismatic leader of the Irish movement, Daniel O'Connell, and a positive view of associations by

Catholic publicists even in the *Vormärz*. Catholic associations and the petition movement in France in the 1840s, the *Association Catholique*, which demanded freedom of religion and education, were also often cited as models.

Structure, Distribution, Range of Activities

Research has definitely established that the political associations of the revolutionary period were a mass phenomenon involving hundreds of thousands of people. It is, however, very difficult to estimate the numbers of associations and their membership as many groups were short-lived and characterized by a fluctuating membership. Nonetheless, it is safe to say that the numbers involved have been underestimated in the past. While, for example, Paschen puts the number of conservative associations in Prussia at 50, new studies have found more than 300 narrowly defined conservative clubs and another 250 military associations.[48] The largest federation of associations in the period, the Central March Association, had, all by itself, over a thousand affiliated societies in the spring of 1849. In total, there were probably several thousands of political associations in the German states at the time. It is more difficult to establish membership figures, as these fluctuated greatly and dual memberships were widespread. An estimate of 800,000 people organized in political associations during the revolutionary period is, however, probably not too high.[49]

Democratic associations were the most widespread, followed by Catholic associations. In general, the constitutionalist liberals had clearly fewer associations, with a few regional exceptions. Only in Prussia were conservatives able to set up a network of associations worth mentioning, but it was a substantial one. The labor movement had the fewest associations and were the least densely spread during the revolutionary period, although they were especially prominent in their activity. In spite of the short-lived nature of many of these associations, the figures demonstrate, nonetheless, impressive political interest among the people and a high level of mobilization and politicization in 1848/49.

The social structure of political associations was broader than has previously been assumed. Not only the urban middle class, artisans, journeymen, and workers joined political associations; the rural population was also involved to a remarkable extent. In southwestern Germany, Lower Franconia, Thuringia, and Silesia, democrats in particular were successful in gaining extensive peasant support, and the majority of democratic associations were located in villages. However, the core membership of these associations was made up of small businessmen and artisans. Prominent among the leadership were intellectuals and members of the educated middle class; in the countryside, democratically-oriented village school teachers and pastors. Constitutionalist-liberal associations had a clearly bourgeois profile and were restricted mostly to the cities. Their membership consisted mainly of businessmen, civil servants, and master artisans. Conservative associations differed from liberal ones in that they tended to be more successful in gaining members from the ranks of small business, artisans, and even the lower classes.

Workers and journeymen made up the membership of the workers' associations, while the educated middle class and intellectuals played an important role in their executive committees, as was the case with the democrats. It is noteworthy that among the artisan members of workers' associations, certain trades dominated—particularly printers, shoemakers, tailors, and cabinet-makers. This is an indication of economic problems, especially in the so-called "mass crafts," but also of organizational experience and early trade union endeavors, for example, among the printers. The Pius Associations had quite a socially heterogeneous membership which ranged from the lower classes to the well-off bourgeoisie and also spread, to a considerable extent, into the countryside. Core membership of these groups, however, was made up of city dwellers, especially from the middle class and small business. The clergy often played a leading role in the Pius Associations, while state officials were found in that role much less frequently. This brief sketch indicates that in spite of a certain amount of overlapping, a social profile of the developing political parties was emerging. This was especially true of the labor movement and of the constitutional liberals and least true of the Catholic associations, in whose ranks the Catholic religion had an integrating effect across social and cultural barriers. Among the new and, for many contemporaries, most disturbing phenomena of political associations was female participation. Even in the *Vormärz* there had been women's associations, which supported political aims with charity work such as associations for the support of the Polish insurgents. The revolutionary period brought with it a considerable quantitative increase in this kind of activity and an extension of women's activities into new fields. A wide range of women's associations appeared, supporting in many ways male political efforts, taking on a complementary or encouraging function, and often creating free space for women's own activity as well. Included among these were women's associations that made flags for gymnastic clubs or civic guards, or those which encouraged the purchase of domestically produced goods.

Within the democratic political spectrum, women's associations were established with statutes, executive committees, and agendas. They, too, supported the political activities of the (male) democratic associations and fulfilled an important task in their helping persecuted democrats and their families. Furthermore, those taking part in meetings of such democratic women's associations are said to have read political newspapers and discussed current events. Even women's gymnastic societies were set up. It was certainly not by chance that women in the executives of such associations were especially likely to be related to or married to democratic men. Women's associations during the revolutionary period were able to achieve a respectable size, as for example the Mainz women's association Humania with 1,647 members in the summer of 1849. There were also associations in smaller communities including a democratic reading circle of rural women, "who bring to us milk, butter, and cheese in the market here," as one urban correspondent wrote.[50] Often female members of the free churches were founders of such associations, being accustomed to a freer and more equal role in their congregations.[51] Still, the associations did not strive for equal political rights for women.

Consideration was also given to allowing female participation in (male) democratic associations. Although there apparently never was formal membership for women, they were accepted as spectators at events and regular meetings of some democratic associations. In the democratic association in Mainz, for example, one hundred seats in the front rows were reserved for women. As Ludwig Bamberger later described it: "Over time we introduced the custom of allowing the female element in, and this was, understandably, as useful for our propaganda as it was pleasant. The ladies sat at first on the front benches, the executive's podium, and the speaker's platform. They did not participate actively in the meeting, but their passive assistance did its share."[52] For conservative contemporaries, women's political activity was dubious: "The major newspapers must be read regardless of what has to be done in the kitchen and cellar," criticized one commentator.[53] Nonetheless, there is evidence that women were present as spectators in the public events of the Catholic Conventions and at the congress of liberal constitutionalist associations in Kassel in November 1848. Especially remarkable is the resolution by the second Catholic Convention in Breslau to allow women as non-speaking members of Pius Associations. Such involvement was, however, extremely controversial in Catholic associations and generally women's activities were much more restricted to charity and social work than among the democrats.

Associations were not founded continually, but in successive waves. The first major boom took place in May–June 1848 in connection with elections for the Frankfurt National Assembly and the first democratic congress. A weaker wave followed between August and October which was succeeded by the largest wave in December–January and March–April 1849. Association congresses like the democratic congresses and the Catholic Conventions as well as calls for new associations had a signal effect. Furthermore, events such as elections or the campaign for the imperial constitution led to the establishment of new associations, and in reaction to victories of the counter-revolution there was occasionally an increase in the formation of associations.

In the winter of 1848/49, many associations were also established in rural areas, whereby it can be assumed that the seasonal cycle of farm work played a decisive role. New associations and related activity in rural communities became more common when there was little to do in the fields. As was reported of one association in rural Nassau at the end of October 1849: "Since longer evenings have encouraged the people to come together, to talk of common weals and woes, our democratic association has also sprung back to life, while during the summer, which the people of Nassau must use for their difficult struggle with nature to wring from their mountains the necessities of life, it just had a phantom existence."[54]

Very significant for the spread of political associations was the extent to which they managed to establish branches in rural areas. In this, the democrats were most successful, followed by the Pius Associations. Regional integration of political associations also depended to a great extent on establishing such village associations. Associations therefore showed quite varied density and were characterized by a distinct regionalization. Overall, there were dense zones of political associations in a broad belt from Silesia in the east, through Saxony, the Thuringian states, Franconia and Hesse to the Rhineland in the west as well as in the southwest, including the left bank of the Rhine north to the middle Rhine region. Throughout the north, by contrast, there were only a few associations, generally restricted to the larger cities. The federations of association of the revolutionary period did not, in general, extend into Austria, and where ties did develop to Austrian associations, they generally remained weak. An exception to this were the Catholic associations in Germany, which included a number of Austrian associations. This was an expression of the Pius Associations' greater- German sympathies, in contrast to other political currents. Equally, it indicates an increasing isolation of Austria within association networks and flows of communication.

Political party "strongholds" also developed. Democratic associations were concentrated in Saxony (280 associations, 75,000 members in April 1849),[55] in the Rhine-Main region, in Rhine-Hesse (120 associations, 14,000 members in May 1849),[56] and in the Palatinate (173 associations, up to 18,000 members in April 1849),[57] in Thuringia, Baden, Lower Franconia (306 associations at the beginning of July 1849)[58] and in Hohenzollern. Apart from these, there were also relatively dense networks in Upper Hesse, Middle Franconia, Silesia, parts of the Rhine province and in Württemberg, especially in the Jagst and Neckar districts. In these regions, democratic associations had a strong presence in the villages. In large portions of northern Germany, in Lower Bavaria and in Prussia's eastern provinces, especially Pomerania, however, democratic associations were not able to establish a foothold. In a report to the second democratic congress in Berlin in October 1848, a delegate expressed his resignation at the situation in Mecklenburg: "The Mecklenburgers are said to be political barbarians. It is not quite that bad, but we are certainly far behind,"[59] and a Schleswig-Holstein reporter even wrote: "Nowhere else is the situation so poor as in Schleswig-Holstein."[60]

Workers' associations, because of their limited numbers, were not able to achieve blanket coverage, but did have their strongholds. The center of the labor movement during the revolutionary period, as indicated by the density of associations and their activity, was located in Saxony, with 55 local associations in total. This was followed by Middle and Lower Franconia, the Rhine province, Württemberg, and the region between Hamburg/Holstein and Hanover/Braunschweig. As a rule, the labor movement was concentrated in cities and manufacturing regions.

Catholic association strongholds included, on the one hand, Silesia, with its influential central association in Breslau (110 branches in 1849) and, on the other, Austria, with the large associations of Linz and Vienna. The numerous associations in Baden, however, were apparently very short-lived. Other concentrations of Catholic associations were in the Rhine province, Westphalia, in Rhine-Hesse and in Nassau (about 50 associations in Rhine-Hesse and Nassau in spring 1849) as well as in Old Bavaria (about 60 affiliates of the main association in Munich). It is difficult to estimate the regional spread of the constitutionalists, who, in April 1849, had a strong presence particularly in Saxony (about 50 associations), the Hessian states including Nassau (about 70 associations), Braunschweig (about 20 associations), Baden (about 30 associations), Württemberg, the Rhine Province, and Westphalia

(74 associations in autumn 1848).[61] Conservative associations were widespread in Prussia's eastern provinces, especially Pomerania, but there were few of them in the Rhine province and in Westphalia.

In their strongholds, political associations often achieved a remarkably high level of mobilization and very large memberships. This was especially true of democratic associations. The Saxon democratic Fatherland Association in Crimmitschau had 1,200 members from a population of 7,000 in April 1849 and in Lichtenstein-Callenberg 540 members from a population of 2,300 in September 1848—that is 66 percent and 90 percent of adult males respectively.[62] The figures are similar for Rhine-Hesse. Ludwig Bamberger could quite justifiably state in his New Year's speech to the democratic association in Mainz in 1848/49: "Our entire state is a democratic association. The fortunate predisposition of the people, which we have met everywhere, has certainly made the greatest contribution to this fantastic blooming of political life in our province. Certainly, however, this predisposition would not have taken on its solid and lively form without our energetic work. There is no longer a difference between city and country. Everywhere the same political ability, everywhere the same enlightened conditions, and all this increased hundredfold in its effectiveness by a closely organized connection of all elements."[63] In the canton of Nieder-Olm in Rhine-Hesse, there were 19 democratic associations with altogether 1,400 members from a population of 19,700 in April 1849. The association in Worms had 1,300 members from a population of 9,450 in February 1849, and in Ober-Olm, there were 256 members of the democratic association out of 1,300 inhabitants in April 1849.[64]

This enormous success in mobilization and organization achieved by early political associations was often based on regional or local traditions, influenced by historical experience—for example, French rule on the left bank of the Rhine— or by the consequences of economic and cultural ties. These defined the special political culture of a region and formed different regional identities, often quite distinct from one another. Typical of this were, for example, anti-Prussian sentiments in the Rhineland, which were tied to a feeling of cultural superiority—encouraging a tendency towards political opposition. Among the inhabitants of Rhine-Hesse, this attitude was directed towards the inhabitants of the core provinces of Hesse-Darmstadt on the right bank of the Rhine. "You don't have to go to Pomerania, you only have to go to Darmstadt to convince yourself of the low level of political life that still exists in certain parts of the German fatherland," wrote the *Mainzer Zeitung* in 1848.[65]

Early political associations drew their integrative power to a great extent from these regional identities. The clashes between such identities, however, hampered cooperation and establishment of political programs at an inter-regional level. For these reasons as well, to stay with the Hessian example, the democratic associations of Hesse-Darmstadt were only united at the state level relatively late. Together with religion, economic factors, social structures and cultural orientation, local and regional identities and traditions formed important structural dimensions of socio-moral milieus, which provided a framework for political actors.[66] Political associations in Germany arose on the basis of such milieus and dense networks of relations within a communal and regional environment. They were the preconditions for the expansion of party organization. These milieus were not static, evolving instead through social interaction and experience, whereby their fundamental patterns proved to be long-lived.

Membership in a political association often meant more than shared political convictions. Especially Catholic and democratic associations, as well as the organizations of the labor movement, tended to become all-encompassing emotionally laden, and ideologically shaped experiential communities in which sociability and a culture of celebration formed important aspects of everyday organizational life. This broad community ideal went as far as to include settling personal disagreements by association mediators. "Whoever has a complaint or a problem seeks advice or help in the association. All personal self-cultivation and self-expression, now mostly directed toward political aspirations, is based on this. Thus organized democracy has become a true church."[67]

Democrats often saw themselves as "brothers" and as "members of a family." Quasi-religious traits, as in the quote above, were especially prominent in celebrations and other events sponsored by the associations. The memorial services for Robert Blum organized by democratic associations throughout Germany are an example of this. Local democratic associations in urban areas were often part of a network of organizations, which also included gymnastic clubs, democratic reading circles and democratic women's associations. Democratic associations might meet regularly in taverns, that were an established part of the democratic milieu, their owners often association members.

The structure of the national federations was loose, decentral, and federalist for all political currents. Only the more radical democrats endeavored more to form a strict, centralized organization. The attempt of the Democratic Central Committee to achieve a real centralization of the affiliated associations failed, however. As a rule, the emerging party organization consisted of a national umbrella association to which state or district federations or individual associations belonged. Established leading committees, as with the Central March Association and the Democratic Central Committee, were the exception. Generally, federations of associations were "led" by set or rotating steering committees, whose members came from one local club. These leading organs only had administrative or executive powers. In this respect, coordinating and programmatic initiatives of the central committee of the Central March Association went further than those of other federations. The general meeting of all affiliated associations was most likely to be the decision-making body in all early party organizations. The founding congress of the National Association and the second Catholic Congress in Breslau show, however, that majority decisions could not be enforced in the face of resistance by powerful affiliated associations: Either individual associations threatened, as with the National Association, to withdraw their affiliation, or they simply ignored the resolutions.

State and district organization was often tighter. The degree of centralization differed considerably, both by region and by political tendency. Federations of democratic clubs were the best organized, conservative ones the weakest. Especially tightly organized, for instance, was the democratic district federation in Rhine-Hesse, which had an additional, cantonal level of organization, with cantonal federations, cantonal conventions, and cantonal statutes. This district federation was headed by a steering committee in Mainz, that later evolved into the democratic provincial committee. This committee would organize the march of armed units into the Palatinate during the campaign for the imperial constitution. Bamberger later quite justifiably called this committee "a sort of people's government."[68] But in Rhine-Hesse as well, the regional convention had final decision-making powers, not the central office or the steering committee.

Weak organizational structure was due to problems of communication and techniques of organization but also to the self-understanding and self-esteem of the individual associations. Even the tone of a letter from the Upper Hesse democratic regional central office raised the ire of some associations: "Could not these demands serve as a perfect model for a regimental command?" was the ironic comment.[69] Local associations, regardless of political tendency, generally placed great value on their independence (in as far as they were not branches of larger groups) and were very sensitive about seeming to be under the tutelage of the central office of a federation of associations. For such reasons, or because they had not yet committed themselves politically, many associations did not join a federation. A loose, decentral, and regionalistic federal structure therefore suited political associations of the revolutionary era very well.

The organizational level of federations of association varied considerably. In any case, it was not membership in a certain federation, but rather the political standpoint of the association itself, which defined its affiliation to a political "party" in the eyes of many contemporaries. The fact that many associations were short-lived, and their activities very different, makes precise statements difficult. Level of organization was generally highest in district federations, which were often able to include all political associations of a curtain current and achieve a considerable echo at regional conventions. For example, more than 85 percent of affiliated associations sent delegates to the regional conventions of Rhine-Hessian democrats. At the national level, on the other hand, level of organization was clearly lower. It was probably highest for the Workers' Fraternization and the Catholic Association of Germany. In the Central March Association, conflicts between republicans and moderate democrats hindered a more extensive participation of all democratic associations. The National Association probably had the lowest level of organization, as it seems that less than a third of all constitutionalist associations joined.

Democratic associations also had the best connections to parliamentary deputies and their caucuses. Only in the Central March Association was this connection institutionalized, although as a matter of principle each federation sought to establish relations with sympathetic parliamentary deputies. Both in the National Assembly as well as in the parliaments of the individual states, deputies quickly formed parliamentary caucuses, which soon established programs and instituted party discipline. Programmatic and organizational consolidation generally followed the establishment of extra-parliamentary organizations. As, in the course of the revolution, political parties were increasingly differentiated, they competed with each other in new elections and in by-elections. Winning elections came to require the support of a political organization and the regional press.

Deputies' view of their own role thus changed—they felt themselves under greater obligation to their constituency and presented accounts of their activities at public meetings. The various party associations organized campaigns for "their" candidates. At lower levels of political representation, municipal government for example, they strove to have their own candidates elected. The extension of the franchise in 1848 thus proved to be an engine of party formation. Campaign organization—up to detailed campaign instructions—was furthest developed among the democrats.

Petitions to the legislatures of the individual states and to the National Assembly, increasingly initiated and organized in mass form by the associations, also intensified relations with deputies and their caucuses. Such organized petitions made up a considerable share of all petitions received by state parliaments and the National Assembly. This was a way for extra-parliamentary organizations to support and legitimate arguments presented in the parliaments. Especially successful in this respect were Catholic associations and the democrats. Petition movements initiated by political organizations marked the beginning of the agitation of political parties and of mass mobilization on certain controversial subjects.

The press played a decisive role in the interaction between parliamentary caucuses and extra-parliamentary organizations and the formation of proto political parties. Freedom of the press, and an increased demand for the latest news, led to the appearance of countless newspapers. For the first time, unrestricted reporting was possible throughout Germany and there existed a broad, interested public. While most of these newspapers did not last very long, still they contributed to the development of a political press. As many from the lower classes, especially in rural districts, were illiterate, the reading of newspaper reports out loud was an important aspect of the meetings of many political associations. Newspapers thus increased the attractiveness of associations, especially in the country, where they were often the only source of current news. Newspapers often became "organs" of party organizations, in that they printed statements and reports of association events. In this way, they could be used for the communication of different associations of the "party" with each other, for the party's self-representation in the public sphere, for election campaigns, and for the process of reaching agreement about political strategies and issues. Newspapers made possible permanent ties between associations in the first place and the rise of proto-parties. Such party organs influenced the policy of "their" party associations though their articles to a great extent, and it was not by chance that many editors held leading positions in political associations.

Attempts by party associations to bring out their own publications, such as the *Newsletter of the German National Association*, were, on the other hand, generally less successful. Many party newspapers, in the form of newsletters, arose in a parliamentary context. Thus, for example, some parliamentary caucuses in the Frankfurt National Assembly put out parliamentary newsletters in an attempt to influence public opinion.[70] It was not uncommon for newspapers to be formed as both a business venture and as a mouthpiece of a certain political current, so that even the name of the newspaper was used synonymously with a certain "party." In most cases, however, newspapers developed into party organs only in the course of the process of political differentiation—not least because this could also prove economically advantageous in association strongholds. Occasionally newspapers included their function as organ of an association in the title page.

It proved helpful for a party association to have connections to a number of newspapers. Because newspapers were still largely regional in nature, this was especially important for national federations of associations in order to reach a wider audience. A good example of this was the Central March Association, whose central office put together a list of 257 newspapers in February 1849 that were willing to print association statements, 53 of which had already published such statements.[71] The list was incomplete, however, and it seems that democratic-oriented newspapers and member association also printed statements of the Central March Association on their own initiative. The success of the Central March Association was doubtless due to its dense network of mostly regional publications. Constitutionalist liberals also recognized quite early the value of newspapers in party formation, like the Elberfeld Constitutional Club, which proposed in May 1848 that associations of the same standpoint should create a "constitutional-monarchist party" through mutual subscription to their publications.[72]

A Look at Future Developments

Political associations became an object of renewed intensive police surveillance even during the revolutionary period. Liberal March ministries banned oppositional democratic associations. The democratic associations in Baden were prohibited on 22 July 1848, and in the neighboring Grand Duchy of Hesse such a ban was at least given consideration. The September uprising in Frankfurt in 1848 gave rise to the edict by the Reich ministries of the interior and justice of 3 October 1848 and a strengthening of surveillance measures.[73] After the failed campaign for the imperial constitution, these measures were expanded to generalized prohibitions of all political associations, not just the democrats or the workers' associations, as happened, for example, in Bavaria in February 1850 and in Hesse-Darmstadt in October 1850. In July 1854, in accordance with a resolution of the German Confederation, associations were forbidden whose aims did not correspond to existing laws or which endangered public order and safety.[74]

Of equal consequence to such prohibitions was a strict police surveillance of political associations and restriction of their activities. This included limits on rights of assembly and freedom of the press, prohibition of associations maintaining relations with each other, and restrictions on the franchise. Without a free press, a free political discourse, without agitation possibilities and united action by like-minded associations, political associations lost all reason to exist. This became especially clear with those Pius Associations which, after the second Catholic Convention in Breslau, had stayed clear of general political discussion and activity. Either they began to resemble even more traditional church associations or they wasted away and finally dissolved themselves as they had been deprived of the basis of their public effectiveness.

It would, however, be wrong to put prohibitions and decline at the end of an account of party formation in the revolutionary era without mentioning continuities and new departures. Against a background of long-term developments, prominence should rather be given to the formation of structures of political communication at the national level, the beginnings of a political mass society and the acceptance in principle of party organization as a political tool even within the conservative camp. In its basic features, the party system of the revolutionary period retained a defining role for parties and parliament in Germany well into the twentieth century.

It was especially organizational experience in political associations in 1848/49 which had a long-term effect. The "forty-eighters" were no "lost generation." The year 1848 was rather an era of upheaval which made possible the rise of a new political elite. Thus, for example, the political careers of many delegates to the National Assembly were only interrupted during the period of reaction, not terminated. Revolutionary experience distinguished an entire generation of politicians in the era of the foundation of the German Empire. Political milieus and networks on which political associations in 1848/49 were based proved to be remarkably stable. They survived the reaction era and formed the starting point for a rebirth of political parties at the beginning of the 1860s. Ludwig Bamberger reported in his memoirs on the new start in Rhine-Hesse: "The party organization, which we had created before, survived in its tradition the reactionary period of the [18]50s. As I, after eighteen years, campaigned for the customs parliament under quite different conditions and with a totally different political tendency, it was the foundations of those old associations and their methods which contributed to a great extent to my success and thus brought me the fruits of a labor long past … "[75]

Liberal and democratic party organizations which appeared again in the new conditions of the 1860s, while surrendering the old model of a federation of associations in favor of a centralized organizational structure, were still based on networks at the regional and local levels. Noticeable in this context was the remarkable continuity of associations in the labor movement: almost half of the new associations of 1860-64 had predecessors in the revolutionary period.[76] Liberals and democrats often made explicit references to the imperial constitution of 1849 and to the *Paulskirche*. In other respects, continuity was clear, well into the second half of the century: a dislike of strict organization remained characteristic of liberal parties, while democrats preferred stronger organizational structures. Political Catholicism retained, even in the German Empire of 1871, its combination of parliamentary caucus and extra-parliamentary association.

However, political Catholicism in 1848 had not achieved the unity and strength of purpose that it would have during the *Kulturkampf*. The Pius Associations were not yet the party associations of the majority of Catholics. The democratic association in Mainz was able to point out spitefully in December 1848 that it had twice as many Catholic members as the local Pius Association.[77] This would change in the following years. Quite early on, contemporaries came to see political Catholicism as the "winner" of the revolution. Ludwig August von Rochau's judgment is representative of many: "Ever since the March revolution of 1848 has put Germany's public affairs in motion, nobody has made better use of the time and the opportunity than the Catholic Church."[78] In the 1860s, political Catholicism, supported by its association network, was able, through its labor policies, to expand its voter reservoir. The social heterogeneity of Catholic associations as well as supporters among the Catholic rural population, remained defining characteristics of the Center Party.

Conservatism formed itself during the revolution of 1848/49 into a party organization of remarkable strength and one with an electoral clientele that included members of the lower classes. Even during the revolutionary period, conservatives gained support in the military and veterans' associations, which increased further in the course of the wars of German unification, forming an anti-revolutionary force. Among the long-term "losers," on the other hand, were the democrats. While in southwestern Germany democratic parties re-formed in the 1860s, they were never able to regain their old strength. This related to the total collapse of bourgeois republicanism as a political force and the disappearance of interest in plebiscitary-democratic concepts.[79] This development is perhaps one of the most important and significant discontinuities resulting from the failure of the revolution. The democrats were also the losers in the process of the formation of the German Empire. From this second blow, the democratic parties never recovered. In the long run, they could only maintain a political presence in alliance with the liberals or the social democrats.

Notes

1. *Frankfurter Gemeinnützige* Chronik 5, No.7 (1845): 53, quoted in Ralf Roth, *Stadt und Bürgertum in Frankfurt am Main. Ein besonderer Weg von der ständischen zur modernen Bürgergesellschaft 1760-1914* (Munich, 1996), 323.

2. Cf. Thomas Nipperdey, "Verein als soziale Struktur im späten 18. und frühen 19. Jahrhundert," in *Gesellschaft, Kultur, Theorie* (Göttingen 1976), 174-205, here 174.

3. Carola Lipp, "Verein als politisches Handlungsmuster. Das Beispiel des württembergischen Vereinswesens von 1800 bis zur Revolution von 1848-1849," in Étienne François (ed.), *Geselligkeit, Vereinswesen und bürgerliche Gesellschaft in Frankreich, Deutschland und der Schweiz, 1750-1850* (Paris 1986), 275-97, here, 275.

4. Wolfgang Hardtwig, "Strukturmerkmale und Entwicklungstendenzen des Vereinswesens in Deutschland 1789-1848," *Historische Zeitschrift* Beiheft, N.S. 9, (1984): 11-54, here 49.

5. Cornelia Foerster, *Der Preß- und Vaterlandsverein von 1832/33. Sozialstruktur und Organisationsformen der bürgerlichen Bewegung in der Zeit des Hambacher Festes* (Trier, 1982), 181.

6. Cf. Dieter Langewiesche, "Die Anfänge der deutschen Parteien. Partei, Fraktion und Verein in der Revolution von 1848/49," *Geschichte und Gesellschaft* 4 (1978): 324-61, here, 328-29.

7. Cf. Dieter Langewiesche, "Die politische Vereinsbewegung in Würzburg und in Unterfranken in den Revolutionsjahren 1848/49," *Jahrbuch für fränkische Landesforschung* 37 (1977): 195–233.
8. In Manfred Botzenhart, *Deutscher Parlamentarismus in der Revolutionszeit 1848-1850* (Düsseldorf, 1977), 324ff.; these have been classified as democratic attempts at organization.
9. *Rheinisches Volksblatt* (Darmstadt) 37, 25 March 1848, emphasis in the original.
10. *Nassauische Allgemeine Zeitung* (Wiesbaden) 168, 18 July 1849.
11. Letter of Friedrich Theodor Vischer to David Strauß of 3 April 1849, in: A. Rapp (ed.), *Briefwechsel zwischen David Strauß und Friedrich Theodor Vischer* (Stuttgart, 1952), Vol. 1, 225–26.
12. Democratic flyer (Trier), 2-5 October 1848, quoted in Langewiesche, "Die Anfänge der deutschen Parteien," 340.
13. *Mainzer Zeitung* 166, 16 June 1848.
14. *Mainzer Zeitung* 300, 11 November 1848, "Der zweite Demokraten-Kongreß VI." For the committee report, see Gerhard Becker, "Die 'soziale Frage' auf dem zweiten demokratischen Kongreß 1848," *Zeitschrift für Geschichtswissenschaft* 15 (1967): 260–80, here, 273–75.
15. According to the Mainz delegate and provisional chairman of the congress, Ludwig Bamberger, *Mainzer Zeitung* 300, 11 November 1848.
16. *Wage, Deutsche Reichstagsrundschau*, 1848 3rd issue (Stadt- und Universitätsbibliothek Frankfurt a.M. S 25/169 [3]), 36.
17. In the lithographed "Verzeichnis der Vereine in Deutschland, welche sich bis zum 31 März 1849 dem Central-März-Vereine angeschlossen haben" a total of 951 associations are listed: Bundesarchiv Außenstelle Frankfurt (BAF) Zsg 9/1131. This list is, however, not complete. Cf. Michael Wettengel, "Der Centralmärzverein und die Entstehung des deutschen Parteiwesens während der Revolution von 1848/49," *Jahrbuch zur Liberalismus-Forschung* 3 (1991): 34–81, esp. 43.
18. BAF ZSg 9/1131.
19. *Neue Deutsche Zeitung* (Frankfurt a.M.) 94, 21 April 1849, reprinted in: Günter Hildebrandt (ed.), *Opposition in der Paulskirche. Reden, Briefe und Berichte kleinbürgerlich-democratischer Parlamentarier 1848/49* (East Berlin, 1981), 300.
20. BAF DB 54/74 (RMI), fol. 14rs communication of 11 October 1848.
21. *Neue Würzburger Zeitung* 154, 3 June 1848, quoted in Langewiesche, "Die politische Vereinsbewegung in Würzburg und Unterfranken," 209.
22. Paul Wentzcke and Wolfgang Klötzer (eds.), *Deutscher Liberalismus im Vormärz. Heinrich von Gagern, Briefe und Reden 1815-184*, (Göttingen, 1959), 133.
23. *Nassauische Allgemeine Zeitung* (Wiesbaden) 214, 19 November 1848.
24. Joseph Hansen and Heinz Boberach (eds.), *Rheinische Briefe und Akten zur Geschichte der politischen Bewegung 1830-1850*, 2 vols in 3 (Cologne and Bonn, 1919–76) Vol. 2 pt. 2, 41.
25. *Nassauische Allgemeine Zeitung* (Wiesbaden) 81, 5 April 1849.
26. *Darmstädter Journal* 54, 5 May 1848.
27. *Constitutionelle Club-Zeitung* (Berlin) 19, 24 June 1848, quoted in: Hartwig Gebhardt, *Revolution und liberale Bewegung. Die nationale Organisation der konstitutionellen Partei in Deutschland 1848/49* (Hamburg, 1974), 35.
28. *Kurze geschichtliche Darstellung der Gründung des Nationalen Vereins auf dem 3., 4. und 5. Novbr. 1848 zu Cassel stattgehabten Congresse von Abgeordneten politischer Vereine Deutschlands* (Kassel, 1848), 21.
29. *Nassauische Allgemeine Zeitung* (Wiesbaden) 207, 11 November 1848.
30. Ibid., 214, 19 November 1848, emphasis in original.
31. Ibid., 132, 6 June 1849.
32. *Neue Preußische Zeitung* ("*Kreuzzeitung*") (Berlin) Supp. 2 53, 31 August 1848, "Die Bildung einer konservativen Partei und der Verein für König und Vaterland," quoted in: Botzenhart, *Deutscher Parlamentarismus in der Revolutionszeit*, 392. Emphasis in the original.
33. See Eckhard Trox, *Militärischer Konservatismus. Kriegervereine und "Militärpartei" in Preußen zwischen 1815 und 1848/49* (Stuttgart, 1990), 289–90; Wolfgang Schwentker, *Konservative Vereine und Revolution in Preußen 1848/49. Die Konstituierung des Konservatismus als Partei* (Düsseldorf, 1988) 321–22.

34. Statutes of the Pius Association of Mainz, 1848, § 11, reprinted in: Ernst Heinen, *Katholizismus und Gesellschaft. Das katholische Vereinswesen zwischen Revolution und Reaktion (1848/49-1853/54)* (Idstein, 1993), 79-81, here 81.

35. "Katholiken Nassau's," Limburg, 23, March 1848, reprinted in: H.H. Schwedt, "Die katholische Kirche nach der Säkularisation," in *Herzogtum Nassau 1806-1866*, (Wiesbaden, 1981), 275-82, here 279.

36. Dom- und Dözesanarchiv Mainz Abt. 41/II.3; these included four Austrian central associations. Cf. Franz Schnabel, *Der Zusammenschluß des politischen Katholizismus in Deutschland im Jahre 1848*, (Heidelberg, 1910), 45.

37. See P. Mazura, *Die Entwicklung des politischen Katholizismus in Schlesien von seinen Anfängen bis zum Jahre 1880*, (Breslau, 1925), 8ff., 15-16. Equally extensive or even larger were the Austrian associations, especially in Vienna and Linz; cf. Heinen, *Katholizismus und Gesellschaft*, 30.

38. *Nassauische Allgemeine Zeitung* (Wiesbaden) 178, 29 July 1849, emphasis in the original.

39. *Kölnische Zeitung* 145, 19 June 1849, quoted in Heinen, *Katholizismus und Gesellschaft*, 66; cf. also, Jürgen Herres, *Städtische Gesellschaft und katholische Vereine im Rheinland 1840-1870* (Essen, 1996), 311.

40. *Katholische Sonntagsblätter zur Belehrung und Erbauung* (Mainz) 37, 16 September 1849, emphasis in the original.

41. Andreas Gottschalk to Moses Hess in Brussels, Cologne, 26 March 1848, in Hans Fenske (ed.), *Vormärz und Revolution 1840-1849* (Darmstadt, 1976), 275.

42. *Der Bund der Kommunisten. Dokumente und Materialien, Vol. I: 1836-1849,* (East Berlin, 1970), 754. In his *Neue Rheinische Zeitung* [New Rhineland News] Marx sought, above all, to advance the democratic movement and introduced coverage of the labor movement only at the beginning of 1849.

43. Program of the Berlin Workers' Central Committee, June 1848, reprinted in Fenske, *Vormärz und Revolution*, 312-13.

44. Central Committee circular to all workers and workers' associations in Germany, Leipzig, 18 September 1848, reprinted in Horst Schlechte (ed.), *Die Allgemeine Deutsche Arbeiterverbrüderung 1848-1850. Dokumente des Zentralkomitees für die deutschen Arbeiter in Leipzig* (Weimar, 1979), 338-40, here 339.

45. Ibid.

46. Frohlinde Balser, *Sozial-Demokratie 1848/49-1863. Die erste deutsche Arbeiterorgnisation "Allgemeine deutsche Arbeiterverbrüderung" nach der Revolution*, 2 vols., 2nd edition (Stuttgart, 1965), Vol. 1, 72ff.

47. Diary of Moritz Hallbauer, in Ludwig Bergsträsser (ed.), *Das Frankfurter Parlament in Briefen und Tagebücher* (Frankfurt, 1929), 149-322, here 167.

48. Cf. Joachim Paschen, *Demokratische Vereine und preußischer Staat. Entwicklung und Unterdrückung der demokratischen Bewegung während der Revolution von 1848/49* (Munich 1977), 90-91, with Schwentker, *Konservative Vereine und Revolution*, 321-22, and Trox, *Militärischer Konservatismus*, 23-24, 289-90, who also points out that Paschen's figures for Catholic and democratic associations may well be incorrect.

49. Cf. Hans Fenske, *Deutsche Parteiengeschichte. Von den Anfängen bis zur Gegenwart* (Paderborn, 1994) 77-78.

50. *Mainzer Zeitung* 67, 20 March 1849.

51. See Sylvia Paletschek, *Frauen und Dissens. Frauen im Deutschkatholizismus und in den freien Gemeinden 1841-1852* (Göttingen, 1990).

52. Ludwig Bamberger, *Erinnerungen*, ed. Paul Nathan (Berlin, 1899), 80.

53. *Nassauische Allgemeine Zeitung (*Wiesbaden) 241, 21 December 1848.

54. *Freie Zeitung* (Wiesbaden) 259, 31 October 1849.

55. Rolf Weber, *Die Revolution in Sachsen 1848/49* (East Berlin, 1970), 251.

56. Michael Wettengel, *Die Revolution von 1848/49 im Rhein-Main-Raum: Politische Vereine und Revolutionsalltag im Großherzogtum Hessen, Herzogtum Nassau und in der Freien Stadt Frankfurt* (Wiesbaden, 1989), 335.

57. Michael Wettengel, "Das liberale und demokratische Vereinswesen in der Pfalz während der Revolution von 1848/49," *Jahrbuch zur Geschichte von Stadt und Landkreis Kaiserslautern* 22/23 (1984/85): 73-90, here 77-78.
58. Langewiesche, "Die politische Vereinsbewegung in Würzburg und in Unterfranken," 217, 232-33.
59. Hauptstaatsarchiv Düsseldorf Reg. Düsseldorf 8806, *Verhandlungen des zweiten demokratischen Congresses zu Berlin, Beilage der Volksblätter* (Berlin), 9.
60. Ibid., 8.
61. With the exception of the Rhine province and Westphalia, figures are for April 1849. See Gebhardt, *Revolution und liberale Bewegung*, 96ff.; for associations in Hesse and Nassau, Wettengel, *Die Revolution von 1848/49 im Rhein-Main-Raum*, 363 ff.; for the Rhine Province and Westphalia Marcel Seyppel, *Die Demokratische Gesellschaft in Köln 1848/49. Städtische Gesellschaft und Parteientstehung während der bürgerlichen Revolution* (Cologne, 1991), 161.
62. Weber, *Die Revolution in Sachsen*, 252.
63. *Mainzer Zeitung* 3, 4 January 1849.
64. Wettengel, *Die Revolution von 1848/49 im Rhein-Main-Raum*, 297.
65. *Mainzer Zeitung* 211, 31 July 1848.
66. On the term milieu, see Rainer Lepsius, "Parteiensystem und Sozialstruktur. Zum Problem der Demokratisierung der deutschen Gesellschaft," in: Gerhard A. Ritter (ed.), *Die Deutschen Parteien vor 1918* (Cologne, 1973), 56-80; more recently also Michael Vester et. al, *Soziale Milieus im gesellschaftlichen Strukturwandel. Zwischen Integration und Ausgrenzung* (Cologne, 1993) 124ff.
67. *Mainzer Zeitung* 339, 27 December 1848.
68. Bamberger, *Erinnerungen*, 157.
69. *Wetterauer Volksblatt* (Friedberg) 8, 27 January 1849.
70. Langewiesche, "Die Anfänge der deutschen Parteien," 335-36; Ludwig Bergsträsser, "Entstehung und Entwicklung der Parteikorrespondenzen in Deutschland im Jahre 1848/49," *Zeitungswissenschaft* 8, no. 1 (15 January 1933): 12-25; for a review of the literature see Martin Henkel and Rolf Taubert, *Die deutsche Presse 1848-1850. Eine Bibliographie* (Munich, 1986).
71. BAF ZSg 8/33, No. 23, "Verzeichniß."
72. *Neue Rheinische Zeitung* (Cologne) 4, 4 June 1848.
73. See Wolfram Siemann, *"Deutschlands Ruhe, Sicherheit und Ordnung." Die Anfänge der politischen Polizei 1806-1866* (Tübingen, 1985), 226ff., 232ff., 357ff., 407, 429.
74. "Bundesbeschluß über Maßregeln zur Aufrechterhaltung der gesetzlichen Ordnung und Ruhe im Deutschen Bunde, insbesondere das Vereinswesen betreffend, vom 13 Juli 1854," reprinted in: Ernst Rudolf Huber (ed.), *Dokumente zur deutschen Verfassungsgeschichte*, Vol. 2 of *Deutsche Verfassungsdokumente 1851-1900*, 3rd edition (Stuttgart, 1986), 7-8; cf. Fenske, *Deutsche Parteiengeschichte*, 81-82.
75. Bamberger, *Erinnerungen*, 79.
76. See Offermann, "Die regionale Ausbreitung der frühen deutschen Arbeiterbewegung," 445ff.; Andreas Biefang, *Politisches Bürgertum in Deutschland 1857-1868. Nationale Organisationen und Eliten*, (Düsseldorf, 1994), 431ff.
77. *Mainzer Zeitung* 320, 5 December 1848.
78. Ludwig Augst von Rochau, *Grundsätze der Realpolitik. Angewendet auf die staatlichen Zustände Deutschlands*. pt. 2 (from 1869), edited by Hans-Ulrich Wehler (Frankfurt, 1972), 326.
79. Cf. Biefang, *Politisches Bürgertum in Deutschland*, 43ff., whom I have to thank for important insights.

Fighting between republicans and parliamentarians in Frankfurt a.M. on 30 March
(Illustrirte Zeitung, Leipzig, no. 252, 29 April 1848, 283)

A sitting of the Revolution Club in Paris

Chapter 23

ORGANIZATION AND "MODERNIZATION" IN THE REVOLUTIONS OF 1848

Edward Berenson

$\mathbf{A}$t the centennial celebration of the Revolutions of 1848—and for two decades afterwards—historians still treated the events of 1848 as something of an embarrassment. The year 1848 remained the "turning point that didn't turn," the episode that marked the failure of liberalism and democracy and the frustration of nationalism with a human face. Marxists, newly prominent in the postwar academic world, leveled perhaps the harshest judgments. The Master himself had dismissed 1848 as little more than a farcical reincarnation of 1789; and his disciples continued to view the later revolutions as revealing the weakness of a bourgeoisie that took refuge behind the political power of feudal lords. In the realm of culture, Marxist critics tended to agree that 1848 saw the end of a literature critically engaged with social class. After the revolutions, novelists withdrew into the safe bourgeois haven of art for its own sake. Above all, historians saw the Revolution of 1848 as a short-lived affair. In France, it ended in June; in Germany the following fall. Throughout Eastern Europe, the revolutions were doomed in the summer of '48, though it took another year or so to finish them off.

Now, at the 150th anniversary of the Revolutions of 1848, the picture looks considerably different. In France, where historiography on 1848 was à la mode from the early 1960s to the mid-1980s, when it succumbed to the bicentennial celebration of the Great Revolution, virtually nothing of the old view remains. Thanks to the pioneering work of Philippe Vigier and Maurice Agulhon, and to others inspired by them, 1848 no longer looms as the failure of socialism and democracy, the precocious defeat of a nascent working class. Instead, 1848 has become the "apprenticeship of the Republic," as Agulhon put it, the years when France's still largely rural population prepared for the republican and democratic regimes they have enjoyed, save for the brief interlude of Vichy, since the 1870s.

This new perception of the French Revolution of 1848 emerged from a large body of work that, like Agulhon's, focused on rural France. Rather than ending their narratives with the defeat of Parisian workers in June, historians extended their efforts to the whole of the country and the whole of the Second Republic (1848-52). In doing so, they saw that the Revolution, far from collapsing in the cataclysm of the June Days, persisted into 1849, 1850, and 1851. During those years, peasants, village artisans, and small-town members of the middling classes expressed allegiance to a radical republicanism that called itself *démocrate-socialiste*. The scholarly spotlight thus shifted away from the democratic failures of spring 1848 to the development of left-wing sentiment in the provinces. There, the legislative election of May 1849 revealed a "red France" that spanned a large number of rural departments in the Center and the South. It has become a commonplace of the new historiography that this election established political tendencies in provincial France that have remained remarkably consistent almost to our own time. Thus, rather than being a pale, even comical, reenactment of an earlier and greater revolution, 1848 in France now appears to be a harbinger of the future. It provided France with an apprenticeship in modern democratic politics and pointed French men and women toward their political destiny.

There have been similar developments in the historiography of the German revolutions of 1848-49, although they have been considerably more recent and have by no means formed anything like the new orthodoxy they have become in France. For reasons having to do with the "German Question" and the related debate over the *Sonderweg*, the problems of national unity, and the liberal and democratic failures have retained their allure. Still, a new body of work has pushed the analysis of the revolution beyond the earlier terminal dates in 1848 and beyond the Frankfurt Parliament and reasons for its collapse. Like the French literature of the 1960s, '70s, and '80s, recent work on Germany has focused on the politicization of artisans, peasants, and small-town members of the middle classes, a development that extended well into 1849. This new work has brought to light a vast panoply of local democratic organizations that recruited tens of thousands of people and influenced hundreds of thousands more. Jonathan Sperber, Michael Wettengel and others have shown that people grouped themselves not just according to trade and guild for immediate economic purposes but in the interests of fundamental changes in German government and society.[1]

Underlying much of the historiography of France and Germany is the problem of modernization. Even if the question is not always asked explicitly, historians want to know to what extent, if at all, the revolutions of 1848 contributed to the modernization of the countries they study. In particular, they have been interested in the role of organizations in that process, since organizations seem to be quintessentially modern political forms. Organizations, it is often claimed, make the difference between "primitive rebels" (E. Hobsbawm) whose protests, however political their implications, rarely produce lasting results.

Modernization, of course, is an extremely slippery concept. Historians do not always say what they mean by it, and it is not uncommon for them to imply that a linear trajectory exists from the "traditional" era—always by definition prior to the modernizing developments they are concerned with—to a time of modernity usually located sometime in the twentieth century."[2] The realities of history seldom, however, follow such neat paths of development, especially during revolutionary periods. Eras like 1848 tend to exhibit what Ernst Bloch called the "simultaneity of the unsimultaneous," the coexistence of new forms of politics and culture with older modes of belief, action, and organization.[3] In these situations, the old and new do not remain stably juxtaposed to each other, but each continuously shapes and reshapes the other, producing hybrid forms of politics and culture that can be seen as neither "traditional" nor "modern."

As Sperber makes clear in *Rhineland Radicals*, and I tried to show in my own work on 1848, elements of "tradition" and "modernity" become especially intertwined when it comes to religion.[4] In many regions of rural France, it was precisely the remaining elements of "tradition," namely a populist religiosity, that enabled republican activists to attract peasants to a progressive democratic ideology. The peasants' anticlerical religiosity possessed an incipiently democratic character, with its distrust of authority and belief in an egalitarian Jesus. Republicans who themselves spoke of a fraternal Jesus, of Jesus as the world's first socialist, could make common cause with peasants with whom they otherwise shared very little. Religion provided the bridge that enabled two such apparently diverse groups to span wide social and cultural differences to forge a political alliance.

Despite the difficulties inherent in modernization theory, for historians the concept of modernization cannot but hold powerful appeal. We are, after all, fundamentally concerned with change over time, and we want to know how such change occurred. It is clear, moreover, that Western societies in the mid-nineteenth century differed enormously from those with which we are familiar today. And it is equally evident that there has been considerable progress in industry, agriculture, medicine, means of transportation and communication, and many other realms. But by calling these developments "modernization" we give them a positive connotation that spills over onto their social and political consequences, sanitizing them and threatening to downplay the problems they have caused. Still, the concept of modernization retains its intuitive allure, and nowhere has it been more instructive than in the work of Charles Tilly.

Although in recent years, Tilly has renounced the concept of modernization and the teleology it implies, his older work has powerfully influenced the historiography of 1848, especially among Anglophone historians. For that reason, it remains important to consider the way Tilly once examined what he called the process of modernization. The critique I propose to offer applies not so much to Tilly himself, who should not be faulted for ideas he no longer holds, but to a historiography his earlier writings helped to shape.

In a seminal article published some twenty-five years ago, Tilly argued that as a result of the Revolution of 1848, protest modernized in France.[5] Even as late as the

1840s, Tilly wrote, "the predominant forms of collective violence in France were rather old-fashioned: the tax revolt, the food riot, the anti-conscription rebellion … the forcible invasion of fields or forests … the attack on machines and urban rebellion." But by the 1860s, such traditional forms of collective violence had all but vanished. Instead, French men, and to some extent women, engaged in strikes, demonstrations, and "similar complex, organized actions."[6] The key to such modernization, Tilly wrote, were the organizations forged by the revolutionaries of 1848.

The pre-1848, or traditional, forms of popular protest, Tilly maintained, featured mostly *communal* contenders. By this he meant small groups recruited largely from a particular locality and consisting of members of kinship alliances and religious congregations, residents of given village or local marketing region. Modern protest, by contrast, involved *associational* contenders: "complex, large, wide-ranging specialized groups recruiting through voluntary adherence and/or personal qualifications."[7] These included political parties, secret societies, industrial firms, and trade unions.

The collective violence that communal groups engaged in tended to remain localized and uncontrolled. It obeyed no coordinated leadership but rather swayed to the rhythms of market schedules, religious or communal festivals, planting and harvest cycles, and the like. Communal actions tended, therefore, to be spontaneous or nearly so; the food riot exemplifies this kind of collective violence. As for associational contenders, their collective actions took place, for the most part, without reference to natural phenomena. Recognized leaders scheduled protests and demonstrations, organizing them in advance and keeping them disciplined and under control. A massive urban demonstration, planned in advance and involving scuffles with the police typifies the associational protest.

Although Tilly's categories are to some extent ideal types, that designation does not absolve them of criticism. Most apparent are chronological difficulties. If protest did not modernize until 1848, how can we explain the existence of the secret societies that figured so prominently among France's oppositional groups of the 1820s and 30s? The actions these associations carried out were disciplined, coordinated, and possessed a clear political purpose. There was nothing communal or spontaneous about them. They can, however, be considered local, since most such organizations existed only in a single city. Still, it seems clear that associational forms of collective protest were quite common in urban France throughout the first half of the nineteenth century.

Beyond the Carbonari and other secret societies, there were fledgling trade unions that organized strikes and republican societies that coordinated large-scale demonstrations. Most notable among them were the Parisian insurrectionary demonstrations of 1832 and 1834 and the uprisings of Lyonnais silk workers that gripped the city in 1831 and again in 1834. The Lyon rebellions grew out of a conflict between workers' associations on the one hand and merchant-capitalist organizations on the other. The contenders in this case were nothing if not associational. Granted, all these events were urban phenomena and involved France's two largest and most advanced cities. Although Tilly did not say so, it may be that his argument for the modernization of protest at the mid-century applies most closely to rural France.

Before turning to the rural situation, it will be useful to consider how modern, according to Tilly's schema, were the forms of protest and collective violence undertaken by the Parisian revolutionary organizations created in the wake of the February revolution. Three kinds of organizations figured most prominently among the new revolutionary associations. (I will ignore existing organizations like the National Guards, which retained a largely anti-revolutionary role after February 24 despite the infusion of working-class members.)

First, there were the trade associations composed chiefly of skilled artisans. These groups achieved formal recognition by the Provisional Government, which invited them to send delegates to a sort of workers' parliament known as the Luxembourg Commission. Led by Louis Blanc, the Commission enjoyed little real legislative power, and its nearly continuous deliberations prevented delegates from participating in other more explicitly revolutionary formations. As an organization it played essentially no role in the revolutionary agitation of spring 1848. Blanc's commission did, however, make a crucial contribution to what can be termed the formation of a revolutionary working-class ideology. In the midst of massive unemployment exacerbated by the revolution, the Luxembourg made the "*droit au travail*," the right to employment, a central workers' demand. This demand had been formulated by Fourierists in the 1840s; in the wake of 1848, the Luxembourg Commission declared that the new Republic owed workers a job.

The ideological work performed by the Luxembourg Commission points to another limitation of Tilly's schema. By focusing exclusively on collective violence, he downplayed one of the most basic requirements of revolutionary protest: the development of an ideology that impels people to join organizations and moves them to act. In fairness, Tilly did observe that between 1848 and 1851 most contending groups expressed an ideological motivation, but he never considered the significance of that ideology as an independent variable. It is true that effective protest requires organizations; but without an oppositional ideology, organizations would have no reason to exist.

Beyond the Luxembourg Commission, other purely working-class organizations, albeit informal ones, were the National Workshops. Established to provide a meager dole for the unemployed—and to keep them off the streets—the National Workshops were a bastardized version of Louis Blanc's state enterprises. Unlike the productive firms Blanc envisioned, the Workshops offered working men little meaningful labor and did nothing to permit them to exercise their individual trades.

Were the National Workshops modern organizations, according to Tilly's ideal types? It is difficult to say. Tilly did not envision that the state would create organizations engaging in oppositional collective violence. Although designed in part to keep workers out of revolutionary trouble, the Workshops served instead as a breeding for violent protest. By bringing workers together without providing them anything useful to do, these organizations gave their members a structure in which to express anti-government resentment. But since their leaders were state officials, there was no deliberate preparation for collective protest. Demonstrations could not, therefore, be planned, disciplined, and controlled.

The June insurrection, for which the Workshops had inadvertently prepared their members, may have benefited from some *ad hoc* organization. But the June Days represented a largely spontaneous eruption of collective violence. As such, they exhibited both "traditional" and "modern" features. Their essentially unplanned and undisciplined character makes them resemble Tilly's communal forms of collective violence, but their close relationship to a large-scale and fairly complex organization, the National Workshop, gives them an associational flavor. It may be that protest did not so much modernize during the French Revolution of 1848 as become muddied by a melding of long-standing and relatively novel organizational forms. Protest bore witness to the simultaneity of the unsimultaneous.

Still, it is perhaps unfair to base such a judgment on government-sponsored forms of organization like the Luxembourg Commission and the National Workshops. Both, after all, owed their existence to a state, that their members ultimately came to oppose. A purer example of revolutionary organizations were the scores of political clubs established in the aftermath of February 1848. Inspired by the Jacobin Clubs of the French Revolution, the club movement of 1848 brought together revolutionaries suspicious of the relative moderation of the Provisional Government and anxious to push it further to the left. Whereas the Luxembourg associations occupied themselves mainly with bread and butter issues, the clubs focused almost exclusively on political concerns. The latter's membership, itself largely working class, undertook to influence the Provisional Government, organize political demonstrations, prepare elections, and debate ideological points. The clubs constituted themselves at once as rivals and collaborators of the new revolutionary regime. They were rivals in the sense that they questioned this government's exclusive right to form policy, and collaborators in that they sought not to circumvent the government but to shape its behavior and orientation.

At the zenith of the club movement in April 1848, activists had established some 225 popular societies comprising perhaps 100,000 members. About 60 percent of these clubs belonged to a federation directed, in theory at least, by a *Club des Clubs*. The largest and most prominent of these popular societies were those led by key oppositional figures from the July Monarchy (1830-48). These included Auguste Blanqui's Central Republican Society, Etienne Cabet's Central Fraternal Society, Armand Barbès's Club of the Revolution, and François Raspail's Society of the Friends of the People. Important as well was the Society of the Rights of Man, whose leadership was collegiate and enjoyed less notoriety. Under the pre-revolutionary regime, Blanqui and Barbès had been underground conspirators with considerable jail time to their credit, while Cabet had been and remained the theorist of a pacific communism steeped in unorthodox Christian sentiment. Raspail was a radical (and unlicensed) physician who ministered to the poor and styled himself a philosopher of socialist democracy.

Attracting as many as five thousand participants, many of them little more than tourists of the revolution, Blanqui's club held passionate debates that pitted insurrectionaries and moderates against one another. Meetings exhibited little organization and lacked even the rudiments of an agenda. Cabet and Raspail's clubs, by contrast, served largely as lecture halls for two men known as much for their ideological and intellectual systems as for their political activism. People came to meetings not to debate issues but to hear the great men speak. Like Blanqui, they routinely attracted four to five thousand people, and like him, their followers were mostly working class.

The Society of the Rights of Man attracted genuine participants rather than debaters and listeners. Its leaders prided themselves on their hierarchic Jacobin discipline, and they announced the intention to exert force, if need be, to shape the Republic's policy. Barbès's club differed from most of the other prominent societies in having a membership chiefly composed of middle class revolutionaries.

Although women attended many of these meetings, most of the prominent clubs refused to allow them to speak. But feminists and other women revolutionaries were not to be denied a voice: activists such as Jeanne Deroin, Adèle Esquiros, and Suzanne Voilquin formed their own women's clubs. The most prominent among them were Société de la Voix des femmes, an organization that coalesced around a feminist newspaper of the same name; the Club de l'Emancipation des Femmes, the Union des Femmes, and the Vesuvians. The latter advanced a particularly radical platform, advocating military service for women and equality in marriage, including the notion that men should share the household chores. All of these feminist clubs demanded full legal equality for women, and Jeanne Deroin later dramatized that demand by declaring herself a candidate for the National Assembly.

Despite the prominence of the "name" clubs in the spring of 1848, they were in many ways atypical. Most popular societies brought together not thousands, but dozens of members, virtually all of whom came from the immediate neighborhood. In their meetings, the mostly working-class participants discussed local issues and aired their grievances. Although many of these smaller clubs had officially affiliated themselves with the Club des Clubs, in reality there was little coordination among the two hundred-odd popular societies. They formed a movement only in the loosest sense.

The club movement's first major political effort was the massive demonstration of March 17. Organizers demanded that the Provisional Government postpone for several months the upcoming election of a Constituent Assembly. Left-wing republicans feared that hastily-called elections would give them insufficient time to proselytize in the provinces and thus award local conservatives an advantage. Club leaders also wanted the Government to put off elections of National Guard leaders and countermand its order to garrison regular army troops in Paris. Although the club movement succeeded in mobilizing an impressive number of demonstrators, perhaps as many as 200,000, it achieved only minimal political objectives. To attract such a large crowd, club leaders softened the tone of their demands, leaving it unclear to many marchers whether they were in the streets to defend or oppose the Provisional Government. As a result, the Government agreed only to push the elections back by a week or two. It refused, moreover, to bar regular troops from the capital, enhancing in the process its ability to resist future challenges. The clubs' apparent victory in mobilizing hundreds of thousands of demonstrators proved Pyrrhic at best.

With the national elections scheduled for April 23, Club leaders faced the need to shift overnight from organizing demonstrations to preparing an electoral campaign. This they were ill-equipped to do. All French politicians were new to the experience of managing elections under universal manhood suffrage, perhaps the Revolution's most important gain, and radical republicans found themselves at a particular disadvantage. For them, revolutionary activity meant demonstrations, insurrections, conspiracy, mass meetings, and the intimidation of political leaders. It had nothing to do with the mundane day-to-day discipline of choosing candidates, developing and circulating effective campaign propaganda, teaching people the importance of voting, and getting their own supporters to the polling stations.

Club leaders found it difficult enough to accomplish all these crucial electoral tasks within their own Parisian neighborhoods. To do so in the all-important provinces proved impossible. The absence of an effective umbrella organization linking the capital's 200 clubs prevented radical leaders from agreeing on a common slate of candidates. As a result, club members divided their electoral energies among far too many political hopefuls, splitting the radical vote and allowing their enemies to win seats that should have gone to the left. In the provinces, where the overwhelming majority of France's newly-enfranchised voters lived, club members proved particularly inept. Because republican—especially radical republican—candidates tended to be less well known than local landowners and other conservative notables, leftists desperately needed to build support for their provincial candidates. But the club leaders' unfamiliarity with the political horizon outside Paris led them to dither for weeks over the effort to choose electoral emissaries for the countryside. As a result, only a tiny number of clubists ever set foot outside the capital. For this and many other reasons, the national results proved even more disastrous for the left than the Parisian ones.

In the aftermath of this first sobering experience with universal suffrage, the clubs returned to their more familiar pastimes: ideological debate and demonstrations. Women's organizations, meanwhile, pressed for voting rights, the legalization of divorce, the right to work, and the ability to participate in the National Workshops. Like the members of the Provisional Government, most male club members opposed, even ridiculed, the feminist demands. Not that support from male organizations would have mattered a great deal. By mid-April, the entire club movement was already waning.

Conservative and moderate forces dominated the newly-elected Constituent Assembly, and the moderate members of the Provisional Government, soon to be reduced to a five-man Executive Commission, now felt emboldened to act against the left. Moderates easily defeated demonstrations the clubs organized on April 16 and May 15, sending prominent club leaders into exile. And by early June, the club movement was in shambles, having vacillated for three months between demonstrations that failed to change government policy and elections that it was woefully unprepared to contest. In part, the demonstrations had foundered over the clubs leaders' ambivalence toward the Provisional Government itself. On the one hand, many of them saw it as only lukewarmly republican and in need of a revolutionary shakeup; on the other, they sought to support it against its anti-republican adversaries and only to nudge it gradually to the left. The clubs lacked the revolutionary single-mindedness that further radicalization would have required.

After the government dissolved the National Workshops on June 21, the clubs possessed neither the means nor the legitimacy to channel the working-class anger that resulted. Miserable and impatient for change, working people reverted to largely spontaneous revolutionary violence. Most recognized leaders on the left either remained aloof from the June Days or openly opposed the uprising. When government troops and adjunct forces put the rebellion down, the clubs succumbed as well. They could not survive the sweeping repressive measures instituted in the aftermath of June.

Peter Amann argues that the club movement failed because it represented a collection of transitory organizations stuck uneasily between their underground insurrectionary traditions and their new and untested role as mass democratic parties.[8] As such, they were neither traditional nor modern, or to use Tilly's terms, neither communal nor associational. The clubs, Amann suggests, had advanced beyond the largely spontaneous rebellion of the food riot or forest invasion, but they never achieved the organizational maturity that would have enabled them to pose a serious threat to the moderate government, either in the streets or the polling booth. For him, the clubs represent "a characteristic revolutionary phenomenon of a society in transition to modernity … They are inconceivable in a society of rank, paternalism, and deference; they are obsolete in a world of assembly lines, recognized labor unions, and mass parties."[9]

Amann is certainly right that the clubs of 1848 could not exist in a world of rank and deference, but whether they are excluded in the "modern" society he depicts is another matter. Do they differ so fundamentally from the Soviets of 1917 or from the German Workers and Soldiers Councils that appeared a year later? Not unlike the clubs of 1848, both found themselves caught between revolutionary insurrectionism and mass electoral democracy. The Soviets succumbed to the forces of a disciplined, elite revolutionary party, the German councils to the establishment of regular procedures and institutions of democracy. Even as military might obviously played a crucial role in the Soviets' demise, so too was force central in the defeat of the Parisian clubs.

Beyond these questions, there is the problem of how Amann defines tradition and modernity. The French Revolution of 1789 certainly did a great deal to shatter the society of rank, paternalism, and deference. Why is it, then, that a revolution occurring more than half a century later still created organizations that remained in many ways unmodern? Clearly, the term "tradition" is far too crude a designation to describe France of 1640 and France of 1840. Nor does it account for the vast differences in a given period between urban and rural France, and for the widely different pace at which city and country changed.

There is, moreover, a problem with how Amann defines the modern. If assembly lines, powerful labor unions, and mass parties characterize political modernity, can our own contemporary Western societies be called modern? In an age of silicon and biotechnology, assembly lines have declined in importance. Large labor unions still exist of course, but in many western countries they encompass only a fraction of the working population. In Germany, unions remain powerful, but only in a sort of neo-corporatist arrangement with industry and the state. As for mass parties, their influence, too, is sharply on the decline as voters show considerably less party loyalty than their parents and grandparents had. Amann's image of modernity seems strangely anachronistic, based as it is on conditions more characteristic of the first half of the twentieth century than of our own fin-de-siècle.

The club experience of 1848 subverts Tilly's polarities of tradition and modernity even more than those of Amann. If "protest modernized" during the Revolution of 1848, it is difficult to explain the nature of the clubs. Their mainly local orientation and membership defies Tilly's model of associational modernity, as does their difficulty in coordinating electoral contests and their inability to discipline the insurrectionary anger of the Parisian working class. The Parisian clubs seem both communal and associational, fostering collective actions at once "localized [and] uncoordinated" and "large in scale, deliberately scheduled, and organized in advance."[10] On the basis of the club experience, Tilly's picture of 1848 as the point of transition from traditional to modern is difficult to sustain.

In Tilly's defense, it can perhaps be argued that because the clubs were born and died so early into the revolutionary years, it stands to reason that they would not become fully modern. But an analysis of political protest, organization and collective violence from July 1848 to December 1851 does not seriously modify the critique of the modernization model. Although different from the Parisian clubs, the new organizations established in the wake of June do not, for the most part, fit Tilly's associational model. They too were hybrid and largely informal constellations, neither "traditional" nor "modern" in form. In many ways, the political organizations of the period after June were unique to 1848, shaped not according to the impulses of political "modernization" but to the particular conditions and experiences of France's Second Republic.

With the defeat of the urban workers, left-wing republican leaders finally resolved to undertake what Club leaders had been unable to accomplish: the republicanization of the countryside. To do so, they created new organizations specially designed for that purpose. Those organizations were premised on an ideological alliance that brought democrats and socialists together in an effort to create a unified revolutionary party. Democrats now claimed that to believe in democracy inevitably made one a socialist, and socialists maintained that they were necessarily democrats as well. As Cabet put it, "there are no real democrats who are not socialists and there are no real socialists who are not democrats and republicans … republic, democracy, socialism are one in the same."[11] Members of the new coalition called themselves *démocrates-socialistes* (*démoc-socs* for short) and agreed to work together to spread their progressive gospel in the provinces.

Leaders of the new coalition created two new organizations to pursue this goal. The one, *Propagande démocratique et sociale européenne* [European Democratic and Social Propaganda], undertook to blanket the provinces with left-wing propaganda;

the other, *Solidarité républicaine* [Republican Solidarity], represented the first French effort to establish a centralized national political party. In their structure, both organizations mimicked the hierarchical order of the French state. They each established a central committee that resembled a cabinet in Paris, and copying the prefectoral system, both sought to open main branches in every department capital and sub-branches in every arrondissement and canton in the country. The two organizations maintained a strict division of labor in which *Propagande démocratique* concentrated on propaganda distribution, *Solidarité républicaine* on political organizing. The former constituted itself as a business enterprise and was able to escape political repression. The latter, openly a political organization, succumbed early to Louis Napoleon's assault against his republican opposition.

Propagande démocratique explicitly dedicated itself to the political education of the French peasantry. Its board of directors, composed of three deputies to the Constituent Assembly, one former club president, and four newspaper editors, decided which writings, images, songs, and other forms of propaganda the organization would disseminate. Publishing nothing itself, *Propagande démocratique* acted as a commercial intermediary between writers and publishers on the one hand and local démoc-soc activists on the other. The latter, many of whom were booksellers, café proprietors, and shopkeepers would buy *Propagande démocratique*'s literature at modest prices and make it available to the artisans and cultivators who frequented their establishments.

Though *Propagande démocratique* displayed no interest in making a profit, it nevertheless became a solid commercial venture. It lasted from November 1848 to the coup d'état—a long time for a démoc-soc association—and was considered a business success by the government officials who surveyed it. The organization kept afloat financially by selling large quantities of low-priced materials. It sold more than a million copies of Felix Pyat's "Toast aux paysans," nearly forty thousand of Proudhon's "Les Malthusiens" as a "considerable number" of the "Evangile social-iste," a text illustrating the common démoc-soc belief that the Gospels provided the basis of modern socialist politics.[12]

In the spring of 1849, Louis Napoleon's police considered *Propagande démocratique* the most dangerous oppositionist organ in the country, "a real force within the state."[13] The government, however, was virtually powerless to act against it. The repressive legislation instituted after the June Days restricted the operations of private organizations that met regularly for political purposes. But the new laws could not touch an organization like *Propagande démocratique*, whose statutes and operations were purely commercial. Police officials lamented that the organization carried on its work "apart from all conspiracies and apart from all secret societies … The *petits livres* are its barricades."[14]

Even more ambitious was the effort on the part of *Solidarité républicaine* to establish itself as a political party national in scope. Its leaders' intention was to create branches of the organization in every French department to contest elections, politicize the peasantry, and prepare to take power by legal means. In January 1849, *Solidarité* established a "shadow cabinet" that paralleled the government ministries;

like the ministry of the Interior, it asked departmental representatives to submit regular reports to Paris outlining the political situation in their regions.

Only in major cities like Marseille and Dijon did widely-known republican leaders direct *Solidarité républicaine* committees. In provincial towns, the organization's governing boards were cross-class alliances of bourgeois professionals and civil servants, shopkeepers and skilled artisans. Where *Solidarité républicaine* committees existed in small towns, peasants occasionally belonged as well.

Solidarité's records show that by the end of January 1849 the organization had established itself in sixty-two of France's eighty-six departments, with a total of 353 branches. The police estimated a national membership of over thirty thousand people. It was precisely this nationwide network of *Solidarité républicaine* committees that so frightened the government of Louis Napoleon. Never had a French government faced an opposition that had organized so successfully in the provinces. "Right in the heart of the State," wrote the General Prosecutor of Aix, "an organization rivaling that of the State has extended its tentacles throughout the entire surface of France."[15]

Although the government doubtless exaggerated its opponent's power, *Solidarité* clearly represented a threat that had to be addressed. Armed with the laws against clubs and "secret societies" enacted in the wake of the June Days, Louis Napoleon moved quickly to dissolve *Solidarité républicaine*. Police raided the national headquarters at the end of January 1849 and officially outlawed the organization shortly thereafter. Despite these repressive measures, many of *Solidarité*'s provincial committees remained intact, and they met discretely to plan the démoc-socs' local electoral campaigns for the crucial legislative contests of May 1849. Thanks in part to *Solidarité*'s efforts, radical republicans succeeded in winning some 35 percent of the vote nationwide and heathy majorities in wide areas of central, southeastern, and southern France. Although the démoc-socs received strong support from the working-class quarters of Paris and Lyon, the bulk of their votes came from the provinces. The efforts on the part of *Propagande démocratique* and *Solidarité républicaine* to reach France's rural population had clearly paid off.

Repression prevented *Solidarité républicaine* from becoming the national party its leaders had sought to make it, but they clearly anticipated the kind of mass political organization characteristic of the late nineteenth and early twentieth centuries. In Tilly's terms, *Solidarité républicaine* was highly modern in design, even if its effect lasted only a few months. As for *Propagande démocratique et sociale européenne*, it too looked toward the future with its centralized administration and innovative commercial structure. But its inability to organize those exposed to its literature limited the group's effectiveness, making it as much an educational society as a political one. Despite their limitations, both *Solidarité républicaine* and *Propagande démocratique* contributed to France's republican apprenticeship.

Even though the démoc-socs constituted a minority, albeit a heathy one, in the new Legislative Assembly, their relative success in May 1849 terrorized the government. If the "reds" could capture a substantial number of peasant votes, what was to stop them from eventually winning a majority? The answer, for Louis Napoleon, was additional repressive measures. A series of legislative acts, liberally interpreted by the government, gave officials wide latitude to act against the démoc-socs. By the middle of 1849, all overtly left-wing societies had been abolished.

In the face of such repression, radical republicans turned to a series of informal organizations and organizers to continue their effort to reach deeply into rural France. After the banning of political clubs and electoral committees, local activists established cafés as centers of propaganda and organization. Sympathetic café proprietors would subscribe to démoc-soc newspapers, and in the course of an evening of drink and talk, literate townsmen would read aloud to all those assembled in the locale. In this way, the démoc-socs kept their ideas alive and made new converts to their cause.

As for the dissemination of propaganda, the démoc-socs began by giving their materials to the rural peddlers or *colporteurs*, who, for centuries, had traveled the countryside on foot selling various forms of popular literature. It did not take the government long to outlaw such colportage; the démoc-socs responded by turning to other, more informal means of disseminating their ideas. Activists recruited salesmen, stagecoach drivers, postal and railroad employees, insurance agents, and others who traveled for a living to distribute démoc-soc propaganda during the normal course of their professional activities. This is precisely what the colporteur had done, but the new propagandists did it much less conspicuously. Police could keep track of professional colporteurs, whose numbers were relatively small and who, as merchants, had to make their presence known. But gendarmes could not survey everyone who traveled for a living, and judges refused to apply the anti-colportage laws to those who distributed literature informally. As a result, these anonymous voyagers forged crucial links in the démoc-socs' nationwide propaganda network much more efficiently than the colporteurs ever did.

Indeed, the growing French system of commerce and communication as a whole provided a cover under which démoc-soc doctrines and organization could spread. Just as road and canal construction, railroad building, and postal reform stimulated French economic growth, so these developments also facilitated ideological diffusion and the extension of organizational links. Literature traveled along newly constructed railroad lines, and from terminal points by coach and foot into the surrounding villages. Since the courts refused to apply the anti-colportage law to literature sent through the mails, démoc-socs were free to send newspapers and other literature to local activists throughout the country.

In addition to bringing propaganda into the provinces, those who circulated throughout France's expanding networks of commerce and communication helped coordinate electoral activities by telling locals for whom to cast their ballots and instructing them about the procedures and mechanics of voting. Travelers also gathered information about the political situation in the provinces they frequented, and on their return to Paris or to regional capitals reported to démoc-soc leaders.

Provincial newspapers played a particularly important role in these informal political and organizational activities. Remnants of the press freedoms established in 1848 permitted left-wing editors to continue publishing their journals and to market subscriptions to them. Subscription salesmen were particularly well-placed to act as propagandists and political organizers. Their task was to travel throughout the region the newspaper served with the goal of widening its circulation and, in turn, spreading the ideas and principles the journal represented. A subscription list found in the possession of one Pierre Arambide, a traveling representative of the *Démocrat du Var*, revealed that some 40 percent of his subscribers were collectivities such as cafés, mutual aid societies, and *chambrées* (social clubs frequented by peasants and artisans). This information confirms the importance of such informal organizations in the creation of a démoc-soc network and demonstrates the centrality of the newspaper in their activities.

In many ways, newspapers became *ad hoc* political parties during the latter years of the Second Republic. They provided crucial political and electoral information, and they alone could openly publicize the names of démoc-soc candidates and urge people to vote accordingly. During an era in which government repression frustrated the effort to establish a mass political party, the démoc-soc press stepped in to assume a leading political role.

Still, as repression deepened after 1850, even newspapers found it increasingly difficult to maintain their political freedom. The government was bent on stamping out all remaining political opposition, whether the laws permitted it or not. Under these circumstances, a growing share of démoc-soc activity had to move underground. In the final year of the Republic, the secret society became a key element of left-wing organization.

During the first part of the nineteenth century, the secret society had been one of the most important forms of oppositionist political activity. Royalist members of the *Chevaliers du Roi* struggled against the Napoleonic empire; Carbonari fought the Bourbon restoration; and a small legion of republican and socialist societies—Families, Seasons, Reformed Carbonari, Voraces, Communists—challenged the July Monarchy. These societies staged elaborate initiation rituals with blindfolded initiates, oaths on daggers, and the threat of death to anyone who revealed the organization's existence.

With the establishment of democracy and full civil liberties in February 1848, the secret society no longer seemed necessary. But with the repression that followed the June Days, activists began to resurrect the underground organization. By the end of 1851, they covered much of what had become the "red" part of France: the Center, Southeast, and Mediterranean regions.

The secret "Montagnard" societies devoted themselves to a pair of goals: defense of the republic by arms if necessary, and propagation of démoc-soc ideology. Hierarchic in structure, these clandestine bodies were organized by commune; within each commune, society affiliates formed ten-member cells called *décuries*, each with its own elected leader. Communes with widespread participation grouped their décuries into hundred-member formations led by a centurion. In well-organized departments like the Nièvre or the Hérault, the secret societies of the various communes corresponded with one another and even held periodic meetings of the department's communal leaders. In the central French departments of the Yonne and the Nièvre, societies were composed mostly of artisans but included some wine growers. In southern France, secret societies tended to enroll at least as many peasants as artisans. Leaders of these organizations came, for the most part, from the ranks of the artisanate and the modest village middle-class. But peasants did play leadership roles, especially in regions where a large membership formed a great many décuries, each with its own head.

Unlike secret societies of the pre-1848 period, the Montagnard organizations did little to prepare their members for armed combat. In many respects they resembled the above-ground informal organizations that had earlier taken shape in cafés, chambrées, and mutual aid societies. Secret society leaders used these organizations to recruit peasants and rural artisans to the démoc-soc cause, transmit propaganda, and prepare for the fabled elections of 1852. Since the constitution limited Louis Napoleon to a single term, démoc-socs saw the presidential and parliamentary elections scheduled for that year as the moment when they could win a majority and assume political control. One obstacle to that outcome was a new electoral law of May 1850 that disenfranchised about one-third of all French voters, mostly peasants and artisans. To overcome that obstacle, secret society members resolved to "march to the voting station with a gun in one hand and a ballot in the other." They were prepared, in other words, to use force, but only to reconquer the universal suffrage that would enable them to take power legally.

The need to maintain secrecy, and the aura of conspiracy that surrounded the Montagnard organizations enhanced their ability to socialize members and ensure their loyalty. Leaders conveyed the seriousness of their efforts through initiation rituals that help wed new members to the cause. Many of these rituals reflected the populist religiosity evident in a great many rural communities. Members referred to the initiation rite as a "baptism" and saw themselves as joining a sort of religious brotherhood devoted to political goals. As one peasant described the initiation ceremony, "One of the society members touched [the new recruit's] bared head with a cold instrument which he knew was a weapon even though he was told it was the hand of Christ." The leader then said, "I baptize you in the name of the Mountain." In some cases the leader declared, "In the name of the Christ of the Mountain, I receive you as a Montagnard and as a brother."[16]

These secret organizations were to prove enormously effective. So thoroughly had they instilled a republican commitment in their members that when Louis Napoleon obliterated the constitution with his coup d'état of December 2, 1851, the secret societies rebelled. Indeed, as Ted Margadant has shown, violent resistance to the coup occurred essentially *only* where secret societies existed.[17] The more extensive the Montagnard organization, moreover, the larger the scale of the rebellion. Since secret societies took root entirely within the "red" areas of France, there is a general correlation between the electoral strength of the démoc-socs and the centers of insurrection.

But at the level of individual departments, the relationship is not so close. Even in departments in which every elected representative sat on the left, if secret societies were feeble or absent, no more than minor rebellions occurred. Conversely, within departments that elected only a minority of left-wing representatives, regions with a strong Montagnard presence sent a great many rebels into the field. The underground organization was a sine qua non of insurrection in December 1851. Leaders mobilized more than 100,000 rebels, making it the largest rural uprising in nineteenth-century France.

How "modern" were these and other organizations that emerged after June 1848? As we have seen, *Solidarité républicaine* and *Propagande démocratique et sociale européenne* appeared to anticipate the kinds of political formations typical of the fin-de-siècle. Repression, however, limited their effectiveness. To compensate, démoc-socs established a variety of informal organizations, *ad hoc* in character and necessarily less hierarchic and disciplined than the national organizations had been. These informal associations little resembled the mass parties of the late century, appearing more consistent with the unstructured associational life of the pre-1848 period. Still, they differed from what had existed previously in their ability to introduce artisans and cultivators to the democratic and socialist ideas destined to prevail later on. Though there was little distinctly new in the informal associations of the Second Republic, they nonetheless gave a great many ordinary people a significant republican apprenticeship.

As for the secret societies, their relation to the poles of "tradition" and "modernity" is even more complex. On the one hand, they looked back toward conspiratorial organizations of the early nineteenth century, with their archaic initiation rituals and quasi-religious ethos. Secret societies, moreover, often mobilized an entire commune, much as the food riot and forest invasion had done in centuries past. On the other hand, like the political formations of a later era, the Montagnards were highly disciplined and capable of mobilizing large numbers of people for a particular event. In addition, the insurrection they led departed significantly from the violent peasant *jacqueries* of earlier times. Rebels showed more interest in seizing symbols of political power—city hall, subprefectures, and the like—than in pillaging the rich and avenging social frustration, two characteristics of "traditional" upheavals. As Louis Napoleon's judicial representative at Aix put it, "There have been none of the murders, the pillages, and other horrors that one might justly expect … indeed a certain moderation, a certain legality—you will excuse the term—can be seen in the acts and the speeches of the leaders."[18]

Most of those who have analyzed the rural commitment to the left evident in central and southern France attribute it in large part to the organizational efforts of urban republicans, whether members of the middle class or the skilled artisanate. Through a network of largely informal organizations, démoc-soc activists introduced rural dwellers to an ideology whose origins lay in the urban world. It goes without saying that not all peasants were receptive to such a new set of beliefs. Démoc-soc activists could succeed only where socio-economic and cultural conditions were right: where an expanding market system had made it increasingly difficult for small-holding peasants and rural artisans to maintain a semblance of economic independence, and where popular religion and popular culture had created a *mentalité* consistent with egalitarian democracy.

Not all historians have accepted this view. Eugen Weber has denied the existence of such a politicized rural population, and, more recently, Peter McPhee has challenged what he terms the "diffusion" argument altogether.[19] McPhee maintains that many of his fellow Anglophone scholars have exaggerated the influence of urban republicans, exaggerated the extent to which they "diffused" their ideology. In doing so, he writes, they have slighted the peasants' own independent political life. For him, the démoc-socs' organizational efforts cannot account for more than a small part of the peasants' commitment to the left; despite the démoc-socs' best efforts, organizers failed in many regions to affect peasant views. Far more important to the explanation of political choice, he writes, were the "social relations of production," the economic conjuncture, and the rural dwellers' memories of the French Revolution.[20]

Although McPhee correctly identifies a "diffusion thesis" in much of the recent literature on 1848, he mars his argument by turning his scholarly opponents into straw men. No serious historian of the period neglects what McPhee calls the social relations of production. Virtually all stress the significance of socioeconomic, geographic, and other material considerations in determining which people were most and least likely to be susceptible to the démoc-soc message. Most scholars have found the economic conjuncture important as well, but note that by itself it determined little. Peasants who suffered from heavy debt and especially poor market conditions in 1849 did not automatically vote for the left. Some individual or organization had first to convince them of the far from evident proposition that casting a paper ballot could do them good. Someone, that is, had to introduce them to the theory and procedures of democracy. Next, organizers had to help them formulate their grievances in terms of the démoc-socs' ideological perspective and then persuade them that their party possessed the wherewithal to address their grievances and help them find a better life.

As for memories of the French Revolution, McPhee himself admits that these are far from self-evident phenomena. Memories are shaped and reshaped by family and group dynamics and by larger political forces. In making their case for the democratic and social republic of 1848, organizers and propagandists mobilized memories of the dechristianization of the Years II and III, the White Terror, and a variety of other events. They emphasized some things over others and encouraged forgetting no less than memory. Perceptions of the French Revolution helped determine the nature of political choice in 1849-51 in part because activists and organizers molded those perceptions in particular ways.

It is certainly true, as McPhee maintains, that peasants brought certain political predilections to the situation facing them in 1849; they were not empty vessels waiting to be filled by démoc-soc politics. But during the Second Republic, propagandists and organizers shaped those predilections into a set of political commitments and modes of political behavior that were largely new. It is in this sense that the French Revolution of 1848 pointed toward republics to come.

The German Revolution, by contrast, has seemed mired in the past. Because the German states failed to make the turn toward "modernity"—that is, toward a single, unified nation with representative institutions and political freedoms—it has long appeared as though nothing innovative occurred. In the social sphere, historians have emphasized the backward-looking nature of the workers' associations, marked by their opposition to capitalism and freedom of trade. The medieval guild, not the modern labor union—so scholars have argued—served as their organizational model. Peasants have appeared in a similar light, as historians focused on their widespread hostility to the capitalist market and the liberal politics identified with it.

In recent years, this view has come under increasing attack as historians have begun to examine the diversity of political experiences during the Revolution of 1848-49. Already in the mid-1960s, Paul Noyes demonstrated that a great many workers distanced themselves from the guilds.[21] Journeymen saw their interests as distinct from those of the master craftsmen who employed them, and after March 1848 journeymen formed their own separate organizations. They sought the right to establish themselves as independent workers and adopted such socialist demands as the creation of producers' cooperatives—collective enterprises owned jointly by all their workers and aided by the state.

That journeymen moved to create their own organizations revealed one of the most emblematic features of the German Revolutions of 1848-49. Throughout the German states, the drive for organization was at least as powerful as its counterpart in France. Middle-class liberals, democrats, feminists, master artisans, journeymen, factory workers—all created their own associations. The "Vereinsmensch" or "association man" became a recognized figure of the Revolution, an individual who believed "organization" would be a panacea for all his ills.

This gendered term masks the women's organizations that also began to appear after March 1848. In western Germany, activists like Louise Otto and Kathinka Zitz-Halein worked actively for women's rights, and as Gabriella Hauch has shown, even in the Habsburg lands the Revolution spawned a variety of women's clubs.[22] Under the leadership of Caroline Perin, Vienna's Democratic Women's Association pressed for the equality of women through education and the solidarity of all women regardless of class. Though short-lived, the Democratic Women's Association became the model for similar organizations elsewhere in Austria and even brought women into the streets. In October 1848, a large contingent of Association members marched to the Reichstag where they presented a petition to the parliament's horrified members.

Although even the most radical men opposed this nascent women's movement, male workers and democrats claimed an expanded public role for themselves. So many activists extolled the virtues of organization that the newspaper *Die Barrikaden* felt compelled to satirize their exuberance: "When one person cannot perform a task through his own power, bring in two who can easily support each other, and where two are too few, perhaps four will suffice … Thus in recent times arose the associations—associations for all possible and impossible purposes."[23]

Among workers, there were, in fact, too many organizations. Leaders of the established guilds formed associations to defend their privileges and request government aid against mass production and the capitalist market. Some journeymen sought organizations oriented to their individual crafts, while others attempted to create all-German societies that would bring workers together across the different trades. Still others hoped to join workers who belonged to guilds to the growing numbers of those who did not. In addition, workers from individual cities or regions formed separate congresses, each with its own distinct orientation and demands. Working-class leaders intended their quest for organization to bring workers together; instead the proliferation of associations emphasized the differences among them and helped keep them apart. Those divisions diluted the effectiveness of organized German workers and weakened them in the face of liberals and conservatives alike

It is important to stress that the workers' weakness stemmed more from disunity than from the antimodern character many historians have ascribed to them. Although some associations represented guild masters who sought to turn back the clock, most workers' congresses of the revolutionary years revealed both backward- and forward-looking designs.

Essentially all German workers wanted to halt, or at least to control, advances in mass production that threatened their livelihood as skilled craftsmen. Although workers can hardly be faulted for attempting to avoid obsolescence, in this demand they presented themselves as obstacles to "progress." Still, many of the journeymen's associations understood that certain new techniques and technologies were inevitable; they merely sought regulations that would give them time to adapt.

Workers' organizations also sought to prohibit cheap English and Belgian goods from penetrating German borders. Although this demand might be seen as backward-looking, it found endorsement in the widely popular views of Friedrich List, who believed that the progress of German industry depended on keeping foreign products from entering the confederation. Protectionism, moreover, was far from uncommon throughout Europe during this period; a great many otherwise liberal businessmen had no trouble supporting tariffs and other similar market constraints.

Although journeymen tended to oppose efforts by master craftsmen to maintain strict limits on the freedom to enter a profession, they did not believe that anyone should be permitted to exercise a trade. All workers in a given field, they argued, ought to have the requisite skill and training. In taking such a stance, journeymen sought to preserve high standards of production as much as to oppose the unfettered capitalist market.

If the workers' positions on trade, technology, and the market revealed a certain resistance to economic change, on other issues they anticipated the organized labor movement of the future, which, it should be noted, has rarely embraced technological change and free trade. In particular, a great many workers in 1848 wanted the state to guarantee them a job, endorsing the French revolutionary demand for the *droit au travail*. They also advocated considerable state intervention into the economy: progressive taxation; unemployment, old age, and disability benefits; state-funded education; payments to widows; subsidies for producers' cooperatives; and the like.

In addition, the journeymen's organizations of 1848, like the labor movement of the late century, began to speak no longer of individual trades but of workers as a unified whole. They developed a certain consciousness of themselves as members of a working class and adopted the new-fangled language of socialism, even as they denounced "capitalism" both for exploiting workers and for threatening the persistence of the handicraft trades. Like their French counterparts, German workers' organizations embodied the simultaneity of the unsimultaneous, combining elements of "tradition" and "modernity" in their exploration of the political possibilities briefly open to them in 1848-49.

The diversity of the German workers' movement mirrors the diversity of the German Revolutions themselves. In some regions, the revolution quickly succumbed to conflicts between peasants and artisans on the one hand and liberals and democrats on the other. For the first two groups, opposition to the advance of mass production and free markets outweighed the potential gains of liberalism and democracy. They came to see middle-class revolutionaries as more menacing than monarchs and aristocrats. But in other regions, recent historiography has revealed a vital democratic movement, one that thrived on support from the lower classes and threatened conservative and liberal officials until the Prussian military intervention of May 1849.

The Rhineland was perhaps the most important of these revolutionary regions; thanks to the work of Jonathan Sperber, Michael Wettengel, and a few others, we now understand the dynamics of its potent democratic forces. Most of the Rhineland had been attached to the French republic and Napoleonic empire from the mid-1790s to 1814. From its involvement with the French Revolution, the Rhineland retained not only the experience of revolutionary upheaval, but the legacy of the legal changes Napoleon had introduced. The French Revolution had abolished the guild system in the Rhineland, and there were no significant efforts to revive it in 1848. As a result, many of the conflicts that divided master artisans from journeymen in the rest of Germany had little bearing here. Most master artisans, like other skilled workers, were subject to the merchant capitalists who assigned them work and controlled access to the market. Artisans of all kinds had far more in common with one another than with the non-producing entrepreneurs on whom they depended. And long-standing hostility toward merchant capitalists helped open considerable numbers of working people to oppositionist politics after March 1848.

During the *Vormärz*, the people of the Rhineland, as elsewhere in Germany, enjoyed only a meager associational life. Government restraints prevented most residents, whether of the working or middle classes, male or female, from engaging openly in political activity. A variety of social organizations did exist, however, and some political discussion could take place. Still, most peasants and members of the urban lower classes remained innocent of any organized political life.

This is not to say, of course, that peasants and urban workers were innocent of all political expression. Villagers regularly did battle with state officials over their presumed right to pasture animals and gather wood in government controlled forests. The peasants' ardent efforts to defend their "rights" constituted a politics of sorts, even if their demands had nothing to do with the more formal political discourse of the era. Similarly, artisans who worked for merchant capitalists, regularly—and sometimes violently—expressed their "right" to independence and a decent standard of living. Such forms of incipient politics, or "pre-politics" as Sperber calls them, largely conform to what Tilly calls traditional forms of collective action. They tended to be communal and unorganized, lacking in anything more than an immediate material objective.

With the legalization of political organizations in the spring of 1848, it became possible for activists to harness popular demands to the more formal political programs and objectives sparked by the March revolution. Although constitutional monarchists and Catholics established their own associations, it was the democrats who undertook to organize most actively. Like their French counterparts, Rhenish leftists began their efforts in the principal cities. There they recruited artisans and members of middling groups disappointed with the moderate to conservative tone of the Frankfurt National Assembly and of the governments established in the individual German states.

Although German democrats suffered nothing so severe as the suppression of the Parisian workers in June, the Rhineland's radicals followed an organizational trajectory similar to that of the French démoc-socs. By the fall of 1848, most Rhenish democrats had become convinced that they needed to turn away from the cities and focus on the territories where most inhabitants lived, namely the rural areas of the three Rhineland regions—the Prussian Rhineland, Rhine-Hessen (part of the Grand Duchy of Hessen-Darmstadt), and the Palatinate (a province of Bavaria). Activists established most of their democratic societies in precisely these rural regions; that they created more than three-quarters of the Rhineland's democratic organizations between fall 1848 and winter 1849 reveals a persistence of revolutionary activity often unacknowledged in earlier historical accounts. In this too, the Rhenish revolution resembled its neighbor in France.

The Rhenish situation mirrored the French one in yet another important respect: the division between north and south. The largely inegalitarian social structure of the northern Rhineland, with its division between prosperous farmers and landless day laborers, contrasted with the more equal, and generally modest, distribution of land and resources in the South. There were, of course, exceptions to this generalization. Wine-growers and peasants in highland regions tended to be desperately poor in both the northern and southern Rhineland. As for industry and manufacture, factories and other large-scale concerns had begun to appear in the Prussian Rhineland, which boasted a wide variety of artisanal enterprises. The South, by contrast, was largely rural and agricultural, although, there too, village and small-town artisans dotted the landscape. Similar generalizations hold for northern and southern France: a highly unequal social structure with prosperous farming and growing industry in the North contrasted with smallholding peasants, few landless laborers, and a small artisanate in the South.

There were, of course, enormous political and religious differences between France as a whole and the Rhineland as a whole. But given the similarities in social structure and economic relations between both northern regions on the one hand

and the two southern regions on the other, it cannot be a pure coincidence that analogous political situations arose in the 1848 revolutions. In both France and the Rhineland, the economically "modern" North embraced "traditionalist" politics, while the "backward" South rejected established political ideas and turned to democracy and socialism.

The nature of the Rhineland's democratic development between August 1848 and May 1849 starkly reveals the political division between North and South. The Prussian (northern) Rhine Province, with three times the population of the Palatinate and Rhine-Hessen combined, had fewer than one-third the number of democratic clubs as the two Rhineland regions of the South. Focusing exclusively on rural areas makes the divergence between North and South more dramatic still: Only one-third of the Prussian Rhineland's democratic clubs existed in rural areas, and most of those took root in the suburbs of major cities or near important manufacturing centers. In the Palatinate, by comparison, 140 of the 173 democratic associations took shape in rural parts of the province. Every single country town in the Palatinate boasted a democratic club, as did each cantonal seat. So deep was the democrats' penetration that 20 percent of the villages possessed their own separate club. The democrats proved even more successful in Rhine-Hessen, where more than 60 percent of the villages formed democratic clubs.[24]

The presence of such large numbers of rural democratic clubs suggests that in a formal sense, at least, the Rhineland's radical movement was more advanced than its French counterpart. As we have seen, repression prevented the démoc-socs from establishing formal political organizations in rural France. Activists had to be content with creating informal associations housed in cafés, inns, chambrées, and ultimately secret societies. In the Rhineland, by contrast, even after what was once routinely thought to be the end of the revolution in September or November 1848, democrats could operate openly and without major legal obstacles. It should also be noted that Rhenish efforts to organize province-wide associations and even an all-German congress of democratic clubs proved more successful than similar French endeavors, which succumbed rapidly to government repression.

In terms of membership, the Rhineland's rural democratic clubs, like France's informal démoc-soc societies, consisted mainly of peasants and artisans. Urban radicals made the initial efforts to establish them and then relied on small-town and village intermediaries such as tavern proprietors and school teachers to recruit peasant members. These intermediaries were intimately familiar with rural culture and, as Sperber makes clear, knew how to draw on religious sensibilities and other aspects of village culture to help bring rural people into the democratic fold.

Although the Rhenish democratic clubs sponsored rallies and demonstrations, their most important task was the political education of their newly-minted rural members. As in France, middle and lower-middle class leaders read newspapers aloud to the assembled peasants and artisans. They did so not only because many of these lower-class members were illiterate, but because the papers were written in a style accessible only to well-educated readers. Leaders, therefore, had both to read articles and explain what they meant.

Crucial as their educative function was, clubs would not have built such widespread support if they had done nothing else. They also helped solve disputes among members and between members and local authorities. Even more important, they participated in aspects of "traditional" village culture and helped turn the charivari and other "folkloric" manifestations into expressions of democratic sentiment. Increasingly, the charivari targeted government officials, conservatives, clergymen, and other of the democrats' political opponents as objects of its ridicule and wrath. In transforming the content of such spontaneous demonstrations—planned charivaris were oxymoronic and seemed never to work—democratic activism revealed both "traditional" and "modern" features. On the one hand it operated within the context of an established popular culture replete with unplanned outbursts and symbolic forms of expression. But on the other it looked forward to the future with its deliberate efforts to politicize a group of people by transmitting a message that was anything but traditional.

In addition to their ability to mix folklore and politics, democratic activists used the villagers' religious orientation and animosities to convert them to the democratic cause. Activists tended to be most successful in places where the peoples' religious affiliation differed from that of their king. Thus, in the Prussian Rhineland, Catholics—especially those who eschewed religious orthodoxy—were more susceptible to the democratic message than Protestants, who shared the king's confession. In the Palatinate, it was Protestant villagers, at odds with Bavaria's Catholic king, who tended to side with the left. Among France's Protestants, religion played a similar role; there, the Calvinist minority—especially in the South—largely supported the démoc-socs.

One final point of comparison between the French and Rhenish Revolutions of 1848 is the way they both culminated in rural insurrections in the South. In both cases, organization was central to the geography of collective violence. As Margadant has shown for southern France, the existence of Montagnard societies was closely correlated with centers of rebellion in December 1851. Sperber has demonstrated much the same thing for the Palatinate. Villages with active People's Associations were far more likely to engage in violence against Bavarian state officials and support the short-lived Provisional Government than those without such organizations. Given socioeconomic environments and religious situations hospitable to the left, political developments in southern France and the southern Rhineland revealed a strong relationship among political organization, left-wing voting, and ultimately a violent attempt to preserve democratic gains. Here again, Germans went further than the French: nothing Louis Napoleon's opponents accomplished in 1851 equaled the establishment in May 1849 of a Palatinate provisional government.

How "modern" were these outcomes? As usual for 1848, they demonstrated a dialectic of the old and the new. The outbreak of revolutionary violence in 1849 and 1851 was, in both cases, largely unplanned. But without the deliberate, disciplined organizing of the previous years, it would never have occurred. The goal of that violence, moreover, was not, as in the past, to pillage the rich or to restore a mythical golden age. It was to establish the new, egalitarian, and popular regimes the revolutions of 1848 had promised but failed to make good.

Notes

1. Jonathan Sperber, *Rhineland Radicals. The Democratic Movement and the Revolution of 1848-1849* (Princeton, 1991); Michael Wettengel, *Die Revolution von 1848/49 im Rhein-Main-Raum. Politische Vereine und Revolutionsalltag im Grossherzogtum Hessen, Herzogtum Nassau und in der Freien Stadt Frankfurt* (Wiesbaden, 1989).

2. For a problematic use of modernization, see Eugen Weber, *Peasants into Frenchmen: The Modernization of Rural France* (Stanford, 1976). For critical analyses of modernization theory see Dean C. Tipps, "Modernization and the Comparative Study of Societies," *Comparative Studies in Society and History*, 15 (1972): 199-229; Joseph R. Gusfield, "Tradition and Modernity," *American Journal of Sociology*, 72 (1966): 351-62. See also the discussion in Sperber, *Rhineland Radicals*, pp. 480-81.

3. Ernst Bloch, *Erbschaft dieser Zeit* (Frankfurt, 1973). English trans. by Neville and Stephen Plaice, *Heritage of Our Times* (Cambridge, 1991); *Vom Hasard zur Katastrophe; Politische Aufsätze 1934-1939* (Frankfurt, 1972).

4. Edward Berenson, *Populist Religion and Left-Wing Politics in France, 1830-52* (Princeton, 1984).

5. Charles Tilly, "How Protest Modernized in France, 1845-1855," in William Aydelotte, (ed.), *The Dimensions of Quantitative Research in History* (Princeton, 1972), 192-255. For Tilly's later work see, in particular, "Did the Cake of Custom Break?" in John M. Merriman, (ed.), *Consciousness and Class Experience in Nineteenth-Century Europe*. (New York, 1979); *European Revolutions, 1492-1992* (Cambridge, MA, 1993); *Popular Contention in Great Britain, 1758-1834* (Cambridge, MA, 1995).

6. Tilly, "How Protest Modernized," 195-96.

7. Ibid., 198.

8. Peter Amann, *Revolution and Mass Democracy. The Parisian Club Movement in 1848* (Princeton, 1975).

9. Ibid., xiii.

10. Tilly, "How Protest Modernized," 199.

11. *Bibliothèque nationale. Cabinet des estampes.* Vinck collection of lithographs. Cabet's speech before the banquet of 22 September 1848.

12. *Archives nationales* BB18 1449. Minister of Interior to Minister of Justice, 10 February 1849.

13. *Archives, Préfecture de la Police.* AA 432, 2 March 1849.

14. Ibid.

15. *Archives nationales*. BB18 1472. Procureur Générale, Aix, to Minister of Interior, 10 January 1849.

16. *Archives départementales.* Var 4M 19/1.

17. Ted W. Margadant, *French Peasants in Revolt: The Insurrection of 1851* (Princeton, 1979).

18. Cited in Philippe Vigier, *La Seconde République dans la région alpine*, 2 vols. (Paris, 1963), Vol. 2, 334.

19. Eugen Weber, *Peasants into Frenchmen*. See also, Weber, "The Second Republic: Politics and the Peasants," *French Historical Studies* 11 (1980): 521-50 and "Comment la Politique Vint aux Paysans: A Second Look at Peasant Politicization," *American Historical Review* 87 (1982): 357-89; Peter McPhee, *The Politics of Rural Life. Political Mobilization in the French Countryside, 1846-1852* (Oxford, 1992).

20. McPhee, *The Politics of Rural Life*, 167.

21. Paul Noyes, *Organization and Revolution. Working-Class Associations in the German Revolutions of 1848-49* (Princeton, 1966).

22. Gabriella Hauch, *Frau Biedermeier Auf Den Barrikaden. Frauenleben in der Wiener Revolution 1848* (Vienna, 1990), esp. ch. 4.

23. 15 September 1848. Quoted in Noyes, *Organization and Revolution*, 125.

24. Sperber, *Rhineland Radicals*, 186-87.

*University Square in Vienna in the night of 13-14 March, drawn by R. Swoboda
(Illustrirte Zeitung, Leipzig, no. 248, 1 April 1848, 218)*

Chapter 24

POWER AND IMPOTENCE OF THE PRESS IN 1848

France and Germany in Comparison

Ursula E. Koch

Formation of Different Media Cultures

Before we approach the subject of the press (printed matter of all types) in France and Germany during the revolution, two fundamental conditions in these two countries need to be called to mind, the roots of which lay in the Middle Ages. These conditions created different frameworks and thus two different "cultures of communication," in their respective communication systems, that have remained distinctive down to the present day. Nonetheless, a reciprocal relation existed from the beginning, whereby, from 1789 onwards, the impulses came primarily from France.

France and the Press of Its Capital City as the "Fourth Estate"

France had been a centralized state since the time of Louis XIV and, from the revolution of 1789 onwards, a united nation. In the nineteenth century, Paris was not only the capital of France, and one rich in tradition, but also, as the poet and journalist Heinrich Heine, who had been living there from 1831, enthused, capital of "the entire civilized world."[1] Although the French press had been subject since 1789 to a constant alternation between constitutionally anchored freedom of opinion and government repression, in Paris, as the "most significant source of radical political opposition," it developed into a so-called "fourth estate."[2]

Notes for this section begin on page 614.

Parisian journalists played a significant role in the overthrow of the Bourbon King Charles X in the "three glorious days" of the July revolution (1830). Under his successor, Louis Philippe (1773-1850), the Duke of Orléans and head of the younger line of the ruling house, some of them then went on to brilliant careers, such as Adolphe Thiers (1797-1877), ofttimes a government minister and twice prime minister. Others, disappointed republicans, with the weapons of a publicist went to war against the "*roi bourgeois*," who had, as a "pear" become a "standing joke" (Heinrich Heine). Among them was Charles Philipon (1800-1862), founder of the weekly *La Caricature politique, morale et littéraire* (1830-1835), which defined the age with its lithographs, and the satirical daily, which was to last nearly a hundred years, *Le Charivari* (1832-1926), as well as the most important artist of the two papers, Honoré Daumier.[3]

Certainly, with the tightened leash from November 1830 onwards, and especially the "hellish" law introduced on 9 September 1835 after a number of violently repressed uprisings and a failed assassination attempt on the head of state, the government sought to bring an end to Parisian "press insolence." Despite the revised Charter of 14 August 1830, the law not only reintroduced prior censorship for pictures, but also increased the number of crimes against the censorship laws that could be punished with imprisonment or banishment as well as the advance deposits publishers had to pay to cover possible fines. For greater Paris (three departments) this amounted to 100,000 Francs for all periodicals which appeared more than twice a week. The "newspaper stamp," which had previously been introduced, a "tax on knowledge," was preserved. Opponents of the July Monarchy—which was based on the propertied bourgeoisie—from both the left and the right, either developed useful strategies of avoidance and survival, or were suppressed or stopped publication because of the high costs.

In spite of all the obstacles, the French press was noteworthy for its pioneering innovation. At the end of 1835 a small translation office for foreign correspondents and newspapers, founded three years earlier, became the powerful *Agence Havas*, supported by the government. Soon, its founder Charles-Louis Havas (1783-1858)could count all the major dailies in the capital among his loyal subscribers. An "impoverished monotony" of foreign reports, according to the novelist and authority on the Paris press Honoré de Balzac (1799-1850), was the unavoidable consequence.[4]

Two daily newspapers, *La Presse* and *Le Siècle*, which both first appeared on 1 July 1836, introduced the age of the press as a business. Their founders, Emile de Girardin and Armand Dutacq, doubled the number of advertisements and halved the price for an annual subscription (from 80 to 40 Francs). With exciting serialized novels by successful authors, including Balzac, Alexandre Dumas the elder (1802-1870), Eugène Sue (1804-1857), and George Sand (1804-1876), these papers and their growing competition sought to capture the attention of the reading public.

In 1846, Paris (with over a million residents) was the most important newspaper city in Europe, with twenty-six dailies that could be subscribed to, bought in the streets, or enjoyed in one the countless reading circles, reading clubs, and cafés. Nearly half of the total circulation of 180,000, however, came from the fours leaders in the field: *Le Siècle* (34,966), *La Presse* (22,409), and the two supporters of the July monarchy, *Le Constitutionnel* (23,170) and *Le Journal des Débats* (9,844) founded in 1819 and 1789 respectively, whose significance for politics, literature, and society was often pointed out.[5] The range of opinions extended from the clerical (*L'Univers*; circulation of 4,158) and "legitimist," that is, supporter of "Henry V" (*Gazette de France*; circulation of 2,946), to the "radical" (that is, republican) and early socialist opponents of the government, above all *Le National* (4,280), *La Democratie pacifique* (1,665) and *La Réforme* (1,860), with their leading figures Armand Marrast, Victor Considérant, and Ferdinand Flocon.

The range of "national" newspapers available was supplemented both by a provincial press (led by Lyon) which boomed in the years between 1830 and 1848, and by a number of journals, almanacs, and pamphlets. Two of these journals stand out for their quality and long life. The magazine *La Revue des deux Mondes*, founded in 1829, still exists. The general weekly *L'Illustration* founded in 1843 along the lines of *The Illustrated London News*, at the same time as the *Illustrirte Zeitung* (Leipzig), would last 101 years. Between these three papers there was an active exchange of clichés.

Pointing the way toward 1848 were also early attempts, starting in the 1830s, at a feminist press (apart from numerous fashion magazines) and the colorful range of early socialist monthlies and weeklies. Etienne Cabet, for example, was a publicist (*Le Populaire de 1841*) who had become a communist in exile in England before returning to France in 1839. In his sociophilosophical novel *A Voyage to Icaria*, which was already in its fifth edition in 1848 and was also translated into German in that year, he propagated the idea of a society of collectivist property, labor, and education. Especially original was the "organ of the working class" *L'Atelier*[The Workshop], founded in 1840. The trans-regional monthly, which also had some liberal bourgeois among its 440 subscribers, was produced by seventeen skilled workers, including seven typesetters. Following the example of Philippe Joseph Benjamin Buchez (1796-1865), a social politician, *L'Atelier* sought to bind together three currents originating in different eras: Catholicism, Saint-Simonism, and democracy.

The opposition movement implicit in these newspapers started to emerge in May 1847. As a consequence of national economic and financial crisis, a mass movement of all opposition groups arose, including over seventy reform banquets with 17,000 participants altogether. They demanded a reform of the franchise, the parliament, and indeed the entire French social order as described by the parodied motto "*Enrichissez-vous!*"[6]

Germany: A Loose State Structure without a Capital

In the territorially and confessionally divided "Holy Roman Empire of the German Nation," which Napoleon I had brought to an end in 1806, there had been a number of newspaper cities since the seventeenth century (1605). As printed newspapers were subject to more or less strict control by the spiritual and temporal rulers or in the laws and regulations of the city governments, expression and exchange of opinions took place above all in pamphlets and periodicals.

The German Confederation, which appeared after the Congress of Vienna of 1815, was characterized by regionalism. The Confederate Diet which met in Frankfurt am Main, was not a representative body, but rather a congress of delegates of thirty-four (for a time thirty-seven) "sovereign princes" and four "free cities"—Hamburg, Bremen, Lübeck, and Frankfurt—under the leadership of Austria.

Neither Vienna nor Berlin, both with populations over 400,000, and the capitals of the two absolutist great powers of Austria and Prussia, were home to a German "trans-regional" press in 1848. Its bases were to be found instead in the trading city of Augsburg, absorbed into the kingdom of Bavaria in 1806, with its "independent" *Allgemeine Zeitung*, read throughout Europe (circulation: 10,400) produced by the Tübingen publishing house of Cotta, and Cologne, which had become Prussian in 1815, with its *Kölnische Zeitung* (circulation: 9,500), which was read throughout northern Germany.

Following the model of Napoleon I, the Austrian statesman Klemens Prince von Metternich (1773-1859) and his closest advisor Friedrich von Gentz, at first a revolutionary and then an ultra-conservative publicist, (ennobled in Sweden in 1804), placed the political press in a strait-jacket. Legislation passed on 20 September 1819 and extended in 1824 for the purpose of preventing "revolutionary intrigues" included, among other things, the following drastic repressive measures: 1. prior censorship for all printed matter under 20 sheets (320 octavio pages); 2. the possibility of imprisonment, banishment, or prohibition on practicing their occupation (limited to five years) for insubordinate journalists. Along the lines of "Confederate law supersedes state law," especially southern German constitutional states were repeatedly called to order.

After the "three glorious days" in Paris (27 to 29 July 1830), some German princes experienced a fear of revolution and the press experienced a new lease on life. "Freedom of the press" became one the most important catchwords of the *Vormärz*. Especially strong resistance to censorship appeared in the Grand Duchy of Baden and in Bavarian Rhine Palatinate. There, in Zweibrücken, the German Fatherland Association for the Support of the Free Press was established at the end of January 1832. Its founders were two journalists who had come into conflict with the authorities: Johann Georg August Wirth and Philipp Jakob Siebenpfeiffer.[7] Among its many tasks, the Press Association organized the "National Festival of the Germans" (30,000 participants) in front of the ruins of the Hambach Castle—since restored. In Neustadt on the Weinstraße, the black-red-gold "tricolor" flew for the first time. A month after the Hambach Festival, on 28 June 1832, the Karlsbad Decrees were tightened, because of a "pathological state of public opinion." One page fliers and caricatures (steel and copper engraving, lithographs) on the one hand, and printed matter over twenty sheets on the other, were subject to prior censorship for the first time. Newspapers and journals were required to have a "concession" (license). An "information office" established in Mainz in 1833, with about fifteen secret agents, monitored not only "the journalism and writers" of the German Confederation (for example, the authors of the Young Germany movement) but also all writers in exile throughout Europe. Opposition journalists were left with the possibility of "smuggling ideas" (language, distribution) or escaping into harmless entertainment.

With Friedrich Wilhelm IV's ascension to the Prussian throne (7 June 1840), enactment of relatively liberal censorship regulations (24 December 1841) and a (temporary) end to prior censorship of pictures (May 1842), many contemporaries became more hopeful. Thus, for example, the series of leaders published in the *Königlich Preußische Staats-Kriegs- und Friedenszeitung* (from 1850 *Königsberger Hartungsche Zeitung*), "Inländische Zustände" [domestic conditions], was both popular and controversial. In the *Rheinische Zeitung für Politik, Handel und Gewerbe* (3,000 subscribers), founded on 1 January 1842, the "radical bourgeois" Karl Marx (1818-1883) earned his spurs as a journalist. However, after the Prussian king—angered at a caricature—tightened the leash once again on 3 February 1843—the Cologne paper was closed down on 31 March 1843.

Nonetheless, supervision by the individual states and the Confederation found its limits in the 1840s. In the Hanseatic cities of Hamburg and Bremen, in the Prussian Rhineland, in the Kingdom of Saxony with its publishing and trade fair center of Leipzig, and especially in the Grand Duchy of Baden, some papers could publish "quite freely." Only one will be mentioned here, the liberal *Deutsche Zeitung*, founded by the professor of history and literature Georg Gervinus (1805-1871), one of the "Göttingen Seven," in Heidelberg. Even a few radical democratic newspapers and journals risked publication. The *Triersche Zeitung* was credited with a "mainly socialist tendency." In September 1847, the Mainz informant Wilhelm Fischer, in a memorandum "on the German newspaper press," came to the following pessimistic conclusion on the situation. "For the serious observer of the intellectual movement in the German world, it is both an interesting and instructive phenomenon that in spite of all restrictions under which they groan, the German press has become a power which can no longer be repressed using any conceivable means."[8]

Flyers, pamphlets, calendars, and "*Groschenhefte*" (the most popular author was Adolf Glaßbrenner), serious and satirical, illustrated by famous (for example, Theodor Hosemann) and unknown artists, as well as political poems by well-known "censorship refugees" (Georg Herwegh, Ferdinand Freiligrath) spread in books and feuilletons, and finally satirical magazines founded in Berlin (*Berliner Charivari*), Düsseldorf (*Düsseldorfer Monatshefte*), Hamburg (*Mephistopheles*), Leipzig (*Charivari*), Munich (*Fliegende Blätter, Leuchtkugeln*), and Stuttgart (*Eulenspiegel*) were signs of a new age.

In 1846/47, Baden, Saxony and even Prussia expressed serious doubts about the positive "effects" of a censorship they held to be "weak with age." At the "First United Diet" of the eight provincial diets of Prussia in Berlin (11 April to 26 June 1847), the estate of the cities demanded its immediate abolition.

Probably it was not only the "social question" which had led to a "deep-seated unrest" (according to a Metternich informant) in the Prussian capital, but also the extensive range of newspapers and journals on offer in the fifty reading cafés and in the *Zeitungshalle* opened in 1847. This reference library, which charged an entrance fee, carried more than 600 periodicals in fourteen languages and offered its readers from all classes, including numerous opposition intellectuals, the opportunity to meet, discuss, and hold speeches in its tastefully decorated rooms.

Admittedly, only four subscription newspapers (total circulation: 40,000) appeared in the city: The organ of the liberal bourgeoisie (circulation: 20,000), the *Königlich privilegirte Berlinische Zeitung von Staats- und gelehrten Sachen* (known after its publisher as the *Vossische Zeitung* or Aunt Voss) founded in 1617; the *Berlinische Nachrichten von Staats- und gelehrten Sachen* (known as the *Haude- und Spenersche Zeitung*), the paper of the court, high-ranking state officials, the rural nobility, and pastors' families, founded in 1740; the *Allgemeine Preußische Zeitung*, close to the government and founded in 1819; and the more recently founded *Berliner Zeitungshalle* (1846).

Only three of the nineteen political dailies in the Habsburg monarchy appeared in the imperial city of Vienna: the official *Wiener Zeitung*, founded in 1703, with its monopoly on advertisements and announcements, as well as the two semi-official papers, the *Österreichischer Beobachter* and the *Wanderer*. The conservative-moderate *Jahrbücher der Literatur*, founded in 1817 at Metternich's instigation, followed his line. However, it did not prove attractive to its target readership, liberals. In *Vormärz* Vienna it was more cultural journalism than political journalism which blossomed, for example in Adolf Bäuerle's journal *Allgemeine Theaterzeitung und Unterhaltungsblatt für Freunde der Kunst, Literatur und des geselligen Lebens* (1806-1860), popular among young and old, or in Moritz Gottlieb Saphir's "journal of humor and seriousness, art, theater, conversation and customs," *Der Humorist* (1837-1855).

Brilliance and Misery of Parisian Journalists

From the February Revolution to the June Uprising

The banning of a reform banquet arranged for 22 February in Paris led to unrest and then to a general uprising. On 24 February, at lunch time, the editor of the daily *La Presse*, Emile de Girardin, went to the Tuileries and demanded—with success—the king's abdication. With the proclamation of the republic on the same evening, Louis Philippe fled to England.

Most members of the Provisional Government, like the poet and foreign minister Alphonse de Lamartine,[9] came from, or were close to, the world of the press. Provisional secretaries of state were the socialist journalist Louis Blanc (creator of the well-known phrase "the organization of labor") and the editors-in-chief of the dailies *Le National* (Armand Marrast) and *La Réforme* (Ferdinand Flocon). Soon Flocon, who at one time translated German ballads, became minister of war and Marrast, a "man of wit," the mayor of Paris. The new rulers not only announced the "right to work" and to form associations, but also approved universal manhood suffrage (women had to wait until 1944!) and freedom of the press, celebrated as the "tool of civilization." On 4 and 6 March, the newspaper stamp, security deposit, and the September Laws, "disapproved of by all Frenchmen," were abolished. From 22 March onwards, all press offenses were tried by jury.

On 6 March, the five-day old "newspaper for ideas and facts" *La Liberté*, wrote, "Monopolies, privileges and capitalism are at an end! The rule of equal rights for all begins!" These enthusiastic words were immediately followed by acts. *La Liberté* reduced its staggered subscription prices (1, 3, 6, 12 months) by more than half (for one year, in Paris, 18 Francs); a single issue cost—unique at the time—only five centimes ("un sou").

The results of elections (22/23 April) for the constituent assembly (9 million instead of 250,000 voters) confirmed the political role of republican journalists. The first president of the constitutional assembly, opened on 4 May, was Armand Marrast (until August). The "clan," the "clique," or the "dynasty" of the newspaper *Le National* was victorious, as contemporaries joked. Altogether, of the delegates elected, 11.4 percent were full-time and 10 percent part-time "hack journalists."[10]

Included among them were quite different characters such as the former editor-in-chief of the *Charivari*, Michel Altaroche, and the head of the Parisian workers' paper *L'Atelier*, Anthime Corbon. For Corbon, "serious life" had already begun at the age of seven. As a member of the constitutional committee and as chairman of the commission, he was at the beginning of a political career which he would conclude as a highly honored senator.

Some of the legitimist press organs ceased publication. Others, such as France's oldest newspaper, *La Gazette de France*, founded in 1631, transformed their anachronistic subtitle into a more contemporary one. After 25 February, it was no longer the "Newspaper of loyal royal principles and national liberties," but the "Newspaper of equal rights for all and universal suffrage." After a short break, not least for tactical reasons, the mouthpiece of Catholicism, *L'Univers* (which hoped for more freedom for the church), as well as the four "majors," *Le Journal des Débats, Le Constitutionnel, La Presse* ("Trust! Confidence!"), and *Le Siècle* also adapted to the new times. Even *Le Moniteur Universel*, from 1799 onwards the "state newspaper" of all the following governments, became "more colorful," "more epic," and described itself, starting on 26 February, as the "official organ of the French republic."

As was to be expected, one found expressions of unlimited joy in *La Démocratie pacifique* in its slogan published on 25 February in bold type: "The republic of 1792 destroyed the old order. The Republic of 1848 must create a new one." Two days later, *L'Atelier*, which had changed from a monthly to a weekly, stated with satisfaction: "Workers! We no longer live in the shadows, we are no longer a lower class!"

As a consequence of freedom of the press won for the third time at the barricades, the number of wall-posters, pamphlets, and newspapers, springing up like mushrooms, became "countless." The press researcher Eugène Hatoin speaks of a "true flood."[11] Seven hundred eighty-nine political and 400 apolitical titles were said to have appeared between 24 February 1848 and the coup of 10 December 1851: above all in Amiens, Bordeaux, Dijon, Lille, Marseille, Toulouse, Valenciennes, and, naturally, in Paris.

Many of these new publications, quite distinct in terms of frequency of appearance (daily, once or twice a week), paper (white, pink, dark red), format (from duodecimo to poster size, especially popular was large format folio), numbers of pages and columns, price policy (Paris, departments), political current, and target readership, never brought out more than a few issues.[12] Others, "old" and "new," saw their circulation and number of editions rise rapidly for a time due to increasing demand and a purchase of rapid printing presses. Among these was *La Liberté*, edited by Alexandre Dumas the Elder from April to June (street sales of over 80,000) and *La Presse* (60,000 to 70,000).

Politicians, clergymen, professors, lawyers, famous or soon to be famous artists, poets, and writers led, "inspired," or edited press organs of all types. In the first and penultimate numbers of their newspaper *Le Salut public*, two seventeen-year-olds, Charles Baudelaire, the future author of *Les Fleurs du mal*, and Champfleury (i.e., Jules Husson) later prominent as a caricature researcher, announced, three days after the proclamation of the republic: "24 February is humanity's most important day!" "Experienced" pressmen, including a number of "previous political prisoners," personified continuity despite all the changes. Apart from them, hundreds of unknown and amateur men and women jumped into the journalistic adventure. To ease their work, the business of lithographic correspondence bloomed (for example *La Correspondance de Paris* or *Le Bulletin de Paris*).

The newly won freedom of opinion and strong competition led to bitter press feuds, especially in Paris. On 4 June, *Le Bonhomme Richard* wrote: "I have read ninety newspapers which our February revolution brought about; I discovered nothing but madness, lies, slander, and evil intent in them."

The large number of new newspapers did not bring with them an equally large number of new, original titles. This explains the number of newspapers with the same or similar titles which gave rise to some confusion. Very popular was the noun "republic" and the adjective "republican."[13] June brought a new, multifaceted "republican wave."[14] At the same time, a true flood of newspapers covered the land which contained the word "people" in their titles.[15] A larger group of newspapers made express reference to the French Revolution in their titles.[16]

Even with their first editions, *L'Ami du Peuple en 1848* and *Le Bonnet rouge* ("organ of a proletarian, written for his friends") raised "childish fears among certain people." The second issue of *L'Ami du Peuple en 1848* (28 February) was publicly burned on the Place Saint-Michel. "In a brutal manner," newspaper boys were forbidden to cry out *Le Bonnet rouge* (no. 2, 15–18 June). Street sales of *L'Aimable Faubourien* [The Friendly Suburbanite], subtitled "Journal de la Canaille," were also stopped. This paper was aimed at "the democratic France of 1792 and 1848," that is, at "the thinkers and the fighters, the voluntary soldiers of the revolution."

It is probable that the latter belonged to the working-class press. In fact, the working-class press held first place between February and June 1848 in terms of numbers: 171 titles for the period from 24 February to 17 June 1848. It, too—like the bourgeois press—was characterized by its variety. Financing was secured through subscription, partnerships or sales of shares. Individual issues of many papers cost—following the example of *La Liberté*—five centimes. The circulation of especially popular papers were quite impressive: between 5,000 and 50,000. Leading by

Figure 1, *Newspapers in Revolutionary Paris*

far was *Le Père Duchène* (up to 80,000). For illiterates, there were public newspaper readings, for example in the workers' library.[17]

Two especially important categories of the workers' press in 1848 should be mentioned briefly here: 1. Newspapers for corporations and associations, and 2. Club publications. Belonging to the first category was France's oldest mouthpiece of an official representation of workers, *Le Journal des Travailleurs,* which appeared twice weekly from 4 to 25 June. In its first edition, the paper founded by members of the "government committee for workers" meeting in the Luxembourg Palace wrote, "Unemployment is the most terrible plague of our current social system." The second group drew on the tradition of the clubs of the revolutionary period.

Of the circa 450 clubs, naturally including a "Club of Publicists," some, like the "Club de L'Atelier," the "Club de la Démocratie pacifique," and the "Club des Amis du Peuple" arose from a journalistic enterprise. In other cases, it was the club which first appeared (for example "Club du Peuple") and then the newspaper (*L'Accusateur public*). On 26 April, sixty clubs followed a call by the "Club of the Revolution" (main speaker Armand Barbès) and united into the "Club of Clubs."

At the beginning of 1848, nearly 5 percent of the population of Paris was German (more than 62,000) with an infrastructure in existence for over thirty years. Hence it is not surprising that German workers also founded a club and a "German Democratic Society" and, on 28 May, took part in the general newspaper frenzy with the *Pariser Abend-Zeitung*. The extent to which German workers felt bound to their host country can be seen in a letter to the editor, in which some of them, "in the name of a large number of like-minded people" addressed to the "citizen editor" of *L'Atelier* (no. 11) on 12 April:

> We were extremely pleased to see that you have spoken out against the deportation of foreigners … German workers fought on the side of French workers in 1830, 1839 and 1848. They have made a great contribution to growth of production in Paris, Lyon, and Marseille. One cannot chase them away, neither with force nor with cunning …

The letter ended with the words "Long live the republic! … Friends, French brothers, you can count on the understanding and the feeling, on the pen and the hand, of the Germans who are living in your midst!"

Some press organs specialized in reporting on club life, for example the "Daily newspaper of public assemblies," *La Voix des Clubs*, which appeared from 8 to 26 March, always with up-to-date club statistics. It was continued in April as *La Sentinelle des Clubs*. In the first edition (8 March) one might read "Clubs mean thought translated into action, the working out of public opinion; it is the word of the masses, it is the republic which gains an audience through thousands of voices."

Some hundreds of men as well as an extraordinary personality like George Sand gained an "audience" for themselves in 1848 with the spoken and written word but so did politicized women among the common people. On 19 March, Eugénie Niboyet, a socially committed writer, journalist, and translator, active in Lyon and Paris for over thirty years, founded the daily *La Voix des Femmes* [The Voice of Women]. The "Socialist Political Journal for the Interests of all Women" (subtitle) defined itself in its first edition: "*La Voix des Femmes* is the first and only serious tribune from which women may express themselves: their moral, intellectual, and material interests will be defended here with vigor." And further along in the text: "All currents in the women's press flow together in this newspaper."

In fact, the editorial staff, a collective, was pluralistic. It united Saint-Simonian workers, including Désirée Veret-Gay (from 1832 to 1834 co-editor of the later-renamed monthly *La Femme Libre*), nearly illiterate working-class women and a number of representatives of the socially active republican bourgeoisie. The print-shop also belonged to a woman, the widow (de) Lacombe, who was also very active in 1848. *La Voix des Femmes*, which was soon transformed into a joint-stock company, cost ten centimes per edition. Its four folio pages contained official texts of laws and decrees, reports from the provinces and from abroad, mixed news, a press review, a feuilleton, an article on social conditions, including two texts by Bettina von Arnim on "Poverty in Germany,"[18] as well as a long series on the rights of women in the existing society.

The editorial rooms also served as a public meeting place of the "Central Committee of the Society of the Voice of Women" from 9 to 5, as well as an advice and support office; moreover, the newspaper supported numerous women's associations. On 20 June, *La Voix des Femmes* (no. 46) appeared for the last time, after the paper had published for a month on and off and toward the end only irregularly. The condescending stance of George Sand, who was worshipped by the editorial staff, and the derision they met with everywhere, may well be two of many reasons for its closure.

On 18 June, the weekly *La Politique des Femmes,* intended as a successor to *La Voix des Femmes*, appeared, although only intermittently because of the June uprising. The editorial staff was made up of a group of women under the leadership of Désirée Gay, at this time delegate of the "Women's Society for Mutual Education." Among the four co-workers known by name was Jeanne Deroin, president of the Association of Working Women's Clubs, and a section head in the National Workshops, H. Sénéchal. After a second edition, on 5 August, a third start was made on 21 August with *L'Opinion des Femmes*, this time by the public school teacher Jeanne Deroin. The brief self-description of the paper, which appeared with interruptions until August 1849, was as follows: "What does 'women's opinion' mean? It is the judgement which allows one half of humankind to consider the laws forced on them by the other half of humankind."[19]

The first protest against the February revolution in the form of establishing a newspaper came with *L'Assemblée Nationale*, founded on 1 March by former high state officials of the July monarchy. It was followed by the legitimist newspaper *L'Opinion publique* (circulation: 6,000) in May and *Le Lampion*, the "torch," founded by the future editor of *Le Figaro*, Villemessant (i.e. Hippolyte Cartier).

Extremely successful—this success being credited to curiosity—also or especially among workers were some Bonapartist periodicals, after Louis Napoléon Bonaparte (1808-1873), who had been in exile in London (until 24 September), and on 4 June 1848 was elected to the National Assembly in four departments at the same time. The "political and literary daily newspaper" *Le Napoléonien* (12 June 1848 to January 1849) managed a circulation of 45,000, followed by the "journal of the younger and old guard," *Le petit Caporal* (The Little Corporal, nickname of his great uncle; circulation of 30,000). A further title drawing on the Napoleonic cult was *La Redingote grise* [The Grey Uniform].

During elections and by-elections for the National Assembly, Parisian newspapers of all political currents played a coordinating role. Each paper published either its own list of candidates or that of an allied publication.

The great questions in domestic politics were: Who is the people? Which revolution? Which republic? That of the bourgeois "blues" represented in the national assembly, or that of the "democratic and social" reds called for by "exalted" workers and their leaders? The following are just a few of the catchwords which appeared in many newspaper headings of declarations of principle: "Freedom, Equality, Fraternity; Tolerance, Human Dignity, Unity, National Consciousness; Social Progress, Right to Work, Organization of Work, Free Public Education, Happiness and Prosperity for All."

Due to the "mission" of the revolutionaries, republican France's foreign policy was defined by the "springtime of the peoples." There was the dream of a "solidarity" or a "holy" alliance of the "democratic peoples" (*La Réforme, L'Alliance des peuples*), of a "great European league" (*Le Banquet social*), of a "great European democracy" (*Le National*), of the "United States of Europe," with a common army, currency, tax and metric system (*La Presse*); the talk was of a "world republic" (*La Démocratie pacifique*) or of "universal harmony" (the title of a paper which updated a term of the philosopher Leibniz). Both bourgeois and workers' presses often dedicated columns specifically to the European revolutions (Germany, Italy, Poland, Hungary). *L'Illustration* applied itself with enthusiasm to the role of a "weekly review," which, however, became ever more conservative.

The reaction of Paris journalists to two canards formed the high point of Franco-German reporting, which were not without their comic aspects. On 21 March a telegram alleged that the king of Prussia had fled to Vienna! Four days later a second telegram from Metz to the Paris stock market alleged that a republic had been proclaimed in Berlin and the king together with his ministers had been arrested.

Against this backdrop, the republican papers raised cries of jubilation. On 22 March *La Démocratie Pacifique* announced: "Around the German republic, as the true core of the European republic, the restored nations will group themselves on their naturally given land, and before the end of the year this work will be completed." Two days later *La République* proclaimed that "Germany is the brain, and France the heart of humanity!" On 27 March Alexandre Dumas wrote in *La Liberté* in an appeal to "the Prussians and the Austrians": "Hail, you blond children of the north: you are the sons of Hermann of the Cherusci; we are the sons of Vercingetorix. We fought against Caesar's cohorts. You defeated the legions of Augustus. Hence we are brothers!"[20]

Lost Illusions

Just eleven days after the national assembly had taken up its work there was a break with the "people of Paris." A demonstration (150,000 participants) organized by the radical-democratic clubs on 15 May, the insurrectional occupation of the assembly chambers, and the arrest of some ringleaders (including the journalists Barbès and Raspail) were commented on as follows by *L'Accusateur Public* (no. 4) on 21 June: "From now on the facts can no longer be covered up: Two classes are facing each other. The one wishes to destroy the other." The Parisian workers' uprising which broke out on 23 June, after the announcement of the closing of the National Workshops, violently suppressed four days later, confirmed this prophecy: 3,600 dead, 1,600 imprisoned, 11,000 deported.

The new head of government, General Louis-Eugène Cavaignac, declared martial law for Paris until the end of October, had the clubs closed temporarily, and suspended (until 6 August) eleven newspapers.[21] With the decree of 9 August (reintroduction of security deposits: 24,000 Francs in Paris) and the "Law for the Protection of the Republic" of 11 August, freedom of the press was once again restricted. Those who were "poor" were "silenced" (according to *Le Peuple Constituant*) or, as an alternative, raised prices or reduced the number of pages or the frequency of publication (*L'Atelier*). An ordinance of 21 August suspended *La Vraie République*, *Le Père Duchène*, and *Le Lampion* for a second time as well as Proudhon's *Le Représentant du Peuple*. Three days later, the royalist *Gazette de France* suffered the same fate. The latter then appeared for two months under the cover name *L'Etoile de France*. All the newspapers banned were accused of increasing the danger of a civil war through their strong attacks on the state, the family, and property.

In this period of repression, a newspaper was founded which was based on a totally new concept: *L'Evénement* [The Event]. In its test issue of 30/31 July, its title was explained: "Our basic idea is simple, but no one has thought of it up to now; we will organize the news, not according to form but according to its importance." "Inspiration" for the paper, which first appeared on 1 August 1848, was France's most important poet, Victor Hugo (1802-1885), who had been elected to the National Assembly on 4 June. It was edited by his sons Charles and François in cooperation with a few authors who were friends of the family. In the three years of its existence, it shifted—like Victor Hugo himself—ever more to the left. Initially, however, the newspaper supported Louis Napoléon and thus contributed to his triumphal election as president of the Republic (5.5 million votes) on 10 December.

From December 1848 to January 1849, a six-volume bibliographic obituary of all printed matter which had "been born, died, aborted, survived, revived or transformed" from 22 February 1848 to Louis Napoléon's swearing in (20 December) appeared with the title *The Gravedigger of the Press*. In this "mass grave" were the press organs for the people, 75 percent of which had not survived the June uprising. Nonetheless, the final hour of the press had not yet rung, as shown by two examples. Proudhon's *Représentant du Peuple* survived, although with longer interruptions, in three new successors (*Le Peuple*, *La Voix du Peuple*, and *Le Peuple de 1850*) until 13 October 1850. From 23 October 1849 to 5 December 1851, the political weekly *La Feuille du Village* spread, in two series, republican ideas throughout the country. Its editor was a publicist, agronomist, and deputy of the extreme left, Pierre Joigneaux.

Admittedly, in 1849, the anti-republican press, a heterogeneous community of interests, was gaining ground both in Paris and in the provinces. The "Journal of Order," *Le Dix décembre* (15 April to 17 June 1850), with the battle cry "Long live the emperor," and *Le Pays* (the fatherland) were the most important new Bonapartist publications. Both were edited by a loyal follower of Louis Napoléon: Adolphe Granier de Cassagnac. *L'Appel au Peuple* (test issue of 10 April) and *Le Journal du Peuple* (8 May to 23 July) did not call for an uprising, but fought against the "terrible doctrine of socialism" and "always and everywhere the revolution."

New marketing concepts were developed. Thus, for example, the "Newspaper for everyone" *Le Bien-Etre* [The Good Feeling], which appeared from 1 March to 13 May 1849 (six issues) promised its subscribers a pension under certain conditions. The daily *Le Bienfaisant* [The Benefactor]—which was brought out by a group of priests, workers, and "men of the world" from 29 October to 22 November and was aimed at two groups of subscribers—reflected the principle, still popular in France today, of mutual aid. The one group of subscribers who could afford 1.20 Francs a month, kept their copies. The other received a copy only to read (two hours) and paid half the price. These "second-class subscribers" could claim free treatment from doctors who had ties to the directors of the paper. All subscribers could buy medicine in the General Reciprocal Apothecary and in its branches at a reduced price.

And there was more. Depending on social status, the subscribers could choose between three different issues. The daily was for people in the big cities, for the educated, and for people with time. The edition which appeared three times a week, which "simplified the debates and summed up events of the day," was intended for "small town residents and the petite bourgeoisie." The weekly edition (with woodcuts, lithographs, anecdotes, and stories in a simple language), sometimes translated into German (Alsace), was directed at the rural population.

The "newspaper of the lovers of order," *La Bourgeoisie* (test edition in May) contained one of the earliest analysis of newspaper readership, although limited to Paris:

> Politically interested readers can be divided as follows. There are 60,000 direct subscriptions for political newspapers and 40,000 subscriptions for reading rooms. Furthermore, 200,000 copies of newspapers of all political currents are sold on the street daily. The number of irregular readers, that is, those who have no subscription but who read here or there, in cafés, reading rooms, associations, or through friends or acquaintances, is approximately 300,000. According to this estimate, the total readership of political newspapers in Paris is about 600,000.[22]

At about the same time, the republic entered its final phase. Alexis de Tocqueville (1805-1859), the famous political scientist, conservative deputy, and soon-to-be minister, commented on the results of the elections for the legislative assembly (13 May), in which neither Lamartine nor Armand Marrast had a seat, as follows: "The opponents of the republic have the majority; both the revolutionary left and the monarchical right are waiting for the opportunity to abolish the constitution."[23]

The right of all citizens to "freely express [their opinions] in the press," granted them in the constitution of 4 November, was restricted step by step after the most recent unrest in Paris (13 June). Legislation of 27 July 1849 extended the number of press offenses (slandering the president of the republic, inciting the military to disobedience) and subjected all forms of colportage to licensing by the prefects. The law of 16 July 1850 reintroduced a stamp tax and ended anonymity for political, ideological, and religious newspaper articles. The number of press trials rose rapidly: from 546 in 1849 to 632 in 1850. *L'Atelier, La Réforme, La Démocratie pacifique, La Liberté* and other journals stopped publishing.

Three weeks after the coup of 2 December 1851, press offenses were transferred from trial by jury to criminal justice. In the "press charter" of February/March 1852 (which included a number of decrees), not only were concession requirements and prior censorship for pictures re-established, but also—as a new measure for the "protection of public security"—a system of "cautions" was established. After two such cautions, the government could close a publication, temporarily or even permanently. *Le National*, *La République*, and *L'Evénement*, renamed *L'Avènement du Peuple* ("The people take the power of government"), on 19 September 1851, were victims of the coup. Flocon, Girardin, Victor Hugo, Pierre Joigneaux, Pierre Leroux, and many others went into exile. Three quarters of the republican journalists were arrested, banished, or deported to Africa. In his well-known pamphlet "Napoleon the Small," published in Brussels on 5 August 1852, that is, on the day he arrived on Jersey, Victor Hugo summed up the new regulations in one line: "I allow you to speak. But I order you to keep quiet." Thirty years would have to pass before the "most liberal press laws in the world" would be passed, on 29 July 1881, that is, in the Third Republic, which, in a somewhat modified form, are still valid today.

The Resistable Rise of the German Press

The German Press: Beneficiary of the February Revolution

From 27 February onward, masses of people were packed in front of newspaper offices, in reading cafés, and reading rooms. Public readings spread the news and commented, "often accompanied by illegal acclamations," on the "extraordinary news from Paris." In Frankfurt, newspapers were cut into pieces so that more than one person could read them at the same time. In the introduction to their second half-year volume of 1848, the *Illustrirte Zeitung* wrote: "The revolt started in France and quickly spread through the regions of Germany, from its loveliest rivers to its furthest borders …" Reason enough for this was to be found locally: in one place, a late feudal agrarian structure; in another, unemployment and starvation; in many places, dissatisfaction with local and national political circumstances.

The "March days" brought with them total liberation from state and economic chains on the press for the first time, even if only temporarily. Grand Duke Leopold of Baden took the first step on 1 March. On 3 March the Confederate Diet allowed its members the possibility of ending censorship. On 4 March, the Free City of Frankfurt am Main and Grand Duke Ludwig II of Hessen-Darmstadt decided in favor of a legislative ending of censorship. They were followed by the Kingdom of Saxony and the Free City of Hamburg on 9 March. The Bavarians were promised freedom of the press after student unrest in February (the Lola Montez affair) and the storming by the people of Munich of King Ludwig I's (1786-1868) arsenal on 6 March. It was only officially granted on 4 June, after the king's abdication (20 March), by his son Maximilian Joseph II (1811-1864). In Austria, freedom of the press, like in Paris, was a true child of the revolution. The popular uprising in Vienna (13 March) led Prince Metternich to retire. He fled to London—like King Louis

Philippe. On 14 March, the abolition of censorship was announced in a special edition of the *Wiener Zeitung*, to great cheers. Admittedly, two months passed before two ordinances (18 May) regulated the press: "No concession, no security deposit, no deposit copies, lifting of controls on colportage …"

Events in Vienna, on the one hand, and the mass meetings of students, artists, academics, businessmen, artisans, and workers since 6 March, totally extraordinary for Berlin, on the other, led King Friedrich Wilhelm IV to sign a "Law on the Press" on 17 March in Potsdam. On 18 March this document, supplemented on 4 April by the ending of security deposits and a special regulation for the Rhine provinces (reintroduction of trial by jury) was announced in Berlin in special editions and wall posters. Nonetheless, because of a "misunderstanding" (two shots set off without orders at a crowd assembled in front of the palace), a short but bitter civil war (256 barricade fighters killed directly or indirectly, including "working women" and one child) broke out in Berlin. It ended with an initial victory for the people.

On 20 March the grand old lady of the Berlin press, the more than 230 year old *Vossische Zeitung* (no. 67) published a "Supplement of Happiness," of which 12,000 copies were sold within five hours. On 24 March, the one-and-a- half-year old *Berliner Zeitungs-Halle* (in which Theodor Fontane would predict a "great German republic" on 31 August) took on the motto: "Everything for the people—Everything by the people." On 2 April the German Confederation suspended all the special legislation passed since 1819. However, Ernst August of Hanover only legalized the abolition of censorship, which had already been authorized on 18 April, after a twenty-five day delay.

On 21 December 1848, after the counter-revolution had long begun, the '"Basic Rights of the German People" were proclaimed in the *Paulskirche*. Article IV declared: "The freedom of the press, may not, under any circumstances and in no way … be restricted, suspended, or annulled." In the constitution of the German people (28 March 1849), which never went into force, freedom of opinion was also guaranteed (article 4, § 143), something which in France had been held to be the "most valuable human right" since 1789.

The Press Explosion—A Phenomenon of the Cities

The "accomplishments of March"—freedoms of the press, assembly, and association, free elections for the first all-German National Assembly and, with various electoral regulations, for the parliaments of the individual states—led to a lively public life. Respected newspapers in the major cities and established weeklies, the so-called homeland newspapers, forced until then into political restraint, enlarged their formats, increased their print runs, expanded their generally pluralistic "public forums," and often took sides in political debates.

In nearly all regions "more newspapers were founded … than had existed before," between 1848 and 1850.[24] As in France, in Germany there was a lack of titles. While there were very few "republicans," there were all the more newspapers which named themselves after the people [*Das Volk*]: *Das Volk, Das Volksblatt, Der Volksbote, (Die) Volksstimme* or *(Der) Volksfreund*, etc. (c. 40!). *Deutsche Volkszeitung* was the name of a Mannheim newspaper (26 March to 29 April) whose editor-in-chief, Julius Fröbel, familiar with the teachings of French early socialism, listed fifteen "proven friends of the people" as co-editors. Among them were the two lawyers and publicists Gustav von Struve and Friedrich Hecker, who a little later, on 12 April, would proclaim the republic in Baden.

The real boom in founding newspapers was, however, restricted to the cities, that is, to the regional centers of political or economic power and social communication. The figures for Vienna are impressive, as it had suffered especially severely from censorship: 181 periodicals of all political currents, including 86 dailies. At the time, on 3 July 1848, one of the leading newspapers of the Habsburg monarchy was founded: *Die Presse*—its motto was "Equal rights for all," and its editor and publisher was August Zang. Among the democratic press was, for example, the "People's Newspaper for Unrestricted Liberty and Reform," *Der Ohnehose,*—which pilloried "profiteers" in its Sunday supplement, the *Arbeiter-Zeitung*, and the *Politischer Courier*, brought out by students, with the appeal (Theodor Körner) from 1813: "A Passage for Freedom." In 1848 (on 14 April), the *Wiener Kirchenzeitung* also appeared. This publication of the Catholic federalist party appeared three times a week and would later become the leading Austrian antisemitic publication.

The Prussian capital of Berlin also experienced an explosion of printed matter: 135 very different newspapers and journals arose between March 1848 and November 1849, including around 100 of a political nature. The titles of the publications founded at the time—as everywhere—reflected the revolution and counterrevolution. The palette of only short-lived new papers ranged from the "Today's Entertainment Paper" *Die Barrikaden* (2 July to 25 December), *Die Republik* (14 October to 11 November) and *Das Volk*, to the "Political Newspaper for Constitutional Germany", *Die Deutsche Reform*, up to the arch-conservative "Organ for Prussia's Women and Girls" *Gott mit uns!* (1849).

The year of birth of a modern political press in Berlin also saw a rise in club and association journals for example the *Club-Blatt*, as well as a modest—when compared with Paris—press for workers. The first real workers' newspaper was the "Organ of the Workers' Central-Committee," *Das Volk*, which appeared starting in June 1848. The editor, and at the same time the founder, of the oldest umbrella organization of German workers' associations and trade associations, the *Arbeiterverbrüderung*, was the typesetter Stephan Born, a friend of Marx and Engels. Admittedly, in his newspaper he drew less on Karl Marx and more on Louis Blanc (organization of work by the state) and Buchez (production associations based on self-help). From 3 October to 29 June 1850, the successor of *Das Volk*, *Die Verbrüderung*, appeared in Leipzig.

Only three of the newly founded Berlin daily newspapers were granted a longer life. The publisher of the *National-Zeitung* (1848-1938), Bernhard Wolff, was for a time an apprentice under Charles Havas and was the first to make use of the telegraph. Out of the telegraph service, established on 28 November 1849, arose the famous international telegraph news agency WTB (Wolffsches Telegraphisches Bureau). The long-time editor-in-chief of the *Volks-Zeitung* (1849-1944), which originated as the *Urwähler-Zeitung*, was Aaron Bernstein, who would always be a full supporter of the "forty-eighters." The *Neue Preußische Zeitung* (1848-1939), inspired and in part written by the future founder of the empire, Otto von Bismack, was known as the *Kreuz-Zeitung* after the iron cross that appeared on its masthead. The *Kreuz-Zeitung* saw it as its duty to strictly oppose the "unleashed spirits of rebellion." Against the "foreign" and "un-German" institutions (National Assembly), the "destructive leveling forces of the age," it upheld the monarchy by grace of God and the existing legal order.

Berlin was flooded with about 2,000 flyers, some illustrated, and with placards that often rose on top of one another from the ground "in huge formats" and transformed corner houses "into open books." One of the most fruitful producers of flyers was the "Dages-Schriftsteller mit'n jroßen Bart," [newspaper journalist with the big beard—in Berlin dialect (Ed.)] Aujust Buddelmey(i)er, in reality the doctor Adalbert Cohnfeld. The most interesting publicist in Berlin at the time, from the communication studies point of view, was doubtlessly the former lieutenant, actor, and "man of the people," Friedrich Wilhelm Held. He was one the first to employ simultaneously the mass effects of media available at the time—newspapers (*Lokomotive*), placards, and rhetoric—for his principles: the combination of democracy, socialism, and "Germanism" (nationalism). Prerequisite for the creation of what was, for Berlin, an extraordinarily broad public was not only the freedom to edit and print a publication, but also the possibility of street sales ('flying bookseller').

Apart from Vienna and Berlin, four other important newspaper cities deserve mention: Cologne, Munich, Leipzig, and Frankfurt am Main. Cologne, the Catholic stronghold of the Rhine province and one of Prussia's more important economic centers, had eight newspapers at the beginning of 1848, with twenty new papers being founded up to 1850. Leading by far was the workers' press with ten newspapers.

One of the most important Prussian newspapers of the revolutionary period was the *Neue Rheinische Zeitung*. The successor of the *Rheinische Zeitung*, which had been closed down by the authorities in 1843, appeared daily except Sundays in large folio format from 1 June 1848 to 19 May 1849. Both its editor-in-chief Karl Marx, who had returned from exile (he wrote c. 150 pieces for the newspaper), as well as his full-time staff—Friedrich Engels, the writer Ernst Dronke (*Aus dem Volk & Polizeigeschichten*), and the journalist Wilhelm Wolff—were members of the Communist League, founded in 1847 and banned in 1852. Feuilleton authors included Georg Weerth, who was writing social reportage in the *Vormärz*, as well as the poet Ferdinand Freiligrath. Numerous correspondents sent reports from Paris, London, or Brussels. After its original liberal financial backer had been frightened away by the newspaper's support for the Paris June rebels, Marx purchased the paper (with the aid of the inheritance of his wife, Jenny, née von Westphalen), as "personal property." When Marx, who was not successful in regaining Prussian citizenship, lost his residency permit on 11 May 1849 because of "incitement to violent rebellion," the *Neue Rheinische Zeitung* (6,000 subscribers, subtitled "Organ of Democracy") stopped publication with a famed, final edition totally in red (no. 301).

Less elitist and intellectual than the *Neue Rheinische Zeitung* was the *Zeitung des Arbeitervereins* (circulation between 1,400 and 1,800), which initially appeared occa-

Figure 2, *Newspapers in Revolutionary Germany*

sionally from 23 April 1848 and then from 2 July to 22 October twice a week. It was succeeded by two competing publications, *Freiheit, Brüderlichkeit, Arbeit,* from 26 October to 31 December 1848 and 8 February to 24 June 1849, and *Freiheit, Arbeit,* from 14 January to 24 June 1849. The *Neue Kölnische Zeitung für Bürger, Bauern und Soldaten* (10 September 1848 to July 1849) was founded by the former Prussian officer Friedrich Anneke, a founding member of the Workers' Association, and Lieutenant Friedrich Beust, as counter-pole to the bourgeois-constitutional *Kölnische Zeitung* (circulation 17,400). Its motto was: "Affluence, Liberty and Education for All." Its aim was a social republic. When Anneke was imprisoned from July to December, his wife Mathilde Franziska took over the paper, under a new, harmless title of *Frauen-Zeitung,* in September (27 and 28), because of a ban after the declaration of martial law.

As a brief aside, the only "true" women's newspapers of the revolutionary period appeared from 21 April 1849 to 1851 in Saxony (near Leipzig) and following a further year in Gera in Thüringia. The *Frauen-Zeitung*, brought out by the poet and women's rights activist (though she did not demand the franchise) Louise Otto, was printed with the motto: "I am recruiting citizenesses for the realm of freedom!" In 1865, Louise Otto-Peters, who had married in the meantime, founded the General German Women's Association, together with Auguste Schmidt.

Back at Cologne, from 1848, newspapers for devout Catholics appeared for the first time, after a number of unsuccessful attempts. The most important was the *Rheinische Volkshalle*, founded on 1 October, and continued a year later as *Deutsche Volkshalle*.

When the "sun of freedom" rose over the landscape of the Munich press, six dailies were being published. Shortly thereafter there were sixteen. Of these children of the revolution, which generally had little chance of survival, one would later become the largest daily in southern Germany: the *Neueste Nachrichten aus dem Gebiete der Politik* first appearing on 9 April 1848(circulation 12,000; from 1887 onwards *Münchner Neueste Nachrichten*). Very popular was the illustrated "Paper for Unrestricted Freedom and the People's Welfare," *Gradaus!!*. Soon "the most severe press feuds were underway" in Munich. The people of Munich, organized in conservative (for example the *Neue Münchner Zeitung*), Catholic (the first Pius Association was established on 28 March 1848), constitutional-liberal, democratic, and workers' associations accused each other in pamphlets and newspapers "of practising journalistic grave-digging of the state and the nation."[25]

For Munich (and Bavaria) it is also possible to provide more exact information on the background and education of the journalists. Seventy percent came from the educated bourgeois middle class; about 80 percent had had academic training, for example as teachers or doctors. The rest were workers, artisans or businessmen without school diplomas.

In the industrial and trade fair city of Leipzig, around 300 periodicals and probably well over 1,000 flyers, placards and the like appeared between 1 January 1848 and 31 December 1849. Louise Otto wrote for one of the three *Volksfreunde* (subtitled: "Saxon Paper for All the Interests of the People"; lasting from 5 April to 27 September 1848). The *Deutsche Volkszeitung* (April) was the "Organ of the Serving Girls Association"; the *Leipziger Arbeiter-Zeitung* (1 May to 22 July 1848) was published by the Workers' Association and edited by workers, for workers. From 1 April the daily *Vaterlandsblätter—Constitutionelle Staatsbürger-Zeitung* appeared, the product of a fusion. It was headed by the journalist Robert Blum, who had been active in Leipzig from the 1830s, and who would continue his work as a deputy in Frankfurt.

In Frankfurt am Main, meeting-place of the pre-parliament and the National Assembly, parliamentary parties developed for every political current from the extreme right, moderate liberals, to the extreme left. Each of these groups had use of a newspaper to express its views. The left, for example, used as their platform the *Deutsche Reichstags-Zeitung*, founded in Frankfurt on 21 May 1848, edited and published by Robert Blum. His language was rich in imagery and carried his readers along with it. He continually made references to the French revolution. As is well-known, Robert Blum was executed a few months later, during the October uprising in Vienna, despite his parliamentary immunity.

A bitter opponent of the *Deutsche Reichstags-Zeitung* was the conservative pastor Karl Jürgens, whose *Flugblätter aus der Deutschen Nationalversammlung* appeared from 14 June 1848. Of the more than thirty newspapers and journals, the short-lived *Allgemeine Arbeiter-Zeitung* (18 May to 10 June), founded by journeymen, and the *Frankfurter Journal*, founded in 1665, deserve mention. Finally, a special role was played by the *Deutsche Zeitung*, the forum of the "professorial guard of the Frankfurt parliament,"[26] which moved from Heidelberg to Frankfurt on 1 October 1848. After the failure of the Frankfurt experiment, though, the paper, whose subscriptions had fallen from 4,000 to 1,700, closed in September 1850.

Lost Illusions

Like in France, the wheel of history in Germany also turned rapidly backwards. After the failure of the revolution and its efforts to unite Germany "from the bottom up," one state after another reinstated restrictions on the freedom of the press. On 20 December 1848, prior censorship was reintroduced in Austria and a ban placed on colportage. On 4 March 1849, the young emperor Franz Joseph enacted a constitution with civil liberties, but then the state of martial law declared for Vienna (until 1853) put a de facto end to press freedom. On 6 November 1850, the advertisement tax was reintroduced; on 6 July 1851, the caution system; and on 27 May 1852 license requirements and security deposits for political periodicals with the exception of official ones.

In Prussia, the imposed constitution of 5 December 1848 dealt with the press in articles 24 to 26 in the spirit of the *Paulskirche*. The revised constitution for the Prussian state of 31 January 1850 also guaranteed "every Prussian" the right "to freely express his thoughts in words, writing, print, and pictorial presentation" in article 27. The second paragraph, however, watered this down significantly and was phrased as follows: "Censorship may not be introduced; all other restrictions on press freedom only through legislation."

The Prussian press law of 12 May 1851 therefore did not openly re-establish censorship. It was instead reintroduced through the back door in fifty-six carefully phrased paragraphs which dealt with press regulations and criminal proceedings, and punishment of press offences. License regulations and security deposits, reintroduced in 1849, were retained, and the deposit copy and (along the lines of French press regulations) the position of the legally "responsible" editor introduced. Finally, in July 1852, new legislation restored the newspaper stamp, which had only been abolished on 1 January 1849. Street sales were and remained forbidden.

In Bavaria, as well, the wheel turned quickly backwards. Already on 22 June 1848, Maximilian II Joseph demanded that his ministers take stricter measures against "disagreeable" publications. On 17 March 1850 a "Law for Protection against the Misuse of the Press" was enacted, which laid down fines and imprisonment, especially for slandering the government, the chambers, authorities, municipal assemblies, and the courts. In all three states, it should be mentioned, the governments sought to supplement the above-mentioned repressive measures with "positive" press guidance, be it financial aid (journalists, newspapers) or through a privileged news policy.

Numerous publications closed their doors. Courageous opposition journalists had to expect fines and imprisonment. Many democratic and communist journalists went into exile in 1849, in Switzerland, in England (for example, Karl Marx), and especially in America (for example the Annekes). Other journalists and publishers turned away from politics, temporarily or permanently.

In 1854, the revived German Confederation enacted the "General Federal Regulations Concerning the Circumstances of the Misuse of the Press." Concessions could be withdrawn by the authorities, the use of the mails by a press publication had to be approved in advance, and the name of the publisher, printer, and responsible editor had to be listed in the masthead. As well, a deposit copy had to be submitted to the police before general distribution. As a consequence of this legislation, attacks both on the state of residence and the authorities of other states could be prosecuted and punished throughout the German Confederation.

Twenty years would have to pass before the "Imperial Press Code" of 1 July 1874 would establish that: "Freedom of the press is only subject to those restrictions set and approved in current legislation." Nonetheless, because of the criminal code, persecution was commonplace, even without the oft-extended "Law against activities by Social Democrats endangering public safety" (1878-1890). As the "basic right" to freedom of expression (article 118), anchored in the Weimar constitution (1919), was soon restricted by the Law for the Protection of the Republic, it would not be wrong to state that only the constitution of the Federal Republic of Germany of 1949, in article 5(1), made the right of "freely expressing and spreading one's opinions in word, writing and picture," which had been first introduced in continental Europe in 1789, inviolable.

Resurrected from the Ruins: Political Cartoons

Daumier, Cham, Bertall, and All the Others

It is impossible to imagine French communicative culture up to the present without its "laughing" at politics and politicians. Hence, in republican Paris—apart from revolutionary and counter-revolutionary flyers (in part in the form of series)—a large number of humorist-satirical periodicals bloomed, and generally faded quickly, in part with and in part without illustrations.[27]

A series of new publications were grouped around the fixed star of *Le Charivari*.[28] Working for all these publications was the blue-blooded *Charivari* artist Cham (from 1843; his real name was Count Amédée Charles Henry de Noé). Like Bertall, he also worked for *L'Illustration* and published a considerable number of albums. As an artist, Cham was not the equal of his teacher Daumier, but he was certainly the most popular illustrated chronicler of his age.

Figure 3, *Le Charivari 9 March 1848 Honoré Daumier (1808-1879):*
Dernier conseil des ex ministres (Final sitting of the former ministerial council)

Under the shocked excellencies one can recognize Adolphe Thiers (with glasses),
ofttimes a minister and even prime minister under King Louis Philippe.

Le Charivari, owned from 1843 onwards by Armand Dutacq (*Le Siècle*), switched from political opposition to social criticism and erotic "moral pictures" after the passing of the "September laws." Daumier's typology of French society in the form of entertaining series (e.g., the big-time rogue "Robert Macaire") and contributions from his artist colleagues Edouard de Beaumont, J.J. Grandville, Paul Gavarni, Henry Monnier, Charles Joseph Traviès, Charles Vernier, and Cham turned the "matador of the small press" into an institution at home and abroad. In 1844, Balzac wrote of the daily lithography: "This collection will doubtless one day be one of the most valuable of our age."[29]

With the abolition of the prior censorship of pictures, a new age began for *Le Charivari*. Politics and new forms of drawing lent page three, dedicated to cartoons, a new shine. With the "representatives represented here"—a series which ran from November 1848 to August 1850—Honoré Daumier popularized the satirical portrait ("*portrait-charge*"). This was distinguished by having an over-large head, made characteristic through certain details, on a small body—like in carnival parades.

Daumier greeted with enthusiasm the long-desired republic on 9 March. A radiant young woman with Phrygian cap and flowing gown appears as shining light of freedom and chases away the completely overrun royal ministerial council. (See figure 3.) No less enthusiastic was *Le Charivari*'s celebration on 22 March of the Franco-German springtime: "France and Germany are now one and the same nation." In a cartoon on 24 March, the absolute German princes were forced to swallow the "constitutional medicine." (See figure 4).

Figure 4, *The absolute kings are forced to swallow the bitter medicine of a constitution.*

Among Europe's rulers one recognizes Friedrich Wilhelm IV of Prussia (right) and the mentally retarded Emperor Ferdinand I of Austria (left), who was replaced by his nephew Franz Joseph at the end of 1848. In the middle, the king of Hanover, Ernst August II, who had abolished a liberal constitution in 1837 and, in civilian clothes, King Friedrich August II of Saxony. He had ended his reactionary course in 1848 and appointed opposition leaders to the government. The "constitutional medicine," however, was, not always taken. Austria, for example, remained an absolute monarchy until 1861.

In the question of "which republic?," the subject of much public discussion, *Le Charivari* came out in support of the "republic of respectable people." The victory of the national guard and soldiers of the army, under the command of General Cavaignac, over rebellious Paris workers was interpreted by the paper in a leader (27 June) as a victory "of nineteenth- century civilization" over the "new barbarians." On the cartoon page appeared an entire series with the title "Memories of the Days of June 1848" (See figure 5). Only Daumier would continue to show in future—and this extremely rarely—the allegorically represented republic with a Jacobin cap.

In fact, *Le Charivari* and its sister paper *Le Journal pour rire* were noticeable for their virulent anti-socialism. Their barbs were directed especially at Pierre Leroux, whom Marx called a "genius," and at Proudhon, called by bourgeois contemporaries the "apostle of socialism," "leveler," "barbarian," "Satan," or "raging fool." Cham not only dedicated numerous single cartoons and series (illustrated broadsheets) to the latter, but also three albums: Proudhoniana, the Proudhon Bank, and Proudhon on vacation.

Chez Aubert Pl. de la Bourse   Imp.Aubert & C.ᵉ

Figure 5, *In memory of the days of June 1848.*

A barricade is taken by the mobile guard.

During the June uprising, the mobile guard was a militia rapidly thrown together with recruits liable for compulsory service. They were to support the regular army in fighting against the rebels.

Two further main targets of satire were the ringleader "Ratapoil," a Bonapartist dreaming of an empire created by Daumier, and women calling for equal social and political rights.

In *Le Charivari, Le Canard, Le Journal pour rire,* and elsewhere, both rebellious and seductive "warrior women" ("Vésuviennes") were made fun of, as were their "socialist" fellow women insisting on divorce rights at public meetings. Well-known names are among the mockers, above all Cham and Honoré Daumier. Daumier's forty-part series "the blue stockings," which appeared in 1844, may have led his pupils to decorate the editor of the women's paper *La Voix des Femmes* Eugénie Niboyet with an enormous beard on 22 June 1848. At about the same time, the "journal of the petticoats," *La République des femmes* published a "women's Marseillaise of 1848" and summed up the alleged demands of the "warrior women" in a parody of the sentimental revolutionary song "Le chant du départ": "We will carry out what they didn't dare do in 1793/we will kill our husbands with a new decree!/… Forward! We will free the world/from the tyrants who have been ruling too long!/War against the bearded!/We will cut their beards off! We will cut everything off!" The author was a journalist of *Le Journal pour rire*!

Of all the above-mentioned satirical journals, only *Le Charivari* and *Le Journal pour rire* survived. *Le Charivari* took the usual path of switching to moral pictures and reporting on foreign policy and from abroad. *Le Journal pour rire*, continued from 1855 to 1933 as *Journal amusant,* ended its interest in politics and became the forefather of the illustrated humorous family magazine "à la française."

The Political Humor Magazine—A Child of the 48 Revolution

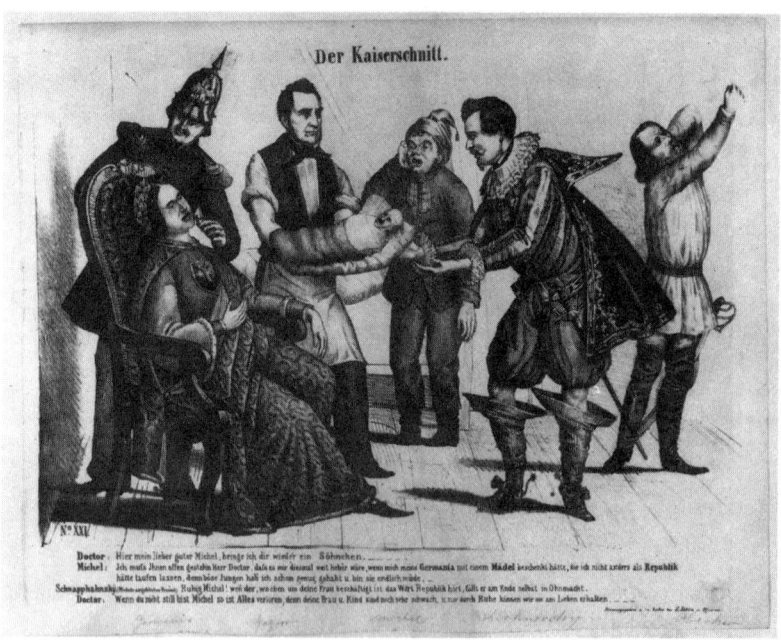

Figure 6, *Offenbach (June/July 1848)*

Anonymous artist: The Caesarean

Germania remains on her throne after a difficult birth. Friedrich Wilhelm IV is holding a bottle of smelling salts under her nose. The president of the Frankfurt National Assembly Heinrich Freiherr von Gagern here transformed into a doctor is giving Prince Lichnowsky (on the Catholic right-wing), derided as 'Schnapphahnsky' (Heine), the baby, which has the face of the Archduke Johann, elected as Imperial Regent. The father, Michel (the German everyman) and the leader of the republicans Friedrich Hecker make their dismay known.

Felag von J.B. Simon, in Frankfurt %.

Figure 7, *J.B. Simon, Frankfurt am Main (8 July 1848)*

When Germany and France go arm in arm, we can put our century in its place! (Bravo!)

The cartoon refers to a speech of the Viennese writer and delegate Alfred Wiener during the defense debate. The energetic play on the Schiller quotation from Don Carlos, is contrasted with the speaker's shaky pin legs. Although in Berlin and Paris there had been diplomatic feelers for an alliance of Germany and France against Russia from April 1848, nothing came of them.

In Germany, the "crazy year" not only brought forth many thousands of illustrated pamphlets and flyers, but also a new medium, the political humor magazine. Illustrated humorous-satirical-ironic weeklies or monthlies, which had already begun appearing shortly before 1848, turned away from their forced tranquillity. Thus, for example, the *Fliegende Blätter*, which had six competitors in 1848, replaced its Biedermeier pair "Baron Beisele" and "Hofmeister Dr. Eisele" with the up-to-date figures of "Barnabas Wühlhuber" and "Casimir Heulmaier." [The names are a play on "Wühler," a right-wing epithet for leftists, and "Heuler," a left-wing epithet for rightists (Ed.)] The Hamburg magazine *Mephistopheles* was clearly based on *Le Charivari* (for example, Daumier's portrait series). As to the illustrators of the *Düsseldorfer Monatshefte*, as officers of the civic guard they were even directly active in political events.

Cartoon journals appeared everywhere—thirty-five in Berlin alone.[30] In Vienna, at least the titles were oriented on the French, Prussian and Bavarian capitals.[31] For the Frankfurt press, 1848/49 was a true high point. Not only the well-designed weekly *Der Satyr*, subtitled "Loose Sheets from the German Empire," appeared here, but also the parliamentary satire *Thaten und Meinungen des Herrn Piepmeyer*. In fact, the Frankfurt deputies (among them 6.4 percent publicists by profession) were no less the target of German caricatures than their French colleagues. Sometimes they were mocked in the form of portrait caricatures, sometimes as "standing figures" with more or less forbearance.

The hero of *Vormärz* cartoons, the "German Michel," shown as dreamer, fool, warrior, and philistine, and today still very much alive, celebrated a grandiose comeback. One saw, for example, the cartoon titles and subtitles: "How the German Michel falls into a rage," "Michel sweeps clean" or "Where the German Michel goes hunting."[32]

The figure of Germania was also revived. Soon she was seen as a statue, or storming forward. Her dress was varied: cap of liberty, imperial crown, a crown of oak leaves, torn chains, raised or lowered sword, shield with a single or double eagle. Both national figures, which also appear together in some illustrations, were taken up by cartoonists for every day politics and trivialized. (See figure 6.) Their presentation in the form of single or a series of cartoons reflected or satirized public debate: republic or constitutional monarchy, greater Germany or small Germany, centralism or federalism, Germany and its neighbors (Ill. 7), labor and women's questions, revolution and counter-revolution.

Only a few of these weeklies survived the massive closure of publications: the prototype of the humorous "family magazine" *Fliegende Blätter* (until 1944), which became apolitical, the *Münchener Punch* (until 1871) and the prototype of the purely political satirical journal *Kladderadatsch* (until 1944) (see figure 8).

Kladderadatsch in der Sylvesternacht
am Grabe seiner bereits verstorbenen oder doch nächstens versterbenden Zeitgenossen.

Also ist im Strom der Zeiten
Wiederum ein Jahr verflossen,
Und ich steh' an den beschnei'ten
Gräbern meiner Zeitgenossen.

Alle fast, die hier vermittern,
's war nicht viel an euch verloren,
Denn ihr war't von faulen Müttern
Schon von Anfang todt geboren.

Doch dort hinten seh' ich eine
Neue Schaar von frischen Grüften,
Und die neuen Leichensteine
Schon geschmückt mit frischen Schriften.

Auch um Euch und Euresgleichen
Wird man Thränen nicht vergießen,
Wenn sich über euren Leichen
Erst des Grabes Pforten schließen.

Rechte Constitutionelle,
Dumme Schwaben, blinde Hessen,
Die bandjüdisch nach der Elle
Nur das Schön' und Große messen!

Oder hergelaufne Schweizer,
Aemtergeile Aposteln —
Die Nation, für ein Paar Kreuzer
Ist sie feil zu allen Thaten!

Wenn ihr Geble nun auch nächsten
Untergeht, so ist's kein Schade —
Traf man euch im Leben höchstens
Doch nur — auf der Retirade! —

Aber weiter dort ruht Einer,
Der im Leben gut gerungen;
Denn er starb im Kampf, von seiner
Feinde Uebermacht bezwungen.

Auch im Jenseits noch wird seines
Ruhmes Ewige Lampe flacken,
Und wird beißend hellen Scheines
Leuchten den verdammten Rackern —

Hundsgemeinen Wuchers Söhner,
Die vom Blut des Volkes saugen,
Daß vom Salz der heißen Thränen
Uebergehn die trief'gen Augen.

Mußtest Du im Tod verbluten,
So will ich Dir sein ein Rächer;
Will, wenn auch mit andern Ruthen
Geißeln die verdammten Schächer!

Nun wohlauf nd meine Seiten
Mit dem Racheschwert umgürt' ich,
Laß uns für einander streiten —
Denn ich bin Dir ebenbürtig. —

Streiten in dem Reich der Geister,
Ich von unten, Du von oben —
Satanas, der alte Meister,
Soll schon seine Diener loben!

Figure 8, Wilhelm Scholz, "Kladderadatsch on New Year's Eve, at the grave of its contemporaries, who have already died, or who are near death."

At the Berlin "newspapers' cemetery" repose the satirical colleagues Freie Blätter *(of Adolf Glaßbrenner),* Berliner Großmaul, Berliner Krakehler, *and* Tante Voss mit dem Besen. *Among the "contemporaries near death" are* Die ewige Lampe, *the moderate* Deutsche Reform *and the* Constitutionelle Zeitung.

Notes

1. Heinrich Heine, *Sämtliche Schriften in zwölf Bänden*, K. Briegleb (ed.), vol. 5, (Munich, 1976), 133-34.
2. The quote is from Heinrich Best, *Die Männer von Bildung und Besitz. Struktur und Handeln parlamentarischer Führungsgruppen in Deutschland und Frankreich 1848/49* (Düsseldorf, 1990), 239. The term "fourth estate" (sometimes falsely translated into German as "fourth power"), much discussed today, originated with the English politician and publicist Edmund Burke (1729-1797) and was taken up again by Honoré de Balzac in 1840.
3. The quote from Heine is from a series (26 articles) which appeared in the *Augsburger Allgemeine Zeitung*, published in part as a book with the title *Französische Zustände*. The liberal daily *Le Charivari* was continued in June 1926 as a radical right-wing satirical weekly and had two further successors between 1957 and 1987.
4. See, *Revue parisienne* no. 2, 25 August 1840. *L'Illustration*, No. 258, compared on 5 February 1848 the Parisian press, with no foreign correspondents and which based their commentary generally on censored newspaper quotations, to the London press (559).
5. Figures given are from Charles Ledré, *La presse à l'assaut de la monarchie 1815-1848* (Paris, 1960), 244.
6. This statement was credited to the extremely unpopular university professor and foreign minister François Guizot (1840-1848) and in full was "enrich yourselves through work and savings!"
7. Wirth had published the daily *Deutsche Tribüne* starting in July 1831, Siebenpfeiffer the daily *Der Bote aus dem Westen*, and then *Der Westbote*, starting in April 1831. Both papers were prohibited by the Confederation in March 1832. After the attack on the Frankfurt police headquarters, Wirth was imprisoned for two years, then placed under police supervision, and escaped to Strasbourg in 1837. Siebenpfeiffer was sentenced to two years imprisonment on 8 November 1833, but was able to escape to Switzerland one week later. Since 1987 a foundation offers the Siebenpfeiffer prize for fearless commitment and fulfilling a journalistic duty to inform.
8. Quoted in F. Th. Hoefer, *Pressepolitik und Polizeistaat Metternichs* (Munich, 1983), 179.
9. Alphonse de Lamartine (1790-1869) "inspired" the newspaper *Le Bien public* from May to December 1848, after which he published the paper *Le Conseiller du Peuple* from April 1849 to November 1851.
10. See Best, *Männer von Bildung und Besitz*, 63 and 71. The disrespectful remark is from the satirical paper *Le Bossu* (The Hunchback) which appeared in London, No. 3, 7 October 1848. See on the powerful position of *Le National* also *Le Bossu*, No. 2, 30 September 1848, and *Le Censeur républicain*, No. 1, 14 May 1848.
11. See Eugène Hatin, *Bibliographie historique et critique de la presse périodique française* (Paris, 1866) (reprint Hildesheim, 1965), 436-37.
12. See Hatin, *Bibliographie historique* 436-525, and *passim*. The Bibliothèque historique de la Ville de Paris has about 150 volumes of newspapers from the Second Republic. This unique collection provided numerous dates and facts for this chapter and for an essay which appeared in French: Ursula E. Koch, "La presse et son public à Paris et à Berlin (1848/49). Une étude exploratoire," in Ilja Mieck, Horst Möller, and Jürgen Voss (eds.), *Paris und Berlin in der Revolution 1848. Paris et Berlin dans la Révolution de 1848* (Sigmaringen, 1995), 19-78.
13. The evening newspaper *La République*, post-dated to 26 February, arose in the middle of torn out cobblestones. Its founder, Eugène Bareste, who had earlier worked for *La Presse*, turned to all citizens and on 5 March (no. 9) compared the task of journalists with a "holy mission," which was to be carried out with "sagacity, sense of justice, political conviction, and above all strength of character." *La République Française*, edited by the theoretical economist Frédéric Bastiat, is correctly dated to 26 February. On 5, 13, and 26 March appeared *La République des Arts* (the republic of the arts), the *Bulletin de la République*, which was sent by the government to all mayors in the form of posters until 6 May, and *La Vraie République* (the true republic), which appeared with the masthead motto "Liberty, Equality, Fraternity." The latter (highest circulation 20,000), edited by the "intellectual proletarian" Théophile Thoré, listed three prominent people as co-workers in its masthead: the professional revolutionary Armand Barbès, recently released from prison, Pierre Leroux, creator

of the term "socialist" (1833), and the writer George Sand, who appeared in a number of left-wing press organs in 1848, also writing for *Le Bulletin de la République*, *La Commune de Paris*, *La Montagne de la Fraternité*, *Le Travail*, *Le Volcan*, and *Le Spectateur Républicain*.

14. *La jeune République démocratique et sociale* and *La République possible* only produced test editions. *La République Rouge* (four issues) distanced itself from the "blue" or "tricolor" republic of "respectable people." As for Proudhon, the red flag was also "the flag of humanity" for the republic.

15. On 27 February 1848, the radical-democratic daily *Le Peuple Constituant* (Motto: "Vox populi, Vox Dei: to which we bow") opened the running. Its founder was "a famous old man," the philosopher and publicist Félicité de la Mennais, a former clergyman who had left the Catholic church. The "workers' daily," *Le Représentant du Peuple* (circulation of between 10,000 and 18,000), that began to be published on 1 April, gained a lot of attention. The "people's representative" was the tribune of the publicist and competitor with Marx, Pierre-Joseph Proudhon (1809-1865). The autodidact was the author of the famous essay, translated into German in 1844, "Qu'est-ce que la propriété?" (1840) which he answered with "property is theft." George Sand's short-lived (9 to 23 April) weekly *La Cause du Peuple* (The People's Cause) contained her "Letter to the People," which had already appeared in March and a "socialism course in three chapters." *L'Apôtre du Peuple* supported—which was somewhat unusual—women's endeavors towards emancipation; for *Les Archives du Peuple*, the people seemingly only consisted of men, that is of the "totality of all enfranchised citizens." Also deserving mention are Etienne Cabet's newly founded newspaper *Le Populaire*, and finally *L'Ami du Peuple en 1848* (a reference to Jean-Paul Marat's *L'Ami du Peuple*), the editor of which was the well-known biologist, chemist, and ultra-left publicist Francois-Vincent Raspail.

16. *La Carmagnole*, *La Guillotine*, *Le Robespierre*, *Le Bonnet rouge* (The Red Cap of Liberty), *Le Père Duchène* (a revival of the title of the same name of Jacques-René Hébert), *Le nouveau*, and *Le vieux Cordelier de 1848* (in memory of Camille Desmoulin).

17. In Paris, about 25 percent of twenty year old recruits were illiterate; in the provinces 42.65 percent in 1845 and 38.94 percent in 1850.

18. These were excerpts translated by the editorial staff of Bettina von Arnim's (1785-1859) legendary indictment *Dies Buch gehört dem König*, in which the inhumane conditions before the gates of Berlin were described (1843). The articles appeared in No. 2 and No. 4 of 22 and 24 March 1848. In No. 25 and 26 (16 and 18 April) Eugénie Niboyet introduced Bettina von Arnim to her readership, as many of them did not know "how famous she is."

19. No. 2 appeared on 22 September 1848; from January to August 1849, *L'Opinion des Femmes* was a monthly.

20. More details in Koch, "Paris und Berlin," 56-57. See also R. Pillorget, "Berlin en Mars 1848, vu par la presse parisienne," in Mieck et al. (ed.), *Paris und Berlin*, 269-78.

21. *La Vraie République*, *Le Père Duchène*, *La Liberté*, *L'Assemblée Nationale*, *Le Lampion*, *Napoléon Républicain*, *La Presse*, among others. They—and the press altogether—were credited with the "misunderstandings between bourgeoisie and the masses." When Emile de Girardin protested against the "rule of the saber," he was given eleven days solitary confinement.

22. The Paris press historian P. Albert believes these figures to be quite probable.

23. Quoted in A. Castelot and A. Decaux, *Histoire de la France et des Français au jour le jour*, Vol. 7 (Paris, 1977), 252.

24. Quoted in Martin Henkel and Rolf Taubert, *Die deutsche Presse 1848-1850* (Munich, 1986), 13. The two authors present, for the first time, a complete bibliography (without Austria). Up to 1849, 1,700 different newspapers and journals were said to have been founded.

25. Quoted in H. Starkulla, "Zur Geschichte der Presse in Bayern," in *50 Jahre Verband Bayerischer Zeitungsverleger e.V. 1913-1963* (Munich, 1963), 25.

26. See Kurt Koszyk, *Deutsche Presse im 19. Jahrhundert* (Berlin, 1966), 112.

27. Without illustration were, for example, *La Foudre* [The Flash], March 1848 and the "political, humorist, and satirical paper of the popular singer" *La République Lyrique* (July 1848 to July 1849). With cartoons were *Le Canard* (9 April to 18 June 1848), the daily *Le Pamphlet* (24 May to 9 November 1848: circulation 11,000), with texts by Champfleury and drawings by Bertall (actually

Count Albert d'Arnoux), *Le Diable rose* (15 to 29 June 1848), and the "Comic Sunday Revue" *Le Caricaturiste* (3 June 1849 to 30 June 1850) as well as *La Silhouette*. Also deserving of mention are the *Revue comique à l'usage des Gens sérieux* (the comic revue for serious people) brought out by Bertall and the caricaturist and art photographer Gaspard Félix Nadar from November 1848 to December 1849, and the anti-republican satirical weekly *Le Bossu*, published by a former French upper civil servant, and illustrated by Paul Gavarni among others.

28. Among them are the weekly *Le Journal pour rire*, founded by Charles Philipon shortly before the outbreak of the revolution on 5 February 1848, *Punch in Paris* (February to June 1850) and the daily *La Caricature* (April 1850 to June 1851). The weekly magazine *Punch* called itself "the London Charivari." It lasted until 1992.

29. Honoré de Balzac, "Monographie de la presse parisienne," in *Oeuvres complètes*, Vol. 26 (Paris, 1976), 234–94.

30. Among others, *Der Teufel in Berlin, Der Satyr, Berliner Krakehler* (20,000 copies, many reprints), *Berliner Großmaul, Tante Voss mit dem Besen*, and *Kladderadatsch*.

31. *Wiener Katzenmusik, Wiener Charivari*, subtitled "political daily for mockery and seriousness with cartoons," *Satan, Der Wiener Krakehler, Der Kladertratsch, Fliegende Blätter*.

32. The three cartoons are mentioned in: *Politische Karikaturen des Vormärz (1815-1848)*, Exhibition catalogue (Karlsruhe, 1984), 99–100.

Part IV

SOCIETY IN UPHEAVAL

Chapter 25

BOURGEOISIE, PETIT BOURGEOISIE, WORKERS

Class Formation and Social Reform in Germany and France

Heinz-Gerhard Haupt and *Friedrich Lenger*

"A specter is haunting Europe—the specter of Communism."[1] This introductory sentence to the *Communist Manifesto* gained special significance when it was published in the same week that the Parisian February revolution broke out. While the specter of communism was not very clearly defined at the beginning of 1848, Marx and Engels point out, with some justice, that an accusation of communism was often used to stigmatize the opposition. They were not content with developing the demands of communism, but instead focused much more of their exposition on the class theory that was the foundation of their program. A division of society "into two great hostile camps, into two great classes directly facing each other: Bourgeoisie and Proletariat," was not postulated here for the first time, but gained new significance in view of the ever more clearly expressed socialist demands in the revolution of 1848/49.[2]

For an understanding of the revolution of 1848 in France and Germany, as will be explored in greater depth below, the clash between bourgeoisie and proletariat in the narrow sense is of secondary importance, and therefore this chapter will not provide a balanced treatment of the bourgeoisie, working class, and petit bourgeoisie. Rather it is necessary to begin with the small artisanal producers, who not only dominated the urban landscape at the middle of the century, but who also determined those actions and organizations that characterized the revolution. The beginnings of a modern capitalist bourgeoisie and a proletarian working class will receive attention only from the perspective of this artisanal core, and in reference to it. Formation of these classes was not very advanced in continental Europe in 1848.

Nonetheless, it is beyond question that demands for reform of society played a key role in the course of the revolution. It was, after all, also a social revolution.

Examining movements for social reform in the revolution of 1848/49 against the backdrop of class formation processes, it is necessary to emphasize one fundamental difference between France and Germany. In France, social demands played an incomparably more central role in the course of the revolution. This was in part the result of a revolutionary tradition and the more highly developed program of a socialist labor movement. Above all, however, the simultaneiety of the national question, the constitutional question, and the social question created a quite different constellation of problems in Germany than in France. While it can be argued that the process of nation-building had not yet been concluded in France in the middle of the century, its existence as a nation-state was as much beyond question as—after a very short time—its republican constitution. To this extent, France was more "modern," and this is also true of the nature of production. Their corporate past colored the language of French revolutionaries, but not the nature of their demands.[3]

In Germany, things were different. For this reason, too, a comparative treatment of these two lands means beginning with Germany, to present the more complex circumstances first—and this all the more so as the decentralized German urban landscape had no center comparable to Paris. "As Paris rules France because of political centralization," wrote Karl Marx in the *Neue Rheinische Zeitung*, "so the workers rule Paris in moments of revolutionary earthquakes."[4] The lack of such a center made a concentration of revolutionary forces more difficult in Germany and lessened the necessity of programmatic conflicts and their resolutions.

The German Case

The Importance of Urban Artisans

About ten years ago, Hans-Ulrich Wehler applied the term dual revolution to German history, thus underlining the simultaneity of political revolution and the beginning of industrialization in the mid-nineteenth century.[5] There are good reasons of economic history to date the beginning of the industrial revolution in Germany to the mid-1840s, but for an understanding of the revolution of 1848/49, its beginnings play at best only a subordinate role. In the mid-nineteenth century there were only the first signs of industrial entrepreneurs and a modern factory proletariat. The latter was not only numerically insignificant, it also hardly participated in the organizations, protests, and struggles of the revolution. This was as true for workers in the railway industry—the driving force of the industrial revolution in Germany—as it was for the early textile workforce.

Within urban society, which one must always have in view for an analysis of relations between the bourgeoisie, the petit bourgeoisie, and the working class, crafts, outwork, and the commercial bourgeoisie dominated. At least nominally independent small scale producers characterized the production sector of urban areas, and for the journeymen, whose numbers were much smaller than those of masters, their status as waged laborer was often overlayed by their dependence on the domestic rights of the master and was, moreover, understood as simply tempo-rary. The ratio between masters and journeymen varied from one craft to another and by city size, and the always considerable number of unskilled workers was not constant. On the other hand, well-trained and politically active groups of workers in larger enterprises, as for example in engineering or printing, were an exception.

Altogether, the class structures of an industrial society had little shaping force in mid-century cities.[6] At least at the socioeconomic level, the revolution did not bring any changes. Indeed, the effects of the agrarian crisis of 1846/47, still very noticeable in 1848, led rather in the opposite direction. On the one hand, the high level of unemployment among journeymen in most cities meant that the only way out was to set up in business for themselves.[7] On the other, the crises of the late 1840s accelerated a structural crisis in craft branches, as outworking spread and craftsmen became increasingly subject to merchants. Here, too, however, the conse-quence was pseudo-self-employment, not a clear rise of class conflict between workers and employers.[8] The question of processes of class formation cannot, there-fore, be limited to the economic level.[9]

When examining in depth relations between bourgeoisie, petit bourgeoisie, and workers in the cities, one is faced with two problems. On the one hand, as men-tioned above, regional and local variations make generalizations difficult. This is as much true of economic and social conditions as it is of the constellations of con-flict, also influenced by confessional and dynastic considerations, in the numerous individual states. On the other hand, new regional studies have not only made clear the extent to which rural society was also increasingly influenced by political orga-nizations in the course of the revolution, but at the same time have directed atten-tion to the still poorly researched small towns as well.[10] For both problems there are no simple solutions; all that can be done is to keep them in mind.

Urban artisans, however, must be placed at the center of attention. In larger cities they formed more than a tenth of the population and thus dominated, with their families, urban social structure. In occupational terms, and to some extent via family ties, some of them were closely connected to retailers and tavern-keepers, further core groups of urban society. Above all, however, urban artisans bound together the three social groups mentioned in the title, and this not only as the core of the petite bourgeoisie. The journeymen formed the core of the working class, but a significant and—in the crisis situation of the late 1840s—growing proportion of the self-employed were barely distinguishable, in terms of income and way of life, from the working class. Above all tailors, shoemakers, and furniture-makers were increasingly employed as outworkers for merchants and large retailers, so that the difference between masters and journeymen (the latter now frequently married) became less meaningful.[11]

Thus, while in some especially large branches the difference between master, journeyman, outworker, and worker faded, on the other hand, a small minority of artisan masters belonged to the local bourgeoisie. This is true in terms of income for some foodstuff, construction, and luxury goods artisans, as well as in reference to municipal parliaments.[12] Socially and culturally, however, barriers existed, at least in the associations in the larger cities, dominated by the educated professional middle class. Even the richest brewer in Munich was out of place there.[13] Self-employed artisans were part of the bourgeoisie in legal terms as well, as they formed the core of the older body of urban burghers, whose legal privileges, like the guild institutions outside Prussia, generally continued to exist.

Lothar Gall has argued that this *Vormärz* group of urban burghers formed the core of the bourgeoisie and, at the same time, was the key social group supporting early liberalism. Craftsmen and the economically rising commercial bourgeoisie, according to a brief version of his thesis, not only formed the core of an (urban) bourgeois society characterized by self-employed artisans and political participation, they were also bound together in a protectionist alliance to the extent that the commercial bourgeoisie supported artisan interests in guild organization. Altogether, Lothar Gall sees the urban society of the first half of the nineteenth century as something like the social substratum of a "classless society of burghers," which he described, some twenty years ago, as the objective of German early liberalism. Another part of Gall's argument is that this objective was shattered by the class conflicts arising in the revolution of 1848/49.[14]

This concept, as briefly outlined above, has a number of weaknesses. In its double fixation on the legal status of urban burghers and independence of artisans, it completely ignores the educated professional bourgeoisie. Up until now, it has been empirically tested primarily in southwest German cities and only confirmed in part. One can hardly speak of alliances between commercial bourgeoisie and artisans in those places, for example, where some of the artisans had become outworkers dependent on merchant capitalists. In any case, this view of prerevolutionary urban society is all too harmonizing, as it ignores those groups without civic rights. The porters, stevedores, dockworkers, and other day-laborers, for example, are not included. Also the decline of a large number of the core groups of urban artisans into dependent, outworking status and the impoverishment of a majority of them is overlooked. To this extent, the concept reflects a tendency towards exclusion, very strong within the society of urban burghers itself, which was expressed in dogged resistance to freedom of residence and occupation, and which underlined an affinity between the urban society of burghers and economic arrangements of guild craftsmen.[15]

Nonetheless, it must be admitted that the early liberal objective of a "classless society of burghers"—a society of small commodity producers, that was not conceived of as legally and socially egalitarian, but open to anyone who could work and educate himself up into it—was a vision of society that was neither restricted to southwest Germany, nor to the liberal bourgeoisie during the *Vormärz*. With the assistance of education, one would be able to gain admission to this "classless society of burghers." And the artisans' and workers' educational associations in the 1840s, not seldom founded by bourgeois liberals, doubtless propagated this idea, even when at the same time some of them functioned as centers for the exchange of early socialist ideas.[16]

The Political Public Sphere

With the March Revolution, the political public sphere expanded suddenly, and new possibilities and forms of interest articulation arose. Artisans were involved in the actions and organizations of the revolution to a great degree. Sixty percent of the victims of the March 1848 barricade fighting in Berlin were artisans, as were a similar proportion of the inhabitants of Constance, who were sought by the police for participation in Hecker's uprising. In the later phase of the revolution as well, it was above all artisans and workers who sought to defend the revolution, on the barricades in Dresden for example. "Artisan" in this context could refer both to master craftsmen and to journeymen. Among the victims of the Berlin barricade fighting journeymen clearly dominated, while in Constance, masters made up the majority of participating artisans. In both places and elsewhere as well, tailors, shoemakers, and cabinet makers dominated, that is artisans from those branches where outworking had made significant inroads, increasing craftsmen's dependence on merchant capitalists.

Beyond barricade fighting, artisans were also active in establishing political associations or were among the participants in protests "in the streets"—which, when they were purely artisan protests, were often directed against Jewish shop owners.[17] A distinction needs to be made between these different levels of action when considering the processes of class formation during the revolution. In this, we would first like to examine how the totally new possibilities for elaboration and articulation of social visions in the narrow sense—that is, in the sense of models of economic and social structures—were used during the revolution.

Certainly, artisans joined together in a movement involving sending petitions and holding congresses, designed to implement their ideas of a just economic and social order. Connecting these demands, generally put forward at the regional or even the national level, to specific urban milieus from which they arose has only been possible up to now in a few individual cases. Nonetheless, the general agreement of demands raised and the broad support for these demands in petitions endorsing them allows, in the final analysis, the draft of a general artisan and trade ordinance put forward by a general Artisan and Trade Congress in Frankfurt (15 July to 18 August 1848) to be seen as generally quite representative. A greater number of protests came only from the artisans in the Palatinate, who preferred to hold fast the freedom of occupation guaranteed in Rhenish Law.[18]

"German soil," as was written in an accompanying letter to the Frankfurt National Assembly that emphasized the relations between the tensions and problems of the *Vormärz* society and the revolution, "German soil was prepared and made receptive for the revolution mainly by a severe neglect of the tradesman class and the drought thus arising, by the exhaustion of all sources of the great German trade life. It required major mass impoverishment in order to overthrow the deeply lodged, all too confident rulers and to open the road to freedom for the oppressed people, the impoverished artisans and tradesmen." These freedoms should certainly not include occupational freedom. The congress demanded its complete abolition, "to the extent that it exists in Germany." The artisans gathered in Frankfurt explained further their "solemn protest, signed and sealed by millions of unfortunates … The specialist ... knows and experiences himself how the lack of restraint creates a tyranny of the individual, of the capitalists against the masses, and gives to the individual that which was taken from the totality of those entitled."[19] The anticapitalism expressed here was primarily directed against commercial capital that had degraded a portion of the artisans into the dependence of outworkers, and, furthermore against factory owners, whose production artisans were not able to compete with and whose competition was felt to be "dishonest."

A general artisan and trade ordinance had to provide protection from both commercial capital and factory competition. The latter was to be reduced by special taxation and restrictions on production, and the sale of craft products by non-artisans was simply to be prohibited. The draft proposed compulsory guild membership in the cities that "the few craftsmen necessary in the countryside" would have to join.[20] Apart from a three- to five- year apprenticeship, a three-year-itinerary was set for journeymen. In this respect, the draft was modeled on older guild regulation. At the same time, these regulations would have to be reformed.

Thus, while only master artisans could independently pursue a craft, with the exact number allowed to be determined by demand, the power to decide on a temporary ban on establishing any more such businesses was to be left to the municipal authorities, not to the guilds. In other areas, as well, attempts were made to prevent abuses by the guilds that had long been the subject of complaints. Thus, journeymen who had failed a master's exam in one place could take it again elsewhere, and a craftsman who was a recognized master in one town would even be allowed to move to another and exercise his craft as a master there. Thus the possibilities for a local guild to keep out unwanted competition via the master's exam was greatly reduced. Finally, the draft also contained quite future-oriented elements such as a planned establishment of sales halls by the guilds with the aim of collectively ensuring market access for small scale masters.[21]

To what extent was the economic and social structure envisaged in the draft quoted above acceptable for workers and the bourgeoisie? Mention has already been made of a possible protectionist alliance of trade bourgeoisie and artisans in southwestern cities during the *Vormärz*. Its implicit objective of "a classless society of burghers"—dominant beyond southwest Germany—did in no way necessarily imply occupational freedom. Even given the dominance of this social vision, there also existed deviating views within the *Vormärz* bourgeoisie that were strongest in the Prussian Rhine Province and, in part, in Saxony, another region with a high level of economic development.[22]

Hence it is not surprising that artisan demands in the revolution of 1848/49 did not meet with full agreement everywhere. In Württemberg, for example, many artisans left trade associations in the second half of 1848 and founded their own associations, because in the trade associations they were not able to carry through their ideas oriented on guild models.[23] In the economics committee of the very bourgeois National Assembly, the wish for regulation expressed in the draft also could not gain a majority. On the other hand, in the committee there was also no majority in favor of unlimited occupational freedom, and the imperial constitution only reserved for later legislative action a regulation of freedom of occupation and settlement.[24] Thus artisan ideas could not gain a consensus, but neither did they push the bourgeoisie and artisans into different political camps—all the less so as the question of protective tariffs tied together a large proportion of businessmen, artisans and workers in a trade policy mass movement.[25]

In the sense described above, the core demands of the artisans for a guild-regulated economy had only a limited political explosive force. This can be seen, on the one hand, in the fact that demands for restrictions on freedom of establishment could be articulated in all political camps; in conservative and Catholic associations, the guilds were especially popular, but even the emerging labor movement was not totally free of such sympathies. Hence it is, on the other hand, not surprising to find artisans in all political associations, independent of political current. This was true of conservative, constitutionalist, democratic, and Catholic associations as well as for organizations of the labor movement.

Conservative associations, concentrated mostly in Prussia, were able to gain some artisans—mostly masters—as members, especially in the countryside surrounding Berlin as well as in the provinces of Pomerania and Saxony. While there were almost no journeymen in the Prussian Associations, the Patriotic Associations or the League for King and Fatherland, master craftsmen could make up as much as 50 percent of total membership. This figure was occasionally even higher in the Catholic Pius Associations, as the bourgeoisie was only weakly represented there, while the liberal constitutionalist associations had a somewhat exclusive character in some places. Here, too, however, the level of artisan membership often lay between a fifth and a quarter, including a respectable number of journeymen.

Artisans played, finally, an even more important role in most urban democratic associations. In Nördlingen, artisans and tradesmen made up two thirds of membership, in Dresden more than half. Among these artisan members numerous were always self-employed and certainly not only impoverished, small scale independent masters. The destitution of the latter seemed to have a mobilizing effect, but their political orientation can neither be traced back to their socioeconomic situation nor to their basic attitudes concerning trades policy.[26]

The social vision of artisans and the bourgeoisie, in summary, were certainly not identical. Their differences, however, were not based on an insurmountable gap between the two groups; indeed they did not even lead to a recognizable crystallization of political parties. In their relations with workers, artisan ideas also initially did not imply a break. Characteristically, it was not different reform objectives, but conflict concerning the patriarchal authority of masters over journeymen that led to an independent journeymen's organization at the national level. Even at the so-called Hamburg pre-congress, journeymen were refused a voice, and at the Frankfurt artisan and trade congress, a majority resolved after a very controversial discussion: "you are the sons of the masters, who represent the fathers, who alone have the right to decide here; if that were not the case then this congress would break up, anarchy would take its place—such a relationship is necessary, like that of children and household members to the family father."[27]

The patriarchalism vehemently defended there was also expressed during the revolution in numerous conflicts over keys to the master's house or the hours when it would be locked. These disputes arose especially in those places where, as for example in Frankfurt, the guild tradition was still totally unbroken.[28] Apart from a necessary differentiation and weighting of conflicts between masters and journeymen on their domestic dependence, it must also be remembered that the vast majority of artisan masters had to do without journeymen or apprentices and thus probably had little interest in such disputes. In relation to their economic and sociopolitical ideas, there was little to distinguish journeymen, who were holding a parallel congress in Frankfurt, from the masters. "We found," they wrote in the introduction to their resolutions, "that we could agree with the masters especially in the important points. ..."[29]

The Rise of the Labor Movement

By no means the least of these points of agreement between masters and journeymen was understanding the "curse of free competition" as the cause of the artisans' precarious situation, and looking to the guilds for its improvement, with decision-making restricted to apprentices, journeymen and masters.[30] The use of the term "workers' congress" to describe the Frankfurt journeymen's meeting was, to this extent, misleading. It was much more appropriate for Stephan Born's previous efforts to coordinate the work of numerous workers' and artisans' associations. At the center of these efforts, which self-consciously and aggressively employed the term "worker," was the organization of workers and the association of labor, as was made clear at the latest in the resolutions of the Workers' Congress that met in Berlin from 23 August to 3 September. "It is above all necessary for workers to form themselves into a living community, which is simultaneously a politically inspired body, among the other citizens, and bring this to the attention of the statesmen, so that labor my be included as a form of property in the basic law of the state."[31]

A number of demands were made on the state, but at the center of them was self-help, in the form of producers' cooperatives. "In order, however, for capital to be robbed of its oppressive power, it is necessary that the workers, thus organized, themselves create a capital in order, in this way, to be able to compete with the capital of the speculators. The means to achieve this was found by the congress in the free association of workers and the establishment of an association fund."[32] With self-help, the path to artisan self-employment was to be collectively assured, which reflected the wishes of the predominantly artisanal membership. The popularity of cooperative ideas, which had already appeared in the demands of the artisan and trade congress, are therefore not surprising. They were certainly not limited to the Workers' Fraternization that arose from the Berlin workers' congress. Remarkable and something that can hardly be overvalued is, however, that this plan included "all workers." "Female workers are not excluded from these regulations and enjoy the same rights with the same obligations."[33]

With this program, the Workers' Fraternization had distanced itself from the ideas of the Frankfurt journeymen's congress. However, here, too, only a minority wished to do without master's exams and restrictions on numbers of apprentices. In any case, the programmatic homogeneity of the Workers' Fraternization should not be overestimated, nor should a thorough radicalization of "the" workers be derived from the standpoints of individual, prominent spokesmen. In the leadership around Stephan Born there were some members of the Communist League, but in general the organization was more of a loose confederation of different artisans' and workers' associations. For all intents and purposes, the affiliation of the organization arising from the Frankfurt journeymen's congress at the beginning of 1849 helped raise its membership to 15,000 by 1850, but doubtless also increased the range of standpoints represented. Still, the Workers' Fraternization criticized the strategy of the first printers' and cigar makers' unions, that took for granted that their situation could be improved by banning female labor or new apprentices for a period of ten years.[34]

"The General German Workers' Congress in Berlin," stated a circular from the central committee of the Workers' Fraternization in September 1848, "does not assume conflicts of interest between master and journeyman, as handed down to us from the medieval guild system; for it, there are only the modern social antagonisms of capitalists and workers."[35] The signatories of this circular, a majority of whom were members of the Communist League, hence did not see class lines running between masters and journeymen, instead placing both in opposition to capitalists. Consequently, the Workers' Fraternization did not exclude masters, any more than the "trade unions" of cigarmakers and printers excluded employers in these trades. Class formation among artisans in general was therefore not very marked, and the numerous strikes during the course of the revolution also did not necessarily present a break with older forms of dispute, at least within traditional crafts.[36]

Nonetheless, the view of society emerging ever more clearly in the labor movement, whose most important organization was doubtless the Workers' Fraternization, differed fundamentally in two points from that of the artisan movement. First, with their demands for freedom of residence and an end to any restrictions on marriage and special municipal citizenship rights, the adherents of the labor movement clearly rejected exclusionist features of the guilds and the urban society of burghers. Second, in its associational structure the labor movement pointed the way to a future social democracy, to an alternative structure of society. This latter point should not, however, be overestimated.

In spite of the numerous personal connections with France of some leading members of the emerging labor movement, concepts relating to associations and their wider-ranging effects remained well behind the French model. Moreover, demands for producers' cooperatives were not specific to a socialist labor movement. Even in the 1850s and 1860s, such cooperatives still held a central position in the liberal program as well.[37] To this extent it would be anachronistic to credit them with considerable explosive force in 1848/49.

The social objectives of bourgeoisie, artisans, and the labor movement in the revolution of 1848/49 demonstrate considerable differences, without, however, leading to a sharp, class-based polarization insofar as future economic structures were concerned. This is most noticeable in the democratic movement, to which workers' associations belonged in many places, but which equally enjoyed substantial support from master craftsmen and sections of the bourgeoisie. Considerable regional distinctions existed, naturally, but the evidence suggests that in the German Revolution of 1848/49 neither economic and social circumstances, nor social objectives in the narrower sense, necessarily drove bourgeoisie, petite bourgeoisie, and workers into different political camps.

Nonetheless, to turn this argument on its head and say that class formation was without significance for the revolution would be completely mistaken. In Cologne, for example, the "demands of the people," including the "securing of work and ensuring of humane living conditions for all," put forth on 3 March 1848 with the support of a crowd of five thousand, were already raising fears among the liberal bourgeoisie.[38] In other places, throughout March 1848, greater emphasis was placed on efforts toward unanimity, but this did not change the fact that, sooner or later, splits between liberals and democrats occurred everywhere.[39] Contradictory governmental and social objectives were of fundamental importance to these splits, tied to the different aims of constitutional monarchy and republic, and very important for the further course of the revolution. In short, democrats were willing to apply a politically egalitarian society of citizens to social demands as well, while the constitutionalist liberals preferred a franchise based on property and, moreover, wanted to preserve the monarchy.

"The constitutional monarchy, like the pure monarchy, is supported by capital, by the representation of [special] interests. Hence with the overthrow of the monarchy, capital is overthrown as well."[40] With these words, the journal of the Workers' Fraternization underlined, in 1850, the close, indeed indissoluble ties between form of government and form of society. This also meant "that the workers' associations called forth by socialism, under the auspices of the grace of God, and the related rule of capital are not in a position to resolve the social question …"[41] The political revolution had to be pushed forward and therefore an alliance with the democratic movement seemed to be only logically consistent. For the majority of democrats, the republic and the social question were not so closely tied together, even when their critics asserted "republic equals social revolution equals rule of the proletariat."[42]

Behind this gap between liberals and democrats stood, however, less differences in their envisaged economic and social orders in the narrow sense, and much more a rejection of claims by the lower classes on the part of the liberals, no matter whether these claims related to political participation or social assistance. Such a rejection came even before the emerging labor movement's development into a party of social democracy, something in any case only recognizable at the organizational level after the split between liberal constitutionalists and democratic republicans had already occurred in many places. Responsible for the fears of a part of the bourgeoisie, apart from the Paris June uprising, was rather above all spontaneous action by the lower classes.

Here—without being class specific—claims were raised to an extent not seen before, which could have called into question liberal bourgeois claims to political rule as well as property rights. Lower class claims were often, but certainly not always, met by the civic guards, recruited mainly from property owners.[43] This was, however, a constellation of conflict that was a continuation of *Vormärz* protest, although becoming much more obvious in the revolution. "When it is a matter of protecting property," wrote the Württemberg liberal Julius Hölder to a friend after the Stuttgart hunger riots of 1847, "in the end there is nothing to do but shoot."[44]

It would be an exaggeration to see only material interests behind the liberals' vehement rejection of political and social claims to participation by the lower classes. Such considerations played a role in, for example, conflicts over the extent and payment for emergency public works programs, which, in comparison to France, were only modest.[45] It was just as much a problem of perception. The manner in which constitutionalist liberals registered the intentions of the democratic movement, which was certainly not aiming at social revolution, or the labor movement, points to fears among bourgeois groups of social groups foreign to them, groups whose inferior legal status had not yet been called into doubt at the very important municipal level.

This feeling of alienation was especially obvious in the large cities, where lower class poverty characterized entire districts.[46] Smaller cities, such as Düsseldorf, also had their districts dominated by unskilled and occasional laborers, but it would seem plausible that the milieu of smaller cities set limits to the possibilities for cultural distancing.[47] Here, too, the attitude of the civic guard was more difficult to predict. When they were ordered out against protesting boatmen and dockworkers in Mainz in mid-May 1848 to secure the barges of the steamboat corporations, the guardsmen, "solid citizens," refused. Asked by Ludwig Bamberger for their reasons "they took the side of the group to be proceeded against and … declared that these people were quite justified."[48]

In summary, it may be said that the economic and social development of the classes of an industrial society had advanced little in Germany up to the mid-nineteenth century and this process received no noticeable acceleration during the revolution itself. Nonetheless, during the revolution different objectives concerning the economic and social order were articulated. However, as on the one hand the proponents of unlimited freedom of occupation were a minority, even in the ranks of the bourgeoisie, and, on the other, even the emerging labor movement remained attached to older artisan models, the model of a reformed guild system propagated by the artisan movement was not a point of controversy that would have led to splits between bourgeoisie, petite bourgeoisie, and workers.

More controversial were workers' demands for political and social participation. Their reflection in the alternatives of republic and monarchy were the lines along which constitutionalist liberals and the democratic movement split. This split occurred relatively early, in spite of all local dissimilarities. Differences in program existed earlier, as is well-known, and demands by some republicans for a social republic must have accentuated them. However, more significant for the defensive attitude of the liberal bourgeoisie, apart from the Parisian June uprising, was, no doubt the numerous protest in the "streets," in which the tensions of *Vormärz* society found their expression. These tensions were not, however, class tensions in the narrower sense of the word.

The social question was of decisive importance for the momentous separation of liberals and democrats. However, this separation was one of political conviction, not class membership, in spite of differences in the social composition of the political associations. This can be seen not least in how diverging political orientations of bourgeoisie, petit bourgeoisie, and workers were to be found in quite similarly structured cities. Regional constellations of conflict, as the campaign for the imperial constitution would once again reveal, were more important here than simply class membership. In the Palatinate or in Baden, it was still possible for the prorevolutionary movement to be a popular one, uniting bourgeoisie, petit bourgeoisie, and workers in the summer of 1849.

France

The historiography of the French Revolution of 1789 has already shown that political and economic upheavals need not necessarily occur simultaneously, and that a change in political, legal, and mental conditions creates the presuppositions for capitalist industrialization. For France in the middle of the nineteenth century, the term "double revolution" is also less applicable for explaining the special features of the societal situation and the dynamics of political transformation. The "take-off"—to use W.W. Rostow's both problematic and expressive metaphor—should be placed rather in the 1860s than during the mid-century revolution. It was only at this point that the creation of a national market for goods, capital, and labor had made conspicuous progress, investment in both producers' and consumers' goods industries had increased, and the levels of enterprise size had come to include large scale production. All these processes had begun in the 1840s, but were not yet defining for society. Maurice Agulhon indeed spoke of an "anteriority of democracy to modernity" in France and thus emphasized the introduction of a universal manhood suffrage over the development of a modern bourgeois capitalist society.[49]

The generally agrarian society in France was, in fact, definitely not organized along class lines. Indeed one could argue that with the lack of a national market, because of numerous market restrictions and non-market social relations, important preconditions of class formation in parts of mid-nineteenth century French society were still lacking. The working population at the time was concentrated more in the crafts than in modern industrial production, which defined workers' living conditions only in the textile factories in Normandy and Alsace or in the coal mines of northern and southern France. As actors in the political and social struggles of the revolutionary period, these proletarians, often unskilled and mostly illiterate, and moreover primarily employed in factories located in the countryside, appeared only rarely on the political stage.

Politically active were rather more the broad lower classes in the cities, especially in Paris and Lyon, as well as parts of rural society.[50] As in Germany, numerous, especially smaller and mid-sized, towns have not been yet sufficiently examined for the revolutionary period, so that broader statements are often generalizations of the few well-known cases. It would appear at times as if the quite influential work of Maurice Agulhon in France had paralyzed the research élan for the revolutionary period and as if this monopoly of interpretation explains the significance that works on the 1848 revolution by American authors in particular have gained in France.

The working classes were not completely excluded from ownership of the means of production. This was, in fact, still the rule in numerous, often only formally independent small enterprises. In Paris, for example, the number of independent masters rose between 1851 and 1872 from 55,100 to 100,000 and thus much quicker than the urban population as a whole—although this rise can also be credited to changes in statistical units. In any case, in 1847/48, 50.4 percent of all Paris enterprises had fewer than two employees, 38.7 percent had between two and ten, and only 10.9 percent had more than ten. About 20 percent of the population of Rouen, and 32 percent of the population of Paris, belonged to this world of trade and commerce in the 1880s; in the smaller towns the figures may have been even greater.[51]

The boundaries between these craftsmen and retailers with their own businesses on the one hand, and the bourgeois strata and the working population on the other, were fluid. In those branches in which the opening of shops and workshops demanded more capital, affluence was more easily achieved and independence maintained over a longer period of time than in those in which the capital base was thin. A part of the petit bourgeoisie, whom Adeline Daumard called the "bourgeoisie populaire" of Paris, was nonetheless successful in passing on their shop or workshop to their children, bequeathing money and property at their deaths and placing their children in bourgeois circles professionally or through marriage.[52]

The majority of craft workshops and retail stores were characterized by high fluctuation, insecure living conditions and economic instability. The living conditions of their owners, in spite of their possession of the means of production, approached those of the proletariat. Frequent shifts between nominal or real ownership of a business and dependency on a wage were not the exception, but were rather widespread, especially in the mass crafts. Moreover, there were neither government regulations nor guild practices to structure the lower middle class, as was the case in Germany. The organization of the lower middle class was not discussed, as in Germany, in terms of a conflict between occupational freedom and a corporate, guild order. Neither the class formation of the working class nor that of the petit bourgeoisie had been completed by the middle of the century. Whether working from the class theories of Karl Marx or those of Max Weber, hybrid social forms and societal mixed zones characterized the society of the middle of the century more than did clear delineations and structurally homogeneous ensembles.

This impression is confirmed by an examination of the urban middle and upper classes. An industrial bourgeoisie was certainly not dominant, except perhaps in Mulhouse or in other, smaller textile cities. Domestic and international trade, money-lending, ownership of landed property, and small scale production were the most important sources of income, with professional employment as lawyer or doctor(*les capacités*) playing an increasingly significant role in the 1840s. In general, ties with the land and land ownership seem to have been greater here than in Germany.

The bourgeois middle class could also, to an extent that varied locally, include better off master craftsmen and shopkeepers, especially bakers and butchers, dealers in tropical products and merchant contractors in the garment trades. The sealing off of access to the bourgeois strata from below, which can be observed in a number of cities in the second half of the nineteenth century, had, circa 1850 not yet put an end to the fluid transitions from artisan affluence to a bourgeois lifestyle.[53] Similar to German municipal law, though with some significant distinctive features, the property-based franchise divided various elements of the bourgeoisie and placed the rich property-owning bourgeoisie among the ranks of the society of notables. Exercising a mediating role between city and country, the urban and rural notables had a common pool of marriage partners, and similar investment practices and political privileges; their ranks included the nobility and the bourgeoisie. While part of the urban middle classes enjoyed the right to vote in municipal elections, where the franchise was less exclusive than at the national level, the majority of the middle bourgeoisie demanded a modification of the franchise, pushing for the elimination of this barrier that they held to be unjust.[54] Even if socioeconomic similarities had already existed between the various sections of the bourgeoisie—which was not the case—such similarities would have been obscured by continuing differences in political rights.

Within the lower classes, various social groups and claims could be bound together in the term and ideal of the "*peuple*," to which all non-monopolists belonged. Excluded were, of course, not only aristocrats and bourgeois notables, but also financiers, businessmen, and increasingly in the wake of urbanization landlords, state officials, and members of the police. The *peuple* included above all the area of small commodity production, based locally on neighborhood relations and personal contacts. This group was, for its part, also not free of conflict. Struggles between journeymen and masters continued. Contrasts became especially virulent when, as in 1820 in the Paris chair-making industry, traditional rights were restricted due to pressure from merchant contractors.[55] However, conflicts between masters and journeymen did not have to occur, as can be seen in the Lyon uprisings of the 1830s in which masters and journeymen defended themselves against the demands of merchant contractors in a struggle concerning piecework, known as the "*tarif*."[56] Such common grounds seem to have been greater in France than in Germany, or, to put it differently, the social relevance of the gap between masters and business owners, on the one hand, and assistants and journeymen on the other, was smaller.

This was reflected in politics as well. Demands for a "moral economy" could be supported by both workers and owners of businesses who were being pushed by merchant contractors toward new divisions and organizations of labor. The slogan of the organization of labor or of "association" could bridge the gap between workers and small scale independent businessmen. These different visions came together in the demand for the establishment of a republican system of government, which was to have both a political and social function.

Before 1848, the republic was the common slogan for oppositional bourgeois journalists, doctors, lawyers, and property owners on the one hand, and a broad lower class including masters, journeymen, and workers on the other. With this slogan, the bourgeoisie was able to place itself at the head of lower class movements relatively easily. In Toulon, before 1848, workers begged a republican doctor to head their association. This slogan was able to include various social groups as a range of sometimes quite dissimilar definitions were bound to the term "republic," their contrasting natures only becoming obvious in the revolution itself. While for the moderate bourgeoisie the republic meant above all an extension of the franchise and better education, socialist authors related it to ideas of an egalitarian property ownership structure. It was only in the course of the revolution of 1848 that the various interpretations of the republic separated into distinct, and at least temporarily opposing, organizations.[57]

Those who preferred to bring an end to the revolution with the new constitution were opposed by the démocrates-socialistes of 1849, who wanted to create the foundations of a social republic through such government measures as the provision of credit, the income tax, free education, tax reductions and waivers, or nationalization, and the recognition and fostering of mutual benefit societies [*sociétés de secours mutuels*]. A few, inspired by socialism went even further, such as the *Société des corporations réunies* [the society of the united craft corporations] in Paris, which, drawing on guild vocabulary, demanded in 1848 an economic and social system based on producers' cooperatives. "The Society of the United Craft Corporations," it was stated in the *Journal des travailleurs* [The Workers' News]- "has as its sole goal the abolition of the exploitation of man by man, via the immediate association of producers, and via the creation of workshops of associated workers."[58]

Social groups and classes certainly did not separate clearly into distinct political positions, as alleged by Karl Marx and as has still recently been suggested by Christophe Charles in his social history of France.[59] Depending on region or local conditions, the bourgeoisie remained active in the group of the "démo-socs" or masters supported demands raised by the *Journal des travailleurs* for the establishment of producers' cooperatives. Even within the working class there were political differences. It is well-known, for example, that both the Paris insurgents of June 1848 and the mobile guard that fought against them, came from the same socioprofessional milieu. However, among the former, metal construction and leather workers predominated, and among the latter workers in small trades and in luxury goods production. Not class, rather at most a difference in age, separated the two, as the members of the mobile guard were younger on average.[60]

Political options were also not directly tied to class situation during the the 1848 revolution in France, all the more as one cannot speak of a political homogeneity of social groups. The social mixture reflected in some political camps was not reduced in the course of the revolution. Of the victims of the political repression that followed Louis-Napoléon's coup in 1851, most of whom were from southern France, 14 percent were lawyers and businessmen, journalists and pharmacists, teachers and surveyors. However, they remained a minority compared to the 5,423 peasants, 1,850 agricultural workers, and 131 gardeners, who made up 27 percent of those arrested. The majority of those demonstrating for the preservation of the republic, however, came more from among artisans than from the factory, and among the 48 percent of those arrested who came from this sector, tailors and shoe-makers, construction workers and furniture-makers formed the majority. Whether this occupational structure exactly reflects the extent and strength of political activity or rather those who were held by the authorities to be republican-oppositional can remain an open question here. Central in any case is that the political activists or those held to be republicans came from various social milieus and classes.[61]

Rather like in Germany, revolutionary events had a marked effect on the political reaction of social groups, without, however, their developing a common political stance. Demands for a "right to work," for an egalitarian distribution of property, and for social equality—"wealth must be distributed among all; misery impossible" was one formula[62]—raised by the popular movement contributed to many, if not all property owners, having a believable image of the horror of the "reds." Condemnation of insurgents in the revolution as the element of disintegration among the people, or—as Marx aptly put it the "scum"—doubtless contributed to a bourgeois counter-reaction, which, however, was not uniform politically. Clear political differences existed, between the political objectives of the Legitimists, Orléanists, and Bonapartists in spite of a common rejection of socialist forces.

The dynamics of the revolutionary events, the rapid formation of a broad network of associations, newspaper and public meetings, their restriction and finally their prohibition and the persecution of their activists and spokesmen also temporarily separated socialists from the democratic movement. When the "démo-socs," for example, called for uprisings to fight the government's breach of the constitution in June 1849, the lower classes in the larger cities remained quiet. Only in the countryside and in the provincial cities was there a reaction. To the extent that the "démo-socs" were then persecuted, the various positions within the opposition came closer, under the umbrella of republicanism, and established a republican milieu in which journeymen artisans, small masters, and workers in the cities and in the countryside, socialists and democrats worked together, often in secret societies.[63]

In contrast to Germany, it is noticeable how radical socialist demands were worded and how widespread they were among the lower classes. Clubs and secret societies, cooperatives and workers' associations were to be found in large cities, but in small ones as well. Possibly contributing to this was the political learning process which these groups had already experienced in the French Revolution, when they were able to actively participate in political life. However, a continuity of occupational organizations, practice in resistance and in the formation of political and social counter-models in times of political crises, the strong tradition of insurrection and attempted coups can also explain why lower-class political and social demands in France were more wide-ranging than those in Germany. Finally, close ties to the republican bourgeois milieu, participation in a political sociability should be mentioned among the politicizing structures in France.

Moreover, the *peuple* were not—as in Germany—concerned with, or divided on, the question of organization. In politics, the republican form of government was widely accepted among the *peuple*, as was, in economic terms, a society of small producers supported by loans from the government, following the model of the French Revolution. To this extent, in the 1848 revolution a social milieu encompassing petit bourgeois and workers developed that united democratic and socialist demands in the demand for the realization of the republic. This milieu only shattered in the 1890s with the dogmatization of the labor movement.[64] This milieu cannot be clearly categorized according to class, but as an integrative force it had important consequences for the formation of class structures in France.

Conclusion

Both case studies have drawn on common elements as "tertium comparationis." They have discussed H.U. Wehler's thesis of the "dual revolution" and demonstrated its limits. The idea of class lines that separated not only social milieus but also political camps has been shown to have only a restricted explanatory power as well. In the urban societies of both countries—insofar as is known—it was social heterogeneity that characterized political organization and political options rather than polarization along class lines. This was due not least to a process of differentiation that accompanied the development of the bourgeoisie in general and a continued existence of the residential and working conditions of small producers. Such a heterogeneity describes the developmental level of both societies on the eve of deepseated industrial transformations; this heterogeneity nonetheless did not lead to the formation of clear political camps and social divisions.

As a result of these findings, one could be inclined to give up the recourse to class structures themselves and emphasize more strongly the heuristic force of comparisons at a lower level of aggregation. Such comparisons could begin with individuals, local groups or occupations, or include social and political practices. Nonetheless, comparisons that draw on class theories and class contexts retain their importance. Even there where it leads to taking into consideration the limitations of class processes and to question the simultaneity of economic, social, and political developments,—as E.P. Thompson has argued for English society in the eighteenth century—it still allows a better understanding of the dynamic of social relations and changes than other competing theories.

Notes

1. Karl Marx and Friedrich Engels, *Manifesto of the Communist Party* (New York, 1982), 8. For the following, cf. Wolfgang Schieder, *Karl Marx als Politiker*, (Munich, 1991), 38.

2. Marx and Engels, *The Communist Manifesto*, 9.

3. On this point, see, most recently, Heinz-Gerhard Haupt, "Zum Fortbestand des Ancien Règime im Europa des 19. Jahrhunderts: Zünfte und Zunftideale," in Manfred Hettling and Paul Nolte (eds.), *Nation und Gesellschaft. Historische Essays* (Munich, 1996), 221-30.

4. Karl Marx, *The Class Struggles in France*, in Karl Marx and Frederick Engels, *Collected Works* Vol. 10 (New York, 1979-), 45-145, here 53.

5. See Hans-Ulrich Wehler, *Deutsche Gesellschaftsgeschichte*, Vol. 2: *Von der Reformära bis zur industriellen und politischen "Deutschen Doppelrevolution"' 1815-1845/49* (Munich, 1987), 587ff.

6. The best overview is Jürgen Kocka, *Arbeitsverhältnisse und Arbeiterexistenzen. Grundlagen der Klassenbildung* (Bonn, 1990).

7. In this, Munich seems to have been an exception. See Karl-Joseph Hummel, *München in der Revolution von 1848/49* (Göttingen, 1987), 451-83.

8. In summary, see Friedrich Lenger, *Sozialgeschichte der deutschen Handwerker seit 1800* (Frankfurt, 1988), 49-58 and 69-70.

9. This is also true in comparative perspective; see for example, Friedrich Lenger, "Beyond Exceptionalism: Notes on the Artisanal Phase of the Labor Movement in France, England, Germany and the United States," *International Review of Social History* 36 (1991): 1-23, esp. 6-10.

10. See, above all, Jonathan Sperber, *Rhineland Radicals. The Democratic Movement and the Revolution of 1848/49* (Princeton, 1991) and Michael Wettengel, *Die Revolution von 1848/49 im Rhein-Main-Raum. Politische Vereine und Revolutionsalltag im Großherzogtum Hessen, Herzogtum Nassau und in der Freien Stadt Frankfurt* (Wiesbaden, 1989).

11. See Lenger, *Sozialgeschichte*, (n. 8).

12. See Friedrich Lenger, *Zwischen Kleinbürgertum und Proletariat. Studien zur Sozialgeschichte der Düsseldorfer Handwerker 1816-1878* (Göttingen, 1986), esp. 40-64 and the figures in Lothar Gall (ed.), *Stadt und Bürgertum im Übergang von der traditionalen zur modernen Gesellschaft* (Munich, 1993).

13. See Ralf Zerback, "Zwischen Residenz und Rathaus. Bürgertum in München 1780-1820," in Lothar Gall (ed.), *Vom alten zum neuen Bürgertum. Die mitteleuropäische Stadt im Umbruch 1780-1820* (Munich, 1991), 605-53, here, 633.

14. In relation to this brief summary of a complex line of argument, see, apart from the collection of essays mentioned in notes 12 and 13, above all Lothar Gall, *Bürgertum in Deutschland* (Berlin, 1989); as well as Lothar Gall, "Liberalismus und 'bürgerliche Gesellschaft.' Zu Charakter und Entwicklung der liberalsn Bewegung in Deutschland," in Lothar Gall (ed.), *Liberalismus* (Cologne, 1976), 162-186.

15. See the extensive critique in Friedrich Lenger, "Bürgertum, Stadt und Gemeinde zwischen Frühneuzeit und Moderne," *Neue Politische Literatur* 40 (1995): 14-29.

16. See, for example, John Breuilly and Wieland Sachse, *Joachim Friedrich Martens (1806-1877) und die Deutsche Arbeiterbewegung* (Göttingen, 1984).

17. See Lenger, *Sozialgeschichte* (n. 8), with further references, and the essay by Manfred Gailus, "The Revolution of 1848 as 'Politics of the Streets," Chapter 33 in this volume.

18. See the analysis of the petitions by Manfred Simon, *Handwerk in Krise und Umbruch. Wirtschaftliche Forderungen und Sozialpolitische Vorstellungen der Handwerksmeister im Revolutionsjahr 1848/49* (Cologne, 1983).

19. All quotations from *Entwurf einer allgemeinen Handwerker- und Gewerbe-Ordnung für Deutschland. Berathen und beschlossen von dem deutschen Handwerker- und Gewerbe-Congreß zu Frankfurt am Main in den Monaten Juli und August 1848* (Hamburg, 1848), reprinted in Dieter Dowe and Toni Offermann (eds.), *Deutsche Handwerker- und Arbeiterkongresse 1848-1852. Protokolle und Materialien* (Berlin, 1983), 178-97, here 179ff.

20. Ibid., 182.

21. For a summary, see Lenger, *Sozialgeschichte* (n. 8), 76-77.

22. See Elisabeth Fehrenbach, "Rheinischer Liberalismus und gesellschaftliche Verfassung," in Wolfgang Schieder (ed.), *Liberalismus in der Gesellschaft des deutschen Vormärz* (Göttingen, 1983), 272-94 and R. Muhs, "Zwischen Staatsreform und politischen Protest. Liberalismus in Sachsen zur Zeit des Hambacher Festes," in ibid., 194-238 as well as Rudolf Boch, *Grenzenloses Wachstum? Das rheinische Wirtschaftsbürgertum und seine Industrialisierungsdebatte 1814-1857* (Göttingen, 1991).

23. Dieter Langewiesche, *Liberalismus und Demokratie in Württemberg zwischen Revolution und Reichsgründung* (Düsseldorf, 1974), 216.

24. See Hubert Sedatis, *Liberalismus und Handwerk in Südwestdeutschland. Wirtschafts- und Gesellschaftskonzeptionen des Liberalismus und die Krise des Handwerks im 19. Jahrhundert* (Stuttgart, 1979) esp. 87-92.

25. Heinrich Best, *Interessenpolitik und nationale Integeration. Handelspolitische Konflikte im frühindustriellen Deutschland* (Göttingen, 1980).

26. The figures come from Lenger, *Sozialgeschichte*, (n.8), 70ff.

27. *Verhandlungen des ersten deutschen Handwerker- und Gewerbe-Congresses gehalten zu Frankfurt a.M. vom 14. Juli bis 18. August*, in G. Schirges (ed.) *Im Auftrag des Congresses*, (Darmstadt, 1848), reprinted in Dowe and Offermann (eds.) *Deutsche Handwerker- und Arbeiterkongresse*, (n.19) 46-177, here, 59.

28. See, for example, Wettengel, *Revolution*, (n. 6), 154-55.

29. *Beschlüsse des allgemeinen deutschen Arbeiterknogresses zu Frankfurt am Main. Gefaßt in den Monaten Juli, August und September 1848* (Dresden, 1848) reprinted in Dowe and Offermann (ed.) *Deutsche Handwerker- und Arbeiterkongresse*, (n. 19), 210-17, here, 211.

30. *Denkschrift über den Entwurf einer allgemeinen deutschen Gewerbe-Ordnung des Handwerker- und Gewerbe-Congresses. Verfaßt von dem allgemeinen deutschen Arbeiter-Congreß zu Frankfurt am Main in den Monaten August und September 1848* (Darmstadt, 1848), reprinted in Dowe and Offermann (eds.) *Deutsche Handwerker- und Arbeiterkongresse*, (n. 19), 218-33, here 220.

31. *Beschlüsse des Arbeiter-Kongresses zu Berlin. Vom 23. August bis 3. September 1848* (Berlin, 1848), reprinted in ibid., 237-49, here 239.

32. Ibid., 248.

33. Ibid., 242.

34. Lenger, *Sozialgeschichte*, (n. 8) 81ff.

35. "Rundschreiben des Zentralkomitees an sämtliche Arbeiter und Arbeitervereine Deutschlands," reprinted in *Die Allgemeine deutsche Arbeiterverbrüderung 1848-1850. Dokumente des Zentralkomitees für die deutschen Arbeiter in Leipzig,* edited and introduced by Horst Schlechte, (Weimar, 1979), 338ff., here 339.

36. This point is much disputed in the research: see, for example, Jürgen Kocka, *Lohnarbeit und Klassenbildung. Arbeiter und Arbeiterbewegung in Deutschland 1800-1875* (Bonn, 1983), 174 and Gailu's essay in this volume.

37. See Heinz-Gerhard Haupt and Friedrich Lenger, "Liberalismus und Handwerk in Frankreich und Deutschland um die Mitte des 19. Jahrhunderts," in Dieter Langewiesche (ed.), *Liberalismus im 19. Jahrhundert. Deutschland im europäischen Vergleich* (Göttingen, 1988), 305-31.

38. Quoted in Marcel Seyppel, *Die Demokratische Gesellschaft in Köln 1848/49. Städtische Gesellschaft und Parteientstehung während der bürgerlichen Revolution*, (Cologne, 1991), 49.

39. See, for the following as well, Dieter Langewiesche, "Republik, konstitutionelle Monarchie und 'soziale Frage'. Grundprobleme der deutschen Revolution von 1848/49," *Historische Zeitschrift* 230 (1980): 529-48, as well as the regional studies by Sperber and Wettengel mentioned in n. 10.

40. *Die Verbrüderung. Correspondenzblatt aller deutscher Arbeiter*, 26 March 1850 (reprint, Leipzig 1975).

41. Ibid.

42. Langewiesche, "Republik," (n. 39), 542.

43. On social protest see Gailus's chapter in this volume; on the behavior of the civic guard, which varied considerably from place to place, the regional studies by Sperber and Wettengel mentioned in n.10 are very instructive.

44. Quoted in Dieter Langewiesche (ed.), *Das Tagebuch Julius Hölders 1877-1880. Zum Zerfall des politischen Liberalismus in Württemberg und im Deutschen Reich* (Stuttgart, 1977), 300-1.

45. See P.-P Sagave, 1848: "Ateliers nationaux à Paris et travaux d'utilitié publique à Berlin," in Ilja Mieck, Horst Möller, and Jürgen Voss (ed.), *Paris und Berlin in der Revolution 1848* (Sigmaringen, 1995), 153-60.

46. See as one example on conditions in Berlin, Rüdiger Hachtmann, "Die soziale Unterschichten in der großstädtischen Revolution von 1848. Berlin, Paris und Wien im Vergleich," ibid., 107-35, who introduces the term, not employed here, of the "culture of poverty" (Oscar Lewis) to describe the feelings of alienation mentioned here.

47. See Lenger, *Kleinbürgertum*, (n. 12), 135-43.

48. Quoted in Wettengel, *Revolution*, (n. 10), 165; see also, on the Mainz civic guard, Sperber, *Rhineland Radicals*, (n. 10), 172.

49. Maurice Agulhon, "The Heritage of the Revolution and Liberty in France," *Review* 12 (1989): 405-22, here 407; P.K. O'Brian and C. Keyder, *Economic Growth in Britain and France, 1780-1917: Two Paths to the Twentieth Century* (London, 1978).

50. See Ronald Aminzade, *Ballots and Barricades: Class Formation and Republican Politics in France, 1830-1871* (Princeton, 1993), 63-104; Mark Traugott, *Armies of the Poor: Determinants of Working Class Participation in the Parisian Insurrection of June 1848*, (Princeton, 1985); Maurice Agulhon, *Les Quarante-Huitards* (Paris, 1975); Maurice Agulhon, *The Republican Experiment, 1848-1852*, trans. Janet Lloyd (Cambridge, 1983).

51. Joan Scott, "Men and Women in the Parisian Garment Trades. Discussions of Family and Work in the 1830s and 1840s," in Pat Thane (ed.), *The Power of the Past* (Cambridge, 1984); Gerard Noiriel, *Workers in French Society in the 19th and 20th Centuries*, trans. Helen McPhail (New York, 1990), 10-11; B.M. Ratcliffe, "Manufacturing in the Metropolis. Toward a new understanding of the Parisian Economy during the Restoration and the July Monarchy," in Ilja Mieck (ed.), *Paris und Berlin in der Restauration 1815-1820*, (Sigmaringen, 1996), 113-72.

52. Adeline Daumard, *La bourgeoisie parisienne, de 1815 à 1848* (Paris, 1963); Geoffrey Crossick and Heinz-Gerhard Haupt, *The Petite Bourgeoisie in Europe 1780-1914* (London, 1995), 64ff.

53. See Christoph Charles, *Histoire sociale de la France au XIXe siècle*, (Paris, 1991), 41ff.

54. See Pierre Rosanvallon, *Le sacre du citoyen. Histoire de suffrage universal en France* (Paris, 1992).

55. Rémi Gossez (ed.), *J.E. Bédé. Un ouvrier en 1820* (Paris, 1984).

56. Robert J. Bezucha, *The Lyon uprising of 1834. Social and Political Conflict in the Early July Monarchy* (Cambridge, 1974); Maurice Agulhon, *Une ville ouvrière au temps du socialisme utopique: Toulouse de 1815 à 1851* (Paris, 1970).

57. Rémi Gossez, *Les ouvriers de Paris 1: L'organisation 1848-1851* (La Roche sur Yon, 1957); William H. Sewell, *Work and Revolution in France: The Language of Labor from the Old Regime to 1848* (Cambridge, 1980); R. Huard, *Le mouvement republicain en Bas-Languedoc 1848-1881* (Paris, 1982).

58. Alain Faure and Jacques Rancière (eds.), *La parole ouvrière 1830-1851* (Paris, 1976), 314.

59. Charles, *Histoire sociale*, (n. 53), 60ff.

60. P. Caspard, Aspects de le lutte des classes en 1848: le recrutement de la garde nationale mobile, *Revue Historique* 511 (1974): 81-106; Rémi Gossez, "Diversité des antagonismes sociaux vers le milieu du XIXe siècle," *Revue économique* 7 (1956): 439-58; Charles Tilly and Lynn Lees, "Le peuple de Juin 1848," *Annales E.S.C.* 29 (1974): 1061-91.

61. Agulhon, *The Republican Experiment*, 163; see also Ted Margadant, *French Peasants in Revolt: The Insurrection of 1851* (Princeton, 1979); Peter Jones, *Politics and the Rural Society: The Southern Massif Central c. 1750-1880* (Cambridge, 1983); Peter McPhee, *The Politics of Rural Life: Political Mobilization in the French Countryside, 1846-1852* (Oxford, 1992).

62. Faure and Rancière (eds.), *La parole ouvriere*, (n. 58), 313.

63. Bernard Moss, "June 13, 1849: The Abortive uprising of French Radicalism," *French Historical Studies* 13 (1984): 390-414; Mary Lynn Stewart-McDougall, *The Artisan Republic: Revolution, Reaction and Resistance in Lyon, 1848-1851* (Montreal, 1984).

64. Philip Nord, *The Republican Movement. Struggles for Democracy in Nineteenth-Century France* (Cambridge and New York, 1995).

Chapter 26

WOMEN'S SPACES IN THE MEN'S REVOLUTION OF 1848*

Gabriella Hauch

* For Antonio Honorio Grieco, poet of life and a friend who died much too young on 27
  October 1996 in San José, Costa Rica.

Vienna, 13 March 1848: Margaretha Schambor, a washerwomen, dies in the
fighting in the suburbs.

Frankfurt, 18 May 1848: following protests, 200 seats are reserved for women in
the spectator's gallery of the *Paulskirche* for the opening of the Frankfurt National
Assembly.

Mainz, Lemberg, Prague, Milan in the spring of 1848: women prepare flags
in the national colors for the newly founded national guard.

Berlin, Paris in the summer of 1848: (petit) bourgeois feelings are outraged at
George Sand, Lola Montez and Louise Aston appearing in public in men's clothing,
smoking cigars.

Berlin, 14 September 1848: the Democratic Ladies' Club discusses child-rearing
along democratic principles at its first meeting.

Paris, April 1849: Jeanne Deroin announces her candidacy for the national assembly on the list of the democratic-socialists.

Dresden, 15 March 1850: Pauline Wunderlich is sentenced to life imprisonment
in a high security prison for her participation in the barricade fighting in Dresden
from 3 to 9 May 1849.

These examples from 1848 and 1849 show the amazing variety of women's lives
and activities. The fears and hopes arising from the revolution marked the broad

Notes for this section begin on page 676.

spectrum of women's motivations and interests. These, like the models for their action, were imbued by the simultaneous existence of traditional and modern elements, which manifested themselves not only in the socioeconomic, cultural and political aspects of this age, but in gender relations as well. These different aspects of the revolution already had their own unique and distinct development; adding gender relations makes the course of the revolution still less uniform and more jagged. To understand this mixture of non-homogeneity and non-simultaneity a careful combination of gender with other categories, such as class, religion, region, ethnicity, nation, and age is necessary—not only to comprehend the respective political, cultural-discursive, and socioeconomic conditions, but also to come closer to the forms of expression of women's different lives. Some fantasies formulated by the new women's movement should assist in reflecting on such a context, as 150 years after the activity, hopes and demands of female eighteen forty-eighters, we are still waiting for a true democratic participation of women in power, the public sphere, and political life.

Although even older literature contains references to the role of women in the revolutionary process, it was only with the introduction of gender as a category of research that women were systematically included in a historic retrospective, and with new theses and viewpoints that the sociopolitical and historical relevance of gender relations was made apparent. In experimenting with discourse analysis, and the introduction of an understanding of politics that calls into question the dichotomy of public and private, as well as the "male gender text" (Nancy Fraser) of citizenship, new traces can be outlined with respect to the construction of "male" and "female" as the constitutive duality of modernity, and to the historical unfolding of the effects of this duality.

In the first phase of women's historiography certain texts formed the core of research interest as part of a larger feminist search for traces of women's agency in history: works by early French female socialists and writers in the *Vormärz*, editions of women's journals such as Louise Otto's *Frauen-Zeitung*, and (auto) biographies of exceptional women. With the extension and development of women's historiography in the direction of gender studies, micro and regional studies began to appear most frequently, such as those about Württemberg, Frankfurt and Vienna. Works on groupings defined by ideological orientation, that analyzed, for instance, the early female socialists in France, female Chartists in England, or the gender-specific significance of religious dissent, also impressively demonstrate that women and gender relations could become an intrinsic factor in the historiography of the European years of revolution 1848/49—if they are examined.

International women's research into the revolution of 1848/49 long stood in the shadow of the great French Revolution. In spite of the considerable number of gaps in research concerning women in 1848/49, work has currently come to a halt, at least in Europe. Revolution as an object of research has experienced a "recession" in recent years, because of a political disavowal of social utopias tied to revolutions, combined with a discussion of the end of certainty at the academic level. Moreover, in feminist research revolution has often been subsumed under war. Although it is still true to say that a feminist standpoint is the best guarantee for the inclusion of gender relations in historiography—and women as theme in historical retrospective is still tied to this—gender-specific themes are increasingly found in the work of male historians.★

In descriptions of the time, the majority of the heroes of 1848/49 were male, young, and handsome. The breach between fathers and sons manifest in the revolution of 1848/49 had its counterpoint in fraternity, which promised a newly constructed future of liberty and equality based on common convictions. Countless contemporary writings, in using these terms, reflect not only a specific structure of the forty-eighters' social and political networks—"brother worker," "sons of the movement." or "fathers of the people"—but also underline the inscription of masculinity in the project of modernity and its concept of politics and law, that is the dominance of masculinity qua gender.

The female trio of mother-companion-beloved stood more off to one side of the male trio of fathers-sons-brothers than facing them. Mothers were given a central role in revolutionary semantics, not only in 1848/49, but companions and women who were beloved, because they were defined in reference to the male, could hardly serve as pendants to sons and brothers. Premodern patriarchal differences, based on status, were set down in the German codes of civil law, the French *Code Civil*, or the British Reform Act as legalized gender differentiation. The ideal "male-citizen" became the head of the family and the individual capable of politics and bearing arms; citizenship became a legal and social category restricted to men.

In the mid-nineteenth century, these rules and conditions reflected above all the life-worlds of the (grand) bourgeois and (enlightened) noble strata. In many countries in Europe there was no freedom of marriage for the lower classes, and they were certainly far removed from family wages. Such segregation applied to the Jewish population. The "atypical" worlds of families privileged by property and education, whose women led the intellectual-artist salons of the *Vormärz*, should not disguise the view of the vast majority, especially discriminated by exceptional taxes, numerus clausus in founding families etc.

The construction of (male) politics of the modern, which appeared so solid, and the "dichotomization of gender character" (Karin Hausen) displayed contradictions from its creation and provoked resistance. In view of socially and regionally distinct legal structures, difficulties in source material and the fictions that surround women and gender relations, it seems sensible for research practice to bundle non-homogeneity and non-simultaneity along the lines of the questions to be posed. Fundamental to this is the concept of space, that refers not only to geographical places, but also to the network of social relations in and outside institutions that is spread throughout society and that simultaneously structures and constitutes it.

How did this exclusion of women function, in view of the political institutions of modernity that were conceived by men as a male space, as accomplishments of the March revolution? What consequences did women draw from this, and what kind of institutionalized female spaces did they create for themselves? How were gender relations orchestrated in the intermediary spaces outside of institutionalized politics? What role did gender relations and the commitment of women to the nationalist movement play? What status did mothers have in contemporary discourse? With what positive and negative effects were wives confronted, as companions of their politically active husbands, and how did the connection between politics and love in the form of the beloved manifest itself? Violent struggles did exist in the intermediary spaces, in which gender levels mixed. How did women fight and how was the "armed woman," the female martyr of the revolution, construed? And finally, how was she treated, as loser, by the victorious counter-revolution?

These questions form the guidelines of the following expedition through the European revolutionary landscape of 1848/49. In viewing a few of its arenas—determined by the state of research and with no claims to being exhaustive—the formative power of gender relations in events, presentation, social and national movements and biographies will be discussed. At the center of this chapter is the thematization of women who defined themselves as eighteen forty-eighters and who saw in the breaking open of the political system and of political culture a chance to move closer to the fulfillment of their own hopes and desires.

In the Galleries—Women and Institutionalized Male Spaces: Political Associations, Suffrage, and Parliament

> "When they talk about the people, women aren't included."
> — Louise Otto, 1849

When Louise Otto, publisher of the *Frauen-Zeitung* in Saxony, expressed her outrage at women's exclusion from political life in April 1849, women had already lost the struggle for a political definition of liberty, equality, and citizenship throughout Europe. This gender-specific definition of position, which has defined the modern political system up to the present, was accompanied by women's resistance from the beginning. This first manifested itself with Olympe des Gouge's *Droits des Femme* (1791) and Mary Wollenstonecraft's *Vindication of the Rights of Women* (1792). Even in the French Revolution, in 1793, women were excluded from political associations, and women's clubs were forbidden. This exclusion was accompanied by the construction of woman as politically incompetent.

In the period after the Paris July Revolution of 1830, in which a great number of women had once again taken part, many women sought to influence the discourse on citizenship and hence sociopolitical reality in their favor, as Michèle Riot-Scacey has shown with the biographies of Désiree Gay, Jeanne Deroin and Eugénie Niboyet and their publications in *L'Apostolat des femmes*, the Saint Simonian women's journal. Not only in France, gender-specific power structureswere so formed that ability to bear arms was restricted to men and rights of citizenship defined in male terms. In 1833, a law on public education established boys' schools throughout France and also the second-class nature of girls' education. In the English Reform Act of 1832, the franchise was restricted to men, although women, such as Mary Smith, a single landowner in Yorkshire, had been demanding it for themselves for years. The first women's association for female suffrage, founded in Sheffield by the Quaker Anne Knight and seven women Chartists, was also already active.[1]

Similar currents can be seen throughout Europe. With the construction of armed masculinity and with the anchoring of gender differentiation in the civil codes, women were excluded from citizenship; they became the subordinate sex. Public revaluation of the model of a social-charitable femininity, the rising popularity of Mary as Mother of God, the increasingly biologically and anthropologically determined "scientific" justifications of the inferiority of women, had as much an effect on the consolidation of the network of dichotomized gender character as did the demands of the emerging labor movement for a family wage for members of the lower classes. The basis for the discourse on the "privatization" of women with regard to voluntary association was anchored in the law, which from the beginning, with the exception of France, had excluded women from the culture of political associations. The female portion of the bourgeois public sphere became charity, as is made clear in the case of the Habsburg Monarchy in the Society of Noble Women for the Encouragement of the Good and the Useful, initiated by the government in 1811.

As a consequence of the Paris February Revolution, a wave of uprisings overran large parts of Europe from March 1848 onwards, carried by demands for civil liberties. Everywhere, however, the franchise and the right to be a parliamentary representative remained reserved to men, and the parliaments, that formed the social and gender-specific power structures of the political public sphere in the name of liberty, equality, and fraternity, thus became exclusively male spaces.

Only in France were women organized in the 250 newly-founded socialist and republican clubs of the first few months after the February Revolution—the "Club des Amis Fraternals," the "Club de la Montagne" or the "Club de Républicains-Socialistes." However, they first had to fight against male resistance for a right to be heard.[2] Unlike in most other countries, women (and men) in France could look back on a tradition of political self-organization—not only during the French Revolution, but also in the early socialist organization of male and female workers and in the revolution of 1830.

In the states of the German Confederation or the Habsburg Monarchy, women were admitted to public sessions of political clubs as spectators in 1848/49, but not as members with voting and speaking rights. Gender relations were generally only differently structured within the religious oppositional movement of German Catholicism.[3] Female members of the congregations had both the right to vote and to speak. Among the "enthusiastic spectators" of the Democratic Club in Berlin, on the other hand, a "garland of democratic women"[4] was lacking, just as the Democratic Club in Mainz in "the course of time … had introduced the custom of admitting the female element, and this was, understandably, as useful for our propaganda as it was pleasant. The ladies sat in the front rows … next to the speakers' platform. They did not actively participate in the meeting, but their passive assistance contributed its share."[5] In these reminiscences of two eighteen forty-eighters, it is clear that after a phase of male experimentation, women of differing status were included in their organizational forms and functioned as decorative spectators to the serious matter of (male) politics.

In this structure, gender relations in the liberal and democratic movement of 1848 are made manifest. The growing willingness to include women in the sphere of politics did not remain restricted to the left or the democratic milieu, although they were most confronted with female expectations. In a "letter to a club," "a lady" in Vienna demanded political rights and participation by women in the left's organization, as their political opponents had already granted women "a decisive voice."[6]

The world of the lower classes was structured differently; however, the necessity of working to ensure a livelihood, which broke down gender barriers, did not imply an increase in gender equity. It was not only the Association of Journeymen Printers and Typesetters in Vienna that set down in its statutes the "abolition of female labor with machines and other manipulations."[7] In Berlin, too, a third of all journeymen and workers, represented by their professional associations, demanded in petitions the prohibition of or at least drastic restrictions on women's waged labor.[8] Female manufacturing and industrial labor was not of equal value; rather, it represented unskilled and low wage competition to skilled journeymen in the guilded, patriarchal tradition.

Moreover, the emerging labor movement focused on bourgeois lifestyles in its blueprints for the future, and there women's place was in the family. This remained, in view of restrictions on marriage for the lower classes, a dream. Apart from the French early socialists, however, the Workers' Central Committee, founded in Berlin in April 1848, and later the Workers' Fraternization established their own women's "sections," which were to concentrate on the "cause of women workers."[9] From the beginnings of the labor movement there had been a considerable gap, in the question of gender equality, between theory—although it too was characterized by structural errors—and the mentalities and actions of its protagonists.

Corresponding to their status in politically and occupationally oriented associations, women and their rights were not a subject of debates on the franchise and parliament—unless they themselves spoke out, as in Paris and Vienna in 1848. Many European countries had not yet formulated the franchise in gender-specific terms (unlike in the Reform Act of 1832) as voting rights were still based on status and not on the individual. In March 1848, the publisher of the first feminist daily newspaper, *La Voix des femmes*, as well as diverse petitions and letters from women's organizations, demanded that the provisional government grant women the franchise for the elections on 25 April.[10] They looked for female candidates, promoted the candidacy of the "femme scandaleuse," George Sand, and supported Pauline Roland, a teacher in a village in Boussac. Their candidacies were, however, rejected, as was woman suffrage. One year later, in April 1849, Jeanne Deroin stood on the list of the Démocrates-socialistes, which had the emancipation of women in its program. In the election meetings, however, she came to know the open resistance of her fellow party members who proclaimed the "civil and political equality of the sexes," but who behaved quite differently in everyday life.

"Do not imagine that we are not filled with a lively interest in the emancipation of humanity … We claim equality of political rights. Why should women not be elected to the Reichstag?"[11] demanded "one woman in the name of many" in Vienna in 1848, breaking the silence surrounding woman suffrage in public discourse. Censors and informants controlled political culture in the *Vormärz* to such an extent that the Habsburg Monarchy was called the "China of Europe." Perhaps the vehemence and radicalism of the struggle in Vienna in 1848, including the struggle for female emancipation, lay in a combination of this culture with social, political, and economic non-simultaneities, expressed by Karl Marx in his argument that in Vienna in 1848, a struggle with the bourgeoisie occurred before the proletariat had been formed as a political class. After mass demonstrations, petitions, the establishment of "committees of public safety," and the May Revolution, the franchise was granted to workers on 10 June. Female voting rights, were, however, not discussed in this movement. "Women of the national guard," countered in a four-page flyer: "It would be mistaken to call the franchise universal when at least half of the subjects are excluded from its use."[12] That they were "as filled by a great love of liberty as men," protested against the idea of an allegedly "spiritually lower" female intelligence and demanded "the undeniable, inalienable, innate and irredeemable rights of the female sex," and the granting, as for men, of the vote and the right to be elected to legislative office. The "petitioners," as they called themselves, referred in their argumentation to gender-specific status treatment as well, which even denied voting rights to property-owning women.

When the constitutional committee finally came to discuss the franchise in its "exile" in Kremsier on 12 February 1849, the civil liberties achieved in the March Revolution were long since passé. stating that "If one wants to implement democracy in every respect, then women must be allowed to vote as well," the deputy Franz Freiherr von Hein argued logically in the sense of gender qualifications, but against a franchise for workers. The democratic deputies Rudolf Brestel and Adolf Fischhof only supported an "equality of classes": "In relation to women, the laws of man do not run against the laws of nature. Female agitation on this aspect never took place, they are represented in and outside the family by their men and wish for nothing more."[13]

Already in March, the adage of women's lack of interest in politics was being countered by their demands to be admitted, at least as spectators, to the sittings of the parliaments, such as the Frankfurt National Assembly or the Reichstag in Vienna. Contemporary reports by women demonstrate that the opinions Fischhof expressed were prejudices. Countless women not only showed political interest, but also bitterness at their restricted possibilities. Clothilde Koch-Gontard, the wife of a Frankfurt businessman, snuck her way into the preparliament in April 1848, as did Malwine von Meysenburg, who with other women followed the debates hidden in the pulpit.[14] Both took part daily in the parliamentary sessions, but found it "very painful to only be a women, forced to remain an onlooker but with feelings and full of energy" as Koch-Gontard phrased it.[15] Similar feelings were expressed by Louise Zimmermann, who provided the most extensive description of the Frankfurt "women's gallery" and who painted a lively portrait, especially of the lack of space and of the heat because of a rising number of female spectators.[16] These spectators did not sit still in the galleries and in the stalls, but made themselves heard in the debates—as, for example, in August 1848, when the question of an amnesty for the fugitive Friedrich Hecker was on the agenda and the gallery was cleared, against the fierce resistance of the women there.[17]

Contemporary commentary on the female spectators underlines various facets of gender specific role-assignment. Apart from paternalistic hymns of praise for "the" politically interested women, whose "educated husband… [explain] didactically the current circumstances"[18]—or "It is a pleasant sign of the times when even women master the political topics of the day,"[19]—there were martial proclamations such as "If you women were at the rudder, things would surely have been very different."[20] Women also defined themselves, on the basis of their peaceful-balanced social character, as "more suitable to be regarded as parliamentarians."[21]

Besides this respectable bourgeois discourse, however, an erotic relationship between deputies and female spectators formed the focus of interest in contemporary commentaries, because the presence of women violated the allegedly gender-neutral integrity of the male space of institutionalized politics. An end to unlimited access to Reichstag sittings was demanded in Vienna using this argument.[22] In this demand, women spectators were changed into "makeup addicts … of the greatest flamboyance who parade around, play with their opera glasses, flirt—in short, like in the theater."[23] The behavior of the women, who were ignoring child-raising and housework through their activities in the Reichstag, and were thus allegedly a threat to the state, was cited in the southern German newspapers as a warning example.[24] Above all, "the daughters [became] immoral and unrestrained," just in the manner of their mothers, "who occupied themselves with politics and spend the whole day in the gallery." The social make-up of female spectators can no longer be reconstructed; however, working women would have had no time during the day to attend the sessions.

Still, the appearance of Anna Bachmann from Vienna in the Reichstag, in which she spoke out against the dissolution of the "committees of public safety" established by the democrats, was described as especially spectacular:

> Thy speech was great—"Amen" from the best men,
> Sublime woman!!—even if contemporaries are silent,
> Posterity will worship thy name.

In spite of Jakob Nitschner's euphoric celebration of her public appearance in his poem "To Anna Bachmann,"[25] female spectators were not usually taken note of. Fears and economic necessity accompanied the cultural norms and the passage of laws for the regulation of gender relations. Through the presence of women, the institutional spaces seemed to lose their asexuality—and from them, chaos and anarchy threatened to disturb or even destroy serious politics.

The discourse on the inclusion and exclusion of women from the emerging male space of institutional politics was, from the outset, characterized neither by gender equity nor by asexuality, but by the dual gender character. Women themselves held different opinions about their exclusion from the institutions. When they referred to this political dichotomy, they sought at the same time not only to overcome it through collective demands or, like George Sand and Louise Asten, with spectacular individual careers, but to create separate female spaces.

"Joining Forces Especially for Ourselves": Institutionalized Women's Spaces: Associations, Newspapers, Projects

> "Our political aims are the same as those of men.
> But our standpoint is different,
> Each of us has to preserve her originality."
> — *La Politique des femmes*, Paris, 18 June 1848

With the exception of France, the first women's associations in Europe in the early nineteenth century helped to stabilize the system, were loyal to the monarchy and patriotic, and of a charitable nature. Among these were the "Society of Noblewomen for the Encouragment of the Good and the Useful," founded in 1811 for female members of the upper aristocracy, the "Lemberg Women's Benevolent Association,"[26] founded in 1816, and the "Benevolent Association of the Isrealite Women of Vienna,"—which are to be distinguished from associations founded by bourgeois or noble women in Germany during the wars of liberation or to support Polish emigrants. Feminist research has long ascribed not just a private character, but also a public-political one to the expansion of women's field of activity beyond that defined by family, servants, companions or households, and the taking over of responsibility for other matters. With this understanding of politics, the fluid transition between public and private has been redefined in gender-specific terms. For the *Vormärz* and 1848, this has been shown in detail above all in studies of Württemberg made under the direction of Carola Lipp.

If one excludes France, England. and Germany for a short period during the Hambach Festival as well as within religious-free-thinking women's associations, no explicitly political activity in associations focusing on women can be found. This reflects the effects of a ban on women's political activity. The women's associations, with statutes, programs, and registered members, must be understood as bourgeois counterpoints to the political culture of the rather noble salons, which often offered the only opportunity in the *Vormärz*, in view of state repression, to discuss matters openly and in which a few exceptional women functioned as organizers and participants.

This mixture also defined the founding of *political women's associations* in 1848 and 1849. Only after they were excluded by men from male associations—in this period of social change in which wishes and demands, could be expressed openly and clearly for the first time because of "freedom of the press"—did women begin to organize themselves. The motto in Berlin: "Let us make use of the existing right of free association for ourselves as well and, joining forces, create something especially for ourselves."[27] Gender-specific segregation was not initially planned. With the founding of women's associations, with their demands and intentions as female individuals and as subjects of democratic, republican or socialist currents, women defined themselves as eighteen forty-eighters. To describe associations as institutionalized women's spaces, not only is their gender composition important, but also their intentions. Women organized themselves on the basis of a common program in a democratic associational structure, open to women of all classes and confessions to fight against social discrimination, to improve their professional, political or legal position and to gain a greater range of choices independent of family ties.

Because of the heterogeneous source material it is difficult to characterize the Democratic Women's Associations as women's spaces. Especially in Germany, many of these associations were *support groups* within the democratic associational milieu. This is not to call their political character into question, but they arose for the care of other men, women, and children and not from a desire by women to become active for themselves. Most of these support groups were only founded after the revolution had failed. One of the most well-known example of these is Humania, founded in Mainz on 16 May 1849 by Kathinka Zitz, to which 1648 women belonged.[28] It and similar grouops set up support networks to aid prisoners and their families, supported refugees and organized escape routes and emigration in the USA.[29] The Concordia Mannheim Women's and Maidens' Association smuggled red neckerchiefs to the prisoners they were caring for and were warned by the authorities to take care, otherwise the would be "brought before court as traitors."[30]

In the lands of the German Confederation, it is above all the approximately thirty-five women's associations of the free-thinking or German Catholic congregations, a number of which had been founded even before the March and April Revolutions, that can be placed within the associational spectrum of women's emancipation.[31] The German Catholic reform movement, that organized 100,000-150,000 people in the years around the revolution, had a membership that was 40 percent female. It defined itself as a democratic-social movement, which bound together criticism of religion and female emancipation. All other political-democratic women's association in German speaking regions were founded in the later summer and autumn of 1848. On 14 September 1848, for example, "a number of emancipated ladies" under the leadership of Lucie Lenz succeeded in founding a Democratic Women's Association in Berlin. The founding membership was made up of thirty women, a number that had risen to "100 to 150 present" at meetings up to the beginning of October, although male spectators were included in this figure.[32] One month later, on 12 November 1848, all political associations in Berlin were banned, including the two women's associations, in the wake of a declaration of martial law. The short life of these associations prevented a further differentiation in program. The Vienna Democratic Women's Association had already been banned by this time, and its president Karoline Perin imprisoned since 4 November 1848. On 31 October 1848, revolutionary Vienna had surrendered to the imperial troops. Using the Berlin Women's Association as example, the press loyal to the emperor spoke of the reprehensibility of women's political activity: "Berlin copies everything from Vienna. Vienna had a club of such undignified women, and immediately Berlin also had to have one. The Berlin Club of Women Democrats is now occupied with setting up soup kitchens; if they do not over-salt the soup and put bombs instead of dumplings in the bowls."[33]

In all democratic movements, and especially in early socialist movements in France, and among the Chartists in England, numerous activists recognized the necessity of including women in discussions and activities not only as a female complement. In the Vienna newspaper *Wahrheit* in May, women were called upon to throw away their knitting needles and sun-umbrellas and instead to take up a pen and write down their demands[34]—a notion that many men only approved of if it did not go beyond the framework of bourgeois morality. The majority of the protagonists of female emancipation and of women's rights in the countries of the German Confederation also stayed within these boundaries. Exalted women who swam against the current, such as Louise Aston and George Sand, were rejected as much as the term "emancipation," which implied sexual permissiveness and the masculinization of women, personified by those women who "not seldom fight for the emancipation of their allegedly oppressed sex with a cigar in their mouths, whip in hand and armed with such attributes of male power and customs ..." as was written in the Frankfurt journal *Didaskalia*.[35]

In opposition to the dominant discourse, the majority of those in the 1848 women's movement drew other consequences from gender differences. Female complementarity of the "other" sex was held by them to be the basis for their definition of gender equity and implied a natural claim to equal political rights and opportunities in education and employment. With the rededication and rephrasing of the discourse in their associations and journals, moreover, they countered the construction of a public-male-political and a private-female-family area. This found not only approval among eighteen forty-eighters, but also provoked resistance and criticism: in print in the form of caricatures, pamphlets, and poems, and legally with a ban on women's associations and in everyday life with manifest violence.

The latter was experienced by "ladies"[36] gathered in Vienna on 28 August 1848, who had met, wearing black-red-gold ribbons on their left breasts, in the salon of the public gardens to discuss program, demands, and statutes of the Vienna Democratic Women's Association. The meeting was stormed by men, including many national guardsmen—that is, by the educated and property owning middle class.[37] They broke windows, occupied the room, jumped on the tables, insulted the women and threatened to box their ears. Under loud vocal protest, which had all the "signs of a infernal charivari," the women retreated, but not without agreeing to meet again in the late afternoon of the same day. Then, the initiators took precautions and a "group of the weaker sex" succeeded in keeping out curious trouble-makers.

The panicky reaction by these men to women's making use of their right of freedom of association must be seen as an episode in the gender-specific defensive struggle against the (women's) emancipation movement arising from bourgeois modernity. Similar scenes were experienced by members of the "Club des femmes" in Paris, when, at a discussion on divorce laws on 6 June 1848, there was trouble and the police had to clear the hall. This was reason enough for the authorities to dissolve the club.[38] The fact that men loudly disturbed a meeting of servant girls in Leipzig in April 1848 also leads to the conclusion that aggressive resistance was not isolated.[39]

The Vienna Democratic Women's Association, unlike its Berlin sister organization, had defined its objectives and formulated three tasks:

1) a political one, to enlighten oneself through reading and educational lectures on the welfare of the fatherland, to spread the democratic principle in all female circles, to spark a love of liberty in the child's breast from the beginning of his upbringing, and at the same time to strengthen the German element;
2) a social one, to work towards equal rights for women through the founding of public schools and institutes of higher education to reform female education and to enoble the situation of poorer girls through loving elevation;
3) a humane one, to express the deeply-felt thanks of the women of Vienna for the blessings of liberty through the attentive care of all victims of the revolution.[40]

The program united equal rights, political education of women, motherly charity towards female members of the lower social classes, and solidarity with the aims of the revolutionary movement as well as nationalistic tones! Especially the third point underlines the radical-democratic nature of the association, which was founded a few days after the split in the cross-class Viennese 1848 movement in the August conflicts. Nonetheless, discussion of the program was not without frictions. Frau Bouvard, the daughter of a sexton, called the other association members "political sleepy-heads" in one of the first meetings.[41] The cause of the argument was a petition on the ministerial council to cancel the semi-annual rents that were due, which was rejected by the majority as an undemocratic attack on private property. Bouvard left the meeting with "Your association in a chimera! You all put on sleeping caps…while the poor starve!"

No matter who supported which position, this clearly shows that, from the outset, sociopolitical questions also divided politically committed women. In September, moreover, a pamphlet appeared in Vienna which raised another factor that possibly also divided women: *Wai! Geschrien!, jetzt fangen die Jüdinnen a schon an* [Cry Woe! Now the Jewesses are Starting].[42] In it, "German" women were called on to become active in the Democratic Women's Association and to prevent Frau Wertheimer, a Jew, from becoming president of the association. While many female Jews from the wealthy ennobled urban finance bourgeoisie, especially with their salons in the *Vormärz*, had had an important role in semi-public politics, they did not appear as Jews, demanding their emancipation like many others in the struggles of 1848.[43]

Egalitarian intercourse between members of various classes and different marital status was set down in the statutes, as their paragraph 10 states: "One simply says 'Mrs.' and 'Miss.' Married women are not given preference over unmarried ones." The statutes also foresaw the foundation of an empire-wide organizational network. Even more than these, the activities of the Vienna Democratic Women's Association in the two months of its existence speak for its egalitarian intentions.[44] The group joined in organizing the funerals for the victims of the August uprising, planned as a reconciliation between the classes. Some hundreds of women marched to the Reichstag in Vienna on 17 October to present a petition with 1,000 signatures for the callup of the home guard. This appearance created "naturally an almost ludicrous impression,"[45] since most deputies had hoped that the women would volunteer to work as nurses in the case of potential fighting.

The male democratic association, on the other hand, reacted positively to the existence of a women's association, accepting it as a partner. Apart from eight other "free-thinker associations"—including liberal, worker and artisan associations and the German Catholic association—the democratic association also invited the democratic women's association to a meeting in the Odeon on 10 September to discuss counter-measures in view of the worsening political-military situation.[46] The women's association was also a member of the central committee of democratic-free thinking associations in Vienna, founded on 30 September.[47] During the discussions in the Odeon, which usually took place in front of thousands of people, the women of the association were both sponsors of the meeting and spseakers in it—for them, the time had passed when they served only as decorative props.

One reason for this close relation between the democratic association and the democratic women's association may be family ties. This is suggested by those members known by name. Karoline Perin, for example, was the longtime companion of Alfred J. Becher, a leading democrat and publisher of the journal *Der Radikale*. Amalie Hempel, correspondent for the Berlin *Zeitungshalle*,[48] was the long-time companion of Hermann Jellinek, and Fräulein Eckhardt was the sister of Ludwig Eckhardt[49] who was also a committed democrat. Nonetheless, Karoline Perin and the Vienna Democratic Women's Association were held in suspicion by some eighteen forty-eighters: "They did not bring us any benefits, and instead hurt us in founding the women's club," was an opinion sometimes expressed after the defeat.[50] Nonetheless, the short-term acceptance of the association as an equal partner in the political democratic association spectrum in Vienna was unique in Europe in 1848/49, at least according to the current state of research.

Apart from appropriating organizational forms created by men, political women's associations were characterized by a common program. Included here was a demand for the end of a gender-specific monopoly on education—one of the main points of the old free-thinking women's movement. In those months free of censorship in Vienna, demands were raised for free access to universities. "We want to become lawyers … we want to become doctors," wrote one woman to the Women's Club in Vienna.[51] In the same year, in England, Queens College was founded, which allowed women a university education, and this was followed, one year later, by the establishment of Bedford College in London.[52] The Hamburg Institute of Higher Learning for the Female Sex (1850-1852)[53] was founded in Hamburg, and a Girls' Secondary School (1849)[54] established in Prague.

Unlike previous, confessionally linked educational institutions for girls, the Hamburg Institute was open to all confessions. Women and girls, from the bourgeois and noble strata, enjoyed an education in the new spirit of the age, with a focus on pedagogy in preparation for the work in education, the only kind acceptable for women in these social circles. Because it was close to the democratic associational milieu both in policy and personnel, however, it was closed for political reasons in 1852.

The Prague Girls' Secondary School was a creation of the Spolek Slovanek (Slav Women's Association) founded in September by bourgeois Czechs, who formed the core of the national Czech women's movement. Until it was closed on 29 November 1850, providing financing for the school, that opened in 1849 with forty-three pupils and eight "Misses" was the center of the association's activities. The aim the members set themselves was a social, but not a political emancipation of women. This understood, this emancipation was seen as part of the emancipation of the Czech nation, which for them was a precondition for a reconciliation with the Germans:

> Women, we are human beings, we have minds, we have souls, we should not be placed so much below men! … My sisters, dear Czechs, I do not believe we should become involved in politics … We should only be taking on the work that men have nothing to do with … namely to ennoble and educate our female hearts … this, and nothing less, is due us. This will close the gap between the Czech and German nationalities.[55]

In Honorata Zapová's appeal it becomes clear that the subordinate position of women was to be changed but not the division of roles between men and women. The example of the second Prague women's association, the Slovanská Dennice (Slavic Morning Star),[56] founded in October 1848, also underscores contemporaries' awareness of the close connection between women's education and Czech national consciousness since the group founded a library and organized lectures. The planned establishment of women's clubrooms was, however, a scandal in Prague's bourgeois milieu. Even some women thought this so unbecoming and immoral that they resigned from the Spolek Slovanek.[57]

Social questions were another main area of interest for women's associations. These were seen, above all, from a motherly-charitable point of view, which played a role in all women's associations at this time. The women extended their familial responsibility for children onto a responsibility for the poor and weak in society, including the persecuted. Hence they created institutions of political charity. Housewives' responsibility for their servants was as much a part of this, most women's associations therefore demanded the establishment of "Servant-Bureaus" as employment search and refuge outside their place of work. From the collection lists of numerous women's associations in the German Confederation, measures to assist victims of political persecution and their families can be followed in detail.[58] Only the Vienna Democratic Women's Association distanced itself from such activities and canceled a charity event for excavators affected by pay reductions and unemployment. Instead they formulated the problem politically and demanded a reversal of the pay cuts from the responsible minister.

Self-organization of women from the lower classes is only known for France. In *L'Opinion des femmes*, which appeared in Paris for the first time on 21 August

1848, a whole series of women's organizations was listed—including washerwomen, midwives, teachers and many other professional groups—that had been founded in the first weeks after the February Revolution to ensure and improve women's living and working conditions.[59] From June 1848 onwards, these associations were supported by the government. After the dissolution of the national workshops, they provided a glimmer of hope for many and enjoyed considerable popularity.

At the end of 1849, 80 to 100 associations came together into a union, following the detailed plans of Jeanne Deroin, in which every branch produced its product directly for associated workers in other branches. When government authorities began to see in this alternative labor organization as a political secret society, it was banned in 1849 and 1850. Deroin, Pauline Roland, and Louise Nicaud, delegates of a washerwomen's association, were arrested and taken to court. The idea that producers' cooperatives as self-help projects were especially useful for women was also propagated by Louise Otto in the *Frauen-Zeitung*, which appeared from April 1849 to 1852 in Meißen and Gera.[60]

The few servant girls' meetings in Leipzig,[61] Mainz,[62] and Vienna organized by working women were not quite so spectacular. The newspaper report on the Vienna meetings underlines the way in which women's activities were reported in 1848 and 1849. A demand by those assembled for a "right of association" was reinterpreted by the author of the article: "This applied mostly to lovers which the women [the servants' employers] did not wish to tolerate."[63] The status of servants, as single and not bound to a family, combined with their legal dependence on the head of the household and his right to employ corporal punishment to them, predestined them for being described as loose women. This line of interpretation—that women were free to decide themselves on a husband—was discussed very seriously by women in 1848.

Especially in view of the example of France, it becomes clear that in establishing female spaces, possibilities of articulation and exchange of information, and thus the publication of newspapers and pamphlets played a significant role. In France, newspapers were central, such as *La Voix des femmes,* which first appeared in Paris on 20 March 1848, or *L'Opinion des femmes.* The women from the *Voix* founded a "society" in connection with the newspaper and invited women for discussions. Organization of diverse committees" was initiated by the editorial staff or its immediate circles.[64] The "Panorama" column in Louise Otto's *Frauen-Zeitung* shows how far a network of women's associations and women's initiatives with political ambitions had developed within the German Confederation following the March Revolution of 1848. Very little is known of the inner life of democratic women's associations, their social composition, their activities, and their associational life. Generally, individual names were mentioned in relation to sensational actions, the names of president or those of women who were portrayed or themselves left written traces.

Specific legal demands for equality were rare in 1848/49. It was all the more surprising that in the 1840s some of the first calls for legal equality for women came from Switzerland, the last country in Europe to give women the vote. In 1847, a group of widows and single women succeeded in having the legal requirement that they have a male guardian [*Geschlechtsbeistandschaft*] abolished in the Canton of

Bern.[65] In the debate on a German constitution in May 1848, hopes were raised that such a constitution would perhaps offer the opportunity of improving women's rights in marriage.

Women were well aware of the contradiction between equality and freedom in a male public space of politics, and inequality and hierarchy in the private space of the family. "It is impossible for him [the free man] to take hold of the crown of liberty with one hand and with the other hand to hold the chains with which he oppresses the no less worthy other half of mankind."[66] However, the free man was capable of this. In this respect, the creation of political women's associations is a facet of early self-determination and part of a specifically female resistance against a male power of definition over the public sphere and politics. "You don't want to hear us, because you are beginning to be afraid of us and it seems to you easier to oppress than to be just. Behind your scorn can be seen your despotism," was Eugénie Niboyet's analysis of the banning of the *Club de femmes* in Paris in 1848.[67]

The Intermediary Spaces: Of Solidarity, Euphoria, and Frustration: On Mothers, Companions, and the Beloved

> "… that you are a woman without a world,
> will suffice to excuse you …"
> Ferdinand Kürnberger to his
> — sister Magdalena, August 1849

In the contemporary discourse "women without a world" meant that women had no "civic personality" (Kant), no head for politics, and lacked as well the ability to develop their own standpoints and opinions. The images, constructions, and fantasies of femininity of many 1848 revolutionaries are marked by this backdrop and can be understood and decoded in countless articles, poems, and letters. However, the large majority of women themselves also participated in the formation of an ideal-typi-cal female gender-character, which they constructed complementary to bourgeois men. The formation of this gender relationship was reflected as much in the sym-bolic language of the revolution as it was in the structure of its movements. To fol-low this trail brings to light facets of women's lives and women's spaces that were more decisive for women, whether for or against the revolutionary movement, than the founding of political women's clubs. Here the social boundaries were, however, fluid and need to be newly defined from case to case. Those from the lower classes were seldom explicitly included in these discourses.

Shortly after the March Revolutions of 1848, there were appeals to women in many parts of the German Confederation to boycott foreign luxury products, espe-cially French fabrics. This idea, which often originated with trade associations, as was the case in Württemberg, led to the informal establishment of women's associ-ations relating to the program of wearing German fabrics.[68] The willingness of women from Württemberg to support the national market and protectionist policies with consumer behavior was shared by many engaged in patriotic and nationalist causes in 1848/49.

In German speaking Europe, the image of the French was related to the Napoleonic wars and to social envy of the aristocratic lifestyle, symbolized by French luxury goods. The campaign, concentrated on textiles, was, not least, also an expression of the crisis of the central European textile industry, as a result of the commercial crisis originating in England. Especially affected, as it concerned their most important product, was the capital of the Habsburg Monarchy, Vienna. In April 1848, 546 Viennese women, headed by fourteen nobles, appealed to the female public with the cry "To the Women of Vienna!" "… following the voice of the heart, which also beats in the female breast, warm and lively for the salvation of the dear fatherland and the well-being of all classes, especially those in need of work … women of all classes are hereby called upon … to no longer purchase any material of foreign manufacture and instead to satisfy their requirements with the domestic industry."[69] Countless other appeals made by women in a similar tone—addressed to the social competencies of women and drawing on their power as that member of the family responsible for purchasing and reproduction—were published in the summer of 1848 as part of collections or lotteries for the building of a "German fleet" or because of the war in Schleswig-Holstein.[70]

Charitable activity in the name of the nation and for the nation should not only to be interpreted as working for others, as a transformation of women's family responsibility into the sphere of public opinion concerning the state and the nation. Rather, a specifically female definition of the "German national character" was oriented toward something uniquely German, constructed out of mentalities and experiences, which only gained justification for existence in contrast with something foreign.

To be "German" meant to develop a (petit) bourgeois lifestyle in opposition to an aristocratic and grand-bourgeois one. "German, that means: nice and simple, in accordance with the husband's income," and to hire only "German governesses and teachers" for the children.[71] This line was tied to a proverbial women's subject, fashion. "The time has come for us to abandon a fashion which stands in contradiction both with our national feelings as with our tastes"[72]—thus the end of the trend-setting function of the "Parisian style fashion journals" was proclaimed. Similar appeals can be found in the German press. "Be German, find your pride in only buying German goods … and do your bit for German industry."[73] It was in this context that a discussion about a German "national costume" took place in 1848.

Reflected in their words is how women of the time, in affirmation of the dual gender character, formed their role as women, rededicated it, without breaking it, and with it entered into the discourse on national identity. This was based on a fundamentally dualist structure. One's own self and the other were constructed through national and gender-specific attributes. With the presentation of their role—defined in contemporary discourse as private, as responsible for family reproduction, but also as part of the 1848 movement, these women articulated a desire to be politically active in their area and underlined the ambivalence of this separation of public and private.

A gender-specific discourse on the nation was not restricted to the "Germans." For many women in Prague, the Czech national movement, openly active following the March Revolution, allowed the possibility of becoming a national factor through their commitment, but also of developing a specifically female Czech national consciousness. The initiator of women's assemblies on 16 and 18 August 1848, Terezie Nätherová, had only developed her political-nationalist commitment in the months in which participation in the Frankfurt "German" National Assembly was discussed in Bohemia. The two women's associations founded in Prague in the autumn of 1848, Spolek Slovanek and Slovanská Dennice, had as their aim to educate women and girls into conscious Czechs through the foundation of educational institutions "on the basis of nationality."[74] Charitable commitment in the name of national emancipation can also be found among Poles, in, for example, the Lemberg Women's Benevolent Association.[75]

Men explicitly encouraged women's commitment in national campaigns. Systematic attempts were made to get women to sign a petition on 15 March 1848 in Prague on national emancipation. The gender-specific facets of nation-building are an important line for understanding the development and dynamic of women's movements in most European regions. This does not mean, however, that the beginnings of the women's movement were per se nationalist or chauvinist.

Apart from the institutions of the revolution and militant struggles yhe image of the revolutions of 1848/49 was defined above all by parades, marches, festivals, and celebrations. Women took part in all these events. Their appearance in them was not uniform, as countless pictures and descriptions show: girls, dressed in white and crowned with flowers, functioned in the Christian-religious tradition as symbols of the purity of revolutionary ideals, but also women dressed as Amazons became living allegories for liberty and equality. Apart from these actresses, however, the large majority of women who took part in these events with their husbands and children should not be overlooked. As spectators they were also a part of the larger revolutionary festival.

In Frankfurt, for example, 7-800 "young ladies … with no distinctions in class" gathered to discuss how they should participate in a reception for the wife of the Imperial Regent. The women did not, however, speak themselves, instead only holding "a vote … in which they accepted or rejected proposals Herr Jucho made to them." In the spirit of the proceedings and corresponding to a division in men's and women's worlds, it was decided to organize an evening candlelight parade of maidens for the Archduchess, as the Archduke had received a torch-light parade from the [male] citizens of the town.[76] Funeral parades were similar. On 4 June 1848, the wives of the members of the democratic association formed their own bloc in a parade in Berlin. On 3 September 1848, the Vienna Democratic Women's Association took part as a group in a funeral demonstration for those who died in the August revolt.[77]

In light of these examples, the deep-seated change that occurred in the three to five months in which civil liberties existed becomes clear. In March, bourgeois women were still only active in student parades as spectators. In Berlin, they advanced to actresses and in Vienna to initiators. Like the other associations that had appealed for this funeral service—intended as a gesture of reconciliation—the Vienna Democratic Women's Association met separately first, and marched "slowly, silently and seriously" through the streets of the district of Währing to the meeting place. There, the group's members took their place in the parade behind the Democratic Association. It was due to the commitment of its members in organizing this event that the Vienna Democratic Women's Association began to be noticed by the press, which up to then had ignored its existence.[78] In Berlin, the women parading were "watched not without a certain surprise," by the spectators "for as much as one recognizes the women's intellectual right, their personal appearance ... lies outside the German character and should therefore not be evoked intentionally."[79] This view shows the extent to which their behavior broke with the previous model in the public space of the streets.

While the Berlin wives of the democratic club provoked surprise with their appearance, Czech women were greeted with applause. Numerous women took part, in national costumes, in the festivals and parades during the Slav Congress from 2 to 12 June 1848 in Prague. Using a national costume, the political symbol of the "national colors" represented authenticity especially for the defensive national movements and expressed the justness of their demands for emancipation. Discussion on the creation of a German national costume, on the other hand, brought no results. In the final days of March, a small group of women from artisan families in Prague had taken part in a festival in uniform dress—with red and white cockades as symbol of the Prague constitutionalists, black mantillas and white scarves.[80] Similar scenes could be observed in Hungary, Croatia, Slovenia, and Lombardy-Venetia. While these instances were, above all, national demonstrations against the rule of "German Austria," the black-red-gold "German colors" were seen in Vienna as liberal counterpoints to the Imperial colors black-yellow, and in Saxony contrasted with the royal green-white. This function is underlined in contemporary descriptions and in poems, and journals contained advertising for "black-red-gold sun umbrellas" appropriate for "the national way of thinking of our ladies."[81] In each region, the appropriate national colors became the colors of fashion.

The cockades lead to the question of both their producers and their donators. Textile crafts, the production of ribbons, cockades and flags with which they adorned both their men and themselves, were part of women's work for the movement. Especially in the production of flags for units of the national guard it becomes clear that the donors, celebrated as "flag-mothers," were not necessarily identical with the producers and that social conflicts could break out between the two groups. In a letter to the editor, a seamstress from Vienna complained that the "twenty-four committee ladies" of the Flag Donation Association, who had nothing to do with their making, had not been able to agree on the appearance and form of a flag in honor of the Vienna university. Because of this dispute, a group of "Hungarian women" were quicker.[82] In this public quarrel, not only social differences between employers and employees becomes clear—widespread in Württemberg as well[83]—but also a national emotionalization of "sewing for the revolution," a women's concern that seemingly leveled all differences.

In the years 1848 and 1849, women entered the space of the political public sphere as donors and producers of decorations—or as decoration themselves—and thus introduced symbols, activities and points of view that had originated in the private sphere. But this was not all. When women participated in political movements as mothers and wives transformed into companions and (potential) lovers, familial and erotic relations between men and women were also staged—something reflected, explicitly and implicitly, in the many descriptions, written mostly by men, but also in correspondence between married couples, diary entries, memoirs, and autobiographies.

The mother in the ideal-typical bourgeois family was assigned many functions in the bourgeois nation-state. She was not only child-bearer, but was also received from politics and scholarship the sociopolitical assignment of being the educator of the next generation. Children meant hope. They were potential beneficiaries and creators of the hoped-for better future and thus carried the hopes of both the family and society. Even the combination of child-bearer and child-rearer, which made women into the "mothers of the nation," did not, however, bring them the rights of citizenship.

Rather, women counterposed to citizenship rights their self-definition as bearers of culture—something already seen in England and France in the 1820s. The tasks and duties of the mother served as a starting-point for raising demands for education, training, and access to public life. Taking care of others, subordinating their own wishes, needs, and hopes, became a feature of the female social character of modernity. Social motherhood transformed itself into female charity in 1848 and 1849, which manifested itself in the countless relief associations as "the national guard of poor relief,"[84] and in political patronage, as when well-off bourgeois women in Vienna donated grants or lunches for politically active students.[85]

Women's child-rearing function was interpreted by contemporaries in quite different ways. This function provided for the justification of the female space of the household, but more as well. For example, the democrat Malwida von Maysenburg—at the time thirty-three, unmarried, and without children and who would later become a teacher at the Hamburge Women's Institute—explained in "The Oath of a Woman," after the defeat of the Dresden uprising in May 1849, the motivations for her choice of profession. She felt "in the depth of [her] heart a noble, flaming desire: the desire to live, in order to raise women as avengers of the murdered freedom, so that they are able to form a generation of free people."[86] The function of avenger was often attributed to women after the defeat of the revolution. However, to become a girls' school teacher in order to take political revenge was the exception, as throughout Europe it was the sons who dominated in the political mother-children-education discourse.[87]

The aim was to become the "free mother of a free son" and to declare proudly "I am a woman," instead of "I am only a woman."[88] The raising of daughters aimed at making them into good, nationally conscious mothers, by which the cycle of a women's career within the framework of the bourgeois family was completed. At the same time, apart from all the revolutionary euphoria of motherhood, voices were raised which rejected this argument of the mother-function as social-charitable women's commitment. In April 1848, some commentators suggested that members of the Association of German Women for the purchase of "German cloth" in Vienna could be neglecting their "child rearing" and "their husbands," both "more important, lovelier German fabric," because of their activity.[89]

In gender-specific discourse, the role of companion was also included in the conception of the wife. Women were not only to be "loyal wives," but, corresponding to the concepts of the early Enlightenment and Romanticism—whose long-term effects shaped the euphoric metaphors—were to use their characteristics and abilities to supplement and support their men, and not vice-versa. A marriage of expediency arising from economic-material reasons was to be replaced by a voluntarily-formed alliance based on intellectual and spiritual agreement. The large majority of women activists in 1848 shared this definition and defined in this difference their claims to liberty and equality in love and marriage. In France, this tradition was justified by early socialist conceptions of love and relationships. Apart from a symbolic presentation of the revolution, discussed primarily by Carola Lipp, the image and the function of companions can be read, above all, in correspondence between deputies and their wives, such as those of Robert and Jenny Blum, Moritz and Emilie Briegleb, Isaac and Antje Brons or Hermann von Beckerath and his wife.[90]

The companion was also assigned a non-legitimated erotic component as the beloved—latent as well as real or metaphorically elevated, immortalized in poetry and novels. The twenty-eight-year-old Ferdinand Kürnberger, a Viennese eighteen forty-eighter who emigrated, was cared for by a "democratic choir leader" during his imprisonment after the defeat of the Dresden uprising in May 1849. To his surprise, she was not only extremely pretty, but also "was educated in the matters of the day and knowledgeable in current political and social questions," and possessed "the authoritative and surprising nature of the female greatness of spirit and power of character in, at the same time, a rare alliance with youth."[91] The lady in question was Fräulein Auguste Schiebe, board member of the Democratic Women's Assistance Association,[92] who organized his escape. Kürnberger fell in love with her, but understood her coded offer to remain incognito in the city only as he was making his escape, and bade farewell with a poem:

> ...
> Where were you, heaven's shining star,
> when she still stood so near to me,
> That I did not hear, nor feel nor see,
> what, alas, now moves me, from afar!
>
> The lovely hand, that held me intertwined,
> The mouth that rained its kisses free,
> The eye, that so warmly gazed at mine
> The voice that pleaded so tenderly
> The enchanting shape, the sweet sight
> Showed me a paradise of love without end,
> Feeling, women's deep might
> With passion over my breast did bend.-

O, that the night fled from me so late!
So late harsh and crude spite has come to heel!
A demon locked my heart's and feelings' gate
That an angel has just now taught me to feel!
...[93]

In his letter, Kürnberger established a direct relation between the confession of his adoration, his (literary) leanings, and the politically like-minded democrat, Auguste Scheibe: "And if I ever cultivated a narrow *Vormärz* prejudice against women's emancipation, in this moment [of their first meeting] it disappeared."[94]

The image of his beloved, euphorically portrayed in his poem, corresponds to the bourgeois role for women. Women embody feelings, love, and warmth. He, as a political fighter, had to learn from her, his angel, how to feel. Far from any consummation, he could follow these fantasies of the ideal beloved-companion through his restless life. In Vienna, he said, he would never "have had the opportunity, with the exception of the Hermann woman, the Weißbach woman, and the infuriating Baroness, to admire the dignity of the female sex in its highest form."

The last-mentioned name refers to Karoline Perin, president of the Vienna Democratic Women's Association. She, too, had to live from the memories of her lover and political companion Alfred J. Becher after the defeat of the Vienna uprising. Becher was summarily executed, like Robert Blum, Wenzel Messenhauser, and Hermann Jellinek. "My dear Lini!" began his farewell letter, "It has come to this, that you are to be made my widow, for I have always seen you as my wife, as you have me as you husband."[95]

The two were among the fourteen people whose surrender Prince Windischgrätz had demanded during the capitulation of Vienna. Politically active and committed, she had caused offense above all with her way of life. Becher, a doctor of law, composer and music critic, widowed like Karoline Perin, lived with her in Vienna from 1845 onwards without getting married. Both were decidedly democratic. The address of the editorial staff of the *Radicalen*, which Becher published, also served as the address of the Democratic Women's Association. Both were the centers of diverse political circles. Contemporaries, including democrats, always supposed that the reason for the common but separate involvement in various associations lay in financial and sexual dependence.[96] Shortly before their planned escape, their hiding place in the Vienna city center was betrayed to the military authorities at the beginning of November. Their revenge was pitiless. "That I cannot see [you] before my death is the bitterest pill that I have to swallow, I begged for it deeply—but you are also a prisoner—and so it was denied me," Becher wrote with resignation shortly before his execution.

Not only in these examples of beloved companions, but more generally, the discourse of the beloved was shaped by the fantasies of the author. This included an eroticization of politics and the movement—as Malwida von Meysenburg phrased it: "A euphoria of delight was in every heart."[97] The euphoric exuberance of feelings was, above all, a feature of metaphors of revolution when civil liberties took the place of a repressive system with strict censorship. "The spark of liberty ignites most purely in her breast, she loved the uprising and its successes with the a woman's complete love"[98] The construction that a woman's world was defined by feelings, love and dedication was transferred to the movement in the context of a special revolutionary situation where the impossible became real.

Numerous literary treatments of the lives of daughters who broke with the conventions of their generally noble or bourgeois background offer further examples of this.[99] The lives of these protagonists of the 1848 revolution could, however, certainly end in tragedy—as shown in the literary biography of Pauline Gritzner, née Marx, known as Blümchen. Against her parent's wishes she followed Maximilian Gritzner, a leading democratic activist in the Vienna Revolution, who, however, kept her away from political activity and turned her into a passive subject: "There was, after all, and association of German women. And me? thought Pauline, why can't I do anything?"[100] The following years of flight, her father's relentless refusal to be reconciled with her, the troubles of life as an émigrée in poverty in the US, and her resignation resulting from this were certainly basic elements that led to her severe psychological problems.

These euphoric relations between the sexes could, however, not hide the fact that many women were frustrated by the new political life of their husbands. Julie and Alexander Pagenstecher, deputy to the Frankfurt National Assembly and personal physician to the imperial regent, provide one example of this. They wrote regularly to each other. He described political events in and around parliament in detail and she functioned as provider of information in Elberfeld and reported to him on who was acting for and who against him. Moreover, she wrote him in detail of events in the Constitutionalist Club in Elberfeld, which distinguishes her as politically interested and informed.[101] In her letter of 4 May 1848, however, there came a change: "… the whole thing is becoming too difficult for me, I wish you would fulfil your mission, which up to now was so glorious, and no more." It is an open question if this request to retire from his political functions can be read in relation to his letter of 18 April, in which he spoke of "wonderful festivals" and wrote "even the ladies are beginning to follow me. But you needn't worry, the admiration has only been platonic, and for anything further one has no time here …"[102]

In May 1848, an "Address of German wives and housewives to their husbands," was published in the Frankfurt journal *Didaskalia*.[103] The gist of their complaint was that their husbands had no time for their children and their families—"disastrous politics has chased the love from your hearts!" A little later, an article appeared in Vienna, "Constitutional Suffering of a Young Woman," which describes the similar troubles of a young newlywed.[104] She complains of visits to her husband of political colleagues, lasting for hours, or even all night, countless club sessions and service in the guard, returning home mostly after midnight and without energy for "conjugal tenderness." "When waking up the first word is newspaper, when going to bed … the last word is newspaper," complained the ladies in Frankfurt.

For these wives, the motivating power of political commitment completely changed their everyday life: "Your political madness has already brought you to the point that you see as a burden, as a hateful barrier to the only thing that you should care for—wife and children!" The seriousness of the situation, in view of an exclusion of women from the male sphere of politics, and the consequences it had for women's relation to these new politics, can be seen in the memoirs of Louise Zimmermann, herself politically active: "They talked, they voted, worked on projects throughout the night ... And I lost him to all this hustle and bustle, to this accursed politics, him, for whom I was a long time the center of his life, who was everything to me. He was my sun, under whose eyes I, an inconspicuous plant, would become gossamer ... I have lost him ..."[105]

In these examples, the women affected did conclude that they had to call into question the male concept of politics or the related role of women, nor that they should develop alternatives to them. Rather they rejected politics, in view of the threat to their intact life-world from "his" political commitment. Resignation replaced a view of life that was quite supportive of the movement. "Women [were] without a world," the socialist Viennese democrat Kürnberger had complained.[106] It did not occur to the "men of the movement" that they in part responsible for this state of affairs. In view of the essays and correspondence that describe women's problems in marriage with politically active men, the globalizing revolution and relationship euphoria, established discursively, must be examined, as well as the quite positive reception of a bourgeois role for women by the women themselves. It is difficult to listen to the waltz "black-red-gold,"[107] composed by Johann Strauß the elder: men lead, set the tempo and direction, women lie in their arms, follow their directions and are led backwards—in three-quarters time.

Intermediary Spaces: Of Desire, Fear, Persecution and Death: On Fighting Women, Heroines, and Martyrs.

> "... today you cannot just sit back and do nothing ...
> Dying is the most that can happen to you."
> — Interrogation Transcript of Margarethe Adams, Frankfurt, September 1848

Margarethe Adams was one of the 585 women interrogated and arrested after the suppression of the Frankfurt uprising of 18 September 1848 for "carrying stones as weapons and building barricades."[108] Women took part in the militant struggles of 1848 and 1849—especially in those insurrections motivated primarily by social and national issues—which helped the March and April Revolutions reach their success and which opposed the counter-revolutionary troops generally to the end. Women were, however, also involved as initiators of plundering and charivaris and in the campaigns of various (revolutionary) armies and armed formations.

These forms of action also mark domains in which the gender levels mixed. At this point, the behavioral norms of women of different social milieus become evident, distinguished by a lack of simultaneity that was the expression of partial modernization and of archaic economic and social systems. At first glance, the attempt to categorize this form of action, looks to the egalitarian level—men and women fought with violence, were punished and also killed for it. However, on the discursive level, one finds little equal treatment.

Women from the lower classes, far from realizing a dream of bourgeois family happiness, encountered women from the bourgeoisie and nobility in these intermediary spaces. The latter ignored the bourgeois image of women which in principle applied to them by negating the restriction to men of bearing arms, thus becoming fighting women and much discussed special cases. In newspaper reports, the authors' perception and fantasies are often fused into a bombastic-emotional discourse on woman as revolution or, visa versa, the revolution as woman, a discourse that spawned the metaphors of women as the desired beloved, the asexual allegory, as well as the feared devourer of men. Beyond the fantastically portrayed amazons of the revolution, the rebellious women from the lower and petit bourgeois strata were successful in gaining action for their life-worlds and their demands.

In traditional society, these women formed a sensitive potential for protest. As mother, daughter, sister, wife or companion, responsible for reproduction, they were the first to notice an approaching situation of dearth. Combined with the traditional codes of behavior that applied to them, this perception could lead to radical forms of ensuring their subsistence. Margarethe Adam's statement draws on this necessity. Subsistence crises, pauperism, and violation of the "moral economy" (Edward P. Thompson) led to plundering, tumults, and bread riots, which heralded, even before the outbreak of the March Revolutions in Europe, the significance of social protest potential involving women.[109]

These militant actions by the urban and rural lower classes—in part initiated together with students, as in Vienna, or following their own dynamics—guaranteed the victory of the bourgeois revolution in Europe. Especially impressive were the days of revolution in Vienna, which led to the flight of State Chancellor Prince Clemens Metternich, the spiritus rector of the repressive *Vormärz* system. In the night of 13-14 March, the gas lines around the city center were set on fire. The ring of fire, that not only symbolically surrounded the center of the empire and the capital, raised fears and was at the same time a symbol for the encircled old powers as well as the new movement filling the night. Women participated in this, as much as they did in the destruction of the consumption tax offices or the plundering of numerous factories in the outlying districts, whose owners were known for especially poor labor conditions and low pay. These "rebellious women," could no longer enjoy the protective function of armed, military masculinity. Instead, soldiers were used against them, and many unknown women were killed.[110] This was not only the case in Berlin, where five women died in barricade fighting on 18 and 19 March,[111] but in all street fighting in 1848/49, from Paris to Prague to Bucharest.

In honor of the "victims of March," a funeral was organized in Vienna. The participation of clergy from all three confessions—Catholic, Jewish, and Protestant—symbolized the philosemitism of the first months of fraternal equality in Vienna, as did the gesture of the Catholic priest Anton Füster to leave the opening words to the Rabbi Noa Mannheimer. This gesture gained political significance in view of the legal and social discrimination against the Jewish population, as well as the anti-

Semitic riots that had also featured in the events of March and had accompanied the social and national protest movements from Easter onwards, or even, as in Bratislava, gave them a pogrom-like character.[112] Mannheimer's speech demanded the emancipation of Jewish men and was part of a contemporary discourse by and about "free men" and "brothers."[113] Female victims were not remembered.

However, Oscar Falke dedicated one verse of his poem, "The Victims of March,"[114] to the only bourgeois victim, the pregnant professor's wife Elisabeth Bauer, who was hit by a bullet as the military was chasing the lower class protesters out of the city center:

> ...
> A woman is among them, not bold and daring,
> She did not tarry 'mid the battle fierce,
> She stood afar, yet with bullets flaring,
> One hastened hence, her timid heart to pierce
> Her pale lips seem still to call
> "Oh Lord, Why take a woman's last breath?
> Even innocent women must fall,
> Who will answer to us for their death?"
> ...

Decisive for this homage was her position as spectator, "afar," "not bold and daring." The same attitude is reflected in the hymn of jubilation published at the same time on "the" women of the March Revolution in Vienna and their supportive, decorative function, from which lower class women also remained excluded.

Quite "bold and daring" were the women of all social milieus who were involved in the so-called barricade-day and barricade-night of 25-26 May 1848 in the streets of Vienna. With the aid of women from all social classes, countless barricades were set up in the Vienna city center. "Women and girls from the educated classes"[115] allegedly dragged "stones and implements in their finest clothes with true enthusiasm."[116] Girls "from one of the best homes, accompanied and supported by their governess ... in their tireless zeal to assist in the building of the barricades [carried], with their tender and spoiled hands, stones, the weight of which took nearly all their strength, up to the second floor, where they could be used as projectiles if necessary."[117] The female residents of the inner city had thrown flowers, ribbons, and jewelry to the demonstrating students in March, and now, as was said, tables, chairs, mattresses and sacks of straw were thrown out of the windows for the barricades.

At the same time, numerous women worked to satisfy physical needs. Bread, meat, beer, wine, water, and cigars were distributed, cooking-fires started in the streets and, according to newspaper reports, women of the better classes served the barricade builders with their own silver cutlery. Whether this report is of an exaggerated topoi intended to illustrate the special dynamic of the revolution or a description of real events is difficult to judge. For women from the better classes, the actions mentioned, be it carrying stones or serving the previously feared "rabble" from the outlying districts with that defining object of the bourgeoisie, meant that they had broken with a bourgeois code of behavior. Similar scenes are found in other reports, which show that women abnegated the norms of their class in the exceptional situation of a revolution, or that they were credited with such behavior. For example, in Heidelberg in March "women of the nobility and wives of high state officials [carried] stones to the roofs and church towers in baskets and aprons."[118]

These well-situated, exceptional women[119] were thus acting for the "good" cause of the nation, reflected the political mainstream of the time and therefore did not violate "the nobility of female dignity."[120] With them, at all the barricades, were above all women from the lower classes. In Vienna, alarmed by students, they marched into the city center on 25 May together with their male colleagues, armed with their tools of their trades, with pick-axes, hammers, and iron bars. For them, physical labor was nothing unusual and did not receive special mention in contemporary reports. What contemporaries found worthy of notice was their public appearance. They were young, wore yellow straw hats, and smoked cigarettes.

The social duality of cultural norms becomes obvious with smoking habits, also a theme in the battle of the sexes carried out in literature and in caricatures. While a cigar was part of the outfit of a lower class woman, bourgeois women who smoked provoked anger and outrage. In the only "ladies' coffee-house" in Vienna, for example, smoking was banned. Through the appearance en masse of the lower classes, the living and working conditions of the lower class milieu also became, directly and indirectly, a subject of discussion in the framework of the social protest movement of 1848'[121] above all "interruptions in work" and poverty, that, under the heading of pauperization, shaped societal sensibility, and led to discussion in the democratic milieu on how to help the female poor in particular.

Josef Hillisch, a printer in Vienna, developed the idea of a "municipal boarding house" that was to be directed by a bourgeois woman and that would provide cheaper foodstuffs through buying in bulk, health and unemployment insurance, as well as evening courses for the working-women residing there and thus secure them a better life.[122] In Berlin, as well, protagonists of the first workers' association developed self-help projects for their female colleagues.[123] The Berlin district committee of the Arbeiterverbrüderung ordered, together with the Berlin Democratic Women's Club, "linen for 1000 shirts," "to create work for [female workers, who] could no longer be employed in the factories." From the project of an "establishment of work-rooms for female workers" arose a producers' cooperative for unemployed seamstresses, probably at the end of October 1848. Intended as a "society of women workers," those employed in it were to decide themselves on the volume of production, and conditions of work and pay "with the aid of an administrative council of women that they themselves elected." The further development of this project ended after the associations involved were prohibited, with the declaration of martial law in Berlin in November.

However, job-creation initiatives were not only begun by private organizations in 1848. Numerous provisional March governments attempted to provide assistance with state or municipal work-programs. In France, the right to work had been a central demand following the French Revolution. After the February Revolution, the provisional government in Paris decided, on 27 February 1848, to establish national workshops [ateliers nationaux] for road work. Women had no access to these institutions; they first had to fight for an equivalent in the form of women's workshops.[124] Désirée Véret, a Saint-Simonian from a proletarian family, published, at the beginning of April in *Voix des Femmes*, a catalog of demands on the Luxembourg Commissions that was responsible for the workshops. In a series of women's meetings, she had rejected the male administration of women's workshops and the pay, which she characterized as a pittance and, above all, developed a model for collective women's work—the women's space of an "association." In June, the national workshops were disbanded and a workers' uprising violently suppressed, thus setting a European-wide signal for dealing with socially rebellious lower classes and an emerging workers' movement, which had its effect in the ministerial council in Vienna as well.

At the beginning of May 1848, the city of Vienna started a job creation program in the form of "excavation work." The construction sites employed 10,343 men and 8,218 women, who received twenty Kreuzer per day, five Kreuzer less than the men. This amount was hardly enough to survive on. For breakfast, ten Kreuzer was standard, for a modest lunch sixteen Kreuzer, and for dinner, six.[125] An immediate resistance was announced to a 25 percent cut in the daily wage for women to fifteen Kreuzer. The minister for public works, Ernst von Schwarzer, reacted to this first women's demonstration with a reference to Paris: "We will not let ourselves be bullied … and the same thing will happen to you as in Paris"[126] and "10,000 workers will be shot before I change my decision."[127] The "large parade of working women [led by] a very powerful working woman" sang "For freedom and for a good loaf of bread, we will march on forth," to the tune of the Marseillaise, as the Galician engineering student, Carl Bobrowski described the otherwise relatively peaceful march.[128] Two days later, after small protest actions, there was a demonstration parade of all excavators, which drew on traditional forms of protest, such as dressing up in Mardi Gras costumes or charivaris, but which was violently stopped by security guards and parts of the national guard with drawn bayonets.

One of the main arguments for taking a hard line against the demonstrators— the beginning of the end of a non class-specific 1848 movement in Vienna—was the unbecoming behavior of the female excavators. "Especially the women behaved like furies: the guard was insulted in the most raw, offensive, and unmoral way" was the justification given by two guardsmen for their actions, which resulted in a woman being badly injured with wounds to the head and throat.[129] A criticism of their brutality, based on the accepted image of the weak female who needed protection, did not apply in this case in the eyes of these guardsmen, as the female excavators had suspended the gender-specific code of conduct by their behavior.

Social protest and its significance within the democratic opposition movement of 1848 and 1849 were combined with national movements in many cities and regions of Europe. The situation in Poland, or in upper Italy, occupied by Austria, in Lombardy or Venice, which were among the richest regions in Europe, was characterized by hunger riots from the spring of 1847 onwards. In April 1848, armed peasants in Venice prevented the transport of polenta, a basic foodstuff, with chants of "Liberty, bread, polenta." At the beginning of January 1848, there were bloody clashes with the military in the wake of a nationally motivated boycott of the Austrian tobacco monopoly. Field Marshal Radetzky reacted with a concentration of troops, which would guarantee the Vienna revolution its months of civil liberties, but underestimated the power of a combination of social protest and national movement. In the "Cinque Giornate" of 18 to 22 March, the garrison from Milan was expelled, with the help of women.[130] "Fuori i Tedeschi," [out with the Germans], was the central slogan.

Czech women, as well, engaged diverse forms of resistance, under a nationalist rubric, against the occupation of Prague by imperial troops under General Windischgrätz during the Whitsun uprising of 12 to 17 June 1848. This resistance was expressed above all in the wearing of red-white cockades. By contrast, Josefa Kubínová's pamphlet "To Bohemia's Female Patriots" was subtitled "whether you speak German or Czech." Here too, the common people and women were in the front rows everywhere," as Honorata Zapová wrote to her husband.[131] However, the rebellious Czech women also doubtless took part in the antisemitic riots.[132]

As in Vienna, Berlin and other cities, not only women from the lower classes, but also women from bourgeois and noble families were active in building barricades and in the fighting, in providing food and drink or functioning as messengers between the lines. Four lost their lives: two female day-laborers, a coo, and a serving girl. Without herself being involved in the fighting, the wife of an innkeeper was killed.[133] The reversal of civil liberties with the declaration of martial law on 20 July 1848 led to resistance from the "nationally" awakened Czech women, which expressed itself in the wearing of cloth accessories in the Czech national colors of red and white.[134]

The women involved in street fighting, or as in Berlin and Vienna in the storming of arsenals, were perceived in the gender-specific discourse as cruel, shameless, and brave and self-sacrificing women. In his nationalist pamphlet on the "Bloody scenes of the Milan Revolution," Franz J. Gaberden underlines above all the cruelties of women. Allegedly they robbed the dead—grenadiers who had fallen were stripped naked and ill-treated.[135] In the lynching of the minister of war, Latour, on 6 October in Vienna, a woman was said to have been especially prominent. After marching orders for the Upper Austrian Richter Grenadiers, stationed in Vienna, against revolutionary Hungary had been made public, an extremely emotionalized mass movement turned to lynch justice. Contemporaries, such as Berthold Auerbach, denied the wide-spread story of "cannibalistic behavior of a few women towards the corpse, as well as the rumor that people had danced on the corpse," as "pure lies."[136] However, the image of raging women became a feature of all traditional militant movements and "women's screeching" was seen in Vienna in the last days of October 1848 as a sign of growing lack of restraint.[137]

The public sphere, as a space "free from instinctual drives," reserved for rationalism, reason, and authority, was upset by the fears, rage and euphoria of these protest actions. Emotions and uncontrollable behavior were seen as expressions of chaos and anarchy and both fascinated and alienated supporters and opponents of the revolutionary movements.

Revolutions are events in which social power structures and moral codes begin to crumble. Both provoke fears. In order to deal with these fears, the causes have to be identified—in this case women took the blame. Often, the Jews or "the masses" were also instrumentalized for this function. The serious, struggling, and politicized popular movement was and remained something for men; women's participation, defined by emotionalism, had a destructive and ruinous effect—the other side of the celebrated gender relations in the well-ordered festivals and parades of the revolution.

"They became drunken Maenaeds [ecstatic female followers of Dionysus, the god of wine] who demeaned our serious popular movement dressed in fantastic costumes and armed with pistols, sabers, muskets and picks. They became perpetually lecherous phrynia [hetaira, prostitutes], who in the dark of the night laid their unchaste boudoir between the barricades and felt cannibalistically good when their abandon, in the most rakish meaning of the word, found the approval of a legion."[138] The ambivalence inherent in women and sexuality was very lively, especially in the fantasy of critics of the 1848 movement. "On 26 May the youths committed so many indecent acts under open skies, that because of syphilis, significant gaps opened in the ranks of the legions," wrote Wenzeslav Dunder.[139] This fantasy, in the spirit of joyful anticipation, of the lack of legionnaires because of syphilis pointedly underlines this ambivalence. Men, symbol of strength and the future, were made weak by sexual diseases picked up when sleeping with women and were no longer able to fight, such that the entire project of a new future threatened to collapse.

Corresponding to their dual image, arising from Christian tradition, as mother and whore, women functioned not only as symbol for the decay of the movement, but also as integrative figure for the just aims of militant struggle. "Whoever supports the revolution, whoever risks his position, he has the backing and sympathy of all women."[140] In this case, women became a moral authority. In the course of the revolution, a few surrendered their role of needing protection and embodied thus all the more, as former members of the "weaker sex," courage and strength. Especially in the final, defensive fighting, they were transformed into the bravest, the most persevering symbols of hope for the just cause.

Also part of this image is the history of the reception of Eugène Delacroix's painting "Liberty guiding the people on the barricades" (1830) which, in 1848, can be traced to Bucharest, to the edge of revolutionary Europe. Bucharest thus becomes recognizable as a revolutionary center. The Rumanian heroine was Ana Ipatescu, the wife of a Rumanian revolutionary. After a call to overthrow the provisional government on 19 June (1 July) 1848, she scaled a coach in the middle of the crowds retreating from the presidential palace, raised two pistols and cried "Be brave children! Death to the traitors!" With this, the masses regained their courage, stormed forwards, the military had to retreat and Ana was carried by cheering crowds on their shoulders into the palace.[141] In using the word children, she declared herself to be the mother of the people, who encourages and protects. In another version, she not only functioned as a model for the masses, but also for the initiators of the demonstration, I.C. Brătianu and Cezar Bolliac.[142]

Some contemporaries hoped that this spectacular event would bring more international attention to their revolution and began to form a myth around Ana Ipatescu: "Become acquainted with her and write her odes and serenades," wrote A.G. Golescu, the revolutionary government's envoy in Vienna, to Bucharest, "perhaps her fire will be ignited in other souls."[143] Her myth mutated from "mother" to "Marianne," and two years later inspired C.D. Rosenthal, painter and Rumanian revolutionary, C.A. Rosetti and his wife, who planned a series of articles for the English Sunday newspapers on the events in Rumania in 1848: "Describe that women Ipatescu, who with loosened hair, half-dressed, storms to the palace with a pistol in her hand. Imagine the scene, create a portrait, fill it with your soul, and it will always be an object of inspiration for our heroines of tomorrow."[144] Rosenthal himself, at the time thirty years old, created a civilized allegory with his "Revolutionary Rumanian."[145] The lace of the broad, not deeply cut blouse repeats the "national colors" of the flag that she is carrying on her left shoulder.

Allegorical presentations of women, successors of the French Marianne, also with bared breast as symbol of the nourishing character of the revolution, are known in the form of the barricade girl, the flag queen, from all revolutionary movements of 1848/49. From the French Marianne, she mutated further to Germania in Berlin or Dresden,[146] and to Slavia or Bohemia in Prague.[147] There was no Austria in Vienna in 1848—this was created, above all by the Social Democrats, only around the turn of the century. In 1848, Caroline was a more common barricade name in Vienna,[148] which is indicative of the later fragility of "Austrian" nation-building. These female figures served especially in the decisive fighting—such as in 1848 in Cracow, Prague, Paris, Milan and Berlin or in 1849 in the campaign for the imperial constitution in numerous regions of the German Confederation and in Hungary—and not only as a model for heroic lithographs or denunciating caricatures, novels and novellas. Generally, situations were also reproduced in which "real existing" women not only animated the courage of the men, maintained their poise and fought, but also killed. Thus, for example, a "virgin" defended a barricade for three days with the "courage of a lion," after her bridegroom had fallen during the Dresden uprising of May 1849, and shot a number of soldiers before she was herself hit by a bullet and died, as a martyr.[149] Not only her death, but also the death of those she killed were concisely shrugged off in the "Panorama" column of the *Frauen-Zeitung*. That is all the more surprising as the *Frauen-Zeitung* not only opposed emancipation in this point as imitation of men,[150] but also explicitly pointed out the equally important place of women in the house, as "sisterly advice, for all those who feel restricted in female circles and who would like to fight with the men for the good of the world."[151] Together with this article, the poem "The Heroic Girl on the Barricades in Dresden" was published[152] without comment on the myth of the heroine cultivated.

...
She fires and not one shot goes astray
As if an angel stood at her side ...
For Germany, my fatherland, you too will die.

This poem contains the female variant of the national myth of a heroic death for the fatherland, propagated since the Napoleonic Wars, together with the revolutionary heroic death. At the discursive level of the revolution of 1848/49, a connection of the ideals of the nation and of liberty—at least within the German Confederation—were immortalized in the deaths of female martyrs. Women sacrificed their power to produce life "on the altar of liberty" by dying and transplanting their function as giver of life to the fatherland.

> From thy grave blooms life so dear,
> And after many turns 'round the sun,
> The joyful harvest time draws near.
> In all hearts what you have done,
> Is engraved in colors, fresh and clear.

Because a female martyr even gave life from the grave and thus nurtured liberty and the fatherland, her role as killer was legitimized. The death of fighting women on the barricades, after they themselves had killed, also contained the facet—in the countless chronicles of these struggles—that a "fallen life [was atoned for through this] hallowed death."[153] The innocent purity of the revolutionary movement, allegorized in the festival parade girls dressed in white, was transferred in fighting and death to the "unfortunate daughter of prostitution," who atoned for and was released from her so impure life.[154]

In spite of this discursive presentation of fighting women, historical women were confronted with an exclusively male "warrior." Even those fighting on the barricades—like men from the lower classes—were never given weapons. They were dependent on self-organization and self-arming. They fought with their work tools, shovels, axes, and bars, as in the storming of the arsenal in Berlin on 31 May 1848,[155] and in Vienna on 6 October 1848, where the men and women taking part, unlike after the storming of the municipal arsenal in March, did not surrender the weapons they had taken. While men from the lower classes took part in the "mobile corps" formed in October for the defense of the city, unlike in the national guard of March, women were excluded. Their protests were dismissed with "echoing laughter."[156] Only in the final days of 28 to 31 October are there contemporary reports of more and more armed women fighting. They had taken their weapons from those who had died or fled, and appeared in women's brigades—one of which was said to have been led by Karoline Perin, wearing a red Marianne cap or a Sansculotte cap—or in mixed bands.[157]

Even in Paris, a women's battalion had been formed by some worker women a few days after the February Revolution. They named themselves after the fire-spitting volcano of Naples "Vésuviennes" and often marched to the City Hall to underline their demands.[158] "Vésuviennes" became an invective which designated crazed, obsessed, and men-killing women. The basis of their manifesto, the "Political Constitution of Women," was equality for men and women, not only legal equality but also equal access to offices in the church and the army—the two institutions which fundamentally define patriarchal modernity. Their program was a radical variant of the discourse of the women's movement of the time. Women who bowed to the will of their men should have their rights of citizenship withdrawn, according to Article 3. The Vésuviennes demanded that housework be divided between men and women and that women be required to serve in the army. With these demands, they were the contemporary women's organization that most radically called into question the dichotomy of gender character and who sought to break one of the major taboos for women, institutionally as well, in demanding the right to bear arms as a sign of their military capability.

Throughout 1848/49, women took two paths to create a place for themselves in the institutionalized male space of the army: as volunteers or by cross-dressing. One possibility of fighting with armed troops, or at least being active among them, arose when women took part together with their husbands. "It was not the war which called me, but love—but I will confess to you—and also hate, the glowing hate arising in a fight for one's life against tyranny and suppressers of holy human rights,"[159] wrote Mathilda Franziska Anneke, ordonnance officer in the Badenese-Palatine campaign.[160] Emma Herwegh also joined up, as scout for the German Legion of Paris in Baden in April 1848.[161] Amalie Struve took part in the Badenese liberation struggle together with her husband, Gustav, and was described by numerous contemporaries as very independent, so that she was far from functioning as an appendage of her husband.[162] Although it was reported that other women fought in these formations—"A number of amazons are also among them," it was said of the German Legion[163]—they were, in fact, more exceptions, who not only led contemporaries to flights of fancy and to fantastic descriptions of their clothing, but also provoked literary outpourings, of which Friedrich Albert Karcher's *Die Freischärlerin* [The Armed Female Volunteer] is a significant example.[164]

In individual cases, gender-specific borders of the male space of the army were broken through 1848/49. One reason for this could be the not yet totally implemented "national" male bearing of arms in the revolutionary armies. At least in the case of the Hungarian "general people's crusade" against Tsarist troops, as proclaimed by Lajor Kossuth, the latter seems to apply. Only very little information is available for the few women, known by name, who fought in the Hungarian army after the defeat of the revolution in Vienna, such as the two Poles Paulina Pfiffner (1825-1853) and Maria Lebstück (1830-1892).[165] Wilhelmine von Beck, a spy for Kossuth, reported of other women who "served in the lines as fighters ... in the infantry, cavalry and artillery."[166] Even if the biographies and subjective motivations of these fighting women cannot be discovered, their position and their commitment must be interpreted as a sign that the male space of the army in the revolutionary campaigns of 1848/49 was not (yet) closed, in gendered terms.

In her commentaries in the *Frauen-Zeitung* on the defense of revolutionary liberties in Hungary, in which women participated, Louise Otto changed her position on fighting women: "We have often declared that we disapprove of sought after and vain amazons ... but when a people is in the position of Hungary today, then things look different. Women also belong in such a crusade. Charpie picking, caring for the wounded, sewing clothes and cooking for the army is not enough ... they will take up the sword or scythe, or the rifle, if they have learned to shoot."[167] Louise Otto, for Ernst Bloch the "red democrat,"[168] raises in this article the possibility that women could kill and asks: "Are men privileged murderers? Does it not matter to a man to kill?" She categorized the Hungarian revolutionary war as one which "against the continued war of the oppressor against the oppressed … [must be carried out] for the victory of freedom for all peoples, and women must be involved." Louise Otto's criticism of "sought-after and vain amazons" was directed at "emancipated" women who fit into no category, such as Louise Aston. Klara Zetkin[169] also placed herself in this tradition of critique. The *Frauen-Zeitung* continually attacked those "Hermaphrodites, like George Sand, Mrs. Aston and consorts, who have abandoned husband and children to wander through the world preaching emancipation,"[170] who wore trousers and smoked, thus becoming caricatures of men.

Armed women were named amazons after the fighting women of Greek mythology. In contrast to the amazons who were part of parades and fraternal festivals, all women willing to fight in the defensive actions of the waning revolution became amazons. During the entire year, the establishment of an amazon corps was discussed, seriously or ironically, in the press of the main urban centers. Uniform designs were published, and more and more women began to demand the establishment of a women's corps, "not just to parade, but to fight." Designs published in the press combined female martiality with the dominance of the dual gender character: "a form of light pike suitable for stabbing and cutting, short, light leather boots, broad leggings of a Turkish cut, a jerkin with belt and a light slouch hat or felt beret with a feather."[171] In spite of the uniforms becoming more similar, unlike a costume, women remained recognizable as such in such clothing, which was tied to a cultural classification.

Things were different for women fighting in men's clothing. The self-evidence of dual genders, which also expresses a dichotomy in optical appearance, has been called into doubt by recent feminist scholarship carried out under the rubric of deconstruction. Thess discussions show that the dual gender character, as one of the first criteria of categorization in the perception of human beings, transports similar cultural attributions while concealing race and forms of third or more genders. Included in this ensemble is clothing as a sign, which can signal a clear membership of a gender in which cultural and biological gender agree. In respect of the amazon costuming of women, an ambivalent simultaneity was demonstrated, in which women could be identified as women but at the same time a function was signaled which did not fit with their gender.

These categories apply only for societies with clearly gender-specific dress regulations and codes. Especially in early modern Europe, feminist research has discovered brash personalities, especially younger women,[172] who lived for years as husbands, undiscovered, and fought as soldiers in the Dutch war of liberation against the Spanish (1568 to 1648). While the Dutch public reacted negatively to women who, as men, had married women, cross-dressing women soldiers, who later returned to their female existence, were celebrated as heroines, although the church and the law banned cross-dressing.

There are parallels to this in 1848. Novellas such as *Caroline, die Wiener Barrikadenheldin, Jäger Karl genannt* (Caroline, Heroine of the Vienna Barricades, called Karl the Ranger) celebrated the life of a courageous young woman who took the side of the revolution, entered the Academic Legion as a man and fought bravely.[173] Caroline's male life as a soldier, however, did not last forever. During the defense of the Milan revolution she was wounded, recognized by a doctor as a woman, and protected from the military court by the "privilege of the female sex." In the defense of Vienna she fell in love with a fellow fighter with whom she successfully fled to Hungary. The message of the novella is that in spite of a superficial confusion of identities, the inner gender, defined by sexuality and emotion, will always win out. A Caroline, who fought as a woman in Hungary, led a rifleman battalion and became well-known in Vienna as "the ranger" was also memorialized by Wilhelmine von Beck.[174] Her model was probably Maria Lebstück, who was arrested after the battle of Vilagos, bore her first child in prison, and later married lieutenant Hoche. She died in the beginning of the 1890s in Vienna.[175]

Traces of traditions of cross-dressing as an external confusion of gender identity can be found in the upside-down world of the carnival. An unrecognized wearing of men's clothes allowed women, their actions corresponding to gender-specific power relations, to enter male spaces, and to take on a different, culturally and socially formed role in mixed gender spaces. It was not for nothing that George Sand "dressed up" to be able to get a cheap seat in the theater.[176] People reacted with repugnance and outrage to the cross-dressing of nineteenth-century feminist rebels, such as George Sand or Louise Aston. Dressing as men was and is related to an increase in possibilities, which, in view of power relations, symbolizes an appropriation of the same.

Looked at the other way—except for sexual-emotional cross-dressing—the man dressed as a woman is only left with jokes and carnival. Female characteristics in men are and were more greatly discriminated against than male characteristics in females. "Virago" was an insult, but less insulting than an "effeminate" man, especially in a time of war and revolution. Biological women could more easily appear with male attributes than biological men with female attributes. Male revolutionaries appearing in dresses would have raised more eyebrows than George Sand or Louise Aston could ever have succeeded in doing.[177]

The defeat of the 1848 and 1849 movement was bound up with death, persecution, imprisonment, banishment or emigration. This affected not only the heroes of the revolution, but also their companions, single female activists and less well-known women combatants. A gender-specific treatment of female eighteen forty-eighters at the institutional level of punishment can only be partially reconstructed, for example in the "life" sentence for Pauline Wunderlich for her part in barricade fighting in Dresden. For this crime, other male combatants were released in a gentlemen's agreement, and only especially "serious cases" sentenced to ten to fifteen years imprisonment. "Why this severity towards P.W. Is she perhaps being punished as a 'deterrent?'" asked Louise Otto in the *Frauen-Zeitung*.[178] In view of the large number of women involved in the Dresden uprising, she was probably right.

To draw a generalized rule from this would, however, be too narrow. Apart from the one line of punishing women especially fiercely for the rebelliousness of their commitment for their own rights and thus setting a signal, the privilege of gender also had its effects at the institutionalized level. As the weaker sex, potentially in need of protection, defense lawyers could sometimes convince judges of women's lesser guilt, as in the case in the trial of Jeanne Deroin and others on the occasion of the ban on associations at the end of 1849. They were accused of forming secret political associations, of attempts at violent revolt and conspiracy against the government. The socialist and feminist activities were especially anticonstitutional, it was emphasized, but the women were only sentenced to six months imprisonment, and their male fellow defendants given much longer sentences.[179]

Apart from sentences and prison terms set down by the courts, women were also often subject to physical humiliation and punishment. Among those female eighteen forty-eighters arrested in Vienna, it is known that the guards pushed Karoline Perin to the ground, kicked her and dragged her through the washroom by her hair after her arrest on 4 November 1848.[180] This and other mistreatment, as well as the execution of her companion Alfred J. Becher, led to a psychological destabilization, as Julius Fröbel, a Frankfurt deputy in prison at the same time as Perin, relates.[181] For this, she was released early but lost custody of her children, and her property was confiscated. On 17 April 1849, she emigrated to Munich. Perin lost everything in the Vienna Revolution: her children, her beloved, and her property. Her friends were dead or had emigrated, and she was humiliated in the Vienna press specifically for her work concerning women. Without integration in a social network, which Malwine von Meysenburg, also a single democrat, found in the Hamburg Women's Institute and in exile in London, she wrote her somewhat edited "memoirs" in exile in Munich, which allowed her to return to Vienna in October 1849.

The violent effects of the triumphal march of the counter-revolutionary troops on women were felt especially by the large mass of lower class women. Rape and mistreatment of sexual organs are not only means of breaking self-confidence, but also the most extreme possibility for men to commit acts of violence on women—independent of social milieu—and to demonstrate power. Rape in wars also turns women's bodies into transmission belts between opposing parties in a patriarchal system. When a man appropriates his enemy's woman, he desecrates the person who has right of disposal over the woman. In the defeat of liberation movements, this fact is expanded by a sadistic reversal of one's own desires for freedom, in the humiliation and destruction of those who allowed themselves the realization of freedom. This, too, occurred in 1848 and 1849, as examples from Vienna show, where women's breasts were cut off, girls and women were horribly mutilated after being raped or died "as a consequence of the violation which she suffered from six Croatians after another."[182] In Frankfurt, too, it was reported in June 1849 that "exploding anger was directed against women and the defenseless." Numerous women and girls, like the waitress, who "did not wish to accept the animalistic lust of a Prussian cuirassier," were killed.[183]

Conclusion and Look into the Future

> "… Recollection must sweeten out
> the bitterness in today's life
> Only from struggle will there sprout
> the joyful future without strife …"
> — Amalie Struve, London, 12 October 1849, dedicated to the "sisters."

When Amalie Struve wrote her *Memoirs of the Struggles for Freedom in Baden* while in exile in London, she looked back on 205 days of solitary confinement in the "Freiburg Tower," her punishment for her part in the republican 1848 movement. Together with her husband, she emigrated to the US, where she continued to be active for women's rights, founded the free German school in New York, and died early, at the age of only thirty-seven, in 1861.[184] The US was the promising destination of many eighteen forty-eighters, including Katharina Zitz and Mathilda Franzeska Anneke, who sit among the pioneers of the women's movement not only in Germany, carrying on with her knowledge, commitment and her experience in the USA. She was active for women's rights, women's education, but also for the abolition of slavery and for voting rights for blacks.

Other 1848 émigrées, such as Malwine von Meysenburg, who ended up in Paris, Emma Herwegh, who supported the Italian liberation struggle from Switzerland, also remained politically active. Among the prominent French female activists of 1848, who were also active in 1830, Pauline Roland was re-arrested in 1852 and deported to Algeria, where she died in December of that year. Jeanne Deroin fled and retired in resignation to a private life. Désiréé Volquin moved with her husband to Geneva and became chair of the women's section of the First International in 1866.[185]

This transfer of women's emancipation after 1848/49 shows that in spite of the defeat, the months of civic freedom, with their possibilities and limits, made defining experiences possible for the women's emancipation movement. With the exception of England and France, where traditions reached back to the eighteenth century, the tendrils of the women's association network spread out in 1848/49 were never completely torn, despite the "bitterness in today's life." In the German Confederation, the *Frauen-Zeitung* ensured continuity, until its prohibition in 1852; the continuity was carried on in the person of its editor, Louise Otto-Peters. In 1865 she founded, together with Auguste Schmidt, the Leipzig Women's Educational Association, which later became the General German Women's Association, in which many women from free-thinking congregations were active after the disbanding of German Catholic associations in 1852.

The beginnings made in the women's emancipation movement in 1848 were most severely interrupted in the Habsburg Monarchy, above all in Vienna. Martial law, as declared in Prague, Milan, and Vienna, as well as in Berlin, meant the withdrawal of civil liberties and the disbanding and banning of all political associations after only a few months' existence. The oppressive mood in Vienna in the years after 1848, with its revived informant system, paralyzed women as well. The German Catholic Henriette Bock wrote to Eugenie Blum about a visit to Vienna in June

1850: "Such a strange mood is present here, it is difficult to describe ... here where everything is again lying in the chains of slaves. Here you see masses of people prostrate before the great idols, the splendor of the churches ... my hands are tied here, as I do not have a single address, it is enough to make me cry."[186] Nonetheless, a line of tradition can be drawn via mothers and fathers and grandmothers and grandfathers who were eighteen forty-eighters, to the founders of women's associations with claims to emancipation, at least in the Cisleithenian part of the monarchy in the last third of the century.

In the center of this review of the months of civic freedom in 1848 and 1849 stood women from various social milieus who defined themselves in sympathy with the 1848 movement and developed various possibilities and strategies to turn the 1848 movement into their movement as well. The conservative potential of women should not be forgotten, nor the important role played by women in the counter-revolution, as, for example, the Arch-Duchess Sophie. Liberal women, too, could also not always keep up with the dynamic of the revolution: "My dear friend! All the best! I shall not write any more, as I have lost my sympathy for your enterprise," wrote Fanny Adelson, who had hosted a liberal salon in Königsberg in the *Vormärz*, to her trusted friend, the democrat Johann Jacoby.[187]

Public action by women, be it the name of the nation, as charity or explicitly political in the name of emancipation, provoked criticism. Here it was a matter of calling into question their life plans, and not (only) the themes toward which they had dedicated themselves. Above all in the discourse on women and gender relations, in the images and imagination that the female world (co-) constructed, the struggle over a gender-specific definition of politics and freedom became clear. Opponents of women's emancipation understood or felt the message of female revolt: the end of their monopoly of power.

Notes

*I would like to thank Edward Berenson, Rüdiger Hachtmann, Jonathan Sperber, and Lothar Maier, as well as Maria Mesner, Karen Offen, Sylvia Paletscheck, and Charlotte Tacke for discussions, tips, and material made available.

1. Marion Ramelson, *The Petticoat Rebellion: A Century of Struggle for Women's Rights* (London, 1967), 72.
2. Helga Grubitzsch and Lauretta Lagpacan, *'Freiheit für die Frauen—Freiheit für das Volk!' Sozialistische Frauen in Frankreich 1830-1848* (Frankfurt, 1980), 106-7.
3. Sylvia Paletschek, *Frauen und Dissens. Frauen im Deutschkatholizismus und in den freien Gemeinden 1841-1852* (Göttingen, 1990).
4. Paul Boerner, *Erinnerungen eines Revolutionärs*, Vol. 2 (Leipzig, 1920), 23.
5. Ludwig Bamberger, *Erinnerungen*, ed. by Paul Nathan (Berlin, 1899), 80.
6. *Der Freimüthige*, Vienna 1848, no. 75, 306.

7. *Die Constitution,* Vienna 1848, no. 19, 276-77.

8. Rüdiger Hachtmann, *Berlin 1848. Eine Politik- und Gesellschaftsgeschichte der Revolution* (Bonn, 1997), 398-99.

9. Ibid., 424.

10. Grubitzsch and Lagpacan, *"Freiheit für die Frauen—Freiheit für das Volk!",* 110-11.

11. *Der Freimüthige,* Vienna 1848, no. 75, 306.

12. *Gleichstellung aller Rechte der Männer mit den Frauen; oder: Die Frauen als Wähler, Deputierte und Volksvertreter* (Vienna, 1848). Pamphlet collection 1848 of the Österreichischen Nationalbibliothek.

13. Anton Springer (ed.), *Protokoll des Verfassungs-Ausschusses im österreichischen Reichstage 1848-1849* (Leipzig, 1885), 187 and 189.

14. Malwida von Meysenburg, *Memoiren einer Idealistin* (1876), ed. by Renate Wiggershaus (Frankfurt, 1985), 124.

15. Clothilde Koch-Gontard, *Briefe und Erinnerungen,* ed. by Wolfgang Klötzer (Frankfurt, 1969) 62ff., 309.

16. Louise Zimmermann, "Bilder aus dem Parlamentsleben," in Stanley Zucker, "Frauen in der Revolution von 1848. Das Frankfurter Beispiel," *Archiv für Frankfurts Geschichte und Kunst* 61 (1987): 210-11.

17. Julie Pagenstecher to her son, 8 August, 9 August, and 23 September 1848, in ibid., 221

18. "Blicke ins Parlament," *Die Sonne,* Stuttgart 1848, no. 19, 73-74, in Gerlinde Hummel-Haasis (ed.), *Schwestern zerreißt eure Ketten. Zeugnisse zur Geschichte der Frauen in der Revolution 1848/49* (Munich, 1982), 36.

19. *Der Freimüthige,* Vienna 1848, no. 113, 457.

20. Georg Weerth, "Proklamation an die Frauen," *Neue Rheinische Zeitung,* Cologne 1849, no 301, title page.

21. "Die Frauen von Bonn an das teutsche Parlament," *Oberrheinische Zeitung* 1848, no. 187, 960, in Hummel-Haasis, *Schwester,* 33.

22. "Der Ständesaal ist kein Theater!" *Wiener Gassenzeitung,* Vienna 1848, no. 39, 154.

23. "Blicke ins Parlament," *Die Sonne,* Stuttgart 1848, no. 19, 73-74, in Hummel-Haasis, *Schwester,* 36.

24. *Nürtlinger Wochenblatt,* 3 March 1848, in Elisabeth Sterr, "'Hat nicht Gott…euch eure Stellung zum Manne angewiesen?' Das Frauenbild in der württembergischen Presse," in Carola Lipp (ed.), *Schimpfende Weiber und patriotische Jungfrauen. Frauen im Vormärz und in der Revolution 1848/49* (Moos and Baden-Baden, 1986), 184 and 186.

25. *Die Constitution,* Vienna 1848, no. 131, 1331.

26. Allgemeines Verwaltungs Archiv, Ob.Pol. Beh., Präs. II, Kt. 34, 1866/1855 Lemberger Frauen-Wohlthätigkeitsverein, Österreichisches Staatsarchiv, Vienna.

27. *Der Klub der Frauen an seine Mitschwestern* (Berlin, 1848), in Hummel-Haasis, *Schwester,* 63.

28. Stanley Zucker, "German Women and the Revolution of 1848. Kathinka Zitz-Halein and the Humania Association," *Central European History* 13 (1980): 237-54.

29. Sources to this point in Hummel-Haasis, *Schwester,* 51-101, 130-44.

30. *Kasteler Beobachter,* Mainz etc. 1848, no. 36, 88, in Hummel-Haasis, *Schwester,* 86.

31. Paletschek, *Frauen und Dissens,* 194ff.

32. Hachtmann, *Berlin 1848,* 515ff.

33. *Die Geißel,* Vienna 1848, no. 79, 330.

34. *Wahrheit,* Vienna 1848, no. 2, 6.

35. Zucker, "Frankfurt," 228.

36. The sources provide different figures: 150 in *Bohemia,* 1848, no. 158, n. pg.; Karl Höger, *Aus eigener Kraft! Geschichte eines österreichisches Arbeitervereins,* (Vienna, 1892), 373, speaks of 400.

37. *Der Frauenaufruhr im Volksgarten,* (Vienna, 1848), pamphlet collection 1848 of the Österreichischen Nationalbibliothek, Vienna. *Neue politische Straßenzeitung,* Vienna 1848, no. 2, 6; *Wiener Gassenzeitung,* Vienna 1848, no. 82, 328.

38. Grubitzsch and Lagpacan, *"Freiheit für die Frauen—Freiheit für das Volk!"* 108.

39. Supplement to the *Mannheimer Morgenblatt,* 1848, no. 108, 588, in Hummel-Haasis, *Schwester,* 172-73.

40. *Statuten des ersten Wiener demokratischen Frauenvereins* (Vienna, 1848), Kriegsarchiv Wien, Zivil- und Militärgouvernement Wien, Politische Erhebungskommission, Post I 100/15. Reprinted in Gabriella Hauch, *Frau Biedermeier auf den Barrikaden. Frauenleben in der Wiener Revolution 1848*, (Vienna, 1990), 235-39.

41. B. von Frankl-Hochwart, "Aus Bechers letzten Tagen. Mit ungedruckten Aufzeichnungen seiner Braut," *Die Zeit*, Vienna 1898, no. 203, 119.

42. *Wai! Geschrien! Jetzt fangen die Jüdinnen a schon an* (Vienna, 1848), Pamphlet collection 1848, Österreichesche Nationalbibliothek, Vienna.

43. Marion Kaplan and Julius Carlebach, "Family Structure and the Position of Jewish Women. A Comment," in Werner E. Mosse, Arnold Pauker, and Reinhart Rürup (eds.), *Revolution and Evolution. 1848 in German-Jewish History* (Tübingen, 1981), 189.

44. Hauch, *Frau Biedermeier*, 144-66.

45. Adolf Streckfuß, *Die Staatsumwälzung der Jahre 1848 und 1849*, 3 vols. (Berlin, 1849), 1278.

46. *Der Radikale*, Vienna 1848, no. 73, 300. Gabriella Hauch, "'Wir hätten ja gern die ganze Welt beglückt'. Demokratische Vereinsgeschichte/n 1848 zwischen geschlechtsspezifischer Konkurrenz und Komplementarität," *Österreichische Zeitschrift für Geschichtswissenschaften* 8, 4. (1998): 471-95.

47. *Wiener Neuigkeiten*, Vienna 1848, no. 99, 397.

48. Wolfgang Häusler, "Hermann Jellinek (1823-1848). Ein Demokrat in der Wiener Revolution," *Jahrbuch des Instituts für Deutsche Geschichte* 5 (1976): 170-71.

49. *Die Geißel*, Vienna 1848, no. 58, 138-39.

50. Ferdinand D. Fenner von Fenneberg, *Geschichte der Wiener Oktobertage. Geschildert und mit allen Aktenstücken belegt* (Leipzig, 1849), 104-5.

51. *Der Freimüthige*, Vienna 1848, no. 131, 552.

52. Bonnie S. Anderson and Judith P. Zinsser, *A History of their Own: Women in Europe from Prehistory to the Present* Vol. 2 (New York, 1988).

53. Paletschek, *Frauen und Dissens*, 218-23.

54. Mirjam Moravcová, "Die tschechischen Frauen im revolutionären Prag 1848/49," in Rudolf Jaworski and Robert Luft (eds.), *1848/49—Revolutionen in Ostmitteleuropa* (Munich, 1996), 92-93.

55. Honorata Zapová, "Vyzvání Ceskám (A Call on all Bohemian Women)," flyer September 1848, in Moravcová, "Die tschechischen Frauen," 91.

56. Ibid., 92-93.

57. Ibid., 92, n. 63.

58. Receipts of the Mainz Women's Association Humania, in Hummel-Haasis, *Schwesterr*, 275-76.

59. Grubitzsch and Lagpacan, *"Freiheit für die Frauen, Freiheit für das Volk!"* 113ff.

60. "Association," *Frauen-Zeitung* 30 November 1850, no. 48, in Ute Gerhard, Elisabeth Hannover-Drück, and Romina Schmitter, *"Dem Reich der Freiheit werb' ich Bürgerinnen." Die Frauenzeitung von Louise Otto* (Frankfurt, 1979), 17-18.

61. Supplement to the *Mannheimer Morgenblatt*, April 1848, no. 108, 588, in Hummel-Haasis, *Schwester*, 172-73.

62. *Saarzeitung*, 1848, no. 93, 2, in Hummel-Haasis, *Schwester*, 173-74.

63. *Satan*, Vienna 1848, no. 4, 29.

64. Grubitzsch and Lagpacan, *"Freiheit für die Frauen, Freiheit für das Volk!"*, 61-115; Karen Offen, "Liberty, Equality and Justice for Women: The Theory and Practice of Feminism in Nineteenth-Century Europe," in Renate Bridenthal (ed.), *Becoming Visible. Women in European History* (Boston, 1987), 335.

65. Beatrice Mesmer, *Ausgeklammert—Eingeklammert. Frauen und Frauenorganisationen in der Schweiz des 19. Jahrhunderts* (Basel, 1988), 79-80.

66. *Didaskalia*, Frankfurt a.M. 1848, in Zucker, "Frankfurt," 233.

67. Grubitzsch and Lagpacan, *"Freiheit für die Frauen, Freiheit für das Volk!"* 108.

68. Sabine Kienitz, "Aecht deutsche Weiblichkeit. Mode und Konsum als bürgerliche Frauenpolitik 1848," in Lipp (ed.), *Schimpfende Weiber*, 76-88.

69. "An die Frauen!" Vienna 1848, in Hauch, *Frau Biedemeier*, 233-24.

70. Eva Kuby, "Politische Frauenvereine und ihre Aktivitäten 1848 bis 1850," in Lipp (ed.), *Schimpfende Weiber*, 248-69.

71. *Der Humorist*, Vienna 1848, no. 83, 374.

72. *Die Constitution*, Vienna 1848, no. 27, 418.

73. *Didaskalia*, Frankfurt a.M. 1848, no. 118, in Zucker, "Frankfurt," 227.

74. *Prazky vecerní list*, Prague 1848, no. 50, 217, in Moravcová, "Die tscechischen Frauen," 88.

75. Allgemeines Verwaltungarchiv, Ob.Pol.Beh., Präs.II, Ft. 34, 1866/1855, Lemberger-Frauen-Wohlthätigkeitsverein und Kt.31, 1511/1856, Lemberger-Frauen-Wohlhätigkeitsverein, Österreichisches Staatsarchiv.

76. *Karlsruher Zeitung*, 4 August 1848.

77. *Politischer Studenten-Courier*, Vienna 1848, no. 66, 268ff.

78. Ibid.

79. Fanny Lewald in P. Goldhammer (ed.), *Augenzeugen der Revolution, Briefe, Tagebücher, Reden, Berichte* (Berlin, 1973), 245.

80. *Bohemia*, Prague 1848, no. 50, 5.

81. *Der Humorist*, Vienna 1848, no. 92, 374.

82. *Die Constitution*, Vienna 1848, no. 21, 312 and no. 24, 363.

83. Tamara Citovics, "Bräute der Revolution und ihre Helden. Zur politischen Funktion des Fahnenstickens," in Lipp (ed.), *Schimpfende Weiber*, 346.

84. *Der Volksfreund*, Vienna 1848, no. 5, 20.

85. *Der Humorist*, Vienna 1848, no. 74, 296.

86. Meysenburg, *Memoiren*, 132.

87. *Der Volksfreund*, Vienna 1848, no. 18, 76.

88. *Didaskalia*, Frankfurt a.M. 1848, no. 329 and no. 334, in Zucker, "Frankfurt," 233.

89. *Satan*, Vienna 1848, unnumbered, 21.

90. Joseph Hansen (ed.), *Rheinische Briefe und Akten zur Geschichte der politischen Bewegung 1830-1850*, Vol. 2, pt. 2, ed. by Heinz Boberach (Cologne and Bonn, 1976).

91. Letter of 11 March 1850 in Ferdinand Kürnberger, *Briefe eines politischen Flüchtlings*, ed. by O.E. Deutsch (Leipzig, 1920), 72-77.

92. Palatschek, *Frauen und Dissens*, 241 and 333.

93. Ferdinand Kürnberger, *Briefe eines politischen Flüchtlings* (Leipzig, 1920), 214-15.

94. Ibid., 74.

95. Alfred J. Becher to Karoline Perin, 23 November 1848, in L.A. Frankl, "Es war einmal," *Neue Freie Presse*, 13 March 1891, no. 9535, 257, n. 492.

96. See Hauch, *Frau Biedermeier*, 155-65.

97. Meysenburg, *Memoiren*, 119.

98. Heinrich Reschauer and Moritz Smets, *Das Jahr 1848. Geschichte der Revolution,* Vol. 2 (Vienna, 1872), 84.

99. "Antoine, die reine Barrikadenbraut," *Der Radikale*, Vienna 1848, no. 5, 19ff.

100. Renate Welsh, *Das Lufthaus* (Graz, 1994), 65.

101. Hansen (ed.), *Rheinische Briefe*, Vol. 2 pt. 2, 68ff., 81ff., 157ff.

102. Ibid, Vol. 2 pt. 2, 70.

103. *Didaskalia*, Frankfurt a.M. 1848, no. 147, in Zucker, "Frankfurt," 235.

104. *Der Omnibus*, Vienna 1848, no. 33, 130.

105. "Erinnerungen Louise Zimmermanns aus dem Parlamentsleben," in Zucker, "Frankfurt," 235.

106. Kürnberger, *Briefe*, 33.

107. *Gold und Larve,* Vienna 1848, no. 10, 40.

108. Zucker, "Frankfurt a.M.," 226.

109. Carola Lipp, "Katzenmusiken, Krawalle und Weiberrevolution," in Lipp (ed.), *Schimpfende Weiber*, 112-30. Hauch, *Frau Biedermeier*, 55-84.

110. Wilhelm M. Hehner, "Wiener Ereignisse," Vienna 1848, 8. *Der Humorist*, Vienna 1848, nos. 72 and 73, 274.

111. Hachtmann, *Berlin 1848*, 181–82.
112. Stefan Rohrbacher, *Gewalt im Biedermeier. Antijudische Ausschreitungen in Vormärz und Revolution (1815-1848/49)* (Frankfurt, 1993), 181ff.
113. "Rede am Grabe der Gefallenen. Gesprochen von Isak Noa Mannheimer, Freitag den 17. März 1848," pamphlet, in *Studia Judaica Austriaca*, Vol. 1, "Das Judentum im Revolutionsjahr 1848" (Vienna, 1974), 40–41.
114. *Politischer Studenten-Courier*, Vienna 1848, no. 33, 139.
115. *Denkbuch der merkwürdigsten Tage Wiens. Eine ausführliche Darstellung aller Ereignisse und Begebenheiten des Jahres 1848 in und um Wien, die Bekanntgabe der erschienenen Proklamationen, gehaltenen Reden und Feierlichkeiten*, (Vienna, 1850), 126.
116. *Der Volksfreund*, Vienna 1848, no. 30, 123.
117. *Der Freimüthige*, Vienna 1848, no. 48, 198.
118. *Deutsche Zeitung*, Vienna 1848, no. 48, 198.
119. A. Röckel, *Sachsens Erhebung und das Zuchthaus zu Waldheim*, (Frankfurt, 1865), 160, in Hummel-Haasis, *Schwester*, 106.
120. *Der Freimüthige*, Vienna 1848, no. 48, 198.
121. *Der Omnibus*, Vienna 1848, no. 4, 15. "Über Wäscherinnen, Blumenmacherinnen, Taglöhnerinnen, Handschuhnäherinnen, Kupferstichmalerinnen, Weißnäherinnen und Putzmacherinnen. Quellen zu diversen Ländern des Deutschen Bundes, vor allem Textilarbeiterinnen in Sachsen (Krise der Heimindustrie)," in Hummel-Haasis, *Schwester*, 170–84.
122. *Die Constitution*, Vienna 1848, no. 165, 800–1.
123. Hachtmann, *Berlin 1848*, 516,
124. Grubitzsch and Lagpacan, *"Freiheit für die Frauen—Freiheit für das Volk!"* 208–15.
125. Wolfgang Häusler, *Von der Massenarmut zur Arbeiterbewegung* (Vienna, 1979), 181.
126. *Der Volksfreund*, Vienna 1848, no. 101, 406
127. *Allgemeine Österreichische Zeitung*, Vienna 1848, no. 142, 1089.
128. Carl Bobrowski to his parents, in Peter Frank-Döfering (ed.), *Die Donner der Revolution über Wien. Ein Student aus Czernowitz (Carl Bobrowski) erlebt 1848* (Vienna, 1988), 125.
129. K. Mellach (ed.), *1848. Protokolle einer Revolution* (Vienna, 1968), 24.
130. Franz J. Gaberden, *Blut-Szenen aus der Mailänder-Revolution. Leiden und Qualen eines gefangen Deutschen* (Vienna, 1848), 5–6.
131. Jelinek, "Honorata z Wisniowskych Zapová, 1894," in Moravcová, "Die tchechischen Frauen," 85.
132. "Trauer-Blatt. Neueste Nachrichten aus Prag. Schreckliches Schicksal der Prager Juden oder Überfall und Plünderung der Judenstadt," Pamphlet collection 1848, Österreichische Nationalbibliothek, Vienna.
133. Pozor, "Prague 1848, no. 92," in Moravcová, "Die tsechischen Frauen," 86, n. 35.
134. *Prags fliegende Blätter—Hauptblatt der Damenmode*, Prague 1848, no. 7, 2, in Moravcová, "Die tchechischen Frauen," 98.
135. Gaberden, *Blut-Szenen*, 5–6.
136. Berthold Auerbach, *Tagebuch aus Wien, Von Latour bis auf Windischgrätz (September bis November 1848)* (Breslau, 1849), 56.
137. Veit Valentin, *Geschichte der deutschen Revolution von 1848-1849*, 2 Vols. (Frankfurt, 1970), 207.
138. Reschauer and Smets, *Das Jahr 1848*, Vol. 2, 282–83.
139. Wenzeslav G. Dunder, *Denkschrift über die Wiener Oktober-Revolution. Ausführliche Darstellung aller Ereignisse aus ämtliche Quellen geschöpft, mit zahlreichen Urkunden begleitet, dann nach eigenen Erlebnissen und nach authentischen Berichten von Augenzeugen und Autoritäten*, (Vienna, 1849), 5.
140. Reschauer and Smets, *Das Jahr 1848*, Vol. 1, 424.
141. L. Predescu, *Enciclopedia Cugetarea. Material Românesc. Oameni si infăptuiri*, (Bucharest, 1940), 442. I would like to thank Lothar Maier for the translation. See also his essay in this volume.
142. A. San, *Revolutia Romana de la 1848* (Bucharest, 1992), 227 (translation by Lothar Maier).
143. Cornelia Bodea (ed.), *1848 a la Romani. O istorie în date si maturii*, Vol. 2 (Bucharest, 1982), 802 (translation by Lother Maier).

144. Bodea, *1848*, 1165.

145. C.D. Rosenthal (1820-1851), "Revolutionary Romania," in Cornelia Bodea, *The Rumanians' Struggle for Unification 1834-1849* (Bucharest, 1970).

146. *Marianne und Germania 1789-1889. Frankreich und Deutschland. Zwei Welten—eine Revue,* exhibition catalog, ed. by Marie-Luise von Plessen (Berlin, 1997).

147. "'Slavia' oder 'Bohemia' auf der Barrikade zwischen Altstädter und Kleinem Ring (Detail)," Lithograph, Prague 1848, in Moravcová, "Die tscechischen Frauen," 86.

148. J.C. Schoeller, "Die Carolinen-Barricade," in Hauch, *Frau Biedermeier*, 131; F. Russ, "Barrikadenmädchen," in ibid., 125.

149. *Frauen-Zeitung*, 19 May 1849, no. 5, 70-71.

150. Ibid., 21 April 1849, no. 1, 39-40 and 42-43.

151. Ibid., 7 July 1849, no. 12, 109-10.

152. Ibid., 7 July 1849, no. 12, 110-11. Further description of these events in Hummel-Haasis, *Schwester,* 108.

153. Röckel, *Sachsens Erhebung*, 161, in Hummel-Haasis, *Schwester*, 107.

154. Henrich Loose, *Der deutsche Reichsverfassungskampf im Jahre 1849, Schlachtenlieder* (Stuttgart, 1852), 10.

155. Hachtmann, *Berlin 1848*, 574-85.

156. *Wiener Gassenzeitung,* Vienna 1848, no. 128, 513.

157. Josef A. von Helfert, *Geschichte Österreichs vom Ausgange des Wiener Oktober-Aufstandes,* Vol. 1 (Leipzig, 1869-1886), 386.

158. Grubitzsch and Lagpacan, *"Freiheit für die Frauen—Freiheit für das Volk!"* 108ff.

159. Mathilde Franziska Anneke, in Martin Henkel and Rolf Taubert (eds.), *Das Weib im Conflict mit den sozialen Verhältnissen* (Bochum, 1976), 64.

160. Manfred Gebhardt, *Mathilda Franziska Anneke. Biographie* (Berlin, 1988).

161. Emma Herwegh, *Zur Geschichte der deutsche demokratischen Legion aus Paris. Von einer Hochverräterin* (Grünberg, 1849), in Hummel-Haasis, *Schwester*, 185-202.

162. Amalie Struve, *Erinnerungen aus den badischen Freiheitskämpfen* (Hamburg, 1850), in Hummel-Haasis, *Schwester*, 203-20.

163. *Mainzer Tagblatt und Fremdenanzeiger*, 1848, no. 120, 2, in Hummel-Haasis, *Schwester*, 202.

164. Inge Buck, "'Aus Liebe zum Vaterland und aus Liebe zu Dir!' Anmerkungen zur Rolle der Flora in der Novella aus der Pfälzer Revolution 1849 'Die Freischärlerin' von F.A. Karchner," in Helga Grubitzsch, Hannelore Cyrus, and Elke Haarbusch (eds.), *Grenzgängerinnen, Revolutionäre Frauen im 18. Und 19. Jahrhundert. Weibliche Wirklichkeit und männliche Phantasien* (Düsseldorf, 1985), 139-52.

165. György Spira, *A magyar farradalom 1848-1849* (Budapest, 1959), 426-27, 649, 654.

166. Wilhelmine von Beck, *Memoiren einer Dame während des letzten Unabhängigkeitskreises in Ungarn,* Vol. 1 (London, 1850), 183-87.

167. Louise Otto, "Der Volkskreuzzug in Ungarn," *Frauen-Zeitung*, 21 July 1849, no. 14, 113.

168. Ernst Bloch, *Das Prinzip Hoffnung,* Vol. 2 (Frankfurt, 1980), 690.

169. Klara Zetkin, *Zur Geschichte der proletarischen Frauenbewegung in Deutschland,* (Frankfurt, 1971), 18.

170. "Anna, Aufruf an deutsche Frauen und Jungfrauen zur Begründung einer echt weiblichen Emancipation," *Frauen-Zeitung*, 21 April 1849, no. 1, 44.

171. *Der Freie Wiener,* Vienna 1848, no. 25, 99.

172. R. Dekker and L. van de Pol, *Frauen in Männerkleidung. Weibliche Transvestiten und ihre Geschichte* (Berlin, 1989).

173. Leopold Storch, *Caroline, die Wiener Barrikadenheldin, Jäger Carl genannt. Revolutionsgeschichte aus Wiens Oktoberkämpfen und dem ungarischen/italienischen Freiheitskriege* (Grimma, 1850).

174. Beck, *Memoiren*, 183-87.

175. *Manchester Guardian*, 6 June 1892, in E. Ethelmer, *Women Free* (London, 1893), 77.

176. George Sand, *Geschichte meines Lebens* (1855) (Frankfurt, 1991).

177. Sophinek Becker, "Transsexuelle—die letzten (echten) Frauen und Männer?" in Sexualberatungsstelle Salzburg (ed.), *Trieb, Hemmung, Begehren, Psychoalalyse und Sexualität* (Göttingen, 1998).

178. *Frauen-Zeitung*, 23 March 1848, no. 12, 241.
179. Grubitzsch and Lagpacan, "*Freiheit für die Frauen—Freiheit für das Volk!*", 113ff.
180. C. Grüner, *Die Geschichte der Oktober-Revolution in Wien, ihrer Ursachen und nächsten Folgen* (Leipzig, 1849), 327.
181. Julius Fröbel, *Briefe über die Wiener October-Revolution mit Notizen über die letzten Tage Robert Blums* (Frankfurt, 1849), 74-75.
182. Grüner, *Geschichte der Oktober-Revolution*, 274-75.; Streckfuß, *Die Staatsumwälzung*, 381.
183. *Karlsruher Zeitung*, 23 June 1849, no. 38, in Hummel-Haasis, *Schwester*, 141.
184. Struve, *Memoiren*, in Hummel-Haasis, *Schwester*, 204-5.
185. Grubitzsch and Lagpacan, "*Freiheit für die Frauen—Freiheit für das Volk!*", 231.
186. Paletschek, *Frauen und Dissens*, 241.
187. Fanny Adelson to Johann Jacoby, Königsberg, April 1848, in Cornelia Schmölders (ed.), *Briefe berühmter Frauen* (Frankfurt, 1993), 320.

Chapter 27

CIVIC GUARDS IN THE EUROPEAN REVOLUTIONS OF 1848

Ralf Pröve

In the years 1848 and 1849, militia-like formations played a central role as opponent or accomplice of the military. Closely bound up with the fate of the revolution, these civic or national guards defined street scenes in European capitals as well as daily life in provincial urban centers. Whether as barricade fighters in Paris, Vienna or Berlin in the spring of 1848, or as living shields in front of the national parliament in Berlin, or in the defense of Vienna in the autumn of the same year, or as volunteer units during the campaign for the imperial constitution in 1849, civic guards and the related question of the so-called "arming of the people" dominated daily life in the revolution and in the debates in the political clubs or parliaments. Supporters and opponents expressed their opinions on the subject in essays, petitions or the flood of daily publications. Interest in the question is also reflected in the wide range of literary treatments of the subject in songs, poems, satirical verses, cartoons, plays, and prose texts.

When the revolution broke out in February 1848 in Paris—encouraged by a broad opposition in which parts of the national guard played a decisive role—and a little later in the German Confederation, nearly every member state proclaimed, together with other wide-ranging reforms, the realization of the "arming of the people." Countless organizations devoted to that end were founded, with quite various names, depending on the region and the state. However, the establishment of a civic guard was not something totally new at this time. The idea of "arming the people" had its roots in Germany in the late enlightenment period and in the patriotism debates, especially of the 1770s and 1780s. With the revolutionary events in Paris, beginning in 1789 and the reform period beginning in Germany a little later, larger militia formations were established for the first time. Not least because of their revolutionary background, such formations were soon disbanded or fundamentally transformed to eradicate their political features.

In France, a conservative transformation of the national guard began under Napoleon in the 1790s. In Germany, civic guards were disbanded with the beginning of the restoration period after 1815 and 1819 respectively. Only following the Paris July Revolution of 1830 were civic militias founded again in the revolutionary centers of Europe. In France, the national guard, disbanded in 1827 because of its criticism of authorities, had to be recalled; in the Principalities of Hessen, Saxony or Brunswick, new civic guards were established.

It was a fundamental problem that the catchword of "arming the people" was not very precise and proposals for putting it into practice varied considerably. In addition, this phrase was interpreted quite differently by representatives of different political currents. Agreement in principle existed only in opposition to an absolutist standing army. Five basic standpoints can be recognized; their explication, in order of increasing radicalization, corresponds to the way that demands for arming the people were put forth, across the passage of time.

In military circles, two camps formed with quite divergent reactions to the military challenges of the day. Supporters of the old order saw in "arming the people" the establishment of a regular draft system drawing on as broad a section of the population as possible. Their aims were only an increase in efficiency for the military, which they felt should continue to function as an independent corporation with special powers. Liberal military reformers in France, Germany or Austria, on the other hand, basically intended to tie the military and society closer together and to create nationally or territorially uniform units, filled with patriotic enthusiasm, instead of a variegated, confused mixture of mercenary troops. They interpreted "arming the people" as, for example, universal conscription and supplementary civic guard bodies such as the [Prussian] *Landwehr*, *Landsturm* or the French national guard, under the command of the army. This interpretation of "arming the people" was criticized both by conservative military men, who feared a "civilianization" of their troops, and by liberals, who painted a picture of a "militarization" of society.

German liberals, such as Carl von Rotteck and Karl Theodor Welcker, totally rejected a standing army as a "hoard of despotism" and put forward the counter-proposal of a national militia for which citizens could volunteer in times of war. Admittedly, not all liberals supported Rotteck's fundamental criticism and pleaded instead for a cautious and slow transformation of the standing army. In those countries that had not established a *Landwehr* on the Prussian model in the first years of the nineteenth century, moderate liberals still held military organizations created in the spirit of military reform to be a worthwhile objective.

Only in the years after 1830, and especially in 1848, did the discussion shift more to the genuinely civilian arena and thus excluded the military completely. Less significant was an increase in the efficiency of the military or the question of society's control of soldiers and officers (for example with the army swearing loyalty to the constitution) or even a cautious transformation along liberal lines. Instead, the military was increasingly contrasted directly with a civic guard. While moderates, however, interpreted "arming the people" as a civic guard of the property-owning bourgeoisie, state officials, and the self-employed, radicals favored a form of "people's guard" that also included workers and day laborers.

This broad spectrum of starting points can be explained by their proponents' various concepts of society and the related semantic range of interpretation of the term "people," which included both an above-below relation as well as an interior-exterior relation. In addition was the specific problem of the concept of citizen [*Bürger*] in German-speaking areas, which included both town burghers or citizens in the sense of the corporate society of the old regime, as well as citizen of a state in the liberal and constitutional meaning of the term. The range of theories was also conditioned by the strange, almost diametrically opposed double function of the civic guards—on the one hand, in the sense of the authorities and conservatives, of ensuring "peace and security" and protecting property, and, on the other hand, from the perspective of the revolutionary movements, of functioning as protectors of constitutions and reforms. The dual function as political-revolutionary and policing elements had its special causes that were not just to be found in the area of politics and constitutions.

Especially the problem of security, subjectively felt and objectively existing, made it obvious for the governments that it was impossible in the long term not to permit civic guards or security associations. The radicalization and politicization of protests, and, especially, a rapidly increasing number of members of "the fourth estate" [the phrase used here in the nineteenth-century German meaning of the working class—ed.], led the government and property owners to see a gap in public safety in the years of crisis during the *Vormärz*. It became increasingly clear that the existing, traditional mechanisms of public order were no longer up to their tasks. The dismantling of the patriarchal household as the lowest level in the structures of social domination, a detachment of people from corporate communities in the cities or manorially or seigneurially dominated agrarian communities in the countryside, robbed old corporate integrative forces of their function.

The state, however, had little possibility of taking on these functions. The "police of absolutism," the military, remained an important factor and was held, especially in conservative circles, to be a guarantee of monarchical order, as a bulwark against potential revolution. However, the military was on the defensive and there was a lack of both money and political will to create a functioning and effective gendarmerie. In the first half of the nineteenth century, the governments were, therefore, still surprisingly dependent on traditional security police forces—which were undergoing a process of disintegration—and premodern corporate patterns of social control.

On the one hand, greater use had to be made of those night-watchmen or market masters and field guards that corporate groups and communities had employed for centuries to preserve peace and order. On the other, residential self-protection (service "in turn" with the possibility of substitution), organized on corporate principles, had to be preserved. Contemporaries found this an unsatisfactory solution, one leading to demands for special bourgeois law enforcement formations.

At the same time, civic guards appeared for many to be the constitutional counter-model to a princely-absolutist military, feared as a bastion of reaction and as a massive threat to all endeavors towards liberty. This dual function of political and public security police contributed decisively to weakening the civic guards in 1848, as social and political tensions were thus transferred directly into them.

In the course of the revolution, three stages of development may be distinguished. In the first phase, which was interpreted as a victory of the protest movement, civic guards were established everywhere. Initially, there were generally only a few signs of confrontations between propertied bourgeoisie and workers, above all in view of the euphoria over the movement's apparent victory. In the second phase, reactionary forces regained ground and civic guards were limited in their rights or even disbanded. At the same time, the formations became arenas for political conflict and a showplace of diverging economic and political interests. In the third phase, finally, the situation came to a head, as during the so-called campaign for the imperial constitution in Germany, or in the struggles in Vienna and Paris, civic guards and military faced each other as direct opponents. Here there were bloody clashes in which sometimes hundreds died.

When the German monarchs allowed an arming of the people in the spring of 1848, the "term 'arming the people' was the first cry of victory that echoed from all sides, and arming the people was the first of the promises and demands whose fulfilment was carried through. Arming the people, the establishment of civic guards, came to be seen as the palladium of all other liberties, as the Minerva behind whose protective shield the recently won liberties of the people [seemed] to be secure," as a resident of Prussia noted. The officer Andreas von Schepeler commented somewhat more ironically on the general enthusiasm for "arming the people." "These days one hears perhaps in most cities in Europe, but certainly in every city in Germany, in every village, indeed in every bar, the high-sounding phrase 'arming the people' bubbling forth from the prayers of the political rosary; it is the catchword of the most vehement public speaker."[1]

Permission for "arming the people"—understood as symbolic gesture, but also as a concession of power-politics—was so tied to the success of the revolution, that, for example in Berlin the events on 18 and 19 March can only be correctly understood against this backdrop. Only when the king agreed to an arming of the people in the early hours of the nineteenth was calm restored. Much more than in 1830, governments had to take into consideration the wishes of the opposition and clearly emphasize political aspects, especially in relation to auxiliary police. Thus, for example, the civic guards in Baden, Hessen-Darmstadt, and Württemberg were supposed to defend "the constitution and the rights and liberties guaranteed by law against internal and external enemies." In Nassau a "people's guard for the guarantee of public liberties" arose, while in Austria the national guard was described as the "shield of the constitution and the law."[2]

One consequence of wide-ranging political concessions was that the previously restricted circle of people qualified to serve was de jure considerably expanded in many states. While, in the Principality of Hessen, all men working for wages and residents without municipal citizenship were excluded according to official statements in 1830, in Prussia, on the other hand, all residents, citizens, and rifle-club members were allowed to join the civic guards. In Austria, all "citizens of the state," in Nassau, "all Nassauers capable of bearing arms," were called to service. Other states, as, for example, the kingdom of Hanover, expressly allowed participation by "non-citizens," but made it dependent on permission from local authorities.[3] However, these concessions were to a great extent lip-service to pacify the lower-class barricade fighters and to channel revolutionary demands. In spite of the remarkable social openness, the civic guards remained institutions of the propertied bourgeoisie or rapidly developed into instruments of the new order, like the mobile guard in Paris.

This mobile guard was established by the government directly following the February Revolution. The national guard was no longer trusted to provide (and to want to provide) protection for the government, as numerous incidents in the 1840s had made obvious: apart from political unreliability, a confused chain of command, low-level of discipline, and impractical alarm plans. Therefore, the new sections of the mobile guard were to take on these functions as a more powerful and dependable arm of the government. Initially planned to have a strength of 24,000 men, 16,000 had been recruited by June 1848. These mobile guardsmen were paid, unlike national guardsmen. The troops were made up of volunteers, especially former soldiers, who were trustworthy in the eyes of the government.

Very quickly it became apparent that the generally excluded lower classes had their own ideas about "arming the people," so that this legal form, legitimized by the authorities, did not remain the only one. Already in April, the radical democrat Friedrich Hecker had armed journeymen artisans, workers, and students in Baden, and then involved this motley formation in a battle with troops of the German Confederation. Hecker's actions offer a relatively early, revolutionary variant of "arming of the people," a counter-example to the civic guard, which confronted the property-owning bourgeoisie with fears of "anarchy" and a "red republic." For the liberal propertied bourgeoisie, it was also unsettling that, at least in the large cities, "wild" or flying corps were increasingly operating—parallel to official formations—in which artisans and workers were involved and which generally evaded intensive control. Again and again, the so-called "rabble" was able to arm itself, as, for example, on 14 June in Berlin during the storming of the arsenal there.

In many cities, the simple "people," protesting and demanding decisive reforms, confronted bourgeois law enforcement formations as opponents. A process of division arose in the civic guards, creating a wing in favor of "order" and one in favor of "movement." The latter supported the "democratic arming of the people," the other, vilified as the "knout guard" the work of the police and the military. In Paris, such divisions—a moderate liberal bloc and a democratic center—was also not unknown in the national guard; in June, only 12,000 of the 190,000 national guardsmen fought on the side of the army. Even the mobile guard suffered political divisions.

The civic guards were not only threatened from "below," by armed workers and social revolutionaries. In the late summer and autumn of 1848, after the signal given by the brutal suppression of the June uprising in Paris, the counter-revolution began, reforms were successively withdrawn, and open military force applied against revolutionaries. Thus the civic guards also came to the attention of the reaction, as not only an arming of the "rabble" but also because the politically insecure and at least indifferent attitude among the civic and national guards had always been a thorn in the side of the old powers. With a series of "autumn decrees," the civic guards, insofar as they had not already been disbanded, were given a new form of organization that stripped them of all political aspects and restricted them to the sector of the auxiliary police. In the following months, either the civic guards were totally banned or promised civic guard legislation was dropped; in any case, the governments managed to disarm the people.

In the wake of the campaign for the imperial constitution, when an attempt was made in Germany in 1849 to ensure the acceptance of the constitution written by the Frankfurt National Assembly, by force if necessary, against its rejection by the most powerful states, especially by the Prussian king, there were bloody clashes with the military. *Landwehr* units and civic guards had openly declared their support for the constitution and called for military action against the "reaction." Thus, for example, the *Landwehr*-committee in Cologne had declared the Prussian (conservative) government to be "illegal,"[4] the civic guards in Karlsruhe and Heidelberg called for a "defensive war," and, in the end, formed a "general command of the people's guard" in Karlsruhe. The revolutionary troops, consisting of people's guards, civic guards, volunteers, and deserting front line soldiers, had little chance against the soon coordinated actions of the Prussian, Hessian, and Württemberg troops. After the revolution had been "liquidated" in Saxony and in the Palatinate, the capitulation of the fortress of Rastatt in Baden on 23 June 1849 meant the final failure of the revolution.

In the spring of 1848 such an end could not necessarily be foreseen. Many conservatives, even the army, tolerated the establishment of civic guards in March and April as a necessary evil, as they initially appeared a suitable means of preventing a further radicalization of the revolution. Even in the early summer, they were still considering increasing the efficiency of the civic guards, strengthening their military aspects and arming them more generously in order to be able to break up riots and demonstrations more energetically in the future. Other conservatives, such as the influential Prussian politician Ernst Ludwig von Gerlach, took exception to the unmilitary picture the civic guards presented, to the men's lack of discipline, and were soon mocking and ridiculing the civic guards and were not sparing with vehement criticism.

Animosity became greater when the civic guards were less and less able or willing to fulfil their police responsibilities in the late summer and autumn of 1848, and were even openly active in political resistance. Thus the conservative Prussian constitutionalist Friedrich Julius von Stahl complained that protection of property was only an excuse for establishing civic guards and that rather "the use of force against the king" was intended. In this manner, the people's army could function as a "parliamentary army," and form a second center of power next to the standing army.[5] When events in Berlin came to a head in October and November, demands were made for an occupation of the city by the army and for the disarming and disbanding of the "shameless civic guards," who, by forgetting their duties, were no longer able to prevent attacks by the "rabble." It was at least necessary, according to a report in the conservative *Kreuzzeitung* of 7 November 1848 "to allow the good spirits in the civic guards to gain the upper hand over the bad elements contained within it." From a "bourgeois formation for the protection of legal order," it had become "a sort of praetorian guard for the party of revolt."

Experience with the civic guards in the following months and the other political developments in the summer and autumn of 1848 were not without their effects on the debate over "arming the people." Above all, three central themes may be distinguished: the question of the areas of responsibility for law enforcement formations, that is, in the narrow sense, the dichotomy of "auxiliary police" and "protector of the constitution"; the question of the potential circle of personnel, and the question of relations with the authorities.

If the civic guards saw themselves above all as auxiliary police, that is if the bourgeoisie saw their task in the preservation of public order, they threatened to become an instrument of the reaction with a change in the political climate. If the guardsmen stuck to the proclaimed function of protecting the constitution, they were in danger of being seen as "revolutionaries" and "subversives." Above all, it was unclear what was meant by "public peace" and "legal order." In a year of rapidly enacted laws and regulations, which were often equally quickly overturned or altered, an unbridgeable gap necessarily arose between police regulation and constitutional liberties. An expert in these difficulties, the Prussian Carl Schwebemeyer, described this problem as follows: "Which role will the civic guard play here? Will it join in with the rebellion? Then it will be acting against its purpose … of protecting public peace and legal order. Will it suppress the rebellion? Then, however, it would be acting according to purpose but against the liberties of the people, and supporting absolutism and tyranny."[6]

This dilemma, relating to the "speed of the revolution," contributed greatly to the above-mentioned split, to the "bad mood" often complained of. Admittedly, such processes were not uniform. Rather, the various political circumstances and socioeconomic conditions in the states, regions, and cities overlapped with the respective specific political developments at the time. Conservatives, in any case, were interested in civic guards oriented towards an exclusive function as auxiliary police, one preventing revolution, as they at first appeared a more flexible instrument for suppressing unrest than the military. When, however, the civic guards lost their ability and also their willingness to suppress demonstrations or protests in the eyes of conservatives, they insisted—parallel to the victories of the reaction—on the disbanding of all such formations.

More difficult was the liberals' standpoint. On the one hand, the propertied bourgeoisie recognized, at the latest in 1830, how useful such formations could be when they themselves became the target of protests and saw their property threatened. Thus they expressly declared their support for the law enforcement aspect, not least in order to gain the support of the princes and adherents of the old order. On the other hand, they did not wish to see themselves degraded to constant henchmen of the police. Especially radical publicists attacked this as an unacceptable restriction. Thus, for example, the editor of the radical newspaper *Locomotive*, Friedrich Wilhelm Alexander Held, ranked the law enforcement aspect as only a "secondary purpose" in July 1848, underlining instead the task of the civic guard as protector of "the people's liberties."[7] The revolutionary writer Karl Gutzkow saw the reasons for disagreements within the civic guard in that "no sooner are the civic guards established, then they are immediately used exclusively as an organ of the police."[8]

When in Prussia during the fall of 1848 a civic guard law was passed that gave greater prominence to the guard's auxiliary police character, the minister of the interior received a number of protest notes, undersigned by hundreds of people. The tenor of these notes was similar. The law did not fulfil the "demands of the people, the rights of citizens, to represent the liberty and constitution of the fatherland with arms." Instead, the civic guard had now "received the hateful requirement to support the police and to fortify a despotic administration." The people were thus "dammed to take up thug's work against themselves."[9]

Apart from this political criticism, there was increasing dissatisfaction among the bourgeoisie about pure security and public order service, which required a lot of time and work. One consequence was the demands for closer cooperation with the police and not a few people sought to evade doing service. Supporters of the civic guard suspected that behind the many authoritarian "requisitions" and the "many tasks" this caused, was a systematic attempt to sabotage the entire institution. Socialists and early communists totally rejected the public order character of the civic guard and demanded full sovereignty and a general political mandate.

The second basic position manifested in the debate over "arming the people" was the question of suitable personnel, which—as already mentioned—had been considerably expanded, at least de jure, at the beginning of 1848. The conservatives wanted only "the good elements" represented in the civic guards, that is the politically conforming propertied and state service bourgeoisie. They strictly rejected any participation by the "rabble," the lower classes. Liberal attitudes toward this problem were, in turn, varied, as they stood between abstract political convictions, on the one hand, and specific personal fears, on the other. Those who feared that unlimited enlistment would lead to subversion directed their voices either against the acceptance in the guard of all men in general who had a certain occupational or social profile (that is journeymen or workers), or only against those held to be unreliable and rebellious.

In political writings of the day, however, voices against an exclusion of certain groups were stronger. Reasons offered included the idea that all citizens had equal rights, but there were also tactical considerations. If workers were excluded, as was written in the *Nationalzeitung*, the civic guard "would be placed in the position of having to oppose the workers."[10] This was related to concerns about a split of the "people" "into two opposing camps," into "a so-called bourgeoisie and a working class,"[11] which would make the civic guard the arena for social struggle and thus incapable of acting, circumstances that would play into the hands of the right-wing.

Dedicated democrats such as Karl Gutzkow even warned quite strongly against leaving the civic guards only to the propertied, to the "vanity of the property owners" and argued for a broad social base for the civic guards.[12] Socialists and early communists, of course, favored "arming the people" over a civic guard. Thus, for example, Friedrich Engels praised the storming of the Berlin arsenal by workers and journeymen as a necessary "self-arming of the people." Especially the "imbalance" of the civic guard against the "people" was responsible for the "unfortunate circumstances."[13]

The third and final focus of discussion was the question of ties to the authorities in the broader sense. Conservatives desired close ties to the local authorities or even to military detachments. This would have assigned the civic guards a passive role, allowing them to form only at the special request of the authorities. Calling out an alarm themselves or independent ability to call up troops, i.e., mobilization of the civic guard at its members' own discretion, was thus to be ruled out. Reactionary critics wanted civil command totally ruled out, as civilians lacked any "military sense."[14] Liberals strictly rejected such restrictions and insisted on an independent position for such formations, allowing for an independent deployment.

As indicated, in the final analysis, the civic guard's readiness for action and willingness to act and their related military and police "value" determined the course of the discussion. The military value, be it as protector of the constitution, or as armed branch of the revolution, was considerably overestimated after the early successes of the civic guards. It was overlooked that the retreating troops were not really defeated, but only withdrawn for reasons of political calculation by governments and generals. The former feared a radicalization of the movement and solidarity with it on the part of previously "peaceful" groups in the population, the latter an infection of their own troops by the revolutionary spark.

This fatal misjudgment by the left did not change the fact that barricade fighting in the narrow streets considerably hindered the normal, tested military tactics of firing from a broad front and in a closed line. As became apparent in the autumn of 1848 and 1849, professional soldiers could not be defeated, especially in the open field, and even in concentrated street fighting, the civic guards could not offer long resistance, as for example in the storming of Vienna by troops under General Windischgrätz or in the Paris uprising in June. These battles lasted only a short time, in spite of the commitment of the voluntary units, because of poor equipment and training as well as their general numerical inferiority. Because the military leadership shied away from the risk of defeat and therefore only took to the field under good conditions and with clearly superior numbers, the reaction achieved victory after victory. Sociopolitical divisions in the revolutionary movement, reflected and concentrated in the civic guards, also led to serious weakening of their military potential.

Their value as policing body also suffered under the various expectations and demands placed on the civic guards. A further problem was the considerable time guardsmen had to spend on guard duty. As the propertied bourgeoisie was not compensated for losses incurred because of absence from shops or factories, willingness to take part sank rapidly, after the early euphoria. Workers and day laborers could only fill the gaps to a certain extent, as the lower classes were greatly dependent on regular income. When a civic guard existed over a number of years, as for example the national guard in Paris or the civic guard in the Principality of Hessen in the 1830s and 1840s, the proper functions of guarding and protection were pushed aside more and more by the needs of representation and social exclusion. If people were looking for a prestigious appearance in public, unpleasant night duty often remained unfulfilled. Especially the more wealthy guardsmen from the economic bourgeois milieu had expensive uniforms and arms made and formed their own, distinct units—which in turn led to social tensions and collided with the basic idea of "arming the people."

Decisive for a weakening and poor functioning of the civilian formations for the preservation of order was, above all, that their deployment had to be based on a certain basic consensus in the respective city. If the group of guardsmen was too small or the extent of unrest too great, attempts to maintain "peace and quiet" generally failed—which opened the road for the military.

The end of the revolution also saw the end of the idea of "arming the people." The governments in Germany and Austria put an end to all such experiments, replacing them with an ever tighter network of gendarmerie. France followed in 1871 and disbanded the national guard. The idea of "arming the people" had fallen into complete disfavor in the eyes of the princes and the restored old governments, as they saw as confirmed the warnings that the old fears of an overthrow of existing order had been quite real—even if not in the sense of power politics. With the catchword "arming the people," weapons had fallen into the hands of radical democrats and "red rabble." "People's armies" that demanded social and political reforms and that seemed willing to enforce their demands with violence had become a new and worrying variant. The armies, not least because of these traumatic experiences, were successively built up by the governments and, in Prussia-Germany, gained a position outside the constitution in the 1860s and in 1871, which contributed greatly to a militarization and secured power for the old elite for another fifty years.

Notes

1. Carl Schwebemeyer, *Die Volksbewaffnung, ihr Wesen und Wirken* (Wriezen n.d. [1848]), 3; A. von Schepeler, *Volksbewaffnung und Republik* (Aachen, 1848), 3.
2. Legislation for the establishment of a civic guard of 3 April 1848 (Baden); almost literally the wording for Hessen-Darmstadt of 15 April 1848. On Württemberg, see the legislation of 1 April 1848, § 15; Law of 11 March 1848 (Nassau); draft of a statute of 8 April 1848 (Austria).
3. Law of 19 March 1848 (Prussia), draft of 8 April 1848 (Austria), § 2; Law of 11 March 1848 (Nassau), § 54; Law of 16 April 1848, § 1 (Hanover).
4. Declaration of 15 November 1848, in Karl Obermann (ed.), *Flugblätter der Revolution. Eine Flugblattsammlung zur Geschichte der Revolution von 1848/49 in Deutschland* (East Berlin, 1970), 350-51.

On the mutinies of *Landwehr* units see Ernst Rudolf Huber, *Deutsche Verfassungsgeschichte seit 1789,* Vol. 2, *Der Kampf um Einheit und Freiheit 1830 bis 1850,* (Stuttgart, 1987), 862-65.

5.   Friedrich Julius Stahl, *Die gegenwärtigen Parteien in Staat und Kircke. Neunundzwanzig akademische Vorlesungen,* (Berlin, 1868), esp. 75-76.

6.   Schwebemeyer. *Die Volksbewaffnung* (n.1), 6.

7.   Friedrich Wilhelm Alexander Held, "Bürgerwehrgesetz-Entwurf bei Gaslicht betrachtet," *Locomotive* 87, 18 July 1848.

8.   Karl Gutzkow, *Deutschland am Vorabend seines Falles oder seiner Größe* (Franfkurt, 1848), 229.

9.   At least some of these notes can be read in the Geheimes preußisches Staatsarchiv Berlin Rep. 77, Titel 244a, no. 1, 161ff.

10. "Was soll die Bürgerwehr?" *Nationalzeitung* no. 21, 21 April 1848, supplement, 1.

11. Schwebemeyer, *Volksbewaffnung,* 4. See also the commentary on draft civic guard legislation in the *Neue Rheinische Zeitung,* 22 July 1848.

12. Karl Gutzkow, *Vor- und Nach-Märzliches,* (Leipzig, 1850), 114. Members of the "bourgeoisie" and the "narrow-minded petit bourgoisie" [*Spießbürgertum*] should be deliberately excluded from the civic guard, and Gutzkow urgently warned against the "veterans of 1813."

13. *Neue Rheinische Zeitung* 20, 20 June 1848.

14. *Bedenken über den Gesetzes-Entwurf der Volksbewaffnung in Württemberg* (Tübingen, 1848), 9. Instead, "leadership" should be taken on by an "excellent, reasonable, energetic, humane, popular-minded military man," Ibid., 12.

Chapter 28

THE ROLE OF THE MILITARY IN THE EUROPEAN REVOLUTIONS OF 1848

Dieter Langewiesche

The revolution began with the euphoria of a general "springtime of the peoples," as contemporaries called their hopes for a revolutionary solidarity of the peoples of Europe. Victorious, however, turned out to be the counter-revolutionary solidarity of the "old powers," which defeated the revolutions in Germany, Italy, Hungary, and the Ottoman Danubian Principalities with military force.[1] Such an end to the revolution was only possible because the military could be set against it. What role did the military play during the revolution in the European states? How did officers and troops adapt to political changes? The patterns of behavior shown by the military in the European revolution will be examined here but not the military course of the revolutionary and national wars in the two years of revolution.[2]

Let us first look at the situation at the beginning of the revolution. Whoever wished to succeed in the revolution needed the support of the military. This applied equally to revolutionaries and counter-revolutionaries, and in all states. Control of the military was most important in those revolutions whose expectations included the establishment an independent nation-state. This was the case in Germany, Italy, the Habsburg Monarch, and the Danubian Principalities of Moldavia and Wallachia. In Denmark, as well, the future form of the nation-state was an open question.[3] States had to be united, confederations of states broken up, and structures of domination superseded.[4]

For every nation the problems were different, and therefore the paths to national unification were as well. However, no matter which paths were taken, all were bound up with the dangers of national wars of unification and secession. In the nineteenth century, no new nation-state was established peacefully. All emerged from war.[5] In the years of revolution, too, this danger was ever present. A major European war was avoided, but there were national revolutionary wars between Denmark and Germany, in Italy, in the Habsburg Monarchy, and in the Danubian Principalities. Only those who controlled the military could survive them. Therefore, taking control of the military was essential for the institutions emerging from the revolution.

The German national revolution was faced with the dual task of simultaneously amalgamating and separating states. Such a Herculean task had never been achieved peacefully. To master it for the first time was the will of the majority in the Frankfurt National Assembly. When the most powerful German states rejected its conceptions of the nation-state, the deputies were faced with the choice: to give in or to go to war against the princes—above all against the Prussian king and the Austrian emperor. This war could only have been a civil war, as the monarchs still retained control of the military and therefore the provisional central power of the *Reich* did not have any regular troops to set against Prussia and Austria. The majority in the National Assembly recoiled at the idea of a civil war against the armies of the monarchs. Their military impotence is reflected in the step by step disbanding of the Assembly during the campaign for the imperial constitution, as more and more delegates left.

In Hungary, the dual problem of integration and disintegration was different and at the same time more crass, as it was more multifaceted. Integration did not mean tying together individual states, as in Germany and Italy. In Hungary, integration meant settling relations between the Hungarian kingdom and its non-Hungarian nationalities, which formed a majority in the Hungarian kingdom and also sought national independence within the Habsburg Empire in 1848/49. These national conflicts were the rock on which the dream of a "springtime of the people" broke, more completely than in any other European state.

The Hungarians were also faced in other ways with the difficult problem of governmental disintegration in the revolutionary years. The Hungarian kingdom, reformed into a liberal nation-state, had to be placed in a new relationship with the Habsburg Monarchy. Thus, the Hungarian nation was faced with a range of conflicts in the revolution, from which arose those military struggles that characterized the Hungarian Revolution—struggles with the Habsburg state and with the non-Magyar nationalities in the Hungarian kingdom. The military question was, therefore, a cardinal problem for the Hungarian Revolution.

This dominance of military aspects applied, if in another way, for Italy as well. Here the problem of integrating of individual states into an Italian nation-state was inextricably bound with the task of liberating upper Italy—Lombardy and Venetia— from Austrian rule, which, throughout Italy, was generally held to be foreign rule.

The Habsburgs lay at the intersection of all lines of national conflict, as the revolutionary attempts to create a German, Italian and Hungarian nation-state all required smashing the Habsburg multinational empire and leaving an Austrian small state in its ruins. Without the use of military force, this would not have been possible.

Faced with this range of problems, democratic dreams of the European "springtime of the peoples" faded, but it is all the more remarkable that attempts to establish nation-states in Germany, Italy, and Hungary, while setting off limited national wars, did not lead to a pan-European war. Many had feared such a war could break out, and many hoped for such a war to create democratic nation-states with force and violence. Looking back after the experience of two world wars, the accomplishment of preventing a European war can be assessed more positively than many contemporaries of the revolution and also many historians have done.

The variety of problems in the European revolutionary centers created different centers of gravity for the national revolutions. In Italy, the revolution was stamped from the beginning by the national war of liberation against Austria. Therefore the Italian Revolution and the Italian armies crystallized around it, while, unlike in Germany and Hungary, no national parliament as national control center appeared. In Hungary, on the other hand, the two came together. With the Hungarian national assembly and the Hungarian government, central political decision-making bodies with a high level of authority existed from the start. At the same time, conflicts with the Habsburgs and the non-Magyar nationalities forced on the military an important, and, in the course of the revolution, ever more central role. In Germany, on the other hand, the Frankfurt National Assembly, as national point of crystallization, was the focus of national events. Only in the final phase of the revolution, when the Prussian and Austrian monarchs rejected the work of the National Assembly in creating a nation-state, did the military become a center of power.

The revolution began with the humiliation of the military elites. The monarchs did not call on them to oppose the revolutionary movements. These were rather victorious and with surprising ease, as the old powers seemed to capitulate without resistance in February/March 1848. Either they retired completely from the political stage—as in France, where the so-called citizens' king abdicated when the citizens withdrew their trust in him—or they took prominent representatives of reforming powers into the government and bowed to the principle of popular sovereignty by allowing constitutions or liberalizing already existing ones. This occurred in the Italian and German states and also in Hungary, where the April laws seemed to introduce a new era. In those places where there were major violent struggles at the beginning of the revolution, especially in the kingdom of the Two Sicilies, Paris, Vienna, Berlin, Milan and Venice, troops were forced, after a brief resistance, to admit defeat and retreat from the disputed cities. The spontaneous revolutionary popular movement thus seemed to have defeated the standing armies.

This surprising success and its apparent ease blinded both sides. Those threatened with a sudden loss of power reacted with conspiracy theories to explain the unexpected. The revolution, they said, had been planned long in advance in secret and been carried through with strict organization. Within the revolutionary movements, on the other hand, there arose a false sense of security and superiority. The victory seemed complete, and everything else only a question of time. Few recognized at the time that these early victories over regular troops were not military, but political in nature. The insecurity of the political leadership, that, in the beginning, wanted to avoid violence, had led to a rapid retreat of the troops from the capitals.

However, everywhere it was an orderly retreat, that could be reversed at any time as soon as the political climate changed.

The military elite hoped for such a change and worked towards it. Through their defeat, which they attributed to the unnecessary softness of the monarchs, they saw their "honor" injured, and in the coalition that seemed to have formed between monarchs and reformers they saw a threat to their previous leading position in state and society. The brother of the Prussian king recognized the danger that an alienation of the monarch from his officer corps could also have for the dynasties. Disapproving his royal brother's accommodating course towards Berlin revolutionaries, and condemned as the "grapeshot prince" by public opinion, he left for London. He thus eased not only public pressure on the monarchy, but at the same time also presented himself as a guarantee for a continuation of the ruling alliance between the Hohenzollern dynasty and the army officer corps. This alliance had to form the foundation of the Prussian state in the future as well—of this he left no doubt in a letter to the commanding general of the Guard Corps in Berlin, in which he explained his stance in the March fighting and was not sparing in his criticism of the king's orders to withdraw the troops. "The terrible change in circumstances … cannot remain without repercussions for the army … what would then be left of Prussia? … You have rescued untarnished the fame, not only the honor and the fame of the Guard Corps, but of the army from the catastrophe which has engulfed us. For this you will go down forever in history, at least in the history of the Prussian Army!"[6]

The rapid early success of the revolution led to a myth of the barricades, a common phenomenon throughout Europe, that deluded at least a part of the revolutionary movement into believing in the existence of a military strength it did not possess. This became quite obvious when the old political leadership groups, believed to be defeated, recovered from the shock of the first wave of revolutions and showed themselves quite prepared to deploy the regular military in a revolutionary civil war. The first such deployments were in Posen [Poznàn], where Polish volunteer units were forced to bow to the superiority of Prussian troops, and in Cracow, which the Austrian command forced into capitulation through bombardment. In the middle of May, the military in Naples demonstrated its unbroken power. While these battles were not seen by the European revolutionary public as a sign of a general turning point in the balance of power, the defeats experienced by the revolution in June 1848 in Prague and Paris and then in October in Vienna against regular troops were signals received throughout Europe.[7]

Everywhere, insufficiently armed revolutionaries proved to be inferior to a massive deployment of regular troops with their modern arms. The army's artillery destroyed the myth of the barricades in the middle of the first year of revolution. What began in Paris in 1830 had become a pan-European experience, was reinforced at the beginning of the 1848 revolution and then, again in Paris, was destroyed after only a few months, before the eyes of a European public. Only the mother country of the revolution did not yet break away from this myth. In the struggles of the Commune in 1870/71, barricades were again set up in Paris.

Nonetheless, the new message of 1848 was that only those in control of the regular army or those able to set up a military force of sufficient strength and with modern weapons could hope to end a revolution victoriously.

Both paths—gaining command of regular troops or creating new military counter-formations—were tried by the revolutionaries and reform-oriented governments of the revolutionized states of Europe in 1848/49. First, it will shown that the attempt to establish military counter-formations was only partially successful in those places where the revolution was bound up with national wars of liberation, that is, in Italy and especially in Hungary. It failed in France and in the German states.

In Paris, where the fate of the French Revolution of 1848 was twice decided—in February against the monarchy and in June against the social republic—sections of the national guard contributed considerably to the fall of the monarchy and to the defeat of troops stationed in Paris in February 1848. This successful deployment of the Paris national guard was one main reason why everywhere in Europe militant revolutionaries in particular placed their hopes in the formation of militia organizations.[8] This conception of a citizens' army seemed to have demonstrated its superiority over the standing army in February 1848, and further successes in the wave of revolutions of March 1848 must have appeared to the revolutionaries as confirmation of this experience.

Within a few weeks, these illusions burst, and this in two respects. First, the militia formations showed themselves to be militarily inferior wherever political leadership deployed regular troops strategically, as nowhere in Europe could the militias and national guards compete with the fighting power of the standing armies. This was due in part to poor training of the volunteers, and not least to their insufficient arms compared to the regular troops. Second, the fighting power of the militias and national guards suffered from the sociopolitical divisions within the revolutionary movements, as these divisions also found their way into the militia organizations. In many places, the disagreements were so strong that armed citizens faced armed citizens.

The national guards and the militias were bastions of the propertied bourgeoisie in those places where they existed before the revolution, and in the years of revolution, as well, the bourgeois national guard generally sought to exclude petit bourgeois and lower-class circles. Even where this was not successful, sociopolitical gaps in the militia remained. This is shown, for example, in Paris, where national guardsmen fought on both sides of the barricades in the decisive struggle for the "social republic" in June 1848. Differences in arms, which guardsmen usually had to supply themselves, also underlined social divisions. The type of arms was an exact reflection of the social position of the individual militia member. It was not, however, only a conflict of the bourgeoisie and the lower classes. The French government established a Mobile Guard in 1848, whose social composition was similar to that of the June insurgents, against whom they were, however, deployed. The Paris June uprising was thus, seen in military terms, also a struggle of the lower classes against the lower classes.[9]

Even in Hungary, which among all the states affected by the revolution made the most determined efforts to establish a militia, the problems of supplying suitable arms proved insurmountable.[10] The number of conscripted national guardsmen reached its highest level in September 1848 at around 400,000 men, of whom only about 150,000 were halfway trained and even fewer, just some 26,000, were more or less properly armed. At most a third of these 150,000 national guardsmen had rifles; the great majority practiced with wooden rifles. Were they to be sent into battle, their only available weapons were stopgaps, recommended by the Hungarian government: sabers, lances, flails, pitchforks, and scythes beaten straight, which would have done no good against regular troops. This was not unique to Hungary, as weapons proved an insoluble problem for militias and volunteer corps throughout Europe.

Poor weapons and social divisions within the militias and national guards considerably weakened their military fighting power. Decisive for the failure of all attempts to establish militias of equal strength to the regular troops was, however, a reason that has been mentioned at most in passing in many studies on the course of the revolution. In these studies it has been argued that the bourgeois–urban activists of the revolution gambled away their chances because they rejected offers of support from urban lower classes and above all from the rural population, which in all continental states formed the largest share of the population, out of fear of the social demands that were raised from within rural and urban lower class circles. Such a shrinking back from peasant revolutionary potential, which could not be fitted into the objectives of a "bourgeois society," can in fact be demonstrated for Vienna or the Polish revolutionary movement, and especially for Italy.

The Hungarian experience indicates, however, that it would be illusory to assume that it would have been possible in 1848/49 to quickly raise a popular army that also included the rural population, even if the revolutionary leadership had so desired. In Hungary, where, unlike in Germany, Austria, France, and Italy, the national guard was organized centrally at the state level, it can be seen that starting in April 1848, especially the rural population was very reserved toward, or openly rejected, the raising of a militia. For this attitude, two causes are decisive, which urban activists of the revolution hardly recognized, or did so only very late.

The "Hungarian peasants and the peasants of the nationalities," who had only recently been relieved of at least part of their feudal burdens, distrusted "a national guard organized by the lords." They saw it as "a new type of tax, a sort of poll-tax."[11] When many of the well-off bought substitutes for their military service, parts of the Hungarian rural population saw this as a further symptom of a continuation of the old, hated recruiting practices of the monarchy. Local authorities sought to overcome these difficulties in relieving national guardsmen drafted into camp service in short intervals of two to four weeks. This rapid change accommodated the living conditions of the rural population, who could not afford to be away from their workplaces for a longer period of time—for this reason, recruitment for the national guard in the months of the agricultural year was especially difficult. However, at the same time a rapid turnover in personnel hindered the development of an effective militia.

A further cause for peasant aversion to service in the militia lay in the rural population being insufficiently included in the process of inner nation-building.[12] As long as the world of the peasants and agricultural workers remained restricted to the village and their horizons ended at the village borders, the rural population was not fully integrated in an idea of the nation for which one was prepared, if necessary, to take on voluntarily oppressive burdens such as armed service. The possibility of establishing a militia as an effective counterforce to the regular armies, of creating a people in arms as a democratic alternative to the existing armies of the princes, hardly existed, given the level of social development in 1848/49 on the European continent. This is true not only for Hungary, but also for Italy, Germany, and even for France.[13] In this respect, Switzerland provided the exception.[14] The socially conditioned hurdle faced by the establishment of national militias in 1848/49, should, therefore, be much more highly rated than is generally the case in the literature—higher, at least, than an alleged "failure" of the revolutionaries in the task of countering armed revolutionary opponents with a popular revolutionary army. Such judgments, that speak of "failure" or even "betrayal" contain a very large dose of illusionary misjudgment of existing potential.

The regular troops could be used as a counter-revolutionary force, but they were certainly not immune to the revolution's attraction. Among the Italian units in the Austrian army in Italy, there were so many desertions that these units were almost totally disbanded. In Baden, troops proved to be so receptive to the revolutionary movement and its ideas that the army was rebuilt from scratch after the revolution. All active and retired officers of the Baden army had to appear before a tribunal from October 1849. Every seventh officer was convicted.[15]

Soldiers used the freedoms created by the revolution. They held meetings, petitioned for better treatment and higher pay, and wore revolutionary symbols. This, however, did not lead to an epidemic of military disobedience. Mass refusal to follow orders only occurred when the soldiers recognized that the "authority" established by the revolution was accepted by a large part of the population. This was the case in Hungary, Italy, and in the last phase of the revolution in Baden. Regular troops did not, however, ally themselves with volunteers, who only found support among a minority of the population. In France, loyalty of the soldiers towards the government of the revolutionary years was reinforced by the cult of Napoleon, which was propagated specifically in the army from the end of 1848 onwards.

When the army was deployed against insurgents, the soldiers did not necessarily have to feel that they were fighting on the side of the counter-revolution. Their actions against the June uprising in Paris were presented by their officers as a struggle by the young republic against its enemies. Things were not different in Germany. When the new imperial military was deployed against insurgents, the soldiers could follow their orders in the conviction that they were fighting for the revolution as represented by the national assembly and the provisional central powers.

Even in the final phase of the German Revolution, in the so-called campaign for the imperial constitution,[16] both sides claimed to be in the service of the new order created by the revolution. Revolutionaries in Baden, Saxony, and the Palatinate fought, gun in hand, to defend the imperial constitution, which was intended as the revolution's permanent home, against refractory princes. The soldiers they faced were told, on the other hand, that they were fighting against anarchy in order to defend the "accomplishments of March." In an appeal on 17 May 1849, for example, the Württemberg ministry of defense struck the pose of defender of the revolution: "People of Württemberg! The king, government and the people stand firmly and steadfast behind the liberties guaranteed in the state and imperial constitutions—which we also recognize and, where necessary, will protect and defend with armed force as laws equally binding for all." Soldiers were promised by the ministerial appeal that "You will never be ordered to take actions which are against the law: I guarantee that with my responsibility!—never acts which are not in agreement with the duties of both citizen and soldier."[17]

Throughout Europe, regular troops remained capable of military action in spite of the deep political and social conflicts that divided the nations in the years of revolution. In other words, the troops subordinated themselves to the political leadership of their respective states. Where such leadership was revolutionary or adapted to the revolutionary movement, as in the leading Italian power of Piedmont-Savoy, or as in Hungary or, initially, in Prussia as well, regular troops fought for the aims of the revolutionary movement. When the leadership was counter-revolutionary, as in France from the middle of 1848 or in Prussia from the autumn of that year, and as in the Habsburg Monarchy and in Russia, the troops fought against the revolution. Circumstances were most difficult for the army in Hungary because of conflicts of loyalty between the counter-revolutionary actions of the Habsburg Monarchy, the national revolutionary government of the Hungarian Kingdom, and the national movements of non-Magyar nationalities in the kingdom of Hungary.

More realistic than the establishment of militias as a counterweight to the regular armies were attempts at subordinating existing troops to the command of the revolutionary governments. Such attempts will be sketched here in a comparison between Germany, Italy, and Hungary. In France, there was no struggle for the loyalty of the army, which always obeyed the government in power. Whether it would have continued in its obedience if the "red republicans" had taken power is an open question.

In Italy, command of the army remained with the princes and governments of the individual states, as no national central power existed and none could be established, in spite of various attempts. The point of unification for the Italian nationalist movement was, therefore, not in a national parliament, but on the battlefields in the struggle against the Austrian army. From the beginning, the kingdom of Piedmont-Savoy took on a leading role in this struggle. Even before the revolution, it had become the center of national hopes and had the strongest army of all the Italian states.

The early victories of the revolution against Austria were won by the popular movements in Milan and Venice. However, the kingdom of Piedmont-Savoy became the leading power as its army seemed to offer the only guarantee against the initially beaten, but not permanently defeated Austrian army. Referendums in Lombardy and Venice decided for the unification of these regions with the Piedmontese kingdom, so that a bloc of states under a monarchical head of state arose in the first year of revolution. It, therefore, inherited the task of extending the process of the formation of an Italian nation-state into central and southern Italy while at the same time providing a defense against the Austrians.

In neither task was it successful. For this, there are many reasons. One lay in Piedmont-Savoy's military weakness. In the defeat of Italian troops by the Austrian army under Radetzky in the battle of Custozza in July 1848, these weaknesses became apparent. They were not only due to the incompetence of Italian military leadership, as is often emphasized in the literature, as important as that was for this and the other defeats that followed. Exacerbating this handicap was a decision by the Italian nationalist movement to force national unification under the protection of the Piedmontese army. This decision implied a central domestic policy choice that restricted the possibilities of the Italian nationalist to act against Austria. When the majority of the Italian unity movement placed its hopes for a nation-state in Piedmont-Savoy in 1848, it also decided for a monarchy as the form of government for the future Italian nation-state, while republican concepts, which were also circulating, were rejected. The choice of monarchy meant, at the same time, that only very limited social reforms were achieved, which were unsatisfactory especially for the rural population, who expected an end to feudal burdens and significant land reform from the revolution.

Radetzky, commander of the Austrian army in Italy, came closer to the social hopes of the rural population in his proclamation than the Italian governments and the bourgeois leadership of the Italian nationalist movement.[18] This contributed considerably to the Austrian army's being able to overcome its initial weaknesses in Italy. In this respect, just as in Hungary and Germany, it is evident that the rural population could not identify with the abstract demand for a democratic nation-state if it did not also include sweeping social reforms. That made a counterattack easier for Austria, and made it more difficult for the Italian army to gain active support from the ranks of the rural population.

Another decision was also made when the Italian nationalist movement handed the Piedmontese army the leading role. The chances for military cooperation between the French republic and the Italian nationalist movement, which still appeared possible in mid-1848, were put to an end when a royal army commander became the head of the national revolution. When the conservative transformation of the French Revolution was sealed by the failure of the Paris June uprising, there was no chance left of French armed assistance for European national movements.[19]

In Germany, the problem of the power of command over the armed forces was different than it was in Italy. While the majority in the Frankfurt National Assembly rejected the democrats' preferred solution of creating a people's army, the German central parliament attempted to bring the armies of the individual states under its command in the middle of the first year of revolution. It ordered the soldiers in the armies of the individual states to take an oath of loyalty to the imperial regent, the provisional head of state of the not-yet established German nation-state. This attempt by the Frankfurt *Paulskirche* to withdraw command of the armies from the individual monarchs by a parliamentary vote and thus to weaken irreparably the position of the old political elite, failed, however, as the two most important German states, Austria and Prussia, rejected such an oath of loyalty to the imperial regent for their armies. The German Central Power therefore remained, in terms of power politics, at the mercy of the individual states—especially Prussia and Austria.

When these two states rejected the will of the German Central Power, as happened in the German-Danish conflict over Schleswig and Holstein and in the fighting in Vienna in October 1848, this was decisive for the fate of the Austrian Revolution, and the German Central Power was faced with the alternative of submitting itself to the dictates of Prussia and Austria or of appealing to the population's readiness to revolt. As the Frankfurt National Assembly and the imperial government were reluctant to make such a revolutionary appeal, they had to bow to the will of the main German powers in conflict situations. This impotence was drastically exposed in the autumn of 1848 when the Austrian authorities allowed the execution of Robert Blum, deputy to the Frankfurt National Assembly, because of his participation in the Viennese October Revolution, in spite of protests by the National Assembly and the imperial government. As the German Central Power did not have an army and rejected revolutionary force, it could only counter this public demonstration of the superior military power of Austria with moral protests.

The Viennese revolutionaries clearly recognized this situation. In October 1848, therefore, they did not look to Frankfurt, to the National Assembly, which could only oppose Austrian troops with political and moral warnings, but hoped instead for military assistance against the Habsburg Monarchy from Hungary. Only the Hungarian government and the Hungarian National Assembly had proven able to reinforce their authority militarily in 1848. On the one hand, they established their own people's army from the autumn of 1848, the Honvéd Army, which absorbed the Hungarian national guard. Above all, however, they gained control over the Hungarian troops of the regular Habsburg army. Hence, a completely different situation arose in Hungary than in Germany. The Hungarian central power was not faced with the alternative: call for a civil war or capitulate to the military force of the counter-revolution. They could oppose the counter-revolution's attack on the national revolution with the fighting ability of a national army. Nonetheless, the Hungarian revolutionary government was also faced with a range of military and military policy problems, only a few of which can be briefly described here.

The complicated military policy situation in Hungary was defined by the varying constitutional relations between the Habsburg royal government and the Hungarian Kingdom, which had become de facto an autonomous state with the emperor's recognition of the April laws of 1848. It thus had control over government functions that had previously been reserved for the Habsburg central administration in Vienna: foreign policy, finances, and the armed forces For the military, there existed from April onwards two high commands: the imperial and the Hungarian, under the Hungarian minister of war. The exact form of this relationship was not defined in the April laws, and was determined by the political and military course of the revolution.

The most significant breach in the military command of the Hungarian government was the appointment of the Croatian nationalist, Jelačić, as governor (Banus) of Croatia-Slovenia. In so doing, the Habsburg court severely restricted Hungary's area of military authority, as Jelačić refused to subordinate himself to the Hungarian government.[20]

As long as Austrian positions in Poland and Italy were under pressure, the Austrian government accommodated Hungarian desires for autonomy. Jelačić's removal from office, however, remained simply a verbal concession to Hungary. It was never put into practice. When the Prague uprising was suppressed and the Italian army defeated, the Austrian counter-offensive began in Hungary as well. Jelačić was officially restored to his office, the autonomy concessions sanctioned in April retracted and, in September, the nearly one-year long national war began, with an invasion of Hungary by Croatian troops under Jelačić. It only ended in August 1849, after Russian troops had moved in to support Austria, with the destruction of the Hungarian Revolution.

In the Hungarian national war, two problems can be recognized that were not unique to the revolutionary national movements in the Habsburg multinational Empire. They could not be solved in the other European revolutions as well.

Apart from France, popular loyalty to the hereditary ruling houses proved to be so effective in all the revolutionized European states that revolutionary restructuring was only possible to a certain degree. Even in Hungary, where the break with the Habsburg Monarchy was obvious from September-October 1848 onwards, the leaders of the revolution long maintained the fiction of a "legal revolution," authorized by the Habsburg Emperor and the Hungarian King. The major military successes of the Hungarian general Arthur Görgey, which brought the Habsburgs to the brink of defeat, were due not least to Görgey's sticking closest to the original Hungarian conception. The Hungarian national war had as its aim the defense of the country and simultaneously the defense of the Habsburg Emperor and the Hungarian King against his enemies.[21]

Görgey's maintenance of the fiction of also defending the rights of Emperor Ferdinand, forced by the Habsburg court to abdicate in December 1848 in his fight against the Austrian army, ensured the loyalty of countless soldiers and officers in the regular army during the struggle against the Habsburg counter-revolution. This long preservation of the idea that the national Hungarian Revolution was taking place under the protection of the will of the emperor, as manifested in the April laws of 1848, on the other hand, forced on the Hungarian leadership considerations that contributed to a weakening of the Hungarian nationalist movement's ability to act itself. Included here is above all the Hungarian government's hesitation in recalling Hungarian troops serving in Italy,[22] as well as the Hungarian army's caution in carrying out military action beyond the country's borders. Both proved to be militarily disastrous.

The Hungarian units in Italy strengthened the Austrian position there and allowed the Habsburg leadership to concentrate militarily on Hungary. Hungary's attempt, too little and too late, to provide the Viennese revolutionaries the assistance they asked for in October 1848,[23] sealed the defeat of the revolution in German Austria. Thus the Hungarian Revolution was completely isolated in Europe. The Frankfurt National Assembly did not come into question as a potential ally because of its military impotence; in Italy the final defeat of the revolutionary national movement was only a matter of time; and the French republic had long become conservative. It took part in the military liquidation of the Italian Revolution in 1849 in the struggle against the Roman Republic. Great Britain, as well, was not a potential ally, as the British government viewed a continued existence of the Habsburgs as indispensable for the European balance of power.

This isolation of Hungary in Europe characterizes in general the European scene of the years of revolution. While the revolutionary and nationalist movements supported each other at most through verbal declarations of sympathy, but often—especially in Hungary—actively fought one another, the old leadership, aiming to preserve existing order, proved capable of overcoming its, in part, contrasting interests in favor of an active anti-revolutionary emergency organization.[24] Command of the military was the most important pillar of this emergency alliance of the European counter-revolution.

Notes

1. This is only one aspect of the vast subject of "counter-revolution," whose range Roger Price explores elsewhere in this volume.

2. For the following, see esp. Sabrina Müller, "Soldaten in der deutschen Revolution von 1848/49" (Ph.D. Diss., Munich, 1996), with extensive literature for Germany; *Handbuch der deutschen Militärgeschichte 1648-1939,* pt. 4/1 (Munich, 1975), pt. 4/2, (Munich, 1976); P. Pieri, *Storia militare del Risorgimento* (Turin, 1962); Alan Sked, *The Survival of the Habsburg Empire: Radetzky, the Imperial Army and the Class War, 1848* (London and New York, 1979); K. Sitzler, *Solidarität oder Söldnertum. Die ausländischen Freiwilligenverbände im ungarischen Unabhängigkeitskreig 1848-49* (Osnabrück, 1980); F. Hauptmann, *Jellačić's Kriegszug nach Ungarn 1848,* 2 vols. (Graz, 1875). Informative on the course of events, although dogmatic in their interpretation, see Heinz Helmert and Hans-Jürgen Usczeck, *Bewaffnete Volkskämpfe in Europa 1848/49* (East Berlin, 1973). See also my essay on which this chapter is based: Dieter Langewiesche, "Die Rolle des Militärs in den europäischen Revolutionen von 1848/49," in W. Bachofer and H. Fischer (eds.), *Ungarn—Deutschland, Studien zu Sprache, Kultur, Geographie und Geschichte* (Munich, 1983), 273-88 as well as other contributions in this volume, esp. on Poland (Hans-Henning Hahn, chapter 7), the Habsburg Monarchy (Jiři Kořalka, chapter 6), the Danubian principalities (Lothar Maier, chapter 8), and Denmark (Steen Bo Frandsen, chapter 12).

3. More exact information can be found in the essays on the respective countries in this volume.

4. From these tasks, Theodore Schieder developed a typology of the establishment of a nation-state. His essays on this are available in one volume: Theodor Schieder, *Nationalismus und Nationalstaat.*

Studien zum nationalen Problem im modernen Europa, ed. by Otto Dann and Hans-Ulrich Wehler (Göttingen, 1991, 1992).

5. See Dieter Langewiesche, *Nationalismus im 19. und 20. Jahrhundert: zwischen Partizipation und Aggression* (Bonn-Bad Godesberg, 1994).

6. Letter of 21 April 1848 in Karl Ludwig von Prittwitz, *Berlin 1848. Das Erinnerungswerk des Generalleutnants Karl Ludwig von Prittwitz und andere Quellen zur Berliner Märzrevolution und zur Geschichte Preußens um die Mitte des 19. Jahrhunderts*, edited and introduced by G. Heinrich (Berlin and New York, 1985), 488-89. This extensive apologia is based on the reports put together by Prittwitz on the fighting in Berlin on 18 and 19 March and sent to the Prince of Prussia in London (xvii).

7. Apart from the literature cited in n. 1, see, for Prague, Stanley Z. Pech, *The Czech Revolution of 1848* (Chapel Hill, 1968); on Vienna, Wolfgang Häusler, *Von der Massenarmut zur Arbeiterbewegung. Demokratie und soziale Frage in der Wiener Revolution von 1848* (Vienna, 1979); for Paris, Roger Price, *The French Second Republic* (London, 1972); Charles Tilly and Lynn H. Lees, "The People of June, 1848," in Roger Price (ed.), *Revolution and Reaction: 1848 and the Second French Republic* (London, 1975), 170-209. In Moldavia, the prince deployed private troops, especially from Albania, against the revolutionaries at the beginning of April. See Lothar Maier's chapter, in this volume. A brief European overview can be found in Geoffrey Best, *War and Society in Revolutionary Europe, 1770-1848* (Leicester, 1982), 273ff.

8. See the essay by Rolf Pröve (chapter 27) and the references in the essay on Poland (Hans-Henning Hahn, chapter 7), Moldavia and Wallachia (Lothar Maier, chapter 8), and Lyon-Hamburg (John Breuilly and Iorweth Prothero, Chapter 16) in this volume.

9. On Paris, see Price, *The French Second Republic*, (n. 7), as well as Tilly and Lees, "The People of June 1848," (n. 7). Concerning the various armed formations in Paris, see P. O'Brian, "The Revolutionary Police of 1848," in Price (ed.), *Revolution and Reaction* (n. 7), 133-49; see also J.M. House, "Civil-Military Relations in Paris 1848," in ibid., 150-69. On Germany and France see the essay by Pröve (chapter 27) in this volume. In Vienna, where, apart from the student Academic Legion, there was a militia in which divisions among the bourgeoisie were often reflected, workers could only arm themselves after the storming of the arsenal in October 1848; Häusler *Von der Massenarmut*, (n.4), 385.

10. A. Urbán, "Die Organisierung des Heeres der ungarischen Revolution vom Jahre 1848," *Annales Universitatis Scientiarum Budapestinensis De Rolando Eötvös Nominatae, Sectio Historica* 9 (1967): 105ff; 13 (1972): 159ff.

11. Ibid., 111. Recruitment for the national guard was most successful in the "larger market regions of the Hungarian plain" (ibid.). The following points are also based on this.

12. A review of the current state of research is provided in Dieter Langewiesche, "Nation, Nationalismus, Nationalstaat: Forschungsstand und Forschungsperspektiven," *Neue Politische Literatur* 40 (1995): 190-236. On the peasants and the agrarian movements in the revolution, see the essays by Christoph Dipper (chapter 18) and Wolfgang Höpken (chapter 19) in this volume.

13. That the French Revolution, initially successful in Paris, failed not least on resistance in the provinces, has been convincingly demonstrated in the research. The example of France also shows, however, that the republicans were able to mobilize the rural population, as seen in the uprising against the coup at the end of 1851. The political mobilization via the larger cities took time, however, which was not available to the revolutionaries. The significance of the factor of time certainly deserves attention in order to avoid forming illusory ideals in retrospect. See the contributions of Pierre Lévêque (chapter 4) and Christoph Dipper (chapter 18) in this volume. On the uprising of 1851 in France and the role of the provinces in it, see especially Ted W. Margadant *French Peasants in Revolt: The Insurrection of 1851*, (Princeton, 1979). It should be remembered that the Habsburg court retreated to the provinces when the situation in Vienna worsened.

14. See the essay by Thomas Christian Müller (chapter 9) in this volume, and R. Jaun, "Vom Bürger-Militär zum Soldaten-Bürger: Die Schweiz im 19. Jahrhundert," in Ute Frevert (ed.), *Militär und Gesellschaft im 19. und 20. Jahrhundert* (Stuttgart, 1997), 48-77.

15. K.-H. Lutz, *Das badische Offizierskorps 1840-1870/71* (Stuttgart, 1996). See also on Baden and for the following esp. Müller, "Soldaten in der deutschen Revolution," (n. 2)

16. See the essay on Germany by Dieter Langewiesche (chapter 5) in this volume.

17. Cited in Müller, "Soldaten in der deutschen Revolution," (n. 2), 138.

18. See Sked, *The Survival of the Habsburg Empire*, (n. 2).

19. See James Chastain, *The Liberation of Sovereign Peoples. The French Foreign Policy of 1848* (Athens, OH, 1988).

20. The national rivalries are analyzed in all studies of the revolution in the Hungarian half of the empire and often the subject of controversy. See, apart from the works mentioned in n. 2, G. Handlery, "Revolutionary Organization in the Context of Backwardness: Hungary's 1848," *East European Quarterly* 6 (1972): 44-61; Z. Tóth, "The Nationality Problem in Hungary in 1848-49," *Acta Historica Academiae Scientiarum Hungaricae* 4 (1955): 235-77; by the same author, "Quelques problèmes de l'état multinational dans la Hongrie d'avant 1848," ibid., 123-49; numerous quotations of sources, translated from Hungarian, are found in I. Barta, "Die Anführer des ungarischen Freiheitskampfes und die Wiener Oktoberrevolution," ibid., 1 (1952): 325-85; Gunther E. Rothenberg, *The Military Border in Croatia 1740-1881* (Chicago, 1966); P. Bödy, "Joseph Eötvös and the Modernization of Hungary 1840-1870," *Transactions of the American Philosophical Society*, N. S. 62, Part 2 (1972): 5-133, esp., chapters 4-5, 46-74; B.C. Fryer, "Balcescu and the National Question in 1849," *East European Quarterly* 12 (1978): 189-208; D. Ghermani, "Sozialer und nationaler Faktor der siebenbürgischen Revolution von 1848 bis 1849 in der Sicht der rumänischen Geschichtswissenschaft nach 1945," *Ungarnjahrbuch* 2 (1970): 108-29; C. Daicoviciu and M. Constantinescu (eds.), *Brève histoire de la Transylvanie* (Bucharest, 1965), chapter 6; J. D. Sucin, "Rumänen und Serben in der Revolution des Jahres 1848 in Banat," *Revue des Études Sud-Est Européennes* 6 (1968): 609-24; E. Arató, "Die Wirkung des Nationalismus auf die Politik der Kräfte der Linken in Österreich und in Ungarn im Frühjahr und im Sommer 1848," *Annales. ... Budapestinensis* 13 (1972): 103-58; by the same author, "Die Bauernbewegungen und der Nationalismus in Ungarn im Frühling und Sommer 1848," ibid., 9 (1967): 61-103; J. Šidak, "The Peasant Question in Croatian Politics of 1848," *Acta Jugoslaviae Historica* 1 (1970): 85-116.

21. See, with further literature, Istvan Deak, "An Army Divided: The Loyalty Crisis of the Habsburg Officer Corps in 1848-49," *Jahrbuch des Instituts für Deutsche Geschichte* 8 (1979): 207-41; and his *The Lawful Revolution. Louis Kossuth and the Hungarians, 1848-1849* (New York, 1979). Görgey's place in Hungarian history is very controversial among Hungarian historians.

22. See Sked, *Survival of the Habsburg Monarchy*, (n. 2).

23. See Wolfgang Häusler, *Das Gefecht bei Schwechat am 30. Oktober 1848* (Vienna, 1977). An extensive range of literature of various viewpoints exists on this point.

24. That the revolution nonetheless meant a deep break in the European system of power has been demonstrated in the more recent literature. Fundamental is Paul W. Schroeder, *The Transformation of European Politics 1763-1848* (Oxford, 1994); brief sketches are provided in the essays by Schroeder, Hans-Hening Hahn, and Anselm Doering-Manteuffel in Peter Krüger (ed.), *Das Europäische Staatensystem im Wandel. Strukturelle Bedingungen und bewegende Kräfte seit der Frühen Neuzeit* (Munich, 1996).

Chapter 29

CHURCHES, THE FAITHFUL, AND THE POLITICS OF RELIGION IN THE REVOLUTION OF 1848

Jonathan Sperber

The shattering of the established order and the rapid transition to a period of greatly expanded political participation in the spring of 1848 would have a substantial effect on the churches and their faithful, although in varied, complex, and often contradictory ways. At the same time, churches and the confessional loyalties and antagonisms that radiated out from them would play a significant role in the course of the 1848 revolution. These two themes, the influence of the revolution on the churches and the influence of the churches on the revolution, will form the basis for considerations in this chapter. Each of these main themes requires some differentiation and refinement.[1]

Most obviously, the revolution brought with it the potential for important changes in church-state relations. Before 1848, most churches were financially supported by the state and exercised power over, for instance, education or marriage, in the name of the state. Such basic civic rights as existed in much of Europe (admittedly, with important exceptions for France and the Low Countries) were connected to membership in an established church. However, this establishment was a two-way street: established churches were also under a greater or lesser (usually greater) degree of state control, the authorities appointing clergy, controlling or at least exercising surveillance over their education and training, and making their influence felt in both administrative and doctrinal aspects of organized religion. Consequently, one of the main religious issues in the 1848 revolution—and, actually, one of the more important issues overall—was the reordering of this relationship. Contemporaries spoke about the independence of the church from the state, meaning a constitutionally defined autonomous position for the established churches, giving them the power and right to administer themselves without special government interference. They also debated the separation of church and state: the restriction or abolition of the role of the church in public education and the ratification and registration of vital events, or the delinking of church membership and citizens' rights.

The revolutionary impulses toward freedom, equality, political participation and representation did not stop at church-state relations, but reverberated within the churches as well. The year 1848 saw demands for a dismantling of hierarchy and a more democratic form of church governance, whether just among the clergy, or including clergy and laity. Centered on the holding of synods or church councils, such demands quickly involved other elements of religious and political life. The state's authority was invoked, thus bringing in the question of church-state relations, since changes in the structure of an established church would require governmental action. Doctrinal and theological controversies, particularly the decades-long clash between rationalists and the neo-orthodox, were mixed with demands for restructuring of the church as well.

Not all churches were established ones. The 1848 revolution would mark a high point for sects, free churches, and more informal gatherings of heterodox religious elements. Such groups had much smaller memberships than the established churches, but the ranks of their adherents had been growing rapidly in the 1840s, and the revolution's potential to shatter existing institutions seemed to offer them an opportunity to challenge their official counterparts. At the very least, these sects and free churches were an important part of the revolutionary scene.

This last consideration already points toward the other main theme of the chapter, the influence of the churches and religion on the revolution. There are two items that might be stressed here. First is a consideration of the role of the clergy in the emergent mass politics of the mid-nineteenth-century revolution. The rapid introduction of a democratic suffrage in most of Europe during the spring of 1848 without the prior existence of well established forms of political organization, such as a mass press or organized political parties, would place a premium on the actions of locally influential men. Priests and pastors fit this description to a greater extent than perhaps any other group.

Secondly, the confessional loyalties and antagonisms associated with the attachment of the faithful to their churches would also play a major role in the politics of the revolution. The 1848 revolution would see the first efforts at the creation of clerical political associations and nascent political parties, sometimes with the assistance of the clergy, sometimes, paradoxically, in opposition to them. Confessional loyalties would also prove important in determining popular responses to major political issues, even ones that were not necessarily explicitly religious in nature. Without wishing to weigh the significance of religious loyalties against other factors in mid-century political life, such as class or nationality, I would say that for a long time historians have not given confessional identities and the political choices stemming from them the attention they deserve.

These five issues—the relationship between church and state, the question of the governance of the churches, the role of sects and free churches, the political activities of the clergy, and the importance of religious loyalties for the politics of the revolution—will be considered in this chapter. I will discuss each of them broadly, taking examples from across the European continent, and conclude with some general observations about the place of religion in the 1848 revolution and the place of the 1848 revolution in the history of religion.

Church and State

Freedom was a major political theme of the 1848 revolution, and the Catholic Church chimed in this chorus by raising the demand for "religious freedom." This demand was widely and broadly formulated from the Italian peninsula to the Hungarian plain, articulated in episcopal memoranda, programs of political clubs, and parliamentary caucuses, in parliaments, the press, and at public meetings, by bishops and the lower clergy, as well as by laymen organized in "Pius Associations for Religious Freedom." Although the exact content of these demands varied from country to country, given the different, prerevolutionary legal circumstances, they typically referred to an end to government control, restrictions or inspection in four areas: (1) the public exercise of religious functions taking place outside of normal church services, such as pilgrimages, processions, or the missions of the Jesuits and the Redemptorists; (2) the admission and establishment of religious orders; (3) the working of the church hierarchy, including such matters as correspondence of the bishops with the Pope, the holding of meetings and conferences among members of the episcopate, the publication and dissemination of pastoral letters, the administration of parish and diocesan property, or the education and appointment of the parish clergy; (4) the role of the church in education.

The effect of such demands was strengthened by the broad support they received, both from the clergy and the faithful. While some skepticism toward these demands did surface, particularly among priests with rationalist ideas, the proponents of state control were never able to organize themselves or to articulate their views effectively. The initiatives toward "religious freedom" were largely successful, the hierarchy of the Catholic Church emerging from both the revolution and the reaction to it in a strengthened and more autonomous position.

The situation among Protestants was quite different, not surprisingly, given the history of a close connection between Protestant Churches and the state. Especially if there was a Protestant monarch and/or a majority Protestant population, calls for greater autonomy for the church were limited to a relatively small group of both pastors and laypeople, typically those with theologically liberal and rationalist ideas. Yet even in Bavaria, one of the few places in Europe where a substantial Protestant population lived under the rule of a Catholic dynasty, the Protestant proponents of independence from the state could make no headway during the revolutionary period, either in parliament or in church synods. The one quite interesting exception to this attitude was in Hungary, where Protestant support for a continued and even expanded autonomy for their church—or, more precisely churches, since

Lutherans, Calvinists and Unitarians were all recognized and established churches in the Hungarian lands of the Habsburg Monarchy—went along with sympathies for an increasingly revolutionary regime that sought to put an end to the privileged power of the Catholic Church as part of its broader program of autonomy within or, ultimately, sought independence from the Catholic Habsburg Dynasty. Smaller, unrecognized churches, such as the Eastern Orthodox in Transylvania, with its Rumanian faithful, were not so much interested in independence (freedom from government control) as in establishment, the ability to receive funds and authority from the government, enjoyed by the more favored Christian confessions, whose members were among the ruling elites, both of the Habsburg regime and of its revolutionary Hungarian opponent.

In February–March 1848, the early phase of the revolution, when emotional enthusiasm and the mystique of freedom were at their height, and different political conceptions, or the groups that articulated them, were still poorly developed, Catholics interpreted freedom of religion as the separation of church and state. The first Catholic political club in Germany, the Mainz Pius Association, described its goal in those terms. Cardinal de Bonauld, Archbishop of Lyon, rallied his clergy to the newly proclaimed French republic at the end of February 1848 by noting "You often used to long for that liberty which makes our brothers in the United States of America so happy. This liberty will now be yours."[2] It did not take long, however, for the negative side of such an approach to become apparent: separation of church and state might liberate the Catholic Church from the heavy hand of state interference, but it would also mean an end to the state's helping hand, in financial and legal matters. Consequently, both clergy and lay activists began to prefer another conception, involving the best of both worlds: retaining the church's legal privileges and financial support, while rejecting any government interference. To describe this state of affairs, they sometimes used a new expression, "independence of the church from the state," and sometimes continued to talk, as previously, about the separation of church and state.

This viewpoint created a potential conflict, since other political forces, particularly the democrats, but more moderate liberals as well, pressed for the separation of church and state. In a conceptually confusing way, although also one characteristic of political discourse in the mid-nineteenth century, they often used the phrase "independence of the church from the state" to describe what they demanded, especially in appealing to a Catholic population. However, the content of this left-of-center agenda was quite different: an end to privileges for established religions, the equality of members of all confessions before the law, and the creation of an essentially secular notion of citizenship. The resulting clash of political agendas provided a problem that parliaments and constituent assemblies in 1848/49 had to resolve.

Historians might wonder, as contemporaries did, whether two such opposing conceptions of the relationship between church and state could be reconciled. In part, this proved possible. Catholics could generally accept equality of confessions, and a secular citizenship, although for activists in southern Germany and the Habsburg Monarchy the emancipation of Jews involved in such new constitutional

712 | *Jonathan Sperber*

arrangements proved hard to swallow. Even the introduction of civil marriage, practiced for decades in France and other predominantly Catholic regions living under the Napoleonic Code, was something that the clergy could live with.

Radicals were more reluctant to accept that state power could not alter the church hierarchy, an attitude seen in the motion of the extreme left of the German National Assembly calling for the abolition of clerical celibacy. The revolutionary government of independent Hungary did try to restructure the church hierarchy or, perhaps more precisely, endorse dissident clergy and laity in their efforts to do so. Yet leftists attempting to attract support in Italy, the Rhineland, and other heavily Catholic regions, could sometimes play down their hostility to the hierarchy for pragmatic reasons, and moderate liberals, such as the once anticlerical Orléanists in France, were even more willing to come to terms with the official church.

There was one area, namely education, where the two conceptions of church-state relations proved to be terminally at odds. To its proponents, separation of church and state implied a secular public school system, with church influence limited, at most, to religious instruction. The combination of establishment and autonomy that proponents of independence of the church from the state desired presented an opposite position: for them, control or at least supervision of public education was as basic to the church as appointments to parishes or administration of diocesan property, so that a secular or even state-controlled school system would be a violation of religious freedom.

This issue of education was the true storm center of the explicit politics of religion in the mid-century revolution. More petitions concerning freedom of religion were submitted to the Frankfurt National Assembly than any other kind, and relations between church and school were constantly present in them, indeed often the occasion for them to be gathered in the first place. While Catholics made up a large majority of the petitioners, there were also tens of thousands of Protestants who submitted similar ones, generally from the ranks of the Pietists and other neo-orthodox Protestants whose thinking about church-state relations was often strikingly similar to that of most Catholics. Church control over education—or, more precisely, over the funds used to finance it—was the main issue for Hungarian Catholics in their often stormy relations with the government in Budapest during 1848/49.

Nowhere, though, was the result of such clerical politics more remarkable than in France, where the Loi Falloux of 1850 (named after the Catholic-conservative politician, Armand de Falloux, Minister of Education in 1849) actually rolled back to a certain extent the secularization of education carried out in the two decades following 1789, granting the church more influence in the administration and inspection of public education, encouraging the use of teaching orders in the public schools, and repealing most limitations on the creation of private, church schools. The passage of this legislation, with the support of once anticlerical liberals, who saw an increased influence of the church on the lower classes via the educational system as a necessity to stem the tide of radicalism and socialism, marked a high point for efforts of the church in the educational arena.

In the end, of the two versions of the restructuring of church-state relations, it was independence that won out over separation. The latter cause was closely connected to revolutionary projects, such as the Roman Republic, the independent Hungarian regime, the German constitution of the Frankfurt National Assembly, or the Kremsier constitution drawn up by the Austrian Constituent Assembly, that did not survive the great confrontations between revolution and counter-revolution during the spring and summer of 1849. A few remnants of separation outlasted the revolutionary period, particularly the creation of a secular citizenship found in the 1848 constitutions of Prussia or Piedmont-Savoy, but on such issues as the introduction of civil marriage, or, most crucially, the connection between church and school, the adherents of separation obtained nothing of what they wished.

The situation was precisely reversed for the supporters of independence, of establishment plus autonomy. The converse to the defeat of the revolutionary project of separation of church and state was the retention of the established position of the churches: the Catholic Church and, frequently, its Protestant counterparts, kept its influence over public education, or even, as in France, extended it, while averting the introduction of civil marriage. Some peculiar links between confession and civic rights, such as "the unity of faith of the *Land* Tyrol," which is the prohibition on non-Catholics from settling there, remained as well. However, almost everywhere—liberal Piedmont-Savoy in Italy, a rare exception—the defeat of the revolutionary movement did not mean an end to the demands expressed at the beginning of the revolution for "freedom of religion." Quite the opposite, on such issues as correspondence of the bishops with Rome, the establishment and activities of religious orders, or the education of the clergy, the church hierarchy had obtained a substantially more autonomous position vis-à-vis the state by 1850 than it had had in 1848, whether such a position was guaranteed by a new constitution, as in Prussia, or by a revived absolutist rule and the negotiation of a Concordat with the Vatican, as was the case in the Habsburg Monarchy. Both revolution and reaction had served the Catholic Church well.

Governance of the Church

Confrontations over church governance ultimately led to many of the same results as did their counterparts concerning church-state relations. The year 1848 saw numerous meetings and conferences, formal and informal, of both laypeople and clergy, some of these ephemeral, others creating institutions that have lasted until the present day. Overall, though, the upshot of all the proceedings was to reinforce the position of the clerical hierarchy and to strengthen the hand of the neo-orthodox element in the churches.

This was perhaps clearest among Protestants, where the church synods held in Bavaria during the year of revolution brought little in the way of changes or even suggestions for changes in the system of church governance. Frustrated theological rationalists in the Pfalz, Bavaria's Rhenish province, were so angered by this state of affairs that they held an informal meeting in July 1848, demanding that the state authorities call a separate synod for the Protestant Church of their province to create a more democratic organizational structure, or they would call such a meeting themselves, and place it under the protection of the Frankfurt National Assembly. In the end, the pre-1848 state of affairs, in which the monarch exercised his power over the church via a government ministry of the interior or of religious affairs, with a basically advisory voice for the pastors and laymen elected to synods, underwent little alteration. The structure of Protestant Church governance in other German states, such as Württemberg and Prussia, also changed little as a result of the 1848 revolution.

If there was not much structural change, the same cannot be said of the personnel administering them. By the 1850s individuals of a neo-orthodox and pietist persuasion were occupying ever more key administrative positions in the established Protestant Churches, pushing out theological liberals and rationalists. Among the Protestants of Hungary who had already had an autonomous church administration from the 1790s onward, one characterized by synods with equal numbers of lay and clerical members, the outcome of the revolution was a movement away from this form of governance. As a consequence of what seemed to the Habsburg authorities to be the overly enthusiastic support of Magyar Protestants for the revolutionary regime, the reaction era government developed a system of state commissars to supervise their potentially subversive subjects and revised synodal membership to guarantee a clerical majority.

The one major informal initiative toward a new Protestant Church, the national conference of German Protestants, held in Wittenberg in September 1848, suggests that the strong postrevolutionary position of theological and political conservatives was a product of the revolutionary era itself. Such conservatives dominated the national conference and in a characteristic move, its members voted to designate 5 November 1848 as a day of prayer and repentance for the sinful revolutionary uprisings of the previous spring. The delegates discussed the idea, first proposed by theological and political liberals five months earlier, of creating a national federation of German Protestant Churches, but never acted on it. Their one successful move in this direction was to bring about the joint sponsorship of all the Protestant Churches for the founding of a national initiative, the "Inner Mission," to bring the Gospel and organized charitable assistance to Central Europe's urban lower classes. Its organizer, the energetic pastor and senior Prussian civil servant Johann Heinrich Wichern, explained his project to the conference as a counter-revolutionary step, combatting the godlessness and socialism among the workers he and many delegates regarded as responsible for the revolution.

Comparable events among Catholics were more complex and ideologically more varied. The initial victories of the revolution were scarcely over when large numbers of parish clergy began demanding the calling of diocesan synods, sometimes with lay participation, sometimes not, to discuss both matters of doctrine and of church governance. At the same time, the episcopate in France, Germany, parts of Italy, and the Habsburg Empire called for national church councils, that would discuss relations with both the state and the papacy, as well as considering questions of doctrine and religious practice.

All such demands, of course, suggested a current of opposition to the hierarchical organization of the Catholic Church, but the theological opinions that accompanied them were strikingly mixed. In central and eastern Europe, the adherents of synods were more often than not supporters of rationalist and Enlightened ideas about religion, such as the parish clergy of the Capital of Linzgau, in southeastern Baden, who called in April 1848 for diocesan and national synods, the election of the bishops by clergy and laity, the elimination of the influence of the "Jesuitical tendency" in the Archdiocese of Freiburg, the introduction of a German language mass, and the abolition of clerical celibacy. More moderate, both in terms of theology and religious practice, were the lower clergy of the Diocese of Vienna. Under the leadership of the neo-Kantian theologian Anton Günther, whose work would be placed on the Index in the following decade, they demanded the calling of a diocesan synod.

Other priests in the Habsburg Monarchy were less restrained than their counterparts in the capital. The Czech clergy in the province of Bohemia demanded the abolition of clerical celibacy and that bishops be elected by parish priests. Still more radical in their aims were those Hungarian priests, led by the pastor of Hatvan, Michael Horváth, who wanted to see the separation of church and state, a democratically elected church hierarchy, a vernacular mass, and the abolition of clerical celibacy. Horváth was named both a bishop and the Minister of Religious and Educational Affairs by the revolutionary Hungarian government of Lajos Kossuth. The national synod he planned for August 1849 to begin the proposed reforms could not be held since the revolutionary government sponsoring it was overthrown. Horváth was forced to flee the country; one of his close clerical collaborators, Imre Szscsvay, was hanged in October 1849 by the victorious forces of order. Interestingly enough, the Hungarians' arch-enemies, the Croatian nationalists, entertained similar ideas about reform of the Catholic Church, one of the Croatian national demands of March 1848 being the abolition of clerical celibacy.

In France, on the other hand, the synodal movement of the lower clergy was decidedly neo-orthodox, calling for the introduction of the Roman liturgy, the encouragement of forms of Marian devotion, and the full subordination to the Pope of the French episcopate, many of whose members still retained older ideas about the national idependence of the Gallican Church. In these efforts, the lower clergy were strongly supported by the prominent Catholic polemicist, the brilliant journalist Louis Veuillot, and his influential clerical-conservative newspaper, *L'Univers*. It might seem odd that these neo-orthodox clergy and laymen, enthusiastic promoters of ideas of hierarchy and authority, "ultramontanists" who made subordination to the Papal head of the ecclesiastical hierarchy the heart of their thinking, should have been encouraging the disaffection of parish priests against their bishops. However, as the frustrated Bishop of Viviers noted a few years later, of such ultramontanists:

> As they practice it, Christian obedience becomes very convenient. It is easy to make eloquent protestations of submission to an authority four hundred leagues distant, and to proclaim each day that all one's writings, one's words and one's most intimate

thoughts are submitted to the Church of Rome, if by this formula one dispenses one-self from all the control of the authority closer at hand.[3]

Ultimately, it was precisely this form of rebellion that was triumphant. Pius IX vetoed all suggestions for the calling of national church councils, possessing any authority to discuss issues of doctrine or governance. A national conference of the German bishops was held in November 1848, beginning a regular series of meetings that continues to the present day; the bishops of the Habsburg Monarchy all gathered in a similar conference the following year. These meetings, however, dealt primarily with church-state relations, issuing demands on central European governments along the lines proposed by adherents of the independence of the church from the state. Insofar as intra-ecclesiastical matters were discussed at all, the proceedings led to a reaffirmation of the Pope's position, rather than a challenge to it.

The diocesan synods so often demanded in the spring of 1848 were never convened, except in France where Pius IX agreed to allow the holding of councils in each church province (an archdiocese and its suffragan dioceses). Mostly, these councils proved to be a forum in which ultramontanists could agitate—once again, with the agile assistance of Veuillot and his newspaper—for their doctrinal, liturgical, and organizational goals. Any conciliar decisions not meeting their approval, such as those passed by Parisian church province under the direction of the rationalist and Gallican Archbishop of Paris, Dominique Sibour, were simply vetoed by the Roman curia.

Thus the demands for councils and synods, originally raised to lead to greater participation in the church, resulted, paradoxically, in the opposite: a reinforcement of the ecclesiastical hierarchy, particularly the position of the Pope, but also of the bishops, provided that they endorsed the supreme position of the Roman pontiff. Here, we can see the effects of the intersection of two kinds of demands for freedom and political participation—for church councils and for independence of the church from the state—that were brought forth, sometimes by the same individuals, and certainly in the same spirit, in the spring of 1848. A church independent of the state would be one in which the hierarchy could run its affairs as it wished. In such a church, there would be no government pressure to hold synods, something the supporters of synods had counted on, but were unable to obtain.

In a similar way, the call for the involvement of laymen and -women in the church, raised by the proponents of synods, ended up working against the goals of their supporters. The laity was involved in religious matters to an unprecedented extent in 1848/49, via petition campaigns to the German, Austrian, and French assemblies, and in meetings of Catholic associations. The two general assemblies of the central European Pius Associations, held in Mainz in October 1848 and in Breslau in May 1849, were largely the work of laymen (with, admittedly, assistance from the parish clergy) and began the regular meetings of German Catholic associations, the *Katholikentage* that continue to the present day. However, all this activity was directed primarily toward assuring the independence of the church from the state, as well as other social and political goals (to be discussed below) that had the practical effect of reinforcing the position of the hierarchy.

Sects and Free Churches

If the revolution, ultimately, seems to have strengthened the position of the established churches that was such a feature of the prerevolutionary scene, one might wish to see if the events of 1848/51 provided a boost for the sects and free churches. These groups were most prevalent in central Europe, where the "Friends of Light" and the "German-Catholics" emerging from the established Protestant and Catholic Churches respectively, counted together some 150,000 members. Both movements had already achieved a loosely federated national structure before 1848 and a joint national synod of the two groups in 1850 provided a further affiliation. Professing beliefs that ranged from Unitarianism to Deism to a spiritualized Hegelian pantheism, members of these free churches were a major presence on the left wing of the 1848 revolution. National leaders of the left, such as Robert Blum or Gustav Struve, were professing German-Catholics, and members of dissident congregations took a leading role in the democratic movement at the local level, in Halle, Breslau, Schweinfurt or Neustadt a.d.W (to name just a few cities). The members of these groups thanked God for the revolution and the initiation of the reign of freedom; their altars were covered with red cloths; the walls of their chapels adorned with pictures of revolutionary heroes such as Lajos Kossuth or Friedrich Hecker.

More than that, the free churches were at the center of a broader network of associations committed to individual moral regeneration as part of the movement toward liberty and political equality. Sectarians took a leading role in founding *Kindergärten*, workers' educational societies, women's clubs, mutual benefit societies, as well as gymnastics and choral societies. The free congregations governed themselves democratically, generally allowing adult women members the vote, and even sometimes permitting them to hold office in councils of the congregations or provincial synods. The opportunities for intense political involvement and social engagement provided by the 1848 revolution served as a hothouse for this broader social movement.

Such sects or free churches were typical of events in predominantly Protestant or mixed Protestant and Catholic countries, while in the Catholic lands of southern and western Europe, they were at the very most marginally present. However, an intellectually and spiritually similar mixture of a rationalized Christianity with a pathos of freedom and social equality pervaded the politics of the left in France and Italy. Proclaiming Jesus Christ to be the first republican, or the first socialist, interpreting the Gospels as inaugurating the doctrine of fraternity, democrats in these countries promoted a Christianized radicalism that combined individual self-regeneration with social transformation, while simultaneously launching a bitter attack on the established Catholic Church for having abandoned these Christian principles.

Historians have often observed that such an ethos of moral regeneration, rationalized Christianity, and anticlericalism was typical of the radicalism of the 1848 revolution. They have sometimes condemned this ethos as naive, and sometimes praised its moral dimension, noting that it enabled leftists to mobilize broad segments of the population, particularly including women, often unaddressed in pre-

vious and subsequent left-wing efforts. While this ethos and the groups that embodied it did indeed provide a basis for commitment and activism, they proved to be
sectarian and marginalizing as well. Efforts to convince lay and clerical rationalists
from the established religions, many of whose spiritual and sociopolitical concerns
paralleled those of members of free churches, to join the dissident movement were
generally unsuccessful. Moreover, the sectarians' rationalist doctrines could be
exploited by the democrats' enemies. There was no better way in 1848 to prevent
left-wing agitators from gaining a hearing among the Catholic, especially rural
population, than by telling them that the radicals were going to force them to
abjure the Pope and become German-Catholics.

Shortly before his death in the fall of 1848, Robert Blum had come to see this
contrast between the ethos of the free churches and the popular belief in orthodox
Christianity as central to the political situation in Germany, in particular to the ever-
growing likelihood of a clash between radicals and counter-revolutionaries. Because,
he said, "our honest work with German Catholicism has not been sufficiently
extensive, so that the mass of the people still hold, with a grip of iron, on to the dog-
mas of a degenerate Christianity, while, on the other hand, their belief in the power
of the ideas of freedom is still so miserably weak and loose … the people do not trust
us free-thinkers."[4] Directly linking the spread of the ethos of the religious radicals,
with popular support for the left, and the maintenance of the orthodox doctrine of
the established churches with consent to the practices of the party of order, Blum
was noting that the minoritarian and sectarian position of the free churches meant
that the democrats would lack the popular support needed in the forthcoming
clashes between the left and the forces of reaction and counter-revolution.

The Clergy and Politics

Robert Blum's appraisal suggests some of the ways in which religious loyalties had
become central to the politics of the 1848 revolution. One reason for that was the
central position of the clergy in a political process characterized by a suddenly
expanded degree of popular participation. The onslaught of mass politics in the
spring of 1848, on the barricades, in the streets, at mass meetings or the polling place
contrasted sharply with the limited suffrage, the few and often censored newspapers,
and the limited, elite or semi-clandestine circles of political action and discussion
that had preceded it. In these circumstances, the clergy, present everywhere, close to
and influential with the popular masses, found themselves in a key position.

This was especially true in eastern Europe, where civil society was still quite
underdeveloped. Particularly among those nationalities lacking an influential aristocracy, the clergy took on the role of political leaders and activists. In Austrian Galicia, the head of the Supreme Ukrainian Council was the Uniate [Greek Catholic]
Bishop of Lemberg, Hryhory Jachymoryč, and the fifty local affiliates that the council created in the province are scarcely understandable without the active support
and leadership of the Uniate clergy. Much was the same in Slovakia, where the

admittedly not-very-effective Slovak national movement in the 1848 revolution was predominantly a creation of Lutheran pastors.

In the easternmost reaches of revolutionary Europe, clergy of the Orthodox Church played a particularly active role. As Lother Maier's account in this volume demonstrates, the active participation of Orthodox priests was absolutely central to the revolution in Moldavia and Wallachia. A leading figure among the more moderate wing of the Rumanian nationalists of Transylvania was the Orthodox bishop Andreiu Şaguna, while his counterpart, the Orthodox Archbishop of Karlowitz Josip Rajačić, was the undisputed leader of the Serb nationalists in the Banat, as his elevation to the rank of Patriarch by the Serbian national assembly in May 1848 testifies. The targeting of Orthodox priests in the Banat for persecution and murder by the Hungarian army in the civil war that raged there in 1848/49, is revealing of the broader role of the clergy in the Serbian national movement, as were the efforts of Patriarch Rajačić to procure Russian intervention against the Magyars.

However, clerical political power in the mid-century revolution was by no means limited to marginal or less developed regions of Europe. The elections held under a broad franchise to constituent assemblies in France, Germany, Austria, and Hungary in the spring of 1848 were a remarkable demonstration of the influence that priests and pastors could exercise in an age of nascent democracy. Whether held in the church or just after Sunday services, these elections frequently yielded candidates chosen by or at least endorsed by the clergy. Sharing their influence to a greater or lesser extent with the aristocracy and more bourgeois notables, men of religion set the initial framework for political life. A particularly revealing example of how this influence was exercised comes from a village in Westphalia in April 1848. Here is an observer's account of the elections to the German and Prussian National Assemblies:

> Early in the morning the congregation gathered in the church. The priest … held the services and following them gave a short speech. He explained that today was the day of the elections and since it was permitted to hold them in the church he requested his parishioners to behave as was appropriate in a sacred place. He called on them to keep in mind the importance of the election. In these great events, God's voice was to be heard; therefore he asked God to enlighten them and guide them in this important business. They would help decide on the entire future position of the Christian religion, of the holy church, of the entire nation, the government, and, finally, of the re-creation of the German Empire. They should only elect thoughtful men who would conscientiously vote for the most worthy candidates. Nothing seems to have been planned in advance. As the election began, everyone sat on the benches in the church; they held no discussions; they did not whisper to each other. Their names were read out, the ballots distributed. Each man wrote down a name on his ballot or had his neighbor write one for him. When the ballots were opened, read aloud, and counted, it turned out that the priest had been elected almost unanimously as an elector for the election of a deputy to Berlin [where the Prussian Constituent Assembly sat]; the elector to Frankfurt [site of the German National Assembly] was the former feudal lord of the village.[5]

Everything about these elections favored clerical influence, from their being held in a church to the lack of any organized political forces to prepare them, leaving the priest's sermon as, in effect, the entire election campaign. However, the steady increase in political organization over the course of the revolution would change this position, offering alternatives both to the priest as political leader and to confessional loyalties as a guide to political behavior. The clergy's influence and, more broadly, the place of religious loyalties in political movements, would by no means disappear, but would be rearticulated in a context characterized by a greater degree of political organization, offering expression to a plurality of political views.

Confessional Loyalties and Confessional Politics in the 1848 Revolution

In other words, discussing the political influence of the clergy leads to a broader consideration of the place of confessional loyalties and confessional politics in the 1848 revolution. A starting point would be to note that many people who held radical or oppositional views were of the opposite confession to the ruling dynasty. Contemporaries were well aware that the Greek-Orthodox villages of Calabria and Sicily were strongholds of radical, insurgent forces, in the fighting against the eminently Catholic Bourbon monarch in Naples. The Protestants of southern France, as a group, quite disproportionately bourgeois, became increasingly strong supporters of the social democratic left in the years 1849/51, out of opposition to the increasingly Catholic-clerical tone of an ever more ascendant conservative politics. State officials observed that the Protestants of Carinthia supported the democrats and were open sympathizers with the revolutionary Hungarian regime, seeing it as a Protestant power opposed to the Catholic Habsburg Dynasty. It is an open question whether the Magyar Protestants were stronger supporters of the revolutionary government than their Catholic counterparts, but Austrian officials certainly thought so, and devoted particular attention to Calvinists in their post-1849 repression.

There are two qualifiers to this picture of confessional loyalties. First, it is obviously not the whole story. Had the French social democrats been limited to Protestant supporters, Sicilian and Calabrian insurgents to Greek Orthodox villages, then neither of these movements would have been a serious threat to their respective governments. While revolutionary forces may have had stronger support among members of religious minorities, most of their adherents belonged to the majority confession.

Secondly, intraconfessional dynamics often disrupted the pattern of oppositional sympathies among members of the confession different from that of the ruling royal house. The neo-orthodox Lutherans of Bavaria, for instance, were strong supporters of the Catholic Wittelsbach dynasty and of a generally conservative politics in 1848, their religious convictions about the need to obey a legally existing and divinely sanctioned authority, outweighing any confessional antagonisms. For rather different reasons, but with the same political outcome, rationalist Catholic priests in Prussia or Baden, two states with Protestant monarchs and a Roman Catholic population (both lay and clerical) that was frequently in opposition to them, tended to support governmental authority, hoping, in vain as it turned out, that a liberal and rationalist state bureaucracy would help them in their struggles against the neo-orthodox element in the Catholic Church.

If confessional differences between a ruling dynasty and population groups tended, all things considered, to predispose the latter to a politics of opposition and revolutionary sympathies, confessional similarities worked in the opposite direction. A particularly good example of this is the political discourse employed by the various central European Catholic clubs, the Pius Associations. At their first national conference in October 1848, the vast majority of the delegates spoke in praise of freedom, and demonstrated, to some extent at least, the revolutionary pathos of the spring of 1848. Summing up this mood, the introduction to the conference proceedings spoke warmly of the "liberation from the Babylonian Captivity in which the all-powerful police state had held the church and Catholic life in chains," "to take possession of the treasure of freedom for the church." The only exception to this praise of freedom at the congress was the representative of the Catholic club of the Tyrol, who warned that the "heroes of freedom" would bring "servitude for the church," reasserted the old Tyrolean motto, "for God, emperor and fatherland," and concluded by distancing himself from the entire revolution: "May the world get out of its storms so that Ttrol does not come into them ..." The Munich Pius Association had refused to take part in the congress altogether; its public statements denounced the dangers of "subversion" and explained the need to "reinforce loyalty to the hereditary royal house ..."[6] It is surely no coincidence that the Catholic associations from states with Protestant monarchs praised the principles of freedom and offered at least a partial assent to the revolution, while those from lands governed by their coreligionists saw instead a world out of joint, a threat of godless subversion, and showed little interest in the blessings of freedom.

Such a perspective was even more pronounced among Protestants. Particularly in Prussia, but also in the other German states with Protestant monarchs, a large majority of the clergy stood squarely against the revolution. They preached sermons calling for loyalty to the monarch, and condemning democrats and subversives; they joined or often founded constitutional-monarchist or outright conservative political clubs and, generally, did their best—with considerable success—to lead their congregations in a counter-revolutionary direction.

Just as was the case with confessional difference, we can also note some modifying factors in this constellation of confessional homogeneity with the monarch leading to conservative attitudes. One factor involves issues of intra-confessional tension. That embattled minority of Protestant pastors or laymen who endorsed rationalist and Enlightened ideas, for instance, were sometimes found on the left, even if they lived in states with a Protestant monarch, such as Prussia, Hessen-Darmstadt, or Baden. Just one example would be Dean Martin Schmidt of Hornberg, in Baden. In 1845, he had organized a conference of rationalist pastors to combat the "attacks of pietist men of darkness"; his open sympathies for the Badenese revolutionaries in 1848/49—for which he was immediately denounced to the authorities by a number of his pietist enemies, following the restoration of order—led the government to dismiss him from his parish.

Also, the presence of a pronounced anticlericalism would weaken the effect of confessionally based loyalties and the clergy promoting them, something seen in 1848/49 in a number of regions of Catholic Europe, from southeastern France to central Italy to Vienna to southwestern Germany. In some ways, though, an even more important exception arose through the political process: with the development of political organizations and the growth of a plurality of political voices (as compared to the univocal environment frequently met, as noted in the previous section, in the spring of 1848), the transformation of confessional loyalties or hostilities into political action became rather more complex.

One way to approach this process of development would be to consider the transition from a politics of religion to a religious politics, from a state of affairs where the clergy sometimes have a substantial influence on political questions, where religious issues are important for political life and confessional loyalties or antagonisms play a substantial role in determining political behavior, to circumstances in which a political party or movement is organized around confessional or religious loyalties. The Christian Democratic parties of twentieth- century Europe would be the prime example of such a religious politics, and their historians often look to the 1848 revolution as an initial moment in their foundation. Such historians note, correctly, that the post-1945 interconfessional character of Christian Democracy was not apparent in 1848; mutual hostility between the Christian confessions was the rule. Therefore, any such early forms of Christian politics would have been confessional in nature. It would be hard to point to an explicitly Protestant politics: politically active pastors and laypeople brought their religious convictions with them to different groupings, from the extreme right through the center to the extreme left, but the local political clubs or nascent, national political parties in which they acted were not specifically Protestant ones.

In France and Italy, this was the case with Catholic priests and lay activists as well. They tended to follow a general political trajectory. In the spring of 1848, they endorsed the revolution, French priests blessing trees of liberty, the lower clergy of Lombardy and Venetia joining the insurrection against Austrian rule in the northern Italian provinces. However, as the revolution continued, the bulk of the clergy and lay activists moved from enthusiasm to skepticism to downright hostility, becoming increasingly identified with the party of order denouncing an anticlerical radicalism.

In so doing, priests and lay activists were following the example of Pius IX himself, who began the revolution as the hero of the Italian national movement, as the symbol of opposition to Austrian rule and to the political disunity of the peninsula. When, in April 1848, though, it became a question of troops from the papal states being committed to an anti-Habsburg war of national liberation, the Pontiff had to realize that he was not just Pope of the Italians, but Pope of the Austrians, as well, perhaps especially Pope of the Austrians. His withdrawal from the war, his subsequent, hopeless efforts at mediation between the Italians and the Austrians, and his increasing alienation from the revolution, culminating in the overthrow of the papal government in November 1848 by Italian democrats, their subsequent proclamation of a Roman Republic, and the Pope's flight from Rome to the protection of the reactionary Bourbon regime of the Two Sicilies, completed this political path, one that was both an example for clergy and lay activists elsewhere in Europe and also complemented their own experiences.

Yet the travails of Pius IX do not provide the whole story of a Catholic politics in the mid-century revolution. Gallican French bishops, for instance, skeptical of papal authority, and not particularly supportive of the Pontiff's temporal power, moved to the right in a similar fashion. The difficulties of creating a clerical politics in 1848 can best be seen in central Europe, where an independent Catholic political movement came closest to being created.

There were certainly informal gatherings of Catholic parliamentary representatives: the Catholic caucus in the Frankfurt National Assembly, the "Rhenish" deputies (that is, actually, Catholic-clerical representatives from the Rhineland and Westphalia, under the leadership of Cologne's Archbishop Johannes von Geissel) in the Prussian National Assembly, or a group of Tyrolean and Galician deputies in the Austrian Constituent Assembly. However, these were less parliamentary caucuses than gatherings of deputies from different caucuses who agreed to take a common line on religious issues, that is on the questions, discussed above, of separation of church and state, and independence of the church from the state. On other political questions, though, they went their separate ways.

At the local level, there were the Pius Associations and other Catholic clubs founded during the revolution: both in the spring of 1848, and, as recent scholarship has demonstrated, in a second wave, during fall 1848 and winter 1849. A considerable number of these groups existed; the most recent estimates are in the neighborhood of some 850 active associations, making them second in number only to the democrats among political groupings in the German states during the 1848 revolution.[7] To take just one regional example, in his admirable study of the 1848 revolution in the Rhine-Main area, Michael Wettengel has found evidence for the existence of some fifty Pius Associations, twice the number of organizations founded by the liberal constitutional monarchists and, in fact, exceeded in extent only by democratic political clubs. This was a remarkable organizational effort, especially since the area had a majority Protestant population.

Overall national figures and this one regional example both suggest that the Pius Associations had the potential to be a considerable political force in the mass politics of the mid-century revolution. If they were not, it was largely because they, too, could not make the transition from a politics of religion to a religious politics. Their political positions and activities were disparate, widely scattered and uncoordinated. Some of these Catholic groups refused to engage in political activity at all, limiting themselves to religious and charitable matters. Others were only willing to take an independent stance on specifically religious issues, either abstaining from other political activity, or cooperating with other groups on the center and right of the political spectrum. (The Pius Association in Trier, that often cooperated with the democrats, is a frequently cited but quite exceptional case.) Only a relatively small number were interested in creating an independent Catholic political force.

However, these efforts, most prevalent in the western provinces of the Prussian Monarchy, proved generally unsuccessful, foundering precisely on the rocks of the politics of confession. This could certainly not have been foreseen at the onset of the revolution. The energetic intervention of the clergy in the newly expanded political process had been extraordinarily successful, priests leading and shaping the elections to the Frankfurt National Assembly and the Prussian National Assembly in the spring of 1848. Clergy and lay activists had founded over the course of the year of revolution a considerable number of Pius Associations; cooperation of these groups with parish priests had produced impressive numbers of signatures on petitions to the assemblies favoring independence of the church from the state and a confessional public education. Seemingly in a strong position as a result of these actions, Catholic parliamentarians and much of the episcopate were increasingly interested by the end of 1848 and the beginning of 1849 in reaching an accord with a Prussian monarch whose conservative government offered firm guarantees for independence of the church from the state and who firmly rejected the Frankfurt National Assembly's offer to make him emperor of a united Germany without Austria, one in which Catholics would be a permanent minority. In taking this stance, however, the Catholic politicians and the bishops were calling on the laity and the lower clergy to abandon their confessionally based opposition to the rule of a Protestant Monarch, an attitude that had been the source of much of the clergy's political authority and of the success of politicians tied to the church.

Consequently, in a series of political events, ranging from the crisis of November 1848, stemming from the confrontation between the crown and the Prussian National Assembly, to the elections to the Prussian parliament of January 1849 to the agitation and uprisings of April-May 1849 (the campaign for the imperial constitution), the Catholic parliamentarians, the leaders of the Rhenish Pius Associations, and the bishops kept finding that a good portion of lay Catholics, and even some of the lower clergy, were refusing to follow their lead, but were instead turning to the political left. For it was the democrats who were now denouncing the king of Prussia, mobilizing Catholic confessional hostility toward a Protestant Monarch, while the leaders of the Pius Associations were unable to do so. Indeed, Catholic activists and parliamentarians themselves, cut off from the confessional loyalties and hostilities that they had previously been able to exploit, were unable to agree on a course of action and found themselves increasingly marginalized in a region where, just a year earlier, they had been the dominant force.

This particular example suggests how clerical influence and confessional politics could interact to their mutual limitation. In the unexpected 'democracy of the spring of 1848, the clergy—particularly Catholic, but Protestant and Eastern Orthodox as well—could play a dominant role, articulating confessionally based political loyalties or enmities, in a situation where there were few others who could compete for the ear of a newly enfranchised public. But with the growth of political organization over the following year, and with the expansion of forms of political agitation, particularly in those areas of western and central Europe with a better developed civil society, alternative voices began to be heard; other claimants on such confessional allegiances presented their cases. In these circumstances, clerical influence could continue to be exercised primarily as part of a broader political movement, one in which confessional and religious concerns, while certainly present, were not paramount. The attempts, admittedly limited primarily to central Europe, and themselves nascent, fumbling and sometimes half-hearted, to create a specifically confessional politics that combined the influence of the clergy, an effective political organization, a high political priority for confessional and religious issues, and a primacy of confessional allegiances, proved unsuccessful. It was, however, a model for the future, one that would be implemented more successfully in subsequent decades.

Some Conclusions

There are four points that might summarize this discussion of churches, the faithful, and the politics of religion in the mid-nineteenth-century revolutions. Each of these points suggests both something of the ways in which 1848 revolution marked a turning point in the history of European revolutions, and also what features were unique to it.

1. The first and most obvious point is that the 1848 revolution was also a revolution in religion. Revolutionaries found it perfectly appropriate to deal with religious issues: the Croatian national demands would include the abolition of clerical celibacy; Palatine Protestants saw nothing inappropriate about appealing to the German National Assembly, if their calls for autonomy within the Protestant Church of Bavaria were not met. Religious issues, particularly the relationship between church and school, although many others as well, played a major role in political agitation and parliamentary debates.

The 1848 revolution also had many of the characteristics of a religious revolution, perhaps more so than any before or since. There were widespread, if ultimately unsuccessful demands for the restructuring of established churches. Unprecedented meetings of both clergy and lay activists took place, that set the pattern for future developments down until the present day. Political groups, even leftist anticlerical ones, expressed their ideas in religious terms, saw the revolutionary process as involving the moral and spiritual regeneration of individuals, and looked to religious institutions, such as the sects and the free churches, to embody these changes.

These efforts were, of course, not unique to the mid-nineteenth century. In particular, the French Revolution of 1789 provided an important predecessor, as the revolutionaries attempted to restructure the established church with their creation of a Civil Constitution of the Clergy. In the most radical, Jacobin phase of the revolution, they tried to create an entire, new, non-Christian religion of reason. The religious pathos of 1848, on the other hand, was distinctly Christian in nature, perhaps a consequence of the revival and new development of Christian practices and beliefs, that can be noted both among Protestants and Catholics in the decades after 1815.

However, this close linkage of religion and revolution would be considerably weakened after 1850. Future European revolutionaries might be ferociously anti-clerical, but they would not consider abolishing clerical celibacy or founding new churches as part of their revolutionary agenda. They might see their revolution as leading to individual moral regeneration, to, for instance, the "new socialist man" envisaged by twentieth-century communist revolutionaries, but such a regeneration was not to be a religious or spiritual one. After 1850, church councils might meet, religious doctrines might be hotly debated, schisms might be threatened, but these events would occur at their own pace and with their own logic, one largely delinked from the outbreak of revolution. Perhaps the one major exception to this rule would be the Nazi regime in Germany (if one considers it a revolutionary one), whose supporters did try both to restructure the existing Christian Churches, particularly the Protestants, and also to found a new, "Nordic" religion.

2. The second conclusion I would suggest concerns the ferment within the churches and among the faithful during the 1848 revolution. It is hard to avoid the impression that the neo-orthodox were most successful in seizing this moment of turmoil and using it to their own advantage. Both Protestant and Catholic rational-ists within the established churches proved unable to deal with the mass politics of religion. Religious radicals, members of sects, and free churches were very active during the revolution, but their activities seem to have frightened off at least as many people as they attracted; they were unable to break the mold of a sectarian existence.

To be sure, it is reasonable to assert that even before the outbreak of the revolution the neo-orthodox were gaining the upper hand over their rationalist counterparts among the clergy and the faithful laypeople of the established churches. However, the revolution enabled the neo-orthodox to press their advantage to decisive effect, by bringing their position both to a mass audience of the sort created by the initial victories of the revolution, and to powerful elites, following the triumph of counter-revolution and reaction. While by no means disappearing from the scene, rationalists would be on the defensive in the following decades; in this same period, the elan of the revolutionary era, the pathos of political and social transformation, could not be maintained among supporters of the sects and free churches. The radical politics articulated in these churches was increasingly secu-larized, articulated in other venues, such as the institutions and associations of the labor movement, leaving the radical religious groups with little content and rela-tively few supporters.

3. The third issue I might note is that the 1848 revolution saw a politics of con-fession, but not a confessional politics. That is, religious issues, generally interpreted and acted upon in confessional fashion, were important in both the popular and the parliamentary politics of the revolution and confessional adherence was crucial to determining political alignments in the revolutionary events. However, if Protestants and Catholics, or Catholics and Greek Orthodox tended to fall out on opposite sides of the political fence, it does not follow that they did so exclusively under the leadership of the clergy or for causes of confessional interest. Often, it was the rad-ical and anticlerical left that was able to exploit confessional tensions for political

advantage, whether among the Catholics of the Rhineland or the Protestants of southern France.

The idea of a confessional politics, of a political party—whether organized as parliamentary caucus, as local political club, or as a regional or national federation of such clubs—based primarily on confessional allegiances, was a new one in 1848. Tentative steps were taken in that direction, but by the end of the revolution they had remained just that—tentative and uncertain, with an unclear future. The subsequent quarter century would see the creation and triumph of Catholic-confessional parties across much of central and western Europe; this outcome was a further development of and massive expansion upon the initial efforts of 1848, occurring after other potential models of the relationship between confession and politics, also tried in 1848, had been eliminated.

4. Finally, the mid-nineteenth-century revolutions were ones in which the pathos of freedom was central to much of the political discourse, never more so than following the initial revolutionary victories of the spring of 1848. It was then that the idea of "religious freedom" made its appearance, as an integral part of the many demands for freedom characteristic of the time. However, as the revolution continued and ultimately gave way to the era of reaction after 1849/51, politically active contemporaries, from all parts of the political spectrum, broke this link between religious and other civic freedoms. They would assert that religious freedom could be enjoyed while others were suppressed, or that an order of civic freedom could include serious infringements on the freedom of religion. In European politics of the second half of the nineteenth century, religious freedom and other civic freedoms increasingly went their separate political ways, adherents of one all too often being enemies of the other. It would take the experiences of the totalitarian regimes of the twentieth century to suggest that freedom of religion is an integral part of civic freedom, that all such freedoms cannot flourish without freedom of religion, and that religious freedom itself requires for its effective exercise the full panoply of civic liberties.

Notes

1. This essay will be concerned with the Christian Churches; developments among the Jewish population will be discussed in the contribution of Reinhard Rürup (chapter 31).
2. Cited in Roger Price (ed.), *1848 in France* (Ithaca and London, 1975), 66-68.
3. Cited in Austin Gough, *Paris and Rome: The Gallican Church and the Ultramontane Campaign 1848-1853* (Oxford, 1986), 206.
4. Hermann Joseph Aloys Körner, *Lebenskämpfe in der Alten und Neuen Welt*, Vol. 2 (New York, 1865), 16-17. Körner's memoirs have frequently been criticized as inaccurate, so it is not impossible that Blum did not use these exact words, or even that Körner made them up completely. Yet even so,

the ideas expressed seem relevant, especially as Körner himself was both a German-Catholic and a democratic political activist.

5. Cited in Wilhelm Schulte, *Volk und Staat. Westfalen im Vormärz und in der Revolution 1848/49* (Münster, 1954), 561.

6. Quotes from Heinz Hürten, *Geschichte des deutschen Katholizismus 1800-1960* (Mainz, 1986), 88-90.

7. More generally, see the essay on political associations by Michael Wettengel (chapter 22), in this volume.

Opening of the Imperial Academy of Sciences in the chambers of the Lower Austrian Diet in Vienna
(Illustrirte Zeitung, Leipzig, no. 246, 18 March 1848, 183)

Assembly of the Congress of Academic Teachers in Jena
(Illustrirte Zeitung, Leipzig, no. 282, 28 November 1848, 353)

Chapter 30

EDUCATIONAL REFORM AS SOCIAL REFORM

The Revolution of 1848 as a Turning-Point in the History of Education

Heinz-Elmar Tenorth

Eighteen Forty-Eight as Memory and Myth in the History of Education

In 1948, before the centenary of the revolution of 1848/49, a discussion arose about exactly which events should be remembered—sessions of the *Paulskirche*, the *Communist Manifesto*, or even—"*dreimal 1848*"[1]—the two previous items plus the first "general asssembly of the Pius-Assocations," the first Catholic convention in May 1848 in Mainz. A Protestant quickly pointed out that the First Evangelical Convention in September 1848 in Wittenberg or the beginnings of the public work of Hamburg social educationalist Johann Heinrich Wichern also needed to be remembered.[2]

A similar questioning arose with respect to the educationally symbolic events of the revolution.[3] Educators' meetings, on the Tivoli in Berlin or in Eiseanach, symbolize, even today, the new revolutionary departure. The 1849 speech of King Friedrich Wilhelm IV, in which he placed the entire blame for the revolution on the "perverted education" in teachers' colleges, symbolizes the collapse of great hopes. Unlike in 1898—when the lasting significance of the "crazy days" and of liberal traditions needed to be underlined vis-à-vis teachers afraid of revolution—the revolution of 1848/49 became a model for the upcoming reform of society and state, schools and public education in both east and west after the Second World War. The nineteenth century has provided the key words for educational reform up to today: schools that are public, non-religious, free and uniform, where equality and democracy function as principles of modern educational organization. Was there however more to look back on than educators' carefully nurtured memories of a new depar-

---

Notes for this section begin on page 746.

ture already held to be a failure in 1849? Does the revolution of 1848 also present a true break in the history of education? It is justified to see it as the point of departure for a modern attempt to reform and democratize society through education?

The Tradition of Modern Educational Reform

The idea of reforming society by reforming education was not first raised in 1848/49, nor was it revived for the last time in 1948. General and egalitarian educational programs can be found in the seventeenth century, e.g., from Comenius. Reform-oriented education and public schooling as a means of developing bourgeois self-consciousness and of countering social crises and collective resignation were already being propagated by Enlightenment educators. From the end of the eighteenth century onwards, national educational plans set the framework for discussions of educational policy both in Germany and in western Europe. The revolutionary restructuring of the French state and society beginning in 1789 was accompanied by detailed educational plans, which, ranging from democratic-liberal options to radical state intervention, already displayed the range of modern educational reforms. In the idea of general education, Prussian reformers articulated a liberal option beginning in 1806, but in educational and social policies conservative government interference held sway after 1810/15. Educational policy in Prussia was not only soon transformed into a defense against revolutionary change and a stabilization of predemocratic conditions, but also into a rigid discipline of teachers and students following the Karlsbad Decrees.

Even if these defensive educational policies of the restoration era contradicted old liberal ideas in their intention, in one respect they confirmed what liberals had presupposed, the "extreme political importance of education." "Correct organization of education," as Schleiermacher said, served both camps as general prevention of all revolutionary changes, as "everything revolutionary" has its roots "in the incorrect organization of the same."[4] The term "reform" thus showed very early on its ambivalence, its modern Janus face, useful for both defensive modernization in a conservative spirit and for emancipation.

In the renewal of public education after 1815, conservative intentions initially dominated. Extension of the educational system took place with the objective of limiting educational ambitions and clearly differentiating between mass and elite education; the state, while taking on financial and administrative responsibility for higher education, generally left expansion of primary education to the communities. Radical or even only liberal attempts at social reform through educational reform therefore only occurred in an isolated and local fashion, e.g. outside Germany in Robert Owen's socialist experiments, or inside Germany but outside government action, in educators' independent associations or in a liberal reform discourse, as seen, for example, in Harkort's "Central Association," founded in 1844.

Between the paternalist pedagogy and an old liberal idea of help through self-help, these educational reforms also remained antirevolutionary and traditional in their core. If one looks at the few exceptions, as for example in the Belgian constitution of 1831—which propagated not only freedom of religion but also freedom of schools and teaching but which, in part, countered such intentions in practice—then one can say that educational reform before 1848 was generally implemented with the intention to pacify and control. In a conflict between freedom and equality, between class privilege and extension of participation, schooling did not follow ideas of general education but rather educational concepts defined in corporate-educational terms, and this more or less continually into the twentieth century.

Does the revolution of 1848/49 nonetheless provide a turning point in the theory and practice of public education? One could say yes even if the reality of education had changed at other times and turning points, and the modern "educational revolution," described by the American sociologist Talcott Parsons, cannot really be dated from the few months of political revolution in 1848/49. In Germany, it is a phenomenon of the first seventy years of the nineteenth century, but it precedes the momentous political revolutionization of German society.[5] However, the impact of this change is more easily understood if the importance of educational policy is seen with respect to the dimensions assigned to it in 1848/49.

Although it had few immediate practical consequences for schooling, the revolution of 1848/49 is of eminent significance for the history of education. From today's perspectives, it makes one aware of the function education can take on in modern society, and it also demonstrates in practice and in theory the controversies that came to be established permanently in lines of conflicts over educational reform. In a four-fold sense at least, the revolution can therefore be described as a break in the history of education—and not in Germany alone:

(1) Normative. Inclusion of articles on education, science and schooling in paragraph 6 in the "basic rights" of the *Paulskirche* constitution repeated in a German context that which had been articulated since the French Revolution on education as a human right.

(2) Political. The structure of education, from preschool to university, was recognized as a public responsibility, becoming at the same time a subject of contention between authoritarian-administrative intervention and democratically-legitimized shaping and construction.

(3) Social. Arising from competing state and social demands placed on the growing generation, educational policy and educational reform became a constant subject of controversy in many forms: in the struggle for cultural hegemony, as instrument of social control or as a means of self-reproduction of one's own class and culture.

(4) Professional. In the social organization of the teaching profession and in the formation of their professional identity a third actor consciously appears from 1848/49, apart from state and society, which would gain a greater say in the structure of education both in theory and in practice.

The origination of a discontinuity in political, social, professional, and theoretical categories can also be credited to the 1848 revolution—in contrast to the discourse around 1800 and the shaping of the school system after 1810 primarily by the state—new and altered conditions for education policy arose. Unlike at the beginning of the nineteenth century, the educational system had taken on an independent form, not only on paper, but also in reality. A qualified teaching staff emerged, both in primary and in the secondary educational sectors. Not only teachers, but also interested lay people had joined together in associations intended to encourage an intensification of civic education and a universalization of popular education both inside and outside of schools as institutions.

In this context, liberal ideas on educational reform were felt to be so strong and so threatening—not only by the Prussian Minister of Religious and Educational Affairs, Eichhorn, but also in Bavaria and Austria—that from the early 1840s onward, control of teachers and schools extended to dismissal from office and a ban on teachers' associations. "Tutelage, nowhere free decisions," was the teachers' diagnosis.[6] The government attributed the crisis in state and society to a politically undesirable effect of intensive educational endeavors. Also in the context of the history of education, the revolution makes manifest an already latent problem that would play a determining role in the future—the ambivalence of education between emancipation and political functionalization.[7]

Educational Questions in the Context of the Revolution

In the events of the revolution beginning in March 1848, the problems of educational policy and reform referred to above did not arise in isolation. They formed part of a general political conflict and struggle; they provided a backdrop for social conflicts, a cause of fears and hopes, motives for forming associations and passing laws. Previous research on the educational history of the revolution has been dominated by a view from the perspective of liberal teachers and the shaping of the public schools.[8] Not only is the professional perspective given more credit than should be allowed; in concentrating on public schools the view also becomes one-sided. Conflicts between different political camps have been too often ignored, as has the role already being played in 1848 by the function of educational policy in the reproduction of social milieus, or for the emancipation of the disadvantaged or groups excluded from power and education, for example, in the women's or workers movements. Beyond the debates in constituent assemblies or the activities of associations, however, especially structural problems, raised or at least made visible in the revolution, are significant.

The following is therefore rather more thematically than chronologically structured, in terms of the systematic importance of the revolution for the role of education in modern society. Only thus can one discuss how the importance of a break, the alleged failure of the revolution, and the long-term setting of the bases for educational policy can be related. While conditions in Germany lie at the center of my considerations, international comparison will show that events in Germany were not unique, but rather related to modern structural questions of educational processes.

Constitutional Debates and the Normative Premises of Educational Policy

In the pre-parliament and then in the debates in the *Paulskirche*, the question of forms of education played an independent role. Consideration was given to compulsory education, universities, academic freedom, the role of the churches, job-training, and further education and the status of teachers. The final version of the constitution, Part VI, §§ 152-158, of the "Basic Rights of the German People" codified the agreements reached during consultations.[9]

These articles certainly did not completely reinvent legal norms for forms of education, but they set accents which, apart from the unavoidable compromises, demonstrate a desire for reform. In the introduction, the central theme of the revolution is specified—freedom: freedom of "scholarship and its teaching"—and followed by a confirmation of "supervision by the state," and the end of church supervision of schools. "Public schools" are expressly given legal status, but the right of private persons to found schools after demonstrating the necessary competence, as, for example, in the Prussian General Code of 1794, was preserved. A reminder of parents' educational duties was also only a repetition of existing legal conditions. A longstanding demand by teachers was met, granting them generally "the rights of state employees" (§156). Finally, a right to free choice of occupation was established (as opposed to compulsory guild membership and mechanisms of professional exclusion), and liberal interpretations of freedom in education confirmed.

Altogether, the articles of the constitution only moderately reflected the demands of established interest groups: despite some teachers' demands, the term "public school" contained neither the primacy nor the sole competence of the state. Rather communities and fathers and their families retained their existing rights. The text of the education articles could be interpreted (as they later were) to mean that "academic freedom" was granted to the universities but not to schools and their teachers. Separation of primary schools from the church was clarified, an emphasis was placed on academic freedom at the university level as well as on the state's role as quality guarantor and supervisory body. However, all details of the shaping of the school or of teaching conditions, and even school organization and financing, remained unregulated, although they had been intensively discussed.

In regional constitutional consultations, especially in Prussia,[10] conflicts related to regulating the school question were perhaps more clearly intentional. In response to Prussia's first draft constitution, the "twenty-three"—a group of liberal educators and politicians around Kapp and Diesterweg—presented, without success, a catalog of demands on which no agreement could be found. It included not only well-known social material and professional demands of teachers, but also gave greater emphasis to the state as supporter of the school system and pleaded—against the church—for "community" teaching and, in respect to equal educational opportunity, for "free" public education.[11]

In general, however, in the text's few and relatively dryly phrased paragraphs, it is extremely difficult to recognize the historical-social problems being worked out.

If one examines related debates in the *Paulskirche* or in constituent assemblies, and, above all, the intense public discussion dedicated to the problem of education, then it becomes clear that the central questions of the revolution were also related to the subject of the parliamentary debates and constitutional articles on education: the "social question," claims to freedom and political participation, and the forming of the people as a united nation. None of the questions found consensus then, nor has any solution found consensus today. However, the majority involved in the education policy discourse (admittedly not a skeptical, critical observer such as Karl Marx) would have agreed with Gustav Thaulow, Hegelian and professor of philosophy and pedagogy in Kiel, that "in epochs, where necessity and pressure call forth the need for reform in a people … the only fundamental means of saving a nation is to be found in the introduction of a national education," and admittedly also "the only means of reconciling God with mankind."[12]

Under the heading of national education, state and society in general were understood as both subject and object of education in public debate and the more prominent plans. Clearly marked by Hegelian ideas, the state was seen as "the spirit, insofar as it been realized in the world up until now";[13] at the same time it was understood as the authority "which takes the education of the entire nation in its hands."[14] The instrument for this—as expressed in Austria[15]—was a "system of public instruction." In plans for national education this extended, although variously structured, from primary and secondary schools up to universities; primary school attendance was generally conceived as obligatory with uniform aims and objectives. Differences existed (according to talent and ability) for secondary education and university, as well as generally for vocational training. In progressive concepts, however, the effects of social differences—"all accidents of class and pecuniary conditions" in Thaulow's words[16]—were not to be allowed to have an effect on an individual's education so that everyone had the opportunity of becoming both free and sensible citizens; as "a person can only become free through schooling and education."[17]

In constitutional debates, and among theorists of state, discussions had taken place, starting in the *Vormärz*, about what exactly was meant by the idea that the state "must bear the responsibility" that everyone experience this freedom and accustom himself "to the equality of all people," so "that the nation as a whole develops a common way of thinking."[18] A liberal view of the state, which only offered the individual freedom of education, was already being juxtaposed with what were almost welfare state ideas, based on educational theories that individual claims to education required a corresponding duty of the state as provider.[19] In this context, apart from founding national schools, the state was to liberate teachers from their supervision by non–specialists, guarantee their rights, and enable them to fulfil their duties competently, so that they could become "indisputably the greatest benefactors of a nation."[20]

The authors of these plans were, of course, not innocent concerning sociopolitical realities. Plans became ever more pragmatic the closer their authors were to the school system, but even the most wide-ranging proposals retained a sober view. For Kapp, for example, it was clear that the state "had not yet understood its own con-

cept";[21] he viewed universities "as national institutions," which had to "place themselves at the head of every intellectual movement" so that "the fundaments of thought
are in advance of the events."[22] Criticism of the existing state and its unwillingness to
place itself at the head of the national movement, to "grab" "the opportunity of this
great moment,"[23] was therefore a significant part of national education plans.

Finally, wide-ranging educational plans, which sought to constitute a "people"
as well as a national educational system, played a significant role, and not only in
Germany. In Germany, educational ideas and pedagogical programs had not infre-
quently had to serve as substitutes for political ambitions and demands since 1800.
During the revolution, national motives also played an important role, in view of the
Danish conflict—as was, for example, the case with Thaulow. Forming a nation
through a public educational system, however, also found greater interest outside
Germany from the middle of the nineteenth century onward.

Among the oppressed peoples of central Europe governed by foreign powers,
efforts towards national liberation were always accompanied by plans for establishing a national education system. In Hungary, for example, demands for free education formed part of the early program of March/April 1848. József Eötvös, the
Minister of Religious and Educational Affairs in the first cabinet, propagated the
"Magyarization" of teaching as a means of forming a Hungarian nation, although
he was only able to implement this program after his return from exile, in his second period of office, after 1867. In that part of Poland occupied by Austria, the language of instruction in secondary schools and at the University of Lemberg was
switched to Polish. Hence, education was understood as an important instrument in
national emancipation and the forming of collective identity. In the Vienna reaction
beginning in fall 1848, educational policy was once again employed as an instrument of sociopolitical control.

In Austria itself, there were no lack of plans for reform and restructuring, nor
of demands for a liberal educational system and for declaring public education "the
first and most holy duty of the state."[24] In view of Austria's backwardness more
important than the aim of a national identity was the objective of social modernization through a reform of education, especially through a reform of secondary
schools and universities along German-Prussian lines. In 1848/49, an independent
Ministry of Education was created for the first time, the dominance of Catholic
clergy in secondary schools and universities was temporarily reduced, and laws
were passed concerning duration and subject matter of secondary school education.
This ambitious educational program had already failed by October 1848, and the
constitution imposed in 1849 restored to the churches their old rights. However,
from this time on, an alternative form of public education existed, which was then
introduced in wide-ranging reform after 1866/67.[25]

Political Conflicts in the Shaping of the Educational System

"The nobles and the wealthy" certainly "would become the greatest opponents of
national education," because of egalitarian programs, Thaulow prophesied in his
national education proposals; due to state claims on education, he also expected

problems with families.[26] Both assumptions were quite realistic. Conservatives sharply rejected demands for equality and for the expansion of educational opportunities. While education was understood, by everyone, as an "organism,"[27] it was not considered in terms of undifferentiated equality as one can find in the twentieth century, in spite of all the rhetoric of unity. Rather, a hierarchy of schools was seen as functional necessary; a differentiation reflecting a hierarchy of professions was expressly justified, by even liberal theoreticians.[28]

Parallel to "men's forms of employment," von Mohl distinguished, for example, "three sections": "simple crafts," for which primary school sufficed, activities that required "an application of natural laws" and that could be learned in technical-secondary schools, and academic education, for which one had to be qualified in "the sciences and scholarship." Justifications of this sort provided seemingly convincing legitimation for existing educational segregation of members of different social classes, well into the twentieth century, against all criticisms of educational policy. So despite the "affluence, education and freedom for all," proposed by the Badenese democratic deputy, Struve, in the Frankfurt pre-parliament,[29] neither the majority of plans nor the reality in the schools achieved this.

Conflicts with parents, as expected by Thaulow, arose in other respects: theoretically in the reflections of educators, and politically in conservative and religious reservations about state schools. For educators, the problem seemed to be resolved in seeing themselves above all as advocates of the child; they expressly rejected claims from the conservative milieu or the church, who claimed the role of spokesmen of parents vis-à-vis the state. Thaulow had seen the conflict but had found a harmonious solution, as for him the "true state" and "true parents" conformed to their plans and intentions: "as the true state only wishes the rights of the children and the true parents cannot but wish anything else ... the conflict arises only through the blindness and obstinacy of the parents."[30]

Thaulow thus reiterated the criticisms of parents and a presentation of the state which had already arisen in the debates on the Prussian General Code and were still held by educational administrators. The state presented itself as "final guardian of those underprivileged and unprotected," in claiming that "the child's own wish, were he capable of deciding, would reasonably be none other: this, however, the state supplements."[31] Admittedly, only the lower classes enjoyed this "supplement" until the end of the nineteenth century.

Nonetheless, the church in particular saw its traditional rights threatened by a secularization of the schools in 1848/49. In the tradition of the teachers' movement, down to the present, a consensus governs that holds that the church, in its administration of schools, should be seen as the main enemy of legitimate public education, and that the Catholic Church—historically—should be seen as a stronghold of prejudice and reaction. Its claims to "the God-given right of teaching and education" and to its own "mission," indeed a demand for "freedom of church and school, of belief and teaching,"[32] as put forward in statements from bishops or in a call for the formation of Catholic associations in 1848, are therefore even today only understood as expressions of clerical defensive struggles.

However, such an interpretation assumes that the state properly conveys universal claims as do teachers their status as the "universal estate" (F. Kapp), that is, of being an altruistic profession above all parties. Political events, from the autumn of 1848 onwards, certainly imply at least that neither the state nor the teachers could be granted such status without reservation. The struggle for cultural hegemony, which the church doubtless forced, is also probably not understood when seen solely from the perspective of the teaching profession. While one can raise questions about the consequences of church administration of schools for the extent to which instruction is determined by subject matter, the conflict presented in the rights of parents remained. The discussion of educational concepts in 1848/49 was even broader than questions of professional competence, and it was not to be resolved by state and teachers declaring themselves guarantors of reason.

The ambivalence in the propagation of parents' rights and claims of educational freedom, as presented by the church, proves to be historical if one glances beyond German borders. In debates on school legislation in France, not only old antirevolutionary emotions against state-controlled school policy arose, but also new concerns about the educational claims of the proletariat. Out of fear of a radical democratic option, the national assembly approved the Lex Falloux in June 1850, in preference to Carnot's (the Minister of Education's) liberal draft law. While promising to secure the "freedom of instruction," it in fact restored the Church's old rights of administering and directing schooling—analogous to the practical consequences of the Belgian constitution of 1831. The deputies were convinced by Thiers's argument, among others: "Catechism or socialism, there is nothing else."[33]

To this extent, the church's struggle for its role in education was already open to a dual interpretation in 1848: as an attempt to preserve old privileges and not to lose cultural hegemony, but also as a reflection of a conflict, arising in the revolution, between the state, the public sphere and the family on the settling of the education question. In regard to attempts to make teaching and education a public responsibility, it was not only strict conservatives who distrusted the state and who saw teachers as the locally present "school gendarmerie"[34] of the authorities.

Educational processes also gained socially differentiated significance in a direct political context, above all in the discussion of voting rights. Even liberals showed a distrust of a universal suffrage that was to give the people, including the unpropertied and uneducated, a share in the business of the state. Conservatives, such as Ranke, vehemently rejected the idea that "artisans and day laborers … suddenly [would gain] a share of state power," "about which they [had] no idea."[35] Plans for national education linked the right to vote to educational programs or, conversely, used the recognition of political rights of participation as a basis for demanding that said educational programs be universal in order "[to give the people] a foothold to enable them to make use of the rights recognized to be theirs," for which, "a certain standard and a certain sort of education is necessary."[36] The people, as "sovereign," needed to be educated—or so the liberals were convinced—and the uneducated excluded from participation in the political process.

The franchise debate during the revolution provides confirmation that education had already been instrumentalized for the purpose of constructing and legitimizing social classes in the *Vormärz*. Based on a symbolic order of certificates and levels of achievement that education had offered, since the introduction of a system of qualification in Germany, class differences were already being constructed parallel to educational levels in 1844. "Educated classes" were distinguished from uneducated and unpropertied, termed the "class of the proletariat."[37] At the same time, education, in its own structure, became the lever for an attempt not only to differentiate between education and work but also to justify value differences between the two. The long-lasting precedence of intellectual work over physical labor thus gained its foundations.

Educational policy, moreover, became interest politics not only between but also within social classes. In a struggle for equal weighing of university entrance for secondary schools specializing in subjects other than ancient language, for example, not only did teachers from diverse technical secondary schools cooperate with clientele of the schools, but even educational theory became an ideology, defensive or offensive.[38] A separation from the lower schools and the disciplinary function attributed to them were the only points of view consistently remaining a consensus among the educated. However, in debates, meetings, and educational plans during the revolution, educational class differences, in the meantime manifest, also became a point of controversy, arising from new calls for equality and for an expansion of access to education.

Educational Reform and Emancipation: Women's and Workers Movements

Wilhelm Weitling, the man who inspired the early communist movement, interpreted the revolution he anticipated as a pedagogic event, indeed as an imposed lesson. In this he meant not so much the many endeavors to establish a new school or the education of the nation, but rather the consequences of revolutionary experience for a social learning process and collective emancipation, provoked by the experience of revolution itself.[39] In 1848/49, such effects could be observed, beyond political discussion in the parliaments, for different social groups as well. These, admittedly, took on different forms and consequences, for example, a first stage of long-term emancipation struggles began, above all in the women's and workers movements, as early form of political instrumentalization of education in social pedagogy or as individualization of educational efforts, for example in adult education and in the foundation and use of libraries.[40] For the long-term consequences of educational policy, emancipation processes based on education are especially instructive.

For the workers' movement, educational questions were eminently significant both internally and externally, even in the *Vormärz*, and were also raised publicly in the revolution. During the Berlin Workers' Congress of 23 August– 3 September 1848, "school demands" were part of a manifesto passed for consideration by the National Assembly, which documents the dual nature of the relevant considerations.[41] They were directed above all at the state, and were very conventional in style when they, for example, assigned instruction to the public schools, and upbringing to parents. Worker demands, however, were quite different from bourgeois ones; for example, in their criticism and rejection of child labor, the demand was made for a ban on private schools or free schooling and vocational education and further training. Their school demands show, finally, how the school was instrumentalized for tasks and problems specific to a milieu, in the intention, for instance, that workers were to be educated into "citizens of the world and the state" in public education.

In these demands, that workers were to be formed into "politically imbued corporations" through educational work, schools and public education processes were assigned a significant role in collective emancipation of the working class itself. Up until then, according to the accompanying manifesto, they were "not truly" recognized "as citizens of the state," because they were without property. "It is above all necessary for workers to form themselves into a living community, which is simultaneously a politically inspired body, among the other citizens, and bring this to the attention of the statesmen, so that labor may be included as a form of property in the basic law of the state. This can only be begun by the workers themselves. Up to now such endeavors have been neglected, but this has been made good by us. ..."[42] Their educational policy demands should be seen in the context of the workers wishing to be recognized as "owners of labor."

Within the working class, especially in the workers' educational associations— which had been established abroad because of political persecution, notably in Switzerland in the 1830s—collective learning came to be seen in this light very early on. The constitution of the proletariat, accordingly, took place as a process, in which educational processes and political articulation were seen as an integrated whole. Apart from mutual benefit societies, various forms of workers' associations could not yet be clearly distinguished by their interpretation of the role of education until 1848. Associations founded by the workers themselves and consciously politically developed were relatively indistinguishable from others, for example the Central Association for the Welfare of the Working Classes,"[43] which, inspired by bourgeois social reformers, served rather the reformist pacification of the workers than preparation for revolutionary changes.[44] In the months of the revolution, differences between the various forms and aims of the organizations became sharper. Suspended during the post-1850 reaction era, they led to a clear separation of workers' movement and bourgeois social reform in the 1860s, and then to a more precise distinction between political action and educational work.

For the women's movement, the events of the revolution were of comparable significance for a discovery and conscious articulation of their own interests.[45] Here, too, emancipation was generally understood as an educational process and collective action interpreted as educational organization. In the tradition of the women's movement, the founding by Louise Otto of the first women's magazine—the *Frauen-Zeitung*, that appeared from 1849 until its prohibition in the fall of 1850— above all represents this break.[46] This magazine and its editor were, however, not alone among women in advocating education as emancipation. Contributions to it documented, apart from the unmistakable conservatism of those involved, a broad participation of women in the controversies of the revolution, the beginning of a politicization, self-confident enjoyment of the rights and role of women and their own attempts at organization, including a myriad of politically and pedagogically determined forms of association and their establishments.[47]

In their awareness of the problems of state and society they unmistakably followed bourgeois-conservative definitions of problems, an approach that dominated their view of the origins of and solutions to social crises in terms of education and training. Thus it was claimed, for example, that "a lack of public education was the cliff against which all modern reform efforts broke"; and it was characteristic of the specific position of the early women's movement that such a diagnosis was followed by calls for a strengthening of the family rather than a program of national education, "as all too often the best seeds sown in the schools are strangled by the thorns and thistles of family life."[48] In this same article, "a neglect of public education" is attributed to "the encroachments of the aristocracy of birth and money" as "they have made the people their slaves," but it is considered that women's educational work primarily should overcome this evil.

"Women of the people" should be enabled, "not only to recognize and fulfil their duties as housewife, but also those as citizen of the state and the world." In other respects, however, clear distinctions were made in educational demands between the "women of the people and those of the so-called higher ranks." The reason for this distinction—"because this education cannot be reconciled with their circumstances,[and] would thus make them dissatisfied and contribute more to their misfortune than their happiness"[49]—can hardly be distinguished from a conservative program of exclusion. As a result, after the revolution, attempts were made to found secondary schools for girls from the upper classes which were sometimes temporarily successful—for example, the foundation of the Institute of Higher Education for the Female Sex (1850-1852) in Hamburg, inspired by the ideas of Friedrich Fröbel.[50] Women's associations for mutual education and instruction therefore remained an important precursor of the women's movement, but did not create the continuity of a feminist and universally determined history.

Teacher Policy in the Revolution: Professional Emancipation and its Consequences

The significance of the revolution of 1848/49 in the history of education has generally been described with regard to the activities of teachers, and documented in their resolutions and plans. For this, there are good reasons. In their meetings, teachers from all types of schools and educational institutions formulated those demands discussed throughout the country in general. With his formula "One fatherland, one nation, one national education," the philologist Hermann Köchly in August 1848 challenged teachers in Dresden to unite and found a "people's school," as an "integrating part of the total national state."[51] For his part, Eduard Hintze, a teacher from Berlin, in his "Appeal to the Prussian Teachers" of 26 April 1848, had put together extensive demands for "reorganization" of "administration, the school, teacher training institutions and teachers' circumstances," so that educational reform could play a part in the constitution of the new state. For teachers, the most important condition for success of the great task of national education was naturally the emancipation of their own profession. Friedrich Kapp emphasized this condition when he emphatically noted at the end of his appeal that "The German teacher hereby declares himself of age and will be able to conquer and secure from this world his self-liberation and thus his inner and outer independence … in a peaceful manner."[52]

Impulses for these demands and wishes came not just from general political and economic circumstances, but also from teachers' professional reality. Limited in their rights, both professionally and politically, economically worse-off than comparable state officials and members of other teaching professions, it was above all elementary school teachers who hoped for extensive changes from the revolution. Starting in the early days of March 1848, they became a conspicuous factor in the revolution.

Teachers not only played an independent role in professional matters; they were part of the bourgeois-liberal movement in the cities, and indispensable in rural areas for their knowledge of the authorities and as peoples' advocates.[53] Teachers' participation rates should not be overestimated, but the level of state persecution and repression after the defeat of the revolution shows the extent to which teachers were politically active. In Saxony, hundreds of teachers were dismissed; in the Palatinate more than 10 percent of teachers were placed under police supervision; 3.3 percent of those charged with active participation in the revolution in 1849 were teachers. Kapp was among the victims of the reaction in Prussia, and among emigrants there were also democratically-minded and democratically organized male and female teachers.[54]

In their own matters, beyond the role of advocating intelligentsia, teachers were, of course, not inactive. In founding numerous associations and in many meetings, they made use of freedoms of the press and of assembly to articulate their interests in all German states. In Saxony teachers' associations enrolled as many as 70 percent of those eligible to join. Regional centers of the teachers' movement were certainly Prussia and Saxony. The most significant resolutions were formulated there, in Berlin by Hintze, teacher at the teachers' college, by Diesterweg, and by the twenty-three. However, Kapp's role in Westphalia, the foundation of the General German Teachers' Association in Eisenach in September 1848 and the "red" Wander's educational policy appeal underline the geographical spread. Teacher policy was based on a number of regional and supraregional meetings and associations.

In the many resolutions, statements, and programs, two clearly distinguishable themes may be recognized. On the one hand, like all other academic professional and interest groups, teachers devoted themselves to the difficulties involved with their own work, problems of social status, pay and training, and a social control of teachers administered by clergy which was experienced as alien to education and degrading. Apart from a group-specific interest policy and increasing their own status, however, teachers and their spokespersons also gave thought to the educational system in general. In their debates, they dealt with themes of general educational policy, shaping principles of educational organizations and their own national education plans. Spokespersons of school policy movements belonged to the liberal and democratic spectrum of developing parties and social camps.[55]

Some of these spokespersons included old liberals, such as the teachers' college director Diesterweg, those moving towards radical democratic ideas, such as Wander in Silesia, a state school teacher long since suspended from his position, left liberal philologists such as Kapp, a Westphalian educator, or Professors Roßmäßler in Leipzig or Thaulow in Kiel. Their texts portray a school system and responsibilities of teachers that could apply to the economic, social, governmental, and moral significance of the education system today. At the same time, even in 1848, teachers' demands were criticized as professional overreach and satirized not only by conservatives contemptuous of liberal and egalitarian educational policies, but also in the bourgeois-liberal press such as the *Vossische Zeitung*. To this extent, the revolution brought to light a conflict between advocacy claims and the self-interest of the teaching profession, which still marks its public image today. Teachers are indispensable for public education but are suspected of only working towards ensuring their own status.

In policy and administration, the government at first accepted and tolerated teachers' educational demands, but soon tied them to collective debates on the constitution or on school legislation. Towards the end of 1848 in Prussia, and after the turn of the year in other states, from Munich to Vienna and Dresden, debate and public activity altered. Born of great hopes, neither new school legislation nor a wide-ranging consideration of education in constitutional texts could be achieved. Teachers found themselves subject to pressures; political discussion in public and among teachers was soon followed by reaction among the authorities and in the church.

In digesting the revolutionary experience and its manifest disappointments obvious conflicts of interests within the teachers' movement and between teachers and clients also becomes noticeable. On the one hand, there was a distancing from their own clientele—typical of the professions—especially from parents, whose own claims were only occasionally given mention in the resolutions of many teachers' conferences in 1848. In view of almost uniform demands for independence from the clergy, for specialization of administration, for better pay and reorganization of training, one could easily overlook internal conflicts of interest in the revolutionary months, which, in retrospect, were all the more obvious: controversies over equal treatment for the ordinary, poorly paid and little respected elementary teachers in rural areas and the better paid and more self-confident teachers of urban schools, as well as differences between upper- and lower-school teachers, between teachers in the Gymnasium and in the technical high schools, between those supportive and those critical of the church. In these respects, the revolution made visible internal conflicts that—similar to controversies at the universities and in differences between professors and unpaid lecturers—provide a foretaste of struggles for position which take place through the mechanism of training and status even today.

The teaching body thus reflects, internally, not only various groups, divided by their status and their occupational position, but simultaneously by educational policy and social camps. The differences between right to left came to light in demands for comprehensive schools, in plans for internal reform of schools and teacher training, in statements on state and community rights. Meetings and associations as well as the later criticism of revolutionary exaggeration, which Diesterweg reproached, or despondent dependence on the state, which Wander complained about, confirm the "heterogeneity of the teachers' movement,"[56] which was already apparent in 1848. In the revolution it became clear that a functional hierarchy among teachers and political attitudes as well had already formed to the extent that a unity of interests within the teaching body no longer represented a realistic aim.[57]

In the premises of their actions, teachers were not only motivated by bourgeois-liberal and democratic ideals, but also by expectations for "rank" and "office"; and their profession began to define their general political standpoint. Rather than taking the side of the proletariat, established teachers interested in improving their station took their place with those who, in a market structured by entitlement, generally viewed their "education" as "property" and less as a personal ideal. The politicization of 1848/49, to this extent, crucially defined both professional and social self-awareness of teachers, and, for the first time, clearly offered options ranging from group orientation to principles of emancipation. The majority of teachers chose the liberal and not the radical-democratic standpoint.

Consequences of the Revolution

The educational movement of 1848/49 remained at first without the consequences desired by teachers and the liberal public. In place of a wide-ranging reorganization of educational administration, teaching conditions and schools, there appeared rigid control, indeed a persecution of teachers, a reactionary return to conservative school ideas, and an almost twenty-year-long domination of a restorative school policy. Nonetheless, the revolution was not without consequence for the history of education, and this can be explained as a pedagogical effect of the revolution. In the struggle for the future of the state, society, and educational organization, the fundamental options were formulated that define, even today, the pedagogical memory of the profession and the nation. These include freedom of educational organization from outside influence, democratization of education, equality of participation, state control, worldliness, secularism, a free and subject-oriented education, as well as the strong conviction that pedagogical reform opened individual carriers, avoided collective crises and, in the final analysis, also prevented revolution.

In contrast to these long-term effects, reactionary endeavors remained short-lived phenomena. Necessity for reform and pressure for modernization in state, society, and education, made visible in 1848/49, could not be ignored in the long-term either in Germany or abroad. In the 1860s—after a military defeat by Prussia—Austria introduced a modern education structure in the form of the imperial elementary school law of 1869. As a consequence of the *Ausgleich*, national schools, as desired by the revolutionaries of 1848, were established in Hungary, under the leadership of Jószef Eözvös, the minister of educational and religious affairs in 1848; and in Prussia there were also changes. Even that symbol of reactionary policy, the so-called *Stiehlschen Regulative* of 1852/53, which organized public school teacher training, had the effect, not of permanently restricting, but rather of raising educational conditions in rural parts of Prussia's eastern provinces to the levels existing elsewhere. After 1865, lesson plans for public schools were also modernized in Prussia to include practical subjects and to free them from the domination of religion. The reaction in educational and pedagogical policy to the experiences and ambitions of the revolution therefore are not only a proof of the dialectic of restoration, but rather of the simultaneity of "modernization and disciplining," even in those states which, still today, are seen as paragons of reaction in educational policy.[58]

From the long-term perspective, the contemporary relevance of the conflicts articulated in the education debates of the time are also surprising. In the struggle between freedom and equality, between state and social milieu, between central control and local autonomy for schools, there are still today no universally accepted solutions; at best, strong assumptions of unity, either for education or for national and collective identity are devalued through historical experience. Finally, as to the "progress" that the revolution was to bring, F.A. Lange, a both distanced and democratically-minded observer, expressed in 1860 his doubts about "the ... dubious relation between the idea of general progress and that of pedagogical progress." His doubts were directed at "the mistaken idea that one can transform to a higher and more noble state any particular condition of the life of the people simply through the introduction of an improved education of the coming generation." Lange insisted that "between general progress and pedagogical progress, only a limited and relative dependence" existed and that the primacy lies outside education, for example in "religious, political, literary" areas. Moreover, to succeed, more was necessary that just "capable teachers"—namely the expectation that "all classes of the people must be stirred by a spirit of life."[59] In the revolution, among other things, it became apparent that such a consensus was as unlikely as the success of attempts to form the nation into a unit through education. Therefore, the liberal vision of the pedagogical inheritance of 1848 is rather more convincing than the fiction of unity.

Notes

1. *Frankfurter Hefte* 3 (1948): 1, 5–8.
2. "Ein viertes Mal '1848-1948,'" *Frankfurter Hefte* 3 (1948): 397–98.
3. See among others, for the Soviet zone of occupation, M. Burrow, "Pädagogische Bestrebungen der Revolution von 1848," *Pädagogik* 3 (1948/pt. 3): 97–113.
4. Schleiermacher, *Vorlesung von 1826*, ed. by Weniger/Schultze Vol. I, 40.
5. Karl-Ernst Jeismann, *Das preußische Gymnasium in Staat und Gesellschaft* Vol. 2 (Stuttgart, 1996).
6. Nacke 1847, quoted in H. König (ed.), *Programme zur bürgerlichen Nationalerziehung in der Revolution von 1848/49* (Berlin, 1971), 20; further references to *Vormärz* educational policy in Jeismann, *Das preußische Gymnasium*, Vol. 2, 555ff.

7. Hartmut Titze, *Die Politisierung der Erziehung* (Frankfurt,1973).
8. For older literature see W. Appens, *Die pädagogischen Bewegung des Jahres 1848* (Elberfeld, 1914); G. Lüttgert, *Preußens Unterrichtskämpfe in der Bewegung von 1848* (Berlin, 1924); for an overview of more recent work, F.-J. Baumgart, *Zwischen Reform and Reaktion. Preußische Schulpolitik 1806-1959* (Darmstadt, 1990).
9. For the debates see Baumgart, *Zwischen Reform und Reaktion*; 169ff; for their part in the constitutional debates, J.-D. Kühne, *Die Reichsverfassung der Paulskirche* (Frankfurt, 1985), 500-22.
10. On these, see Jeismann, *Das preußische Gymnasium*, Vol. 2, 552ff.
11. The text in the version of 21 July 1848 can be found in Diesterweg, *Sämmtliche Werke*, Vol. 7, 416ff.
12. Gustav Thaulow, "Plan einer Nationalerziehung, Kiel 1848," in König, *Programme*, 156-57, § 1, § 5; Thedor Hegener, "Die Unterrichtsfrage vom demokratischen und nationalen Gesichtspunkte aus erörtert" (1848), in ibid., 129ff., who sees national education in the context of the state's "duty to protect against revolution," among other ways, through "inner agreement and unity in the entire state organism" (132).
13. Friedrich Kapp, "Aufruf zur Umgestaltung der deutschen Nationalerziehung," (Hamm 1848), in König, *Programme,* 93ff., quotation § 8, 96.
14. Thaulow, "Plan einer Nationalerziehung," 10.
15. F.S. Exner, "Entwurf der Grundzüge des öffentlichen Unterrichtswesens in Österreich (1848)," in H. Engelbrecht, *Geschichte des österreichischen Bildungswesens*, Vol. 4 (Vienna, 1986), 518.
16. Thaulow, "Plan einer Nationalerziehung," § 35.
17. Ibid., § 26; similarly "schooling" is for Kapp (§ 24) "the most powerful lever of the spirit," admittedly only "in the hands of a gently smiling freedom." Otherwise "unfortunately [it is] the thickest of shrouds in the hands of the sinister medieval forms of despotism, aristocracy and orthodoxy." In the second edition there followed a critique of the Jesuits, who provided an excellent example of this ambivalence: "Aufruf zur Umgestaltung," 291, § 29.
18. Thaulow, "Plan einer Nationalerziehung," § 92, 95; similarly, see Diesterweg.
19. Using the example of Robert von Mohl und Fröbel, see among others, H. Gembries, *Verfassungsgeschichtliche Studien zum Recht auf Bildung im deutschen Vormärz* (Darmstadt and Marburg, 1973), 87ff.
20. Thaulow, "Plan einer Nationalerziehung," § 93.
21. Kapp, "Aufruf," § 8.
22. Kapp, "Aufruf," § 14, in König, *Programme*, 289.
23. Kapp, "Aufruf," § 23, 98.
24. Apart from Adalbert Stifter, who expressed himself thus in 1849 (Engelbrecht, *Geschichte*, Vol. 4, 534), Exner's plans for restructuring higher education also took up such wording.
25. Engelbrecht, *Geschichte*, vol. 4; for Hungary an overview can be found in Hoesch.
26. Thaulow, "Plan einer Nationalerziehung," § 62, 63-67.
27. For example in the August 1848 appeal by Hermann Köchly, employee of a teacher's association; on discussions concerning comprehensive schools, see D. Oppermann, *Gesellschaftsreform und Einheitsschulgedanke*, 2 vols. (text and sources) (Frankfurt, 1982).
28. Robert von Mohl (1849), quoted in L. von Rönne, *Das Unterrichtswesen des preußischen Staates*, Vol. 2, (Berlin, 1855) 3, 5.
29. Quoted in B. Michael and H.-H. Schepp (eds.), *Politik und Schule von der Französischen Revolution bis zur Gegenwart: eine Quellensammlung zum Verhältnis von Gesellschaft, Schule und Staat im 19. u. 20. Jahrhundert* (Frankfurt a.M., 1973), Vol. 1, 356.
30. Thaulow, "Plan einer Nationalerziehung," § 72.
31. L. von Rönne, *Das Unterrichtswesen des preußischen Staates*, Vol. 1 (Berlin, 1855), 560. On the Prussian General Code, Reinhart Koselleck, *Preußen zwischen Reform und Revolution*, (Stuttgart, 1981), esp. 52ff.
32. Michael and Schepp (eds.), *Quellensammlung*, Vol. 1, 371ff., 381.
33. M. von Boehn, *Vom Kaiserreich zur Republik* (Munich, 1921), 291 and J. Schriewer, *Die französischen Universitäten 1945-196*, (Bad Heilbrunn, 1972), 60-61.

34. Friedrich A.W. Diesterweg, "Zur Schulfrage," *Sämtliche Werke*.Vol. 7, 436, quotes such an objection and attempts to disarm it.

35. Quoted in Hans-Ulrich Wehler, *Deutsche Gesellschaftsgeschichte*,Vol. 2 (Munich, 1987), 738.

36. Theodor Hegener, "Die Unterrichtsfrage," (n. 12), in König, *Programme*, 129ff., quote on 132.

37. With mention, among others, of J.G. Hoffmann (1844), see also the rich materials in Ulrich Engelhardt, "*Bildungsbürgertum*". *Begriffs- und Dogmengeschichte eines Etiketts* (Stuttgart, 1986), 104ff. and passim.

38. M. Eckert, *Die schulpolitische Instrumentalisierung des Bildungsbegriffs. Zum Abgrenzungsstreit zwischen Realschule und Gymnasium im 19. Jahrhundert* (Frankfurt, 1984).

39. Wilhelm Weitling, *Garantien der Harmonie und Freiheit* (1842) (Berlin, 1955).

40. For the context: *Handbuch der deutschen Bildungsgeschichte*,Vol. 3 (Munich, 1987), esp. the section on social pedagogy and adult education.

41. Reproduced in K.H. Günther et al., *Quellen zur Geschichte der Erziehung*, (East Berlin, 1978), 245-47; Michael and Schepp,Vol. 1, 368.

42. Michael and Schepp (eds.), *Quellensammlung*,Vol.1, 368.

43. Jürgen Reulecke, "Die Anfänge der organisierten Sozialreform in Deutschland," in Rüdiger vom Bruch (ed.), *Weder Kommunismus noch Kapitalismus. Bürgerliche Sozialreform in Deutschland vom Vormärz bis zu Ära Adenauer* (Munich, 1985), 21-59, esp. 27ff.

44. K. Birker, *Die deutschen Arbeiterbildungsvereine 1840-1870* (Berlin, 1973).

45. See the essay by Gabriella Hauch (chapter 26) in this volume.

46. "*Dem Reich der Freiheit werb' ich Bürgerinnen*". *Die Frauen-Zeitung von Louise Otto*, edited with commentary by Ute Gerhard, Elisabeth Hannover-Drück, and Romina Schmitter (Frankfurt, 1980).

47. See the overview in the introduction to Gerhard et al., "*Dem Reich der Freiheit*," 7-34, esp. 20-22.

48. *Frauen-Zeitung*, no. 31, Saturday 17 November 1849, 172.

49. Ibid., 173.

50. E. Kleinau, "Die 'Hochschule für das weibliche Geschlecht' und ihre Auswirkung auf die Entwicklung des höheren Mädchenschulwesens in Hamburg," *Zeitschrift für Pädagogik* 36 (1990): 121-38.

51. König, *Programme*, 13-14.

52. Kapp, "Aufurf," § 30 (König, *Programme*, 100).

53. Supplementing older literature see also F.-J. Baumgart, "Lehrer und Lehrervereine während der Revolution von 1848/49," in *Mentalitäten und Lebensverhältnisse* (Göttingen, 1982), 173-88; Werner Wedmann, "Schulbildung und Lehrerstand in der Pfalz um die Mitte des 19. Jahrhunderts und die 1848/49er Revolution," *Jahrbuch zur Geschichte von Stadt und Landkreis Kaiserslautern* 22/23 (1984/85): 269-98; U. Jungbluth, "Politische Lernprozesse und die Rolle der Volksschullehrer im Vormärz und der 1848er Revolution im nassauischen Dorfe Nauort," *Nassauische Annalen* 106 (1995): 187-204.

54. Bruce Goldberg, "The Forty-Eighters and the School System in America: The Theory and Practice of Reform,"in Charles L. Brancaforte (ed.), *The German Forty-Eighters in the United States*, (New York, 1989), 203-18; A. Etges, "Erziehung zur Gleichheit. Mathilde Franziska Annekes Töchter-Institut in Milwaukee und ihr Eintreten für die Rechte der Frauen," *Zeitschrift für Pädagogik* 40 (1994): 945-62.

55. D. Krause-Hotop, *Der junge Wander* (Braunschweig, 1989), 291ff; G. Geißler and H.F. Rupp, *Diesterweg zwischen Forschung und Mythos*, (Neuwied, 1996), esp. 109ff; Jeismann, *Das preußische Gymnasium*,Vol. 2, esp. 558ff.

56. Baumgart, *Lehrer*, 180.

57. Anothony J. LaVolpa, *Prussian School Teachers 1763-1848* (Chapel Hill, 1980).

58. F.-M. Kuhlemann, *Modernisierung und Disziplinierung. Sozialgeschichte des preußischen Volksschulwesens 1794-1872* (Göttingen, 1992).

59. Friedrich Albert Lange," Fortschritt," in K.A. Schmid (ed.), *Encyklopädie des gesammten Erziehungs- und Unterrichtswesens*, 2 vols. (Gotha, 1860), 417-19.

Chapter 31

PROGRESS AND ITS LIMITS

The Revolution of 1848 and European Jewry

Reinhard Rürup

Revolutions have played an important, but ambiguous role in the modern history of European Jewry. Granting Jews equal rights began with the revolution of 1789, and it was left to the revolution of 1917 to finally introduce legal equality for Jews in Russia as well, after decades of delay. On the other hand, revolutionary upheavals were tied to antisemitic unrest and riots. In this respect as well, the French revolution of 1789 sent the first signal. In Alsace and Lorraine, where the vast majority of French Jews lived, the revolution did not begin with a fraternization of Christians and Jews, but with attacks on Jewish residents and their property, the fierceness of which deeply shocked the protagonists of enlightenment and progress. At the moment when political and social conditions had begun to shake, an antisemitism vented itself that was both economically and religiously motivated and that had as a precondition mutual unfamiliarity with ways of life.

For relations between Jews and Christians, the revolution did not initially appear to be the beginning of a new era, but rather announced a relapse into times thought to be long past. In historical consciousness, however, local and regional shocks quickly paled in comparison with the fact that the National Assembly drew the practical consequences for Jews from the fundamental principle that the rights of man and citizen applied to all. The emancipation law of 28 September 1791 that granted all Jews living in France citizenship, was seen as an epochal break, as the beginning of a Jewish history in Europe which—in spite of all the obvious counter-tendencies—was characterized by emancipation and integration, by the flowering of Jewish life under the conditions of civil society, until the beginning of National Socialist rule.

In 1848, the process of emancipation and integration was well-advanced in some European countries, while in others it had hardly begun. This reflects the quite distinctive level of political and social development in the different countries. Developed constitutional government existed only in a few west European states; a start had been made in parts of the German Confederation as well, especially in the south and southwest. Most states still had an absolutist government, even when arbitrariness had at least been partially restricted by tendencies toward the rule of law and by clear administrative regulations. The process of defeudalization had begun everywhere, with the exception of Russia, but progress made up to the eve of the revolution was very unequal, and it was especially the delay in this aspect which belonged—together with the immediate crises—to the most significant causes of the revolutionary upheavals.

With the exception of England and Belgium, the industrial revolution was at best still in its initial stages, but was becoming increasingly important in some states or regions in the years immediately before the revolutions. More advanced was the commercialization of living conditions, not least in the agrarian sector. In Germany and Italy, in parts of the Habsburg Monarchy and the Russian Empire, nationalist aspirations had become so significant that they came well to the fore at the outbreak of revolution. In defining the possibilities and limits of the revolutions of 1848 in respect of the introduction of a bourgeois-liberal society, one must be well aware in advance that the supporters of the revolution in the individual states were faced with extremely different tasks. And, in fact, one can hardly speak of a uniform revolutionary process, in spite of the epidemic of revolution spreading through large parts of Europe.

When one looks in greater detail at the situation of Jews on the eve of the revolution, the picture is similarly disparate.[1] While one can speak of a European age of emancipation for the period following 1789 and the Napoleonic era, specific emancipation policies were always a matter for the individual states. Only in France, Holland, and Belgium was full legal equality guaranteed Jews, while in other parts of Europe legal restrictions continued to exist: from Russia, which did not have its own emancipation policy, to the Habsburg Monarchy, which had not moved beyond Joseph II's Edicts of Toleration, and Prussia, which in many ways had retreated from its emancipation legislation of 1812, to England, where it was only a question of certain political rights for the Jewish upper class. Jewish living conditions in Europe in the 1840s, as well, ranged from a traditional Jewish milieu only little affected by modern developments to extensive assimilation and integration in the non-Jewish world, in which religion had become more and more a "private matter." Nonetheless, a debate on emancipation existed which did not stop at national or state borders, and in the 1840s it had become clear that the fate of the Jews was coupled with the development of liberal and democratic movements throughout Europe. At that moment when representatives of the bourgeois movement took over the reigns of government, it was generally felt that the emancipation of the Jews would also have to be completed.

Under these circumstances it was a shock not only for the Jews themselves but also for the liberal public that the revolution of 1848, especially in its early phase, was also defined by numerous anti-Jewish riots. These often occurred in regions where there had already been anti-Jewish unrest in 1819 and in the early 1830s, but these pogrom-like movements extended far beyond such centers. In the European countries affected by revolution, 180 such events have been discovered in which Jews were threatened, attacked, and in some cases even killed, their houses destroyed or plundered.[2] These stretched from French Alsace through southern and central Germany and eastern Prussia to Bohemia, Moravia, and Hungary, and, in Italy, to Rome. The clear centers were in Alsace, with about sixty localities and in the non-Habsburg parts of the German Confederation, with about eighty.

The riots in Alsace must have been especially disturbing, because the legal barriers between Jews and Christians had been completely abolished since 1791, or, taking into consideration the legal restrictions decreed by Napoleon in 1808 for 10 years, at least since 1818. Thus, according to the expectations of theorists of emancipation, the old religious and social tensions should have been broken down in the meantime.[3] Such, however, was obviously not the case. Cultural convergence in Alsace, where Jews lived in relatively closed settlements, had only progressed slowly, as had their turning away from the traditional trades of money-lending and peddling. The vast majority of Jews were still seen by the Christian population as money-lenders and traders. Jews were different and this difference was felt to be annoying or even threatening by sections of the Christian population in 1848 as well. The violent unrest, in the course of which hundreds of Jews fled from the Sundgau for Switzerland (where there were only few Jews and no emancipation legislation), had to be understood as a warning far beyond the borders of France not to expect a reduction in the traditional conflict potential in the short-term.

Popular unrest at the beginning of a revolution reflects prerevolutionary crises. This was also true of 1848, in which a number of crises overlapped. All European countries were affected by the structural crisis, even if to a quite different extent, which accompanied the transformation from a feudal to a modern bourgeois-capitalist society. The commercialization and capitalization of agriculture, the transition from outwork and manufacturing to industrial production, the extension of the transportation network, the tapping of new markets, and the constantly increasing significance of capital caused a "modernization crisis," that was also felt in "backward" regions and sectors of the economy. This crisis was aggravated by the catastrophic harvest failures of 1845 and 1846, which had set off not only an existential crisis in agriculture but also wide-ranging inflationary and hunger crises. While the harvest of 1847 was better and acute supply bottlenecks overcome, the experience of hunger and deprivation was not forgotten. On top of this came the beginning of an international recession in the trade and industrial sectors, which had far-reaching consequences for the labor and capital markets.

In this situation, the still existing feudal burdens and feudal restrictions proved especially oppressive for a majority of people. The popular revolutionary movement, born of economic and social deprivation, displayed both antifeudal and anticapitalist features, especially in rural areas, and not seldom the two were inseparably intertwined. For the Jews, in view of their special position in trade and money-lending, that meant that they—independent of their legal status—could easily, and did, become the preferred object of "popular anger."

In southwestern Germany, the protests and attacks were directed at the ever more oppressive feudal burdens in the principalities and manors, but also at the oft-bewailed "rule of money."[4] "All around us," it was reported from the Badenese village of Mosbach in the Odenwald in mid-March 1848, "numerous masses of people threaten the Israelites, the higher nobility and the feudal lords, and ever more every well-off person altogether" (whereby the reporter adds that: "it almost seems as if the forgotten times of the peasant wars would be repeated here").[5] From Mergentheim in Württemberg it was reported at around the same time that "behind the … persecution of Jews is not simply revenge for alleged or real instances of being taken advantage of, but also a good bit of communism, which has gone to work with unbelievable cheek."[6]

The exact extent, however, to which Jews were attacked because of their special position in the economy and specific practices of "usury," or because of their status as an ethnic-religious minority is difficult to discover in retrospect.[7] Cases have been reported where, as in Ettlingen or Richen, only individual houses, whose owners were held to be especially base "usurers" were victims of the "people's court," while the rest of the Jewish families—the vast majority—were expressly spared.[8] On the other hand, it was apparent that in some towns "a barbarian fury arose against the holders of the Mosaic belief in general," according to a contemporary report.[9]

Obviously, deeply-rooted religious prejudice and fears played a significant role, as was shown not least in that threats against Jews were often tied to church holidays such as Good Friday or Easter. On the other hand there are cases in which collective interest conflicts were a factor, as for example, when Jewish residents were forced to surrender all claims to "use of village property"—as a rule not yet granted, but expected or feared by non-Jewish inhabitants.[10] Finally it should not be overlooked that while in Baden there were no less than thirty-three localities with anti-Semitic unrest, in the other 140 localities where Jews resided things remained peaceful. In Alsace, as well, the proportion of Jewish communities affected by unrest in the Departments of the Haut-Rhin and the Bas-Rhin was around 20 percent.

The cities, too, did not remain unaffected. In a number of German cities there were violent acts which, as a rule, could be quickly suppressed.[11] Among the places affected were Karlsruhe, Heidelberg, and Gießen, but also Berlin or Landsberg, Hirschberg and Gleiwitz. The "excesses" were directed against individual Jews or their firms. Thus, for example, in Heidelberg, a clothes shop was destroyed, whose Jewish owner was held responsible for the crisis in the tailor's craft. In some of the larger cities in the Habsburg Monarchy antisemitic riots had been long-prepared. In Prague and in some other Bohemian cities there had been sporadic attacks on Jewish firms in the textile industry from the mid-1840s, and, in the hunger crisis of 1846/47, on Jewish grain dealers as well. In the spring of 1848, worker unrest in Prague, caused by high prices and unemployment, initially discharged itself in violence against individual Jewish bakers and traders, followed by larger scale riots on 1 and 2 May, in which the massive anti-Jewish propaganda of the previous weeks played an important role.

In Bratislava, there were attacks on houses in which Jews lived located outside the ghetto at the end of March, and at Easter (23/24 April) there were violent riots inside and outside the ghetto, which led to the destruction and plundering of shops and which did not stop at a Jewish children's home and a cemetery building. Here, too, economic tensions were aggravated by anti-Jewish propaganda, so that general discontent was finally directed against Bratislava Jews. In Vienna, however, where the production shops of Jewish businessmen were also affected by the unrest in the outer districts in March, an antisemitic accent was lacking at this time. However, a growing antisemitic mood could be observed in the following months, and at the end of July it was claimed that Vienna was on the brink of a persecution of the Jews— whereby opponents of the revolution had become supporters of this movement.

It is noticeable that unrest against Jews was restricted, almost without exception, to the first weeks and months of the revolution. Antisemitic disturbances began in Alsace and in southwestern Germany in the final days of February, had their high-point in March and in part in April, while in May only a few regions were affected— Hungary above all, but also Silesia and, once again, Alsace. From all the later revolutionary crises—armed struggles in Italy, in Austria or Hungary, the June uprising in Paris or the campaign for the imperial constitution in Germany in 1849—no antisemitic currents are known.

That may well be due for example, to, the rural population no longer playing a significant role in the revolutionary struggles from the spring of 1848 onwards in Germany and that everywhere the severity of the economic and social crises declined in the course of the revolution. It can also be understood as the result of a process of political enlightenment, as not only the new governments but also the liberal and democratic leadership energetically opposed all antisemitic activities. "As soon as the revolution had reached the phase of establishing itself," in Simon Dubnow's interpretation of this development, "the excesses that had accompanied the March revolts came to an end."[12] While the spontaneously arising mass movement was an expression of "passions" and direct interests, the later phases of the revolution were dominated by liberal and democratic programs and strategies, and open discrimination and persecution of Jews did not fit within their frameworks. Contrary tendencies existed at most only in the counter-revolution, as can be seen especially clearly in Vienna.

Jewish liberal and democratic representatives tended to play down the importance of the riots. Leopold Zunz adjudged quite soberly in March: "The storm of the riffraff against the Jews in certain areas will pass without trace like other nonsense, and liberty will remain."[13] In the short-term, developments seemed to confirm his words. Nonetheless, the riots certainly did not remain without consequence. Even during the revolution, not a few governments used such "popular anger" to delay emancipation legislation. Even prominent revolutionary leaders, such as Lajos Kossuth, argued in this spirit when declaring before the Hungarian Reichstag: "If we sought to emancipate the Jews now, we would place them at the mercy of their enemies and give rise to a second St. Bartholomew's Night."[14] In Vienna, Jewish writers were already in March expressing the fear that rapid emancipation would lead to "the spectacle of previously experienced persecution of Jews."[15]

In any case, events of the spring of 1848 had made clear, in a frightening manner, that the Jews in Europe were still at the mercy of more or less spontaneous outbreaks of hate and brutality, even under "modern" conditions. It was, therefore, not without reason that the leading Jewish publisher Ludwig Philippson praised the special value of peaceful developments for Jews under the protection of the state a few years after the revolution: "Altogether, we Jews thankfully recognize that of all the modern factors, it is still the state, and especially the bureaucratic state, which was and is liberal to us, as in every stormy period the people raised themselves against us and in every reaction the aristocracy and upper bourgeoisie—only the peacefully developing state gives us peace, rights, liberty, and it alone grants hope for the future."[16] The Jews had already learned in the *Vormärz* that they could not do without the protection of the state, as restricted and costly as it might be. The revolution had clearly shown that legal security, even when it was only the guarantee of limited rights, was absolutely necessary for Jews, even in a modern society.

Examining the progress made in the legal status of the Jews in 1848/49, one finds a disparate, contradictory picture. At the beginning of the revolution it appeared natural that Jews would receive legal equality without further debate, in spite of antisemitic "excesses." In elections for constituent assemblies, they were granted both the right to vote and to be elected, without a long discussion. Governments and parliaments expressed their support of complete emancipation. Freedom of religion and conscience and independence of political and civil rights from religious confession were among to the central planks of the revolutionary movement. In May 1848, for example, the *Spenersche Zeitung* in Berlin wrote that the "'Jewish Question,' which had raised strong feelings hardly a year ago, now only [belongs] in the political antique chamber."[17] In a debate on emancipation legislation in Baden, it was stated that extensive justification would only be "a waste of time." "There are no more hurdles to be overcome: the mighty call of the times has, with one stroke, overthrown them all."[18] And, in fact, major debates on the emancipation of Jews no longer took place in the parliaments of the revolutionary period—the matter seemed to be settled.

The actual course of legislation contradicts, however, this first impression. Thus, for example, equal rights were promised in the Austrian constitution of 25 April 1848, but the abolition of legal restrictions on Jews was, however, expressly left to the decision of the future Reichstag. A hand-written note from emperor Ferdinand I on the restructuring of the kingdom of Bohemia had already been published on 8 April, in which the Jews were promised "freedom to practice their religion." Beyond that, however, the note just stated that "Citizenship for Jews in Bohemia is to be the object of mature deliberation in the Bohemian Diet, suitable to the time and local conditions."[19] On 5 October 1848, the Austrian Reichstag resolved to abolish the special "Jew tax," but was unable to carry wide-ranging emancipation legislation. Thus it was left to the government to grant full legal equality to Jews (which was thus, admittedly, not permanently guaranteed) in the imposed constitution of 4 March 1849, after the defeat of the revolution.

In Hungary, the "Jewish question" was initially given no consideration in legislative endeavors to establish a new liberal order. Quite the opposite, the Hungarian Diet withdrew the franchise initially granted Jews. The newly elected constituent assembly then voted for a gradual, step-by-step emancipation of the Jews, without, however, passing the corresponding legislation. Only at the end of July 1849, two weeks before the final defeat of the Hungarian Revolution, did the Assembly finally decide to grant full equality to Jews, an act, however, with no practical consequences.

Developments in Italy were much more favorable. While the constitution of the kingdom of Piedmont-Savoy from the beginning of March 1848 contained only toleration clauses for all non-Catholics, Jews were granted equality in civil rights at the end of March and in political rights in June. The provisional government in Lombardy immediately abolished legal restrictions on Jews, and the Republic of Venice also proclaimed, without hesitation, full legal equality for members of all religious confessions. Emancipation provisions were also contained in the liberal constitution of the grand duchy of Tuscany and of the duchy of Modena. In Rome, the walls of the ghetto were torn down on 17 April 1848, and in the republic proclaimed in February 1849, Jews were granted full legal equality. Emancipation of the Jews had become a permanent component of the liberal and national movement in Italy, supported by the bourgeois classes into which a majority of Jews had been assimilated. Admittedly, they shared the fate of the revolutionary movement: with the defeat of the revolution and the re-establishment of the old powers, emancipation of Jews in Italy was also reversed—with the exception of Piedmont-Savoy—to the point of rebuilding the ghetto walls in papal Rome.

A short glance at Switzerland, which did not experience revolution in 1848, but did not remain unaffected by the revolutionary upheavals in Europe, is informative. Emancipation of the Jews had advanced little in Switzerland up to that point, and in May 1848, the *Großer Rat* was still demanding of Jews that they first prove themselves "deserving of emancipation."[20] Hence important rights, such as rights of residency, continued to be reserved for members of Christian confessions in the new federal constitution of 12 November 1848. With good reason, therefore, a Jewish petition of February 1849 could state: "The confederate constitution is, among all the constitutions drawn up in the last year, the only one which sets as condition to the full enjoyment of civil liberties the Christian confession."[21] Only in 1866 and 1872, after a hard struggle, was full legal equality for Jews in Switzerland granted through amendments to the federal constitution.

In Germany, immediate legal equality was granted to Jews only in a few smaller principalities (Hessen-Homburg and Hessen-Nassau, Anhalt-Bernburg and Anhalt-Dessau) in March 1848. Prussia, on the other hand, in a "Decree on the Basis of a Future Constitution" of 6 April, proclaimed equality of rights of citizenship but this was only clearly regulated in the imposed constitution of 5 December 1848. Although the constituent assembly in Prussia also intended full emancipation, it was left as in Austria to counter-revolutionary forces to grant equality. Developments in Bavaria seemed to be following a similar path, where Jews were granted political rights in June 1848 but further improvements were denied them. Only in May 1849, after the end of revolutionary struggles, did the government present unrestricted emancipation legislation that gained the approval of the lower house, but failed in the upper house—after the rise of a major anti-emancipation storm of protest.

Characteristic for the ambiguity of emancipation policies in not a few German states were developments in Baden, the most progressive of the German states in the liberal-democratic sense. Emancipation legislation hastily approved by the lower house in the spring of 1848 only passed into law in February 1849 because of successful foot-dragging by the government and the upper house. The final version only contained equality in political rights, but not in important rights of municipal citizenship. This was not by chance, but was fully intended. The liberal government feared new unrest above all from among the rural population and therefore substituted tactics for principles.

Other German states, in contrast, decided from the start against introducing their own legislation, preferring to await the decision of the Frankfurt National Assembly. There, the principle of full equality met with no resistance worth mentioning—despite a few reservations expressed in the constitutional committee—so that unrestricted legal equality was included in the "Basic Rights of the German People," which was published as imperial legislation on 27 February 1849, in anticipation of the constitution. With the failure of the revolution, however, the legal validity of the "Basic Rights" was a matter of controversy, and on 23 August 1851 it was completely repealed by the Confederate Diet, which in the meantime had been reactivated.

To provisionally summarize, it has been shown that the results of the revolution at the level of emancipation legislation were much more restricted than at first assumed. Apart from Piedmont-Savoy—and Denmark as well—the achievements of the revolution were only short-term or limited in extent. Only some of the smaller German states preserved the legal equality they had granted. In Prussia, equality for Jews was reconfirmed in the revised constitution of 31 January 1850 in Article 12, but this was in part called into question and in part directly undermined by the enactment of a "Christian state" in Article 14. In Austria as well, legal status became unclear once again with the repeal of the constitution in 1851, something only rectified with the introduction of full equality in the constitution of 1867. Hence the revolution in toto did not bring the conclusion of emancipation legislation expected of it at the beginning; in most of Europe this only occurred in the 1860s and in some places only in the early 1870s. Nonetheless, the belief commonly held by contemporaries that the emancipation of Jews was decided at least in principle in the revolution is not incorrect. Even when specific results were not achieved, the discussions in the years that followed were only a sort of rearguard action which, while delaying equality, could no longer prevent it.

Jewish emancipation was no longer first and foremost a question of legislation—this became clear in 1848 and 1849. Beginning in 1830, and in part even earlier, Jews in the European states were pressing with growing force for their rights.

They emphasized the necessary and indivisible ties between the objectives of the bourgeois movement and the emancipatory aspirations of the Jewish population. The Hamburg jurist, Gabriel Riesser, became the most important symbol of the ties between liberal bourgeoisie and Jewish emancipation. In newspapers and journals, in flyers and petitions, Jews no longer begged for their legal equality as a favor; rather they began to demand it as a right withheld from them, based on the ideas of the rights of man and citizen. They demanded assimilation and integration of the Jews, but rejected the idea that emancipation first had to be earned or that it was at the discretion of Christian politics.

With the first revolutionary movements, something completely new took place in 1848, something that decisively changed the position of Jews in the European states. For the first time, Jews appeared as political actors in large numbers, and not seldom even as leaders of general political movements. In Vienna, as in Berlin, Jews were actively involved in the street-fighting that led to the victory of the revolutionary movement in March 1848. Of the first five fatalities of the revolution in Vienna, two were Jews: a student at the polytechnic and a journeyman weaver. In Berlin, the number of Jews among the victims of the March barricade fighting cannot be determined exactly, but there were no less than ten, which translates into a share of at least 4-5 percent of all fatalities (with a share in the population of about 2 percent). Funeral services in Vienna (17 March) and in Berlin (20 March) turned into demonstrations of an overcoming of old religious barriers. In both cities, Christian clergy and Jewish rabbis spoke in ecumenical services. In Alsace, as well, the chief rabbi accompanied the bishop of Strasbourg and Protestant clergy in blessing trees of liberty and celebrating the revolution.

In France, the February Revolution meant a major breakthrough in that among the nine members of the provisional government, two—Adolphe Crémieux (Justice) and Michel Goudchaux (Finance)—were Jews. Crémieux, who worked closely together with Lamartine, was a respected lawyer and politician, who, at the same time, openly supported specific Jewish interests; he later founded the "Alliance israélite universelle" (1860) for the promotion of political and social equality for Jews throughout the world. Goudchaux enjoyed the special confidence of the Parisian commercial and financial bourgeoisie. At the same time as Jews were being persecuted in Alsace, they could rise to the highest offices of the land in the capital.

Outside France, only in Venice did Jews take ministerial office in 1848. In the provisional government formed at the end of March, headed by Daniel Manin, whose ancestors were Jewish but who was himself a Christian, were also two Jews: Isaac Pesaro Maurogonato (Finance) and Leone Pincherle (Agriculture and Trade). Moreover, there were Jews among the closest advisors of Cavour and the Piedmontese king Emanuel II. Jews took part in armed struggles on the side of the insurgents and were elected to the parliaments of a number of states. In Venice, there were three Jews in the first parliament of the revolution; in the second, there were seven. In Rome, three Jews were elected to the constituent assembly after the proclamation of a republic in the spring of 1849, while others were members of the city council and took on important functions in the civic guard and the committee of public safety. After the defeat of the revolution, Jews were among Garibaldi's troops trying to fight their way to the north.

In the German states, there were no Jewish ministers, but a number of deputies who had gained the trust of non-Jewish voters. Even among those invited to the so-called pre-parliament in Frankfurt am Main because of their trans-regional reputation there were no less than six Jews—Berthold Auerbach, Julius Fürst, Johann Jacoby, Ignaz Kuranda, Gabriel Riesser, and Moritz Veit—while seven were elected to the German National Assembly (apart from Jacoby, Kuranda, Riesser, and Veit, also Ludwig Bamberger, Moritz Hartmann, and Friedrich Wilhelm Levysohn; Hartmann and Kuranda were among the Austrian delegates). There were, moreover, ten deputies of Jewish ancestry, who deserve mention in this context to the extent that their background—in part, simply because of their Jewish sounding names—was not unknown to their voters.

Gabriel Riesser, a member of the constitutional committee was elected second vice-president of the National Assembly in Octobe. He also belonged to the delegation, as did Johann Jacoby, that offered the Prussian king the imperial crown in April 1849. Among those deputies who had been baptized as children, Eduard Simson, elected president of the National Assembly in December and head of the "imperial delegation," Moritz Heckscher as justice and foreign minister, and Johann Hermann Detmold as minister of justice and the interior in the "provisional government of the Reich" played very public roles. In 1848, for the first time, Jews were also elected in the parliaments and constitutional assemblies in various states in the German Confederation: Prussia, Bavaria, Brunswick, Mecklenburg-Schwerin, Sachsen-Anhalt, Hessen-Homburg, Frankfurt, Hamburg, and Lübeck.

There were five Jewish deputies in the Prussian constitutional assembly, of whom special mention must be given to Johann Jacoby, one of the most well-known leaders of the democratic camp, Raphael Kosch, elected vice-president in August, and Julius Brill, who as a typesetter was one of the few delegates who could be included in the "laboring classes." Jewish politicians were strongly represented in the constituent assemblies of Hamburg and Frankfurt, while in all other parliaments only one or two Jews had seats. Two Jews were even named to the upper house of the Prussian parliament in 1849.

Jews played an unusually active role, one important for the course of the revolution, in Austria, and that means above all in Vienna. Here, the fact that there were four Jewish deputies in the newly elected Reichstag that met in July 1848 is only of secondary importance. Rather, Jews played a major and at times prominent role in decisive situations in the revolution and in numerous revolutionary institutions. Above all the doctors Adolf Fischhof and Joseph Goldmark became recognized leaders of the revolutionary movement advocating a liberal program. It was Fischhof who first articulated the demands of the revolution in an improvised speech on 13 March; he and numerous other Jews were among the leaders of the popular movement at the time. In Vienna, it was above all Jewish students and young academics (doctors, journalists and jurists) who came out in favor of the revolution—in this they differed little from their fellow students, who, more than in any other land, saw themselves as the avant-garde of the democratic-liberal movement. Four Jews, all with doctorates, were part of the first delegation that negotiated at the behest of the rebels, and when the conflict reached its climax, other Jews took part in the storming of the arsenal. Belonging to the student committee formed at the end of March, which was to play an important role in the further course of the revolution, were, apart from Goldmark as chairman, numerous other Jews, among others Boch, Fischhof, Flesch, Frankl, Kapper, Mannheimer, Tausenau, Taussig, and Unger (most of them also young doctors). Jews were also members of the armed "Academic Legion" and the national guard, which were to defend the aims of the revolution not only against reactionary endeavors, but also against possible uprisings among the proletariat in the Vienna suburbs. Some companies elected Jewish commanders.

The outstanding role that Jews played in the Vienna Revolution was unequalled elsewhere in Europe, as became more obvious when the committee of public safety, the most influential political institution up to the forming of the Reichstag, was founded at the end of May during a phase of radicalization. Fischhof was elected chairman by a large majority, and another Jewish member (Karl Freund) was chosen as one of his two deputies. It was this constellation that led to a petition by the Vienna trade association to the Minister of the Interior for an exclusion of Jews from the committee of public safety because they "no longer wished to be in tutelage to Jews."[22] The struggle against the revolutions increasingly took on an antisemitic tone from the summer, so that even a statement by Minister Schwarzer was circulated that the entire revolution was nothing more that "simply a Jewish revolution."[23] As wrong as such statements were, it is indisputable that a surprisingly large number of Jews enjoyed the trust of the liberal-democratically minded public, and a few, such as Hermann Jellinek and Adolf Chaizes, also that of the armed workers. In the revolutionary struggles in October, Jews once again played a significant role, up to their dying for the revolution (Hermann Jellinek was executed under martial law) or emigrating.

In the non-Habsburg portions of the German Confederation, Jewish participation in the revolution was also not restricted to election rallies and parliamentary work, but the significance of their activities was less than in Vienna. This may be due to the more advanced level of emancipation, but also to the altogether more moderate course of the revolution. In Berlin, young Jewish intellectuals were able to exert a not insignificant amount of influence in the mass meetings and political clubs, and in other cities, too, Jews took on important political functions. Remarkable is their participation in the democratic congresses in Frankfurt and later in Berlin, where the Jewish doctor Sigismund Asch, from Breslau, was elected vice-president. Andreas Gottschalk, a doctor from Cologne baptized in 1847, played a prominent role in the democratic and socialist movement of 1848. Also deserving mention in this context is the outstanding role played by Stephan Born, descended from a Jewish family in Posen, especially in the Workers' Fraternization founded in August. The number of Jews, however, very active in promoting the interests of the liberal bourgeoisie against all democratic-socialist currents in southern Germany, as in Berlin, is also not insignificant.

Important, finally is the high level of participation by Jews in political debates in the daily press, in flyers, journals, and brochures. In Berlin, Bernhard Wolff published the *National-Zeitung*, Aaron Bernstein the *Urwähler-Zeitung*, Heinrich Bernhard Oppenheim the *Reform*, and Karl Weill the *Konstitutionelle Zeitung*; there were numerous other newspapers with Jewish publishers.[24] Contemporary polemics denouncing the "Jewish press" were primarily directed against liberal, democratic, and socialist publications and thus make clear that the majority of Jewish journalists and publishers belonged to the revolutionary camp. However, it offers no basis for an even halfway reliable estimate of the qualitative and quantitative significance of the journalism described at the time as Jewish.

A unique development, deviating from events in other countries, occurred in Hungary. Although Jews there were often pushed aside in the early phases of the revolution, the majority of them identified with the Hungarian liberation movement which they supported in many ways, also through service in the army, after being allowed to sign up. However, their influence remained restricted. There were no Jews in the National Assembly or in important political offices, and in the army there were no Jewish high-ranking officers. It has been quite justifiably said of the Hungarian Revolution that "the Hungarian Jews never gained the decisive influence that, for example, Fischhof and Goldmark had in Vienna, Jacoby had in Berlin, Crémieux had in Paris, and other Jews had in smaller German states."[25] Nonetheless, the major significance of Jews for the Hungarian struggles for liberation were in the end confirmed by the counter-revolution in that they were especially harshly treated by the victorious imperial army and that special reparations payments—2.3 million Gulden (which was later reduced to 1 million) was placed on them. Thus, for the Hungarian Jews, the end of the revolution brought a new form of counter-revolutionary "tax on Jews."

Certainly, not all Jews were supporters of the revolution and even less were all active revolutionaries. From the political point of view as well, the Jewish population in the various countries in Europe did not form a united bloc. Although a revolution that aimed at introducing civil liberties and improving living conditions must have appeared positive in an age of emancipation, given their social circumstances, the number of "apolitical" individuals among Jews was also quite large. In traditional Orthodox milieus the distance from politics was especially marked, while an interest in general sociopolitical conditions and the introduction of liberal norms grew with the level of assimilation. However, it should not be forgotten that there were not only liberals among the highly assimilated groups, but also radical revolutionaries and conservatives. In the stratum of the commercial and financial bourgeoisie, many Jews held the conviction that they would lose more than they would gain in a revolution.

On the basis of his many years of experience with conditions in Germany, Jacob Toury has attempted to develop percentage estimates of the political attitudes of the entire Jewish population in Germany. His estimates are that in 1848/49 about 25 percent were conservative, 25-30 percent loyalist, 30-35 percent moderate liberals, 14 percent radical-democratic, and 1 percent socialist.[26] For Austria, these figures would be shifted considerably over to the right, because of the great number of Orthodox Jews in Bohemia, Moravia and Galicia—in spite of quite different conditions in Vienna. Much the same would be true of Hungary, and even in France, the fundamental distance of Orthodox Jewry from the political struggles in 1848 has been pointed out.

An estimate of the share of the Jewish population politically active in the revolution would produce quite different results everywhere, with a strong shift to the left.[27] For the frequently mentioned thesis that Jews could be found in all political camps individual examples can always be found, but it is noticeable that for the conservatives and for the socialists it is mostly so-called "baptized Jews" who are mentioned—from Friedrich Julius Stahl to Karl Marx. And in fact, relations were not quite so balanced, as the vast majority of politically active Jews belonged to the liberal, and in part to the democratic camp.

Decisive for the further history of Jews in Europe was the fact that following 1848 they were no longer just an object of politics, but, in spite of all still existing and revived restrictions and prejudices, were themselves active in deciding their own fate in the greater political community. With common action for a shared problem, a common history began—the early stages of which had already been seen in the war of liberation against Napoleon. Thus, the revolution of 1848 set off a transformation in the self-understanding and self-awareness of European Jews, the significance of which cannot be overestimated. As was written in a memorandum by Swiss Jews in February 1849 in respect of revolutionary events in Europe: "Israelite honor was glowingly satisfied by the fact that very many Israelites were at the head of the popular movements during that uprising and were elected as deputies, and a number were placed at the head of the highest state authorities …"[28] After centuries of oppression and contempt, the experience of the revolutionary period meant a decisive step on the way to Jews in Europe being able to hold their heads up high. Heinrich Graetz elegantly expressed this feeling when he wrote in his *History of the Jews* about the 1848 revolution: "In all civilized and halfway civilized countries in the world, Jews have shed their slavish image, carry their heads high and no longer allow themselves to be intimidated by the 'hep-hep' cries of the scoundrels."[29]

As much as this is true, one should not overlook the fact that 1848 was also an important date in the formation of modern antisemitism. Even during the revolution, one could already find that explosive mixture of arrogance towards traditional Judaism and fear of modern Judaism. It was a combination of arrogance and fear that fed a new type of malignancy. A "financial power" of Jews was conjured up and it was baldly stated: "Tyranny comes from money and the money belongs to the Jews."[30] In this context, conservative and social-revolutionary standpoints became remarkably close. Although the anticapitalism of these camps resulted from quite different interests and values, they overlapped in an antisemitic criticism of capitalism, in which both groups demanded, instead of the emancipation of the Jews, an "emancipation from the Jews."[31]

Against a backdrop of nationalist mobilization, Jewish "nationality" became simultaneously an object of aggressive polemic. Doubts were raised as to whether

Jews were only just a religious community, and on this basis their equal participation in the nation-state was challenged. No one, however, drew from this the conclusion that Jews should be treated as other nationalities. The Hungarian Reichstag passed at the end of 1849, indeed in direct succession, a law on equal rights for nationalities, that is equality for non-Magyars, and a law on the emancipation of Jews, that is equality for non-Christians.

Even the assimilation of the Jews was no longer held to be desirable in some of the antisemitic polemics of the revolutionary period. "Especially this outwards assimilation allows Jews to have an undermining effect on other nations and religions, which they gradually attempt to dissolve into a primitive mass in political, social, religious and moral respects, in order to exploit this as raw material."[32] Here, anti-liberal currents, the fear of a "primitive mass" of a defeudalized and "decorporatized" society based on the autonomy of the individual is unmistakable. However, this argumentation signifies a qualitative leap in the "Jewish question," as such a fundamental critique of assimilation denied a basis for any emancipation policy and at the same time justifies central positions of modern antisemitism. It is therefore not surprising that the "Jewish question" was also occasionally discussed, even in 1848, as a "racial question." In an age that was marked by bourgeois ideas and interests, in spite of the defeat of liberal and democratic forces, antisemitic currents had, however, no chance to develop fully and have a determining influence on society. It would take a quarter of a century before modern antisemitism appeared as a relevant political factor.

Notes

1. On Jewish history before and during the revolution in general, see Salo W. Baron, "The Impact of the Revolution of 1848 on Jewish Emancipation," *Jewish Social Studies* 11 (1949): 195-248; Reinhard Rürup, "The European Revolutions of 1848 and Jewish Emancipation," in Werner E. Mosse, Arnold Paucker, and Reinhard Rürup (eds.), *Revolution and Evolution. 1848 in German-Jewish History* (Tübingen, 1981), 1-53 (here, too, further literature). On the prehistory see also David Sorkin, "Jewish Emancipation in Central and Western Europe in the Eighteenth and Nineteenth Centuries," in David Englander (ed.), *The Jewish Enigma: An Enduring People* (Milton Keynes, 1992), 81-109. On developments in Germany see, among others, Michael Brenner, "Zwischen Revolution und rechtliche Gleichstellung," in Michael Brenner, Stefi Jersch-Wenzel, and Michael A. Meyer, *Emanzipation und Akkulturation, 1780-1871* (Munich, 1996), 287-325; Rüdiger Hachtmann, "Berliner Juden und die Revolution von 1848," in Reinhard Rürup (ed.), *Jüdische Geschichte in Berlin: Essays und Studien* (Berlin, 1995), 53-84; Dieter Langewiesche, "Revolution und Emanzipation 1848/49," in F.D. Lucas (ed.), *Geschichte und Geist. Fünf Essays zum Verständnis des Judentums* (Berlin, 1995), 11-34; Erik Lindner, "Die Revolution von 1848/49 als innerjüdische Wende," in Erik Lindner, *Patriotismus deutscher Juden von der napoleonischen Ära bis zum Kaiserreich* (Frankfurt, 1997), 229-65; Reinhard Rürup, *Emanzipation und Antisemitismus. Studien zur "Judenfrage" der bürgerlichen Gesellschaft,* (Frankfurt, 1987); Jacob Toury, *Turmoil and Confusion in the Revolution of 1848: The Anti-Jewish Riots in the "Year of Freedom" and their Influence on Modern Antisemitism* (Merhavia, 1968) (in Hebrew).

2. Figures from Jacob Toury, *Soziale und politische Geschichte der Juden in Deutschland 1847-1871. Zwischen Revolution, Reaktion und Emanzipation*, (Düsseldorf, 1977), 290-91; see also Rürup, "European Revolutions," 32-41.

3. See also Daniel Gerson, "Die Ausschtreitungen gegen die Juden im Elsaß 1848," *Bulletin des Leo Baeck Instituts* 87 (1990): 29-44. On the history of emancipation in France and especially in Alsace, see Paula E. Hyman, *The Emancipation of the Jews of Alsace. Acculturation and Tradition in the Nineteenth Century* (New Haven, 1991); Patrick Girard, *Les Juifs de France de 1789 à 1850. De l'émancipation à l'égalité* (Paris, 1976).

4. See especially Michael Anthony Riff, "The Anti-Jewish Aspects of the Revolutionary Unrest of 1848 in Baden and its Impact on Emancipation," *Leo Baeck Institute Year Book* 21 (1976): 27-40.

5. *Karlsruher Zeitung*, 13 March 1848.

6. Ibid, report from Mergentheim, 9 March 1848.

7. Running against the widespread tendency in the research to give a strong emphasis to general economic and social causes of the unrest against the Jews is Stefan Rohrbacher, *Gewalt im Biedermeier. Antijudische Ausschreitungen in Vormärz und Revolution (1815-1848/49)* (Frankfurt, 1993). See also Brenner, "Zwischen Revolution und rechtlicher Gleichstellung," (n. 2) who also emphasizes specific anti-Jewish currents.

8. *Mannheimer Abendzeitung*, 13 March 1848: "Moreover, it is remarkable that when one of the number of those who in Richen were performing these acts of violence attacked the shop of a respectable Israelite, a number of voices called out together: 'Stop, he's not due anything; he's no haggler.'"

9. Ibid.

10. See Rohrbacher, *Gewalt im Biedermeier*, (n. 7), 192ff.

11. On the anti-Jewish unrest in Germany see, apart from Rohrbacher, *Gewalt im Biedermeier*, Manfred Gailus, *Straße und Brot. Sozialer Protest in den deutschen Staaten unter besonderer Berücksichtigung Preußens, 1847-1849* (Göttingen, 1990); Rürup, "European Revolutions," (n.1), 36ff.

12. Simon Dubnow, *Weltgeschichte des jüdischen Volkes*, Vol. 9: *Das Zeitalter der ersten Reaktion und der zweiten Emanzipation*, (Berlin, 1929), 321.

13. Leopold Zunz in a letter to Philipp and Julie Ehrenberg, 17 March 1848, reprinted in Nahum N. Glatzer, "Leopold Zunz and the Revolution of 1848," *Leo Baeck Institute, Year Book* 5 (1960): 132; similarly a letter to Samuel Meier Ehrenberg of 7 April 1848 (ibid.: 139): "in spite of some troubles with and against the Jews, to which I attach no importance, our matter has achieved a decisive victory in civilized Europe, and with this in mind let us celebrate our redemption at the next Passover."

14. Quoted in Dubnow, *Weltgeschichte*, (n. 12), 371.

15. Heinrich Löwe in the *Deutsch-Österreichische Zeitung*, 1 April 1848, quoted in H. Tietze, *Die Juden Wiens. Geschichte, Wirtschaft, Kultur* (Leipzig, 1933), 186.

16. Ludwig Philippson, *Allgemeine Zeitung des Judentums*, 1854, 40, quoted in Ludwig Philippson, *Weltbewegende Fragen in Politik und Religion* (Leipzig, 1868), 413.

17. *Spenersche Zeitung*, 12 May 1848, quoted in Hachtmann, "Berliner Juden," (n.1), 70.

18. *Verhandlungen der Zweiten Kammer der Ständeversammlung des Großherzogthums Baden,* Kommissionsbericht (K. Zittel), 7 April 1848, 7th Supplement, 103-4.

19. Quoted in Friedrich Prinz, *Prag und Wien. Probleme der nationalen und sozialen Revolution im Spiegel der Wiener Ministerratsprotokolle*(Munich, 1968), 116.

20. Quoted in A. Weldler-Steinberg, *Geschichte der Juden in der Schweiz vom 16. Jahrhundert bis nach der Emanzipation* (edited and supplemented by F. Guggenheim-Grünberg), Vol. 2 (Zurich, 1969), 29.

21. Quoted in ibid., 33.

22. Quoted in S. Czaczkes-Tissenboim, "Der Anteil der Juden an der Wiener Revolution 1848," unpublished Ph.D. Diss., Vienna 1926, 229.

23. Quoted in ibid., 168-69.

24. See Peter Pulzer, "Jews and Nation-Building in Germany, 1815-1918," *Leo Baeck Institute Year Book* 41 (1996): 202.

25. J. Einhorn, *Die Revolution und die Juden in Ungarn* (Leipzig, 1851), 118.

26. Jacob Toury, *Die politischen Orientierungen der Juden in Deutschland. Von Jena bis Weimar* (Tübingen, 1966), 98.

27. Ibid., 67. Of the Jews politically active in 1848/49, Toury estimates that 9 percent were conservatives and loyalists, 32 percent moderate liberals, 41 percent radical democrats, and 18 percent socialists.

28. Quoted in Weldler-Steinberg, *Geschichte der Juden in der Schweiz*, (n. 20), Vol. 2, 33.

29. Heinrich Graetz, *Geschichte der Juden von den ältesten Zeiten bis auf die Gegenwart*, Vol. 11 (Leipzig, 1900), 549.

30. Eduard von Müller-Tellering, *Freiheit und Juden. Zur Beherzigung an alle Volksfreunde* (Vienna, 1848), 9. Müller-Tellering was the Vienna correspondent of the *Neue Rheinische Zeitung*.

31. Such statements were even made by liberal politicians such as Karl Mathy. See Riff, "Anti-Jewish Aspects," (n. 4), 38.

32. *Judenverfolgung und Emancipation von den Juden*, 2nd ed. (Münster, 1861), 20.

Public assembly at an isolated poplar in Berlin
(Illustrirte Zeitung, Leipzig, no. 277, 21 October 1848, 257)

The sovereign Lindenclub in Berlin—before martial law
(Illustrirte Zeitung, Leipzig, no. 284, 9 December 1848, 373)

Chapter 32

PUBLIC MEETING DEMOCRACY IN 1848

Wolfram Siemann

The term "public meeting democracy" has not yet established itself in the research on the revolution of 1848/49, although it has already developed clear contours through the academic examination of collective protest during the *Vormärz* and the revolution.[1] Two things are concentrated in the term "public meeting democracy": a special viewpoint and a restricted field, both through which the complexity of revolutionary events can be dissected and analyzed in a new way. Before proceeding to this task, let us offer a few explanatory considerations in advance.

The right to assemble freely and to associate for political purposes was one of the central "March demands"; their proclamation in March and April 1848 eliminated numerous *Vormärz* repressive measures directed mainly against political associations, mass meetings, and festivals. The decision of the Diet of the German Confederation on 5 July 1832, especially with the recent Hambach Festival in mind, had, in no uncertain terms, laid down strict prohibitions of these. At public meetings and festivals, whether "extraordinary" or "permitted," "public speaking of a political nature" was forbidden without exception.[2] The events themselves had to be approved in advance by the responsible authorities. If not completely banned, controls burdened the elementary need to meet or to associate and assemble for political purposes.

With the outbreak of the March Revolution in 1848, the right of free association was quickly introduced in all German states. It expressed itself in numerous forms, so that all forms of association with democratic tendencies could in fact be included in the term "public meeting democracy." Such a broad grasp would not, however, lead to any new understanding and is, in practice, useless. "Public meeting democracy" is distinct from:

- the wide range of political associations and parliamentary parties; these are obviously based on assembly, but aim for permanence and developed established forms, so that they should be included in the "institutionalized revolution" (Langewiesche), that implies more than just "meeting";

- the wider range of societal organizations, or "associations," as people said in the *Vormärz* groups that sought to organize industrial, social, cultural, occupational, religious, artisanal, or agrarian life. These associations also went beyond "meetings" as used here, in consistency and permanence, and often had their roots in the *Vormärz*. On the other hand, they often lacked a clear political aspect, although they also often related to political institutions as lobbying groups did. To be excluded are also the numerous related congresses of the revolutionary period, with which local and regional associations sought to establish national umbrella organizations or at least national platforms, as was the case with artisans, teachers, students, university lecturers, journeymen, doctors, lawyers, members of the major churches, and German Catholics etc.;

- violent gatherings, such as collective protests or the recruitment of armed volunteer corps, because in this case the deliberative element that is part of public meeting democracy plays at most a minor role. Instead, central to these was, "Talk and Revolution," as phrased by Peter N. Stearns in another context.[3]

The public meetings referred to here moved in an extraparliamentary field, and belonged to the "grassroots revolution." "Grass-roots" is understood here—without wishing to imply any sort of value hierarchy—as the socially undifferentiated level of action that can be assigned to the local arena, that is the streets, everyday life, the barricades, festivals, inns. Langewiesche's phrase "spontaneous revolution," or, as he prefers in this volume, "primal revolution," applies only partially to the field of activity under discussion here. For, by analogy with the "institutionalized" revolution, the grassroots revolution could also be characterized by planned and long-term action, as can be seen in some examples of public meeting democracy occurring in the transitional period between spontaneous action and the beginning of organization. Such is the form of the assembly, "in the tents," in the Berlin Tiergarten, for example, described by Manfred Gailus. After the March uprising, it became "an institution;"[4] it became part of the "tradition of mass meetings," which grew and which activists attempted to revive as interest in the revolution waned.[5]

"Public meetings democracy" contains normative elements. It assumes that the meeting served a political purpose—that is, included the political system in the revolutionary process. It was generally accessible and public, was at the same time also the deliberating "revolution of the streets," and incorporated political participation of "the common people" and of women as well. It was a form of expression with which the revolution developed a special dynamics from March onwards.

Choreography and rituals of (mass-) meetings had developed in the age of the European-Atlantic revolutions, from the late eighteenth century onwards, and reveal their imminent systematics only when seen from a European-wide viewpoint. Squares and buildings, where democracy was publicly fought for and practiced during the revolution of 1789 in France were thus lent a distinctive image and were later transformed into tradition-forming memorials—into "sites of memory" as Pierre Nora has put it.[6] Nora interprets them in their broadest sense, including the abstract; in the context of this paper they are understood in the strict material sense as memorial sites, as arenas which were connected with democratic action during the revolution.

Town halls could be understood as early witnesses of "public meeting democracy" in this sense. The French national assembly of 1789 granted wide-ranging rights of municipal self-government to all towns in the countryside—that is, to the smallest rural village, even still-existing manors. This right to have a council and mayor led to the appearance of 38,000 towns halls in France from 1789 onwards—the epitome of local life and local political power.[7] In Germany as well, during the July Revolution of 1830 and to a greater extent in March and April 1848, town halls became the targets of village communities or urban citizens in order to present publicly their first protest and proclamations.

A comparable political function developed, in bourgeois life in France, for the meeting places of eighteenth century elites, the cafés. Cafés did not have the poor reputation that taverns and bars did. Their role is reflected in some characterizations as "workshops of the intellect," as "salons of democracy," as the "true legislative branch in France."[8] These connotations had already been established as a historical model for German parliamentarians when they, too, began to hold caucus meetings in the cafés and restaurants of Frankfurt to prepare for the floor debates in the National Assembly—in the "Café Milani," in the "Casino," "Württemberger Hof," "Nürnberger Hof," "Augsburger Hof," or "Deutschen Hof," in the "Weidenbusch," "Donnersberg" or in the "Westendhall."

They drew on an older tradition and themselves created something new—what else could they have done? No rooms existed that were reserved exclusively for the work of parties and parliamentary parties. On the other hand, restaurants and inns were, from the end of the eighteenth century onwards, meeting places for bourgeois associations—with names like "Casino," "Harmonie" or "Museumsgesellschaft." Every municipality used public inns as a forum for public politics in 1848.

The extent to which public politics at the regional level was defined by the national level has also been examined in French scholarship as part of modern research into memorial sites. In German scholarship on the revolution, the postulate of "fundamental politicization" points in a similar direction. In France, however, unlike in Germany, the revolution transformed the geographical framework, in that it irrevocably redefined the local world by establishing departments.[9] In the German states, inherited units of administration, the church districts, the village, town and state borders were retained and functioned as filters against the grasp of the nation-state.

Research into Anglo-Saxon and Irish history of the era before 1848 also points to new forms of struggle to practice freedom of assembly. Thus the "public meeting" was also "a relatively recent development" in England in the early nineteenth century.[10] There it functioned as an instrument for the exertion of extraparliamentary pressure. These public meetings gained "the informal status of an organ for the direct expression of political demands at the grassroots level."[11] They are therefore comparable to the "grassroots revolution" in Germany, as is the exercise of the right of freedom of assembly inherent in them. Public meetings, with their petitions and proclamations, appear, in the extreme case, as competitors to the legitimacy of national parliaments in both countries and to the legitimacy of the legislatures of the individual German states.

Such assemblies presented an important "alternative form of action to the legally guaranteed possibilities of participation,"[12] or, as the *Morning Chronicle* put it in 1823, formed a "safety valve" for the constitution. In England and Ireland there existed, apart from this, a traditional form of assembly, the so-called country meeting, in which clergy, gentry, and freeholders gathered to allow local notables to speak, in honor and respect. These assemblies, too, changed their character and transformed themselves into propagandistic demonstrations, presenting an alternative to the elitist-restrictive franchise. "Petition and debate" developed into methods of exerting influence on the parliament from outside. The petition, in this respect, functioned as a "tie between parliament and public."[13] In 1831 alone, 8,961 petitions were addressed to parliament.

In comparison to the mass meetings held in Ireland during the 1840s, similar events in *Vormärz* Germany appear as miniatures and even the largest of them, the Hambach Festival with its estimated 30,000 participants, seems small. Headed by the champion of political and religious independence, Daniel O'Connell (1775-1847), a series of assemblies were held which the *Times* disparagingly described as "monster meetings." More than forty nationalist mass demonstrations took place in 1843, on average two per week, preferably on Sundays or church holidays. In a deliberately calculated strategy, meetings were held near historical sites and provincial towns in order to reach the largest possible proportion of the rural population.

The extent of planning to prepare assemblies with more than 500,000 or even 800,000 reliably witnessed participants and to carry them out following an established ritual and course is amazing. A special event, probably the largest, took place on 15 August in Tara and included forty town-music groups from throughout Ireland—with a number of altars from which open-air masses were celebrated. O'Connell paid attention to even the smallest details including the instruction: "Let me speak with the wind."[14] Political mass meetings and popular festivals were closely connected in this respect and had an inestimable effect on the emerging Irish national self-understanding.

For the formation of "public meeting democracy" in the major cities, English research can also point to London as model. In the mid-nineteenth century there were struggles in most British cities for the right of access to "public places" to hold meetings there. The most severe conflicts took place in London in the presence of the central government. The struggle for the right of assembly forms a bridge in the history of English radicalism between the Chartist movement of the 1840s and the reform movement of the 1860s. These conflicts also exposed class boundaries, as civic parks were carefully patrolled by watchmen in the 1840s and 1850s, who, like the police, were uniformed and cooperated with them. The "park-keepers" became part of "working-class demonology" with prominent places, such as Hyde Park and Trafalgar Square, becoming objects of the struggle. Control of the streets embodied, at the same time, a victory of the united bourgeois and plebeian public spheres.[15]

Against this European background, it is all the more interesting to look for the beginnings of a "public meeting democracy" in the German Revolution. Such an examination leads unavoidably to the history of regions and localities—but how to choose among them? It is impossible, given the current state of research on regional history, to present a synthesis. Access can therefore initially only be inductive and begin with especially promising examples, rich in source material and events, to provide the basis for a model. Elements of "public meeting democracy" will therefore be developed in the following, initially using the example of Trier in the revolution of 1848/49.[16]

The revolution created, here as elsewhere, typical media and arenas in order to fulfil an important requirement: communication. To get news and to exchange it, to prepare actions, to form opinions—all this took place in an unchanging scenario. The public places were streets, squares, and inns. The "street as mass medium" (Bernd Jürgen Warneken) united the various social groups, as it was used both for bourgeois parades and for lower class demonstrations. In Trier, the revolution took place in the main streets of the city; the *Hauptmarkt* was the "most important gathering place for the people, where many often gathered especially on Sunday afternoons when the shops were closed."[17] The market as meeting place concentrated communication; it served as a place to exchange opinions and often as starting point for conflicts.

The *Hauptmarkt* also embodied authority in the government buildings and, above all, the main guardhouse located there. On the market cross, which dominated the square, was a bust of Friedrich Wilhelm IV. This prominent square served meetings with different purposes, all of which implicitly raised the claim to political participation because of the presence of the authorities. In March 1848, a victim of the revolution was carried through all the surrounding streets to the *Hauptmarkt*. At the beginning of October 1848, the population countered a parade of soldiers with a demonstration in which songs were sung directly in front of the main guardhouse. Funeral ceremonies for Robert Blum also passed the *Hauptmarkt* on the way to St. Gangolf's church.

The ambivalence of assembly and conflict could be seen on the *Hauptmarkt*. Apart from demonstrations, protest actions with a high level of symbolism had their beginnings there. At the beginning of May, for example, the main guardhouse—the symbol of political power—was systematically plundered and destroyed. The people took over the square in a most drastic manner. And even soldiers (!) recruited from the vicinity made their sympathies for this form of attack on the government apparent. As the bust of Friedrich Wilhelm IV on the *Hauptmarkt* was knocked down, they did not intervene, but instead commented on this revolutionary act by publicly smoking cigars in full view of the rioters. That was a rejection of *Vormärz* police ordinances, that had regulated everyday life down to the tiniest detail.

The arena of Prussian domination contrasted with the center of municipal power and of the public sphere: the *Kornmarkt*. The building of the bourgeois

Casino society—which is still standing today—was located there, as was the city hall, where the prerevolutionary town council met. On this square the assemblies took place which sent deputations on 19 March and in May.

In general, the news of the March Revolution in Berlin was heard, above all, in meetings in the streets. The Trier *Volksblatt* of 10 May 1848 reported, with an eye for the dynamics of "public meeting democracy": "Everyone was taken by an indescribable sensation. Masses of people could be seen in the squares and streets of the city having the newspaper read to them. Students, journeymen, and normal workers, according to the reports, have fought and won. With a certain voracity the lower classes swallowed the news."[18]

Only many individual details can produce an image that underlines how communication functioned here and the extent to which socially mixed sections of the population participated in it. Newspapers and posters on street corners were read out loud. For Trier it has been shown that the citizens held discussions in front of government posters in the first days of May. After barricades had been built in May, the citizens deliberately showed themselves in the streets to demonstrate that they had not been arrested. Face-to-face oral communication took on revolutionary tones, as the chief tax collector bitterly complained: "For a long time now, state officials, have been most outrageously insulted, through countenances, words, gestures, wherever they go. Every cad feels the need to hurdle unpunished insults and threats at state officials in passing."[19]

Inns developed into distinct sites of revolutionary culture. For Trier, inns have been identified for all political currents. One public beer garden was especially prominent, as it had been the focus of public life before the revolution, for the choral societies and the carnival balls. A ball was held here in honor of Ludwig Simon. One feature of Trier was the Roman amphitheater, which was especially popular for public meetings because of its backdrop, built in a circle, and because of its acoustics.

The boundaries between city and country were certainly not clear-cut. Peasants outside Trier came into the city, especially on Sundays, to catch up with the latest news. They also came as bearers of news, although in their own traditional, symbolic way. Jonathan Sperber reports of attacks on that symbol of Prussian rule, the eagle. Hunsrück peasants from Lingerhahn proclaimed the republic and secession from Prussia; the nearby town of Langenfeld was the target of their message. Their leader was dressed as Napoleon![20]

The newspapers in fact reported, as for example in the *Trier'sche Zeitung* of 14 May 1848, on a "participation of all classes of the population." That was in reaction to the first major public meeting in Trier on 12 March 1848. Its circumstances raise doubts about the dominant role of spontaneity. Intentionally, the large Helfferschen Hall was selected. Sunday was chosen for the meeting, as it allowed non-residents from the vicinity to travel to Trier in order to attend. The organizers sought to attract as broad a public as possible. It would be worth examining, by comparing the calendar of the revolution for all the important sites in Germany, the extent to which workdays, holiday, and Sundays determined the timing of revolutionary events.

One thousand people, just a third of those trying to get in, found a seat in the hall; 500 signed a petition. This meeting with a rather bourgeois character was followed by marches through the streets, in which workers, journeymen, boatmen, reservists, and many pupils took part. The bourgeois order of the assembly contrasts with this archaic spontaneous gathering, although the bourgeois placed themselves at the head of the march in order to maintain order. A series of citizens' meetings assemblies in March throughout the Rhine-Main region followed the same script, as liberals and democrats appeared in at the meeting place with "March demands" already written up, and had them acclaimed by those assembled.[21]

In his book *Straße und Brot*, Manfred Gailus has shown how "public meeting democracy" had first to fight for its domain, the "freedom of movement," to gain the space for public meetings, demonstrations, festivals, parades, and memorial services.[22] The core of this open-air democratic politics, he found, were the permanently debating "standing" street clubs. A contemporary (Robert Springer) reported that in the avenue "Unter den Linden" a form of street parliament called the "Linden club" met regularly in the evening, so that this place was taken from the refined ice-cream eaters and Madeira sippers and democratized for the broad masses of people.[23] The people of Berlin had conquered, temporarily, their own Hyde Park Corner.

The postrevolutionary government's dealing with these sites of public meeting democracy demonstrated their high level of symbolic and practical communication value. The authorities were all the more determined to regain control of the streets. In Berlin a police force was set up, and put on the beat—winning back for the authorities these sites of democracy.[24] The reconquest in Trier took place in November 1848, also in a symbolic manner. A government poster strictly prohibiting the tax-boycott campaign was put up on the market cross in the *Hauptmarkt* and guarded by two soldiers. Attempts to tear it down were put a stop to with strokes from their sabres. The struggle for the meeting place extended into the beginning of 1851, when a pillory was set up with the name of the fugitive Ludwig Simon and his death sentence was symbolically carried out by breaking a lance. Under cover of night, the pillory was decorated with roses and thus, for a short time, returned to the political opposition.

With the political repression of the reaction era, the basic elements of public meeting democracy as it had been practiced disappeared. These had come to be: announcements in the press and in wall-posters, a prominent, dramatic cause, preference for Sundays as date for the meetings, selection of a large hall or, better still, an open-air site for the meeting, participation by all classes, singing of patriotic songs, a set program, a political speech followed by demonstrations, petitions, and marches. A proximity to popular festivals was likely. Altogether, such meetings articulated themselves as "crystallization points of mass communication."[25]

Recent scholarship on the revolution has more closely investigated the regional and municipal levels, as underlined in Dieter Langewiesche's second report on the state of research. Local focal points are receiving increasing attention, and a series of regional and city studies for the revolution confirm this impression. It must be asked how far the concept of "public meeting democracy" can provide an instrument to integrate and analyze, in comparative fashion, the numerous individual observations of local revolutionary action. Seven theses will provide the outline of such an effort:

1. Public meeting democracy allows for an understanding of participation in the revolution as learning process, primarily through its function as focal point of local communication;

2. The concept provides modern observers with indicators of the extent of fundamental politicization, sometimes doubted, but which can becomes more apparent in this context;

3. It provides information, beyond written reports, transmitted on a metalevel (rituals, "scripts," choreography, symbols) on the deeper motivation of participants and betrays what, specifically, the revolution meant for them. These original "meanings" turned the sites of public meeting democracy into "lieux de mémoire"—the best example of which is the Berlin Friedrichshain, where the "victims of March" were buried and where a cult developed around them through repeated meetings.[26]

4. Public meeting democracy, as part of the grassroots revolution, also contained elements of continuity and predictability—comparative studies are needed to examine this point in greater detail—which extended in part beyond the radius of the "spontaneous revolution." This applies especially to the early phase of the revolution, when associations had not yet established a set structure, but where it was necessary to find the desired candidate for the elections to the state parliaments and the Frankfurt National Assembly through a series of local political assemblies. New, more differentiated election studies show the importance of local meetings in public, in the coffee houses and restaurants. Through them, one confirmed one's own political convictions and recognized one's opponents as a "party."[27]

5. Public meeting democracy shows that the politics of the streets was not only the preserve of social protest, but allowed a broad spectrum of public expression of opinion, by concentrating them in each town's Hyde Park Corner, known to the local population and a place where people gathered.

6. Public meeting democracy went beyond the original "political counterpublic sphere" of the outbreak of the revolution in giving rise to a new formation of opinion, which brought into contact, and, in the end, split apart "bourgeois," "rural," and "proletarian" elements. Such public meeting democracy included, among other things, extraparliamentary pressure on parliament, as for example in the meeting on 17 September 1848 on the Frankfurt Pfingstweide, which recalls English and Irish "public meetings." This gathering, attended by more than 10,000, released a complex dynamic because the radical republicans used it as forum. In part unintentionally, the Pfingstweide assembly set off a political crisis by bringing together the local democratic-republican association, the workers' association, individual deputies of the *Paulskirche*, the Frankfurt civic guard, and finally the National Assembly, its provisional central powers and the Prussian troops brought in from the federal barracks in Mainz, into a chain of actions, incalculable in advance.

This lively assembly activity from the grassroots level finally led to spontaneous uprisings and barricade fighting in Frankfurt—with disastrous consequences for the public reputation of the democratic movement. The assembly on the Pfingstweide functioned, at the same time, as a catalyst for a series of urban struggles throughout the Rhein-Main region. Unintentionally, it "laid the foundations for the victory of the counter-revolution in this region."[28] An increase in meetings and dynamic did not necessarily result in an increase in democracy and participation. Comparable assemblies took place during the campaign for the imperial constitution in the spring of 1849, for example in Heilbronn and Reutlingen;

7. Public meeting democracy sometimes displayed forms that arose from archaic patterns of political participation, such as charivaris or carnival masquerades, and sometimes modern forms, including lectures, discussions, passing resolutions. It is not always clear to distinguish between traditional, backward-looking forms and modern expectations. The dual nature of the revolution, also diagnosed in other aspects, can also be seen in public meeting democracy. Nowhere else, however, did the range of expectations come together in physical contact and confrontation. The postrevolutionary memory of this form of democratic public life was correspondingly divided. Judgements ranged between the poles of anarchy and liberty. To have expressed oneself politically in such a lively but also exhausting form remained a treasure of experience. In the "New Era," beginning in 1858, after a decade of reaction, this experience would be a potential that could be activated at any time and led the liberal and democratic movements to new departures.

Notes

1. See the research report by Dieter Langewiesche, "Die deutsche Revolution von 1848/49 und die vorrevolutionäre Gesellschaft: Forschungsstand und Forschungsperspektiven," Part II, *Archiv für Sozialgeschichte* 31 (1991): 331-443, here 406-11.

2. See the "ten articles" of 5 July 1832 in Ernst Rudolf Huber (ed.), *Dokumente zur deutschen Verfassungsgeschichte*, Vol. 1 (Stuttgart, 1978), 134.

3. See Langewiesche, "Forschungsstand," 355.

4. Manfred Gailus, *Straße und Brot. Sozialer Protest in den deutschen Staaten unter besonderer Berücksichtigung Preußens, 1847-1849* (Göttingen, 1990), 400.

5. Ibid., 406.

6. See in summary Pierre Nora, *Zwischen Geschichte und Gedächtnis* (Berlin, 1990).

7. Maurice Agulhon, "La mairie," in Pierre Nora (ed.), *Les lieux de mémoire*, Vol. 1: *La République* (Paris, 1984), 168.

8. B. Lecoq, "Le café," in Pierre Nora (ed.), *Les lieux de mémoire*, Vol .3: *Les Frances*, Pt. 2 (Paris, 1992), 855.

9. See Th. Gasnier, "Le local. Une et divisible," in ibid., 464-525.

10. For this and the following, see A. Wirsching, *Parlament und Volkes Stimme. Unterhaus und Öffentlichkeit im England des frühen 19. Jahrhunderts* (Göttingen and Zurich, 1990), esp. 85-92.

11. Ibid., 86.

12. Ibid., 89.

13. Ibid., 91.

14. This is shown in the Munich dissertation, still in progress, of M.A. Schwaiger, "Nationale Mobilisierung einer Agrargesellschaft. Die 'Catholic Association', die 'Loyal National Repeal Association' and 'Young Ireland' 1801-1848."

15. A. Taylor, "'Commons-Stealers', 'Land-Grabbers', and 'Jerry-Builders': Space, Popular Radicalism and the Politics of Public Access in London, 1848-1880," *International Review of Social History* 40 (1995): 383-407.

16. Developed in the investigation of G. Luz-y-Graf, "1848/49 in Trier und Umgebung. Revolution und Revolutionskultur einer Stadt und ihres Umlandes," *Examsarbeit* (Trier, 1995); in progress as a dissertation.

17. *Trier'scher Anzeiger*, 21 November 1848.

18. "Geschichte der Bewegung in Trier," *Volksblatt*, 11 August 1848.

19. Quoted, Landeshauptarchiv Koblenz (403 6583, fol. 238-241) in Luz-y-Graf, "1848/49 in Trier," 136.

20. Jonathan Sperber, *Rhineland Radicals. The Democratic Movement and the Revolution of 1848-49* (Princeton, 1991), 167.

21. See Michael Wettengel, *Die Revolution von 1848/49 im Rhein-Main-Raum. Politische Vereine und Revolutionsalltag im Großherzogtum Hessen, Herzogtum Nassau und in der Freien Stadt Frankfurt* (Wiesbaden, 1989), 51-62.

22. Gailus, *Straße und Brot*, 350-418, esp. 357ff.

23. See Langewiesche, "Forschungsstand," 408.

24. See Albrecht Funk, *Polizei und Rechtsstaat. Die Entwicklung des staatlichen Gewaltmonopols in Preußen 1848-1918* (Frankfurt, 1986).

25. Wolfgang Kaschuba and Carola Lipp, *1848—Provinz und Revolution. Kultureller Wandel und soziale Bewegung im Königreich Württemberg* (Tübingen, 1979), 174.

26. See Manfred Hettling," Das Begräbnis der Märzgefallenen 1848 in Berlin," in Manfred Hettling and Paul Nolte (eds.), *Bürgerliche Feste. Symbolische Formen politischen Handelns im 19. Jahrhundert* (Göttingen, 1993), 95-123, esp. 118.

27. See Raimund Waibel, *Frühliberalismus und Gemeindewahlen in Württemberg (1817-1855). Das Beispiel Stuttgart,* (Stuttgart, 1992), esp. 378-91.

28. See Wettengel, *Die Revolution von 1848/49 im Rhein-Main-Gebiet*, 269-74, esp. 273.

Speaker in front of the Lower Austrian Diet on 13 March, drawn by R. Swoboda
(Illustrirte Zeitung, Leipzig, no. 248, 1 April 1848, 218)

Funeral for fallen workers in Vienna on 3 September
(Illustrirte Zeitung, Leipzig, no. 273, 23 September 1848, 193)

Chapter 33

THE REVOLUTION OF 1848 AS "POLITICS OF THE STREETS"

Manfred Gailus

Without the spontaneous, mostly action-oriented and often violent "politics of the street," there could have been no revolution in the mid-nineteenth century—although, of course, the revolution in 1848 in western and central Europe was not totally subsumed by such "street politics." The streets and central squares, taken over by mass gatherings, ordered parades, and debating meetings, but also by angered crowds in popular uprisings and spectacular unrest, seemed to many contemporaries to be the experience of the revolution, to be its true symbol. More decisive than the short-term, occasional barricade fighting were, admittedly, permanent forms of occupying the streets and the new political impulses that arose from these newly conquered spaces in which the political public sphere could be played out. The "streets"—the politicized public sphere of the streets, during the revolution, understood in the broadest possible sense of the term—can be seen as the central mass medium for a majority of contemporaries, much more than the "tavern" or the press, freed from censorship and powerfully expanding.

"Politics of the streets" or "street politics" has a dual meaning. On the one hand it refers to a collective occupation of the streets (their public space) for the articulation of complaints, the formation of group identity through consultation and self-representation, and, finally, the enforcement of objectives through influence on the government arising from group action. This street politics "from the bottom up" always corresponds—and this has only recently been underlined—to a dominant, ruling, street politics "from the top down," based on power, through which the authorities or government seek to subjugate public spaces for their own purposes.[1]

This chapter will investigate popular street politics, particularly in German cities, as it developed in the context of the 1848 revolution. The focus will therefore be that level of the revolution characterized by Dieter Langewiesche as the "spontaneous or primal" revolution, in contrast to an "institutionalized" one.[2] Street politics in the sense employed here encompasses the entire spectrum of collective manifestations that have, up to now, generally been included in the concept of "social protest." This conceptual transformation in the direction of street politics seems to me appropriate in order to end the traditionally dominant analytical separation of social and political spheres which also dominates research into revolutions, and not to its advantage. An understanding of politics limited to institutionalized forms has also proven to be inappropriate to sufficiently comprehend revolutionary events at the beginning of the democratic-parliamentary era.

Street politics is not necessarily violent, including explicitly non-violent manifestations as well—for example mass meetings, demonstrations or public political events and festivals. Street politics is not per se to be attributed to an emerging political-parliamentary left, and admittedly even less to the right, although both sides practiced or exploited it at times. It followed its own laws and rules, although not independent of the more or less developed institutionalized politics of associations, parties, and parliaments. Street politics is not the invention or monopoly of modern revolutions—it has a long prehistory and its own cycle of ups and downs, while admittedly reaching a peak in the revolutionary era.[3]

Temporal and Geographical Structures

Let us start with temporal structures. The use of public space in the sense of street politics was, in the restrictive conditions of *Vormärz* regimes, de facto hardly possible other than as a "disturbance of public peace and order." Until the beginning of the revolution in March 1848, there was no legal space for street politics, and hence very little chance of practicing nonviolent forms of action such as public meetings and mass demonstrations. Equally, there was a lack of generally accepted, institutionalized "rules of the game" for dealing with fundamental social conflicts in the areas of subsistence problems, claims to public assistance or labor conditions. Those subjects generally excluded from any form of participation were often left only with the risky path of direct self-help, direct action, the "tumults" to which the authorities generally reacted with the quite disproportionate means of a "tumult control," usually military. Just the rise in intensity of protest from the mid-1840s onward indicates that the political and social legitimacy of the *Vormärz* regimes was waning. The food riots of 1847—more than two hundred such cases have been demonstrated—resulting from failed harvests, inflation, and massive supply problems, permanently shattered *Vormärz* "peace and order." In retrospect, these conflicts seem to precede so closely the spontaneous revolution developing from March 1848 that, in the context of street politics, there are good reasons to speak of a period of two and a half years (January 1847 to July 1849) as an integrated period of activity and experience. At no other time in the nineteenth century was there a comparable intensity of a street politics "from the bottom up."

The dynamic of the German Revolution was greatly determined by the cycles of street politics. In detail, the above-mentioned period can be divided into four phases. The first two were the "1847 experience," which arose above all from country-wide subsistence conflicts in April and May 1847, followed almost a year later by the "intoxication of freedom" in March and April 1848. These were the exceptional months, in which nearly a third of all cases of conflict fell, with a de facto collapse of the old public order creating traumatic effects for the old elite of the ancien régimes and, to almost the same extent, for the new bourgeois leadership. For the period May to November 1848, a "revolutionary everyday life" became established with a medium level of protest intensity, in retrospect a very short period, in which the beginnings of a new popular culture of revolution developed and could define political events mostly through the counterweight of having occupied public space. Finally, there followed a phase of decline of the spontaneous revolution, in which its room for action was increasingly limited by the restrictive measures of the advancing counter-revolution. Even before the end of 1848, a resolute, restrictive politics "from the top down" gained influence, a dynamic that did not experience a fundamental change even through the mass movement that flared up in the context of the campaign for the imperial constitution in May 1849.[4]

Second, let us consider the geographical structures and topography of street politics. The preferred arena of the spontaneous revolution was, not surprisingly, the urban environment. While city-dwellers only made up a quarter of the total population in 1848, two-thirds of all unrest and actions of street politics occurred in urban centers. There was doubtless no lack of cause for conflict in rural-agrarian milieus, as more than 130 peasant riots and nearly 70 rebellions by agrarian lower classes clearly demonstrate, but in general rural conflicts were quite restricted, compared to urban environments, due to generally unfavorable conditions for open collective protest. Only for a short period, in March 1848, did the level of unrest in the villages approach that of the towns and cities. After that, things became "quiet" once again in the countryside, at least as far as concerns the direct actions under discussion here.[5]

The centers of street politics were the major cities. In Berlin alone there were 125 actions, in Cologne forty-six, in Breslau forty-five, followed by Munich (twenty-four), Mainz (twenty-two), Königsberg (twenty-one), Hamburg (twenty) and Kassel (twenty). Admittedly, if one examines the number of actions in relation to population, a number of mid-sized towns appear more troubled than larger cities: Trier (7.37 cases per 10,000 residents), Münster (7.2), Düsseldorf (6.92), Darmstadt (6.67), Mainz (5.95), and Kassel (5.56). The high level of conflict in Rhineland-Westphalia expresses first and foremost a vehement "opposition to the Berlin tutelage system" (Veit Valentin). A large part of these confrontations resulted from antipathies of self-confident Rhinelanders, the majority of whom were Catholic, who rebelled against their semi-colonial status—which they felt humiliating—and against numerous, unreasonable demands by a strict authoritarian, Protestant regime from regions east of the Elbe and which were seen as backward. Smaller towns with a resident court, such as Darmstadt or Kassel, favored a greatly politicized public climate—through authority being concentrated in restricted urban space, through the physical closeness of the people to the high politics of the monarchs, through the state authorities and their institutions of power—which especially encouraged certain forms of street politics such as charivaris, demonstrations, and mass meetings. The relative peacefulness of centers of manufacturing and early industry, on the other hand, is noticeable—for example in Chemnitz (.59 cases per 10,000 residents), Elberfeld (1.79), Barmen (.28), Iserlohn (1.82), Remscheid (1.67), Solingen (1.67), and Krefeld (.83).

In regards to the geographical distribution of conflicts, I would like to restrict myself to a few remarks. With an almost equal share of the population, the level of street politics action was almost evenly distributed between Prussia (excluding Posen) and the "third Germany." The level of protest in Prussia is slightly above average but is, admittedly, clearly surpassed by that in some mid-sized and smaller states such as the grand duchies of Hessen, Baden, and Weimar or the principality of Hessen. If one wished to single out a noticeably dense region of unrest, this would doubtless be the Rhine-Main area, above all Hessen-Darmstadt, which has been quite superbly examined by Michael Wettengel. Especially in the catchment area of this relatively densely populated, highly urbanized medium-sized state, and in regions bordering on it, the variety of effects of a special geographic location and mentality came together, as it had been an especially fruitful port of entry into Germany for "French ideas" since 1789. During the crisis of 1830/32 caused by the French July Revolution, the Rhine-Main area also lay at the center of the main German zones of conflict.

Decisive was the historical-geographic function of this region as a bridge between east and west, as well as the aura of Frankfurt am Main as a political center of national significance. Moreover, mention must above all be given to Mainz, combative and once a Jacobin republic; a city in which a strong democratic tradition was apparently preserved through generations and which in 1848 had a major cause for conflict on its doorstep with the Confederate fortress controlled by the Prussian military. Especially in Mainz, as well as the grand-ducal residence of Darmstadt, a variety of clashes in street politics during the revolutionary period were a nearly endemic phenomenon.[6]

Who against whom? At first glance, the protest statistics of about fifteen hundred actions of street politics show an almost bewildering, often overlapping, chaotic confusion of lines of conflict, collective solidarity, and phobias, a traditional society that had suddenly been set in motion and that, as it must have appeared at least to the many worried contemporaries, threatened to fall apart at the seams. All those who had been able to consolidate or form new identity groups in *Vormärz* society had to reassure themselves anew in an extremely accelerated process of intensive self-examination—at a time when "a lot" or "everything" seemed to be at stake— who or what they were in the total context of society or what they aimed to be, not least by marking themselves off sharply against "the others," by abrupt about-faces in their orientation, breaks in group relations, the omnipresent power of identity-defining confrontations.

Other groups, in contrast, perceived themselves for the first time as a special identity group at that moment when "a lot" or "everything" seemed to be at stake.

Much deeper than in the years and decades before, the few months of revolutionary crisis sharpened the perception of images of the self and the other, of "friend" and "enemy." Prussian subjects, Hanoverians, the inhabitants of Bavaria or Württemberg, the Saxons, the inhabitants of Anhalt, or of Schleswig-Holstein, and other disparate sections of the population discovered, more than before, that they were "German"—in contrast to Frenchmen, Italians, Danes, Poles or Russians. "Subjects" discovered that they were free and equal citizens or at least that this was their wish. "Country people" discovered that they were country people and ascribed to themselves a certain quiescence, staunchness, placidness, and a growing distrust towards excited, arrogant, all-knowing educated and enlightenment-rabid town people. The poor and unpropertied saw their poverty, their social subordinate ranking, more distinctly compared to the rich and well-off, and they saw themselves encouraged to articulate their collective feelings, wishes, and voices in public. The well-off feared—often in worries expressed with remarkable exaggeration—the calls by the "have-nots" for a redistribution of property, not so often raised in reality, and by response gathered together and segregated themselves as "property owners," as a special class of people vis-à-vis the unpropertied much more strictly than ever before.

Having grown distrustful through a range of experience and willing to employ self-help, consumers of permanently limited financial means cast a sharp glance at the business practices of foodstuff producers and traders, who quickly fell under the public suspicion of being "profiteers," and were attacked. The younger generation—pupils, students, apprentices, shop assistants—discovered their youth and articulated it, naturally often in grossly exaggerated claims on the establishment of the older generation, the successful, and the powerful, on the well-established parental generation, those who were satisfied with their status. And "locals" discovered "strangers." Residents of a town, of a state, of the emerging nation asserted their rights of birth, their inherited "homeland qualities" and claims that allegedly could be derived from them over illegitimate competitors for meager resources, that is over "strangers." Moreover "Christians" once again recognized that they were different from "the Jews," because of commonalties of religion and culture and that every strange belief had to be punished for this or that general evil. Catholics dared to defend themselves more fiercely against Protestant tendencies to exploit their majority position, and at times the reverse also occurred. Women discovered their exclusion or reduced position on the basis of their sex in most spheres of public life and began to rebel against it. The moderns, the "friends of progress," distanced themselves from "reactionaries," from the conservatives. The "dyed in the wool Prussians" saw themselves more and more a special class and drew closer together, because they felt Prussian values and virtues threatened, and in general all those loyal to the king identified more exactly than before the enemies of the king and attacked them when the time seemed ripe. The emphatically pious, finally, saw an uprising against the "godless" approaching. They recognized in an increasingly falling away from faith the main cause of modern confusion, and they constituted themselves as the pious in order to take the field against a further advance of "godlessness" by new means.[7]

All of these and an abundance of further conflicts arose in a society for the moment freed of its old authorities, in part euphorically engaging in a new departure, together, and in part violently breaking apart, and found a first step towards resolution in the actions of street politics. They "fed," so to speak, street politics and, in a second, slightly delayed development, the newly emerging associations of the revolutionary period. In this unrest, these lines of conflicts seldom appeared in pure form, but generally rather in complicated blends and overlaps. The ubiquity of conflict in March and April 1848 quickly swung back to a median level—this was then "everyday revolutionary life." Admittedly, one cannot exactly weigh and measure these confrontations. In practice, this means that the conflicts, put simply, need to be ordered, structured, and then described in frequency and regional dissemination. This will be attempted by means of a distinction that differentiates between fifteen disparate conflict groups.

Rural Protests and Subsistence Conflicts

Among rural protests, peasant unrest (132 cases, representing circa 9 percent of the total) and rebellions by the agrarian lower classes (sixty-eight, representing about 5 percent) dominated. Peasant unrest was a disproportionate phenomenon in the south and southwest, with some rather weak runners into central Germany and Silesia. In no other state did such actions define the image of protest as in Bavaria (thirty-two cases, circa 22 percent of all Bavarian protests). They were also important in Württemberg, in the grand duchy of Hessen, and in Baden. In Prussia, on the other hand, they remained weak; only Silesia stood out with eighteen cases. Peasant unrest was extremely "fixated on March." About two-thirds of all conflicts occurred in March 1848; thereafter, they dropped off considerably.

Among all the protests of the revolutionary period, peasant unrest was "antifeudal" in the strictest sense of the term. As local rebellions of potential propertyholders, peasant protests aimed above all at the complete establishment or fulfillment of peasant property claims and at an extensive-as-possible village autonomy. In northern and northeastern Germany, peasant property-holders, with few exceptions, oriented themselves against the revolution relatively early on, as they feared actions by the poor and unpropertied rural population, which was subsistence-oriented and aimed at sharing of resources and redistribution. In the total context of the spontaneous revolution, peasant groups were, moreover, the only property-owning group (apart from a few more well-off master craftsmen) that did not shrink from violent direct action. In general, from a north-German-Prussian perspective, I judge the chances of a contribution supporting the revolution or even furthering it from rural districts more skeptically than is generally accepted, in spite of some successes for the democratic association movement among the rural population, starting in the fall of 1848.[8]

This is already apparent in the uprisings of the agrarian lower classes in the countryside. Not only did they not conform to peasant aims, they were indeed often fundamentally antipeasant oriented and certainly did not encourage peasant support for the revolution in those places where they occurred or where they were feared. Symptomatic were foodstuff marches, endemic phenomena of a social war between propertied and unpropertied, forms of "social piracy," especially in the territories east of the Elbe. These could already be observed during the food price crisis in the spring of 1847 and were repeated in 1848. A large part of the poor village population—men, women, and children—gathered together in large marches in which potatoes, grain, and other items were demanded with threats. In other places the people went further, demanding rights to common wood and kindling, and pushing for retention or restoration of common pastureland. Occasionally calls for smallholdings or job creation schemes could be heard. Such a rural line of confrontation was more widespread in northern and northeast German territories, and in general it was common in those regions where a commercialization of agriculture was more advanced and agrarian reform had been more rapidly introduced.[9]

In the context of the revolution, these rural, subsistence-oriented rebellions occurred mostly in conformity with the preceding unrest over high food prices. One hundred forty-two such conflicts (about 10 percent of all cases), concentrated especially in 1847 and returning in March and April 1848—more faintly and concealed somewhat by high politics—point to problems of subsistence and provision among the urban lower classes, above all. Their survival was, in part, acutely endangered in the spring of 1847 and their constant struggle for survival was certainly not ended with the better harvests and lower prices from the late summer of 1847. In a broader view, about 210 cases of food price protests have been discovered for 1847 alone, something that documents deep splits in the communities throughout the country. It is quite obvious that severe social tensions arose from this dense network of confrontations between mostly urban consumers and agrarian producers, extending into "1848," which greatly defined the behavior of the other side in the conflict—estate owners, peasants, bakers, millers, wholesalers, market dealers, and related groups during the revolutionary era.

Tense relations between peasants, whose sacks of potatoes and grain were emptied by force in the markets in 1847, and poor urban consumers were quite evident. This, too, belonged to the "1847 experience" and was not forgotten in 1848 when urban democrats entered into the countryside with the intention of propagating prorevolutionary enlightenment. If one includes workers' actions, over 110 protests resulting from the context of a meager existence and constant struggle for survival (attacks on machinery, pay conflicts, tumults, unemployment protests) then one has altogether a significant block of subsistence-oriented street-politics actions, which make up almost a quarter of eruptions of the spontaneous revolution. They point to struggles by a significant portion of the urban and in part also rural lower classes, which I have characterized under the symbolic term "bread" as a central plank of street politics. Those who wished—at other levels, in associations or parliaments—to promote the revolution, and those who wished to stop or reverse it, had to deal with this very crucial impetus and motive for action in the total context of the spontaneous revolution.[10]

Political Protests

Local Protests

The second major bloc of the spontaneous revolution was formed by that occupation of the streets aimed directly at politics—politics as understood in the narrower
sense of the word as general matters of public concern. This was above all the
politicized charivaris (more than 9 percent), unrest connected to municipal politics
and directed against the exclusive rule of the local notables (8 percent), and urban
mass action related to major political themes, for example uprisings and barricade
fighting, mass meetings and large demonstrations or revolutionary festivals in the
major cities. In total they form a share of nearly 35 percent of all actions. The charivaris of the revolutionary period arose, in regard to their symbolic repertoire, from
the traditional popular culture of censure customs, but appeared quite detached
from this in an urbanized, modernized and, in part, also politically instrumentalized
variant. As a rule, these symbolic censure actions were directed at local notables and
other authority figures: mayors, officials of municipal government or city councilors, political deputies, unpopular journalists or judges with a reputation for handing down severe verdicts, "hard-hearted" doctors, "reactionary" teachers and pastors,
and "miserly" businessmen and manufacturers regarded as uncharitable.

Quite obviously, these expressive, often extremely slapstick and colorful forms
of political street theater were a suitable form of action for the "little people," which
reflected their social circumstances and allowed them to appear themselves as actors
on the political stage and to articulate their political sympathies and antipathies. A
distinct picture of geographic distribution of these politicized censure customs cannot be formed, but they seem to dominate altogether in western and southwestern
regions, compared to the north and northeast. Proverbial was the "fever for charivaris" that dominated the streets of Berlin in the spring of 1848. In the short period
between 20 and 26 May alone, fifteen cases have been demonstrated. The most
prominent target was Ludolf Camphausen, who, as Prussian Prime Minister at the
time, had called for the return of the prince of Prussia to Berlin, who had fled after
the barricade fighting and was extremely unpopular among the masses. On at least
three consecutive days he had to suffer loud protests from the streets outside his
office in the Wilhelmstraße. A few days later his brother Otto, who at the time was
working as his assistant, wrote to Ludolf's wife in Cologne:[11]

> Ludolf is in quite a good mood and well-disposed today; on the days before, especially
> on Friday (26 May) his nerves suffered considerably. Even when he took the charivari
> directed at him on the first three days of the week with equanimity, as in fact it was per-
> formed only by street urchins and riffraff, still, the prospect of such a visit was not very
> inviting, and on Thursday apparently they intended a major coup, which it later
> emerged was not the case. On Friday, I insisted that Ludolf shift his bedroom to the back
> and that we work in the back during the evening. Both not because a direct danger
> threatened, as in my view such does not exist at this time because the radical party
> would be making a big mistake with a personal attack on the minister, but to evade the
> repulsive noise from the streets.

Suspicions of political instigators of the charivari, as raised here by Otto Camphausen with his reference to the democratic association, have not been proven. The repertoire, at times seemingly archaic-backward and crude, and the danger of a violent escalation, made this form of street politics—and this can be demonstrated for Berlin—seem suspicious to the enlightened, educated "friends of the people" who set the tone in the politically radical democratic clubs. They distanced themselves from such activity, seen as "medieval." Already at the end of May 1848, charivaris were formally banned in Berlin with reference to the relevant criminal laws of the Prussian General Code. However, charivaris did not completely disappear from the stage of street politics up to the end of the year.[12]

Municipal government unrest was de facto charivaris expanded to the level of local government. No longer were individual, unpopular persons targets of the actions, but rather representatives of *Vormärz* municipal power, and occasionally their demonstrative nouveau riche behavior, seen as immoral. Such actions were carried out with the same moral impetus of symbolic censure and public ostracism as seen in charivaris. These actions were directed against real or alleged local corruption, against a municipal monopoly of power altogether seen as corrupt, and often led to an occupation of city halls or other public buildings. In numerous towns and cities this unrest formed the real start of the revolution; the following are a few of the more significant actions: the storming of the city hall in Cologne (3 March), and similar unrest in Breslau (6 March, 16-19 March, 16-17 April), Dresden (8 March), Lübeck (11 March), Hamburg (13 March), Königsberg (13 March), Erfurt (14 March), Elberfeld (18 March), Aachen (20-21 March, 15-17 April), and in Krefeld (20-21 March).

These events, too, were extremely "March-fixated," with 47 percent of all municipal unrest in March 1848. The most noticeable concentration is to be found in Hessen-Darmstadt. Within Prussia, these uprisings were widespread in the two western provinces, and almost totally absent in regions east of the Elbe. Almost always, these protests led to a rapid change in the leadership of municipal government. Typical was an immediate change in personnel, as the discredited careerists were forced to resign and were replaced by popular, oppositional "men of the people." At the same time, popular demands for effective assistance, for a securing of subsistence, for guarantees of affordable food supplies and employment through job creation, articulated in the course of such actions, had sweeping effects on the subsequent decisions of the newly restaffed organs of municipal government.

High Politics

Finally, let us consider actions concerning high politics. Referred to here are those confrontations that went beyond narrow local horizons, which just through their size, and often through extreme violence, sent an inter-regional or even national signal. These were major events of street politics which through their direct relation to the controversial political questions of the day, reached the level of high politics. With 252 cases (more than 17 percent), these manifestations formed the second largest group in street politics. They were foremost a product of a metropolitan milieu and common especially in those places where there existed a developed system of associations supporting the revolution, especially democratic clubs and workers' associations. In Prussia, such manifestations were especially widespread in Berlin, in the Province of Saxony and in the Rhine Province.

After a first highpoint in March 1848, a second, rising wave of these actions appears in the autumn of 1848 (September—November), followed by a significant drop and a final peak in May 1849 in the context of the campaign for the imperial constitution. Individual characteristics of these manifestations of high politics included first and foremost, naturally, major barricade fighting and regional attempts at uprisings, the true symbolic event of the revolution: for example, the Berlin street fighting of 18-19 March, the Baden revolts in April and September, the September crisis in Frankfurt am Main with its violent struggles, furthermore in May 1849 the uprisings and attempts at uprisings in the Palatinate and in Baden, in Dresden, in some Rhenish-Westphalian cities such as Elberfeld or Iserlohn which were suppressed by force.

A major feature of street politics continued to be mass meetings, large rallies with often many tens of thousands participants—seen by contemporaries as a new and in principle nonviolent political mass medium that surprisingly quickly conquered the main streets and squares of the large cities, but extended to the smaller cities and even into the countryside. Moreover, parades or marches must be mentioned—a political form of expression on the road to modern mass demonstrations, the repertoire and symbolic language of which were often dominated by traditional elements of occupational-corporative parades: bands, Sunday best or guild clothing, military marching formation, procession-like dignity, usually also strictly hierarchical order of status and professional groups. Finally, political revolutionary festivals must be mentioned, groping attempts to counter an inherited cycle of public festivals, strongly authoritarian-monarchical in nature, with a national and democratic festival culture based on the revolution.

Special emphasis must be given here to attempts to revitalize the Hambach tradition in memory of the Hambach Festival of 1832, or an attempt by students, as part of a national student gathering in Eisenach (June 1848) to draw on the tradition of the Wartburg Festival of 1817. Further opportunities were offered by, for example, homage ceremonies in honor of the Imperial Regent at the beginning of August 1848, memorial services for Robert Blum (November 1848), and finally—but only possible behind closed doors in many parts of the country—ceremonies in January 1849 to celebrate the constitution and in March 1849 on the anniversary of the revolution. In Berlin above all, memorial services for those who fell in March founded a new memorial tradition. Admittedly, one should not overestimate the effects of all these celebrations. They had hardly been established when the counter-revolution ejected them from the streets and squares—the time in which they could develop was extremely short. Equally, it should not be forgotten that at the same time and during the course of the revolution as well, patriotic-military and monarchist festival traditions continued unbroken in many parts of the country, just as if a "revolution" had never happened.[13]

Nowhere in German speaking regions, with the exception of Vienna, did street politics develop so powerfully and in such varied ways as in Berlin. A series of mass meetings, beginning on 6 March in the well-known assembly area "In den Zelten" (in the Tiergarten, outside the city walls) and leading up to the barricade fighting of 18 and 19 March, formed the start of an occupation of the streets. Initially, in April, reconquered public space was used above all for subsistence oriented actions that targeted an improvement in living standards. Widespread were classical bread riots, unemployment protests (demands for municipal job creation), worker and journeymen unrest (central demand: increase in pay and shortened working hours). Up to the end of July, this taking of the streets continued unbroken and allowed the development of a diverse revolutionary culture, which found its characteristic expression in mass meetings and demonstrations, in "storm petitions" and mass delegations to the ministries in the Wilhelmstraße and other centers of power, in festivals and revolutionary celebrations, in charivaris and in "standing" street clubs, which for a time met every evening Unter den Linden, debating in small groups, in a number of newly founded newspapers and the opening up of old newspapers to commentary from their readers in the form of oft published "incomings" (letters to the editor), in a booming trade in political pamphlets and daily distribution of flyers, in placard actions by competing political associations, and in some heroes of the revolution, known throughout the city and achieving broad popularity (for example the writer and journalist F.W. Held, the veterinarian L. Urban, the pasty-cook A.F. Karbe, the iron-wares dealer Müller, known as "Lindenmüller").

Admittedly, the failed attempt to storm the arsenal on 14 June in order to arm the people marked the beginning of a change in the dynamics of an occupation of the streets. These events, in which the civic guard proved itself to be a less than reliable law enforcement organization in the view of many from the growing party of supporters of peace and order, accelerated plans by municipal and state authorities to create a new police force, which began to patrol in the capital at the end of July 1848 and had, as its main task, breaking up every assembly on the streets. Clashes between the police and people in the streets were notorious, from then on, and marked an important turning-point towards a general authoritarian retaking of occupied public space.[14]

Public Meetings and Demonstrations

Let us now examine more closely public meetings, mass demonstrations, and revolutionary celebrations as the core of Berlin street politics. The frequency of major public meetings in Berlin can be approximately reconstructed. They reached a high level above all in the spring of 1848. In March nine open-air mass meetings took place, in April fifteen, in May eleven, and in June only two. Even before the counter-revolution banned them, this new political medium of the revolution had become hackneyed. However, in the spring and summer of 1848 these mass meetings indeed served as a form of popular counter-parliament, open to everybody, as an early public school for democracy in authoritarian Prussia. The speakers' platforms were controlled by the leading members of the democratic associations, the young civil servants and journalists, the writers, lawyers and other academics, who were joined by some influential Berlin revolutionary characters, sometimes bizarre and somewhat dubious phenomena, whose demagogic talents made them into city celebrities within a few weeks. They were also joined by a few exceptional representatives of the early labor movement.

Generally the meetings dealt with issues of high politics: questions of the franchise, the planned recall of the prince of Prussia, the Prussian draft constitution. Occasionally, social problems were discussed, which certainly corresponded to the pressing demands of many of the audience—"little people" with a meager standard of living. Viewing these mass meetings beyond the perspective of the platform, their popular festival character, which also defined many of these, becomes noticeable. Reports of marquee assemblies speak of countless food traders who did a good business, of a rise in gaming tables with dice games, of games of chance, of "the devil of gambling," which, to the displeasure of political organizers spread more and more on such occasions and threatened to override the true sense of these meetings.

From a number of mass demonstrations and revolutionary celebrations, about ten to twelve major parades are prominent with a level of participation reaching ten to a maximum of some fifty thousand. Especially the demonstration in honor of the "victims of March" in Friedrichshain (4 July) and the major demonstration of 6 August in memory of the war of liberation were showcases for supporters of the revolution in the streets. The march to Friedrichshain was prompted by a student committee in order to counter an increasing public slandering of the "revolution" and its fallen "heroes." It was directly related to an important parliamentary debate scheduled for that time on "recognizing the revolution," as a extra-parliamentary march to support the parliamentary left.

The parade, which formed on the Gendarmenmarkt, bore the clear characteristics of a occupational-corporate march in its strictly hierarchical ordering according to status-groups. Contemporary descriptions emphasize the great number of flags, emblems, and symbols. The democratic club carried its new association flag made of red silk with the inscription "Democratic Club" and "18 and 19 March!" Book printers carried a black-red-gold banner, prominent because of its "colossal size," with the inscription "Free Press." Journeyman carpenters appeared with a standard in the German colors. The parade was led by civic guardsmen and the civic guard cavalry followed by members of the artisan associations; finally came the left-wing caucus in the Prussian parliament, about 150 deputies, followed by the many political associations as well as delegations of political clubs from neighboring towns. Mention was also made of the families of the "victims of March," delegates of the trades and guilds of the city; finally, large numbers of diverse workers' associations and groups and, toward the end of the parade, a group of unemployed with their own white flag with the inscription "The Unemployed Workers."

Estimates on numbers of participants in this parade, one of the largest of the revolutionary period, range between forty- and eighty-thousand people. At the cemetery in Friedrichshain twelve people spoke, one from each section of the parade. The speeches given were full of pathos; noticeable were the strongly religious metaphors used by a number of speakers; and throughout one could hear an effusive-exagger-ated self-confirmation of the joy of revolution. Their incantations were directed at the legacy of the fallen, the endangered unity of the bourgeoisie and the workers which needed to be preserved, the good harmony between the revolutionary capi-tal and the much more conservative provinces, which needed to be maintained in the future. The parade that took place two months later, on 6 August—the day of the officially ordered homage to the Austrian Imperial Regent, Archduke Johann—to the war of liberation monument on the Kreuzberg showed, in comparison to the Friedrichshain parade, a clear reduction in the prorevolutionary camp. Some associ-ations such as the "constitutionalist club" and the artisan associations had in the meantime consciously retreated "from the streets" and held separate celebrations indoors. Altogether the number of participants had fallen considerably compared to June and the parade had a more proletarian face. Among the hundreds of flags, par-ticularly noticeable were the magnificently decorated trade union flags and the Ger-man colors, while Prussian flags were absent. Many German flags had the Prussian colors in bands or in small fields. For the first time, observers noticed red flags in the parade, for them an especially noteworthy innovation.

Step by step, the space for street politics was restricted from the late summer of 1848 onwards, and old, prerevolutionary laws increasingly enforced. Especially in the form of countless police ordinances, an attempt was made once again to strictly regulate life on the streets. Certainly, smoking in the street, banned in Berlin up to the beginning of the revolution, remained permitted. However, public behavior and public expression of opinion was increasingly subject to controls. From July 1848, the number of people charged with lèse-majesté began to rise again. Radical speak-ers at popular assemblies were repeatedly accused of or charged with high treason. Authors of placards or pamphlets were once again persecuted. In general, free or "wild" placarding, which had developed spontaneously in March and which had lent the Prussian capital a greatly changed, and in the eyes of many a disorderly, but, in any case, "revolutionary" appearance, came under attack from the authorities with the aim of having the police totally prevent such uncontrolled activity.

The authorities also endeavored to restrict "street literature," especially the itin-erant trade of the "flying booksellers." Sale in the streets of newspapers, pamphlets, flyers and placards had become a not insignificant source of income for writers, journalists, publishers, printers, and street vendors—the latter mostly children. At times, up to thirty-five humorist-satirical journals were being published, sold above all in the streets. Starting at the end of July, "flying traders" were arrested and con-victed by the new police force by the dozens, publishers and print-shop owners brought to court for illegal distribution. Mass meetings as well, from March onwards a self-evident customary right of the revolution, were subject to new police con-trols. On 8 July, the new chief of police, von Bardeleben, announced that organiz-ers of mass meetings not licensed by the police would be subject to a fine of five to fifty talers. A number of leaders of the democratic association, who felt themselves provoked by this directive and organized unlicensed popular assemblies, were brought before the police courts at the end of August.

Finally, the permanent street clubs were broken up. With names such as "Linden-Club" and "Club on the political corner," spontaneous debating clubs had formed, meeting every evening in central locations in the city, especially on popular central points on the boulevard Unter den Linden, to exchange opinions and views on the politics of the day. In many respects, these standing street clubs involved a transfer to the city center of the previous mass meetings in the tents, which had become hackneyed political routine. An announcement by the chief of police on 31 July forbade such street gatherings on Unter den Linden. During the following weeks, every evening there were "proper games of tag" on numerous city-center streets as groups were broken up by the police and reformed immediately further down the street.

For Karl Varnhagen von Ense, a critical contemporary observer, Berlin had become "a capital of constables, as constables have become its main feature. The entire city is a constable-city. Wherever you look, you see constables. They amble through the streets with folded arms, they are standing on all the street corners, everywhere you run across constables ..." Action was taken where there was no reason, wrote Varnhagen further, passers-by were eyed suspiciously, and people who wanted to stop to look at something were told to move on. He felt reminded of the pre-revolutionary period, of vagrancy police and night-watchmen, police spies and gendarmes, bloodhounds, and bailiffs.[15]

Counter-Revolutionary Endeavors

A third large block of street politics, which will only briefly be mentioned here, includes counter-revolutionary endeavors, insofar as they can be established as actions. These were in essence "repression conflicts" (clashes arising mostly from offensive operations by the armed forces) and the "throne and altar" unrest, limited mostly to Prussia (militant attacks by fanatic "friends of the king," mostly from the lower classes, on liberal and democratic representatives of the revolution). Taken together, these two forms of street politics made up almost exactly a quarter of all registered conflicts of the revolutionary period. The high-point of "repression conflicts"—at 19 percent the largest single group—signaled very exactly the gradual revitalization of the temporarily paralyzed party of order and their temporarily restrained military units and police formations. Clashes of this sort rose, from a nadir in March, relatively continually and reached a first peak in October and November 1848, culminating then again in May 1849 in the regional centers of the campaign for the imperial constitution.

In Prussia they were common, apart from Berlin, especially in the strongly anti-Prussian-democratic southern borderlands of the province of Saxony and in the Rhineland. Furthermore, they appeared more often in some garrison towns and residential cities such as Mainz and Darmstadt (grand duchy of Hessen) or Ulm and Stuttgart (Württemberg). More authentic in the sense of a street politics "from the bottom up" were certain forms of spontaneous and civilian counter-revolution, that is those violent actions for "throne and altar," which, above all in Prussia, were also able to define the dynamics of the revolution. Of the eighty-one "throne and altar" disturbances, seventy occurred in Prussia, especially in the provinces of East and West Prussia, Pomerania, and Brandenburg. Towns with royal residences near the capital, such as Charlottenburg and Potsdam, provincial centers such as Königsberg and Stettin, commercial centers such as Elbing and Danzig, proved to be preferred arenas for such violent attacks. In general, the participants were primarily plebeian-proletarians and the old middle class, classes permeated by "true Prussian convictions," who attacked democratic and liberal associations and their leading spokesmen—those who were identified with "the revolution" and its consequences, with continued "unrest" and widespread insubordination and who were thus held to be dangerous. In certain regional milieus, such "trouble-makers," as un-Prussian strangers, were faced with a sharp, and sometimes physical public-moral contempt and even at times expulsion.[16]

Conclusion

For the lower classes, street politics was a self-evident, socially and culturally suitable form of action. If they wanted to gain an independent and effective hearing, then this had to be done in the collective, direct, expressive manner described above. Thus they were able to create a counter-discourse and, for a time, local alternative centers of power. The occupied streets were used in many ways: as a site of social contact, communication, as a place to gather and exchange opinions, as a site for public petitions against distress, a place for public ridicule, for collective censure of unpopular people from the rich and powerful, as a tribune for formulating collective wishes, requests and desires, as a place of pressing demands and threats, as well as moral pressure, and, not least a place of threats and violence against private persons and the authorities. In their generally narrow, more direct than indirect, non-representative (in the literal sense of the word) grasp of politics, they understood their forms of action mostly as direct self-help. Characteristic elements of their political mentality were the "here" and "now" of their form of action, the implicit claim to be able to have in their hands the direct results of their desires, so to speak, on the evening of the same day.

Forms and aims of the actions of street politics are difficult to separate. That which was disputed above all, was the specific: the objects of daily life and survival, those things held to be vital for a halfway dignified life, sufficient food, regular work, sufficient income, clear rights and legitimate claims to resources that ensured a comfortable existence. Less disputed was the abstract, the indirect, the distant, such as determining a new political system, even when this question naturally touched the lives of many. Expressed in positive terms, the unwritten program of street politics, articulated more through action and the spoken word, can be characterized as a collective desire for an ensemble of goods, resources, rights, and norms, which can be paraphrased with the two symbolic terms "bread" and "street." These were the two central points towards which the "self-defined" [*eigensinnig*] actions of the masses were directed.

"Street" in this sense means more than a temporary occupation of public space for protests. Rather it signifies unrestricted and independent participation in public affairs. The topos "street" is used here in the broader sense of the sum of all customary rights of popular modes of using of public space, claims "from the bottom up" to the disputed territory of an emerging civil society—which could be more strictly regulated or used in a more liberal manner as a political tribune, as a parliament of the masses. Equally the topos "bread" refers to more than simply a conflict for affordable foodstuffs during periods of high prices. Rather, much more broadly, the premarket economy's "principle of nourishment" (*Nahrungsprinzip*) was at stake, a value system in which the authorities' and municipalities' common responsibilities of supply were inseparably included. In these subsistence-oriented collisions, long-term conflicts broke out concerning the proper operation and use of social resources, above all essential foodstuffs, between the two quite contrary aims of private marketing and general claims to security.

Without these "self-defined" protests, rebellions, and demonstrations of large masses in the streets, which here has been generally described as street politics, there could have been no revolution of 1848. This consideration may be expanded in the other direction: the eruptive movements of street politics, in the final analysis, had to be set on the path of an institutionalized revolution of associations and parliaments, in order to transform at least a part of their energies spent, their expressively articulated desires into permanent successes. It was exactly this point, this "translation" of the concerns of the masses, expressed in the context of street politics, into verbal programs for a new order worth striving for, open to discourse and being set down on paper, that a key problem of the revolution lay. In putting together the sometimes parallel, sometimes contrary endeavors of street politics, it appears that a respectable mass basis for a democratic and social republic was certainly present. However, who was to bring about this transformation of street politics in such a short time? Required here was a "great leap forward" in political culture—indeed, a miracle. Certainly, the generally very limited possibilities available to democratic associations and the new labor movement were greatly overtaxed in trying to bring about such a transformation. In relation to the revolution as a whole, the results of street politics therefore remain extremely contradictory.

Initially they contributed significantly—already in 1847 and then quite decisively in March and April 1848—to a delegitimization of the old regime. They made obvious, much more than all other parallel endeavors, the waning ability of the old elite to overcome pressures of social problems. Secondly, they proved, in spite of all the risks contained in every sort of direct action, quite effective for a large part of the population in the short-term—and this was their view point—and in the end an indispensable means of collective self-help, for there were doubtless "successes": subsidized food supply and generally increased efforts in private and public welfare, increased wages and in general better work conditions, noteworthy municipal and state measures against wide-spread underemployment and unemployment. As long as the revolutionary occupation of the streets maintained a certain level, all sections of society paid these problem areas an unusually high amount of attention. However, at the same time, the actions of street politics proved to be, because of their nature, incompatible with the political culture of liberal and democratic reform movements, to a great degree. Strict recognition of state monopoly in the use of force as well as sacrosanct respect towards modern private property would equally have meant the end of that—in the short-term quite effective—form of popular self-help. In the end, the revolutionary crisis did not lead to an effective alliance between the lower classes and the middle classes open to reform, but rather encouraged the old elite of the Ancien Régime and decisive sections of a rising bourgeois middle class to move closer together.

Notes

1. On the subject of "streets" and "public order" as a permanently disputed political terrain of civil society, see also B.J. Warneken (ed.), *Massenmedium Straße. Zur Kulturgeschichte der Demonstration* (Frankfurt, 1991); Thomas Lindenberger, *Straßenpolitik. Zur Sozialgeschichte der öffentlichen Ordnung in Berlin 1900 bis 1914* (Bonn, 1995); Thomas Lindenberger and Alf Lüdtke (eds.), *Physische Gewalt. Studien zur Geschichte der Neuzeit* (Frankfurt, 1995).

2. Dieter Langewiesche, "Die deutsche Revolution von 1848/49 und die vorrevolutionäre Gesellschaft: Forschungsstand und Forschungsperspektiven," Part 2, *Archiv für Sozialgeschichte* 31 (1991): 331-443, here 333.

3. Overviews of "social protest" and "street politics" can be found in Arno Herzig, *Unterschichtenprotest in Deutschland 1790-1870* (Göttingen, 1988); Manfred Gailus and HeinrichVolkmann (eds.), *Der Kampf um das tägliche Brot. Nahrungsmangel, Versorgungspolitik und Protest, 1770-1990* (Opladen, 1994); Wolfgang von Hippel, *Armut, Unterschichten, Randgruppen in der Frühen Neuzeit* (Munich, 1995). A. Würgler, *Unruhen und Öffentlichkeit. Städtische und ländliche Protestbewegungen im 18. Jahrhundert* (Tübingen, 1995) has impressively demonstrated that bourgeois/middle class groups in the eighteenth century could also exploit street politics. On the revolution of 1848/49 as "street politics," see Manfred Gailus, *Straße und Brot. Sozialer Protest in den deutschen Staaten unter besonderer Berücksichtigung Preußens, 1847-1849* (Göttingen, 1990), esp. 29-42, 350-430.

4. Here and in the following I am drawing, where not otherwise noted, on my own research in Gailus, *Straße und Brot*. Statistics are based on 1,486 cases of protest taken from a systematic analysis of five major daily newspapers of the revolutionary period.

5. This is true at least of peasant unrest, and less so for peasant participation in rural association movements; see also for a critique on this point, Langewiesche, "Die deutsche Revolution von 1848/49," 412-13.

6. In greater detail with extensive references: Gailus, *Straße und Brot*, 72-106. For a model regional study of the revolutionary period for the Rhine-Main area, MichaelWettengel, *Die Revolution von 1848/49 im Rhein-Main-Raum. Politische Vereine und Revolutionsalltag im Großherzogtum Hessen, Herzogtum Nassau und in der Freien Stadt Frankfurt* (Wiesbaden, 1989).

7. The lines of confrontation and conflict referred to here form an (incomplete) cross-section of the collected material in the protest sample of my research for 1847/49.

796 | *Manfred Gailus*

8. Gailus, *Straße und Brot*, 113-20; see also, more extensively on the agrarian movement, the essay of Christoph Dipper (chapter 18) in this volume.

9. To name some relevant new regional studies for northern Germany: Josef Mooser, *Ländliche Klassengesellschaft 1770-1848. Bauern und Unterschichten, Landwirtschaft und Gewerbe im östlichen Westfalen* (Göttingen, 1984), esp., 246-80; Bernd Parisius, *Vom Groll der "Kleinen Leute" zum Programm der kleinen Schritte. Arbeiterbewegung im Herzogtum Oldenburg, 1840-1890* (Oldenburg, 1985), esp. 16-60; G. Schildt, *Tagelöhner, Gesellen, Arbeiter. Sozialgeschichte der vorindustriellen und industriellen Arbeiter in Braunschweig, 1830-1880* (Stuttgart, 1986), 111-21.

10. Most recently on subsistence unrest during the 1840s and the revolutionary period: Manfred Gailus, "Nahrungsmangel, Versorgungspolitik und Protest in Deutschland (ca. 1770-1873)," unpublished MS Berlin 1996. Furthermore on attitudes of artisan journeymen and workers in the revolutionary period: Jürgen Bergmann, *Wirtschaftskrise und Revolution. Handwerker und Arbeiter 1848/49* (Stuttgart, 1986).

11. Quoted in Joseph Hansen (ed.), *Rheinische Briefe und Akten zur Geschichte der politischen Bewegung 1830-1850*, Vol. 2.2, ed. By Heinz Boberach (Cologne, 1976), 180.

12. On the distancing of Berlin democrats from charivaris, see also R. Springer, *Berlin's Strassen, Kneipen und Clubs im Jahre 1848* (Berlin, 1850), 85; and A. Streckfuss, *1848. Die März-Revolution in Berlin. Ein Augenzeuge erzählt*, ed. by Horst Denkler and Irmgard Denkler (Cologne, 1983), 337.

13. See for greater detail Gailus, *Straße und Brot*, 149-52, 170-79.

14. Ibid., 364-413. On the Berlin revolutionary culture of flyers and placards see also S. Weigel, *Flugschriftenliteratur 1848 in Berlin. Geschichte und Öffentlichkeit einer volkstümlichen Gattung* (Hamburg, 1977); further, cf. comparisons between Paris and Berlin can be found in Ilja Mieck, Horst Möller, and Jürgen Voss (eds.), *Paris und Berlin in der Revolution 1848* (Sigmaringen, 1995).

15. Karl August Varnhagen von Ense, *Tagebücher*, Vol. 5 (Leipzig, 1861/62), 134ff., and 138-41.

16. For more detail on the spontaneous counter-revolution, see Gailus, *Straße und Brot*, 431-94; furthermore for associations, see Wolfgang Schwentker, *Konservative Vereine und Revolution in Preußen 1848/49. Die Konstituierung des Konservatismus als Partei* (Düsseldorf, 1988); Eckhard Trox, *Militärischer Konservatismus. Kriegervereine und "Militärpartei" in Preußen zwischen 1815 und 1848/49* (Stuttgart, 1990), esp. chapter 5.6.3. "Öffentliche Umzüge und Kriegerfeste," 225-28.

Torchlight parade in honour of the delegates in Frankfurt a.M.
(Illustrirte Zeitung, Leipzig, no. 255, 20 May 1848, 331)

Torchlight parade in honour of the President of the Constitutional Assembly, Freiherr Heinrich von
Gagern, in Frankfurt a.M. on 31 May (Illustrirte Zeitung, Leipzig, no. 259, 17 June 1848, 391)

Chapter 34

REVOLUTIONARY FESTIVALS IN GERMANY AND ITALY

Charlotte Tacke

Seldom have there been so many celebrations as in the years of revolution. The movement of the political public sphere, the hope of change and increasing differentiation of political opinion found its expression in the streets. Both in Paris, Rome, Berlin or Vienna and in the small towns and villages the revolutionary spark ignited in a culture of festivals. Not only did the bourgeoisie celebrate, the petit bourgeoisie and the rural strata also took part, every group according to its custom, in the great festival: revolution.

In order to escape the historiographically privileged view of the festival of revolution as a festival of the bourgeoisie which took place in the (major) cities,[1] a regional, comparative approach was chosen for this contribution. While restricting comparison to two regions in Germany and Italy, cannot do justice to either national or continent-wide diversity, it can present the richness of the social and political impetus. Especially for Germany and Italy, a regional approach is justified by the tangle of local, regional, and national loyalties particularly noticeable in the revolution. The two grand duchies of Baden and Tuscany experienced similar processes of radicalization in the course of the revolution, which in both cases culminated in a declaration of a republic in the early months of 1849. Furthermore, Tuscany was not directly affected by the struggles of the war of independence like the north and the south of Italy, where the festival atmosphere was often saddened by events of the war.

The temporal framework of this comparison has been shifted slightly. While the February uprising in Paris provided the starting signal for the revolution in Baden and the spring of 1848 marked a break between the *Vormärz* and the revolution both in intensity as well as in the symbolic and ritual expression of the festival cultures,

---

the political and national awakening had already begun in Italy in 1846/47. The political substance of these early festivals seems less revolutionary. However, accelerated change in festival culture before March 1848 and the continuities in festival culture from 1847 to the autumn of 1848 justify a glance at festivals before 1848.

The political starting point was different in the two countries. While the grand duchy of Baden had been a constitutional monarchy since 1818, Tuscany had never experienced a constitutional regime. In Baden, the constitution became the central symbol of the liberal movement, which had already developed its own bourgeois political festival culture and symbolism in the *Vormärz*. Especially the constitutional festivals of 1843 demonstrated, through their success in attracting people from both city and country, their well-developed communication structures and their bourgeois-optimistic symbolism, a strongly liberal, if not fundamentally oppositional movement.[2] In Tuscany, on the other hand, the festival culture remained restricted to representation of the monarchy and the court well into the second half of the 1840s. Only in 1846, when the liberal movement saw in the election of Pius IX a symbol of Italian rebirth and independence, and later, when it was able to force political reforms on the individual states, did the festival culture also take on new forms and extent.

The Tuscan Festivals

From 1846 onwards, the occasions for political festivals in Tuscany increased rapidly. In the center of these often stood the new Pope as symbol of liberal hopes. The election of Pius IX, the amnesties he announced, and the relevant anniversaries were celebrated in countless big and small towns in Tuscany with festive church services, parades, artillery salutes, speeches, and public entertainment.

The *Guardia Civica* became the central symbol of political reform. The civic guard outwardly symbolized national unity against the common enemy of Austria and also promised, in its form of recruitment, social equality of male citizens, even if it was hierarchically structured internally. "With the *Guardia Civica*, we will ensure the independence of the government and the people, force our enemies to respect us; we will raise a masculine and active youth and protect our liberties from open attack."[3] It is therefore not surprising that Leopold II's permitting a *Guardia Civica* in September was the occasion for countless small and large festivals in the city and in the country.

In Florence, more than 20,000 people gathered on 5 September—this, at least, was the number given by the sympathizing newspaper *L'Alba*—on the various squares in the city and marched in ordered rows to the Palazzo Pitti, to express their thanks to the Grand Duke. They carried with them more than sixty banners with inscriptions such as "Viva Leopold II," "Viva Pio IX," "Viva la Indipendenza Italiana," "Unione," and "Fratellanza." They had stuck red and white cockades in their hats, while the Romans and Piedmontese living in the city were wearing cockades in the colors of their own countries. The women—in windows and on the balconies—also wore red and white cockades on their chests and waved flags and sashes in the national colors.

With calls of "Viva l'Italia" and "Viva la Guardia Civile," they tossed flowers and laurels on the men marching past. Special greetings were given to a group of 500 men from the "contado," the rural region surrounding the city, who were cheered along with enthusiastic cries of "Viva i contadini." After the crowds had cheered the Grand Duke and the princes on the terrace of the Palazzo Pitti, they marched past the palace of the Papal Nuncio to give three cheers to the Pope. At five o'clock in the afternoon, the Archbishop held a solemn Te Deum in the cathedral; later he blessed the crowd. The parade also passed the Jewish quarter and thus underlined liberal demands for freedom of religion. The closeness of the national movement to the Catholic Church, however, excluded integration of Jews in the movement.[4]

Although separated from one another, city dwellers and peasants, locals and foreigners, men and women together celebrated a national festival. Social differences were emphasized rather than evened out. The national enthusiasm, moreover, left much room for stressing local and regional loyalties. The latter was demonstrated in a parade that presented the *Guardia Civica* as a matter for urban, Catholic male citizens; other groups were included in the national enthusiasm but were assigned a subordinate role in the new order.

The celebrated unity of people and ruler was certainly not as idyllic as the enthusiasm of the journalists suggested. This unity would not only appear questionable in the future. Even on 4 September, as consultations on the establishment of the *Guardia Civica* began, police presence was doubled in case of a negative decision by the committee. Only later could the reporters ask why it was felt necessary to monitor public order. Was it not a true popular festival, celebrating the existing public order?[5]

In the countryside too—"in every corner of Tuscany"[6]—the establishment of the *Guardia Civica* was celebrated, even if often with some delay. Rural festivals usually did not develop spontaneously as a parade of men through the community, but were prompted by the Catholic clergy in connection with the Sunday service. "Everywhere, religious festivals preceded secular ones, and religious feelings mixed with patriotic ones."[7] The rural population was both mobilized and controlled.

On the evening of 10 September, the priest of S. Donnino a Brozzi and the Vicar of S. Andrea summoned the people in the church with church-bells. With "brief, but warm and emotional words," they praised the reforms of the prince, and "so that no undesired unrest would arise from the ignorance of some of current events, they declared to the people what they could expect from the *Principe*."[8] Following, the Te Deum intoned and "thousands of voices rose in this moment towards the heavens for Italy's fortunes." Often the "Salvum fac popolum tuum Domine" of the Te Deum was repeated. Religious deliverance was charged with a national spirit. "Hearts were stirred, knees bent to the ground to pray for deliverance from foreign rule by the highest lord of the peoples."[9]

Apart from church services, sermons, and Te Deums, further symbols and rituals of the Catholic Church were placed in the service of the national cause: banners were raised, the blessed sacrament was presented for worship, and the people blessed. Sometimes the differences between festival parade and procession were blurred. In Castiglion Fiorentino people marched to the church with Tuscan, papal and national flags, including the bishop, who was visiting the town, as well as the chapter, the entire clergy, and the theological college. Behind the state officials of the various branches of the administration and civil institutions, there followed a group of women and girls, led by a noblewoman. A youth choir with red and white sashes sang festive songs. In the church, the Bishop intoned the Te Deum, and all the people joined in.[10]

The presence of clergy and, above all, of women and girls in this parade, as well as the festive songs and the parade to the church, resemble more a procession than a festive parade, especially since it may be assumed that the clergy was marching in its vestments. In Borgo San Lorenzo, the parade assembled in front of the crucifix after the service to place the national flag, so that the people "would undertake no magnanimous act without before praying for divine help in front of the miraculous image of the Savior."[11]

Not only were national festivals enriched with religious elements; the reverse was also true as religious festivals came to resemble secular ones. On the occasion of the festival of the "Vergine del Rosario," the people of Sesto and Colonnata organized a procession on the first Sunday in October 1847 in which the monstrance was paraded. The priest spoke "warm words over the holy body on the fatherland and on religion, on the valuable institutions arising from them and on reforms and numerous charitable deeds."[12] After the Te Deum, he blessed the faithful. The two parishes then marched, with banners and music, through the village, sang national hymns and gave three cheers for Leopold II, Pius IX, Gioberti, the *Guardia Civica*, for religion, and Italian independence. Similarly, 300 youths, on the occasion of the festival of San Felice in San Lucchese, wore tricolor cockades in the procession and carried numerous banners with the inscriptions "Viva Leopoldo II" and "Viva Pio IX." After the service, the entire village was illuminated, music was played and cheers given for the Grand Duke and the Pope.[13]

The closeness of the movement to the Catholic Church, and the hopes it placed in the Pope, allowed for a broad mobilization of the rural population by the clergy. Clerics also provided a certain guarantee that the movement in the countryside would not get out of control. Again and again they preached the necessity and Christian duty of the preservation of peace. In Florence, the Minister of the Interior Cosimo Ridolfi called on the crowds in the Piazza Pitti to respect order—so that crafts, trade, and industry could flourish. "Only order creates power, wealth, and virtue."[14] In Montaione, on the other hand, the priest preached in the church and emphasized the necessity of "proper respect for our holy religion, never-ending honor of the Holy Father, the honest feeling of dependence, thankfulness and obedience towards our Principe, the practice of civic virtues, and the love of order."[15]

Behind these words stood a liberal fear of the people, a bourgeois fear of the lower classes, and an urban fear of the rural population. On 11 October 1847, a crowd of over 300 youths from the countryside marched to Porto Ferraio (Isola

d'Elba) to be registered in the *Guardia Civica* and to put on "an enthusiastic demonstration in honor of this patriotic institution." They carried Tuscan flags and drums
and gave three cheers to the Grand Duke, the Pope, and Italy. Thirty of them were
"armed with totally antiquated, damaged, and rusted rifle lacking both flints and
munitions." This assembly of the "classe campagnola" displeased some citizens of the
town, who feared a "clash between the rural population and citizens of the town,"
and who alarmed the military to prevent the youths from entering the city. In the
church and in the processions, these young men were welcome guests; in a spontaneous festival, and especially an armed one, they seemed unpredictable.[16]

In the spring of 1848, the festivals in Tuscany differed little from those of previous years. At most a few tendencies had been strengthened. As before, constitutional proclamations were accompanied by festive parades and church services. The
dense sequence of constitutions made them appear a national event. This was
expressed in the symbolism of the festivals. While in 1847 the colors of the grand
duchy still outweighed the national colors, in February 1848 the tricolor dominated. In a festive parade on 18 February in Florence, the participants no longer
wore red and white, but red-white-green cockades instead, and the banners "were
mostly tricolored."[17]

The national mood still allowed room for local and regional loyalties, however.
These were no longer attached first and foremost to dynastic loyalties, but to historical traditions. The reforms were celebrated as a renaissance of the Florentine
Republic. "Liberty was not born in Florence this morning; it returned after a cen-
tury-long exile!"[18] In this appeal to history, the city and region assigned themselves
a prominent place in the coming nation. It was seen as a loose confederation of separate "republics." Specific ideas of its political and social structure remained unex-
pressed. History, in its ambiguity, allowed a consensus beyond different political
ideas and social position.

The tangle of different loyalties was especially clearly expressed in a banner that
had already appeared in the autumn of 1847 at a festival in a village in Mugello in
honor of the *Guardia Civica*. It consisted of a yellow cloth with a tricolor star. Within
the star was placed the allegory of armed Italia, which symbolized above all the
threat to the nation from abroad. The white point was decorated with religious symbols, the green with symbols of the grand duchy and the red with an allegory of liberty with symbols of the press, the *Guardia Civica*, and the urban communities.[19]

Harmony and unity as festive symbolism could only cover over social and political differences for a short time. When the news of the revolution in Vienna began
to circulate in Florence on 19 March, the city erupted in delight. For the chronicler of the Florentine Revolution, Conte Luigi Passerini de' Rilli, the distinction
between "Patricians, bourgeoisie, and commoners" melted away in a common festival of joy.[20] Five days later, however, the harmony had been disrupted. The people
celebrated in their own fashion, something which certainly did not fit the tastes of
the bourgeoisie. A "mob" had marched to the residence of the Austrian Minister,
torn down the coats of arms, dragged it through the city, and then burned it on the
Piazza del Granduca (today the Piazza della Signoria) and the Piazza Pitti. "The

people then continued to march through Florence the entire evening, sang abusive songs against Austria and the hated minister, and forced citizens to place lights in their windows. In this way, many houses were illuminated."[21] A gap emerged between the bourgeoisie and the people, highlighted by the festive illumination.

The Badenese Festivals

In Baden, the movement and the outbreak of revolution were expressed in a number of spontaneous festivals or symbolic acts. Especially young men from the lower classes used the streets to attract attention and express their still diffuse political interests and feelings towards social abuses. They drew on a symbolic repertoire made up of a colorful mixture of traditional popular culture and the political language of the French Revolution. In Heidelberg a "number of sections" of local and out-of-town apprentice artisans marched through the town between eight and nine in the evening on 28 February. They sang songs of liberty and chanted "up with freedom."[22] They marched passed the house of the privy councillor Gelius, demanded "out with you!", hurled insults at him, "and then they marched on."

When the notables of Ettenheim organized a masked ball in the Pflugswirtshaus for 4 March—it was carnival—"disapproving and threatening remarks from the commoners" could already be heard some days before. On the evening, 150 "in part young men and mostly unmarried lads" gathered in front of the Badischen Hof, an inn that lay at the gates of the city, marched from there with torches into the city and then out again to the inn. In the course of their March they passed by the Pflugswirtshaus and the civic guard watch and sang "loudly the well-known song of liberty or death."[23]

These events—of which there are many other examples—are full of elements of traditional popular culture: young men, who ganged up together under protection of darkness, drank alcohol, marched through the city to bring charivaris against unpopular people. In 1848, these unpopular people were no longer competing youths who had violated the code of honor, but rather mostly officials and representatives of state power.[24] The symbols used were changing. While traditional forms were in part preserved—the people cursed, yelled, drummed on a watering-can or otherwise made noise—new elements were also included imported directly from France: the tricolor, the tree of liberty, the Marseillaise and other songs of liberty. Activists from the lower classes rapidly absorbed a new, revolutionary system of symbols.

The novelty of this symbolism was apparent in the fact that it had not been standardized. Although the black-red-gold tricolor had already been declared the colors of the German Confederation on 9 March, three days later red-yellow (Badenese) flags with black diagonal strips were still appearing.[25] It could also be that the transformation of the Badenese flag into a tricolor can be interpreted as a sign of local and regional trajectory in the protests. The mass meetings held everywhere in the first days of March certainly contributed to spreading revolutionary symbolism.

It was not just in Ettenheim, where the youth mob was explicitly directed against the celebrating notables, or in charivaris, where representatives of state power were denounced, that festive culture itself expressed the social conflicts of the revolution and various models of social structure. In their symbolism and ritual forms, festivals were political events that expressed quite definite social views.

When concessions by the Badenese government were announced on 1 March 1848, these two worlds met in shared rapture. In Mannheim, reported the progovernmental *Karlsruher Zeitung*, this news "was most happily received." One thousand five hundred to 1800 "people, to whom women had distributed tricolored (black-red-gold) sashes," streamed to the train station—probably because they hoped to hear the latest news from Karlsruhe there. "Some concern was caused by the mass of proletarians," who, also carrying tricolor sashes, marched singing through the streets. Bourgeois joy at the government's concessions was dampened, thoughts were given to security measures, and it was hoped "that a civic guard will be organized today, so that every danger can be prevented."[26]

Bourgeois with black-red-gold sashes and "proletarians" with black-red-gold sashes faced each other from the beginning as strangers, as opponents threatening civic order—although the republic had only hesitatingly appeared on the political stage and no barricades had yet been set up in Baden. Political conflict had been predefined by social conflict. A connective festive culture that encouraged unity had not yet been developed. Quite the opposite, in fact: festive culture tended to highlight social differences.

The tricolor, as the Mannheim example shows, was taken up as a symbol by all political currents and social groups and could only be clearly interpreted in connection with other symbols or symbolic practices. The black-red-gold flag appeared in three different social and political contexts in March 1848. In Rüslingen "a number of lads and a few citizens—the so-called rabble," hung a black-red-gold banner on the tree of liberty in front of the parish church at eight in the evening on 12 March, sang songs of liberty until twelve and organized a march along the main street to the high town. "The civic guard patrolled the entire night."[27] In Heidelberg, on 22 March at half past twelve in the afternoon, a black-red-gold flag was raised on the market square accompanied by music. Master baker Leonhard Kitzhaupt reminded the people that they had been awakened after such a very long "very deep sleep." "The citizens should now," he warned, "remain true to this awakening, obey and honor the law and not be drawn into unconsidered actions which are against the laws and regulations."[28] A few days later, on 26 March at twelve o'clock, a "raising of the German flag" took place in Rastatt in the federal fortress. All the troops of the garrison, authorities of the Grand Duchy and the municipality, the mayor and city council, the citizens committee, the civic corps and the people of the town gathered and accompanied the flag in a festive parade to the castle. The people, "some armed, some not," formed a guard of honor and the flag was raised, accompanied by music, drums and three cheers "which was joyfully repeated by all the troops and the mass of people," while the troops presented arms.[29]

All these events took place after 9 March. The black-red-gold flag had already been declared the colors of the German Confederation by the Confederate Diet and Baden was no longer a symbol of the opposition. The banners in Rüslingen were raised under protection of darkness, while the same ceremony took place in Heidelberg and Rastatt in the middle of the day. In Rüslingen this event was attributed to the "rabble"; in Heidelberg the burghers were involved; and, in Rastatt, the entire town and the administration were united with the military. While the young men sang songs of liberty, the bourgeoisie in Heidelberg did not sing themselves, but raised their flag accompanied by music. In Rastatt, on the other hand, military music was played. In Rüslingen, the banner was decorated with a tree of liberty, evoking the revolutionary symbol drawn from the French Revolution. In Rastatt, it was drawn from a revolutionary tradition as the "colors of the former German Imperial banner," and placed within the context of the former empire and the order of the German states.

In Heidelberg the question of which tradition was being drawn on remained open. The baker's reference to an awakening of the people placed it closer to the French tricolor; the warning to maintain order, however, separates it from the "rabble." The events in Rüslingen and Heidelberg were watched over by the police, because they were seen as a threat to public order. In Rüslingen, moreover, the civic guard patrolled. The two flags in Rüslingen and Heidelberg were interpreted as political symbols of internal opposition. The tricolor in Rastatt outwardly symbolized national unity and attempted to paper over domestic conflicts. "From our fortress flies the banner of the German nation and announces from now on a new age of power and honor, like the unity of the German people. May victory, fortune, unity and peace of all the German tribes from the Alps to the Eider [sic!] and from the Rhine to the Vistula ever bloom under the wings of this holy banner!"[30]

The national impetus of the black-red-gold banner, directed outward, did not, however, have a unifying effect. Reference to the symbolism of the French Revolution, open in Rüslingen and indirect in Freiburg, given the rumour circulating in the spring of 1848 that Baden would become part of the French Republic, points to another nation. Blended in the tricolor were quite different social, political, and national ideas. None of the three events was able to speak for all levels of the population, disassociating themselves instead more or less clearly from one another. The common symbols could achieve at most a frail consensus on the basis of suppressed misunderstandings, in assuming against better judgement that everyone carrying a tricolor was following the same hopes.

In the mass meetings, described by contemporaries as festivals and which drew on the festive culture for many of their symbols and rituals, attempts were made to suppress social conflict in favor of a common political aim. Like in the *Vormärz* festivals, one can read out of the reports of mass meetings in March and April 1848 the confidence that bourgeois order could be extended to all classes. While making claims to being popular festivals, their structure was bourgeois. The mass meetings drew, with their rituals and symbolism, on the bourgeois, liberal festivals of the *Vormärz* and radiated their optimism that they could create a "classless society of burghers." The towns were festively decorated, the people marched in ordered parades to the meeting point. "An imposing parade of at least 3,000 people marched [in April 1848 in Waldshut] through the streets, led by a group of miners in traditional costumes and weapons, with their state banner, and in the middle of the parade the German flag waved, and a large musical choir raised the mood to joyful enthusiasm. All the streets we marched through were richly decorated and gave silent witness to the excellent spirit which enlivened Waldhut's worthy citizens."[31]

The letter of Mayor Rée of Offenburg, reporting on a mass meting to the responsible district office, described it as a "gathering of all friends of the fatherland for the protection of public order, unfortunately disturbed in many parts of our country, and the rights of the people."[32] This report explicitly tied the maintenance of public order to the rights of citizens and thus expressed the revolutionaries' ambivalent attitude. The mass meeting aimed at the preservation of public (social) order as much as at the representation of revolutionary politics.

The political unity of the people was thus presented as social unity. This is clearly reflected in the different use of language in the various source material. Newspaper articles and memoirs describing the mass meetings of March and April 1848 emphasized their unity and order, especially when they identified with the aims of the mass meetings. Newspapers reports of a mass meeting in Offenburg describe a fantastic meeting and the countless national flags "earlier frowned upon, but now flying from government buildings."[33] The crowds marched from the train station in orderly lines with music and black-red-gold flags to the town hall. Adolf Kußmaul, a doctor, noticed especially the picturesque traditional, costumes of the countryfolk and compared the meeting with "a lovely popular festival."[34] People had put on their Sunday best and even a skeptical observer saw "only well-dressed city dwellers and countryfolk," "among them no roughs, no rabble, no drunks."[35] At night, things remained peaceful. For the bourgeois observer, unity in political aims and hopes was expressed in the peace and order of the festival. "Thus the meeting concluded in exemplary peace and order, unhindered and unsupervised by police and military, carrying copious seeds for the future in their hands."[36]

This assessment, which even in the *Vormärz* had become standard for bourgeois descriptions of such festivals, reflected more the bourgeois program and attempts at legitimation than reality. First, the meeting was under the surveillance of the police, who saw it more as a "demonstration,"[37] than a "popular festival"; and second, the police saw more disorderly behavior than order among the participants. The local magistrate reported "fifty wagons full of people" from Kehl, Hanau, and the surroundings of Offenburg, who were driven into the city and of whom "*quite a few* were armed with muskets, double-barrelled guns and well-sharpened scythes."[38] From Oberkirch, 130 men arrived "mostly with guns and twenty men with scythe-like weapons."[39] Although some participants were armed, this fact cannot be interpreted as an intention to begin an armed struggle, but more as underlining the radical demand for arming of the people; what becomes clear are the different views among the participants.[40] The one saw picturesque traditional costumes and flags, the other scythelike weapons and rifles.

While the radical spokesmen renounced using the word "republic"[41] at the mass meeting in Offenburg, out of political considerations and to maintain the unity of the movement, the police reported on the return of Offenburg participants, who entered their town "with loud cheers of 'long live liberty,' 'long live the republic.'"[42] The festive rituals also appeared in another light to the police. While the people honored above all the official festive order, police reports spoke of traditional "brawling."[43] They repeatedly mentioned the noisy disturbance of young men yelling, singing loudly, shouting, and being annoying—performing a charivari was only the extreme form of celebrations seen as disturbance of the peace. They touched on the raw nerve of bourgeois ideals, which had stylized order and peace as central values. It was not by chance that the terms "Ruhestörung" and "Krawall" [literally "disturbance of rest" and "big noise" -ed.] refer to noise disturbance in the true meaning of the word, but were applied to the disturbance of public order.

Even at the beginning of the revolution, when the political positions of the opposition still appeared open to compromise and the joy at the political upheaval that seemed to be coming united the various political camps, two cultures faced each other. The noisemakers were socially and politically excluded. State officials continually point out in their reports that those causing disturbances were "dissolute riffraff," "citizens from the lower classes," "common rabble", "the lowest class and riffraff" or the "lowest class of people."[44]

Political festivals, including republican ones, occurred within the framework of a bourgeois festive culture formed in the *Vormärz*, but they were accompanied by a popular festive culture, which threw a threatening shadow of the lower classes jeopardizing bourgeois festive and revolutionary culture. The republicans attempted to educate the popular masses and to use the festival in the *Vormärz* tradition as a means of enlightenment and education. Their opponents used references to disturbances at republican festivals as a means of political exclusion. Political conflicts between republicans and conservatives were, however, not expressed in different festive cultures, like social exclusion, but occurred instead in nearly identical ritual forms of bourgeois festive order. The formation of political camps was reflected at best in the use of symbols. While individual symbols, such as the tricolor, were used by all political currents and social classes, other symbols and occasions openly competed with each other. Depending on the symbolism used, the festivals of the revolution could emphasise unity or conflict.

Italian Rebellion

While the Badenese mass meetings were celebrations, war stood at the center of Italian festivals: the "holy crusade against the enemy."[45] In the spring and summer of 1848 it still superseded domestic political conflicts. "War, war against the Austrian is the only thought, the only necessity of the moment."[46] Occasions for celebrations came from outside, celebrations for domestic political reasons were seldom. This was all the more true as Pius IX had distanced himself from the national movement in

April and was no longer available as a unifying symbol. The religious symbols did not, however, lose in significance. Depending on the occasion, a Te Deum or a requiem was sung.

Joy and sorrow went hand in hand. Joy at successes in the war and sorrow because of the dead could, however, be united in the sense of "dying for the fatherland,"[47] as long as the war remained distant and relatively abstract. Sorrow and joy led to conflicts, however, when the war demanded immediate sacrifices. The dead of the uprising in Sicily were forgotten with the victory gained with the constitution. "Yesterday we mourned between the graves of Santa Croce the horrible deaths of Italians killed by the swords of the enemy; today we celebrate in the Cathedral of Santa Maria del Fiore the emancipation of the Italians from the ignominious yoke of the same enemy … Holy and sincere was our pain. Holy and sincere is this joy."[48]

In March, the anti-Austrian uprising in Milan was accompanied by joyful festivals; festivals were organized for Tuscan volunteers for the war of independence.[49] The news of heavy losses among the Tuscan volunteers was met with consternation in Florence, "because we all have either family members, relatives or friends among them."[50] While this sorrow changed into "indescribable joy" as the news spread of Austria's defeat near Goito, a shadow hung over their joy. On 2 June, Carlo Alberto's victory was remembered with a Te Deum in the cathedral. The next day a requiem was held for those who had died at Mantua. "The funeral dirges were followed by hymns of victory, from the graves of Italian soldiers rose the life and power of the nation." *La Patria* allowed that the city should mourn its sons, but this should only be done in "a manly way." For them, it was less a matter of mourning the deaths of their own sons, than to mourn the loss of the strongest fighters for the birth of Italy.[51]

It was in this spirit that Passerini described the reaction of an old man from the crowd, who was said to have cried out with tears in his eyes: "I have lost my only son in the battle on the 29th, but long live Italy."[52] This reaction, however, does not appear to have been typical. National rhetoric was one thing, private mourning another. The *Gonfaloniere* had ordered an illumination of the city for 4 July to celebrate the victory once again. Apart from a few public buildings, only a limited number of private people followed this request. Some had even called publicly for non-observance in order not to disturb the mourning of many Florentines. The money for illuminations should be given to the poor, they said.[53] Public celebration and private sorrow could not be brought into harmony.

When the victories became defeats and Carlo Alberto negotiated a truce with the Austrians at the end of July 1848, the festivals changed into demonstrations. When news of the truce reached Florence on 30 July, a crowd marched through the city to Palazzo Vecchio. They carried a tricolor with a black ribbon and demanded: "Down with the government!" Some drafted a decree in the name of the people which announced the overthrow of the Lorraine dynasty and the establishment of a provisional government. The decree remained, however, without consequence. Although observers reported no violent acts, the parade through the city was described as "frightening agitation" and as a "tumult." This banding together of the people and the possibility of a republic was seen by moderates as a threat, indeed as a revolution. "The demonstrations, or perhaps it would be better to say the revolution, took on an imposing character."[54] And in fact, the time of unifying festivals was past. In view of defeats and failure of neo-Guelf hopes, there was no longer any occasion for festivals that would unite bourgeoisie and the people. The alternative of a "republic" separated the social and political camps.

National Festivals in Baden

Only two events during the revolution of 1848/49, the election of Archduke Johann von Austria as imperial regent and the assassination of Robert Blum in Vienna, gave rise to "national" festivals in Baden. All the other festivals related to local and regional events. While the imperial regent was to a great extent able to bridge political and confessional differences—unlike in the Rhineland—Robert Blum became a martyr for the republican cause after his violent death.

Celebrations in honor of the imperial regent took place in July and August 1848. The citizens of Karlsruhe spontaneously organized a festival on 30 June after news arrived of the election of Johann as imperial regent. In Rastatt and Freiburg, Archduke Johann's arrival in Frankfurt and his introduction into the parliament were celebrated on 16 and 18 July. In most other towns in Baden, homage ceremonies ordered by the imperial minister of war took place on 6 and 7 August including the military stationed there, in which the troops swore loyalty to the imperial regent. Unlike in Prussia and the north German states, the government in Baden had ordered homage by the military. Apart from the archduke, the (Badenese) military served as a national symbol of integration, especially as the ceremony took place at the same time as the army's departure for Schleswig-Holstein. Celebrations for the imperial regent also drew on various events and celebrated quite different national symbols.

When news of the election of the imperial regent reached Karlsruhe, the city put on its "party dress." All bells in the city were rung, the civic guard artillery fired canons from the gates of the city, and "sprightly music" could be heard throughout the town: the report of the festival in the *Karlsruher Zeitung* expressed the journalist's emphatic joy at the political event, but even more at what he saw as the social unity of the citizens of Karlsruhe in this "popular festival." "Differences of class and dress disappeared, person to person we passed on our joy and gave each other our hand. We were what we are and want to be: we were brothers." When a parade formed in the evening which marched to the palace decorated with "German flags" and green branches to include the Grand Duke in "such a wonderful celebration of patriotic fraternity," and to bring him "greetings from the heart," from a "free but loyal people," "nearly the entire city" had gathered. "I was led by a dragoon, I led a gunner, at his side was an academic gentleman, then a smith from Keßler's factory, a rifleman, and a man from the fire department. Differences in class had not disappeared; they could still be read from the dress of the participants—rather social and political conflicts were forgotten in this common festival and replaced by gestures of friendship: people went arm in arm and shook each other by the hand."[55]

Whether this social unity was real and would be preserved beyond the festival is another question, but obviously the joy and hopes of the citizens were genuine. There was hardly a sentence in the report of the festival not marked by the highly emotional power of the events, and the choice of words expressed joy and happiness in all of their variations. Thus they hoped to preserve this unity for the future. Or was this perhaps an incantation for the future against their better judgement? "These fraternal feelings will not escape, and whatever may happen, we stand firm for liberty, justice and order." It would seem reasonable to read in this trilogy of "liberty, justice, and order" a bourgeois adaptation of the French "liberté, égalité, fraternité." These hopes for the future make clear that the celebrated fraternity and equality confronted the hegemonic claims by the bourgeoisie to political and social leadership, and to the shaping of the revolution.

While participants in the festival included bourgeois, artisans, and workers, it was dominated by the bourgeoisie. It remained within the rituals of *Vormärz* bourgeois festivals, underlining unity in the differences, and did not for one moment endanger bourgeois order. Quite the opposite: apart from a promise of social peace in bourgeois order, it contained no impulse for change. Even when the spontaneity of the festival was especially underlined, it was not a popular celebration but remained in bourgeois hands.

In Catholic Freiburg, the introduction of the imperial regent to the Frankfurt parliament was celebrated on 16 July with a service in the Freiburg cathedral, which interpreted the "feeling of great joy and jubilation"[56] in confessional terms. In the election of a member of the Austrian Catholic dynasty, the Catholics felt themselves strengthened vis-à-vis Prussian Protestantism.[57] The fact that he also received tumultuous applause from Karlsruhe Protestants shows, however, that the anti-Prussian element that could be seen in the person of the imperial regent had a stronger unifying force in southern Germany than did confessional tensions. This was different in Prussian Rhineland, where conflicts between Catholics and Protestants were vented in public on this occasion.[58] Moreover, a church service was seen as a symbol of order, as the "most suitable form" to celebrate "the destruction of anarchistic endeavors."

Before and after the service in Freiburg, the festival was a secular one. A ball in the museum and a concert by the *Liedertafel*, proceeds from which were to be given to the poor of the city, placed it in an urban bourgeois tradition. It is remarkable how attempts were made at national occasions to bind different territorial—local, regional, and national—loyalties. The parade of the citizens to the service consisted of three sections, each separated by a marshal with a flag. The first section, which was preceded by a German flag, included academics, the deputy rector, and professors of the university (with their own university banner), the director and professors of the lyceum, and the director of the school for the blind. The second section, consisting of the "rest of" the grand duchy's civil administration, marched behind a Badenese flag. The third section followed with a municipal flag. At its head was the mayor and city council, teachers from the secondary school, trade school, and primary school as well as the citizens' committee and municipal officials. They were followed by citizens and residents with guild flags "as orderly as the groups before." Residents of the town who did not belong to a guild were asked to join "any guild at their own discretion."[59]

The ordered nature of the parade shows that changes were underway in Freiburg, but that they were still being repressed into old ritual forms. Both the nation as well as some citizens and residents who did not fit in the old political and social order could no longer be included in the categories of municipal parades. It would seem that the organizers of the festival faced the problem of how they could include the nation in the traditional parade order. The division into three sections was new and a product of the revolution; otherwise, it would not have been necessary to remind citizens and residents to maintain the customary order when lining up. Before the revolution, the university and secondary school would have been placed among the civic corporations. Civic and territorial order was reflected by the officers and the institutions they represented. An attempt was therefore made to present the nation in the same categories, even if it could not be personified by its own institutions of state. Although they, like those in the second section, were officials of the grand duchy, academics were apparently most suitable for this role, probably as they embodied national values in education and culture.

Possible alternatives, for example abstaining from local and territorial ties in favor of the nation or having the citizens and residents who did not fit in the civic order represent the nation, were unimaginable for the organizers. The nation arose as a new, extra level next to the city and the grand duchy. It did not compete with the old political and social order and loyalties. Other, new forms of political organization were still beyond the horizon. Unity and liberty were understood by man, and not only in Freiburg, within the framework of traditional civic order.

Celebrations of homage for the imperial regent by the Baden military, which took place in numerous large and small towns on 6 August, arose not from civic but from governmental and military initiative and was the only form of official celebration during the revolution. While military in their orientation, the festivals were not restricted to the troops. In numerous cases they included the civic guards and were accompanied by a large part of the urban population. The cities were festively decorated—"without being asked" as was expressly stated in Freiburg[60]—with black-red-gold banners and flags for the occasion. Surrounding the central celebration were a series of smaller ceremonies by the citizens: banquets, church services, religious parades and militia parades.

As military celebrations the homages developed a relatively large aura and integrative force. It was not the nation's domestic political circumstances that were remembered but Germany's outward strength and independence. The war in Schleswig-Holstein, for which troops were being mobilized at the time, provided the opportunity to celebrate the nation's outward strength and greatness and to suppress domestic political conflict. In the language of the military, the "high goals" of the war were replaced by military duties and (male) honor. While General v. Röder honored the "venerable colors of the one, great united fatherland" in his speech to the troops in Freiburg, he also called on the soldiers above all to be prepared to "test the power of German male oath on the enemies of our German brothers requesting help in Schleswig-Holstein."[61] In Karlsruhe and Freiburg, soldiers paraded past at the end of the ceremony to the music of "Was ist des Deutschen Vaterland" and "Schleswig-Holstein meerumschlungen."[62] In Donaueschingen, the presence of troops scheduled to leave for Schleswig-Holstein the next day lent the ceremony a special solemnity. The outward greatness and strength of the nation allowed different political camps to move closer together.

This wartime truce on domestic conflict did not, however, last long. Even before acceptance of the Malmö armistice by the National Assembly on 16 September triggered renewed mobilization and radicalization and Struve's failed attempt three days later to proclaim a republic in Baden, the fronts between the political camps had hardened. While the mass meetings in March and April seemed to cover over political disagreement with open symbolism, unambiguous political symbols were now on the agenda. The people of Oberkirch went to Achern in a wagon decorated with flags on 10 September, on their return they gave three cheers for Hecker, the symbol of the Badenese republic.[63] In Weinheim, during a mass meeting, a portrait of Hecker decorated with chains of flowers was hung near the school house.[64]

The organizers had registered the meeting with the authorities and had promised "to maintain peace and order" and to make sure that nobody came armed. They assigned fifty men to be marshals, "who were marked by red bands on their arms."[65] Was it by chance that the red color of the republic was chosen as a symbol for the marshals? Compared to Hecker, red only played a subordinate role as a symbol of recognition for the republicans and appears for the first time in the sources here.

Next to Friedrich Hecker came Robert Blum. While Hecker was above all the symbol of the Badenese Revolution, Robert Blum stood for a more abstract, republican, transregional solidarity. In November and December, the police observed "republican party" memorial ceremonies for Robert Blum in twenty-three cities and towns in Baden alone.[66] The course of the celebration was similar in all cases and was oriented in its ritual form of expression towards both traditional Christian rites of passage and towards *Vormärz* bourgeois festivals. Republican associations also placed great value on order in their festivals, although celebrating in Robert Blum a symbol of armed revolt. On the one hand, the bourgeois leaders of the republicans could not imagine another form of festival; on the other, they attempted more or less consciously to discipline their supporters and to educate them in the spirit of bourgeois order. For them, too, traditional tumults and excesses were not an acceptable form of political struggle.

The celebrants gathered as a rule in an inn and marched from there with torches, flags with a black ribbon, often with a portrait of Robert Blum, and in many cases accompanied by funeral music, to the cemetery, or, if they were able to find a sympathetic clergyman, to the church. Then, the deceased was commemorated with songs, speeches, and a review of his life. After the mourners marched back to the inn, where they held political speeches and drank. The number of participants varied: in Renchen about 150, in Heidelberg, Bruchsal and Rastatt around 500, in Wiblingen 800, and in republican Constance 1,000.[67] Participants came from the university-educated middle class, the middle class of the towns, or were journeymen artisan. In rare cases they were joined by state officials, who were then reported by police spies. Civic guards or gymnastic or music associations were also occasionally present. The celebrations took place in an urban environment, but sometimes country people went to the next largest city to take part.

The location of the celebration spoke a clear, if initially ambiguous language. Most funeral marches connected inn and cemetery or inn and church. While the festival parades generally met at the city hall, suggesting an apolitical nature and claims to their representing the entire citizenry, political parties met in inns. These they had to themselves and thus were able to speak "openly," without attracting the attentions of political opponents or the police. It was not only in Frankfurt or other major cities that inn customers were divided along political lines, and it is not by chance that one of the first measures of the reaction was to close these places, which were seen as "gathering places for revolutionary parties."[68] Naturally people drank in the inns as well.[69]

Church and cemetery, on the other hand, were public and sacred places. It was not just the death of Robert Blum that was transferred from the profane to the sacred world through rites of passage. Also expressed was a claim by the participants to a transition from the world of arguments between political parties to a world of republican harmony. The inn was profane and political. The parade symbolized a transition from one world to the other. At the end of the parade stood the sacred place, at which politicians became martyrs and the political party became a consecrated following with claims of general representation. It is not by chance that most political speeches were held in the inns, while in the church or cemetery especially the life of the deceased was recalled. The solemnity of the place not only forbade politics, but even raised it into religion.

The parade was hence a sacred ritual. (Party) political symbols were never employed. Apart from black-red-gold flags and banners of the cities and guilds, wrapped in black ribbons and thus already assigned to "the other world," no political symbols appeared. The participants did not sing, for example, songs of liberty, but followed the funeral music in silence. In Rastatt everybody wore "black and white cockades on their head covering as [a sign of] mourning"[70]; there are no references to red scarves or flags. Hecker, too, was neither named nor symbolically represented. In several cases, the portrait of Blum was carried on an embroidered pillow at the front of the procession.

This symbolism recalls *Vormärz* constitutional festivals, in which a copy of the constitution was carried in a similar place of honor.[71] There is also, however, an analogy to the traditional funeral march, in which the deceased himself was accompanied by the mourners in his last passage through the community. Finally, there are undertones of processions and veneration of the saints, in which the image of a saint or martyr was carried through the streets. The funeral marches for Robert Blum expressed all these aspects simultaneously and drew from them their sacred solemnity.

The claim to general representation and unity, which the sacred place represented, was also underlined by the celebrations involving Catholics, Protestants, and German Catholics, in which, although seldom, there were pastors from all Christian confessions willing to hold services in Protestant or Catholic churches, as well as in the prayer-rooms of the German Catholics. Thus the confessions mixed because participants were motivated more by their political attitudes and less by their confession. However, the number of pastors participating in such celebrations was limited. Pastors supporting Blum had to expect everything from sanctions to suspension.[72]

Use of the space and ritual of the church and the attempt "to play with the misuse of religious things in the festive parade of a politically red demonstration,"[73] in effect exploiting religion to give politics a transcendental consecration, met with the "strong disapproval,"[74] or mockery of political opponents: "In the end, our democratic association will become a prayer circles."[75] A member of the congregation of the Protestant Trinity church in Mannheim held the view that "religious services for the purpose of a political party demonstration" contradicted the moral and religious welfare of the congregation. Such a funeral ceremony was not consistent with evangelical rites. As a place of peace and Christian unity, the church had to be preserved from becoming "a place of political demonstrations." "What will it mean for the effectiveness of the pastor, when he appears as a party man?"

Presenting the church as a place of unity and as an institution above all parties is of course hypocritical. Political church services were daily occurrences during the revolution. The birthday of the Grand Duke, homage for the imperial regent, as well as burial of the dead from battles between republicans and government troops were celebrated with church services, which only the participants saw as apolitical, but which opponents must have seen as a provocation. What they rejected was not so much the political character of the celebration in itself, but the oppositional, republican convictions of the celebrants.

Just as a festival was only a festival when it took place within the framework of bourgeois order, and lower-class festivals were dismissed as tumults or excesses; only festivals that celebrated existing order were seen as unifying celebrations. Republican festivals, on the other hand, were dismissed as political demonstrations. The public of the revolution was bourgeois and moved within a framework of the existing order; to this extent, however, it was highly political.

Revolution and Festivity in Tuscany

On 20 October 1848, a tree of liberty was planted in Livorno.[76] The radicalization of the movement, which had achieved its first highpoint in the naming of a democratic government and finally peaked in the proclamation of the republic, also found its expression in a transformed festive culture. The symbols changed, stressing much more social and political conflict than bourgeois order. The social composition of the celebrants changed: the people took over the streets. The centers of celebration also changed: while most of the celebrations, and the largest of them had up until then taken place in Florence, radical Livorno became the festival center par excellence. The locations themselves were symbols of social and political contrasts.

The news of the resignation of the old government reached Livorno in the middle of the night of 12-13 October. At four in the morning, the people were awakened by bell ringing and shots. "Work will be stopped today. The poor worker, the day laborer will no longer think of his family, his wife, his children because he senses that he has a fatherland, and this fatherland is Italy."[77] At ten o'clock a crowd marched through the city, accompanied by music from the *Guardia Civica* with a tricolor at its head. The reporter from the newspaper *Il Popolano* saw in this parade of "thousands of citizens" both a political festival and a demonstration. What was new in the demonstrations in October, however—and this distinguished them from festival parades—was that the participants carried banners on which they expressed their political demands.[78]

A few days later, the demand that Montanelli and Guerrazzi form a government was underlined with a new demonstration. "Well-ordered," many thousands marched through Livorno; they stressed, however, that this would be the "last peaceful demonstration." The tree of liberty planted on 20 October gave expression to the revolutionary mood in the city that had already experienced bloody tumults and uprisings. "Agitation increased because of the silence of the central government." The difference between festival, demonstration, and uprising was only one of degree.

The naming of the new government was celebrated in numerous cities and some villages. The manner in which their joy was expressed varied from place to place. In Florence, about 15,000 people marched to the Palazzo Pitti to express their thanks to the Grand Duke, who presented himself on the balcony of the palace to the applause of the crowd. The newspaper *L'Alba*, which supported the government, felt it necessary to report that "everything was peaceful and without unrest." "This provides renewed proof that the new ministers were not forced on us by a seditious and rebellious minority."[79]

In Livorno, Montevarchi, and Arezzo, hate of political opponents was also expressed in the festive pleasures. Although it was stressed that participants came from all classes and social groups "so that one could, without exaggeration, speak of the entire population," conservatives were excluded by publicly burning their newspaper, *La Patria*. While some saw in this "just desserts,"[80] others felt it an "attack on the holiest of all liberties, even on the bulwark of liberty."[81]

In Pistoia the festival took on the character of a procession. The supplement to the newspaper *L'Alba* in which the names of the new ministers was printed was attached to a pole decorated with flowers and laurels carried in the middle of national flags through the streets of the town.[82] Although the Pope and the Catholic Church was no longer available as symbol and pioneer of the movement, religion still remained a central element of the celebrations. Even some of the clergy still placed themselves at the service of the movement. In Montepulciano the Bishop led a Te Deum; the clergy and religious corporations took part in the festival.[83] In the small village of Gello, near Pistoia, the priest put out the blessed sacrament for adoration on the occasion of the formation of the government, explained to the peasants the significance of divine Providence and prayed for assistance from the heavens. Finally he intoned the Te Deum and blessed the believers.[84]

Even after the announcement of a constituent assembly, the flight of the Grand Duke and the proclamation of a republic in January and February 1849, religious rites remained a part of the festivals and celebrations, mixing together with the new symbols of the republic, which in the wake of radicalization spread ever further. In the churches the Te Deum was sung, while on the streets the first red caps and flags appeared and numerous trees of liberty were planted and blessed. "Even in its enthusiasm and joy, the people preserve its entire dignity and its respect for religion."[85] Following a democratic banquet in which democrats from Livorno and Florence dined on macheroni al sugo and roast beef, "holy trees of liberty were planted" in all the squares of Florence, "crowned with flowers, overhung with tricolor banners and Jacobin caps."[86] The tree of liberty on the Piazza Strozzi was blessed by a priest to the applause of the people. "Faith and Liberty": these words of the priest caused, according to L'Alba, a "shudder of emotion" among those present.[87] In the Florence cathedral, Guerrazzi even laid red camellia in front of the statue of the Madonna before the Te Deum.[88]

Symbols of the French republic were supplemented by some local ones, which legitimized the republic through the tradition of the city-state. "Over the euphoric masses stood the colossus of the warrior David, which the great spirit of Michelangelo had placed before the republican palace."[89] In Grosseto, a festive Te Deum was sung. "Here there is no-one who does not wear the republican emblem on his chest."[90] In Pisa, trees of liberty were set up and, "as the first action of a republican people," a Te Deum was sung.[91] In Montepulciano, symbols of the republic and of the church were even mixed with those of popular culture. On two squares, trees of liberty were set up. "The Bishop spoke to the people and showed that our religion is most compatible with the republic and called for unity and harmony ... Numerous cheers and large crowds from the countryside—it was a lovely final carnival day ... Long live the Italian Republic!"[92] In Castello, banners decorated the tree of liberty: "Viva la Repubblica," "Viva il Vangelo." "Men, women and priests cheered and rejoiced for joy," as *Il Lampione* reported. "Such are the countryfolk when they are not seduced and sold by the lords."[93]

The clergy, however, was split; there were only a few willing to fulfil republican wishes for religious legitimacy. Even in January, the Florentine Archbishop refused to hold a Te Deum for the proclamation of the constituent assembly in Rome. The rest of the clergy in the city followed their leader. After the celebrants had sung the Te Deum without the help of clergy, they marched to the house of the Archbishop for a charivari. However, they were dissuaded from this action by one of "the best citizens," as the republican newspaper *L'Alba* reported, who demanded that they not spoil such a holiday through violence against persons. Here, too, peace and order was the concern of the "best" republicans.[94] However, around midnight there were further incidents. This time, a crowd succeeded in stealing the papal coat of arms. It was then burned on the Piazza Duomo to the sound of whistles and insults. For monarchists, the republic had lost all legitimacy because of this "rabble."[95]

On the other hand, priests in the countryside who publicly supported the republic had to expect attacks from their congregation. At the festival of St. John there was a "large gang of people and peasants" who insulted the priest of St. Jacopo in Trecento near Montespertoli, a "very good priest," and forced him to flee "this drunken mob" to Florence.[96] He was the only priest in the region who had interpreted the Bible in the spirit of the new liberties. In Florence, the priests who had fled their "reactionary" faithful received a festive reception. A republican priest from Santa Lucia was greeted with torches, banners, and cheers and led through the city in a "triumphal procession."[97] The republic could not abstain from using religious symbols and rituals. In these festivals, however, the contrast between city and countryside was especially clear. Apart from a few cities such as Siena and Empoli where there were antirepublican demonstrations or tumults, it was above all the countryside that was opposed to the republicans. Trees of liberty were planted in the cities; they had to be defended against an onslaught from the countryside.

On the evening of 21 February, a few days after the Grand Duke had fled, the people of Florence heard shots from the hills near the city. Initially various rumors spread: some thought them to be an uprising by reactionary peasants, others thought that the rural population was holding festivals to set up trees of liberty accompanied by rifle shots. However, even after the peasants had marched against the city, issuing cheers for the Grand Duke, and at the gates of the city were forced to flee by the *Guardia Civica* or were arrested, the Florentines could not agree whether this was an "attack by the reaction"[98] or a "festive boisterousness."[99] *Il Popolano* reported that the "Campagnoli" had wanted to burn the trees of liberty and put back up the symbols of the Grand Duke's sovereignty.[100] The government, too, saw "order and freedom" in danger; this all the more as the peasants, with their cries of "Viva i Tedeschi," betrayed not only their support for the reaction but also of the enemy.[101]

Count Passerini, on the other hand, saw defenseless peasants who had been taken in by the rumor that the Grand Duke was in the Medici villa Poggio a Caiano near the city. This was the reason they marched festively with cheers for the Grand Duke to Florence; he had not heard cheers for the enemy. That would also have robbed the peasants of legitimacy in the eyes of the monarchists. In his eyes, the celebrants were totally defenseless. Their arms only served to set off shots in celebration, and none of those arrested had been carrying knives or similar weapons. If the republicans saw in this a victory against reaction, then they desired only to demonstrate their superiority and prove that they had the support of the *Guardia Civica* and the population. "But this too is wrong; when so many of the national guard took up arms, then it was not to defend the government but to protect their property. A misleading rumor had spread that the peasants or ultramontane enemies would push their way into the city and could begin plundering."[102]

Although monarchists and republicans argued about whether it was a festival or a tumult, they both agreed in the end that the peasants presented a danger to the city, whether they wanted to overthrow the republic or attack the property of the citizens. Bourgeois order had to be protected in any case. The social contrasts found ever greater expression in festive culture. The sometimes bloody confrontations between city and countryside made clear that social conflict had not been eradicated with political transformation. Quite the contrary, to the extent that the revolution was radicalized and the majority of the clergy left the movement, the republic lost its possibilities of influencing the rural population. All political camps drew on religion as an integrative symbol and sign of their legitimacy. It could, however, only serve as a social connecting tie. The revolution and the republic were matters for the cities and overlooked the needs of the rural population. It was not the Grand Duke who was a symbol of social tensions, but the city and urban property owners.

Mass Meetings in Baden

Such attitudes towards the "common" people were also strengthened in the wake of the radicalization of the Badenese Revolution. In the mass meetings of the people's associations from March to May 1849, which preceded the Badenese Revolution and culminated in the great Offenburg meeting of 13 May, autonomous symbols of the republic first appeared in revolutionary festivals. In the mass meeting of 6 March 1849 in Königshafen, the police noted for the first time, apart from the black-red-gold flag, "a red panel with the words 'Long Live the Republic.'" Moreover, many participants "wore totally red ribbons on their jackets."[103] Twenty local associations marched into Adelsheim for a mass meeting on 20 April—"only those from Sutzbach displayed blood-red." Nearly all of the houses in the town were decorated with garlands and German flags, but also "decorated portraits of Hecker, Blum, and Windisch-Grätz on the gallows had to serve the celebration."[104] At the mass meeting in Offenburg were "many red caps, like those worn by the Jacobins"; the Bühl delegation had acquired "a number of red flags" for this occasion.[105]

　　While the police were seeing red, even the most radical member of the Badenese republic shut his eyes. Johann Philipp Becker and Christian Esselen described the Offenburg meeting in the history of the southern Baden Revolution from 1849 in the style of a bourgeois festival report. "In the middle of the festively decorated city … a large crowd had gathered in the early afternoon around two to have the gospel of freedom preached to them from the tribune. One saw the contented urban burghers next to the craftsman, whose brow was creased by the burden of labor and privation; the strong peasant from the Black Forest stood in his most handsome costume with beribboned hat listening next to the soldiers, in whose eyes one could read the joy that he was no longer the enemy of his friends and family."[106]

　　In his report on the Badenese Revolution, written in 1850, Franz Raveaux even denied the presence of red flags. "The town itself was festively decorated with German flags and green branches. From the train station to the meeting place, I saw only tricolor German flags; however many of the young people, especially gymnasts and farm servants, had stuck red feathers and bands to their hats and the cry of 'long live Hecker' could often be heard, but nowhere among the thousands of flags could I discover a red one." It would seem that they shut their eyes to the red symbols, on the one hand in order to underline a harmony among all social classes, and on the other not to come under the suspicion of Jacobinism. Raveaux was obviously under pressure to offer justification when he added to his description: "This may provide more credit for the movement than it received from the so-called good press at the time."[107]

However, it was less the red symbolism and more the social composition of the mass meetings in the spring of 1849 that allowed their opponents to dismiss them as unrepresentative mobs. For this reason as well, Becker and Esselen painted an idyllic portrait of celebrating burghers, artisans, peasants, and soldiers, that is, all the socially respected groups in the population: the lower classes are absent from their descriptions. The red symbolism was credited to young lads—even when an entire town was united behind a red flag. Young lads, however, like women and children, were not held to be politically mature citizens; their political pronouncements were not taken seriously either by the left or the right.

Quite the opposite, the legitimacy of a mass meeting was often called in to question through references to its social composition. The police reported a mass meeting in Buppingen on 6 May, attended by 400 to 500 people, but qualified its political potential by pointing out that present were "mostly young people from eighteen to twenty, lads and children." Few adult men were to be seen and the figures mentioned "included onlookers of both sexes" and children.[108] A police report from Todtnau of 29 April was similar. The meeting had not met the expectations of the democrats as only 300 people were present "of whom hardly 100 belonged to the local parish, among them were 150 women and school children, the rest were men and single lads from Todtnau itself and its parish."[109] The *Karlsruher Zeitung*, loyal to the government, also called into question the success of the mass meeting with reference to its social composition. No one would have seen the public meeting as a mass meeting if it had not been advertised as such. It had consisted of only a few hundred lads, "and many women and children, but only a small number of people of middle and mature age."[110]

Women

Until the summer of 1848, female participation was an established part of Tuscan festive culture, even if only in a subordinate role. Women and men, however, occupied separate domains in the new national order symbolized by the festivals. While men were active in forming the new order, women were given the role of supportive, loving, and decorative companion. Above all the war against the common enemy allocated the two sexes different, but complementary roles in the national movement. "And you, o women, you, in you the love for the fatherland must almost be stronger … Remember, that you are lovelier and more dear under the national colors; remember, that the love of your husband and sons is stronger when it is blessed by a love of the fatherland which you have been able to awaken in their hearts. Reaffirm your love in discussions in the circle of the family, in the moment of joy, of sacrifice or regret."[111]

Volunteers in the war as well as the *Guardia Civica* could count on special attention from women—at least according to nationalist rhetoric. In Florence, Siena, and Grosseto, women embroidered flags for the *Guardia Civica*;[112] in Fucecchio, girls and women carried a sign at the constitutional festival on which they challenged "their husbands, brothers and sweethearts" to sign on as volunteers.[113] The women of Florence embraced tired soldiers "fraternally" and gave them something to drink.[114] Again and again, and in different variations, the image of manly warrior and supportive, loving wife was staged, and the nation presented as a harmony of the sexes as well.

The central position of the church in particular allowed women an established place in Italian festive culture. Women were not only present during the weekly church service and the Te Deum, they were often included in the ranks of numerous festive parades directly preceding or following church services, especially in the small towns and villages. In these processions, women did not march singly or at their husbands' sides. Instead—corresponding to the separation of the sexes during the service—they were segregated from them and marched as a closed group. They were festively dressed or wore white hats and were decorated with flowers and tricolors, as in Vicopisano during a festival for the *Guardia Civica*.[115] In the larger towns, especially in Florence, where the festival parades were much more secular and both temporally and geographically separated from the church, women were relegated to the role of spectators. They decorated the windows and terraces and waved or cheered the men marching by.[116]

The more the unifying elements of the church and the war faded into the background, the more festivals from the summer, were radicalized and celebrated as democratic or republican festivals, and the more women disappeared from the streets; they were, at least, no longer registered by observers, even when it must be assumed that they were still present at festive church services. No report of a festival from October 1848 mentions women as participants or spectators. It was no longer the unifying nation that stood in the foreground, symbolizing society as a binding public and private domain, but the republic. The public domain of politics, however, remained closed to women. One exception was provided by the festive opening of the constituent assembly in Florence; women were allowed in as spectators from the tribunes.[117] Presented and legitimized here was not party politics, but a representation of all the people arising from universal (male) elections, with separate domains for the two sexes.

In Baden, figures given for mass meetings were continually qualified by a reference to "curious women."[118] It was completely unthinkable that women would participate for political reasons or that they would, as in Oberkirch, "even" join a festive parade through the streets of Oberkirch after returning from a mass meeting in Achern.[119] All political camps were united in this exclusion of women from political discourse.

For the Offenburg mass meeting on 19 March 1848, an appeal appeared in the *Karlsruher Beobachter* "to all the women and and maidens of Karlsruhe," in which men going to Offenburg explained the necessity of the meeting to their women. "From the north and the south, from the lake and from the Tauber come enthusiastic masses, selected by the trust of their fellow citizens or voluntarily joining in ... and from your midst, your fathers and brothers, the men of your love, they, too, do not wish to be absent on this festive day!" Women were included in a "common love of the newly emerging fatherland," but they were not to participate actively in "the holy struggle for the preservation and development of the newly achieved highest good," but rather to support "the men of Baden" with their love and not hold them back with female timidity and fears from their political struggle. "That is why we are marching to our sister city, and believe and trust us, Germany's genius will be with us! We send you this as a word of reassurance for your perhaps worried natures—as our deepest conviction, do not be timid, do not be afraid!"[120]

Festive parades for mass meetings—the parade in Oberkirch being the exception—were made up only of men. At most, women stood to one side and watched; hence the accusation of curiosity. Women were only allowed in a political parade in an allegorical role. As virgins dressed in white they underlined, on the one hand, the purity of the political movement and, on the other, the dichotomy of the sexes. Especially during funeral parades for Robert Blum there were girls dressed in white with black sashes as a symbol of mourning. In Heslach, thirty-two virgins marched in the parade; twenty wore black and twelve white. Those dressed in white held a portrait of Robert Blum on a small cushion.[121] In Rastatt eight girls in white dresses and black crêpe carried a portrait of Robert Blum on a "decorated cushion, surrounded by two banners in the national colors," probably also made by women.[122] In Waldhut, all the male participants wore black clothes of mourning; only twelve girls were dressed in white.[123] The girls were integrated in the parade as part of a (sacred) range of symbols, but not as political individuals.

Only in "apolitical" festivals, which were not oppositional, but rather were to express the unity of all the people, were women welcomed as spectators. Their presence served to represent bourgeois order and harmony. While men of all classes shook each other by the hand and celebrated fraternal harmony during the Karlsruhe festival on the occasion of the election of Archduke Johannes to imperial regent, a "female tear [glittered] in the eyes of the women who had brought their small children with them and looked securely into the happy crowd."[124]

This observation clearly underlines the separation of bourgeois festivals into a public, male sphere and the female sphere of the family. If a reference to women had been absent, the festival would have appeared to be a purely male gathering. Men were active, representing their women and children in public; women looked on and expressed their sympathy with a quiet tear. Their presence was decisive for the success of a festival. Festivals claimed to represent the entire society, even if only a minority was active in it. Above all, however, participation by women and children underlined a trust in bourgeois order. They could securely move through the crowds although, it had to be added, all social classes were present.[125] These were "popular festivals" and not political festivals.

Hence Raveaux also attempted to remove the political and exclusive taint from the Offenburg mass meeting of 1849 in describing it as a popular festival in which "countless people [were] gathered: the Black Foresters in their original costumes … in between, gymnasts, soldiers, women, and girls."[126] This distinction between political demonstration and popular festival on the basis of sex was redoubled in social separation. At popular festivals that represented bourgeois order, "ladies" were present; at political demonstrations, women were present. Republican demonstrations were politically and socially excluded; bourgeois order faced the uprisings of the rabble. While republicans based their actions on an ability of the people to be educated and attempted to combine the republic and bourgeois order, most of the bourgeoisie felt a republic was incompatible with bourgeois order. The political conflict was socially based. Not only Hecker and Struve with their revolutionary uprisings failed on this dilemma, but also the Badenese republic.

Revolutionary Events and Social Conflicts

To great cheers, the tree of liberty was chopped down on 12 April 1849 in Florence and replaced by the Grand Ducal insignia, long before the Grand Duke had returned from exile. From the balcony of the Palazzo della Signoria there once again flew the tricolor with the Grand Ducal coat of arms and the Florentine lily. "It is impossible to describe the enthusiasm that spread through the people as the flag appeared which has become the symbol of better times."[127] Well into the night "the people" marched through the streets with torches and candles, carrying portraits of the Grand Duke and Pius IX. Two days later, people from the rural districts came into the city to celebrate the restoration. This time, the peasants celebrated the same event as the urban population had before; but once again "public safety," had to be secured, once again city dwellers had to be protected from the rural population.

The entry of Austrian troops into the city was not cheered, but rather met "with dignity." Only a few peasants and youths were said to have greeted the troops with laurels and myrtle. The Austrians had hoped, reports Conte Passerini, to be festively received by the Florentines, but the cheers for the Austrians and the emperor came from the rural population, not from city-dwellers.[128] The common enemy—Austria—still symbolized the desire for national unity and independence: it was, however, subordinated to political efficacy. On 28 July the Grand Duke, who returned to Florence accompanied by Austrian troops, was given a large reception. All the bells of the city and surrounding villages rang festively, the city was decorated and the people cheered. Only a few whistles could be heard.[129]

The people of Karlsruhe only prepared a festive greeting for the republican state committee because they saw themselves confronted with a political vacuum in May 1849 after the Grand Duke and the government had fled. Accompanied by "music"

and the "cheers of the citizens, the privy councilors and court jewellers, police officers and gendarmerie," the revolutionary government entered Karlsruhe on 14 May
1849. The cheers were not for the republic, however—one has to agree with Becker's
and Esselen's assessment here—but rather for the lesser evil. The people of Karlsruhe
were motivated by "a fear of anarchy and communism which, in the opinion of the
citizens of Karlsruhe, was unavoidable without a Grand Ducal government."

They demanded of the committee that it come to the residential city "to govern temporarily, that is to keep in check the proletariat, the gymnasts, and volunteers, and the rebellious soldiers, and to protect the interests of citizens."[130] Only
thus can one explain why the people of Karlsruhe—and it was seemingly the same
people—gave an at least equally enthusiastic greeting to the advancing Prussian
troops on 25 June. "Last night at three the Royal Prussian troops entered the city
and brought its residents the long-hoped for release from a state of lawless confusion and repression that was daily more insufferable."[131]

In Italy and Germany festivals and celebrations accompanied the revolution
and drove it onward. In the variety of occasions, rituals, and places, the broad spectrum of revolutionary festive culture becomes clear. Revolutionary and reactionary,
republican and liberal, lower class and bourgeois, "rabble" and state officials, men
and sometimes even women, celebrated in inns, in the streets and in the churches
quite different events of the revolution. Common to all these festivals were their ritualized forms and use of symbolic forms of expression, which lent the individual
event an overriding significance. Drinking together in the inns, performing a charivari in front of the house of a government official or clergyman, singing in front of
deputies' hotels, parades through decorated streets, the Te Deum in the church,
funeral addresses in the cemetery or greetings for victorious generals are quite different forms of festive culture with quite varied social and political significance; all
of them, however, drew on a quite similar fund of symbolic and ritualized language.

To do justice to this variety of social and political languages, the political festival culture of the revolution cannot be reduced to being bourgeois festivals. The
shadow of the *Vormärz*, with its dominant bourgeois festivals, has led especially
German historiography to examine the festivals of the revolution as an expression
of bourgeois culture.[132] Only those planned and ordered rituals of the bourgeoisie
were perceived as festivals, while similar, but often spontaneous and unordered rituals of the lower classes were portrayed as excesses or caterwauling.[133] With this
division of festive culture, however, the revolution is understood as a purely bourgeois one, directed first and foremost against the old order and its elites. Social
protest by the lower classes can then at best be seen as deviation or disruption; conflicts between bourgeois and popular cultures, between the city and the countryside, which occurred to a great extent in the streets and in symbolic form and
decisively defined and determined the course of the revolution, are not analyzed.
Above all, however, such a division follows the ideas of conservative bourgeois contemporaries, who presented their own festivals as unifying, ordered and paradigmatic, but denounced those of their lower class opponents as tumult, disturbances
and revolutionary excess.

In both countries, the ritual forms used by the opposing social groups did not differ greatly. People gathered, organized a parade that tied together symbolically significant places and linked the parade to them; music was played; people sang and wore integrative or political symbols; people met in the inns or for a banquet and drank, held speeches and gave toasts, sang and celebrated. However, rituals and symbolism in the traditional and bourgeois festive culture were given contrasting meanings and directed against one another. The young apprentices of the urban or rural lower classes celebrated in the evening or at night; the bourgeoisie during the day as a rule, if they did not turn night into day with a torchlight parade and illuminations. The former sang "loudly," disturbed the peace in the true sense of the word, yelled, made noises and screamed; the latter sang harmonious songs, paraded behind music groups presenting well-studied tones or otherwise remained quiet. The former shot off their pistols, the latter gave a well-ordered artillery salute. The lads reprimanded and rebuked; the bourgeoisie gave toasts to deserving men and their actions. The ones performed charivaris; the others serenaded deserving men. Young men were provocative in their spontaneous disorder, noise, and vandalism: the bourgeoisie demanded above all order in their festivals. Conflicts between the various interpretations of order were reflected in bourgeois perception of women in the streets. In bourgeois festivals, well-dressed ladies served as decoration and symbols of order, at political festivals they were not wanted. If they were perceived at all at such occasions, they were defamed as common women.

In Tuscany, moreover, social conflict was presented and perceived as a contrast of city and country. In Baden, the rural population took part in urban festivals; they marched festively to the next town to participate in the festivals and mass meetings. In the eyes of the bourgeoisie, they were unpredictable, but as such were not much different from the urban lower classes, especially as their demands did not deviate greatly from those of the urban population. Social conflict was expressed in Baden rather as a conflict between above and below and less between city and country. The rural population was included in political mobilization to a great degree, although circumstances were different in Prussia.[134] In Tuscany, the revolution took place above all in the city. Rural festivals did not, as a rule, arise spontaneously, but were initiated and controlled by the clergy and rural notables. Ties to the Catholic Church and a mixture of religious and political rituals guaranteed both broad participation among the population and their social control. The more radical the movement became, however, the more political conflict appeared with social differences. The city was in the hands of the republicans; the countryside belonged to the reaction.

The Italian movement's closeness to the Catholic Church makes clear another distinction in the symbolism of the revolution. Even when the revolutionary symbolism in Baden was partly oriented to Christian rituals, it was much more secular than in Tuscany. The church played a subordinate role as festival location and in significance. Church services in connection with political festivals were seldom, compared to the *Vormärz*. In the case of homage for the imperial regent, in which Catholicism also could give expression to a political stance against Prussia and for

Austria, church services were assigned an important role. The republicans only drew on religious symbolism with the death of Robert Blum. For the rite of passage, the church had a monopoly; other forms of ritual presentation of death were not available, even when funerals served as explicit political demonstrations.

In Italy, on the other hand, there was hardly a festival that did not draw on the repertoire of Catholic rituals and symbols. Secularized rituals were not available, because a festive culture comparable to that of *Vormärz* Germany was absent. The connection of reform and the Catholic Church, moreover, was reasonable as long as Pius IX was stylized as symbol of new national beginnings and a large part of the Catholic clergy supported the movement. The symbolic connection of the movement with the Catholic Church was so strong that it was preserved even though the Pope and the vast majority of the clergy increasingly turned against the movement. Political articulation was not possible in Italy in 1848/49 without church rituals and symbols, although here, like in Germany, independent, revolutionary republican symbols appeared which drew on the repertoire of the French Revolution.

Badenese and Tuscan festivals were quite similar in festive presentations of national ideals and aims. Common to both was, above all, that the nation was constantly celebrated and symbolized, but remained very vague as to its future form and structure. The nation was first and foremost outward unity. Festivals and celebrations that focused on the struggle against a common enemy and presented national unity as setting external boundaries were much more able to cover over social differences and domestic conflicts than other festivals. That was only possible, however, as long as there was still hope for a victorious end to the war; afterwards the movement became more radical. Festivals became political demonstrations. Domestic conflict over the alternative of monarchy or republic shattered national unity.

In both countries, national loyalties were paralleled by regional and local ones. Festivals were, as a rule, occasioned by local and regional events. This was especially true of Baden. Apart from festivals in honor of the imperial regent and the funerals for Robert Blum, all festivals arose from regional events. It is especially remarkable that the National Assembly, as the political representation of the nation, was not honored with any festivals in Baden. In Tuscany, uprisings and political reforms in other regions were honored with a Te Deum, but these festivals also served above all to underline the necessity of reform in their own region. The region was always the focus of the festivals. In both grand duchies, regional colors mixed with the tricolor. There were no plans for a national centralized state along French lines; at most the nation was interpreted as a loose confederation of individual regions. Urban traditions, moreover, defined the festive culture. In Baden the republic was celebrated as urban bourgeois order; in Florence, the republic even appeared as a resurrection of the historical city-state. The nation was not subordinated to the city or region, but paralleled them as an ancillary authority. The question of which political and governmental powers it would receive remained open. Unity and liberty were celebrated in both countries; in both countries, however, festivals underlined above all the ambivalence and multiple meanings of this slogan.

Notes

1. See Maurice Agulhon, *Les Quarante-huitards* (Paris, 1975); Manfred Hettling, "Das Begräbnis der Märzgefallenen 1848 in Berlin," in Manfred Hettling and Paul Nolte, *Bürgerliche Feste. Symbolische Formen politischen Handelns im 19. Jahrhundert* (Göttingen, 1993), 95–123; Luciano Nasto," Le feste civili a Roma (1846-1848)," *Rassegna storica del Risorgimento* 3 (1992): 315–38. An exception is Jonathan Sperber, "Festivals of National Unity in the German Revolution of 1848-1849," *Past and Present* 136 (1992): 114–38.

2. See Paul Nolte, "Die badischen Verfassungsfeste im Vormärz. Liberalismus, Verfassungskultur und soziale Ordnung in den Gemeinden," in Nolte and Hettling, *Bürgerliche Feste*, 63–94.

3. *L'Alba*, 6 September 1847.

4. *L'Alba,* 8 September 1847.

5. *La Patria*, 8 October 1847.

6. *L'Alba*, 21 October 1847.

7. *La Patria*, 21 October 1847.

8. *L'Alba*, 22 September 1847.

9. *La Patria*, 12 October 1847.

10. *L'Alba*, 22 September 1847.

11. *La Patria*, 12 October 1847.

12. *La Patria*, 8 November 1847.

13. *L'Alba*, 8 September 1847.

14. *La Patria*, 8 October 1847.

15. *L'Alba*, 2 November 1847.

16. *La Patria*, 21 October 1847.

17. *La Patria*, 18 February 1848.

18. Ibid., 17 February 1848; see also *Il Popolano*, 19 February 1848.

19. *La Patria*, 10 November 1848.

20. *Diario inedito del Conte Luigi Passerini de' Rilli, Il quarantotto in Toscana*, ed. by F. Martin (Florence, 1918), 6.

21. Ibid., 11.

22. Generallandesarchiv Karlsruhe (subsequently, GLA) 236/2244 (29 February 1848).

23. GLA 236/2245 (20 April 1848).

24. See Manfred Gailus, *Straße und Brot. Sozialer Protest in den deutschen Staaten unter besonderer Berück-sichtigung Preußens, 1847-1849* (Göttingen, 1990), 151; Wolfgang Kaschuba, "Ritual und Fest. Das Volk auf der Straße," in Richard van Dülmen (ed.), *Dynamik der Tradition* (Frankfurt, 1992), 240–67.

25. GLA 236/2244 (8 March 1848).

26. *Karlsruher Zeitung* (subsequently, *Kztg*), 4 March 1848.

27. GLA, 236/2244 (13 March 1848).

28. GLA, 236/2244 (22 March 1848).

29. *Kztg*, 27 March 1848.

30. Ibid.

31. Ibid., 14 April 1848.

32. GLA 236/8195 (11 March 1848); see also Paul Nolte, *Gemeindebürgertum und Liberalismus in Baden 1800-1850. Tradition-Radikalismus-Republik* (Göttingen, 1994), 319–20.

33. *Wochenblatt für die Amtsbezirk Offenburg, Oberkirch, Achern, Rheinbischofsheim, Kork, Gengenbach, Haslach und Wolfach* (subsequently, *Wbl*), 24 March 1848.

34. Adolf Kußmaul, *Jugenderinnerungen eines alten Arztes*, (Stuttgart, 1899), 402.

35. *(Augsburger) Allgemeine Zeitung*, 26 March 1848, quoted in Nolte, *Gemeindebürgertum*, 320.

36. *Wbl*, 24 March 1848.

37. GLA, 236/2244 (20 March 1848).

38. GLA, 236/8195 /19 March 1848); emphasis in the original.

39. GLA, 236/2244 (20 March 1848).

40. See also Nolte, *Gemeindebürgertum*, 238.
41. See also ibid., 320.
42. GLA, 236/2244 (20 March 1848).
43. GLA, 236/2244 (4 March 1848).
44. GLA, 236/2245 (20 June 1848 and 22 April 1848), GLA, 236/2244 (4 March 1848), GLA, 236/2247 (3 May 1848).
45. *L'Alba*, 28 March 1848.
46. *La Patria*, 28 March 1848.
47. *La Patria*, 4 February 1848.
48. *La Patria*, 5 February 1848.
49. See, for example, *L'Alba*, 28 March 1848.
50. *Diario Passerini*, 42.
51. *La Patria*, 5 June 1848.
52. Ibid., 43.
53. *Diario Passerini*, 48.
54. Ibid., 79.
55. *Kztg*, 1 July 1848.
56. GLA, 236/2245 (16 July 1848).
57. See also Clemens Rehm, *Die katholische Kirche in der Erzdiözese Freiburg während der Revolution 1848/49* (Munich, 1987), 123-24.
58. See Sperber, "Festivals of National Unity."
59. GLA, 236/2245 (16 July 1848).
60. *Kztg*, 9 August 1848.
61. Ibid.
62. *Kztg*, 8 August 1848 and 9 August 1848.
63. GLA, 236/2245 (12 September 1848).
64. GLA, 236/8195 (8 September 1848 and 11 September 1848).
65. GLA, 236/8195 (30 August 1848).
66. See GLA, 236/2245 and 2246.
67. GLA, 236/2246 (19 November 1848, 27 November 1848, 29 November 1848, 3 December 1848, 4 December 1848, and 17 December 1848).
68. See, for example, for Mannheim, GLA, 236/2247 (30 June 1849).
69. GLA, 236/2246 (29 November 1848).
70. GLA, 236/2246 (27 November 1848).
71. See Paul Nolte, "Die badische Verfassungsfeste im Vormärz. Liberalismus, Verfassungskultur und soziale Ordnung in den Gemeinden," in Hettling and Nolte (eds.), *Bürgerliche Feste*, 71.
72. See Rehm, *Die katholische Kirche*, 141.
73. *Süddeutsche Zeitung*, quoted in *Kztg*, 14 December 1848.
74. *Kztg*, 29 November 1848.
75. *Kztg*, 8 December 1848.
76. *Il Popolano*, 20 October 1848.
77. *Il Popolano*, 14 October 1848.
78. *L'Alba,* 10 October 1848 and 15 October 1848.
79. *L'Alba*, 31 October 1848.
80. *Il Popolano*, 31 October 1848.
81. *La Patria*, 30 October 1848.
82. *L'Alba*, 31 October 1848.
83. Ibid.
84. *Il Monitore Toscano*, 16 November 1848.
85. *Il Lampione*, 21 February 1849.
86. *Diario Passerini*, 270.; *L'Alba*, 28 February 1849.
87. *L'Alba*, 28 February 1849.
88. *Diario Passerini*, 295-96.

89. *Il Popolano*, 15 February 1848.

90. *L'Alba*, 25 February 1849.

91. *Il Lampione*, 21 February 1849.

92. *L'Alba*, 25 February 1849.

93. *Il Popolano*, 28 February 1849.

94. *L'Alba*, 23 January 1849; *Il Popolano*, 3 February 1849.

95. *Diario Passerini*, 211ff.; quote, 213.

96. *Il Lampione*, 23 April 1849.

97. *L'Alba*, 25 February 1849.

98. *Il Popolano*, 23 February 1849.

99. *Diario Passerini*, 278.

100. There were similar troubles in Prato and Pistoia; see also *Diario Passerini*, 280; *L'Alba*, 22 February 1849.

101. Appeal by the provisional government, quoted in *Diario Passerini*, 281.

102. *Diario Passerini*, 280.

103. GLA, 236/2247 (6 March 1849).

104. GLA, 236/8195 (23 April 1849).

105. GLA, 236/8195 (11 May 1849).

106. Johann Philipp Becker and Christian Essellen, *Geschichte der süddeutschen Mai-Revolution des Jahres 1849* (Geneva, 1849), 65-66.

107. Franz Raveaux, *Mittheilungen über die Badische Revolution* (Frankfurt, 1850), 11.

108. GLA, 236/8195 (7 May 1849).

109. GLA, 236/2247 (29 April 1849)

110. *Kztg*, 6 May 1849.

111. *Il Poplano*, 8 August 1848.

112. *La Patria*, 2 October 1847 and 7 March 1848; *Il Poplano*, 18 August 1848.

113. *La Patria*, 9 March 1848.

114. *L'Alba*, 15 October 1847.

115. *L'Alba*, 22 September 1847.

116. *L'Alba*, 8 September 1847.

117. *Il Lampione*, 26 March 1849.

118. GLA, 236/2247 (6 March 1849).

119. GLA, 236/2246 (10 September 1848).

120. *Karlsruher Beobachter*, 19 March 1848.

121. GLA, 236/2246 (4 December 1848).

122. GLA, 236/2246 (27 November 1848).

123. GLA, 236/2246 (1 December 1848).

124. *Kztg*, 1 July 1848.

125. See similar reports in *La Patria*, 12 October 1847.

126. Raveaux, *Mittheilungen*, 10.

127. *Diario Passerini*, 386.

128. Ibid., 465.

129. Ibid., 487ff.

130. Becker and Essellen, *Geschichte*, 92.

131. *Kztg,* 27 June 1848.

132. See Dieter Düding et. al. (eds.), *Öffentliche Festkultur. Politische Feste in Deutschland von der Aufklärung bis zum Ersten Weltkrieg* (Reinbeck bei Hamburg, 1988); Hettling and Nolte (eds.), *Bürgerliche Feste*; M. Maurer, "Feste und Feiern als historische Forschungsgegenstand," *Historische Zeitschrift* 253, (1991): 101-30; Ute Schneider, *Politische Festkultur im 19. Jahrhundert. Die Rheinprovinz von der französischen Zeit bis zum Ende des Ersten Weltkrieges (1806-1918)* (Essen, 1995), 123-35; Sperber, "Festivals of National Unity."

133. See also, Gailus, *Straße und Brot*; Kaschuba, "Ritual und Fest."

134. See Gailus, *Straße und Brot*, 431ff.

Chapter 35

"SPEAKING IS A DEED FOR YOU."

Words and Action in the Revolution of 1848

Willibald Steinmetz

Innovation or Repetition?

"**Y**ou could go crazy when you read the newspapers, with all those details about the French Republic. The words 'citoyen,' 'peuple,' 'nation' you find at the top of a mass of decrees; you find yourself thinking back to 1793."[1] Princess Melanie noted this in her diary as the first news of the Paris February Revolution reached the court in Vienna. Metternich's wife was not the only one who saw the language of 1848 simply as a repetition, nor was the feeling of *déja entendu* limited to aristocratic circles and opponents of the revolution. It was not restricted to a particular party or country.

Thus, for example, Georg Herwegh was writing at the end of February from Paris, in spite of all his enthusiasm, that people were slowly getting tired of Lamartine's speeches because he had "the history of the Girondists too much in mind and is working, *like nearly everyone, according to models* of the first revolution."[2] In Germany, accusations of repetition were joined by those of delayed and clumsy imitation of foreign models. Karl August Varnhagen, for example, could find nowhere in German newspapers a tone appropriate to the situation: "As if they, like the government, had slept for thirty years, those manners of speaking now awaken which could have been used against Bonaparte, against Bourbon, against Orléans France. How moderately and pure the new French government speaks, how magnanimously and far from any bragging! We, on the other hand, brag and boast as if we had to take over their behavior and the slogans they had rejected!"[3]

Notes for this section begin on page 861.

Only England seemed to be immune to the danger of being infected by French revolutionary phrases. The language of the Chartists did not follow a foreign model, but drew on an indigenous radical tradition extending back into the seventeenth century.[4] "And 'le droit de l'homme' was," as the London correspondent of the *Grenzboten* remarked "very little understood in good old England. Even the liberals here are not able to recognize such a principle; man as individual is nothing for them."[5] Admittedly, the English radicals also could not avoid the effect of a wearing out of political slogans.

Especially the Chartist leaders were forced to discover that the arguments and methods of agitation they had used since the Reform Act of 1832 could not be re-employed at will. The English parliament, at least, and the upper classes who were the main target of mass petitions and the threatening language of demonstrations, would no longer be alarmed. Quite the opposite, they "wanted to watch this English mob-assembly, like a play, and they advised the American philosopher Emerson not to miss the opportunity of seeing a Chartist meeting, something best done from the top of an omnibus."[6] The governments and ruling classes on the continent were not yet so relaxed in March and April 1848, but they, too, regained their composure after a few months and soon began to make jokes about the manner of expression of the popular speakers publicly and with increasing confidence.

Was the language of revolution of 1848 therefore only borrowed from the past? Was it only a matter of an already out-of-date "second edition" at the time of its appearance—fit for the "crude farce" into which the revolution had degenerated, in the eyes of its most pitiless critic?[7] Or were contemporaries fooled by the seeming parallels? Were there long-term, if perhaps less obvious changes in the use of language? Or to rephrase the question, can semantic innovations and new forms of linguistic use be discovered which accompanied or determined the sociopolitical break?

The results of research into the history of concepts allow—as far as the German speaking countries are concerned—partial answers to these questions. This will be detailed in the first section of this paper on the basis of selected terms and semantic fields. Less favorable is the level of research in France and other countries affected by the revolution. For the period around 1848, hardly any ground-work is available.[8] Comparisons can therefore be made only in certain points. There is much to be said, however, for the argument that, especially in France, the struggles of 1848/50 followed the linguistic patterns of earlier revolutions and reactions much more than in Germany. In Germany, too, it will be shown, that the revolution of 1848, compared with the so-called "era of transition" [*Sattelzeit*], was rather poor in coining new words. The disputed principles had already been defined to a great extent and those neologisms that appeared often retained the character of a short-lived slogan.

To provide a comprehensive answer to the question of continuity and discontinuity in the language of revolution, studies on individual terms or words are not sufficient. It is also necessary to identify typical associations of terms and longer chains of argumentation that were used, more or less successfully, by various groups. The search should not only be oriented to prominent nouns, as has usually been the case, but also needs to be extended to other parts of speech. The object of the analysis therefore needs to be sentences or longer text passages. In other words, what is called for is what has been long pursued as research on "languages" among Anglo-American historians.[9]

In the second section of this paper an attempt will be made to describe some of the "languages" used in German politics around 1848.[10] This will show that there were clearer discontinuities than are recognizable for individual terms. Older forms of argumentation and speaking, which were still often used in the first few months of the revolution, began to lose their persuasiveness. Here we are dealing with, on the one hand, the revolutionary rhetoric of freedom, and on the other the language of historically developed rights. Other, more recent semantic combinations, however, were increasingly employed during the struggles and consolidated into a new kind of political idiom which only later on became known under the heading of "Realpolitik" and which for the purposes of this paper will be denoted as the "language of hard facts."

If it is not an easy undertaking to establish a transformation in language and to date it to a specific event, then it is even more difficult to name the reasons for this transformation. Why did some terms change and others not? Why were some patterns of argumentation retained and others replaced by new ones? One answer, as abstract as it is simple, would be that certain words or manners of speech remained attractive for political action as long as they could be politically exploited in the form of gaining consent, building up alliances, soothing one's conscience, maintaining personal dignity and the like. More simply put, politicians chose their words so that they were successful in a particular situation. On the other hand, they avoided formulations with which they, in their experience, gained nothing or caused offense. Admittedly, this says nothing about what success was and where the line was drawn between what could and should not be said. Both depended on a number of factors: first, naturally on the intentions, temperament, and authority of the speaker; then, on the desires and basis for judgement of the audience; moreover, on the probable effect of what was said on a third party not present; furthermore on the customs and rules of the institutions in which the speaking or writing took place; finally on the distortions to which that actually said was subject to in oral or written transmission.

An abstract model for explaining change in the use of language needs to take into consideration the interaction of all these factors, as well as many others. Even if this is possible, there remain a few cases that cannot be explained, which have to be credited to the actor's individual manner of speaking or otherwise to chance. Nonetheless, one need not stop at a simple description. A first approach to the problem could be an attempt to describe how the limits of the sayable had been defined in various fields of communication, how they were maintained, and how individuals managed to overcome them.

In the third section, as an example, closer inspection will be given to one area of action decisive for the acceptance or rejection of political idioms in the revolutionary period. Here I am referring to leading politicians' dealings with the public outside parliaments and cabinets, that is with "citizens" [*Bürger*] and the "people" [*Volk*]. Other communicative domains should be examined in the same way, for example the secret consultations of the monarch with his advisors and, especially, parliamentary debates. The tactics applied in parliament will be the subject of a few remarks, using the *Paulskirche* as example, in the final section.

Both in their dealings with the public and in parliamentary debates, German politicians in 1848 quickly learned that which their British and French colleagues had already long mastered. The Germans were well informed about political conditions in western Europe in the *Vormärz*—one reason for their catching up very quickly. Theoretically schooled in foreign models and prepared in practice through their work in city councils and in voluntary associations, the Germans learned within a matter of weeks how to mobilize or assuage the masses, how to create resonance within the public, how to exploit standing orders and unwritten rules of parliamentary debate for their own purpose.

The German Revolution of 1848 was hence not only—as has been pointed out—a process of learning and politicization for the previously "silent" or those with only restricted rights of participation, such as peasants, workers, women or Catholics.[11] It demanded as well, and indeed especially from the political elite, the monarchs, ministers, advisors, diplomats, political professors, and public speakers, new forms of rhetoric and written expression. In personal statements from this circle of people one can discover a high level of conscious appreciation of their own and their opponents' speaking abilities. The actors not only planned beforehand what they wanted to say, they also reflected on the proper choice of words, on good and bad speeches, and on the reasons for the success or failure of their verbal strategies. This essay is based to a great extent on these critical observations offered by contemporaries. They serve as a guidepost to the conventions of speech and their violation, to that which was heard a thousand times before and that which remained "unheard of," to controversial terms and to the limits of the sayable.

This essay can do no more than provide an initial sketch of the problem. Before I move on to individual examples, I would like to summarize the initial hypothesis. When asking about continuity and change in political language in 1848 it is sensible to distinguish between three levels. On the level of the meaning of the individual word (semantics), the revolution of 1848/49 did not produce much which was new; repetitions set the pattern. On the level of longer chains of argumentation and typical sentences ("languages"), on the other hand, there were more discontinuities. Older political idioms lost their attractiveness and new ones were adopted. Finally, the reaction of politicians to the sudden change in communicative structures was also new. At the level of linguistic pragmatics, the innovation of 1848/49 consisted especially of many actors simultaneously becoming aware of how to do things with words.

Concepts and Catchwords

When contemporaries perceived so many repetitions in the speeches and writings of the revolutionary period, it was because they first turned their attention to the vocabulary as the most obvious field of linguistic change. Yet, at the level of individual words and terms, innovation in the revolutionary years did, in fact, remain limited.

As far as the most controversial political terms are concerned, the spectrum of their meaning was more or less established: "Popular sovereignty" and the "monarchical principle," "revolution" and "reaction," "citizen" and "subject," "people" and "nation," "constitution" and "historical rights," "freedom" and "equality," "republic" and "democracy"—all these terms had become ideologically charged, at the latest, during the Restoration, and had served since then as instruments in party political disputes. What these terms could mean, and especially what they meant *for* those parties which had a predilection for using them, was quite clear to the educated public. Sufficient reference books and treatises existed, above all the Rotteck-Welcker *Staats-Lexikon*, which provided information from the respective party standpoint. Existing meanings were played with in 1848, ambiguities were exploited or a more extreme definition attributed to one's opponent than he originally intended. Such linguistic play is, however, part of the field of linguistic pragmatics. Permanent semantic transformations did not arise through this as a rule; at the most an increase in the range of meaning in one or two cases.

An overlayering of several meanings made some terms so complex that they became unusable for precise description, for example in legal texts. This was, for example, the fate of the German word "*Bürger*" and the numerous compound words derived from it.[12] Even in the *Vormärz* parliaments of the individual states, there had been endless debates about citizenship. Such discussions always centered on the question of who should have priority in making a "citizen", whether it should be the state's or the municipalities' task to define the right to permanent residence and political rights. Was there to be a kind of universal citizenship for all residents in the state [*Staatsbürgertum*]? Or should the state accept only those as citizens who already enjoyed residential and/or political rights [*Bürgerrecht*] in the municipalities? The results of these debates varied from state to state, and in Prussia even from province to province. Thus, in Baden, the traditional "localism in regard to residential rights" [*bürgerrechtlicher Lokalismus*] was abolished in 1831 and replaced by a uniform citizenship, defined by the state.[13] In the Prussian Rhine Province, the trend ran in the other direction. Here the Prussian government was successful in 1845, after years of contention, in including the principle of local differentiation in the new law on municipal government and thus in undermining the general "citizenship" [*Staatsbürgertum*] of all residents maintained in high esteem in the Rhineland since the Napoleonic era. A manifest expression of this was the striking of the word "Bürger" from the final legislative draft by the government, after the provincial diet itself had only dared to use it, in parentheses, as a clarification of the word "member of the community."[14]

In view of the diverging legal definitions in the German states it is not surprising that the question of the rights of German citizens [*deutsches Reichsbürgerrecht*] was among the most insoluble problems in the Frankfurt National Assembly and gave rise to week-long, and, in the end, fruitless debates. This contention was not, however, new in the true sense, but was only a continuation of that discussed *in extenso* in the individual states. It was no accident that deputies from all parties complained of the boredom of precisely these debates.[15] There arose neither a new definition nor a redefinition, nor were the terms unclear in and of themselves.

The solution, which was finally anchored in the Frankfurt imperial constitution, initially left the conflict of priorities between the rights of all German citizens [*Reichsbürgerrecht*], the rights of the citizens of the individual German states [*Staatsbürgerrecht*], and the rights of inhabitants of municipalities [*Gemeindebürgerrecht*] up in the air. The defining paragraphs referred to a law on legal residence, that was to be worked out later, and in the rest of the text almost no use was made of the word "Bürger," which was replaced with a term no less open to interpretation, namely "German." If one occasionally has the impression, when reading this debate, that even the professors in the *Paulskirche* themselves could not completely understand what individual speakers meant with terms such as "Bürger," "Staatsbürger," "Reichsbürger" etc. in the heat of the argument, there can be no doubt that it would have been possible for them to reach a clear understanding of the various definitions after reading the stenographic reports of the proceedings if they had wanted to reach an understanding.

Lack of clarity in terminology was, therefore, not the problem, at least among the educated. Difficulties, however, arose when terms became overloaded with meaning. Apart from the word "Bürger" this was also true of other terms, for example "*Stand*" [order, estate, occupation—ed.], "sovereignty," "constitution." Whenever a text—an address, a law, a diplomatic note—had to be agreed upon, great efforts were made to find an alternative less pregnant in meaning. This strategy of evasion, of searching for a formulation as open in meaning as possible, was used by members of nearly all parties in 1848/49, depending on the situation. This occurred for various reasons. In avoiding highly ideologized and politicized basic concepts, possible options were left open, alliances with former opponents made possible or one's true opinion veiled in order to gain time.

While the meaning of the most important political terms was generally established long before 1848, so that the respective words could only be paraphrased in the case of dispute but not redefined, the social terms were still relatively fluid in the *Vormärz*. They remained so during the revolution. This was primarily due to the "labor question" only becoming a pressing theme in Germany after 1840. It gave rise to the spread of new antitheses: "employer" and "employee," "labor" and "capital," "producer" and "consumer," "bourgeoisie" and "proletariat." Many of these were translated or borrowed from foreign languages, especially from French. There were, however, genuine German neologisms, due above all to the unsurpassed wealth of the German language in word combinations as well as in suffix and prefix constructions. The new words spread quickly, because at the beginning they were not definitely attached to a certain party or group. Hence the semantic field of social terms remained in motion during the entire revolution and for a long time after.

A genuine German creation was, for example, the word "Bürgertum."[16] Only towards the end of the 1840s did it gradually gain acceptance to refer to the characterization of a social group. In so doing, it competed with the older words "Bürgerstand" or "Bürgerklasse," as well as "Mittelstand" or "Mittelklasse." The new term had the advantage vis-à-vis the older ones of not recalling either the reactionary "principle of a corporate social order" or the socialist "class struggle." It was therefore quite useful for expressing a desire for social balance and the hope of an inclusion of as broad a section of the population as possible in political participation.

A claim to legal equality was contained in the word "Bürgertum"—indeed that was its original sense. At the same time, however, as formed from the word "Bürger," the idea that not everyone could belong was raised without being too pointed. In the years of revolution, the new, social meaning of "Bürgertum" appeared, still curiously intertwined with the older, political and legal meaning of the word. A few years later, the older meaning had become almost incomprehensible. This was thus a semantic innovation, but one for which an individual process or event of the revolution cannot be made responsible.

Parallel to the rise of the term "Bürgertum," socialist authors and observers of France made a distinction between "bourgeoisie" and "proletariat" popular in Germany. These terms did not have a harmonizing effect, emphasizing instead antagonisms in society. Those using them wanted either to warn of a spread of economic conflicts or—less often—to raise a call for active struggle and division. Petitions to the German artisan and trade congress, which took place in Frankfurt from 13 July to 18 August 1848, provide a good example of how especially the new, borrowed word "proletariat" quickly penetrated the language of German tradesmen and the specific function it fulfilled.[17] As long as it was a question of specific demands by individual branches or "trades," the petitions were able to do without naming large social groups, as the simple job-title was sufficient. If, however, motives or fears were mentioned which should lead the delegates to act, the new vocabulary came into play.

"Proletariat" in this case was a code for a social form of existence which they saw having already become reality in England and France and which they feared for Germany in the near future. The trade associations of the city of Amberg in the Upper Palatinate, for example, protested against freedom of occupation because "it would create a economic law of the jungle which would make the poor intelligent tradesman a slave of the capitalist who had learned no trade, destroy the middle class, create, as a logical consequence, a large proletariat, place wealth in the hands of the few, in short would lead to the rule of an aristocracy of money."[18] As the quote shows, there were in Germany often other, more graphic terms than the foreign word "bourgeoisie" for those whom the small master craftsmen would describe as their enemies, those who benefitted from unlimited freedom of occupation and labor-saving machinery.

Often petitions simply spoke accusingly of the "rich," the "propertied," the "owners." Or they chose a neutral job title—"manufacturer," "factory owner," "merchant." Thus, they could ascribe the guilt for exisiting abuses to individuals, and avoid attacking an entire social stratum, most of whose members, they hoped, would see the evil of their ways and improve their behavior. The masters were faced with the threat of social degradation, but did not believe in its inevitability. They employed fragments of socialist vocabulary, without taking on the theory. Their own ideal image of society was, rather, that of good Aristotelians. Their aim was the "improvement of the order or class of craftsmen [*Handwerkerstand*], a middle class or order [*Mittelstand*] that holds the balance between the rich and poor classes [*Reichen- und Armenklasse*], and that forms loyal, industrious, affluent citizens for the state."[19]

The consciously propagated self-description as a "middle class" or "middle order" by the artisan masters and tradesmen in the revolutionary period proved in the long term to be a successful piece of linguistic politics. After the mid-nineteenth century it was rarely the case that other groups claimed this term, traditionally a positive one, for themselves, and when they did so, they almost always included master artisans in their ranks. The revolution, while not being the cause of this narrowing of the social meaning of "middle class," had established and spread it through frequent use. Here, too, it was a matter, moreover, of a specifically German development. This becomes apparent both in a comparison with the English case, where "middle class" continued to embody a broad social class, including rich industrialists, as well as with the French case, where the term "classe moyenne" had become discredited after 1848 because in party politics it was attributed to the ruling class of the July Monarchy and remained banned from the political-social vocabulary for a number of decades.

Let us now turn to a third field of terminology: the names for political parties and for general political tendencies. Here, the revolution most clearly had direct effects on the use of terms. This is especially true of Germany. In many places it was only in 1848 that the external preconditions were given for an open avowal of political preferences and for polemics against political opponents. For the first time as well, a center was created, in the form of the Frankfurt National Assembly, that offered at least the chance of a nationally uniform use of definitions of position. In comparison to this, there was a high level of continuity in France. There, the assignment of party names to certain ideas, persons, and groups remained relatively stable. Contributing to this were continued dynastic affiliation, were the identification of most of the actors with certain phases of the revolution of 1789 and finally an unbroken parliamentary tradition from 1815 onwards. Among the new terms, only "démocrate-socialiste" and "rouge" proved durable. New names for movements or alliances such as "partageux" [dividers up—i.e., communists], "parti de l'ordre" [the party of order], "les partis honnêtes" [the parties of respectable men] remained tied to a specific situation and only experienced a short-term popularity.

The development of party names in England was unaffected by revolutionary events. Chartist unrest did not produce any significant changes either. "Radicals" and "republicans" had existed in England for a long time, and the use of these words did not change because of the revolution on the continent. The transition from "Whig" to "liberal" and "Tory" to "conservative" occurred gradually and cannot be ascribed to any one specific date. The terms "democrat," "socialist," "communist" gained increasing usage around 1848 as borrowings from French, but were therefore seen as un-English, even among Chartists, and were only occasionally used in domestic politics, and then for purposes of polemic rather than self-definition.

In Germany, on the other hand, the revolution caused considerable confusion in the semantic field of party names. Heinrich Laube's observation that "a true St. Vitus's dance of terms" had begun applies here.[20] One reason for this was the great number of arenas in which "revolutionary" and "reactionary," "radical" and "conservative," "decisive" and "moderate" could take on quite different meanings. There was no center to provide a yardstick for the entire country. The Frankfurt National Assembly did not fulfil this role. A consistent use of party names was especially difficult when those names indicated a certain position within the course of time, such as "conservative" or "progressive", or a simple relation of more or less, such as "moderate" and "decisive". The same problem occurred with definitions based on locality, such as "left" and "right".[21] Someone sitting in Frankfurt on the extreme right and who was seen as "dyed in the wool Prussian," such as Vincke, could, at the same time, be a popular ministerial candidate in Berlin, one committed to the "German cause." The label "conservative" covers a broad spectrum of positions. As a description of their own standpoint, it was used by the prince of Prussia and the Gerlach brothers, as well as by the Rhineland liberals Mevissen and Beckerath or by Wilhelm Stahl from the *Württemberger Hof.*[22] These were more or less the groups that were in the habit of describing themselves as "right-thinking" [*gutgesinnt*]. "Conservative" could be no more than a relative definition of position in specific situations, given the circumstances of 1848/49. Some supporters of antirevolutionary policy close to the Prussian court were angered that the majority in the *Paulskirche* adorned themselves with the resonant attribute "conservative." They could do nothing about it, however, as the word was too much associated with a broad political tendency for one specific group to have monopolized it. The young Karl Friedrich von Savigny, for example, was outraged that someone in Frankfurt "specifically Bassermann, the so-called conservative," would go as far as "perhaps declaring Hanover a territory to be under the direct rule of the future German empire [*ein offenes Reichsland*]."[23] On the other hand, Radowitz enthused to the Prussian king of the endless "advantages to be gained from this wonderful circumstance that this central German assembly presents a conservative majority."[24]

Apart from this issue of the existence of multiple political arenas, the "achievements" of March were themselves responsible for some party names suffering in distinctive quality. The word "constitutional" provides the best example of this. Before 1848, it stood for a relatively exactly defined position in the individual states, but after 1848 this was no longer the case. It has often been observed how similar the demands and concessions were throughout Germany. All at once "black-red-gold" was seen everywhere, everyone was "patriotic" and "German," everyone was somehow "constitutional," and even "democratic" was no longer an insult after voting was everywhere possible "on the broadest foundation."[25] Or, as Heinrich Laube put it under the impression of the mood in Frankfurt on the eve of the opening of the preparliament: "All were still brothers in the bustle; the slogans were still general, and thus shared in common; the decisive phrases, the ones that would divide people, had not yet been discovered, or at least not spoken out loud; the great future of the fatherland embraced them all."[26]

This uniformity of slogans often led to their being interchangeable. This, too, created confusion, for example in the names of the countless local clubs and associations that were being founded everywhere. What did it mean specifically, when, for example, a "democratic-constitutionalist club" was founded in Königsberg, "whose wish is for the development of the monarchy in state and municipality strictly on the basis of democratic principles?"[27] As an observer of Königsberg remarked succinctly: "The constitutional democratic monarchy is for me an Irish bull [a confusion of terms—ed.]."[28] Ideally, party names should indicate the basic political positions of those active for the party. For the word "constitutional," and to an extent for "democratic," that was no longer the case during the revolution. The semantic function of referring to substance retreated in favor of the pragmatic function of ensuring group cohesion and identification of the opponent. Only the specific situation allowed one to decide to whom these terms referred.

While the revolution made some previously strict partisan terms so elastic and ubiquitous that they even became unusable for polemical purposes, there were other terms that only fully developed their usefulness for verbal warfare in the struggles of 1848/49. In a dismissal of enemies, moreover, a lack of exactitude was no disadvantage. The cruder the characterization of the enemy camp, the better. In defining the enemy to the right, the most effective label was "reactionary." Apparently no one dared support "reactionaries." Those suspected of "reaction," such as the prince of Prussia before his return from English exile, found themselves forced to clearly dismiss such accusations. All protestations that one was "not reactionary" increased further the defamatory effect of the word.

Without success, Ludwig von Gerlach sought to break through this circle and return to the word its original apolitical or even positive sense in order, as he said, to "warn the faithful against joining in the use of contemporary slogans, that the radicals have so arrogantly made into common currency."[29] At least he was successful in keeping the program point "no reaction" out of the prospectus for the newly founded conservative newspaper, the *Kreuz-Zeitung*.[30] Only in private circles and in letters was it still possible to use the word without inhibition and, for example, to wish for "a beneficial reaction."[31]

Among friends, even liberal deputies to the *Paulskirche* occasionally expressed themselves in a similar vein, for example Wilhelm Stahl, who saw "the entire future of Germany [dependent on] a reasonable, that is conservative or reactionary electoral law."[32] To say such things publicly, from the tribune of the National Assembly, was, however, totally impossible. "Reactionary" remained a negative label throughout Germany, even in the old Prussian provinces loyal to the king. Those who were stuck with the label had great difficulty in losing it again.[33]

There were more effective means than words to fight one's political opponents at the other end of the political spectrum, on the left: police surveillance, threat of indictment, house searches, imprisonment. That naturally does not mean that there was a lack of insults for the left: "agitator," "barricadist," "red," "nihilist," "revolutionary," "leveler," "anarchist," "scum"—there were no limits to the possibilities. For a self-definition, it was decisive which title was tolerated by the authorities and even the "right-thinking" people. Clearly beyond the limit of the sayable throughout Germany was the self-definition "communist." Even in revolutionary circles it was not advisable to stand out as a communist agitator. "If someone would appear here as a communist," reported Johann Schickel about the Mainz Workers' and Citizens' Association, "he would certainly be stoned to death, although these cattle haven't the vaguest clue of what communism is."[34]

The term "republican," on the other hand, was a borderline case. In southwestern Germany, especially in Baden, it was possible, and sometimes even advisable, up until the defeat of the revolution, to describe oneself as a republican without much ceremony. The Rhineland Prussian Jacob Venedey was quite enthusiastic when, on his arrival in Mannheim at the beginning of May 1848, he was greeted by the local gymnasts with the cry "long live the republican Venedey": "I can say what I think here quite openly, and that does not hurt me, but helps …"[35] In his home state, Venedey would have had to be more careful. The Prussian police observed quite closely public language and immediately noted when people such as Andreas Gottschalk and Friedrich Anneke declared themselves to be "firm republicans" at a meeting of the Cologne Workers' Association in June 1848, and addressed those present "for the first time not only as brothers, but also as republicans."[36]

Admittedly, a profession of republicanism could be varyingly interpreted. Purely theoretical remarks on the republic as the best form of government were relatively innocuous. People living in the city-states could also describe themselves as such without much problem.[37] Those who aimed at a republic for a united Germany could say so in meetings and in the newspapers, as long as they did not call into question the continued existence of the monarchies in the individual states. Nonetheless, caution was advisable. The left in the *Paulskirche* did not call themselves "republicans," preferring the title "radical-democratic" party. As the delegate Reinstein explained to his voters, this they did "for the very simple reason that the republic can also be an aristocracy, that can also be a bad constitution."[38] The true reason was probably the same that motivated the second democratic congress in Berlin at the end of October 1848. While demanding the "democratic-socialist republic," they abstained from using the term "republican" for the party, "as many in the provinces could be offended by it."[39] Not only in the provinces, especially in the north and east of Germany, but even more in the courts, in most state administrations and governments as well as among the military, "republic" stood for everything they feared. The word was the embodiment of everything they were fighting against politically. With the victory of these forces over the alleged or true "republicans" of 1848, there was a general distancing from this term.[40] Thus a "devaluation" of this term began in Germany, which, in the twentieth century, with respectful distance to the revolution, allowed it to be used by almost everybody.[41] The example of the word "republic" underlines again that did not change significantly the potential meaning of individual words in 1848. What changed was the functional and argumentative context in which words were used.

This overview of some of the more enduring names for parties and political tendencies has shown that major political principles were not sufficient to define the great number of actual mergers, parliamentary parties, and occasional coalitions in Germany in 1848/49. In part the terms were too elastic ("conservative," "constitutionalist," "democratic," "liberal"); in part they had the character of a crude insult ("reactionary," "communist," "republican," "ultramontane"). In day-to-day politics, therefore, numerous group and party names were necessary. These were drawn from certain meeting rooms, fraternities, places ("Gothaer"), historical events ("Central March Association"), flags and symbols ("Black-Yellow," "Men wearing smocks"), single issues ("Party of the Hereditary Emperor"), or foreign models ("Doctrinaires"); surprisingly few, compared with England, were derived from persons ("the Hecker crowd"). The language of the revolution was boundless in its wealth in such coinages. Many of them lasted only a short while and were not permanently included in the German political vocabulary. Where, however, unsolved problems or mutual bias was described, the words retained their power. Especially the national question produced differences that were not quickly forgotten. "Small German" continued to oppose "Greater German," and "south German," "north German."

With terms for parties or groups arising from a specific situation, we have left the level of basic terminology and have arrived at catchwords. Even contemporaries noticed how certain expressions and slogans became familiar quotations within a few weeks and sometimes, through overuse, became equally quickly ridiculous. A sure indicator for a term becoming worn out was its being qualified with the attribute "so-called," the use of distancing inverted commas, the existence of parody, puns, and ironic references to it, as well as illustration of catchwords in caricatures.[42] Such signals initially served understanding among like-minded people. In setting the others' catchwords on a proscription list, so to speak, one ensured that one's own use of the language would remain pure. Through a continued exposition, one could hope, furthermore, to destroy the magic of certain words and sayings in the opposing camp as well.

It is not possible to individually list all the slogans and neologisms that arose and often quickly became obsolete during the revolution. Otto Ladendorf's *Historisches Schlagwörterbuch,* which appeared more than fifty years after the revolution, listed numerous expressions, for example "idle stroller," "Waldeck's Charter," "brawl," or "on the basis of legality" the political meaning of which, gained in 1848, had disappeared by the end of the century.[43] Other coinages dated by Ladendorf to 1848, for example Wilhelm Jordan's "healthy national egoism," or Dahlmann's "the saving deed,"[44] became detached from the context of their origin and became part of enduring political idiom, which, however, had little to do with the hopes of 1848. Simple collections of references such as Ladendorf's do not provide much help for the identification of such idioms.[45] Even with the methodologically more demanding history of concepts one runs up against limits here. Therefore, the examination in the following section will be extended to typical sentences and forms of argumentation.

The "Languages" of the Revolution and their Ups and Downs

Contemporary observation provides the first clue to the linguistic peculiarities of individuals or parties. Notice was taken above all of extremes. On the one hand the endless repetition of worn out phrases, on the other hand the "unheard of," the liberating or provoking expression of that which no one had dared say before. While repetitions point more to a "language" of the past, a violation of the conventions of speech, when it proved useful and attracted imitation, could quickly become the accepted coinage of political discussion. The stage of transition from unusual to normal, that is the actual process of a change in the language, escaped the notice of most contemporaries, especially when a new turn of phrase became broadly accepted.

One of the most effective means of discrediting the commonplaces of political opponents was caricature and ironic quotation. A good example is the well-known satire from the vicinity of the Frankfurt National Assembly, the *Deeds and Opinions of Herrn Piepmeyer*.[46] It appeared from the summer of 1848 in individual papers in Frankfurt as a comic strip whose protagonist was a mediocre back-bench deputy named Piepmeyer. Constantly trying to increase his popularity, he shifted "in view of the most recent events of the day," sometimes to the left and sometimes to the right.[47]

In his manner of speech and habits, he always followed those models which seemed to promise the most success. In the beginning, he grows a beard and prepares himself for the role of tribune of the people; his idol is obviously Robert Blum. "P. practiced a speech with the corresponding manners of speech and gestures. I interpellate the Ministry! We wish to do justice to the desires of the people! From my standpoint. The gentlemen of this side of the house—the gentlemen of that side of the house—The Convention, gentlemen, the Convention! Reaction, obvious reaction! A disloyal Camarilla, a brutal Soldateska! Not an inch of German soil! Bravo! The breaking celestial eye of freedom! Bravo!!"[48] When, after many failed attempts, Piepmeyer is finally called on to speak, he criticizes "bureaucratic interference … which recalls the worst days of the Metternich police state," warns of the "undeniable reaction," and asks the minister what he "intends to do to preserve for the German people the accomplishments of March …?"[49]

The story ends with Piepmeyer's seeing that after the election of an emperor the time for a tribune of the people has passed, shaving off his beard, and, on 1 April 1849, travelling to Berlin "to become something."[50] The effect of this satire in the *Paulskirche* was such that "Piepmeierei" and "Piepmeiern" themselves became catchword descriptions of unprincipled parroting of phrases popular on the left and semi-left. If Heinrich Laube provides a good witness, then the fear of "the horrible, even if only quietly whispered word 'Piepmeyer' within the ranks of the 'betters' [was] a correction against drifting into the rhetoric of the left."[51]

As the days of March became increasingly distant, every form of pathos became the object of ridicule. In the language of the left, the dualistic juxtaposition of good and evil powers is especially noticeable in this respect. Hardly any speech was given without a profession or warning that one wanted to and must take responsibility for the "revolution," the "people," and especially for "liberty." Warnings were continually given not to underestimate the sinister machinations of the enemy. It was therefore necessary to always be on guard and take action when required. It was not seldom that borrowings were made from religious vocabulary in order to illustrate the struggle of good and evil.

One characteristic stylistic form of the left, often used as part of such juxtapositions, was the genitive construction. This feature was even noticed by contemporaries. Jakob Radike's *Lehrbuch der Demagogie* (Handbook of Demagoguery), published in 1849, provides a few examples. On the one hand are expressions such as "fuel for the revolution," "arsenal of liberty," "highest triumph of liberty," "dawn of liberty," "dramatic rage of the people in insurrection"; and on the other hand it includes the "poisoned breath of absolutism," "the pestilent miasma of despotism," the violent stroke of reaction," "in the pay of the camarilla," "dragon seed of the old governmental jugglers," "the enemy party showing its teeth," "pacifier of consolation."[52]

There is a lot to be said for assuming that this stylistic form was encouraged by a study of French revolutionary eloquence, but this cannot be proven. Robert Blum, at least, had his wife send him Lamartine's *History of the Girondists* and Mignet's *History of the French Revolution* to Frankfurt, requesting expressly "only those volumes which refer to the Constituent Assembly."[53] Other wordings that tended towards pathos such as the call for "permanence" or the slogans the "organization of labor" and "the fatherland is in danger" can be recognized as direct translations from the French. Accusations by opponents that this form of rhetoric was "a completely artificial composition," "established along the lines of speeches given in the French Convention,"[54] are confirmed by the private writings of radical democrats, characterized by a tone totally without pathos, and much more jocular-cynical or resigned. This, tone, however, expressed even more clearly the sharpness of the friend-enemy classification.

The radical democratic pathos of liberty doubtless met with a strong resonance among broad sections of the population in the first months of the revolution. The language in most petitions was affected by this, especially in the introductory and concluding sentences. In the *Paulskirche* and other newly elected assemblies, the "constitutionalist" deputies had, at first, little with which to oppose this left-wing rhetoric of a political profession of faith. Only those who adapted themselves to it, complained the deputies of the center, and right-wing parties, were seen as "popular."[55]

The more the work in the national assembly was concentrated on the actual constitutional decisions, the less effective became professions of popular sovereignty and the newly won freedom. Left-wing deputies soon realized that a simple assertion of principles no longer had much effect on the majority: "And were an angel from heaven to descend to the tribune and announce the gospel of freedom with thunder and lightening, even the majestic thunder would not awaken the philistines, even the flashing lightening would not penetrate the blinkers the philistines cover their eyes with."[56] In the caucus meetings of the *Deutscher Hof*, the pathos of sentences such as "we have to take the revolution in our hands" were met by open criticism from party leaders.[57]

The time had come for a transformation of one's own demands into juridical terminology. Here the left, again following the French revolutionary model, preferred a declamatory style. The derivation of all power from the "people" and the basic rights were to be formulated in the present tense and thus "established" as already existing. In this way, the concepts of natural rights were translated into legal language. As many individual rights as possible were to be "unconditionally" articulated, that is without restriction or legislative qualification, to protect them from later "reactionary" reinterpretation. The imperial constitution finally passed in Frankfurt bears, at least in some parts, the signature of the left-wing minority. While the pathos of liberty, copied from the French, lost a good deal of its effectiveness for speeches in the course of the revolution, the captivating simplicity of the French constitutional language retained its appeal well beyond 1848/49.

When searching for elements of a specific pathos in the liberal parties of the center-right, both Greater German and Small German, one initially notices some frequently used adjectives and adverbs: "noble," "dignified," "magnanimous," "powerful," "manly," "bold," "finally." Characteristic and arising in connection with this is furthermore a vocabulary of the "saving deed."[58] Included here were especially verbs such as "create," "build," and "found." Finally we find, in a certain contrast to professions of a willingness to act, a continual raising of historical necessity, which allegedly lay in the "things" or the "nature of things" and made certain actions necessary.[59] Common reference point of such formulations was almost always the longed for German unity. All of these elements formed themselves into a specific linguistic style only in the course of consultations in the *Paulskirche*. It had no recognizable foreign models. Famous remarks such as those of Heinrich von Gagern in the debate on provisional central powers contributed to establishing this style: "Gentlemen! I will take a bold step and say to you: we have to create the provisional central power ourselves. (Long, sustained, tumultuous cheers.)"[60]

In the first months, the emphatic call for "powerful" action often stood alone. The closer the completion of the German constitution seemed to come, the more often sentences appeared in which one saw the course of action predetermined by the "gravity of events" or the "genuine powers." With such expressions the Small German liberals hinted at that which they did not yet dare speak out loud: their willingness to compromise with the princes, especially the Prussian king. This "practical" or "realistic" form of argumentation was, for the majority in the *Paulskirche*, not just something for the speaker's platform. It also fills private letters and memoranda intended for internal use. Thus, for example, Wilhelm Beckerath wrote to his wife: "… with its noble self-awareness, the majority comprehends its grand task. It recognizes that the unity of Germany must be created as a consequence of a necessity arising from the events, namely by the German parliament."[61] The Prussian representative to the provisional German Central Power, Ludolf Camphausen, wrote in his memorandum on the German question, that "We must let the natural gravity take its effect and effectively encourage it. Only Prussia is able to create unity in Germany."[62]

Unlike the pathos of liberty of the left, the language of "deeds" and "facts" employed by the liberals initially seemed detached from any ideology. For this reason, it was more difficult for contemporaries to recognize the typical links. In newspaper and party correspondence, the left restricted its criticism to ironic quotations of individual phrases. The criticism remained, moreover, greatly personalized. A target was, for example, Gagern's conduct of negotiations, which contrasted with his emphasis on dignity and his self-presentation as "noble": "…the 'noble' [Gagern] is an expert on 'boldness' and can clearly distinguish it from 'impudence'; boldness for him and impudence for the others!"[63] The attack was extended further to the entire party of the hereditary emperor and "its false pathos with the banal phrases of historical actions and similar expression of enthusiasm." However, they did admit that the pathos was effective among its supporters: "Bassermann cried until his eyes were red, and as Riesser ended, the right fell on him, drunk with enthusiasm, Gagern hugged and kissed his friend, and Arndt could not stop prattling. Parson Mauritius, according to informed sources, is said to have immediately written the verse on his blackboard: 'Gagern gives, according to a club decision/Riesser a noble kiss.'"[64]

If the success of a language can be measured by how long it defines the political culture of a country, then the *Paulskirche* liberals were certainly more successful than their colleagues on the left. While the rhetoric of the left seemed not only to belong to an alien tradition after 1849, but also to an age long passed, the speeches on the irresistible "power of the facts" and the necessity of "historical deeds" long echoed in Germany. They were taken up and raised into an ideology by the advocates of "Realpolitik" and found, in the eyes of the Borussian historical tradition, their embodiment in the person and works of Bismarck.[65] The transformation of the language which began in 1848/49 anticipated the actual style of action in the era of the formation of the German Empire and provided its justification in advance. It was, therefore, the allegedly idealistic professors in the *Paulskirche*, at least the Small German liberals among them, who laid the foundations for the language of authoritative Realpolitik.

That the talk of historic powers and great acts could already have had practical effects in 1849 is witnessed by none other than Bismarck himself. In April 1849, in the middle of the struggle for the recognition of the imperial constitution, he wrote that the "giddiness of the *Paulskirche*" had also infected men around the Prussian government, "even people like Arnim, Boitz[enburg] and Schwerin," namely "after the people had rejected any compromise and sought to impose on us their official anarchy *par droit de souverain*." This was "a sign of the mad contagion with which Satan has impregnated the air."[66]

The quotation indicated which language was still being spoken at the court of Friedrich Wilhelm IV. It was a language centered on an older understanding of sovereignty, based on historical law and divine right, a language that rejected every attack on the monarchical principle as sacrilegious. In its dualistic juxtaposition of good and evil and its often religious coloring, this language had a considerable resemblance to that of the left. It was as given to professions of faith and as principled, but, of course in the opposite direction. The language, however, could hardly be heard in public in 1848. Even after the revolution was defeated, it remained restricted to smaller circles of traditional conservative politicians.

In the parliaments of 1848/49, even the minority of those who strictly insisted on the "legal foundations" and supported cooperation with the monarchs, certainly did not have in mind the Prussian king's idea that he ruled by the grace of God. Referring to historical rights, as Siemann has shown for the *Paulskirche*, could serve different purposes.[67] It could be used to defend the "variety" of ancient personal or political rights against "mechanical leveling". Respect for the "given", however, did not necessarily exclude "organic progress," and that, in the end, meant legislative intervention. This argumentation was thus opposed not only to the left's assertion of inalienable human rights based on reason, but also to the idea of the divine and therefore inviolable rights of the princes.

Rather than to the substance of ancient rights, the discourse of "legal foundations" could also refer, and indeed in most cases did refer, only to the process of transition from old to new constitutional structures. This transition was to take place as far as possible in legal form, which is why efforts needed to be made to gain the agreement of the monarchs. Whether agreement needed to be gained for every step, either in advance or belatedly, was a matter of dispute among supporters of a legal process. Heinrich von Gagern's "bold step" signaled a decision in this dispute in favor of a minimal solution. The initiative was to lie with the assembly, the monarchs only given a hearing in the end. This was justified with arguments of practicality.

Following this decision, historical-legal arguments lost significance in the *Paulskirche*, at least when it was not a question of the content of the constitution, but of the political course for the future. Many of the so-called "doctrinaires," accused by the left of "hanging on like leeches to the written word and constitutional law,"[68] began ever more themselves to give preference to the language of hard facts, from which "practical" politics had primarily to be derived.[69]

A parallel process, the transition from historical-legal argumentation to that of practicality, can be observed for some of the English Whigs during the debates on electoral reform in 1831/32. Tied to this was also, at the time, an emphasis on a willingness to take reforming steps. Around the mid-nineteenth century, it had already become a commonplace of English political discussion that "facts" were to be given precedence over historical rights in the decision-making processes.[70] It is rather unlikely that the German liberals' new form of argumentation was encouraged by a knowledge of English circumstances. An early reception of a positivism arising in France at about the same time is also unlikely. Here, too, it is rather more a matter of a parallel development. Possible, however, is stimulation by the "cult of facts" of the intellectually related French doctrinaires.[71]

Decisive for the "turn toward Realpolitik" in Germany seems to be something else, however: the direct experience that one could more successfully argue in parliamentary and official negotiations if one's standpoint was based on a recognition of the "facts" as they were. This argument was successful because it was open to the left and right. It allowed alliances with the radical democrats and with the Prussian king. Sticking to the "facts," one could agree provisionally and without loss of face, even when the "legal base" was undermined and principles remained disputed. For this reason, the new political language was attractive for all political actors, especially for the liberals in the *Paulskirche*. That their project failed nonetheless lay, not least, in the many communicative fields and channels that could not be controlled from Frankfurt and in which the catchwords of the *Paulskirche* had no or only little validity. One of these communication fields, the relationship between political actors and the public, will be more closely examined in the next section.

Dealing with the Public: Mobilization and Pacification, "Stirring Up" and Provocation.

While all speakers in the Frankfurt parliament at least claimed to follow the ideals of rational discussion, the actors behaved quite differently vis-à-vis the public. Some politicians had no difficulty in directly approaching citizens and the people, either in the form of speeches or in written propaganda. Others felt they owed it to their social position or political role to speak to the "people" only indirectly, through reports in the media or through a middleman. To a certain extent this was a matter of personal ability and temperament, and thus eludes attempts at systematization. Friedrich Wilhelm IV, for example, enjoyed speaking publicly in an informal manner; other monarchs would have been horrified even by the thought.[72] Regular patterns of behavior, however, can be observed.

Probably the most important dividing line ran between functionaries and private people. Before 1848 it was normal in Germany for functionaries to be subjected to certain restrictions in speech outside their institutions. This was especially true of holders of higher offices. For a prince, a minister, a deputy to a state parliament, it was generally held to be unseemly to appear before a broader public at one's own initiative, without a formal cause and corresponding compulsion, and to freely express one's opinion. Extreme reserve in choice of words was also called for in writing on the political questions of the day, in one's character as civil servant or deputy.

Those who felt bound by the norms of institutional communication naturally had a difficult time in a revolutionary situation. For them, the possibility of direct agitation was more or less ruled out. They had to find other means and ways to gain the support of "the public". All political forces were faced with this challenge in Germany in 1848. At the beginning, the radical democrats and republicans were at an advantage because they had held practically no important offices or political functions before 1848 and could use the new freedom relatively unrestrained. The liberals believed they had to show more consideration. Probably most difficult was the learning process for the monarchs and their conservative or reactionary advisors. They, too, found paths of communication after a few months in which they could speak, or let someone else speak out, publicly, something which "officially" remained taboo for them. In general, the revolution led to an increase in competence and refinement in this field. The means by which this occurred for parties and individuals will be explained in the following.

Let us begin with the liberals. As long as they were in the opposition, they were faced with a similar dilemma everywhere in Europe. They desired far-reaching reform, but without a revolution. They needed, however, the threat of revolution to move reluctant monarchs and cabinets towards reform. In this situation the temptation to stir up public dissatisfaction was great, which could then be used as an argument. This could be achieved by prompting, from parliament, the "citizens" or the "people" to demonstrate their dissatisfaction. However, such prompting could only be done in a veiled manner, as a direct appeal to the public was everywhere, even in England, held to be a violation of the unwritten rules of parliamentary speech.

Another possibility was to initiate an extraparliamentary campaign. Here, too, certain forms had to be maintained, as the aim was to gain a hearing from the governments and princes. Speeches to voters, petitions from "respectable" citizens, addresses from city councilmen, as well as press reports on all these activities were allowed, in moderation and in consideration of existing censorship. Going beyond this was, as a rule, to go beyond the limits of the permissible. In any case, it was a difficult linguistic balancing act to call forth a powerful public movement without this being too noticeable and moreover to ensure that expressions of discontent by the "people" were dispensed in proper measure. Protest had to be neither too weak nor was it to shift into a truly revolutionary mood. Liberal argument had therefore always to be ambiguous. It had to mobilize and pacify simultaneously; it had to create a certain public opinion, but at the same time had to present "public opinion" as if it were an unstoppable, self-driven power.

Of all the European liberals, the English had most successfully applied this double strategy. The Reform Act of 1832 and the abolition of the Corn Laws were achieved in this manner. It was, therefore, not surprising that the French opposition politicians during the July Monarchy looked across the English Channel for inspiration for their actions. To be more exact, this inspiration came to them in the summer of 1846 in the form of Richard Cobden. He had shown that far-reaching reform without revolution was possible. He had demonstrated how to organize a campaign and increase agitation to that point where the parliamentary majority yielded and the government fell on the question.

After his victory, Cobden needed a rest and traveled in triumph throughout Europe, everywhere promoting free trade. In Paris, Cobden was literally passed around among the opposition leaders. They consulted him "as to the way of managing such things."[73] Cobden recalled later that he had encouraged Odilon Barrot in his plans for an extraparliamentary campaign for electoral reform, but was, at the same time, astonished at how harmless and restricted the opposition plans for reform were.

And, in fact, Barrot and his friends were not successful in ensuring in the form of action they had chosen, the banquets of 1847, that all speakers stuck to moderate toasts and demands. Ledru-Rollin, Louis Blanc, Arago and other republicans put on appearances, refused to drink to the "institutions of July," and instead offered toasts to the Convention and to the rights of man and citizen. The radicalization of the banquets provided Guizot with an excuse to counterattack. He knew England well enough to see through the moderate opposition's game with the argument of a threatening revolt. Through his provocative appearances in parliament, he placed the opposition before the alternative of either continuing their extraparliamentary agitation with the danger of joining those who openly sought revolution, or returning to parliamentary mode of conduct and swallowing a certain defeat.

Initially Guizot's strategy seemed to work. With his ban on banquets in Paris, he pushed provocation to a head. To maintain the right of freedom of assembly, the majority of opposition deputies decided to let the banquet take place after all. Moderate deputies failed in their attempt to limit participation by the people as much as possible and to organize the banquet—in arrangement with the government!—simply as a symbolic retreat before the threat of force. Once the popular movement was authorized, it could no longer be kept in check by a few leaders.

The events that finally led to the Journées of 22 to 24 February 1848 presented types of linguistic action that did not call for imitation. On the one hand, it became obvious what risks were bound up with an extraparliamentary campaign involving the people. It had become apparent that no one could credibly threaten revolution who let it be known from the beginning that at the decisive moment he would shy away from open struggle. On the other hand, Guizot's example made clear that one could only provoke one's opponents when willing to make full use of one's forces, that is to accept bloodshed if necessary. Both lessons were learned in Germany. The German liberals were, from the beginning, more cautious, and the German monarchs and their advisors considerably more uncompromising after a few months of "self-effacement."[74]

While the French parliamentary opposition had helped to set off the revolution with its reform offensive, German liberals were overtaken by events. Before they had the chance to mobilize a broad public for their own aims, they were called into the governments throughout the country in order to subdue attempts to go further. In the eyes of the courts and the old elite, the leading liberals were acceptable as ministers because they were not directly responsible for unrest among the population. They recommended their persons and program to the kings at the moment of crisis as the only possibility of having a pacifying effect on the "people." In this, however, they committed themselves from the start to a course of pacification. They left mobilization to others.

In one German state, the grand duchy of Baden, the liberal opposition politicians were rhetorically on the brink of following the example of French reformers and justifying from parliament a more radical strategy that included the people. On 23 February, when fighting in Paris had already broken out, there were tumultuous scenes in the Badenese lower chamber during a debate on censorship.[75] Karl Mathy triggered it off in recommending "unruliness" as a strategy, after not having achieved much with "tameness." And he added that this unruliness "should not be [limited] to the chambers of parliament." This partial sentence was immediately criticized as a "revolutionary statement" and as a "call from here to the people for revolution." In spite of the tumult, Mathy did not withdraw his words—a sign of how fluid the conventions of speech had become. It is both ironic and symptomatic for the rapid change of attitude of most leading liberals in the revolution that the same Karl Mathy who called for "wild" action, became only one week later the spokesman for those who defended orderly parliamentary debate against the demands of the "radicals" assembled outside. This energetic counteraction occurred, as the deputy Buhl wrote to Gustav Mevissen, in the hope "that, in the interest of the country, we will succeed in retaining our leadership which is naturally only possible when we have the people behind us."[76]

The grand duchy of Baden and the regions bordering on it were an exception in the German revolution to the extent that the liberals there were forced, immediately at the outbreak of disturbances, into a literal race with the republicans for the support of the people. They had to leave the parliamentary chambers and campaign for their position, which was to a great extent identical with that of the government. Such a campaign had to be carried out in what were, in part, already "republicanized" municipalities. Once again it was Karl Mathy who played an important role. Together with others, he was sent by the Interior Ministry to the Lake [Constance] District "to calm down the excitement there."[77] In his reports to State Councilor Bekk, Mathy drew a vivid portrait of the techniques he used to influence the people in the spirit of the government. Always using the quickest means of transport ("express coach," "steamboat"), he hurried from place to place, spoke from balconies to public assemblies, sought a dialog with the people in the streets, called mayors and notables together for meetings and did not shy away from direct verbal duels with his republican antagonist, Josef Fickler.

Measured against the forms accepted in Karlsruhe, Mathy and some Badenese officials made use of a quite unorthodox language in these weeks. Mathy reported of the newly-named District Director Peter that in an assembly he had expressly spoken "as a citizen," and concerning Peter's appeal to the residents of the Lake District: "His proclamation may not meet with total acceptance in the capital city; some points might cause offense, but only this language can awaken trust in the Lake District and provide the movement with a regularized bed in which it can flow."[78] The norm—that an office holder should not publicly express his political views—was temporarily suspended in revolutionary Baden.

In the first weeks of the revolution, liberals benefitted from already having built up an extensive correspondence and contact network in the *Vormärz*. The constant exchange of letters and their proximity to the centers of decision-making provided the liberals with an advantage in information, compared to the republicans. In the unclear situation of March and April 1848, when the press had not yet fully developed, reliable information was as decisive for the formation of public opinion among citizens in the provinces as were rousing ideas. Only a minority probably had truly set political convictions in the spring of 1848. In Baden, the people were perhaps more "republican" minded than elsewhere in Germany, but here, too, most citizens adopted a wait-and-see policy. They adapted to the prevailing slogans of the day and turned to those who they felt had the strongest battalion at the moment. It was probably this phenomenon which some contemporaries interpreted as "conceptual confusion."

Only among the rebellious peasants in some regions of southern and western Germany does it seem to have been a matter of a true ignorance of the terms.[79] For republicans and so-called "agitators," the habitual opportunism of the people was a problem. Very clearly, even in its diction, this problem is expressed in a letter from a communist agitator: "Let me know how things look with the march of the volunteers, as that is very necessary so that you know the spirit in which to make propaganda. Because if we don't retain the upper hand or if the revolution doesn't take place as we would like, it is always better to try to teach the people as scientifically as before, than to encourage them to join in the struggle. We would have again that same old song that the people were being used as a means where they should be the end."[80] Those who could credibly report on the actual course of events in the capitals in this confused situation had a clear advantage in their arguments. The liberals had the necessary knowledge, but they could only exploit it when they, like Karl Mathy in Baden, actually risked coming face to face with the public. Leading liberals in other parts of Germany only went this far, however, in exceptional cases.

In Prussia, Austria and the smaller states in northern and central Germany, liberals were at great pains to preserve form vis-à-vis the princes. This went so far that at times—for example at the beginning of March in Cologne—they did not even dare to use the word "demand," and, instead, in an effort "to moderate the harshness," left it as a petition.[81] As much as possible, liberals stayed away from "republican" mass meetings, rather seeking support from the more restricted bourgeois public of the town councils. In Vienna, five weeks after the overthrow of Metternich, a north German speaker who had talked of a "storm petition" in the Aula, was even placed before a tribunal by the national guard and students which was to consider his deportation.[82]

The limits of the sayable vis-à-vis the throne and the authorities thus remained much more restricted in the north and east than in the southwest. A trust in the monarchs' willingness to reform had also not yet disappeared. Prussian liberals such as David Hansemann, with the impressions of the February Revolution still fresh in mind, hoped that a direct call on the people by the king would work wonders, as in 1813, insofar as only the most important reform promises were made "frankly and clearly."[83] Even just a few hours before fighting on the barricades broke out, Friedrich Wilhelm IV still possessed an aura which prevented members of the bourgeois delegation in the Berlin palace from contradicting him.[84]

Although the words of the king were still credited with a certain magic power, a mistrust towards the language of the monarch and his ministers, peppered with hidden reservations, was widespread. The first royal charter of 14 March confirmed these suspicions especially in Prussia. David Hansemann saw in it only "the old system of Prussian cunning, which was never shrewd and is very dumb today."[85] The years of a policy of qualified concessions, however, had led some liberal deputies in the provincial diets to adopt a similar style. Especially Ludolf Camphausen was a master at making the hard core of what he wanted to demand or to say nearly disappear in a cloud of well-sounding phrases.

There was nearly a split within Rhineland liberals because of a text of a speech in Bonn by a Rhenish deputy on 11 March which had been considerably revised under Camphausen's influence. Hansemann sharply criticized "the Camphausen policy which believes that you can achieve something with euphemisms," and did not want to distribute "the opus."[86] In their aims, there was little to distinguish the two Rhinelanders, but differences arose in questions of tactics. While Hansemann championed an energetic and open argumentative use of popular demands, Camphausen wished to remain courteous in tone with the king and avoid all those "revolutionary" emotive words to which Friedrich Wilhelm was so allergic. Camphausen believed that he could deal with the king without use of threats of revolution. He did not see radical statements as helpful, but rather as troublesome for his own argumentation.

This attitude and his talent for linguistic veiling made Camphausen the best possible prime minister for Friedrich Wilhelm IV in the unusual situation following the days of March. The king needed a politician who saved him from having to define more exactly promises already made. Camphausen protected him at least from corresponding demands from the Berlin National Assembly. The prime minister was a master in the verbal defusing or prevention of "revolutionary" resolutions, whereby he also made clever use of the agenda. In the delicate question of the return from exile of the prince of Prussia, Camphausen was so successful that Friedrich Wilhelm was full of praise: "You maneuver masterly. I think better than a Thiers on horseback would, who thinks himself the successor of Napoleon. Congratulations!"[87]

In the debate on recognition of the March Revolution on 9 June, a compromise wording was passed by a small majority, which, while at least partially satisfying the king, was subject to scorn and derision in the press and among the public. Efforts to hide one's own standpoint behind a pretentious style were too obvious: "The Assembly, recognizing that the high significance of the great events of March which we, in connection with royal approval, have to thank for the current constitutional situation, agreeing that the contribution of the fighters for the same is incontrovertible and, moreover, not seeing its task in passing judgement, but in agreeing on a constitution with the crown, will now continue to the next item on the agenda."[88] "The devil take this dissembler!" was Varnhagen's comment on this sort of politics. He put into words what many felt.[89]

Camphausen's work amounted to nothing more than keeping open the possibility of future agreement between the king and a majority in the Assembly through such maneuvers. He had remained a man of the limited public of the *Vormärz* Prussian provincial diets. From his circles, only his Rhineland correspondent Claessen occasionally advised him to employ a policy that used at least the impatient manifestations of popular will as an argument.[90] The task of creating a positive resonance in public opinion was left by Camphausen's and Hansemann's cabinet to the "moderate" newspapers and associations. Vis-à-vis the national assembly, the members of the government always presented themselves as agents of the king. They made no energetic attempt to base themselves on the Assembly, against the monarch. Here, too, they slipped into a role familiar to them from the provincial diets.

While the liberal Prussian ministers thus only hesitatingly went beyond the accepted patterns of dealing with various publics, the extremists on both sides learned very quickly in this respect. For quite contrasting reasons, they worked on frustrating the endeavors of the ministers for an undisturbed consultation between king and national assembly. In Prussia, the right was clearly the stronger and more active; the influence of the extraparliamentary left on political events at the top was rather more indirect.

Those few extremist republicans and the leaders of the labor movement in the larger Prussian cities were too well aware of the weakness of their position to try their luck with short-term action. As early as May 1848, Stephan Born was writing to Karl Marx that as much as possible he was preventing the Berlin proletariat from starting "useless brawls" so that no "senseless noise" would be made.[91] Similar warnings were made by Andreas Gottschalk to the Cologne workers: "Do not forget that you alone are not strong enough ... that a provincial town can never make a revolution, but only a riot, a revolt."[92]

Agitators such as Born and Gottschalk saw their main task in first educating and gathering their forces. For this reason, they worked within the democratic association movement and used its infrastructure and forms of action: exchange of letters, centralized organization, press, oral propaganda, festivals, protests, collection of signatures. Up to the end of 1848 they generally remained, as the police were forced to recognize, within the limits of permissible expression of opinion.[93] For the rest, they hoped for a violent disciplining by the reaction as a stimulus; they were waiting for the others to attack first. Reactionary-minded observers generally had an exaggerated idea of the willingness of the so-called "agitators" to use violence—or they consciously exaggerated it, as this was in many cases the purpose of corresponding statements in the letters and memoranda of reactionaries.

Unlike the ministers, the court, the camarilla, and the army had no hesitation in exploiting the argument of a threatening radicalization of the revolution for their own purposes. They waited impatiently for all news of even the most insignificant incident in order to blow it up, and confront the ministers with it, as a great danger for security and order. Seemingly paradoxically, it was especially the reactionaries who were permanently working with the threat of a revolution. The court and the army followed a strategy of escalation. The king raised warnings and constantly pushed for measures which he knew would have a provocative effect on the more radical part of the population of Berlin. The State Treasury was to be removed from Berlin, the ministers withdrawn to Potsdam, the army stationed in the capital.

Friedrich Wilhelm and his informal advisers consciously calculated (indeed, they outright yearned for it) that the so-called "agitators" and the "riffraff" from elsewhere, a large number of whom had allegedly gathered in Berlin, would use the return of the prince of Prussia or other acts of the government as a reason for violent action. In his private correspondence with friends and family members—which included the Tsar of Russia and the Kings of Hanover and Saxony—Friedrich Wilhelm IV repeatedly indulged in civil war scenarios and made it obvious that he wished for a fight. Leopold von Gerlach prayed for a war against republican France, and, as he could not have it, he hoped at least for the proclamation of a republic in Berlin. "If it comes to a conflict with ministries, rabble, constituent assembly, all the better."[94]

Successful appeasement by the ministers or shrewd restraint by the radicals was repeatedly greeted with regret. "Unfortunately," Berlin had remained peaceful once again; it was still not possible to form a reactionary government. "Only after the sovereign people have been Cavaignacked would something like that be possible."[95] From the provinces, the military inquired, when "to be sure of public opinion," "the right time to intervene would come." "Is a public parade with red flags sufficient? Or do their intentions need to be pronounced through violence?"[96] Similar planning was to be found throughout the summer of 1848 in correspondence between Friedrich Wilhelm IV and Josef Radowitz. To his friend, the king frankly admitted that he "would actually most prefer the most open rebellion of the Berlin Assembly."[97]

In public announcements, all this naturally could not be said; appearances had to be maintained that the king and the army were only worried about the preservation of peace and order so that the work of drafting a constitution could make progress. In the barracks, at the court, in the salons and soirées, however, the desire of the court and military party war for a civil war was ever more openly blurted out. Through indiscretion, the camarilla—acting on the behalf of the king, who had to content himself with dropping hints—created support for the coming coup, at least among those groups that counted. Many in Berlin society saw through this game, and that disturbed to a certain extent the plans of those who needed an excuse for a coup. Or to be more exact, all the talk made it more difficult to convincingly present a coup, whenever it came, as a measure for ensuring peace and order.

The left in the National Assembly and the forces that supported it well understood the dilemma of the camarilla. Deputies such as Johann Jacoby saw that it was necessary to hold the "people" back from violent demonstrations which could be interpreted as acts of intimidation. The reaction should not be provided with any excuse for intervention. For those who had previously only been mobilized or "stirred up," this was a new experience: "The leaders of the democratic clubs are making every possible effort to stir down [a newly invented terminus technicus!], and up to now they have been fairly successful, to the disappointment of the opposing party."[98] Thus the democratic left also concentrated on pacification—and cut themselves off from the public resonance they would have needed in the case of a civil war. The extent to which the Prussian democrats still believed in the sense of a revolutionary strategy in the summer and autumn of 1848 is unclear. In the eastern provinces the "handful of liberals left over," as they described themselves, felt themselves placed in the defensive to the extent that they no longer dared celebrate out loud victories in parliamentary divisions.[99] If at all, only a violent coup against the national assembly could have led once again to a revolutionary situation; even in this case, left-wing deputies were warned that they should "not count on special sympathy among the mass of people"; this advice suggesting that they concentrate on the constitution and on improving their own image through educational work.[100]

For a number of months, the parliamentary left and its supporters in the clubs were relatively successful in the business of self-appeasement. The Pfuel ministry was unable to find a legal pretext to transfer the Assembly out of Berlin and worked together with the majority reasonably well. This enraged the king and his circle so much that they only interpreted this insistence on legality as a betrayal of agreements and as cowardice. "I have been brought to the point of despair because I am losing all trust in mankind! Because as soon as a man becomes a minister, he becomes a coward and pours oil on troubled waters! The same thing has happened to Pfuel! ... And how poorly he speaks in the chamber, how weak and foolish! ... Fritz is furious, but has to hold himself back, because he cannot chuck the minister out straight away."[101]

There was no clear winner in the conflict between the court party and the parties of the left. The dissolution of the national assembly took place without leading to greater unrest among the people; that was a disgrace for the democrats. In the view of German public opinion, the event looked all too much like a coup, which is why Brandenburg's government felt it necessary to sweeten the change with the granting of a liberal constitution, including a democratic franchise; that was a disappointment to the king and his supporters.

After indiscretion and intrigue had led to only a partial victory, the Prussian camarilla had no other alternative but to transform itself into a party and to seek public support. The groundwork had already been laid in 1848. The foundation of the newspaper, the *Kreuzzeitung*, was the first step, establishment of King and Fatherland Associations in the provinces the second.[102] In these actions, Ernst von Gerlach and Hermann Wagener oriented themselves on the constitutional and democratic movements, whose financial strength and organizational capabilities they considerably overestimated. For Wagener, the effectiveness of the opponents' network of associations was due, among other things, to an allegedly consciously chosen structure that could best be described as conspiratorial democratic centralism, and which he thought well worth imitating: "... the slogans are given from above, and every association believes it can decide independently, but is only the tool of its unknown leader."[103]

With the newspaper and the associations, an infrastructure had already been created before the coup which would prove useful in supporting the new course. After the coup, as a first step, it was important to counterpose to the left's tax boycott campaign, professions of loyalty from the countryside. Experience gained in the meantime provided the means of creating an impression of broad public approval, even when this was in fact weak. Bismarck wrote to his brother: "Make sure that from there letters approving the transfer are sent to the ministry and the Berlin newspapers, a lot of single letters, even if only a few are signed, if possible from every town, even with only one signature, the latter will not be printed; you must blow your own trumpet."[104]

The final step on the road to forming a party was effective speaking in parliament. Gerlach, up to then more active in writing, lacked experience compared to the liberals and to the naturally talented Bismarck. In the debate on Camphausen's motion of August 1849 to subordinate in advance the Prussian chambers to the future imperial constitution, Gerlach spoke, as he remarked in his diary, "for the newspapers and the country, as the chamber is too little the country ..."[105] In the chamber his speech fell through, and there was a large majority for Camphausen whose tactical cleverness and ability with words could once again blossom in the restrictive conditions of the postrevolutionary era.

It is not possible simply to generalize from the considerations raised with the Prussian example. Not everywhere were liberals, once they had entered the government, as restrained in mobilizing public approval. Not everywhere, too, was there a king or camarilla who easily accepted the risk of a civil war as the ultima ratio of their policies. And finally, not everywhere was the democratic left so weak as to become defensive simply out of fear of pushing the reaction into violent action and abandoning the extraparliamentary domain to extremists. In spite of these special features, the Prussian case was in some respects typical for most German states.

Nearly everywhere, liberals renounced the use of a threat of revolution from the beginning and tried to tone down the language of expressions of "public opinion" and to push these back into an ordered structures of institutional communication. Nearly everywhere, reactionary forces, after some months of retreat, learned how to reconquer territory without loud declarations in important parts of the public, how, in an exaggerated description of opposing "agitators," to drive moderates to even greater restraint, and how to induce the shrillest counter-reaction with provocative gestures. In the end, almost all democrats and liberals were sooner or later faced with the alternative of either working together in parliament and adapting their form of expression at least to the extent that alliances with the center remained possible, or to stick strictly to their radical language and thus to rob themselves of a parliamentary forum.

The Politics of Language between Revolution and Reaction

"Speaking is a deed for you." Thus wrote Wilhelm Arendt to his friend Droysen, who could not force himself to take the speaker's platform in the *Paulskirche*.[106] Arendt was right: speaking on the floor of the first German parliament was an act. But in parliamentary business, other forms of oral and written linguistic action also counted, on which, in fact, Droysen worked very assiduously: negotiations in closed committees, preparatory caucus meetings, informal discussions, clapping applause and "hissing" disapproval, writing letters and passing on news to the press, editing minutes and formulating motions. One decisive deed of the deputies, in the course of which they did not have to say a word, was, finally, voting in the divisions, and whether a change in attitude was brought about by a speech proceeding the division is difficult to discover. Were the major speeches not really all that important? What else could Arendt have been referring to when he encouraged his friend to speak up and thus to act?

Expressions of skepticism about the significance of parliamentary speeches can also be found in the literature on "political rhetoric." One can often read that speeches on the floor only serve as justifications of respective party viewpoints to a broader public, as the results of divisions are already certain as a rule. For this situation the somewhat disparaging term "speech out the window" was coined. In linguistics, the more neutral term "trialogical communication" is used, in which those formally addressed are not identical with the true addressees, the public outside listening or reading.[107] Such observations may be true for the present day, but for the Frankfurt parliament and other assemblies in 1848 it is not totally accurate, as these often had changing majorities. In the *Paulskirche*, this was especially true for the most difficult questions: the question of the parliament's own authority, and the question of the head of state and the relationship of the assembly to the individual states. When these questions were debated, that is in the first weeks and then in the final months, the results could certainly not be calculated in advance. One rousing speech in the chamber might well prove decisive for the results.

Apart from this, it is also fundamentally incorrect to measure the effectiveness of a parliamentary speech by whether or not it leads to a change in voting behavior. For an analysis of possible effects of speeches it is not sufficient to view them using a model of an intentional, hermetic act. A speaker sets a goal, speaks for a time and, in the end, has persuaded his listeners or not, as the case may be.

It seems to me more sensible to view speeches as composite acts. Metaphorically speaking, it is a matter of offering a number of individual bits of language. A speaker introduces a surprising argument here and repeats there a phrase already applauded a hundred times; here he throws an apt catchword into the discussion and there uses a well-known term in an unusual context. Equally, the listeners do not react to the speech as a whole, but to individual parts. They enthusiastically take in some phrases and indignantly reject others; one argument is well received, because it could perhaps prove useful or finally puts into words what everyone had been thinking; another is censured because it calls into question the beliefs of the majority and thus cannot be accepted unchallenged. Viewed in this manner, a good speaker would be one whose language is accepted or even taken on by many, even if he is part of the minority when it comes to a vote. A parliamentary speech is thus an act at least in the sense that the speaker tries to make certain manners of speech acceptable to others, or even obligatory.

Which language could gain acceptance in parliament, however, did not depend solely on the inner convictions of the deputies themselves. Rather, they also directed their manner of speech and their willingness to agree at the image they thought they presented in the eyes of those present and more distant observers. From their own writings one can discover that hardly any politician in the revolutionary period was totally free of considerations related to his public. Each had different publics that were held to be relevant. Prince Wilhelm of Prussia, for example, was most interested in the effect his appearance before the Prussian National Assembly would have "in the eyes of the Army."[108] For most parliamentarians, what the voters, friends, and family at home thought of them was not insignificant. That made it more difficult to deviate in parliament from previously declared principles. Whoever did so risked his reputation. The desire to remain consistent and true to oneself often stood counter to the situation in the assembly.

Especially in the *Paulskirche*, with its large galleries, a special dynamic developed. Many delegates experienced their time in Frankfurt as a unique period and the assembly itself as a microcosm. By comparison, the outer world became ever more distant. The reactions of those present, their "hisses" or "tumultuous bravos" gained more weight in such a situation than the delayed, much filtered echo from outside.[109] Between the moral dictates of remaining true to one's principles and efforts to be "popular" in and around the *Paulskirche* or at least not to be "impossible," conflicts could easily arise. Desire for popularity and maintaining consistency as a matter of honor were strong motivating factors. Doubtless they were often more effective than rational argument. Most of the tricks of parliamentary tactics consisted of activating one of these two motives and using it as a means of applying pressure.

Even in the preparliament, patterns of "left-wing" and "right-wing" tactics appeared, recognizable to contemporaries. The tactical repertoire of the left was based above all on making the deputies fully aware of the impression they were making on a public that always favored the most radical solution. Useful for this was the continually demanded roll call vote, in which the "half-hearted" or "apostates," and the "traitors to the people's cause" could be exposed.[120] Depending on their strength of numbers, such tricks were assisted by a public cheering the left in the galleries and in the streets—whether manipulated and staged, as many right-wing deputies complained, or of their own free will and convictions. Robert Blum and his friends knew that the gallery, and here especially the "fanatic" women were "a powerful lever" in their hands.[111] They thus put into practice the recommendations of the author of the article "oratory, parliament" in the *Staats-Lexikon* of 1848, written during the *Vormärz*.[112]

The reporting of public reactions in the stenographic proceedings contributed further to strengthening the impression of a public which was, in terms of party preferences, not neutral. A suspicion that Wigard and his editorial staff intentionally distributed the "bravos" and "applause" unequally could not change the situation.[113] The public accusation that the left appealed "only" to the people in the gallery and that therefore their behavior was demagogic and undignified was rather more counterproductive. It enabled the left to present itself even more as the advocate of the people.[114] Moreover, the right cut themselves off from any recourse to similarly "undignified" means of mobilizing support.

In the first months, the "right" and those still undecided delegates reacted with a strategy of evasion. They tried, above all, to prevent situations arising where the tactical repertoire of the "left" could be applied. Depending on the situation, this meant skipping over motions by the left directly to the day's agenda. Subjects that allowed repetition of "popular" demands, going on about principles or attacks on the government should not even be raised, if possible. If a discussion could not be avoided, its being transferred to a committee or commission was the next best strategy. If this, too, did not seem advisable, because a decision was unavoidable, the possibility remained of toning down the wording of the resolution. The parties of the center-right had, in experienced southern German Diet members such as Friedrich Bassermann and Heinrich von Gagern, sufficient talent to challenge the left's gifts of phrasing. The result was arguments about words such as "before" or "in that."[115]

Such quibbling over terms was not the sort of material that allowed fiery appeals by the left to the gallery, and from the standpoint of the right and the undecided, this was already a partial victory. The search for phrasing as open to interpretation as possible was not only—as has been described above—a consequence of ideological weight borne by certain fundamental concepts such as "citizen" or "sovereignty." In the *Paulskirche*, the flexibility of the language was also an end in itself. It enabled the center parties to avoid having to take a clear stand in constitutional questions, to offend either princes or the "people" and thus to keep the process of negotiation going.[116]

The tactic of leaving questions open everywhere and not expressing things could admittedly lead to confusion among the still uncoordinated groups of the center and moderate right. One example of this was Gagern's proposal that the National Assembly should "indicate" the person of the Imperial Regent. Numerous "conservative" deputies supported the motion in the mistaken belief that the final choice remained reserved for the government. They were bitterly disappointed when another understanding of the word came to be accepted in the course of the debate.[117] In the early days of the Assembly, some resolutions were passed which, because of poor preparation on the "right" and clever use of the public by the "left," were more radical in phrasing than could be expected given the majorities in the parliament.

This changed in the course of the summer and autumn of 1848. In part in order to rationalize debate, in part because they did not wish to be taken by surprise any longer, all sides carefully prepared for the floor sessions in caucus meetings, in the course of which the "right-wing" majority became aware of its own strength. Moreover, the "right" had also found the means and ways of at least temporarily annulling the most important instrument of their opponent's tactics, pressure from the Frankfurt public. Occasions for this were offered by "insulting" statements from the left against persons or German "tribes" as well as the tumults that generally followed calls to order; furthermore, above all, the events of the September uprising in Frankfurt. Whether a party strategy was behind restrictions on the public and a strict interpretation of the standing orders by Gagern's presidency, as the left suspected,[118] or whether the motives of the "right-wing" majority actually corresponded to reasons given in public need not be discussed here.[119] Only the effect should be underlined here: a narrowing of the base for resonance which the left required for their parliamentary politics of language. That is the reason, and perhaps the most important one, that the left's rhetoric of profession, so successful at first, was increasingly seen as hollow, pompous, and absurd.

For those who wished for German unity under Prussian leadership, the road to a completion of their project now seemed open. It was sufficient, they believed, to let the "facts" speak for themselves. Droysen sketched the tactical guidelines. "We will work out as quickly as possible the articles on the upper and lower houses, extend the provisional central power into the first German parliament, and on the jurisdiction of the Reich vis-à-vis the states, *we must say as little as possible, so that the facts can decide.*"[120]

It was exactly those problems on which Droysen wished to "say as little as pos-sible" that were most talked about from January 1849 onwards and on which Ger-man unity failed in the end: the question of the head of state and relations between the Reich and individual states. The numerous tactical expressions in the debates on the Austrian question and the hereditary empire cannot be followed in detail here. In terms of the politics of language, the break up of the center right along regional and religious lines necessitated a new change in behavior, both on the right and the left. Characteristic for the final phase in the *Paulskirche* deliberations was above all a growing discrepancy between the more or less secret advance agreements, on the one hand, and floor debates on the other.

While in the caucuses, in private meetings, and in the corridors of the *Paulskirche* a very pragmatic "barter system"[121] for coalitions and short-term alliances developed, speakers on the platform could make no mention of all this. They had to continue to speak as if only rational grounds and their long cherished convictions, long a matter of public knowledge, were decisive for them. Newly dis-covered emotional ties to their own homeland, to the royal house or to religion were not sufficient to justify outwardly a change of opinion. Even expressing the suspicion that someone had sacrificed his formerly "holy" principles for a short-term advantage brought loud protestations from the person referred to. An appeal to an opponent's "point of honor," to his consistency of principles, became the pre-ferred tactical method on all sides. Using this method, attempts could be made in the chamber to break up coalition agreements achieved only with great difficulty before a division.[122] This did not always succeed, but the constant mutual warnings in general contributed to the *Paulskirche* deputies becoming, to a certain extent, prisoners of their previously declared convictions. An escape from this situation was only possible when a majority was successful in agreeing to "stick to the facts," and in defending this policy from the speaker's platform using arguments of expediency. This was the reason, perhaps the decisive one, that the above-mentioned "language of hard facts" became ever more attractive for the Small German liberals in the course of the constitutional deliberations.

In the heat of parliamentary debate, however, the supporters of the Gagern program apparently forgot that the "genuine" powers with which they wanted to "create" a new Germany, especially the Prussian king, pursued a quite different lin-guistic politics. In the vicinity of the king, plans for reaction continued to be made openly. Among other things, the representatives of the Prussian government offi-cially maintained the diplomatic, qualified language of the Camphausen style.[123] They were playing for time and continued with the tactics they had employed from the beginning in dealing with the revolution. Instead of expressing themselves clearly, they intentionally chose veiled phrasing, open to a wide range of interpre-tation, in which the things were given "a certain misty suspension."[124]

In so doing, hopes were kept alive without making concessions to revolution-ary vocabulary. The king himself was a master in this respect, as was shown in his March 1848 expressions: "agreement on a constitution," elections "on the broadest basis," and on "Prussia's merging into Germany." Friedrich Wilhelm IV was well aware, as were his informal advisors, the Gerlach brothers, "how dangerous word-concessions are."[125] His vague statements, however, could not be interpreted at will, and therefore he had to become at least a constitutional king in Prussia in the end. The king, too, was to a certain extent a prisoner of his word of honor which he had solemnly given in his initial shock.

Returning to the question raised at the beginning, of whether the revolution of 1848 led to innovations in the language of politics, the answer may now—in regard to Germany—be given more exactly. In the semantic sense, very little changed in the meaning of words; to this extent contemporary views quoted at the beginning were correct. However, the altered circumstances and communicative structures lent the words a new potential force, and the actors quickly learned how to pursue political goals with them. In an interaction between the tactical use of language and uncontrollable circumstances, older "languages" were pushed aside and new ones arose. This took place to a great extent behind the backs of contemporaries and was certainly not sudden. The revolution was only the midwife of the new, and people only became aware of it later. Directly tangible for all participants, on the other hand, was the experience that one can not only act with words, but than one can also become the victim of one's own words. In this sense, the revolution of 1848 was also a revolution in the language of politics.

Notes

1. Diary of Princess Melanie c. 7 March 1848. *Aus Metternich's nachgelassenen Papieren*, ed. By Prince R. Metternich-Winneberg, Vol. 7 (Vienna, 1883), 534. For friendly tips and a critical reading of this manuscript, I would like to thank Rudolf Muhs, Johannes Paulmann, und Peter Wende.
2. Georg Herwegh to Johann Jacoby (?), 28 February 1848, in *J. Jacoby, Briefwechsel 1846-1849*, ed. by E. Silberner (Hanover, 1974), 395.
3. Karl-August Varnhagen von Ense, *Journal einer Revolution. Tagesblätter 1848/49*, ed. by Hans Magnus Enzensberger (Nördlingen, 1986), 70 (entry of 8 March 1848). See also Jacob Venedey, *Die Wage. Deutsche Reichstagsschau* (Frankfurt, 1848), 44, on the "aping" of French terms among the democrats.
4. See Gareth Stedman Jones, "Rethinking Chartism," in his *Languages of Class. Studies in English Working-Class History* (Cambridge, 1983), 90-178, esp. 102ff.; James A. Epstein, "The Constitutionalist Idiom," in his *Radical Expression. Political Language, Ritual and Symbol in England, 1790-1850* (New York and Oxford, 1994), 3-28.
5. Amely [Bölte], "Aus London," *Die Grenzboten* 7/1 Vol. 2 (1848), 167. On the author see: U. Schmidt-Brümmer, "Zwischen Gouvernantentum und Schriftstellerei: Amalie Bölte in England," in Peter Alter and Rudolph Muhs (eds.), *Exilanten und andere Deutsche in Fontanes London* (Stuttgart, 1996), 198-224.
6. Amely [Bölte], "Plaudereien aus London," *Die Grenzboten* 7/1, Vol. 1 (1848), 584.
7. See the famous opening sentences of Karl Marx, *The Eighteenth Brumaire of Louis Bonaparte*, in Karl Marx and Frederick Engels *Collected Works*, Vol. 11 (New York, 1977-), 103-97, here 103.

8. The only monograph I am aware of on language during the French Revolution of 1848 is D. Oehler, *Ein Höllensturz der Alten Welt. Zur Selbsterforschung der Moderne nach dem Juni 1848* (Frankfurt, 1988). This work is based above all on literary sources and deals with the semantics of the class struggle and its suppression after June 1848. See also: William H. Sewell, Jr., *Work and Revolution in France. The Language of Labor from the Old Regime to 1848* (Cambridge, 1980), esp. 243-76; U. Spree, "Der 'Bürger' in der Sprache der Revolution," in Ilja Mieck, Horst Möller, and Jürgen Voss (eds.), *Paris und Berlin in der Revolution 1848* (Sigmaringen, 1995), 89-106. For the transition from Second Empire to Third Republic, a lexicological study is available, which also contains some references to usages around 1848: J. Dubois, *Le vocabulaire politique et social en France de 1869 à 1872* (Paris, 1962). For a contemporary critic of French socio-political vocabulary from a democratic-republican viewpoint, see F. Wey, *Manuel des Droits et des Devoirs. Dictionnaire Démocratique* (Paris, 1848).

9. The methodological approach of the history of concepts does not in principle exclude a synchronic analysis of networks of terms and "languages"—as must be said in view of so much unfair criticism. That so little has been done in this direction for German speaking countries lies in the decision of the editors of *Geschichtliche Grundbegriffe*, taken for practical reasons, to choose the form of a dictionary. An instructive comparison of German and Anglo-American methods of historical language analysis is offered by the contributions in Hartmut Lehmann and Melvin Richter (eds.), "The Meaning of Historical Terms and Concepts, New Studies on Begriffsgeschichte," German Historical Institute Washington, Occasional Papers No. 15, 1996, esp. the papers by J.G.A. Pocock and Reinhart Koselleck.

10. Useful for the identification of typical sentences and networks of terms in 1848 is H. Grünert, *Sprache und Politik. Untersuchungen zum Sprachgebrauch der Paulskirche* (Berlin, 1974). The study suffers, however, from an all too schematic application of a theoretically derived model of political argumentation.

11. See, among others Hans-Werner Hahn, "Adelsherrschaft und bäuerliche Protestbewegung im Solmser Land. Ein Beitrag zur Geschichte der Revolution von 1848/49," *Nassauische Annalen* 103 (1992): 263-94; Wolfgang Kaschuba and Carola Lipp, *1848—Provinz und Revolution. Kultureller Wandel und soziale Bewegung im Königreich Württemberg* (Tübingen, 1979); Manfred Gailus, *Straße und Brot. Sozialer Protest in den deutschen Staaten unter besonderer Berücksichtigung Preußens, 1847-1849* (Göttingen, 1990); Carola Lipp (ed.), *Schimpfende Weiber und patriotische Jungfrauen. Frauen im Vormärz und in der Revolution 1848/49* (Bühl-Moos, 1986); Jonathan Sperber, *Rhineland Radicals, The Democratic Movement and the Revolution of 1848-1849* (Princeton, 1991); Thomas Mergel, "Ultramontanism, Liberalism, Moderation: Political Mentalities and Political Behaviour of the German Catholic Bürgertum, 1848-1914," *Central European History* 29 (1996): 151-74.

12. In general, on this point, see Reinhart Koselleck, Ulrike Spree, and Willibald Steinmetz, "Drei bürgerliche Welten? Zur vergleichenden Semantik der bürgerlichen Gesellschaft in Deutschland, England und Frankreich," in Hans-Jürgen Puhle (ed.), *Bürger in der Gesellschaft der Neuzeit. Wirtschaft—Politik—Kultur* (Göttingen, 1991), 14-58.

13. See for details Paul Nolte, *Gemeindebürgertum und Liberalismus in Baden 1800-1850. Tradition—Radikalismus—Republik* (Göttingen, 1994), 85-99; quotation on 95.

14. The text of the law of 1845 on municipal government in the Rhineland is in Chr. Engeli and W. Haus (eds.), *Quellen zum modernen Gemeindeverfassungsrecht in Deutschland* (Stuttgart, 1975), 284-309. See also the modified draft of the provincial diet of 1843 in *Verhandlungen des siebenten Rheinischen Provinzial-Landtags etc.* (Coblenz, 1843), 284-300, here 285. The corresponding debates in: *Sitzung-Protokolle des Siebenten Rheinischen Provinzial-Landtages* [1843] (Coblenz, 1844), 61-62.

15. See also the debates themselves: *Sten. Ber.* 1: 731-749. Furthermore two comments: R. Haym to his parents, 6 July 1848: "From the tribune, thundered down one speaker after another. The debates on the first paragraph of the 'basic rights of the German people' are as sterile and boring as possible." Hans Rosenberg (ed.), *Ausgewählter Briefwechsel Rudolf Hayms* (Stuttgart 1930, reprint, Osnabrück 1967), 50. Report by the delegate Reinhard to his voters, 7 July 1848: "Professors, the seeds you've sown are flourishing. But if the majestic parliament wishes to have a coat of arms made, then I sug-

gest a turtle." Günter Hildebrandt (ed.), *Opposition in der Paulskirche. Reden, Briefe und Berichte klein-bürgerlich-demokratischer Parlamentarier 1848/49* (East Berlin, 1981), 54.

16. On this point in greater detail: Willibald Steinmetz, "Die schwierige Selbstbehauptung des deutschen Bürgertums: begriffsgeschichtliche Bemerkungen in sozialhistorischer Absicht," in R. Wimmer (ed.), *Das 19. Jahrhundert. Sprachgeschichtliche Wurzeln des heutigen Deutsch* (Berlin, 1991), 12-40.

17. *Die Petitionen an den Deutschen Handwerker- und Gewerbe-Kongreß in Frankfurt 1848*, ed. by Werner Conze and Wolfang Zorn, revised by Rüdiger Moldenhauer (Boppard, 1994).

18. Petition of the Trades Association of the city of Amberg in the Upper Palatinate, 19 July 1848, ibid., 19.

19. Memorandum of the butchers' guild of Jena, 20 July 1848, ibid., 101.

20. H. Laube, *Das erste deutsche Parlament*, Vol. 1 (Leipzig, 1849, reprint Aalen 1978), 185.

21. One example from the early days of the revolution: Karl von Canitz and Dallwitz to Max von Gagern, Berlin, 12 March 1848, on the Rhineland delegates who had taken part in the Heidelberg negotiations: "… they belong to a relatively small minority and represent in the combined diets, in constitutional language, the extreme left." G. Dallinger, *Karl von Canitz und Dallwitz. Ein preußischer Minister des Vormärz. Darstellung und Quellen* (Cologne, 1969), 155.

22. See K.-H. Börner (ed.), *Prinz Wilhelm von Preußen an Charlotte. Briefe 1817-1860* (Berlin, 1993), 220-21; Helmut Diwald (ed.), *Von der Revolution zum Norddeutschen Bund. Politik und Ideengut der preußischen Hochkonservativen 1848-1866. Aus dem Nachlaß von Ernst Ludwig von Gerlach*, Vol. 1: *Tagebuch 1848-1866* (Göttingen, 1970), 107; Joseph Hansen, *Gustav von Mevissen. Ein rheinisches Lebensbild*, Vol. 2 (Berlin, 1906), 462, 474-75; Joseph Hansen and Heinz Boberach (eds.), *Rheinische Briefe und Akten zur Geschichte der politischen Bewegung 1830-1850*, Vol. 2: 1846-50, 2. Hälfte (Cologne and Bonn, 1976), 195 (Beckerath); "Briefe Wilhelm Stahls aus der Paulskirche," M. von Gerber (ed.), *Historisch-politisches Archiv zur deutschen Geschichte des 19. und 20. Jahrhunderts* 1 (1930): 5-132, here 31.

23. Karl Friedrich von Savigny to his parents, 17 July 1848, in Willy Real (ed.), *Karl Friedrich v. Savigny 1814-1875. Briefe, Akten, Aufzeichnungen aus dem Nachlaß eines preußischen Diplomaten der Reichsgründungszeit*, Vol. 1 (Boppard, 1981), 370-71.

24. Joseph von Radowitz to the king, 21 November 1848, in W. Möring (ed.), *Josef von Radowitz. Nachgelassene Briefe und Aufzeichnungen zur Geschichte der Jahre 1848-1853*, (1922, reprint, Osnabrück, 1967), 66.

25. See also Veit Valentin, *Geschichte der deutschen Revolution von 1848-1849*, Vol. 1 (Berlin, 1930/31, reprint Cologne, 1970) 339, 371.

26. Laube, *Parlament*, Vol. 1, 18.

27. Gustav Dinter to Johann Jacoby, 14 September 1848, in Jacoby, *Briefwechsel*, 507.

28. Ludwig Walesrode to Johann Jacoby, 20 September 1848, ibid., 510.

29. Diary of Ernst Ludwig v. Gerlach, 14 May—28 May 1848, in Diwald (ed.), *Nachlaß von Ernst Ludwig von Gerlach*, Vol. 1, 97.

30. See H.-Chr. Kraus, *Ernst Ludwig von Gerlach. Politisches Denken und Handeln eines preußischen Altkonservativen* (Göttingen, 1994), 414.

31. Prinz Wilhelm to Charlotte, London, 27/28 May 1848, in Börner (ed.), *Prinz Wilhelm*, 300.

32. Wilhelm Stahl to Carl Friedrich Gerber, 14 February 1849, in Stahl, *Briefe*, 79.

33. See for example Bismarck, who explained his poor chances in the election in Havelland in Brandenburg in that "the vague description as reactionary seems to stick especially to me." Otto von Bismark, *Die Gesammelten Werke*, Vol. 14, pt. 1 (Berlin, 1933), 122.

34. Johann Schickel to Karl Marx, 14 April 1848, *Marx Engels Gesamtausgabe [MEGA]*, Vol. 3 pt. 2, 421.

35. Jakob Venedey to Johann Jacoby, Mannheim, 7 May 1848, in Jacoby, *Briefwechsel*, 450.

36. Hansen/Boberach, *Rheinische Briefe*, Vol. 2/2, 210, 282. See also 315ff.

37. See the following anecdote told by Arnold Duckwitz: "One time, while taking a walk, a member of the left met me and began to speak to me. We walked along together and spoke, as was always the

case at the time, about politics, and I made no secret of the fact that I was a republican. That pleased the gentleman considerably, who believed that I was a republican of his sort, while I was only thinking of the Republic of Bremen." Arnold Duckwitz, *Denkwürdigkeiten aus meinem öffentlichen Leben von 1841-1866. Ein Beitrag zur bremischen und deutsche Geschichte* (Bremen, 1877), 228.

38. Report of the deputy Reinstein to his voters, 20 July 1848, *Der deutsche Bürger* (Naumburg), 28 July 1848, in Hildebrandt, *Opposition*, 65. See the Marxist mockery of the programme of the "so-called" radical-democratic party in the *Neue Rheinische Zeitung* of 7 June 1848, in Marx and Engels, *Collected Works*, Vol. 7, 48-52. See also, from the other direction, the no less mocking remarks of Fürst v. Lichnowsky in the *Paulskirche* on 24 June 1848, in *Sten. Ber.*, Vol. 1, 540-41.

39. G. Lüders, *Die demokratische Bewegung in Berlin im Oktober 1848*, 167, quoted in Valentin, *Geschichte der Deutschen Revolution*, Vol. 2, 256. On the disputes at the democratic congress on which "republic" should be the goal, see Joachim Paschen, *Demokratische Vereine und preußischer Staat. Entwicklung und Unterdrückung der demokratischen Bewegung während der Revolution von 1848/49* (Munich, 1977), 103-4.

40. See also the caricature in A. Gessler and K.-H. Grahl (eds.), *Seine Feinde zu beissen. Karikaturen aus der deutschen bürgerlichen Revolution von 1848/49*, (Berlin, 1962), 130. (The original, according to the publisher's reference, is in *Deutsche Reichsbremse. Beiblatt zum Leuchtturm*, Leipzig 1849.) Portrayed are two cleaning ladies talking to each other, and the one says: "Can you believe it! I can say that I was always for the republic, but now, where I see that the lords have our best in mind and mix with the people, now I've become a constitutionalist as well."

41. See Dieter Langewiesche, *Republik und Republikaner. Von der historischen Entwertung eines Politischen Begriffs*, (Essen, 1993).

42. See, for example, in the *Kladderadatsch*, Vol. 1, (1848, reprint Berlin 1898), the weekly title pages and the series "Illustrirte Phrasen aus dem Jahre 1848," 39, 64, 71, 80, 88, 96, 108, and "Illustrirte Schlagworte der Gegenwart," 104, 108.

43. Otto Ladendorf, *Historisches Schlagwörterbuch. Ein Versuch* (Strasbourg, 1906), 39, 43, 181, 262ff.

44. Ibid., 106-7, 269-70.

45. Useful are examinations of the vocabulary of specific groups or parties such as, for example: Wulf Wülfing, *Schlagworte des Jungen Deutschlands. Mit einer Einführung in die Schlagwortforschung* (Berlin, 1982). See also for the period after 1848, [August Reichensperger], *Phrasen und Schlagwörter. Ein Noth- und Hülfsbüchlein für Zeitungsleser*, (Paderborn, 1863). This small dictionary is a critique of typical liberal commonplaces from a Catholic standpoint.

46. [J.H. Detmold], *Thaten und Meinungen des Herrn Piepmeyer, Abgeordneten zur constituirenden Nationalversammlung zu Frankfurt am Main* (Frankfurt, n.d. [1850]).

47. Ibid., 17-18.

48. Ibid., 16.

49. Ibid., 31-32.

50. Ibid., 48-49.

51. Laube, *Parlament*, Vol. 2, 114.

52. Jacob Radike, *Lehrbuch der Demagogie* (Leipzig, 1849); here quoted from an advertisement in *Die Grenzboten* 8/2, Vol. 3 (1849), 99-100.

53. Robert Blum to his wife Jenny, 15 May 1848, in Ludwig Bergsträsser (ed.), *Das Frankfurter Parlament in Briefen und Tagebüchern. Ambrosch, Rümelin. Hallbauer, Blum* (Frankfurt, 1929), 368.

54. Rudolf Haym to David Hansemann, 29 May 1848, in Haym, *Briefwechsel*, 41 (here in reference to Blum).

55. For example, Julius A. Ambrosch to Ignaz von Olfers, 29 September 1848, in Bergsträsser (ed.), *Parlament*, 27; Ernst Moritz Arndt to Moritz August von Bethmann-Hollweg, 16 June 1848, in H. Meisner and R. Geerds (eds.), *Ernst Moritz Arndt. Ein Lebensbild in Briefen* (Berlin, 1898), 437.

56. Report of the deputy Reinhard to his voters, 4 July 1848, in Hildebrandt (ed.), *Opposition*, 51.

57. See the description in the diary of Gustav Moritz Hallbauer, 20 November 1848, in Bergsträsser (ed.), *Parlament*, 164.

58. Dahlmann, in *Sten. Ber.*, Vol. 6, 4097.

59. See the observations by Grünert, *Sprache und Politik*, 202, 240, 296. Possible intellectual roots of this use of the language in Fichte's philosophy of action and Hegelian historical philosophy cannot be explored here.

60. *Sten. Ber.*, Vol. 1, 521. The dictates of necessity as a motive for action is, incidentally, much more pronounced with the previous speaker Mathy, from whom Gagern borrowed the expression "bold step." See ibid., 520.

61. Beckerath to his wife, 30 May 1848, in Hansen and Boberach (eds.), *Rheinische Briefe*, Vol. 2/2, 193.

62. Camphausen's memorandum, 14 December 1848, in Erich Brandenburg, *Untersuchungen und Aktenstücke zur Geschichte der Reichsgründung* (Leipzig, 1916), 290-300, here 295.

63. *Neue Deutsche Zeitung*, 10 November 1848, in Hildebrandt (ed.), *Opposition,* 186-87.

64. *Parteikorrespondenz der Linken*, 22 March 1849, ibid., 259; see also ibid., 261: "The nation has had it with the 'saving deed.'"

65. See, among others, Karl-Geog Faber, "Realpolitik als Ideologie. Die Bedeutung des Jahres 1866 für das politische Denken in Deutschland," *Historische Zeitschrift* 203 (1966): 1-45; G. Plumpe, "Einleitung," in G. Plumpe and E. McInnes (eds.), *Bürgerlicher Realismus und Gründerzeit 1848-1890* (Vol. 6: Hansers Sozialgeschichte der deutschen Literatur,) (Munich, 1996), 17-83, here, 30-41; P. Stemmler, "'Realismus' im politischen Diskurs nach 1848. Zur politischen Semantik des nachrevolutionären Liberalismus," in ibid., 84-107; U. Gerhard, "Aus 'luftiger Höhe' zum 'Boden der Tatsachen'—Bemerkungen zur Kollektivsymbolik in Deutschland Mitte des 19. Jahrhunderts," in *Das Selbstverständnis der Germanistik. Aktuelle Diskussionen. Vorträge des Germanistentages* Vol. 2 (Berlin, 1987), (Tübingen), 205-27.

66. Bismarck to his brother, 18 April 1849, in Otto von Bismarck, *Gesammelte Werke*, Vol. 14/1, 127.

67. Wolfram Siemann, *Die Frankfurter Nationalversammlung 1848/49 zwischen demokratischem Liberalismus und konservativer Reform. Die Bedeutung der Juristendominanz in den Verfassungsverhandlungen des Paulskirchenparlaments* (Bern, 1976).

68. Moritz Hartmann to Frl. …, 30 May 1848, in Hildebrandt, *Opposition,* 13.

69. "Doctrinaire," that is sticking to constitutional forms, and "practical" had become antithetical terms for two styles of argumentation in the summer of 1848. See H. Büttner to Max Duncker, Elbing, 11 November 1848: "Duncker, you truly do not lack courage, but by all which is holy to you and me, do not be a doctrinaire…Your speech on the central power in June of this year was not doctrinaire, I quite agreed with it, but Gagern was more practical. See to it [in view of events in Berlin—WS], where Gagern perhaps does not, that the German National Assembly 'takes a bold step.'" J. Schultze (ed.), *Max Duncker. Politischer Briefwechsel aus seinem Nachlaß* (Stuttgart, 1923), 6.

70. See G.C. Lewis, *A Treatise on the Methods of Observation and Reasoning in Politics,* (London, 1852).

71. See Pierre Rosanvallon, *Le Moment Guizot* (Paris, 1985), 155-62, here 159.

72. See David E. Barclay, *Frederick William IV and the Prussian Monarchy, 1840-1861* (Oxford and New York, 1995), 12, 49, 54-5, 127.

73. Richard Cobden (c. 1856), quoted in John Morley, *The Life of Richard Cobden,* Vol. 1 (London, 1881), 419. See on this point, and for the following, A. Jardin, "La chute du régime de Juillet," in M. Valensise (ed.), *François Guizot et la culture politique de son temps* (Paris, 1991), 203-217.

74. See in unsurpassed plainness: Ernst August of Hannover to Friedrich Wilhelm IV, 6 June 1848: "Blood has to flow, and believe me that as much I am an enemy of such measures, in the end I have to admit that without bloodshed there will be no peace here in Germany." K. Haenchen (ed.), *Revolutionsbriefe 1848. Ungedrucktes aus dem Nachlaß König Friedrich Wilhelms IV. von Preußen* (Leipzig, 1930), 110.

75. *Verhandlungen der Stände-Versammlung des Großherzogtums Baden im Jahre 1848, Protokolle der Zweiten Kammer*, Zweites Protokollheft, 23 Feb. 1848, quoted in Hans Fenske (ed.), *Vormärz und Revolution 1840-1849* (Vol. 4: "Quellen zum politischen Denken der Deutschen im 19. und 20. Jahrhundert"), (Darmstadt, 1976), 263-64. The following quotation is from this source.

76. L. Buhl to G. Mevissen, 2 March 1848, in Hansen, *Mevissen*, Vol. 2, 336.

77. Staatsrat Bekk to the Minister of the Interior, 13 March 1848, in L. Mathy (ed.), *Aus dem Nachlaß von Karl Mathy. Briefe aus den Jahren 1846-1848* (Leipzig, 1898), 127.

78. Ibid., 137.

79. See Rainer Wirtz, "Die Begriffsverwirrung der Bauern im Odenwald 1848. Odenwälder 'Excesse' und die Sinsheimer 'republikanische Schilderhebung,'" in Detlev Puls (ed.), *Wahrnehmungsformen und Protestverhalten. Studien zur Lage der Unterschichten im 18. und 19. Jahrhundert* (Frankfurt, 1979), 81-104 and, by the same author *"Widersetzlichkeiten, Excesse, Crawalle, Tumulte und Skandale." Soziale Bewegung und gewalthafter sozialer Protest in Baden 1815-1848* (Frankfurt, 1981), 179-84.

80. F.A. Bergmann to the central office, Regensburg, April 1848, in *Marx Engels Gesamtausgabe*, Vol. 3/2, 428.

81. A. Nacken to Ludolf Camphausen, 4 March 1848, in Joseph Hansen (ed.), *Rheinische Briefe und Akten zur Geschichte der politischen Bewegung 1830-1850*, Vol. 2: 1846-1850, 1. Hälfte (Bonn, 1942), 515.

82. See the description in Laube, *Parlament*, Vol. 1, 152-53.

83. David Hansemann to Minister v. Bodelschwingh, 1 March 1848, in Hansen, *Rheinische Briefe*, Vol. 2/1, 477-82, here 480.

84. See the description in F. von Raumer, *Briefe aus Frankfurt und Paris 1848-1849*, Vol. 1 (Leipzig, 1849), 10.

85. Hansemann to Mevissen, 16 March 1848, in Alexander Bergengrün, *David Hansemann* (Berlin, 1901), 417.

86. Ibid. For details see Jürgen Hofmann, *Das Ministerium Camphausen-Hansemann, Zur Politik der preußischen Bourgeoisie in der Revolution von 1848/49* (East Berlin, 1981), 35 ff.

87. Friedrich Wilhelm IV to Camphausen, 5 June 1848, in Erich Brandenburg (ed.), *König Friedrich Wilhelms IV. Briefwechsel mit Ludolf Camphausen* (Berlin, 1906) 149. See also the preceding letter from Camphausen in which he explains his tactics to the king. See as well, *Sten. Ber. über die Verhandlungen der zur Vereinbarung der preußischen Staats-Verfassung berufenen Versammlung*, Vol. 1 (Berlin, 1848), 114 (session of 5 June 1848).

88. Ibid., 184.

89. Varnhagen, *Journal*, 165 (entry 16 June 1848), See also Friedrich Engels in the *Neue Rheinische Zeitung* of 17 June 1848, in Marx and Engels, *Collected Works*, Vol. 7, 83: "This muddled and unprincipled amendment, which pays obeisance to all sides…this bitter-sweet pap is the 'formulation' on the 'basis' of which the Camphausen Government 'stands' and is able to stand."

90. Heinrich Claessen to Camphausen, 26 May 1848: "Using the current storm as a purifying force in this direction I would see as allowed and as intelligent." Hansen/Boberach (eds.), *Rheinische Briefe*, Vol. 2/2, 176.

91. Stephan Born to Karl Marx, 11 May 1848, *MEGA* Vol. 3/2, 445.

92. Andreas Gottschalk speaking to the Cologne Workers' Association, 26 June 1848, in Hansen and Boberach (eds.), *Rheinische Briefe*, Vol. 2/2, 277.

93. Report of the State Procurator Hecker to Justice Minister Maercker, 22 July 1848, in ibid., 320.

94. Leopold v. Gerlach to his brother Ludwig, 19 May 1848, in Diwald (ed.), *Nachlaß von Ernst Ludwig von Gerlach*, Vol. 2, 519.

95. Leopold v. Gerlach to his brother Ludwig, 20 July 1848, in ibid., 551.

96. Report of the Commander of the 15th *Landwehr* Brigade, Major General Kaiser, to the General Command of the VIII Corps, Cologne, 24 June 1848, in Hansen and Boberach (eds.), *Rheinische Briefe*, Vol. 2/2, 274.

97. Friedrich Wilhelm IV to Josef Radowitz, 13 June 1848, in Radowitz, *Briefe*, 55.

98. Johann Jacoby to Ludwig Moser, 2 September 1848, in Jacoby, *Briefwechsel*, 497.

99. Jakob van Riesen to Johann Jacoby, Elbing, 10 September 1848, ibid., 502-3.

100. Karl Reinhold Jachmann to Johann Jacoby, Kobulten, 22 September 1848, ibid., 512.

101. Prinz Wilhelm to Charlotte, 27 September 1848, in Börner (ed.), *Prinz Wilhelm*, 311-12.

102. See Wolfgang Schwentker, *Konservative Vereine und Revolution in Preußen 1848/49. Die Konstitutierung des Konservatismus als Partei* (Düsseldorf, 1988).

103. Hermann Wagener to Otto Frhr. v. Manteuffel, 20 September 1848, in H. v. Poschinger, *Unter Friedrich Wilhelm IV: Denkwürdigkeiten des Ministers Otto Freiherrn v. Manteuffel*, Vol. 1, (Berlin, 1901), 13.

104. Bismarck to his brother, 12 November 1848, in Bismarck, *Gesammelte Werke*, Vol. 14/1, 118. See also, Leopold v. Gerlach to his brother Ludwig, 26 November 1848, in Diwald (ed.), *Aus dem Nachlaß Ernst Ludwig von Gerlachs*, Vol. 2, 609: "It is strange that no loyalist address dares to wish for a return to the old state of affairs, which is certainly the case on a large scale, and is expressed in train compartments. I do not wish to see them return, but certainly such requests would be a most useful counter-opposition, when thinking as a minister."

105. Ernst Ludwig v. Gerlach, diary, 17 August 1849, in ibid., vol. 1, 196.

106. Wilhelm Arendt to Droysen, 13 July 1848, in R. Hübner (ed.), *Johann Gustav Droysen. Briefwechsel*, Vol. 1: 1829-1851 (Stuttgart, 1929, reprint Osnabrück, 1967), 448.

107. Walther Dieckmann, "Probleme der linguistischen Analyse institutioneller Kommunikation," in his *Politische Sprache, politische Kommunikation: Vorträge, Aufsätze, Entwürfe* (Heidelberg, 1981), 208-45.

108. Prinz Wilhelm to Charlotte, 9 June 1848, on his appearance in uniform: "I would have embarassed myself completely if I had taken off the coat I usually wear." Börner (ed.), *Prinz Wilhelm*, 302.

109. From outside came the accusation "that you […] in Frankfurt are sitting on an insulated chair from which only you can see what a Bassermann draws for you and only hear what they convince each other of." H. Büttner to Duncker, 9 March 1849, Duncker, *Briefwechsel*, 12.

110. See also Raumer, *Briefe*, Vol. 1, 73; Laube, *Parlament*, Vol. 1, 90-91.

111. Robert Blum to his wife Jenny, 25-27 June 1848: "The women are fanatic here in the south and demonstrations of their interest are sometimes unbelievable. During a lively debate, a significant speech, the clapping, waving of handkerchiefs, throwing flowers and blowing kisses or sending bouquets never stops … When I was recently speaking about the Central Power and at the end became very serious and solemn, the women's section was swimming in tears and hundreds of hands sobbingly reached towards me as I came down from the platform … so the matter remained purely political, but it is a powerful lever, which you shouldn't have anything against." Bergsträsser, *Parlament*, 376-77.

112. Georg Friedrich Kolb, "Redekunst, parlamentarische," in Carl von Rotteck and Carl Welcker (eds.), *Das Staats-Lexikon. Encyklopädie der sämmtlichen Staatswissenschaften für alle Stände*, Vol. 11 (Altona, 1848), 378-89, here 389.

113. Laube, *Parlament*, Vol. 1, 216-17; Stahl, *Briefe*, 65.

114. See the report of deputy Reinstein to his voters, 26-27 June 1848, *Der deutsche Bürger*, 7 July 1848, in Hildebrandt, *Opposition*, 39-40.

115. See Wolfram Siemann, *Die deutsche Revolution von 1848/49* (Frankfurt, 1985), 81.

116. The left initially interpreted this behavior as a lack of courage, see the report of deputy Tzschucke to his voters, *Meißner Blätter*, 10 and 13 June 1848, in Hildebrandt, *Opposition*, 19-20; report of the deputy Reinstein to his voters, 5 June 1848, *Der deutsche Bürger*, 13 June 1848, in ibid., 24. That tactical considerations were behind it for some is shown, for example, by Haym to David Hansemann, 18 July 1848, in Haym, *Briefwechsel*, 52ff.

117. See Beckerath to Valentin Heilmann, 25 June 1848, in Hansen and Boberach (eds.), *Rheinische Briefe*, Vol. 2/2, 279; Raumer, *Briefe*, Vol. 1, 141-42.

118. They used the term "terrorize." See F. Nägele, report to the voters, 26 June 1848, *Heilbronner Tageblatt*, 28 June 1848: "The right wing terrorizes, although they are rather certain of victory. … they terrorize, as they refuse to be bound by the agenda." B. Mann (ed.), *Heilbronner Berichte aus der deutschen Nationalversammlung 1848/49. Louis Hentges, Ferdinand Nägele, Adolph Schoder* (Heilbronn, 1974), 29.

119. On this point, see Gilbert Ziebura, "Anfänge des deutschen Parlamentarismus. Geschäftsverfahren und Entscheidungsprozeß in der ersten deutschen Nationalversammlung 1848/49," in Gerhard A. Ritter and Gilbert Ziebura (eds.), *Faktoren der politischen Entscheidung. Festgabe für Ernst Fraenkel zum 65. Geburtstag* (Berlin, 1963), 185-236, esp. 197-203; furthermore, Manfred Botzenhart, *Deutscher Parlamentarismus in der Revolutionszeit 1848-1850* (Düsseldorf, 1977), 439ff. and 489-93.

120. Droysen to Wilhelm Arendt, 10 August 1848, in Droysen, *Briefwechsel*, 460 (my emphasis).

121. Ambrosch to v. Olfers, 19 February 1849, in Bergsträsser (ed.), *Parlament*, 80.

122. Wilhelm Stahl to Carl Friedrich Gerber, 11 March 1849, in Stahl, *Briefe*, 85.

123. A prime example in this respect was the Prussian note of 23 January 1849. It was—under Camphausen's influence—so cleverly phrased that Droysen believed to have discovered signs of hope in it. The text of the note in P. Roth and H. Merck (eds.), *Quellensammlung zum Deutschen Öffentlichen Recht seit 1848*, Vol. 2 (Erlangen, 1850-52), 253ff. For Droysen's assessment and Wilhelm Arendt's much more critical judgement see Droysen, *Briefwechsel*, 517 ff. See also the "left-wing" view, *Neue Deutsche Zeitung*, 4 February 1849, in Hildebrandt, *Opposition*, 234-35.

124. Th. Mundt, *Die Staatsberedsamkeit der neueren Völker* (Berlin, 1848) 386, here not referring to a specific incident, but as characterizing public speaking in Germany in general. Mundt puts this "misty suspension" of official German political language down to the "language of bureaucrats" and the "preaching style."

125. Leopold v. Gerlach to his brother Ludwig, 20 July 1848, in Diwald (ed.), *Nachlaß Ernst Ludwig von Gerlach*, Vol. 2, 551.

Chapter 36

ON THE LOOSE

The Impact of Rumors and *Mouchards* in the Ardèche during
the Second Republic[1]

John Merriman

More than merely an occasional force in history, rumor has perhaps been an inherent part of the political process itself. The intersection between rumor and the evolution of public opinion, and the impact of rumors on the shaping of government
policies, largely remains to be studied. Yet, the history of France in the ancien régime,
during the Revolution, and in the nineteenth and twentieth centuries offers fascinating glimpses of the role of rumor. Rumors that King Louis XVI was profiting
from the hoarding of grain before the Revolution may well have helped prepare the
French Revolution; certainly, the impact of the Great Fear on the night of 4 August
1789 is beyond dispute, or at least should be. Richard Cobb frequently returns to the
role of rumor during the waxing and waning of popular movements during the
Revolution and Empire.[2] More recently, Bronislaw Baczko has considered the significance of wild rumors about Robespierre-the-king sweeping Paris, which he
argues influenced the fall of the Incorruptible One on the Ninth of Thermidor.[3]

I have elsewhere tried to demonstrate the power of rumor in France in 1829
and 1830, when, before the July Revolution of 1830, a frightening and sometimes
devastating series of arson attacks in Normandy sparked widely believed rumors.[4]
To liberals, bands of brigands armed with matches were trying to frighten *censitaires*
into voting for the candidates of the Polignac ministry; to conservatives, the fires
were the work of those in the pay of liberals, trying to frighten electors into joining the rapidly expanding liberal forces challenging the Restoration politics. Alain
Corbin has splendidly evoked the role of rumor in the atrocious murder of a
Poitevin noble during the Franco-Prussian War in 1870, even if subsequent rumors
had it wrong that the latter had been eaten by his murderers.[5]

During *la semaine sanglante* in May 1871, rumors spread rapidly on the Versaillais side that *les pétroleuses* were torching buildings, including the Bank of France. Rumors of German atrocities, including rapes and murder, against civilians during World War I probably contributed to the firm resolve with which the French home front held on in 1914 and thereafter.[6] The impact of powerful rumors—even the most bizarre—did not end in France with the era of the mass press, nor were they confined to the country's rural world. In 1969, the "rumor of Orléans" had it that Jewish shopkeepers were kidnapping girls and selling them into slavery.[7] This particular rumor generated a boycott against Jewish shopkeepers.

We do not have a general study of rumor—*les on-dit, les rumeurs, les bruits,*—in modern French history. I will here expand the consideration of rumor to include not only "*les on-dit*" that began in small, distant villages, or in cabarets in small towns, or at the octroi of larger ones, but also briefly consider what one might call "official rumors"—some of it simply misinformation, or what Cobb calls "political rumors," set running by politicians. Rumors became "official" when they reached subprefectures, prefectures, and the corridors of the ministries of interior, justice, and war in Paris. There, manipulated at different levels of the administrative, judicial, and military hierarchies, they helped shape the government's contention that the Montagnards stood on the verge of insurrection in 1852. Both kinds of rumors, which were easily conflated by officials looking to confirm their worst fears and determined to destroy the Republic, helped shape government policy in 1850 and 1851. They thus contributed to move conservative public opinion toward acceptance of, indeed eagerness for, the destruction of the Republic. Thus, Louis Napoleon Bonaparte's regime would later insist that the coup d'état had been necessary to save France from socialist-inspired civil war.

I also want to consider the role that *mouchards*, or police spies, played in propagating rumor during the Second Republic, in shaping the confrontation between the government of Louis Napoleon Bonaparte and the Montagnards. To be sure, the French monarchy had frequently relied on police spies during the ancien régime, including none other than Brissot himself.[8] For these particular *mouchards*, convinced that what they were doing was extremely important and would be therefore pleasing to those who employed them, accentuated the diffusion of official rumors. Thus, it is possible, I think, to pluck rumors from the air in which they seemed to float, and place them squarely in the context of the social and political reality of the Second Republic. In this *ballon d'essai*, I can only scratch the surface, drawing on some examples I have recently marshalled from the Ardèche, where rumors, Montagnard secret societies, and police spies abounded, and whose archives include some extremely rich reports from three police spies.

First, what do we mean by rumor? A rumor can be defined as "a common talk or opinion, a widely disseminated belief having no discernible foundation or source," or "a statement or report current without any known authority for its truth," which, however distorted, may have some foundation in reality. Thus, a rumor is news that is diffused and widely believed, whether true or false.[9] Rumors are not, then, the same thing as oral communication, which, at the time of the Second Republic, still remained the principal source of news for most people. Nor are they necessarily the same thing as misinformation, though misinformation, diffused directly or indirectly by state authorities, could itself be a source of rumors and, in turn, be shaped by them.

Certainly, we need to know much more about the language, representation, and receptivity of rumor, for example about the relationship between French and patois in regions in which the latter greatly held sway among ordinary people. Historians might also want to determine to what extent the role of rumor declined with the emergence of more institutionalized mass political life (mass circulation newspapers, political parties, universal manhood suffrage, then universal suffrage, and so on) during the French Third Republic.[10]

To be sure, several of major studies of the Revolution of 1848 and the Second Republic in France have noted the importance of rumor, notably Ted Margadant's study of the resistance to the coup d'état, and that of Peter McPhee on Roussillon.[11] At a minimum, we can say that one of the results of rumors during the Second French Republic was to increase social conflict during the period and to encourage supporters of the government to anticipate and accept a violent end to the republic, as well as to keep Montagnards in a state of anxious readiness. Thus, both "official" rumor and popular rumor served to drive Montagnards and the regime and its supporters further apart as the destruction of the Second Republic loomed near.

Rumors thus operated as a powerful force by helping define the "view of the other" for the two principal political forces of the Second Republic: the *démoc-socs*, or Montagnards, of the left, and the government of Louis Napoleon Bonaparte, backed by many conservatives who would welcome his coup d'état with a sense of relief. Long ago, J. Dagnan noted that although the Bonapartist state had at its disposal the most technologically advanced means of communication—the telegraph—it fell back on the power of rumor.[12] Rumors convinced many conservatives that Montagnards were blood-thirsty fanatics poised to launch a major insurrection throughout much of France, after which they would turn against property and social hierarchy. By mid-1850, many administrators and magistrates believed that a massive plot existed to seize power, and in 1851, the year "1852" was whispered fearfully as promising a Montagnard takeover, whether by the ballot-box or through insurrection.

Rumors spread in provincial France during the Second Republic by the familiar conduits that traditionally carried news of all kinds along valley routes, upland footpaths, *chemins vicinaux*, on upgraded departmental and national roads, and by steamboats and, then, railroads. They were carried by commercial travelers, journeymen, peddlers, and seasonal migrants leaving and returning to the Massif Central, the Limousin, the Pyrénées, and the Alpine region, among others. They were related by and to peddlers working fairs and markets, and selling door to door in the countryside. Rumors accompanied journeymen on the tour de France; *colporteurs* brought not only published material with them to be read, but songs to be sung, *les images d'Épinal*, viewed and discussed. Yet, it is far more difficult to assess the number of people who believed rumors, or to chart the path of rumors with anything like the accuracy of Georges Lefebvre's study of the Great Fear.

The role of rumor after the Revolution of 1848 should be placed in the context of—and indeed was part of—the massive political mobilization that followed the revolution.[13] Rumors themselves reflected the degree of social and political conflict intensified by the revolution of 1848, accentuated by the economic crisis of 1846-47 that the revolution re-ignited following the brief recovery. The violence of the June Days, the subsequent attempted insurrections in 1849, and the heated rhetoric of the left contributed to this social polarization, expanding the power of rumor.

Nowhere did rumors—both "official rumors" and popular rumors—run more rampant than in an increasing number of prefectures of southern France. And yet, while convincing themselves that each arrest, discovery of Montagnard propaganda, and, sometimes, a cache of powder revealed a plot being secretly organized, prefects, subprefects, and *procureurs* themselves accentuated the power of rumor. Rumors surrounded and helped invent the "Complot de Lyon" of 1850, and various other "uncovered," largely imaginary plots large and small to overthrow the regime, such as those of the Southeast, Béziers, Perpignan, and perhaps the most pathetic invention of all, the "plot" surrounding a banquet in the Ardèchois village of Laurac in October 1851, which helped provide an excuse for the government to declare a state of siege in the Ardèche, along with five other departments. Prefects and magistrates thus elevated rumor to the status of fact, and then shaped policy accordingly, preparing the way for the coup d'état less than two months later.

However, some rumors aided the Montagnard cause, none more powerful (and ultimately accurate) than that picturing the regime as poised in 1851 to overthrow the republic. The Montagnards viewed officials of the centralized state as ruthless plotters against the great hopes of the republic who were fully capable of turning France back over to the great property-owners and to the hierarchy of the Catholic Church. McPhee considers rumors that the victory of the Montagnards and the establishment of a "democratic and social republic" was not far away to have been an important part of the *démoc-socs'* "language of justice and retribution," one greatly informed by rural life.[14] These rumors may have manifested a millenarian quality. Furthermore, some rumors probably added to the ranks of the left, for example convincing some peasants that under a "social" republic, only the rich would have to pay taxes. In the final attempt to defend hope for the "democratic and social republic," rumor would play a role in swelling the ranks of the insurgents in early December 1851.

The power of rumor was immediately apparent in the wake of the February Revolution, among great political uncertainty, as *commissaires* named by the new revolutionary authority assumed power and delegates from the Club of Clubs arrived in some regions to attempt to mobilize support for the republican left as the elections of April 23 approached. Rumors of leftist alleged misdeeds and plots quickly mobilized conservatives of all persuasions, probably contributing no small amount to the coalescence of France's notables, frightened by the potential move of the revolution to the left.[15]

From the beginning of the republic, the collective memory of the French Revolution and its accompanying violence remained closely linked to rumors among conservatives. Certainly, the claim by some radical republicans that the emerging Montagnard party had inherited the mantle of 1793 contributed to rumors that a violent insurrection of the left was not far away, even before the June Days. Shouts of "*Vive la guillotine!*" and "*Vive '93!*" were taken to augur a return of the scaffold, as in Bédarieux—where three gendarmes would be killed during the insurrection following the coup d'état—when an electoral meeting in April 1848 "cheered the memory of 1793 and called for a red flag."[16]

Such shouts and revolutionary songs such as *Le Chant du départ* and *Ça ira* were easily transformed by rumor into real acts of violence, or into certain projects for the future. Rumors accompanying news of the June Days had something of the impact of the Great Fear of 1789 in some places. Reports by *commissaires de police*, gendarmes, and secret police were, of course, not always very reliable; senior authorities did not just simply believe *anything* they heard. But by the last months of 1851, virtually any rumor seem to have been routinely taken as fact, or at least treated as such to encourage support from public opinion and to justify continued systematic political repression. For example, in 1850 the subprefect of Tournon assured the prefect of the Ardèche that a banquet of 3,000 people was being organized to celebrate the anniversary of the February Revolution. In fact, the eighty people picnicking at Crussol were out-numbered by the 100 troops sent from Valence to disperse them. Officials took "the smallest excursion among friends [*camarades*]," to be part of a massive conspiracy.[17]

Later that year, another banquet was rumored but never held near the vineyard town of St. Péray on the Rhône. Another "*on me dit que*" had a small banquet having taken place in remote St. Romain de Lerps, and yet another planned for the following weeks. The subprefect concluded, "I scarcely believe these meetings in the fields. People could have been mistaking hunters for socialists." Even the prefect knew that the very location of St. Romain de Lerps made any such gathering highly unlikely: "You have to climb for an hour to reach St. Romain de Lerps, which consists of a church, the rectory, an inn and the house of the mayor who is a blacksmith. What effect would a banquet in such a place have? My arrondissement is perfectly calm."[18] A year later, such rumors were taken to be fact that a massive Montagnard conspiracy was afoot.

Officially orchestrated rumors of Montagnard conspiracy were something of a self-fulfilling prophesy. The centralized repression may have cut apart the radical apparatus in much of France, but it also forced Montagnards in much of the Midi and some parts of the Center to organize secret societies.[19] Increasingly, many of the rumors that swept regions focused on these Montagnard organizations and particularly on the belief that their insurrection was near, if not at hand. In April, 1850, Minister of the Interior Baroche summarized the "numerous warnings," however vague, imprecise, and, in some cases, already known, that had arrived in his ministry, which "lead one to believe in the existence of plots for insurrection in the departments of the East and the Midi," which which awaited only the orders [*mot d'ordre*] from Marseille, Toulon, Lyon, and other major Montagnard centers."[20]

Such rumors that Montagnard leaders had given the password for an armed uprising to be prepared drew on fears among high officials and local elites that *démoc-socs* were stocking gunpowder and bullets and forging knives. The *Commissaire extraordinaire* of the sixth military division commanding the state of siege in the Lyon region went so far as to claim that from August 1850 to the end of March 1851, "from St. Étienne there have been sent to the department of the Ardèche alone 20,000 firearms, rifles and especially pistols."[21] In August 1850, a denunciation offered by three members of a so-called "sociey of order," reached the prefect of the Ardèche. Based on rumors that a Montagnard insurrection was in the works, it warned that "To prevent an imminent armed uprising and to strike a salutary terror against anarchy, it is necessary to proceed immediately to search the house of Meyssat." Specifically, they promised that a search would turn up under the counter on the first floor or in a room up the stairs the seal of the secret society and "an extensive correspondence setting in motion a vast conspiracy." As for the *cave*, the "men of order" advised that what appeared to be an empty barrel contained munitions. After listing leaders of the secret society who should be arrested immediately, the letter warned that if "no measure is taken within three days, we will take our concerns higher up, and we will be heard. Our safety demands it." However, a thorough police search turned up nothing suspicious.[22]

In June, 1850, officials in the Ardèche were tipped off that many leaders of the Montagnard secret societies had met in Montélimar, including about twenty from the department. Since this meeting, he could assert that there had been "considerable movement in the villages, meetings on Saturdays, [and] new affiliations." Members thereafter let their mustaches grow. Beards and mustaches were, at least in the Bas Vivarais, sometimes taken to indicate that he who sported one was a Montagnard and so was the gesture of tugging at one's ear with the thumb and index fingers of the right hand.[23] According to a police informant, the insurrection had been set for June 10, "at nightfall, the *tocsin* will everywhere be sounded, [the insurgents] will meet, take the arms of the national guard, and those in public storehouses, then depart, march all night to arrive the next morning in Privas, to the number of twelve to fifteen thousand men. There, they will seize the adminstration of the department and the public treasury, dispatch the prefect or take him hostage...and subsequently, in concert with other departments, proclaim Ledru Rollin president, and after this president has been installed in Paris, take, under his direction, great measures of public safety."[24]

In the hills above Aubenas and Vals, Antraigues had become a minor center of *démoc-soc* activity. In November, 1850, a police *confidente* related that "I have received a confidential report that there exists a conspiracy to set fire to the prefecture and the barracks on the night of the 19-20 or 20-21 and to liberate the prisoners." Even as he wrote, it appeared that a "large number of socialists" from other corners of the department were heading toward Antraigues and other places preparing for "some sort of surprise attack,—the result of the extraordinary intrigues of the secret societies, who, as you know, are infiltrating all our villages."[25]

The postman from Vernoux who delivered mail to the village of Bouffres had bragged that he had distributed more than forty pounds of gunpowder to Montagnards on his rounds, and that they were many *servatines* [*chevrotines*: small bullets for hunting game] in Vernoux. In Privas, Bouvier, a tinsmith, had called for calm, and patience: "when the time comes, we will make them dance a famous dance [hanging from a pole]; we have guns and we have ammunition, if you need some, we will pass some along."[26] The quest for the goods on Montagnards could, however, lead to some fairly elementary mistakes. In November, 1849, the commissaire de police of Annonay reported that some of the glove makers were wearing the *bonnet rouge* of the sans-culottes of the Revolution. It then had to be pointed out that such woolen red caps produced in Annonay were normal winter headwear for mountain people. Likewise, rumor transformed gunpowder being prepared for the Ardèchois passion of hunting into preparation for bloody insurrection.[27]

In February, 1850, at the time of the anniversary of the 1848 Revolution, an outing by about twenty workers from Vallon led to "*le bruit*" that near the famous natural bridge Pont d'Arc itself "they had sworn to remain faithful to their cause." The workers, when interrogated, insisted that they had gone out on a Sunday "for a pleasant outing, and not with other intentions," although, to be sure, such initiations almost certainly did occur, even if not necessarily that particular day.[28] Large gatherings of Montagnard leaders from the Ardèche, Haute-Loire, and Drôme were rumored on several occasions during that same year. In September, a rumor circulated that the prefect had asked that the Ardèche be put under the state of siege, but that the departmental *Conseil Général* had refused to permit this (as if that body would have had any such leverage). Again, such a *bruit*, no matter what its origins, probably helped propagate the belief among people of means that only by a strong, authoritarian move could the Montagnards be defeated.[29] And when a rumor had Annonay becoming the center of insurrection in November, the commander of the Gendarmerie claimed that such rumors "are only disseminated for the purpose of sowing unrest.[30]

In June, in the hills of the Ardèche "an individual, an outsider, had come to the village of St. Étienne de Boulogne and had harangued the public as people were leaving mass, calling on 'le peuple' to remain ready to soon take up arms, and overthrow the government." An investigation failed to verify this event, but, in any case, the rumor was launched. A brief investigation revealed that a man from Ucel, across the Ardèche River from Aubenas, had indeed been in St. Étienne-de-Boulogne on 9 June 1850; he had stood in the middle of the village square drinking *eau de vie* and handing out swigs to those whom he met, but no more than this.[31] Similarly, in September a police report arrived in Privas that "assured" the prefect that in Pouzin in the Rhône Valley a woman—*la crieuse public*, appropriately enough—had shouted a warning that all those who had gunpowder and weapons should hide them, because the police were undertaking house searches. When asked who had told her to shout out such a message, she had replied that "a man had paid her to do so." Gendarmes who went by asked her who had her shout that and she said that she did not know him, that was the end of the investigation, but probably not the rumors of Montagnard mobilization that followed the incident.[32]

Even the absence of apparent Montagnard activity sparked rumors among conservatives that an underground plot was in the works.[33] And when Montagnard

activity seemed to rise again between June and December 1850: "It is difficult not
to see in this the work of a master plan, if not a conspiracy." The "discovery" of the
"complot de Lyon" in October, 1850 centered on the political activities of Alphonse
Gent, a former member of the National Assembly, who spent a great deal of time in
Lyon, making many trips to see other Montagnards in various towns in the Southeast.[34] The idea of giving or receiving a "password" in cafés, *chambrées* [private male
drinking and social clubs in parts of the Midi], or at the market or fair, or in other
"permanent centers of disorder," "disguised [political] clubs, dens of demagogy," and
so on, remained the core of plot hypotheses.[35]

And when the local Montagnard leader Mazon was arrested and taken away
with a heavy chain around his neck that same month amid considerable "agitation,"
rumor had emissaries going out from Largentière to organize a mobilization to free
him: "the rumors of a rescue of the prisoners have been verified in such a serious
way that I have had to take all necessary precautions to guard against such an eventuality, whose realization, if not probable seems at least possible."[36] A day later, the
procureur ordered Mazon freed (at which point he went into hiding somewhere
between Thueyts and Prades above Aubenas), fearing precisely such an eventuality.
In this case, too, authorities accused the Montagnards of starting rumors that they
believed served their interests: "the reds have circulated the rumor that the local
authorities have been frightened by the obvious movement of armed men in the
hills, and that they gave up Mazon in order to prevent Largentière from being
burned down and its inhabitants massacred."[37]

In late 1851, the justice of the peace of the canton of Aubenas related a series
of "*on me dit que*": that secret gatherings were being held all over the department,
"where letters are being read that incite this agitation. It has been claimed for some
time now that the triumph of socialism is imminent. Since people are sure that
general Changarnier will vigorously crush the rebellion, they want the departments to take the initiative, and seven generals have been designated in advance as
the leaders of the movement to inspire confidence," including, absurdly enough,
General Cavaignac.[38]

Several incidents in the Ardèche of Montagnard resistance to gendarmes accentuated official certainty and elite fears that a popular insurrection lay not far away.
Gendarmes raiding a Montagnard gathering in the largely Protestant commune of
Salavas led to the freeing of prisoners and the flight of a number of "suspects" into
the hills, where they were protected by the population, and the inevitable attempts
of authorities to link this "conspiracy" with the "complot de Lyon."[39] Yet, the *procureur général* of Nîmes complained of the incomplete and vague nature of the
reports coming out of the Bas Vivarais.[40]

The aggressive presence of gendarmes at *fêtes votives* [festivals celebrating patron
saints] in the Ardèche generated two cases of popular resistance that further convinced authorities that secret societies were organized and ready for 1852. When
gendarmes tried to break up a brawl in the largely Protestant village of Labastide-
de-Virac on 3 August, "Protestant democrats" chased them away and, as in the
Salavas incident, "suspects" disappeared into the hills. A week later, in Laurac, just off

the road from Aubenas to Alès and only a few kilometers from Largentière, two brigades of gendarmes moved in to break up a Montagnard "banquet" organized by local activists, at which fifty or sixty people challenged prefectoral decrees by singing "demagogic songs." A crowd then moved against the gendarmes, hurling bottles and rocks, to which the gendarmes replied with swords and guns, but had to be rescued by the arrival of the subprefect with loyal national guardsmen from Largentière. On 31 August at Vinezac, a few kilometers up the road toward Aubenas, villagers assailed gendarmes who prevented their *fête* from even beginning. Troops rescued the gendarmes, firing shots, and arresting several people.[41]

Two weeks earlier, a Montagnard supposedly *had* confessed that a *démoc-soc* plot existed to storm Largentière, put to death various officials, and pillage the place. After admitting in a letter that it would be difficult legally to prove that a plot actually existed before the banquet at Laurac, the seizure of letters in rural communes seemed to provide proof that secret societies existed. Only a sizable military presence could help the authorities turn the corner, reassuring the "men of order."[42] When the *procureur-général* of Nîmes expressed doubts that sheer military force could overwhelm political opposition and suggested that the proliferation of such incidents as had occurred in Laurac and Vinezac could be counter-productive because they acclimated the local population to resist the forces of order, the Minister of Justice insisted that the wide-spread organization of secret societies in the district necessitated such an aggressive show of force.[43]

Thus, in order to get the goods on the Montagnard secret societies, three police spies were sent into the Ardèche, one for each arrondissement, but while they apparently had no contact with each other, they knew of each others' existence. Sent to the Bas Vivarais by orders of unspecified Parisian authorities, each was put in contact with the prefect ("I belong to you, body and soul") and two subprefects of the department. Yet, they had no "official" authority. "I am in no way an agent with official standing," wrote one of them, "Arnaud," traveling as a wine merchant, "I must be and remain foreign to all authority, and if the occasion is sufficiently urgent, the authorities may treat me like the other criminals caught red handed…we must have recourse to the ruse."[44] Letters from the prefect and subprefects were to be sent care of the hotels in which they were staying, or *poste restante*, or even to neighboring localities.

When they were not writing to ask for more money, the three *mouchards* planted themselves in cafés, where they spent their time in idle chatter. They seem to have knowingly treated the rumors they heard as fact, and threats and playful pleasantries as one and the same. They did so, in part, because (as Richard Cobb insisted in the case of the *commissaires de police* of the Revolutionary and Napoleonic eras[45]) they tended to report what they believed their superiors wanted to hear. In the Second Republic, *commissaires de police* tended to be more cautious and accurate in their reporting, because they had to limit their investigations to the town to which they were assigned. "Arnaud" claimed that in Annonay a Montagnard hairdresser, had told other socialists in the glove-making town, that "if we take action, we will make those famous gloves with the skin of the prefect. It was said to him, is this a joke? He replied: no, this is very serious; he will not leave Privas alive. We don't ever want to be caught." In the arrondissement of Largentière, the *mouchard* Vigier traveled with a passport in the name of Antoine Ballard, thirty-six years of age, commercial bookkeeper [*comptable d'une maison de commerce*]. In the meantime, another agent, a former café proprietor from Avignon, had been posted in Annonay. Vigier's trek took him from Thueyts above Aubenas on the road to Le Puy to the largely Protestant communes in the cantons of Le Vans, Joyeuse, and Vallon in the Bas Vivarais. The subprefect hoped to link the secret societies directly to the Laurac affair, construed to have been part of a specific Montagnard plot. Compounding the difficulties of Vigier's assignment was the fact that the secret agent on the loose in Privas and its region had been totally compromised by his own foolish comportment, and was widely considered to be a *mouchard*.[46]

How was Vigier to become a well-informed informant, after receiving a quick crash course from the subprefect on the Montagnards of the Bas Vivarais? The subprefect knew that it would take at least some time for him to be able to pass on useful information to the subprefect, who would, in turn, send it to Privas: "if he endeavors to acquire little by little the confidence of the reds, and he will accomplish this, I do not doubt, if he works at it seriously."[47]

The local gendarmerie and police *commissaires* were not let in on Vigier's mission. Thus, Vigier encountered an occupational hazard of his métier—a gendarme arrested him in the village of Mayras. He stood accused of being a Montagnard propagandist. After all, he had with him a list of local "demagogues" and their addresses, and pamphlets like "The People Will Take Revenge," as well as a list of his expenses. But Vigier could not hide his indignity at being arrested, nor his sense of self-importance in working for higher authorities than the gendarme who arrested him. Even his description to the subprefect of his arrest could not have been complete without the comment that he had been thrown in the jail because he was taken to be "a very dangerous man, inciting the masses to rebellion." Thus, Vigier told the gendarme taking him to Aubenas that he had been sent from Paris: "I let him know that I had business in Jaujac, on the orders of authorities, but he did not want to believe any of it." After being freed by order of the subprefect, Vigier did not want to be turned loose in Aubenas, fearing that the Montagnards would find him out, and was packed off in a coach to Largentière.[48]

After this episode, Vigier began a tour that took him to Montréal, Laurac, Rosières, Joyeuse, Lablachère, Les Assions, Les Vans, Berrias, and St. André-de-Crozières; all of the stops were to be completed by the time he was to meet with the subprefect in eight days.[49] From Laurac, one of his first stops, Vigier reported that the "party" of Montagnards "is not extinguished, but there are men who are not well intentioned," a significant minority of the population, including a certain Dussère "known as *le penitent blanc*," who, although not a radical, had twenty-three bullets and two "little packets of hunting powder," in a drawer in his armoire. As for gunpowder, all the Montagnards, he claimed, were in perfect agreement that it could be produced so quickly that it was perhaps not wise to stock up, since it could be seized in searches. In the wake of the state of siege, Vigier believed that "a kind of secret society has existed in principle, but since the state of siege was imposed, it no longer exists, or at least no longer appears to exist." The Montagnards appeared somewhat demoralized, frozen in their tracks—"everyone is afraid"—with a couple of their leaders in hiding.[50] In and around Privas, republicans and *démoc-socs* believed that the effect of the siege would be to "democratize the Ardèche even more by annoying it. They expect that the peasants will be furious and that they vote in the elections for whomever they please."[51]

But rumors that Vigier was a police spy circulated. Furthermore, the subprefect complained that his reports "tell us nothing new, and only repeat what I have already said to him myself. [Yet] his evaluations are, in general, accurate enough," but of the relations that he has with the demagogues, "those are boasts that he has attempted to exaggerate." For example, some of the stories he passed along at the time of a Montagnard banquet to celebrate the anniversary of the February Revolution could be dismissed as "pure invention." The *mouchard* had exaggerated the number of members of the Montagnard secret society to be 900, while the subprefect held to an also inflated total of "five or six hundred, of whom only three hundred could be counted on." His passing on rumors of alleged Montagnard plans for insurrection including a fanciful account of the execution of the prefect on the *place* de L'Airette in Aubenas (which would have, for one thing, entailed bringing him over the difficult Col d'Escrinet from Privas simply to be hung in Aubenas).[52]

Vigier's downfall came after his return from the canton of Vallon, as well as a quick trip to Montpellier for family matters. After his report that several gendarmes in the canton of Aubenas had been publicly singing Montagnard songs could not be verified by their commanders, he asked to be put at the disposition of the prefect in Privas or elsewhere, however not in the arrondissement of Largentière. Furthermore, the subprefect criticized Vigier's "lack of caution"; the *mouchard* had apparently related his arrest to gendarmes in Vallon, where he had no reason to do so, and had revealed his identity as a secret agent to the *commissaire de police* there. By then, "the reds are stating opnely that he is a government agent," telling him this to his face. "People are talking openly about this matter, and Vigier is strolling in public with the *commissaire de police*, which discredits him even more." In the opinion of the subprefect, Vigier was intelligent, yet very lazy. Vigier, however, continued to boast of his energy on behalf of the Bonapartist cause: "I have had intimate relations with the mistress of Lemairoux, I am going to resume these and attempt to find out, via this intermediary, where the fugitives have their lair." He could keep a secret, but only up to a point. Again, Vigier's need to be important got the best of him; he had proudly revealed his mission to gendarmes in order to learn information about the Montagnards in the villages he was supposed to be infiltrating; he did so in order to avoid the expense and bother of more travelling to new places, and of hobnobbing with people to whom he believed himself superior, and whom he disparagingly referred to as the "vile multitude."[53]

It must be said that Vigier was educated: few French speaking Ardèchois and certainly precious few police spies used words like "the coryphaeus" to describe a leader of the Montagnards of Largentière. However, Vigier had gone to Montpellier against the wishes of the subprefect, while insisting that his purpose was to learn more about the Montagnards in and around in the *chef-lieu* [departmental capital] of the Hérault. While the subprefect had kept "the silence of death about this man and his mission," now even a modest *commissaire de police* stepped forward to complain about Vigier. The subprefect concluded that it was necessary to send Vigier out of the arrondissement: "he cannot do any more good here … he is too compromised." That, as far as we know, was the end of the Vigier's mission in the Ardèche.[54]

What had Vigier accomplished? Despite his obvious incompetence, the essence of his reports reached Paris, through the intermediary of the prefect, helping confirm the image that the Ardèche was on the verge of a Montagnard insurrection. His reports confirmed what was already known about Montagnard strength in the Bas Vivarais. He identified Montagnards, leaders and followers, adding some new names, complete with detailed descriptions, to the growing list in secret files in Largentière and in Privas. He assessed their degree of radicalization (for example, carefully noting those who could be defined, rightly or wrongly, as "*partageux*," and those who remained fully respectful of property). Village by village, Vigier estimated the percentage of *démoc-socs* among the population: three-fifths in Salavas, three-quarters in Vallon, at least two-thirds in lovely Balazuc, half in Ruoms, and so on. These were good guesses. Vigier recognized that the state of siege had indeed driven Montagnard activity further underground in the Ardèche, and believed that the arrondissement of Largentière might well rise up if an insurrection occurred in Paris or Lyon. In October, Vigier reported that the Montagnards of Largentière "are convinced that the decisive crisis will occur before January 1, and that a violation of the constitution will bring about an uprising [that] must open the doors of prisons to those accused or condemned of political crimes in the Ardèche and everywhere else."[55]

But, in the end, Vigier added little that was new, sometimes simply repeating information that the subprefect had provided him at the outset of his small adventure, and he even got some things flat wrong. The subprefect did not share his optimistic assessment of Joyeuse, nor his pessimistic view of Les Vans, at least from the point of view of the authorities concerned with such things. His reports nonetheless added to the willingness of the administration to convey to Paris the continued existence of secret societies—though he greatly exaggerated the number of members—to which authorities responded by attributing secret preparations, including the stocking of gunpowder in Vallon and other places to plans for armed insurrection in 1852. Rumor helped determine and later justify official policy.

In Privas, "Arnaud" did not do much better, and seemed almost obsessed with providing careful physical descriptions of Montagnards. He thus described the long-haired man accompanying a Montagnard at the "republican café" as "[wearing] bourgeois clothing that is shabby, and talking politics with the goal of bring others into a general conversation, probably in order to get me to participate and to learn who I am." This preoccupation with physical descriptions at a time when police depended on *signalements* [written descriptions of features] is to be expected. When, in the early days of his stay in Privas, the *mouchard* maintained the discretion of attentive silence so as to avoid suspicion while seeking acceptance as a politically reliable *habitué*, a peasant on market day who was a little drunk chastised him for using a white handkerchief for his cold, repeating several times, "A bas les blancs! Vivent les rouges!" Integrating himself into the small world of Montagnards took time: "Yesterday was a good one for increasing my popularity, which I do with extreme moderation at the end complete confidence will be obtained." His attendance at a rural festival helped build confidence—a confidence, of course, that was completely misplaced—among "*les rouges*." In September 1851, Arnauld left Privas with two or three printshop workers and spent some hours there. "I played *boules* with the peasants; at times we addressed each other familiarly [nous nous tutoyâmes parfois], and we drank, danced and sang with a primitive independence." Ever playing the role of a bourgeois socialist, Arnaud could not resist cautioning the young workers to help keep the *fête* on a reasonable, restrained track, as a vigorous water game led to a fight and to the intervention of several gendarmes.

He then naively claimed that his attendance at the *fête* had demonstrated to all that he was a Montagnard, not a *mouchard*. Police spies, after all, had to be actors (and, as such, risked having the same status as actors, if even that). Excluded from citizenship (or rather subjectship, as it were) until the French Revolution because they were reviled as dishonest and untrustworthy for their facility in adopting different personnae, the *mouchards* were in the end trusted neither by the Montagnards upon whom they spied, nor, by virtue of their failures, by those to whom they reported.[56]

Flushed with excitement and emboldened by some sense of triumph, Arnaud wrote, "It seems to me that I constantly have a demagogue on my shoulders, I will continue to write you about this kind of terror in our department." He then fell ill with a fever, which he was unsure whether to blame on the air, the water, or the heat of the Ardèche; in any case, he soon found himself covered with red splotches. Sick or not, in a letter to the prefect he unctuously expressed pleasure at the harsh measures taken by the government: "Arbitrariness itself loses its name when confronted by the orgies and the criminal designs of the demagogues." A prefectorial wall poster underlining the illegality of wearing the color red (Arnaud's red splotches did not count)—identified with the Montagnards—gave Arnaud the chance to report to the prefect more conversations, including one *rouge* who boasted, "As for me, I will wear my red robe to have this kid [*chevreau*, also the name of the prefect] hobbled."[57]

Yet though he took care to grow a Montagnard beard, Arnaud was increasingly assumed to be a police spy. In mid-September, Montagnards informed him that the *commissaire de police*—whom Arnaud believed was jealous of him—had identified him as "an agent of the government [*pouvoir*]," and he had to talk his way out again. For one thing, as he pointed out himself, he may have attracted attention because a wine merchant—his purported profession—did not usually stay in one place for such a long time. How would he deal with the leading *démagogues* who suspected him, besides conspicuously reading *La Feuille du village*, which had been banned by decree? He would really put on a show: "Let me as well fear the *mouchards*! … From that time on, I will crush with my republican pride those who raise doubts…It is something like an actor's role that I am developing, with an aplomb and an accent of conviction that will persuade them!"After such bravado, Arnaud's moment came in the Café Meyssac (where he apparently limited himself to drinking *sirop* with water) when a well-dressed man with two other Montagnards in tow entered, announcing, "I have come because I was told that there is a *mouchard* here. I would be very happy to see his face." To which Arnaud claimed to have replied, "In Paris we are accustomed to see thieves be the first to shout 'Stop thief!' Everyone knows this and the insolent fellow lets his head fall and remains silent."[58]

As for the *mouchard* sent to the arrondissement of Tournon, his reports "tell us nothing new, and only say what I myself, have alaready said to the agent." Local authorities already suspected the various mutual aid societies among the glove-workers of Annonay of helping to mobilize Montagnards, whom he counted at about five to six hundred. His embellished reports on his relations with local Montagnards in order to make him look good.[59]

The rare and sometimes fascinating letters from the Ardèche's three *mouchards* do not help us resolve one interesting problem, that of accent and, for that matter, language. It was difficult enough finding some degree of acceptance—at least for a time—as a Montagnard. In the Ardèche, a strong Languedocien accent was prevalent among the upper classes in the Bas-Vivarais, and patois almost universally spoken among ordinary people, particularly in the countryside. In the mountains of the Ardèche toward the Haute-Loire, another accent and another (Auvergnat) patois could be heard, while the accent of the arrondissement of Tournon was somewhat different still.[60] At a minimum, the *mouchards'* urban references (Arnaud's quote about thieves in Paris, for example) attracted no small degree of suspicion that even claims of holding positions as commercial travelers could not allay. In short, to repeat, we need to know more about language.

The Ardèche was certainly not alone in being awash with rumors and fear in late 1851. By March of that year, the Gers "has been taken over by fear of the reds: this fear leads to the most childish alarms, people constantly believing they are on the brink of the most serious trouble," amid discussion of a possible revision of the constitution to allow Louis Napoleon to stand for another term as president. At the time of the return of the National Assembly in November, rumors of a coup d'état were rampant in the Gers, contributing to a growing anxiety among people of means and fear that perhaps, as *l'Opinion* editorialized, "we need to resign ourselves to legality, as to the inflictions that God sends us," and that 1852 would be the year of Montagnard "revenge, expropriations, and pillage."[61] In Roussillon, the "men of order informed their apocalyptic vision of 1852 with symbols of a natural world in chaos."[62] Amid such panic, *Le Constitutionnel* publicly called into question the need for new elections. "Legality" would require elections in 1852 "in the face of terrifying organization of all the forces of socialism." On 27 August it suggested that any solution which crushed the left would be preferable to "the dangers of that sort of legality." Auguste Romieu in *Le Spectre rouge de 1852* proposed such a solution:

> the social order has as its sole and real support, not your ridiculous collection of law codes, but the strong ramparts where authority remains with its flag, ramparts alive with

strong hearts, bristling with bayonets and artillery … Do not despair. Blood and tears will flow … As for the soldiers' leader, his task is simple. He must resolutely make himself a total dictator.[63]

Writing eighteen years after the coup d'état, Eugène Ténot's two books on the resistance to the coup—written to rehabilitate the insurgents pictured by official Bonapartist accounts and propaganda as blood-thirsty monsters—recalled both the pervasive fear of "1852" and mounting rumors reaching into other European states that a coup d'état was imminent:"At the moment when the National Assembly was about to resume its labors, there was no noise but that about the Coup d'État, which had failed to occur during the prorogation. The newspapers entertained their readers with it; in political circles it was the subject of every conversation … The singularly violent language of the Napoleonic press against the Assembly and against the Constitution, at the same time as against the Republican party, was not of a nature to allay the general apprehensions."[64]

The coup d'état of December 2, of course, generated massive resistance in which well over 100,000 people took arms in France. The secret societies, as Margadant has clearly demonstrated, lay behind the widespread resistance to the coup in the Midi. The secret societies of the Bas Vivarais, based in perhaps as many as fifty communes, spearheaded the local insurrection in defense of the republic. The Montagnard secret societies in the Ardèche rose up to defend the republic, particularly but not exclusively from communes (notably Salavas and Chomerac) where there were many Protestant families for whom the history of the wars of religion remained alive.[65] A column of several thousand Montagnards from the canton of Vallon marched on Largentière, their numbers drawn from Lablachère, Lagorce, Balazuc, and other beautiful but impoverished villages. In the darkness before dawn on the morning of 7 December, they turned back in panic when confronting a small armed infantry regiment on the outskirts of the subprefecture.[66]

On the side of the Montagnards, early rumors of insurgent successes certainly encouraged continued resistance in the Bas Vivarais, as well as some other regions of the Midi.[67] Rumors in some places convinced people that armed defense of the "democratic and social republic" was sweeping the entire nation, or exaggerated the number and success of insurgents in neighboring departments, or in the same department. In one village in the Drôme, insurgents confidently told a local notary that "Crest, Valence, and Lyon were in the power of the insurgents." Likewise, a political fugitive in another village predicted that "before dawn [on the eighth] 50,000 people would reach Loriol from the departments of the Drôme and the Ardèche."[68]

However, the most salient legacy of the role of rumors during and after the insurrection was to provide an official interpretation of the coup d'état as having been necessary to save France from social armageddon in 1852. The aggressive rhetoric of the Montagnards certainly played a part in the propagation of rumors about the threat they posed to social order. Corbin cites an example from the Haute-Vienne, where an insurgent in Saint-Auvent "proposed to re-establish the guillotine for the rich and the government officials: they would catch the 'whites';

once again the movement would take the form of a *fête* in the course of which they would command that food and drink brought to them."[69] For administrators and the upper classes, armed resistance, leading to the death of several gendarmes in Bédarieux, were taken to demonstrate what would have been in store for France's social and political elite had not Louis Napoleon Bonaparte intervened. Baroche, giving a speech as the results of the (first) plebiscite were announced to Louis Napoleon on 31 December, summarized the Bonapartist canon shaped by officially orchestrated rumors: "Let France be at last delivered from those men always ready for murder and pillage; from those men who, in the nineteenth century, bring horror into civilization, and seem, while awakening the saddest remembrances, to carry us back five hundred years into the past."[70]

We return to the Ardèche to conclude. In the period following the coup d'état, officials assessing the political situation in the Ardèche blamed rumors and "false news" for the mobilization in the countryside of early December 1851. The prefect claimed that Ardèchois peasants had been "misled" as to the goals of the government before the coup. "Poorly enlightened, in addition, and having no easy and habitual communication with the centers of population from where real news originals…they let themselves be led into the most glaring error. The false news propagated by the leaders of the secret societies, with the help of the taverns and the bad press, has misled the ignorant, made them believe in the infallability of [their] success, and led them into an armed uprising."[71] All of this was quite ironic, in that rumor had itself been a weapon of the government in the Ardèche, as other departments.

In August 1852, the prefect decided to grant freedom to a *démoc-soc* implicated in the resistance to the coup—under the supervision of a priest from his mountain village—in exchange for information that would lead to the arrest of several Montagnards. The one-time *démoc-soc* had attracted the prefect's attention by informing him that several of those implicated in the resistance were still in the uplands of the Ardèche, preparing and distributing gunpowder in preparation for a new insurrection that had been commanded in Paris, and that was to occur by the end of August. The soldiers of this insurrection would be drawn among peasants, especially Protestants. An amnesty for some insurgents anticipated for August 15, "the rumor of which has been spread," was to swell the ranks of the insurgents: "Should it occur, the secret societies will make one final attempt."[72] A friend of the newly proclaimed Second Empire, the schoolteacher of St. Just, wrote "In my village, I combat these rumors, with all my strength, but my duties as teacher leave me with little time to chat and scarely permit me to work against them in the café, I am powerless against them."[73]

A certain irony—however unintended—may be found in the teacher's complaints that rumors were circulating in the Ardèche that were hostile to Napoleon III. During the Second Republic, the government of Louis Napoleon Bonaparte had benefitted more than their Montagnard opponents from rumor. Building on elite fears of growing Montagnard influence, particularly but not exclusively in regions where secret societies had proliferated, the Bonapartists had manipulated and encouraged rumor to their advantage, preparing the way for the coup d'état.

Notes

1. The author is Charles A. Seymour Professor of History at Yale University. He would like to thank Carol Merriman, Elinor Accampo, Susan P. Connor, Paul Hanson, Carole Lacherey, and Heinz-Gerhard Haupt for comments on earlier versions of the paper, one of which was presented at the Kolloquium, Europa in den Revolutionen von 1848, Academie Frankenwarte, Würzburg, Germany, October 1996, and a shorter version at the Consortium on Revolutionary Europe, Baton Rouge, Louisiana, February 1997.

2. See, for example, his "La Monteé à Paris," in *Paris and its Provinces 1792-1802* (London, 1975), 26-27.

3. Georges Lefebvre, *The Great Fear of 1789: Rural Panic in Revolutionary France* trans. Joan White (New York, 1973); Bronislaw Baczko, *Ending the Terror: the French Revolution after Robespierre*, trans. Michel Petheram (Cambridge, 1994); Richard Cobb, *The Police and the People: French Popular Protest, 1789-1820* (Oxford, 1970). See also Arlette Farge and Jacques Revel, *The Vanishing Children: Rumor and Politics before the French Revolution* (Cambridge MA, 1991), 95, who underline the fact that "rumour was an intrinsic part of the city's life"; Arlette Farge, *Subversive Words: Public Opinion in Eighteenth-Century France*, trans. Rosemary Morris (University Park, PA, 1995); Daniel Roche, *The People of Paris: an Essay in Popular Culture in the Eighteenth Century*, trans. Marie Evans (Berkeley, 1987); and Paul Hanson "Rumor and its Resonance in the French Revolution," paper presented at the Consortium on Revolutionary Europe, Baton Rouge, Louisiana, February 1997.

4. John M. Merriman, "The Norman Fires of 1830: Incendiaries and Fear in Rural France," *French Historical Studies* 9 (1976): 451-66.

5. Alain Corbin, *Le village des cannibales* (Paris, 1990). In fact, such incidents seem to have been extremely rare. For another, see Peter McPhee, "Un meurtre dans le Sud de la France en 1830: violence, mémoire et tradition démocratique," *Bulletin du Centre d'histoire contemporaine du Languedoc Méditerranéen* 56 (June 1995): 3-30.

6. On atrocities believed to have been perpetrated by German troops and the reaction of the French population, see Ruth Harris, "The 'Child of the Barbarians': Rape, Race and Nationalism in France during the First World War," *Past and Present* 141 (November, 1993): 170-206.

7. Edgar Morin, *The Rumor of Orléans*, trans. Peter Green (New York, 1971); Edith Thomas, *The Women Incendiaries*, trans. James and Starr Atkinson (New York, 1966)

8. See Robert Darnton, *The Literary Underground of the Old Regime* (New York, 1985).

9. *Webster's Third New International Dictionary* (1986). Baczko writes that a "false rumour is a real social fact," and "the more a public rumour is false, implausible and fantastic, the more its history promises to be rich in lessons," and that one can use the study of rumor to learn of the "conditions that make its emergence and circulation possible, about the state of mind, the mentalités and the imagination of those who accepted it as true." Baczko, *Ending the Terror*, 3. Thanks to Susan Connor for alerting me to these particular quotes.

10. Richard Cobb, *The Police and the People*, 322, writes of World War II: "Then also rumour found ready credence even in the highest places: the B.B.C. informed its listeners in 1944, a few months before the invasion that French children in the Nord had been so reduced by famine that, if they had the slightest fall, they broke a limb."

11. Ted W. Margadant, *French Peasants in Revolt: The Insurrection of 1851* Princeton, 1979); Peter McPhee, *Les Semailles de la République dans les Pyrénées-Orientales 1846-1852* (Perpignan, 1995). See McPhee's criticism of the "trickle-down" studies of Agulhon, Margadant, and this author in McPhee, *The Politics of Rural Life: Political Mobilization in the French Countryside 1846-1852* (Oxford, 1992). See also Alain Corbin, *Archaïsme et modernité en Limousin au XIXe siècle, 1845-1880*, 2 vols. (Paris, 1975).

12. J. Dagnan, *Le Gers sous la Second République*, 2 vols. (Auch, 1928-39), 509. Yet, use of the telegraph could also propagate rumors, which reached Paris from provincial officials with great speed.

13. See Maurice Agulhon, *La République au village* (Paris, 1970) [English-language edition, *The Republic in the Village*, trans. Janet Lloyd (Cambridge, 1982)]. For dissenting views, see Eugen Weber's

entertaining but impressionistic *Peasants into Frenchmen: The Modernization of Rural France, 1870-1914*, (Stanford, 1977) and Peter Jones, *Politics and Rural Society: The Southern Massif Central c. 1750-1880* (Cambridge, 1985). For a nuanced look at Montagnard ideology, see Edward Berenson, *Popular Religion and Left-Wing Politics in France, 1830-1852* (Princeton, 1984).

14. McPhee, *The Politics of Rural Life*, 223.

15. André-Jean Tudesq, *Les grands notables en France*, 2 vols. (Paris, 1964), still a classic study. A rumors circulating in June had British guns being unloaded on the coast of the Vendeé (A.N. BB30 364).

16. McPhee, *Politics*, 128, citing Roger Price, *The French Second Republic: A Social History* (London, 1972), 126.

17. ADA 5M 10, Subprefect of Tournon, 29 January 1850; Elie Reynier, *La Seconde République dans l'Ardèche (1848-1852)*(Privas, 1948), 89.

18. ADA 5M 10, Subprefect of Tournon,19 September 1850.

19. Margadant, *French Peasants in Revolt*, especially chapter 6; Merriman, *Agony of the Republic*, chapters 2-7.

20. ADA 5M 10, circular of the Minister of the Interior (J. Baroche) to prefects, 6 April 1850. Two months later, he wrote prefects that "I am assured that the greater part of the former clubbists and the leaders of the revolutionary party are seeking to spark a movement on the occasion of the completion of the new electoral register." Soldiers for this insurrection would be drawn from men who had lost the right to vote by the law of 31 May 1850. This in itself was a frightening thought, because the law had eliminated voters who had not resided in one place for a specific period of time, thus raising the spectre of a revolt by those perceived as *marginaux*. The minister called yet again on his prefects to observe the comings and goings of suspected Montagnards and to report the various rumors circulating in the provinces (Ministry of the Interior circular, 29 June 1850)

21. Reynier, *La Seconde République*, 103-4.

22. ADA 5M 10, letter and police report of 17 September 1850. Furthermore, a search of a workshop whose workman had also been denounced by a secret police agent for allegedly having made knives for a noted Montagnard turned up but two knives ordered from a cutler.

23. Writing of Bourg St. Andéol and its region, Arnaud wrote, "The men of this region are all big and hardy, with mustaches and beards that strike terror." (5M 10 Arnaud, 18 September 1851).

24. ADA 5M 10, n.d.

25. ADA 5M 10.

26. ADA 5M 10, police spy, 18 and 19 August 1850.

27. Reynier, *La Second République*, 88-89.

28. ADA 5M 10, Lt. Gend. Largentière, 23 February 1850.

29. ADA 5M 10, undated report of police spy from September 1850.

30. ADA 5M 10, Captain Gend., 29 November 1850.

31. ADA 5M 10, Gendarmerie report, 19 June 1850 and *procès-verbal*.

32. ADA 5M 10, police report of September 1850.

33. Philippe Vigier,*La Second République dans la région alpine* 2 vols. (Paris, 1963), 280-86. "the insurrectional parties here are more ready to act than at any time since the revolution of February."

34. Vigier, p. 287; McPhee, *The Politics of Rural Life*, 207.

35. Dagnan, *Le Gers*, 430.

36. ADA 5M 10, subprefect of Largentière, 28 November, 1850.

37. ADA 5M 10, subprefect of Largentière, 27 November 1850.

38. ADA 5M 10, n.d.

39. Margadant, *French Peasants in Revolt*, 208, citing reports in ADA 10M 13.

40. ADA 5M 10, 16 September 1850.

41. Margadant, *French Peasants in Revolt*, 208, citing reports in ADA 5M 13.

42. Ibid., 210.

43. A.N. BB30 394, 10 September 1851.

44. ADA 5M 10, Arnaud, letter of 11 September 1851. Arnaud apparently knew the prefect, asking that letters to him be sent by the brother of the *fonctionnaire*, whom he apparently also knew.

45. See n. 2.

46. ADA 5M 10, Subprefect of Largentière, 29 September 1851.

47. ADA, 5M 10, Subprefect of Largentière, 3 October 1851. Some of the news reported the prefect of the Ardèche might not have wanted to hear, as when the *mouchard* working the arrondissement of Tournon compared the prefect's reputation in Annonay with that of Privas: in the latter, Montagnards joked about the prefect's name, while in Annonay, "they regard you as a very adroit scoundrel, very fine, a swine who respects nothing and to whom all means are good" (report of 2-7 October 1851).

48. ADA 5M 10, gendarmerie report, 13-14 October and Subprefect, 14 October, 1851.

49. ADA 5M 10, Subprefect, 18 October 1851.

50. ADA 5M 10, summary report for October.

51. ADA 5M 10, Arnaud, 16 September 1851.

52. ADA 5M 10, Vigier, 28 October and Subprefect, 28 November 1851.

53. The *mouchard* working the arrondissement of Tournon reflected such prejudices, as well." Annonay "was a city of workers, and, thus of rioters." In contrast, Arnaud revealed more grudging respect for those upon whom he was spying, at least those of Bourg St. Andéol: "Real men live in Bourg St. Andéol! They are calm, reflective, democratic, but with a fire that smolders under the ashes. Here, I see nothing but ignorant prattlers, pretentious orators of the countryside and the taverns: in Bourg, there are workers, who are kept busy and do not waste their energy in a weekly drinking bout, they even go to bed at an early hour," reading newspapers and anticipating 1852—"They stroll, they play *boules*." 5M 10, Arnaud, 20 September 1851; Tournon police spy, 2-7 October 1851

54. ADA 5M 10, gendarmerie lieutenant of Aubenas, 31 October and Subprefect of Largentière, 14 November 1851. The *mouchard* in the arrondissement of Tournon had consulted with the mayor of Annonay.

55. ADA, 5M 10, report, n.d., [October] 1851.

56. Thanks to Elinor Accampo for pointing out this connection to me. See Lynn Hunt, ed., *The French Revolution and Human Rights: A Documentary History* (New York, 1995), 90.

57. ADA 5M 10, Arnaud, letters of 9, 15, 16, and 17 September 1851.

58. A.D.A. 5M 10, Arnaud, 16, 19, 23, and 24 September 1851. Yet, 21 September he claimed that a *rouge* had told him that the *commissiare de police* [presumably of Privas] had identified him as an agent of the Montagnards. In any case, the *commissaire de police* gave him twenty-four hours to leave the Ardèche, but was apparently convinced that he could not be sent away if he had a fever.

59. ADA 5M 10, Subprefect of Tournon, 13 October 1851.

60. The *mouchard* working the arrondissement of Tournon had been a café owner in Avignon, though where he came from originally, we cannot say. His accent would have been somewhat similar to that of Ardèchois, but not quite the same and he did not speak the same patois, though might have understood some of it, if he was indeed originally from the Vaucluse, where a Provençal-based patois was spoken among ordinary people.

61. Dagnan, *Le Gers*, 608-9.

62. McPhee, *Politics*, 223.

63. Ibid., 224.

64. Eugène Ténot, *Paris in December, 1851, or, The Coup d'État of Napoleon III* (Paris, 1870), translation of *Paris en décembre 1851: Étude historique sur le coup d'état* (Paris, 1868), 42-47. See also his *La province en décembre* (Paris, 1869).

65. Margadant, *French Peasants*, 139-142.

66. Ibid., 295.

67. Ibid., 256. In Paris, too, false rumors momentarily increased popular defiance. As resistance spread on the central right bank, "rumors of bad news from Louis Napoleon—mostly false—were received with avidity" (Ténot, *Paris*, 169-170, 180-181, 185, giving many examples). The army diffused false rumors to justify the massacre of civilians following incidents in which shots were allegedly fired from houses, for example on the boulevards Montmartre and Bonne-Nouvelle. To Ténot, "The impression produced in Paris by this fatal event was immense, beyond all that may be

imagined. The news spread rapidly, augmented by popular rumor. The unspeakable fright of those who escaped was transmitted to the masses, and it congealed them … The revolutionary movement, which was initiated in the first half of the 4th day of December with so much power that it seemed as if it was to carry the entire city with it, was therefore broken" (Ténot, *Paris*, 225, 236-37).

68. For Margadant, "These inaccurate and exaggerated accounts of insurgency were a natural concomitant of the oral communications networks through which villagers exchanged information with townspeople. By democratizing their leadership to include semiliterate and illiterate peasants, and by renouncing written means of communication within the underground, Montagnard organizers had encouraged the circulation of unconfirmed rumors in the countryside … Many branch leaders were themselves unaccustomed to verifying political information in the newspapers. Instead of dominating the flow of news by virtue of their superior literacy, militants often shared with everyone else a penchant for numerical exaggeration, emotionalism, and wishful thinking. Bourgeois Republicans in the towns might await precise, written news from Paris before deciding whether to support a *prise des armes*, but artisans and peasants in the bourgs and villages often responded with enthusiasm to oral messages heralding a general uprising" (*French Peasants*, 256-57). One might well quarrel, as would Peter McPhee, with this characterization of rural people as depending on instruction from slick urban bourgeois republicans, but the role of rumor in swelling the ranks of insurgents remains worthy of note.

69. Corbin, *Archaïsme*, Vol. 2, 835. Thus, Morny addressed his prefects on 10 December, the anniversary of Louis Napoleon's election as president; "You have just experienced in 1851 the social war which was to have broken out in 1852. You will have recognized it by its typical features of murder, brigandage, and incendiarism" (Margadant, *French Peasants*, 312, citing Adrien Dansette, *Louis Napoléon à la conquête du pouvoir* (Paris, 1961), 366).

70. Ténot, *Paris*, 247-248.

71. A.N., F1c III Ardèche 7, Prefect of the Ardèche, 14 July 1852.

72. A.N. F1c III Ardèche 7, Prefect, 4 August 1852.

73. A.N. F1c III Ardèche 7, Boiron, *instituteur* of St. Just, 1 February 1853, writing to the prefect. Four years later, on 7 July 1857, the prefect reported of rumors based in Aubenas, the center of "perverse men, incorrigible spirits," waiting for the right time to stir up trouble again. Fearing of the effects of these rumors on the countryside, he ordered the arrest of two "propagators of false news."

Part V

CONSEQUENCES OF THE REVOLUTION OF 1848

Manifest

der

Kommunistischen Partei.

Veröffentlicht im Februar 1848.

Proletarier aller Länder vereinigt euch.

London.

Gedruckt in der Office der „Bildungs-Gesellschaft für Arbeiter"
von J. E. Burghard.
46, LIVERPOOL STREET. BISHOPSGATE.

Manifesto of the Communist Party. Published in February 1848.
Title page of the first (23 page) edition

Chapter 37

ON THE TRADITION OF 1848 IN SOCIALISM

Beatrix Bouvier

The events of 1989/90 in central and eastern Europe refuted all those analyses that regarded revolutions or fundamental transformations in contemporary Europe as unimaginable.[1] Whether or not the view that these far-reaching changes should be characterized as revolutions, as is widely held, has not yet been confirmed and depends both on later historiographical analysis of the still incomplete process of transformation, and how revolution is ultimately to be defined. The common use of the term and academic definitions are based to a great extent on the so-called "classic" revolutions in Europe, to which those of 1848 belong.

As memories of historical revolution depend on the context in which one lives, those of 1989/90 and a look back to those of 1848 are similarly influenced by their central demands of liberty and the achievements of a liberal, bourgeois, western-style democracy. These demands expressed a wish to be connected to a united Europe whose process of formation is in part determined by historically developed values. And thus one cannot forget that the events of 1848 themselves were of a European dimension. This dimension existed relatively early on in the consciousness of all the different varieties of socialists, even when they, in part, were tied to other connotations than today's idea of Europe.

The anniversary of the revolution is being celebrated in a reunited Germany, a state that, in many respects, corresponds to what more than a few of the 1848 revolutionaries aimed for: a united parliamentary republic, democratically and socially structured. If one looks back for milestones in past revolution anniversaries or commemorations, it becomes clear that the path leading through the nineteenth and twentieth centuries from the 1848 revolution to today's conditions was everything but direct.

Notes for this section begin on page 914.

Especially as memories of 1848—like those of other revolutions—were defined by the time in which they arose, *a* tradition of 1848 does not exist. Equally, there was or is no one European socialism, even ignoring for a moment the split between the traditions of freedom and democracy on the one hand, and authoritarianism on the other. The various lines of development were already becoming clear during the revolution of 1848. Socialists and the corresponding parties (also to be understood as a movement, in line with the concept of "party" of the early nineteenth century) saw 1848 as a European event; a consequence, among other things, of the simultaneous revolutions occurring in numerous European countries, albeit with nationally specific features. General agreement existed among contemporaries and later analysts that there were centers of the revolution and a peripheral region.

In the center of revolutionary events stood, Berlin, but above all Paris, among other places, that lit the spark with its February revolution and that sounded the bell for the end of the revolution—not only in France—with the defeat of the July uprising. The "June days" in particular were significant, in the eyes of socialists, and they were certainly not seen as an isolated event of the French Revolution of 1848.

Revolutions, uprisings, and rebellions had occurred earlier, not least in France, and would occur later, if one includes the uprising of the Paris Commune of 1871—imperative for a socialist understanding of revolution and tradition. Socialists, socialist movements, and currents also existed before 1848. The development of the terms "revolution" and "socialism" or "socialist" begin to be defined over the course of the "great" French Revolution and continued to be influenced by economic and social upheavals in western Europe at the beginning of the nineteenth century.[2] Before 1848, the meaning of the term "revolution" remained ambiguous and approached that of the "great crisis." Equally early on, the counter-term "evolution" split off, which, in the political sense, had the same meaning as "gradual reform." Adjectives tied to the term "revolution" or various aspects of revolution were thus considerably differentiated, so that "political revolution" was restricted to the violent overthrow of a state structure, while "social revolution" related to society, understood as distinct from the state. Society, for its part, was differentiated according to class criteria, so that a distinction could be made between the terms "bourgeois" and "proletarian" revolutions.

Marx and Engels only extended inherited semantics, without themselves developing a stringent theory of revolution. Surprisingly, the term "bourgeois revolution" does not appear in their works to the extent that one could expect. It characterized above all a sequence of revolutions by the bourgeoisie within European history. The "proletarian revolution" was to be their direct successor. This was initially expected in England, where the industrial revolution was most advanced. However, on the eve of the revolution of 1848, these expectations shifted to Germany, as, according to the *Communist Manifesto*, Germany stood on the eve of a bourgeois revolution and conditions in Germany were such that this could only be an overture to a proletarian revolution.[3]

This diagnosis, or perhaps better, this assumption, was shared by other socialists, such as Moses Heß for example, or, somewhat more cautiously Stephan Born, who wrote in the spring of 1848 that the revolution was not a social one, but rather completely of political nature, and could not be anything else as the conditions for a "social transformation" did not yet exist.[4] The actual course of the revolution of 1848/49 reinforced this interpretation. Consequently, the "proletarian revolution" remained a term of expectation for Marx as well, into which the experiences of the following decades were added. It is not the aim of this paper to develop Marx's and Engels's conceptual universe, but to recall their influence on ideas and theories about the German and European workers' movement that was organizing in the nineteenth century.

The term "socialism" refers back to the period before the revolution. While in England and France it was formed as a modern conception of socialism in the wake of the rise of independent social theories and movements, in Germany it was mainly taken over from the western European discussion. Those called socialists were, at the beginning, only supporters of English and French social theory, and socialism was the content of these systems. At the beginning of the 1840s, "socialism" in Germany was a collective noun for radical social reforms and their supporters. In the reception of the western European discussion of socialism in Germany, Lorenz Stein played a decisive role. With his epochal work of 1842 on *Socialism and Communism in Today's France* he provided a new basis for discussion in Germany, so that, with him, a scholarly discussion of socialism began in Germany. His view of socialism as an organized body of knowledge [*Wissenschaft*] stimulated discussion in Germany until 1848.

Interest in the topic was increased by the appearance of the first social critics who presented themselves as socialists. For them, Stein's book was a sort of key experience, notably for Moses Heß and Karl Grün, whose ideas "scientific [or scholarly] socialism," were derided by Marx and Engels as "true" socialism. In the *Communist Manifesto* of 1848 the term "true socialism" was so established that it remained in use as a designation in the Marxist tradition until the end of the twentieth century. A short time later, Marx and Engels also distanced themselves from the early French and English socialists. Admittedly, this did not mean that they denied their ideas the character of an organized body of knowledge. They sought rather to make a distinction in the claim of having achieved an especially scientific (or scholarly) quality with the "materialist-critical" form.

With the outbreak of the revolution of 1848, the discussion concerning socialism, up to then rather theoretical, especially in Germany, found an echo in practical politics. Socialism became a catchword in day-to-day politics, taken up by various sides. At the same time, the terms "democracy" and "socialism" became permanently connected.[5] At the beginning this was a method of social reform policy; a prime example being the Badenese radical democrat Friedrich Hecker, who, even before the outbreak of the revolution, spoke in the parliament of Baden about socialism as the idea of a social welfare state. At the Heidelberg meeting of the "fifty-one friends of the fatherland" on 5 March 1848 he described himself as one of the first "social-democrats."

The difficulties entailed in transforming a social-reformist concept of socialism into a specific program for the democratic movement could be seen in the two national democratic congresses. Even the most cautious phrasing, for example that of the Cologne labor leader Andreas Gottschalk, was controversial. Only the delegates of the workers' associations seemingly saw in it the principle of a democratic and social republic. Stephan Born's proposal for an alliance between the "democratic parties" and the Berlin Workers' Congress was rejected at the second democratic congress in October 1848. Many bourgeois democrats seemingly feared that they would be encouraging a social evolution through an alliance with the workers' associations.

The catchword "social democracy" shifted in the course of the revolution to the labor movement, especially to Stephan Born's *Arbeiterverbrüderung* [Workers' Fraternization]. Members of the group saw themselves as "social-democratic" to distinguish the democratic labor movement from bourgeois democracy. Karl Marx, however, saw in it only an ideology of "republican petty-bourgeois," "who now call themselves red and social-democratic because they cherish the pious wish of abolishing the pressure of big capital on small capital, the big bourgeois on the petty bourgeois."[6] They lacked, however, a revolutionary class consciousness. As, however, the workers and their movement claimed "democracy" and "socialism" for themselves in the revolutionary period, it is reasonable to assume that this association was an expression of their desire for emancipation and of their—quite diverse—conceptions.

When the (German) labor movement began to get organized at the beginning of the 1860s, its members drew on their experiences in the revolutionary period of 1848/49 both personally and ideologically, without this being simply a resumption of old traditions. It was more the revolution of 1789 that continued to influence the thinking and conceptions of socialists of all currents. It determined assumptions on the course of revolutionary processes as well as those on the rise and character of a modern state. It became the paradigm of revolution per se, and the idea that the historic constellation of 1789 and the following years would repeat themselves at the next stage of social development was part of fundamental assumption that was long influential. For all its constantly reiterated "scientific" reinforcement, this basic assumption remained, pre-scientific in nature.

This assumption marked the writings of Marx and Engels on revolution. This was true of their writings from the revolution itself, for example the series of articles in the *Neue Rheinische Zeitung*, such as "The Bourgeoisie and the Counterrevolution," as well as those written directly after the revolution, such as *Class Struggles in France, 1848 to 1850*, or *The Eighteenth Brumaire of Louis Bonaparte*, in which the function of the revolution of 1789 as a gauge for revolutionary development is especially obvious. The "great" revolution had completed its task, against which the epoch from 1848 to 1850 was nothing more than a parody. The new, the hoped for, the predicted revolution of the nineteenth century, the social or proletarian revolution, was not to draw "its poetry" from the past, but was nonetheless compared to it.[7] This view, together with the writings on revolution, became the core of a store of quotations in the nineteenth century labor movement, kept alive for decades as part of the preservation of tradition and recharged with differing degrees of contemporary relevance. In the twentieth century, this form of preservation of tradition has been taken on and continued above all by the communist wing of the labor movement.[8]

Nonetheless, the revolution of 1848 was a turning-point, especially with the impulses coming from the French Revolution which developed the idea of the revolution as an expression of a class struggle. In spite of numerous differentiations, this early view was preserved up to the end of "real existing" socialism, as can be seen from this balance sheet on 1848, published in 1990:

> The European revolution is held to be the first revolution in history in which the proletariat as a class more or less consciously, that is above all with a variety of its own demands, intervened … Nonetheless, the identification of an intervention by the proletariat in the bourgeois revolution of 1848/49 requires more precise definition. Active proletarian involvement was known only in two European countries: France and Germany, where—to varying degrees—modern capitalist conditions had already developed. On the rest of the continent, the third estate had certainly not broken apart, as the proletariat existed only sporadically, and, as a consequence of the massive predominance of agriculture and the still unanswered agrarian question, the peasantry was still the main army to fight the battles of the bourgeois revolution. The most developed capitalistic country, England, where a mass industrial proletariat was active and had formed itself as a political force in Chartism, remained, for various reasons, exempted from the waves of revolution.[9]

The prominence of "workers," and of socialist and communist groups or "parties," as well as the temporary participation of "workers" in the French government, had fed the hopes of a further development of the revolution, its transformation into the "social revolution" which, according to the assumed cycle of revolutions, should follow the bourgeois-democratic revolution. With and after the suppression of the Paris June uprising this assumption shifted to a hope in the future. For decades it continued to be renourished.

This understanding of the participation of the "proletariat" or the "workers" in the revolution of 1848 is, as a rule, independent of the sociostructural conditions of the time. It was and furthermore is, as a rule, an understanding based on developments in metropolitan centers as Paris, Berlin or Vienna. Moreover, it overlooks the possibility that a number of revolutions took place parallel to one another in 1848. Even the Parisian workers, whom a contemporary such as Karl Marx almost always described as the "proletariat," were only to a very limited extent factory workers. Predominantly were still self-confident, artisanally trained workers and craftsmen in small- and medium-sized workshops.[10] Their general aspiration to their own, independent business or workshop was threatened by numerous new developments, as the prosperity of the July Monarchy benefited mostly large firms. A fall in real wages was periodically accompanied by under-employment, which in times of crisis became mass unemployment. In the perception of contemporaries, the various factors were interwoven into a whole. At the same time, the French capital, with its dense social and economic structure, provided good soil for a radical social movement, as could be observed in the period between 1789 and 1871.

The social dynamite contained in this mixture was certainly not limited to Paris or France, but was also true of other European countries, or their capitals, such as Berlin. In the economic crisis of 1846/47 which followed a boom, old crisis phenomena overlapped with the new economic cycle. The direct effects of the crisis, with its various causes, were divergent in the different countries and cities. It would, however, be safe to say that it was neither the undeniable poverty of broad sections of the population nor hunger riots nor an uprising of impoverished masses that led to the events in Paris and Berlin in February and March 1848. Significant for both was the criticism of a broad bourgeois public sphere. Nonetheless, participation by the lower classes in the revolutionary events should not be underestimated.[11]

While socioeconomic conditions were similar in the above-mentioned major cities, the political and social attitudes of the "lower social strata" are still less comparable, even when contemporary demands such as those for producers' cooperatives and national workshops would suggest this and point to the conceptions of the modern labor movement.[12] However, the differences were great, and they in turn point to later conflicts between the labor movements in France and Germany, which in part arose from distinct political traditions. These include, for example, the abolition of the monarchy and establishment of a republic, not as a political goal anchored in the broad popular masses in Berlin (and Vienna) but rather, a turn to the republic as ideal form of government. In Paris, neither the "great" revolution nor the first republic had been forgotten. They were, one might say, easily available as demands of the lower classes, because Louis Philippe's increasing loss of legitimacy was accompanied by a discrediting of the monarchical form of government.

On top of this came differences in conceptions of revolution. While a large part of all classes in Berlin, basing themselves on the tradition of the Prussian reform movement, looked toward a "revolution from the top down," "the idea among the Paris lower classes of a revolution from the bottom up, supported by the broad popular masses [was] self-evident."[13] Just as the tradition of the Prussian reform movement and the wars of liberation in the late nineteenth century belonged to an understanding of tradition of the German labor movement, equally the different concepts of revolution continued to have an effect, as for example in the debate between August Bebel and Jean Jaurès at the Amsterdam Congress of the Second International.

The defeat of the revolution of 1848 could above all encourage the tendency to see in a revolution "from the bottom up" something that was doomed to failure and to continue to look for one from above. This continued view "from the top down" was admittedly more characteristic of the bourgeoisie and the middle classes than of the Berlin lower classes; in the wake of the events of 1848, they lost hope in the understanding and ability to reform of the powers that be. Even during the revolution, they began to look for a "revolution from the bottom up," for the creation of a modern social welfare state, or the development of a socialist society.[14]

In France as well, the revolution ended in defeat, a result, however, that did not produce the same consequences, as the traditions and myths of the victorious "great" revolution were much too deeply rooted. This, too, an important distinction in the later labor movement, was in the background of the political struggle within the Second International. While for the one side the "success" continued to live and to be effective at least as myth, the members of the German labor movement saw defeats, including the defeat of the French June uprising and, later, the Paris Commune. "Doctrines" of revolutionary and political strategies were drawn from this view of defeat.

In the lower classes of Berlin—unlike in Paris—social discontent was, moreover, not related to the same goals. Early socialist theories were less widespread, and in view of *Vormärz* repression those organizations that fell under their influence, as for example German artisan communism, had originated abroad. The willingness to absorb new ideological concepts was, however, great and became apparent after the bans on the press, assembly, and association had been lifted following the March Revolution. Above all for the months between March and June 1848, a radical transformation in attitudes and modes of behavior has been established.[15] Demands no longer reflected the old guild ideals, and the rituals of industrial action also changed within a few months. While at the beginning they recalled earlier journeyman strikes, only a little time later they already had features of modern labor conflicts.

With the abolition of the prohibition on association, the Workers' Central Committee was set up in April, from which arose the Workers' Fraternization in the summer of 1848. In its structure and program, which was certainly not oriented on the guild tradition, it was one of the most important roots of the "modern" German labor movement. Concrete issues included the establishment of institutions that could negotiate collective bargaining agreements, the creation of a ministry of labor, the replacement of indirect taxes by a progressive income tax, free schooling and free public libraries, employment of the unemployed in state institutions, the establishment of model workshops by the state and the care of "all those who are helpless" and "invalids of labor," measures, that is, which, in today's Employment Promotion Act, are the responsibility of the state. Their demands certainly did not aim at a restoration of guild-like economic structures, but rather at the extension of freedom of occupation and the easing of trade restrictions. It was due to the Central Committee, and especially to Stephan Born as its most outstanding spokesman, that there were almost no attacks on machines, unlike in Vienna.[16]

If we look at the demands of the Parisian February Revolution, the Berlin parallels to a ministry of labor or employment and to the national workshops are evident. National workshops were demanded above all by groups of journeyman among whom the traditions of journeying about was still widespread and who were also champions of *Vormärz* artisan radicalism. Even when an orientation on the French model is obvious, the traditions of Prussian miners played a significant role.[17] Nonetheless, the effects of the February revolution in Paris were doubtless quite considerable.[18] Here it cannot be overlooked that a positive connotation by the Berlin lower classes of France as the mother country of revolution corresponded to a negative estimation among broad circles of the bourgeoisie. They were related to one another, and on both sides there grew an identification, among the proletariat and lower classes one with the French model. Once again one sees in the revolution of 1848t he seeds of modes of behavior that would remain valid over time and decades later become fully visible.

In addition to this arose processes of radicalization among the Berlin lower classes in 1848, who hoped in vain that not only bourgeois-liberal demands would be fulfilled, but also those for an improvement of their social condition. As, however, the pressure from the lower social strata in Paris was comparatively greater, social concessions in the February Revolution were correspondingly more extensive. Developments aligned relatively quickly, so that socialist ideas increasingly fell on fertile ground in German speaking regions. Nonetheless, considerable differences continued to exist; an uprising comparable to the "June days" in Paris did not take place in Berlin in the summer of 1848.

Independent of whether one sees the June insurrection as an attempt at a social revolution or only as a spontaneous reaction to the decision to close the national workshops, the strongly rooted socialist ideas and the relatively strict military organization of the national workshops point to another dimension than that of a purely spontaneous reaction. In Berlin, workers and journeymen gave precedence to the establishment of quasi-trade union organizations. While they were not exclusively intended to be social special interest groups, during the months of the revolution Stephan Born and other spokesmen of the Central Committee were very cautious about political action in order to not to endanger unnecessarily the recently established organization. This relatively rapid organizational development of the German labor movement was interrupted for a decade after the revolution, but restarted above all toward the end of the nineteenth century. Here, nothing corresponded to the French developments, and this difference, already visible during the revolution of 1848, contributed later to misunderstandings and conflicts between the representatives of the German and French labor movements.

This contrasts with the contemporary observation that developments and events conditioned one another, that they were mutually dependent. The impetus normally came from Paris. This is much more true for the "June days" than for the February Revolution, the June uprising finding an echo in the lower classes which led to the core of the social democratic tradition in Germany decades later. Included in this tradition was the idea that the "workers" did not fight on the streets of Paris for themselves and their French interests, but for all workers, that nothing separated them and that they had common interests. Another part of it was the idea that the gap between bourgeoisie on the one hand, and the workers, lower classes or proletariat, on the other, had widened since then. The gap was not exclusively due to this, but events of the revolution had contributed greatly to its becoming greater. That the structures of prejudice became established in the bourgeoisie did correspond, on the other hand, to the elements of a class consciousness and representation of their own interests that were formed during the revolutionary period.

Decisive was the defeat of the Paris June uprising. When fighting broke out, all critical comments in the publications of those groups to be included in a later labor movement were put aside in favor of unrestricted solidarity. It was a solidarity that they all supported. The self-evident solidarity with the vanquished, the defeated, was repeated a quarter of a century later in the context of the Paris Commune of 1871, the brutally suppressed uprising following the Franco-Prussian War, that contemporaries and later socialists saw as an attempt as a proletarian revolution. Once again it was the defeat, which, like that after the June insurrection of 1848, led to cross-border solidarity and contributed to the formation of a socialist tradition. Included here, admittedly, was a distancing, conditioned by the times, which—as shortly after June 1848—was expressed as "lessons" of the defeat. These "lessons" were of great significance for debates on strategies for the road to a socialist future, on reform and revolution, and were also important indicator for the rapidly forming national distinctiveness of the European labor movements.

The June uprising of 1848 led to discussions of common grounds and gaps between the bourgeoisie and the proletariat, which discussion in principle never ended. Simultaneously in the decades after the revolution, the idea of internationalism grew, and not only among the refugees of the wave of revolutions of 1848. This "modern" internationalism is a product of the events of 1848, not to be separated from, for example, the German and Italian movements for national unity. In the middle of the 1860s, the International Workingmen's Association (IWA) was established—the first attempt at European cooperation between labor organizations, which, according to the preamble of its charter, was based on the "consideration that the emancipation of the working class itself must be taken by force ..."[19]

Surprisingly quickly, a number of groups formed, which in their variety of goals, motivations, influences, and traditions reflected national and local conditions. Nonetheless, the IWA remained "a great soul in a weak body."[20] This specific form of internationalism failed in the 1870s after the Franco-Prussian War and the establishment of a German nation-state. The idea of a reconciliation of peoples in the spirit of international fraternity, with its roots in 1848, no longer had a chance. Nations and national parties had to find another form of international cooperation.

In view of nationalism and chauvinism during and after the Franco-Prussian War, the attitude of the recently established German labor movement to the war and to the Paris Commune was remarkable. Above all the defeat in the "bloody weeks of May" led—as in the June insurrection of 1848—to unrestricted solidarity with the communards. This international solidarity, "dangerous" in the eyes of the opponents of the labor movement, contributed greatly to the accusation—still effective in the twentieth century—that the social democrats were "traitors to the Fatherland." Nonetheless, German social democrats continued to support this international solidarity, as could be seen at first in 1848 and then in 1871. They expressed this solidarity with the "March days": a day of double remembrance of 18 March 1848 and 18 March 1871, which was considered very important for the German labor movement before the First World War and was only gradually replaced by May Day.

With the "March days," the German social democrats recalled the "revolutionary" events of 1848 and 1871, which by chance had taken place on the same day, the 18th of March. When the 18th of March began to be commemorated at the beginning of the 1870s, about one year after the end of the Paris Commune and a quarter of a century after the revolution of 1848, it was still under the influence of the defeat of 1871. In the course of the following decades direct ties with the events of 1871 weakened. Commemoration shifted to the revolution of 1848 and to a greater emphasis on national events. This transformation doubtless was related to the development of German social democracy and its dominating role within European socialism. Equally important was the formation and development of an understanding of history and tradition, which dated their origins to 1848 and increased the interpretation of further developments on this basis.

From this viewpoint, the separation of the labor movement and the bourgeoisie was inevitable; in addition, it was solely the labor movement that not only had accepted but also preserved the common inheritance of 1848, while the bourgeoisie had "betrayed" it. At the same time, the extent to which an understanding of revolution was transformed becomes clear in the development of the commemoration up to the First World War. The earlier revolutions, especially the French defeat of June 1848 and the Paris Commune of 1871, became to a great extent expressions of an obsolete barricade fighting. Such fighting was now seen as part of the past; what had previously been predecessors and models became a sort of photographic negative image of another, positive development, in which 1848 was the starting point of democratic socialism and social democracy in Germany.

Solidarity with the people, with the "fighters," who as vanquished could always count on the pity from the others remained unaffected. While this form of unconditional solidarity was originally also influenced by the idea that the June insurgents and communards had fought on behalf of the international proletariat, this idea retreated in the course of time, as it became mixed with a feeling of superiority, for non-Germans difficult to tolerate, which drew on German social democrats' own successes and led to the view that they could dispense with the once so important models and themselves become role-models for others.

This German understanding of history and tradition remained embedded in the discussion about revolutionary cycles and the meaning of the "bourgeois-democratic revolution" of 1848. With the Russian Revolutions of 1905 and 1917, such considerations gained new virulence through the question of a completion or further development of the "bourgeois-democratic revolution." After the final split of the labor movement during and after the First World War, a tradition comparable to the period before 1914, as had been established with the commemoration of 18 March, was no longer possible.[21]

In the early 1870s, the 18th of March was celebrated by both factions of the German labor movement, the Lassalleans and the "Eisenachers," initially separately and with different emphases. It was the Lassalleans who, in 1872, for the first time, used the double commemoration as an occasion to recall the two "revolutions"; the "Eisenachers," on the other hand, concentrated above all on the so-called "bloody weeks of March" of 1871 and on the communards as the champions of all proletarians. The first highpoint for the new revolutionary celebration was the twenty-fifth anniversary of the revolution of 1848. Weeks before, celebrations were announced in social democratic newspapers in which the feelings of liberty of 1848 and those who had fallen in the March Revolution were to be recalled. The commemoration of the Commune, in turn, was an expression and recognition of the struggle for liberty and equality as well as for socialism. As "principle," this was to be valued more highly than the Berlin March days, in which "the proletariat" only pulled the bourgeoisie's "constitutional chestnuts" out of the fire. Rather the fighters should be honored who believed that they were fighting for liberty and that this had been victorious.

Around 18 March 1873, there were events in numerous places in which speeches were given; the events often ended with tableaux vivants presenting the Communards' struggle. A central event of this revolutionary anniversary, which fell on a working day, was doubtless the demonstration march to the Friedrichshain in Berlin, in which over twenty thousand workers were said to have taken part. The "Marseillaise" was sung, and wreaths with red ribbons were placed on the graves. The police forced the removal of the ribbons, and in the course of the day there was rioting, in which two policemen were injured, numerous people were arrested, and a few of them later sentenced.

Demonstration marches or "promenades" on 18 March to the Friedrichshain became as established as the annual mass meeting, which was often banned because of its "glorification of violence." Harassment, increasing persecution, and the anxious behavior of the bourgeoisie during the *Kulturkampf*, strengthened the conviction of social democrats that they alone were the champions of liberty, because the bourgeoisie was ashamed of its "revolutionary youth." During the era of the Anti-Socialist Laws, the extent to which this specific form of international solidarity could be used as a weapon against the social democrats became clear, who in turned systematically exploited the 18th of March for propaganda.

The fiftieth anniversary of the 1848 revolution in 1898 was also almost exclusively a matter for the labor movement, which claimed a historically incontestable right to the German March Revolution. The proletariat had paid the "blood money of the March Revolution" and therefore celebrated the revolution "as the action with which its class struggle began."[22] During the fiftieth anniversary, the need for commemoration obscured the fact that the understanding of revolution had long-since been transformed. It is not surprising, however, that the Commune did not play a significant role; in the years before and after it received little mention. At the so-called March commemorations, specific historic events were often replaced by a general symbol of the month of March, in which the widespread belief in the course of human development following natural laws found its expression.

In contrast to this, the great significance of 1848 for German social democracy was presented on a broad level in 1898, in newspapers, magazines, illustrations, pictures, and caricatures, which constantly emphasized the European context of this movement. Mention was given to the revolutions in Vienna, in Hungary, to the Chartist movement in England, but it was above all the French development that was recalled. Hence, for the anniversary of the March Revolution not only saw the second edition of Wilhelm Blos's *History of the German Revolution of 1848* published, but also Louis Héritier's long-awaited *History of the French Revolution*, edited by Eduard Berstein.

Karl Kautsky, a vehement critic of revisionism and an important theoretician of the period, summarized the developments of the previous fifty years in 1898, begin-

ning with socialist currents in the *Vormärz* as follows: with the revolutionary movement of 1848, the road was not only made free for capitalism, but also for the proletariat. Kautsky concluded by stating that capitalism had entered its last phase, in
which a new phase of proletarian socialism would begin. In the new century, the
struggle for power within the state would come to the fore. This retrospective on
the occasion of the anniversary of the revolution provided grounds for feelings of
pride; out of a "mass of workers" in the "stormy March movement" arose a "great
proletarian army." In this retrospective the previous fifty years appear to be a single
great and direct victory lap.[23]

While Héritier's book on the February revolution of 1848, which the German
social democrats published on its fiftieth anniversary has since then sunk into obscu-
rity, this same can not be said of its editor, Eduard Berstein, the leading representative of a quite controversial "revisionism" of the time, who later achieved great
honors as the theoretician of "democratic socialism." His investigation of the 1848
French Revolution of was the spark for the development of revisionism, which he
expounded in his *Evolutionary Socialism* of 1899. His distancing himself from Marx's
interpretations, which had only recently been reprinted in the form of *The Class
Struggles in France, 1848 to 1850*, increased. His estrangement from the Marxist
interpretation was related by Bernstein to his own evaluation of the French revolution. This amounted to a positive view of the February Revolution, the bourgeois
republic, and the work of the Luxembourg Commission committee under Louis
Blanc as the "center" or "core" of the "workers' movement."

Basically his assessments were a comment on the themes of revolution and
reform. These were, like revisionism altogether, not a subject limited to German
social democracy. Without this being recognizable in its specific points as a debate
about the revolution of 1848, the debate on strategy towards the end of the nineteenth century, known as the "revisionism controversy," was one of the major
themes of the Second International. It was bound up with conflicts that were virulent in the national parties and took place both internally and at the congresses of
the International, with the aid of 'reinforcements." German, French, and Franco-
German debates about "revisionism" provide a very vivid example of this.

Differences existed in the heterogeneous Second International from the beginning. After the break-up of the First International there had been constant attempts
to found a new organization, although no agreement could be reached, even concerning its form. As, however, the labor movements in most European countries
were growing in strength, in spite of factional disputes, splits, and persecution by the
authorities, conditions for a refounding of the International seemed promising in
the second half of the 1880s. Competing initiatives defined the image of the international workers' congress, and called for the anniversary of the great French Revolution on 14 July 1889, which has been called the "birth date" of the Second
International.[24] Even before the meeting it had become clear that differences and
rivalries were not only a question of issues, but of leadership and influence.

Without being officially established, without setting a name and a form of organization, the Second International existed until 1900 only in the form of its con-

gresses. Resolutions were neither coordinated, nor supervised, but it was nonetheless a recognized institution. It gained in authority and its discussions were echoed elsewhere. In 1900, the International Socialist Bureau (ISB) was founded, which was manned by two delegates from each country and had a permanent office in Brussels. This was followed in 1904 by the Interparliamentary Socialist Commission, which was to coordinate socialists' parliamentary work.

Looking at the years between 1889 and 1914, one can distinguish two phases. The first, a sort of transitional phase, extended to the "revisionism crisis" of the turn of the century, while the second heralded the structural changes of the twentieth century. While the second was distinguished by debates on imperialism, colonialism, the national question and, above all, war and peace, other debates and struggles were characteristic of the first years. These included initially a struggle with anarchism, already virulent in the First International, which ended with the exclusion of anarchists. Equally characteristic and, compared to the second phase, still traditional, was the widespread and quite emotional expectation of a revolution. The definition of what a "revolution" should be and the setting of the means for its realization were admittedly extremely contradictory. They included the long-discussed question of whether economic emancipation could be ensured with political emancipation or whether complete emancipation was only possible after a seizure of political power.

The debates at the congresses showed that agreement could be found for specific social demands and practical activities, but that placing reforms in a comprehensive strategic concept raised the question of the extent to which the struggle for reform was an end in itself or a means of accelerating the collapse of capitalist society. In these debates, German social democrats, who formed the largest section, were very quickly able to carry the day with their views, especially those on Marxism. There, the dictum from the *Communist Manifesto* that at the end of a long road stood the revolution, written on the eve of the 1848 revolution still held true. This was, however, qualified by later hints from Friedrich Engels that the revolution was not a logical necessity, at least in Germany, as the party there thrived much better by legal means than by illegal ones and "subversion."[25]

The struggle with anarchism only covered over the fundamental differences between those who wished to take the road of reform and those who thought a violent break with the existing social system inevitable. The so-called "revisionism crisis" in the transition from the first phase of the development phase of the International to the second was by far the most visible expression of a struggle between reform and revolution. This struggle reached a first highpoint shortly after the fiftieth anniversary of the revolution, when, in the summer of 1899, Alexandre Millerand became the first socialist in Europe to become a member of a bourgeois cabinet. In view of a threatened coup from the right, socialists and bourgeois radicals had formed a parliamentary alliance, and Millerand justified his step with the threat to the republic.

It was well known that he championed an overcoming of capitalism through a slow process, not through a revolutionary step. His joining the cabinet, which also contained a bitter opponent of the Paris Commune—General Galliffet—led to angry protests in the international labor movement. A short time later, German social democrats quarreled at the Hanover convention about the views of Eduard Bernstein, who had become "an international symbol of a revolt against the currents of revolutionary socialism."[26] Bernstein had broken with a socialist dogma; his proposals were rejected in 1899 in Hanover and again in 1903 in Dresden with the revisionism resolution.

The international discussion of reform and revolution took place via revisionism at the Amsterdam congress. This congress of the Second International of 1904 became famous because of the verbal exchange between August Bebel and Jean Jaurès, who had supported Millerand's actions. While the discussion was about various strategies, it became clear that the distinct traditions of 1848 also played a role. Especially because the Guesdistes claimed the Dresden revisionism-resolution for themselves, Jaurès turned against their internationalization. He pointed out that, thanks to reformist tactics in France, the republic had been saved. This was countered by Babel that one could be quite envious of the French because of their republic, their universal suffrage, and their liberties, but the social democrats did not want to have their heads beaten in for them. And with their reference to their own electoral successes, he felt in necessary to add that the German social democrats would "have made something completely different"[27] out of such liberties and rights. What they would have done, however, he did not say. It had angered him that Jaurès felt he had the right to judge and criticize the internal situation of German social democracy.

It was above all the "political impotence" of German social democrats which Jaurès found questionable; it was a large party but it was defined by a contrast between apparent power and real influence. It had neither the tradition nor the structural mechanisms that would allow it to translate its millions of votes into political action. Jaurès became even more blunt. What German social democracy lacked was a revolutionary tradition. The German proletariat had "not won the universal suffrage at the barricades. It had received it from above. And while one could not imagine taking something from those who had won it, because they could easily win it back, one could imagine taking something from above which had been granted from above."[28] Just as German social democrats did not have the means for revolutionary action and a strength arising from a revolutionary tradition, they also did not have parliamentary strength, as the German parliament was at best a "half" parliament.

This criticism angered Bebel, and he objected that the French republic was also only a class society and had nothing corresponding to German social welfare legislation. Admittedly, Babel did not take up possible positive and negative effects of this criticized lack of revolutionary tradition, but rather emphasized only the negative consequences of the June uprising. He also did not mention that the revolutionary movement of 1848/49, apart from national peculiarities, had otherwise always been compared to the epochal revolution of 1789.

This debate clarified both the way in which 1848 played a role for how the German and French labor movements viewed themselves, and their different conditions for development and structural circumstances. Their paths led in different directions, and a lack of understanding and awareness of these different paths increased in the twentieth century. In Amsterdam, the Dresden resolution was also approved by the International. The representatives of reformist thought were still not able to form a majority. Nonetheless, it could not be overlooked that the German Social Democratic Party, as the leading party within the socialist movement, was only revolutionary in its words, in theory. In practice it had always taken the path of reform. The French socialists, on the other hand, pressed much more urgently for political action.

This confrontation between reform and revolution continued to follow the labor movement and thus influenced the tradition of the commemoration of the revolution of 1848. At the next major anniversary in 1923, the situation had changed radically compared to the nineteenth century. The labor movement had also split organizationally. Neither the experience of the Russian Revolution—quite apart from the First World War—nor that of the German November Revolution could lead to a common understanding of the revolution of 1848. Germany was a constantly threatened republic, and had, in Friedrich Ebert, for the first time a Social Democratic president. This republic, with the Social Democratic Party of German (SPD) as its champion, had good reasons to create its own tradition with a commemoration of 1848, as predecessor of the Weimar Republic, so to speak. Hence it was not the 18th of March that was recalled. The local event originally planned just for Frankfurt was extended to a national celebration, to which President Ebert traveled in a railway salon carriage.

The meeting on 18 May began in the Frankfurt Römer with short speeches by dignitaries, but more important was the accompanying music. The young composer Paul Hindemith had been asked to play the piece by Joseph Hayden which contained the melody Hoffmann von Fallersleben had selected for the *Deutschlandlied*. This rather reserved interpretation of the national anthem seemed to have had its effect on the mostly academic celebration.[29] From the Römer, in front of which a sort of popular festival was taking place, a march with a black-red-gold flag from 1848 left for the *Paulskirche*, where another academic celebration was held with the Heidelberg Professor Alfred Weber as speaker.

In the German labor movement, the tradition of 18 March was broken off with the First World War, and it was not revived. In the deeply split labor movement, no common views of history were possible because of the most recent past. A glance in a "reader" for workers on 1848, published for the anniversary, makes clear which "revolutionary historical" ideology was dominant for many.[30] With the exception of a contribution by Paul Frölich, at the time a member of the Reichstag for the Communist Party of German (KPD), later the Socialist Workers' Party (SAP) and after 1945 member of the SPD, this reader was a collection of extremely different texts from the nineteenth century. They are juxtaposed without introduction or commentary.

The reader includes texts by Franz Mehring on the Berlin and Vienna Revolutions from his *History of Social Democracy*. These are followed by long passages from the *Communist Manifesto*, remarks by both Bakunin and Marx and Engels on the German and French Revolutions, especially the June uprising. An excerpt from

Ferdinand Lassalle's speech before the assizes seems almost out of place in this collection. Much more familiar, on the other hand, are the poems to be found in almost every brochure or March-newspaper of the nineteenth century: Heinrich Heine's *Eighteenth March*, Georg Herwegh's *Eighteenth March 1873*, which symbolized the double commemoration, as well as Ferdinand Freiligrath's *The Dead to the Living*. All in all, it was a collection that did not much differ from earlier ones.

Only Paul Frölich's essay, "German Social Democracy and the Revolution of 1848," allows the collection to be situated politically. It is above all a critique of Eduard Bernstein's *How a Revolution Failed*, which appeared in 1921, and a comparison with his much-discussed brochure of 1899. While the one was responsible for revisionism, the other, written against the backdrop of the most recent revolution, was at the "origin of anti-Bolshevist theory." Bernstein had examined once again, and much more critically, the French Revolution of 1848 and had come to the conclusion that the June uprising could have been avoided if the workers had better come to terms with and "accepted" the "bourgeois republic." In contrast, Frölich emphasized the inevitability of insurrection in 1848 (and in 1871, 1905, and 1919) because the bourgeoisie was fundamentally "reactionary" and Bernstein's view of a reciprocity between revolutionary action and the behavior of the bourgeoisie was unacceptable from the outset. "Naturally, this view leads to a fundamental rejection of all revolutionary struggle, in as far as it is directed against the bourgeoisie. Thus Bernstein also places himself fundamentally on the historic ground of the bourgeoisie."[31]

Frölich saw Bernstein's and Social Democracy's ostensibly anti-revolutionary stance, as one of the motives for its anti-Bolshevism. Not without good reason he cited, with reference to the most recent events, its "fear of the costs" of a revolution, and its fear of the economic consequences of a "proletarian terror." As positions like those of Bernstein would earlier have been unchallenged in the SPD, their way into the present had been almost inevitable. It was only a small step away from justifications of Cavaignac to Noske's attacks on the workers. The incompatibilities visible in this pattern of argument remained preserved, although admittedly appearing in 1948 in another constellation in a changed form.

When it came to celebrating the centenary of the revolution of 1848, this took place once again after the catastrophe of a world war and a transformed international political situation. In France, these commemorations took place against the backdrop of the widespread impression that the social demands of the February Revolution would finally be implemented. All the demands worked out by the Luxembourg commission under Louis Blanc were published in a multi-volume edition on the occasion of the anniversary. In Germany, on the other hand, the question of the causes and consequences of National Socialism and war inevitably formed the backdrop to the commemorations, thus raising questions for which historians could not have an answer. The international ideological split was not yet concluded, but just as predictable was the division of Germany, whose existence as a state had not yet been restored.

In view of this, the century-old question of dictatorship and democracy was also raised in the anniversary, the roots of which were important subjects in the two future German states, which allowed different possibilities of approach to 1848. The breaks and refractions that could be discovered in the past century were expressed by, for example, the historian Friedrich Meinecke in a "secular observation," published by the municipal government of greater Berlin on the occasion of the anniversary celebrations in March 1848. The bourgeois historian, in the Weimar Republic at first republican by rational argument [*Vernunftrepublikaner*] and then member of the German Democratic Party (DDP), felt it necessary to allow revolutions a historic right "in certain cases." The "new world" had to be victorious sooner or later, in his view. The authoritarian state was to be replaced by "some" form of democracy. This, Meinecke saw as the task of his day, without admittedly describing democracy in greater detail. Democracy, as "cure" was already a magic word in 1848, which for Meinecke was nothing other than the "negation of the authoritarian state." It was necessary in 1848—and still in 1948—to give due attention to the elementary interests of people and social groups, as the problem of "social restructuring" had divided the "nation." This was to be overcome, and peace secured, through new forms of cooperation between the peoples. For Meinecke, the lasting legacy of 1848 was to "eradicate the roots of war" and thus to consummate the revolution of 1848. Finally purified, the Germans should reach the goals of their "desires": national unity in a democratic "communal state."

In the Western Zone, the present-day relevance of a view of 1848 could appear differently. An anniversary brochure by Hermann Martens dealt with liberty as the greatest good. Social differences and the demands for social leveling were problems not to be denied, but secondary in comparison to the alternative of democracy or dictatorship. This alternative could be traced back to 1848, went from "socialism and democracy" to "socialism or democracy" and, especially in the Weimar Republic, was declared to be a "fateful question" for the workers. In other countries one found a democratic road to socialism, but in Germany the labor movement was so deeply split that the question of democracy or dictatorship had become the overriding one. It had brought about a parting of the ways at present.

When a commemoration of 1848 was already used to serve the establishment of a democratic tradition in 1923, then this was all the more pressing in 1948. In view of the political situation, there were extremely distinct possibilities in a commemoration of 1848 for drawing on the revolution of 1848—to use it for propaganda purposes or to secure a democratic tradition in Germany. There were examples of both. Meetings, events and also popular brochures were one possibility, but going via the schools with their central educational function should not be forgotten.

This took on different forms in East and West. The political significance of the revolution of 1848 in the Soviet Occupation Zone was made obvious in the KPD appeal of 1945 for the completion of the bourgeois-democratic revolution of 1848 in which, on the one hand, an inclusion of the broader classes was sought and, on the other, a fundamental socioeconomic "anti-fascist-democratic" transformation was intended. In the light of this appeal, it was obvious that the centenary was going to be commemorated.

In this context, it should not be forgotten that the centenary coincided with an anniversary of the November Revolution. Otto Grotewohl laid down how the two were to be tied together in his foreword to a publication on the November revolution, the contents of which he had presented to the executive of the Socialist Unity Party of German (SED: formed by the coerced merger of the social democrats and communists in the Soviet zone of occupation—ed.).[32] "1848 is not only the one hundredth anniversary of the failed bourgeois revolution of 1848. The revolution of 1918 will have its thirtieth anniversary on 9 November 1948. In the scales of history, the November revolution of 1918 weighs as little as the March revolution of 1848. Both did not achieved a fundamental change of the face of Germany in the progressive sense."[33] In this speech, drafted by the SED party institute of higher education, premises were formulated for the treatment of the 1848 revolution which would remain valid for about a decade. It amounted to an emphasis on failure, without naming other factors.

Nonetheless, it was concerned with "lessons," with historical legitimacy for contemporary reconstruction, for revolutionary transformation, for which the support of as many people as possible was sought. Students, academics and especially artists were approached to "draw on" the revolutionary-democratic tradition of 1848 and to place themselves at the service of the new order. In the spring of 1948, a number of exhibitions were opened in Berlin, organized by the municipal government, the German Administration for Public Education, the Cultural League and the "Permanent Committee for Unity and a Just Peace." Not The obvious motto for these exhibitions ,"1848—a Revolution and Its lessons," was used by the one put on by the Administration for Public Education, but other exhibitions concentrated at least partially on themes of cultural history. The most popular exhibition proved to be the one in the Berlin *Stadtschloß*, damaged in the war but still standing. The DEFA had also taken up this subject and brought out a film, *Once again 1848,* directed by Gustav Wangenheim.

In Berlin, a center of the "March Revolution," it was quite reasonable to revive the tradition of commemorating the 18th of March. The function it was to be assigned was already clear before the founding of the SED—the forced unification of SPD and KPD—when at a common public rally of the two parties on the anniversary of the March revolution the "necessity" of the unity of the labor movement was "unanimously" stressed. For 1948, events were politically prepared and directed according to a central plan worked out by the central office of the SED. The beginning of this was marked, for example, with a festive occasion in the German State Opera for the centenary of the publication of the *Communist Manifesto.* There were also commemorations at the graves of the "victims of March" in the Berlin Friedrichshain, with Wilhelm Pieck as speaker. There had been considerable controversy within the Berlin municipal government and in the city council, because representatives of the SPD, the Christian Democratic Union (CDU), and the Liberal Party of Germany (LPD: known in the western zones as the Free Democratic Party or FDP—ed.) rejected the form planned by the SED. As they could not prevent the event, a commemoration was held in front of the ruins of the

Reichstag in West Berlin on 18 March, with Franz Neumann (SPD) and Jakob Kaiser (CDU), among others, as speakers.

The finale of the series of events planned and staged by the SED—which were not restricted to Berlin—was a congress of the German People's Council on 18 May, which was to commemorate the opening of the German National Assembly in Frankfurt am Main one hundred years previously. This was also intended to form a counterpoise to a corresponding event in Frankfurt am Main, where, since 1923, commemorations had been held on 18 May instead of on 18 March. Something comparable to East German centralism did not admittedly exist in the Western Zone. Not everywhere was it felt necessary to undertake something. In Bavaria it was felt that this revolution no longer had any relevance for the present, and in Hamburg the authorities refrained from organizing public events, because in 1848 "there was no significant transformation" there.

Things were different in Frankfurt am Main, where on the 18th of May the rector of the university, Walter Hallstein, held a commemorative speech in the assembly hall on the subject of "Scholarship and Politics." In comparison to this conventional academic event, Fritz von Unruhe, as commemorative speaker in the *Paulskirche*, represented much more clearly traditions on which in particular quite a number of social democrats, such as the Mayor of Frankfurt Walter Kolb, sought to draw in this anniversary year. He had demonstrated his republican convictions quite early, had already been honored in the Weimar Republic for his tireless work for peace, and, as he was threatened by the National Socialists, he had to emigrate before 1933. This, too, could be seen as a legacy of 1848, a legacy, admittedly, which had little chance of being accepted in the new Federal Republic.

Events with, as a rule, directly recognizable political (or only seemingly apolitical) aims were and are one common form of anniversary commemoration, brochures another. They were especially necessary after the years of National Socialism for their combination of spreading knowledge and political education. Thus a comparison with 1848 also served to encourage the youth to participate in the reconstruction of a democratic state. A quite social-democratic viewpoint was expressed, for example, by Walter G. Oschilewski.[34]

His descriptions are comparable to those common in social democratic publications before the First World War. They are interspersed with the revolutionary poetry of Ferdinand Freiligrath, and he recalls above all the tradition of the "walk" to the graves of the "victims of March." His classification of the revolution as a link in the chain of the "struggle of the old feudal social order with the new bourgeois-capitalist one"—including numerous Marx quotations— also corresponded in style and diction to the nineteenth century. His conclusions recall Friedrich Meinecke in that he wrote of a necessary transformation of the old authoritarian state into a new "communal state" that was already a motivating factor in the revolution of 1848 and still had to be realized. To this must be added the constructive ideas of a socialist formation of society. It corresponded to social-democratic concepts to see in them a democracy based on a recognition of personal liberty, securing of human rights and the right to work with a fair wage. Like the KPD/SED—but for other reasons—he also called for a completion of the revolution. "This struggle for German unity, for the formation of a socialist economy, for liberty and the recognition of human dignity no longer occurs on the barricades in the twentieth century, but, in the wake of political renewal and development of public opinion, as a never-ending process in the hands of a new society."[35]

This was a clear distinction from that which the SED understood and practiced as the completion of the 1848 revolution by an "anti-fascist-democratic transformation." To lend this fundamental restructuring historical legitimacy and to derive from the 1848 revolution a unity of the nation-state, at the time still vehemently advocated by the SED, a leitmotif of brochures was published in the Soviet occupation zone. There was still, admittedly, no binding historical ideal based on Marxism-Leninism, in which the revolution of 1848 would later be embedded, but the beginnings of such were already visible and propagated. Often falling back on Marx and Engels, who, of course, were also used by the social democrats, was an obvious move. Just as the social democrats had seen themselves as the only and "true" heir of the 1848 revolution in the nineteenth century, so the SED took on this role after the Second World War, claiming this for itself, and for the "working class" it allegedly represented.[36] Not only from the viewpoint of the SED, and historians sympathetic to it did the developments after the defeat of 1848 lead to national and democratic traditions in Germany growing apart. To lead them back together was an important goal, for which the SED claimed a monopoly and was thus able to attract the support of non-Communists. As was briefly and self-confidently stated in 1948: "To put it briefly, the revolution had two tasks: First to break the power of the nobility in state and society, and second to create a unified German nation-state. Of these two tasks, one has been completed in a part of Germany, in the Soviet occupation zone—up to now, the other has remained unfulfilled, and its resolution is more pressing than ever."[37]

Alfred Meusel's expression "two tasks" was also introduced into schooling in the Soviet Zone in the anniversary year of 1948. These tasks were to be treated in history lessons in the context of a "struggle for unity in German history." In this, developments in the nineteenth century were placed in the foreground, but it was also necessary to tie them to the present.[38] The restructuring of the schools had not yet been completed; not all teachers, especially in the secondary schools, had been exchanged. For Greater Berlin, the allied command council had, in fact, only allowed history lessons again starting 1 September 1948. These should be entrusted to teachers who could guarantee to give them in an "anti-Nazi," "anti-militaristic," and "democratic" spirit.

The aim of history lessons was still cautiously defined at this time. History lessons had nothing to do with "empathizing with the past." Apart from imparting knowledge, an understanding for the inner relations and patterns of history was to be awakened and—most importantly—had to achieve a reference to current events. Such a reference, as shown in the example of the revolution of 1848, was to the struggle for German unity.[39]

As new school books were not immediately available, workbooks and material had to be worked out successively or put together ad hoc.[40] For additional information, teachers were referred to more extensive study materials on which the workbooks had been based. This material was so broad and varied that it had to be carefully selected, in view of the number of lesson-hours available. For developments in Europe between 1815 and 1849, eighteen hours were available, six of which were dedicated to the German Revolution of 1848/49. "Sources" for the school included descriptions of events, visual aids, such as pictures and cards, statistics, documents such as speeches, letters, more easily read newspaper articles and also assessments of events. The "description of events" was generally based on reports of those living at the time—which later came to be called eyewitness reports—or on the lively presentation by Wilhelm Blos, popular in the nineteenth century. All that in some way related to economic or social aspects drew on the work of Jürgen Kuczynski, and assessments generally came from Marx and Engels.

If one looks at the further reading lists in the workbooks, most of the material, apart from Kuczynski's works, a study by Hans Mayer of Georg Büchner, and the above-mentioned brochure by Meusel, was written in association with the labor movement in the nineteenth and early twentieth centuries. Veit Valentin's history of the German Revolution, from 1930/31, was probably held to be the historiographically standard work. The material in the workbook is divided into six large chapters, beginning with the prehistory (the Wartburg Festival, the Hambach Festival, Germany in the *Vormärz* according to Karl Marx, Badenese liberalism, the Heidelberg Assembly) and ends with the campaign for the imperial constitution and the victory of reaction in 1849.

The text talks of "popular uprisings" in the spring of 1848, especially those in Vienna, Berlin, and Baden, of peasant unrest and the Frankfurt preparliament, of the "struggles in the parliaments" (Frankfurt National Assembly and the Prussian National Assembly) as well as the "counter-strike" by the forces of reaction (in Vienna and Germany). One chapter is dedicated to "German views" of non-German events. These include articles by Karl Marx from the *Neue Rheinischen Zeitung* on Poland, Hungary, and Italy. Neither the Parisian February Revolution nor the June uprising—as spark for the revolution and for the counter-revolution in the normal pattern of argument for the labor movement of the nineteenth century and for Marx and Engels—receive mention. At this time they were ignored in the Soviet zone, as they did not correspond to the national aspects important at the time, but to an international tradition of the German labor movement.

In the western zones, as well, teaching material and source material for the teachers had to be put together anew. Even where social democrats were actively involved, as, for example, in Hesse or Brunswick, materials for teachers were not comparable. In Brunswick, the pedagog and historian Georg Eckert drew directly on the traditions of the labor movement, which included a recollection of the ideas and, above all, of the revolutionary poetry of the *Vormärz*.[41] Names such as Heine, Gutzkow, and Büchner were once just as familiar as Freiligrath or Herwegh. Doubtless selection was not made on artistic-aesthetic criteria, but on those of value as historical source. With literary documentation, the range of idea of the bourgeoisie in the 1830s and 1840s and the diversity of opposition currents was to be shown.

The words of Ludwig Uhland expressed the political message of aiming at a new Germany of unity and liberty. Eckert's adaptation of the revolution of 1848/49 remained embedded in the European context, even when he focused on the German events.[42] "Lessons" and political messages for the present could not be found in Eckert's work, but it did contain, in the form of key words, the negative consequences of the revolution and the ways in which the revolution was important for the "German labor movement." Especially on this issue, Eckert developed a standpoint uncommon in the labor movement until then and which only later began to gain acceptance among social democrats and sympathetic historians (also in contrast to GDR-interpretations). Marx and Engels and the Communist League no longer stand in the foreground, but Stephan Born and the Workers' Fraternization with their demands, which anticipated much of what would later become trade union ideals. The influence of Marx and Engels was certainly not denied, but they had not significantly influenced the course of the revolution. Depending on the teacher's previous knowledge, such a presentation had to have long-term effects.

A brochure for teachers published by the Hessian Ministry of Educational and Religious Affairs did without the wider range noticeable in Eckert.[43] For the Hessian Minister of Educational and Religious Affairs, Erwin Stein (CDU), a member of a social democratic cabinet, a look back at 1848 was only of limited value. The schools were accordingly requested to commemorate the 18th of May in a ceremony or a youth meeting "from today's standpoint and with a view to the future." The celebrations should be based on certain themes; participation by the students should also be encouraged. If one examines the themes, one sees that they focused mainly on the Frankfurt Parliament and its leading representatives, on poets such as Ernst Moritz Arndt and Ludwig Uhland and in all variations on the importance of personal and political freedom as a precondition of just social relations.

In this interpretation, the influence of the American occupying power is noticeable, which from the beginning invested considerable energy in the Hessian educational system. In the view of the Hessian Minister of Educational and Religious Affairs, 1848 should make clear that the solutions and slogans of 1848 were no longer applicable to the present, where once again a state was to be created in freedom and the "people" were to be imparted a "democratic way of life." For him, the breaks with the past century were too great, the task for the future of preparing the road to a European "community of nations" too important, for too much contemplation of the past to be helpful.

Even these few examples show that, unlike in the Soviet Zone and future GDR, there was hardly any unified reference back to the tradition of 1848 in the Western Zones and then in the Federal Republic, just as there could be no unified view of history. Nonetheless a common tenor can be discovered in the context of the centenary: this was the search for a permanent peace and the anchoring of a social welfare democracy in a state dedicated to freedom and to the values of Western civilization. Even when in the Soviet Zone and early GDR there was not yet an established Marxist historiography, historians followed the guidelines and resolutions of the SED from the beginning—in this case the resolution of January

1848, in which the assessment and appreciation of 1848/49 was established. The very noticeable emphasis on "national unity" in 1948 disappeared in time, but, well into the 1960s, they stuck to an emphasis of the negative consequences of the revolution as a "failed" revolution.

In its function as a conscience-forming and politically stabilizing institution, DDR-historiography formulated and repeated, almost like a prayer-wheel, the "lessons" according to which social changes in the Soviet zone/GDR could also be seen as a fulfillment of the legacy of 1848/49. The revolution was defined as a high-point in the struggle of the "masses" against a still semi-feudal Prussia; in a political test of strength the bourgeoisie proved itself incapable of taking on a leading role. From the end of the 1960s and beginning of the 1970s the viewpoint widened, and "positive" effects were included with the "negative" consequences.

The revolution was increasingly placed, in the context of a periodization, in a cycle of revolutions. The focus of research was, naturally, on Marx and Engels as well as on the groups and persons associated with them, on the significance of the "working class" and the labor movement in general. This research was also embedded in the discussion arising in the 1970s of "tradition and legacy." The commemoration of the 125th anniversary of the revolution of 1848 during the most successful phase of the GDR in its efforts towards international recognition must also be located in this debate. There were now indestructible historical lines of tradition, "which [unite] the socialist present in the German Democratic Republic with the revolutionary events in the middle of the nineteenth century."[44]

The "lessons" were assumed to be known, but special reference was made to their further development through Leninism, as the victory of the "working class" in the twentieth century was unthinkable without this theory. The "deep" historical meaning of 1848 lay in its having created the conditions for the development of the modern proletariat, that force "which today defines the age."[45] The revolution of 1848/49, was, according to this viewpoint, the first great test for this class, whose "irresistible rise" began then, which "led to the defeat of reaction and brought the GDR to the heights of historical progress of our age." And in the DDR, one did not wish to be denied this legacy, this revolutionary line of tradition, by social democratic historians from the Federal Republic who—it was assumed—thought they could create for the Federal Republic a "positive" historical line of tradition in their research of the 1970s. This mutual challenge has, in the meantime, become irrelevant.

If one looks only at the commemorations of the revolution in this century, the world has once again changed fundamentally for the sesquicentennial of 1848. That which was seen as the legacy to be fulfilled, has been achieved, on the one hand, and is threatened on the other. National unity in a liberal-democratic state is achieved; admittedly, when one sees in the demands of 1848 the origins of the social welfare state, just the term itself—unlike at the 125th anniversary—seems to have taken on negative connotations among its opponents. Not only is it subject to critical examination, many have called it into question completely. The labor movement, which, in the sense of democratic socialism, saw itself as the heir of the revolution of 1848, has been said by many to be at an end, at least in its traditional form, as, for example, in the talk of an end of the social-democratic century. The strain of socialism realized in the GDR has been discredited, certainly for the foreseeable future. Thus it must remain open as to whether the commemoration of 1848 will be more than a historical reminiscence on origins, hopes, and demands that in the twentieth century have come to be seen as almost irreversible.

Notes

1. See Charles Tilly, *European Revolutions, 1492-1992* (Cambridge, MA, 1993), 1-4.
2. See the articles on revolution (by Reinhart Koselleck) and on socialism (by Wolfgang Schieder) in *Geschichtliche Grundbegriffe. Historisches Lexikon zur politisch-sozialen Sprache in Deutschland*, Vol. 5 (Stuttgart, 1984), 749-88 and 923-96.
3. Karl Marx and Friedrich Engels, *Manifesto of the Communist Party* (New York, 1948), 44.
4. See Stephan Born, "Die Moralischen und die Unmoralischen, die Freien und die Despoten (3 June 1848)," reprinted in Eduard Bernstein (ed.), *Documente des Socialismus*, vol. 1 (Berlin, 1902; reprint, Frankfurt 1968), 78.
5. See also for the following *Geschichtliche Grundbegriffe*, Vol. 5, 970ff.
6. Karl Marx and Frederick Engels *Collected Works* (New York, 1977-) Vol. 10, 279.
7. Karl Marx, *The Eighteenth Brumaire of Louis Napoleon*, in ibid., Vol. 11, 103-97, here 106.
8. See for example Walter Schmidt, *Bürgerliche Revolution und proletarische Emanzipation in der deutschen Geschichte* (Berlin, 1990), 187ff, 241ff.
9. Walter Schmidt, "Proletariat und bürgerliche Revolution 1848/49. Die europäische Arbeiterbewegung in der Achtundvierziger Revolution—Versuch eines historischen Vergleichs," in Manfred Kossok and E. Kross (eds.), *Proletariat und bürgerliche Revolution (1830-1917)* (Vaduz, 1990), 101-2.
10. A. Wirsching, "Arbeiter und Arbeiterbewegung in Paris in vergleichende Perspektive," in Ilja Mieck, Horst Möller, and Jürgen Voss (eds.), *Paris und Berlin in der Revolution 1848* (Sigmaringen, 1995), 161-84; Rüdiger Hachtmann, "Die sozialen Unterschichten in der großstädtischen Revolution von 1848. Berlin, Wien und Paris im Vergleich," in ibid., 107-36; Heidrun Homburg, "Kleingewerbe in den Hauptstädten Paris-Berlin. Wirtschaftliche Rahmenbedingungen und konjunkturelle Entwicklung im Vorfeld der Revolution von 1848," in ibid., 137-51.
11. On the terminology see Jürgen Kocka, *Weder Stand noch Klasse. Unterschichten um 1800* (Bonn, 1990); also, see Hachtmann, "Die sozialen Unterschichten," 108.
12. For this and for the following, see Hachtmann, "Die soziale Unterschichten," 112ff.
13. Ibid., 114.
14. See ibid., 115.
15. Ibid., 117.
16. Ibid., 120.
17. On a comparison of job creation measures in Paris and Berlin, see also P.-P. Sagave, "1848: Ateliers nationaux à Paris et travaux d'utilité publique à Berlin," in ibid., 153-59.
18. See W. Kreutz, "Das Bild der Pariser Februarrevolution in Deutschland," in ibid., 241-68.
19. Quoted in Annie Kriegel, "Die Internationale Arbeiterassoziation (1864-1876)," in Jacques Droz (ed.), *Geschichte des Sozialismus*, Vol. 2 (Frankfurt, 1975), 187.
20. Ibid., 92.
21. For an overview see also Beatrix W. Bouvier, "Die Märzfeiern der sozialdemokratischen Arbeiter: Gedenktage des Proletariats—Gedenktage der Revolution. Zur Geschichte des 18. März," in

Dieter Düding et al. (eds.), *Öffentliche Festkultur. Politische Feste in Deutschland von der Aufklärung bis zum Ersten Weltkrieg* (Reinbeck, 1988), 334-51.

22. Quoted in ibid., 339.
23. See also *Mai-Zeitung 1898*; quoted in U. Achten (ed.), *Zum Lichte empor. Mai-Festzeitungen der Sozialdemokratie 1891-1914* (Berlin and Bonn, 1980), 80.
24. In overview, for this and the following, K.-L. Günsche and K. Lantermann, *Kleine Geschichte der Sozialistischen Internationale* (Bonn, 1977); Georges Haupt, *Programm und Wirklichkeit. Die internationale Sozialdemokratie vor 1914* (Neuwied and Bonn, 1970); Julius Braunthal, *Geschichte der Internationale*, Vol. 1 (Hanover, 1961).
25. Thus the tone of his oft-quoted remarks in the introduction to Marx's *Class Struggles in France*, in Robert Tucker (ed.), *The Marx-Engels Reader* (New York, 1978), 556-73.
26. Braunthal, *Geschichte*, Vol. 1, 269.
27. See *Kongreß-Protokolle der Zweiten Internationale*, Vol. 1. (Amsterdam, 1904), 38.
28. Ibid., 38.
29. See the description in Edwin Redslob, *Von Weimar nach Europa* (Berlin, 1972), 175-76.
30. *1848. Ein Lesebuch für Arbeiter* (Berlin, 1923).
31. Ibid., 119.
32. Otto Grotewohl, *Dreißig Jahre später. Die Novemberrevolution und die Lehren der Geschichte der deutschen Arbeiterbewegung* (Berlin, 1948).
33. Ibid., 5.
34. Walter G. Oschilewscki, *Die Märztage 1848 von Berlin* (Berlin, 1948).
35. Ibid., 42.
36. As, for example, the tone of O. Jensen, *Die bürgerliche Revolution 1848* (Weimar, 1948).
37. Alfred Meusel, *Die deutsche Revolution 1848. Mit einem Beitrag von F. Albin, Marx und Engels und die Revolution von 1848* (Berlin, 1948), 23.
38. See also *Geschichte in der Schule. Zeitschrift für den Geschichtsunterricht*, Vol. 1 (1948), Issue 1/2.
39. See also the essay by A. Kloss, in ibid., 39ff.
40. E. Hadermann, "Das Arbeitsheft 'Die deutsche Revolution 1848 bis 1849' im Geschichtsunterricht der Oberschule," *Geschichte in der Schule*, Vol. 1 / 2, (1949 Nr. 4). This work book was put together by I.M. Lange and H.F. Schötzki and published by the Verlag Volk und Wissen in 1948.
41. Georg Eckert, *Das junge Deutschland und die Revolutionsdichtung des Vormärz* ("Beiträge zum Geschichtsunterricht. Quellen und Unterlagen für die Hand des Lehrers") (Brunswick, 1948).
42. Georg Eckert, *Die Revolution von 1848/49* ("Beiträge zum Geschichtsunterricht. Quellen und Unterlagen für die Hand des Lehrers") (Brunswick, 1947).
43. *1848. Die revolutionäre Bewegung und ihr Erbe* ("Der Deutsche Lehrer. Gedanken und Anregungen zur Lösung der Erziehungsaufgaben der Gegenwart," Nr. 6/7) (Wiesbaden, 1948).
44. Walter Schmidt, *Die Revolution von 1848 als historisches Erbe* (East Berlin, 1972).
45. Ibid., 11.

Chapter 38

1848 IN EUROPEAN COLLECTIVE MEMORY

Robert Gildea

Our perspective on any historical event is conditioned not only by historical scholarship but also by collective memory, by the collective construction of the past related more to political controversy and power struggles than the scholarly scrutiny of historical documents. I shall explore, in admittedly sketchy fashion, the ways in which the revolutions of 1848 have been remembered collectively, through the commemoration of given heroes and events, funeral rites, statues, the naming of public places, processions to shrines and mass rallies, and political debates, which crystallized around the celebration of key anniversaries. Such commemoration often serves to promote a founding myth of a political movement, a story of its origin and purpose, in order to define it against competing movements, to unite it, and to establish the legitimacy of its claims. Here myth is understood of course not as fiction or fairy-tale but as a shared construction of the past that fulfils these political purposes of definition, binding, and legitimation.

There was no single, objective view of the 1848 revolutions but only competing views, constructed and sustained by different political communities, seeking to justify their own agendas. For democrats, 1848 was a democratic revolution par excellence, which ensured, through the processes of democracy, liberty, equality, and fraternity. For socialists, on the other hand, 1848 represented the betrayal of democratic ideals by a bourgeoisie intent only on maintaining its class domination at the expense of the proletariat. For patriots, 1848 was the springtime of peoples, when emergent nationalities threw off the yoke of the old multinational empires. For emancipationists, finally, 1848 meant the emancipation of slave labor, at least in the French colonies.

The paradox of these myths, by which politicians and activists found in 1848 the heroes and defining moment of their own movements, was that in all cases 1848

Notes for this section begin on page 936.

failed them. The year was full of promise, but the promise was not realized. The democrats lost their liberty and sometimes democracy too; the socialists were crushed and persecuted; the champions of national liberation were sacrificed at the altar of *Realpolitik*; and the emancipationists were confronted by colonial oppression and racism. At best, 1848 continued to hold out a mirror to their aspirations, presenting them with an ideal that might one day be fulfilled. At worst, it saddled political communities with a historical burden that outweighed the benefits of legitimation afforded by the founding myth and encouraged them to seek a principle of legitimation elsewhere.

It must be said, of course, that changing events altered the way in which the revolutions of 1848 were regarded by any or all of these political movements. Ideals that were shattered at one moment nevertheless remained ideals, with a power to inspire, and in different circumstances the realization of those ideals could become feasible. This chapter seeks to trace changes in collective memory over the 150 years that followed the revolutions, concentrating on the fiftieth, 100th and—in so far as it is yet possible to judge—the 150th anniversaries of 1848.

The Democratic Myth

The first myth constructed around the revolution of 1848 was the democratic myth. Democratic movements traced their foundation to 1848 and argued that its central achievement was to find a path to democracy between stifling authoritarianism and violent revolution. The emphasis was different from country to country. In France the democratic myth proclaimed that the revolution of 1848 fulfilled the promises of the revolution of 1789 and yet was the antithesis of the Terror of 1793. In Germany, where fear of French-style revolution was so intense that revolution was virtually prevented from breaking out at all, 1848 was cultivated as a reminder by democrats that even in authoritarian and then Nazi Germany there was still an indigenous democratic moment.

For French democrats democracy meant bringing back the republic that had originally been founded in 1792, but republicanism was discredited in the early part of the nineteenth century in France by its identification with revolutionary dictatorship, the guillotine, the Terror, and civil war. French republicans, an endangered species, understood that they would have to demonstrate that the republic was compatible with liberty if it were ever to gain acceptance at a future date. They argued therefore that democracy in the form of universal suffrage would make the violent seizure of power unnecessary, and that if the people were consulted, political strife would subside as the people came together in fraternal union in support of the republic. That republic, they insisted, would not terrorize its opponents but establish a regime of liberty, justice, and respect for rights, and seek to win over doubters by weight of numbers and force of argument.

The agenda of the republicans was clear even before the revolution of 1848. François Raspail, who was born under one republic and wished to die under another, told his opponents in 1835: "The republic we desire is not that of '93. It is the republic where discussion will replace war and the improvement of mankind will make the scaffold redundant."[1] Shortly after taking power in 1848, the provisional government of the republic announced the abolition of the death penalty for political crimes and called elections under universal manhood suffrage to a Constituent Assembly. Victor Hugo, in his manifesto to the electors of the Seine, said that the republic must not restart "those two fatal and inseparable machines, the *assignat* printing-press and the pivot of the guillotine," that had discredited the first republic, but become "the holy communion in the democratic principle of all French people now, and of all peoples one day."[2]

Whether to trust in free elections and fraternity to secure the republic was not rather naïve is open to debate. The elections of 1848 returned a majority of conservatives and class war broke out in the streets. On the anniversary in 1848 of the proclamation of the first French republic [1792], Raspail told Ledru-Rollin, who had been Minister of the Interior in the provisional government, "All your policy is based on fraternity, and the policy of a people of brothers has only to lift a finger and thrones collapse."[3] Ironically Raspail was speaking from prison, Ledru-Rollin would be driven into exile the following year, and the much vaunted people threw themselves into the arms of Louis-Napoleon Bonaparte. The democratic agenda failed to understand that universal suffrage would not necessarily play into the hands of republicanism. It failed to deal adequately with its enemies, royalists or Bonapartists. And it failed to see that as the working classes became disillusioned and class struggles sharpened, the rhetoric of fraternity would look increasingly threadbare.

Despite these errors of judgement, republicans of 1848 clung to the view that the regime of 1848 was an immense improvement on that of 1793 and that democracy would replace repression by liberty, civil strife by fraternity. Ledru-Rollin, elected to the National Assembly of the Third Republic in 1874, praised the "Republic of clemency" of 1848, so unlike the first Republic, which had become an armed camp, and blamed the monarchists and Bonapartists for not giving it a chance.[4] Louis Blanc, who had chaired a commission on labor questions in 1848, likewise stressed the "magnanimity" and "generosity" of the revolutionaries of 1848.[5] He admitted, when a monument to Ledru-Rollin was unveiled in 1878, that the provisional government had not had enough faith in the republic and had sometimes lacked boldness and energy. But he insisted that universal suffrage was "the saving principle that checks insurrections and riots, and dispenses from violent efforts."[6] "Before this powerful voice of the country," he reiterated at Raspail's funeral, "all parties must withdraw and fall silent. We expect this act of patriotism from them. The country wishes it; the country commands it."[7]

The men who founded the Third Republic and steered it between the reefs of popular revolution and monarchist and Bonapartist reaction took a more realistic view of the ethos of 1848. In 1904 a Société d'Histoire de la Révolution de 1848 was founded, sponsored by Henri Brisson and Armand Fallières, respectively speakers of the Chamber of Deputies and Senate, the socialist deputies Alexander Millerand and Jean Jaurès, and the in-house historian of the Radical Party, Alphonse

Aulard. At its general assembly in the Sorbonne on 24 February 1905, the society's president, Adolphe Carnot, member of a great republican dynasty, brother of the assassinated president and a leader of the center-left Alliance démocratique, provided a perceptive but critical defense of 1848.

> There were at that time surges of universal fraternity which were ahead of their time but had an influence of the development of the aspirations of modern peoples towards harmony and general peace. We must not lose the lessons of a period so full of generous hopes, which were often illusions, but which also sometimes led to great reforms and beautiful creations. Swept along by their own generosity, the emancipators of 1848 were too ready to believe the hypocritical promises of their opponents. The republic and liberty fell victim to this confidence and, during a cold December night, were strangled by the prince president who had sworn an oath to defend them. The present republic has returned in part to the great ideas of the Second Republic. But it must not forget to learn the lessons of history. On the one hand it must take precautions against the maneuvers of reaction, while on the other it must moderate dangerous impatience and unrealizable utopias by expanding both general and civic education.[8]

History cruelly demonstrated that the maneuvers of reaction would easily get the better of the generous ideals of 1848. The democratic myth, as we shall see, was appropriated by reformist socialists such as Léon Blum, who opposed joining the Third International in 1920 on the grounds that Bolshevism represented the dictatorship of the proletariat, the eclipse of liberty, and a return to the Terror. Yet the noble ideals that had inspired the republic did not prevent its abolition by the Vichy regime in 1940 and Blum himself spending five years in the prisons of Vichy and Nazi Germany. When he delivered a lecture at the Sorbonne for the 100th anniversary of the revolution in 1948 he was pessimistic. "We are still confronted by the same problems, the same difficulties, the same anxieties and sometimes without the same hopes," he said, "so that one might say that [in 1848] humanity never lost such an opportunity, that it never toppled from so high up." He criticized the members of the provisional government of 1848 for being the "victims of a psychosis," of being so obsessed by the need to exorcise the memory of the Terror that they lacked the confidence to take decisive action, called elections before educating the masses in republican ways, and were afraid to alienate the bourgeoisie by social reforms but alienated the working classes who were their staunchest supporters.[9]

By the time of the 150th anniversary in 1998 the republic was politically secure and its survival not in doubt. Celebration of the revolution was a low-key affair, centering on an exhibition in the National Assembly inspired by its speaker, Laurent Fabius, and organized by the leading historian of the republic, Maurice Agulhon. Fears of 1793 had long been laid to rest. Commemoration was confined to the grand setting of the Palais-Bourbon and did not spill onto the streets. Fabius echoed Blum's reproach of the "generous and sometimes unrealistic idealism" of the revolutionaries, their "magnificent surge of fraternity" halted by the June Days and coup of 2 December. But the brief of the exhibition was not reality but image, and the image of the republic given maximum prominence was the neo-classical Marianne of Jean-Léon Gérôme honored by the provisional government of the republic in

1848: statuesque, more crown of laurels than red bonnet scarcely visible, sword pointing down and lifted arm offering an olive branch in the other.[10] The issue in 1998, however, was not whether the republic was still violent but whether it could still stimulate any enthusiasm among the French people.

While for a long time the main purpose of the democratic myth of 1848 in France was to purge the heinous associations of the republic of 1793, in Germany it served to recall that Germans were capable not only of revolution but of freedom. Revolutions in France throughout the nineteenth century and then in Russia in 1917 drove German in to the arms of authoritarian and repressive governments for eighty-one of the ninety-seven years between 1848 and 1945. Democrats searching for a founding myth were loath to turn to the violent revolution of 18 March 1848 in Berlin which was, as we shall see, appropriated by the socialists, but the opening of National Assembly in the *Paulskirche* of Frankfurt on 18 May 1848 offered an altogether more respectable heritage. When Imperial Germany collapsed in the defeat of 1918, Friedrich Ebert, the social-democratic chancellor of the new Republic, announced that "The great German Revolution will bring Germany neither a new dictatorship nor servitude, but will firmly establish German freedom … Political freedom is democracy on the secure foundations of a constitution and the law."[11]

Weimar democracy in fact hovered between Communist revolution and Nazi counter-revolution and in May 1923, as civil war threatened, Ebert went to the *Paulskirche* with the leading politicians of the republic to head the commemoration of the seventy-fifth anniversary of the opening of the Assembly. Greeted by a crowd of 30,000, he argued that on 18 May 1848, escaping from reactionary government, "the German people took its destiny into its own hands." Although the revolution was defeated, he asserted, the ideals of "Unity, Freedom, and Fatherland," lived on, so that when the German people once again took control of its destiny in 1918, it was to the Frankfurt Assembly that the architects of the Weimar Republic like himself turned for inspiration.[12]

The purpose of Ebert's speech was to establish the legitimacy of the constitutional, parliamentary republic and to give honor and respectability to the revolution of 1848. Needless to say, the Nazis and Communists rejected both, the monument to Ebert placed on the façade of the *Paulskirche* in 1926 was demolished by the Nazis in 1933, and the church was reduced to rubble by Allied bombing. The postwar mayor of Frankfurt, Walter Kolb, interpreted the destruction of the church as a divine punishment for Germany's betrayal of democracy and had it rebuilt in time for the centenary of 1848 with materials brought from all over the country as a "credo of German democracy." It was thought fitting that the speeches should be made by a German poet, Fritz von Unruh, who had fled the Third Reich in 1933 and campaigned for democracy in the United States, and by the chancellor of the University of Chicago who greeted the reintegration of Germany with the "spiritual life of the world."[13]

The idea that democracy in Germany was not home-grown but was imposed by victorious foreigners after 1945 died hard. Speaking in the *Paulskirche* for the

150th anniversary of the opening of the National Assembly, however, Federal President Herzog riposted that there was indeed an indigenous democratic tradition in Germany, symbolized by two great events, the Frankfurt Assembly and the collapse of the Berlin Wall. He admitted that "the history of freedom in our nation has often been one of experiment, losing the thread, of mistakes and defeats," but for their own self-confidence and identity Germans must honor the right tradition. In this respect 1848 was central as the moment when all the principles underpinning Germany's current political existence—the rights of man, democracy, and the common will to unite the diverse regions and movements—had been laid down. Though Germans were suffering the dislocations and disappointments of reunification, he urged, they should not throw in their lot with extremist parties who had already destroyed German democracy once, but learn the lesson of 1848, when people also in crisis put their faith in parliamentary leaders and democratic solutions.[14] In both France and Germany democratic republics were firmly established, but the appropriation of the democratic myth of 1848 by the political establishment ran the risk that ordinary citizens would no longer respond to it.

The Socialist Myth

The socialist view of the 1848 revolutions held that the democratic claim that liberty and fraternity could be established purely by the democratic process was nothing but a political illusion. It argued that the democratic rhetoric of fraternity concealed the reality of bourgeois class interests and that democratic revolution against absolutism and feudalism became bourgeois betrayal and bourgeois repression when the working classes started to assert their own interests.

For socialists the defining moment of the 1848 revolution was the June Days in Paris, when the working classes were provoked into insurrection and then ruthlessly suppressed by the fraternity-preaching bourgeoisie. Pierre-Joseph Proudhon recalled that two weeks after his election to the French Constituent Assembly in June 1848, the proletarians who had returned him were brutally massacred. "The memory of the June Days will leaden my heart with an eternal remorse," he wrote. It was a "disastrous apprenticeship," both for himself and the workers, which dispelled illusions about the political process. "Fighters of June!" he warned, "In March, April, and May, instead of organizing yourselves for labor and liberty ... you ran to the government, you asked it to provide what you alone could give yourselves, and postponed the revolution by three stages."[15]

The young Jules Vallès, who witnessed columns of insurgents of June being marched off in chains for deportation, was haunted for the rest of his life by the June Days. He was obsessed by the idea of writing a history of it, but so great was his emotion that he was never able to put pen to paper. The hero of *L'Insurgé*, Vallès's fictional account of the Commune (1886) is also trying to write a history of the June Days. As a journalist in Paris in 1871, Vallès interpreted the revolutionary ferment in Paris that led up to the Commune in the light of the June Days.

It was in June and the same men who have just dishonored Paris, the Jules Favres, the Pagès's, all the traitors, trotted through the barricaded and smoking streets behind Cavaignac's mare and spat on the wounds of the defeated. In the cellar of the Tuileries, beneath the barracks, in the Panthéon, the prisoners were swimming in blood and excrement. Sometimes they were asked through a skylight, "Who wants bread?" And when a pale face appeared it was blown apart by a rifle shot.[16]

The suppression of working-class revolution served the elaboration of the founding myth of socialism. Socialism sprang from the June Days, said Vallès, like the ball from a cannon. A brief alliance between middle- and working-classes had been constructed in Paris, bringing in the republic and a number of social reforms, but was not even attempted in Germany, where the middle classes threw themselves into the arms of monarchy, army, bureaucracy, and aristocracy at the first whiff of popular revolution. Workers' demands were rejected, workers' insurrections were crushed, and socialists were able to define 1848 as the martyrdom of the proletariat, which must according to the logic of the socialist gospel eventually result in its resurrection.

The ferocity of the repression of the June Days served the French socialist myth well; by contrast Engels regretted that the people of Berlin, far from putting up a fight, had opened the gates of Berlin to the Prussian army in November 1848.

A well-contested defeat is a fact of as much revolutionary importance as an easily-won victory. The defeats of Paris in June 1848, and of Vienna in October, certainly did far more in revolutionizing the minds of the people of those two cities than the victories of February and March. The Assembly and the people of Berlin would probably have shared the fate of those two towns above-named; but they would have left behind themselves, in the minds of the survivors, a wish of revenge, which in revolutionary times is one of the highest incentives to energetic and passionate action.[17]

As a result of this non-event, socialists looking for a revolutionary event in Berlin to commemorate fastened on the initial insurrection of 18 March 1848, when crowds gathering in the castle square to applaud concessions made by the king were cleared by royal troops, and artisans who threw up barricades were fired upon.

The elements of the socialist collective memory were thus democratic illusion and bourgeois betrayal, the martyrdom of the proletariat, and lastly the socialist revolution that had remained unfulfilled in 1848 but now became the goal for all future revolutions. For Karl Marx, as for French socialists, the Paris Commune was seen as popular retribution for the repression of the June Days carried out by the men of order. On 18 March 1871, he asserted, "the ghosts of the victims, assassinated at their hands from the Days of June 1848 down to the 22 January 1871, arose before their eyes."[18] Unfortunately the bourgeoisie was again triumphant and, for Marx, as far as the repression they indulged in was concerned, "1848 was only child's play compared with their frenzy in 1871."[19]

The June Days were joined by the Paris Commune in the litany of proletarian martyrdoms. The Communard Benoît Malon, in exile in Switzerland, spoke of *The Third Defeat of the French Proletariat*, following the Lyons rising of 1832 and the June Days.[20] Even after the Commune, the French socialist leader Jules Guesde proclaimed that "the fighters of June were the first to resort to arms for the social Republic. Their glorious and bloody defeat marks the violent entry of the proletariat, as a distinct party, onto the stage."[21] It was not until his newspaper, *L'Égalité*, went into a second series in 1880 and he started to build the *Parti Socialiste Français* that he concentrated on the cult of the Paris Commune rather than on the June Days.

In Germany, the Berlin barricades of March 1848 were briefly joined by the Paris Commune in the *Märzfeier* organized by the Social Democratic Party to define its ideals and legitimacy, but by the 1890s the cult of the Paris Commune weakened in Germany and 1848 once again became the sole object of the March festivals.[22] Only the socialists remained loyal to the cult of 1848 as a violent and popular revolution. Franz Mehring claimed in *Die Neue Zeit* in 1898 that the ruling classes had tried to eliminate "the extraordinary year" [1848] from the history books and pretended that concessions in 1848 had been made out of the goodness of Frederick William's heart rather than wrung out of him by the people on the barricades of 18 March. "The now class-conscious proletariat is the sole true heir legacy of the March fighters, and this class alone dares to celebrate the fiftieth anniversary of the March Revolution as it deserves to be: candidly, unreservedly, bearing in mind all its consequences."[23]

At precisely the same time as the fiftieth anniversary of the 1848 revolution was being celebrated by socialists, however, doubts were being expressed in socialist circles about the lessons of 1848. Questions were raised first, given the spread of democracy throughout Europe in the shape of elections under universal manhood suffrage, as to whether fighting on the barricades, 1848-style, was the best way to achieve a socialist revolution; and second, whether 1848 and indeed 1871 were not premature and reckless and demonstrated the need to build organization and class-consciousness among the proletariat to be certain of success. In all European socialist movements the debate between the revolutionary and reformist strategies was also a debate about the interpretation of the events of 1848.

Engels set the cat among the pigeons on the eve of fiftieth anniversary with his introduction to the 1895 edition of Marx's *Class Struggles in France*. "The time of surprise attacks," he argued, "of revolutions carried through by small conscious minorities at the head of unconscious masses, is past." Both 1848 and 1871 had failed because the proletariat was unprepared for revolution. "Long, persistent work," he said, was necessary to build up class consciousness and organization among the proletariat. Street-battles could never be won by the masses, for though towns had grown, so had armies, and these could now be mobilized more speedily by railway. Moreover barricades were rendered obsolete by the advent since 1848 in Germany of universal suffrage. This, concluded Engels, opened the way for the peaceful, legal coming to power of social democracy.

By 1898 the French had fifty years' experience of democracy, and one wing of the socialist movement was convinced that power could be achieved through elections. Marking the fiftieth anniversary of 1848, the democratic socialist Alexandre Millerand warned that the revolution had at that point been premature, and opposed by the mass of the peasantry who had voted Louis-Napoleon Bonaparte president of the republic. "Our first task is to teach, to instruct, to enlighten," he warned, while the second (particularly important as the Dreyfus Affair raged) was to remain united.[24] Millerand did not carry all socialists with him, particularly when he accepted office in a bourgeois so-called "government of republican defense" against the forces of anti-Dreyfusard reaction. Jules Guesde argued that "ministerialism" would alienate the masses who would then "allow through the first saber as, after the collapse of the Second Republic in the blood of June, they permitted the 2 December of M. Louis Bonaparte."[25] For Guesde the unity of the Socialist Party had to built around the doctrine of class struggle and revolution, and he continued to cultivate the heroic myth of the June Days and Paris Commune rather than, like the democratic socialists, criticize them as premature.

Engels was cited as an authority by Eduard Bernstein, when in 1898 the latter tried to persuade the Stuttgart congress of the German Social Democratic Party (SPD) to abandon the doctrines of violent revolution and the dictatorship of the proletariat. Far from acclaiming the barricade fighters in their anniversary year, he was influenced by the current thinking about crowd psychology of Scipio Sighele and Gustave Le Bon. He argued that crowds were inherently unstable, suggestible, and prone to criminal activities and atrocities like the massacres of St. Bartholomew and of September 1792.[26] Appropriating the discourse of evolutionism, he asserted moreover that democracy was an inevitable stage in the development of society and must be the instrument of the gradual socialization of society; the dictatorship of classes belonged to "a lower civilization," and was "a reversion, a political atavism."[27] Stefan Born, who had founded the General German Workers' Brotherhood in 1848, but had fled to Switzerland after the Dresden rising of 1849 and started a new career as an academic, concurred that theories of evolution undermined doctrines of class struggle leading to a perfect socialist society, and claimed that ideas were more important than material forces. "Social revolutionaries become social reformers," he concluded fifty years after the event, "that is the trend of the times."[28]

A contrary view was taken by Rosa Luxemburg and Lenin. They argued that democratic concessions were fragile and illusory, granted by reactionary governments and ruling classes and liable to be withdrawn at any moment if it seemed as though the socialist movement might benefit. Moreover, they claimed, an objective reading of Marx and Engels demonstrated that they adhered to a revolutionary interpretation of 1848. Rosa Luxemburg replied to Bernstein that the advent of democracy was not inevitable; on the contrary, it was now being abandoned by the bourgeoisie "for fear of the growing labor movement." She accused Bernstein of "saying goodbye to the mode of thought of the revolutionary proletariat, to dialectics, and to the materialist conception of history."[29]

The analysis of Lenin, during the 1905 revolution, was likewise based squarely on the purported original reading of the 1848 revolution in Germany by Marx and Engels. Since the German bourgeoisie had thrown itself into the arms of the monarchy, army, and feudal aristocracy, who then turned their bayonets on the people, the same was likely to happen in Russia. The Union of Liberation, inspired by the strategy of French democrats in 1848, had launched a banquet campaign in

1904 at which orators demanded a Constituent Assembly elected by universal suffrage. One of the young lawyers who helped to organize the banquets was Alexander Kerensky.[30] "Constitutional illusions and school exercises in parliamentarism become merely a screen for the bourgeois betrayal of the revolution," riposted Lenin in 1905, and bourgeois force would have to met by the force of a democratic dictatorship of the proletariat and peasantry. Likewise "petty-bourgeois illusions about the unity of the people and the absence of a class struggle within the people," which ensured that the 1848 revolution was "not consummated" in a socialist sense, must be avoided. In Russia the workers would be led by an "independent proletarian party" dedicated to "the complete victory of the revolution."[31] In *State and Revolution* written in August 1917, Lenin renewed the attack on "the petty-bourgeois democrats, those sham socialists who replaced the class struggle by dreams of class harmony," and who had betrayed the French Revolution of 1848. He cited the *Communist Manifesto* to justify class struggle and the dictatorship of the proletariat, and argued that "all his life Marx fought against this petty-bourgeois socialism now revived in Russia by the Socialist-Revolutionary and Menshevik Parties."[32]

Whereas for democratic socialists in Germany, as we have seen, the 1918 revolution was the fulfillment of the democratic hopes of 1848, for Rosa Luxemburg no faith could be placed in a national assembly if the bourgeoisie and feudal class decided to defend their privileges by force; existing workers' and soldiers' councils must be transformed into a soviet regime. "The species embodied by Lamartine, Garnier-Pagès, Ledru-Rollin, namely the species of petit-bourgeois illusionists and babblers of AD 1848, has not died out," she ranted, "it has reappeared—without the luster and talent and allure of newness—in a boring, pedantic, scholarly German edition written by Kautsky, Hilferding, and Haase."[33] After the workers' and soldiers' councils voted to support a national assembly, Luxemburg helped to found the German Communist Party, claimed the authority of the *Communist Manifesto* of 1848 and argued that with their aim of destroying capitalism "we stand on the same ground that Marx and Engels occupied in 1848 and from which in principle they did not deviate."[34]

But Engels had also pointed out that the lack of revolutionary decisiveness manifested in Germany in 1848 boded ill for the success of revolution in the future. After the defeat of the Communist rising of January 1919 and shortly before her murder, Rosa Luxemburg was led to much the same conclusion:

> The heroic action of the proletariat of Paris in 1848 has become the living source of class energy for the whole International. The wretchedness of the German March Revolution, by contrast, has weighed down the whole modern German development like a ball and chain. It has produced after-effects extending from the special history of official German Social Democracy up to the latest events of the German revolution—right up to the dramatic crisis we have just witnessed.[35]

For Communists the failed revolution of 1918 was explained by the burden of the failed revolution of 1848, but the defeat of the Third Reich and the patronage of Soviet Communism offered an opportunity in 1948 for realizing the hopes of those who subscribed to the revolutionary message of 1848. In the Soviet-controlled eastern zone of Germany the Dresden Socialist Unity Party, which fused communists and some socialists, announced that "the new Germany has the duty of making up for the neglect of the 1848 revolution," and organized a 50,000 strong demonstration in honor of the March fighters. Unlike in 1848, it argued, the working class was now class-conscious, led by a united socialist party, and in a position, linked to wider progressive forces in Germany, to "undertake the completion of the historical tasks of the March fighters ... against imperialists and reactionaries."[36]

French Communists were similarly keen to claim the mantle of the revolutionaries of 1848 from what they called the "American party" which now ran France, and to assert that the ideals of 1848 were now realized in the Soviet bloc. At a mass rally in Paris, André Marty insisted that the Prague coup of the Czech Communist leader Gottwald was only trying to prevent their revolution failing in the same way as the French one had failed in 1848. "The dream of 1848 has come true," he asserted, "because in the USSR, over a sixth of the globe, there is no more exploitation of man by man, because the socialist regime has been born. It has crushed the Hitlerian hordes and, over the ruins of Berlin, the Red Army has raised the flag of the insurgents of 1848 that the fascists stole."[37] Totalitarian communism made a bid to appropriate the myth of the failed revolution that needed to be completed by decisive action, and in a short space of time would also seek to appropriate the myth of national liberation for its own ends.

The collapse of communism in Europe removed the primary exponents of the revolutionary interpretation of 1848. In Germany the sacred date of 18 March was still an issue in 1998, although not for the SPD. The Berlin senate, controlled by a coalition between the Christian Democratic Union (CDU) and the SPD, was extremely reluctant to organize any commemoration at all in 1998.[38] In the end the minister president of Baden-Württemberg, Erwin Teufel, laid a wreath at the monument to the victims of the March Revolution, but revolutionary protest was confined to the 18 March Initiative of Günter Grass and Christa Wolf. They paraded 300-strong to demand that 18 March be established as a public holiday and hung signs reading "18 March Square" over those signaling "Brandenburg Gate Square" since an official renaming had been rejected by the Berlin senate.[39] The French Communist Party (PCF) marked the 150th anniversary of the publication of the *Communist Manifesto* by a debate in Paris in June on its future path. Regrets were expressed for the Stalinist period and an address by Ababacar Diop, leader of the "sans-papier" or non-regularized immigrants under threat of expulsion, gave some indication of new battles to be fought on behalf of "modern slaves" other than Marx's proletariat. No mention however was made of the June Days as the masses bowed to the false consciousness of World Cup hysteria.

The Myth of National Liberation

One of the most enduring myths of the 1848 revolutions was that it ushered in the springtime of peoples, the liberation of nations from subservience to the great dynastic empires, and that it looked to apply the principle of fraternity to the international community by forming a brotherhood of free nations. In his address to foreign powers of 2 March 1848 Lamartine declared that the treaties of 1815 were no longer valid and that France would come to the help of peoples who wished to recover their freedom. Unfortunately Lamartine was also keen to lay to rest the ghost of the expansionist First Republic, and in so doing rendered illusory promises of military support to nations seeking independence. "To return after fifty years to the principle of 1792, to the idea of conquering an empire," Lamartine declared, "would be to go not forwards but backwards in time ... The world and we ourselves wish to march towards fraternity and peace."[40] As a result the old empires were able to reassert their domination over subject peoples, and the French themselves intervened in 1849 to restore the Pope to Rome, whence he had been driven by revolutionary nationalists under Mazzini and Garibaldi.

A hundred years later Frenchmen, who had always defended the liberating and civilizing mission of France, were still beating their breasts about the missed opportunity. In his Sorbonne lecture Léon Blum argued that 1848 was a honeymoon period when "movements for national liberation coincided exactly with movements for democratic liberation," that this was the moment to have created a "Federation of free democracies in Europe." Since the policy of non-intervention in Spain followed by Blum's government of 1936 had been discredited along with the appeasement of fascist powers, and the Soviet Union had renewed its grip on eastern Europe, Blum now argued that the French should have intervened decisively in European affairs in 1848, without thought of conquest but to support democratic and national liberation. Instead of this the Russian tsar and Austrian emperor had been permitted to reestablish their reactionary empires.[41] By extension, he suggested, such an interventionist policy after 1918 might have ensured a benevolent French patronage of nascent democracies in central and eastern Europe, instead of the totalitarian empires of Nazi Germany or the USSR.

The collective memory of national liberation was developed after the victory of the Austrian and Russian empires in 1849 by nationalist leaders such as Mazzini and Kossuth who had been driven into exile. Mazzini enjoyed the support of the Friends of Italy Society in London, where in 1852 he ranted against the papacy, nobles and the kingdom of Piedmont.[42] Kossuth, who had declared the Habsburg Dynasty deposed and issued a Hungarian Declaration of Independence, launched himself on a tour of England and the United States in 1851/2, seeking international recognition for his Declaration of Independence and financial and even military support to make it a reality. In England he flattered the British love of liberty, played on his Protestantism, and saw himself acclaimed as a new Cromwell.[43] In Birmingham he announced to cheers that "As long as Hungary shall not be restored to its sovereign liberty and independence, as long as Italy shall not become free, the foot of Russia will rest on Europe's neck ... The cause of Hungary is the cause of civil and religious liberty."[44] In the United States, Kossuth praised the American Declaration of Independence and the republican constitution, but was powerless to persuade the Americans to reconsider the Monroe Doctrine and intervene in Europe.[45]

Revolutionary nationalists were brushed aside by the power-politics of national unification undertaken from above by the Italian and German states. Mazzini continued to struggle for a popular revolution and constituent assembly to found an Italian republic on the model of 1848/9 and to denounce the "diplomatization" of the Risorgimento. He languished in prison in 1870 when Rome was finally occupied by Piedmontese armies, refused to accept a royal pardon for his patriotism, and, though acclaimed by the people when he died in 1872, received no tribute from either government or parliament. Kossuth likewise attacked the *Ausgleich* by which Hungary became part of a dual monarchy with Austria, preferring a republic and refusing to accept anything but full independence for Hungary. He was *persona non grata* to Francis Joseph, died in exile in Turin in 1894, and though the crowds turned out in hundreds of thousands for his burial in Budapest, at the wish of the emperor the Hungarian government and parliament did not participate. The street along which the cortège passed was named after him in 1894, but the square outside the Parliament building did not take his name until after the First World War.

The gulf between revolutionary nationalism and official nation-building was clearly articulated when the fiftieth anniversary of 1848 revolutions was marked in 1898. Official Italy celebrated the anniversary of the *Statuto*, or constitution granted by Charles Albert of Piedmont, which later became the constitution of a united Italy. The socialist leader Turati challenged the official celebrations in Milan by demanding the full realization of the political and civil rights granted by the constitution. Meanwhile the official procession to commemorate the Five Days in March 1848 during which the Milanese drove out the Austrian forces was countered by a popular demonstration.[46] Two months later, popular discontent and strike action in Milan was suppressed by military force in the so-called *Fatti di Maggio*, precipitating a major constitutional crisis.

In the German Reichstag a confrontation took place on the anniversary of the uprising of 18 March between Robert von Puttkamer, the Prussian minister of the interior, the socialist leader August Bebel, and the doyen of the National Liberal Party Rudolf von Bennigsen. Puttkamer declared that the revolution had been caused by an "foreign rabble" who had stirred up "our good and loyal people" against their king and had wantonly interrupted the process of reform. Bebel protested at the use of the term "rabble" to describe those who had died for their ideals on the barricades and argued that "without the 18 March there would be no German Reich, without the German Reich there would be no German Reichstag, and I might add, without the German Reichstag there would be no war minister responsible to it." He concluded that had King Frederick William kept his promises of 18 March instead of ordering his soldiers to shoot, German unification would have been possible without Bismarck and without the war of 1870.[47]

This provoked Rudolf von Bennigsen to intervene, attacking Bebel for opposing the war of 1870, which had been crucial for German unification, and arguing that the 18 March had not had the slightest influence on Germany's rise to greatness. "Its foundations," he said, "were not the Berlin street-fighting but the great national movement in which participated the whole German people, including notables, governments, and princes." He underlined that the Frankfurt Assembly, which brought together the best elements in the German nation, must be credited with the first serious attempt at unification, but that the role of the future King William, who had to flee Berlin after 18 March, and of the Otto von Bismarck, who had fiercely opposed the street-fighting, were absolutely central to the success of unification.[48] For most Germans, 1898 was marked less by commemoration of the March 1848 revolution than by celebration of the tenth anniversary of the accession of Kaiser William II on 16 June, and the funeral of Bismarck in August. In Austria, to complete the picture, the festivities of 1898 were devoted not to revolution but to the fiftieth anniversary of the accession of the Emperor Franz Joseph, praised in one commemorative work as a "savior and restorer" who had steered the monarchy away from revolution towards peace and stability.[49]

In Imperial Germany the socialists were pilloried as antipatriotic enemies of the Reich. When they came to power in the Weimar Republic they needed to convince nationalists that they were in a position to protect Germany's interests. In 1923, with the Ruhr occupied by French forces, Friedrich Ebert argued in his *Paulskirche* speech that the concepts of "unity, freedom, and fatherland" that guided the Frankfurt Assembly were also "the essence and guiding star of the struggle for existence we are forced to carry on today on the Rhine, Ruhr, and Saar."[50] Unfortunately, nationalists and Nazis persuaded the German people that Fatherland and Unity was best secured by sacrificing freedom, including the existence of the republic.

In 1948, after the collapse of the Third Reich, there was arguably greater harmony between the aspirations of the nationalists of 1848 towards national liberation and international brotherhood and those of the architects of a new Europe. However there were significant differences from country to country, depending on whether aspirations towards national liberation that were on the agenda had been realized, or were frustrated and remained a painful memory.

In Germany, which was occupied militarily by the Allies and divided by the developing Cold War between capitalist west and communist east, the debate on 1848 was likewise divided. In the west, intellectuals and politicians looked nostalgically at 1848 as an opportunity to combine the freedom and unity of the German nation that had been squandered. Friedrich Meinecke argued that March 1848 inflicted not just a physical but a political and psychological defeat on the Prussian military monarchy and that it might have turned the "authoritarian state" into a "partnership state," but did not.[51] Theodor Heuss said that repression following the 1848 revolution had favored only American democracy as Germans emigrated to the United States, but conceded that the myth of German unity and self-government had been passed down to subsequent generations.[52]

The journalist Ernst Friedländer regretted that the Germans had no national day of celebration on a par with the French Bastille Day or American Independence Day. He argued that in 1848 the German people had been united and had the princes on the run, but that deeds had failed to match spirit and concluded that 1848 remained a "standstill revolution." Echoing Friedrich Ebert he reflected that "the Germans tried to grasp destiny in their hands and it eluded them." German unity had come from the hands of Bismarck, for the people but not by the people. The one lesson to learn was that freedom was more important than unity and that current Soviet propaganda ostensibly in favor of a democratic and united Germany in fact promised a "Soviet-totalitarian mass existence and in no sense a German existence."[53]

For the Communists of the eastern zone, like their Soviet master, the division of Germany was a temporary affair contingent on military occupation. The goal was a united democratic Germany and in this respect the lesson of 1848 was there to be learned. The commemoration of 18 March 1848 coincided with the second German Peoples Congress in Berlin, attended by 2,000 delegates. Otto Grotewohl of the official Socialist Unity Party (SED) called for the delegates to fulfil the vision of those who had fought in March 1848 and found a democratic and united Germany. He rejoiced that some delegates had come from the western zones and argued that German unity served not just a class or a party but the German nation as a whole.[54] This attempt to appropriate a legitimacy derived from 1848 to set up a Germany that would clearly be a one-party state under the protection of the USSR was necessarily doomed to failure.

The Austrians, who had lost an empire and suffered annexation by the Third Reich, drew few lessons from a revolution that had threatened the integrity and great-power status of that empire. Their main response was amnesia, believing fervently that "nothing had happened" there in 1848. *Neues Österreich* reported that "the reminder that a hundred years ago blood was spilt in Vienna for human rights, freedom and democracy, disturbs the operetta-like image we have of the "good old time," in which thirty years ago the "good old" Emperor Franz died."[55] From their troubled present they preferred to look back to a golden age of imperial rule.

Nationalities that had struggled to free themselves from the Habsburg Empire in 1848 took a very different view. In Italy, the lessons of national unity and independence to be learned from 1848 were indeed much clearer after the defeat of fascism and with the challenge of communism to be faced. The centenary of the Five Days of Milan took on new significance after the expulsion of a new wave of Germanic invaders in 1945. A plaque in the piazza della Scala in Milan linked the republican heroes and martyrs of the Five Days fighting for "justice, liberty, and independence" to the partisan struggle of 1943/45 culminating in the "victorious insurrection of 25 April 1945," an interpretation that neatly brushed aside the fascist episode as a foreign imposition, not a home-grown product. A new constitution was voted in 1948, on the centenary of the *Statuto*, taking on a new sheen after the fascist interlude. The Italian parliament celebrated 100 years of existence, the speaker of the new Chamber of Deputies hailing his predecessor, Vicenzo Gioberti, elected speaker of the Turin parliament on 8 May 1848, and praising the parliament's stalwart defense of civil and democratic liberties against the reaction of 1898 and against fascism.[56] Given that disunity had often left Italy vulnerable to foreign intervention, and the new threat came from the Communist bloc, Prime Minister De Gasperi, who had built a four-party anti-Communist coalition, opened the twenty-seventh Congress for the History of the Risorgimento in Milan by insisting that the lesson of 1848 was that Italians must remain united in their defense of liberty.[57]

Hungary had achieved independence in truncated form in 1918, and the statue erected to Kossuth in Budapest in 1927 depicted him as a defeated leader. Another national hero of 1848, the poet Petöfi, was honored by a statue in 1882. When the reactionary Hungarian government entered the war against the Soviet Union in 1941, Communists, Socialists, and trade-unionists expressed their opposition to the war and desire for an independent, democratic Hungary by turning to the national heroes. Wreaths were laid at the statues of Petöfi and Kossuth on 15 March 1942, leading to the arrest of 600 Communists, but mass celebrations of the fiftieth anniversary of Kossuth's death planned for 20 March 1944 were curtailed by the German invasion of the previous day.[58]

As in eastern Germany, the Communists who gained influence in Hungary after the war sought to demonstrate that they alone gave expression to the aspirations of 1848 for national liberation and made a bid for the myth of Louis Kossuth. A new statue, surrounded by peasants, workers, and soldiers, was dedicated to him in 1952 and the Communist education minister Jósef Révai, inaugurating it, said that:

> Although he was not a son of his people, he realized that without the liberation of the serfs the nation was exposed to oppression. We respect Kossuth for his unshakable loyalty to the cause of Hungarian independence, for refusing to give way to despair even after the defeat of the revolution and shameful agreement of 1867. We respect Kossuth for the fact that he was clearly aware in 1848 of the relationship between the struggle for freedom of the Hungarian people and the similar struggle of other peoples in Europe.[59]

What Révai failed to point out was that Kossuth's struggle was as much against the Russians as against the Austrians, so that when the Hungarians rose against Communist and Soviet rule in 1956, they immediately reappropriated their national heroes of 1848 and orchestrated the revolutionary movement around their shrines. The demonstration of 23 October in Budapest began at the statue of Petöfi, where one of his poems was recited. It moved to the statue of Josef Bem, the Polish general who had led the struggle against the Russians in 1849, erected in 1934, where another a poem of Petöfi was read out:

> Magyars rise, your country calls!
> Meet this hour, whate'er befalls!
> Shall we freemen be, or slaves?
> Choose the lot your spirit craves![60]

As dusk fell the immense statue of Stalin at the entrance to the city woods was brought down, and the crowds marched to Kossuth Square, in front of the parliament building, demanding the return of Imre Nagy to power. From there they went to the radio station, and when security forces fired on them they seized control of the station, subsequently renaming the national radio Radio Kossuth.[61] The crushing of the Hungarian Revolution represented for one of the Social Democratic leaders the revenge of the "red tsars," the heirs of those that had crushed Hungary in 1849.[62]

The reunification of Germany in 1990 provoked widespread fears that the Bismarckian Reich with its militarism and expansionist designs would be resurrected. This specter the Germans were keen to exorcise, both for others and themselves. The mantle of the revolution of 1848, when the German nation had sought unity and freedom, and had not (with the exception of a small clash with Denmark) embarked on expansion was clearly an attractive one. So was the European dimension of 1848, in which subject peoples had to some extent helped each other in the struggle against the authoritarian, multinational empires, for a united Germany contained within the framework of the European Union was felt to be a more acceptable quantity than a great power allying, for example, with Russia.

By the same token, those keen on broadening and deepening European integration and popularizing the European idea saw the European vision of 1848 as a rich source of legitimation. Rudolf Scharping, for example, an SPD deputy in the Bundestag, urged the parliament to celebrate 1848, as a "Europe-wide movement of peoples towards freedom … If, 150 years later, Europe wishes to move close together," he said, "it must be a Europe of the people."[63] In his *Paulskirche* speech, moreover, President Herzog argued that only in a united democratic Europe would democracy have a chance of meeting the undemocratic challenges of globalization. The fascination of the Frankfurt National Assembly with freedom and democracy, he concluded, must now be translated into efforts to democratize decision-making in Europe.[64]

Celebrations of 1848 were scarcely conducted on a European scale in 1998. Moreover commemorations on a national level were challenged by local or regional commemorations claiming the heritage of 1848 for their own. In Germany there was a noticeable difference between the enthusiasm of south and west Germany, with its democratic tradition, to mark the event, and Berlin where, as we have seen, the senate showed a marked reluctance to do anything. Even sharper was the clash in Italy, where the Five Days of Milan were the subject of two different commemorative events. The official celebration, in the piazza Tricolore, portrayed them as the first act of popular participation in the "great struggle for national independence," while in the piazza XXIV Maggio the Northern League claimed it as the founding act not of Italian unity but of Milanese autonomy and Lombard self-government.[65] Explaining the failure of the war against Austria in 1848 the Tuscan radical Montanelli had said, "We fought as Piedmontese, as Tuscans, as Neapolitans, as Romans, not as Italians."[66] A century and a half later, in the context of the regionalist challenge to the nation-state, that same fragmentation was being celebrated.

The Emancipationist Myth

The final founding myth of 1848 concerns only one country, France. It relates to the abolition of slavery in the French colonies by a decree of the provisional government on 27 April 1848. This was associated with the name of Victor Schoelcher, an Alsatian journalist and philanthropist who chaired a commission of the Constituent Assembly which pressed for abolition and was later elected deputy for Martinique. Slavery had in fact been abolished by the Convention in 1794, but this date was never celebrated because it was short-lived, abrogated by Napoleon Bonaparte in 1802. Very little was made of the matter in 1898, but to mark the centenary on 27 April 1948 lectures were given at the Sorbonne by three black politicians. They were selected as models of assimilated colonial peoples who subscribed to the myth of the liberating and civilizing mission of a nation that conferred citizenship on all who adopted its values, but while two went through the routine admirably, one was much more critical.

Gaston Monnerville, who originated from French Guiana and was now president of the Council of the Republic (the upper house of parliament), suavely located the emancipation of the slaves in the republican tradition of liberty, equality, and fraternity, and argued that the liberating gesture had been repaid by the rallying of Félix Éboué, Governor of Chad, to the Free French in 1940 and confirmed by the foundation of the French Union in 1946, which was to guide the colonies to democratic self-government. Léopold Sédar Senghor, deputy for Senegal and later its president, said that despite his reservations he had confidence that the constitution of 1946 would be of benefit for colonial peoples.

The third speaker, Aimé Césaire, was a communist deputy for Martinique who was less likely to flatter French self-congratulation because Communist ministers had been expelled from the government the previous year and because demonstrations in the Martiniquais capital Fort-de-France were broken up by the police. Césaire argued that Victor Schoelcher and the decree on emancipation had been systematically marginalized by accounts of the 1848 revolution, which amounted to a form of racism, that slavery demonstrated the coexistence of civilization and barbarism in the French nineteenth century, and that while "the colonial question has been put, it is a long way from being resolved."[67] Elsewhere he likened the transport of African peoples to slave plantations in the Americas to deportation of the Jews to Nazi concentration camps, and called the bourgeoisie of France, Spain, Britain, and Holland who had constructed capitalism on the back of slavery "innocent Himmlers of the system."[68]

The emancipationist myth aligned the generosity of the French nation with the gratitude of the emancipated black, who, having been given his liberty, was keen to assimilate French values. It was suggested that emancipated blacks would naturally side with France, given its liberating and civilizing mission incarnate in the Resistance, against oppressive and barbaric powers like Germany. Thus when the remains of Schoelcher were transferred to the Panthéon in 1949 they were accompanied by those of Félix Éboué. Whether the populations of France's Empire felt that gratitude in practice is another matter.

For the 150th anniversary of emancipation, Jacques Chirac invited an élite of assimilated French citizens to the Élysée and was pictured with the goalkeeper Serge Lama. He produced a homily on France's liberating and civilizing mission, reminding his audience that the emancipation decree applied the first article of the Declaration of Rights of Man and the Citizen of 1789, "men are born and remain free and equal in rights." He underlined the "open and generous attitude" of the French nation, prepared to welcome those who wished to join it and, in return for the rights of citizenship, despite their own culture and traditions, were prepared to accept the French system of values. This, he said, was "the French model of integration."[69]

For the inhabitants of Martinique and Guadeloupe, where the movement for independence from French rule was gathering pace, this restatement of old platitudes was seen as a slap in the face. They were keen to develop their own myth of slavery and emancipation in order to justify their political claims. Thus Martiniquais were quick to point out that on their island abolition had been the fruit of struggle, not generosity, a measure taken by the local French authorities before the arrival of the decree from Paris in direct response to the slave insurrection of 22 May 1848. Guadaloupians called for a boycott of the commemorative ceremonies, on the grounds that by honoring the virtue of Schoelcher the French were shuffling off responsibility for crime of slavery which they had restored and continued much longer than other nations like the British.

More forcefully than Aimé Césaire in 1948, the International Committee of Black People, based in Guadeloupe, asked Laurent Fabius, president of the National Assembly, to have the Assembly adopt a resolution that slavery was a crime against humanity in the same way that the Shoah was, and to apologize for it. "Let us be clear," said their spokesman, "that the genocide of the Jews has been recognized, the crime has been condemned, and the pain of it taken into account. But for the slave there has been nothing. Nothing. The life of a black man does not have the same value as that of the white man." Visiting the village of Champagney (Haute-Saône) where the cahier de doléance in 1789 had called for the abolition of slavery, prime minister Jospin admitted that "in the human tragedy represented by slavery the former colonial powers have to take their share of responsibility." The inversion of the emancipationist myth, however, thrown back at the French by pro-independence leaders who equated slavery with the Holocaust, illustrates the irreconcilability of collective memories and the fragility of the ideologically inspired interpretations of 1848.[70]

Conclusion

Three general points may be made in conclusion. First, the collective memories of 1848 were diverse, elaborated by a number of political movements—democratic, socialist, and nationalist—which sought to define and legitimate themselves against the authoritarian empires that dominated in Europe. To some extent, while in opposition, they allied with each other, but they were also rivals and if one movement achieved power it tried to impose its version of events on its rivals as the received wisdom. Thus the democrats sought to win socialists over to the idea of the democratic, not revolutionary, path to power. On other occasions, those already in power appropriated the myth fostered by the opposition and use it for its own ends. In this way the ideal of national liberation was taken up by states such as Piedmont or Prussia for the sake of nation-building, and purged of any revolutionary connotations.

Second, there was a powerful tension between the 1848 revolutions as a rich source of founding myths to define and legitimate political communities, and the burden of failed revolution that threatened to undermine as much as it inspired. Revolutionary movements were tempted to look alternatively to 1789, 1871 or 1917 for founding myths, either because they were more successful revolutions or because (as with 1871) the martyrdom was more spectacular. The German people was more likely to be defined with reference to successful moments of nation-state building such as Sedan Day 1870 rather than to 1848, when combined national and democratic aspirations ended in failure. Similarly the diverse peoples of the Habsburg Monarchy cultivated the accession of Franz Joseph rather that the revolution that had tried to unseat the dynasty and divide the empire. And yet the when reunification took place in 1990 the German nation was happy to revive a democratic and fraternal nationalist myth that offered an alternative to the militaristic and aggressive national myths of the Second and Third Reichs.

This brings us to the third point: that collective memories of the 1848 revolutions changed over time. In 1898 the democratic heirs of 1848 had learned the lessons of failure and were in power in France, socialists were divided over 1848 according to whether they were likely to achieve power democratically or not, and national liberationists had been brushed aside by nation-building led by states. In 1948 democrats in western Europe were reflecting on their resurrection from the dead and questioned the generosity of their predecessors, the socialist myth was taken up by communist parties, while the myth of national liberation was taken up in Italy to whitewash its fascist past and by communists in East Germany and Hungary, where it was hotly contested by democratic nationalists in 1956. In 1998 both communism and the socialist myth were dead, Germans struggled to learn democratic and nationalist lessons of 1848 afresh, Italians realized that 1848 could sustain regionalist demands, while the French, assuming that they had no more to learn as a democratic nation-state, saw the emancipationist myth blow up in their faces.

Notes

A version of this essay has been published in R.J.W. Evans and H.P. von Strandmann (eds.) *The Revolutions in Europe 1848-1849* (Oxford: Oxford University Press, 2000).

1. *Le Réformateur*, 10 January 1835
2. Victor Hugo, *A ses Concitoyens* (Paris, 1848).
3. François Raspail, *Remerciements* in *Discours du citoyen Ledru-Rollin prononcés au banquet du Châtelet, 22 Sept. 1848* (Paris, 1849), 19.
4. Alexandre Ledru-Rollin, *Discours politiques et écrits divers* Vol. 2 (Paris, 1879), 483
5. Louis Blanc, speech the Revolution of February 1848, 24 February 1877, in *Discours politiques, 1847-1881* (Paris, 1882), 247, *Histoire de la Révolution de 1848*, Vol. 1 (Paris, 1880), chapter 6: "Caractère généreux de la Révolution de février."
6. Louis Blanc, speech of 24 February 1878 in *Discours politiques*, 299.
7. Ibid., 291. Speech of 13 January 1878.
8. *La Révolution de 1848. Bulletin de la Société d'Histoire de la Révolution de 1848. Deuxième Année*, 1905-6, 2.
9. Léon Blum, lecture of 24 February 1948, in *L'Oeuvre* 6/2 (Paris, 1963), 420-8. On the commemoration of 1848 in France see Timothy Baycroft, "Commemorations of the Revolution of 1848 and the Second Republic," *Modern and Contemporary France* 6/2 (May 1998): 155-68.
10. France. Assemblée Nationale, *Les Révolutions de 1848. L'Europe des Images* (Paris, 1998). I am grateful to Tom Gretton for this reference.
11. Friedrich Ebert, *Schriften, Aufzeichnungen, Reden*, Vol. 2 Dresden, 1926), 120-21.
12. Dieter Rebentish, *Friedrich Ebert und die Paulskirche. Die Weimarer Demokratie und die 75-Jahrfeier der 1848er Revolution* (Heidelberg, 1998), 10. I am grateful to Hartmut Pogge von Strandmann for this reference.
13. *Frankfurter Neue Presse*, 19 May 1948.
14. *Frankfurter Allgemeine Zeitung*, 19 May 1998.
15. P.-J. Proudhon, *Les Confessions d'un Révolutionnaire* [Oct. 1849], *Oeuvres complètes*, Vol. 7 (Paris, 1927), 167-9.
16. *Le Cri du Peuple*, 22 February 1871.
17. Friedrich Engels, *Revolution and Counter-Revolution in Germany in 1848* (London, 1896), 96. Written in March 1852.
18. Karl Marx, *The Paris Commune of 1871* ed. by Christopher Hitchens, (London, 1971), 86.
19. Karl Marx, *The Civil War in France* (London, 1933), 10.
20. Benoît Malon, *La Troisième Défaite du Prolétariat français* (Neuchâtel, 1871).
21. *L'Égalité*, first series, 25 June 1878.
22. Vernon L. Lidtke, *The Alternative Culture. Socialist Labor in Imperial Germany* (New York and Oxford, 1985), 77.
23. *Die Neue Zeit* 16 (1897-8): 739.
24. *La Petite République*, 27 February 1898
25. *Congrès général des organisations socialistes françaises tenu à Paris du 3 au 8 décembre 1899* (Paris, 1900), 186.
26. *Die Neue Zeit*, 10 November 1897, 1 March 1898, in Henry and J.M. Tudor, *Marxism and Social Democracy. The Revisionist Debate, 1896-1898* (Cambridge, 1988), 110-18, 220-21.
27. Eduard Bernstein, *Evolutionary Socialism: A Criticism and Affirmation* (London, 1909), 146.
28. Stephan Born, *Erinnerungen eines Achtundvierzigers* (Leipzig, 1898), 295.
29. Rosa Luxemburg, *Reform or Revolution* [1900] (London, 1986), 64.
30. Paul Miliukov, *Political Memoirs, 1905-1917*, ed. By Arthur P. Mendel (Ann Arbor, 1967), 12; Alexander Kerensky, *The Kerensky Memoirs* (London, 1966), 45.
31. Lenin, *Two Tactics of Social-Democracy in the Democratic Revolution* [July 1905], in *Selected Works* (Moscow, 1968), 141, 142, 145.
32. Ibid., 279, 286.
33. *Die Rote Fahne*, 20 November 1918, in Rosa Luxemburg, *Selected Political Writings*, ed. by Robert Looker (London,, 1972), 263.

34. Rosa Luxemburg, *Ich war, ich bin, ich werde sein! Artikel und Reden zur Novemberrevolution* (Berlin, 1958), 99.

35. Luxemburg, *Selected Political Writings*, 305.

36. *Sächsische Zeitung*, 17, 19 March 1948.

37. *L'Humanité*, 25 February 1948.

38. *Die Zeit*, 26 February 1998, "Blamabel und unwürdig. In Sachen 1848 reagiert der Berliner Senat hilflos."

39. *Süddeutsche Zeitung*, 19 March 1998.

40. Comité national du centenaire de 1848, *Documents diplomatiques du gouvernement provisoire et de la commission du pouvoir exécutif* 1 (Paris, 1953), 8.

41. Lecture of 24 February 1848, *L'Oeuvre*, Vol. 6/2: 425-29.

42. Emilia Morelli, *Mazzini in Inghilterra* (Florence, 1938), 162-66. Meeting of the Society, 24 March 1852.

43. *Kossuth* (London, 1851), iv-v.

44. *Authentic Life of his Excellency Louis Kossuth, Governor of Hungary, with a full report of his speeches delivered in England* (London, 1851), 117. Speech of 12 November 1851.

45. John H. Komlos, *Kossuth in America, 1851- 1852* (Buffalo, 1973).

46. Alfredo Canavero, *Milano e la crisi di fino secolo, 1896-1900* (Milan, 1976), 155-57; Louise A. Tilly, *Politics and Class in Milan, 1881-1901* (New York and Oxford, 1992), 260-61.

47. *Stenographische Berichte über die Verhandlungen des Reichstags. IX Legislatur Periode. V. Session 1897/8. Zweiter Band* (Berlin, 1898), 1591, 1600-1.

48. Ibid., 1606-7; speech also in Adolf Kiepert, *Rudolph von Bennigsen* (Hannover and Berlin, 1903), 215-17.

49. Carl Klopfer, *Unser Kaiser. Ein Gedankbuch der fünfzigjährigen Regierung, zugleich ein Lebens- und Charakterbild Kaiser Franz Joseph* (Vienna, 1898), 4.

50. Rebentisch, *Friedrich Ebert*, 11.

51. Friedrich Meinecke, *1848. Ein Säkularbetrachung* (Berlin, 1948), 9.

52. Theodor Heuss, *1848. Werke und Erbe* (Stuttgart, 1948), 161-2, 167.

53. *Die Zeit*, 18 March 1948.

54. *Leipziger Volkszeitung,* 18 March 1948; *Sächsische Zeitung*, 19 March 1948.

55. *Neues Österreich*, 1 January 1948.

56. Segretario Generale della Camera dei Deputati, *Il Centenario del Parlamento, 8 maggio 1848-8 maggio 1948* (Rome, 1948), 18.

57. *Corriere della Sera*, 20 March 1948

58. C.A. Macartney, *October Fifteenth. A History of Modern Hungary, 1929-1945* Vol. 2 (Edinburgh, 1957), 104-5, 247. I am grateful to Robert Evans for information concerning the statues of Kossuth, Petöfi, and Bem in Budapest.

59. British Hungarian Friendship Society, *Kossuth, Architect of Hungarian Freedom, 1802- 1894* (London, 1953), 8.

60. Laslo Beke, *A Student's Diary: Budapest, October 16—November 1 1956* (London, 1957), 28.

61. François Fejtö, *Behind the Rape of Hungary* (New York, 1957); Paul E. Zinner, *Revolution in Hungary* (New York and London, 1963).

62. Béla K. Király and Paul Jónas, *The Hungarian Revolution of 1956 in Retrospect* (Boulder, 1978), 12.

63. *Die Zeit*, 19 February 1998.

64. *Frankfurter Allgemeine Zeitung*, 19 May 1998.

65. *Corriere della Sera*, 18, 19 March 1998.

66. Quoted in Robert Gildea, *Barricades and Borders. Europe 1800-1914* (Oxford, 1996), 98.

67. Gaston Monnerville, Léopold Sédar Senghor, Aimé Césaire, *Commémoration du Centenaire de l'Abolition de l"Esclavage. Discours prononcés à la Sorbonne le 27 avril 1948* (Paris, 1948), 4-5, 22, 27-28.

68. Aimé Césaire, introduction, in Émile Terson (ed.), *Victor Schoelcher, Esclavage et Colonisation* (Paris, 1948), 17-18.

69. *Libération*, 24 April 1998; *Le Monde*, 24 April 1998.

70. *Le Monde*, 25, 26-7, 28 April 1998.

SELECT BIBLIOGRAPHY

I. European and National Histories

Accademia nazionale dei Lincei, ed. Il 1848 nella storia d'Europa, 2 Vols., Rome: 1949

Agulhon, Maurice. 1848 ou l'apprentissage de la République, 1848-1852. 2nd ed. Paris: 1992. English edition, The Republican Experiment. Trasnlated by Janet Lloyd. Cambridge: 1983.

_____. Les Quarante-huitards. Paris, 1975

Anăniloaie, Nichita and Dan Berindei, eds. Revolutia de la 1848 în ţările române. Culegere de studii. Bucharest: 1974.

Apih, Josip, Slovenci in 1848, leto [Slovenia in 1848]. Ljubijana: 1888.

Barrié, Ottavio. L'Inghilterre e il problema italiano nel 1848-49. Dalla rivoluzione alla seconda restaurazione. Milan: 1965.

Baumgart, Franzjörg. Die verdrängte Revolution. Darstellung und Bewertung der Revolution von 1848 in der deutschen Geschichtsschreibung vor dem Ersten Weltkrieg. Düsseldorf: 1976.

Berindei, Dan. Revoluţia Română din 1848-1849. Consideratii si reflexii. Cluj-Napoca: 1997.

Bertrand, Louis. Histoire de la démocratie et du socialisme en Belgique depuis 1830. 2 vols. Brussels: 1906/7.

Biele, J.J. De pen in aanslag. Revolutionairen rond 1848. Bussum: 1968.

Bjorn, Claus. "Fra reaktion til grundlov 1800-1850." in O. Olsen (ed.). Danmarks Historie. 10 Vols. Copenhagen: 1977-90.

Blanc, Louis. Histoire de la révolution de 1848. 2 vols. Paris: 1849.

Blom, J.H.C. and E. Lamberts, eds. Geschiednis van de Nederlanden. Rijswilk: 1993.

Bodea, Cornelia. The Rumanians' Struggle for Unification. 1834-1849. Bucharest: 1970.

Bodea, Cornelia, ed. 1848 la Români. O istorie în date şi mărturii. 2 vols. Bucharest: 1982.

Boogman, J.C. Rondom 1848. Bussum: 1978.

Booms, Hans and Marian Wojciechowski, eds. Deutsche und Polen in der Revolution 1848-1849. Dokumente aus deutschen und polnischen Archiven. Boppard: 1991.

Candeloro, Giorgio. Storia dell'Italia moderna. 8 vols. Vol. 3: La Rivoluzione nazionale. 1846-1849. Milan: 1960.

Cherubini, Giovanni, Giorgio Mori, and Franco Della Peruta, eds. Storia della società italiana. 23 vols. Vol. 17. Il movimento nazionale e il 1848. Milan: 1981/91.

Della Peruta, Franco. Democrazia e socialismo nel Risorgimento. Rome: 1965.

De Luna, Frederick. The French Republic under Cavaignac. Princeton: 1969.

Deme, Laszlo. The Radical Left in the Hungarian Revolution of 1848. Boulder: 1976.

De Ridder, A. La crise de la neutralité belge de 1848. Brussels: 1928.

Documente privind Revoluția de la 1848 în țările române. B. Țara românească. 12 martie 1848-21 aprilie 1850. Bucharest: 1983.

Droz, Jacques. Les Révolutions Allemandes de 1848. Paris, 1957.

Dunk, Hermann von der. Der Deutsche Vormärz und Belgien 1830-1848. Wiesbaden: 1966.

Epstein, James and Dorothy Thompson, eds. The Chartist Experience: Studies in Working-Class Radicalism and Culture. 1830-1860. London: 1982.

Erbe, Michael. Belgien, Niederlande, Luxemburg. Geschichte des niederländischen Raumes. Stuttgart: 1993.

Ernst, A., A. Tanner, and A. Weishaupt, eds. Die konflikthafte Entstehung des schweizerischen Bundesstaates 1798-1848. Zurich: 1998.

Fetjö, François, ed. 1848 dans le monde. le printemps des peuples. 2 vols. Paris: 1948.

⸻ The Opening of an Era. 1848. An Historical Symposium. With an Introduction by A.J.P. Taylor. London: 1948.

Geschichte der Schweiz und der Schweizer. With essays by François de Capitani, Roland Ruffieux, Georges Andrey. Basel: 1986.

Girard, Louis. La IIᵉ République. Paris: 1968.

Godechot, Jacques. Les révolutions de 1848. Paris: 1971.

Goldstein, Robert. Political Repression in 19th Century Europe. London: 1983.

Grew, Raymond. A Sterner Plan for Italian Unity. The Italian National Society and the Risorgimento. Princeton: 1963.

Handbuch der Schweizer Geschichte. 2 vols. With contributions by Andreas Staehelin, Daniel Frei, Jean-Charles Biaudet, Erwin Bucher. Zurich: 1972/77.

Helfert, Josef Alexander Freiherr von. Geschichte der österreichischen Revolution im Zusammenhang mit der mitteleuropäischen Bewegung der Jahre 1848-1849. 2 vols. Freiburg/Breisgau: 1907/09.

⸻. Geschichte Österreichs vom Ausgange des Wiener Oktober-Aufstandes 1848. 4 vols. Prague and Leipzig: 1869/86.

Hildbrand Th. and A. Tanner, eds. Im Zeichen der Revolution. Der Weg zum schweizerischen Bundesstaat 1798-1848. Zurich: 1998.

Hitchens, Keith. The Romanians, 1774-1866. Oxford: 1996.

Illustrierte Geschichte der deutschen Revolution 1848/49. Authors' Collective: Walter Schmidt, Gerhard Becker, Helmut Bleiber, Rolf Dlubek, Siegfried Schmidt, Rolf Weber. East Berlin: 1973. 2nd ed., 1975.

Jaworski, Rudolf and Robert Luft eds. 1848/49—Revolutionen in Ostmitteleuropa. Munich: 1996.

Jorgensen, A.D., et. al. Danmarks Riges Historie. 8 vols. Copenhagen, 1896/98.

Joyce. Patrick. Visions of the People: Industrial England and the Question of Class. Cambridge: 1991.

Kazbunda, Karel. Ceské hnutí roku 1848 [The Czech Movement of 1848]. Prague: 1929.

Kiszling, Rudolf. Die Revolution im Kaisertum Österreich 1848-49. 2 vols. Vienna: 1948.

Klima, Arnost. "The Bourgeois Revolution of 1848-49 in Central Europe." In Roy Porter and Mikulas Teich (eds.). Revolution in History. Cambridge: 1986.

Kolejka, Josef. Národy habsburské monarchie v revoluci 1848-1849 [The Peoples of the Habsburg Monarchy in the Revolution of 1848-1849]. Prague: 1989.

Kořalka. Jiři. Tschechen im Habsburgerreich und in Europa 1815-1914. Vienna and Munich: 1991.

Kossock, Manfred, ed. Revolutionen der Neuzeit. East Berlin, 1982.

Lademacher, Horst. Die belgische Neutralität als Problem der europäischen Politik. 1830-1914. Bonn: 1971.

_____. Die Niederlande. Politische Kultur zwischen Individualität und Anpassung. Berlin: 1993.

Lamartine, Alphonse de. Histoire de la révolution de 1848. 2 vols. Paris: 1849.

_____. La France parlementaire. 5 vols. Paris: 1865.

Langewiesche, Dieter. "Die deutsche Revolution von 1848/49 und die vorrevolutionäre Gesellschaft. Forschungsstand und Forschungsperpektiven." Archiv für Sozialgeschichte 21 (1981): 458-98; 31 (1991): 331-43

_____. Europa zwischen Restauration und Revolution 1815-1849. 3rd ed. Munich: 1993.

Langewiesche, Dieter, ed. Demokratiebewegung und Revolution 1847 bis 1849. Internationale Aspekte und europäische Verbindungen. Karlsruhe: 1998.

_____. Die deutsche Revolution von 1848/49. Darmstadt: 1983.

Mack, Karl-Heinz, ed. Revolutionen in Ostmitteleuropa 1848-1849. Vienna: 1996.

Mieck, Ilja, Horst Möller, and Jürgen Voss, eds. Paris und Berlin in der Revolution 1848. Sigmaringen: 1995.

Mosse. Werner E., Arnold Pauker, and Reinhard Rürup, eds. Revolution and Evolution. 1848 in German-Jewish History. Tübingen: 1981.

Murat, Inès. La Seconde République, 1848-1851. Paris: 1987.

Näf, Werner. "Der Schweizerische Sonderbundskrieg als Vorspiel der deutschen Revolution von 1848." Basler Zeitschrift für Geschichte und Altertumskunde. 19/1 (1921): 1-105.

_____. Die Schweiz in der deutschen Revolution 1847-1849. Ein Kapital schweizerisch-deutscher Beziehungen in den Jahren 1847-1849. Frauenfeld: 1929.

Niederhauser, Emil. 1848. Sturm im Habsburgerreich. Budapest and Vienna: 1990.

Pech, Stanley Z. The Czech Revolution of 1848. Chapel Hill: 1969.

Pierard, L. Histoire de la Belgique. Paris: 1948.

Pirenne, Henri. Histoire de la Belgique. 5 vols. Vol. 4-5: L'Europe et l'indépendance belge. Brussels: 1990.

Polišenký, Josef. Revoluce a kontrarevoluce v Rakousku 1848. Prague: 1975. English-language edition, Aristocrats and the Crowd in the Revolutionary Year 1848. Translated Frederick Snider. Albany: 1980.

Porzio, Guido. La guerra regia in Italia nel 1848-49. Rome: 1955.

Price, Roger. Documents on the French Revolution of 1848. Basingstoke, 1996.

_____. The French Second Republic: A Social History. London, 1972.

Price, Roger, ed. Revolution and Reaction: 1848 and the Second French Republic. London: 1975.

Rapant, Daniel. Slovenské povstanie roku 1848-49 [The Slav Uprising of 1848-49]. 5 vols. Turciansky Sväty´ Martin and Bratislava: 1937/67.

Roberts, Ian W. Nicholas I. and the Russian Intervention in Hungary. New York and London: 1991.

Robertson, Priscilla. Revolutions of 1848. A Social History. Princeton: 1952.

Rota, Ettore, ed. Il 1848 nella storia italiana ed europea. 2 vols. Milan: 1948.

Rürup, Reinhard. Emanzipation und Antisemitismus. Studien zur "Judenfrage" der bürgerlichen Gesellschaft. Göttingen: 1975. Reprint, Frankfurt: 1987.

Saville. John. 1848. The British State and the Chartist Movement. Cambridge: 1987

Schmidt, Hans. Die polnische Revolution des Jahres 1848 im Großherzogtum Posen. Weimar: 1912.

Seip, Anne-Lise, et. al. Aschehougs Norgeshistorie. 10 vols. Vol. 8. Nasjonen bygges 1830-1870. Oslo: 1979.

Seip, Jens Arup. Utsikt over Norges historie. 2 vols. Oslo: 1974/81.

Sejerstedt, Francis, et. al. Norges historie. 14 vols. Vol. 10 Den vanskelige frihet 1814-50. Oslo: 1976/79.

Sewell, William H., Jr. Work and Revolution in France: The Language of Labor from the Old Regime to 1848. Cambridge: 1980.

Šidak, Jaroslav. Studije iz hrvatske povijesti za revolucije 1848-49 [Studies on Croatian History during the Revolution of 1848/49]. Zagreb: 1979.

Siemann, Wolfram. Die deutsche Revolution von 1848/49. Frankfurt: 1985.

Société d'Histoire de la Révolution de 1848 et des Révolutions du XIXᵉ siècle, ed. Maintien de l'ordre et polices en France et en Europe au 19e siècle. Paris: 1967.

Sperber, Jonathan. The European Revolutions, 1848-1851. Cambridge: 1994.

Springer, Anton. Geschichte Österreichs seit dem Wiener Frieden 1809. Part 2: Die österreichisches Revolution. Leipzig: 1865.

Stadelmann, Rudolf. Soziale und politische Geschichte der Revolution von 1848. Munich: 1948. 3rd ed., 1973.

Stan, Apostol. Revoluţia română de la 1848. Bucharest: 1992.

Storia della società italiana. Vol. 15. Il movimento nazionale e il 1848. Milan: 1986.

Stuke, Horst, and Wilfried Forstmann eds. Die europäischen Revolutionen von 1848. Königstein/Ts: 1979.

Szakály. F., et. al. Hungary and Eastern Europe. Research Report. Budapest: 1980.

Taylor, Alan J.P. The Italian Problem in European Diplomacy (1847-1849). Manchester: 1934.

Taylor, M. "Rethinking the Chartists: Searching for Synthesis in the Historiography of Chartism." Historical Journal 39 (1996):

Try, Hans, et. al. Norges historie. 14 vols. Vol. 11. To kulturer. En stat 1851-1884. Vol. 11. Oslo: 1976/79.

Valentin, Veit. Geschichte der Revolution von 1848-49. 2 vols. Berlin: 1930/31. Reprint Cologne, 1970.

Vigier, Philippe. La Seconde République. Paris: 1967.

Vovelle, Michel. Die Französische Revolution—Soziale Bewegungen und Umbruch der Mentalitäten. Munich, 1982. English-language edition. The Fall of the French Monarchy, 1787-1792. Translated Susan Burke. Cambridge: 1983.

Wagner, R., ed. Die Revolutionsjahre 1848-49 im Königreich Galizien-Lodomerien (einschließlich Bukowina). Munich: 1983.

Wandruszka, Adam and Peter Urbanitsch, eds. Die Habsburgermonarchie 1848-1918. Vol. 1: Die wirtschaftliche Entwicklung. Vienna: 1973. Vol. 3. Die Völker des Reiches. Vienna: 1980. Vol. 4. Die Konfessionen. Vienna, 1985.

Wehler, Hans-Ulrich. Deutsche Gesellschaftsgeschichte. Vol. 2: Von der Reformära bis zur industriellen und politischen "Deutschen Doppelrevolution," 1815-1845/49. Munich: 1987.

Weisser, Henry. British Working-Class Movements and Europe 1815-1848. Manchester: 1975.

Witte. E., and J. Craeybeckx, Politieke geschiedenis van Belgie sinds 1830. Spanningen in een burgerlijke democratie. 3rd. ed. Antwerp, n.d.

Wollstein, Günther. Deutsche Geschichte 1848/49. Stuttgart: 1986.

Zöllner, Erich, ed. Revolutionäre Bewegungen in Österreich. Vienna: 1981.

II—Specialized Studies

Abrahamsson, A. "Ljus och frihet till näringsfång. Om tidningsväsendet. arbetarrörelsen och det sociala medvetandets ekologi—exemplet Stockholm 1838-1869." Ph.D. Dissertation, Stockholm: 1990.

Adler, Laure. Les premières journalistes (1830-1850). Paris: 1979.

Agulhon, Maurice. La République au village. Paris 1970. English language edition. The Republic in the Village. Translated Janet Lloyd. Cambridge: 1982.

Amann, Peter H. Revolution and Mass Democracy: The Paris Club Movement in 1848. Princeton: 1975.

Aminzade, Ronald. Ballots and Barricades. Class Formation and Republican Politics in France. 1830-1871. Princeton: 1993.

Antes, Claudia, and Elke Schunder. Frauenrechtsbewegung und Publizistik 1848 in Frankreich. Frankfurt: 1992.

Aráto, E. "Die Bauernbewegung und der Nationalismus im Frühling und Sommer 1848." Annales Universitatis Scientiarum Budapestiensis. Sectio Historica 9 (1967): 61-103; 11 (1970): 45-68.

Bachem, Karl. Vorgeschichte. Geschichte und Politik der deutschen Zentrumspartei. Zugleich ein Beitrag zur Geschichte der katholischen Bewegung sowie zur allgemeinen Geschichte des neueren und neuesten Deutschland 1815-1914. 9 vols. Cologne: 1929.

Balser, Frolinde. Sozial-demokratie 1848/49-1863. Die erste Arbeiterorganisation "Allgemeine deutsche Arbeiterverbrüderung" nach der Revolution. 2 vols. 2nd ed. Stuttgart: 1965.

Barclay, David. Frederick William IV and the Prussian Monarchy 1840-61. Oxford: 1995.

Baron, Salo W. "The European Revolutions of 1848 and Jewish Emancipation." Jewish Social Studies 11 (1949): 195-248.

Bastid, Paul. Doctrines et institutions politiques de la Seconde République. 2 vols. Paris: 1945.

Belchem, John. Popular Radicalism in Nineteenth-Century Britain. London: 1996.

Bellanger, Claude, Jacques Godechot,, Pierre Guiral, and Fernand Terrou. Histoire générale de la presse française. 3 vols. Paris, 1969.

Benoit, Joseph. Confessions d'un Prolétaire. Paris: 1968.

Berenson, Edward. Populist Religion and Left-Wing Politics in France. 1830-1852. Princeton: 1984.

Bergier, Jean-François. Die Wirtschaftsgeschichte der Schweiz. Zurich: 1983.

Bergmann, Jürgen. Wirtschaftskrise und Revolution. Handwerker und Arbeiter 1848/49. Stuttgart: 1986.

Bernardello, Adolfo. "Burocrazia, borghesia e contadini nel Veneto austriaco." Studi storici 17/4 (1976): 127-52.

Best, Heinrich. Die Männer von Bildung und Besitz. Struktur und Handeln parlamentarischer Führungsgruppen in Deutschland und Frankreich 1848/49. Düsseldorf: 1990.

Best, Heinrich. Interessenpolitik und nationale Integration 1848/49. Handelspolitische Konflikte im frühindustriellen Deutschland. Göttingen: 1980.

Best, Heinrich, and Wilhelm Weege. Biographisches Handbuch der Abgeordneten der Frankfurter Nationalversammlung 1848/49. Düsseldorf: 1996.

Bezucha, Robert J. "The French Revolution of 1848 and the social history of work," Theory & Society 12 pt. 4 (1983): 469-84.

Bjørklund, Oddvar. Marcus Thrane. sosialistleder i et u-land. Oslo: 1970.

Blanqui, Adolphe. Des classes ouvrières en France pendent l'année 1848. Paris: 1849.

Boldt, Werner. Die Anfänge des deutschen Parteiwesens. Fraktionen. politische Vereine und Parteien in der Revolution 1848. Darstellung und Dokumentation. Paderborn: 1971.

Borgetto, M. La notion de fraternité dans le droit public français. Paris: 1992.

Borusso, Edoardo. "Agricultura e questione contadina nella Lombardia della Restaurazione." Studi storici 20 (1979): 799-832.

Botzenhart, Manfred. Deutscher Parlamentarismus in der Revolutionszeit 1848-1850. Düsseldorf: 1977.

Bouillon, Jacques. "Les démocrates-socialistes aux élections de 1849." Revue française de sciences politiques 6 (1956): 71-95.

Braun, Rudolf. Sozialer und kultureller Wandel in einem ländlichen Industriegebiet. Erlenbach-Zurich: 1965. English-language edition. Industrialisation and Everyday Life . Translated Sarah Hanbury Tenison. Cambridge: 1990.

Brenner, Michael, Stefi Jersch-Wenzel, and Michael A. Mayer. Emanzipation und Akkulturation. 1780-1871. Munich: 1996.

Breuilly, John, and Wieland Sachse. Joachim Friedrich Martens (1806-1877) und die Deutsche Arbeiterbewegung. Göttingen: 1984.

Brunello, Piero. Ribelli, questuanti e banditi. Proteste contadine in Veneto e in Friuli 1814-1866. Venice: 1981.

Bucher, Erwin. Die Geschichte des Sonderbundskriegs. Zurich: 1966.

Bull, Edvard. Arbeiderbevegelsens historie i Norge. Arbeiderklassen blir til 1850-1900. Vol. 1. Oslo: 1985.

Burian, Peter. Die Nationalitäten in "Cisleithanien" und das Wahlrecht der Märzrevolution 1848/49. Zur Problematik des Parlamentarismus im alten Österreich. Graz and Cologne: 1962.

Chorley, Katherine. Armies and the Art of Revolution. Boston: 1943.

Colling, Claudia and Mirtide Gavelli. Passi di danza, passi di parata. Feste civili e patriottiche a Bologna 1796-1870. Bologna: 1994.

Compte-rendus des séances de l'Assemblée nationale constituante. Paris: 1850.

Corbin, Alain. Archaïsme et modernité en Limousin au XIXe siècle. 1845-1880. 2 vols. Paris: 1975.

————. "L'histoire de la violence dans les campagnes françaises au XIXe siècle. Esquisse d'un bilan." Ethnologie française 21 (1991): 224-36

Corfus, Ilie. L'agriculture en Valachi durant le première moitié du XIXe siècle. Bucharest: 1983.

Coupe, William A. German Political Satires from the Reformation to the Second World War. Part 1. 2 vols. New York: 1992.

Craig, Gordon A. The Triumph of Liberalism: Zürich in the Gold Age. New York: 1988.

Craveri, P. Genesi di una costituzione. Libertà e socialismo nel dibattito costituzionale del 1848. Naples: 1985.

Dann, Otto. "Die Anfänge politischer Vereinsbildung in Deutschland." In Ulrich Engelhardt, Volker Sellin, and Horst Stuke, eds. Soziale Bewegung und politische Verfassung. Beiträge zur Geschichte der modernen Welt. Stuttgart: 1976.

Daumard, Adeline. La bourgeoisie parisienne de 1815 à 1848. Paris: 1963.

Deak, Istvan. The Lawful Revolution: Louis Kossuth and the Hungarians, 1848-1849. New York: 1979.

Dessal, M. L'accueil fait en Belgique à la révolution de 1848. Rennes: 1939.

Die Evangelischen Kirchen und die Revolution von 1848 (=Zeitschrift für bayerische Kirchengeschichte 62 [1993]).

Dietrich, Stefan J. Christentum und Revolution. Die christlichen Kirchen in Württemberg 1848-1852. Paderborn, 1996.

Dipper, Christof. Die Bauernbefreiung in Deutschland 1790-1850. Stuttgart, 1980.

Djakow W.E. S. Kieniewicz, W. Sliwowska, eds. Wiosna Ludów w Królestwie Polskim. Organizacja 1848 roku. Wroclaw: 1994.

Donnard J.-H. "Gobineau et le 'modèle suédois.'" Acta Regiae … Gothoburgensis. Humaniora. 29. Gothenburg and Paris: 1988.

Dowe, Dieter. Aktion und Organisation. Arbeiterbewegung. sozialistische und kommunistische Bewegung der preußischen Rheinprovinz 1820-1852. Hanover: 1970.

Dowe, Dieter and Toni Offermann, eds. Deutsche Handwerker- und Arbeiterkongresse 1848-1852. Protokolle und Materialien. Berlin: 1983.

Düding, Dieter. Organisierter gesellschaftlicher Nationalismus in Deutschland (1808-1847). Bedeutung und Funktion der Turner- und Sängerbewegung für die deutsche Nationalbewegung. Munich: 1984.

Erba, A. L'esprit laïque en Belgique sous le gouvernement libéral doctrinaire. Louvain: 1967.

Fasel, George. "The Wrong Revolution. French Republicanism in 1848." French Historical Studies 8 (1974): 645-77.

Feldman, Jósef. Sprawa polska w roku 1848. Cracow: 1933.

Fenske, Hans. Deutsche Parteigeschichte. Von den Anfängen bis zur Gegenwart. Paderborn: 1994.

Fiume, Giovanna. La crisi sociale del 1848 in Sicilia. Messina: 1982.

Frandsen, Steen Bo. Opdagelsen af Jylland. Den regionale dimension i Danmarkshistorien 1814-1864. Aarhus: 1996.

Franz. Eckhart G. "Die hessische Arbeitervereine im Rahmen der politischen Arbeiterbewegung der Jahre 1848-1850." Archiv für hessische Geschichte und Altertumskunde N.S. 33 (1975): 167-262.

Fuchs, Eduard. Die Karikatur der europäischen Völker von 1848 bis zur Gegenwart. Berlin: 1903.

Funk, Albrecht. Polizei und Rechtsstaat. Die Entwicklung des staatlichen Gewaltmonopols in Preußen 1848-1914. Frankfurt: 1986.

Gabe, Walter. Hamburg in der Bewegung von 1848/49. Heidelberg: 1911.

Gailus, Manfred. Straße und Brot. Sozialer Protest in den deutschen Staaten unter besonderer Berücksichtigung Preußens 1847-1849. Göttingen: 1990.

Gall, Lothar, ed. Stadt und Bürgertum im Übergang von der traditionalen zur modernen Gesellschaft. Munic:, 1993.

Gamby, E. Pär Götrek och 1800-talets svenska arbetarörelse. Stockholm: 1987.

Gasslander, O. "J.A. Gripenstedt." Ph.D. Dissertation Lund, 1949.

Gebhardt, Hartwig. Revolution und liberale Bewegung. Die nationale Organisation der konstitutionellen Partei in Deutschland 1848/49. Hamburg: 1974.

Geiger, Ruth-Esther. Zeitschriften 1848 in Berlin. Die Zeitschrift als Medium bürgerlicher Öffentlichkeit und ihr erweiterte Funktionszusammenhang in der Berliner Revolutionsmonaten von 1848. Berlin: 1980.

Gemeinsame deutsch-polnische Schulbuchkommission, ed. Die deutsch-polnischen Beziehungen 1831-1848:Vormärz und Völkerfrühling. Braunschweig: 1979.

Gerard, P.A.F. Etudes historiques et critiques de la constitution belge. Brussels: 1869.

Gerhard, Ute. "Über die Anfänge der deutschen Frauenbewegung um 1848. Frauenpresse, Frauenpolitik und Frauenvereine." In Karin Hausen, ed. Frauen suchen ihre Geschichte. Historische Studien zum 19. und 20. Jahrhundert. Munich: 1983.

Gerson, Daniel. "Die Ausschreitungen gegen die Juden im Elsaß 1848." Bulletin des Leo Baeck Instituts 87 (1990): 29-44.

Gessler, Alfred, and Karl-Heinz Grahl, eds. Seine Feinde zu beißen. Karikaturen aus der deutschen bürgerlichen Revolution von 1848/49. Berlin: 1962.

Ginsborg, Paul. Daniele Manin and the Venetian Revolution of 1848-49. Cambridge: 1979.

———. "Peasants and Revolutionaries in Venice and the Veneto, 1848." Historical Journal 17 (1974): 503-50.

———. "Rivoluzione. guerra d'indipendenza e reazione in Italia." In Nicola Tranfaglia and Massimo Firpo, eds. La Storia. I grandi problemi dal Medioevo all'Età Contemporanea. 10 vols. Turin: 1986/93.

Godechot, Jacques. Les constitutions de la France depuis 1789. Paris: 1995.

Goodway, David. London Chartism, 1838-48. Cambridge: 1982.

Gossez, Rémi. Les ouvriers de Paris .Vol 1. L'organisation 1848-1851. La Roche sur Yon: 1957.

Gough, Austin. Paris and Rome. The Gallican Church and the Ultramontane Campaign 1848-1853. Oxford: 1986.

Grankvist, Rolf. Thranitterbevegelsen i Trondelag. Trondheim: 1996.

Grooch, Brison D. Belgium and the February Revolution. The Hague: 1963.

Grünert, Horst. Sprache und Politik. Untersuchungen zum Sprachgebrauch der Paulskirche. Berlin: 1974.

Hachtmann, Rüdiger. Berlin 1848. Eine Politik- und Gesellschaftsgeschichte der Revolution. Bonn: 1997.

———. "Berliner Juden und die Revolution von 1848." In Reinhard Rürup, ed. Jüdische Geschichte in Berlin. Essays und Studien. Berlin: 1995.

Hahn, Hans Henning. "Polen im Horizont preußischer und deutscher Politik im 19. Jahrhundert." Jahrbuch für die Geschichte Mittel- und Ostdeutschlands 35 (1986): 1-19.

Halder, Winfried. Katholische Vereine in Baden und Württemberg 1848-1914. Ein Beitrag zur Organisationsgeschichte des südwestdeutschen Katholizismus im Rahmen der Entstehung der modernen Industriegesellschaft. Paderborn: 1995.

Hallgarten, Wolfgang. Studien über die deutsche Polenfreundschaft in der Periode der Märzrevolution. Munich and Berlin: 1928.

Hardtwig, Wolfgang. "Strukturmerkmale und Entwicklungstendenzen des Vereinswesens in Deutschland 1789-1848." Historische Zeitschrift. Beiheft. N.S. 9 (1984): 11-54.

Harms, Ute. "… Und das nennen sie eine 'Republik'!!!" Politische Karikatur in Hamburg um 1848. Hamburg: 1988.

Harris, James F. The People Speak! Anti-Semitism and Emancipation in Nineteenth-Century Bavaria. Ann Arbor: 1994.

Hauser, Christoph. Anfänge bürgerlicher Organisation. Philhellenismus und Frühliberalismus in Südwestdeutschland. Göttingen: 1990.

Häusler, Wolfgang. "Österreich und die Polen Galiziens in der Zeit des "Völkerfrühlings" (1830-1849)." In Walter Leitsch and Maria Wawrykowa, eds. Polen-Österreich. Aus der Geschichte einer Nachbarschaft. Vienna and Warsaw, 1988.

Häusler, Wolfgang. Von der Massenarmut zur Arbeiterbewegung. Demokratie und soziale Frage in der Wiener Revolution von 1848. Vienna and Munich: 1979.

Heinen, Ernst. Katholizismus und Gesellschaft. Das Katholische Vereinswesen zwischen Revolution und Reaktion (1848/49-1853/54). Idstein: 1993.

Henkel, Martin and Rolf Taubert. Die Deutsche Presse 1848-1850. Munich: 1986.

Herres, Jürgen. Städtische Gesellschaft und katholische Vereine im Rheinland 1840-1870. Essen: 1996.

Hettling, Manfred. "Das Begräbnis der Märzgefallenen 1848 in Berlin." In Manfred Hettling and Paul Nolte, eds. Bürgerliche Feste. Symbolische Formen politischen Handelns im 19. Jahrhundert. Göttingen: 1993.

Hitchens, Keith. Orthodoxy and Nationality: Andrieu Saguna and the Rumanians of Transylvania. 1846-1873. Cambridge MA: 1977.

Hoefer, Frank Thomas. Pressepolitik und Polizeistaat Metternichs. Die Überwachung von Presse und politischer Öffentlichkeit in Deutschland und den Nachbarstaaten durch das Mainzer Informationsbüro (1833-1848). Munich: 1983

Hofmann, Jürgen. Das Ministeriums Camphausen-Hansemann. Zur Politik der preußischen Bourgeoisie in der Revolution 1848/49. East Berlin: 1981.

Hoor, Ernst. Erzherzog von Österreich als Reichsverweser. Vienna: 1981.

Hooykaas, G.J., ed. De briefwisseling van J.R. Thorbecke. 4 vols. The Hague: 1975-1993.

Huard, Raymond. La Préhistoire des partis. Le Parti républicain en Bas-Languedoc. 1848-1881. Paris: 1982.

Hummel, Karl-Joseph. München in der Revolution von 1848/49. Göttingen: 1987.

Hummel-Haasis, Gerlinde, ed. Schwestern, zerreißt Eure Ketten. Zeugnisse zur Geschichte der Frauen in der Revolution von 1848/49. Munich: 1982.

Hymans, L.. Histoire parlementaire de la Belgique. 2 vols.. Brussels, 1858.

Hymans, L. L'Eglise et les libertés belges. Brussels: 1858.

Isenghi, Mario. L'Italia in piazza. I loughi della vita pubblica dal 1848 ai giorni nostri. Milan: 1994.

Jedin, Hubert. ed. Handbuch der Kirchengeschichte. Vol. 6./1. Die Kirche zwischen Revolution und Restauration. Freiburg, Basel, and Vienna: 1971.

Jeismann, Karl-Ernst. Das preußische Gymnasium in Staat und Gesellschaft. 2 vols. Stuttgart: 1996.

Jelavich, Barbara. "The Russian Intervention in Wallachia and Transylvania. September 1848 to March 1849." Rumanian Studies 4 (1979).

Jensen, Hans. De danske Staenderforsamlingers Historie 1830-1848. 2 vols. Copenhagen: 1931-34.

Jones, P.M. Politics and Rural Society: The Southern Massif Central c. 1750-1880. Cambridge: 1985.

Kann, Robert A. The Multinational Empire; Nationalism and National Reform in the Habsburg Monarchy, 1848-1918. New York: 1950.

Kaschuba. Wolfgang. "Ritual und Fest. Das Volk auf der Straße." In Richard van Dülman, ed. Dynamik der Tradition. Frankfurt: 1992.

Kieniewicz, Stefan. Spoleczenstwo polskie w powstanie poznańskim. 2nd revised ed. Warsaw: 1960. First edition, 1935.

Kleßmann, Christoph. "Zur Sozialgeschichte der Reichsverfassungskampagne von 1849." Historische Zeitschrift 218 (1974): 283-337.

Koberdowa, Irena. Polska Wiosna Ludów. Warsaw: 1967.

Koch, Rainer. "Die Agrarrevolution in Deutschland 1848. Ursachen, Verlauf. Ergebnisse." In Dieter Langewiesche (ed.). Die Deutsche Revolution von 1848/49. Darmstadt: 1983.

Koch, Ursula E. Der Teufel in Berlin. Von der Märzrevolution bis zu Bismarcks Entlassung. Illustrierte politische Witzblätter einer Metropole 1848-1890. Cologne: 1991.

Koch. Ursula E., and Pierre-Paul Sagave. "Le Charivari." Die Geschichte einer Pariser Tageszeitung im Kampf um die Republik (1832-1882). Cologne: 1984.

Kölz, Alfred. Quellenbuch zur neueren schweizerischen Verfassungsgeschichte Ihre Grundlinien vom Ende der Alten Eidgenossenschaft bis 1848. Bern: 1992.

König, Helmut, ed. Programme zur bürgerliche Nationalerziehung in der Revolution von 1848/49. Berlin: 1971.

Kossmann, Ernst Heinrich. The Low Countries, 1780-1940. Oxford: 1978.

Koszyk, Kurt. Deutsche Presse im 19. Jahrhundert. Berlin: 1966.

Kozik, Jan. The Ukrainian National Movement in Galicia: 1815-1849. Edmonton: 1986.

Krey, Ursula. Vereine in Westfalen 1840-1855. Strukturwandel, soziale Spannungen, kulturelle Entfaltung. Paderborn: 1993.

Kühne, Jörg-Detlef. Die Reichsverfassung der Paulskirche—Vorbild und Verwirklichung im späteren deutschen Rechtsleben. Frankfurt: 1985.

Lamprecht, Helmut , ed. Deutschland Deutschland. Politische Gedichte vom Vormärz bis zum Gegenwart. Bremen: 1969.

Langewiesche, Dieter. "Die Anfänge der deutschen Parteien. Partei, Fraktion und Verein in der Revolution von 1848/49." Geschichte und Gesellschaft 4 (1978): 324-61.

_____. "Die politische Vereinsbewegung in Würzburg und in Unterfranken in den Revolutionsjahren 1848/49." Jahrbuch für fränkische Landesforschung 37 (1977): 195-233.

_____. "1848/49: Die Revolution in Hamburg—eine vergleichende Skizze." In: Das Alte Hamburg (1500-1848/49). Vergleichende Beziehungen. Hamburg: 1989.

_____. Liberalismus in Deutschland. Frankfurt: 1988.

_____. Liberalismus und Demokratie in Württemberg zwischen Revolution und Reichsgründung. Düsseldorf: 1974.

_____. "Republik, konstitutionelle Monarchie und 'Soziale Frage.' Grundprobleme der deutschen Revolution von 1848/49." Historische Zeitschrift 230 (1980): 529-48.

_____. "Revolution und Emanzipation 1848/49: Möglichkeiten und Grenzen." In Franz D. Lucas, ed. Geschichte und Geist. Fünf Essays zum Verständnis des Judentum. Berlin: 1995.

Langewiesche, Dieter, ed. Revolution und Krieg. Zur Dynamik historischen Wandels seit dem 18. Jahrhundert. Paderborn: 1989.

Lenger, Friedrich. Sozialgeschichte der deutschen Handwerker seit 1800. Frankfurt, 1988.

_____. Zwischen Kleinbürgertum und Proletariat. Studien zur Sozialgeschichte der Düsseldorfer Handwerker 1816-1878. Göttingen: 1986.

Le trasformazioni della festa. Secolarizzazione. politicizzazione e sociabilità nel XIX secolo (Francia. Italia. Spagna). Special issue, Memoria et Ricerca 5 (1994).

Lévêque, Pierre. Une société en crise: La Bourgogne au milieu du XIXe siècle (1846-1852). Paris: 1983.

Lindner, Erik. "Die Revolution von 1848/49 als innerjüdischer Wendepunkt." In Erik Lindner, Patriotismus deutscher Juden von der napoleonischen Ära bis zum Kaiserreich. Frankfurt: 1997.

Lipp, Carola. "Verein als politisches Handlungsmuster. Das Beispiel des württembergischen Vereinswesen von 1800 bis zur Revolution 1848-1849." In Ètienne François, ed. Geselligkeit, Vereinswesen und bürgerliche Gesellschaft in Frankreich. Deutschland und der Schweiz, 1750-1850. Paris: 1986.

_____. "Württembergische Handwerker und Handwerkervereine im Vormärz und in der Revolution 1848/49." In Ulrich Engelhardt, ed. Handwerker in der Industrialisierung. Lage, Kultur und Politik vom späten 18. bis ins frühe 20. Jahrhundert. Stuttgart: 1984.

Lipp, Carola, ed. Schimpfende Weiber und patriotische Jungfrauen. Frauen im Vormärz und in der Revolution 1848/49. Moos and Baden-Baden: 1986.

Livois, René de. Histoire de la presse française. 2 vols. Paris: 1965.

Lorenz, Einhart, ed. Marcus Thrane. Arbeidere. forén dere! Oslo: 1969.

Maillard, H. La théorie du droit au travail en France. Paris: 1912.

Mannonni, S. Une et indivisible. Vol. 2. Milan: 1996.

Margadent. Ted W. French Peasants in Revolt: The Insurrection of 1851. Princeton: 1979.

McPhee, Peter. "La mainmorte du passé?. Les images de la Révolution française dans les mobilisations politiques rurales sous la Seconde République." In Michel Vovelle, ed. L'image de la Révolution française. Vol. 2. Paris: 1990.

_____. Les Semailles de la République dans les Pyrénées Orientales 1846-1852. Perpignan: 1995.

_____. The Politics of Rural Life. Political Mobilization in the French Countryside. 1846-1852. Oxford and New York: 1992.

Merriman, John. The Agony of the Republic: the Repression of the Left in Revolutionary France, 1848-51. London: 1978.

_____. The Margins of City Life: Explorations on the French Urban Frontier, 1815-1851. Oxford and New York: 1991.

_____. The Red City: Limoges and the French Nineteenth Century. New York: 1985.

Moses, Claire Goldberg. French Feminism in the Nineteenth Century. Albany, New York: 1984.

Mosse, Werner E., Arnold Pauker, and Reinhard Rürup, eds. Revolution and Evolution 1848 in German-Jewish History. Tübingen: 1981.

Müller, Michael G., and Bernd. Schönemann, Die "Polen-Debatte" in der Frankfurter Paulskirche. Darstellungen, Lernziele, Materialien. Frankfurt: 1995 (1991).

Nasto, Lucianno. "Le feste civili a Roma (1846-1848)." Rassegna storica del Risorgimento 79 (1992): 315-38.

Nicollet, C. L'idée républicaine en France. Paris: 1982.

Nilsson, Göran B. André Oscar Wallenberg. 3 vols. Stockholm: 1984/94.

Nipperdey, Thomas. "Kritik oder Objektivität? Zur Beurteilung der Revolution von 1848." In Wolfgang Klötzer, Rüdiger Moldenhauer, and Dieter Rebentisch, eds. Ideen und Strukturen der deutschen Revolution 1848. Archiv für Frankfurts Geschichte und Kunst 54 (1974): 143-62.

Noyes, Paul. Organization and Revolution. Working-Class Associations in the German Revolutions of 1848-49. Princeton: 1966.

Nybom, T. "The Swedish Social Democratic State in a Tradition of Peaceful Revolution." In Konflikt og samarbejde. Festskrift til Carl-Axel Gemzell. Copenhagen: 1993.

Oehler, Dolf. Ein Höllensturtz der Alten Welt. Zur Selbsterforschung der Moderne nach dem Juni 1848. Frankfurt: 1988.

Offermann, Toni. "Die regionale Ausbreitung der frühen deutschen Arbeiterbewegung 1848/49-1860/64." Geschichte und Gesellschaft 13 (1987): 419-47.

Orton, Lawrence D. The Prague Slav Congress of 1848. Boulder CO: 1978.

Owsińska, Anna. Powstanie palatynacko-baden'skie 1949 r. oraz udzial w nim Polaków. Wroclaw: 1985.

Paletschek, Sylvia. Frauen und Dissens. Frauen im Deutschkatholizismus und in den freien Gemeinden 1841-1852. Göttingen: 1990.

Palmer, S.H. Police and Protest in England and Ireland, 1780-1850. New York: 1988.

————. "Power Coercion and Authority: Protest and Repression in 1848 in England and Ireland." Consortium on Revolutionary Europe 2 (1989).

Paschen, Joachim. Demokratische Vereine und preußischer Staat. Entwicklung und Unterdrückung der demokratischen Bewegung während der Revolution von 1848/49. Munich: 1977.

Paupié, Kurt. Handbuch der österreichischen Pressegeschichte 1848-1959. 2 vols. Vienna: 1960.

Perenyi. J. "Revolutionsuppfattningens anatomi. 1848 års revolutioner i svensk debatt." Ph.D. Dissertation, Uppsala: 1979.

Ponteil, Felix. Les institutions de la France de 1814 à 1870. Paris: 1966.

Procacci, Giovanna. Gouverner la misère. Paris: 1993.

Pryser, Tore. Klassebevegelse eller folkebevegelse? En sosialhistorisk undersokelse av thranittene i Ullensaker. Oslo: 1997.

————. Thanerørsla i norske bygder. Oslo: 1977.

Quarck, Max. Die erste deutsche Arbeiterbewegung. Geschichte der Arbeiterverbrüderung 1848/49. Ein Beitrag zur Theorie und Praxis des Marxismus. Leipzig: 1924. Reprint, Glashütten: 1970.

Raginel. A. Histoire des votes des représentants du peuple dans nos Assemblées Nationales depuis la Révolution de Février 1848. Paris: 1851.

Rath. R. John. The Viennese Revolution of 1848. Austin: 1957.

Regnault, E. Histoire du Gouvernement provisoire. Paris: 1850.

Rehm, Clemens. Die katholische Kirche in der Erzdiözese Freiburg während der Revolution 1848/49. Freiburg and Munich: 1987.

Reichardt, Rolf, ed. Französische Presse und Pressekarikaturen 1789-1992. Mainz: 1992.

Rerup, Lorenz. Slesvig og Holsten efter 1830. Copenhagen: 1982.

Riff, Michael Anthony. "The Anti-Jewish Aspects of the Revolutionary Unrest of 1848 in Baden and its Impact on Emancipation." Leo Baeck Institute Year Book 21 (1976): 27-40.

Riot-Sarcey, Michèle. La Démocratie a l'épreuve des femmes. Trois figures critique de pouvoir, 1830-1848. Paris: 1994.

Rizzi, Franco. La coccarda e le campane. Communità rurali e Repubblica romana nel Lazio (1848-1849). Milan: 1988.

Robert, Vincent. "Cortèges et manifestations à Lyon (1848-1914)." DES. Lyon II, 1991.

Robijns, M.J.F. Radicalen in Nederland (1840-1851). Leiden: 1967.

Rohrbacher, Stefan. Gewalt in Biedermeier. Antijüdische Ausschreitungen in Vormärz und Revolution (1815-1848/49). Frankfurt: 1993.

Rosanvallon, Pierre. Le sacre du citoyen. Histoire du suffrage universel en France. Paris: 1992.

Rürup, Reinhard. "The European Revolutions of 1848 and Jewish Emancipation." In Werner Mosse, Arnold Pauker, and Reinhard Rürup, eds. Revolution and Evolution. 1848 in German-Jewish History. Tübingen: 1981.

Rütten, Raimund, Ruth Jung, and Gerhard Schneider, eds. Die Karikatur zwischen Republik und Zensur. Bildsatire in Frankreich 1830 bis 1880. Marburg: 1991.

Scharff, Alexander. "Schleswig-Holstein in der europäischen und nordischen Geschichte." In Alexander Scharff. Gesammelte Aufsätze. Stuttgart: 1969.

Schieder, Theodor. "Das Problem der Revolution im 19. Jahrhundert." In Theodor Schieder. Staat und Gesellschaft im Wandel unserer Zeit. Munich: 1958.

Schirrmeister, Karl-Günther. "Menschenrechte in den Petitionen an die Deutsche Nationalversammlung 1848/49." Ph.D. Dissertation, Mainz: 1970.

Schlechte, Horst, ed. Die Allgemeine deutsche Arbeiterverbrüderung 1848-1850. Dokumente des Zentralkomitees für die deutschen Arbeiter in Leipzig. Weimar: 1979.

Schmidt, Wolfgang. Die Revolution von 1848/49 in Hamburg. Hamburg: 1983.

Schnabel, Franz. Der Zusammenschluß des politischen Katholizismus in Deutschland im Jahre 1848. Heidelberg: 1910.

Schneider, Ute. Politische Festkultur im 19. Jahrhundert. Die Rheinprovinz von der französischen Zeit bis zum Ende des Ersten Weltkrieges (1806-1918). Essen: 1995.

Schraepler, Ernst. Handwerkerverbände und Arbeitervereine 1830-1853. Die politische Tätigkeit deutscher Sozialisten von Wilhelm Weitling bis Karl Marx. New York and Berlin: 1972.

Schwentker, Wolfgang. Konservative Vereine und Revolution in Preußen 1848/49. Die Konstituierung des Konservatismus als Partei. Düsseldorf: 1988.

Seillière, Ernest. L'Académie des sciences morales et politique et le redressement moral de la France après les événements de 1848. Paris: 1941.

Seyppel, Marcel. Die Demokratische Gesellschaft in Köln 1848/49. Städtische Gesellschaft und Parteientstehung während der bürgerlichen Revolution. Cologne: 1991.

Simon, Manfred. Handwerk in Krise und Umbruch. Wirtschaftliche Forderung und sozialpolitische Vorstellungen der Handwerksmeister im Revolutionsjahr 1848/49. Cologne: 1983.

Sked, Alan. The Survival of the Habsburg Empire. Radetzky. the Imperial Army and the Class War. London and New York: 1979.

Slagstad, R. "Frederik Stangs ideologiske lederskep." Nytt norsk tidsskrift (Oslo) 2 (1992).

Soldani, Simonetta. "Contadini. operai e 'popolo' nella rivoluzione del 1848-49 in Italia." Studi storici 14 (1973): 557-613.

Şotropa, Valeriu. Proiectele de constituţie, programele de reforme şi petiţiile de drepturi diu ţările române în secolul al XVIII.-1 ea şi prima jumătate a secolului al XIX.-1 ea. Bucharest: 1976.

Sperber, Jonathan. "Festivals of National Unity in the German Revolution of 1848-1849." Past and Present 136 (1992): 114-38.

_____. Rhineland Radicals: The Democratic Movement and the Revolution of 1848-1849. Princeton: 1991.

Spira, György. Kossuth and Posterity. Budapest: 1980.

Spuller, E. Histoire parlementaire de la Seconde République. Brussels: 1891.

Stewart-McDougall, Mary. The Artisan Republic: Revolution, Reaction and Resistance in Lyon 1848-1851. Gloucester: 1984.

Stuurman. S. Wacht op onze daden. Het liberalisme en de vernieuwing van de Nederlandse staat. Amsterdam: 1992.

Svanberg, V. Rydbergs romanfragment "Benoni Strand" och femtitalsliberalismen. Samlaren: 1921.

Tanner, Albert. Arbeitsame Patrioten und wohlanständige Damen. Bürgertum und Bürgerlichkeit in der Schweiz. Zurich: 1995.

Tchernov, I. Associations et sociétés secrètes sous la Deuxième République. Paris: 1905.

Thompson, Dorothy. "Seceding from the Seceders: The Decline of the Jacobin Tradition in Ireland, 1790-1850." In Dorothy Thompson. Outsiders: Class. Gender and Nation. London: 1993.

Tilly, Charles. "Food Supply and Public Order in Modern Europe." In Charles Tilly, ed. The Formation of National States in Western Europe. Princeton: 1975.

_____. "How Protest Modernized France." In William Aydelotte, ed. The Dimensions of Quantitative Research in History. Princeton: 1972.

Tocqueville, Alexis de. De la démocratie en Amérique. Oeuvres complètes. 18 vols. Paris: 1951/85

_____. Écrits et discours politiques. Oeuvres complètes. 18 vols. Paris: 1951/85.

_____. Recollections. In J.P. Mayer and A.P. Kerr, ed. Translated by George Lawrence. Garden City, NY 1970. (French 1st ed. 1893).

Toury, Jacob. Die politischen Orientierungen der Juden in Deutschland. Von Jena bis Weimar. Tübingen: 1966.

_____. Soziale und politische Geschichte der Juden in Deutschland 1847-1871. Zwischen Revolution, Reaktion und Emanzipation. Düsseldorf, 1977.

Traugott, Mark. Armies of the Poor: Determinants of Working-Class Participation in the Parisian Insurrection of June 1848. Princeton: 1985.

Trox, Eckhard. Militärischer Konservatismus. Kriegervereine und "Militärpartei" in Preußen zwischen 1815 und 1848/49. Stuttgart: 1990.

Tudesq, André-Jean. Les grands notables en France (1840-1849). Etude historique d'une psychologie sociale. 2 vols. Paris: 1963.

_____. L'élection présidentielle de Louis-Napoléon Bonaparte, 10 décembre 1848. Paris, 1965.

Vamman, Hans. "Casino 1848." Historisk Tidsskrift (1988): 252-79.

Vigier, Philippe. La Seconde République dans la région alpine. 2 vols. Paris: 1963.

_____ "Lyon et l'évolution politique de la province française au XIXᵉ siècle. Quelques direction de recherche." Cahiers d'Histoire 12 (1967).

Vincent, Robert. "Cortèges et manifestations à Lyon (1848-1914)." DES. Lyon II, 1991.

Visalli, Vittorio. Lotta e martirio del popolo calabrese (1847-1848). Cosenza: 1928.

Volkov, Shulamit. Die Juden in Deutschland, 1780-1918. Munich: 1994.

Waibel, Raimund. Frühliberalismus und Gemeindewahlen in Württemberg (1817-1855); das Beispiel Stuttgart. Stuttgart: 1992.

Weber, Eugen. Peasants into Frenchmen: The Modernization of Rural France. 1870-1914. Stanford: 1976.

_____. "The Second Republic, Politics, and the Peasant." French Historical Studies 11 (1980)

Weber, Rolf. Die Revolution in Sachsen 1848/49. East Berlin: 1970.

Weigel, Sigrid. Flugschriftenliteratur 1848 in Berlin. Geschichte und Öffentlichkeit einer volkstümlichen Gattung. Stuttgart: 1979.

Weisser, Henry. April 10: Challenge and Response in England in 1848. Lanham: 1983.

Wettengel, Michael. "Der Centralmärzverein und die Entstehung des deutschen Parteiwesens während der Revolution von 1848/49." Jahrbuch zur Liberalismus-Forschung 3 (1991): 34–81.

_____. Die Revolution von 1848/49 in Rhein-Main-Raum. Politische Vereine und Revolutionsalltag im Großherzogtum Hessen. Herzogtum Nassau und in der Freien Stadt Frankfurt. Wiesbaden: 1989.

Widmer, Sigmund. "Das ist die Freiheit!" "Das ist Barbarei!" Sonderbundskrieg und Bundesreform von 1848 im Urteil Frankreichs. Bern: 1948.

Wigard, Franz, ed. Stenographischer Bericht über die Verhandlungen der deutschen constituierenden Nationalversammlung. 9 vols.. Stuttgart: 1848/49.

Wirsching, Andreas. "Arbeiter und Arbeiterbewegung in Paris in vergleichender Perspektive." In Ilja Mieck et. al., eds. Paris und Berlin in der Revolution 1848. Sigmaringen: 1995.

Wolf, Sylvia. Politische Karikaturen in Deutschland 1848/49. Munich: 1982.

Yanagisawa, Osamu. "Die sozio-ökonomischen Forderungen der preußischen Landbevölkerung im Jahre 1848 im Spiegel der Petitionsnachweisung." In Wirtschaftskräfte und Wirtschaftswege. Vol. 3: Auf dem Weg zur Industrialisierung. Festschrift für Hermann Kellenbenz. Stuttgart: 1978.

Zucker, Stanley. Kathinka Zitz-Halein and Female Civic Activism in Mid-Nineteenth-Century Germany. Carbondale and Edwardsville: 1991.

LIST OF ILLUSTRATIONS AND MAPS

pg. 340 *top*: Shot-maker behind a barricade [in Berlin], drawn by R. Kretschmer (Illustrirte Zeitung, Leipzig, no. 250, 15 April 1848, 254)

    bottom: The Palais des Prinzen von Preußen in Berlin (Illustrirte Zeitung, Leipzig, no. 251, 22 April 1848, 267)

pg. 370 *top*: Assembly in tents on 20 April in Berlin (Illustrirte Zeitung, Leipzig, no. 253, 6 May 1848, 302)

    bottom: Dissolution of the Prussian Constitutional National Assembly in Mielentz'schen Saale in Berlin, on 14 November (Illustrirte Zeitung, Leipzig, no. 283, 2 December 1848, 365)

pg. 400: Public Assembly at the Franciskanerkeller in the Au district of Munich (Illustrirte Zeitung, Leipzig, no. 271, 9 September 1848, 165)

pg. 442 *top*: Scene from the riots at the Waldenburg Castle (Illustrirte Zeitung, Leipzig, no. 251, 22 April 1848, 271)

    bottom: Scene from the Magyar camp (Illustrirte Zeitung, Leipzig, no. 278, 28 October 1848, 277)

pg. 474 *top*: Sitting of the preparatory parliament in the St. Paulskirche in Frankfurt a.M. (Illustrirte Zeitung, Leipzig, no. 255, 20 May 1848, 330)

    bottom: Clearing of the rostrum in the national assembly hall after the attack by the clubbists on 15 May (Illustrirte Zeitung, Leipzig, no. 257, 3 June 1848, 371)

pg. 479: Formation of the Frankfurt National Assembly Constituencies of Delegates to the Heidelberg Assembly, Pre-Parliament and The Committee of Fifty

pg. 488: Strongholds of the Rights and Left in the Assemblée nationale constituante

pg. 494: Political Conflict Groups in the Frankfurt National Assembly: Left and Centre-Left: Constituency of the Delegate: Group Membership as per Voting Behaviour

pg. 498: Election of the Emperor in the Frankfurt National Assembly. Constituency of delegates summoned

pg. 506 *top*: Lamartine's victory over the red flag through a speech to the people on 25 February (Illustrirte Zeitung, Leipzig, no. 246, 18 March 1848, 187)

    bottom: Sitting of the provisional government of the French republic in the Paris city hall (Illustrirte Zeitung, Leipzig, no. 249, 8 April 1848, 238)

pg. 528: Festival parade of Berlin clubs to Kreuzberg on 6 August (Illustrirte Zeitung, Leipzig, no. 270, 2 September 1848, 149)

pg. 558 *top*: Fighting between republicans and parliamentarians in Frankfurt a.M. on 30 March (Illustrirte Zeitung, Leipzig, no. 252, 29 April 1848, 283)

    bottom: A sitting of the Revolution Club in Paris (Illustrirte Zeitung, Leipzig, no. 252, 29 April 1848, 283)

pg. 584: University Square in Vienna in the night of 13 - 14 March, drawn by R. Swoboda (Illustrirte Zeitung, Leipzig, no. 248, 1 April 1848, 218)

pg. 593: Newspapers in Revolutionary Paris

pg. 603: Newspapers in Revolutionary Germany

pg. 607: Honoré Daumier, Dernier conseil des ex-ministres (Le Charivari, 9 March 1848, U.E. Koch/P.-P. Savage, ≤Le Charivari", Cologne 1984, Ill. 41)

CONTRIBUTORS

Dieter Dowe is director of the Historical Research Center of the Friedrich-Ebert Foundation in Bonn-Bad Godesberg. He has written on the early German labor movement and socialist movements. His publications include *Aktion und Organisa-tion:Arbeiterbewegung, sozialistische Bewegung und kommunistische Bewegung in der preußis-chen Rheinprovinz 1820-1852* (1970) and *Deutschse Handwerker- und Arbeiterkongresse 1848-1852. Protokolle und Materialien*, coedited with Toni Offerman (1983).

Heinz-Gerhard Haupt is Professor of Modern History at the University of Biele-feld. His publications include *Die Kleinbürger: eine Europäische Sozialgeschichte des 19. Jahrhunderts*, edited with Geoffrey Crossick (1998); *Sozialgeschichte Frankreichs seit 1789* (1989); *Nationalismus und Demokratie: zur Geschichte der Bourgeoisie im Frankre-ich der Restauration* (1980); *Die Pariser Kommune : Erfolg u. Scheitern einer Revolution*, coauthored with Karin Hausen (1979).

Dieter Langewiesche is Professor of History at the University of Tübingen, and currently serving as *Prorektor* of the newly created University of Erfurt. He has writ-ten extensively on the social and political history of the nineteenth century. Among his works are *Liberalismus in Deutschland* 4th ed. (1995); *Europa zwischen Restauration und Revolution 1815-1849* 3rd ed.(1993);"Republik, konstitutionelle Monarchie und 'soziale Frage'. Grundprobleme der deutschen Revolution von 1848/49," *Historische Zeitschrift* (1980); *Zur Freizeit des Arbeiters: Bildungsbestrebungen und Freizeitgestaltung österreichischer Arbeiter im Kaiserreich und in der Ersten Republik* (1980); *Liberalismus und Demokratie in Württemberg zwischen Revolution und Reichsgründung* (1974).

Jonathan Sperber is Professor of History at the University of Missouri, Colum-bia. Among his publications are *Popular Catholicism in Nineteenth Century Germany* (1984); *Rhineland Radicals: the Democratic Movement and the Revolution of 1848-1849* (1991); *The European Revolutions, 1848-1851* (1994); *The Kaiser's Voters: Electors and Elections in Imperial Germany* (1997); *Revolutionary Europe, 1780-1850* (2000). He is currently working on a study of the uses of property in the nineteenth century.

John Belchem is Professor of History and Head of the School of History at the University of Liverpool. His extensive publications on British popular politics include *Popular Radicalism in Nineteenth-Century Britain* (1996) and *"Orator" Hunt: Henry Hunt and English Working-Class Radicalism* (1985). His research interests now focus on Liverpool, Celticism and the Irish Sea region.

Edward Berenson is Professor of History and French Studies and Director of the Institute of French Studies at New York University. He is the author of *Populist Religion and Left-Wing Politics in France* (1984) and *The Trial of Madame Caillaux* (1992) His current work is devoted to the origins of the mass media in France.

Heinrich Best is Professor of Sociology and Dean of the Faculty for Social and Behaviorial Sciences at the University of Jena. His main research areas are the comparative study of political elites and the methodology of historical sociology. He is author or coauthor of three major works on the revolutions of 1848/49: *Interessenpolitik und nationale Integration 1848/49* (1980); *Die Männer von Bildung und Besitz* (1990); and, *Biographisches Handbuch der Abgeordneten der Frankfurter Nationalversammlung*, coauthored with Wilhelm Weege, 2nd ed. (1997).

John Breuilly is Professor of Modern History at the University of Birmingham. His major publications include *Nationalism and the State* 2nd ed., (1993), *Labour and Liberalism in 19th Century Europe* (1992), and *The Formation of the First German Nation State 1800-1871* (London, 1996). His current research interests: applying concepts of modernization to the history of the German lands c.1800-1930 and writing a comparative cultural history of the bourgeois elites of mid-nineteenth century Hamburg, Lyon and Manchester.

Beatrix Bouvier is Professor of History at the Darmstadt Institute of Technology. She has written extensively on French and German history of the nineteenth and twentieth centuries. Her most recent major work is *Ausgeschaltet! : Sozialdemokraten in der sowjetischen Besatzungszone und in der DDR ;1945–1953* (1996).

Christoph Dipper is Professor of Modern and Contemporary History at the Darmstadt Institute of Technology. His scholarly interests include agricultural history, the comparative social history of Italy and Germany, and the history of the Holocaust. Among his works are *Die Bauernbefreieung in Deutschland 1790-1848* (1980); *1848 Revolution in Deutschland*, coedited with Ulrich Speck (1998).

Steen Bo Frandsen Vice-Director of the Danish Institute of Science and Art in Rome. He has done research on Danish-German relations since the end of the eighteenth century, and on regional history in nineteenth century Denmark and Italy. Among his publications are *Dänemark. Der kleine Nachbar im Norden* (1994); and *Opdagelsen af Jylland. Den regionale dimension i Danmarkshistorien 1814-1864* (1996).

Manfred Gailus is lecturer (*Privatdozent*) at the Institute of Historical Sciences of the Berlin Institute of Technology. His research has centered around social protest in eighteenth and nineteenth century Germany, and nationalism, Protestantism and Nazism in twentieth century Germany. Among his works are *Straße und Brot. Sozialer Protest in den deutschen Staaten unter besonderer Berücksichtigung Preußens 1847-1849* (1990); *Der Kampf um das tägliche Brot. Nahrungsmangel, Versongungspolitik und Protest 1770-1990* (1994); and *Bruderkampf im eigenen Hause. Studien zur nationalsozialistischen Duchdringung des protestantischen Sozialmilieus in Berlin 1930-1950* (2000).

Robert Gildea is Reader in Modern History and Fellow at Merton College, Oxford University. His recent publications include *The Past in French History* (1996) and *France since 1945* (1996). Her is currently writing a book on France under the German occupation regime, 1940-1945.

Rüdiger Hachtmann is Lecturer (*Privatdozent*) at the Institute of Historical Sciences of the Berlin Institute of Technology. His major publications include *Industriearbeit im Dritten Reich. Untersuchungen zu den Lohn- und Arbeitsbedingungen 1933 bis 1945* (1989) and *Berlin 1848. Eine Politik und Gesellschaftsgeschichte der Revolution* (1997). Current research interests include the "culture of poverty" in the first half of the nineteenth century and mass tourism in twentieth century dictatorial regimes.

Hans Henning Hahn is Professor of Modern East European History at the University of Oldenburg. His scholarly interests center on the history of Poland in the eighteenth through the twentieth centuries. Among his publications are *Außenpolitik in der Emigration. Die Exildipolomatie Adam Jerzy Czartoryskis 1830-1840* (1978; Polish edition, 1987); ed., *Historische Stereotypenforschung. Methodische Überlegungen und empirische Befunde* (1995); "Die Revolution von 1848 als Strukturkrise des europäischen Staatensystems," in Peter Krüger (ed.), *Das europäische Staatensystem im Wandel* (1996).

Gabriella Hauch is Associate Professor at the Ludwig Boltzmann Institute of social and cultural history at the University of Linz. She also teaches at the Universities of Vienna Salzburg and Linz. Her publications include *Frau Biedermeier auf den Barrikaden. Frauenleben in der Wiener Revolution 1848.* (1990). Current research interests include a studies of female slave laborers and their children in the Linz branch of the *Reichswerke Hermann Göring* and of the gendered populism of the Austrian Freedom Party.

Wolfgang Höpken is Professor of East- and Southeast European History at the University of Leipzig. His research interests lie in the nineteenth and twentieth century of the region, with a particular focus on the history and function of nationalism. His most publications include *Öl ins Feuer? Schulbücher, ethnische Stereotypen und Gewalt in Südosteuropa* (1996); *Eliten in Südosteuropa. Rolle, Kontinuität, Brüche, in Geschichte und*

Gegenwart, coauthored with H. Sundhaussen(1998); and *Ethnische und politische Gewalt in Südosteuropa und Lateinamerika,* coauthored with M. Riekenberg (1999).

Karl-Joseph Hummel is Director of the Institute of Contemporary History in Bonn. His major publications include *München in der Revolution von 1848/49* (1987) and *Deutsche Geschichte 1933-1945* (1998).

Ursula Koch is Professor of Communications at the University of Munich. Her research interests include the history of the media and journalism in Germany and France, and the study of political cartoons and stereotypes. Among her books, and exhibitions, are *Berliner Presse und europäisches Geschehen 1871* (1978; awarded the Prix Strasbourg); *Der Teufel in Berlin. Von der Märzrevolution bis zu Bismarcks Entlassung. Illustrierte politische Witzblätter einer Metropole (1848-1890)* (1991); *Marianne et Germania dans la caricature (1550-1997)/ Marianne und Germania in der Karikatur (1550-1999)* (1997/99) and, with Albert Pierre, *Les médias en Allemagne* (2000).

Jiři Kořalka was Researcher at the Institute of History of the Czechoslovak Academy of Sciences, 1955-74, 1992-93, and head historian of the Hussite Museum, Tábor, 1975-91, now emeritus. His major publications include *Tsechen im Habsburgerreich und in Europa 1815-1914* (1991) and *František Palacký* (1998).

Horst Lademacher is Professor of Netherlands Studies and Modern and Contemporary History at the University of Münster. His scholarship has centered on the history of the labor movement, on the regional history of the Rhineland, on the history of the ColdWar, and on the history of the Low Countries. Among his major publications are *Die belgische Neutralität als Problem der europäischen Politik: 1830–1914* (1971); *Von den Provinzialständen zum Landschaftsverband : zur Geschichte der landschaftlichen Selbstverwaltung der Rheinlande* (1973); *Moses Hess in seiner Zeit* /(1977); *Geschichte der Niederlande : Politik—Verfassung—Wirtschaft* (1983); *Zwei ungleiche Nachbarn: Wege und Wandlungen der deutsch-niederländischen Beziehungen im 19. und 20. Jahrhundert* (1990) *Tradition und Neugestaltung: zu Fragen des Wiederaufbaus in Deutschland und den Niederlanden in der frühen Nachkriegszeit* ed. (1991); *Krieg und Kultur: die Rezeption von Krieg und Frieden in der Niederländischen Republik und im Deutschen Reich 1568–1648,* ed. (1998)

Friedrich Lenger is Professor of Medieval and Modern History at the University of Gießen. His major publications include *Zwischen Kleinbürgertum und Proletariat: Studien zur Sozialgescschichte der Düsseldorfer Handwerker 1816-1878* (1986); *Sozialgeschichte der Deutschen Handwerker seit 1800* (1988) and *Werner Sombart (1863-1941). Eine Biographie* (1994).

Pierre Lévêque is Professor emeritus at the University of Burgundy. His research centers on the social and political history of nineteenth and twentieth century France. His major publications include *Une société provinciale: La Bourgogne sous la* *monarchie de Juillet* (Paris, 1983); *Une société en crise: La Bourgogne au milieu du xixe siècle (1846-1852)* (1983); *Histoire des forces politiques en France* 3 vols. (1992/97).

Lothar Maier is Professor of East European History at the University of Münster. His scholarly interests include the history of German-Russian economic relations, nineteenth century Russian, Polish and Rumanian history, and the history of the Russian Revolution of 1917. Among his major publications is *Rümänien auf dem Weg zur Unabhängigkeitserklärung, 1866-1877. Schein und Wirklichkeit liberaler Verfassung und staatlicher Souveränität* (1989).

John Merrimann is Charles Seymour Professor of History at Yale University. His books include *The Agony of the Republic: The Repression of the Left in Revolutionary France, 1848-51* (1978); *The Red City: Limoges and the French Nineteenth Century* (1985); *The Margins of City Life* (1991); and *A History of Modern Europe* (1996).

Thomas Christian Mueller is a researcher (*wissenschaftlicher Assistent*) at the Center for Research into Social and Economic History at the University of Zürich. His scholarship is centered on the social history of modern Switzerland and Germany, the history of the press, and the role of political exiles in the first half of the nineteenth century. His doctoral dissertation on German exile politics in Switzerland, 1830-48, and the smuggling of political writings across the Swiss German border, is due to appear in press, shortly.

Goran B. Nilsson is Professor emeritus of the interdisciplinary study of technology and social change at Linköpings University. His *opus magnum* is a three-volume biography of the Swedish banker, political and journalist, A. O. Wallenberg (1816-1886).

Giovanna Procacci teaches the history of sociology in the Faculty of Political Sciences at the University of Milan. Her main fields of scholarship are the origins of social sciences, poverty and social welfare policy, and citizenship theory and social rights. Her major publications include *Gouverner la misère* (1993); "Against Exclusion: the Poor and the Social Sciences," in M. Rhodes and Y. Meny (eds.), *The Future of European Welfare* (1998) and "Poor Citizens: Social Citizenship versus Individualization of Welfare," in C. Crouch, K. Eder and D. Tambini, (eds.) *Citizenship, Markets and the State* (1999).

Ralf Pröve is Lecturer [*Privatdozent*] at the Humboldt University in Berlin and at the University of Potsdam. His publications include *Stehendes Heer und Ständische Gesellschaft im 18. Jahrhundert: Göttingen und seine Militärbevölkerung 1713-1756* (1995); *Wege ins Ungewisse: Reisen in der Frühen Neuzeit* (1997); and three co-edited works, *Agrarische Verfassung und politische Struktur. Studien zur Gesellschaftgeschichte Preußens 1700-1913* (1998); *Landsknechte, Soldatenfrauen und Nationalkrieger: Militär Krieg und Geschlechterordnung im historischen Wandel* (1998) and *Leben und Arbeiten auf märkischen Sand: Wege in die Gesellschaftsgeschichte Brandenburgs 1700-1914* (1999).

His book-length study of political participation and civic formations of order in German municipalities from the end of the eighteenth to the middle of the nineteenth centuries is forthcoming.

Roger Price is Professor of History at the University of Wales, Aberystwyth. His major publications include *The French Second Republic* (1972); *An Economic History of Modern France, c. 1730-1914* (1981); *The Modernisation of Rural France: Communication Networks and Agricultural Market Structures in 19th Century France* (1983); *A Social History of 19th Century France* (1988); *The Revolutions of 1848* (1989); *A Concise History of France* (1993); *Napoleon III and the Second Empire* (1997). A book on state and society during the Second Empire is forthcoming.

Iorweth Prothero is Senior Lecturer at the University of Manchester. His scholarship is focused on nineteenth century labor movements, dissident religion, and culture in Britain and France. His most recent major work is *Radical Artisans in England and France, 1830-1870* (1997).

Reinhard Rürup is Professor of Modern History at the Berlin Institute of Technology. His publications include *Emanzipation und Antisemitismus. Studien zur "Judenfrage" der bürgerlichen Gesellschaft* (1975; 2nd. ed. 1987); *Deutsche Geschichte im 19. Jahrhundert, 1815-1871* (2nd. ed., 1992), *Revolution and Evolution. 1848 in German Jewish History*, co-edited with Werner Mosse and Arnold Paucker (1981) and *Jüdisches Leben auf dem Lande. Studien zur deutsch-jüdischen Geschichte*, coedited with Monika Richarz (1997).

Anne-Lise Seip is Professor of Modern History at the University of Oslo. Her scholarship is centered on intellectual history and the history of social welfare. Her major works include *Vitenskap og virkelighet* (1975); *Om velferdsstatens framvelst* (1981); *Eilert Sundt* (1983); *Sosialhjelpstaten blir til. Norsk sosialpolitikk 1740-1920* (1984); *Veiene til velfedsstaten. Norsk sosialpolitikk 1920-1975* (1994); and a volume in the general history of Norway series, *Nasjonen bygges 1830-1870* (1997). She is currently working on a history of the University of Oslo at the beginning of the nineteenth century.

Wolfram Siemann is Professor of Modern and Contemporary History at the University of Munich. His scholarship has encompassed the history of the revolution of 1848, the history of the political police, the history of publication and the book trade, and the history of nationalism and nation-building. Among his major publications are *"Deutschlands Ruhe, Sicherheit und Ordnung." Die Anfänge der politischen Polizei 1806-1866* (1985); *Die Deutsche Revolution von 1848/49* (1985); 7th ed., 1997; English-language edition, *The German Revolution of 1848-49* (1998); *Gesellschaft in Aufbruch: Deutschland 1849-1871* (1990); 4th ed. 1997; *Vom Staatenbund zum Nationalstaat. Deutschland 1806-1871* (1995).

Simonetta Soldani is Professor of Contemporary History at the University of Florence. Her main scholarly interests have been the history of European Revolutions of the nineteenth century and of the Italian Risorgimento, and the making of the nation state and citizenry in modern Italy. Her publications includei "La Grande guerra lontano dal fronte," in G. Mori (ed.), *Storia d'Italia* (1986); *L'educazione delle donne. Scuole e modelli di vita nell'Italia contemporanea*, (1989); *Fare gli italiani. Scuola ecultura nell'Italia contemporanea*, coauthored with Gabriele Turi (1993); *L'istruzione agraria in Italia, 1860-1928*, coauthored with A. P. Bidolli (1999); "From divided memory to silence. The Italian Jubilees of 1848," in Axel Koerner (ed.), *1848. A revolution?* (1999).

Willibald Steinmetz is a *Deutsche Forschungsgemeinschaft* scholar at the University of Bochum. His main fields of interest are the comparative history of political languages and modern social and legal history. He is author of *Das Sagbare und das Machbare: Zum Wandel politischer Handlungsspielräume—England 1780-1867* (1993) and editor of the forthcoming *Private Law and Social Inequality in the Industrial Age: Comparing Legal Cultures in Britain, France, Germany and the United States.*

Charlotte Tacke, after receiving her doctorate from the European University Institute in Florence, is currently working on her Habilitation at the University of Bielefeld, a comparative history of hunting in Germany and Italy. Her publications include *Denkmal im sozialen Raum. Nationale Symbole in Deutschland und Frankreich im 19. Jahrhundert* (1995); "National Symbols in France and Germany in the Nineteenth Century," in Heinz-Gerhard Haupt, Michael G. Müller, and Stuart Woolf (eds.), *Regional and National Identities in Europe in the Nineteenth and Twentieth Centuries* (1998); and "Die Kultur des Nationalen. Sozial- und kulturgeschichtliche Ansätze bei der Erforschung des europäischen Nationalismus im 19. Und 20. Jahrhundert," coauthored with Heinz-Gerhard Haupt, in Wolfgang Hardtwig and Hans-Ulrich Wehler, (ed.) *Kulturgeschichte Heute* (1998).

Heinz–Elmar Tenorth is Professor of Education at the Humboldt University in Berlin. His scholarship has been on the history of education. His major publications include, *Geschichte der Erziehung. Einführung in die Grundzüge ihrer neuzeitlichen Entwicklung* (1992) and *Erziehungsstaaten. Historisch vergleichende Analysen ihrer Denktraditionen und nationalen Gestalten*, coedited with Dietrich Benner and Jürgen Schriwer (1998).

Michael Wettengel is a section director [*Referatsleiter*] at the German Federal Archives, in Koblenz. He has written extensively on the regional history of Hessen and on the history of political parties and organizations. His major publication is *Die Revolution von 1848/49 im Rhein-Main-Raum* (1989).

INDEX

in Great Britain 29, 255
in Ireland 244
in Italy 60-62, 71, 77, 347-48
in the Netherlands 262-65, 283
in the Polish lands 150, 172, 182-83
in southeastern Europe 458,
in Switzerland 227-31
Nazis and Nazism 906, 909, 917, 929, 933
Negri, Costache 193
Neofit (Metropolitan) 199-200
Neo-Guelfism 74
Nesselrode, Count Karl Robert von 193, 193,
201
Neumann, Franz 909
Neustadt 588, 717
neutrality
Belgian 261, 272, 281, 283, 522
Swiss 213, 228, 231-32, 272, 402-3
New York 245-46, 675
newspapers and the periodical press 5-6, 8, 18,
26, 28, 32, 36, 43, 344, 500, 585–616, 663,
672, 690, 709-10, 718, 757, 779, 830, 898
in Belgium 273, 276-78, 521, 522
in Denmark 291, 293, 297-300, 304, 306
feminist and women's 647, 653
in France 565, 587, 594-96,
642, 644, 652-53, 666, 923
in Germany 587, 603-4, 640,
642, 651, 653, 661, 669,
671, 673, 675, 741-42, 923
in the Habsburg monarchy 649
in France 38-39, 43, 93, 95-96, 99-101,
104-8, 111-15, 277, 377-78, 381,
384, 388, 395, 410, 428, 481, 488,
512, 515, 534, 569, 571-72, 579,
585-612, 633, 715, 870-71, 881,
884, 888 n. 68
in Germany 27, 36, 44, 47, 124, 136-38,
140-41, 229, 270, 346, 382, 389-91,
408, 410-11, 423, 501, 535, 537-39,
542-43, 546, 548, 551-52, 585-612,
620, 646, 651, 655, 660, 689, 744,
754, 760, 772, 789-91, 805, 807,
820, 822, 830, 839-40, 842, 848,
850, 852-53, 855-56, 894, 900-1,
906
in Great Britain 249-52, 254, 669, 770,
831
in the Habsburg monarchy 30, 43, 147,
156, 158, 160-62, 412, 590, 600-1,
605, 611, 649, 675
in Italy 65, 67, 70, 73, 79-80, 800-1,
803, 816-18
in Moldavia and Wallachia 190, 192, 199
in the Netherlands 266, 268-70
in Norway 314-18, 320-22
in Sweden 326-32, 334-36
in Switzerland 213, 215, 227, 229-31,
233, 236
Niboyet, Eugénie 101, 594, 610, 642, 654
Nicaud, Louise 653

Niebuhr, Barthold G. 264
Nicholas I, Tsar 40, 175, 187, 197, 201
Nîmes 876-77
Nitschner, Jacob 646
nobility 6, 8, 20, 32-34, 351, 358, 360, 418,
641, 651, 663, 665, 667, 719, 754, 910
in Belgium 273, 282
in Denmark 291
in France 92, 105, 113, 425, 436, 493,
632, 645
in Germany 34, 36, 358, 405, 418, 420-
21, 493, 578, 651, 661, 742, 922,
924
in Great Britain 770
in the Habsburg crown lands 20, 36, 45,
146, 151, 159, 655, 718
in Hungary 20, 27, 148, 159-60, 443-
523, 456, 458-59, 463
in Italy 60-61, 78, 431, 802-3, 927
in Moldavia and Wallachia 187, 188-94,
199-205, 207-8
in the Netherlands 266, 271
in Norway 341
in the Polish lands 30-31, 146, 148,
152, 172-73, 159, 172-73, 177-78
in southeastern Europe 443-47, 453-65
in Sweden 325, 331, 333-34
in Switzerland 212, 220-222
Noé, Count Amédee Charles Henry de *see*
Cham
Noer, Prince von 308
Nördlingen 625
Normanby, Constantine Henry Phipps Lord 38
notables 719, 825
in France 92, 94, 97, 102, 104-5, 107,
109, 111, 114, 116, 395, 426, 427-
28, 438, 482-83, 486, 498, 872
in Germany 632
in Italy 433
Noske, Gustav 906
Novara, battle of 38, 80, 180
Nuremberg 404, 538, 542

O

O'Brien, Bronterre 249
O'Brien, Smith 244
O'Connell, Daniel 243-44, 246, 543, 770
O'Connor, Feargus 246, 248, 254, 543
Oberkirch 807, 813, 821
Ochsenbein, Ulrich 217
Odobescu, Ioan 199-200
Offenburg 424, 532, 807-8, 819
officer corps 34, 684, 694
in Denmark 298
in France 35, 381, 383, 386, 565, 700
in Germany 35, 130, 387, 603, 611,
686, 697, 700
in the Habsburg monarchy 31, 35, 39,
164, 704, 760